Computer Fundamentals and Microsoft Office 2013

Custom Edition

D1198064

CENGAGE
Learning·

Australia • Brazil • Japan • Korea • Mexico • Singapore • Spain • United Kingdom • United States

CENGAGE
Learning·

**Computer Fundamentals and Microsoft Office
2013, Custom Edition**

Discovering Computer Fundamentals: Your Interactive Guide to the Digital
World, First Edition
Gary B. Shelly| Misty E. Vermaat

© 2012 Cengage Learning. All rights reserved.

New Perspectives on HTML and CSS: Brief, 6th Edition
Patrick M. Carey

© 2012 Cengage Learning. All rights reserved.

Microsoft® Office 2013: Brief, 1st Edition
Gary B. Shelly| Misty E. Vermaat
© 2014 Cengage Learning. All rights reserved.

Senior Project Development Manager:
 Linda deStefano

Market Development Manager:
 Heather Kramer

Senior Production/Manufacturing Manager:
 Donna M. Brown

Production Editorial Manager:
 Kim Fry

Sr. Rights Acquisition Account Manager:
 Todd Osborne

For product information and technology assistance, contact us at
Cengage Learning Customer & Sales Support, 1-800-354-9706

For permission to use material from this text or product,
submit all requests online at **cengage.com/permissions**
Further permissions questions can be emailed to
permissionrequest@cengage.com

This book contains select works from existing Cengage Learning resources and
was produced by Cengage Learning Custom Solutions for collegiate use. As such,
those adopting and/or contributing to this work are responsible for editorial
content accuracy, continuity and completeness.

Compilation © 2014 Cengage Learning

ISBN-13: 978-1-285-91393-3

ISBN-10: 1-285-91393-0

Cengage Learning
5191 Natorp Boulevard
Mason, Ohio 45040
USA
Cengage Learning is a leading provider of customized learning solutions with
office locations around the globe, including Singapore, the United Kingdom,
Australia, Mexico, Brazil, and Japan. Locate your local office at:
international.cengage.com/region.

Cengage Learning products are represented in Canada by Nelson Education, Ltd.
For your lifelong learning solutions, visit **www.cengage.com/custom.**
Visit our corporate website at **www.cengage.com.**

Printed in the United States of America

Brief Table of Contents

Microsoft Powerpoint 2013

Chapter One

Introduction to Computers

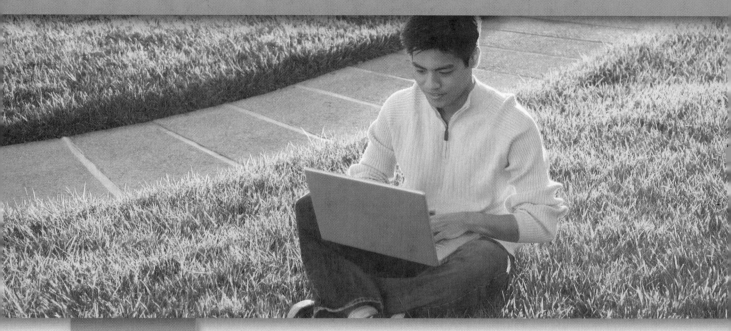

Objectives

After completing this chapter, you will be able to:

1. Explain why computer literacy is vital to success in today's world

2. Describe the five components of a computer: input devices, output devices, system unit, storage devices, and communications devices

3. Discuss the advantages and disadvantages that users experience when working with computers

4. Discuss the uses of the Internet and World Wide Web

5. Distinguish between system software and application software

6. Differentiate among types, sizes, and functions of computers in each of these categories: personal computers (desktop), mobile computers and mobile devices, game consoles, servers, mainframes, supercomputers, and embedded computers

7. Explain how home users, small office/home office users, mobile users, power users, and enterprise users each interact with computers

8. Discuss how society uses computers in education, finance, government, health care, science, publishing, travel, and manufacturing

A World of Computers

Computers are everywhere: at work, at school, and at home (Figure 1-1). Mobile devices, such as many cell phones, often are classified as computers. Computers are a primary means of local and global communication for billions of people. Employees correspond with clients, students with classmates and teachers, and family with friends and other family members.

Through computers, society has instant access to information from around the globe. Local and national news, weather reports, sports scores, airline schedules, telephone directories, maps and directions, job listings, credit reports, and countless forms of educational material always are accessible. From the computer, you can make a telephone call, meet new friends, share photos and videos, share opinions, shop, book flights, file taxes, take a course, receive alerts, and automate your home.

In the workplace, employees use computers to create correspondence such as e-mail messages, memos, and letters; manage calendars; calculate payroll; track inventory; and generate invoices. At school, teachers use computers to assist with classroom instruction. Students use computers to complete assignments and research. Instead of attending class on campus, some students take entire classes directly from their computer.

Figure 1-1 People use all types and sizes of computers in their daily activities.

People also spend hours of leisure time using a computer. They play games, listen to music or radio broadcasts, watch or compose videos and movies, read books and magazines, share stories, research genealogy, retouch photos, and plan vacations.

Many people believe that computer literacy is vital to success. **Computer literacy**, also known as **digital literacy**, involves having a current knowledge and understanding of computers and their uses. Because the requirements that determine computer literacy change as technology changes, you must keep up with these changes to remain computer literate.

This book presents the knowledge you need to be computer literate today. As you read this first chapter, keep in mind it is an overview. Many of the terms and concepts introduced in this chapter will be discussed in more depth later in the book.

What Is a Computer?

A **computer** is an electronic device, operating under the control of instructions stored in its own memory, that can accept data, process the data according to specified rules, produce results, and store the results for future use.

Data and Information

Computers process data into information. **Data** is a collection of unprocessed items, which can include text, numbers, images, audio, and video. **Information** conveys meaning and is useful to people.

As shown in Figure 1-2, for example, computers process several data items to print information in the form of a cash register receipt.

DATA

2 Medium Sodas	$1.49 each
1 Small Turkey Sub	$3.49 each
1 Caesar Salad	$4.49 each
1 Bag of Chips	$0.99 each
3 Cookies	$0.39 each
Amount Received	$20.00

PROCESSES

- Computes each item's total price by multiplying the quantity ordered by the item price (i.e., 2 * 1.49 = 2.98).
- Organizes data.
- Sums all item total prices to determine order total due from customer (13.12).
- Calculates change due to customer by subtracting the order total from amount received (20.00 - 13.12 = 6.88).

INFORMATION

Arrow Deli
10 Park Street
Maple River, DE 20393
(734) 555-2939

QTY	ITEM	TOTAL
2	Medium Sodas	2.98
1	Small Turkey Sub	3.49
1	Caesar Salad	4.49
1	Bag of Chips	0.99
3	Cookies	1.17

Total Due	13.12
Amount Received	20.00
Change	6.88

Thank You!

Figure 1-2 A computer processes data into information. In this simplified example, the item ordered, item price, quantity ordered, and amount received all represent data. The computer processes the data to produce the cash register receipt (information).

Information Processing Cycle

Computers process data (input) into information (output). Computers carry out processes using instructions, which are the steps that tell the computer how to perform a particular task. A collection of related instructions organized for a common purpose is referred to as software. A computer often holds data, information, and instructions in storage for future use. Some people refer to the series of input, process, output, and storage activities as the **information processing cycle**. Recently, communications also has become an essential element of the information processing cycle.

The Components of a Computer

A computer contains many electric, electronic, and mechanical components known as **hardware**. These components include input devices, output devices, a system unit, storage devices, and communications devices. Figure 1-3 shows some common computer hardware components.

Input Devices

An **input device** is any hardware component that allows you to enter data and instructions into a computer. Five widely used input devices are the keyboard, mouse, microphone, scanner, and Web cam (Figure 1-3).

A computer keyboard contains keys you press to enter data into the computer. A mouse is a small handheld device. With the mouse, you control movement of a small symbol on the screen, called the pointer, and you make selections from the screen.

A microphone allows a user to speak into the computer. A scanner converts printed material (such as text and pictures) into a form the computer can use.

A Web cam is a digital video camera that allows users to create movies or take pictures and store them on the computer instead of on tape or film.

Output Devices

An **output device** is any hardware component that conveys information to one or more people. Three commonly used output devices are a printer, a monitor, and speakers (Figure 1-3).

A printer produces text and graphics on a physical medium such as paper. A monitor displays text, graphics, and videos on a screen. Speakers allow you to hear music, voice, and other audio (sounds).

Figure 1-3 Common computer hardware components include the keyboard, mouse, microphone, scanner, Web cam, printer, monitor, speakers, system unit, hard disk drive, external hard disk, optical disc drive(s), USB flash drive, card reader/writer, memory cards, and modem.

System Unit

The **system unit** is a case that contains electronic components of the computer that are used to process data (Figure 1-3 on the previous page). The circuitry of the system unit usually is part of or is connected to a circuit board called the motherboard.

Two main components on the motherboard are the processor and memory. The **processor**, also called the **CPU** (**central processing unit**), is the electronic component that interprets and carries out the basic instructions that operate the computer. **Memory** consists of electronic components that store instructions waiting to be executed and data needed by those instructions. Most memory keeps data and instructions temporarily, which means its contents are erased when the computer is shut off.

Storage Devices

Storage holds data, instructions, and information for future use. For example, computers can store hundreds or millions of customer names and addresses. Storage holds these items permanently.

A computer keeps data, instructions, and information on **storage media**. Examples of storage media are USB flash drives, hard disks, optical discs, and memory cards. A **storage device** records (writes) and/or retrieves (reads) items to and from storage media. Storage devices often function as a source of input because they transfer items from storage to memory.

A USB flash drive is a portable storage device that is small and lightweight enough to be transported on a keychain or in a pocket (Figure 1-3). The average USB flash drive can hold about 4 billion characters.

A hard disk provides much greater storage capacity than a USB flash drive. The average hard disk can hold more than 320 billion characters. Hard disks are enclosed in an airtight, sealed case. Although some are portable, most are housed inside the system unit (Figure 1-4). Portable hard disks are either external or removable. An external hard disk is a separate, freestanding unit, whereas you insert and remove a removable hard disk from the computer or a device connected to the computer.

An optical disc is a flat, round, portable metal disc with a plastic coating. CDs, DVDs, and Blu-ray Discs are three types of optical discs. A CD can hold from 650 million to 1 billion characters. Some DVDs can store two full-length movies or 17 billion characters (Figure 1-5). Blu-ray Discs can store about 46 hours of standard video, or 100 billion characters.

Some mobile devices, such as digital cameras, use memory cards as the storage media. You can use a card reader/writer (Figure 1-3) to transfer stored items, such as digital photos, from the memory card to a computer or printer.

Figure 1-4 Most hard disks are housed inside the system unit.

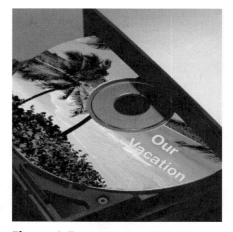

Figure 1-5 A DVD in a DVD drive.

Communications Devices

A **communications device** is a hardware component that enables a computer to send (transmit) and receive data, instructions, and information to and from one or more computers or mobile devices. A widely used communications device is a modem (Figure 1-3).

Communications occur over cables, telephone lines, cellular radio networks, satellites, and other transmission media. Some transmission media, such as satellites and cellular radio networks, are wireless, which means they have no physical lines or wires.

Advantages and Disadvantages of Using Computers

Society has reaped many benefits from using computers. A **user** is anyone who communicates with a computer or utilizes the information it generates. Both business and home users can make well-informed decisions because they have instant access to information from anywhere in the world. Students, another type of user, have more tools to assist them in the learning process.

Advantages of Using Computers
The benefits from using computers are possible because computers have the advantages of speed, reliability, consistency, storage, and communications.
- **Speed:** When data, instructions, and information flow along electronic circuits in a computer, they travel at incredibly fast speeds. Many computers process billions or trillions of operations in a single second.
- **Reliability:** The electronic components in modern computers are dependable and reliable because they rarely break or fail.
- **Consistency:** Given the same input and processes, a computer will produce the same results — consistently. Computers generate error-free results, provided the input is correct and the instructions work.
- **Storage:** Computers store enormous amounts of data and make this data available for processing anytime it is needed.
- **Communications:** Most computers today can communicate with other computers, often wirelessly. Computers allow users to communicate with one another.

Disadvantages of Using Computers
Some disadvantages of computers relate to the violation of privacy, public safety, the impact on the labor force, health risks, and the impact on the environment.
- **Violation of Privacy:** In many instances, where personal and confidential records stored on computers were not protected properly, individuals have found their privacy violated and identities stolen.
- **Public Safety:** Adults, teens, and children around the world are using computers to share publicly their photos, videos, journals, music, and other personal information. Some of these unsuspecting, innocent computer users have fallen victim to crimes committed by dangerous strangers.
- **Impact on Labor Force:** Although computers have improved productivity and created an entire industry with hundreds of thousands of new jobs, the skills of millions of employees have been replaced by computers. Thus, it is crucial that workers keep their education up-to-date. A separate impact on the labor force is that some companies are outsourcing jobs to foreign countries instead of keeping their homeland labor force employed.
- **Health Risks:** Prolonged or improper computer use can lead to health injuries or disorders. Computer users can protect themselves from health risks through proper workplace design, good posture while at the computer, and appropriately spaced work breaks. Two behavioral health risks are computer addiction and technology overload. Computer addiction occurs when someone becomes obsessed with using a computer. Individuals suffering from technology overload feel distressed when deprived of computers and mobile devices.
- **Impact on Environment:** Computer manufacturing processes and computer waste are depleting natural resources and polluting the environment. **Green computing** involves reducing the electricity consumed and environmental waste generated when using a computer. Strategies that support green computing include recycling, regulating manufacturing processes, extending the life of computers, and immediately donating or properly disposing of replaced computers.

Green Computing
For more information, visit the Computer Concepts CourseMate Web site at www.cengagebrain.com, navigate to the Chapter 1 Web Link resource for this book, and then click Green Computing.

Networks and the Internet

A **network** is a collection of computers and devices connected together, often wirelessly, via communications devices and transmission media. When a computer connects to a network, it is **online**. Networks allow computers to share **resources**, such as hardware, software, data, and information. Sharing resources saves time and money.

The **Internet** is a worldwide collection of networks that connects millions of businesses, government agencies, educational institutions, and individuals (Figure 1-6). More than one billion people around the world use the Internet daily for a variety of reasons, including the following: to communicate with and meet other people; to conduct research and access a wealth of information and news; to shop for goods and services; to bank and invest; to participate in online training; to engage in entertaining activities, such as planning vacations, playing online games, listening to music, watching or editing videos, and books and magazines; to share information, photos, and videos; to download music and videos; and to access and interact with Web applications. Figure 1-7 shows examples in each of these areas.

The Internet

For more information, visit the Computer Concepts CourseMate Web site at www.cengagebrain.com, navigate to the Chapter 1 Web Link resource for this book, and then click The Internet.

Figure 1-6 The Internet is the largest computer network, connecting millions of computers and devices around the world.

Figure 1-7 Home and business users access the Internet for a variety of reasons.

People connect to the Internet to exchange information with others around the world. E-mail allows you to send and receive messages to and from other users (read Ethics & Issues 1-1 for a related discussion). With instant messaging, you can have a live conversation with another connected user. In a chat room, you can communicate with multiple users at the same time — much like a group discussion. You also can use the Internet to make a telephone call.

Businesses, called access providers, offer access to the Internet free or for a fee. By subscribing to an access provider, you can use your computer and a modem to connect to the many services of the Internet.

The **Web**, short for World Wide Web, is one of the more popular services on the Internet. The Web contains billions of documents called Web pages. A **Web page** can contain text, graphics, animation, audio, and video. The nine screens shown in Figure 1-7 on the previous page are examples of Web pages.

Web pages often have built-in connections, or links, to other documents, graphics, other Web pages, or Web sites. A **Web site** is a collection of related Web pages. Some Web sites allow users to access music and videos that can be downloaded, or transferred to storage media in a computer or portable media player. Once downloaded, you can listen to the music through speakers, headphones, or earbuds, or view the videos on a display device.

Anyone can create a Web page and then make it available, or publish it, on the Internet for others to see. Millions of people worldwide join online communities, each called a **social networking Web site** or **online social network**, that encourage members to share their interests, ideas, stories, photos, music, and videos with other registered users. Hundreds of thousands of people today also use blogs to publish their thoughts on the Web. A **blog** is an informal Web site consisting of time-stamped articles in a diary or journal format, usually listed in reverse chronological order. As others read the articles in a blog, they reply with their own thoughts (to learn more about creating and using blogs, complete the Learn How To 1 activity on page 34). Podcasts are a popular way people verbally share information on the Web. A **microblog**, such as Twitter, allows users to publish short messages, usually between 100 and 200 characters, for others to read. A **podcast** is recorded audio stored on a Web site that can be downloaded to a computer or a portable media player such as an iPod.

A **Web application** is a Web site that allows users to access and interact with software from any computer or device that is connected to the Internet. Examples of software available as Web applications include those that allow you to send and receive e-mail messages, prepare your taxes, organize digital photos, create documents, and play games.

Web sites such as social networking Web sites, blogs, and Web applications are categorized as Web 2.0 sites. The term **Web 2.0** refers to Web sites that provide a means for users to share personal information (such as social networking Web sites), allow users to modify the Web site contents (such as some blogs), and/or have software built into the site for users to access (such as Web applications).

Ethics & Issues

For the complete text of the Ethics & Issues boxes found in this chapter, visit the Computer Concepts CourseMate Web site at www.cengagebrain.com and then navigate to the Chapter 1 Ethics & Issues resource for this book.

ETHICS & ISSUES 1-1

What Should Be Done about Identity Theft?

Using e-mail and other techniques on the Internet, scam artists are employing a technique known as phishing to try to steal your personal information, such as credit card numbers, banking information, and passwords. For example, an e-mail message may appear to be a request from your bank to verify your Social Security number and online banking password. Instead, the information you submit ends up in the hands of the scammer, who then uses the information for a variety of unethical and illegal acts. Sadly, the result often is identity theft. You can help to deter identity theft in several ways: 1) shred your financial documents before discarding them, 2) do not click links in unsolicited e-mail messages, and 3) enroll in a credit monitoring service. Consumer advocates often blame credit card companies and credit bureaus for lax security standards. Meanwhile, the companies blame consumers for being too gullible and forthcoming with private information. Both sides blame the government for poor privacy laws and light punishments for identity thieves. But while the arguments go on, law enforcement agencies bear the brunt of the problem by spending hundreds of millions of dollars responding to complaints and finding and processing the criminals.

Who should be responsible for protecting the public from online identity theft? Why? Should laws be changed to stop it, or should consumers change behavior? What is an appropriate punishment for identity thieves? Given the international nature of the Internet, how should foreign identity thieves be handled? Why?

? FAQ 1-1

What U.S. Web sites are visited most frequently?

A recent survey found that Google's Web site is visited most frequently, with Microsoft and Yahoo! not far behind. The chart to the right shows the five most frequently visited Web sites, as well as the approximate number of unique visitors per month.

For more information, visit the Computer Concepts CourseMate Web site at www.cengagebrain.com, navigate to the Chapter 1 FAQ resource for this book, and then click Top Web Sites.

An **FAQ** (frequently asked question) helps you find answers to commonly asked questions. Web sites often post an FAQ section, and each chapter in this book includes FAQ boxes related to topics in the text.

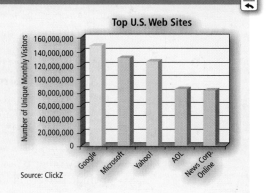

Source: ClickZ

Computer Software

Software, also called a **program**, is a series of related instructions, organized for a common purpose, that tells the computer what task(s) to perform and how to perform them. You interact with a program through its user interface. Software today often has a graphical user interface. With a **graphical user interface** (**GUI** pronounced gooey), you interact with the software using text, graphics, and visual images such as icons. An icon is a miniature image that represents a program, an instruction, or some other object. You can use the mouse to select icons that perform operations such as starting a program.

The two categories of software are system software and application software. Figure 1-8 shows an example of each of these categories of software, which are explained in the following sections.

Figure 1-8 Today's system software and application software usually have a graphical user interface.

System Software

System software consists of the programs that control or maintain the operations of the computer and its devices. System software serves as the interface between the user, the application software, and the computer's hardware. Two types of system software are the operating system and utility programs.

Operating System An **operating system** is a set of programs that coordinates all the activities among computer hardware devices. It provides a means for users to communicate with the computer and other software. Many of today's computers use Microsoft's Windows, the latest version of which is shown in Figure 1-8, or Mac OS, Apple's operating system.

When a user starts a computer, portions of the operating system are copied into memory from the computer's hard disk. These parts of the operating system remain in memory while the computer is on.

Windows

For more information, visit the Computer Concepts CourseMate Web site at www.cengagebrain.com, navigate to the Chapter 1 Web Link resource for this book, and then click Windows.

Utility Program A **utility program** allows a user to perform maintenance-type tasks usually related to managing a computer, its devices, or its programs. For example, you can use a utility program to transfer digital photos to an optical disc. Most operating systems include several utility programs for managing disk drives, printers, and other devices and media. You also can buy utility programs that allow you to perform additional computer management functions.

Application Software

Application software consists of programs designed to make users more productive and/or assist them with personal tasks. A widely used type of application software related to communications is a Web browser, which allows users with an Internet connection to access and view Web pages or access programs. Other popular application software includes word processing software, spreadsheet software, database software, and presentation software.

Many other types of application software exist that enable users to perform a variety of tasks. These include personal information management, note taking, project management, accounting, document management, computer-aided design, desktop publishing, paint/image editing, audio and video editing, multimedia authoring, Web page authoring, personal finance, legal, tax preparation, home design/landscaping, travel and mapping, education, reference, and entertainment (e.g., games or simulations).

Software is available at stores that sell computer products (Figure 1-9) and also online at many Web sites.

Figure 1-9 Stores that sell computer products have shelves stocked with software for sale.

Installing and Running Programs

When purchasing software from a retailer, you typically receive a box that includes an optical disc(s) that contains the program. If you acquire software from a Web site on the Internet, you may be able to download the program; that is, the program transfers from the Web site to the hard disk in your computer.

The instructions in software are placed on storage media, either locally or online. To use software that is stored locally, such as on a hard disk or optical disc, you usually need to install the software. Web applications that are stored online, by contrast, usually do not need to be installed.

Installing is the process of setting up software to work with the computer, printer, and other hardware. When you buy a computer, it usually has some software preinstalled on its hard disk. This enables you to use the computer the first time you turn it on. To begin installing additional software from an optical disc, insert the program disc in an optical disc drive. To install downloaded software, the Web site typically provides instructions for how to install the program on your hard disk.

Once installed, you can run the program. When you instruct the computer to **run** an installed program, the computer loads it, which means the program is copied from storage to memory. Once in memory, the computer can carry out, or **execute**, the instructions in the program so that you can use the program. Figure 1-10 illustrates the steps that occur when a user installs and runs a program.

Installing and Running a Computer Program

Step 1: INSTALL
When you insert a program disc, such as a photo editing program, in the optical disc drive for the first time, the computer begins the procedure of installing the program on the hard disk.

optical disc

Step 2: RUN
Once installed, you can instruct the computer to run the program. The computer transfers instructions from the hard disk to memory.

instructions transfer to memory

Step 3: USE
The program executes so that you can use it. This program enables you to edit photos.

Figure 1-10 This figure shows how to install and run a computer program.

Software Development

A **programmer**, sometimes called a **developer**, is someone who develops software or writes the instructions that direct the computer to process data into information. Complex programs can require thousands to millions of instructions.

Programmers use a programming language or program development tool to create computer programs. Popular programming languages include C++, Visual C#, Visual Basic, JavaScript, and Java. Figure 1-11 shows a simple Visual Basic program.

```
Public Class frmPayrollInformation

    Private Sub btnCalculatePay_Click(ByVal sender As System.Object, ByVal e As System.
    EventArgs) Handles btnCalculatePay.Click
        'This procedure executes when the user clicks the
        'Calculate Pay button. It calculates regular
        'and overtime pay and displays it in the window.

        ' Declare variables
        Dim strHoursWorked As String
        Dim strHourlyRate As String
        Dim decHoursWorked As Decimal
        Dim decHourlyRate As Decimal
        Dim decRegularPay As Decimal
        Dim decOvertimeHours As Decimal
        Dim decOvertimePay As Decimal
        Dim decTotalPay As Decimal

        ' Calculate and display payroll information
        strHoursWorked = Me.txtHoursWorked.Text
        strHourlyRate = Me.txtHourlyRate.Text
        decHoursWorked = Convert.ToDecimal(strHoursWorked)
        decHourlyRate = Convert.ToDecimal(strHourlyRate)

        If decHoursWorked > 40 Then
            decRegularPay = 40 * decHourlyRate
            Me.txtRegularPay.Text = decRegularPay.ToString("C")
            decOvertimeHours = decHoursWorked - 40
            decOvertimePay = (1.5 * decOvertimeHours) * decHourlyRate
            Me.txtOvertimePay.Text = decOvertimePay.ToString("C")
            decTotalPay = decRegularPay + decOvertimePay
            Me.txtTotalPay.Text = decTotalPay.ToString("C")
        Else
            decRegularPay = decHoursWorked * decHourlyRate
            Me.txtRegularPay.Text = decRegularPay.ToString("C")
            Me.txtOvertimePay.Text = "$0.00"
            Me.txtTotalPay.Text = decRegularPay.ToString("C")
        End If
    End Sub
End Class
```

Figure 1-11 Some of the instructions in a program.

✔ **QUIZ YOURSELF 1-2**

Instructions: Find the true statement below. Then, rewrite the remaining false statements so that they are true.

1. A resource is a collection of computers and devices connected together via communications devices and transmission media.

2. Installing is the process of setting up software to work with the computer, printer, and other hardware.

3. Popular system software includes Web browsers, word processing software, spreadsheet software, database software, and presentation software.

4. The Internet is one of the more popular services on the Web.

5. Two types of application software are the operating system and utility programs.

Quiz Yourself Online: To further check your knowledge of pages 8 through 13, visit the Computer Concepts CourseMate Web site at www.cengagebrain.com, navigate to the Chapter 1 Quiz Yourself resource for this book, and then click Objectives 4 – 5.

Categories of Computers

Industry experts typically classify computers in seven categories: personal computers (desktop), mobile computers and mobile devices, game consoles, servers, mainframes, supercomputers, and embedded computers. A computer's size, speed, processing power, and price determine the category it best fits. Due to rapidly changing technology, however, the distinction among categories is not always clear-cut. This trend of computers and devices with technologies that overlap, called **convergence**, leads to computer manufacturers continually releasing newer models that include similar functionality and features. For example, newer cell phones often include media player, camera, and Web browsing capabilities. As devices converge, users need fewer devices for the functionality that they require. When consumers replace outdated computers and devices, they should dispose of them properly (read Ethics & Issues 1-2 for a related discussion).

Figure 1-12 summarizes the seven categories of computers. The following pages discuss computers and devices that fall in each category.

ETHICS & ISSUES 1-2

Should Recycling of Electronics Be Made Easier?

Experts estimate that about one billion computers have been discarded to date. The discarded items often are known as e-waste. As technology advances and prices fall, many people think of computers, cell phones, and portable media players as disposable items. These items often contain several toxic elements, including lead, mercury, and barium. Computers and mobile devices thrown into landfills or burned in incinerators can pollute the ground and the air. A vast amount of e-waste ends up polluting third world countries. One solution is to recycle old electronic equipment, but the recycling effort has made little progress especially when compared to recycling programs for paper, glass, and plastic.

Some lawmakers prefer an aggressive approach, such as setting up a recycling program that would be paid for by adding a $10 fee to the purchase price of computers and computer equipment, or forcing computer manufacturers to be responsible for collecting and recycling their products. California already requires a recycling fee for any products sold that include certain electronic equipment. Manufacturers have taken steps, such as offering to recycle old computers and using energy efficient and environmentally friendly manufacturing techniques, but some claim that consumers should bear the responsibility of disposing of their old computer parts. While some companies have

set up recycling programs, many claim that forcing them to bear the cost of recycling programs puts the company at a competitive disadvantage when compared to foreign companies that may not be forced to maintain a recycling program.

Why is electronics recycling not as popular as other types of recycling? How can companies make it easier to recycle electronics while being compensated fairly for the cost of recycling? Should the government, manufacturers, or users be responsible for recycling of obsolete equipment? Why? Should the government mandate a recycling program for electronics? Why or why not?

Categories of Computers

Category	Physical Size	Number of Simultaneously Connected Users	General Price Range
Personal computers (desktop)	Fits on a desk	Usually one (can be more if networked)	Several hundred to several thousand dollars
Mobile computers and mobile devices	Fits on your lap or in your hand	Usually one	Less than a hundred dollars to several thousand dollars
Game consoles	Small box or handheld device	One to several	Several hundred dollars or less
Servers	Small cabinet	Two to thousands	Several hundred to a million dollars
Mainframes	Partial room to a full room of equipment	Hundreds to thousands	$300,000 to several million dollars
Supercomputers	Full room of equipment	Hundreds to thousands	$500,000 to several billion dollars
Embedded computers	Miniature	Usually one	Embedded in the price of the product

Figure 1-12 This table summarizes some of the differences among the categories of computers. These should be considered general guidelines only because of rapid changes in technology.

Personal Computers

A **personal computer** is a computer that can perform all of its input, processing, output, and storage activities by itself. A personal computer contains a processor, memory, and one or more input, output, and storage devices. Personal computers also often contain a communications device.

Two popular architectures of personal computers are the PC (Figure 1-13) and the Apple (Figure 1-14). The term, PC-compatible, refers to any personal computer based on the original IBM personal computer design. Companies such as Dell and Toshiba sell PC-compatible computers. PC and PC-compatible computers usually use a Windows operating system. Apple computers usually use a Macintosh operating system (Mac OS).

Two types of personal computers are desktop computers and notebook computers.

Figure 1-13 PC and PC-compatible computers usually use a Windows operating system.

Figure 1-14 Apple computers, such as the iMac, usually use a Macintosh operating system.

Desktop Computers

A **desktop computer** is designed so that the system unit, input devices, output devices, and any other devices fit entirely on or under a desk or table. In some models, the monitor sits on top of the system unit, which is placed on the desk. The more popular style of system unit is the tall and narrow tower, which can sit on the floor vertically.

Mobile Computers and Mobile Devices

A **mobile computer** is a personal computer you can carry from place to place. Similarly, a **mobile device** is a computing device small enough to hold in your hand. The most popular type of mobile computer is the notebook computer.

display

keyboard

hinge

optical disc drive

Figure 1-15
On a typical notebook computer, the keyboard is on top of the system unit, and the display attaches to the system unit with hinges.

Notebook Computers

A **notebook computer**, also called a **laptop computer**, is a portable, personal computer often designed to fit on your lap. Notebook computers are thin and lightweight, yet can be as powerful as the average desktop computer. A **netbook**, which is a type of notebook computer, is smaller, lighter, and often not as powerful as a traditional notebook computer. Most netbooks cost less than traditional notebook computers, usually only a few hundred dollars. Some notebook computers have touch screens, allowing you to interact with the device by touching the screen, usually with the tip of a finger.

On a typical notebook computer, the keyboard is on top of the system unit, and the display attaches to the system unit with hinges (Figure 1-15). These computers weigh on average from 2.5 to more than 10 pounds (depending on configuration), which allows users easily to transport the computers from place to place. Most notebook computers can operate on batteries or a power supply or both.

Tablet PCs Resembling a letter-sized slate, the **Tablet PC**, or tablet computer, is a special type of notebook computer you can interact with by touching the screen with your finger or a digital pen. One design of Tablet PC, called a convertible tablet, has an attached keyboard. Another design, which does not include a keyboard, is called a slate tablet (Figure 1-16) and provides other means for typing. Tablet PCs are useful especially for taking notes in locations where the standard notebook computer is not practical.

Mobile Devices

Mobile devices, which are small enough to carry in a pocket, usually store programs and data permanently on memory inside the system unit or on small storage media such as memory cards. You often can connect a mobile device to a personal computer to exchange information. Some mobile devices are **Internet-enabled**, meaning they can connect to the Internet wirelessly. Because of their reduced size, the screens on handheld computers are small.

Figure 1-16
The iPad is a widely used slate tablet.

Popular types of mobile devices are smart phones and PDAs, e-book readers, handheld computers, portable media players, and digital cameras.

Smart Phones and PDAs Offering the convenience of one-handed operation, a **smart phone** (Figure 1-17) is an Internet-enabled phone that usually also provides personal information management functions such as a calendar, an appointment book, an address book, a calculator, and a notepad. In addition to basic phone capabilities, a smart phone allows you to send and receive e-mail messages and access the Web — usually for an additional fee. Many models also function as a portable media player and include built-in digital cameras so that you can share photos or videos. Many smart phones also offer a variety of application software such as word processing, spreadsheet, and games.

Many smart phones have keypads that contain both numbers and letters so that you can use the same keypad to dial phone numbers and enter messages. Others have a built-in mini keyboard. Some have touch screens, and some include a stylus. Instead of calling someone's smart phone or cell phone, users often send messages to others by pressing buttons on their phone's keypad, keys on the mini keyboard, or images on an on-screen keyboard. Types of messages users send with smart phones include text messages, instant messages, picture messages, and video messages.

- A **text message** is a short note, typically fewer than 300 characters, sent to or from a smart phone or other mobile device.
- An **instant message** is a real-time Internet communication, where you exchange messages with other connected users.
- A **picture message** is a photo or other image, sometimes along with sound and text, sent to or from a smart phone or other mobile device. A phone that can send picture messages often is called a **camera phone**.
- A **video message** is a short video clip, usually about 30 seconds, sent to or from a smart phone or other mobile device. A phone that can send video messages often is called a **video phone**.

A **PDA** (personal digital assistant), which often looks like a smart phone, provides personal information management functions such as a calendar, an appointment book, an address book, a calculator, and a notepad. A PDA differs from a smart phone in that it usually does not provide phone capabilities and may not be Internet-enabled, support voice input, have a built-in camera, or function as a portable media player.

E-Book Readers An **e-book reader** (short for electronic book reader), or e-reader, is a handheld device that is used primarily for reading e-books (Figure 1-18). An **e-book**, or digital book, is an electronic version of a printed book, readable on computers and other digital devices. Most e-book readers have a touch screen and are Internet-enabled.

Figure 1-18
An e-book reader.

Handheld Computers A **handheld computer**, sometimes referred to as an **Ultra-Mobile PC** (**UMPC**), is a computer small enough to fit in one hand. Industry-specific handheld computers serve mobile employees, such as parcel delivery people, whose jobs require them to move from place to place.

Portable Media Players A **portable media player** is a mobile device on which you can store, organize, and play digital media (Figure 1-19). For example, you can listen to music; watch videos, movies, and television shows; and view photos on the device's screen. With most, you download the digital media from a computer to the portable media player or to media that you insert in the device.

Figure 1-19 The iPod, shown here, is a popular portable media player.

earbuds

Portable media players usually include a set of earbuds, which are small speakers that rest inside each ear canal. Some portable media players have a touch screen; others have a touch-sensitive pad that you operate with a thumb or finger, to navigate through digital media, adjust volume, and customize settings.

Digital Cameras A **digital camera** is a device that allows users to take pictures and store the photographed images digitally, instead of on traditional film (Figure 1-20). Although digital cameras usually have some amount of internal storage to hold images, most users store images on small storage media such as memory cards. Digital cameras typically allow users to review, and sometimes modify, images while they are in the camera.

Often users prefer to download images from the digital camera to the computer. Or, you can remove the storage media such as a memory card from the digital camera and insert it in a card reader in or attached to the computer.

Figure 1-20 With a digital camera, users can view photographed images immediately through a small screen on the camera to see if the picture is worth keeping.

Digital Cameras
For more information, visit the Computer Concepts CourseMate Web site at www.cengagebrain.com, navigate to the Chapter 1 Web Link resource for this book, and then click Digital Cameras.

! INNOVATIVE COMPUTING 1-1

Wii a Welcome Medical Skill Builder

A patient awaiting laparoscopic procedures may be less tense knowing that the surgeons have honed their dexterity and coordination using a Nintendo Wii. Preliminary studies have found that doctors can improve

their fine motor control by playing video games that emphasize subtle hand movements used in minimally invasive surgeries. Researchers are developing Wii surgery simulators that will allow doctors to practice their skills at home or in break rooms at hospitals.

The Wii game system is finding a medical home in other nontraditional places. Physical therapists urge arthritic patients to use Wiihabilitation to build endurance and increase their range of motion. Therapeutic recreation with the Wii's sports games may help patients recovering from strokes, fractures, and combat injuries.

Researchers in a testing lab in California are experimenting with using the Wii's motion-activated controls in non-gaming applications, such as allowing doctors to explain X-ray images to patients.

For more information, visit the Computer Concepts CourseMate Web site at www.cengagebrain.com, navigate to the Chapter 1 Innovative Computing resource for this book, and then click Medical Wii.

Game Consoles

A **game console** is a mobile computing device designed for single-player or multiplayer video games (Figure 1-21). Standard game consoles use a handheld controller(s) as an input device(s); a television screen as an output device; and hard disks, optical discs, and/or memory cards for storage. The compact size and light weight of game consoles make them easy to use at home, in the car, in a hotel, or any location that has an electrical outlet. Three popular models are Microsoft's Xbox 360, Nintendo's Wii (pronounced wee), and Sony's PlayStation 3. Read Innovative Computing 1-1 for a look at how Nintendo Wii applications are being used in the medical field.

A handheld game console is small enough to fit in one hand. With the handheld game console, the controls, screen, and speakers are built into the device. Some models use cartridges to store games; others use a memory card or a miniature optical disc. Many handheld game consoles can communicate wirelessly with other similar consoles for multiplayer gaming. Two popular models are Nintendo DS Lite and Sony's PlayStation Portable (PSP).

In addition to gaming, many game console models allow users to listen to music, watch movies, keep fit, and connect to the Internet.

handheld game console

game console

Figure 1-21 Game consoles provide hours of video game entertainment.

Servers

A **server** controls access to the hardware, software, and other resources on a network and provides a centralized storage area for programs, data, and information (Figure 1-22). Servers support from two to several thousand connected computers at the same time.

People use personal computers or terminals to access data, information, and programs on a server. A terminal is a device with a monitor, keyboard, and memory.

Figure 1-22 A server controls access to resources on a network.

Mainframes

A **mainframe** is a large, expensive, powerful computer that can handle hundreds or thousands of connected users simultaneously (Figure 1-23). Mainframes store huge amounts of data, instructions, and information. Most major corporations use mainframes for business activities. With mainframes, enterprises are able to bill millions of customers, prepare payroll for thousands of employees, and manage thousands of items in inventory. One study reported that mainframes process more than 83 percent of transactions around the world.

Servers and other mainframes can access data and information from a mainframe. People also can access programs on the mainframe using terminals or personal computers.

Figure 1-23 Mainframe computers can handle thousands of connected computers and process millions of instructions per second.

Supercomputers

A **supercomputer** is the fastest, most powerful computer — and the most expensive (Figure 1-24). The fastest supercomputers are capable of processing more than one quadrillion instructions in a single second.

Applications requiring complex, sophisticated mathematical calculations use supercomputers. Large-scale simulations and applications in medicine, aerospace, automotive design, online banking, weather forecasting, nuclear energy research, and petroleum exploration use a supercomputer.

Figure 1-24 This supercomputer, IBM's Roadrunner, can process more than one quadrillion instructions in a single second.

Embedded Computers

An **embedded computer** is a special-purpose computer that functions as a component in a larger product. A variety of everyday products contain embedded computers:

• Consumer electronics
• Home automation devices
• Automobiles
• Process controllers and robotics
• Computer devices and office machines

Because embedded computers are components in larger products, they usually are small and have limited hardware. Embedded computers perform various functions, depending on the requirements of the product in which they reside. Embedded computers in printers, for example, monitor the amount of paper in the tray, check the ink or toner level, signal if a paper jam has occurred, and so on. Figure 1-25 shows some of the many embedded computers in cars.

Adaptive cruise control systems detect if cars in front of you are too close and, if necessary, adjust the vehicle's throttle, may apply brakes, and/or sound an alarm.

Advanced airbag systems have crash-severity sensors that determine the appropriate level to inflate the airbag, reducing the chance of airbag injury in low-speed accidents.

Tire pressure monitoring systems send warning signals if tire pressure is insufficient.

Cars equipped with wireless communications capabilities, called telematics, include such features navigation systems, remote diagnosis and alerts, and Internet access.

Drive-by-wire systems sense pressure on the gas pedal and communicate electronically to the engine how much and how fast to accelerate.

Figure 1-25 Some of the embedded computers designed to improve your safety, security, and performance in today's automobiles.

Examples of Computer Usage

Every day, people around the world rely on different types of computers for a variety of applications. To illustrate the range of uses for computers, this section takes you on a visual and narrative tour of five categories of users: a home user, a small office/home office (SOHO) user, a mobile user, a power user, and an enterprise user.

Home User

In an increasing number of homes, the computer is a basic necessity. Each family member, or **home user**, spends time on the computer for different reasons. These include personal financial management, Web access, communications, and entertainment (Figure 1-26).

On the Internet, home users access a huge amount of information, conduct research, take college classes, pay bills, manage investments, shop, listen to the radio, watch movies, read books, file taxes, book airline reservations, make telephone calls, and play games. They also communicate with others around the world through e-mail, blogs, instant messages, and chat rooms. Home users share ideas, interests, photos, music, and videos on social networking Web sites.

With a digital camera, home users take photos and then send the electronic images to others. Many home users have a portable media player, so that they can listen to downloaded music and/or podcasts at a later time through earbuds attached to the player. They also usually have one or more game consoles to play video games.

Today's homes typically have one or more desktop computers. Some home users network multiple desktop computers throughout the house, often wirelessly. These small networks allow family members to share an Internet connection and a printer.

Home users have a variety of software. They type letters, homework assignments, and other documents with word processing software. Personal finance software helps the home user with personal finances, investments, and family budgets. Other software assists with preparing taxes, keeping a

household inventory, setting up maintenance schedules, and protecting computers against threats and unauthorized intrusions.

Reference software, such as encyclopedias, medical dictionaries, or a road atlas, provides valuable information for everyone in the family. With entertainment software, the home user can play games, compose music, research genealogy, or create greeting cards. Educational software helps adults learn to speak a foreign language and youngsters to read, write, count, and spell.

FAQ 1-3

How many households do not use the Internet or related technologies?

A recent survey estimates that 18 percent of U.S. households have no Internet access. Furthermore, about 20 percent of U.S. heads of households have never sent an e-mail message. The chart to the right illustrates the lack of experience with computer and Internet technology.

For more information, visit the Computer Concepts CourseMate Web site at www.cengagebrain.com, navigate to the Chapter 1 FAQ resource for this book, and then click Experience with Technology.

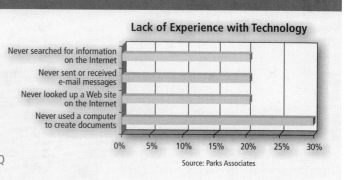

Lack of Experience with Technology

Never searched for information on the Internet
Never sent or received e-mail messages
Never looked up a Web site on the Internet
Never used a computer to create documents

0% 5% 10% 15% 20% 25% 30%

Source: Parks Associates

personal financial management

Web access

entertainment

communications

Figure 1-26 The home user spends time on a computer for a variety of reasons.

Small Office/Home Office User

Computers assist small business and home office users in managing their resources effectively. A **small office/home office (SOHO)** includes any company with fewer than 50 employees, as well as the self-employed who work from home. Small offices include local law practices, accounting firms, travel agencies, and florists. SOHO users typically use a desktop computer. Many also use smart phones.

SOHO users access the Internet — often wirelessly — to look up information such as addresses, directions, postal codes, flights (Figure 1-27a), and package shipping rates or to send and receive e-mail messages, or make telephone calls. Many have entered the e-commerce arena and conduct business on the Web. Their Web sites advertise products and services and may provide a means for taking orders.

To save money on hardware and software, small offices often network their computers. For example, the small office connects one printer to a network for all employees to share.

SOHO users often work with basic business software such as word processing and spreadsheet programs that assist with document preparation and finances (Figure 1-27b). They are likely to use other industry-specific types of software. An auto parts store, for example, will have software that allows for looking up parts, taking orders and payments, and updating inventory.

Figure 1-27a (Web access)

Figure 1-27b (spreadsheet program)

Figure 1-27 People with a home office and employees in small offices typically use a personal computer for some or all of their duties.

Mobile User

Today, businesses and schools are expanding to serve people across the country and around the world. Thus, increasingly more employees and students are **mobile users**, who work on a mobile computer or device while away from a main office, home office, or school (Figure 1-28). Some examples of mobile users are sales representatives, real estate agents, insurance agents, meter readers, package delivery people, journalists, and students.

notebook computer

Tablet PC

handheld game console

smart phone

Figure 1-28 Mobile users have a variety of computers and devices so that they can work, do homework, send messages, connect to the Internet, or play games while away from a wired connection.

Mobile users often have a mobile computer and/or mobile device. With these computers and devices, the mobile user can connect to other computers on a network or the Internet, often wirelessly accessing services such as e-mail and the Web. Mobile users can transfer information between their mobile devices and another computer. For entertainment, the mobile user plays video games on a handheld game console and listens to music or watches movies on a portable media player.

The mobile user works with basic business software such as word processing and spreadsheet software. With presentation software, the mobile user can create and deliver presentations to a large audience by connecting a mobile computer or device to a video projector that displays the presentation on a full screen.

Power User

Another category of user, called a **power user**, requires the capabilities of a powerful desktop computer, called a workstation. Examples of power users include engineers, scientists, architects, desktop publishers, and graphic artists (Figure 1-29). Power users typically work with multimedia, combining text, graphics, audio, and video into one application. These users need computers with extremely fast processors because of the nature of their work.

The power user's workstation contains industry-specific software. For example, engineers and architects use software to draft and design floor plans, mechanical assemblies, or vehicles. A desktop publisher uses software to prepare marketing literature. A graphic artist uses software to create sophisticated drawings. This software usually is expensive because of its specialized design.

Power users exist in all types of businesses. Some also work at home. Their computers typically have network connections and Internet access.

Figure 1-29 This graphic artist uses a powerful computer to develop computer games.

Enterprise User

An enterprise has hundreds or thousands of employees or customers that work in or do business with offices across a region, the country, or the world. Each employee or customer who uses a computer in the enterprise is an **enterprise user** (Figure 1-30).

Many large companies use the words, **enterprise computing**, to refer to the huge network of computers that meets their diverse computing needs. The network facilitates communications among employees at all locations. Users access the network through desktop computers, mobile computers, and mobile devices.

Enterprises use computers and the computer network to process high volumes of transactions in a single day. Although they may differ in size and in the products or services offered, all generally use computers for basic business activities. For example, they bill millions of customers or prepare payroll for thousands of employees. Some enterprises use blogs to open communications among employees and/or customers.

Enterprises typically have e-commerce Web sites, allowing customers and vendors to conduct business online. The Web site showcases products, services, and other company information. Customers, vendors, and other interested parties can access this information on the Web.

The marketing department in an enterprise uses desktop publishing software to prepare marketing literature. The accounting department uses software for accounts receivable, accounts payable, billing, general ledger, and payroll activities.

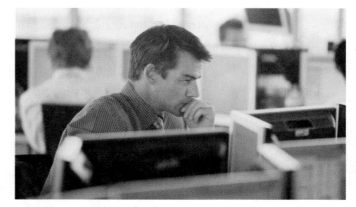

Figure 1-30 An enterprise can have hundreds or thousands of users in offices across a region, the country, or the world.

Enterprise Computing
For more information, visit the Computer Concepts CourseMate Web site at www.cengagebrain.com, navigate to the Chapter 1 Web Link resource for this book, and then click Enterprise Computing.

Enterprise users work with word processing, spreadsheet, database, and presentation software. They also may use calendar programs to post their schedules on the network. And, they might use smart phones or other mobile devices to maintain contact information. E-mail programs and Web browsers enable communications among employees, vendors, and customers.

Many employees of enterprises today telecommute. **Telecommuting** is a work arrangement in which employees work away from a company's standard workplace and often communicate with the office through the computer. Employees who telecommute have flexible work schedules so that they can combine work and personal responsibilities, such as child care.

Computer Applications in Society

The computer has changed society today as much as the industrial revolution changed society in the eighteenth and nineteenth centuries.

People interact directly with computers in fields such as education, finance, government, health care, science, publishing, travel, and manufacturing. In addition, they can reap the benefits from breakthroughs and advances in these fields. The following pages describe how computers have made a difference in people's interactions with these disciplines. Read Looking Ahead 1-1 for a look at how embedded computers may improve the quality of life.

↗ LOOKING AHEAD 1-1

Embedded Computers May Improve Quality of Life

The weather forecast may be as close as your fingertips if plans to integrate embedded computers in everyday objects become a reality. Researchers are envisioning an umbrella with an embedded cell phone in the handle that will dial and then download the local forecast. The handle will glow green for good weather and flash red for imminent storms.

Dancers can pin a small flower with an embedded motion-detecting computer to their clothes. When they move, the embedded computer senses action and then synchronizes the tempo of music to this movement. Other embedded computers woven into clothing can monitor heart and breathing rates.

Wearing hidden embedded computers can help the elderly and people recovering from accidents and surgeries monitor their walking stride and pace. When their steps are uneven, the embedded computer can sound a warning and perhaps prevent a fall. Other embedded computers can give subtle feedback on the quality of physical activity.

For more information, visit the Computer Concepts CourseMate Web site at www.cengagebrain.com, navigate to the Chapter 1 Looking Ahead resource for this book, and then click Embedded Computers.

Education

Education is the process of acquiring knowledge. In the traditional model, people learn from other people such as parents, teachers, and employers. Many forms of printed material such as books and manuals are used as learning tools. Today, educators also are turning to computers to assist with education (Figure 1-31).

Many schools and companies equip labs and classrooms with computers. Some schools require students to have a mobile computer or mobile device to access the school's network or Internet wirelessly.

Students use software to assist with learning or to complete assignments. To promote education by computer, many vendors offer substantial student discounts on software.

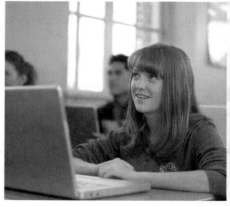

Figure 1-31 In some schools, students have mobile computers on their desks during classroom lectures.

Sometimes, the delivery of education occurs at one place while the learning occurs at other locations. For example, students can take a class on the Web. More than 70 percent of colleges offer distance learning classes. A few even offer entire degrees online.

Finance

Many people and companies use computers to help manage their finances. Some use finance software to balance checkbooks, pay bills, track personal income and expenses, manage investments, and evaluate financial plans. This software usually includes a variety of online services. For example, computer users can track investments and do online banking. With **online banking**, users access account balances, pay bills, and copy monthly transactions from the bank's computer right into their computers (Figure 1-32).

Investors often use **online investing** to buy and sell stocks and bonds — without using a broker. With online investing, the transaction fee for each trade usually is much less than when trading through a broker.

Figure 1-32 An online banking Web site.

Government

A government provides society with direction by making and administering policies. To provide citizens with up-to-date information, most government offices have Web sites. People access government Web sites to file taxes, apply for permits and licenses, pay parking tickets, buy stamps, report crimes, apply for financial aid, and renew vehicle registrations and driver's licenses.

Employees of government agencies use computers as part of their daily routine. Military and other agency officials use the U.S. Department of Homeland Security's network of information about domestic security threats to help protect our nation. Law enforcement officers have online access to the FBI's National Crime Information Center (NCIC) through in-vehicle computers, fingerprint readers, and mobile devices (Figure 1-33). The NCIC contains more than 52 million missing persons and criminal records, including names, fingerprints, parole/probation records, mug shots, and other information.

Figure 1-33 Law enforcement officials have in-vehicle computers and mobile devices to access emergency, missing person, and criminal records in computer networks in local, state, and federal agencies.

Health Care

Nearly every area of health care uses computers. Whether you are visiting a family doctor for a regular checkup, having lab work or an outpatient test, or being rushed in for emergency surgery, the medical staff around you will be using computers for various purposes:

- Doctors use the Web and medical software to assist with researching and diagnosing health conditions.
- Doctors use e-mail to correspond with patients.
- Pharmacists use computers to file insurance claims.
- Robots deliver medication to nurse stations in hospitals.
- Hospitals and doctors use computers and mobile devices to maintain and access patient records.

- Computers and computerized devices assist doctors, nurses, and technicians with medical tests (Figure 1-34).
- Computers monitor patients' vital signs in hospital rooms and at home.
- Surgeons implant computerized devices, such as pacemakers, that allow patients to live longer.
- Surgeons use computer-controlled devices to provide them with greater precision during operations, such as for laser eye surgery and robot-assisted heart surgery.

Figure 1-34 Doctors, nurses, technicians, and other medical staff use computers and computerized devices to assist with medical tests.

Two forms of long-distance health care are telemedicine and telesurgery. Through **telemedicine**, health-care professionals in separate locations conduct live conferences on the computer. For example, a doctor at one location can have a conference with a doctor at another location to discuss a bone X-ray. Live images of each doctor, along with the X-ray, are displayed on each doctor's computer.

With **telesurgery**, a surgeon performs an operation on a patient who is not located in the same physical room as the surgeon. Telesurgery enables surgeons to direct robots to perform an operation via computers connected to a high-speed network.

Science

All branches of science, from biology to astronomy to meteorology, use computers to assist them with collecting, analyzing, and modeling data. Scientists also use the Internet to communicate with colleagues around the world.

Breakthroughs in surgery, medicine, and treatments often result from scientists' use of computers. Tiny computers now imitate functions of the central nervous system, retina of the eye, and cochlea of the ear. A cochlear implant allows a deaf person to listen. Electrodes implanted in the brain stop tremors associated with Parkinson's disease. Cameras small enough to swallow — sometimes called a camera pill — take pictures inside your body to detect polyps, cancer, and other abnormalities (Figure 1-35).

How a Camera Pill Works

Step 1

A patient swallows a tiny capsule that contains a miniature disposable camera, lights, a transmitter, and batteries. The camera is positioned at the clear end of the capsule.

Step 3

The doctor transfers the data on the recording device to a computer so that it can be processed and analyzed.

Step 2

As the capsule moves through the inside of the patient's body, the camera snaps about 50,000 pictures, which are transmitted to a recording device worn as a belt on the patient's waist.

 Figure 1-35 This figure shows how a camera pill works.

Publishing

Publishing is the process of making works available to the public. These works include books, magazines, newspapers, music, film, and video. Special software assists graphic designers in developing pages that include text, graphics, and photos; artists in composing and enhancing songs; filmmakers in creating and editing film; and journalists and mobile users in capturing and modifying video clips.

Many publishers make their works available online (Figure 1-36). Some Web sites allow you to copy the work, such as a book or music, to your desktop computer, mobile computer, smart phone, or other mobile device.

Figure 1-36 Many magazine and newspaper publishers make the content of their publications available online.

Travel

Many vehicles manufactured today include some type of onboard navigation system. Some mobile users prefer to carry specialized handheld navigation devices (Figure 1-37).

In preparing for a trip, you may need to reserve a car, hotel, or flight. Many Web sites offer these services to the public. For example, you can order airline tickets on the Web. If you plan to drive somewhere and are unsure of the road to take to your destination, you can print directions and a map from the Web.

Figure 1-37 This handheld navigation device gives users turn-by-turn voice-prompted directions to a destination.

Manufacturing

Computer-aided manufacturing (**CAM**) refers to the use of computers to assist with manufacturing processes such as fabrication and assembly. Often, robots carry out processes in a CAM environment. CAM is used by a variety of industries, including oil drilling, power generation, food production, and automobile manufacturing. Automobile plants, for example, have an entire line of industrial robots that assemble a car (Figure 1-38).

Figure 1-38 Automotive factories use industrial robots to weld car bodies.

Instructions: Find the true statement below. Then, rewrite the remaining false statements so that they are true.

1. A desktop computer is a portable, personal computer designed to fit on your lap.

2. A personal computer contains a processor, memory, and one or more input, output, and storage devices.

3. Each enterprise user spends time on the computer for different reasons that include personal financial management, Web access, communications, and entertainment.

4. A home user requires the capabilities of a workstation or other powerful computer.

5. Mainframes are the fastest, most powerful computers — and the most expensive.

6. With embedded computers, users access account balances, pay bills, and copy monthly transactions from the bank's computer right into their personal computers.

Quiz Yourself Online: To further check your knowledge of pages 14 through 27, visit the Computer Concepts CourseMate Web site at www.cengagebrain.com, navigate to the Chapter 1 Quiz Yourself resource for this book, and then click Objectives 6 – 8.

Chapter Summary

Chapter 1 introduced you to basic computer concepts. You learned about the components of a computer. Next, the chapter discussed networks, the Internet, and computer software. The many different categories of computers, computer users, and computer applications in society also were presented.

This chapter is an overview. Many of the terms and concepts introduced will be discussed further in later chapters. For a history of hardware and software developments, read the Timeline feature that follows this chapter.

Computer Usage @ Work

Transportation

What is transportation like without computers? Delivery drivers use clipboards to hold their records. Human navigators use paper maps to track routes for pilots. Ship captains rely solely on experience to navigate through shallow waters. Today, the transportation industry relies heavily on computer usage.

As presented in this chapter, many vehicles include onboard navigation systems to help you navigate from one location to another. These systems also usually provide other services such as dispatching roadside assistance, unlocking the driver's side door if you lock the keys in your vehicle, and tracking the vehicle if it is stolen.

The shipping and travel industries identify items during transport using bar codes, which are identification codes that consist of lines and spaces of different lengths. When you ship a package, the shipping company, such as UPS or FedEx, places a bar code on the package to indicate its destination to a computer. Because a package might travel to its destination by way of several trucks, trains, and airplanes, computers automatically route the package as efficiently as possible.

When you travel by airplane, baggage handling systems ensure that your luggage reaches its destination on time. When you check in your baggage at the airport, a bar code identifies the airplane on which the bags should be placed. If you change planes, automated baggage handling systems route your bags to connecting flights with very little, if any, human intervention. When the bags reach their destination, they are routed automatically to the baggage carousel in the airport's terminal building.

Pilots of high-technology commercial, military, and space aircraft today work in a glass cockpit, which features computerized instrumentation, navigation, communication, weather reports, and an autopilot. The electronic flight information shown on high-resolution displays is designed to reduce pilot workload, decrease fatigue, and enable pilots to concentrate on flying safely.

Boats and ships also are equipped with computers that include detailed electronic maps, help the captain navigate, as well as calculate the water depth and provide a layout of the underwater surface so that the captain can avoid obstructions.

As you travel the roadways, airways, and waterways, bear in mind that computers often are responsible for helping you to reach your destination as quickly and safely as possible.

For more information, visit the Computer Concepts CourseMate Web site at www.cengagebrain.com, navigate to the Chapter 1 Computer Usage @ Work resource for this book, and then click Transportation.

Companies on the Cutting Edge

APPLE Innovative Industry Products

Apple recently sold a record 5.2 million of its latest iPhone models in one quarter, establishing the company's appeal to both consumer and corporate cell phone users. Apple is noted for introducing innovative products, starting with the Apple II, which was the first mass-marketed personal computer, in 1977 and the Macintosh, which featured a graphical user interface, in 1984.

Steve Jobs and Steve Wozniak founded Apple in 1976 when they marketed the Apple I, a circuit board they had developed in Jobs's garage. Under Jobs's direction as CEO, Apple developed the OS X operating system; iLife for working with photos, music, videos, and Web sites; and iWork, a collection of business programs. Apple also is leading the digital media revolution with its iPod portable media players, iPad tablet computer, and iTunes online store, which is the most popular Web site selling music. More than 10 million downloads occur each day from Apple's App Store, for a total download count exceeding 7 billion.

AMAZON Retailer Focused on Consumers

Online shoppers can find practically any product they desire on Amazon.com. Billing itself as the "Earth's most customer-centric company," it offers books, movies, electronics, clothing, toys, and many other items.

Jeff Bezos founded Amazon in 1995 knowing that book lovers would gravitate toward a Web site offering the convenience of browsing through millions of book titles in one sitting. He fulfilled orders for customers in every U.S. state and 45 additional countries during the first 30 days of business, all shipped from his Seattle-area garage.

The company has grown to permit third parties to sell products on its Web site. Its Kindle portable reader wirelessly downloads more than 450,000 books along with blogs, magazines, and newspapers to a high-resolution electronic paper display. Recently, it launched Kindle Singles, which are Kindle books with up to 30,000 words, the equivalent of two chapters of a typical book.

For more information, visit the Computer Concepts CourseMate Web site at www.cengagebrain.com and then navigate to the Chapter 1 Companies on the Cutting Edge resource for this book.

Technology Trailblazers

BILL GATES Microsoft Founder

When Bill Gates stepped down from his day-to-day activities at Microsoft in 2008, his action marked the end of an era that shaped the computer world. He remains the company's chairman and advisor, but he now devotes much of his time directing the Bill & Melinda Gates Foundation, a philanthropic organization working to help people worldwide lead healthy, productive lives. His foundation currently is awarding $3 billion in grants to improve education and graduation rates via technology, with an emphasis on online learning.

Gates learned to program computers when he was 13 years old. Early in his career, he developed the BASIC programming language for the MITS Altair, one of the first microcomputers. He founded Microsoft in 1975 with Paul Allen, and five years later they licensed the first operating system, called PC-DOS, to IBM for $80,000. This decision to license, rather than sell, the software is considered one of the wisest business decisions Gates ever made. Today, Microsoft's Windows and Office products dominate the software market.

TOM ANDERSON MySpace Cofounder and President

Having more than 11 million friends is all in a day's work for Tom Anderson, the current president and one of the founders of MySpace, one of the world's largest online social networks. Every MySpace account includes Anderson as a default first friend who is invited to view each personal network.

When Anderson's own rock group failed, he needed a place to post his songs. He started MySpace in 2003 with his friend, Chris DeWolfe, as a free tool to help musicians promote their songs and allow music lovers to create their own Web pages devoted to sharing their favorite music with like-minded admirers. Two years later they sold the business to Rupert Murdoch's News Corporation for $580 million. Anderson graduated from the University of California – Los Angeles in 2001 with a master's degree in film and from the University of California – Berkeley in 1998 with a bachelor's degree in English and rhetoric.

For more information, visit the Computer Concepts CourseMate Web site at www.cengagebrain.com and then navigate to the Chapter 1 Technology Trailblazers resource for this book.

Chapter Review

The Chapter Review reinforces the main concepts presented in this chapter.

To listen to an audio version of this Chapter Review, visit the Computer Concepts CourseMate Web site at www.cengagebrain.com and then navigate to the Chapter 1 Chapter Review resource for this book.

1. **Why Is Computer Literacy Vital to Success in Today's World?** **Computer literacy**, also called digital literacy, involves having current knowledge and understanding of computers and their uses. As computers become an increasingly important part of daily living, many people believe that computer literacy is vital to success. Because the requirements that determine computer literacy change as technology changes, you must keep up with these changes to remain computer literate.

2. **List and Describe the Five Components of a Computer.** A **computer** is an electronic device, operating under the control of instructions stored in its own memory, that can accept data, process the data according to specified rules, produce results, and store the results for future use. The electric, electronic, and mechanical components of a computer, or **hardware**, include input devices, output devices, a system unit, storage devices, and communications devices. An **input device** allows you to enter data or instructions into a computer. An **output device** conveys information to one or more people. The **system unit** is a case that contains the electronic components of a computer that are used to process data. A **storage device** records and/or retrieves items to and from **storage media**. A **communications device** enables a computer to send and receive data, instructions, and information to and from one or more computers.

3. **What Are the Advantages and Disadvantages That Users Experience When Working with Computers?** A **user** is anyone who communicates with a computer or utilizes the information it generates. Advantages of using a computer include speed, reliability, consistency, storage, and communications. The disadvantages include violation of privacy, public safety, impact on the labor force, health risks, and impact on the environment.

Visit the Computer Concepts CourseMate Web site at www.cengagebrain.com, navigate to the Chapter 1 Quiz Yourself resource for this book, and then click Objectives 1 – 3.

4. **How Are the Internet and World Wide Web Used?** The Internet is a worldwide collection of networks that connects millions of businesses, government agencies, educational institutions, and individuals. People use the Internet to communicate with and meet other people; conduct research and access information and news; shop for goods and services; bank and invest; participate in online training; engage in entertaining activities; download music and videos; share information, photos, and videos; and to access and interact with Web applications. The **Web**, short for World Wide Web, contains billions of documents called Web pages.

5. **What Are the Differences between System Software and Application Software?** **Software**, also called a **program**, is a series of related instructions, organized for a common purpose, that tells the computer what tasks to perform and how to perform them. The two categories of software are system software and application software. **System software** consists of the programs that control or maintain the operations of a computer and its devices. Two types of system software are the **operating system**, which coordinates activities among computer hardware devices, and **utility programs**, which perform maintenance-type tasks usually related to managing a computer, its devices, or its programs. **Application software** consists of programs designed to make users more productive and/or assist them with personal tasks. Popular application software includes a Web browser, word processing software, spreadsheet software, database software, and presentation software.

Visit the Computer Concepts CourseMate Web site at www.cengagebrain.com, navigate to the Chapter 1 Quiz Yourself resource for this book, and then click Objectives 4 – 5.

6. **What Are the Differences among the Types, Sizes, and Functions in the Following Categories: Personal Computers (Desktop), Mobile Computers and Mobile Devices, Game Consoles, Servers, Mainframes, Supercomputers, and Embedded Computers?** A **personal computer** is a computer that can perform all of its input, processing, output, and storage activities by itself. A **mobile computer** is a personal computer that you can carry from place to place, and a **mobile device** is a computing device small enough to hold in your hand. A game console is a mobile computing device designed for single-player or multiplayer video games. A **server** controls access to the hardware, software, and other resources on a network and provides a centralized storage area for programs, data, and information. A **mainframe** is a large, expensive, powerful computer that can handle hundreds or thousands of connected users simultaneously and can store huge amounts of data, instructions, and information. A **supercomputer** is the fastest, most powerful, and most expensive computer and is used for applications requiring complex, sophisticated mathematical calculations. An **embedded computer** is a special-purpose computer that functions as a component in a larger product.

7. **How Do the Various Types of Computer Users Interact with Computers?** Computer users can be separated into five categories: home user, small office/home office user, mobile user, power user, and enterprise user. A **home user** is a family member who uses a computer for a variety of reasons, such as personal financial management, Web access, communications, and entertainment. A **small office/home office** (**SOHO**) includes any company with fewer than 50 employees or a self-employed individual who works from home and uses basic business software and sometimes industry-specific software. **Mobile users** are employees and students who work on a computer while away from a main office, home office, or school. A **power user** can exist in all types of businesses and uses powerful computers to work with industry-specific software. An **enterprise user** works in or interacts with a company with many employees and uses a computer and computer network that processes high volumes of transactions in a single day.

8. **How Does Society Use Computers in Education, Finance, Government, Health Care, Science, Publishing, Travel, and Manufacturing?** In education, students use computers and software to assist with learning or take distance learning classes. In finance, people use computers for **online banking** to access information and **online investing** to buy and sell stocks and bonds. Government offices have Web sites to provide citizens with up-to-date information, and government employees use computers as part of their daily routines. In health care, computers are used to maintain patient records, assist doctors with medical tests and research, file insurance claims, provide greater precision during operations, and as implants. All branches of science use computers to assist with collecting, analyzing, and modeling data and to communicate with scientists around the world. Publishers use computers to assist in developing pages and make their works available online. Many vehicles use some type of online navigation system to help people travel more quickly and safely. Manufacturers use **computer-aided manufacturing** (**CAM**) to assist with manufacturing processes.

Visit the Computer Concepts CourseMate Web site at www.cengagebrain.com, navigate to the Chapter 1 Quiz Yourself resource for this book, and then click Objectives 6 – 8.

Key Terms

You should know the Key Terms. The list below helps focus your study.

To see an example of and a definition for each term, and to access current and additional information from the Web, visit the Computer Concepts CourseMate Web site at www.cengagebrain.com and then navigate to the Chapter 1 Key Terms resource for this book.

application software (12)	FAQ (11)	network (8)	social networking
blog (10)	game console (18)	notebook computer (16)	Web site (10)
camera phone (17)	graphical user interface	online (8)	software (11)
communications device (6)	(GUI) (11)	online banking (25)	storage device (6)
computer (3)	green computing (7)	online investing (25)	storage media (6)
computer literacy (3)	handheld computer (17)	online social network (10)	supercomputer (19)
computer-aided	hardware (4)	operating system (11)	system software (11)
manufacturing (CAM)	home user (20)	output device (5)	system unit (6)
(27)	information (4)	PDA (17)	Tablet PC (16)
convergence (14)	information processing	personal computer (15)	telecommuting (24)
CPU (central processing	cycle (4)	picture message (17)	telemedicine (26)
unit) (6)	input device (4)	podcast (10)	telesurgery (26)
data (4)	installing (12)	portable media	text message (17)
desktop computer (16)	instant message (17)	player (17)	Ultra-Mobile PC (UMPC)
developer (13)	Internet (8)	power user (23)	(17)
digital camera (18)	Internet-enabled (16)	processor (6)	user (7)
digital literacy (3)	laptop computer (16)	program (11)	utility program (12)
e-book (17)	mainframe (19)	programmer (13)	video message (17)
e-book reader (17)	memory (6)	resources (8)	video phone (17)
embedded computer (19)	microblog (10)	run (12)	Web (10)
enterprise computing	mobile computer (16)	server (19)	Web 2.0 (10)
(23)	mobile device (16)	small office/home office	Web application (10)
enterprise user (23)	mobile users (22)	(SOHO) (22)	Web page (10)
execute (12)	netbook (16)	smart phone (17)	Web site (10)

Checkpoint

The Checkpoint exercises test your knowledge of the chapter concepts. The page number containing the answer appears in parentheses after each exercise.

To complete the Checkpoint exercises interactively, visit the Computer Concepts CourseMate Web site at www.cengagebrain.com and then navigate to the Chapter 1 Checkpoint resource for this book.

Multiple Choice Select the best answer.

1. Computer literacy, also known as digital literacy, involves having a current knowledge and understanding of _____. (3)
 a. computer programming
 b. computers and their uses
 c. computer repair
 d. all of the above

2. _____ is/are a collection of unprocessed items, which can include text, numbers, images, audio, and video. (4)
 a. Data b. Instructions
 c. Programs d. Information

3. Millions of people worldwide join online communities, each called _____, that encourage members to share their interests, ideas, stories, photos, music, and videos with other registered users. (10)
 a. a podcast
 b. enterprise computing
 c. a social networking Web site or online social network
 d. a blog

4. _____ consists of the programs that control or maintain the operations of the computer and its devices. (11)
 a. A graphical user interface (GUI)
 b. A communications device
 c. System software
 d. Application software

5. Two types of _____ are desktop computers and notebook computers. (15)
 a. servers
 b. supercomputers
 c. mainframe computers
 d. personal computers

6. Five popular types of _____ are smart phones, PDAs, handheld computers, portable media players, and digital cameras. (17)
 a. mobile devices
 b. notebook computers
 c. desktop computers
 d. tower computers

7. A(n) _____ message is a real-time Internet communication, where you exchange messages with other connected users. (17)
 a. text b. instant
 c. picture d. video

8. Many large companies use the word(s), _____, to refer to the huge network of computers that meets their diverse computing needs. (23)
 a. information technology
 b. telecommuting
 c. enterprise computing
 d. multimedia

Matching Match the terms with their definitions.

_____ 1. information processing cycle (4)

_____ 2. processor (6)

_____ 3. storage device (6)

_____ 4. portable media player (17)

_____ 5. digital camera (18)

a. records (writes) and/or retrieves (reads) items to and from storage media

b. mobile device on which you can store, organize, and play digital media

c. fastest, most powerful computer — and the most expensive

d. electronic component that interprets and carries out the basic instructions for a computer

e. series of input, process, output, and storage activities

f. device that allows users to take pictures and store the photographed images digitally, instead of on traditional film

Short Answer Write a brief answer to each of the following questions.

1. What does it mean to be computer literate? _____ What is a computer? _____

2. Describe two health risks posed by computers. _____ How might computers have a negative effect on the environment? _____

3. What are five common storage devices? _____ How are they different? _____

4. What is a Web application? _____ What are some features of a Web 2.0 site? _____

5. How is hardware different from software? _____ What are two types of system software and how are they used? _____

6. How do computers benefit individuals' health care? _____ How does telesurgery differ from telemedicine? _____

Problem Solving

The Problem Solving exercises extend your knowledge of the chapter concepts by seeking solutions to practical computer problems that you may encounter at home, school, or work. The Collaboration exercise should be completed with a team.

In the real world, practical problems often can be solved in multiple ways. Provide one solution to each of the following problems using available resources, such as articles on the Web or in print, blogs, podcasts, videos, television, user guides, other individuals, and electronics and computer stores. You may need to use multiple resources to obtain an answer. Present your solutions in the form requested by your instructor (brief report, presentation, discussion, or other means).

@ Home

1. **Incorrect Grade Report** Your grade report came in the mail today. On the grade report, your grade point average (GPA) is not what you expect. After computing it manually, you discover that the GPA on your grade report is incorrect. What might be causing the error?

2. **Suspicious Charges** Your credit card company called to inform you that your account has a suspicious charge. Upon further investigation, you realize the charge does not belong to you. What steps will you take to correct the problem?

3. **Problematic Player** After charging your portable media player overnight, you turn it on only to find that it is reporting a low battery. Seconds later, it shuts off automatically. What might be wrong?

4. **Inaccessible Media** You insert an optical disc with digital photos from your most recent family vacation and discover that your computer will not read the optical disc. What might be wrong?

@ Work

5. **Insufficient Disk Space** Recently, you purchased a USB flash drive that you plan to use to store work-related files. When you attempt to store a file on the USB flash drive, the computer displays an error message indicating that the file will not fit. How could a brand new USB flash drive not have enough room to store the first file you attempted to store on it?

6. **Power Outage** The power in your office has been out for the last two hours and has just come back on. When you attempt to start your computer by pressing the power button, nothing happens. What is your next step before calling technical support?

7. **Incorrect Login Credentials** Upon returning to the office from a well-deserved two-week vacation, you turn on your computer. Upon entering your user name and password, an error message appears stating that your password is incorrect. What are your next steps?

8. **Software Installation** You are attempting to install a program on your office computer. After inserting the installation disc and specifying that you would like to begin the installation, your computer appears to begin installing the software. Halfway through the installation process, an error message appears stating that you must have administrative privileges to perform the installation. Why were you not informed immediately upon beginning the installation? What are your next steps?

Collaboration

9. **Computers in Transportation** Your project team has been accepted to present a business proposal to a group of potential investors. Because the presentation will take place in San Francisco, CA, you will need to transport people and ship some materials to that location. Form a team of three people and determine how to use technology to ship materials and how to make travel arrangements. One team member should research the steps required to use a Web site to make flight reservations, one team member should determine the steps necessary to print a UPS shipping label from their computer and track the package while it is en route, and another team member should find directions from San Francisco International Airport to a nearby hotel.

Learn How To

The Learn How To activities step you through fundamental technology skills when using a computer. The Learn How To exercises enable you to become more proficient with these skills.

Premium Activity: To relate this Learn How To activity to your everyday life, see a visual demonstration of the activity, and complete a short assessment, visit the Computer Concepts CourseMate Web site at www.cengagebrain.com and then navigate to the Chapter 1 Learn How To resource for this book.

Learn How To 1: Create and Use Your Own Blog

A blog can contain any information you wish to place in it. Originally, blogs consisted of Web addresses, so that an individual or group with a specific interest could direct others to useful places on the Web. Today, blogs contain addresses, thoughts, diaries, and anything else a person or group wants to share.

Once you have created a blog, you can update it. A variety of services available on the Web can help you create and maintain your blog. One widely used service is called Blogger. To create a blog using Blogger, complete the following steps:

1. Start your Web browser, type `blogger.com` in the Address bar, and then press the ENTER key to display the Blogger home page (Figure 1-39).
2. Click the CREATE A BLOG button on the Blogger home page.
3. Enter the data required on the 'Create Blogger Account' page. Your e-mail address and password will allow you to change and manage your

Figure 1-39

blog. Your Display name is the name that will be shown on the blog as the author of the material on the blog. Many people use their own names, but others use pseudonyms as their "pen names" so that they are not readily identifiable.
4. Click the Continue arrow and then enter your Blog title and Blog address. These are the names and addresses everyone will use to view your blog.
5. Click the Continue arrow to display the 'Choose a template' screen.
6. Choose a template for your blog and then click the Continue arrow.
7. Your blog will be created for you. When you see the 'Your blog has been created!' screen, click the START BLOGGING arrow.
8. From the screen that is displayed, you can post items for your blog, specify settings, change the layout, and view your blog.
9. When you have posted all your information, click the Sign out link at the top right of the screen. You will be logged out.
10. To edit your blog and add or change information on it, visit the Blogger home page and sign in by entering your user name and password. You will be able to post to your blog.
11. Others can view your blog by entering its address in the browser's Address bar and then pressing the ENTER key.

Exercises

1. Start your Web browser and visit blogger.com. Click the 'Take a quick tour' link and go through all the screens that explain about a blog. What did you learn that you did not know? What type of blog do you find most compelling — a group or an individual blog? Why? Submit your answers to your instructor.

2. Optional: Create your own blog. Carefully name it and begin your posts at this time. What is your blog name and address? What is its primary purpose? Is it an individual or group blog? Write a paragraph containing the answers to these questions and any other information you feel is pertinent. Submit this paragraph to your instructor.

Learn How To 2: Use the Computer Concepts CourseMate Web Site for Discovering Computers Fundamentals

The Computer Concepts CourseMate Web site for Discovering Computers Fundamentals provides a variety of activities, exercises, and other resources. To use the site, you first establish a user name and password for your student account and then register this book. Perform the following steps to create a student account and register this book:

1. Start the Web browser.
2. Type www.cengagebrain.com in the Address bar of the Web browser and then press the ENTER key to display the CengageBrain home page.

3. If you do not have an account, follow the on-screen instructions to sign up for a new student account. If you already have an account, log in with your user name and password.

4. Register this book by entering its Access Code in the appropriate text box and then clicking the corresponding button.

5. To open the resources for this book, click the button corresponding to Computer Concepts CourseMate Web site for Discovering Computers.

Exercise

1a. After creating a student account and registering this book as described in the steps above, start your Web browser, type www.cengagebrain.com in the Address bar of the browser, and then press the ENTER key to display the CengageBrain home page.

1b. Log in to your student account with your user name and password.

1c. Open the resources for this book by clicking the button corresponding to Computer Concepts CourseMate Web site for Discovering Computers.

1d. Select Chapter 1 and then click each resource listed below the chapter title to display the content associated with the selected resource.

1e. Write a report that describes the use of each of the Chapter 1 resources for this book. Which resources do you think will prove the most valuable to you when using the book and the Web site? Why? Submit your report to your instructor.

Learn It Online

The Learn It Online exercises are interactive Web exercises designed to reinforce and expand your understanding of the chapter concepts. The descriptions below briefly summarize each exercise.

To complete the Learn It Online exercises, visit the Computer Concepts CourseMate Web site at www.cengagebrain.com, navigate to the Chapter 1 resources for this book, click the link for the exercise you want to complete, and then read the instructions.

1 At the Movies — Computer History in a Barn
Watch a movie to tour the Digibarn Computer Museum and then answer questions about the movie.

2 Student Edition Labs — Using Input Devices and Using Windows
Enhance your understanding and knowledge about input devices and the Windows operating system by completing the Using Input Devices and Using Windows Labs.

3 Practice Test
Take a multiple choice test that checks your knowledge of the chapter concepts and review the resulting study guide.

4 Who Wants To Be a Computer Genius²?
Play the Shelly Cashman Series version of this popular game by answering questions to find out if you are a computer genius. Panic buttons are available to provide assistance during game play.

5 Crossword Puzzle Challenge
Complete an interactive crossword puzzle to reinforce concepts presented in this chapter.

6 Windows Exercises
Step through the Windows 7 exercises to learn how to use help, improve mouse skills, and identify computer information.

7 Exploring Computer Careers
Read about a career as a computer salesperson, search for relevant employment advertisements, and then answer related questions.

8 Web Apps — Google Maps
Learn how to locate businesses in your area, view a location's surroundings via satellite, and find directions from one location to another using Google Maps.

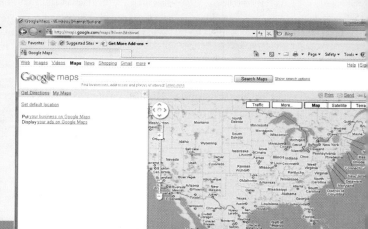

Web Research

The Web Research exercises broaden your understanding of the chapter concepts by presenting questions that require you to search the Web for answers.

1 Search Sleuth

Use one of the search engines listed in Figure 2-8 in Chapter 2 on page 65 or your own favorite search engine to find the answers to the following questions. Copy and paste the Web address from the Web page where you found the answer. Some questions may have more than one answer. If required, submit your answers to your instructor. (1) What company was the first to sell a USB flash drive? (2) What is the significance of the Universal symbol on Apple's Mac application programs? (3) Which retailers offer to dispose of old computers and other electronic products properly to help protect the environment? (4) What are three Illustrative Grant Commitments the Bill & Melinda Gates Foundation has made? (5) According to *Fortune*, at what company do MBA students most want to work when they graduate? (6) Who created the first set of icons for the Macintosh computer? What sound does her Clarus the Dogcow make? (7) What company manufactured the first notebook computer, the UltraLite, in 1989?

2 Green Computing

Computer usage requires electricity, whether to power the system unit and monitor, recharge batteries, or print. In addition, the computer manufacturing process depletes natural resources and often uses toxic chemicals. As you learned in this chapter, many environmentally conscious people practice green computing by attempting to reduce electricity and environmental waste. Examine your computing practices, and determine 10 ways that you can use less power on your computing equipment at home, work, and school. Consider how often you use the printer and the types of documents you print. Examine your monitor, system unit, and printer. Do you see any notation indicating they are environmentally sound? Do they hibernate or go into a power save mode when not being used? Write a 50-word summary of the green computing practices in your life.

3 Social Networking

One of the more popular social networking Web sites is Facebook. This quickly growing service differentiates itself from other online social networks by having widespread privacy controls. In addition, its development platform, called f8, allows developers to create programs (called applications) that users can add to a Web page. Hostels, for example, lets world travelers research and rate hostels and includes photos and descriptions. Visit the Facebook site (facebook.com), click the About link at the bottom of the page, and then read about Facebook's features. What are three of Facebook's top features? What information is given in the recent Facebook blog posts? Visit the AppRate Web site (apprate.com) and then summarize three Facebook application reviews and ratings.

4 Blogs

Blogs profiling the music industry discuss new technologies, legal issues, podcasts, and business news. Visit the CNET blog (blogs.cnet.com) and then read and summarize at least three of the articles in the Most Recent Posts section. Locate the Crave, Gaming and Culture, and Green Tech features and then read and summarize at least one story from each blog. Then visit the iLounge (ilounge.com) Web site and read reviews of at least three new products for the iPhone. Would you purchase any of the products discussed? What books and buyer's guides are available to download from the Library? Which iPod cases and speakers received favorable reviews? Read and summarize at least three stories and associated comments in the News section.

5 Ethics in Action

The Internet has increased the ease with which students can plagiarize material for research paper assignments. Teachers are using online services, such as Turnitin and PlagiarismDetect.com, to help detect plagiarized papers and to help students understand how to cite sources correctly. Visit the Turnitin Web site (turnitin.com) and then write a summary of how this service is used. How does this service attempt to prevent plagiarism through the Turnitin Write Cycle? How prevalent is plagiarism on your campus? What is your school's official policy on disciplining students who submit plagiarized papers? Does your school have an honor code? If required, submit your summary to your instructor.

Special Feature

Timeline
Milestones in Computer History

Visit the Computer Concepts CourseMate Web site at www.cengagebrain.com and then navigate to the Timeline Feature resource for this book.

1937 Dr. John V. Atanasoff and Clifford Berry design and build the first electronic digital computer. Their machine, the Atanasoff-Berry-Computer, or ABC, provides the foundation for advances in electronic digital computers.

1945 John von Neumann poses in front of the electronic computer built at the Institute for Advanced Study. This computer and its von Neumann architecture served as the prototype for subsequent stored program computers worldwide.

1947 William Shockley, John Bardeen, and Walter Brattain invent the transfer resistance device, eventually called the transistor. The transistor would revolutionize computers, proving much more reliable than vacuum tubes.

1937 — **1943** — **1945** — **1946** — **1947** — **1951**

1943 During World War II, British scientist Alan Turing designs the Colossus, an electronic computer created for the military to break German codes. The computer's existence is kept secret until the 1970s.

1946 Dr. John W. Mauchly and J. Presper Eckert, Jr. complete work on the first large-scale electronic, general-purpose digital computer. The ENIAC (Electronic Numerical Integrator And Computer) weighs 30 tons, contains 18,000 vacuum tubes, occupies a 30 × 50 foot space, and consumes 160 kilowatts of power.

1951 The first commercially available electronic digital computer, the UNIVAC I (UNIVersal Automatic Computer), is introduced by Remington Rand. Public awareness of computers increases when the UNIVAC correctly predicts that Dwight D. Eisenhower will win the presidential election.

1952 Dr. Grace Hopper considers the concept of reusable software in her paper, "The Education of a Computer." The paper describes how to program a computer with symbolic notation instead of detailed machine language.

1957 The IBM 305 RAMAC computer is the first to use magnetic disk for external storage. The computer provides storage capacity similar to magnetic tape that previously was used but offers the advantage of semi-random access capability.

1959 More than 200 programming languages have been created.

1959 IBM introduces two smaller, desk-sized computers: the IBM 1401 for business and the IBM 1620 for scientists.

1957 FORTRAN (FORmula TRANslation), an efficient, easy-to-use programming language, is introduced by John Backus.

1952

1953

1957

1958

1959

1960

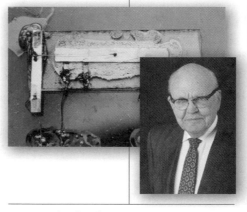

1953 Core memory, developed in the early 1950s, provides much larger storage capacity than vacuum tube memory.

1953 The IBM model 650 is one of the first widely used computers. The computer is so successful that IBM manufactures more than 1,000. IBM will dominate the mainframe market for the next decade.

1958 Jack Kilby of Texas Instruments invents the integrated circuit, which lays the foundation for high-speed computers and large-capacity memory. Computers built with transistors mark the beginning of the second generation of computer hardware.

1960 COBOL, a high-level business application language, is developed by a committee headed by Dr. Grace Hopper.

1965 Dr. John Kemeny of Dartmouth leads the development of the BASIC programming language.

1965 Digital Equipment Corporation (DEC) introduces the first minicomputer, the PDP-8. The machine is used extensively as an interface for time-sharing systems.

1968 In a letter to the editor titled, "GO TO Statements Considered Harmful," Dr. Edsger Dijkstra introduces the concept of structured programming, developing standards for constructing computer programs.

1968 Computer Science Corporation (CSC) becomes the first software company listed on the New York Stock Exchange.

1969 Under pressure from the industry, IBM announces that some of its software will be priced separately from the computer hardware, allowing software firms to emerge in the industry.

1969 The ARPANET network is established, which eventually grows to become the Internet.

1964 The number of computers has grown to 18,000. Third-generation computers, with their controlling circuitry stored on chips, are introduced. The IBM System/360 computer is the first family of compatible machines, merging science and business lines.

1968 Alan Shugart at IBM demonstrates the first regular use of an 8-inch floppy disk.

1964 IBM introduces the term word processing for the first time with its Magnetic Tape/Selectric Typewriter (MT/ST). The MT/ST was the first reusable storage medium that allowed typed material to be edited without having to retype the document.

1970 Fourth-generation computers, built with chips that use LSI (large-scale integration) arrive. While the chips used in 1965 contained up to 1,000 circuits, the LSI chip contains as many as 15,000.

1975 MITS, Inc. advertises one of the first microcomputers, the Altair. The Altair is sold in kits for less than $400 and within the first three months 4,000 orders are taken.

1979 The first public online information services, CompuServe and the Source, are founded.

1979 VisiCalc, a spreadsheet program written by Bob Frankston and Dan Bricklin, is introduced.

1981 The IBM PC is introduced, signaling IBM's entrance into the personal computer marketplace. The IBM PC quickly garners the largest share of the personal computer market and becomes the personal computer of choice in business.

1975 Ethernet, the first local area network (LAN), is developed at Xerox PARC (Palo Alto Research Center) by Robert Metcalfe.

1971 **1975** **1976** **1979** **1980** **1981**

1980 IBM offers Microsoft Corporation cofounder, Bill Gates, the opportunity to develop the operating system for the soon-to-be announced IBM personal computer. With the development of MS-DOS, Microsoft achieves tremendous growth and success.

1981 The first computer virus, Elk Cloner, is spread via Apple II floppy disks, which contained the operating system. A short rhyme would appear on the screen when the user pressed Reset after the 50th boot of an infected disk.

1971 Dr. Ted Hoff of Intel Corporation develops a microprocessor, or microprogrammable computer chip, the Intel 4004.

1976 Steve Jobs and Steve Wozniak build the first Apple computer. A subsequent version, the Apple II, is an immediate success. Adopted by elementary schools, high schools, and colleges, for many students, the Apple II is their first contact with the world of computers.

1980 Alan Shugart presents the Winchester hard disk, revolutionizing storage for personal computers.

1982 3,275,000 personal computers are sold, almost 3,000,000 more than in 1981.

3.275 Million

1982 Compaq, Inc. is founded to develop and market IBM-compatible PCs.

COMPAQ

1982 Hayes introduces the 300 bps smart modem. The modem is an immediate success.

Apple

1984 Apple introduces the Macintosh computer, which incorporates a unique, easy-to-learn, graphical user interface.

1984 Hewlett-Packard announces the first LaserJet printer for personal computers.

1982 **1983** **1984** **1986**

1983 Instead of choosing a person for its annual award, *TIME* magazine names the computer Machine of the Year for 1982, acknowledging the impact of computers on society.

Microsoft®

1986 Microsoft has public stock offering and raises approximately $61 million.

1983 Lotus Development Corporation is founded. Its spreadsheet software, Lotus 1-2-3, which combines spreadsheet, graphics, and database programs in one package, becomes the best-selling program for IBM personal computers.

WWW

1989 While working at CERN, Switzerland, Tim Berners-Lee invents the World Wide Web.

1991 Kodak announces the first digital SLR (single-lens reflex) camera. The Kodak DCS 100 is developed mostly for photojournalism purposes and stores the photos and batteries in a separate unit.

1989 Nintendo introduces the Game Boy, its first handheld game console.

1991 World Wide Web Consortium releases standards that describe a framework for linking documents on different computers.

1992

1991

1989

1988

1988 Microsoft surpasses Lotus Development Corporation to become the world's top software vendor.

1989 The Intel 486 becomes the world's first 1,000,000 transistor microprocessor. It executes 15,000,000 instructions per second — four times as fast as its predecessor, the 80386 chip.

1992 Microsoft releases Windows 3.1, the latest version of its Windows operating system. Windows 3.1 offers improvements such as TrueType fonts, multimedia capability, and object linking and embedding (OLE). In two months, 3,000,000 copies of Windows 3.1 are sold.

993 Several companies introduce mputers using the Pentium ocessor from Intel. The ntium chip contains 1 million transistors and capable of performing 2,000,000 instructions r second.

1994 Jim Clark and Marc Andreessen found Netscape and launch Netscape Navigator 1.0, a Web browser.

1994 Linus Torvalds creates the Linux kernel, a UNIX-like operating system that he releases free across the Internet for further enhancement by other programmers.

993 The U.S. Air Force mpletes the Global sitioning System by unching its 24th Navstar tellite into orbit. Today, GPS ceivers can be found in cars, tebook computers, and art phones.

1994 Apple introduces the first digital camera intended for consumers. The Apple QuickTake 100 is connected to home computers using a serial cable.

1993

1994

1993 Microsoft releases Microsoft Office 3 Professional, the first version of Microsoft Office for the Windows operating system.

1994 Yahoo!, a popular search engine and portal, is founded by two Stanford Ph.D. students as a way to keep track of their personal interests on the Internet. Currently, Yahoo! has approximately 12,000 employees and more than 500 million unique visitors to its Web site.

1993 The White House launches its Web site, which includes an interactive citizens' handbook and White House history and tours.

1994 Amazon is founded and later begins business as an online bookstore. Amazon eventually expands to sell products of all types and facilitates the buying and selling of new and used goods. Today, Amazon has approximately 17,000 employees.

SPECIAL FEATURE

1996 U.S. Robotics introduces the PalmPilot, an inexpensive user-friendly personal digital assistant (PDA).

1995 Sun Microsystems launches Java, an object-oriented programming language that allows users to write one program for a variety of computer platforms.

1996 Microsoft releases Windows NT 4.0, an operating system for client-server networks.

1996

1997

1995

1997 Intel introduces the Pentium II processor with 7.5 million transistors. The new processor, which incorporates MMX technology, processes video, audio, and graphics data more efficiently and supports programs such as movie editing, gaming, and more.

1995 Microsoft releases Windows 95, a major upgrade to its Windows operating system. Windows 95 consists of more than 10,000,000 lines of computer instructions developed by 300 person-years of effort.

1995 eBay, an online auction Web site, is founded. Providing an online venue for people to buy and sell goods, it quickly becomes the world's largest online marketplace as it approaches 100 million active users worldwide.

1997 Microsoft releases Internet Explorer 4.0 and seizes a key place in the Internet arena.

1998 Google files for incorporation and is now the most used search engine, capturing more than 60 percent of the market over other search engines.

1998 Apple Computer introduces the iMac, the next version of its popular Macintosh computer. The iMac wins customers with its futuristic design, see-through case, and easy setup.

1999 Microsoft introduces Office 2000, its premier productivity suite, offering new tools for users to create content and save it directly to a Web site without any file conversion or special steps.

1999 Open source software, such as the Linux operating system and the Apache Web server created by unpaid volunteers, begin to gain wide acceptance among computer users.

1999 Intel introduces the Pentium III processor. This processor succeeds the Pentium II and can process 3-D graphics more quickly. The Pentium III processor contains between 9.5 and 44 million transistors.

1998 **1999**

1998 E-commerce booms. Companies such as Amazon.com, Dell, and E*TRADE spur online shopping, allowing buyers to obtain a variety of goods and services.

1998 Microsoft ships Windows 98, an upgrade to Windows 95. Windows 98 offers improved Internet access, better system performance, and support for a new generation of hardware and software.

1999 Governments and businesses frantically work to make their computers Y2K (Year 2000) compliant, spending more than $500 billion worldwide.

2000 Shawn Fanning, 19, and his company, Napster, turn the music industry upside down by developing software that allows computer users to swap music files with one another without going through a centralized file server.

2001 Microsoft releases major operating system updates with Windows XP for personal computers and servers. Windows XP is significantly more reliable than previous versions, features a 32-bit computing architecture, and offers a new look and feel.

2001 Intel unveils its Pentium 4 chip with clock speeds starting at 1.4 GHz. The Pentium 4 includes 42 million transistors.

2000 Microsoft ships Windows 2000 and Windows Me. Windows 2000 offers improved behind-the-scenes security and reliability.

2001

2000

2000 E-commerce achieves mainstream acceptance. Annual e-commerce sales exceed $100 billion, and Internet advertising expenditures reach more than $5 billion.

2000 Telemedicine uses satellite technology and video conferencing to broadcast consultations and to perform distant surgeries. Robots are used for complex and precise tasks.

2001 Microsoft introduces Office XP, the next version of the world's leading suite of productivity software. Features include speech and handwriting recognition, smart tags, and task panes.

2001 Wikipedia, a free online encyclopedia, is introduced. Additional wikis begin to appear on the Internet, enabling people to share information in their areas of expertise. Although some might rely on wikis for research purposes, the content is not always verified for accuracy.

2000 Dot-com companies (Internet based) go out of business at a record pace — nearly one per day — as financial investors withhold funding due to the companies' unprofitability.

2002 After several years of negligible sales, the Tablet PC is reintroduced to meet the needs of a more targeted audience.

2003 Wireless computers and devices, such as keyboards, mouse devices, home networks, and wireless Internet access points become commonplace.

2002 Digital video cameras, DVD burners, easy-to-use video editing software, and improvements in storage capabilities allow the average computer user to create Hollywood-like videos with introductions, conclusions, rearranged scenes, music, and voice-over.

2003 Microsoft ships Office 2003, the latest version of its flagship Office suite. More than 400 million people in 175 nations and 70 languages are using a version of Office.

2002

2003

2002 Microsoft launches its .NET strategy, which is a new environment for developing and running software applications featuring ease of development of Web-based services.

2003 In an attempt to maintain their current business model of selling songs, the Recording Industry Association of America (RIAA) files more than 250 lawsuits against individual computer users who offer copyrighted music over peer-to-peer networks.

2002 DVD burners begin to replace CD burners (CD-RW). DVDs can store up to eight times as much data as CDs. Uses include storing home movies, music, photos, and backups.

2003 MySpace, an online social network, is founded. MySpace allows users to share information, photos, and videos, as well as stay in touch with their friends and make new friends. MySpace eventually grows to nearly 200 million users, making it one of the more popular and successful online social networks.

2002 Intel ships its revamped Pentium 4 chip with the 0.13 micron processor and Hyper-Threading (HT) Technology, operating at speeds of 3.06 GHz. This new development eventually will enable processors with a billion transistors to operate at 20 GHz.

2004 Companies such as RealNetworks, Microsoft, Sony, and Walmart stake out turf in the online music store business started by Apple Computer.

2004 USB flash drives become a cost-effective way to transport data and information from one computer to another.

USB flash drive

2004 Flat-panel LCD monitors overtake bulky CRT monitors as the popular choice of computer users.

2004 106 million, or 53 percent, of the 200 million online population in America accesses the Internet via broadband.

2004 The smart phone overtakes the PDA as the mobile device of choice.

2004 Major retailers begin requiring suppliers to include radio frequency identification (RFID) tags or microchips with antennas, which can be as small as one-third of a millimeter across, in the goods they sell.

2004 Facebook, an online social network originally available only to college students, is founded. Facebook eventually opens registration to all people and immediately grows to more than 110 million users with more than 10 billion photos, 30 million of which are uploaded daily.

facebook.

2004

2004 Linux, the open source operating system, makes major inroads into the server market as a viable alternative to Microsoft Windows Server 2003, Sun's Solaris, and the UNIX operating systems.

DVD
Linux

2004 Sony unveils its PlayStation Portable (PSP). This handheld game console is the first to use optical discs.

2004 Mozilla releases its first version of the Firefox Web browser. Firefox provides innovative features that enhance the Web browsing experience for users, including tabbed browsing and a Search box. Firefox quickly gains popularity and takes market share away from Microsoft's Internet Explorer.

2004 Apple Computer introduces the sleek iMac G5. The new computer's display device contains the system unit.

Video iPod

2005 Apple releases the latest version of its popular pocket-sized iPod portable media player. First it played songs, then photos, then podcasts, and now, in addition, up to 150 hours of music videos and television shows on a 2.5" color display.

2005 YouTube, an online community for video sharing, is founded. YouTube includes content such as home videos, movie previews, and clips from television shows. In November 2006, Google acquires YouTube.

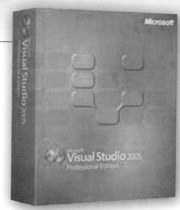

2005 Microsoft introduces Visual Studio 2005. The product includes Visual Basic, Visual C#, Visual J#, Visual C++, and SQL Server.

You Tube ™

Spyware
Spam Pharming
Phishing
Spim Spit

2005 Spam, spyware, phishing, pharming, spim, and spit take center stage, along with viruses, as major nuisances to the 801 million computer users worldwide.

2005

2005 Microsoft unveils Windows XP Media Center Edition 2005. This operating system focuses on delivering media content such as music, digital photos, movies, and television.

2005 Microsoft releases the Xbox 360, its latest game console. Features include the capability to play music, display photos, and network with computers and other Xbox gamers.

2005 Blogging and podcasting become mainstream methods for distributing information via the Web.

Blogging
Podcasting

2006 Sony launches its PlayStation 3. New features include a Blu-ray Disc player, high-definition capabilities, and always-on online connectivity.

2006 Microsoft and Mozilla release new versions of their respective Web browsers. Microsoft's Internet Explorer 7 and Mozilla's Firefox 2 offer easier browsing through the use of tabs and allow search capabilities directly from the toolbar.

2006 Web 2.0, a term coined in 2004, becomes a household term with the increase in popularity of online social networks, wikis, and Web applications.

2006 Text, picture, and video messaging continue to increase as popular communications methods. In addition to people sending informal messages to each other, businesses and other institutions use messaging to allow people to vote in polls, receive targeted advertisements, and view news updates.

2006 Nintendo Wii is introduced and immediately becomes a leader in game consoles. The Wii is being used in revolutionary ways, such as training surgeons.

2006 Intel introduces its Core 2 Duo processor family. Boasting record-breaking performance while using less power, the family consists of five desktop computer processors and five mobile computer processors. The desktop processor includes 291 million transistors, yet uses 40 percent less power than the Pentium processor.

2006

2006 IBM produces the fastest supercomputer, Blue Gene/L. It can perform approximately 28 trillion calculations in the time it takes you to blink your eye, or about one-tenth of a second.

2006 Nintendo releases the Nintendo DS Lite, a handheld game console with new features such as dual screens and improved graphics and sound.

2006 Apple begins selling Macintosh computers with Intel microprocessors.

2007 Video blogs, or vlogs, grow in popularity along with YouTube. Vlogs allow users to video their message instead of entering text via a regular blog. The growth in the popularity of vlogs is attributed to several factors, including the use of video portable media players. Podcasting also increases in popularity for the same reasons. A podcast is distinguished from other digital audio formats by its capability to be downloaded automatically.

2007 Intel introduces Core 2 Quad, a four-core processor made for dual-processor servers and desktop computers. The larger number of cores allows for more energy-efficient performance and optimizes battery performance in notebook computers.

2007 Apple introduces the iPhone and sells 270,000 phones in the first 2 days. iPhone uses iTouch technology that allows you to make a call simply by tapping a name or number in your address book. In addition, it stores and plays music like an iPod. Also, Apple sells its one billionth song on iTunes.

2007 VoIP (Voice over Internet Protocol) providers expand usage to include Wi-Fi phones. The phones enable high-quality service through a Wireless-G network and high-speed Internet connection.

2007 Apple releases its Mac OS X version 10.5 "Leopard" operating system, available in a desktop version and server version. The system includes a significantly revised desktop, with a semitransparent menu bar and an updated search tool that incorporates the same visual navigation interface as iTunes.

2007

2007 Wi-Fi hotspots are popular in a variety of locations. People bring their computers to coffeehouses, fast food restaurants, or bookstores to access the Internet wirelessly, either free or for a small fee.

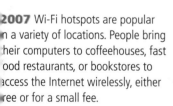

2007 Blu-ray Discs increase in popularity, overcoming and replacing HD DVD in less than one year. A Blu-ray Disc can store approximately 9 hours of high-definition (HD) video on a 50 GB disc or approximately 23 hours of standard-definition (SD) video.

2007 Half of the world's population uses cell phones. More and more people are using a cell phone in lieu of a landline in their home.

2007 Microsoft releases Office 2007. New features include the most significant update to the user interface in more than a decade, including the introduction of the Ribbon, which replaces the toolbars in most of the programs, and the capability to save documents in XML and PDF formats.

2007 Microsoft ships the latest version of its widely used operating system, Windows Vista. Vista offers the Basic interface and the Aero interface, which offers several graphical features, including transparent windows. Internet Explorer 7 is included with Windows Vista.

2008 Microsoft introduces Windows Server 2008, the successor to Windows Server 2003.

2008 Bill Gates retires from Microsoft. He continues as chairman and advisor on key development projects.

2008 Dell offers a hybrid computer. Smaller than a desktop computer but larger than a notebook computer, these hybrid computers contain features comparable to their larger counterparts and can work more easily in a home entertainment environment.

2008 Netflix, an online movie rental company, and TiVo, a company manufacturing digital video recorders (DVRs), make Netflix movies and television episodes available on TiVo (DVRs).

2008

2008 WiMAX goes live! The advantage of this technology is the capability to access video, music, voice, and video calls wherever and whenever desired. Average download speeds are between 2 Mbps and 4 Mbps. By year's end, Sprint has approximately 100 million users on its network.

2008 Smart phones become smarter. Smart phones introduced this year include enhanced features such as touch screens with multi-touch technology, mobile TV, tactile feedback, improved graphics, GPS receivers, and better cameras.

2008 Computer manufacturers begin to offer solid state drives (SSDs) instead of hard disks, mostly in notebook computers. Although SSDs have a lower storage capacity, are more expensive, and slightly more susceptible to failure, they are significantly faster.

2008 Google releases its new Web browser. Google Chrome uses an entirely unique interface and offers other features such as dynamic tabs, crash control, and application shortcuts.

Google Chrome

Firefox 3

2008 Mozilla releases Firefox 3, the latest version of its Web browser. Firefox 3 offers greater security, a more user-friendly interface, and other improvements to enhance the Web browsing experience.

2009 Web applications continue to increase in popularity. Web applications make it easier to perform tasks such as word processing, photo editing, and tax preparation without installing software on your computer.

2009 In June 2009, federal law requires that all full-power television stations broadcast only in digital format. Analog television owners are required to purchase a converter box to view over-the-air digital programming.

2010 Kinect for Xbox 360 changes the way people play video games. Game players now can interact with the game with a series of sensors, as well as a camera, tracking their movements in 3-D.

2009 Microsoft releases the newest version of its Windows operating system, Windows 7. This version provides greater stability and security; a more flexible, user-friendly interface; and requires fewer computing resources to operate.

2009 Microsoft releases Internet Explorer 8, also known as IE8. IE8 offers new features such as InPrivate Browsing, Accelerators, and support for WebSlices.

2009

2010

2009 Intel releases the Core i5 and Core i7 line of processors. These processors offer increased performance for some of the more demanding tasks. Intel also enhances its Core processor family by releasing multi-core processors, designed to increase the number of instructions that can be processed at a given time.

2010 AMD develops a 12-core processor, which contains two 6-core processors, each on an individual chip. Power consumption is similar to that of a 6-core processor but offers reduced clock speed.

2009 Computers and mobile devices promote fitness by offering games and programs to help users exercise and track their progress. These games and programs also are used to assist with physical rehabilitation.

2010 Microsoft releases Office 2010, the latest version of its Office suite. This version is available in multiple editions and continues to help people work more efficiently. Office Web apps, available free to Windows Live users, offer online access to scaled-down versions of Word, PowerPoint, Excel, and OneNote.

2009 Social networking revolutionizes communications. Schools, radio stations, and other organizations develop pages on popular online social networks, such as Facebook, creating closer connections with their stakeholders.

2010 Adobe releases the latest version of its design suite, Adobe CS5. This new suite has many performance and interface enhancements over previous versions and takes advantage of new technologies such as multi-touch.

2011 Individuals and enterprises increase their focus on green computing. Computer manufacturers not only sell more energy-efficient hardware, they also provide easy ways in which customers can recycle their old computers and devices.

2010 Apple releases the iPad, a revolutionary mobile device with a 9.7-inch multi-touch screen. The iPad boasts up to 10 hours of battery life, connects wirelessly to the Internet, and is capable of running thousands of apps.

2010 Hard disk capacity continues to increase at an exponential rate, with the largest hard disks storing more than 2.5 TB of data and information. Solid state storage also is becoming more popular, with storage capacities increasing and prices decreasing.

2011 Netbooks prove to be an attractive alternative to traditional notebook computers. Netbooks are smaller and lighter than traditional notebook computers, while providing nearly the same functionality.

2011

2010

2011 E-books and e-book readers explode in popularity. Many novels, textbooks, and other publications now are available digitally and can be read on an e-book reader, computer, or mobile device.

2011 Decreases in storage costs and increases in Internet connection speeds persuade more users to use cloud storage for their data. Cloud storage also provides users with the convenience of accessing their files from almost anywhere.

2011 A new generation of Web browsers is released to support HTML5, enabling Web pages to contain more vivid, dynamic content.

2011 More than 200 types of mobile devices are using Google Android, an operating system originally designed for mobile devices.

The Internet and World Wide Web

Objectives

After completing this chapter, you will be able to:

1 Identify and briefly describe various broadband Internet connections

2 Describe the types of Internet access providers: Internet service providers, online service providers, and wireless Internet service providers

3 Explain the purpose of a Web browser and identify the components of a Web address

4 Describe how to use a search engine to search for information on the Web

5 Describe the types of Web sites: portal, news, informational, business/marketing, blog, wiki, online social network, educational, entertainment, advocacy, Web application, content aggregator, and personal

6 Recognize how Web pages use graphics, animation, audio, video, virtual reality, and plug-ins

7 Identify the steps required for Web publishing

8 Explain how e-mail, mailing lists, instant messaging, chat rooms, VoIP, FTP, and newsgroups and message boards work

9 Identify the rules of netiquette

The Internet

One of the major reasons business, home, and other users purchase computers is for Internet access. The **Internet**, also called the **Net**, is a worldwide collection of networks that links millions of businesses, government agencies, educational institutions, and individuals. The Internet is a widely used research tool, providing society with access to global information and instant communications.

Today, more than one billion home and business users around the world access a variety of services on the Internet, some of which are shown in Figure 2-1. The World Wide Web, or simply the Web, and e-mail are two of the more widely used Internet services. Other services include chat rooms, instant messaging, and VoIP (Voice over Internet Protocol).

The Internet has its roots in a networking project started by an agency of the U.S. Department of Defense. The goal was to build a network that (1) allowed scientists at different locations to share information and work together on military and scientific projects and (2) could function even if part of the network were disabled or destroyed by a disaster such as a nuclear attack. That network, called ARPANET, became functional in September 1969, linking scientific and academic researchers across the United States.

The original ARPANET consisted of four main computers, one each located at the University of California at Los Angeles, the University of California at Santa Barbara, the Stanford Research Institute, and the University of Utah. Each of these computers served as a host on the network. A host or server is any computer that provides services and connections to other computers on a network. By 1984, ARPANET had more than 1,000 individual computers linked as hosts. Today, more than 550 million hosts connect to this network, which is known now as the Internet.

Figure 2-1　People around the world use a variety of Internet services in daily activities. Internet services allow home and business users to access the Web for activities such as conducting research, reading blogs, or sharing videos; to send e-mail messages; or to converse with others using chat rooms, instant messaging, or VoIP.

The Internet consists of many local, regional, national, and international networks. Both public and private organizations own networks on the Internet. These networks, along with telephone companies, cable and satellite companies, and the government, all contribute toward the internal structure of the Internet.

Each organization on the Internet is responsible only for maintaining its own network. No single person, company, institution, or government agency controls or owns the Internet. The World Wide Web Consortium (W3C), however, oversees research and sets standards and guidelines for many areas of the Internet. More than 350 organizations from around the world are members of the W3C.

Connecting to the Internet

Many home and small business users connect to the Internet via high-speed **broadband** Internet service. With broadband Internet service, your computer or mobile device usually is connected to the Internet the entire time it is powered on. Examples of broadband Internet service include the following:

- **Cable Internet service** provides high-speed Internet access through the cable television network via a cable modem.
- **DSL** (digital subscriber line) provides high-speed Internet connections using regular telephone lines.
- **Fiber to the Premises (FTTP)** uses fiber-optic cable to provide high-speed Internet access to home and business users.
- **Fixed wireless** provides high-speed Internet connections using a dish-shaped antenna on your house or business to communicate with a tower location via radio signals.
- A **Wi-Fi** (wireless fidelity) network uses radio signals to provide high-speed Internet connections to wireless computers and devices.

- A **cellular radio network** offers high-speed Internet connections to devices with built-in compatible technology or computers with wireless modems.
- **Satellite Internet service** provides high-speed Internet connections via satellite to a satellite dish that communicates with a satellite modem.

Employees and students typically connect their computers to the Internet through a business or school network. The business or school network connects to a high-speed broadband Internet service.

Mobile users access the Internet using a variety of services. Most hotels and airports provide wired or wireless Internet connections. Wireless Internet services such as Wi-Fi networks, allow mobile users to connect easily to the Internet with notebook computers, smart phones, and other mobile devices while away from a telephone, cable, or other wired connection. Many public locations, such as airports, hotels, schools, and coffee shops, are **hot spots** that provide Wi-Fi Internet connections to users with mobile computers or devices.

Many home users set up a Wi-Fi network, which sends signals to a communications device that is connected to a high-speed Internet service such as cable or DSL. Instead of using broadband Internet service, however, some home users connect to the Internet via dial-up access, which is a slower-speed technology. **Dial-up access** takes place when the modem in your computer connects to the Internet via a standard telephone line that transmits data and information using an analog (continuous wave pattern) signal. Users may opt for dial-up access because of its lower price or because broadband access is not available in their area.

? | **FAQ 2-1**

How popular is broadband?

According to a study performed by Pew Internet & American Life Project, 63 percent of American adults have broadband Internet connections at home. Adoption of broadband connections increases during good economic times, while some may hesitate to make the switch during an economic downturn. It is believed that once the price of a broadband connection decreases, and broadband is available in more rural areas, its popularity will increase further.

For more information, visit the Computer Concepts CourseMate Web site at www.cengagebrain.com, navigate to the Chapter 2 FAQ resource for this book, and then click Broadband.

Access Providers

An **access provider** is a business that provides individuals and organizations access to the Internet free or for a fee. For example, some Wi-Fi networks provide free access while others charge a per use fee. Other access providers often charge a fixed amount for an Internet connection, usually about $5 to $24 per month for dial-up access and $13 to $120 for higher-speed access. Many Internet access providers offer services such as news, weather, financial data, games, travel guides, e-mail, photo communities, and online storage to hold digital photos and other files. (A file is a named unit of storage.)

Access providers are categorized as ISPs, online service providers, and wireless Internet service providers. An **ISP** (**Internet service provider**) is a regional or national access provider. A regional ISP usually provides Internet access to a specific geographic area. A national ISP is a business that provides Internet access in cities and towns nationwide. National ISPs usually offer more services and have a larger technical support staff than regional ISPs. Examples of national ISPs are AT&T and EarthLink.

In addition to providing Internet access, an **online service provider** (**OSP**) also has many members-only features such as instant messaging or their own customized version of a Web browser. The two more popular OSPs are AOL (America Online) and MSN (Microsoft Network). AOL also provides free access to its services to any user with a high-speed Internet connection.

A **wireless Internet service provider**, sometimes called a wireless data provider, is a company that provides wireless Internet access to computers and mobile devices, such as smart phones and portable media players with built-in wireless capability (such as Wi-Fi) or to computers using wireless modems or wireless access devices. Wireless modems usually are in the form of a USB flash drive or a card that inserts in a slot in a computer or mobile device. Examples of wireless Internet service providers include AT&T, Boingo Wireless, Sprint Broadband Direct, T-Mobile, and Verizon Wireless.

Wireless Modems

For more information, visit the Computer Concepts CourseMate Web site at www.cengagebrain.com, navigate to the Chapter 2 Web Link resource for this book, and then click Wireless Modems.

How Data and Information Travel the Internet

Computers connected to the Internet work together to transfer data and information around the world using various wired and wireless transmission media. Several main transmission media carry the heaviest amount of traffic on the Internet. These major carriers of network traffic are known collectively as the **Internet backbone.**

In the United States, the transmission media that make up the Internet backbone exchange data and information at several different major cities across the country. That is, they transfer data and information from one network to another until reaching the final destination (Figure 2-2).

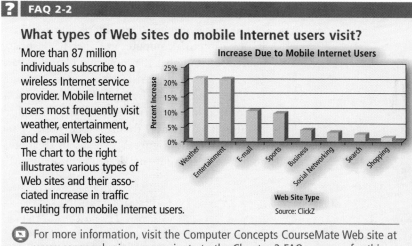

? FAQ 2-2

What types of Web sites do mobile Internet users visit?

More than 87 million individuals subscribe to a wireless Internet service provider. Mobile Internet users most frequently visit weather, entertainment, and e-mail Web sites. The chart to the right illustrates various types of Web sites and their associated increase in traffic resulting from mobile Internet users.

Increase Due to Mobile Internet Users

Web Site Type

Source: ClickZ

For more information, visit the Computer Concepts CourseMate Web site at www.cengagebrain.com, navigate to the Chapter 2 FAQ resource for this book, and then click Mobile Internet.

How a Home User's Data and Information Might Travel the Internet Using a Cable Modem Connection

Step 1
You initiate an action to request data or information from the Internet. For example, you request to display a Web page on your computer screen.

Step 2
A cable modem transfers the computer's digital signals to the cable television line in your house.

Step 3
Your request (digital signals) travels through cable television lines to a central cable system, which is shared by up to 500 homes in a neighborhood.

Step 4
The central cable system sends your request over high-speed fiber-optic lines to the cable operator, who often also is the ISP.

Step 5
The ISP routes your request through the Internet backbone to the destination server (in this example, the server that contains the requested Web site).

Step 6
The server retrieves the requested Web page and sends it back through the Internet backbone to your computer.

Figure 2-2 This figure shows how a home user's data and information might travel the Internet using a cable modem connection.

Internet Addresses

The Internet relies on an addressing system much like the postal service to send data and information to a computer at a specific destination. An **IP address**, short for Internet Protocol address, is a number that uniquely identifies each computer or device connected to the Internet. The IP address usually consists of four groups of numbers, each separated by a period. In general, the first portion of each IP address identifies the network and the last portion identifies the specific computer.

These all-numeric IP addresses are difficult to remember and use. Thus, the Internet supports the use of a text name that represents one or more IP addresses. A **domain name** is the text version of an IP address. Figure 2-3 shows an IP address and its associated domain name. As with an IP address, the components of a domain name are separated by periods.

Figure 2-3 The IP address and domain name for the Google Web site.

The text in the domain name up to the first period identifies the type of Internet server. In Figure 2-3, for example, the www indicates a Web server. The Internet server portion of a domain name often is not required.

Every domain name contains a **top-level domain (TLD)**, which is the last section of the domain name. A generic TLD (gTLD), such as the com in Figure 2-3, identifies the type of organization associated with the domain. Figure 2-4 lists some gTLDs. For international Web sites outside the United States, the domain name also includes a country code TLD (ccTLD), which is a two-letter country code, such as au for Australia or fr for France.

When you specify a domain name, a server translates the domain name to its associated IP address so that data and information can be routed to the correct computer. This server is an Internet server that usually is associated with an Internet access provider.

Examples of Generic Top-Level Domains

Generic TLD	Intended Purpose	Generic TLD	Intended Purpose
aero	Aviation community members	mil	Military organizations
biz	Businesses of all sizes	mobi	Delivery and management of mobile Internet services
cat	Catalan cultural community	museum	Accredited museums
com	Commercial organizations, businesses, and companies	name	Individuals or families
coop	Business cooperatives such as credit unions and rural electric co-ops	net	Network providers or commercial companies
edu	Educational institutions	org	Nonprofit organizations
gov	Government agencies	pro	Certified professionals such as doctors, lawyers, and accountants
info	Business organizations or individuals providing general information	tel	Internet communications
jobs	Employment or human resource businesses	travel	Travel industry

Figure 2-4 In addition to the generic TLDs listed in this table, proposals for newer TLDs continually are evaluated.

The World Wide Web

The **World Wide Web (WWW)**, or **Web**, a widely used service on the Internet, consists of a worldwide collection of electronic documents. Each electronic document on the Web, called a **Web page**, can contain text, graphics, animation, audio, and video. Additionally, Web pages usually have built-in connections to other documents. A **Web site** is a collection of related Web pages and associated items, such as documents and pictures, stored on a Web server. A **Web server** is a computer that delivers requested Web pages to your computer. Some industry experts use the term **Web 2.0** to refer to Web sites that provide a means for users to share personal information (such as social networking Web sites), allow users to modify Web site content (such as wikis, which are discussed later in this chapter), and have application software built into the site for visitors to use (such as e-mail and word processing programs). Read Looking Ahead 2-1 for a look at Web 3.0.

Browsing the Web

A **Web browser**, or **browser**, is application software that allows users to access and view Web pages or access Web 2.0 programs. To browse the Web, you need a computer or mobile device that is connected to the Internet and that has a Web browser. The more widely used Web browsers for personal computers are Internet Explorer, Firefox, Opera, Safari, and Google Chrome.

With an Internet connection established, you start a Web browser. The browser retrieves and displays a starting Web page, sometimes called the browser's home page. Figure 2-5 shows how a Web browser displays a home page.

Another use of the term, **home page**, refers to the first page that a Web site displays. Similar to a book cover or a table of contents for a Web site, the home page provides information about the Web site's purpose and content. Often it provides connections to other documents, Web pages, or Web sites, which can be downloaded to a computer or mobile device. **Downloading** is the process of a computer or device receiving information, such as a Web page, from a server on the Internet.

How a Web Browser Displays a Home Page

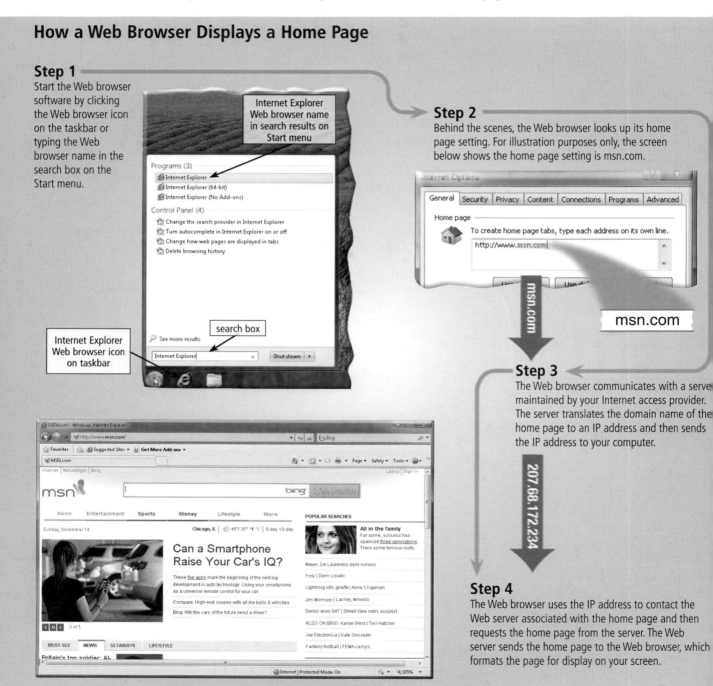

Step 1
Start the Web browser software by clicking the Web browser icon on the taskbar or typing the Web browser name in the search box on the Start menu.

Internet Explorer Web browser name in search results on Start menu

Internet Explorer Web browser icon on taskbar

search box

Step 2
Behind the scenes, the Web browser looks up its home page setting. For illustration purposes only, the screen below shows the home page setting is msn.com.

msn.com

msn.com

Step 3
The Web browser communicates with a server maintained by your Internet access provider. The server translates the domain name of the home page to an IP address and then sends the IP address to your computer.

207.68.172.234

Step 4
The Web browser uses the IP address to contact the Web server associated with the home page and then requests the home page from the server. The Web server sends the home page to the Web browser, which formats the page for display on your screen.

Figure 2-5 This figure shows how a Web browser displays a home page.

Web Addresses

A Web page has a unique address, which is called a **URL** (Uniform Resource Locator) or **Web address**. For example, the home page for the United States National Park Service Web site has a Web address of http://www.nps.gov. A Web browser retrieves a Web page using its Web address.

If you know the Web address of a Web page, you can type it in the Address bar at the top of the browser window. If you type http://www.nps.gov/grsm/planyourvisit/wildlifeviewing.htm as the Web address in the Address bar and then press the ENTER key, the browser downloads and displays the Web page shown in Figure 2-6.

A Web address consists of a protocol, domain name, and sometimes the path to a specific Web page or location on a Web page. Many Web page addresses begin with http://. The http, which stands for Hypertext Transfer Protocol, is a set of rules that defines how pages transfer on the Internet. To help minimize errors, many browsers and Web sites do not require you enter the http:// and www portions of the Web address.

When you enter the Web address, http://www.nps.gov/grsm/planyourvisit/wildlifeviewing.htm in the Web browser, it sends a request to the Web server that contains the nps.com Web site. The server then retrieves the Web page that is named wildlifeviewing.htm in the grsm/planyourvisit path and delivers it to your browser, which then displays the Web page on the screen.

To save time, many users create bookmarks for their frequently visited Web pages. A **bookmark**, or **favorite**, is a saved Web address that you access by clicking the bookmark name in a list. That is, instead of entering a Web address to display a Web page, you can click a previously saved bookmark.

For information about useful Web sites and their associated Web addresses, read the Making Use of the Web feature that follows this chapter.

Figure 2-6 After entering http://www.nps.gov/grsm/planyourvisit/wildlifeviewing.htm as the Web address in the Address bar, this Web page at the United States National Park Service Web site is displayed.

Navigating Web Pages

Most Web pages contain links. A **link**, short for **hyperlink**, is a built-in connection to another related Web page or part of a Web page. Links allow you to obtain information in a nonlinear way. That is, instead of accessing topics in a specified order, you move directly to a topic of interest.

Branching from one related topic to another in a nonlinear fashion is what makes links so powerful. Some people use the phrase, **surfing the Web**, to refer to the activity of using links to explore the Web.

A link can be text or an image. Text links may be underlined and/or displayed in a color different from other text on the Web page. Pointing to, or positioning the pointer on, a link on the screen typically changes the shape of the pointer to a small hand with a pointing index finger. Pointing to a link also sometimes causes the link to change in appearance or play a sound. The Web page shown in Figure 2-7 contains a variety of link types, with the pointer on one of the links.

Each link on a Web page corresponds to a Web address or document. To activate a link, you **click** it, that is, point to the link and then press the left mouse button. Clicking a link causes the Web page or document associated with the link to be displayed on the screen. The linked object might be on the same Web page, a different Web page at the same Web site, or a separate Web page at a different Web site in another city or country.

Most current Web browsers support **tabbed browsing**, where the top of the browser displays a tab (similar to a file folder tab) for each Web page you open. To move from one open Web page to another, you click the tab in the Web browser.

Because some Web sites attempt to track your browsing habits or gather personal information, some current Web browsers include a feature that allows you to disable and/or more tightly control the dissemination of your browsing habits and personal information. Read Ethics & Issues 2-1 for a related discussion.

Tabbed Browsing
For more information, visit the Computer Concepts CourseMate Web site at www.cengagebrain.com, navigate to the Chapter 2 Web Link resource for this book, and then click Tabbed Browsing.

Figure 2-7 This browser window has several open tabs. The current tab shows a Web page that has various types of links.

Should the Government Allow You to Sign Up for a Do-Not-Track List?

When you visit a Web site that includes an advertisement, someone probably is recording the fact that you visited that Web site and viewed the advertisement with your browser. Over time, companies that specialize in tracking who views which online advertisements can amass an enormous amount of information about your online Web surfing habits. Through tracking the Web sites a user visits, the products they buy, and the articles they read, a company may attempt to profile the visitor's beliefs, associations, and habits. Although a user may think he or she is anonymous while navigating the Web, the company can attempt through various means to link the user's true identity with the user's online profile. The company can sell online profiles, with or without the user's true identity, to other advertisers or organizations. Some privacy groups have called for the government to allow consumers to sign up for a do-not-track list modeled after the popular do-not-call list.

Should organizations be allowed to track your Web surfing habits? Why or why not? Should organizations be allowed to associate your real identity with your online identity and profit from the information? Should the government force companies to give you the option of not being tracked? Why or why not? What are the benefits and dangers of online tracking?

Searching the Web

The Web is a worldwide resource of information. A primary reason that people use the Web is to search for specific information, including text, pictures, music, and video. The first step in successful searching is to identify the main idea or concept in the topic about which you are seeking information. Determine any synonyms, alternate spellings, or variant word forms for the topic. Then, use a search tool to locate the information.

Two types of search tools are search engines and subject directories. A **search engine** is a program that finds Web sites, Web pages, images, videos, news, maps, and other information related to a specific topic. A **subject directory** classifies Web pages in an organized set of categories or groups, such as sports or shopping, and related subcategories.

Some Web sites offer the functionality of both a search engine and a subject directory. Google and Yahoo!, for example, are widely used search engines that also provide a subject directory. To use Google or Yahoo!, you enter the Web address (google.com or yahoo.com) in the Address bar in a browser window. The table in Figure 2-8 lists the Web addresses of several popular general-purpose search engines and subject directories.

Ethics & Issues

For the complete text of the Ethics & Issues boxes found in this chapter, visit the Computer Concepts CourseMate Web site at www.cengagebrain.com and then navigate to the Chapter 2 Ethics & Issues resource for this book.

Widely Used Search Tools

Search Tool	Web Address	Search Engine	Subject Directory
A9	a9.com	X	
AlltheWeb	alltheweb.com	X	
AltaVista	altavista.com	X	
AOL Search	search.aol.com	X	
Ask	ask.com	X	
Bing	bing.com	X	
Cuil (pronounced cool)	cuil.com	X	
Dogpile	dogpile.com	X	
Excite	excite.com	X	X
Gigablast	gigablast.com	X	X
Google	google.com	X	X
Lycos	lycos.com	X	
MSN	msn.com	X	X
Open Directory Project	dmoz.org	X	X
WebCrawler	webcrawler.com	X	
Yahoo!	yahoo.com	X	X

Figure 2-8
Popular search engines and subject directories.

Search Engines A search engine is helpful in locating information for which you do not know an exact Web address or are not seeking a particular Web site. Some search engines look through Web pages for all types of information. Others can restrict their searches to a specific type of information, such as images, videos, audio, news, maps, people or businesses, and blogs.

Search engines require that you enter a word or phrase, called **search text**, that describes the item you want to find. Your search text can be broad, such as spring break destinations, or more specific, such as Walt Disney World. Figure 2-9 shows one way to use the Google search engine to search for the phrase, Aspen Colorado ski resorts. The results shown in Step 3 include nearly 150,000 links to Web pages, called hits, that reference Aspen Colorado ski resorts. Each hit in the list has a link that, when clicked, displays an associated Web site or Web page. Most search engines sequence the hits based on how close the words in the search text are to one another in the titles and descriptions of the hits. Thus, the first few links probably contain more relevant information.

How to Use a Search Engine

Step 1
Type the search engine's Web address (in this case, google.com) in the Address bar in the Web browser.

Step 2
Press the ENTER key. When the Google home page is displayed, type `Aspen Colorado ski resorts` as the search text and then point to the Google Search button.

Step 4
Click the Aspen Snowmass link to display a Web page with a description and links to skiing in Aspen.

Step 3
Click the Google Search button. When the results of the search a displayed, scroll through the links and read the descriptions. Poir the Aspen Snowmass link.

Figure 2-9 This figure shows how to use a search engine.

Some Web browsers contain an Instant Search box that, when filled in, uses a predefined or default search engine to perform searches. Using the Instant Search box eliminates the steps of displaying the search engine's Web page prior to entering the search text.

If you enter a phrase with spaces between the words in the search text, most search engines display results (hits) that include all of the words. The following list identifies techniques you can use to improve your searches. To learn more about searching for information, complete the Learn How To 2 activity on pages 88 and 89.

- Use specific nouns.
- Put the most important terms first in the search text.
- Use the asterisk (*) to substitute characters in words. For example, retriev* displays hits containing retrieves, retrieval, retriever, and any other variation.
- Use quotation marks to create phrases so that the search engine finds an exact sequence of words.
- List all possible spellings, for example, email, e-mail.
- Before using a search engine, read its Help information.
- If the search is unsuccessful with one search engine, try another.

Subject Directories A subject directory provides categorized lists of links arranged by subject (Figure 2-10). Using this search tool, you locate a particular topic by clicking links through different levels, moving from the general to the specific.

Types of Web Sites

Thirteen types of Web sites are portal, news, informational, business/marketing, blog, wiki, online social network, educational, entertainment, advocacy, Web application, content aggregator, and personal. Many Web sites fall into more than one of these categories.

Figure 2-10
A subject directory provides categorized lists of links.

Portal A **portal** is a Web site that offers a variety of Internet services from a single, convenient location (Figure 2-11a). Most portals offer these free services: search engine; news; sports and weather; Web publishing; reference tools such as yellow pages, stock quotes, and maps; shopping; and e-mail communications services. Popular portals include AltaVista, AOL, Excite, GO.com, iGoogle, Lycos, MSN, and Yahoo!.

Figure 2-11a
(portal)

Figure 2-11b
(news)

News A news Web site contains newsworthy material including stories and articles relating to current events, life, money, sports, and the weather (Figure 2-11b). Newspapers and television and radio stations are some of the media that maintain news Web sites.

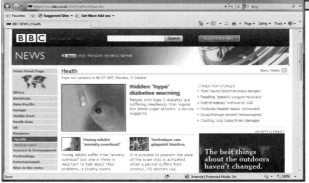

Figure 2-11 Types of Web sites. *(continued on next page)*

Figure 2-11c (informational)

Figure 2-11d
(business/marketing)

Figure 2-11e
(blog)

Figure 2-11f
(wiki)

Wiki

For more information, visit the Computer Concepts CourseMate Web site at www.cengagebrain.com, navigate to the Chapter 2 Web Link resource for this book, and then click Wiki.

Figure 2-11 Types of Web sites. *(continued)*

Informational An informational Web site conta... factual information (Figure 2-11c). Many United States government agencies have informational Web sites providing information such as census da... tax codes, and the congressional budget. Other org... nizations provide information such as public trans- portation schedules and published research finding...

Business/Marketing A business/marketing Web site contains content that promotes or sells products or services (Figure 2-11d). Nearly every enterprise has a business/marketing Web site. Many companies also allow you to purchase their products or services online.

Blog A **blog**, short for Weblog, is an informal Web site consisting of time-stamped articles, or posts, in a diary or journal format, usually listed i... reverse chronological order (Figure 2-11e). A blo... that contains video clips is called a **video blog** or **vlog**. A **microblog** allows users to publish short messages, usually between 100 and 200 character... for others to read. Twitter is a popular microblog... The term **blogosphere** refers to the worldwide collection of blogs, and the **vlogosphere** refers to all vlogs worldwide. Blogs reflect the interests, opinions, and personalities of the author and sometimes site visitors. Blogs have become an important means of worldwide communications.

Wiki A **wiki** is a collaborative Web site that allow... users to create, add to, modify, or delete the Web si... content via their Web browser. Most wikis are oper... to modification by the general public. Wikis usually collect recent edits on a Web page so that some- one can review them for accuracy. The difference between a wiki and a blog is that users cannot mod... original posts made by the blogger. A popular wiki ... Wikipedia, a free Web encyclopedia (Figure 2-11f... Read Ethics & Issues 2-2 for a related discussion.

Online Social Networks An **online social network**, also called a **social networking Web site**, is a Web site that encourages members in its online community to share their interests, ideas, stories, photos, music, and videos with other registered users (Figure 2-11g). Popular social networking Web sites include MySpace and Facebook, with Facebook alone boasting more than 300 million active users. A **media sharing Web site** is a specific type of online social network that enables members to share media such as photos, music, and videos. Flickr, Fotki, and Webshots are popular photo sharing communities; PixelFish and YouTube are popular video sharing communities.

Educational An educational Web site offers exciting, challenging avenues for formal and informal teaching and learning (Figure 2-11h). For a more structured learning experience, companies provide online training to employees; and colleges offer online classes and degrees. Instructors often use the Web to enhance classroom teaching by publishing course materials, grades, and other pertinent class information.

Entertainment An entertainment Web site offers an interactive and engaging environment (Figure 2-11i). Popular entertainment Web sites offer music, videos, sports, games, ongoing Web episodes, sweepstakes, chat rooms, and more.

Advocacy An advocacy Web site contains content that describes a cause, opinion, or idea (Figure 2-11j). These Web sites usually present views of a particular group or association.

Web Application A **Web application**, or **Web app**, is a Web site that allows users to access and interact with software through a Web browser on any computer or device that is connected to the Internet. Some Web applications provide free access to their software (Figure 2-11k). Others offer part of their software free and charge for access to more comprehensive features or when a particular action is requested. Examples of Web applications include Google Docs (word processing, spreadsheets, presentations), TurboTax Online (tax preparation), and Windows Live Hotmail (e-mail).

Figure 2-11g (online social network)

Figure 2-11h (educational)

Figure 2-11i (entertainment)

Figure 2-11j (advocacy)

Figure 2-11k (Web application)

Figure 2-11 Types of Web sites. *(continued on next page)*

Figure 2-11l (content aggregator)

Figure 2-11m (personal)

Figure 2-11 Types of Web sites. *(continued)*

Criteria for Evaluating a Web Site's Content

Evaluation Criteria	Reliable Web Sites
Affiliation	A reputable institution should support the Web site without bias in the information.
Audience	The Web site should be written at an appropriate level.
Authority	The Web site should list the author and the appropriate credentials.
Content	The Web site should be well organized and the links should work.
Currency	The information on the Web page should be current.
Design	The pages at the Web site should download quickly, be visually pleasing, and easy to navigate.
Objectivity	The Web site should contain little advertising and be free of preconceptions.

Figure 2-12 Criteria for evaluating a Web site's content.

Content Aggregator A **content aggregator** is a business that gathers and organizes Web content and then distributes, or feeds, the content to subscribers for free or a fee (Figure 2-11l). Examples of distributed content include news, music, video, and pictures. Subscribers select content in which they are interested. Whenever this content changes, it is downloaded automatically (pushed) to the subscriber's computer or mobile device. **RSS 2.0**, which stands for Really Simple Syndication, is a specification that content aggregators use to distribute content to subscribers.

Personal A private individual or family not usually associated with any organization may maintain a personal Web site (Figure 2-11m). People publish personal Web pages for a variety of reasons. Some are job hunting. Others simply want to share life experiences with the world.

Evaluating a Web Site

Do not assume that information presented on the Web is correct or accurate. Any person, company, or organization can publish a Web page on the Internet. No one oversees the content of these Web pages. Figure 2-12 lists guidelines for assessing the value of a Web site or Web page before relying on its content.

Multimedia on the Web

Most Web pages include more than just formatted text and links. The more exciting Web pages use multimedia. **Multimedia** refers to any application that combines text with graphics, animation, audio, video, and/or virtual reality. Multimedia Web pages often require specific hardware and software and take more time to download because they contain large graphics files or video or audio clips. The sections that follow discuss how the Web uses graphics, animation, audio, video, and virtual reality.

Graphics A **graphic**, or graphical image, is a digital representation of nontext information such as a drawing, chart, or photo. Many Web pages use colorful graphical designs and images to convey messages (Figure 2-13). Read Innovative Computing 2-1 to find out how astronomers share graphics of the universe.

Figure 2-13 This Web page uses colorful graphical designs and images to convey its messages.

Of the graphics formats that exist on the Web, the two more common are JPEG and GIF formats. JPEG (pronounced JAY-peg) is a format that compresses graphics to reduce their file size, which means the file takes up less storage space. The goal with JPEG graphics is to reach a balance between image quality and file size. Digital photos often use the JPEG format. GIF (pronounced jiff) graphics also use compression techniques to reduce file sizes. The GIF format works best for images that have only a few distinct colors, such as company logos.

Some Web sites use thumbnails on their pages because graphics can be time-consuming to display. A **thumbnail** is a small version of a larger graphic. You usually can click a thumbnail to display a larger image.

Animation Many Web pages use **animation,** which is the appearance of motion created by displaying a series of still images in sequence. Animation can make Web pages more visually interesting or draw attention to important information or links.

Audio On the Web, you can listen to audio clips and live audio. **Audio** includes music, speech, or any other sound. Simple applications on the Web consist of individual audio files available for download to a computer or device. Once downloaded, you can play (listen to) the contents of these files. Audio files are compressed to reduce their file sizes. For example, the **MP3** format reduces an audio file to about one-tenth its original size, while preserving much of the original quality of the sound.

Some music publishers have Web sites that allow users to download sample tracks free to persuade them to buy all the songs contained on the CD. Others allow a user to purchase and download an entire CD (Figure 2-14). It is legal to download copyrighted music only if the song's copyright holder has granted permission for users to download and play the song.

To listen to an audio file on your computer, you need special software called a **player**. Most current operating systems contain a player, for example, Windows Media Player. Some audio files, however, might require you to download a player. Players available for download include iTunes and RealPlayer.

Some applications on the Web use streaming audio. **Streaming** is the process of transferring data in a continuous and even flow. Streaming allows users to access and use a file while it is transmitting. For example, streaming audio enables you to listen to music as it downloads to your computer.

Podcasting is another popular method of distributing audio. A **podcast** is recorded audio, usually an MP3 file, stored on a Web site that can be downloaded to a computer or a portable media player such as an iPod. Examples of podcasts include music, radio shows, news stories, classroom lectures, political messages, and television commentaries. Podcasters register their podcasts with content aggregators. Subscribers select podcast feeds they want to be downloaded automatically whenever they connect. Most smart phone users who subscribe to a wireless Internet service provider can listen to streaming audio and podcasts.

How to Purchase and Download Music Using iTunes

Step 1
Display the iTunes program on the screen. Search for, select, and pay for the music you want to purchase from the iTunes Music Store, which is integrated in the iTunes program.

Step 2
Download the music from the iTunes Music Store server to your computer's hard disk.

Step 3a
Listen to the music from your computer's hard disk.

Step 3b
Download music from your computer's hard disk to a portable media player. Listen to the music through earbuds attached to the portable media player.

Figure 2-14 This figure shows how to purchase and download music using iTunes.

Video On the Web, you can view video clips or watch live video. **Video** consists of images displayed in motion. Most video also has accompanying audio. You can use the Internet to watch live and prerecorded coverage of your favorite television programs or enjoy a live performance of your favorite vocalist. You can upload, share, or view video clips at a video sharing Web site such as YouTube. Educators, politicians, and businesses are using video blogs and video podcasts to engage students, voters, and consumers.

Video files often are compressed because they are quite large in size. These clips also are quite short in length, usually less than 10 minutes, because they can take a long time to download. The Moving Pictures Experts Group (MPEG) defines a popular video compression standard, a widely used one called MPEG-4 or **MP4**. Another popular video format is Adobe Flash. As with streaming audio, streaming video allows you to view longer or live video images as they download to your computer.

Virtual Reality **Virtual reality (VR)** is the use of computers to simulate a real or imagined environment that appears as a three-dimensional (3-D) space. VR involves the display of 3-D images that users explore and manipulate interactively. A VR Web site, for example, might show a house for sale. Potential buyers walk through rooms in the VR house by moving an input device forward, backward, or to the side.

Plug-ins Most Web browsers have the capability of displaying basic multimedia elements on a Web page. Sometimes, a browser might need an additional program, called a plug-in. A **plug-in**, or **add-on**, is a program that extends the capability of a browser. You can download many plug-ins at no cost from various Web sites (Figure 2-15).

? | **FAQ 2-4**

How are social networking Web sites and Internet video affecting Internet traffic?

A report from Cisco Systems states that Internet traffic will double every two years until 2012. The volume of Internet traffic is increasing mostly because of Internet videos and social networking. In addition, the increased use of video conferencing by business users accounts for the increase in traffic.

For more information, visit the Computer Concepts CourseMate Web site at www.cengagebrain.com, navigate to the Chapter 2 FAQ resource for this book, and then click Internet Traffic.

Popular Plug-Ins

Plug-In Application		Description	Web Address
Acrobat Reader	Get ADOBE® READER®	View, navigate, and print Portable Document Format (PDF) files — documents formatted to look just as they look in print	adobe.com
Flash Player	Get ADOBE® FLASH® PLAYER	View dazzling graphics and animation, hear outstanding sound and music, display Web pages across an entire screen	adobe.com
Java	Java » Get it Now	Enable Web browser to run programs written in Java, which add interactivity to Web pages	java.com
QuickTime	Get QuickTime Free Download	View animation, music, audio, video, and VR panoramas and objects directly on a Web page	apple.com
RealPlayer	real RealPlayer DOWNLOAD	Listen to live and on-demand near-CD-quality audio and newscast-quality video, stream audio and video content for faster viewing, play MP3 files, create music CDs	real.com
Shockwave Player	Get ADOBE® SHOCKWAVE® PLAYER	Experience dynamic interactive multimedia, 3-D graphics, and streaming audio	adobe.com
Silverlight	Install Microsoft®Silverlight®	Experience high-definition video, high-resolution interactive multimedia, and streaming audio and video	microsoft.com
Windows Media Player	Windows Media Player	Listen to live and on-demand audio, play or edit WMA and MP3 files, burn CDs, and watch DVD movies	microsoft.com

Figure 2-15 Most plug-ins can be downloaded free from the Web.

Web Publishing

Before the World Wide Web, the means to share opinions and ideas with others easily and inexpensively was limited to the media, classroom, work, or social environments. Today, businesses and individuals conve information to millions of people by creating their own Web pages.

Web publishing is the development and maintenance of Web pages. To develop a Web page, you do not have to be a computer programmer. For the small business or home user, Web publishing is fairly easy as lon as you have the proper tools.

The five major steps to Web publishing are as follows:

1. Plan a Web site: Think about issues that could affect the design of the Web site.
2. Analyze and design a Web site: Design the layout of elements of the Web site such as links, text, graphics, animation, audio, video, and virtual reality.
3. Create a Web site: Use a word processing program to create basic Web pages or Web page authoring software to create more sophisticated Web sites.
4. Deploy a Web site: Transfer the Web pages from your computer to a Web server.
5. Maintain a Web site: Ensure the Web site contents remain current and all links work properly.

**Web Page
Authoring Software**

For more information, visit the Computer Concepts CourseMate Web site at www.cengagebrain.com, navigate to the Chapter 2 Web Link resource for this book, and then click Web Page Authoring Software.

E-Commerce

E-commerce, short for electronic commerce, is a business transaction that occurs over an electronic network such as the Internet. Anyone with access to a computer or mobile device, an Internet connection, and a means to pay for purchased goods or services can participate in e-commerce.

Three types of e-commerce are business-to-consumer, consumer-to-consumer, and business-to-business. Business-to-consumer (B2C) e-commerce consists of the sale of goods and services to the general public. For example, Apple has a B2C Web site. Instead of visiting a retail store to purchase an iPod, for example, customers can order one directly from Apple's Web site.

E-retail, short for electronic retail, occurs when businesses use the Web to sell products (Figure 2-16). A customer (consumer) visits an online business through an **electronic storefront**, which contains produc

An Example of E-Retail

Step 1
The customer displays the e-retailer's electronic storefront.

Step 2
The customer collects purchases in an electronic shopping cart.

Step 3
The customer enters payment information on a secure Web site. The e-retailer sends financial information to a bank.

Step 4
The bank performs security checks and sends authorization back to the e-retailer.

Step 7
While the order travels to the customer, shipping information is posted on the Web.

Step 6
The fulfillment center packages the order, prepares it for shipment, and then sends a report to the server where records are updated.

Step 5
The e-retailer's Web server sends confirmation to the customer, processes the order, and then sends it to the fulfillment center.

Step 8
The order is delivered to the customer, who may be required to sign a handheld computer or document to acknowledge receipt.

Figure 2-16 This figure shows an example of e-retail.

descriptions, images, and a shopping cart. The **shopping cart** allows the customer to collect purchases. When ready to complete the sale, the customer enters personal data and the method of payment, which should be through a secure Internet connection.

Consumer-to-consumer (C2C) e-commerce occurs when one consumer sells directly to another, such as in an online auction. With an **online auction**, users bid on an item being sold by someone else. The highest bidder at the end of the bidding period purchases the item. eBay is one of the more popular online auction Web sites.

As an alternative to entering credit card, bank account, or other financial information online, some shopping and auction Web sites allow consumers to use an online payment service such as PayPal or Google Checkout. To use an online payment service, you create an account that is linked to your credit card or funds at a financial institution. When you make a purchase, you use your online payment service account, which transfers money for you without revealing your financial information.

Most e-commerce, though, actually takes place between businesses, which is called business-to-business (B2B) e-commerce. Many businesses provide goods and services to other businesses, such as online advertising, recruiting, credit, sales, market research, technical support, and training.

Google Checkout
For more information, visit the Computer Concepts CourseMate Web site at www.cengagebrain.com, navigate to the Chapter 2 Web Link resource for this book, and then click Google Checkout.

✔ **QUIZ YOURSELF 2-2**

Instructions: Find the true statement below. Then, rewrite the remaining false statements so that they are true.

1. A blog is a Web site that uses a regularly updated journal format to reflect the interests, opinions, and personalities of the author and sometimes site visitors.

2. A Web browser classifies Web pages in an organized set of categories and related subcategories.

3. Business-to-consumer e-commerce occurs when one consumer sells directly to another, such as in an online auction.

4. The more widely used search engines for personal computers are Internet Explorer, Firefox, Opera, Safari, and Google Chrome.

5. To develop a Web page, you have to be a computer programmer.

Quiz Yourself Online: To further check your knowledge of pages 61 through 75, visit the Computer Concepts CourseMate Web site at www.cengagebrain.com, navigate to the Chapter 2 Quiz Yourself resource for this book, and then click Objectives 3 – 7.

Other Internet Services

The Web is only one of the many services on the Internet. The Web and other Internet services have changed the way we communicate. We use computers and mobile devices to send e-mail messages to the president, have a discussion with experts about the stock market, chat with someone in another country about genealogy, and talk about homework assignments with classmates via instant messages. Many times, these communications take place completely in writing — without the parties ever meeting each other.

The following pages discuss these Internet services: e-mail, mailing lists, instant messaging, chat rooms, VoIP (Voice over IP), FTP (File Transfer Protocol), and newsgroups and message boards.

E-Mail

E-mail (short for electronic mail) is the transmission of messages and files via a computer network. Today, e-mail is a primary communications method for both personal and business use.

You use an **e-mail program** to create, send, receive, forward, store, print, and delete e-mail messages. Outlook and Windows Live Mail are two popular desktop e-mail programs.

The steps in Figure 2-17 illustrate how to send an e-mail message using Outlook; Gmail and Windows Live Hotmail are two popular free e-mail Web applications. The message can be simple text or can include an attachment such as a word processing document, a graphic, an audio clip, or a video clip. To learn more about how to attach a file to an e-mail message, complete the Learn How To 1 activity on page 88.

Just as you address a letter when using the postal system, you address an e-mail message with the e-mail address of your intended recipient. Likewise, when someone sends you a message, he or she must have your e-mail address. An **e-mail address** is a combination of a user name and a domain name that

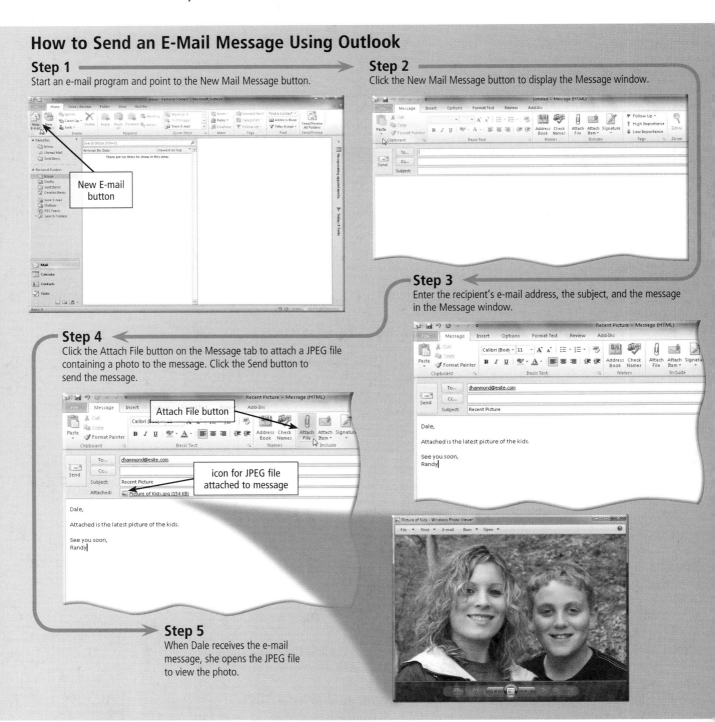

How to Send an E-Mail Message Using Outlook

Step 1
Start an e-mail program and point to the New Mail Message button.

New E-mail button

Step 2
Click the New Mail Message button to display the Message window.

Step 3
Enter the recipient's e-mail address, the subject, and the message in the Message window.

Step 4
Click the Attach File button on the Message tab to attach a JPEG file containing a photo to the message. Click the Send button to send the message.

Attach File button

icon for JPEG file attached to message

Step 5
When Dale receives the e-mail message, she opens the JPEG file to view the photo.

Figure 2-17 This figure shows how to send an e-mail message using Outlook.

identifies a user so that he or she can receive Internet e-mail. A **user name** is a unique combination of characters, such as letters of the alphabet and/or numbers, that identifies a specific user.

In an Internet e-mail address, an @ (pronounced at) symbol separates the user name from the domain name. Your service provider supplies the domain name. A possible e-mail address for Kiley Barnhill would be kbarnhill@esite.com, which would be read as follows: K Barnhill at e site dot com. Most e-mail programs allow you to create an **address book**, or contacts folder, which contains a list of names and e-mail addresses.

When you send an e-mail message, an outgoing mail server that is operated by your Internet access provider determines how to route the message through the Internet and then sends the message. As you receive e-mail messages, an incoming mail server — also operated by your Internet access provider — holds the messages in your mailbox until you use your e-mail program to retrieve them. Most e-mail programs have a mail notification alert that informs you via a message and/or sound when you receive new mail. Figure 2-18 illustrates how an e-mail message may travel from a sender to a receiver using a desktop e-mail program.

E-Mail

For more information, visit the Computer Concepts CourseMate Web site at www.cengagebrain.com, navigate to the Chapter 2 Web Link resource for this book, and then click E-Mail.

? FAQ 2-5

Can my computer get a virus through e-mail?

Yes. A virus is a computer program that can damage files and the operating system. One way that virus authors attempt to spread a virus is by sending virus-infected e-mail attachments. If you receive an e-mail attachment, you should use an antivirus program to verify that it is virus free.

For more information, read the section about viruses and antivirus programs in Chapter 7, and visit the Computer Concepts CourseMate Web site at www.cengagebrain.com, navigate to the Chapter 2 FAQ resource for this book, and then click Viruses.

How an E-Mail Message May Travel from a Sender to a Receiver

Step 1
Using an e-mail program, you create and send a message.

Step 2
Your e-mail program contacts software on your service provider's outgoing mail server.

Step 3
Software on the outgoing mail server determines the best route for the data and sends the message, which travels along Internet routers to the recipient's incoming mail server.

Internet router

Step 4
When the recipient uses an e-mail program to check for e-mail messages, the message transfers from the incoming mail server to the recipient's computer.

Internet service provider's incoming mail server

Internet router

Figure 2-18 This figure shows how an e-mail message may travel from a sender to a receiver.

Mailing Lists

A **mailing list**, also called an e-mail list or distribution list, is a group of e-mail names and addresses given a single name. When a message is sent to a mailing list, every person on the list receives a copy of the message in his or her mailbox. For example, your credit card company may add you to its mailing list in order to send you special offers. To add your e-mail name and address to a mailing list, you **subscribe** to it. To remove your name, you **unsubscribe** from the mailing list.

Thousands of mailing lists exist about a variety of topics in areas of entertainment, business, computers, society, culture, health, recreation, and education.

Instant Messaging

Instant messaging (**IM**) is a real-time Internet communications service that notifies you when one or more people are online and then allows you to exchange messages or files or join a private chat room with them (Figure 2-19). **Real time** means that you and the people with whom you are conversing are online at the same time. Some IM services support voice and video conversations. For IM to work, both parties must be online at the same time. Also, the receiver of a message must be willing to accept messages.

An Example of Instant Messaging

Step 1
Log in to the IM server.

Step 2
The server determines if any of your established friends, family, or coworkers, called buddies, are online.

IM server

Step 3
You send instant messages, voice, and/or video communications to an online buddy.

Step 5
Your online buddy replies.

Step 4
Your instant message, voice, and/or video travels through a messaging server and then to the online buddy's computer.

messaging server

Figure 2-19 This figure shows an example of instant messaging.

To use IM, you may have to install instant messenger software on the computer or device, such as a smart phone, you plan to use. Some operating systems, such as Windows, include an instant messenger. Few IM programs follow IM standards. To ensure successful communications, all individuals on the contact list need to use the same or a compatible instant messenger.

Chat Rooms

A **chat** is a real-time typed conversation that takes place on a computer. A **chat room** is a location on an Internet server that permits users to chat with each other. Anyone in the chat room can participate in the conversation, which usually is specific to a particular topic.

As you type on your keyboard, a line of characters and symbols is displayed on the computer screen. Others connected to the same chat room server also see what you type (Figure 2-20). Some chat rooms support voice chats and video chats, in which people hear or see each other as they chat.

To start a chat session, you connect to a chat server through a program called a chat client. Today's browsers usually include a chat client. If yours does not, you can download a chat client from the Web. Once you have installed a chat client, you can create or join a conversation on the chat server to which you are connected.

Chat Rooms
For more information, visit the Computer Concepts CourseMate Web site at www.cengagebrain.com, navigate to the Chapter 2 Web Link resource for this book, and then click Chat Rooms.

Figure 2-20 As you type, the words and symbols you enter are displayed on the computer screens of other people in the same chat room. To save time many chat and IM users type abbreviations and acronyms for phrases, such as 'r u there?', which stands for 'Are You There?'.

VoIP

VoIP (Voice over IP, or Internet Protocol), also called Internet telephony, enables users to speak to other users over the Internet (instead of the public switched telephone network).

To place an Internet telephone call, you need a high-speed Internet connection (e.g., via cable or DSL modem); Internet telephone service; a microphone or telephone, depending on the Internet telephone service; and Internet telephone software or VoIP router, or a telephone adapter, depending on the Internet telephone service (Figure 2-21). VoIP services also are available on some mobile devices that have wireless Internet service. Calls to other parties with the same Internet telephone service often are free, while calls that connect to the telephone network typically cost about $15 to $35 per month.

Figure 2-21 One type of equipment configuration for a user making a call via VoIP.

FTP

FTP (File Transfer Protocol) is an Internet standard that permits the process of file uploading and downloading with other computers on the Internet. Uploading is the opposite of downloading; that is, **uploading** is the process of transferring documents, graphics, and other objects from your computer to a server on the Internet.

Many operating systems include FTP capabilities. An FTP site is a collection of files including text, graphics, audio clips, video clips, and program files that reside on an FTP server. Many FTP sites have anonymous FTP, whereby anyone can transfer some, if not all, available files. Some FTP sites restrict file transfers to those who have authorized accounts (user names and passwords) on the FTP server.

Newsgroups and Message Boards

A **newsgroup** is an online area in which users have written discussions about a particular subject (Figure 2-22). To participate in a discussion, a user sends a message to the newsgroup, and other users in the newsgroup read and reply to the message.

Some newsgroups require you to enter a user name and password to participate in the discussion. For example, a newsgroup for students taking a college course may require a user name

Figure 2-22 Users in a newsgroup read and reply to other users' messages.

and password to access the newsgroup. This ensures that only students in the course participate in the discussion. To participate in a newsgroup, typically you use a program called a newsreader.

A popular Web-based type of discussion group that does not require a newsreader is a **message board**. Many Web sites use message boards instead of newsgroups because they are easier to use.

Netiquette

Netiquette, which is short for Internet etiquette, is the code of acceptable behaviors users should follow while on the Internet; that is, it is the conduct expected of individuals while online. Netiquette includes rules for all aspects of the Internet, including the World Wide Web, e-mail, instant messaging, chat rooms, FTP, and newsgroups and message boards. Figure 2-23 outlines some of the rules of netiquette. Read Ethics & Issues 2-3 for a related discussion.

NETIQUETTE — Golden Rule: Treat others as you would like them to treat you.

1. In e-mail, chat rooms, and newsgroups:
 - Keep messages brief. Use proper grammar, spelling, and punctuation.
 - Be careful when using sarcasm and humor, as it might be misinterpreted.
 - Be polite. Avoid offensive language.
 - Read the message before you send it.
 - Use meaningful subject lines.
 - Avoid sending or posting flames, which are abusive or insulting messages. Do not participate in flame wars, which are exchanges of flames.
 - Avoid sending spam, which is the Internet's version of junk mail. Spam is an unsolicited e-mail message or newsgroup posting sent to many recipients or newsgroups at once.
 - Do not use all capital letters, which is the equivalent of SHOUTING!
 - Use **emoticons** to express emotion. Popular emoticons include

 | :) | Smile | :\| | Indifference | :o | Surprised |
 | :(| Frown | :\\ | Undecided | | |

 - Use abbreviations and acronyms for phrases:
 | btw | by the way |
 | imho | in my humble opinion |
 | fyi | for your information |
 | ttfn | ta ta for now |
 | fwiw | for what it's worth |
 | tyvm | thank you very much |
 - Clearly identify a spoiler, which is a message that reveals a solution to a game or ending to a movie or program.
2. Read the FAQ (frequently asked questions), if one exists. Many newsgroups and Web pages have an FAQ.
3. Do not assume material is accurate or up-to-date. Be forgiving of other's mistakes.
4. Never read someone's private e-mail.

Figure 2-23 Some of the rules of netiquette.

ʸ ETHICS & ISSUES 2-3

Would Banning Anonymous Comments Reduce Cyberbullying?

Recently, several high-profile cases highlighted the issue of cyberbullying. Cyberbullying is the harassment of computer users, often teens and preteens, through various forms of Internet communications. The behavior typically occurs via e-mail, instant messaging, and chat rooms, and can result in a traumatic experience for the recipient. The bullying may be in the form of threats, spreading of rumors, or humiliation. Usually, the perpetrators of cyberbullying remain anonymous. Many people believe that the anonymous nature of the Internet directly leads to this unscrupulous behavior. Some government officials and advocacy groups have asked for laws that would ban anonymous comments in chat rooms and require that Internet access providers verify and record the true identity of all users. Others have proposed that it be illegal to sign up for an e-mail account or instant messaging account with a fake screen name. Opponents of such plans claim that anonymity and privacy are too important to give up. They state, for example, that the right to be critical of the government in an anonymous forum is a basic right. The rights of everyone should not be infringed upon due to bad behavior of a small group of people.

Would banning anonymous comments reduce cyberbullying? Why or why not? What are the positive and negative aspects of the freedom to remain anonymous on the Internet? What other measures can be taken to reduce cyberbullying? What role can parents play in reducing cyberbullying?

✔ **QUIZ YOURSELF 2-3**

Instructions: Find the true statement below. Then, rewrite the remaining false statements so that they are true.

1. A chat room is a location on an Internet server that permits users to chat with each other.
2. An e-mail address is a combination of a user name and an e-mail program that identifies a user so that he or she can receive Internet e-mail.
3. FTP uses the Internet (instead of the public switched telephone network) to connect a calling party to one or more called parties.
4. Netiquette is the code of unacceptable behaviors while on the Internet.
5. VoIP enables users to subscribe to other users over the Internet.

🖥 **Quiz Yourself Online:** To further check your knowledge of pages 75 through 81, visit the Computer Concepts CourseMate Web site at www.cengagebrain.com, navigate to the Chapter 2 Quiz Yourself resource for this book, and then click Objectives 8 – 9.

Chapter Summary

This chapter presented the history and structure of the Internet. It discussed the World Wide Web at length, including topics such as browsing, navigating, searching, Web publishing, and e-commerce. It also introduced other services available on the Internet, such as e-mail, mailing lists, instant messaging, chat rooms, VoIP, FTP, and newsgroups and message boards. Finally, the chapter listed rules of netiquette.

Computer Usage @ Work

Entertainment

Do you wonder how music on the radio sounds so perfectly in tune, how animated motion pictures are created, or how one controls lighting during a concert? Not only does the entertainment industry rely on computers to advertise and sell their services on the Internet, computers also assist in other aspects, including audio and video composition, lighting control, computerized animation, and computer gaming.

As mentioned in this chapter, entertainment Web sites provide music and movies you can purchase and download to your computer or mobile device; live news broadcasts, performances, and sporting events; games you can play with other online users; and much more.

As early as 1951, computers were used to record and play music. Today, computers play a much larger role in the music industry. For example, if you are listening to a song on the radio and notice that not one note is out of tune, it is possible that software was used to change individual notes without altering the rest of the song.

Many years ago, creating cartoons or animated motion pictures was an extremely time-consuming task because artists were responsible for sketching thousands of drawings by hand. Currently, artists use computers to create these drawings in a fraction of the

time, which significantly can reduce the time and cost of development.

Computers also are used in the game industry. While some game developers create games from scratch, others might use game engines that simplify the development process. For example, LucasArts created the GrimE game engine, which is designed to create adventure games.

During a concert, lighting technicians use computer programs to turn lights off and on, change color, or change location at specified intervals. In fact, once a performance begins, the technicians often merely are standing by, monitoring the computer as it performs most of the work. A significant amount of time and effort, however, is required to program the computer to perform its required tasks during a live show.

The next time you listen to a song, watch a movie, play a game, or attend a concert, think about the role computers play in contributing to your entertainment.

🖥 For more information, visit the Computer Concepts CourseMate Web site at www.cengagebrain.com, navigate to the Chapter 2 Computer Usage @ Work resource for this book, and then click Entertainment.

Companies on the Cutting Edge

GOOGLE Popular Search Engine and Services

Google founders Sergey Brin and Larry Page have done very little advertising, but their Web site has become a household word, largely on favorable word-of-mouth reviews. They launched the Web site in 1998 in a friend's garage with the goal of providing the best possible experience for their loyal users who are looking for information presented clearly and quickly.

Google regularly scans more than one trillion Web pages in search of unique phrases and terms. Its thousands of connected computers deliver organized search results for the hundreds of millions of queries users input daily. Recently, the company updated its Google Earth product to allow users to explore the Moon, and also updated its popular advertising product, AdWords. Among its other services are Google Docs and YouTube.

eBAY World's Largest Online Marketplace

Millions of products are traded daily on eBay auctions, whether it is across town or across the globe. The more than 88 million registered worldwide shoppers generate at least $1.8 billion in annual revenue through purchases on the main Web site, eBay, along with items on Shopping.com, tickets on StubHub, classifieds on Kijiji, and other e-commerce venues.

The shoppers likely pay for their merchandise using PayPal, another eBay service. This merchant service allows buyers to transfer money from savings accounts

or use their credit card without having to expose the account number to the seller. Other eBay companies are Rent.com, which offers listings for apartments and houses, and Shopping.com, which allows consumers to find and compare products. Recently, eBay introduced a program to more easily identify its top-rated sellers. It also invited buyers and sellers to become members of the eBay Green Team, which encourages and promotes environmentally friendly business practices.

For more information, visit the Computer Concepts CourseMate Web site at www.cengagebrain.com and then navigate to the Chapter 2 Companies on the Cutting Edge resource for this book.

Technology Trailblazers

TIM BERNERS-LEE Creator of the World Wide Web

Being the creator of the World Wide Web is an impressive item on any resume, and it certainly helped Tim Berners-Lee become the 3Com Founders Professor of Engineering at the Massachusetts Institute of Technology in 2008. As a professor in the electrical engineering and computer science departments, he researches social and technical collaboration on the Internet.

Berners-Lee's interest in sharing information via Web servers, browsers, and Web addresses developed in 1989

while working at CERN, the European Organization for Nuclear Research, in Geneva, Switzerland. He continued to improve his design of a program that tracked random associations for several years and then became the director of the World Wide Web Consortium (W3C), a forum to develop Web standards, in 1994.

Recently, Queen Elizabeth bestowed the Order of Merit — the highest civilian honor — upon the British-born Berners-Lee.

MARK ZUCKERBERG Facebook Founder and CEO

As one of the youngest self-made billionaires in history, Mark Zuckerberg could have his choice of the finest things in life. Instead, he lives very modestly and walks to Facebook's Palo Alto headquarters.

Both Microsoft and AOL had recruited Zuckerberg during his senior year in high school in New Hampshire. He declined their job offers and decided to attend Harvard. In college, he and some friends developed several projects, laying the foundation that led to Facebook's

eventual start. Harvard administrators claimed these Web sites violated students' privacy. He, however, had instant success launching Facebook from his dorm room, and the Web site's popularity quickly spread to other Ivy League and Boston-area colleges and then worldwide. He left his studies at Harvard University in 2004 and moved to California.

Today, Zuckerberg says he spends the majority of his time running the $15 billion company on very little sleep.

For more information, visit the Computer Concepts CourseMate Web site at www.cengagebrain.com and then navigate to the Chapter 2 Technology Trailblazers resource for this book.

Chapter Review

The Chapter Review reinforces the main concepts presented in this chapter.

To listen to an audio version of this Chapter Review, visit the Computer Concepts CourseMate Web site at www.cengagebrain.com and then navigate to the Chapter 2 Chapter Review resource for this book.

1. What Are the Various Broadband Internet Connections? The **Internet** is a worldwide collection of networks that links millions of businesses, government agencies, educational institutions, and individuals. Many home and small business users connect to the Internet via high-speed **broadband** Internet service. **Cable Internet service** provides high-speed Internet access through the cable television network via a cable modem. **DSL** (digital subscriber line) provides high-speed Internet connections using regular telephone lines. **Fiber to the Premises** (**FTTP**) uses fiber-optic cable to provide high-speed Internet access. **Fixed wireless** high-speed Internet connections use a dish-shaped antenna to communicate via radio signals. A **Wi-Fi** network uses radio signals to provide Internet connections to wireless computers and devices. A **cellular radio network** offers high-speed Internet connections to devices with built-in compatible technology or computers with wireless modems. **Satellite Internet service** communicates with a satellite dish to provide high-speed Internet connections. Some home and small businesses connect to the Internet with **dial-up access**, which uses a modem in the computer and a standard telephone line.

2. What Are the Types of Internet Access Providers? An **access provider** is a business that provides access to the Internet free or for a fee. An **ISP** (**Internet service provider**) is a regional or national access provider. An **online service provider** (**OSP**) provides Internet access in addition to members-only features, such as instant messaging or customized Web browsers. A **wireless Internet service provider** provides wireless Internet access to computers and mobile devices with built-in wireless capability (such as Wi-Fi) or to computers using wireless modems or wireless access devices.

Visit the Computer Concepts CourseMate Web site at www.cengagebrain.com, navigate to the Chapter 2 Quiz Yourself resource for this book, and then click Objectives 1 – 2.

3. What Is the Purpose of a Web Browser, and What Are the Components of a Web Address? A **Web browser**, or **browser**, is application software that allows users to access and view Web pages or access Web 2.0 programs. A **Web address** is the unique address for each **Web page** and consists of a protocol, a domain name, and sometimes the path to a specific Web page or location on a Web page.

4. How Do You Use a Search Engine to Search for Information on the Web? A **search engine** is a program that finds Web sites, Web pages, images, videos, news, maps, and other information related to a specific topic. A search engine is helpful in locating information for which you do not know an exact Web address or are not seeking a particular Web site. Search engines require **search text** that describes the item you want to find. After performing the search, the search engine returns a list of hits, each one a **link** to an associated Web page.

5. What Are the Types of Web Sites? A **portal** is a Web site that offers a variety of Internet services from a single location. A news Web site contains newsworthy material. An informational Web site contains factual information. A business/marketing Web site promotes or sells products or services. A **blog** is an informal Web site consisting of time-stamped articles, or posts, in a diary or journal format, usually listed in reverse chronological order. A **wiki** is a collaborative Web site that allows users to create, add to, modify, or delete the Web site content via their Web browser. An **online social network**, or **social networking Web site**, encourages members to share their interests, ideas, stories, photos, music, and videos with other registered users. An educational Web site offers avenues for teaching and learning. An entertainment Web site offers an interactive and engaging environment. An advocacy Web site describes a cause, opinion, or idea. A **Web application**, or **Web app**, is a Web site that allows users to access and interact with software through a Web browser on any computer connected to the Internet. A **content aggregator** is a business that gathers and organizes Web content and then distributes, or feeds, the content to subscribers for free or a fee. A personal Web site is maintained by a private individual or family.

6. How Do Web Pages Use Graphics, Animation, Audio, Video, Virtual Reality, and Plug-Ins? More exciting Web sites use **multimedia**, which refers to any application that combines text with graphics, animation, video, and/or virtual reality. A **graphic**, or graphical image, is a digital representation of nontext information such as a drawing, chart, or photo. **Animation** is the appearance of motion created by displaying a series of still images in sequence. **Audio** includes music, speech, or any other sound. **Video** consists of full-motion images that are played back at various speeds. **Virtual reality** (**VR**) is the use of computers to simulate a real or imagined environment as a 3-D space. A **plug-in** is a program that extends the capability of a browser.

STUDENT ASSIGNMENTS

7. What Are the Steps Required for Web Publishing? **Web publishing** is the development and maintenance of Web pages. The five major steps to Web publishing are: (1) plan a Web site, (2) analyze and design a Web site, (3) create a Web site, (4) deploy a Web site, and (5) maintain a Web site.

Visit the Computer Concepts CourseMate Web site at www.cengagebrain.com, navigate to the Chapter 2 Quiz Yourself resource for this book, and then click Objectives 3 – 7.

8. How Do E-Mail, Mailing Lists, Instant Messaging, Chat Rooms, VoIP, FTP, and Newsgroups and Message Boards Work? E-mail (short for electronic mail) is the transmission of messages and files via a computer network. A **mailing list** is a group of e-mail names and addresses given a single name, so that everyone on the list receives a message sent to the list. **Instant messaging** (**IM**) is a **real-time** Internet communications service that notifies you when one or more people are online. A **chat room** is a location on an Internet server that permits users to **chat**, or conduct real-time typed conversations. **VoIP** (Voice over IP, or Internet Protocol) enables users to speak to other users over the Internet instead of the public switched telephone network. **FTP** (File Transfer Protocol) is an Internet standard that permits file **uploading** and **downloading** with other computers on the Internet. A **newsgroup** is an online area in which users have written discussions about a particular subject. A **message board** is a popular Web-based type of discussion group that is easier to use than a newsgroup.

9. What Are the Rules of Netiquette? **Netiquette**, which is short for Internet etiquette, is the code of acceptable behaviors users should follow while on the Internet. Keep messages short. Be polite. Use **emoticons**. Read the FAQ if one exists. Do not assume material is accurate or up-to-date, and never read someone's private e-mail.

Visit the Computer Concepts CourseMate Web site at www.cengagebrain.com, navigate to the Chapter 2 Quiz Yourself resource for this book, and then click Objectives 8 – 9.

Key Terms

You should know the Key Terms. The list below helps focus your study.

To see an example of and a definition for each term, and to access current and additional information from the Web, visit the Computer Concepts CourseMate Web site at www.cengagebrain.com and then navigate to the Chapter 2 Key Terms resource for this book.

access provider (58)
add-on (73)
address book (77)
animation (71)
audio (72)
blog (68)
blogosphere (68)
bookmark (63)
broadband (57)
browser (61)
cable Internet service (57)
cellular radio network (58)
chat (79)
chat room (79)
click (64)
content aggregator (70)
dial-up access (58)
domain name (60)
downloading (62)
DSL (57)
e-commerce (74)
electronic storefront (74)
e-mail address (76)
e-mail program (75)
emoticons (81)

favorite (63)
Fiber to the Premises (FTTP) (57)
fixed wireless (57)
FTP (80)
graphic (70)
home page (62)
hot spots (58)
hyperlink (64)
instant messaging (IM) (78)
Internet (56)
Internet backbone (59)
IP address (60)
ISP (Internet service provider) (58)
link (64)
mailing list (78)
media sharing Web site (69)
message board (81)
microblog (68)
MP3 (72)
MP4 (73)
multimedia (70)
Net (56)
netiquette (81)

newsgroup (80)
online auction (75)
online service provider (OSP) (58)
online social network (69)
player (72)
plug-in (73)
podcast (72)
portal (67)
real time (78)
RSS 2.0 (70)
satellite Internet service (58)
search engine (65)
search text (66)
shopping cart (75)
social networking Web site (69)
streaming (72)
subject directory (65)
subscribe (78)
surfing the Web (64)
tabbed browsing (64)
thumbnail (71)
top-level domain (TLD) (60)
unsubscribe (78)

uploading (80)
URL (63)
user name (77)
video (73)
video blog (68)
virtual reality (VR) (73)
vlog (68)
vlogosphere (68)
VoIP (80)
Web (61)
Web 2.0 (61)
Web address (63)
Web app (69)
Web application (69)
Web browser (61)
Web page (61)
Web publishing (74)
Web server (61)
Web site (61)
Wi-Fi (57)
wiki (68)
wireless Internet service provider (58)
World Wide Web (WWW) (61)

Checkpoint

The Checkpoint exercises test your knowledge of the chapter concepts. The page number containing the answer appears in parentheses after each exercise.

To complete the Checkpoint exercises interactively, visit the Computer Concepts CourseMate Web site at www.cengagebrain.com and then navigate to the Chapter 2 Checkpoint resource for this book.

Multiple Choice Select the best answer.

1. _____ offers high-speed Internet connections to devices with built-in compatible technology or computers with wireless modems. (58)
 a. Cable Internet service
 b. A digital subscriber line
 c. A cellular radio network
 d. Fiber to the Premises (FTTP)

2. Instead of using broadband Internet service some home users connect to the Internet via _____, which is a slower-speed technology. (58)
 a. satellite Internet service
 b. cable Internet service
 c. DSL
 d. dial-up access

3. _____ is the process of a computer or device receiving information, such as a Web page, from a server on the Internet. (62)
 a. Uploading b. Social networking
 c. Downloading d. Blogging

4. A _____ is a Web site that allows users to post short text updates, usually between 100 and 200 characters. (68)
 a. podcast
 b. wiki
 c. microblog
 d. portal

5. A _____ is a specific type of online social network that enables members to share photos, music, and videos. (69)
 a. blog
 b. wiki
 c. podcast
 d. media sharing Web site

6. A(n) _____ is a small version of a larger graphic. (71)
 a. thumbnail
 b. wiki
 c. MP3
 d. portal

7. In _____ e-commerce, one consumer sells directly to another. (75)
 a. consumer-to-business
 b. business-to-business
 c. consumer-to-consumer
 d. business-to-consumer

8. The _____ standard permits uploading and downloading of files on the Internet. (80)
 a. FTP
 b. newsgroup
 c. message board
 d. mailing list

Matching Match the terms with their definitions.

_____ 1. home page (62)

_____ 2. search engine (65)

_____ 3. MP3 (72)

_____ 4. e-mail address (76)

_____ 5. emoticons (81)

a. used to express emotions in e-mail, chat rooms, and newsgroups

b. the first page that a Web site displays

c. combination of a user name and a domain name that identifies an Internet user

d. program that finds Web sites, Web pages, images, videos, news, maps, and other information related to a specific topic

e. built-in connection to a related Web page or part of a Web page

f. format that reduces an audio file to about one-tenth its original size

Short Answer Write a brief answer to each of the following questions.

1. Describe three different types of broadband Internet services. _____ What is the difference between a regional ISP and a national ISP? _____

2. How is a Web page different from a Web site? _____ How can you use a Web address to display a Web page? _____

3. What are the differences between blogs, wikis, and podcasts? _____ When might you use each? _____

4. What is a Web application? _____ What are some features and examples of Web applications? _____

5. What is one specification used by content aggregators to distribute content? _____ How might you evaluate the accuracy of a Web site? _____

Problem Solving

The Problem Solving exercises extend your knowledge of the chapter concepts by seeking solutions to practical computer problems that you may encounter at home, school, or work. The Collaboration exercise should be completed with a team.

In the real world, practical problems often can be solved in multiple ways. Provide one solution to each of the following problems using available resources, such as articles on the Web or in print, blogs, podcasts, videos, television, user guides, other individuals, and electronics and computer stores. You may need to use multiple resources to obtain an answer. Present your solutions in the form requested by your instructor (brief report, presentation, discussion, or other means).

@ Home

1. **Slow Internet Connection** You just installed VoIP telephone service in your house. Each time you are on the telephone, however, you notice that your Internet connection slows down significantly. What could be causing this?

2. **No Wireless Connection** When you return home to visit your parents and turn on your new notebook computer, it does not connect automatically to their wireless network. What is your next step?

3. **Incorrect Search Engine** A class project requires that you conduct research on the Web. After typing the Web address for Google's home page and pressing the ENTER key, your Web browser redirects you to a different search engine. What could be wrong?

4. **New Browser Windows** While browsing the Web, each time you click a link, the link's destination opens in a new browser window. You prefer to have each link open in a new tab so that your taskbar does not become cluttered. How will you resolve this?

@ Work

5. **Access Denied** During your lunch hour, you decide to search the Web for possible vacation destinations. After visiting several airline and hotel Web sites, you attempt to visit the Web site for a Caribbean resort. Much to your surprise, the Web browser informs you that the Web site has been blocked. Why might this happen?

6. **Sporadic E-Mail Message Delivery** The e-mail program on your computer has been delivering new messages only every hour, on the hour. Historically, new e-mail messages would arrive and be displayed immediately upon being sent by the sender. Furthermore, your coworkers claim that they sometimes do not receive your e-mail messages until hours after they are sent. What might be the problem?

7. **E-Mail Message Formatting** A friend sent an e-mail message containing a photo to your e-mail account at work. Upon receiving the e-mail message, the photo does not display. You also notice that e-mail messages never display any formatting, such as different fonts, font sizes, and font colors. What might be causing this?

8. **Automatic Response** When you return from vacation, a colleague informs you that when she sent e-mail messages to your e-mail address, she would not always receive your automatic response stating that you were out of the office. Why might your e-mail program not respond automatically to every e-mail message received?

Collaboration

9. **Computers in Entertainment** The drama department at a local high school is considering developing a movie and has asked for your help. The drama teacher would like to incorporate technology wherever possible, in hopes that it would decrease the costs of the movie's production. Form a team of three people to help determine what technology can be used to assist in the movie's production. One team member should research the type of technology that can be used during the filming process. Another team member should research the types of hardware and software available for editing footage, and the third team member should research the hardware and software requirements for creating the media to distribute the finished product.

Learn How To

The Learn How To activities step you through fundamental technology skills when using a computer. The Learn How To exercises enable you to become more proficient with these skills.

Premium Activity: To relate this Learn How To activity to your everyday life, see a visual demonstration of the activity, and complete a short assessment, visit the Computer Concepts CourseMate Web site at www.cengagebrain.com and then navigate to the Chapter 2 Learn How To resource for this book.

Learn How To 1: Attach a File to an E-Mail Message

When you send an e-mail message, it sometimes is necessary to attach a file to supplement the body of the e-mail message. Most e-mail programs allow you to attach a file to your e-mail messages easily, but many do not allow you to attach files exceeding a specified size limit (which varies by your e-mail service). You can attach a file to an e-mail message by completing the following steps:

1. Start your e-mail program and compose a new e-mail message to your recipient. Make sure that you have a descriptive subject and that you explain in the e-mail message that you are attaching a file.
2. To attach a file, locate and click the Attach File button or link. If you are unable to locate this button, you may find an icon with a picture of a paperclip or a menu command to attach a file. Some e-mail programs also may have a text box in the new message window with an adjacent Browse button. In this case, click the Browse button.
3. Locate and click the file you wish to attach and then click the Open (or Insert or Select) button (Figure 2-24).
4. Verify that your e-mail message contains the attachment and then click the Send button.

Figure 2-24

When the recipient opens the e-mail message, he or she also will be able to open the attachment.

Exercises

1. Start your e-mail program. Compose a new e-mail message to your instructor, and attach a file containing your current course schedule. Verify that your message has been received and then close your e-mail program.

2. Locate three free e-mail Web applications. How many file attachments do these e-mail programs allow you to attach to one e-mail message? Is a maximum file size specified for an e-mail attachment? Can you pay to upgrade your e-mail account so that these restrictions are lifted? Submit these answers to your instructor.

Learn How To 2: Search the Web for Driving Directions, Addresses, and Telephone Numbers

In addition to searching the Web for information using search engines such as Google and Yahoo!, some Web sites are designed specifically to search for other information such as driving directions, addresses, and telephone numbers.

Search for Driving Directions

1. Start your Web browser, type mapquest.com in the Address bar, press the ENTER key to display the MapQuest home page, and then click the Directions tab.
2. Type the starting address (or intersection), city, state, and ZIP code (if you know it) in the appropriate text boxes in the Starting Location area of the Directions page.
3. Type the ending address (or intersection), city, state, and ZIP code (if you know it) in the appropriate text boxes in the Ending Location area of the Directions page.
4. Click the Get Directions button to display the driving directions.

Search for the Address and Telephone Number of a Business

1. If necessary, start your Web browser. Type yellowpages.com in the Address bar, and then press the ENTER key to display the Yellow Pages Local Directory home page.

2. Type the name of the business in the Find text box, and type the city, state, and ZIP (if you know it) in the Location text box.
3. Click the FIND button to display the search results.
4. Close your Web browser.

Exercises

1. If necessary, start Internet Explorer by clicking the Start button, and then click Internet Explorer on the Start menu. Type `mapquest.com` in the Address bar, and then press the ENTER key. Search for driving directions between your address and the address of a friend or family member. How many miles are between the two addresses? How long would it take you to drive from your address to the other address? Write a paragraph explaining whether you would or would not use MapQuest to retrieve driving directions. Submit this paragraph to your instructor.

2. Use the Web to search for another Web site that provides driving directions. Use the Web site to search for directions between the same two locations from Exercise 1. Are the driving directions the same as the ones that MapQuest provided? If not, why might they be different? Which Web site did you use? Do you prefer this Web site to MapQuest? Why or why not? Write a paragraph with your answers and submit it to your instructor.

3. Think about a company for which you would like to work. In your Web browser, display the Yellow Pages Web page (yellowpages.com) and then search for the address and telephone number of this company. If Yellow Pages does not display the desired information, what other Web sites might you be able to use to search for the address and telephone number for a company?

Learn It Online

The Learn It Online exercises are interactive Web exercises designed to reinforce and expand your understanding of the chapter concepts. The descriptions below briefly summarize each exercise.

To complete the Learn It Online exercises, visit the Computer Concepts CourseMate Web site at www.cengagebrain.com, navigate to the Chapter 2 resources for this book, click the link for the exercise you want to complete, and then read the instructions.

1 At the Movies — Tell Your Stories via Vlog
Watch a movie to learn about how to post your thoughts to a vlog and then answer questions about the movie.

2 Student Edition Labs — Connecting to the Internet, Getting the Most out of the Internet, and E-mail
Enhance your understanding and knowledge about the Internet and e-mail by completing the Connecting to the Internet, Getting the Most out of the Internet, and E-mail Labs.

3 Practice Test
Take a multiple choice test that checks your knowledge of the chapter concepts and review the resulting study guide.

4 Who Wants To Be a Computer Genius²?
Play the Shelly Cashman Series version of this popular game by answering questions to find out if you are a computer genius. Panic buttons are available to provide assistance during game play.

5 Crossword Puzzle Challenge
Complete an interactive crossword puzzle to reinforce concepts presented in this chapter.

6 Windows Exercises
Step through the Windows 7 exercises to learn about Internet properties, dial-up networking connections, and using Help to understand the Internet.

7 Exploring Computer Careers
Read about a career as a Web developer, search for related employment advertisements, and then answer related questions.

8 Web Apps — Windows Live Hotmail
Learn how to sign up for a free e-mail account, add a contact to your address book, and send an e-mail message.

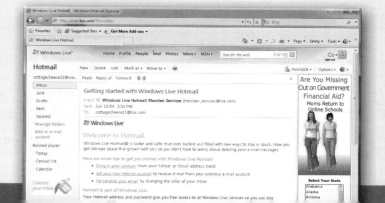

Web Research

The Web Research exercises broaden your understanding of the chapter concepts by presenting questions that require you to search the Web for answers.

1 **Search Sleuth**

Use one of the search engines listed in Figure 2-8 in Chapter 2 on page 65 or your own favorite search engine to find the answers to the following questions. Copy and paste the Web address from the Web page where you found the answer. Some questions may have more than one answer. If required, submit your answers to your instructor. (1) What were the title, date of publication, and purpose of the Internet Engineering Task Force's RFC 1 document? (2) What is the mission of the World Wide Web Consortium (W3C)? (3) What topic does the film *Adina's Deck* address? (4) What are the current figures on the Reporters Without Borders' Press Freedom Barometer? (5) What was eBay's original name, and what was the first item offered for auction? (6) Why did ConnectU sue Facebook in 2008 and 2004? (7) What is the cost to use Google's 411 service?

2 **Green Computing**

EcoSearch is a search engine dedicated to supporting the Earth's natural resources. Visit this Web site (ecosearch.org), use your word processing program to answer the following questions, and then, if required, submit your answers to your instructor. (1) From what company do the search results come? (2) Click the Learn More link on the page. What charities does EcoSearch support? (3) How can you get involved to help EcoSearch? (4) Click the EcoSearch Home link at the bottom of the page to return to the EcoSearch home page. In the text box, type ecosearch donate profits and then click the Search button. Click several of the resulting links and review the information. Write a 50-word summary of the information, including what percent of EcoSearch proceeds is donated to charities and how much money EcoSearch expects to donate each year.

3 **Social Networking**

MySpace is considered one of the pioneering Web sites that helped popularize the online social networking phenomenon. Calling itself "a place for friends," it allows the millions of registered members to create profiles for free and then invite friends to join their networks. The growth of this Web site has helped it emerge as one of the more popular search engines. Visit the MySpace site (myspace.com), type the name of your favorite musical artist or group in the search text box, and then click the Search button. How many search results were found? Visit some of these profiles. Which music videos, playlists, and ringtones are featured? How do you create and edit your own playlists and add a song to your profile? Then click the Safety Tips link at the bottom of the page and read the guidelines for posting information and reporting inappropriate content. Summarize the music profiles you viewed and the guidelines. If required, submit your summary to your instructor.

4 **Blogs**

Many of the best blogs in the blogosphere have received awards for their content and design. For example, loyal blogging fans nominate and vote for their favorite blogs by visiting the Blogger's Choice Awards Web site (bloggerschoiceawards.com). Visit this Web site, click the Best Blog Design, Best Blog About Blogging, and Best Education Blog links, and view some of the blogs receiving the largest number of votes. Then visit other award sites, including the Interactive Media Awards (interactivemediaawards.com), Bloggies (bloggies.com), and the Best of Blogs (thebestofblogs.com). Which blogs, if any, received multiple awards on the different Web sites? Who casts the votes? What criteria are used to judge these blogs?

5 **Ethics in Action**

Some Internet access providers have admitted they monitored their users' Web surfing activities without giving notice of this eavesdropping practice. Embarq and Charter Communications secretly tested advertising technology to gather data about specific Web searches and then display advertisements relating to these searches. Privacy expert claim these Internet access providers' practices violate federal privacy laws, including the wiretapping statute. Locate news articles discussing the Internet access providers' Web eavesdropping. Then locate Web sites that oppose this practice. Summarize the views of the advertisers and the privacy proponents. If required, submit your summary to your instructor.

Making Use of the Web

INFORMATION LITERACY IS DEFINED as having the practical skills needed to evaluate information critically from print and electronic resources and to use this information accurately in daily life. Locating Web sites may be profitable for your educational and professional careers, as the resources may help you research class assignments and make your life more fulfilling and manageable.

Because the Web does not have an organizational structure to assist you in locating reliable material, you may need additional resources to guide you in searching. To help you find useful Web sites, this Special Feature describes specific information about a variety of Web pages, and it includes tables of Web addresses so that you can get started. The material is organized in several areas of interest.

Web Exercises at the end of each area will reinforce the material and help you discover Web sites that may add a treasure trove of knowledge to your life.

Areas of Interest

Fun and Entertainment	Shopping and Auctions
Research	Weather, Sports, and News
Blogs	Learning
Online Social Networks and Media Sharing	Science
Travel	Health
Environment	Careers
Finance	Literature and Arts
Government	

Fun and Entertainment
That's Entertainment

Rock 'n' Roll on the Web

Consumers place great significance on buying entertainment products for fun and recreation. Nearly 10 percent of the United States's economy is spent on attending concerts and buying optical discs, reading materials, sporting goods, and toys.

Many Web sites supplement our cravings for fun and entertainment. For example, you can see and hear the musicians inducted into the Rock and Roll Hall of Fame and Museum. If you need an update on your favorite reality-based television program or a preview of an upcoming movie, E! Online and Entertainment Weekly provide the latest features about actors and actresses. The Internet Movie Database contains reviews of more than one million titles (Figure 1).

Watch the surfers riding the waves and romp with pandas at the San Diego Zoo. Web cams can display live video on Web pages, taking armchair travelers across the world for views of natural attractions, monuments, and cities. Many Web sites featuring Web cams are listed in the table in Figure 2.

Figure 1 Visitors exploring the Internet Movie Database will find the latest news about their favorite television programs and movies.

Fun and Entertainment Web Sites

Entertainment	Web Address
allmusic	allmusic.com
E! Online	eonline.com
Entertainment Weekly's EW	ew.com/ew
Games.com	games.com
Internet Movie Database	imdb.com
Old Time Radio (OTR) — Radio Days: A Radio History	otr.com
Rock and Roll Hall of Fame and Museum	rockhall.com
World Radio Network	wrn.org
Yahoo! Entertainment	entertainment.yahoo.com

Web Cams	Web Address
Camvista	camvista.com
Discovery Kids — Live Cams	kids.discovery.com/cams/cams.html
EarthCam — Webcam Network	earthcam.com
ESRL/GMD Mauna Loa Live Camera	esrl.noaa.gov/gmd/obop/mlo/livecam/index.html
Gatorland	gatorland.com/gatorcam.php
Geocaching — The Official Global GPS Cache Hunt Site	geocaching.com
Panda Cam San Diego Zoo	sandiegozoo.org/zoo/ex_panda_station.html
WebCam Central	camcentral.com
Wild Birds Unlimited Bird FeederCam	wbu.com/feedercam_home.html

For more information about fun and entertainment Web sites, visit the Computer Concepts CourseMate Web site at www.cengagebrain.com and then navigate to the Making Use of the Web Feature resource for this book.

Figure 2 When you visit Web sites offering fun and entertainment resources, you can be both amused and informed.

Fun and Entertainment Web Exercises

1 **Visit the Geocaching site listed in Figure 2.** Find the geocaches within five miles of your home or school and then print a map showing their locations. Then, visit the Discovery Kids — Live Cams Web site and view one of the animal cams in the Live Cams. What do you observe? Visit another Web site listed in Figure 2 and describe the view. What are the benefits of having Web cams at these locations throughout the world?

2 **What are your favorite movies?** Use the Internet Movie Database Web site listed in Figure 2 to search for information about two films, and write a brief description of the biographies of the major stars and director for each movie. Then, visit one of the entertainment Web sites and describe three of the featured stories. At the Rock and Roll Hall of Fame and Museum Web site, view the information about The Beatles and one of your favorite musicians. Write a paragraph describing the information available about these rock stars.

Research
Search and Ye Shall Find

Information on the Web

A recent Web Usability survey conducted by the Nielsen Norman Group found that 88 percent of people who connect to the Internet use a search engine as their first online action. Search engines require users to type words and phrases that characterize the information being sought. Bing (Figure 3), Google, and AltaVista are some of the more popular search engines. The key to effective searching on the Web is composing search queries that narrow the search results and place the more relevant Web sites at the top of the results list.

Keep up with the latest computer and related product developments by viewing online dictionaries and encyclopedias that add to their collections on a regular basis. Shopping for a new computer can be a daunting experience, but many online guides can help you select the components that best fit your needs and budget. If you are not confident in your ability to solve a problem alone, turn to online technical support. Hardware and software reviews, price comparisons, shareware, technical questions and answers, and breaking technology news are found on comprehensive portals. Figure 4 lists popular research Web sites.

Research Web Sites

Research	Web Address
A9.com	a9.com
AccessMyLibrary	accessmylibrary.com
AltaVista	altavista.com
Answers.com	answers.com
Ask	ask.com
Bing	bing.com
ChaCha	chacha.com
CNET	cnet.com
eHow	ehow.com
Google	google.com
HotBot	hotbot.com
Librarians' Internet Index	lii.org
PC911	pcnineoneone.com
Switchboard	switchboard.com
Webopedia	webopedia.com
ZDNet	zdnet.com

For more information about research Web sites, visit the Computer Concepts CourseMate Web site at www.cengagebrain.com and then navigate to the Making Use of the Web Feature resource for this book.

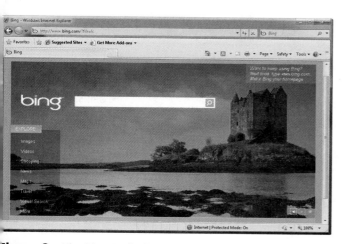

Figure 3 The Bing Web site provides a search engine for images, videos, shopping, news, maps, and travel.

Figure 4 Web users can find information by using research Web sites.

Research Web Exercises

1 Visit two of the research Web sites listed in Figure 4 to find three Web sites that review the latest digital cameras from Kodak and Canon. Make a table listing the research Web sites, the located Web site names, and the cameras' model numbers, suggested retail price, and features.

2 Visit the Webopedia Web site. Search this site for five terms of your choice. Create a table with two columns: one for the term and one for the Web definition. Then, create a second table listing five recently added or updated words and their definitions on this Web site. Next, visit the CNET Web site to choose the components you would buy if you were building a customized desktop computer and notebook computer. Create a table for both computers, listing the computer manufacturer, processor model name or number and manufacturer, clock speed, RAM, cache, number of expansion slots, and number of bays.

Blogs
Express Yourself

Blogosphere Growing Swiftly

Internet users are feeling the need to publish their views, and they are finding Weblogs, or blogs for short, the ideal vehicle. The blogosphere began as an easy way for individuals to express their opinions on the Web. Today, this communications vehicle has become a powerful tool, for individuals, groups, and corporations are using blogs to promote their ideas and advertise their products. It is not necessary to have a background in Web design to be able to post to a blog.

Bloggers generally update their Web sites frequently to reflect their views. Their posts range from a paragraph to an entire essay and often contain links to other Web sites. The more popular blogs discuss politics, lifestyles, and technology.

Individuals easily may set up a blog free or for a fee, using Web sites such as Blogger, Bloglines (Figure 5), and TypePad. In addition, online social networks may have a built-in blogging feature. Be cautious of the information you post on your blog, especially if it is accessible to everyone online.

Figure 5 Bloglines keeps readers abreast of the latest technology, entertainment, and political news in the blogosphere.

Corporate blogs, such as The GM FastLane Blog, discuss all aspects of the company's products, whereas all-encompassing blogs, such as the MetaFilter Community Weblog and others in Figure 6, are designed to keep general readers entertained and informed.

Blogs are affecting the manner in which people communicate and some experts predict they will one day become our primary method of sharing information.

Blogs Web Sites	
Blog	**Web Address**
A List Apart	alistapart.com
Blog.com	blog.com
Blog Flux	topsites.blogflux.com
Blogger	blogger.com
Bloglines	bloglines.com
Blogstream	blogstream.com
Davenetics*Remote Control Revolutionary	davenetics.com
Geek News Central	geeknewscentral.com
GM FastLane Blog	fastlane.gmblogs.com
kottke.org	kottke.org
MetaFilter Community Weblog	metafilter.com
Rocketboom	rocketboom.com
TreeHugger	treehuggertv.com
Twitter	twitter.com
TypePad	typepad.com

For more information about blogs Web sites, visit the Computer Concepts CourseMate Web site at www.cengagebrain.com and then navigate to the Making Use of the Web Feature resource for this book.

Figure 6 These blogs offer information about technology, news, politics, and entertainment.

Blogs Web Exercises

1 **Visit three of the blog Web sites listed in Figure 6.** Make a table listing the blog name, its purpose, the author, its audience, and advertisers, if any, who sponsor the blog. Then, write a paragraph that describes the information you found on each of these blogs.

2 **Many Internet users read the technology blogs to keep abreast of the latest developments.** Visit the Geek News Central and Bloglines blogs listed in Figure 6 and write a paragraph describing the top story in each blog. Read the posted comments, if any. Then, write another paragraph describing two other stories found on these blogs that cover material you have discussed in this course. Write a third paragraph discussing which one is more interesting to you. Would you add reading blogs to your list of Internet activities? Why or why not?

Online Social Networks and Media Sharing
Check Out My New Photos

Online Social Networks and Media Sharing Web Sites Gain Popularity

Do you ever wonder what your friends are doing? What about your friends' friends? The popularity of online social networks has increased dramatically in recent years. Online social networks, such as those listed in Figure 7, allow you to create a personalized profile that others are able to view online. These profiles may include information about you such as your hometown, your age, your hobbies, and pictures. You also may create links to your friends' pages, post messages for individual friends, or bulletins for all of your friends to see. Online social networks are great places to keep in touch with your friends and to network with professionals for business purposes.

If you would like to post pictures and videos and do not require the full functionality of an online social network, you might consider a media sharing Web site, which is a type of online social network. Media sharing Web sites such as YouTube and Phanfare (Figure 8) allow you to post media, including photos and videos, for others to view, print, and/or download. Media sharing Web sites, which may be free or charge a fee, provide a quick, efficient way to share photos of your last vacation or videos of your family reunion.

Online Social Networks and Media Sharing

Online Social Networks	Web Address
Club Penguin	clubpenguin.com
Facebook	facebook.com
LinkedIn	linkedin.com
MySpace — a place for friends	myspace.com
orkut	orkut.com
Windows Live Spaces	spaces.live.com

Media Sharing	Web Address
flickr	flickr.com
Phanfare	phanfare.com
Photobucket	photobucket.com
Picasa	picasa.com
Shutterfly	shutterfly.com
Yahoo! Video	video.yahoo.com
YouTube	youtube.com

For more information about online social networks and media sharing Web sites, visit the Computer Concepts CourseMate Web site at www.cengagebrain.com and then navigate to the Making Use of the Web Feature resource for this book.

Figure 7 Online social networks and media sharing Web sites are popular ways to keep in touch with friends, meet new people, and share media.

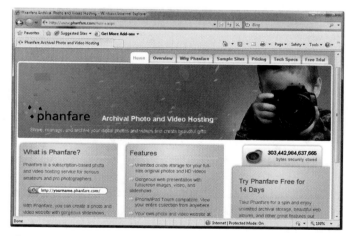

Figure 8 The Phanfare Web site allows users to share their photo and video files with people throughout the world.

Online Social Networks and Media Sharing Web Exercises

1 **Many individuals now use online social networks.** Visit two online social networks listed in Figure 7. (If you are attempting to access an online social network from your classroom and are unable to do so, your school may have restricted use of social networking Web sites.) Compare and contrast these two sites by performing the following actions and recording your findings. First, create a profile on each of these sites. If you find a Web site that charges a fee to sign up, choose another Web site. How easy is the sign-up process? Does either Web site ask for any personal information you are uncomfortable sharing? If so, what information? Once you sign up, make a list of five of your closest friends, and search for their profiles on each of these two sites. Which site contains more of your friends? Browse each site and make a list of its features. In your opinion, which site is better? Explain why.

2 **Media sharing Web sites make it easy to share photos and videos with friends, family, and colleagues.** Before choosing a media sharing Web site to use, do some research. Visit two media sharing Web sites in Figure 7. Is there a fee to post media to these Web sites? If so, how much? Are these Web sites supported by advertisements? Locate the instructions for posting media to these Web sites. Are the instructions straightforward? Do these Web sites impose a limit on the number and/or size of media files you can post? Summarize your responses to these questions in two or three paragraphs.

Travel
Get Packing!

Explore the World without Leaving Home

When you are ready to arrange your next travel adventure or just want to explore destination possibilities, the Internet provides ample resources to set your plans in motion.

To discover exactly where your destination is on this planet, cartography Web sites, including MapQuest and Yahoo! Maps, allow you to pinpoint your destination. View your exact destination using satellite imagery with Google Maps and Bing Maps (Figure 9).

Some excellent starting places are general travel Web sites such as Expedia Travel, Cheap Tickets, Orbitz, and Travelocity. Many airline Web sites allow you to reserve hotel rooms, activities, and rental cars while booking a flight. These all-encompassing Web sites, including those in Figure 10, have tools to help you find the lowest prices and details about flights, car rentals, cruises, and hotels. Comprehensive online guidebooks can provide useful details about maximizing your vacation time while saving money.

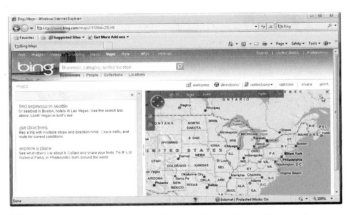

Figure 9 Bing Maps provides location information and satellite imagery for many regions on this planet.

Travel Web Sites

General Travel	Web Address
CheapTickets	cheaptickets.com
Expedia Travel	expedia.com
Kayak	kayak.com
Orbitz	orbitz.com
SideStep	sidestep.com
Travelocity	travelocity.com
Cartography	**Web Address**
Bing Maps	bing.com/maps
Google Maps	maps.google.com
MapQuest	mapquest.com
Maps.com	maps.com
Yahoo! Maps	maps.yahoo.com
Travel and City Guides	**Web Address**
Frommer's Travel Guides	frommers.com
GoPlanit	goplanit.com
U.S.-Parks US National Parks Travel Guide	www.us-parks.com
Virtual Tourist	virtualtourist.com

For more information about travel Web sites, visit the Computer Concepts CourseMate Web site at www.cengagebrain.com and then navigate to the Making Use of the Web Feature resource for this book.

Figure 10 These travel resources Web sites offer travel information to exciting destinations throughout the world.

Travel Web Exercises

1 Visit one of the cartography Web sites listed in Figure 10 and obtain the directions from your campus to one of these destinations: the Washington Monument in Washington, D.C.; the Statue of Liberty on Ellis Island in New York; Disneyland in Anaheim, California; or the Grand Old Opry in Nashville, Tennessee. How many miles is it to your destination? What is the estimated driving time? Use the Google Maps Web site to obtain an overhead image of this destination. Then, visit one of the general travel Web sites listed in the table and plan a flight from the nearest major airport to one of the four destinations for the week after finals and a return trip one week later. Which airline, flight numbers, and departure and arrival times did you select?

2 Visit one of the travel and city guides Web sites listed in Figure 10, and choose a destination for a getaway this coming weekend. Write a one-page paper giving details about this location, such as popular hotels and lodging, expected weather, population, local colleges and universities, parks and recreation, ancient and modern history, and tours. Include a map or satellite photo of this place. Why did you select this destination? How would you travel there and back? What is the breakdown of expected costs for this weekend, including travel expenditures, meals, lodging, and tickets to events and activities? Which Web addresses did you use to complete this exercise?

Environment
The Future of the Planet

Making a Difference for Earth

From the rain forests of Africa to the marine life in the Pacific Ocean, the fragile ecosystem is under extreme stress. Many environmental groups have developed informative Web sites, including those listed in Figure 11, in attempts to educate

Environment Web Sites

Name	Web Address
Central African Regional Program for the Environment (CARPE)	carpe.umd.edu
Earthjustice	earthjustice.org
EarthTrends: Environmental Information	earthtrends.wri.org
Environmental Defense Fund	edf.org
Environmental Sites on the Internet	www.ima.kth.se/im/envsite/envsite.htm
EPA AirData — Access to Air Pollution Data	epa.gov/air/data
Global Warming	globalwarming.org
Green Computing Impact Organization	gcio.org
GreenNet	gn.apc.org
New American Dream	newdream.org
University of Wisconsin — Milwaukee Environmental Health and Safety Resources	uwm.edu/Dept/EHSRM/EHSLINKS
USGS Branch of Quality Systems	bqs.usgs.gov/acidrain

For more information about environment Web sites, visit the Computer Concepts CourseMate Web site at www.cengagebrain.com and then navigate to the Making Use of the Web Feature resource for this book.

Figure 11 Environment Web sites provide vast resources for ecological data and action groups.

worldwide populations and to increase resource conservation. The Environmental Defense Fund Web site (Figure 12) contains information for people who would like to help safeguard the environment.

On an international scale, the Environmental Sites on the Internet Web page developed by the Royal Institute of Technology in Stockholm, Sweden, has been rated as one of the better ecological Web sites. Its comprehensive listing of environmental concerns range from aquatic ecology to wetlands.

The U.S. federal government has a number of Web sites devoted to specific environmental concerns. For example, the U.S. Environmental Protection Agency (EPA) provides pollution data, including ozone levels and air pollutants, for specific areas. Its AirData Web site displays air pollution emissions and monitoring data from the entire United States and is the world's most extensive collection of air pollution data.

Figure 12 A visit to the Environmental Defense Fund Web site provides practical advice about protecting the environment.

Environment Web Exercises

1. **The New American Dream Web site encourages consumers to reduce the amount of junk mail sent to their homes.** Using the table in Figure 11, visit the Web site to learn how many trees are leveled each year to provide paper for these mailings and how many garbage trucks are needed to haul this waste. Read the letters used to eliminate names from bulk mail lists. To whom would you mail these letters? How long does it take to stop these unsolicited letters?

2. **Visit the EPA AirData Web site.** What is the highest ozone level recorded in your state this past year? Where are the nearest air pollution monitoring Web sites, and what are their levels? Where are the nearest sources of air pollution? Read two reports about two different topics, such as acid rain and air quality, and summarize their findings. Include information about who sponsored the research, who conducted the studies, when the data was collected, and the impact of this pollution on the atmosphere, water, forests, and human health. Whom would you contact for further information regarding the data and studies?

Finance
Money Matters

Cashing In on Financial Advice

You can manage your money with advice from financial Web sites that offer online banking, tax help, personal finance, and small business and commercial services.

If you do not have a personal banker or a financial planner, consider a Web adviser to guide your investment decisions. The MSN Money Web site (Figure 13) provides financial news and investment information.

If you are ready to ride the ups and downs of the Dow and the NASDAQ, an abundance of Web sites listed in Figure 14, including Reuters and Morningstar, can help you select companies that fit your interests and financial needs.

Claiming to be the fastest, easiest tax publication on the planet, the Internal Revenue Service Web site contains procedures for filing tax appeals and contains IRS forms, publications, and legal regulations.

Figure 13 The MSN Money Web site contains features and information related to college and family finances.

Finance Web Sites	
Advice and Education	**Web Address**
Bankrate	bankrate.com
ING Direct	ingdirect.com
LendingTree	lendingtree.com
Loan.com	loan.com
The Motley Fool	fool.com
MSN Money	moneycentral.msn.com
Wells Fargo	wellsfargo.com
Yahoo! Finance	finance.yahoo.com
Stock Market	**Web Address**
E*TRADE	us.etrade.com
Financial Engines	financialengines.com
Merrill Lynch	ml.com
Morningstar	morningstar.com
Reuters	reuters.com/investing
Valic	valic.com
Vanguard	vanguard.com
Taxes	**Web Address**
H&R Block	hrblock.com
Internal Revenue Service	www.irs.gov
Jackson Hewitt	jacksonhewitt.com
Liberty Tax Service	libertytax.com

For more information about finance Web sites, visit the Computer Concepts CourseMate Web site at www.cengagebrain.com and then navigate to the Making Use of the Web Feature resource for this book.

Figure 14 Financial resources Web sites offer general information, stock market analyses, and tax advice, as well as guidance and money-saving tips.

Finance Web Exercises

1 Visit three advice and education Web sites listed in Figure 14 and read their top business world reports. Write a paragraph about each, summarizing these stories. Which stocks or mutual funds do these Web sites predict as being sound investments today? What are the current market indexes for the DJIA (Dow Jones Industrial Average), S&P 500, and NASDAQ, and how do these figures compare with the previous day's numbers?

2 Using two of the stock market Web sites listed in Figure 14, search for information about Microsoft, Apple, and one other software vendor. Write a paragraph about each of these stocks describing the revenues, net incomes, total assets for the previous year, current stock price per share, highest and lowest prices of each stock during the past year, and other relevant investment information.

Government
Stamp of Approval

Making a Federal Case for Useful Information

When it is time to buy stamps to mail your correspondence, you no longer need to wait in long lines at your local post office. The U.S. Postal Service has authorized several organizations to sell stamps online.

You can recognize U.S. Government Web sites on the Internet by their gov top-level domain. For example, the Library of Congress Web site is loc.gov (Figure 15). Government and military Web sites offer a wide range of information. The Time Service Department Web site will provide you with the correct time. If you are looking for a federal document, FedWorld lists thousands of documents distributed by the government on its Web site. For access to the names of your congressional representatives, visit the extensive HG.org Web site. Figure 16 shows some of the more popular U.S. Government Web sites.

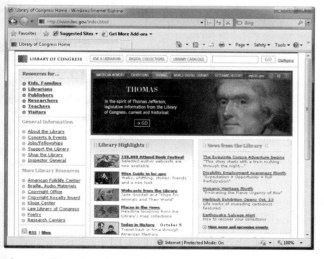

Figure 15 The Library of Congress Web site has resources about American history, world culture, and digital preservation.

Government Resources Web Sites	
Postage	**Web Address**
Endicia	endicia.com
Pitney Bowes	pb.com
Stamps.com	stamps.com
Government	**Web Address**
FedWorld	www.fedworld.gov
HG.org — Worldwide Legal Directories	hg.org
Library of Congress	loc.gov
National Agricultural Library	nal.usda.gov
Smithsonian Institution	smithsonian.org
THOMAS (Library of Congress)	thomas.loc.gov
Time Service Department	tycho.usno.navy.mil
U.S. Department of Education	ed.gov
United States Department of the Treasury	treas.gov
U.S. Government Printing Office	www.access.gpo.gov
United States National Library of Medicine	nlm.nih.gov
United States Patent and Trademark Office	uspto.gov
USAJOBS	usajobs.opm.gov
The White House	whitehouse.gov

For more information about government Web sites, visit the Computer Concepts CourseMate Web site at www.cengagebrain.com and then navigate to the Making Use of the Web Feature resource for this book.

Figure 16 These Web sites offer information about buying U.S.-approved postage online and researching federal agencies.

Government Web Exercises

1 View the three postage Web sites listed in Figure 16. Compare and contrast the available services on each one. Consider postage cost, necessary equipment, shipping services, security techniques, and tracking capability. Explain why you would or would not like to use this service.

2 Visit the HG.org Web site listed in Figure 16. What are the names, addresses, and phone numbers of your two state senators and your local congressional representative? On what committees do they serve? Who is the chief justice of the Supreme Court, and what has been this justice's opinion on two recently decided cases? Who are the members of the president's cabinet? Then, visit two other Web sites listed in Figure 16. Write a paragraph about each Web site describing its content and features.

Shopping and Auctions
Bargains Galore

Let Your Mouse Do Your Shopping

From groceries to clothing to computers, you can buy just about everything you need with just a few clicks of your mouse. More than one-half of Internet users will make at least one online purchase this year. Books, computer software and hardware, and music are the hottest commodities.

The two categories of Internet shopping Web sites are those with physical counterparts, such as Walmart and Fry's Electronics (Figure 17), and those with only a Web presence, such as Amazon and Buy. Popular Web shopping sites are listed in Figure 18.

Another method of shopping for the items you need, and maybe some you really do not need, is to visit auction Web sites, including those listed in Figure 18. Categories include antiques and collectibles, automotive, computers, electronics, music, sports, sports cards and memorabilia, and toys. Online auction Web sites can offer unusual items, including *Star Wars* memorabilia or a round of golf with Jack Nicklaus. eBay is one of thousands of Internet auction Web sites and is the world's largest personal online trading community. In addition, craigslist is a free online equivalent of classified advertisements.

Shopping and Auctions Web Sites	
Auctions	**Web Address**
craigslist	craigslist.org
eBay	ebay.com
Sotheby's	sothebys.com
uBid	ubid.com
U.S. Treasury — Seized Property Auctions	ustreas.gov/auctions
Books and Music	**Web Address**
Amazon	amazon.com
Barnes & Noble	bn.com
BookFinder	bookfinder.com
Computers and Electronics	**Web Address**
BestBuy	bestbuy.com
Buy	buy.com
Fry's Electronics	frys.com
Miscellaneous	**Web Address**
drugstore	drugstore.com
Google Product Search	google.com/products
SmashBuys	smashbuys.com
Walmart	walmart.com

For more information about shopping and auctions Web sites, visit the Computer Concepts CourseMate Web site at www.cengagebrain.com and then navigate to the Making Use of the Web Feature resource for this book.

Figure 17 Fry's is a popular electronic retailer that sells a variety of products.

Figure 18 Making online purchases can help ease the burden of driving to and fighting the crowds in local malls.

Shopping and Auctions Web Exercises

1 **Visit two of the computers and electronics and two of the miscellaneous Web sites listed in Figure 18.** Write a paragraph describing the features these Web sites offer compared with the same offerings from stores. In another paragraph, describe any disadvantages of shopping at these Web sites instead of actually visiting a store. Then, describe their policies for returning unwanted merchandise and for handling complaints.

2 **Using one of the auction Web sites listed in Figure 18, search for two objects pertaining to your hobbies.** For example, if you are a sports fan, you can search for a complete set of Upper Deck cards. If you are a car buff, search for your dream car. Describe these two items. How many people have bid on these items? Who are the sellers? What are the opening and current bids?

Weather, Sports, and News
What's News?

Weather, Sports, and News Web Sites Score Big Hits

Rain or sun? Hot or cold? Weather is the leading online news item, with at least 10,000 Web sites devoted to this field. Millions of people view The Weather Channel Web site (Figure 19) each month.

Baseball may be the national pastime, but sports aficionados yearn for everything from auto racing to cricket. The Internet has millions of pages of multimedia sports news, entertainment, and merchandise.

The Internet has emerged as a major source for news, with more than one-third of Americans going online at least once a week and 15 percent going online daily for reports of major news events. Many of these viewers are using RSS (Really Simple Syndication) technology to be notified when new stories about their favorite topics are available on the Internet. Popular weather, sports, and news Web sites are listed in Figure 20.

Figure 19 Local, national, and international weather conditions and details about breaking weather stories are available on The Weather Channel Web site.

Weather, Sports, and News Web Sites

Weather	Web Address
AccuWeather	accuweather.com
Infoplease Weather	infoplease.com/weather.html
Intellicast	www.intellicast.com
National Weather Service	www.crh.noaa.gov
The Weather Channel	weather.com
Sports	**Web Address**
CBS Sports	cbssports.com
ESPN	espn.com
NASCAR	nascar.com
International Olympic Committee	www.olympic.org
Sporting News Radio	radio.sportingnews.com
Yahoo! Sports	sports.yahoo.com
News	**Web Address**
FactCheck	factcheck.org
Geek.com	geek.com
Google News	news.google.com
MSNBC	msnbc.com
Onlinenewspapers	onlinenewspapers.com
privacy.org	privacy.org
SiliconValley	siliconvalley.com
starting page	startingpage.com/html/news.html
USA TODAY	usatoday.com
Washington Post	washingtonpost.com

For more information about weather, sports, and news Web sites, visit the Computer Concepts CourseMate Web site at www.cengagebrain.com and then navigate to the Making Use of the Web Feature resource for this book.

Figure 20 Keep informed about the latest weather, sports, and news events with these Web sites.

Weather, Sports, and News Web Exercises

1 Visit two of the sports Web sites in Figure 20 and write a paragraph describing the content these Web sites provide concerning your favorite sport. Visit Google News and then search for stories about this sports team or athlete. Then, create a customized news page with stories about your sports interests. Include RSS feeds to get regularly updated summaries on this subject.

2 Visit the Onlinenewspapers and starting page Web sites listed in Figure 20 and select two newspapers from each site. Write a paragraph describing the top national news story featured in each of these four Web pages. Then, write another paragraph describing the top international news story displayed at each Web site. In the third paragraph, discuss which of the four Web sites is the most interesting in terms of story selection, photos, and Web page design.

Learning
Yearn to Learn

Discover New Worlds Online

While you may believe your education ends when you finally graduate from college, learning is a lifelong process. You can increase your technological knowledge by visiting several Web sites (Figure 21) with tutorials about building your own Web sites, the latest news about the Internet, and resources for visually impaired users.

Learning Web Sites	
Learning How To's	**Web Address**
Bartleby: Great Books Online	bartleby.com
AT&T Knowledge Network Explorer	www.kn.pacbell.com/wired
BBC Learning	bbc.co.uk/learning
CBT Nuggets	cbtnuggets.com
HowStuffWorks	howstuffworks.com
Internet Public Library	ipl.org
Learn the Net	learnthenet.com
ScienceMaster	sciencemaster.com
Search Engine Watch	searchenginewatch.com
Wiredguide	wiredguide.com
Cooking	**Web Address**
Betty Crocker	bettycrocker.com
Chef2Chef	chef2chef.net
Food Network	foodnetwork.com

For more information about learning Web sites, visit the Computer Concepts CourseMate Web site at www.cengagebrain.com and then navigate to the Making Use of the Web Feature resource for this book.

Figure 21 The information gleaned from these Web sites can help you learn about many aspects of our existence.

The HowStuffWorks Web site has won numerous awards for its clear, comprehensive articles that demystify aspects of our everyday life. It includes ratings and reviews of products written by *Consumer Guide* editors.

A consortium of colleges maintains the Internet Public Library, which includes subject collections, reference materials, and a reading room filled with magazines and books. Volunteer librarians will answer your personal questions asked in its Ask an IPL Librarian form.

Enhancing your culinary skills can be a rewarding endeavor. No matter if you are a gourmet chef or a weekend cook, you will be cooking in style with the help of online resources, including those listed in Figure 21.

Have you ever wondered how to make a key lime pie? How about learning how to cook some easy, low-calorie dishes? Are you seeking advice from expert chefs? The Food Network Web site (Figure 22) is filled with information related to cooking, grilling, and healthy eating.

Figure 22 The Food Network Web site provides access to healthy recipes, grilling tips, and cookware.

Learning Web Exercises

1 Using one of the Learning How To's Web sites listed in Figure 21, search for information about installing memory in a computer. Write a paragraph about your findings. Then, review the material in the HowStuffWorks Web site listed in Figure 21, and write a paragraph describing articles on this Web site that are pertinent to your major.

2 Visit one of the cooking Web sites listed in Figure 21 and find two recipes or cooking tips that you can use when preparing your next meal. Write a paragraph about each one, summarizing your discoveries. Which Web sites allow you to create your own online recipe book? What are the advantages and disadvantages of accessing these Web sites on the new appliances and gadgets that might someday be in your kitchen?

Science
$E = mc^2$

Rocket Science on the Web

For some people, space exploration is a hobby. Building and launching model rockets allow these at-home scientists to participate in exploring the great frontier of space. For others, space exploration is their life. Numerous Web sites, including those in Figure 23, provide in-depth information about the universe.

Science Web Sites

Periodicals	Web Address
Archaeology Magazine	archaeology.org
Astronomy Magazine	astronomy.com
New Scientist	newscientist.com
OceanLink	oceanlink.info
Science Magazine	sciencemag.org
Scientific American	sciam.com

Resources	Web Address
National Science Foundation (NSF)	nsf.gov
Science.gov: USA.gov for Science	science.gov
Thomson Reuters	scientific.thomson.com/free/

Science Community	Web Address
American Scientist	amsci.org
Federation of American Scientists	fas.org
NASA	www.nasa.gov
Sigma Xi, The Scientific Research Society	sigmaxi.org

For more information about science Web sites, visit the Computer Concepts CourseMate Web site at www.cengagebrain.com and then navigate to the Making Use of the Web Feature resource for this book.

Figure 23 Resources available on the Internet offer a wide range of subjects for enthusiasts who want to delve into familiar and unknown territories in the world of science.

NASA's Web site contains information about rockets, space exploration, the International Space Station, space transportation, and communications. Other science resources explore space-related questions about astronomy, physics, the earth sciences, microgravity, and robotics.

Rockets and space are not the only areas to explore in the world of science. Where can you find the latest pictures taken with the Hubble Space Telescope? Do you know how climate change is affecting the human body? You can find the answers to these questions and many others through the New Scientist Web site (newscientist.com) shown in Figure 24.

The National Science Foundation's Web site features overviews of current topics and an extensive Multimedia Gallery with audio and video files, photos, and paintings.

Science.gov is an outstanding resource for scientific databases and thousands of authoritative science Web sites. The U.S. government science information provided offers 200 million pages of research, with search results ranked by relevance and sorted by topic and year.

Figure 24 The New Scientist Web site covers news about space exploration, the environment, and technology.

Science Web Exercises

❶ Visit the National Science Foundation Web site listed in the table in Figure 23. What are the topics of the latest science news and special reports? Which speeches and lectures are featured? What are the titles of image, video, and audio files in the Multimedia Gallery?

❷ Visit the NASA Web site listed in the table in Figure 23. Click the Missions link and then click the Mission Calendar link. When are the next two launches scheduled? What are the purposes of these missions? Click the Careers @ NASA topic and then write a paragraph describing the internships, cooperative programs, and summer employment opportunities. Then, view two of the science community Web sites listed in Figure 23 and write a paragraph about each of these Web sites describing the information each contains.

Health

No Pain, All Gain

Store Personal Health Records Online

More than 75 million consumers use the Internet yearly to search for health information, so using the Web to store personal medical data is a natural extension of the Internet's capabilities. Internet health services and portals are available to store your personal health history, including prescriptions, lab test results, doctor visits, allergies, and immunizations.

Google Health allows users to create a health profile, import medical records, and locate medical services and doctors. Web sites such as healthfinder.gov (Figure 25) provide free wellness information to consumers. Wise consumers, however, verify the online information they read with their personal physician.

In minutes, you can register with a health Web site by choosing a user name and password. Then, you create a record to enter your medical history. You also can store data for your emergency contacts, primary care physicians, specialists, blood type, cholesterol levels, blood pressure, and insurance plan. No matter where you are in the world, you and medical personnel can obtain records via the Internet or fax machine. Some popular online health databases are shown in Figure 26.

Figure 25 The healthfinder.gov Web site provides advice and tools to prevent illnesses and check drug interactions.

Health Web Sites

Medical History	Web Address
Google Health	google.com/health
Lifestar	mylifestarphr.com
Medem	medem.com
PersonalMD	personalmd.com
Practice Solutions	practicesolutions.ca
Records for Living, Inc — Personal Health and Living Management	recordsforliving.com
WebMD	webmd.com

General Health	Web Address
Consumer and Patient Health Information Section (CAPHIS)	caphis.mlanet.org/consumer
Centers for Disease Control and Prevention	cdc.gov
familydoctor	familydoctor.org
healthfinder	healthfinder.gov
KidsHealth	kidshealth.org
LIVESTRONG.COM	livestrong.com
MedlinePlus	medlineplus.gov
PE Central: Health and Nutrition Web Sites	pecentral.org/websites/healthsites.html
Physical Activity Guidelines	health.gov/paguidelines

For more information about health Web sites, visit the Computer Concepts CourseMate Web site at www.cengagebrain.com and then navigate to the Making Use of the Web Feature resource for this book.

Figure 26 These health Web sites allow you to organize your medical information and store it in an online database and also obtain information about a variety of medical conditions and treatments.

Health Web Exercises

1 **Access one of the health Web sites listed in Figure 26.** Register yourself or a family member and then enter the full health history. Create an emergency medical card if the Web site provides the card option. Submit this record and emergency card to your instructor. If you feel uncomfortable disclosing medical information for yourself or a family member, you may enter fictitious information.

2 **Visit three of the health Web sites listed in Figure 26.** Describe the features of each. Which of the three is the most user-friendly? Why? Describe the privacy policies of these three Web sites. Submit your analysis of these Web sites to your instructor.

Careers
In Search of the Perfect Job

Web Helps Career Hunt

While your teachers give you valuable training to prepare you for a career, they rarely teach you how to begin that career. You can broaden your horizons by searching the Internet for career information and job openings.

First, examine some of the job search Web sites. These resources list thousands of openings in hundreds of fields, companies, and locations. For example, the USAJOBS Web site, shown in Figure 27, allows you to find information for Federal jobs. This information may include the training and education required, salary data, working conditions, job descriptions, and more. In addition, many companies advertise careers on their Web sites.

When a company contacts you for an interview, learn as much about it and the industry as possible before the interview. Many of the Web sites listed in Figure 28 include detailed company profiles and links to their corporate Web sites.

Figure 27 The USAJOBS Web site is the official location for federal jobs and information for job seekers.

Career Web Sites

Job Search	Web Address
BestJobsUSA	bestjobsusa.com
CareerBuilder	careerbuilder.com
Careerjet	careerjet.com
CareerNET	careernet.com
CAREERXCHANGE	careerxchange.com
CollegeGrad.com	collegegrad.com
EmploymentGuide.com	employmentguide.com
Job.com	job.com
Job Bank USA	jobbankusa.com
JobWeb	jobweb.com
Monster	monster.com
USAJOBS	www.usajobs.gov
VolunteerMatch	volunteermatch.org
Yahoo! HotJobs	hotjobs.yahoo.com
Company/Industry Information	**Web Address**
Careers.org	careers.org
Forbes	forbes.com/leadership/careers
Fortune	fortune.com
Hoover's	hoovers.com
Occupational Outlook Handbook	stats.bls.gov/oco

For more information about career Web sites, visit the Computer Concepts CourseMate Web site at www.cengagebrain.com and then navigate to the Making Use of the Web Feature resource for this book.

Figure 28 Career Web sites provide a variety of job openings and information about major companies worldwide.

Careers Web Exercises

1 Use two of the job search Web sites listed in Figure 28 to find three companies with job openings in your field. Make a table listing the Web site name, position available, description, salary, location, desired education, and desired experience.

2 It is a good idea to acquire information before graduation about the industry in which you would like to work. Are you interested in the automotive manufacturing industry, the restaurant service industry, or the financial industry? Use two of the company/industry information Web sites listed in Figure 28 to research a particular career related to your major. Write a paragraph naming the Web sites and the specific information you found, such as the nature of the work, recommended training and qualifications, employment outlook, and earnings. Then, use two other Web sites to profile three companies with positions available in this field. Write a paragraph about each of these companies, describing the headquarters' location, sales and earnings for the previous year, total number of employees, working conditions, benefits, and competitors.

Literature and Arts
Find Some Culture

Get Ready to Read, Paint, and Dance

Brush up your knowledge of Shakespeare, grab a canvas, and put on your dancing shoes. Literature and arts Web sites, including those in Figure 29, are about to sweep you off your cyberfeet.

Literature and Arts Web Sites

Literature	Web Address
Bartleby	bartleby.com
Bibliomania	bibliomania.com
The Complete Review	www.complete-review.com
eNotes	enotes.com
Fantastic Fiction	fantasticfiction.co.uk
Literary History	literaryhistory.com
Nobel Prize in Literature	nobelprize.org/nobel_prizes/literature/laureates/1909/press.html
Project Gutenberg	gutenberg.org
Project MUSE	muse.jhu.edu
Arts	**Web Address**
absolutearts	absolutearts.com
The Children's Museum of Indianapolis	childrensmuseum.org
ARTINFO Gallery Guide	artinfo.com/galleryguide/
The Getty	getty.edu
Louvre Museum	louvre.fr
Montreal Museum of Fine Arts	mmfa.qc.ca
Museumstuff.com	museumstuff.com
The Museum of Online Museums	coudal.com/moom
National Gallery of Art	nga.gov

For more information about literature and arts Web sites, visit the Computer Concepts CourseMate Web site at www.cengagebrain.com and then navigate to the Making Use of the Web Feature resource for this book.

Figure 29 Discover culture throughout the world by visiting these literature and arts Web sites.

The full text of hundreds of books is available online from the Bibliomania and Project Gutenberg Web sites. The Complete Review provides summaries, reviews, and Web links about a variety of books and their authors. The Bartleby Web site features biographies, definitions, quotations, dictionaries, and indexes.

When you are ready to absorb more culture, you can turn to various art Web sites. Many museums have images of their collections online. Among them are the Getty Museum in Los Angeles, the Montreal Museum of Fine Arts, and the Louvre Museum in Paris (Figure 30).

The absolutearts Web site focuses on contemporary art and includes video interviews with artists, art history research, and artists' blogs.

The Museum of Online Museums Web site provides links to museum and gallery Web sites, such as the Museum of Modern Art, The Bauhaus Archive, and The Art Institute of Chicago.

Figure 30 Permanent and temporary exhibitions, educational activities, and a bookstore are featured on the Louvre Museum Web site.

Literature and Arts Web Exercises

1 Visit the Literary History Web site listed in Figure 29 and view one author in the Twentieth Century Literature, Nineteenth Century Literature, British Poets, and African American Literature sections. Read two literary criticism articles about each of the four authors and write a paragraph describing which of these authors is the most interesting to you. What are the advantages and disadvantages of reading literary criticism electronically?

2 Using the arts Web sites listed in Figure 29, search for three temporary exhibitions in galleries throughout the world. Describe the venues, the artists, and the works. Which permanent collections are found in these museums? Some people shop for gifts in the museums' stores. View and describe three items for sale.

The Components of the System Unit

Objectives

After completing this chapter, you will be able to:

1 Differentiate among various styles of system units on desktop computers, notebook computers, and mobile devices

2 Describe the control unit and arithmetic logic unit components of a processor, and explain the four steps in a machine cycle

3 Define a bit and describe how a series of bits represents data

4 Differentiate among the various types of memory: RAM, cache, ROM, flash memory, and CMOS

5 Describe the purpose and types of expansion slots and adapter cards

6 Differentiate between a port and a connector, and explain the differences among a USB port and other ports

7 Describe the types of buses in a computer

8 Understand how to clean a system unit on a computer or mobile device

The System Unit

Whether you are a home user or a business user, you most likely will purchase a new computer or upgrade an existing computer at some time in the future. Thus, you should understand the purpose of each component in a computer. As Chapter 1 discussed, a computer includes devices used for input, processing, output, storage, and communications. Many of these components are part of the system unit.

The **system unit** is a case that contains electronic components of the computer used to process data. System units are available in a variety of shapes and sizes. The case of the system unit is made of metal or plastic and protects the internal electronic components from damage. All computers and mobile devices have a system unit (Figure 4-1).

On desktop personal computers, the electronic components and most storage devices are part of the system unit. Other devices, such as the keyboard, mouse, microphone, monitor, printer, USB flash drive, scanner, Web cam, and speakers, normally occupy space outside the system unit. An all-in-one desktop personal computer is an exception, which houses the monitor and the system unit in the same case. On most notebook computers, including netbooks, the keyboard and pointing device often occupy the area on the top of the system unit, and the display attaches to the system unit by hinges. The location of the system unit on a Tablet PC varies, depending on the design of the Tablet PC. With the slate Tablet PC (shown in Figure 4-23 on page 173), which typically does not include a keyboard, the system unit is behind the display. On a convertible Tablet PC (shown in lower-left corner of Figure 4-1), by contrast,

Figure 4-1 All sizes of computers and mobile devices have a system unit.

the system unit is positioned below a keyboard, and the display attaches to the system unit with a swivel-type hinge, which enables a user to rotate the display and fold it down over the keyboard to look like a slate Tablet PC. The system unit on an Ultra-Mobile PC, a smart phone, and a PDA usually consumes the entire device. On these mobile computers and devices, the display often is built into the system unit. With game consoles, the input and output devices, such as controllers and a television, reside outside the system unit. On handheld game consoles, portable media players, and digital cameras, by contrast, the packaging around the system unit houses the input devices and display.

At some point, you might have to open the system unit on a desktop personal computer to replace or install a new electronic component. For this reason, you should be familiar with the electronic components of a system unit. Figure 4-2 identifies some of these components, which include the processor, memory, adapter cards, drive bays, and the power supply.

The processor interprets and carries out the basic instructions that operate a computer. Memory typically holds data waiting to be processed and instructions waiting to be executed. The electronic components and circuitry of the system unit, such as the processor and memory, usually are part of or are connected to a circuit board called the motherboard. Many motherboards also integrate sound, video, and networking capabilities.

Adapter cards are circuit boards that provide connections and functions not built into the motherboard or expand on the capability of features integrated into the motherboard. For example, a sound card and a video card are two types of adapter cards found in some desktop personal computers today.

Devices outside the system unit often attach to ports on the system unit by a connector on a cable. These devices may include a keyboard, mouse, microphone, monitor, printer, scanner, USB flash drive, card reader/writer, Web cam, and speakers. A drive bay holds one or more disk drives. The power supply allows electricity to travel through a power cord from a wall outlet into a computer.

Figure 4-2 The system unit on a typical personal computer consists of numerous electronic components, some of which are shown in this figure. The sound card and video card are two types of adapter cards.

The Motherboard

The **motherboard**, sometimes called a system board, is the main circuit board of the system unit. Many electronic components attach to the motherboard; others are built into it. Figure 4-3 shows a photo of a current desktop personal computer motherboard and identifies its slots for adapter cards, the processor chip, and memory. Memory chips are installed on memory cards (modules) that fit in a slot on the motherboard.

A computer **chip** is a small piece of semiconducting material, usually silicon, on which integrated circuits are etched. An integrated circuit contains many microscopic pathways capable of carrying electrical current. Each integrated circuit can contain millions of elements such as resistors, capacitors, and transistors. Specific types of processor, memory, and other chips are discussed later in the chapter. Read Innovative Computing 4-1 to find out about chips implanted in animals.

⚠ INNOVATIVE COMPUTING 4-1

Chip Implants Identify Animals

When Fido and Fluffy run away, their safe return home may be based on data stored on a chip that veterinarians have implanted under the skin, usually at the neck or shoulder blades. Other animals can be chipped, including horses, birds, and livestock.

Each chip is numbered uniquely and registered to the owner's name and address. This chip, sometimes called a microchip because it is the size of a grain of rice, contains an antenna and transponder encased in a glass tube. The antenna receives low-frequency radio waves when a scanning device passes over the chip, and the transponder sends a signal with the chip's number back to the scanner.

Shelters and animal control centers routinely scan runaway pets for chips in an attempt to reunite animals with their owners, and some animal hospitals scan pets to determine whether they have been reported lost or stolen. Most shelters require pets to have the implant before the animals are adopted. In addition, breeders, farmers, and animal associations implant the chips to thwart thieves. Researchers also use this technology to track migration of wild animals and fish.

For more information, visit the Computer Concepts CourseMate Web site at www.cengagebrain.com, navigate to the Chapter 4 Innovative Computing resource for this book, and then click ID Chips.

Figure 4-3 Many electronic components attach to the motherboard in a desktop personal computer, including a processor chip, memory modules, and adapter cards.

Processor

The **processor**, also called the **central processing unit** (**CPU**), interprets and carries out the basic instructions that operate a computer. The processor significantly impacts overall computing power and manages most of a computer's operations. On a personal computer, all functions of the processor usually are on a single chip. Some computer and chip manufacturers use the term **microprocessor** to refer to a personal computer processor chip.

Most processor chip manufacturers now offer multi-core processors. A processor core contains the circuitry necessary to execute instructions. The operating system views each processor core as a separate processor. A **multi-core processor** is a chip with two or more separate processor cores. Two common multi-core processors are dual-core and quad-core. A **dual-core processor** is a chip that contains two separate processor cores. Similarly, a **quad-core processor** is a chip with four separate processor cores.

Each processor core on a multi-core processor generally runs at a slower clock speed than a single-core processor, but multi-core processors typically increase overall performance. For example, although a dual-core processor does not double the processing speed of a single-core processor, it can approach those speeds. Multi-core processors also are more energy efficient than separate multiple processors, requiring lower levels of power consumption and emitting less heat in the system unit.

Processors contain a control unit and an arithmetic logic unit (ALU). These two components work together to perform processing operations. Figure 4-4 illustrates how other devices that are connected to the computer communicate with the processor to carry out a task.

Multi-Core Processors

For more information, visit the Computer Concepts CourseMate Web site at www.cengagebrain.com, navigate to the Chapter 4 Web Link resource for this book, and then click Multi-Core Processors.

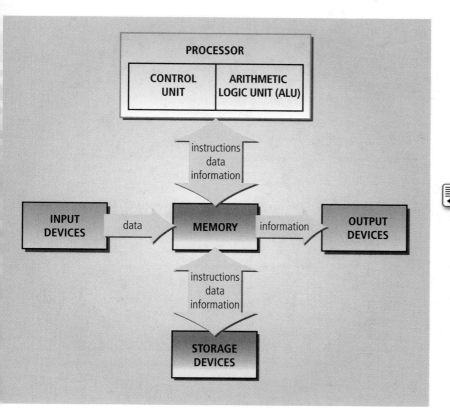

Figure 4-4 Most devices connected to the computer communicate with the processor to carry out a task. When a user starts a program, for example, its instructions transfer from a storage device to memory. Data needed by programs enters memory from either an input device or a storage device. The control unit interprets and executes instructions in memory, and the ALU performs calculations on the data in memory. Resulting information is stored in memory, from which it can be sent to an output device or a storage device for future access, as needed.

The Control Unit

The **control unit** is the component of the processor that directs and coordinates most of the operations in the computer. The control unit has a role much like a traffic cop: it interprets each instruction issued by a program and then initiates the appropriate action to carry out the instruction. Types of internal components that the control unit directs include the arithmetic/logic unit and buses, each discussed in this chapter.

The Arithmetic Logic Unit

The **arithmetic logic unit** (ALU), another component of the processor, performs arithmetic, comparison, and other operations. Arithmetic operations include basic calculations such as addition, subtraction, multiplication, and division. Comparison operations involve comparing one data item with another to determine whether the first item is greater than, equal to, or less than the other item. Depending on the result of the comparison, different actions may occur.

Machine Cycle

For every instruction, a processor repeats a set of four basic operations, which comprise a machine cycle (Figure 4-5): (1) fetching, (2) decoding, (3) executing, and, if necessary, (4) storing. Fetching is the process of obtaining a program instruction or data item from memory. The term decoding refers to the process of translating the instruction into signals the computer can execute. Executing is the process of carrying out the commands. Storing, in this context, means writing the result to memory (not to a storage medium).

The Steps in a Machine Cycle

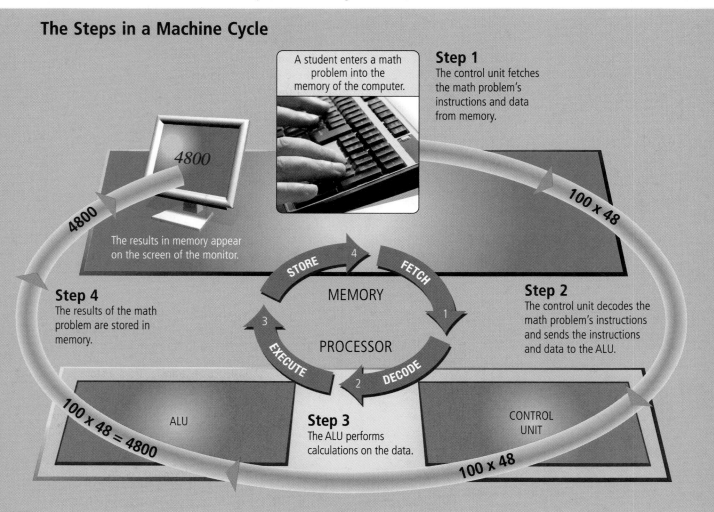

A student enters a math problem into the memory of the computer.

Step 1
The control unit fetches the math problem's instructions and data from memory.

The results in memory appear on the screen of the monitor.

Step 4
The results of the math problem are stored in memory.

STORE 4
FETCH
MEMORY
1
EXECUTE 3
PROCESSOR
2 DECODE

4800

100 x 48

Step 2
The control unit decodes the math problem's instructions and sends the instructions and data to the ALU.

ALU

100 x 48 = 4800

Step 3
The ALU performs calculations on the data.

CONTROL UNIT

100 x 48

Figure 4-5 This figure shows the steps in a machine cycle.

The System Clock

The processor relies on a small quartz crystal circuit called the **system clock** to control the timing of all computer operations. Just as your heart beats at a regular rate to keep your body functioning, the system clock generates regular electronic pulses, or ticks, that set the operating pace of components of the system unit.

The pace of the system clock, called the **clock speed**, is measured by the number of ticks per second. Current personal computer processors have clock speeds in the gigahertz range. Giga is a prefix that stands for billion, and a hertz is one cycle per second. Thus, one **gigahertz (GHz)** equals one billion ticks of the system clock per second. A computer that operates at 3 GHz has 3 billion (giga) clock cycles in one second (hertz). The faster the clock speed, the more instructions the processor can execute per second. The speed of the system clock is just one factor that influences a computer's performance. Other factors, such as the type of processor chip, amount of cache, memory access time, bus width, and bus clock speed, are discussed later in this chapter.

Comparison of Personal Computer Processors

The leading manufacturers of personal computer processor chips are Intel and AMD. These manufacturers often identify their processor chips by a model name or model number.

High-performance desktop personal computers today use a processor in the Intel Core family. Less expensive, basic personal computers today use a brand of Intel processor in the Pentium or Celeron family. The Xeon and Itanium families of processors are ideal for workstations and low-end servers.

AMD is the leading manufacturer of Intel-compatible processors, which have an internal design similar to Intel processors, perform the same functions, and can be as powerful, but often are less expensive.

In the past, chip manufacturers listed a processor's clock speed in marketing literature and advertisements. As previously mentioned, though, clock speed is only one factor that impacts processing speed in today's computers. To help consumers evaluate various processors, manufacturers such as Intel and AMD now use a numbering scheme that more accurately reflects the processing speed of their chips.

If you are ready to buy a new computer, the processor you select should depend on how you plan to use the computer. For detailed personal computer and mobile device purchasing guidelines, read the Buyer's Guide feature that follows Chapter 7.

? FAQ 4-1

Which PC vendors are the most popular with consumers?

Hewlett-Packard (HP) has the highest market share worldwide at approximately 20 percent, with Dell in second place with nearly 13 percent market share. HP accounts for nearly 21 percent of PC sales in the United States. The chart to the right compares the worldwide market share for various PC vendors.

Worldwide PC Market Share

Source: Gartner

HP
Dell
Acer
Lenovo
Toshiba
Others

For more information, visit the Computer Concepts CourseMate Web site at www.cengagebrain.com, navigate to the Chapter 4 FAQ resource for this book, and then click PC Vendor Market.

✔ QUIZ YOURSELF 4-1

Instructions: Find the true statement below. Then, rewrite the remaining false statements so that they are true.

1. A computer chip is a small piece of semiconducting material, usually silicon, on which integrated circuits are etched.

2. Four basic operations in a machine cycle are: (1) comparing, (2) decoding, (3) executing, and, if necessary, (4) pipelining.

3. Processors contain a motherboard and an arithmetic logic unit (ALU).

4. The central processing unit, sometimes called a system board, is the main circuit board of the system unit.

5. The leading processor chip manufacturers for personal computers are Microsoft and AMD.

6. The system unit is a case that contains mechanical components of the computer used to process data.

Quiz Yourself Online: To further check your knowledge of pages 156 through 161, visit the Computer Concepts CourseMate Web site at www.cengagebrain.com, navigate to the Chapter 4 Quiz Yourself resource for this book, and then click Objectives 1 – 2.

Data Representation

To understand how a computer processes data, you should know how a computer represents data. Most computers are **digital**. They recognize only two discrete states: on and off. The two digits, 0 and 1, easily can represent these two states (Figure 4-6). The digit 0 represents the electronic state of off (absence of an electronic charge). The digit 1 represents the electronic state of on (presence of an electronic charge).

The computer uses a binary system because it recognizes only two states. The **binary system** is a number system that has just two unique digits, 0 and 1, called bits. A **bit** (short for binary digit) is the smallest unit of data the computer can process. By itself, a bit is not very informative.

When 8 bits are grouped together as a unit, they form a **byte**. A byte provides enough different combinations of 0s and 1s to represent 256 individual characters. These characters include numbers, uppercase and lowercase letters of the alphabet, punctuation marks, and others, such as the letters of the Greek alphabet.

The combinations of 0s and 1s that represent characters are defined by patterns called a coding scheme. In one coding scheme, the number 4 is represented as 00110100, the number 6 as 00110110, and the capital letter E as 01000101 (Figure 4-7). ASCII (pronounced ASK-ee), which stands for American Standard Code for Information Interchange, is the most widely used coding scheme to represent data (Figure 4-8).

Coding schemes make it possible for humans to interact with a digital computer that processes only bits. When you press a key on a keyboard, a chip in the keyboard converts the key's electronic signal into a

Figure 4-6 A computer circuit represents the 0 or the 1 electronically by the presence or absence of an electronic charge.

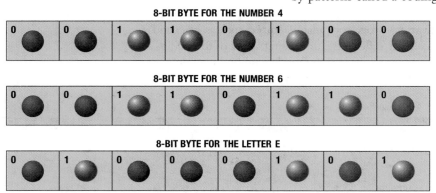

Figure 4-7 Eight bits grouped together as a unit are called a byte. A byte represents a single character in the computer.

Figure 4-8 ASCII is a widely used coding scheme.

ASCII	SYMBOL	ASCII	SYMBOL
00110000	0	01001110	N
00110001	1	01001111	O
00110010	2	01010000	P
00110011	3	01010001	Q
00110100	4	01010010	R
00110101	5	01010011	S
00110110	6	01010100	T
00110111	7	01010101	U
00111000	8	01010110	V
00111001	9	01010111	W
01000001	A	01011000	X
01000010	B	01011001	Y
01000011	C	01011010	Z
01000100	D	00100001	!
01000101	E	00100010	"
01000110	F	00100011	#
01000111	G	00100100	$
01001000	H	00100101	%
01001001	I	00100110	&
01001010	J	00101000	(
01001011	K	00101001	)
01001100	L	00101010	*
01001101	M	00101011	+

scan code that is sent to the system unit. Then, the system unit converts the scan code into a binary form the computer can process and is stored in memory. Every character is converted to its corresponding byte. The computer then processes the data as bytes, which actually is a series of on/off electrical states. When processing is finished, software converts the byte into a human-recognizable number, letter of the alphabet, or special character that is displayed on a screen or is printed (Figure 4-9). All of these conversions take place so quickly that you do not realize they are occurring.

Standards, such as those defined by ASCII, also make it possible for components in computers to communicate successfully with each other.

How a Letter Is Converted to Binary Form and Back

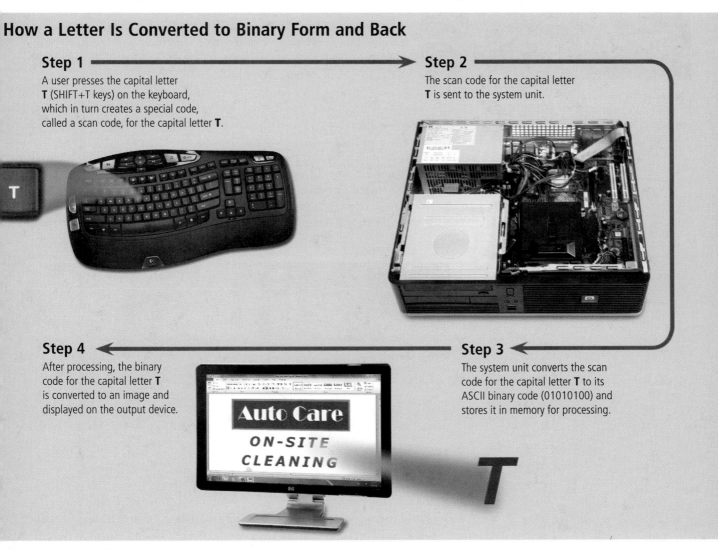

Step 1
A user presses the capital letter **T** (SHIFT+T keys) on the keyboard, which in turn creates a special code, called a scan code, for the capital letter **T**.

Step 2
The scan code for the capital letter **T** is sent to the system unit.

Step 4
After processing, the binary code for the capital letter **T** is converted to an image and displayed on the output device.

Step 3
The system unit converts the scan code for the capital letter **T** to its ASCII binary code (01010100) and stores it in memory for processing.

Auto Care
ON-SITE
CLEANING

Figure 4-9 This figure shows how a letter is converted to binary form and back.

Memory

Memory consists of electronic components that store instructions waiting to be executed by the processor, data needed by those instructions, and the results of processing the data (information). Memory usually consists of one or more chips on the motherboard or some other circuit board in the computer.

Memory stores three basic categories of items: (1) the operating system and other system software that control or maintain the computer and its devices; (2) application programs that carry out a specific task such as word processing; and (3) the data being processed by the application programs and resulting information. This role of memory to store both data and programs is known as the stored program concept.

seat G35

seat G36

Figure 4-10
Seats in an opera house are similar to addresses in memory: a seat holds one person at a time, and a location in memory holds a single byte; and both a seat and a byte can be empty.

Bytes and Addressable Memory

A byte (character) is the basic storage unit in memory. When application program instructions and data are transferred to memory from storage devices, the instructions and data exist as bytes. Each byte resides temporarily in a location in memory that has an address. An address simply is a unique number that identifies the location of the byte in memory. The illustration in Figure 4-10 shows how seats in an opera house are similar to addresses in memory: (1) a seat, which is identified by a unique seat number, holds one person at a time, and a location in memory, which is identified by a unique address, holds a single byte; and (2) both a seat, identified by a seat number, and a byte, identified by an address, can be empty. To access data or instructions in memory, the computer references the addresses that contain bytes of data.

Memory Sizes

Manufacturers state the size of memory (Figure 4-11) and storage devices in terms of the number of bytes the chip or device has available for storage. Recall that storage devices hold data, instructions, and information for future use, while most memory holds these items temporarily. A **kilobyte** (**KB** or **K**) is equal to exactly 1,024 bytes. To simplify memory and storage definitions, computer users often round a kilobyte down to 1,000 bytes. For example, if a memory chip can store 100 KB, it can hold approximately 100,000 bytes (characters). A **megabyte** (**MB**) is equal to approximately 1 million bytes. A **gigabyte** (**GB**) equals approximately 1 billion bytes. A **terabyte** (**TB**) is equal to approximately 1 trillion bytes.

Memory Sizes

Term	Abbreviation	Approximate Number of Bytes	Exact Number of Bytes	Approximate Number of Pages of Text
Kilobyte	KB or K	1 thousand	1,024	1/2
Megabyte	MB	1 million	1,048,576	500
Gigabyte	GB	1 billion	1,073,741,824	500,000
Terabyte	TB	1 trillion	1,099,511,627,776	500,000,000

 Figure 4-11 Terms commonly used to define memory sizes.

Types of Memory

The system unit contains two types of memory: volatile and nonvolatile. When the computer's power is turned off, **volatile memory** loses its contents. **Nonvolatile memory**, by contrast, does not lose its contents when power is removed from the computer. Thus, volatile memory is temporary and nonvolatile memory is permanent. RAM is the most common type of volatile memory. Examples of nonvolatile memory include ROM, flash memory, and CMOS. The following sections discuss these types of memory.

RAM

Users typically are referring to RAM when discussing computer memory. **RAM** (random access memory), also called main memory, consists of memory chips that can be read from and written to by the processor and other devices. When you turn on power to a computer, certain operating system files (such as the files that determine how the desktop appears) load into RAM from a storage device such as a hard disk. These files remain in RAM as long as the computer has continuous power. As additional programs and data are requested, they also load into RAM from storage.

The processor interprets and executes a program's instructions while the program is in RAM. During this time, the contents of RAM may change (Figure 4-12). RAM can hold multiple programs simultaneously, provided the computer has enough RAM to accommodate all the programs.

Most RAM is volatile, which means it loses its contents when the power is removed from the computer. For this reason, you must save any items you may need in the future. Saving is the process of copying items from RAM to a storage device such as a hard disk.

How Program Instructions Transfer in and out of RAM

Step 1
When you start the computer, certain operating system files are loaded into RAM from the hard disk. The operating system displays the user interface on the screen.

Step 2
When you start a Web browser, the program's instructions are loaded into RAM from the hard disk. The Web browser and certain operating system instructions are in RAM. The Web browser window appears on the screen.

Step 3
When you start a paint program, the program's instructions are loaded into RAM from the hard disk. The paint program, along with the Web browser and certain operating system instructions, are in RAM. The paint program window appears on the screen.

Step 4
When you quit a program, such as the Web browser, its program instructions are removed from RAM. The Web browser no longer is displayed on the screen.

Figure 4-12 This figure shows how program instructions transfer in and out of RAM.

Three basic types of RAM chips exist: dynamic RAM, static RAM, and magnetoresistive RAM.

- Dynamic RAM (DRAM pronounced DEE-ram) chips must be re-energized constantly or they lose their contents. Many variations of DRAM chips exist, most of which are faster than the basic DRAM.

- Static RAM (SRAM pronounced ESS-ram) chips are faster and more reliable than any variation of DRAM chips. These chips do not have to be re-energized as often as DRAM chips, thus, the term static.

- A newer type of RAM, called magnetoresistive RAM (MRAM pronounced EM-ram), stores data using magnetic charges instead of electrical charges. Manufacturers claim that MRAM has greater storage capacity, consumes less power, and has faster access times than electronic RAM.

Figure 4-13 This photo shows a memory module being inserted in a motherboard.

RAM

 For more information, visit the Computer Concepts CourseMate Web site at www.cengagebrain.com, navigate to the Chapter 4 Web Link resource for this book, and then click RAM.

RAM chips usually reside on a **memory module**, which is a small circuit board. **Memory slots** on the motherboard hold memory modules (Figure 4-13). To learn more about how to purchase RAM for a computer, complete the Learn How To 1 activity on pages 184 and 185.

RAM Configurations The amount of RAM necessary in a computer often depends on the types of software you plan to use. A computer executes programs that are in RAM. The more RAM a computer has, the faster the computer will respond.

Retail software typically indicates the minimum amount of RAM it requires. If you want the software to perform optimally, usually you need more than the minimum specifications for the software.

Generally, home users running the latest version of Windows and using basic application software such as word processing should have at least 1 GB of RAM. Most business users who work with accounting, financial, or spreadsheet programs, and programs requiring multimedia capabilities should have 2 to 8 GB of RAM. Users creating professional Web sites or using graphics-intensive applications will want 8 GB or more of RAM. The amount of RAM in computers purchased today ranges from 1 GB to 128 GB. Read Ethics & Issues 4-1 for a related discussion.

ETHICS & ISSUES 4-1

How Much Technology Should Be Provided to Students and Teachers?

Around the country and around the world, local and national governments have begun to supply schoolchildren with inexpensive notebook computers, including netbooks. Many school districts in the United States purchase notebook computers for each student and hope to recoup some of the cost by purchasing lower-cost CD-based textbooks. The United Nations endorses a plan known as One Laptop per Child to supply $100 notebook computers to developing countries, some of which already pledged to purchase millions of the devices for schoolchildren. The device, which recharges with a hand crank, includes Wi-Fi networking and a simple, intuitive user interface.

Supporters of these plans maintain that computer literacy and electronic communications are vital skills in today's world, and students should be introduced to computers as early in their school years as possible. Others claim that when students use notebook computers, instructors tend to lecture less, requiring students to engage in more research and independent study. Many people oppose plans to equip every student with a computer because they say that the technology detracts from traditional educational subjects, such as basic reading and math. Some believe that the best approach is to maintain dedicated computer lab rooms rather than allow computers in the classroom. Computers require maintenance, support, and instructional time to teach students how to use the devices. Young children may lack the responsibility to care for and use the computers properly.

Should schools supply computers to all students or teachers or both? Why or why not? What is the appropriate grade level at which to require computer literacy? Why? Should computers be relegated to a dedicated lab room? Why or why not?

Cache

Most of today's computers improve processing times with **cache** (pronounced cash). Two types of cache are memory cache and disk cache. This chapter discusses memory cache.

Memory cache helps speed the processes of the computer because it stores frequently used instructions and data. Most personal computers today have at least two types of memory cache: L1 cache and L2 cache.

- **L1 cache** is built directly in the processor chip. L1 cache usually has a very small capacity, ranging from 8 KB to 128 KB.
- **L2 cache** is slightly slower than L1 cache but has a much larger capacity, ranging from 64 KB to 16 MB. Current processors include **advanced transfer cache**, a type of L2 cache built directly on the processor chip. Processors that use advanced transfer cache perform at much faster rates than those that do not use it. Personal computers today typically have from 512 KB to 12 MB of advanced transfer cache.

Cache speeds up processing time because it stores frequently used instructions and data. When the processor needs an instruction or data, it searches memory in this order: L1 cache, then L2 cache, then RAM — with a greater delay in processing for each level of memory it must search. If the instruction or data is not found in memory, then it must search a slower speed storage medium such as a hard disk or optical disc.

ROM

Read-only memory (**ROM** pronounced rahm) refers to memory chips storing permanent data and instructions. The data on most ROM chips cannot be modified — hence, the name read-only. ROM is nonvolatile, which means its contents are not lost when power is removed from the computer.

Manufacturers of ROM chips often record data, instructions, or information on the chips when they manufacture the chips. These ROM chips, called **firmware**, contain permanently written data, instructions, or information.

Flash Memory

Flash memory is a type of nonvolatile memory that can be erased electronically and rewritten. Most computers use flash memory to hold their startup instructions because it allows the computer easily to update its contents. For example, when the computer changes from standard time to daylight savings time, the contents of a flash memory chip (and the real-time clock chip) change to reflect the new time.

Flash memory chips also store data and programs on many mobile computers and devices, such as smart phones, portable media players, PDAs, printers, digital cameras, automotive devices, digital voice recorders, and pagers. Some portable media players store music on flash memory chips (Figure 4-14). Others store music on tiny hard disks or flash memory cards. Flash memory cards contain flash memory on a removable device instead of a chip.

ROM

For more information, visit the Computer Concepts CourseMate Web site at www.cengagebrain.com, navigate to the Chapter 4 Web Link resource for this book, and then click ROM.

How a Portable Media Player Might Store Music in Flash Memory

Step 1
Purchase and download music tracks from a Web site. With one end of a special cable connected to a USB port on the system unit, connect the other end to the USB port in the portable media player.

Step 2
Instruct the computer to copy the music tracks to a flash memory chip in the portable media player.

flash memory chip

USB port

portable media player

earbuds

Step 3
Plug the earbuds in the portable media player, push a button on the portable media player, and listen to the music through the earbuds.

Music

from the computer

USB port

Figure 4-14 This figure shows how a portable media player might store music in flash memory.

? FAQ 4-3

How much music can I store on a portable media player?

Portable media players that store music on flash memory chips can hold up to 16,000 songs. Portable media players with tiny hard disks have a much greater storage capacity — from 1,000 to more than 80,000 songs.

For more information, visit the Computer Concepts CourseMate Web site at www.cengagebrain.com, navigate to the Chapter 4 FAQ resource for this book, and then click Portable Media Players.

CMOS

Some RAM chips, flash memory chips, and other types of memory chips use complementary metal-oxide semiconductor (**CMOS** pronounced SEE-moss) technology because it provides high speeds and consumes little power. CMOS technology uses battery power to retain information even when the power to the computer is off. Battery-backed CMOS memory chips, for example, can keep the calendar, date, and time current even when the computer is off. The flash memory chips that store a computer's startup information often use CMOS technology.

Memory Access Times

Access time is the amount of time it takes the processor to read data, instructions, and information from memory. A computer's access time directly affects how fast the computer processes data. Accessing data in memory can be more than 200,000 times faster than accessing data on a hard disk because of the mechanical motion of the hard disk.

Today's manufacturers use a variety of terminology to state access times (Figure 4-15). Some use fractions of a second, which for memory occurs in nanoseconds. A **nanosecond** (abbreviated ns) is one billionth of a second. A nanosecond is extremely fast (Figure 4-16). Other manufacturers state access times in MHz; for example, 800 MHz RAM.

While access times of memory greatly affect overall computer performance, manufacturers and retailers usually list a computer's memory in terms of its size, not its access time.

Access Time Terminology		
Term	**Abbreviation**	**Speed**
Millisecond	ms	One-thousandth of a second
Microsecond	µs	One-millionth of a second
Nanosecond	ns	One-billionth of a second
Picosecond	ps	One-trillionth of a second

Figure 4-15 Access times are measured in fractions of a second. This table lists the terms used to define access times.

10 million operations = 1 blink

Figure 4-16 It takes about one-tenth of a second to blink your eye, which is the equivalent of 100 million nanoseconds. In the time it takes to blink your eye, a computer can perform some operations 10 million times.

✔ | **QUIZ YOURSELF 4-2**

Instructions: Find the true statement below. Then, rewrite the remaining false statements so that they are true.

1. A computer's memory access time directly affects how fast the computer processes data.
2. A gigabyte (GB) equals approximately 1 trillion bytes.
3. Memory cache helps speed the processes of the computer because it stores seldom used instructions and data.
4. Most computers are analog, which means they recognize only two discrete states: on and off.
5. Most RAM retains its contents when the power is removed from the computer.
6. Read-only memory (ROM) refers to memory chips storing temporary data and instructions.

Quiz Yourself Online: To further check your knowledge of pages 162 through 168, visit the Computer Concepts CourseMate Web site at www.cengagebrain.com, navigate to the Chapter 4 Quiz Yourself resource for this book, and then click Objectives 3 – 4.

Expansion Slots and Adapter Cards

An **expansion slot** is a socket on the motherboard that can hold an adapter card. An **adapter card**, sometimes called an **expansion card,** is a circuit board that enhances functions of a component of the system unit and/or provides connections to peripherals. A **peripheral** is a device that connects to the system unit and is controlled by the processor in the computer. Examples of peripherals are modems, disk drives, printers, scanners, and keyboards.

Figure 4-17 lists a variety of types of adapter cards. Sometimes, all functionality is built into the adapter card. With others, a cable connects the adapter card to a device, such as a digital video camera, outside the system unit. Some are a card that you insert in a slot on the computer. Figure 4-18 shows an adapter card being inserted in an expansion slot on a personal computer motherboard.

Some motherboards include all necessary capabilities and do not require adapter cards. Other motherboards may require adapter cards to provide capabilities such as sound and video. A **sound card** enhances the sound-generating capabilities of a personal computer by allowing sound to be input through a microphone and output through external speakers or headphones. A **video card,** also called a **graphics card,** converts computer output into a video signal that travels through a cable to the monitor, which displays an image on the screen.

Video Cards

For more information, visit the Computer Concepts CourseMate Web site at www.cengagebrain.com, navigate to the Chapter 4 Web Link resource for this book, and then click Video Cards.

Types of Adapter Cards

Adapter Card	Purpose
CableCARD	Allows viewing of digital cable television channels
Disk controller	Connects disk drives
FireWire	Connects to FireWire devices
HDTV tuner	Allows viewing of HDTV broadcasts on the monitor
MIDI	Connects musical instruments
Modem	Connects other computers through telephone lines, cable television lines, or other transmission media
Network	Connects other computers and peripherals
PC-to-TV converter	Connects a television
Sound	Connects speakers or a microphone
TV tuner	Allows viewing of television channels on the monitor
USB	Connects to USB devices
Video	Connects a monitor
Video capture	Connects an analog video camera or VCR

Figure 4-17 Currently used adapter cards and their functions.

Figure 4-18 An adapter card being inserted in an expansion slot on the motherboard of a personal computer.

Removable Flash Memory

Removable flash memory includes these devices: memory cards, USB flash drives, and PC Cards/ExpressCard modules.

- A **memory card** is a removable flash memory device, usually no bigger than 1.5" in height or width, that you insert and remove from a slot in a personal computer, game console, mobile device (Figure 4-19a), or card reader/writer. Many mobile and consumer devices, such as smart phones, digital cameras, and portable media players use memory cards. Some printers and computers have built-in card readers/writers or slots that read flash memory

Figure 4-19a (memory card)

memory card in camera slot

Figure 4-19 Examples of removable flash memory in use. *(continues on next page)*

Figure 4-19b (USB flash drive)

USB flash drive
in USB port

Figure 4-19c (ExpressCard module)

ExpressCard module in
an ExpressCard slot

Figure 4-19 Examples of removable flash memory in use. *(continued)*

cards. In addition, you can purchase an external card reader/writer that attaches to any computer.

• A **USB flash drive** is a flash memory storage device that plugs in a USB port on a computer or mobile device (Figure 4-19b). (A later section discusses USB ports.)

• Many desktop computers, traditional notebook computers, and Tablet PCs, have a PC Card slot or an **ExpressCard slot,** which is a special type of expansion slot that holds a PC Card or an ExpressCard module, respectively. Most netbooks do not have a PC Card slot or ExpressCard slot. A **PC Card** is a thin, credit card-sized removable flash memory device that primarily is used today to enable traditional notebook computers and Tablet PCs to access the Internet wirelessly. An **ExpressCard module**, which can be used as a removable flash memory device, is about one-half the size of a PC Card and adds memory, communications, multimedia, and security capabilities to computers (Figure 4-19c).

Ports and Connectors

A **port** is the point at which a peripheral attaches to or communicates with a system unit so that the peripheral can send data to or receive information from the computer. An external device, such as a keyboard, monitor, printer, mouse, and microphone, often attaches by a cable to a port on the system unit. Instead of port, the term jack sometimes is used to identify audio and video ports. The front and back of the system unit on a desktop personal computer contain many ports (Figure 4-20). On notebook computers, including netbooks and Tablet PCs, the ports are on the back, front, and/or sides (Figure 4-21).

built-in memory card readers

microphone port

headphones port (or jack)

keyboard port

digital audio (or S/PDIF) out port

serial port

FireWire port

USB ports

FireWire port

side surround sound port

microphone port

speaker port

DVI port

mouse port

digital audio (or S/PDIF) in port

network port

rear surround sound port

center surround sound/subwoofer port

audio in port

S-video port

HDMI port

Figure 4-20 A system unit on a desktop personal computer has many ports on its front and back.

Figure 4-21 Ports on a typical notebook computer.

A **connector** joins a cable to a port. A connector at one end of a cable attaches to a port on the system unit, and a connector at the other end of the cable attaches to a port on the peripheral.

The next section discusses the more widely used ports.

USB Ports

A **USB port**, short for universal serial bus port, can connect up to 127 different peripherals together with a single connector. Devices that connect to a USB port include the following: mouse, printer, digital camera, scanner, speakers, portable media player, optical disc drive, smart phone, PDA, game console, and removable hard disk. Personal computers typically have six to eight USB ports on the front and/or back of the system unit (Figure 4-20). USB ports on mobile devices usually are smaller than those on personal computers. Figure 4-22 shows a variety of USB ports and connectors.

USB Connectors and Ports

	Connector	Port	Where Used
Type A			Desktop computers, traditional notebook computers, netbooks, and Tablet PCs
Type B			Peripherals (printers, scanners, external hard disks, etc.)
Mini-B			Mobile devices (cameras, phones, handheld game consoles)

Figure 4-22 A variety of USB ports and connectors are available.

USB Ports

For more information, visit the Computer Concepts CourseMate Web site at www.cengagebrain.com, navigate to the Chapter 4 Web Link resource for this book, and then click USB Ports.

USB 2.0, or **Hi-Speed USB**, is a more advanced and faster USB, with speeds 40 times higher than that of its predecessor. USB 3.0 is even faster than USB 2.0. Both USB 2.0 and USB 3.0 are backward compatible, which means they support older USB devices as well as newer USB devices. Keep in mind, though, that older USB devices do not run any faster in a newer USB port.

To attach multiple peripherals using a single port, you can use a USB hub. A **USB hub** is a device that plugs in a USB port on the system unit and contains multiple USB ports in which you plug cables from USB devices. Some newer peripherals may attach only to a USB port. Others attach to either a serial or parallel port, as well as a USB port.

FireWire Ports

FireWire

For more information, visit the Computer Concepts CourseMate Web site at www.cengagebrain.com, navigate to the Chapter 4 Web Link resource for this book, and then click FireWire.

Previously called an IEEE 1394 port, a **FireWire port** is similar to a USB port in that it can connect multiple types of devices that require faster data transmission speeds, such as digital video cameras, digital VCRs, color printers, scanners, digital cameras, and DVD drives, to a single connector. A FireWire port allows you to connect up to 63 devices together. The three latest versions, FireWire 800, FireWire 1600, and FireWire 3200, have speeds faster than the original FireWire 400.

You can use a FireWire hub to attach multiple devices to a single FireWire port. A **FireWire hub** is a device that plugs in a FireWire port on the system unit and contains multiple FireWire ports in which you plug cables from FireWire devices.

Other Ports

Some ports not included in typical computers but sometimes used are Bluetooth, SCSI, eSATA, IrDA, and MIDI. For a computer to have these ports, you often must customize the computer purchase order.

Bluetooth Port **Bluetooth** technology uses radio waves to transmit data between two devices. Bluetooth devices have to be within about 33 feet of each other. Many computers, peripherals, smart phones, PDAs, cars, and other consumer electronics are Bluetooth-enabled, which means they contain a small chip that allows them to communicate with other Bluetooth-enabled computers and devices. If you have a computer that is not Bluetooth enabled, you can purchase a Bluetooth wireless port adapter that will convert an existing USB port into a Bluetooth port. Also available are Bluetooth PC Cards and ExpressCard modules for traditional notebook computers and Tablet PCs and Bluetooth cards for smart phones and PDAs.

SCSI Port A special high-speed parallel port, called a **SCSI port**, allows you to attach SCSI (pronounced skuzzy) peripherals such as disk drives and printers. **SAS** (serial-attached SCSI) is a newer type of SCSI that transmits at much faster speeds than parallel SCSI. Some computers include a SCSI port. Others have a slot that supports a SCSI card.

eSATA Port An **eSATA port**, or external SATA port, allows you to connect a high-speed external SATA (Serial Advanced Technology Attachment) hard disk to a computer.

IrDA Port Some devices can transmit data via infrared light waves. For these wireless devices to transmit signals to a computer, both the computer and the device must have an **IrDA port.**

To ensure nothing obstructs the path of the infrared light wave, you must align the IrDA port on the device with the IrDA port on the computer, similarly to the way you operate a television remote control. Devices that use IrDA ports include a smart phone, PDA, keyboard, mouse, and printer.

MIDI Port A special type of port that connects the system unit to a musical instrument, such as an electronic keyboard, is called a **MIDI port**. Short for Musical Instrument Digital Interface, MIDI (pronounced MID-dee) is the electronic music industry's standard that defines how devices such as sound cards and synthesizers, represent sounds electronically. A synthesizer, which can be

a peripheral or a chip, creates sound from digital instructions. A system unit with a MIDI port has the capability of recording sounds that have been created by a synthesizer and then processing the sounds (the data) to create new sounds.

Port Replicators and Docking Stations

Instead of connecting peripherals directly to ports on a mobile computer, some mobile users prefer the flexibility of port replicators and docking stations. A **port replicator** is an external device that provides connections to peripherals through ports built into the device. The mobile user accesses peripherals by connecting the port replicator to a USB port or a special port on the mobile computer.

A docking station is similar to a port replicator, but it has more functionality. A **docking station**, which is an external device that attaches to a mobile computer or device, contains a power connection and provides connections to peripherals; it usually also includes slots for memory cards, optical disc drives, and other devices (Figure 4-23). With the mobile computer or device in the docking station, users can work with a full-sized keyboard, a mouse, and other desktop peripherals from their traditional notebook computer, netbook, or Tablet PC. Read Looking Ahead 4-1 for a look at the next generation of notebook computers.

Tablet PC

docking station

Figure 4-23 To use a slate Tablet PC while working at a desk, insert the Tablet PC in a docking station. Devices such as a keyboard and an optical disc drive can be plugged in the docking station.

↗ **LOOKING AHEAD 4-1**

Bendable Notebook Computers Will Slip in Your Pocket

Today's notebook computers are light and compact, but they will be enormous compared to what is being planned for the retail marketplace in the next 10 years. Top designers at Lenovo and Intel are designing flexible machines weighing less than one pound that are thin enough to fold and place in a pocket. Battery life will be nearly one week, and the 256-core processors will make current computers with quad-core processors seem like they are running at a snail's pace.

Notebook computer users will speak into a microphone, touch the screen, or type on a virtual keyboard that does not have actual keys but can give feedback that a letter or number has been selected. Thin screens will roll out to

any size needed and will be viewed easily outdoors. Users with sight impairments can coat their screens with a synthetic material that will create 3-D shapes for such tactile uses as reading Braille letters and blueprints.

💻 For more information, visit the Computer Concepts CourseMate Web site at www.cengagebrain.com, navigate to the Chapter 4 Looking Ahead resource for this book, and then click Future Notebooks.

Buses

As explained earlier in this chapter, a computer processes and stores data as a series of electronic bits. These bits transfer internally within the circuitry of the computer along electrical channels. Each channel, called a **bus**, allows the various devices both inside and attached to the system unit to communicate with each other. Just as vehicles travel on a highway to move from one destination to another, bits travel on a bus (Figure 4-24).

Buses are used to transfer bits from input devices to memory, from memory to the processor, from the processor to memory, and from memory to output or storage devices. Buses consist of two parts: a data bus and an address bus. The data bus is used to transfer actual data and the address bus is used to transfer information about where the data should reside in memory.

The size of a bus, called the bus width, determines the number of bits that the computer can transmit at one time. For example, a 32-bit bus can transmit 32 bits (4 bytes) at a time. On a 64-bit bus, bits transmit from one location to another 64 bits (8 bytes) at a time. The larger the number of bits handled by the bus, the faster the computer transfers data. Most personal computers today use a 64-bit bus.

Every bus also has a clock speed. Just like the processor, manufacturers state the clock speed for a bus in hertz. Recall that one megahertz (MHz) is equal to one million ticks per second. Today's processors usually have a bus clock speed of 400, 533, 667, 800, 1066, 1333, or 1600 MHz. The higher the bus clock speed, the faster the transmission of data, which results in programs running faster.

A computer has these basic types of buses: a system bus, possibly a backside bus, and an expansion bus. A **system bus**, also called the **front side bus** (FSB), is part of the motherboard and connects the processor to main memory. When computer professionals use the term bus by itself, they usually are referring to the system bus. A **backside bus** (BSB) connects the processor to cache.

An **expansion bus** allows the processor to communicate with peripherals. Some peripherals outside the system unit connect to a port on an adapter card, which is inserted in an expansion slot on the motherboard. This expansion slot connects to the expansion bus, which allows the processor to communicate with the peripheral attached to the adapter card.

processor

bus

memory chips

Figure 4-24 Just as vehicles travel on a highway, bits travel on a bus. Buses are used to transfer bits from input devices to memory, from memory to the processor, from the processor to memory, and from memory to output or storage devices.

Bays

After you purchase a desktop or notebook computer, you may want to install an additional storage device such as a disk drive in the system unit. A **bay** is an opening inside the system unit in which you can install additional equipment. A bay is different from a slot on the motherboard, which is used for the installation of adapter cards. A **drive bay** is a rectangular opening that typically holds disk drives. Other bays house card readers and widely used ports such as USB, FireWire, and audio ports.

An external bay allows a user to access openings in the bay from outside the system unit (Figure 4-25). Optical disc drives are examples of devices installed in external bays. An internal bay is concealed entirely within the system unit. Hard disk drives are installed in internal bays.

card readers

optical disc drives

ports

Figure 4-25 External bays usually are located beside or on top of one another.

Power Supply

Many personal computers plug in standard wall outlets, which supply an alternating current (AC) of 115 to 120 volts. This type of power is unsuitable for use with a computer, which requires a direct current (DC) ranging from 5 to more than 15 volts. The **power supply** is the component of the system unit that converts the wall outlet AC power into DC power.

Built into the power supply is a fan that keeps the power supply cool. Some have variable speed fans that change speed or stop running, depending on temperature in the system unit.

Some external peripherals such as a cable modem, speakers, or a printer have an **AC adapter**, which is an external power supply. One end of the AC adapter plugs in the wall outlet and the other end attaches to the peripheral. The AC adapter converts the AC power into DC power that the peripheral requires.

Ethics & Issues

For the complete text of the Ethics & Issues boxes found in this chapter, visit the Computer Concepts CourseMate Web site at www.cengagebrain.com and then navigate to the Chapter 4 Ethics & Issues resource for this book.

Putting It All Together

When you purchase a computer, it is important to understand how the components of the system unit work. Many components of the system unit influence the speed and power of a computer. These include the type of processor, the clock speed of the processor, the amount of RAM, bus width, and the clock speed of the bus. The configuration you require depends on your intended use. Read Ethics & Issues 4-2 for a related discussion.

The table in Figure 4-26 lists the suggested minimum processor and RAM requirements based on the needs of various types of computer users.

ETHICS & ISSUES 4-2

Is Government Search and Seizure of Computers Ethical?

In the interest of national security, the Department of Homeland Security may search and seize any mobile computer or device from people arriving in the United States. The sometimes random searches may be done without a warrant or even a reason. Additionally, the government has taken computers from schools and libraries in a similar manner. Computers and mobile devices might be taken away for an off-site inspection for any amount of time. Sometimes, the devices are not returned and little or no reason is given for the seizure.

At airports and other points of entry to the country, the government considers computers and mobile devices to be containers, just as a piece of luggage is a container. Computers, therefore, can be searched and seized similarly to luggage without reasonable suspicion. Opponents claim that the data on a computer is like memories stored in the brain. They claim that the government should be able to inspect the hardware, but not the contents of memory or hard disk. Librarians and school administrators claim that the government is invading the privacy of patrons and students.

Is government search and seizure of computers without a warrant ethical? Why or why not? Would you allow a government employee to inspect the data on your mobile computer or device? Why or why not? If memories, thoughts, or intentions in one's mind could someday be deciphered by a computer at a security checkpoint, should the government be allowed to scan them? Why?

Suggested Minimum Configurations by User

User	Processor and RAM
Home	Intel Core i5 or Intel Core i3 or AMD Athlon II or AMD Sempron
	Minimum RAM: 2 GB
Small Office/Home Office	Intel Core i7 or Intel Core i7 Extreme or AMD Phenom II or AMD Athlon II
	Minimum RAM: 4 GB
Mobile	Intel Core i7 Extreme or Intel Core i7 or AMD Phenom II or AMD Turion II
	Minimum RAM: 2 GB
Power	Intel Xeon or Intel Itanium or AMD Opteron
	Minimum RAM: 8 GB
Enterprise	Intel Core i7 or Intel Core i7 Extreme or AMD Phenom II or AMD Athlon II
	Minimum RAM: 4 GB

Figure 4-26 Suggested processor and RAM configurations by user.

Keeping Your Computer or Mobile Device Clean

Over time, the system unit collects dust — even in a clean environment. Built up dust can block airflow in a computer or mobile device, which can cause it to overheat, corrode, or even stop working. By cleaning your computer or mobile device once or twice a year, you can help extend its life. This preventive maintenance requires a few basic products (Figure 4-27):

- can of compressed air — removes dust and lint from difficult-to-reach areas; removes sticky liquid spilled on keyboards
- lint-free antistatic wipes and swabs
- screen cleaning solution or 50/50 mix of rubbing alcohol and water (do not use ammonia-based solutions)
- small computer vacuum (or small attachments on your house vacuum)
- antistatic wristband — to avoid damaging internal components with static electricity
- small screwdriver (may be required to open the case or remove adapter cards)

Before cleaning the exterior of a computer or mobile device, turn it off, and if necessary, unplug it from the electrical outlet, remove its battery, and disconnect all cables from the ports. Use compressed air to blow away dust from any openings on the computer or device case, such as drives, slots, ports, and fan vents. Then, use an antistatic wipe to clean the exterior of the case and a cleaning solution on a soft cloth to clean the screen.

If you do not feel comfortable cleaning the inside of a desktop or notebook computer case, you can have a local professional or computer company clean it for you. Or, if you are familiar with electronics, you can clean it yourself if it will not void a warranty. While working inside the case, be sure to wear an antistatic wristband on your wrist. Use the antistatic wipes to clean inside the walls of the computer case. Vacuum as much dust as possible from the interior of the case, including the wires, chips, adapter cards, and fan blades. Release short blasts of compressed air in areas the vacuum cannot reach. If the motherboard and adapter cards still look dirty, gently clean them with lint-free wipes or swabs lightly dampened with alcohol. When finished, write down the date you cleaned the computer so that you have a record for your next cleaning.

Figure 4-27 With a few products, this computer user keeps his computer clean.

✔ | **QUIZ YOURSELF 4-3**

Instructions: Find the true statement below. Then, rewrite the remaining false statements so that they are true.

1. A bus is the point at which a peripheral attaches to or communicates with a system unit so that the peripheral can send data to or receive information from the computer.
2. An AC adapter is a socket on the motherboard that can hold an adapter card.
3. eSATA ports can connect up to 127 different peripherals together with a single connector.
4. The higher the bus clock speed, the slower the transmission of data.
5. When cleaning the inside of the system unit, wear an antistatic wristband to avoid damaging internal components with static electricity.

Quiz Yourself Online: To further check your knowledge of pages 169 through 177, visit the Computer Concepts CourseMate Web site at www.cengagebrain.com, navigate to the Chapter 4 Quiz Yourself resource for this book, and then click Objectives 5 – 8.

Chapter Summary

Chapter 4 presented the components of the system unit; described how memory stores data, instructions, and information; and discussed the sequence of operations that occur when a computer executes an instruction. The chapter included a comparison of various personal computer processors on the market today. It also discussed how to clean the exterior and interior of a system unit.

Computer Usage @ Work

Sports

While watching your local football team play an out-of-state game on television, you watch various player and game statistics appear on the screen, alerting you to how many yards the offense must travel before making a first down. The camera then focuses on the large, colorful, high-resolution scoreboard at the stadium. While sports such as football have been around for many decades, the integration of computers has added significantly to the viewing experience.

While watching a baseball game, you notice that the scoreboard shows the number of balls and strikes for the player at bat, as well as the speed of each pitch. Behind home plate, an electronic radar gun calculates and records the speed of each pitch. This recorded data, along with the umpire's call (ball or strike) and the player's performance at bat (hit, home run, strike out, etc.) are entered in a computer, which updates the player's batting average automatically. During this entire time, the video display on the stadium's scoreboard plays audio and video to entertain the fans. The computer storing the player and game statistics, audio, and video communicates with the scoreboard and video display using either a wired or wireless connection. (If the computer communicates using wires, the scoreboard and

video display connect directly to a port on a system unit. Recall from the chapter that a port is the point at which a peripheral attaches to or communicates with a system unit.) At the same time, these computers send updated scores and statistics to Web pages and mobile devices.

Computers not only are used to keep track of athlete statistics and communicate with scoreboards, but also in NASCAR to help measure a vehicle's performance before a race. Sensors installed on a car can measure throttle inputs, airflow over the body, the distance between the car's frame and the track, and more. The NASCAR teams then can modify the car so that it achieves maximum performance during a race.

Overall, computers add enjoyment to various sporting events for many individuals. While waiting for a pitcher to throw the next ball or for a football team to start its next play, keep in mind that the integration of computers entertains you with interesting statistics and replays between the action.

For more information, visit the Computer Concepts CourseMate Web site at www.cengagebrain.com, navigate to the Chapter 4 Computer Usage @ Work resource for this book, and then click Sports.

Companies on the Cutting Edge

NVIDIA Visual Computing Technologies Leader

Serious gamers relish software with ultra-realistic graphics, while film producers need high-definition graphics. Both of these creative types of people likely have used a system unit equipped with an NVIDIA processor.

NVIDIA's technological specialty is developing high-performance processors that help generate graphics for personal computers, game consoles, and mobile devices. In the film and entertainment worlds, Sony Pictures, Sportvision, and Weather Central rely on NVIDIA's processor chips to produce imagery and animation. In medicine, the company's processors helped researchers to design a device that stabilizes the heart during bypass surgery and also to develop virtual reality simulations that help burn victims undergoing therapy.

Recently, NVIDIA's CUDA technology was used to enhance the historic *Apollo 11* video of Neil Armstrong walking on the moon.

INTEL World's Leading Chip Manufacturer

Turbochargers have a place in high-performance sports cars, but they have a new home residing in Intel's processors. Some of the company's chips have a turbo mode, which turns cores on and off depending upon when programs demand more processing power, all while conserving energy.

The company's chips have set the standard for personal computers since 1980 when IBM chose the Intel 8080 chip for its new product. Intel now is the world's largest chip manufacturer, with its processors found in approximately 80 percent of the world's personal computers.

Recently, Intel completed its acquisition of Wind River Systems, Inc., a leading software vendor in embedded devices. This acquisition will allow Intel to reach customers outside the traditional PC and server market.

 For more information, visit the Computer Concepts CourseMate Web site at www.cengagebrain.com and then navigate to the Chapter 4 Companies on the Cutting Edge resource for this book.

Technology Trailblazers

JACK KILBY Integrated Circuit Inventor

Jack Kilby is credited with being one of the more influential people in the world. He was awarded more than 60 patents during his lifetime, but none changed society as much as the one for his integrated circuit, or microchip, that made microprocessors possible. His Nobel Prize in physics, awarded in 2005, recognized his part in the invention of the integrated circuit.

Kilby started his work with miniature electrical components at Centralab, where he developed transistors for hearing aids. He then took a research position with Texas Instruments and developed a working model of the first integrated circuit, which was patented in 1959. Kilby applied this invention to various industrial, military, and commercial applications, including the first pocket calculator. Kilby died in 2005, but his legacy lives on.

GORDON MOORE Intel Cofounder

Moore's Law is a prediction made in 1965 by one of Intel's founders, Gordon Moore, that the number of transistors and resistors placed on a computer chip would double every year. This doubling would have a proportional increase in computing power and decrease in cost. This forecast proved amazingly accurate for 10 years, and then Moore revised the estimate to doubling every two years. A recent breakthrough in chip technology using photolithography, which uses light to imprint circuits on a chip, could perpetuate his estimate.

Moore cofounded Intel in 1968 with the conviction that silicon chips would change the world. His lifelong interest in technology is continuing with his contributions to the Large Binocular Telescope, the world's most technologically advanced optical telescope, in southeastern Arizona.

For more information, visit the Computer Concepts CourseMate Web site at www.cengagebrain.com and then navigate to the Chapter 4 Technology Trailblazers resource for this book.

Chapter Review

The Chapter Review reinforces the main concepts presented in this chapter.

🔊 To listen to an audio version of this Chapter Review, visit the Computer Concepts CourseMate Web site at www.cengagebrain.com and then navigate to the Chapter 4 Chapter Review resource for this book.

1. How Are Various Styles of System Units on Desktop Computers, Traditional Notebook Computers, and Mobile Devices Different? The **system unit** is a case that contains electronic components of the computer used to process data. System units are available in a variety of shapes and sizes. The case of the system unit protects the internal electronic components from damage. All computers and mobile devices have a system unit. On desktop personal computers, most storage devices also are part of the system unit. On most notebook computers, including netbooks, the keyboard and pointing device often occupy the area on top of the system unit, and the display attaches to the system unit by hinges. The location of the system unit on a Tablet PC varies, depending on the design of the Tablet PC. On mobile computers and devices, the display often is built into the system unit. With game consoles, the input and output devices, such as controllers and a television, reside outside the system unit. On handheld game consoles, portable media players, and digital cameras, by contrast, the packaging around the system unit also houses the input devices and display.

2. What Are the Control Unit and Arithmetic Logic Unit Components of a Processor, and What Are the Four Steps in a Machine Cycle? The **processor**, also called the **central processing unit (CPU)**, interprets and carries out the basic instructions that operate a computer. The processor significantly impacts overall computing power and manages most of a computer's operations. Processors contain a control unit and an arithmetic logic unit, which work together to perform processing operations. A **control unit** directs and coordinates most of the operations in the computer, and an **arithmetic logic unit** (ALU) performs arithmetic, comparison, and other operations. The machine cycle is a set of four basic operations — fetching, decoding, executing, and storing — that the processor repeats for every instruction. Fetching obtains a program instruction or data item from memory. Decoding translates the instruction into signals the computer can execute. Executing carries out the commands. Storing writes the result to memory (not to a storage medium).

💻 Visit the Computer Concepts CourseMate Web site at www.cengagebrain.com, navigate to the Chapter 4 Quiz Yourself resource for this book, and then click Objectives 1 – 2.

3. What Is a Bit, and How Does a Series of Bits Represent Data? Most computers are **digital** and recognize only two discrete states: off and on. To represent these two states, computers use the **binary system**, which is a number system that has just two unique digits — 0 (for off) and 1 (for on) — called bits. A **bit** (short for binary digit) is the smallest unit of data a computer can process. Grouped together as a unit, 8 bits form a **byte**, which provides enough different combinations of 0s and 1s to represent 256 individual characters. These characters include numbers, uppercase and lowercase letters of the alphabet, punctuation marks, and others, such as letters of the Greek alphabet. The combinations are defined by patterns, called coding schemes, such as ASCII.

4. What Are the Various Types of Memory? **Memory** consists of electronic components that store instructions waiting to be executed by the processor, data needed by those instructions, and the results of processing the data (information). The system unit contains volatile and nonvolatile memory. **Volatile memory** loses its contents when the computer's power is turned off. **Nonvolatile memory** does not lose its contents when the computer's power is turned off. RAM is the most common type of volatile memory. **RAM** (random access memory), also called main memory, consists of memory chips that can be read from and written to by the processor and other devices. The three basic types of RAM chips are dynamic RAM (DRAM), static RAM (SRAM), and magnetoresistive RAM (MRAM). ROM, flash memory, and CMOS are examples of nonvolatile memory. **ROM** (**read-only memory**) refers to memory chips storing permanent data and instructions that usually cannot be modified. **Flash memory** can be erased electronically and rewritten. **CMOS** (complementary metal-oxide semiconductor) technology uses battery power to retain information even when the power to the computer is turned off.

💻 Visit the Computer Concepts CourseMate Web site at www.cengagebrain.com, navigate to the Chapter 4 Quiz Yourself resource for this book, and then click Objectives 3 – 4.

5. What Are the Purposes and Types of Expansion Slots and Adapter Cards? An **expansion slot** is a socket on the motherboard that can hold an adapter card. An **adapter card**, sometimes called an **expansion card**, is a circuit board that enhances functions of a component of the system unit and/or provides a connection to a **peripheral** such as a modem, disk drive, printer, scanner, or keyboard. Several types of adapter cards exist. A **sound card** enhances the sound-generating capabilities of a personal computer. A **video card**, also called a **graphics card**, converts computer output into a video signal that displays an image on the screen.

6. What Is the Difference between a Port and a Connector, and What Are the Differences among a USB Port and Other Ports? A **port** is the point at which a peripheral attaches to or communicates with a system unit so that the peripheral can send data to or receive information from the computer. A **connector** joins a cable to a port. A **USB port** (short for universal serial bus port) can connect up to 127 different peripherals together with a single connector. A **FireWire port** can connect multiple types of devices that require faster data transmission speeds. Other ports are Bluetooth, SCSI, eSATA, IrDA, and MIDI. **Bluetooth** technology uses radio waves to transmit data between two devices. A **SCSI port** attaches the system unit to SCSI peripherals, such as disk drives and printers. A **eSATA port** connects a high-speed external SATA hard disk to a computer. An **IrDA port** allows wireless devices to transmit signals to a computer via infrared light waves. A **MIDI port** connects the system unit to a musical instrument.

7. What Are the Types of Buses in a Computer? A **bus** is an electrical channel along which bits transfer within the circuitry of a computer, allowing devices both inside and attached to the system unit to communicate. The size of a bus, called the bus width, determines the number of bits that the computer can transmit at one time. The larger the bus width, the faster the computer transfers data. A computer has a **system bus**, also called the **front side bus** (FSB); possibly a **backside bus** (BSB); and an **expansion bus**.

8. How Do You Clean a System Unit on a Computer or Mobile Device? Before cleaning the exterior of a computer or mobile device, turn it off, and if necessary, unplug it from the electrical outlet, remove the battery, and disconnect all cables from the ports. Use compressed air to blow away dirt from any openings on the case, such as drives, slots, ports, and fan vents. Use an antistatic wipe to clean the exterior of the case and a cleaning solution on a soft cloth to clean the screen. While working inside the case, be sure to wear an antistatic wristband. If you do not feel comfortable cleaning the inside of the case, you can have a professional or computer company clean it for you. Use a vacuum and compressed air to remove dust inside the case.

Visit the Computer Concepts CourseMate Web site at www.cengagebrain.com, navigate to the Chapter 4 Quiz Yourself resource for this book, and then click Objectives 5 – 8.

Key Terms

You should know each key term. The list below helps focus your study.

To see an example of and a definition for each term, and to access current and additional information from the Web, visit the Computer Concepts CourseMate Web site at www.cengagebrain.com and then navigate to the Chapter 4 Key Terms resource for this book.

AC adapter (175)
access time (168)
adapter card (169)
advanced transfer cache (167)
arithmetic logic unit (160)
backside bus (174)
bay (175)
binary system (162)
bit (162)
Bluetooth (172)
bus (174)
byte (162)
cache (167)
central processing unit (CPU) (159)
chip (158)
clock speed (161)
CMOS (168)
connector (171)
control unit (159)

digital (162)
docking station (173)
drive bay (175)
dual-core processor (159)
eSATA port (172)
expansion bus (174)
expansion card (169)
expansion slot (169)
ExpressCard module (170)
ExpressCard slot (170)
FireWire hub (172)
FireWire port (172)
firmware (167)
flash memory (167)
front side bus (174)
gigabyte (GB) (164)
gigahertz (GHz) (161)
graphics card (169)
Hi-Speed USB (172)
IrDA port (172)

kilobyte (KB or K) (164)
L1 cache (167)
L2 cache (167)
megabyte (MB) (164)
memory (163)
memory cache (167)
memory card (169)
memory module (166)
memory slots (166)
microprocessor (159)
MIDI port (172)
motherboard (158)
multi-core processor (159)
nanosecond (168)
nonvolatile memory (164)
PC Card (170)
peripheral (169)
port (170)
port replicator (173)
power supply (175)

processor (159)
quad-core processor (159)
RAM (164)
read-only memory (ROM) (167)
SAS (172)
SCSI port (172)
sound card (169)
system bus (174)
system clock (160)
system unit (156)
terabyte (TB) (164)
USB flash drive (170)
USB hub (172)
USB port (171)
video card (169)
volatile memory (164)

Checkpoint

The Checkpoint exercises test your knowledge of the chapter concepts. The page number containing the answer appears in parentheses after each exercise.

To complete the Checkpoint exercises interactively, visit the Computer Concepts CourseMate Web site at www.cengagebrain.com and then navigate to the Chapter 4 Checkpoint resource for this book.

Multiple Choice Select the best answer.

1. On _____, the display often is built into the system unit. (157)
 a. desktop personal computers
 b. mobile computers and devices
 c. notebook computers
 d. all of the above

2. The _____ is the component of the processor that directs and coordinates most of the operations in the computer. (159)
 a. register
 b. arithmetic logic unit
 c. control unit
 d. machine cycle

3. Each processor core on a multi-core processor generally runs at _____ clock speed than a single-core processor. (159)
 a. a faster b. the same
 c. twice the d. a slower

4. The term decoding refers to the process of _____. (160)
 a. obtaining a program instruction or data item from memory
 b. translating an instruction into signals a computer can execute
 c. carrying out commands
 d. writing a result to memory

5. ROM chips, called _____, contain permanently written data, instructions, or information. (167)
 a. memory cache b. registers
 c. transistors d. firmware

6. A(n) _____ is a socket on the motherboard that can hold an adapter card. (169)
 a. expansion slot
 b. parallel port
 c. drive bay
 d. front side bus

7. A(n) _____, which is an external device that attaches to a mobile computer or device, contains a power connection and provides connections to peripherals; it usually also includes slots for memory cards, optical disc drives, and other devices. (173)
 a. docking station
 b. port replicator
 c. peripheral
 d. expansion bus

8. A(n) _____ is part of the motherboard and connects the processor to main memory. (174)
 a. expansion bus
 b. system clock
 c. memory module
 d. front side bus

Matching Match the terms with their definitions.

_____ 1. processor (159)
_____ 2. memory module (166)
_____ 3. read-only memory (ROM) (167)
_____ 4. expansion slot (169)
_____ 5. port replicator (173)
_____ 6. backside bus (174)

a. external device that provides connections to peripherals through ports built into the device
b. interprets and carries out the basic instructions that operate a computer
c. connects the processor to cache
d. small circuit board on which RAM chips usually reside
e. socket on the motherboard that can hold an adapter card
f. memory chips storing permanent data and instructions
g. most common type of volatile memory

Short Answer Write a brief answer to each of the following questions.

1. What are two types of designs of Tablet PCs? _____ What are the differences in the designs of the two types of Tablet PCs? _____

2. What is the motherboard? _____ What is a computer chip? _____

3. What is memory cache? _____ How are the two types of cache (L1 cache and L2 cache) different? _____

4. What are four types of removable flash memory devices? _____ How are they different? _____

5. What is compressed air used for with regards to caring for your computer? _____ How should you prepare for cleaning your computer? _____

Problem Solving

The Problem Solving exercises extend your knowledge of the chapter concepts by seeking solutions to practical computer problems that you may encounter at home, school, or work. The Collaboration exercise should be completed with a team.

In the real world, practical problems often can be solved in multiple ways. Provide one solution to each of the following problems using available resources, such as articles on the Web or in print, blogs, podcasts, videos, television, user guides, other individuals, and electronics and computer stores. You may need to use multiple resources to obtain an answer. Present your solutions in the form requested by your instructor (brief report, presentation, discussion, or other means).

@ Home

1. **Malfunctioning Speakers** While working on a homework assignment, you decide to listen to one of your favorite music CDs through your computer speakers. The media player program on your computer automatically starts when you insert the CD. Although it looks like the CD is playing, no sound is coming from your speakers. What might be causing this? What is the first step that you will take to correct this problem?

2. **Removing Germs** While recovering from an illness, you realize that by using your computer during your illness, you probably left some germs behind on the keyboard and mouse. How will you clean these devices so that your family members will not become sick?

3. **Numerous Memory Types** You have decided to purchase additional memory for your computer in order to better support the latest version of the Windows operating system. At the local computer store, you notice that not only are different types of memory for sale, but different sizes are available. What will you do to ensure that you get the proper memory for your computer?

4. **Missing Songs** During the past several months, you downloaded more than 1,000 songs to your portable media player. Tonight, when you turn on your portable media player, it is not able to locate any of your songs and an error message displays on the screen. What might be causing this?

@ Work

5. **Printer Port Problem** A colleague received a new printer and has delivered her old printer to your desk for your use. When attempting to plug the printer in a port on the back of your computer, you see that the connector will not fit in any of the available ports. You also notice that even the ports that are in use will not accept the connector. What steps will you take so that you can use the printer?

6. **USB Device Not Working** You purchased a new USB external hard disk so that you can take work home. After plugging the hard disk in a USB port on your computer, the other USB devices stopped working, and the external hard disk does not work. You return to the store to exchange the hard disk, but the same problem occurs with the new device. Why might this be happening? What steps will you take to resolve this problem?

7. **Incorrect System Date and Time** While using your computer, you notice that the date and time are incorrect. You correct the date and time settings, continue using your computer, and then power it off before leaving work. When you arrive to work the next morning and turn on the computer, the date and time once again are incorrect. What might be causing this, and what is the first step you might take to solve this problem?

8. **Dirty Fan** While using your computer, you notice that the fan that removes the hot air from the inside of the computer has stopped running. You immediately turn off your computer to prevent it from overheating and notice that the fan is coated with dust. How will you clean the fan?

Collaboration

9. **Computers in Sports** You serve as an assistant coach for your former high school's football team. The head coach, who has a computer that is more than five years old, informs you that he would like to create a program that will allow him to keep track of his players' statistics. For instance, he would like to track the quarterback's number of passing yards, rushing yards, and completions. Form a team of three people to determine the requirements for implementing his request. One team member will research the types of application software that can track this data, another team member will determine the specifications for a computer capable of running the software and storing the data, and the other team member will determine the best way to collect the data during the game.

Learn How To

The Learn How To activities step you through fundamental technology skills when using a computer. The Learn How To exercises enable you to become more proficient with these skills.

Learn How To 1: Purchase Memory for a Computer

One of the less expensive and more effective ways to speed up a computer, make it capable of processing more programs at the same time, and enable it to handle graphics, gaming, and other high-level programs is to increase the amount of memory. The process of increasing memory is accomplished in two phases — purchasing the memory and installing the memory. To purchase memory for a computer, complete the following steps:

1. Determine the amount of memory currently in the computer. The amount of memory in your computer is displayed in the Welcome Center when Windows starts.
2. Determine the maximum amount of memory your computer can contain. This value can change for different computers, based primarily on the number of slots on the motherboard available for memory and the size of the memory modules you can place in each slot. On most computers, different size memory modules can be inserted in slots. A computer, therefore, might allow a 128 MB, 256 MB, 512 MB, 1 GB, or 2 GB memory module to be inserted in each slot. To determine the maximum memory for a computer, in many cases you can multiply the number of memory slots on the computer by the maximum size memory module that can be inserted in each slot.

 For example, if a computer contains four memory slots and is able to accept memory modules of 128 MB, 256 MB, 512 MB, 1 GB, or 2 GB in each of its memory slots, the maximum amount of memory the computer can contain is 8 GB (4 x 2 GB).

 You can find the number of slots and the allowable sizes of each memory module by contacting the computer manufacturer, looking in the computer's documentation, or contacting sellers of memory such as Kingston (kingston.com) or Crucial (crucial.com) on the Web. These sellers have documentation for most computers, and even programs you can download to run on your computer that will specify how much memory your computer currently has and how much you can add.
3. Determine how much memory you want to add, which will be somewhere between the current memory and the maximum memory allowed on the computer.
4. Determine the current configuration of memory on the computer. For example, if a computer with four memory slots contains 1 GB of memory, it could be using one memory module of 1 GB in a single slot and the other three slots would be empty; two memory modules of 512 MB each in two slots with two slots empty; one memory module of 512 MB and two memory modules of 256 MB each in three slots with one slot empty; or four memory modules of 256 MB each in four slots with no slots empty. You may be required to look inside the system unit to make this determination. The current memory configuration on a computer will determine what new memory modules you should buy to increase the memory to the amount determined in Step 3.

 You also should be aware that a few computers require memory to be installed in the computer in matching pairs. This means that a computer with four slots could obtain 512 MB of memory with two memory modules of 256 MB each in two slots, or four memory modules of 128 MB each in four slots.
5. Determine the number of available memory slots on your computer and the number and size memory modules you must buy to fulfill your requirement. Several scenarios can occur (in the following examples, assume you can install memory one module at a time).
 a. Scenario 1: The computer has one or more open slots. In this case, you might be able to purchase a memory module that matches the amount of memory increase you desire. For example, if you want to increase memory by 2 GB, you should purchase a 2 GB memory module for insertion in the open slot. Generally, you should buy the maximum size module you can for an open slot. So, if you find two empty slots and wish to increase memory by 2 GB, it is smarter to buy one 2 GB module and leave one empty slot rather than buy two 1 GB memory modules and use both slots. This allows you to increase memory again without removing currently used modules.
 b. Scenario 2: Many other combinations can occur. You may have to perform arithmetic calculations to decide the combination of memory modules that will work for the number of slots on the computer and the desired additional memory.
6. Determine the type of memory to buy for the computer. Computer memory has many types and configurations, and it is critical that you buy the kind of memory for which the computer was designed. It is preferable to buy the same

type of memory that currently is found in the computer. That is, if the memory is DDR3 SDRAM with a certain clock speed, then that is the type of additional memory you should place in the computer. The documentation for the computer should specify the memory type. In addition, the Web sites cited in Step 2, and others as well, will present a list of memory modules that will work with your computer. Enough emphasis cannot be placed on the fact that the memory you buy must be compatible with the type of memory usable on your computer. Because so many types and configurations exist, you must be especially diligent to ensure you purchase the proper memory for your computer.

7. Once you have determined the type and size of memory to purchase, buy it from a reputable dealer. Buying poor or mismatched memory is a major reason for a computer's erratic performance and is one of the more difficult problems to troubleshoot.

Adding memory to a computer can extend its usefulness and increase its processing power.

Exercise

1. Assume you have a computer that contains 1 GB of memory. It contains four memory slots. Each slot can contain 128 MB, 256 MB, 512 MB, 1 GB, or 2 GB memory modules. Two of the slots contain 512 MB memory modules. What memory chip(s) would you buy to increase the memory on the computer to 4 GB? What is the maximum memory on the computer? Submit your answers to your instructor.

Learn It Online

The Learn It Online exercises are interactive Web exercises designed to reinforce and expand your understanding of the chapter concepts. The descriptions below briefly summarize each exercise.

To complete the Learn It Online exercises, visit the Computer Concepts CourseMate Web site at www.cengagebrain.com, navigate to the Chapter 4 resources for this book, click the link for the exercise you want to complete, and then read the instructions.

1 At the Movies — The Leopard with a Time Machine
Watch a movie to learn about Apple Computer's "Time Machine" software, which allows users to travel through time by scrolling through different windows that represent days, to help them find the files that they need and then answer questions about the movie.

2 Student Edition Labs — Understanding the Motherboard and Binary Numbers
Enhance your understanding and knowledge about the motherboard and binary numbers by completing the Understanding the Motherboard and Binary Numbers Labs.

3 Practice Test
Take a multiple choice test that checks your knowledge of the chapter concepts and review the resulting study guide.

4 Who Wants To Be a Computer Genius²?
Play the Shelly Cashman Series version of this popular game by answering questions to find out if you are a computer genius. Panic buttons are available to provide assistance during game play.

5 Crossword Puzzle Challenge
Complete an interactive crossword puzzle to reinforce concepts presented in this chapter.

6 Windows Exercises
Step through the Windows 7 exercises to learn about installing new hardware, setting the system clock, using Calculator to perform number system conversion, and power management.

7 Exploring Computer Careers
Read about a career as a computer engineer, search for related employment advertisements, and then answer related questions.

8 Web Apps — Google Docs
Learn how to create, edit, and share documents, presentations, and spreadsheets using Google Docs.

Web Research

The Web Research exercises broaden your understanding of chapter concepts by presenting questions that require you to search the Web for answers.

❶ Search Sleuth

Use one of the search engines listed in Figure 2-8 in Chapter 2 on page 65 or your own favorite search engine to find the answers to the following questions. Copy and paste the Web address from the Web page where you found the answer. Some questions may have more than one answer. If required, submit your answers to your instructor. (1) In nanometers, what is the current size of a quad-core processor? (2) What company holds the trademark for the term, FireWire? (3) What is the relationship between the names of the Itanium processors and the steamship *Titanic*? (4) What Intel chip powered the Busicom calculator? (5) What is the admission price to visit the Intel Museum in Santa Clara, California? (6) What term did Dr. Werner Buchholz coin while designing the IBM Stretch computer? (7) How was a Steckerverbindung used in an Enigma machine?

❷ Green Computing

Greenpeace International's *Guide to Greener Electronics* ranks the major technology hardware companies in their manufacturing and recycling efforts. The goal is to urge these computer, television, mobile devices, and game console manufacturers to reduce the use of toxic chemicals and to implement recycling policies. View the *Guide* (greenpeace.org/electronics) and then use your word processing program to answer the following questions. Then, if required, submit your answers to your instructor. (1) The *Guide* has been updated every three months since June 2006. What is the version of this most current *Guide*? (2) Which company is at the top of the list for its better toxic waste, recycling, and climate change practices? What is this company's score, and why did this company receive this ranking? (3) Which company received the lowest ranking? Why? (4) What criteria are used to score the manufacturers? (5) Review the Toxics News links and read the article discussing the rankings from the previous year. Compare the companies' rankings between the past year and the current year. (6) How does Greenpeace obtain the data for its analysis? (7) What are Greenpeace's definitions of PVC-free and BFR-free?

❸ Social Networking

Business creativity helps drive innovation and invention of new products. Oddpodz is an online meeting place for creative people to share ideas with like-minded professionals. This Web site includes a blog, a marketplace for unique products, job postings, and a forum to discuss current topics. Visit the Oddpodz Web site (Oddpodz.com) and then read the FAQs to get an overview of the Web site and to learn the definitions of an Oddpodz. Browse the company profiles in the Creative Services Marketplace. Read the profiles of some new members, who are called citizens, and view some of the creative projects featured. Read several articles in the Cylibrary about the advice given to plan a business. Review the topics in the blog, especially those discussing current advertising campaigns. Summarize the information you read and viewed.

❹ Blogs

Technology news blogs offer information about new products, trends, and issues facing information technology professionals. Visit several technology blogs, including those from CNET (news.cnet.com), Geekzone (geekzone.co.nz/blogindex.asp), Good Morning Silicon Valley (blogs.siliconvalley.com/gmsv), Lifehacker (lifehacker.com), TechnoClicks (technoclicks.com), and WordPress (wordpress.com/tag/technology/). What are bloggers discussing in their more recent posts? What top news stories are featured? What products are reviewed? What questions are members asking about computer chips, flash memory, Bluetooth, and green computing products? Which stories have generated more than 20 comments?

❺ Ethics in Action

Law enforcement agencies use handheld wireless devices to access commercial databases. For example, Massachusetts state police stationed at Logan International Airport use the LocatePLUS Holdings Corporation's database, which has information on 98 percent of Americans. Police say accessing this information helps them perform their jobs more efficiently. Privacy experts, in contrast, say that information collected for one purpose, such as checking credit or registering motor vehicles, should not be available in other contexts. View online sites that provide information about commercial databases for sale. Write a report summarizing your findings, and include a table of links to Web sites that provide additional details.

Input and Output

Objectives

After completing this chapter, you will be able to:

1 Identify the keys and buttons commonly found on desktop computer keyboards, and describe how keyboards for mobile computers and devices differ from desktop computer keyboards

2 Describe different mouse types

3 Describe various types of touch screens and explain how a touch-sensitive pad works

4 Describe various types of pen input

5 Explain other types of input, including various game controllers, other input for smart phones, how resolution affects the quality of a picture captured on digital cameras, voice and video input,

scanners and reading devices, various biometric devices, and terminals

6 Explain the characteristics of LCD monitors, LCD screens, and CRT monitors

7 Summarize the various types of printers: ink-jet printers, photo printers, laser printers, multifunction peripherals, thermal printers, mobile printers, and plotters and large-format printers

8 Identify the purpose and features of speakers, headphones, and earbuds; data projectors; and interactive whiteboards

9 Identify input and output options for physically challenged users

What Is Input?

Input is any data and instructions entered into the memory of a computer. As shown in Figure 5-1, people have a variety of options for entering data and instructions into a computer.

An **input device** is any hardware component that allows users to enter data and instructions into a computer. The following pages discuss a variety of input devices.

touch-sensitive pad

touch screen

keyboard

mouse

input

biometric device

RFID reader

MICR

magnetic stripe
card reader

Figure 5-1 Users can enter data and instructions into a computer in a variety of ways.

Keyboard and Pointing Devices

Two of the more widely used input devices are the keyboard and the mouse. Most computers include a keyboard or keyboarding capabilities.

The mouse is a **pointing device** because it allows a user to control a pointer on the screen. In a graphical user interface, a **pointer** is a small symbol on the screen whose location and shape change as a user moves a pointing device. A pointing device can select text, graphics, and other objects; and click buttons, icons, links, and menu commands.

The following pages discuss the keyboard and a variety of pointing devices.

game controller

graphics tablet

stylus

microphone

devices

Web cam

bar code reader

scanner

optical mark recognition

The Keyboard

Many people use a keyboard as one of their input devices. A **keyboard** is an input device that contains keys users press to enter data and instructions into a computer (Figure 5-2).

All desktop computer keyboards have a typing area that includes the letters of the alphabet, numbers, punctuation marks, and other basic keys. Many desktop computer keyboards also have a numeric keypad on the right side of the keyboard.

Most of today's desktop computer keyboards are enhanced keyboards. An enhanced keyboard has 12 or more function keys along the top and a set of arrow and additional keys between the typing area and the numeric keypad (Figure 5-2). Function keys are special keys programmed to issue commands to a computer.

Keyboards with media control buttons allow you to control your media player program, access the computer's optical disc drive, and adjust speaker volume. Internet controls allow you to open an e-mail program, start a Web browser, and search the Internet. Some keyboards include buttons and other features specifically for users that enjoy playing games on the computer.

Desktop computer keyboards often attach via a cable to a USB port on the system unit. Some keyboards, however, do not have any wires connecting the keyboard to the system unit. A wireless keyboard, or cordless keyboard, is a battery-powered device that transmits data to the system unit using wireless technology, such as radio waves (Bluetooth) or infrared light waves (IrDA).

Regardless of size, many keyboards have a rectangular shape with the keys aligned in straight, horizontal rows. Users who spend a lot of time typing on these keyboards sometimes experience repetitive strain injuries (RSI) of their wrists and hands. For this reason, some manufacturers offer ergonomic keyboards, which have a design that reduces the chance of wrist and hand injuries.

The goal of **ergonomics** is to incorporate comfort, efficiency, and safety in the design of the work place. Employees can be injured or develop disorders of the muscles, nerves, tendons, ligaments, and joints from working in an area that is not designed ergonomically.

Ergonomics

For more information, visit the Computer Concepts CourseMate Web site at www.cengagebrain.com, navigate to the Chapter 5 Web Link resource for this book, and then click Ergonomics.

Figure 5-2 On a desktop computer keyboard, you type using keys in the typing area and on the numeric keypad.

Keyboards for Mobile Computers and Mobile Devices On notebook and some handheld computers, smart phones, and other mobile devices, the keyboard is built in the top of the system unit. To fit in these smaller computers and devices, the keyboards usually are smaller and have fewer keys than desktop computer keyboards.

A variety of options are available for typing on a smart phone (Figure 5-3). Many can display an on-screen keyboard, where you press the on-screen keys using a stylus or your finger. Some smart phones have one key for each letter of the alphabet, often called a mini-keyboard. Other phones have keypads that contain fewer keys than there are letters in the alphabet. For these phones, each key on the keypad represents multiple characters, which are identified on the key.

Figure 5-3 Users have a variety of options for typing on a phone.

Mouse

A **mouse** is a pointing device that fits comfortably under the palm of your hand. With a mouse, users control the movement of the pointer. As you move a mouse, the pointer on the screen also moves. Generally, you use the mouse to move the pointer on the screen to an object such as a button, a menu, an icon, a link, or text. Then, you press a mouse button to perform a certain action associated with that object.

Most desktop computer users today have some type of **optical mouse**, which uses devices that emit and sense light to detect the mouse's movement. Some use optical sensors, and others use a laser. The latter, often referred to as a **laser mouse**, usually is more expensive than the former (Figure 5-4).

The mobile user who makes presentations may prefer a mouse that has additional buttons for running a slide show and controlling media, similar to a remote control. An **air mouse** is a newer type of motion-sensing mouse that, in addition to the typical buttons, allows you to control objects, media players, and slide shows by moving the mouse in predetermined directions through the air. For example, raising the mouse up might increase the volume on your media player.

Figure 5-4 This mouse uses a laser to detect movement of the mouse. It also includes buttons you push with your thumb that enable forward and backward navigation through Web pages.

A mouse connects to a computer in several ways. Many types connect with a cable that attaches to a USB port or a mouse port on the system unit. A wireless mouse, or cordless mouse, is a battery-powered device that transmits data using wireless technology, such as radio waves (Bluetooth) or infrared light waves (IrDA). Read Ethics & Issues 5-1 for a related discussion.

ETHICS & ISSUES 5-1

Are Employers Responsible for Computer-Related Repetitive Strain Injuries?

When you consider the causes of workplace injuries, you might not put clicking a mouse or using a cell phone in the same category with lifting a bag of concrete, but perhaps you should. According to the chairman of a National Academy of Sciences panel that investigated workplace injuries, every year one million Americans lose workdays because of repetitive strain injuries (RSIs), including the latest malady known as cell phone elbow. RSI is caused when muscle groups perform the same actions over and over again. Once, RSIs were common among factory workers who performed the same tasks on an assembly line for hours a day. Today, these injuries, which often result from prolonged use of a computer mouse and keyboard or overuse of cell phones and other mobile devices, are the largest job-related injury and illness problem in the United States and are almost completely avoidable with proper computer and mobile device use. OSHA proposed standards whereby employers would have to establish programs to prevent workplace injuries with respect to computer use. Yet, Congress rejected the standards, accepting the argument that the cost to employers would be prohibitive and unfair. Some argue that it is each employee's responsibility to be aware of preventative measures against RSI.

Should the government establish laws regarding computer use? Why or why not? Are employees, employers, or the government responsible for repetitive strain injuries? Why? Who should be responsible for the costs of prevention and medical care? Why?

Ethics & Issues

For the complete text of the Ethics & Issues boxes found in this chapter, visit the Computer Concepts CourseMate Web site at www.cengagebrain.com and then navigate to the Chapter 5 Ethics & Issues resource for this book.

Trackball

A **trackball** is a stationary pointing device with a ball on its top or side (Figure 5-5). To move the pointer using a trackball, you rotate the ball with your thumb, fingers, or the palm of your hand. In addition to the ball, a trackball usually has one or more buttons that work just like mouse buttons.

Touchpad

A **touchpad** is a small, flat, rectangular pointing device that is sensitive to pressure and motion (Figure 5-6). To move the pointer using a touchpad, slide your fingertip across the surface of the pad. Some touchpads have one or more buttons around the edge of the pad that work like mouse buttons. On most touchpads, you also can tap the pad's surface to imitate mouse operations such as clicking. Touchpads are found most often on notebook computers, including netbooks and many Tablet PCs.

Pointing Stick

A **pointing stick** is a pressure-sensitive pointing device shaped like a pencil eraser that is positioned between keys on a keyboard (Figure 5-7). To move the pointer using a pointing stick, you push the pointing stick with a finger. The pointer on the screen moves in the direction you push the pointing stick. By pressing buttons below the keyboard, users can click and perform other mouse-type operations with a pointing stick.

Figure 5-5 A trackball.

Figure 5-6 Most notebook computers have a touchpad that allows users to control the movement of the pointer.

Figure 5-7 Some notebook computers include a pointing stick to allow a user to control the movement of the pointer.

Touch Screens and Touch-Sensitive Pads

A **touch screen** is a touch-sensitive display device. Touch screens that recognize multiple points of contact at the same time are known as multi-touch. Users can interact with touch screens by touching areas of the screen. Because touch screens require a lot of arm or hand movements, you do not enter large amounts of data using a touch screen. Instead, users touch words, pictures, numbers, letters, or locations identified on the screen. Some touch screens also respond to finger motions such as sliding your finger to drag an object or pinching your fingers to zoom in or out. The latest version of the Windows operating system provides increased support for computers with touch screens. Support for touch screens makes it easier for users to interact with the operating system.

With some smart phones, portable media players, and other mobile devices, you can touch the screen to perform tasks such as dialing phone numbers, entering text, and making on-screen selections. Some handheld game consoles also have touch screens. A **kiosk**, which is a freestanding computer, usually includes a touch screen (Figure 5-8).

A recently developed touch screen, called **Microsoft Surface**, is a 30-inch tabletop display that allows one or more people to interact with the screen using their fingers or hands (Figure 5-9). The Microsoft Surface display also allows devices that are not digital, such as an everyday paintbrush, to be used as an input device.

Figure 5-8 This traveler checks in using an airport kiosk.

Figure 5-9 Guests explore photos of hotel amenities by touching and dragging them across the Microsoft Surface display.

Multi-Touch Screens
For more information, visit the Computer Concepts CourseMate Web site at www.cengagebrain.com, navigate to the Chapter 5 Web Link resource for this book, and then click Multi-Touch Screens.

Touch-Sensitive Pads

Portable media players that do not have touch screens typically have a **touch-sensitive pad**, which is an input device that enables users to scroll through and play music, view pictures, watch videos or movies, adjust volume, and/or customize settings. Touch-sensitive pads typically contain buttons and/or wheels that are operated with a thumb or finger. For example, users rotate a **Click Wheel** to browse through a portable media player's song, picture, or movie lists and press the Click Wheel's buttons to play or pause media, display a menu, and perform other actions (Figure 5-10).

touch-sensitive pad

Figure 5-10 You use your thumb to rotate or press buttons on a Click Wheel.

Pen Input

With **pen input**, you touch a stylus or digital pen on a flat surface to write, draw, or make selections. The flat surface may be a screen on a monitor or mobile device, a signature capture pad, or a graphics tablet (Figure 5-11). A **stylus** is a small metal or plastic device that looks like a tiny ink pen but uses pressure instead of ink. A **digital pen**, which is slightly larger than a stylus, typically provides more functionality than a stylus, featuring electronic erasers and programmable buttons. Most digital pens, often simply called pens, are pressure-sensitive.

Some desktop and mobile computers and nearly all mobile devices have touch screens that recognize pen input and thus include a pressure-sensitive digital pen or stylus.

To capture a handwritten signature, a user writes his or her name on a **signature capture pad** with a stylus or pen that is attached to the device. Software then transmits the signature via a cable connected to a USB or serial port on the computer. Signature capture pads often include a magnetic stripe card reader and work with POS terminals, both discussed later in the chapter.

To use pen input on a computer that does not have a touch screen, you can attach a graphics tablet to the computer. A **graphics tablet** is a flat, rectangular, electronic, plastic board. Architects, mapmakers, designers, artists, and home users create drawings and sketches by using a pressure-sensitive pen on a graphics tablet.

Figure 5-11 You use a stylus or a pen to write, draw, or make selections on a screen, signature capture pad, or graphics tablet.

Other Types of Input

In addition to the keyboard, mouse, and pointing devices just discussed, users have a variety of other options available to enter data and instructions into a computer. These include other input for smart phones, game controllers, digital cameras, voice input, video input, scanners and reading devices, biometric input, and terminals.

Other Input for Smart Phones

Previously discussed input devices such as mini-keyboards, keypads, touch screens, and a stylus are used with smart phones and PDAs. In addition to these input methods, a variety of alternatives for entering data and instructions is available for smart phones and mobile devices (Figure 5-12).

obtain maps and directions on the phone by attaching this navigation receiver to your vehicle's window

speak into the microphone that wirelessly communicates with the phone

take a picture using the digital camera built into the back of the phone

use one end of the stylus to write on the phone's screen and the other end as a ballpoint pen

transfer data and instructions to and from the computer and phone by connecting it to the computer with a cable

enter text-based messages via a wireless keyboard

Figure 5-12 Besides a touch screen and basic stylus, users have a variety of other options for entering data and instructions into a smart phone.

You can talk directly into the smart phone's microphone or into a Bluetooth headset that wirelessly communicates with the smart phone to receive audio. Some smart phones have digital cameras that take pictures and touch-sensitive pads that enable you to interact with media, such as music and photos. Others can receive navigation signals to provide users with maps and directions.

You also can transfer, or synchronize, data and information from a computer to a phone. With some phones, you synchronize wirelessly; with others, you attach the phone to the computer via a cable or a cradle that has a cable connected to the computer.

Figure 5-13
A variety of game controllers.

Game Controllers

Video games and computer games use a **game controller** as the input device that directs movements and actions of on-screen objects (Figure 5-13). Game controllers include gamepads, joysticks and wheels, light guns, dance pads, and a variety of motion-sensing controllers.

Gamepads A **gamepad**, which is held with both hands, controls the movement and actions of players or objects in video games or computer games. On the gamepad, users press buttons with their thumbs or move sticks in various directions to trigger events. Gamepads communicate with a game console or a personal computer via wired or wireless technology.

Joysticks and Wheels Users running game software or flight and driving simulation software often use a joystick or wheel to control an airplane, vehicle, or player. A **joystick** is a handheld vertical lever mounted on a base. You move the lever in different directions and press buttons to control the actions of the simulated vehicle or player. A **wheel** is a steering-wheel-type input device that you turn to simulate driving a car, truck, or other vehicle. Most wheels also include foot pedals for acceleration and braking actions. Joysticks and wheels typically attach via a cable to a personal computer or game console.

Light Guns A **light gun** is used to shoot targets and moving objects after you pull the trigger on the weapon. Light guns typically attach via a cable to a game console or personal computer.

Dance Pads A **dance pad** is a flat electronic device divided into panels that users press with their feet in response to instructions from a music video game. These games test the user's ability to step on the correct panel at the correct time, following a pattern that is synchronized with the rhythm or beat of a song. Dance pads communicate with a game console or a personal computer via wired or wireless technology.

Motion-Sensing Game Controllers Motion-sensing game controllers allow the user to guide on-screen elements by moving a handheld input device in predetermined directions through the air. Sports games, for example, use motion-sensing game controllers, such as baseball bats and golf clubs, as their input device. These types of controllers communicate with a game console or a personal computer via wired or wireless technology.

A popular general-purpose, motion-sensing game controller is Nintendo's Wii Remote. Shaped like a television remote control and operated with one hand, the **Wii Remote** is a motion-sensing input device that uses Bluetooth wireless technology to communicate with the Wii game console. Users point the Wii Remote in different directions and rotate it to control on-screen players, vehicles, and other objects.

Other Game Controllers Other popular game controllers include musical instruments and balance boards. Controllers that resemble musical instruments, such as guitars, drums, and keyboards, work with music video games that enable game players to create sounds and music by playing the instrument. Fitness games often communicate with a balance board, which is shaped like a weight scale and contains sensors that measure a game player's balance and weight. Musical instrument and balance board controllers communicate with game consoles via wired or wireless technology.

Game Controllers

For more information, visit the Computer Concepts CourseMate Web site at www.cengagebrain.com, navigate to the Chapter 5 Web Link resource for this book, and then click Game Controllers.

Digital Cameras

As discussed in Chapter 1, a **digital camera** is a mobile device that allows users to take pictures and store the photographed images digitally, instead of on traditional film. The three basic types of digital cameras are studio cameras, field cameras, and point-and-shoot cameras. The most expensive and highest quality of the three is a studio camera, which is a stationary camera used for professional studio work. Often used by photojournalists, a field camera is a portable camera that has many lenses and other attachments. As with the studio camera, a field camera can be quite expensive. A point-and-shoot camera is much more affordable and lightweight and provides acceptable quality photographic images for the home or small business user. Figure 5-14 illustrates how one model of a point-and-shoot digital camera works.

How a Digital Camera Might Work

Step 1
Point to the image to photograph and take the picture. Light passes into the lens of the camera.

Step 2
The image is focused on a chip called a charge-coupled device (CCD).

Step 3
The CCD generates an analog signal that represents the image.

Step 4
The analog signal is converted to a digital signal by an analog-to-digital converter (ADC).

Step 5
A processor in the camera adjusts the quality of the image and usually stores the digital photo on media inserted in the camera.

Figure 5-14 This figure shows how a digital camera might work.

Often users prefer to download, or transfer a copy of, the images from the digital camera to the computer's hard disk, where the photos are available for editing with photo editing software, printing, faxing, sending via e-mail, including in another document, or posting to a Web site or photo community for everyone to see.

One factor that affects the quality of digital camera photos is its resolution. **Resolution** is the number of horizontal and vertical pixels in a display device. A digital camera's resolution is defined in pixels. A **pixel** (short for picture element) is the smallest element in an electronic image. The greater the number of pixels the camera uses to capture a picture, the better the quality of the picture. Digital camera resolutions range from about 4 million to more than 16 million pixels (MP).

Voice Input

Voice input is the process of entering input by speaking into a microphone. Uses of voice input include instant messaging that supports voice conversations, chat rooms that support voice chats, VoIP, and voice recognition. Recall that VoIP (Voice over IP) enables users to speak to other users over the Internet. **Voice recognition**, also called **speech recognition**, is the computer's capability of distinguishing spoken words. Voice recognition programs recognize a vocabulary of preprogrammed words. The vocabulary of voice recognition programs can range from two words to millions of words.

Audio Input Voice input is part of a larger category of input called audio input. **Audio input** is the process of entering any sound into the computer such as speech, music, and sound effects. To enter high-quality sound into a personal computer, the computer must have a sound card. Users enter sound into a computer via devices such as microphones, tape players, CD/DVD/Blu-ray Disc players, or radios, each of which plugs in a port on the sound card.

Some users also record live music and other sound effects using external music devices such as an electronic keyboard (Figure 5-15), guitar, drums, harmonica, and microphones. Music production software allows users to record, compose, mix, and edit music and sounds.

Figure 5-15 An electronic keyboard can be connected to a computer, allowing users to record and store music in the computer.

Video Input

Video input is the process of capturing full-motion images and storing them on a computer's storage medium such as a hard disk or optical disc. Some video devices use analog video signals. A **digital video (DV) camera**, by contrast, records video as digital signals instead of analog signals. Many DV cameras have the capability of capturing still frames, as well as motion. To transfer recorded images to a hard disk or optical disc, users connect DV cameras directly to a USB port or a FireWire port on the system unit. After saving the video on a storage medium, such as a hard disk or DVD, you can play it or edit it using video editing software on a computer. For additional information about digital video, read the Digital Video Technology feature that follows this chapter.

Web Cams A **Web cam**, also called a **PC video camera**, is a type of digital video camera that enables a home or small business user to capture video and still images, send e-mail messages with video attachments, add live images to instant messages, broadcast live images over the Internet, and make video telephone calls (Figure 5-16). During a **video telephone call**, both parties see each other as they communicate over the Internet. The cost of Web cams usually is less than $100.

Figure 5-16 This student uses a notebook computer, which has a built-in Web cam, to watch a video of a lecture for her online class.

You can configure some Web cams to display their output on a Web page. This use of a Web cam attracts Web site visitors by showing images that change regularly. Home or small business users might use Web cams to show a work in progress, weather and traffic information, employees at work, photos of a vacation, and countless other images.

Video Conferencing A **video conference** is a meeting between two or more geographically separated people who use a network or the Internet to transmit audio and video data (Figure 5-17). To participate in a video conference using a computer, you need video conferencing software or use a video conferencing Web application, along with a microphone, speakers, and a video camera attached to or built into a computer. As you speak, members of the meeting hear your voice on their speakers. Any image in front of the video camera, such as a person's face, appears in a window on each participant's screen.

As the costs of video conferencing hardware and software decrease, increasingly more business meetings, corporate training, and educational classes will be conducted as video conferences.

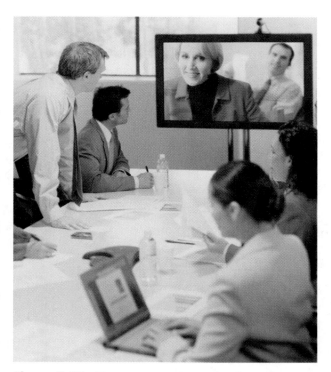

Figure 5-17 To save on travel expenses, many large businesses are turning to video conferencing.

Scanners and Reading Devices

Some input devices save users time by capturing data directly from a source document, which is the original form of the data. Examples of source documents include time cards, order forms, invoices, paychecks, advertisements, brochures, photos, inventory tags, or any other document that contains data to be processed.

Devices that can capture data directly from a source document include optical scanners, optical readers, bar code readers, RFID readers, magnetic stripe card readers, and magnetic-ink character recognition readers.

Optical Scanners An optical scanner, usually called a **scanner**, is a light-sensing input device that reads printed text and graphics and then translates the results into a form the computer can process. A **flatbed scanner** works in a manner similar to a copy machine except it creates a file of the document in memory instead of a paper copy (Figure 5-18). Once you scan a picture or document, you can display the scanned object on the screen, modify its appearance, store it on a storage medium, print it, fax it, attach it to an e-mail message, include it in another document, or post it on a Web site or photo community for everyone to see.

Figure 5-18
A flatbed scanner.

Many scanners include OCR (optical character recognition) software, which can read and convert text documents into electronic files. OCR software converts a scanned image into a text file that can be edited, for example, with a word processing program.

Optical Readers An optical reader is a device that uses a light source to read characters, marks, and codes and then converts them into digital data that a computer can process. Two technologies used by optical readers are optical character recognition and optical mark recognition.

- **Optical character recognition (OCR)** involves reading typewritten, computer-printed, or hand-printed characters from ordinary documents and translating the images into a form the computer can process. Most **OCR devices** include a small optical scanner for reading characters and sophisticated software to analyze what is read. OCR devices range from large machines that can read thousands of documents per minute to hand-held wands that read one document at a time.

 Many companies use OCR characters on turnaround documents. A **turnaround document** is a document that you return (turn around) to the company that creates and sends it. For example, when consumers receive a bill, they often tear off a portion of the bill and send it back to the company with their payment (Figure 5-19). The portion of the bill they return usually has their payment amount, account number, and other information printed in OCR characters.

- **Optical mark recognition (OMR)** devices read hand-drawn marks such as small circles or rectangles. A person places these marks on a form, such as a test, survey, or questionnaire answer sheet.

this portion is returned with payment

CHASE Continental Airlines

| PAYMENT DUE DATE | NEW BALANCE | MINIMUM DUE |
| 03/14/11 | $1,165.15 | $23.00 |

ACCOUNT NUMBER:24085 6105 0824 8058
Enter Amount Enclosed In Boxes Below

$

name and address printed using OCR characters

ISAAC NARO
1227 SOUTH HI ST
LOS ANGELES CA 90055

new balance

minimum due

OCR characters

P.O. BOX 52064
PHOENIX AZ 85072-2064

4081610509248852001165150000230004 ◄ OCR characters

Continental Airlines

Continental Airlines Visa® Signature Card from Chase
ACCOUNT NUMBER: 24085 6105 0824 8058

| NEW BALANCE | REVOLVING LINE BALANCE | NON REVOLVING LINE BALANCE | STATEMENT CLOSING DATE |
| $1,165.15 | $1,165.15 | $0.00 | 02/18/11 |

| REVOLVING LINE | AVAILABLE REVOLVING LINE | CASH ACCESS LINE | AVAILABLE CASH |
| $25,000 | $23,834 | $25,000 | $23,834 |

ONEPASS® MILEAGE SUMMARY

| Miles Earned This Statement | Total Miles Earned Since 01/09 |
| 1,014 | 100,497 |

Here is your Account Summary:

	TOTAL
Previous Balance	$471.50
(-) Payments, Credits	471.50
(+) Purchases, Cash, Debits	1,165.15
(+) FINANCE CHARGES	0.00
(=) New Balance	1,165.15
Total Minimum Payment Due by 03/14/11	$23.00

Figure 5-19 OCR characters frequently are used with turnaround documents. With this bill, you tear off the top portion and return it with a payment.

Bar Code Readers A **bar code reader**, also called a bar code scanner, is an optical reader that uses laser beams to read bar codes (Figure 5-20). A **bar code** is an identification code that consists either of a set of vertical lines and spaces of different widths or a two-dimensional pattern of dots, squares, and other images. The bar code represents data that identifies the manufacturer and the item. A newer type of bar code, called a 2-D bar code, can store much more data than the traditional linear bar code.

Manufacturers print a bar code either on a product's package or on a label that is affixed to a product.

Figure 5-20 A bar code reader uses laser beams to read bar codes on products such as food and boarding passes.

RFID Readers **RFID** (radio frequency identification) is a technology that uses radio signals to communicate with a tag placed in or attached to an object, an animal, or a person. RFID tags, which contain a memory chip and an antenna, are available in many shapes and sizes. An **RFID reader** reads information on the tag via radio waves. RFID readers can be handheld devices or mounted in a stationary object such as a doorway.

Many retailers see RFID as an alternative to bar code identification because it does not require direct contact or line-of-site transmission. Each product in a store would contain a tag that identifies the product (Figure 5-21). As consumers remove products from the store shelves and walk through a checkout area, an RFID reader reads the tag(s) and communicates with a computer that calculates the amount due.

Other uses of RFID include tracking times of runners in a marathon; tracking location of soldiers, employee wardrobes, airline baggage, and misplaced or stolen goods; checking lift tickets of skiers; managing inventory; gauging temperature and pressure of tires on a vehicle; checking out library books; and tracking payment as vehicles pass through booths on tollway systems.

Figure 5-21 RFID readers read information stored on an RFID tag and then communicate this information to computers, which instantaneously compute payments and update inventory records. In this example, the RFID tag is embedded in a label attached to the tire.

Magnetic Stripe Card Readers A **magnetic stripe card reader**, often called a magstripe reader, reads the magnetic stripe on the back of credit cards, entertainment cards, bank cards, and other similar cards. The stripe contains information identifying you and the card issuer (Figure 5-22). Some information stored in the stripe includes your name, account number, the card's expiration date, and a country code.

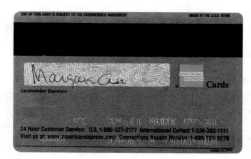

Figure 5-22 A magnetic stripe card reader reads information encoded on the stripe on the back of your credit card.

When a consumer swipes a credit card through a magstripe reader, it reads the information stored on the magnetic stripe on the card. If the magstripe reader rejects the card, it is possible that the magnetic stripe is scratched, dirty, or erased. Exposure to a magnet or magnetic field can erase the contents of a card's magnetic stripe.

MICR Readers **MICR** (magnetic-ink character recognition) devices read text printed with magnetized ink. An **MICR reader** converts MICR characters into a form the computer can process. The banking industry almost exclusively uses MICR for check processing. Each check in your checkbook has precoded MICR characters beginning at the lower-left edge (Figure 5-23).

When a bank receives a check for payment, it uses an MICR inscriber to print the amount of the check in MICR characters in the lower-right corner. The check then is sorted or routed to the customer's bank, along with thousands of others. Each check is inserted in an MICR reader, which sends the check information — including the amount of the check — to a computer for processing.

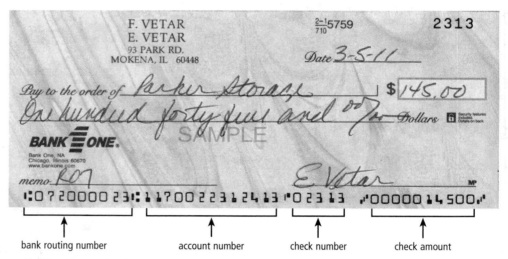

bank routing number account number check number check amount

Figure 5-23 The MICR characters preprinted on the check represent the bank routing number, the customer account number, and the check number. The amount of the check in the lower-right corner is added after the check is cashed.

Biometric Input

Biometrics is the technology of authenticating a person's identity by verifying a personal characteristic. Biometric devices grant users access to programs, systems, or rooms by analyzing some physiological (related to physical or chemical activities in the body) or behavioral characteristic. Examples include fingerprints, hand geometry, facial features, voice, signatures, and eye patterns.

The most widely used biometric device today is a fingerprint reader. A **fingerprint reader** captures curves and indentations of a fingerprint (Figure 5-24). To save on desk space, some newer keyboards and notebook computers have a fingerprint reader attached to them, which allows users to log on to programs and Web sites via their fingerprint instead of entering a user name and password.

A face recognition system captures a live face image and compares it with a stored image to determine if the person is a legitimate user. Some buildings use face recognition systems to secure access to rooms. Law enforcement, surveillance systems, and airports use face recognition to protect the public. Read Ethics & Issues 5-2 for a related discussion.

Figure 5-24 A fingerprint reader.

How Often Should You Be Monitored in Public Locations?

Customers with yearly passes for a theme park in Japan enjoy a unique method of entering the park. A biometric face recognition system recognizes the customer's face and allows the visitor entry into the park. At large sporting events, airports, and other public areas, face recognition systems scan visitors' faces and compare the visitors' faces to wanted or known criminals. Those who match a known criminal's face are detained so that authorities can make a final determination if the person should be removed from the location or arrested. Some local governments support placing face recognition systems on streets and scanning everybody who walks by. Supporters state the use of these systems, rather than authorities trying to recognize criminals, is more efficient in finding wanted criminals and allows law enforcement personnel to focus their efforts elsewhere.

Opponents of the systems claim that they are an invasion of privacy and even may violate the fourth amendment to the Constitution, which provides protection from unreasonable searches. They also claim that the systems result in an increase in innocent people being detained because the systems are imperfect. In fact, at one large sporting event, more than a dozen people were detained, but none was found to be a match to a known criminal.

Would you mind constant monitoring by face recognition systems? Why? Which types of criminals should face recognition systems be used to locate? Why? How would you react if you were improperly detained due to a mistake made by a face recognition system?

Biometric devices measure the shape and size of a person's hand using a hand geometry system. Because their cost is more than $1,000, larger companies typically use these systems as time and attendance devices or as security devices.

A voice verification system compares a person's live speech with their stored voice pattern. Larger organizations sometimes use voice verification systems as time and attendance devices. Many companies also use this technology for access to sensitive files and networks.

A signature verification system recognizes the shape of your handwritten signature, as well as measures the pressure exerted and the motion used to write the signature. Signature verification systems use a specialized pen and tablet.

High security areas use iris recognition systems. The camera in an iris recognition system uses iris recognition technology to read patterns in the iris of the eye (Figure 5-25). These patterns are as unique as a fingerprint. Iris recognition systems are quite expensive and are used by government security organizations, the military, and financial institutions that deal with highly sensitive data. Some organizations use retinal scanners, which work similarly but instead scan patterns of blood vessels in the back of the retina.

Biometric Input

For more information, visit the Computer Concepts CourseMate Web site at www.cengagebrain.com, navigate to the Chapter 5 Web Link resource for this book, and then click Biometric Input.

Figure 5-25 An iris recognition system.

Terminals

A **terminal** is a computer, usually with limited processing power, that enables users to send data to and/or receive information from a host computer. Special-purpose terminals perform specific tasks and contain features uniquely designed for use in a particular industry. Three special-purpose terminals are point-of-sale (POS) terminals, automated teller machines, and DVD kiosks.

- The location in a retail or grocery store where a consumer pays for goods or services is the point of sale (POS). Most retail stores use a **POS terminal** to record purchases, process credit or debit cards, and update inventory.

 Many POS terminals handle credit card or debit card payments and thus also include a magstripe reader. Some have fingerprint readers (discussed in the next section) that read your fingerprint, which is linked to a payment method such as a checking account or credit card. Once the transaction is approved, the terminal prints a receipt for the customer. A self-service POS terminal allows consumers to perform all checkout-related activities (Figure 5-26). That is, they scan the items, bag the items, and pay for the items themselves.

- An **automated teller machine** (**ATM**) is a self-service banking machine that connects to a host computer through a network (Figure 5-27). Banks place ATMs in convenient locations, including grocery stores, convenience stores, retail outlets, shopping malls, sports and concert venues, and gas stations.

 Using an ATM, people withdraw cash, deposit money, transfer funds, or inquire about an account balance. Some ATMs have a touch screen; others have special buttons or keypads for entering input. To access a bank account, you insert a plastic bankcard in the ATM's magstripe reader. The ATM asks you to enter a password, called a personal identification number (PIN), which verifies that you are the holder of the bankcard. When your transaction is complete, the ATM prints a receipt for your records.

touch screen with graphical user interface

bar code reader reads UPC labels

Figure 5-26 Many grocery stores offer self-serve checkouts, where the consumers themselves use the POS terminals to scan purchases, scan their store saver card and coupons, and then pay for the goods.

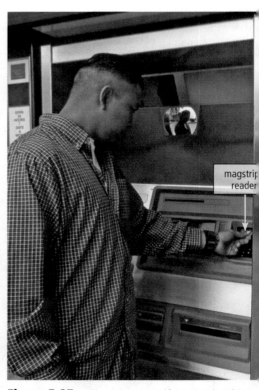

magstripe reader

Figure 5-27 An ATM is a self-service banking terminal that allows customers to access their bank accounts.

- A **DVD kiosk** is a self-service DVD rental machine that connects to a host computer through a network (Figure 5-28). The DVD kiosks, some of which can hold more than 600 DVDs, are located nationwide at retail stores, fast-food restaurants, grocery stores, airports, and other convenient public locations

 A DVD kiosk is associated with a particular vendor. To rent a movie online, for example, a customer visits the vendor's Web site, establishes an account or connects to an existing account, selects the desired movie, and then chooses a nearby DVD kiosk where the movie will be picked up. Customers also usually can select movies directly on the DVD kiosk via a touch screen or some other input device on the kiosk. After presenting identifying information and swiping a credit card through the reader, the DVD kiosk dispenses the rented movie to the customer. When finished viewing the movie, the customer returns it to any of the vendor's nationwide DVD kiosks, at which time the customer's account is charged a fee based on the time elapsed.

Figure 5-28 A DVD kiosk is a self-service DVD rental machine.

✔ **QUIZ YOURSELF 5-2**

Instructions: Find the true statement below. Then, rewrite the remaining false statements so that they are true.

1. A digital camera allows users to take pictures and store the photographed images digitally, instead of on traditional film.

2. A fingerprint reader captures curves and indentations of a signature.

3. After swiping a credit card through an MICR reader, it reads the information stored on the magnetic stripe on the card.

4. Video games and computer games use a Web cam as the input device that directs movements and actions of on-screen objects.

5. Many smart phones today have POS capabilities.

6. RFID is a technology that uses laser signals to communicate with a tag placed in an object, an animal, or a person.

⌨ **Quiz Yourself Online:** To further check your knowledge of pages 195 through 205, visit the Computer Concepts CourseMate Web site at www.cengagebrain.com, navigate to the Chapter 5 Quiz Yourself resource for this book, and then click Objective 5.

What Is Output?

Output is data that has been processed into a useful form. That is, computers process data (input) into information (output). Users view or watch output on a screen, print it, or hear it through speakers, headphones, or earbuds. While working with a computer, a user encounters four basic types of output: text, graphics, audio, and video (Figure 5-29). Very often, a single form of output, such as a Web page, includes more than one of these types of output.

An **output device** is any hardware component that conveys information to one or more people. Commonly used output devices include display devices; printers; speakers, headphones, and earbuds; data projectors; and interactive whiteboards.

Figure 5-29 Four types of output are text, graphics, audio, and video.

Display Devices

A **display device** is an output device that visually conveys text, graphics, and video information. Desktop computers typically use a monitor as their display device. A **monitor** is a display device that is packaged as a separate peripheral. Some monitors have a tilt-and-swivel base that allows users to adjust the angle of the screen to minimize neck strain and reduce glare from overhead lighting. With some, you can rotate the screen. Adjustable monitor stands allow you to adjust the height of the monitor. Some have integrated speakers and/or a built-in Web cam. Monitor controls permit users to adjust the brightness, contrast, positioning, height, and width of images.

Most mobile computers and devices integrate the display and other components into the same physical case.

GRAPHICS

VIDEO

Most display devices show text, graphics, and video information in color. Some, however, are monochrome. Monochrome means the information appears in one color (such as white, amber, green, black, blue, or gray) on a different color background (such as black or grayish-white). Some mobile devices use monochrome displays because they require less battery power.

Types of display devices include LCD monitors and LCD screens, plasma monitors, and CRT monitors. The following sections discuss each of these display devices.

LCD Monitors and LCD Screens

An **LCD monitor** is a desktop monitor that uses a liquid crystal display to produce images (Figure 5-30). These monitors produce sharp, flicker-free images. LCD monitors have a small footprint; that is, they do not take up much desk space. LCD monitors are available in a variety of sizes, with the more common being 19, 20, 22, 24, 26, 27, and 30 inches — some are 45 or 65 inches. Most are **widescreen,** which are wider than they are tall. You measure a monitor the same way you measure a television, that is, diagonally from one corner to the other.

speakers

Figure 5-30 This widescreen LCD monitor has built-in speakers.

Widescreen LCD Monitors

 For more information, visit the Computer Concepts CourseMate Web site at www.cengagebrain.com, navigate to the Chapter 5 Web Link resource for this book, and then click Widescreen LCD Monitors.

Mobile computers and mobile devices often have built-in LCD screens (Figure 5-31). Many are widescreen; some are touch screen. Notebook computer screens are available in a variety of sizes, with the more common being 14.1, 15.4, 17, and 20.1 inches. Netbook screens typically range in size from 8.9 inches to 12.1 inches, and Tablet PC screens range from 8.4 inches to 14.1 inches. Portable media players usually have screen sizes from 1.5 inches to 3.5 inches. On smart phones, screen sizes range from 2.5 inches to 4.1 inches. Digital camera screen sizes usually range from 2.5 inches to 4 inches. Read Innovative Computing 5-1 to find out about another use of LCD screens.

notebook computer

PDA

smart phone

portable media player

digital camera

handheld game console

Figure 5-31 Many people use their computers and mobile devices to view photos or watch downloaded videos and home movies. To learn about creating and uploading videos to YouTube, complete the Learn How To 1 activity on pages 228 and 229.

Get the Picture with Digital Frames

Put away your photo albums filled with vacation pictures, baby portraits, and wedding reception candids. With digital photo frames, you constantly can display all the photos that capture the best times of your life.

Digital photo frames are becoming main stream as they drop in price and increase in quality. A correlation exists between price, photo quality, and features, so the higher priced frames generally have clearer displays with accurate color. They also have adjustments for brightness, contrast, tint, and color and may use rechargeable batteries instead of electricity to power the display and dissolve from one photo to the next. Look for frames with a resolution of at least 640 × 480.

Some frames integrate Wi-Fi so that you can send your photos to the frame via your home network or download them from photo sharing Web sites. Once the photos are stored, you can add transitions and set the mood by timing the presentation to your favorite songs.

For more information, visit the Computer Concepts CourseMate Web site at www.cengagebrain.com, navigate to the Chapter 5 Innovative Computing resource for this book, and then click Digital Frames.

LCD Technology and Quality A **liquid crystal display** (**LCD**) uses a liquid compound to present information on a display device. Computer LCDs typically contain fluorescent tubes that emit light waves toward the liquid-crystal cells, which are sandwiched between two sheets of material.

The quality of an LCD monitor or LCD screen depends primarily on its resolution, response time, brightness, dot pitch, and contrast ratio.

• Resolution is the number of horizontal and vertical pixels in a display device. For example, a monitor that has a 1440 × 900 resolution displays up to 1440 pixels per horizontal row and 900 pixels per vertical row, for a total of 1,296,000 pixels to create a screen image. A higher resolution uses a greater number of pixels and thus provides a smoother, sharper, and clearer image. As the resolution increases, however, some items on the screen appear smaller.

With LCD monitors and screens, resolution generally is proportional to the size of the device. That is, the resolution increases for larger monitors and screens. For example, a widescreen 19-inch LCD monitor typically has a resolution of 1440 × 900, while a widescreen 22-inch LCD monitor has a resolution of 1680 × 1050. LCDs are geared for a specific resolution.

• Response time of an LCD monitor or screen is the time in milliseconds (ms) that it takes to turn a pixel on or off. LCD monitors' and screens' response times range from 3 to 16 ms. The lower the number, the faster the response time.

• Brightness of an LCD monitor or LCD screen is measured in nits. A nit is a unit of visible light intensity. The higher the nits, the brighter the images.

• Dot pitch, sometimes called pixel pitch, is the distance in millimeters between pixels on a display device. Average dot pitch on LCD monitors and screens should be .30 mm or lower. The lower the number, the sharper the image.

• Contrast ratio describes the difference in light intensity between the brightest white and darkest black that can be displayed on an LCD monitor. Contrast ratios today range from 500:1 to 2000:1. Higher contrast ratios represent colors better.

Ports and LCD Monitors A cable on a monitor plugs in a port on the system unit. LCD monitors use a digital signal to produce a picture. To display the highest quality images, an LCD monitor should plug in a DVI port, an HDMI port, or a DisplayPort. A DVI (Digital Video Interface) port enables digital signals to transmit directly to an LCD monitor. An HDMI (High-Definition Media Interface) port combines DVI with high-definition (HD) television and video. The DisplayPort is an alternative to DVI that also supports HDMI.

DVI

 For more information, visit the Computer Concepts CourseMate Web site at www.cengagebrain.com, navigate to the Chapter 5 Web Link resource for this book, and then click DVI.

Plasma Monitors

A **plasma monitor** is a display device that uses gas plasma technology, which sandwiches a layer of gas between two glass plates (Figure 5-32).

Plasma monitors offer screen sizes up to 150 inches wide and richer colors than LCD monitors but are more expensive. Like LCD monitors, plasma monitors can hang directly on a wall.

Figure 5-32
Large plasma monitor can measure up to 15 inches wide.

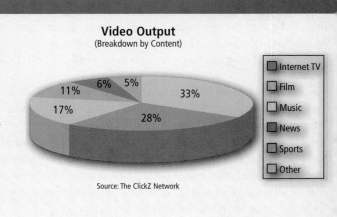

? FAQ 5-3

What type of video content do users view on display devices?

Music videos and newscasts are the most widely viewed video content on display devices, as shown in the chart to the right.

For more information, visit the Computer Concepts CourseMate Web site at www.cengagebrain.com, navigate to the Chapter 5 FAQ resource for this book, and then click Video Output Content.

Video Output
(Breakdown by Content)

Internet TV
Film
Music
News
Sports
Other

Source: The ClickZ Network

CRT Monitors

A **CRT monitor** is a desktop monitor that contains a cathode-ray tube (Figure 5-33). A cathode-ray tube (CRT) is a large, sealed glass tube. The front of the tube is the screen. A CRT's viewable size is the diagonal measurement of the actual viewing area provided by the screen in the CRT monitor. A 21-inch monitor, for example, may have a viewable size of 20 inches.

Figure 5-33 The popularity of CRT monitors is declining.

CRT monitors produce a small amount of electromagnetic radiation. Electromagnetic radiation (EMR) is a magnetic field that travels at the speed of light. Excessive amounts of EMR can pose a health risk. To be safe, all high-quality CRT monitors comply with a set of standards that defines acceptable levels of EMR for a monitor. To protect yourself even further, sit at arm's length from the CRT monitor because EMR travels only a short distance.

✔ **QUIZ YOURSELF 5-3**

Instructions: Find the true statement below. Then, rewrite the remaining false statements so that they are true.

1. A lower resolution uses a greater number of pixels and thus provides a smoother image.
2. An output device is any type of software component that conveys information to one or more people.
3. Types of pixels include LCD monitors, LCD screens, plasma monitors, and CRT monitors.
4. You measure a monitor diagonally from one corner to the other.

Quiz Yourself Online: To further check your knowledge of pages 206 through 211, visit the Computer Concepts CourseMate Web site at www.cengagebrain.com, navigate to the Chapter 5 Quiz Yourself resource for this book, and then click Objective 6.

Printers

A **printer** is an output device that produces text and graphics on a physical medium such as paper. Many different types and styles of printers exist with varying speeds, capabilities, and printing methods. Figure 5-34 presents a list of questions to help you determine the printer best suited to your needs.

The following pages will help you to answer these questions by discussing various ways to produce printed output, as well as many different types of printers.

1. What is my budget?
2. How fast must my printer print?
3. Do I need a color printer?
4. What is the cost per page for printing?
5. Do I need multiple copies of documents?
6. Will I print graphics?
7. Do I want to print photos?
8. Do I want to print directly from a memory card?
9. What types of paper does the printer use?
10. What sizes of paper does the printer accept?
11. Do I want to print on both sides of the paper?
12. How much paper can the printer tray hold?
13. Will the printer work with my computer and software?
14. How much do supplies such as ink, toner, and paper cost?
15. Can the printer print on envelopes?
16. How many envelopes can the printer print at a time?
17. How much do I print now, and how much will I be printing in a year or two?
18. Will the printer be connected to a network?
19. Do I want wireless printing capability?

Figure 5-34 Questions to ask when purchasing a printer.

Producing Printed Output

Although many users today print by connecting a computer to a printer with a cable, a variety of printing options are available as shown in Figure 5-35.

Today, wireless printing technology makes the task of printing from a notebook computer, smart phone, or digital camera much easier. Two wireless technologies for printing are Bluetooth and infrared. With Bluetooth printing, a computer or other device transmits output to a printer via radio waves. With infrared printing, a printer communicates with a computer or other device using infrared light waves.

Instead of downloading photos from a digital camera to a computer, users can print these digital photos using a variety of techniques. Some cameras connect directly to a printer via a cable. Others store photos on memory cards that can be removed and inserted in the printer. Some printers have a docking station, into which the user inserts the camera to print photos stored in the camera.

Finally, many home and business users print to a central printer on a network. Their computer may communicate with the network printer via cables or wirelessly.

Figure 5-35 Users print documents and photos using a variety of printing methods.

Nonimpact Printers

A **nonimpact printer** forms characters and graphics on a piece of paper without actually striking the paper. Some nonimpact printers spray ink, while others use heat or pressure to create images. Commonly used nonimpact printers are ink-jet printers, photo printers, laser printers, thermal printers, mobile printers, plotters, and large-format printers.

Ink-Jet Printers

An **ink-jet printer** is a type of nonimpact printer that forms characters and graphics by spraying tiny drops of liquid ink onto a piece of paper. Ink-jet printers have become a popular type of color printer for use in the home. Ink-jet printers produce text and graphics in both black-and-white and color on a variety of paper types (Figure 5-36). A reasonable quality ink-jet printer costs less than $100.

As with many other input and output devices, one factor that determines the quality of an ink-jet printer is its resolution. Printer resolution is measured by the number of dots per inch (dpi) a printer can print. Most ink-jet printers can print from 1200 to 4800 dpi.

The speed of an ink-jet printer is measured by the number of pages per minute (ppm) it can print. Most ink-jet printers print from 12 to 36 ppm. Graphics and colors print at a slower rate.

Figure 5-36 Ink-jet printers are a popular type of color printer used in the home.

The print head mechanism in an ink-jet printer contains ink-filled cartridges. Each cartridge has fifty to several hundred small ink holes, or nozzles. The ink propels through any combination of the nozzles to form a character or image on the paper. When the ink cartridge runs out of ink, you simply replace the cartridge. Most ink-jet printers use two or more ink cartridges: one containing black ink and the other(s) containing colors. Consider the number of ink cartridges a printer requires, along with the cost of the cartridges, when purchasing a printer. To reduce the expense of purchasing cartridges, some users opt to purchase refilled cartridges or have empty cartridges refilled by a third party vendor.

Photo Printers

A **photo printer** is a color printer that produces photo-lab-quality pictures (Figure 5-37). Some photo printers print just one or two sizes of photos, for example, 3 × 5 inches and 4 × 6 inches. Others print up to letter size, legal size, or even larger. Many photo printers use ink-jet technology. With models that can print letter-sized documents, users connect the photo printer to their computer and use it for all their printing needs.

Most photo printers are PictBridge enabled, so that you can print photos without a computer. **PictBridge** is a standard technology that allows you to print photos directly from a digital camera by connecting a cable from the digital camera to a USB port on the printer.

Photo printers also usually have a built-in card slot(s) so that the printer can print digital photos directly from a memory card. Some photo printers have built-in LCD color screens, allowing users to view and enhance the photos before printing them.

prints 4 × 6, 5 × 7, 8 × 10, 8½ × 11, and panoramic sizes

Figure 5-37 Photo printers print in a range of sizes.

Photo Printers

For more information, visit the Computer Concepts CourseMate Web site at www.cengagebrain.com, navigate to the Chapter 5 Web Link resource for this book, and then click Photo Printers.

Laser Printers

A **laser printer** is a high-speed, high-quality nonimpact printer (Figure 5-38). Laser printers for personal computers ordinarily use individual sheets of paper stored in one or more removable trays that slide in the printer case.

Laser printers print text and graphics in high-quality resolutions, usually ranging from 1200 to 2400 dpi. While laser printers usually cost more than ink-jet printers, many models are available at affordable prices for the home user. Laser printers usually print at faster speeds than ink-jet printers. Printer manufacturers state that a laser printer for the home and small office user typically prints black-and-white text at speeds of 15 to 62 ppm. Color laser printers print 8 to 40 ppm. Laser printers for large business users print more than 150 ppm.

Depending on the quality, speed, and type of laser printer, the cost ranges from a few hundred to a few thousand dollars for the home and small office user, and several hundred thousand dollars for the large business user. Color laser printers are slightly higher priced than otherwise equivalent black-and-white laser printers.

Operating in a manner similar to a copy machine, a laser printer creates images using a laser beam and powdered ink, called **toner**. Black-and-white laser printers use one toner cartridge. Color laser printers use multiple cartridges — one for black and one or more for colors. When the toner runs out, you replace the toner cartridge.

black-and-white
laser printer

color laser printer

Laser Printers

For more information,
visit the Computer Concepts
CourseMate Web site at
www.cengagebrain.com,
navigate to the Chapter 5
Web Link resource for this
book, and then click Laser
Printers.

Figure 5-38 Laser printers are available in both black-and-white and color models.

? FAQ 5-4

How do I dispose of toner cartridges?

Do not throw them in the garbage. The housing contains iron, metal, and aluminum that is not biodegradable. The ink toner inside the cartridges contains toxic chemicals that pollute water and soil if discarded in dumps. Instead, recycle empty toner cartridges. Many stores that sell new toner cartridges also allow you to recycle your old ones. Recycling programs in which some schools and organizations participate offer discounts or cash to customers who bring in depleted cartridges. If you are unable to find a recycling program in your area, contact your printer manufacturer to see if it has a recycling program.

For more information, visit the Computer Concepts CourseMate Web site at www.cengagebrain.com, navigate to the Chapter 5 FAQ resource for this book, and then click Recycling Toner Cartridges.

Multifunction Peripherals

A **multifunction peripheral**, also called an **all-in-one device**, is a single device that looks like a printer or copy machine but provides the functionality of a printer, scanner, copy machine, and perhaps a fax machine (Figure 5-39). Some use color ink-jet printer technology, while others include a black-and-white or color laser printer. An advantage of these devices is they are significantly less expensive than if you purchase each device separately. If the device breaks down, however, you lose all four functions, which is the primary disadvantage.

Figure 5-39
This multifunction peripheral is a color printer, scanner, copy machine, and fax machine.

Thermal Printers

A **thermal printer** generates images by pushing electrically heated pins against heat-sensitive paper. Basic thermal printers are inexpensive, but the print quality is low and the images tend to fade over time. Self-service gas pumps often print gas receipts using a built-in lower-quality thermal printer. Many point-of-sale terminals in retail and grocery stores also print purchase receipts on thermal paper.

Some thermal printers have high print quality and can print at much faster rates than ink-jet and laser printers. A dye-sublimation printer, sometimes called a **digital photo printer**, uses heat to transfer colored dye to specially coated paper. Professional applications requiring high image quality, such

as photography studios, medical labs, and security identification systems, use dye-sublimation printers. These high-end printers cost thousands of dollars and print images in a wide range of sizes.

Dye-sublimation printers for the home or small business user, by contrast, typically print images in only one or two sizes and are much slower than their professional counterparts. These lower-end dye-sublimation printers are comparable in cost to a photo printer based on ink-jet technology (Figure 5-40).

Figure 5-40 The printer shown in this figure uses dye-sublimation technology to create photographic-quality output for the home or small office user.

Mobile Printers

A **mobile printer** is a small, lightweight, battery-powered printer that allows a mobile user to print from a notebook computer, or smart phone or other mobile device while traveling (Figure 5-41). Barely wider than the paper on which they print, mobile printers fit easily in a briefcase alongside a notebook computer. Mobile printers mainly use ink-jet or thermal technology.

Figure 5-41
A mobile prin

Plotters and Large-Format Printers

Plotters are sophisticated printers used to produce high-quality drawings such as blueprints, maps, and circuit diagrams. These printers are used in specialized fields such as engineering and drafting and usually are very costly.

Using ink-jet printer technology, but on a much larger scale, a **large-format printer** creates photo-realistic-quality color prints. Graphic artists use these high-cost, high-performance printers for signs, posters, and other professional quality displays (Figure 5-42).

 Figure 5-42 Graphic artists use large-format printers to print signs, posters, and other professional quality displays.

Impact Printers

An **impact printer** forms characters and graphics on a piece of paper by striking a mechanism against an inked ribbon that physically contacts the paper. Impact printers are ideal for printing multipart forms because they easily print through many layers of paper. Two commonly used types of impact printers are dot-matrix printers and line printers.

A **dot-matrix printer** produces printed images when tiny wire pins on a print head mechanism strike an inked ribbon (Figure 5-43). When the ribbon presses against the paper, it creates dots that form characters and graphics. Dot-matrix printers typically use continuous-form paper, in which thousands of sheets of paper are connected together end to end. The pages have holes along the sides to help feed the paper through the printer. The speed of most dot-matrix printers ranges from 375 to 1100 characters per second (cps), depending on the desired print quality.

A **line printer** is a high-speed impact printer that prints an entire line at a time. The speed of a line printer is measured by the number of lines per minute (lpm) it can print. Some line printers print as many as 3,000 lpm.

continuous-form paper

Figure 5-43 A dot-matrix printer produces printed images when tiny pins strike an inked ribbon.

Other Output Devices

In addition to monitors and printers, other output devices are available for specific uses and applications. These include speakers, headphones, and earbuds; data projectors; and interactive whiteboards.

Speakers, Headphones, and Earbuds

An **audio output device** is a component of a computer that produces music, speech, or other sounds, such as beeps. Three commonly used audio output devices are speakers, headphones, and earbuds. Most personal computers and mobile devices have a small internal speaker that usually emits only low-quality sound. Thus, many users attach surround sound **speakers** or speaker systems to their computers to generate higher-quality sounds (Figure 5-44). Most surround sound computer speaker systems include one or two center speakers and two or more satellite speakers that are positioned so that sound emits from all directions. Speakers typically have tone and volume controls, allowing users to adjust settings. To boost the low bass sounds, surround sound speaker systems also include a subwoofer. In many cases, a cable connects the speakers or the subwoofer to a port on the sound card. With wireless speakers, however, a transmitter connects to the sound card, which wirelessly communicates with the speakers.

Many users opt for a wireless music system, where you can play any optical disc or media file on your computer and transmit the audio to a home or office stereo or television. You also can plug a portable media player, such as an iPod, into the computer to hear its songs on the stereo or television speakers.

In a computer laboratory or other crowded environment, speakers might not be practical. Instead, users can listen through wireless headphones or earbuds or plug the device into a port on the sound card, in a speaker, or in the front of the system unit. With headphones or earbuds, only the individual

subwoofer

satellite speakers

satellite speakers

center speaker

Figure 5-44 Most personal computer users attach high-quality surround sound speaker systems to their computers.

Earbuds

For more information, visit the Computer Concepts CourseMate Web site at www.cengagebrain.com, navigate to the Chapter 5 Web Link resource for this book, and then click Earbuds.

wearing the headphones or earbuds hears the sound from the computer. The difference is that **headphones** cover or are placed outside of the ear, whereas **earbuds**, or **earphones**, rest inside the ear canal.

A **headset** is a device that functions as both headphones and a microphone. Computer and smart phone users wear a headset to free their hands for typing and other activities while talking or listening to audio output.

Portable media players usually include a set of earbuds. As an alternative, you can listen to audio fr the portable media player through speakers in a vehicle or on a stereo system at home or work. Or, y can purchase speakers specifically designed to play audio from a portable media player.

Electronically produced voice output is growing in popularity. **Voice output** occurs when you hear person's voice or when the computer talks to you through the speakers on the computer. In some pro- grams, the computer can speak the contents of a document through voice output. On the Web, you ca listen to (or download and then listen to) interviews, talk shows, sporting events, news, recorded music and live concerts from many radio and television stations. Some Web sites and programs, such as medi players, dedicate themselves to providing voice output, such as those that allow you to listen to and the purchase and download songs. VoIP allows users to speak and listen to others over the Internet using their computer or mobile device.

Data Projectors

A **data projector** is a device that takes the text and images displaying on a computer screen and projects them on a larger screen so that an audience can see the image clearly. Some data projectors are large devices that attach to a ceiling or wall in an auditorium. Others, designed for the mobile user, are small portable devices that can be transported easily (Figure 5-45).

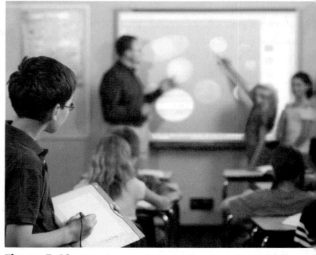

computer

data projector

Figure 5-45 Data projectors can produce sharp, bright ima

Interactive Whiteboards

An **interactive whiteboard** is a touch-sensitive device, resembling a dry-erase board, that displays the image on a connected computer screen. A pre- senter controls the computer program by clicking a remote control, touching the whiteboard, drawing on or erasing the whiteboard with a special digital pen and eraser, or writing on a special tablet. Notes written on the interactive whiteboard can be saved directly on the computer. Interactive whiteboards are used frequently in classrooms as a teach- ing tool (Figure 5-46), during meetings as a collaboration tool, and to enhance delivery of presentations.

Interactive whiteboards, which are hung on the wall or mounted on a stand, range in size from 48 to 94 inches. A widely used interactive whiteboard is the SMART Board.

SMART Board

For more information, visit the Computer Concepts CourseMate Web site at www.cengagebrain.com, navigate to the Chapter 5 Web Link resource for this book, and then click SMART Board.

Figure 5-46 Teachers and students can write directly on a interactive whiteboard, or they can write on a wireless slate that communicates with the whiteboard.

Putting It All Together

Many factors influence the type of input and output devices you should use: the type of input and output desired, the hardware and software in use, and the anticipated cost. Figure 5-47 outlines several suggested input and output devices for various types of computer users.

Suggested Input and Output Devices by User

User	Input Device	Output Device
Home 	• Enhanced keyboard or ergonomic keyboard • Mouse • Stylus for smart phone or other mobile device • Game controllers • Color scanner • 7 MP digital camera • Headphones that include a microphone (headset) • Web cam • Fingerprint reader	• 19- or 20-inch color LCD monitor, or 17-inch LCD screen on notebook computer • Ink-jet color printer; or • Photo printer • Speakers • Headphones or earbuds or headset
Small Office/Home Office	• Enhanced keyboard or ergonomic keyboard • Mouse • Stylus and portable keyboard for smart phone or other mobile device, or digital pen for Tablet PC • Color scanner • 8 MP digital camera • Headphones that include a microphone (headset) • Web cam	• 20- or 22-inch LCD monitor • LCD screen on smart phone or other mobile device • Multifunction peripheral; or • Ink-jet color printer; or • Laser printer (black-and-white or color) • Speakers
Mobile	• Wireless mouse for notebook computer • Touchpad or pointing stick on notebook computer • Stylus and portable keyboard for smart phone or other mobile device, or digital pen for Tablet PC • 7 or 8 MP digital camera • Headphones that include a microphone (headset) • Fingerprint reader for notebook computer	• 17-inch LCD screen on notebook computer • 8.9-inch screen on a netbook • LCD screen on smart phone or other mobile device • Mobile color printer • Ink-jet color printer; or • Laser printer, for in-office use (black-and-white or color) • Photo printer • Headphones or earbuds or headset • Data projector
Power	• Enhanced keyboard or ergonomic keyboard • Mouse • Stylus and portable keyboard for smart phone or other mobile device • Pen for graphics tablet • Color scanner • 9 to 12 MP digital camera • Headphones that include a microphone (headset) • Web cam	• 30-inch LCD monitor • Laser printer (black-and-white or color) • Plotter or large-format printer; or • Photo printer; or • Dye-sublimation printer • Speakers • Headphones or earbuds or headset
Enterprise	• Enhanced keyboard or ergonomic keyboard • Mouse • Stylus and portable keyboard for smart phone or other mobile device, or digital pen for Tablet PC • Touch screen • Color scanner • 9 to 12 MP digital camera • OCR/OMR readers, bar code readers, or MICR reader • Microphone • Video camera for video conferences • Fingerprint reader or other biometric device	• 20- or 22-inch LCD monitor • LCD screen on smart phone or other mobile device • High-speed laser printer • Laser printer, color • Line printer (for large reports from a mainframe) • Speakers • Headphones or earbuds or headset • Data projector • Interactive whiteboard

Figure 5-47 This table recommends suggested input and output devices for various types of users.

Input and Output Devices for Physically Challenged Users

The ever-increasing presence of computers in everyone's lives has generated an awareness of the need to address computing requirements for those who have or may develop physical limitations. The **Americans with Disabilities Act** (**ADA**) requires any company with 15 or more employees to make reasonable attempts to accommodate the needs of physically challenged workers. Read Ethics and Issues 5-3 for a related discussion.

Besides voice recognition, which is ideal for blind or visually impaired users, several other input devices are available. Users with limited hand mobility who want to use a keyboard have several options. Keyboards with larger keys are available. Still another option is the on-screen keyboard, in which a graphic of a standard keyboard is displayed on the user's screen. As the user clicks letters on the on-screen keyboard, they appear in the document at the location of the insertion point. An option for people with limited hand movement is a head-mounted pointer to control the pointer or insertion point (Figure 5-48). To simulate the functions of a mouse button, a user works with switches that control the pointer. The switch might be a hand pad, a foot pedal, a receptor that detects facial motions, or a pneumatic instrument controlled by puffs of air.

⋎ ETHICS & ISSUES 5-3

Should Web Sites Be Held Accountable for Accessibility Levels for Physically Challenged People?

The World Wide Web Consortium (W3C) has published accessibility guidelines for Web sites. The guidelines specify measures that Web site designers can take to increase accessibility for physically challenged users. Among its guidelines, the W3C urges Web site designers to provide equivalent text for audio or visual content, include features that allow elements to be activated and understood using a variety of input and output devices, and make the user interface follow principles of accessible design. A recent report found that most Web sites do not meet all of the W3C guidelines. This failure is disappointing, because many physically challenged users could benefit from the Web's capability to bring products and services into the home. Ironically, a survey discovered that more than 50 percent of the

Web sites hosted by disability organizations also fail to meet the W3C guidelines. Critics contend that these Web sites neglect the needs of their users and fail to lead by example. The Web site supporters contend, however, that many sponsoring organizations lack the funding necessary to comply with the guidelines.

Should the government require that all Web sites meet the W3C accessibility guidelines? Why or why not? Do Web sites hosted by disability organizations have a moral obligation to meet the guidelines? Why? What can be done to encourage people and organizations to make their Web sites more accessible?

camera/receiver

reflective tracking surface attached to brim of hat

Figure 5-48 A camera/ receiver mounted on the monitor tracks the position of the head-mounted pointer, which is reflective material that this user is wearing on the brim of her hat. As the user moves her head, the pointer on the screen also moves.

For users with mobility, hearing, or vision disabilities, many different types of output devices are available. Hearing-impaired users, for example, can instruct programs to display words instead of sounds. Read Looking Ahead 5-1 for a look at a tongue-powered input device.

Visually impaired users can change Windows settings, such as increasing the size or changing the color of the text to make the words easier to read. Instead of using a monitor, blind users can work with voice output. That is, the computer reads the information that appears on the screen. Another alternative is a Braille printer, which outputs information on paper in Braille (Figure 5-49).

Figure 5-49 A Braille printer.

LOOKING AHEAD 5-1

Tongue May Become Joystick to Control Devices

Thousands of people are paralyzed from the neck down due to spinal cord damage, but they have full control of their tongue because it is controlled by a cranial nerve, not the spinal cord. For these people, Georgia Institute of Technology's Tongue Drive System may be the input device that helps them control their lives.

In the Georgia Tech prototype, the tongue serves as a joystick. A magnet less than one-eighth of an inch wide is surgically implanted under the tip of the tongue, and when a person moves his or her tongue, sensors on each cheek record the magnet's movements in one of six directions: left, right, forward, backward, single-click, and double-click. This data is sent to a receiver on top of the person's head, which, in turn, transmits a signal wirelessly to a computer that controls an electronic device. For example, if the tongue moves forward and to the left, lights in the room could turn on or a wheelchair could roll forward.

In a future development of the Tongue Drive System, an individual tooth could be designated as a specific letter, so teeth could function, in effect, as a keyboard.

For more information, visit the Computer Concepts CourseMate Web site at www.cengagebrain.com, navigate to the Chapter 5 Looking Ahead resource for this book, and then click Tongue Joystick.

Instructions: Find the true statement below. Then, rewrite the remaining false statements so that they are true.

1. A laser printer generates images by pushing electrically heated pins against heat-sensitive paper.
2. A photo printer creates images using a laser beam and powdered ink, called toner.
3. An ink-jet printer is a type of impact printer that forms characters and graphics by spraying tiny drops of liquid nitrogen onto a piece of paper.
4. Many personal computer users attach surround sound printer systems to their computers to generate a higher-quality sound.
5. Multifunction peripherals require more space than having a separate printer, scanner, copy machine, and fax machine.
6. The Americans with Disabilities Act (ADA) requires any company with 15 or more employees to make reasonable attempts to accommodate the needs of physically challenged workers.

💻 **Quiz Yourself Online:** To further check your knowledge of pages 211 through 221, visit the Computer Concepts CourseMate Web site at www.cengagebrain.com, navigate to the Chapter 5 Quiz Yourself resource for this book, and then click Objectives 7 – 9.

Chapter Summary

Input is any data and instructions you enter into the memory of a computer. This chapter described the various techniques of entering input and several commonly used input devices. Topics included the keyboard, mouse and other pointing devices, touch screens, pen input, other input for smart phones, game controllers, digital cameras, voice input, video input, scanners and reading devices, biometric input, and terminals.

Computers process and organize data (input) into information (output). This chapter also described the various methods of output and several commonly used output devices. Output devices presented included display devices; printers; speakers, headphones, and earbuds; data projectors; and interactive whiteboards.

Computer Usage @ Work

Space Exploration

Watching the television closely, you hear the announcer count the seconds until the spacecraft lifts off from its launch pad: "Three, two, one, and we have liftoff." The engines ignite and the glow from the burning fuel illuminates the night sky as it begins its journey toward the International Space Station. As you sit back and watch, mesmerized by the thought that a group of astronauts are accomplishing something of which you only could dream, hundreds of individuals and computers are working behind the scenes to ensure a safe mission.

Because space exploration is fraught with danger, it is extremely important that all decisions be made with precision and that personnel become aware of problems before the problems become too serious. For instance, space vehicles contain a plethora of sensors that measure environmental variables such as temperature, velocity, position, and altitude. If the sensors return readings outside an acceptable range, computers correct any problems or notify mission managers as necessary. Employees work around the clock monitoring the output from the spacecraft sensors while it is in flight and communicating to astronauts any actions required to ensure a continued safe mission.

In addition to keeping the spacecraft safe while in orbit, computers also help guide the spacecraft into and out of orbit. To reach the International Space Station, spacecraft can be launched safely only during specified launch time frames. Once the spacecraft is launched, it must travel in a precise direction at an exact velocity to ensure a successful mission. As the mission nears completion and a capsule containing the astronauts reenters the atmosphere, onboard computers position the capsule precisely so that the extreme temperatures at the reentry interface do not cause catastrophic damage. Furthermore, these onboard computers help to ensure that the capsule touches down in a safe location.

With billions of dollars spent on space travel, computers play a vital role in guaranteeing the safety of the space vehicle, the astronauts, and those of us on Earth.

💻 For more information, visit the Computer Concepts CourseMate Web site at www.cengagebrain.com, navigate to the Chapter 5 Computer Usage @ Work resource for this book, and then click Space Exploration.

Companies on the Cutting Edge

LOGITECH Personal Interface Products Leader

Design and innovation drive the development of Logitech products, and the company continues to win top industry awards for its imaginative personal peripheral, Internet communications, home entertainment, gaming, and digital music devices. Logitech has sold millions of mouse devices and wireless products in practically every country in the world.

Stanford computer science students Daniel Borel and Pierluigi Zappacosta, along with Giacomo Marini, founded Logitech in 1981 at Borel's father-in-law's farm in Apples, Switzerland. The company's name is derived from logiciel, which is the French word for software.

Many of Logitech's latest ventures have capitalized on consumers' growing interest in their digital homes. Recently, Logitech announced its one millionth Logitech Vid customer after only three months of being available publicly. Logitech Vid is Logitech's free video conferencing software.

HP Hardware and Software Products Leader

One of the more famous real estate parcels in the United States is the birthplace of the Silicon Valley: the garage where Stanford University friends William Hewlett and David Packard developed various electronic products. Their first success in 1938 was an oscillator used to test sound equipment.

Today HP (Hewlett-Packard) has become the world's top manufacturer of ink-jet and laser printers, multifunction peripherals, desktop and notebook computers, and servers. It also is a leading software company with products for networking and storage management.

Recently, HP introduced the first workstation with a six-core AMD Opteron processor, delivering high productivity for multi-threaded programs. HP also ranked ninth in the 2009 FORTUNE 500 ranking.

For more information, visit the Computer Concepts CourseMate Web site at www.cengagebrain.com and then navigate to the Chapter 5 Companies on the Cutting Edge resource for this book.

Technology Trailblazers

DOUGLAS ENGELBART Creator of the Mouse

The ubiquitous mouse is a staple for desktop computers, but its evolution to becoming the most widely used pointing device was a slow process. Douglas Engelbart conceived the idea of the mouse in 1950 to help humans work more efficiently. Fourteen years later he developed the first prototype with the goal of making it easier for people to move a cursor around a computer screen. In 1974, engineers at Xerox refined Engelbart's prototype and showed the redesigned product to Apple's Steve Jobs, who applied the concept to his graphical Macintosh computer. The final product did not gain worldwide acceptance for another 10 years.

Engelbart is continuing his pursuits of helping people work smarter. His Bootstrap Institute is a California-based company that promotes collaboration, creativity, and competition to solve problems.

URSULA BURNS Xerox Chairman and CEO

When Ursula Burns was nominated to chair Xerox Corporation in 2010, two milestones were reached: she became the first African-American woman to lead a major American company and the first woman to succeed another woman in that role.

She began working at Xerox 30 years earlier as a mechanical engineering summer intern. After earning her bachelor's and master's degrees in that field, she worked in various areas of the corporation, including office network printing, global research, product development, manufacturing, and planning.

When Burns was named Xerox's president in 2007, her leadership role expanded to include the information technology, corporate marketing, and human resources departments.

Forbes and *Fortune* have named Burns as one of the most powerful women in the world. She serves as advisor to several educational and community organizations, including FIRST (For Inspiration and Recognition of Science and Technology) and the White House's STEM (Science, Technology, Engineering, and Math) program.

For more information, visit the Computer Concepts CourseMate Web site at www.cengagebrain.com and then navigate to the Chapter 5 Technology Trailblazers resource for this book.

Chapter Review

The Chapter Review reinforces the main concepts presented in this chapter.

To listen to an audio version of this Chapter Review, visit the Computer Concepts CourseMate Web site at www.cengagebrain.com and then navigate to the Chapter 5 Chapter Review resource for this book.

1. **What Keys and Buttons Commonly Are Found on Desktop Computer Keyboards, and How Do Keyboards for Mobile Computers and Devices Differ from Desktop Computer Keyboards?** A **keyboard** is an input device that contains keys users press to enter data and instructions into a computer. Desktop computer keyboards have a typing area that includes letters of the alphabet, numbers, punctuation marks, and other basic keys. An enhanced keyboard also has function keys programmed to issue commands, a numeric keypad, arrow keys, and additional keys and buttons. On mobile computers and devices, the keyboard is built into the system unit. Keyboards on these devices usually are smaller and have fewer keys than desktop computer keyboards. Some smart phones have a mini-keyboard or on-screen keyboard.

2. **What Are the Different Mouse Types?** An **optical mouse** uses devices that emit and sense light to detect the mouse's movement. A **laser mouse** uses a laser to detect movement. An **air mouse** is a motion-sensing mouse that you can move through the air. A wireless, or cordless, mouse transmits data using wireless technology.

3. **What Are the Various Types of Touch Screens, and How Does a Touch-Sensitive Pad Work?** A **touch screen** is a touch-sensitive display device that you interact with by touching areas of the screen. A **kiosk** is a freestanding computer that includes a touch screen. **Microsoft Surface** is a tabletop display that allows users to interact with the screen using their fingers or hands. A **touch-sensitive pad** enables users to scroll through and play music, view pictures, watch videos or movies, adjust volume, and/or customize settings on a portable media player or other mobile device. Touch-sensitive pads typically contain buttons and/or wheels that are operated with a thumb or finger.

4. **What Are the Various Types of Pen Input?** With **pen input**, you touch a **stylus** or a **digital pen** on a flat surface to write, draw, or make selections. A **signature capture pad** captures handwritten signatures. A **graphics tablet** can be connected to a computer that does not include a touch screen in order to use pen input.

Visit the Computer Concepts CourseMate Web site at www.cengagebrain.com, navigate to the Chapter 5 Quiz Yourself resource for this book, and then click Objectives 1 – 4.

5. **What Are Other Types of Input?** Video and computer games use a **game controller** as the input device. Game controllers include a **gamepad**, which controls the movement and actions of players or objects in video games or computer games; a **joystick**, which is a handheld vertical lever mounted on a base; a **wheel**, which is a steering-wheel-type input device; a **light gun**, which is used to shoot targets; and a **dance pad**, which users press with their feet in response to instructions. The **Wii Remote** is a type of motion-sensing game controller. For smart phones, you can talk directly into the microphone or headset. Some smart phones have digital cameras and touch-sensitive pads. A digital camera's **resolution** is the number of horizontal and vertical pixels in a display device. **Video input** is the process of capturing full-motion pictures and storing them on a computer's storage medium. A **Web cam** is used for video input. A **video conference** is a meeting between two or more geographically separate people who use a network to transmit audio and video data. A **scanner** is a light-sensing input device that reads printed text and graphics and translates the results into a form a computer can process. An optical reader is a device that uses a light source to read characters, marks, and codes and converts them into digital data. **OCR (optical character recognition)** devices use a small optical scanner and software to analyze characters from ordinary documents. **OMR (optical mark recognition)** devices read hand-drawn marks on a form. A **bar code reader** uses laser beams to read bar codes. An **RFID device** reads information on an embedded tag via radio waves. A **magnetic stripe card reader** reads the magnetic stripe on the back of credit cards and other similar cards. **MICR** (magnetic-ink character recognition) devices read text printed with magnetized ink. Biometric input can include fingerprints, hand geometry, facial features, voice, signatures, and eye patterns.

Visit the Computer Concepts CourseMate Web site at www.cengagebrain.com, navigate to the Chapter 5 Quiz Yourself resource for this book, and then click Objective 5.

6. **What Are the Characteristics of LCD Monitors, LCD Screens, and CRT Monitors?** A **display device** is a commonly used **output device** that visually conveys text, graphics, and video information. An **LCD monitor** is a desktop monitor that uses a liquid crystal display. A **liquid crystal display (LCD)** uses a liquid compound to present information on a display device. A **CRT monitor** is a desktop monitor that contains a cathode-ray tube. The popularity of CRT monitors is declining.

Visit the Computer Concepts CourseMate Web site at www.cengagebrain.com, navigate to the Chapter 5 Quiz Yourself resource for this book, and then click Objective 6.

7. What Are Various Types of Printers? A **printer** is an output device that produces text and graphics on a physical medium. An **ink-jet printer** forms characters and graphics by spraying tiny drops of ink onto paper. A **photo printer** produces photo-lab-quality pictures. A **laser printer** is a high-speed, high-quality printer that operates in a manner similar to a copy machine. A **multifunction peripheral** is a single device that looks like a computer or copy machine but provides the functionality of a printer, scanner, copy machine, and possibly a fax machine. A **thermal printer** generates images by pushing electrically heated pins against heat-sensitive paper. A **mobile printer** is a small, battery-powered printer used to print from a notebook computer, or mobile device. **Plotters** are used to produce high-quality drawings in specialized fields. A **large-format printer** creates large, photo-realistic-quality color prints. A **dot-matrix printer** is an impact printer that produces an image when tiny wire pins on a print head strike an inked ribbon. A **line printer** prints an entire line at a time.

8. What Are the Purposes and Features of Speakers, Headphones, and Earbuds; Data Projectors; and Interactive Whiteboards? **Speakers** are a type of **audio output device** added to computers to generate higher-quality sounds. Only the individual wearing headphones or earbuds hears the sound from the computer. The difference is that **headphones** cover or are placed outside of the ear, whereas **earbuds** rest inside the ear canal. A **data projector** takes the text and images displaying on a computer screen and projects them on a larger screen for an audience. An **interactive whiteboard** is a touch-sensitive device, resembling a dry-erase board, that displays the image on a connected computer screen.

9. What Are Input and Output Options for Physically Challenged Users? **Voice recognition** is an input option for visually impaired users. Input options for people with limited hand mobility include keyboards with larger keys, on-screen keyboards, and head-mounted pointers. Hearing-impaired users can instruct programs to display words instead of sounds. Visually impaired users can change Windows settings to make words easier to read. Blind users can use voice output and a Braille printer.

Visit the Computer Concepts CourseMate Web site at www.cengagebrain.com, navigate to the Chapter 5 Quiz Yourself resource for this book, and then click Objectives 7 – 9.

Key Terms

You should know each key term. The list below helps focus your study.

To see an example of and a definition for each term, and to access current and additional information about the term from the Web, visit the Computer Concepts CourseMate Web site at www.cengagebrain.com and then navigate to the Chapter 5 Key Terms resource for this book.

air mouse (191)
all-in-one device (215)
Americans with Disabilities Act (ADA) (220)
audio input (198)
audio output device (217)
automated teller machine (ATM) (204)
bar code (201)
bar code reader (201)
biometrics (202)
Click Wheel (193)
CRT monitor (210)
dance pad (196)
data projector (218)
digital camera (197)
digital pen (194)
digital photo printer (215)
digital video (DV) camera (199)
display device (207)
dot-matrix printer (217)
DVD kiosk (205)
earbuds (218)
earphones (218)
ergonomics (190)
fingerprint reader (202)

flatbed scanner (200)
game controller (196)
gamepad (196)
graphics tablet (194)
headphones (218)
headset (218)
impact printer (217)
ink-jet printer (213)
input (188)
input device (188)
interactive whiteboard (218)
joystick (196)
keyboard (190)
kiosk (193)
large-format printer (216)
laser mouse (191)
laser printer (214)
LCD monitor (208)
light gun (196)
line printer (217)
liquid crystal display (LCD) (209)
magnetic stripe card reader (201)
MICR (202)
MICR reader (202)

Microsoft Surface (193)
mobile printer (216)
monitor (207)
mouse (191)
multifunction peripheral (215)
nonimpact printer (213)
OCR devices (200)
optical character recognition (OCR) (200)
optical mark recognition (OMR) (200)
optical mouse (191)
output (206)
output device (206)
PC video camera (199)
pen input (194)
photo printer (214)
PictBridge (214)
pixel (198)
plasma monitor (210)
plotters (216)
pointer (189)
pointing device (189)
pointing stick (192)
POS terminal (204)
printer (211)

resolution (198)
RFID (201)
RFID reader (201)
scanner (200)
signature capture pad (194)
speakers (217)
speech recognition (198)
stylus (194)
terminal (204)
thermal printer (215)
toner (214)
touch screen (193)
touch-sensitive pad (193)
touchpad (192)
trackball (192)
turnaround document (200)
video conference (199)
video input (199)
video telephone call (199)
voice input (198)
voice output (218)
voice recognition (198)
Web cam (199)
wheel (196)
widescreen (208)
Wii Remote (197)

Checkpoint

The Checkpoint exercises test your knowledge of the chapter concepts. The page number containing the answer appears in parentheses after each exercise.

To complete the Checkpoint exercises interactively, visit the Computer Concepts CourseMate Web site at www.cengagebrain.com and then navigate to the Chapter 5 Checkpoint resource for this book.

Multiple Choice Select the best answer.

1. An ergonomic keyboard _____. (190)
 a. has a design that reduces wrist and hand injuries
 b. transmits data using wireless technology
 c. is used to enter data into a biometric device
 d. is built into the top of a handheld computer

2. A _____ is a small metal or plastic device that looks like a tiny ink pen but uses pressure instead of ink. (194)
 a. touch screen
 b. stylus
 c. trackball
 d. pointing stick

3. Architects, mapmakers, designers, artists, and home users create drawings and sketches on a _____. (194)
 a. trackball
 b. smart terminal
 c. graphics tablet
 d. touchpad

4. _____ is the computer's capability of distinguishing spoken words. (198)
 a. Voice input
 b. VoIP
 c. MIDI
 d. Voice recognition

5. RFID is a technology that uses _____ to communicate with a tag placed in or attached to an object, an animal, or a person. (201)
 a. a thin wire
 b. pixels
 c. radio signals
 d. light waves

6. The speed of an ink-jet printer is measured by the number of _____ it can print. (213)
 a. lines per page (lpp)
 b. dots per inch (dpi)
 c. characters per second (cps)
 d. pages per minute (ppm)

7. The primary disadvantage of multifunction peripherals is that _____. (215)
 a. if the multifunction peripheral breaks down, all functions are lost
 b. they all use laser-printer technology
 c. they are significantly more expensive than purchasing each device separately
 d. all of the above

8. Basic _____ are inexpensive, but the print quality is low and the images tend to fade over time. (215)
 a. laser printers
 b. thermal printers
 c. dot-matrix printers
 d. line printers

Matching Match the terms with their definitions.

_____ 1. kiosk (193)
_____ 2. turnaround document (200)
_____ 3. biometrics (202)
_____ 4. POS terminal (204)
_____ 5. headset (218)

a. technology of authenticating a person's identity by verifying a personal characteristic
b. a device that functions as both headphones and a microphone
c. self-service banking machine that connects to a host computer through a network
d. freestanding computer that includes a touch screen
e. a document that you return to the company that creates and sends it
f. used by most retail stores to record purchases, process credit or debit cards, and update inventory

Short Answer Write a brief answer to each of the following questions.

1. How are an optical mouse, an air mouse, and a wireless mouse different? _____ How is a trackball used? _____

2. How does a signature capture pad work? _____ How is an RFID reader used? _____

3. What is a DVD kiosk? _____ How might a DVD kiosk function for a customer? _____

4. What type of monitor emits electromagnetic radiation? _____ What can you do to protect yourself from electromagnetic radiation from a monitor? _____

5. How does an ink-jet printer work? _____ What are the differences between dye-sublimation printers used by professionals as compared to home or small business users? _____

Problem Solving

The Problem Solving exercises extend your knowledge of the chapter concepts by seeking solutions to practical computer problems that you may encounter at home, school, or work. The Collaboration exercise should be completed with a team.

In the real world, practical problems often can be solved in multiple ways. Provide one solution to each of the following problems using available resources, such as articles on the Web or in print, blogs, podcasts, videos, television, user guides, other individuals, and electronics and computer stores. You may need to use multiple resources to obtain an answer. Present your solutions in the form requested by your instructor (brief report, presentation, discussion, or other means).

@ Home

1. **No Media Controls** You have purchased a new keyboard for your three-year-old computer. When you connect the keyboard to your computer's USB port, you are able to type, but the media controls do not work. What could be the problem?

2. **Smeared Printouts** Each time you print a picture on photo paper using your photo printer, the photo comes out of the printer smeared. What is one step you can take that might prevent the ink from smearing while the photo is printing?

3. **Dim Screen** While using your notebook computer, the screen suddenly becomes dim. You set the brightness to its highest setting before it dimmed, and wonder why it suddenly changed. After resetting the brightness to its highest setting, you continue working. What might have caused the screen to dim?

4. **Malfunctioning Earbud** While listening to music on your portable media player, one side of your earbuds suddenly stops working. What might have caused this?

@ Work

5. **Fingerprint Not Recognized** To increase security, your company now requires employees to log into their computers using a fingerprint reader instead of entering a user name and password. This past weekend, you cut the finger you use to log in, and your computer now does not recognize your fingerprint. As a result, you are unable to access your computer. What are your next steps?

6. **Access Denied** Your company uses security badges with embedded RFID tags to authenticate the rooms to which employees have access. This badge also grants employees access to the company's parking lot. When arriving at work one morning, you wave your badge in front of the RFID reader, but the gate that allows access to the parking lot does not rise. In addition, a red light blinks on the RFID reader. What are your next steps?

7. **Unrecognizable Characters** Because of budget cuts, you and your coworkers no longer have printers connected to your computers and must print to a printer connected to the company network. You started to print a 40-page document, but realized immediately that you needed to make one more change to the document, so you cancelled the print job. After making the correction and printing the document again, you walk to the printer only to find the printer printing many pages with unrecognizable characters. What might be wrong?

8. **Monitors Reversed** You have two monitors set up on your desk at work: the monitor on the left is your primary monitor and displays the taskbar, and you typically use the monitor on the right to display your e-mail program. When you arrive at work and log into Windows, you realize that the monitor on the right is now the primary monitor. What might have happened?

Collaboration

9. **Computers in Space Exploration** The space tourism industry is gaining worldwide attention. Many more people might express interest in experiencing outer space if prices become more reasonable and safety concerns are minimized. Computers help ensure safety by helping the space vehicles to fly with great precision, but human intervention also is necessary. Form a team of three people and determine how computer output can provide enough information to ensure a safe experience. One team member should research current space exploration and data returned from space vehicles that proved useful. Another team member should research how space vehicles collect this data and present it in a useful form, and the other team member should think of additional ways that computer output can assist in space exploration. Write a brief report summarizing your findings.

Learn How To

The Learn How To activities step you through fundamental technology skills when using a computer. The Learn How To exercises enable you to become more proficient with these skills.

Premium Activity: To relate this Learn How To activity to your everyday life, see a visual demonstration of the activity, and complete a short assessment, visit the Computer Concepts CourseMate Web site at www.cengagebrain.com and then navigate to the Chapter 5 Learn How To resources for this book.

Learn How To 1: Make a Video and Upload It to YouTube

As digital video cameras become smaller and more affordable, many individuals are choosing to create digital recordings of everyday events. In the past, video cameras were bulky, expensive, and required big VCR tapes. Video cameras now are digital and small enough to take anywhere. They also have the capability to transfer video footage to a computer, allowing you to reuse tapes. The increase in individuals storing videos on their computer has prompted companies to develop media sharing Web sites, such as YouTube, for people to post their videos online for others to view. This is especially helpful when you would like to share a video of a memorable event, such as your child's first steps, with a relative across the country who was unable to experience it in person.

Transferring a Video from a Digital Video Camera to a Computer

1. Connect the digital video camera to a computer using the provided USB or FireWire cable. If the camera does not have a cable and stores the digital video on a memory card, remove the memory card from the camera and then insert it into the computer.
2. You can transfer the video from the digital video camera to a computer in one or more of the following ways, depending upon the type of camera you own:
 a. Start the program that came with the digital video camera and follow the manufacturer's instructions for importing the video to a hard disk.
 b. When the digital video camera or memory card is displayed as a removable disk in Windows, copy the video file(s) to a hard disk.
 c. Open Windows Live Movie Maker and click the 'Import from device' command on the Movie Maker menu to import video from the digital video camera.
3. Your video should be less than 10 minutes, less than 2 GB in size, and one of the following file formats: .AVI, .MOV, .WMV, or .MPG. If your video does not meet these requirements, you either should create your video again or use software such as Windows Live Movie Maker to change its file format or reduce its length or size.
4. Double-click the video on the computer to make sure that it plays in its entirety and that you can hear audio.
5. If you would like to free space on a digital camera's media, delete the original video file(s) from the digital video camera or memory card.
6. Disconnect the digital video camera from the computer or remove the memory card from the computer.

Log into YouTube

1. Start a Web browser, type youtube.com in the Address bar, and then press the ENTER key to display the YouTube - Broadcast Yourself Web page.
2. Click the Sign In link.
3. Type your user name and password, and then click the Sign In button. If you do not have a YouTube account, click the Sign up for YouTube! link and follow the instructions to sign up for a new YouTube account.

Upload the Video

1. Click a Upload button to display the Video File Upload Web page.
2. Click the Upload Video button to display the 'Select file to upload' dialog box. Locate the video on your computer that you wish to upload and then click the Open button.
3. If necessary, change the title of the video to one you prefer.
4. Enter the description and tags for this video. If you would like to make it easy for people to find your video, enter a detailed description and several tags.
5. Select a video category from the Category drop-down list.
6. If you want to make the video private, click the 'Private (Viewable by you and up to 25 people)' option button.

7. Click the Save Changes button.
8. YouTube will save your changes once the video is finished uploading.

View the Video

1. Point to your user name at the top of the Video File Upload Web page and then click My Videos.
2. Click the Play button to preview the video. Once the video has finished playing, click the Sign Out link to sign out of YouTube.

Exercise

1. Use a digital video camera to create a short video that is less than 20 seconds in length. Save the video to your computer and then sign into YouTube. Upload the video you just created (if you do not have a digital video camera, upload a sample video that is included with Windows or another video on your computer that is not protected by copyright). Once the video has finished uploading, preview it and then send the Web address to your instructor.

Learn It Online

The Learn It Online exercises are interactive Web exercises designed to reinforce and expand your understanding of the chapter concepts. The descriptions below briefly summarize each exercise.

To complete the Learn It Online exercises, visit the Computer Concepts CourseMate Web site at www.cengagebrain.com, navigate to the Chapter 5 resources for this book, click the link for the exercise you want to complete, and then read the instructions.

1 At the Movies — Video Editing on Your Computer
Watch a movie to learn about simple editing tips for converting raw video footage into interesting videos.

2 Student Edition Labs — Peripheral Devices
Enhance your understanding and knowledge about the motherboard and binary numbers by completing the Peripheral Devices Lab.

3 Practice Test
Take a multiple choice test that checks your knowledge of the chapter concepts and review the resulting study guide.

4 Who Wants To Be a Computer Genius²?
Play the Shelly Cashman Series version of this popular game by answering questions to find out if you are a computer genius. Panic buttons are available to provide assistance during game play.

5 Crossword Puzzle Challenge
Complete an interactive crossword puzzle to reinforce concepts presented in this chapter.

6 Windows Exercises
Step through the Windows 7 exercises to learn about your computer, Accessibility options, Magnifier, and adjusting the sound on a computer.

7 Exploring Computer Careers
Read about a career as a graphic designer/illustrator, search for related employment advertisements, and then answer related questions.

8 Web Apps — YouSendIt
Learn how to use YouSendIt to create an e-mail message with an attachment and add options such as premium delivery, password-protected secure delivery, certified delivery with tracking, and return receipt.

Web Research

The Web Research exercises broaden your understanding of the chapter concepts by presenting questions that require you to search Web for answers.

1 **Search Sleuth**

Use one of the search engines listed in Figure 2-8 in Chapter 2 on page 65 or your own favorite search engine to find the answers to the following questions. Copy and paste the Web address from the Web page where you found the answer. Some questions may have more than one answer. If required, submit your answers to your instructor. (1) Which Haruhi Suzumiya games have been released for the Nintendo Wii? (2) Which two companies worked in partnership with Kodak to develop kiosks with digital image-making software? (3) Which countries have adopted the ENERGY STAR program? (4) What invention relating to the printing industry did Lord Kelvin patent in 1867? (5) Which output devices did Donald Bitzer design for the PLATO IV computer assisted instruction system at the University of Illinois? (6) Which country has imposed a maximum limit of 100 decibels on all headphones and earbuds sold?

2 **Green Computing**

Digital cameras use more battery power than film cameras because they operate electronic image sensors, LCD viewfinders, and flashes. They also write images to storage devices. The battery packs discharge whether you snap photos or not, but you can help extend your digital camera's battery life by following some conservation tips. View online Web sites, including The Battery Bank (batterybank.net), MalekTips (malektips.com/digital_camera_battery_help_and_tips.html), and Associated Content (associatedcontent.com) that provide information about charging battery packs, using cameras, and storing batteries. How do nickel cadmium (Ni-Cd), nickel metal hydride (Ni-MH), and lithium ion (Li-ion) batteries differ in charging time and discharge? How should batteries be stored if cameras are used infrequently? How does conditioning affect "memory effect"? Write a report summarizing your findings, and include a table of links to Web sites that provide additional details.

3 **Social Networking**

Each day, more than 100,000 people register for Friendster, which is one of the top three online social networking Web sites in the world. The San Francisco-based company is popular in more than 75 countries, particularly in Asia. Its mobile Web site, m.friendster.com, allows the more than 110 million registered users to receive and send messages using their smart phones. Visit the Friendster Web site (friendster.com). Follow the instructions to create a Friendster account, log in, and then click the Explore link at the top of the home page. Who are some musicians, athletes, and artists featured in the Fan Profiles section? Click the Classifieds link and then select a city in the Location area. What types of computer listings are shown in the Services area? Click the About Us link at the bottom of the page and then click the Testimonials link. What do members like about Friendster? Summarize the information you read and viewed.

4 **Blogs**

Whether you are listening to the radio, watching television, or drinking a beverage at the local coffee shop, the world of sports is likely to surface. People are passionate about their favorite athletes and sporting events, from the community Little League game to the NFL Super Bowl. Visit several sports blogs, including those from Fanblogs (fanblogs.com), BC Sports (blogcritics.org/sports), Deadspin (deadspin.com), Full Throttle (fullthrottle.cranialcavity .net), ESPN (sports.espn.go.com/espn/blog), and Fox Sports (community.foxsports.com/blogs). What are the more popular discussions? Which college football and basketball teams are featured? Who are the professional athletes receiving much discussion? Which NASCAR teams are analyzed?

5 **Ethics in Action**

"Netomania" is not a recognized disorder, but this popular name for Internet Addiction Disorder (IAD) may be affecting some Internet users who spend many hours gaming, blogging, shopping, and social networking. People may be addicted when they spend up to 10 hours a day online, they occasionally binge for extended Internet sessions, and they suffer withdrawal symptoms when they have not been online for some time. Some researchers, however, believe the Internet problem is just a symptom of other psychiatric disorders, such as manic depression. View online sites that provide information about IAD, including the Center for Internet Addiction Recovery (netaddiction.com). Write a report summarizing your findings, and include a table of links to Web sites that provide additional details.

Digital Video Technology

Everywhere you look, people are capturing moments they want to remember. They shoot movies of their vacations, birthday parties, activities, accomplishments, sporting events, weddings, and more. Because of the popularity of digital video cameras and mobile devices with built-in digital cameras, increasingly more people desire to capture their memories digitally, instead of on film. As shown in Figure 1, people have the ability to modify and share the digital videos they create. When you use special hardware and/or software, you can copy, manipulate, and distribute digital videos using your personal computer and the Internet. Amateurs can achieve professional quality results by using more sophisticated hardware and software. This feature describes how to select a video camera, record a video, transfer and manage videos, edit a video, and distribute a video.

Digital recordings deliver significant benefits over film-based movie making. With digital video cameras, recordings reside on storage media such as a hard disk, optical disc,

or memory card. Unlike film, storage media can be reused, which reduces costs, saves time, and provides immediate results. Digital technology allows greater control over the creative process, both while recording video and in the editing process. You can check results immediately after capturing a video to determine whether it meets your expectations. If you are dissatisfied with a video, you can erase it and recapture it, again and again. Today, many mobile devices, such as smart phones and PDAs, allow you to capture video.

As shown in Figure 1, digital video cameras, and mobile devices function as input devices when they transmit video to a personal computer. You can transmit video by connecting the video camera or mobile device to your personal computer using a USB or FireWire port, or by placing the storage media used on the camera or mobile device in the computer. Some cameras and devices also can transmit wirelessly to a computer or to the media sharing Web sites.

Figure 1 A variety of input, output, and storage devices are used by home users to process and edit digital video.

When you transmit video that was captured with a digital video camera or mobile device to a computer, you can edit the video using video editing software. If desired, you often can preview the video during the editing process on a television. Finally, you save the finished result to the desired media, such as an optical disc or, perhaps, e-mail the edited video or post it to a media sharing Web site. In this example, an optical disc drive also can be used to input video from an optical disc. Also in the example shown in Figure 1 on the previous page, a mobile device that includes a video camera sends a video directly to a media sharing Web site.

Digital video technology allows you to input, edit, manage, publish, and share your videos using a personal computer. With digital video technology, you can transform home videos into Hollywood-style movies by enhancing the videos with scrolling titles and transitions, cutting out or adding scenes, and adding background music and voice-over narration. The following sections outline the steps involved in the process of using digital video technology.

① Select a Video Camera

Video cameras record in either analog or digital format. **Analog formats** include 8mm, Hi8, VHS-C, and Super VHS-C. **Digital formats** include Mini-DV, MICROMV, Digital8, DVD, Blu-ray, and HDV (high-definition video format). Some digital video cameras record on an internal hard disk. Others may allow you to record directly on an optical disc drive. Digital video cameras fall into three general categories: high-end consumer, consumer, and webcasting and monitoring (Figure 2). Consumer digital video cameras are by far the most popular type among

consumers. High-end consumer models may support the Blu-ray or HDV standards. A video recorded in high-definitio can be played back on a high-definition display. Many mobile devices allow you to record video that you later can transmit to your computer or e-mail from the device. Some devices allow you to upload video directly to video sharing Web sites Digital video cameras provide more features than analog video cameras, such as a higher level of zoom, better sound, c greater control over color and lighting.

② Record a Video

Most video cameras provide you with a choice of recording programs, which sometimes are called automatic settings. Each recording program includes a different combination of camera settings, so that you can adjust the exposure and other functions to match the recording environment. Usually, several different programs are available, such as point and-shoot, point-and-shoot with manual adjustment, sports, portrait, spotlit scenes, and low light. You also have the ability to select special digital effects, such as fade, wipe, and black an white. If you are shooting outside on a windy day, then you can enable the windscreen to prevent wind noise. If you are shooting home videos or video meant for a Web site, then the point-and-shoot recording program is sufficient.

③ Transfer and Manage Videos

After recording the video, the next step is to transfer the video to your personal computer or to the Internet. Mos video cameras connect directly to a USB or FireWire port on a personal computer (Figure 3). Transferring video with

high-end consumer

consumer

webcasting and monitoring

Figure 2 The high-end consumer digital video camera can produce professional-grade results. The consumer digital video camera produces amateur-grade results. The webcasting and monitoring digital video camera is appropriate for webcasting and security monitoring.

personal computer

USB or FireWire

digital video camera

DVD/Blu-ray Disc recorder

Figure 3 A digital video camera is connected to the personal computer or DVD/Blu-ray Disc recorder via a USB or FireWire por No additional hardware is needed.

digital camera or mobile device is easy, because the video already is in a digital format that the computer can recognize. Many mobile devices include a special cable used to connect the device to a personal computer or allow you to transfer the videos to a media sharing Web site or your own Web site.

Some people own analog format video tapes that require additional hardware to convert the analog signals to a digital format before the video can be manipulated on a personal computer. The additional hardware includes a special video capture card using a standard RCA video cable or an S-video cable (Figure 4). **S-video** cables provide sharper images and greater overall quality. A personal computer also can record video to an optical disc, or it can be connected to an external DVD/Blu-ray Disc recorder to record videos. Video conversion services often specialize in converting older analog video to a variety of digital formats.

When transferring video, plan to use approximately 15 to 30 GB of hard disk storage per hour of digital video. High-definition formats may require much more storage per hour. A typical video project requires about four times the amount of raw footage as the final product. At the high end, therefore, a video that lasts an hour may require up to 120 GB of storage for the raw footage, editing process, and final video. This storage requirement can vary depending on the software you use to copy the video from the video camera to the hard disk and the format you select to save the video. For example, Microsoft's Windows Live Movie Maker can save 15 hours of standard video in 10 GB when creating video for playback on a computer, but saves only 1 hour of video in 10 GB when creating video for playback on a DVD. A high-definition video file may require more than 40 GB per hour.

The video transfer requires application software on the personal computer (Figure 5). The Windows Live Movie Maker software, available as a free download from Microsoft's Web site, allows you to transfer the video from

Figure 5 Some video editing software allows you to transfer a video from any video source to a hard disk.

a video camera. Depending on the length of video and the type of connection used, the video may take a long time to transfer. Make certain that no other programs are running on your personal computer while transferring the video.

The frame rate of a video refers to the number of frames per second (fps) that are captured in the video. The most widely used frame rate is 30 fps. A smaller frame rate results in a smaller file size for the video, but playback of the video will not be as smooth as one recorded with a higher frame rate.

When transferring video, the software may allow you to choose a file format and a codec to store the video. A video **file format** holds the video information in a manner specified by a vendor, such as Apple or Microsoft. Six of the more popular file formats are listed in Figure 6. The 3GP format is widely used on mobile devices.

File formats support codecs to encode the audio and video into the file formats. A **codec** specifies how the audio and video is compressed and stored within the file. A particular file format may be able to store audio and video in a number of

Figure 4 An analog camcorder or VCR is connected to the personal computer via an S-video port on a video capture card.

Popular Video File Formats

File Format	File Extensions
Apple QuickTime	.MOV or .QT
DivX	.DIVX
Microsoft Windows Media Video	.WMV or .ASF
MPEG-4 Part 4	.MP4
Real RealMedia	.RM or .RAM
3GP	.3GP or .3G2

Figure 6 Apple, DivX, Microsoft, and Real offer the more popular video file formats.

different codecs. Figure 7 shows some options available for specifying a file format and video quality settings in a video capture program. The file format and codec you choose often is based on what you plan to do with the movie. For example, if you plan to upload your video to the YouTube video sharing Web site, the best choices are DivX and MPEG-4 file formats. Many users find that they are unable to play their own or others' videos, and the problem often is that the proper codec is not installed on the user's personal computer. Video conversion software often allows the user to convert a video in a less popular format to a better supported format. Many of these programs are available as freeware.

After transferring the video to a personal computer or the Internet, and before manipulating the video, you should store the video files in appropriate folders, named correctly, and backed up. Most video transfer application software helps manage these tasks.

4 Edit a Video

Once the video is stored on your hard disk or the Internet, the next step is to edit, or manipulate, the video. If you used a video capture card to transfer analog video to the computer (Figure 4 on the previous page), the files

may require extra initial processing. Some Web sites allow you to perform minor editing and other tasks on the Web site. When you use a video capture card, some of the video frames may be lost in the transfer process. Some video editing programs allow you to fix this problem with **frame rate correction** tools.

The first step in the editing process is to split the video into smaller pieces, or scenes, that you can manipulate more easily. This process is called splitting. Most video software automatically splits the video into scenes, thus sparing you the task. After splitting, you should delete unwanted scenes or portions of scenes. This process is called pruning.

After creating the scenes you want to use in the final production, you edit each individual scene. You can crop, or change the size of, scenes. That is, you may want to delete the top or a side of a scene that is irrelevant. You also can resize the scene. For example, you may be creating a video that will be displayed on a media sharing Web site. Making smaller video, such as 320 × 200 pixels, instead of 640 × 480 pixels, results in a smaller file that transmits faster over the Internet. Some media sharing Web sites recommend smaller video resolutions, such as 320 × 200 pixels, and some will perform the conversion for you automatically.

Figure 7 Video editing software allows you to specify a combination of file format and video quality settings when saving a video

If a video has been recorded over a long period, using different cameras or under different lighting conditions, the video may need color correction. Color correction tools analyze your video and match brightness, colors, and other attributes of video clips to ensure a smooth look to the video (Figure 8).

You can add logos, special effects, or titles to scenes. You can place a company logo or personal logo in a video to identify yourself or the company producing the video. Logos often are added on the lower-right corner of a video and remain for the duration of the video. Special effects include warping, changing from color to black and white, morphing, or zoom motion. Morphing is a special effect in which one video image is transformed into another image over the course of several frames of video, creating the illusion of metamorphosis. You usually add titles at the beginning and ending of a video to give the video context. A training video may have titles throughout the video to label a particular scene, or each scene may begin with a title.

The next step in editing a video is to add audio effects, including voice-over narration and background music. Many video editing programs allow you to add additional tracks, or layers, of sound to a video in addition to the sound that was recorded on the video camera or mobile device. You also can add special audio effects.

The final step in editing a video is to combine the scenes into a complete video (Figure 9). This process involves ordering scenes and adding transition effects between scenes. Video editing software allows you to combine scenes and separate each scene with a transition. Transitions include fading, wiping, blurry, bursts, ruptures, erosions, and more.

Figure 8 Color correction tools in video editing software allow a great deal of control over the mood of your video creation.

Figure 9 Scenes are combined into a sequence on the bottom of the screen.

5 Distribute the Video

After editing the video, the final step is to distribute it or save it on an appropriate medium. You can save video in a variety of formats. Video recorded on a mobile device often requires conversion to a more widely accepted format.

Video also can be stored in digital formats in any of several optical disc formats or on a media sharing Web site. **Optical disc creation software**, which often is packaged with video editing software, allows you to create, or master, optical discs. You can add interactivity to your optical disc creations. For example, you can allow viewers to jump to certain scenes using a menu.

You also can save your video creation in electronic format for distribution over the Web, via e-mail, or to a mobile device. Some cameras include a button that allows users to upload directly to a media sharing Web site. Popular media sharing Web sites, such as YouTube (Figure 10), have recommendations for the best file format and codecs to use for video that you upload to them (Figure 11). Your video editing software must support the file format and codec you want to use. For example, Apple's iMovie software typically saves files in the QuickTime file format.

Professionals use hardware and software that allow them to create a film version of digital video that can be played in movie theaters. This technology is becoming increasingly popular. The cost of professional video editing software ranges from thousands to hundreds of thousands of dollars. Video editing software for the home user is available for a few hundred dollars or less. Some Hollywood directors believe that eventually all movies will be recorded and edited digitally.

After creating your final video for distribution or for your personal video collection, you should back up the final video file. You can save your scenes for inclusion in other video creations or create new masters using different effects, transitions, and ordering of scenes.

Figure 10 Media sharing Web sites allow you to share your videos with acquaintances or the entire world.

Figure 11 Media sharing Web sites, such as YouTube, provide tools that simplify the process of uploading videos to the site.

Storage

After completing this chapter, you will be able to:

1 Describe the characteristics of an internal hard disk including capacity, platters, read/write heads, cylinders, sectors and tracks, and revolutions per minute

2 Discuss the purpose of network attached storage devices, external and removable hard disks, and hard disk controllers

3 Describe the various types of flash memory storage: solid state drives, memory cards, USB flash drives, and ExpressCard modules

4 Describe cloud storage and explain its advantages

5 Describe the characteristics of optical discs

6 Differentiate among various types of optical discs: CDs, archive discs and Picture CDs, DVDs, and Blu-ray Discs

7 Identify the uses of tape, magnetic stripe cards, smart cards, microfilm and microfiche, and enterprise storage

Storage

Storage holds data, instructions, and information for future use. For example, all types of users store digital photos; appointments, schedules, and contact/address information; correspondence, such as letters, e-mail messages; tax records; and Web pages. A home user also might store budgets, bank statements, a household inventory, records of stock purchases, tax information, homework assignments, recipes, music, and videos. In addition or instead, a business user stores reports, financial records, travel records, customer orders and invoices, vendor payments, payroll records, inventory records, presentations, quotations, and contracts. Other users store diagrams, drawings, blueprints,

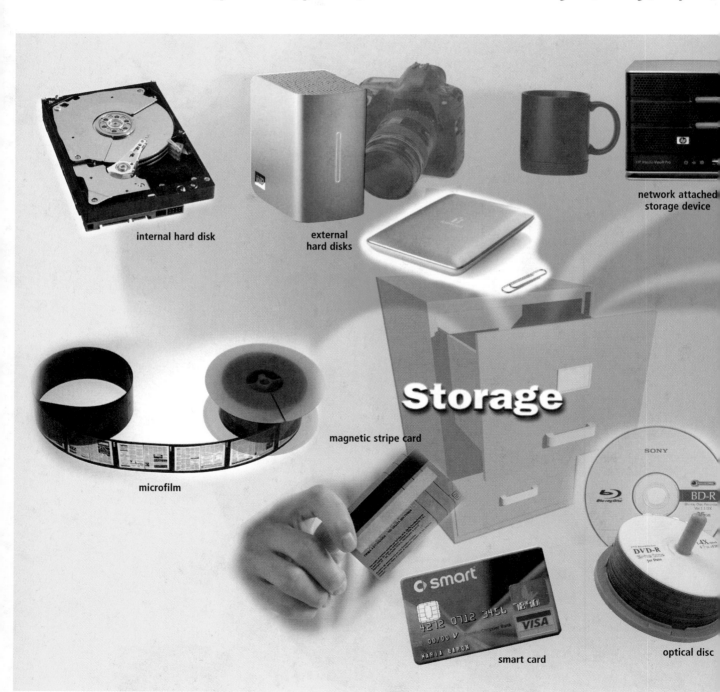

internal hard disk

external
hard disks

network attached
storage device

microfilm

magnetic stripe card

smart card

optical disc

Figure 6-1 A variety of storage options.

designs, marketing literature, corporate newsletters, and product catalogs. All computers also store system and application software.

Storage requirements among users vary greatly. Home users typically have much smaller storage requirements than enterprise users. For example, a home user may need 320 GB (billion bytes) of storage, while enterprises may require 50 PB (quadrillion bytes) of storage.

A **storage medium** (media is the plural), also called **secondary storage**, is the physical material on which a computer keeps data, instructions, and information. Examples of storage media are hard disks, solid state drives, memory cards, USB flash drives, ExpressCard modules, optical discs, smart cards, magnetic stripe cards, and microfilm. Cloud storage is another storage option, in which the actual storage media used is transparent to the user. Figure 6-1 shows a variety of storage options.

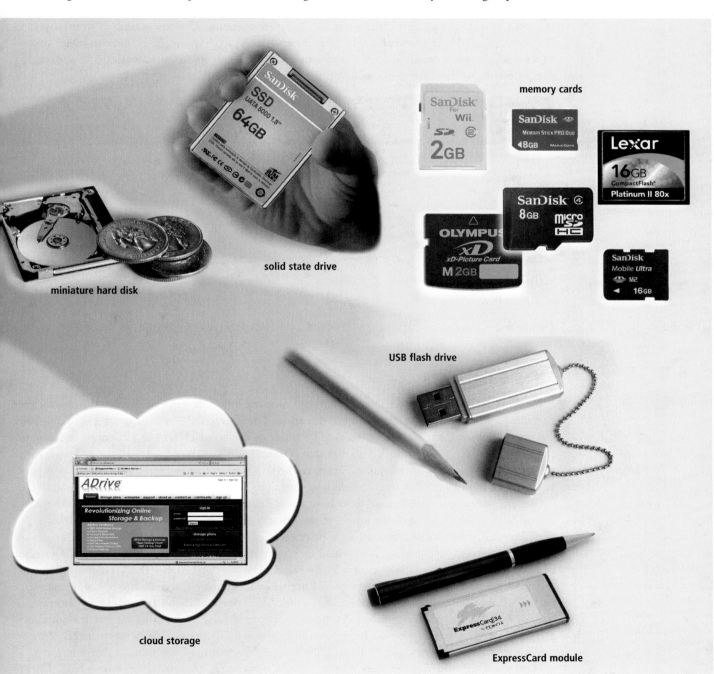

miniature hard disk

solid state drive

memory cards

USB flash drive

cloud storage

ExpressCard module

Capacity is the number of bytes (characters) a storage medium can hold. Figure 6-2 identifies the terms manufacturers use to define the capacity of storage media. For example, a reasonably priced USB flash drive can store up to 4 GB of data (approximately four billion bytes) and a typical hard disk has 320 GB (approximately 320 billion bytes) of storage capacity.

A **storage device** is the computer hardware that records and/or retrieves items to and from storage media. **Writing** is the process of transferring data, instructions, and information from memory to a storage medium. **Reading** is the process of transferring these items from a storage medium into memory. When storage devices write data on storage media, they are creating output. Similarly, when storage devices read from storage media, they function as a source of input. Nevertheless, they are categorized as storage devices, not as input or output devices.

The speed of storage devices is defined by access time. **Access time** measures the amount of time it takes a storage device to locate an item on a storage medium. The access time of storage devices is slow, compared with the access time of memory. Memory (chips) accesses items in billionths of a second (nanoseconds). Storage devices, by contrast, access items in thousandths of a second (milliseconds) or millionths of a second (microseconds).

Storage Terms

Storage Term	Approximate Number of Bytes	Exact Number of Bytes
Kilobyte (KB)	1 thousand	2^{10} or 1,024
Megabyte (MB)	1 million	2^{20} or 1,048,576
Gigabyte (GB)	1 billion	2^{30} or 1,073,741,824
Terabyte (TB)	1 trillion	2^{40} or 1,099,511,627,776
Petabyte (PB)	1 quadrillion	2^{50} or 1,125,899,906,842,624
Exabyte (EB)	1 quintillion	2^{60} or 1,152,921,504,606,846,976
Zettabyte (ZB)	1 sextillion	2^{70} or 1,180,591,620,717,411,303,424
Yottabyte (YB)	1 septillion	2^{80} or 1,208,925,819,614,629,174,706,176

Figure 6-2 The capacity of a storage medium is measured by the number of bytes it can hold.

Hard Disks

A **hard disk** is a storage device that contains one or more inflexible, circular platters that use magnetic particles to store data, instructions, and information. The system unit on most desktop and notebook computers contains at least one hard disk. The entire device is enclosed in an airtight, sealed case to protect it from contamination. A hard disk that is mounted inside the system unit sometimes is called a fixed disk because it is not portable (Figure 6-3). With respect to a storage medium, the term portable means you can remove the medium from one computer and carry it to another computer.

Current personal computer hard disks have storage capacities from 160 GB to 2 TB and more. Home users store documents, spreadsheets, presentations, databases, e-mail messages, Web pages, digital photos, music, videos, and software on hard disks. Businesses use hard disks to store correspondence, reports, financial records, e-mail messages, customer orders and invoices, payroll records, inventory records, presentations, contracts, marketing literature, schedules, and Web sites.

Traditionally, hard disks stored data using **longitudinal recording**, which aligned the magnetic particles horizontally around the surface of the disk. With **perpendicular recording**, by contrast, hard disks align the magnetic particles vertically, or perpendicular to the disk's surface, making much greater storage capacities possible. Experts estimate that hard disks using perpendicular recording provide storage capacities about 10 times greater than disks that use longitudinal recording.

Hard disks are read/write storage media. That is, you can read from and write on a hard disk any number of times. Read Ethics & Issues 6-1 for a related discussion.

Perpendicular Recording

 For more information, visit the Computer Concepts CourseMate Web site at www.cengagebrain.com, navigate to the Chapter 6 Web Link resource for this book, and then click Perpendicular Recording.

hard disk
mounted inside
system unit

close-up of
hard disk

Figure 6-3 The hard disk in a desktop
computer is enclosed inside an airtight,
sealed case inside the system unit. (In this
and other hard disk photos in the book,
the top plate is removed from the hard
disk for illustration purposes.)

? FAQ 6-1

To what degree are hard disk capacities increasing?

Hard disk capacities have increased at an exponential
rate. Advancements in technology, such as perpendic-
ular recording and enhanced read/write heads that
can read and write denser areas on the platter, have
resulted in a hard disk's capability of storing increas-
ing amounts of data and information in a fixed
amount of space. The chart to the right illustrates
that the maximum hard disk size is growing.

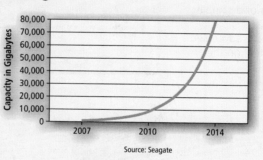

Source: Seagate

For more information, visit the Computer Concepts
CourseMate Web site at www.cengagebrain.com,
navigate to the Chapter 6 FAQ resource for this
book, and then click Hard Disk Capacity.

Ethics & Issues

For the complete text of
the Ethics & Issues boxes
found in this chapter, visit
the Computer Concepts
CourseMate Web site at
www.cengagebrain.com
and then navigate to the
Chapter 6 Ethics & Issues
resource for this book.

⅄ ETHICS & ISSUES 6-1

Should the Government Require Hard Disks to Be Cleaned?

An IT professional recently purchased a
hard disk on an auction Web site only to
find private banking records of several
million people. Fortunately, the purchaser
notified authorities, rather than use the
data for nefarious purposes. In other
incidents, taxpayer data and secret police
tactics appeared on hard disks purchased
on auction Web sites, donated to charitable
organizations, or recovered from discarded
computers. Most people do not realize that
deleting files from a computer does not
render the data permanently inaccessible.
Deleted files can be recovered easily by a
smart criminal or digital forensics examiner.
 Experts recommend that special util-
ity software, known as a wiping utility,

be used to clean the contents of a hard
disk before it leaves possession of the
owner. The government sets various disk
wiping standards. For example, one stan-
dard requires that the software wipe the
drive seven times, while a more stringent
standard requires fourteen. Experts also
recommend the use of full disk encryp-
tion, which is the process of encoding data
and information into an unreadable form.
Others recommend that any hard disk that
at any time contained sensitive information
be destroyed by a service company that
specializes in hard disk destruction. Some
companies now offer a service that allows
you to keep a hard disk if it fails while
covered by a warranty. Typically, companies

require that you return the damaged hard
disk when you receive the replacement.
Some people are not comfortable with this
service, for fear of confidential information
on the damaged hard disk falling into the
wrong hands.

Should the government require that hard
disks on sold, donated, or discarded com-
puters be cleaned, encrypted, or destroyed?
Why or why not? Would you make an extra
effort to clean or encrypt the contents of
hard disks on sold, donated, or discarded
computers? Why or why not?

Characteristics of a Hard Disk

Characteristics of a hard disk include capacity, platters, read/write heads, cylinders, sectors and tracks, revolutions per minute, transfer rate, and access time. Figure 6-4 shows sample characteristics of a 1 TB hard disk. The following paragraphs discuss each of these characteristics.

1 TB disk can store any of the following:
- 500,000,000 pages of text
- 285,000 digital photos
- 250,000 songs
- 120 hours of digital video

Sample Hard Disk Characteristics

Advertised capacity	1 TB
Platters	4
Read/write heads	8
Cylinders	16,383
Bytes per sector	512
Sectors per track	63
Sectors per drive	1,953,525,168
Revolutions per minute	7,200
Transfer rate	300 MBps
Access time	8.5 ms

Local Disk (C:) Properties

Security | Previous Versions | Quota
General | Tools | Hardware | Sharing

My Book

Type: Local Disk
File system: NTFS

Used space:	700,344,934,400 bytes	652 GB
Free space:	299,857,305,600 bytes	279 GB
Capacity:	1,000,202,240,000 bytes	931 GB

actual disk capacity

Drive C:

Disk Cleanup

☐ Compress this drive to save disk space
☑ Allow files on this drive to have contents indexed in addition to file properties

OK Cancel Apply

Figure 6-4 Characteristics of a sample 1 TB hard disk. The actual disk's capacity sometimes is different from the advertised capacity because of bad sectors on the disk.

The capacity of a hard disk is determined from whether it uses longitudinal or perpendicular recording, the number of platters it contains, and the composition of the magnetic coating on the platters. A platter is made of aluminum, glass, or ceramic and is coated with an alloy material that allows items to be recorded magnetically on its surface. The coating usually is three millionths of an inch thick.

Magnetic disks store data and instructions in tracks and sectors (Figure 6-5). A track is a narrow recording band that forms a full circle on the surface of the disk. The disk's storage locations consist of pie-shaped sections, which break the tracks into small arcs called sectors. On a hard disk, a sector typically stores up to 512 bytes of data.

On desktop computers, platters most often have a size of approximately 3.5 inches in diameter. On notebook computers, mobile devices, and some servers, the diameter is 2.5 inches or less. A typical hard disk has multiple platters stacked on top of one another. Each platter has two read/write heads, one for each side. The hard disk has arms that move the read/write heads to the proper location on the platter (Figure 6-6).

The location of the read/write heads often is referred to by its cylinder. A cylinder is the vertical section of a track that passes through all platters (Figure 6-7). A single movement of the read/write head arms accesses all the platters in a cylinder. If a hard disk has two platters (four sides), each with 1,000 tracks, then it will have 1,000 cylinders with each cylinder consisting of 4 tracks (2 tracks for each platter).

sectors

track

cluster

Figure 6-5 Tracks form circles on the surface of a hard disk. The disk's storage locations are divided into pie-shaped sections, which break the tracks into small arcs called sectors.

While the computer is running, the platters in the hard disk rotate at a high rate of speed. This spinning, which usually is 5,400 to 15,000 revolutions per minute (rpm), allows nearly instant access to all tracks and sectors on the platters. The platters may continue to spin until power is removed from the computer, or more commonly today, they stop spinning or slow down after a specified time to save power. The spinning motion creates a cushion of air between the platter and its read/write head. This cushion ensures that the read/write head floats above the platter instead of making direct contact with the platter surface. The distance between the read/write head and the platter is about two millionths of one inch.

How a Hard Disk Works

Step 2
A small motor spins the platters while the computer is running.

Step 3 When software requests a disk access, the read/write heads determine the current or new location of the data.

Step 1
The circuit board controls the movement of the head actuator and a small motor.

Step 4
The head actuator positions the read/write head arms over the correct location on the platters to read or write data.

Figure 6-6 This figure shows how a hard disk works.

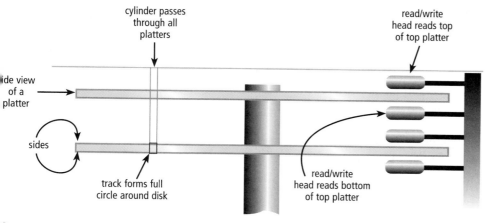

cylinder passes through all platters

read/write head reads top of top platter

side view of a platter

sides

track forms full circle around disk

read/write head reads bottom of top platter

Figure 6-7 A cylinder is the vertical section of track through all platters on a hard disk.

As shown in Figure 6-8, this close clearance leaves no room for any type of contamination. Dirt, hair, dust, smoke, and other particles could cause the hard disk to have a head crash. A head crash occurs when a read/write head touches the surface of a platter, usually resulting in a loss of data or sometimes loss of the entire disk. Thus, it is crucial that you back up your hard disk regularly. A **backup** is a duplicate of a file, program, or disk placed on a separate storage medium that you can use in case the original is lost, damaged, or destroyed. Chapter 7 discusses backup techniques. Access time for today's hard disk ranges from approximately 3 to 12 ms (milliseconds).

Figure 6-8 The clearance between a disk read/write head and the platter is about two millionths of an inch. A smoke particle, dust particle, human hair, or other contaminant could render the disk unusable.

RAID

Some personal computer manufacturers provide a hard disk configuration that connects multiple smaller disks into a single unit that acts like a single large hard disk. A group of two or more integrated hard disks is called a **RAID** (redundant array of independent disks). RAID is an ideal storage solution for users who must have the data available when they attempt to access it.

Network Attached Storage

For more information, visit the Computer Concepts CourseMate Web site at www.cengagebrain.com, navigate to the Chapter 6 Web Link resource for this book, and then click Network Attached Storage.

NAS

A **network attached storage** (NAS) device is a server connected to a network with the sole purpose of providing storage (shown in Figure 6-1 on page 238). Any user or device connected to the network can access files on the NAS device. These devices often use a RAID configuration. In the past, enterprises were the primary users of NAS. With the introduction of smaller, less expensive NAS devices, however, some home and small business users opt to add up to 6 TB or more of hard disk storage space to their network with a NAS device.

External and Removable Hard Disks

An **external hard disk**, shown in the left picture in Figure 6-9, is a separate freestanding hard disk that connects with a cable to a USB port or FireWire port on the system unit or communicates wirelessly. As with the internal hard disk, the entire hard disk is enclosed in an airtight, sealed case. External hard disks have storage capacities of up to 4 TB and more. Some external hard disk units include multiple hard disks that you can use for different purposes, if desired.

A **removable hard disk** is a hard disk that you insert and remove from a drive. A removable hard disk drive, shown in the right picture in Figure 6-9, reads from and writes on the removable hard disk. Removable hard disks have storage capacities up to 1 TB or more.

External and removable hard disks offer the following advantages over internal hard disks (fixed disks):

- Transport a large number of files
- Back up important files or an entire internal hard disk (several external hard disk models allow you to back up simply by pushing a button on the disk)
- Easily store large audio and video files
- Secure your data; for example, at the end of a work session, remove the hard disk and lock it up, leaving no data in the computer
- Add storage space to a notebook computer, including netbooks and Tablet PCs
- Add storage space to a desktop computer without having to open the system unit or connect to a network

gure 6-9 Examples of external and removable hard disks.

iniature Hard Disks

Both internal and external hard disks are available in miniature sizes. These tiny hard disks ve form factors of 1.8 inch, 1 inch, and 0.85 inch. Devices such as portable media players, gital cameras, and smart phones often have internal miniature hard disks, which provide greater orage capacities than flash memory (Figure 6-10). External hard disks that are smaller in size and pacity, which also contain miniature hard disks, are sometimes called a **pocket hard drive** because ey enable mobile users easily to transport photos and other files from one computer to another igure 6-11). Miniature hard disks have storage capacities that range from 4 GB to 250 GB.

gure 6-10 This miniature hard disk is used in portable edia players and other small devices, enabling users to ore music, videos, movies, and any other type of files the disk.

Figure 6-11 Users easily can transport data from one computer to another with a pocket hard drive.

Hard Disk Controllers

A **disk controller** consists of a special-purpose chip and electronic circuits that control the transfer of data, instructions, and information from a disk to and from the system bus and other components in the computer. That is, it controls the interface between the hard disk and the system bus. A disk controller for a hard disk, called the hard disk controller, may be part of a hard disk or the motherboard, or it may be a separate adapter card inside the system unit.

In their personal computer advertisements, vendors usually state the type of hard disk interface supported by the hard disk controller. Thus, you should understand the types of available hard disk interfaces. In addition to USB and FireWire, which can function as external hard disk interfaces, four other types of hard disk interfaces for use in personal computers are SATA, EIDE, SCSI, and SAS.

- SATA (Serial Advanced Technology Attachment) uses serial signals to transfer data, instructions, and information. The primary advantage of SATA interfaces is their cables are thinner, longer, more flexible, and less susceptible to interference than cables used by hard disks that use parallel signals. SATA interfaces also support connections to optical disc drives. External disks use the eSATA (external SATA) interface, which is much faster than USB and FireWire.
- EIDE (Enhanced Integrated Drive Electronics) is a hard disk interface that uses parallel signals to transfer data, instructions, and information. EIDE interfaces can support up to four hard disks at 137 GB per disk. EIDE interfaces also provide connections for optical disc drives and tape drives.
- SCSI interfaces, which also use parallel signals, can support up to eight or fifteen peripheral devices. Supported devices include hard disks, optical disc drives, tape drives, printers, scanners, network cards, and much more. Some computers have a built-in SCSI interface, while others use an adapter card to add a SCSI interface.
- SAS (serial-attached SCSI) is a newer type of SCSI that uses serial signals to transfer data, instructions, and information. Advantages of SAS over parallel SCSI include thinner, longer cables; reduced interference; less expensive; support for many more connected devices at once; and faster speeds. In addition to hard disks, SAS interfaces support connections to optical disc drives, printers, scanners, digital cameras, and other devices. Experts predict that SAS eventually will replace parallel SCSI.

Maintaining Data Stored on a Hard Disk

Most manufacturers guarantee their hard disks to last approximately three to five years. Many last much longer with proper care. To prevent the loss of items stored on a hard disk, you regularly should perform preventive maintenance such as defragmenting or scanning the disk for errors. To learn more about how to maintain a hard disk, complete the Learn How To 1 activity on pages 266 and 267. Chapter 7 discusses these and other utilities in depth.

eSATA

For more information, visit the Computer Concepts CourseMate Web site at www.cengagebrain.com, navigate to the Chapter 6 Web Link resource for this book, and then click eSATA.

✔ QUIZ YOURSELF 6-1

Instructions: Find the true statement below. Then, rewrite the remaining false statements so that they are true.

1. Hard disks contain one or more inflexible, circular platters that magnetically store data, instructions, and information.
2. SATA is a hard disk interface that uses parallel signals to transfer data, instructions, and information.
3. Storage media is the computer hardware that records and/or retrieves items to and from a storage device.
4. Users can move an internal hard disk from computer to computer as needed by connecting the disk to a USB port or FireWire port on the system unit.

Quiz Yourself Online: To further check your knowledge of pages 238 through 246, visit the Computer Concepts CourseMate Web site at www.cengagebrain.com, navigate to the Chapter 6 Quiz Yourself resource for this book, and then click Objectives 1 – 2.

Flash Memory Storage

As discussed in Chapter 4, flash memory is a type of nonvolatile memory that can be erased electronically and rewritten. Flash memory chips are a type of **solid state media**, which means they consist entirely of electronic components, such as integrated circuits, and contain no moving parts. The lack of moving parts makes flash memory storage more durable and shock resistant than other types of media such as magnetic hard disks or optical discs.

Types of flash memory storage include solid state drives, memory cards, USB flash drives, and ExpressCard modules.

Solid State Drives

A **solid state drive** (**SSD**) is a storage device that typically uses flash memory to store data, instructions, and information (Figure 6-12). With available sizes of 3.5 inches, 2.5 inches, and 1.8 inches, SSDs are used in all types of computers including servers, desktop computers, and mobile computers and devices such as portable media players and digital video cameras. Storage capacities of current SSDs range from 16 GB to 256 GB and more.

SSDs have several advantages over magnetic hard disks.

- Access times of SSDs are about 0.1 ms, which is more than 80 times faster than a hard disk.
- Transfer rates of SSDs are faster than comparable hard disks.
- SSDs generate less heat and consume less power than hard disks.
- Manufacturers claim that SSDs will last more than 50 years, which is much greater than the 3 to 5 year hard disk stated lifespan.

The disadvantages of SSDs are they currently have a higher failure rate than hard disks, and their cost is much higher per gigabyte. As the price of SSDs drops, experts estimate that increasingly more users will purchase computers and devices that use this media.

Solid State Drives

For more information, visit the Computer Concepts CourseMate Web site at www.cengagebrain.com, navigate to the Chapter 6 Web Link resource for this book, and then click Solid State Drives.

Figure 6-12 As the price of SSDs drops, experts estimate that increasingly more users will purchase computers and devices that use this media.

Memory Cards

Memory cards enable mobile users easily to transport digital photos, music, or files to and from mobile devices and computers or other devices. As mentioned in Chapter 4, a **memory card** is a removable flash memory device, usually no bigger than 1.5 inches in height or width, that you insert and remove from a slot in a computer, mobile device, or card reader/writer (Figure 6-13).

Common types of memory cards include **CompactFlash (CF)**, **Secure Digital (SD)**, **Secure Digital High Capacity (SDHC)**, **microSD**, **microSDHC**, **xD Picture Card**, **Memory Stick**, and **Memory Stick Micro (M2)**. The table in Figure 6-14 compares storage capacities and uses of

Figure 6-13 Many types of computers and devices have slots for memory cards.

hese flash memory storage media. Depending on the device, manufacturers claim memory cards an last from 10 to 100 years.

To view, edit, or print images and information stored on memory cards, you transfer the contents o your desktop computer or other device. Some printers have slots to read flash memory cards. f your computer or printer does not have a built-in slot, you can purchase a **card reader/writer**, vhich is a device that reads and writes data, instructions, and information stored on memory cards. Card reader/writers usually connect to the USB port or FireWire port on the system unit. The type f card you have will determine the type of card reader/writer needed.

SDHC Cards

For more information, visit the Computer Concepts CourseMate Web site at www.cengagebrain.com, navigate to the Chapter 6 Web Link resource for this book, and then click SDHC Cards.

Various Memory Cards

Media Type		Storage Capacity	Use
CompactFlash (CF)		512 MB to 100 GB	Digital cameras, smart phones, PDAs, photo printers, portable media players, notebook computers, desktop computers
Secure Digital (SD)		512 MB to 8 GB	Digital cameras, digital video cameras, smart phones, PDAs, photo printers, portable media players
SDHC		4 to 32 GB	Digital cameras
microSD		1 to 2 GB	Smart phones, portable media players, handheld game consoles, handheld navigation devices
microSDHC		4 to 16 GB	Smart phones, portable media players, handheld game consoles, handheld navigation devices
xD Picture Card		256 MB to 2 GB	Digital cameras, photo printers
Memory Stick PRO Duo		1 to 16 GB	Digital cameras, smart phones, handheld game consoles
Memory Stick Micro (M2)		1 to 16 GB	Smart phones

Figure 6-14 A variety of memory cards.

USB Flash Drives

A **USB flash drive**, sometimes called a thumb drive, is a flash memory storage device that plugs in a USB port on a computer or mobile device (Figure 6-15). USB flash drives are convenient for mobile users because they are small and lightweight enough to be transported on a keychain or in a pocket. Current USB flash drives have storage capacities ranging from 512 MB to 64 GB, with the latter being extremely expensive.

Figure 6-15 A close-up of the flash memory and circuitry inside a USB flash drive.

? | **FAQ 6-2**

Can airport security screening equipment damage or erase the data on my mobile media or hard disk?

The Transportation Security Administration's Web site states that their screening (X-ray) equipment will not damage or erase the data stored on flash memory mobile media, optical discs, or hard disks. Although your media is equally safe whether you carry it onto the airplane or leave it in checked baggage, packing it with your carry-on items is a better safeguard against physical damage. If you are uneasy about your media passing through the airport screening equipment, you may be able to request that the items be manually (hand) searched. It is important to note that the equipment used to screen checked baggage will not harm electronic media, but it may damage undeveloped film. As a safeguard, you should carry all film onto the airplane and request a manual search.

💻 For more information, visit the Computer Concepts CourseMate Web site at www.cengagebrain.com, navigate to the Chapter 6 FAQ resource for this book, and then click Airport Screening Equipment.

ExpressCard Modules

An **ExpressCard module** is a removable device, about 75 mm long and 34 mm wide or L-shaped with a width of 54 mm, that fits in an ExpressCard slot (Figure 6-16). ExpressCard modules can be used to add memory, storage, communications, multimedia, and security capabilities to a computer. ExpressCard modules commonly are used in notebook computers.

two sizes of ExpressCard modules

Figure 6-16 ExpressCard modules are available in two sizes.

Cloud Storage

Some users choose cloud storage instead of storing data locally on a hard disk or other media. **Cloud storage** is an Internet service that provides hard disk storage to computer users (Figure 6-17).

Types of services offered by cloud storage providers vary. Figure 6-18 identifies a variety of cloud storage providers. Read Innovative Computing 6-1 to find out about another type of cloud storage.

Fee arrangements vary. For example, one cloud storage service provides 25 GB of storage free to registered users; another charges $5 per month for 150 GB of storage. For enterprises, cloud storage services typically charge for storage on a per gigabyte basis, such as 5 cents per gigabyte.

INNOVATIVE COMPUTING 6-1

Digital Books Are a Good Read

It is time to dust off your library card, because thousands of libraries are stocking their digital shelves with electronic books that you can download from anywhere you have computer access. Just locate a participating library's Web site, download the desired book files to your personal computer, and then transfer the files to your portable media player or smart phone. For patrons who do not want to download files, some libraries are lending a Playaway, which is a small device that stores 80 hours of digitized audio books.

Another set of books is available for reading at the British Library's Online Gallery. Software called Turning the Pages allows readers to browse some of the rarest books in the world and magnify details on the pages. The books include the *Gutenberg Bible*, Lewis Carroll's original *Alice in Wonderland*, and *The Diamond Sutra*, the oldest book in existence, printed in China in 868 A.D.

For more information, visit the Computer Concepts CourseMate Web site at www.cengagebrain.com, navigate to the Chapter 6 Innovative Computing resource for this book, and then click Online Libraries.

Figure 6-17 An example of one Web site that provides cloud storage.

Cloud Storage Providers

Web Site Names	Type of Storage Provided	Other Services
Box.net, IDrive, Windows Live SkyDrive	Backup or additional storage for any type of file	
Flickr, Picasa	Digital photos	Photo editing and photo management
YouTube	Digital videos	
Facebook, MySpace	Digital photos, digital videos, messages, and personal information	Social networking
Google Docs, Office Web Apps	Documents, spreadsheets, presentations	Productivity suite
Gmail, Windows Live Hotmail, Yahoo! Mail	E-mail messages	
Amazon EC2, Amazon S3, Nirvanix	Enterprise-level storage	Web services, data center services

Figure 6-18 Some of the more widely used cloud storage providers.

Cloud Storage

For more information, visit the Computer Concepts CourseMate Web site at www.cengagebrain.com, navigate to the Chapter 6 Web Link resource for this book, and then click Cloud Storage.

Users subscribe to a cloud storage service for a variety of reasons:
- To access files on the Internet from any computer or device that has Internet access
- To allow others to access their files on the Internet so that others can listen to an audio file, watch a video clip, or view a photo — instead of e-mailing the file to them
- To view time-critical data and images immediately while away from the main office or location; for example, doctors can view X-ray images from another hospital, home, or office
- To store offsite backups of data
- To provide data center functions, relieving enterprises of this task

Read Ethics & Issues 6-2 for a related discussion.

ETHICS & ISSUES 6-2

Is Data Stored in the Cloud Free from Prying Eyes?

At an ever increasing rate, companies and individuals store Web sites and data in the cloud. For example, those who utilize Web-based e-mail store their sent and received e-mail messages in the e-mail provider's cloud environment. Those who use corporate or private e-mail servers do not store their communications in the cloud. Important legal rulings highlight the differences between the two approaches for storing e-mail. Law enforcement agencies consider e-mail stored in the cloud to belong to the company that owns the cloud service, often an Internet access provider. E-mail stored on a private e-mail server, however, is the property of the company or individual who owns the server. When the law enforcement officials need to read someone's e-mail on a private e-mail server, they must obtain a warrant that outlines exactly the information being sought. In the cloud, however, law enforcement officials simply may need to request the information from the company that owns the cloud service. The user might not be notified of the search until up to 90 days later; further, the search may occur without limitations and may include continuous monitoring of an individual's e-mail. While the government takes a liberal approach to viewing one's e-mail in the cloud, individuals who secretly read others' e-mail messages may be subject to felony computer crimes.

Should data kept in the cloud be treated the same way legally as items that are kept in one's home? Why? Should the government be able to access your data in the cloud without your knowledge or permission? Why or why not? What types and amount of personal data are you comfortable storing in the cloud? Why?

QUIZ YOURSELF 6-2

Instructions: Find the true statement below. Then, rewrite the remaining false statements so that they are true.

1. A USB flash drive is a flash memory storage device that plugs in a parallel port on a computer or mobile device.
2. CompactFlash and Memory Sticks are two types of flash memory cards.
3. Cloud storage is a storage device that typically uses flash memory to store data, instructions, and information.
4. An ExpressCard module is a removable RAID device that fits in an ExpressCard slot.

Quiz Yourself Online: To further check your knowledge of pages 247 through 252, visit the Computer Concepts CourseMate Web site at www.cengagebrain.com, navigate to the Chapter 6 Quiz Yourself resource for this book, and then click Objectives 3 – 4.

Optical Discs

An **optical disc** is a type of optical storage media that consists of a flat, round, portable disc made of metal, plastic, and lacquer. These discs usually are 4.75 inche in diameter and less than one-twentieth of an inch thick.

Optical discs primarily store software, data, digital photos, movies, and music. Some optical disc formats are read only, meaning users cannot write (save) on the media. Others are read/write, which allows users to save on the disc just as they save on a hard disk.

Nearly every personal computer today includes some type of optical disc drive installed in a drive bay. On some, you push a button to slide out a tray, insert the disc, and then push the same button to close the tray; others are slot loaded, whic means you insert the disc in a narrow opening on the drive (Figure 6-19).

Figure 6-19 A slot-loaded optical disc drive.

With some discs, you can read and/or write on one side only. Manufacturers usually place silk-screened label on the top layer of these single-sided discs. You insert a single-sided disc the drive with the label side up. Other discs are double-sided. Simply remove the disc from e drive, flip it over, and reinsert it in the drive to use the other side of the disc. Double- led discs often have no label; instead, each side of the disc is identified with small writing ound the center of the disc. Some drives use **LightScribe technology**, which works with ecially coated optical discs, to etch labels directly on the disc (as opposed to placing an hesive label on the disc).

Optical discs store items by using microscopic pits (indentations) d lands (flat areas) that are in the middle layer of the disc. A high-owered laser light creates the pits. A lower-powered laser light ads items from the disc by reflecting light through the bottom the disc. The reflected light is converted into a series of bits the mputer can process.

Manufacturers claim that a properly cared for high-quality optical sc will last 5 years but could last up to 100 years. Figure 6-20 offers me guidelines for the proper care of optical discs.

Many different formats of optical discs exist today. Figure 6-21 entifies a variety of optical disc formats and specifies whether a user n read from the disc, write to the disc, and/or erase the disc. The llowing sections describe characteristics unique to each of these disc rmats.

Optical Disc Formats

Optical Disc	Read	Write	Erase
CD-ROM	Y	N	N
CD-R	Y	Y	N
CD-RW	Y	Y	Y
DVD-ROM BD-ROM	Y	N	N
DVD-R DVD+R BD-R	Y	Y	N
DVD-RW DVD+RW DVD-RAM BD-RE	Y	Y	Y

Figure 6-21 Manufacturers sell CD-ROM, DVD-ROM, and BD-ROM media prerecorded (written) with audio, video, and software. Users cannot change the contents of these discs. Users, however, can purchase the other formats of optical discs as blank media and record (write) their own data, instructions, and information on these discs.

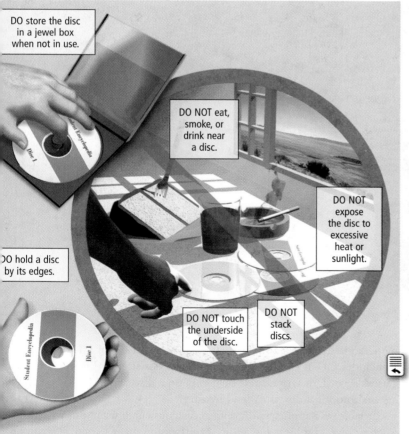

DO store the disc in a jewel box when not in use.

DO NOT eat, smoke, or drink near a disc.

DO NOT expose the disc to excessive heat or sunlight.

DO hold a disc by its edges.

DO NOT touch the underside of the disc.

DO NOT stack discs.

ure 6-20 Some guidelines for the proper care of optical discs.

? **FAQ 6-3**

Can I clean a disc?

Yes, you can remove dust, dirt, smudges, and fingerprints from the surface of an optical disc. Moisten a nonabrasive cloth with warm water or rubbing alcohol (do not use ammonia-based solutions) and then wipe the disc in straight lines from the center outward. You also can repair scratches on the bottom surface with a specialized disc repair kit.

For more information, visit the Computer Concepts CourseMate Web site at www.cengagebrain.com, navigate to the Chapter 6 FAQ resource for this book, and then click Cleaning and Repairing Discs.

CDs

A **CD-ROM**, or compact disc read-only memory, is a type of optical disc that users can read but not write (record) or erase — hence, the name read-only. Manufacturers write the contents of standard CD-ROMs. A standard CD-ROM is called a single-session disc because manufacturers write all items on the disc at one time. Software manufacturers often distribute programs using CD-ROMs (Figure 6-22).

A typical CD-ROM holds from 650 MB to 1 GB of data, instructions, and information. To read a CD-ROM, insert the disc in a **CD-ROM drive** or a CD-ROM player. Because audio CDs and CD-ROMs use the same laser technology, you may be able to use a CD-ROM drive to listen to an audio CD while using the computer.

Figure 6-22 Encyclopedias, games, simulations, and many other programs are distributed on CD-ROM.

CD-Rs and CD-RWs Many personal computers today include either a CD-R or CD-RW drive, or a combination drive that includes CD-R or CD-RW capabilities, as a standard feature. Unlike standard CD-ROM drives, users record, or write, their own data on a disc with a CD-R or CD-RW drive. The process of writing on an optical disc is called **burning**.

A **CD-R** (compact disc-recordable) is a multisession optical disc on which users can write, but not erase, their own items such as text, graphics, and audio. Multisession means you can write on part of the disc at one time and another part at a later time. Each part of a CD-R can be written on only one time, and the disc's contents cannot be erased.

A **CD-RW** (compact disc-rewritable) is an erasable multisession disc you can write on multiple times. To write on a CD-RW disc, you must have CD-RW software and a **CD-RW drive**. A popular use of CD-RW and CD-R discs is to create audio CDs. For example, users can record their own music and save it on a CD, purchase and download songs from the Web, or rearrange tracks on a purchased music CD. The process of copying audio and/or video data from a purchased disc and storing it on digital media is called **ripping**.

Archive Discs and Picture CDs

Many people use archive discs or Picture CDs to preserve their photos. When you post and share photos online on a photo sharing community, you can choose to save your collection of online photos on an **archive disc**, which stores photos in the jpg file format (Figure 6-23). The cost of archive discs is determined by the number of photos being stored. One service, for example, charges $9.99 for the first hundred pictures.

A Kodak **Picture CD** stores digital versions of film using a jpg file format. Many photo centers offer Picture CD service for consumers when they drop off film to be developed. The additional cost for a Picture CD is about $3 per roll of film.

Most optical disc drives can read an archive disc and a Picture CD. You can print copies of the photos from the disc on paper with an ink-jet printer. If you do not have a printer to print the images, many stores have kiosks at which you can print pictures from an archive disc, a Picture CD, or other media.

How an Archive Disc Works

Step 1
Upload your digital photos to a photo sharing community for others to view.

Step 2
Select the photos to be stored on the archive disc and then place your order.

Step 3
Pick up your archive disc at a designated store or receive it in the mail. At home, edit and/or print images from the archive disc on your ink-jet or photo printer, or view the images on a monitor or television screen. At a store, edit and/or print images from the archive disc at a kiosk.

archive disc ➝

Figure 6-23 This figure shows how an archive disc works.

DVDs and Blu-ray Discs

Although the size and shape of a CD and DVD are similar, a DVD stores data, instructions, and information in a slightly different manner and thus achieves a higher storage capacity. DVD quali also far surpasses that of CDs because images are stored at higher resolution.

A **DVD-ROM** (digital versatile disc-read-only memory or digital video disc-read-only memory is a high-capacity optical disc on which users can read but not write or erase. Manufacturers write the contents of DVD-ROMs and distribute them to consumers. DVD-ROMs store movies, music huge databases, and complex software (Figure 6-24).

To read a DVD-ROM, you need a **DVD-ROM drive** or DVD player. Most DVD-ROM drives a can read audio CDs, CD-ROMs, CD-Rs, and CD-RWs. Some drives, called DVD/CD-RW drives, are combination drives that read and write DVD and CD media Many of today's computers include these combination drives.

A DVD-ROM uses one of three storage techniques. The first involves making the disc denser by packing the pits closer together. The second involves using two layers of pits. For this technique to work, the lower layer of pits is semitransparent so that the laser can read through it to the upper layer. This technique doubles the capacity of the disc. Finally, some DVD-ROMs are double-sided.

A newer, more expensive DVD format is Blu-ray, which is a higher capacity and better quality than standard DVDs, especia for high-definition audio and video. A **Blu-ray Disc** (BD) has storage capacities of 100 GB, with expectations of exceeding 20(GB in the future. Blu-ray Disc drives and players are backward compatible with DVD and CD formats. Figure 6-25 compares t current storage capacities of DVD and Blu-ray media. Another high density format, called **HD VMD** (Versatile Multilayer Disc potentially will contain up to 20 layers, each with a capacity of 5 GB. Current HD VMDs have capacities of 40 GB and more.

A mini-DVD that has grown in popularity is the UMD, which works specifically with the PlayStation Portable (PSP) handheld game console. The **UMD** (Universal Media Disc), which has a diameter of about 2.4 inches, can store up to 1.8 GB of games, movies, or music. Similarly, the mini Blu-ray Disc, which is used primarily in digital video recorders, stores approximately 7.5 GB.

Blu-ray

For more information, visit the Computer Concepts CourseMate Web site at www.cengagebrain.com, navigate to the Chapter 6 Web Link resource for this book, and then click Blu-ray.

DVD drive

DVD ➡

Figure 6-24 A DVD-ROM is a high-capacity optical disc.

DVD and Blu-ray Storage Capacities

Sides	Layers	DVD	Blu-ray
1	1	4.7 GB	25 GB
1	2	8.5 GB	50 GB
2	1	9.4 GB	50 GB
2	2	17 GB	100 GB

Figure 6-25 Storage capacities of DVDs and Blu-ray Discs.

Recordable and Rewritable DVDs Many types of recordable and rewritable DVD formats are available. DVD-R, DVD+R and BD-R allow users to write on the disc once and read (play) it ma times. **DVD-RW, DVD+RW,** and **DVD+RAM** are three competing rewritable DVD formats. Similarly, **BD-RE** is a high-capacity rewritable DVD format. To write on these discs, you must have a compatible drive or recorder.

Rewritable DVD drives usually can read a variety of DVD and CD media. Before investing in equipment, check to be sure it is compatible with the media on which you intend to record.

Other Types of Storage

In addition to the previously discussed types of storage, other options are available for specific uses and applications. These include tape, magnetic stripe cards and smart cards, microfilm and microfiche, and enterprise storage.

Tape

One of the first storage media used with mainframe computers was tape. **Tape** is a magnetically coated ribbon of plastic capable of storing large amounts of data and information at a low cost. Tape no longer is used as a primary method of storage. Instead, business users utilize tape most often for long-term storage and backup.

A **tape drive** reads and writes data and information on a tape. Although older computers used reel-to-reel tape drives, today's tape drives use tape cartridges. A tape cartridge is a small, rectangular, plastic housing for tape (Figure 6-26). Tape cartridges that contain quarter-inch-wide tape are slightly larger than audiocassette tapes.

Business users sometimes back up personal computer hard disks to tape, often using an external tape drive. On larger computers, tape cartridges are mounted in a separate cabinet called a tape library.

Tape storage requires sequential access, which refers to reading or writing data consecutively. As with a music tape, you must forward or rewind the tape to a specific point to access a specific piece of data. Hard disks, flash memory storage, and optical discs all use direct access. Direct access means that the device can locate a particular data item or file immediately, without having to move consecutively through items stored in front of the desired data item or file. When writing or reading specific data, direct access is much faster than sequential access.

Figure 6-26 A tape drive and a tape cartridge.

Magnetic Stripe Cards and Smart Cards

A **magnetic stripe card** is a credit card, entertainment card, bank card, or other similar card, with a stripe that contains information identifying you and the card (shown in Figure 6-1 on page 238). Information stored in the stripe includes your name, account number, and the card's expiration date. A magnetic stripe card reader reads information stored on the stripe.

A **smart card**, which is similar in size to a credit card or ATM card (Figure 6-27), stores data on a thin microprocessor embedded in the card. Smart cards contain a processor and have input, process, output, and storage capabilities. When you insert the smart card in a specialized card reader, the information on the smart card is read and, if necessary, updated. Uses of smart cards include storing medical records, vaccination data, and other health care or identification information; tracking information, such as customer purchases or employee attendance; storing a prepaid amount of money, such as for student purchases on campus; and authenticating users, such as for Internet purchases or building access. In addition, a smart card can double as an ID card. Read Ethics & Issues 6-3 for a related discussion.

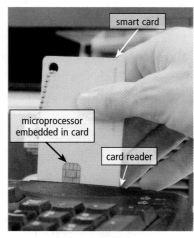

Figure 6-27 This user inserts the smart card to access the computer.

ETHICS & ISSUES 6-3

Should the World Become a Cashless Society?

Do you toss your loose change in a jar with the hopes of making a special purchase with the savings someday? This habit may become futile if the world goes cashless. One form of payment that could end the need for cash is the smart card, which can store a dollar amount on a thin microprocessor and update the amount whenever a transaction is made. Advocates claim that smart cards would eliminate muggings and robberies, make it difficult to

purchase illegal goods, and reduce taxes by identifying tax cheats. Also, payment using biometrics, such as fingerprints, is becoming more common. Several high-profile security breaches at credit reporting and credit card companies, however, have heightened concerns over privacy. In a recent survey, most Americans said that they would not use a smart card even if privacy was guaranteed. Another survey shows that most Americans believe that fingerprints are a

trustworthy form of identification. A cash purchase usually is anonymous. Yet, a smart card purchase preserves a record of the transaction that could become available to other merchants, advertisers, government agencies, or hackers.

Should the world become a cashless society? Why or why not? Would you be comfortable using a smart card or fingerprint instead of cash for all transactions? Why?

Figure 6-28 Images on microfilm can be read only with a microfilm reader.

Media Life Expectancies*
(when using high-quality media)

Media Type	Guaranteed Life Expectancy	Potential Life Expectancy
Magnetic disks	3 to 5 years	20 to 30 years
Optical discs	5 to 10 years	50 to 100 years
Solid state drives	50 years	140 years
Microfilm	100 years	500 years

*according to manufacturers of the media

 Figure 6-29 Microfilm is the medium with the longest life.

Microfilm and Microfiche

Microfilm and microfiche store microscopic images of documents on roll or sheet film. **Microfilm** is a 100- to 215-foot roll of film. **Microfiche** is a small sheet of film, usually about 4 × 6 inches. A computer output microfilm recorder is the device that records the images on the film. The stored images are so small that you can read them only with a microfilm or microfiche reader (Figure 6-28).

Microfilm and microfiche use is widespread, with many companies allowing you to search through and view microfilm images online. Libraries use these media to store back issues of newspapers, magazines, and genealogy records. Some large organizations use microfilm and microfiche to archive inactive files. Some banks use them to store transactions and canceled checks. The U.S. Army uses them to store personnel records.

The use of microfilm and microfiche provides a number of advantages. They greatly reduce the amount of paper firms must handle. They are inexpensive and have the longest life of any storage media (Figure 6-29). Read Looking Ahead 6-1 for a look at long-term storage.

↗ **LOOKING AHEAD 6-1**

Rosetta Project a Storage Solution

The Rosetta Stone unlocked the secret of understanding Egyptian hieroglyphics. Created in 186 B.C., the carved stone contains translations of one hieroglyphic passage into three languages. Today, more than 2,500 human languages exist, but 50 to 90 percent of them are expected to become extinct by the end of this century. In an effort to preserve these languages using long-term storage technology, thousands of people collaborated on the Rosetta Project to create the Rosetta Disk.

Measuring only 3 inches wide, the nickel Rosetta Disk contains 15,000 etched pages documenting more than 1,000 known languages in the world. Each page is .019 inches wide, approximately the width of 5 human hairs. The pages are readable when the Disk is magnified 1,000 times. For protection, the Disk is housed in a 4-inch spherical container.

Five prototype Disks were created. The original Disk is attached to the European Space Agency's Rosetta Space Probe that was launched in 2004 and is expected to land on a comet in 2014. The Probe will measure the comet's molecular composition and then orbit the sun for millions of years.

For more information, visit the Computer Concepts CourseMate Web site at www.cengagebrain.com, navigate to the Chapter 6 Looking Ahead resource for this book, and then click Long-Term Storage.

Enterprise Storage

A large business, commonly referred to as an enterprise, has hundreds or thousands of employees in offices across the country or around the world. Enterprises use computers and computer networks to manage and store huge volumes of data and information about customers, suppliers, and employees.

To meet their large-scale needs, enterprises use special hardware geared for heavy use, maximum availability, and maximum efficiency. One or more servers on the network have the sole purpose of providing storage to connected users. For high-speed storage access, entire networks are dedicated exclusively to connecting devices that provide storage to other servers. In an enterprise, some storage systems can provide more than 185 TB of storage capacity. Optical disc servers hold hundreds of optical discs.

An enterprise's storage needs usually grow daily. Thus, the storage solutions an enterprise chooses must be able to store its data and information requirements today and tomorrow. Read Ethics & Issues 6-4 for a related discussion.

ETHICS & ISSUES 6-4

Who Should Be Looking at Your Medical Records?

A medical transcriber based in a foreign country and hired by a U.S. medical center threatened to post private medical records to the Internet if she was not paid more. With the widespread use of computers and an explosion in data storage capacity around the world, private information, such as medical records, requires increased diligence by companies, governments, and individuals to maintain this privacy. The government would like most Americans' health care records available in privacy-protected electronic format by 2014. Although these records will be stored by a corporation or the government, individuals probably will have complete control, or ownership, of these electronic records.

The Health Insurance Portability and Accountability Act (HIPAA) sets rigorous standards for medical record privacy. The law does not cover financial records, education records, or employment records — each of which may contain medical information about you. Your medical information also may be examined by insurance companies, government agencies, the Medical Information Bureau (MIB), employers, and the courts. You also inadvertently may pass on medical information to direct marketers when you participate in informal health screenings or surveys. Some people have found that discussing medical conditions via Internet chat rooms or newsgroups has resulted in unwanted attention, and they later regret the disclosures. Proponents of greater electronic access to medical records claim that more access means that physicians can be better prepared when they see patients, physicians will make fewer errors, and insurance companies can better root out fraud.

Should more limits be placed on what other people can do with your medical information? Why or why not? What are the advantages of increased access to medical records? What are the disadvantages?

Putting It All Together

Many factors influence the type of storage devices you should use: the amount of data, instructions, and information to be stored; the hardware and software in use; and the desired cost. The table in Figure 6-30 outlines several suggested storage devices for various types of computer users.

Categories of Users

User	Typical Storage Devices	User	Typical Storage Devices
Home	• 500 GB hard disk • Cloud storage • Optical disc drive • Card reader/writer • USB flash drive	Power	• 2.5 TB hard disk • Cloud storage • Optical disc drive • Portable hard disk for backup • USB flash drive
Small Office/Home Office	• 1 TB hard disk • Cloud storage • Optical disc drive • External hard disk for backup • USB flash drive	Enterprise	• Desktop Computer - 1 TB hard disk - Optical disc drive - Smart card reader - Tape drive - USB flash drive • Server or Mainframe - Network storage server - 40 TB hard disk system - Optical disc server - Microfilm or microfiche
Mobile	• 250 GB hard disk • Cloud storage • Optical disc drive • Card reader/writer • Portable hard disk for backup • USB flash drive		

Figure 6-30 Recommended storage devices for various users.

Instructions: Find the true statement below. Then, rewrite the remaining false statements so that they are true.

1. A CD-RW is a type of optical disc on which users can read but not write (record) or erase.
2. A DVD-RAM is a single-session disc that stores digital versions of film using a jpg file format.
3. DVDs have the same storage capacities as CDs.
4. Optical discs are written and read by mirrors.
5. Microfilm and microfiche have the shortest life of any media.

🖥 **Quiz Yourself Online:** To further check your knowledge of pages 252 through 259 visit the Computer Concepts CourseMate Web site at www.cengagebrain.com, navigate to the Chapter 6 Quiz Yourself resource for this book, and then click Objectives 5 – 7.

Chapter Summary

Storage holds data, instructions, and information, which includes pictures, music, and videos, for future use. Users depend on storage devices to provide access to their storage media for years and decades to come.

This chapter identified and discussed various storage media and storage devices. Storage media covered included internal hard disks; external and removable hard disks; solid state drives; memory cards; USB flash drives; ExpressCard modules; cloud storage; CDs, DVDs, and Blu-ray Discs; tape smart cards; and microfilm and microfiche.

Computer Usage @ Work

Meteorology

With the television tuned to the local weather station, you anxiously are awaiting to see the projected path of a hurricane in the tropics. Having experienced hurricanes in the past, you rely heavily on the accuracy of weather forecasts so that you can adequately prepare if a storm travels through the area. Computers allow meteorologists to better estimate the severity and path of storms, enabling people to make potentially life-saving preparations.

The National Hurricane Center uses multiple computer models to determine a storm's path. These models consider factors such as the storm's current strength, the effects of nearby weather systems, the storm's central pressure, and whether the storm may travel over land. These models also may consider previous storms that traveled a similar path. Historical weather and storm data are stored on large storage devices by the National Weather Service. While these models are not 100 percent accurate, they do ensure that everyone who may be affected by the storm has enough time to prepare.

Violent, rotating thunderstorms potentially can spawn tornadoes, which sometimes cause catastrophic damage. For this reason, it is important for everyone to closely watch or listen to the weather during the storm. Meteorologists can monitor weather systems on multiple radars and send additional severe weather warnings automatically to weather radios. Computer technology enables these messages to be broadcast automatically only to weather radios in areas that may be affected.

In addition to computers helping us stay safe during severe storms, they also assist with day-to-day weather forecasting. Several years ago, meteorologists could predict the weather for only a few days into the future. Beyond that point, the forecast was very uncertain. Meteorologists presently are able to predict the weather, including temperature and chance of precipitation, one week or more into the future with much greater accuracy because computers create models using historical weather data and behavior to predict the future path of various weather systems.

News and weather stations also post their weather forecasts online. In fact, several Web sites have interactive radars that allow visitors to zoom in and view how weather is affecting their immediate neighborhood.

The meteorology field has made significant advancements because of computer technologies. Weather forecasts are more meaningful, which not only helps us prepare on land but also helps to protect those traveling by air or by sea.

🖥 For more information, visit the Computer Concepts CourseMate Web site at www.cengagebrain.com, navigate to the Chapter 6 Computer Usage @ Work resource for this book, and then click Meteorology.

Companies on the Cutting Edge

SEAGATE TECHNOLOGY Storage Solutions Supplier

The average household with a broadband Internet connection will need nearly 1 TB of storage for its personal media collections, and Seagate has the storage solutions for practically every digital need. The company offers more than 40 products for the personal computing, consumer electronics, and enterprise computing fields.

Seagate has been at the forefront of the digital storage world since it developed the first 5.25-inch hard disk for the personal computer in 1980. In 2008 it shipped its one billionth hard disk, making the company's

production for the past 30 years a total of 79 million terabytes. Seagate expects to ship its two billionth hard disk by 2013.

Seagate recently introduced the FreeAgent DockStar network adapter. This device allows users to access their digital media from anywhere in the world and share these files with anyone. The FreeAgent DockStar network adapter also enables users to link their digital content to online social networks such as Facebook, Twitter, and MySpace.

SANDISK CORPORATION Flash Memory Storage Supplier

The number of flash memory card formats is growing, and only one company has the rights to design, develop, manufacture, and market every one of them: SanDisk. The company is the world's largest supplier of flash memory storage products and also has lines of portable media players.

The company was founded in 1988, and one of its earliest flash drives was used on a U.S. space shuttle three years later. Today SanDisk is developing rewritable 3-D memory products that will store data vertically, and

company executives believe this technology will replace flash products in the next decade.

SanDisk recently introduced the world's fastest 32 GB SDHC card. The 32 GB SanDisk Extreme SDHC card boasts read and write speeds of 30 megabytes per second. The increased speeds enable photographers to take pictures quickly without having to wait long for the card to record the images. In addition, computer users also are able to transfer data to and from the card quickly.

For more information, visit the Computer Concepts CourseMate Web site at www.cengagebrain.com and then navigate to the Chapter 6 Companies on the Cutting Edge resource for this book.

Technology Trailblazers

AL SHUGART Storage Expert

Al Shugart said that his real goal in life was to have fun, and he spent his life doing the things that gave him the most pleasure. The day after receiving his bachelor's degree in engineering physics in 1951, he landed a job at IBM doing what he loved to do: fixing broken items and developing new technology. He was promoted to supervisor of the product development team that developed the first removable hard disk drive.

Shugart then left IBM, became vice president of Memorex, and then started Shugart Associates and

began developing floppy disks. In 1979 he founded Seagate Technology with a friend. As his company grew to become the world's largest hard disk manufacturer, he had fun placing his dog, Ernest, on the ballot for a Congressional seat.

Shugart served as president and CEO of Al Shugart International, a venture capital firm in California, until his death in 2006.

MARK DEAN IBM Inventor

Web 2.0 applications demand large, inexpensive storage, and Mark Dean is hard at work helping to meet this need. As vice president of IBM's Almaden Research Center lab in California, Dean is responsible for developing innovative products.

Dean joined IBM after graduating from Stanford University with a degree in electrical engineering. He led a team that developed the first CMOS microprocessor to operate at one gigahertz and has more than

40 patents or patents pending that are used in more than 40 million personal computers manufactured each year. Three of his patents are among the nine registered for the architecture of the original personal computer.

Dean is the first African-American to be appointed to IBM Fellow, the company's highest level of technical merit. He also was inducted in the National Inventors Hall of Fame.

For more information, visit the Computer Concepts CourseMate Web site at www.cengagebrain.com and then navigate to the Chapter 6 Technology Trailblazers resource for this book.

Chapter Review

The Chapter Review section reinforces the main concepts presented in this chapter.

To listen to an audio version of this Chapter Review, visit the Computer Concepts CourseMate Web site at www.cengagebrain.com and then navigate to the Chapter 6 Chapter Review resource for this book.

1. What Are the Characteristics of an Internal Hard Disk? A **hard disk** is a storage device that contains one or more inflexible, circular platters that use magnetic particles to store data, instructions, and information. The system unit in most desktop and notebook computers contains at least one hard disk. **Capacity** is the number of bytes (characters) a storage medium can hold. Hard disk capacity is determined from whether it uses **longitudinal recording** or **perpendicular recording**, the number of platters it contains, and the composition of the magnetic coating on the platters. A platter is made of aluminum, glass, or ceramic and is coated with a material that allows items to be recorded magnetically on its surface. Each platter has two read/write heads, one for each side. The location of a read/write head often is referred to by its cylinder, which is the vertical section of a track that passes through all platters. Magnetic disks store data and instructions in tracks and sectors. A track is a narrow recording band that forms a full circle on the surface of the disk. The disk's storage locations consist of pie-shaped sections, which break the tracks into small arcs called sectors. While the computer is running, the platters rotate at 5,400 to 15,000 revolutions per minute (rpm), which allows nearly instant access to all tracks and sectors on the platters.

2. What Is the Purpose of Network Attached Storage Devices, External and Removable Hard Disks, and Hard Disk Controllers? A **network attached storage** (NAS) device is a server connected to a network with the sole purpose of providing storage. Any user or device connected to the network can access files on the NAS device. These devices often use a **RAID** (redundant array of independent disks) configuration. A group of two or more integrated hard disks is called a RAID. An **external hard disk** is a separate freestanding hard disk that connects with a cable to a USB or FireWire port on the system unit or communicates wirelessly. External hard disks have storage capacities up to 4 TB or more. A **removable hard disk** can be inserted or removed from a drive. Removable hard disks have storage capacities up to 1 TB. A **disk controller** consists of a special-purpose chip and electronic circuits that control the transfer of data, instructions, and information from a disk to and from the system bus and other components in the computer. A hard disk controller may be part of a hard disk on the motherboard, or it may be a separate adapter card inside the system unit. In addition to USB and FireWire, which can function as hard disk interfaces, four other types of hard disk interfaces for use in personal computers are SATA (Serial Advanced Technology Attachment), EIDE (Enhanced Integrated Drive Electronics), SCSI, and SAS (serial-attached SCSI).

Visit the Computer Concepts CourseMate Web site at www.cengagebrain.com, navigate to the Chapter 6 Quiz Yourself resource for this book, and then click Objectives 1 – 2.

3. What Are the Various Types of Flash Memory Storage? Flash memory chips are a type of **solid state media,** which means they consist entirely of electronic components and contain no moving parts. A **solid state drive** (SSD) is a storage device that uses flash memory to store data, instructions, and information. Although SSDs currently have a higher failure rate than hard disks and are more expensive, experts estimate that as the price of SSDs drops, increasingly more users will purchase computers and devices that contain this media. A **memory card** is a removable flash memory device that you insert and remove from a slot in a computer, mobile device, or card reader/writer. Common types of memory cards include **CompactFlash (CF), Secure Digital (SD), Secure Digital High Capacity (SDHC), microSD, microSDHC, xD Picture Card, Memory Stick,** and **Memory Stick Micro (M2).** A **USB flash drive** is a flash memory storage device that plugs in a USB port on a computer or mobile device. An **ExpressCard module** is a removable device that fits in an ExpressCard slot. ExpressCard modules add storage or other capabilities to a computer and commonly are used in notebook computers.

4. What Is Cloud Storage, and What Are Its Advantages? **Cloud storage** is an Internet service that provides storage for computer users. Types of services offered by cloud storage providers vary. Available for all sizes of users, with various degrees of storage services available for home and business users, cloud storage fees vary, depending on the user's storage requirements. Advantages include accessing files on the Internet from any computer or device with Internet access; storing large audio, video, and graphics files on the Internet instantaneously; allowing others to access their files on the Internet; viewing time-critical data and images immediately; storing off-site backups of data; and providing data center functions.

Visit the Computer Concepts CourseMate Web site at www.cengagebrain.com, navigate to the Chapter 6 Quiz Yourself resource for this book, and then click Objectives 3 – 4.

Chapter Review

5. What Are the Characteristics of Optical Discs? An **optical disc** is a type of storage media that consists of a flat, round, portable disc made of metal, plastic, and lacquer. These discs usually are 4.75 inches in diameter and less than one-twentieth of an inch thick. Optical discs primarily store software, data, digital photos, movies, and music. Some are read only, which means users cannot write (save) on them; others are read/write, which allows users to save on the disc just as they save on a hard disk. Optical discs store items by using microscopic pits (indentations) and lands (flat areas). A high-powered laser light creates the pits, and a lower-powered laser light reads items by reflecting light through the bottom of the disc. The reflected light is converted into a series of bits the computer can process.

6. What Are the Various Types of Optical Discs? A **CD-ROM** is an optical disc that users can read but not write (record) or erase. A **CD-R** is a multisession disc on which users can write, but not erase. A **CD-RW** (compact disc-rewritable) is erasable and can be written on multiple times. An **archive disc** is used to store photos from a photo sharing community in the jpg file format. A **Picture CD** stores digital versions of film using a jpg file format. A **DVD-ROM** is a high-capacity disc which users can read but not write on or erase. A **Blu-ray Disc** (BD) currently has storage capacities of 100 GB. The **HD VMD** (Versatile Multilayer Disc) is a high-density format with a capacity of 40 GB or more. A mini-DVD that has grown in popularity is the UMD (Universal Media Disc), which works specifically with the PlayStation Portable handheld game console. Similarly, the mini Blu-ray Disc is used primarily in digital video recorders. DVD-R, DVD+R, BD-R formats can be written on once. **DVD-RW**, **DVD+RW**, and **DVD+RAM** are three competing high-capacity rewritable DVD formats. **BD-RE** is a high-capacity rewritable DVD format.

7. How Are Tape, Magnetic Stripe Cards, Smart Cards, Microfilm and Microfiche, and Enterprise Storage Used? **Tape** is a magnetically coated ribbon of plastic capable of storing large amounts of data and information at a low cost. A **tape drive** reads and writes data and information on tape. Business users utilize tape most often for long-term storage and backup. A **magnetic stripe card** is a credit card, entertainment card, bank card, or other similar card with a stripe that contains information identifying you and the card. A magnetic stripe card reader reads information stored on the stripe. A **smart card**, which is similar in size to a credit or ATM card, stores data on a thin microprocessor embedded in the card. Smart cards contain a processor and have input, process, output, and storage capabilities. **Microfilm** is a 100- to 215-foot roll of film. **Microfiche** is a small sheet of film, usually about 4 × 6 inches. Microfilm and microfiche greatly reduce the amount of paper firms must handle, are inexpensive, and have the longest life of any storage media. Enterprises use special hardware to meet their large-scale needs, including servers, entire networks, and optical disc servers. In an enterprise, some storage systems can provide more than 185 TB of storage capacity.

Visit the Computer Concepts CourseMate Web site at www.cengagebrain.com, navigate to the Chapter 6 Quiz Yourself resource for this book, and then click Objectives 5 – 7.

Key Terms

You should know each key term. The list below helps focus your study.

To see an example of and a definition for each term, and to access current and additional information from the Web, visit the Computer Concepts CourseMate Web site at www.cengagebrain.com and then navigate to the Chapter 6 Key Terms resource for this book.

Checkpoint

The Checkpoint exercises test your knowledge of the chapter concepts. The page number containing the answer appears in parentheses after each exercise.

To complete the Checkpoint exercises interactively, visit the Computer Concepts CourseMate Web site at www.cengagebrain.com and then navigate to the Chapter 6 Checkpoint resource for this book.

Multiple Choice Select the best answer.

1. _____ measures the amount of time it takes a storage device to locate an item on a storage medium. (240)
 a. Capacity
 b. Access time
 c. A storage medium
 d. Reading

2. A group of two or more integrated hard disks is called a _____. (244)
 a. backup
 b. platter
 c. RAID
 d. portable hard disk

3. A _____ consists of a special-purpose chip and electronic circuits that control the transfer of data, instructions, and information from a disk to and from the system bus and other components in the computer. (246)
 a. pocket hard drive
 b. removable hard disk
 c. magnetic disk
 d. disk controller

4. A _____ is a memory storage device that plugs in a USB port on a computer or mobile device. (250)
 a. smart card
 b. USB flash drive
 c. UMD
 d. Memory Stick

5. Users subscribe to a cloud storage service to _____. (252)
 a. access files from any computer that has Internet access
 b. allow others to access their files
 c. store offsite backups of data
 d. all of the above

6. _____ technology works with specially coated optical discs to etch labels directly on the disc. (253)
 a. LightScribe
 b. SATA
 c. LightSaber
 d. SCSI

7. _____ storage requires sequential access. (257)
 a. Hard disk
 b. Tape
 c. Memory card
 d. DVD

8. A(n) _____ card is a credit card, entertainment card, bank card, or other similar card, with a stripe that contains information identifying you and the card. (257)
 a. Secure Digital High Capacity
 b. magnetic stripe
 c. Secure Digital
 d. microSDHC

Matching Match the terms with their definitions.

_____ 1. backup (244)

_____ 2. external hard disk (244)

_____ 3. solid state media (247)

_____ 4. solid state drive (247)

_____ 5. card reader/writer (249)

a. media which consist entirely of electronic components, such as integrated circuits, and contain no moving parts

b. device that reads and writes data, instructions, and information stored on memory cards

c. portable, large-capacity magnetic medium that can store from 100 MB to 750 MB of data

d. duplicate of a file, program, or disk placed on a separate storage medium that you can use in case the original is lost, damaged, or destroyed

e. a storage device that typically uses flash memory to store data, instructions, and information

f. a separate freestanding hard disk that connects with a cable to a USB port or FireWire port on the system unit or communicates wirelessly

Short Answer Write a brief answer to each of the following questions.

1. What is longitudinal recording? _____ What is the benefit of perpendicular recording over longitudinal recording? _____

2. What is network attached storage? _____ How much hard disk storage can home and small business users add to their network with a NAS device? _____

3. How is a single-session disc different from a multisession disc? _____ What is a CD-RW? _____

4. Why do users use memory cards? _____ Name five types of memory cards and describe some of the characteristic of each card. _____

5. What is one difference between microfilm and microfiche? _____ What are some uses of microfilm and microfiche? _____

Problem Solving

The Problem Solving exercises extend your knowledge of the chapter concepts by seeking solutions to practical computer problems that you may encounter at home, school, or work. The Collaboration exercise should be completed with a team.

In the real world, practical problems often can be solved in multiple ways. Provide one solution to each of the following problems using available resources, such as articles on the Web or in print, blogs, podcasts, videos, television, user guides, other individuals, and electronics and computer stores. You may need to use multiple resources to obtain an answer. Present your solutions in the form requested by your instructor (brief report, presentation, discussion, or other means).

@ Home

1. **Old Movies** During the past two decades, you have been recording home movies on VHS tapes. It is becoming more difficult to locate blank VHS tapes, and you are worried that if your current VCR breaks, it will be hard to find a store that sells them new. A friend suggests that you copy these movies to an optical disc. What steps will you take to convert these movies?

2. **Possible Head Crash** When you turn on your computer, you hear a clicking sound coming from inside the computer. Furthermore, you realize that Windows is not starting automatically. You talk to a friend who said that your hard disk might have experienced a head crash. What might have caused this?

3. **Missing Cable** You are attempting to install a new 1 TB hard disk in your computer. You have found the empty bay for the new hard disk, but you cannot locate the cable that connects it to the computer. What are your next steps?

4. **Memory Card Problems** For the past two years, you have been using the same Secure Digital (SD) memory card to take pictures with your digital camera. When you insert the SD memory card in your computer's card reader to transfer the pictures, your computer does not display the contents of the card. When you put the card back into your digital camera, you can see that the pictures still are stored on the card. What might be wrong?

@ Work

5. **Disk Not Recognized** The information technology manager at your company has purchased external hard disks for employees to use to back up their files. When you connect the external hard disk to the USB port on your computer, the computer displays a message stating that it cannot recognize the device. What might you do to correct this problem?

6. **File Will Not Open** Your computer is unable to open a file on an optical disc that you just inserted into the optical disc drive. You have been able to access other files on the same disc, but one file in particular is not opening. What might be causing this?

7. **Backing Up Data** It has been several years since your office computer was upgraded, and you just received an e-mail message stating that you finally will receive a new computer next week. The e-mail message also stated that all employees will be responsible for backing up their data. What files will you back up?

8. **Optical Disc Problem** Your colleague gives you an optical disc containing some video files. When you insert the disc in your computer, the disc burning software asks if you would like to finalize the disc. How will you respond?

Collaboration

9. **Computers in Meteorology** Your environmental sciences instructor is teaching a lesson about how computers have advanced the meteorology field. Form a team of three people to prepare a brief report about how computers and meteorology are connected. One team member should research how meteorologists predicted weather patterns before computer use became mainstream. Another team member should create a timeline illustrating when and how computers were introduced to the meteorology field, and the third team member should research the types of computer hardware and software required for a typical news station to forecast and present the weather.

Learn How To

The Learn How To activities step you through fundamental technology skills when using a computer. The Learn How To exercises enable you to become more proficient with these skills.

Premium Activity: To relate this Learn How To activity to your everyday life, see a visual demonstration of the activity, and complete a short assessment, visit the Computer Concepts CourseMate Web site at www.cengagebrain.com and then navigate to the Chapter 6 Learn How To resource for this book.

Learn How To 1: Maintain a Hard Disk

A computer's hard disk is used for the majority of storage requirements. It is important, therefore, to ensure that each hard disk on a computer is operating at peak efficiency, both to use the available storage space effectively and to make disk operations as fast as possible.

Two tasks that maximize disk operations are removing unused or unnecessary files and folders by using the Disk Cleanup utility program and consolidating files and folders into contiguous storage areas using the Disk Defragmenter utility program. Defragmenting allows your system to access stored files and folders more efficiently.

A. Cleanup Disk

To clean up the disk by removing any programs and data that are not required for the computer, complete the following steps:

1. Click the Start button on the Windows taskbar and then click Computer on the Start menu.
2. When the Computer window opens, right-click the hard disk icon for drive C (or any other hard disk you want to select) and then click Properties on the shortcut menu.
3. If necessary, click the General tab in the disk drive Properties dialog box to display the General sheet.
4. Click the Disk Cleanup button in the General sheet to display the Disk Cleanup Options dialog box.
5. The Disk Cleanup dialog box is displayed and contains a message that indicates the amount of space that can be freed up is being calculated.
6. After the calculation is complete, the Disk Cleanup dialog box specifies the amount of space that can be freed up and the files to delete, some of which are selected automatically (Figure 6-31). Select those items from which you wish to delete files.
7. Click the OK button in the Disk Cleanup dialog box.
8. A dialog box asks if you are sure you want to perform these actions. Click the Delete Files button. The Disk Cleanup dialog box illustrates the progress of the cleanup. When the cleanup is complete, the dialog box closes.

Figure 6-31

B. Defragment Disk

After removing all the unnecessary files from the hard disk, the next step in disk maintenance is to defragment all the files on the disk. When a file is stored on disk, the data in the file sometimes is stored contiguously, and other times is stored in a noncontiguous manner. The greater the amount of data on a disk, the more likely files will be stored noncontiguously. When a file is stored in a noncontiguous manner, it can take significantly longer to find and retrieve data from the file. One of the more useful utilities to speed up disk operations, therefore, is the defragmentation program, which combines all files so that no files are stored in a noncontiguous manner. To use the defragmentation program, complete the following steps:

1. If necessary, click the Tools tab in the Properties dialog box for the hard disk to be defragmented.
2. Click the Defragment now button in the Tools sheet to open the Disk Defragmenter window (Figure 6-32). This window displays the Disk Defragmenter schedule, when Disk Defragmenter was run last, and when Disk Defragmenter is scheduled to run next.
3. Click the Defragment disk button. The defragmentation process begins. During the defragmentation process, the Stop operation button replaces the Defragment disk button. The defragmentation process can consume more than one hour in some cases, depending on the size of the hard disk and the amount of processing that must occur. You can cancel the operation at any time by clicking the Stop operation button in the Disk Defragmenter window.
4. When the process is complete, the Defragment disk button will replace the Stop operation button.
5. Click the Close button to close the Disk Defragmenter window.

Proper disk maintenance is critically important so that disk operation is as efficient as possible.

Learn How To

Exercises

Caution: The exercises for this chapter that require actual disk maintenance are optional. If you are performing these exercises on a computer that is not your own, obtain explicit permission to complete these exercises. Keep in mind that these exercises can require significant computer time and the computer may be unusable during this time.

Disk Defragmenter window

Defragment disk button

Close button

Figure 6-32

1. Display the Properties dialog box for a hard disk found on the computer. Display the General sheet. What is the capacity of the hard disk? How much space is used? How much free space is available? Click the Disk Cleanup button. How much space can be freed up if you use the Disk Cleanup program? Click the OK button to clean up the disk. How long did it take to perform the disk cleanup? Submit your answers to your instructor.

2. Display the Properties dialog box for a hard disk found on the computer. Display the Tools sheet. Click the Defragment now button. In the Disk Defragmenter window, click the Defragment disk button. How could you tell when the defragmentation process was completed? How long did defragmentation require? Submit your answers to your instructor.

Learn It Online

The Learn It Online exercises are interactive Web exercises designed to reinforce and expand your understanding of the chapter concepts. The descriptions below briefly summarize each exercise.

To complete the Learn It Online exercises, visit the Computer Concepts CourseMate Web site at www.cengagebrain.com, navigate to the Chapter 6 resources for this book, click the link for the exercise you want to complete, and then read the instructions.

❶ At the Movies — Thumb-drive (USB Flash Drive) Encryption

Watch a movie to learn how people who store personal and confidential information on USB flash drives can use third-party programs to password-protect the files so that others cannot access them and then answer questions about the movie.

❷ Student Edition Labs — Maintaining a Hard Drive (Hard Disk) and Managing Files and Folders

Enhance your understanding and knowledge about maintaining a hard disk and managing files and folders by completing the Maintaining a Hard Drive and Managing Files and Folders Labs.

❸ Practice Test

Take a multiple choice test that checks your knowledge of the chapter concepts and review the resulting study guide.

❹ Who Wants To Be a Computer Genius²?

Play the Shelly Cashman Series version of this popular game by answering questions to find out if you are a computer genius. Panic buttons are available to provide assistance during game play.

❺ Crossword Puzzle Challenge

Complete an interactive crossword puzzle to reinforce concepts presented in this chapter.

❻ Windows Exercises

Step through the Windows 7 exercises to learn about the Recycle Bin, working with files, the hard disk, and Disk Cleanup.

❼ Exploring Computer Careers

Read about a career as a computer technician, search for related employment advertisements, and then answer related questions.

❽ Web Apps — TurboTax Online

Learn how to use TurboTax Online to create an account, start a new tax return from scratch, review your tax return, and then print and file your tax return.

Web Research

The Web Research exercises broaden your understanding of chapter concepts by presenting questions that require you to search the Web for answers.

1 Search Sleuth

Use one of the search engines listed in Figure 2-8 in Chapter 2 on page 65 or your own favorite search engine to find the answers to the following questions. Copy and paste the Web address from the Web page where you found the answer. Some questions may have more than one answer. If required, submit your answers to your instructor. (1) What album did Hillsong United release in 2008 on a flash drive embedded in a rubber wristband? (2) What country uses the MyKad smart card for national identification? (3) What product did HP develop in 2004 based on the efforts of engineer Daryl Anderson? (4) What products are available for sale at the SanDisk Plaza? (5) For what storage medium are phase change alloys used? (6) What company introduced using a hard disk for accounting projects in 1956?

2 Green Computing

Data storage is doubling every 18 months according to some computer industry experts, and consumers and businesses are turning to environmentally sound methods of backing up and storing files. Accessing hard disks consumes 80 percent of a storage system's electrical consumption, so companies have developed products that reduce a system's energy usage. Businesses invest in cooling systems that dissipate the heat generated when servers and storage hardware operate. Locate Web sites that describe these products and how they operate efficiently to conserve energy. How much energy savings do they claim to make in one year? To what extent are carbon dioxide and other greenhouse gases reduced? How do they maximize the use of power and cooling resources? Review your search results and then write a 50-word summary of your findings.

3 Social Networking

Privacy on social networking Web sites such as MySpace and Facebook is an international concern, and the Electronic Privacy Information Center (epic.org/privacy/socialnet) features news, policies, and resources discussing safeguarding and controlling personal information. At least one-fourth of hiring managers admit to researching job applicants' "digital dirt" by searching social networks and blogs, and some employers search social networking Web sites for profiles of current employees. Visit the Reputation Defender (reputationdefender.com) and Defend My Name (defendmyname .com) Web sites and read about the services offered. Then view the standards posted on the MySpace and Facebook Web sites regarding privacy and allowable content. Summarize the information you read and viewed.

4 Blogs

Exercise and nutrition advice is available from experts who post firsthand experiences in their blogs. These authorities may be people who share a particular experience, such as losing weight or training for a marathon, or who have specialized training in the fitness field. For example, noted author Lou Schuler discusses nutrition, weight training, and issues of particular interest to men (malepatternfitness.com). Other popular fitness blogs are featured by The Families .com (fitness.families.com/blog) and Diet-Blog (diet-blog.com). Athlete Blog Central (yardbarker.com/athletes) lists blogs that professional and amateur athletes and their fans write. Visit these sites and read the posts. Which stories received more than 25 comments? Which food, exercises, and programs are featured?

5 Ethics in Action

The United States Federal Bureau of Investigation used a controversial program until January 2005 to monitor and store the e-mail and Internet activity of suspected criminals. Originally called Carnivore, the surveillance program was renamed DCS1000. The program was designed to track the activities of potential terrorists, spies, drug traffickers, and organized crime ring members. FBI agents needed to obtain a court order to monitor an individual, but privacy advocates claim the software tracked people not covered under the court order. View online sites that provide information about DCS1000 or Carnivore, including HowStuffWorks (howstuffworks.com/carnivore.htm). What commercial software has replaced Carnivore? Write a report summarizing your findings, and include a table of links to Web sites that provide additional details.

Operating Systems and Utility Programs

Objectives

After completing this chapter, you will be able to:

1 Define system software and identify the two types of system software

2 Describe each of these functions of an operating system: starting and shutting down a computer, providing a user interface, managing memory, coordinating tasks, configuring devices, establishing an Internet connection, monitoring performance, providing file management and other utilities, updating automatically, controlling a network, and administering security

3 Summarize the features of several stand-alone operating systems: Windows, Mac OS, UNIX, and Linux

4 Identify various server operating systems

5 Briefly describe several embedded operating systems: Windows Embedded CE, Windows Phone, Palm OS, iPhone OS, BlackBerry, Google Android, Embedded Linux, and Symbian OS

6 Explain the purpose of several utility programs: file manager, search utility, image viewer, uninstaller, disk cleanup, disk defragmenter, backup and restore utilities, screen saver, personal firewall, antivirus programs, spyware and adware removers, Internet filters, file compression, media player, disc burning, and personal computer maintenance

System Software

When you purchase a personal computer, it usually has system software installed on its hard disk. **System software** consists of the programs that control or maintain the operations of the computer and its devices. System software serves as the interface between the user, the application software, and the computer's hardware.

Two types of system software are operating systems and utility programs. This chapter discusses the operating system and its functions, as well as several types of utility programs for personal computers.

start and shut down the computer

administer security

control a network

update automatically

operating system functions

provide file management and other utilities

Figure 7-1 Most operating systems perform similar functions, which are illustrated with the latest version of Windows in this figure.

Operating Systems

An **operating system** (**OS**) is a set of programs containing instructions that work together to coordinate all the activities among computer hardware resources. Most operating systems perform similar functions that include starting and shutting down a computer, providing a user interface, managing programs, managing memory, coordinating tasks, configuring devices, establishing an Internet connection, monitoring performance, providing file management and other utilities, and automatically updating itself and certain utility programs. Some operating systems also allow users to control a network and administer security (Figure 7-1).

Although an operating system can run from an optical disc and/or flash memory mobile media, in most cases, the operating system is installed and resides on the computer's hard disk. On handheld computers and many mobile devices, the operating system may reside on a ROM chip.

provide a user interface

manage programs

manage memory

establish an Internet connection

monitor performance

coordinate tasks and configure devices

Different sizes of computers typically use different operating systems because operating systems generally are written to run on a specific type of computer. For example, a mainframe computer does not use the same operating system as a personal computer. Even the same types of computers, such as desktop computers, may not use the same operating system. Some, however, can run multiple operating systems. When purchasing application software, you must ensure that it works with the operating system installed on your computer or mobile device.

The operating system that a computer uses sometimes is called the platform. With purchased application software, the package or specifications identify the required platform (operating system). A cross-platform program is one that runs the same on multiple operating systems.

Operating System Functions

Many different operating systems exist; however, most operating systems provide similar functions. The following sections discuss functions common to most operating systems. The operating system handles many of these functions automatically, without requiring any instruction from a user.

Starting and Shutting Down a Computer

Booting is the process of starting or restarting a computer. When turning on a computer that has been powered off completely, you are performing a **cold boot**. A **warm boot**, by contrast, is the process of using the operating system to restart a computer. With Windows, for example, you can perform a warm boot by clicking a menu command (Figure 7-2).

When you install new software or update existing software, often an on-screen prompt instructs you to restart the computer. In this case, a warm boot is appropriate.

Each time you boot a computer, the kernel and other frequently used operating system instructions are loaded, or copied, from storage into the computer's memory (RAM). The kernel is the core of an operating system that manages memory and devices, maintains the computer's clock, starts programs, and assigns the computer's resources, such as devices, programs, data, and information. The kernel is memory resident, which means it remains in memory while the computer is running. Other parts of the operating system are nonresident, that is, these instructions remain on a storage medium until they are needed.

When you boot a computer, a series of messages may appear on the screen. The actual information displayed varies depending on the make and type of the computer and the equipment installed. The boot process, however, is similar for large and small computers.

Although some users leave their computers running continually and never turn them off, others choose to shut them down. Shut down options including powering off the computer, placing the computer in sleep mode, and hibernating the computer. Both sleep mode and hibernate are designed to save time when you resume working on the computer. **Sleep mode** saves any open documents and programs to RAM, turns off all unneeded functions, and then places the computer in a low-power state. **Hibernate**, by contrast, saves any open documents and programs to a hard disk before removing power from the computer.

Figure 7-2 To reboot a running computer, click the Shut down button arrow and then click Restart.

Providing a User Interface

You interact with software through its user interface. That is, a **user interface** controls how you enter data and instructions and how information is displayed on the screen. Two types of user interfaces are graphical and command-line (Figure 7-3). Operating systems sometimes use a combination of these interfaces to define how a user interacts with a computer.

Graphical User Interface Most users today work with a graphical user interface. With a **graphical user interface (GUI)**, you interact with menus and visual images such as buttons and other graphical objects to issue commands (Figure 7-3a). Many current GUI operating systems incorporate features similar to those of a Web browser.

Windows 7 offers two different GUIs, depending on your hardware configuration. Computers with less than 1 GB of RAM work with the Windows 7 Basic interface. Computers with more than 1 GB of RAM that have the required hardware may be able to work with the Windows 7 Aero interface, also known as **Windows Aero**, shown in Figure 7-3a, which provides an enhanced visual look, additional navigation options, and animation.

Command-Line Interface To configure devices, manage system resources, and troubleshoot network connections, network administrators and other advanced users work with a command-line interface. In a **command-line interface**, a user types commands or presses special keys on the keyboard to enter data and instructions (Figure 7-3b). Some people consider command-line interfaces difficult to use because they require exact spelling, grammar, and punctuation.

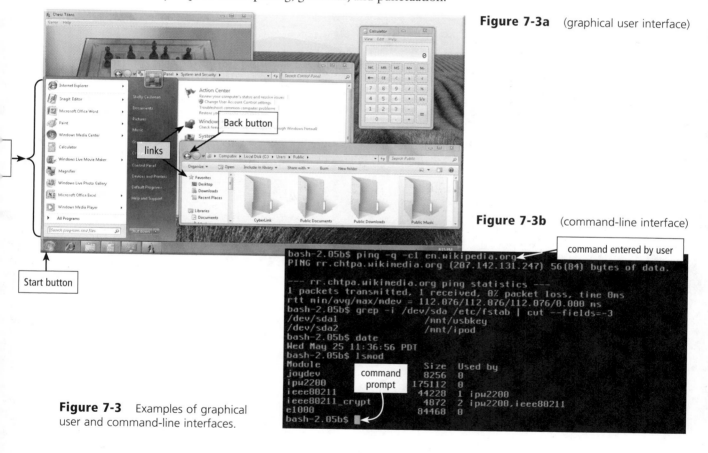

Figure 7-3a (graphical user interface)

Figure 7-3b (command-line interface)

Figure 7-3 Examples of graphical user and command-line interfaces.

Managing Programs

Some operating systems support a single user and only one running program at a time. Others support thousands of users running multiple programs. How an operating system handles programs directly affects your productivity.

A single user/single tasking operating system allows only one user to run one program at a time. Smart phones and other mobile devices often use a single user/single tasking operating system.

A single user/multitasking operating system allows a single user to work on two or more programs that reside in memory at the same time. Users today typically run multiple programs concurrently. It is common to have an e-mail program and Web browser open at all times, while working with application programs such as word processing or graphics.

When a computer is running multiple programs concurrently, one program is in the foreground and the others are in the background. The one in the foreground is the active program, that is, the one you currently are using. The other programs running but not in use are in the background. In Figure 7-4, the Windows Live Movie Maker program is in the foreground, and three other programs are running in the background (Windows Media Player, Microsoft PowerPoint, and Chess Titans).

The foreground program typically is displayed on the desktop but the background programs often are hidden partially or completely behind the foreground program. You easily can switch between foreground and background programs. To make a program active (in the foreground) in Windows, click its program button on the taskbar. This causes the operating system to place all other programs in the background.

foreground program

taskbar

program button

background programs

Figure 7-4 The foreground program, Windows Live Movie Maker, is displayed on the desktop. The other programs (Windows Media Player, Microsoft PowerPoint, and Chess Titans) are in the background.

A **multiuser** operating system enables two or more users to run programs simultaneously. Networks, servers, mainframes, and supercomputers allow hundreds to thousands of users to connect at the same time, and thus are multiuser.

A **multiprocessing** operating system supports two or more processors running programs at the same time. Multiprocessing involves the coordinated processing of programs by more than one processor. Multiprocessing increases a computer's processing speed.

Managing Memory

The purpose of **memory management** is to optimize the use of random access memory (RAM). RAM consists of one or more chips on the motherboard that hold items such as data and instructions while the processor interprets and executes them. The operating system allocates, or assigns, data and instructions to an area of memory while they are being processed. Then, it carefully monitors the contents of memory. Finally, the operating system releases these items from being monitored in memory when the processor no longer requires them.

Virtual memory is a concept in which the operating system allocates a portion of a storage medium, usually the hard disk, to function as additional RAM. As you interact with a program, part of it may be in physical RAM, while the rest of the program is on the hard disk as virtual memory. Because virtual memory is slower than RAM, users may notice the computer slowing down while it uses virtual memory.

The operating system uses an area of the hard disk for virtual memory, in which it swaps (exchanges) data, information, and instructions between memory and storage. The technique of swapping items between memory and storage is called paging. When an operating system spends much of its time paging, instead of executing application software, it is said to be thrashing. If application software, such as a Web browser, has stopped responding and the hard disk's LED blinks repeatedly, the operating system probably is thrashing.

Instead of using a hard disk as virtual memory, Windows users can increase the size of memory through **Windows ReadyBoost**, which can allocate available storage space on removable flash memory devices as additional memory cache. Users notice better performance with Windows ReadyBoost versus hard disk virtual memory because the operating system accesses a flash memory device, such as a USB flash drive or SD memory card, more quickly than it accesses a hard disk.

Coordinating Tasks

The operating system determines the order in which tasks are processed. A task, or job, is an operation the processor manages. Tasks include receiving data from an input device, processing instructions, sending information to an output device, and transferring items from storage to memory and from memory to storage.

A multiuser operating system does not always process tasks on a first-come, first-served basis. Sometimes, one user may have a higher priority than other users. In this case, the operating system adjusts the schedule of tasks.

Sometimes, a device already may be busy processing one task when it receives a second task. This occurs because the processor operates at a much faster rate of speed than peripheral devices. For example, if the processor sends five documents to a printer, the printer can print only one document at a time and store as many documents as its memory can handle.

While waiting for devices to become idle, the operating system places items in buffers. A **buffer** is a segment of memory or storage in which items are placed while waiting to be transferred from an input device or to an output device.

The operating system commonly uses buffers with printed documents. This process, called **spooling**, sends documents to be printed to a buffer instead of sending them immediately to the printer. If a printer does not have its own internal memory or if its memory is full, the operating system's buffer holds the information waiting to print while the printer prints from the buffer at its own rate of speed. By spooling documents to a buffer, the processor can continue interpreting and executing instructions while the printer prints. This allows users to work on the computer for other

Spooling
For more information, visit the Computer Concepts CourseMate Web site at www.cengagebrain.com, navigate to the Chapter 7 Web Link resource for this book, and then click Spooling.

tasks while a printer is printing. Multiple print jobs line up in a **queue** (pronounced Q) in the buffer. A program, called a print spooler, intercepts documents to be printed from the operating system and places them in the queue (Figure 7-5).

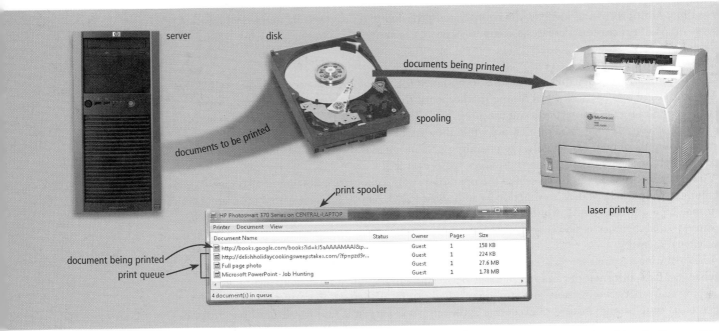

Figure 7-5 Spooling increases both processor and printer efficiency by placing documents to be printed in a buffer on disk before they are printed. This figure illustrates three documents in the queue with one document printing.

Configuring Devices

A **driver** is a small program that tells the operating system how to communicate with a specific device. Each device on a computer, such as the mouse, keyboard, monitor, printer, and scanner, ha its own specialized set of commands and thus requires its own specific driver. When you boot a computer, the operating system loads each device's driver.

If you attach a new device to a computer, such as a printer or scanner, its driver must be installe before you can use the device. Today, most devices and operating systems support Plug and Play. **Plug and Play** means the operating system automatically configures new devices as you install them. With Plug and Play, a user can plug in a device, turn on the computer, and then use the device without having to configure the system manually.

Establishing an Internet Connection

Operating systems typically provide a means to establish Internet connections. For example, Windows includes a Set Up a Connection or Network wizard that guides users through the process of setting up a connection between a computer and an Internet access provider (Figure 7-6).

Some operating systems also include a Web browser and an e-mail program, enabling you to begin using the Web and comm nicate with others as soon as you set up the Internet connection. Some also include utilities to protect computers from unauthori intrusions and unwanted software such as viruses and spyware.

Figure 7-6 To connect to a network using Windows, click the Star button, click Control Panel, click Network and Internet, click Network Sharing Center, and then click 'Set up a new connection or network' t open the window shown here.

Monitoring Performance

Operating systems typically contain a performance monitor. A **performance monitor** is a program that assesses and reports information about various computer resources and devices (shown in Figure 7-1 on pages 270 and 271).

The information in performance reports helps users and administrators identify a problem with resources so that they can try to resolve any problems. If a computer is running extremely slow, for example, the performance monitor may determine that the computer's memory is being used to its maximum. Thus, you might consider installing additional memory in the computer. Read Looking Ahead 7-1 for a look at a future type of health-based performance monitor.

⤢ LOOKING AHEAD 7-1

Contact Lenses Monitor Glaucoma

The future looks good for contact lenses that will help study and treat glaucoma. Biomedical engineers at the University of California – Davis are developing lenses that measure eye pressure and then flow if the readings are abnormal.

Glaucoma occurs when the fluid pressure inside the eye increases. This intraocular pressure can result in total blindness if the optic nerve, which sends messages from the eyes to the brain, is damaged. Doctors can measure the amount of pressure and then perform surgery to correct the blockage in the back of the eye that prevents the fluid from draining. As an alternative to the pressure measurement, the new contact lenses can perform the fluidic resistance evaluation for the drainage network of the eye, which prevents dangerously high levels in the early glaucomatous eyes.

Lasers, too, are expected to become part of a doctor's means of detecting glaucoma. A high-resolution laser can measure 28 million areas of the optic nerve, and then software can create a 3-D view of the eye and assess signs of the disease.

💻 For more information, visit the Computer Concepts CourseMate Web site at www.cengagebrain.com, navigate to the Chapter 7 Looking Ahead resource for this book, and then click Contact Lenses.

Providing File Management and Other Utilities

Operating systems often provide users with the capability of managing files, searching for files, viewing images, securing a computer from unauthorized access, uninstalling programs, cleaning up disks, defragmenting disks, diagnosing problems, backing up files and disks, and setting up screen savers. A later section in the chapter discusses these and other utilities in depth.

Updating Software Automatically

Many popular programs, including most operating systems, include an **automatic update** feature that automatically provides updates to the program. With an operating system, these updates can include fixes to program bugs (errors), enhancements to security, modifications to device drivers, access to new or expanded components such as desktop themes or games, and even updates to application software on the computer such as a Web browser or an e-mail program.

Many software makers provide free downloadable updates, sometimes called a **service pack**, to users who have registered and/or activated their software. With operating systems, the automatic update feature automatically alerts users when an update is available; further, it can be configured to download and install the update automatically. Users without an Internet connection usually can order the updates on an optical disc for a minimal shipping fee. To learn about keeping Windows up-to-date, complete the Learn How To 2 exercise on pages 298 and 299.

Controlling a Network

Some operating systems are designed to work with a server on a network. A **server operating system** is an operating system that organizes and coordinates how multiple users access and share resources on a network. Resources include hardware, software, data, and information. For example, a server operating system allows multiple users to share a printer, Internet access, files, and programs.

Some operating systems have network features built into them. In other cases, the server operating system is a set of programs separate from the operating system on the client computers that access the network. When not connected to the network, the client computers use their own operating system. When connected to the network, the server operating system may assume some of the operating system functions.

The network administrator, the person overseeing network operations, uses the server operating system to add and remove users, computers, and other devices to and from the network. The network administrator also uses the server operating system to install software and administer network security.

Administering Security

Computer and network administrators typically have an **administrator account** that enables them to access all files and programs on the computer or network, install programs, and specify settings that affect all users on a computer or network. Settings include creating user accounts and establishing permissions. These permissions define who can access certain resources and when they can access those resources.

For each user, the network administrator establishes a user account, which enables a user to access, or **log on** to, a computer or a network (Figure 7-7). Each user account typically consists of a user name and password. A **user name**, or **user ID**, is a unique combination of characters, such as letters of the alphabet or numbers, that identifies one specific user. Many users select a combination of their first and last names as their user name. A user named Henry Baker might choose H Baker as his user name.

A **password** is a private combination of characters associated with the user name that allows access to certain computer resources. Some operating systems allow the computer or network administrator to assign passwords to files and commands, restricting access to only authorized users.

To prevent unauthorized users from accessing computer resources, keep your password confidential. While users type a password, most computers hide the actual password characters by displaying some other characters, such as asterisks (*) or dots. After entering a user name and password, the operating system compares the user's entry with a list of authorized user names and passwords. If the entry matches the user name and password kept on file, the operating system grants the user access. If the entry does not match, the operating system denies access to the user.

The operating system records successful and unsuccessful logon attempts in a file. This allows the computer or network administrator to review who is using or attempting to use the computer. The administrators also use these files to monitor computer usage.

To protect sensitive data and information as it travels over a network, the operating system may encrypt it. Encryption is the process of encoding data and information into an unreadable form. Administrators can specify that data be encrypted as it travels over a network to prevent unauthorized users from reading the data. When an authorized user attempts to read the data, it automatically is decrypted, or converted back into a readable form.

Figure 7-7 Most multiuser operating systems allow each user to log on, which is the process of entering a user name and a password into the computer.

QUIZ YOURSELF 7-1

Instructions: Find the true statement below. Then, rewrite the remaining false statements so that they are true.

1. A buffer is a small program that tells the operating system how to communicate with a specific device.
2. A warm boot is the process of using the operating system to restart a computer.
3. A password is a public combination of characters associated with the user name that allows access to certain computer resources.
4. The program you currently are using is in the background, and the other programs running but not in use are in the foreground.
5. Two types of system software are operating systems and application programs.

Quiz Yourself Online: To further check your knowledge of pages 270 through 278, visit the Computer Concepts CourseMate Web site at www.cengagebrain.com, navigate to the Chapter 7 Quiz Yourself resource for this book, and then click Objectives 1 – 2.

Types of Operating Systems

When you purchase a new computer or mobile device, it typically has an operating system preinstalled. As new versions of the operating system are released, users upgrade their existing computers and mobile devices to incorporate features of the new version. Purchasing an operating system upgrade usually costs less than purchasing the entire operating system.

New versions of an operating system usually are backward compatible. That is, they recognize and work with application software written for an earlier version of the operating system (or platform). By contrast, the application software may or may not be upward compatible, meaning it may or may not run on new versions of the operating system.

The three basic categories of operating systems that exist today are stand-alone, server, and embedded. The table in Figure 7-8 lists names of operating systems in each category. The following pages discuss a variety of operating systems.

Categories of Operating Systems

Category	Operating System Name
Stand-alone	• DOS • Early Windows versions (Windows 3.x, Windows 95, Windows NT Workstation, Windows 98, Windows 2000 Professional, Windows Millennium Edition, Windows XP, Windows Vista) • Windows 7 • Mac OS X • UNIX • Linux
Server	• Early Windows Server versions (Windows NT Server, Windows 2000 Server, Windows Server 2003) • Windows Server 2008 • UNIX • Linux • Solaris • NetWare
Embedded	• Windows Embedded CE • Windows Phone 7 • Palm OS • iPhone OS • BlackBerry • Google Android • Embedded Linux • Symbian OS

Figure 7-8 Examples of stand-alone, server, and embedded operating systems. Some stand-alone operating systems include the capability of configuring small home or office networks.

FAQ 7-2

Which operating systems have the most market share?

The Windows operating system family currently dominates the operating system market with more than 93 percent market share. The Mac operating system is in second place with nearly 5 percent market share. The chart to the right illustrates the market share for various operating systems.

For more information, visit the Computer Concepts CourseMate Web site at www.cengagebrain.com, navigate to the Chapter 7 FAQ resource for this book, and then click Operating System Market Share.

Operating System Market Share

☐ 93% ☐ 5% ☐ 1% ☐ 1%

☐ Windows
☐ Mac
☐ Linux
☐ Other

Source: Market Share by Net Applications

Stand-Alone Operating Systems

A **stand-alone operating system** is a complete operating system that works on a desktop computer, notebook computer, or mobile computing device. Some stand-alone operating systems are called client operating systems because they also work in conjunction with a server operating system. Client operating systems can operate with or without a network. Other stand-alone operating systems include networking capabilities, allowing the home and small business user to set up a small network. Examples of currently used stand-alone operating systems are Windows 7, Mac OS X, UNIX, and Linux.

Windows 7

In the mid-1980s, Microsoft developed its first version of Windows, which provided a graphical user interface (GUI). Since then, Microsoft continually has updated its Windows operating system, incorporating innovative features and functions with each new version. **Windows 7** is Microsoft's fastest, most efficient operating system to date, offering quicker program start up, built-in diagnostics, automatic recovery, improved security, enhanced searching and organizing capabilities, and an easy-to-use interface (Figure 7-9).

Most users choose one of these Windows 7 editions: Windows 7 Starter, Windows 7 Home Premium, Windows 7 Ultimate, or Windows 7 Professional.

- Windows 7 Starter, designed for netbooks and other small notebook computers, uses the Windows 7 Basic interface and allows users easily to search for files, connect to printers and devices, browse the Internet, join home networks, and connect to wireless networks. This edition Windows typically is preinstalled on new computers and not available for purchase in retail store
- Windows 7 Home Premium, which includes all the capabilities of Windows 7 Starter, also includes Windows Aero with its Aero Flip 3D feature and provides tools to create and edit high definition movies, record and watch television shows, connect to a game console, and read from and write on Blu-ray Discs.
- Windows 7 Ultimate, which includes all features of Windows 7 Home Premium, provides additional features designed to keep your files secure and support for 35 languages.
- With Windows 7 Professional, users in all sizes of businesses are provided a secure operating environment that uses Windows Aero where they easily can search for files, protect their computers from unauthorized intruders and unwanted programs, use improved backup technologies, securely connect to Wi-Fi networks, quickly view messages on a powered-off, specially equipped notebook computer, easily share documents and collaborate with other users, and watch and record live television.

Windows 7 adapts to the hardware configuration on which it is installed. Thus, two users with the same edition of Windows 7 may experience different functionality and interfaces.

Windows 7

 For more information, visit the Computer Concepts CourseMate Web site at www.cengagebrain.com, navigate to the Chapter 7 Web Link resource for this book, and then click Windows 7.

Figure 7-9 Windows 7 h new interface, easier naviga searching techniques, and i security.

Mac OS X

Since it was released with Macintosh computers in 1984, Apple's **Macintosh operating system** has set the standard for operating system ease of use and has been the model for most of the new GUIs developed for non-Macintosh systems. The latest version, **Mac OS X**, is a multitasking operating system available only for computers manufactured by Apple (Figure 7-10).

Mac OS X

For more information, visit the Computer Concepts CourseMate Web site at www.cengagebrain.com, navigate to the Chapter 7 Web Link resource for this book, and then click Mac OS X.

Figure 7-10 Mac OS X is the operating system used with Apple Macintosh computers.

UNIX

UNIX (pronounced YOU-nix) is a multitasking operating system. Several versions of this operating system exist, each slightly different. Although some versions of UNIX have a command-line interface, most versions of UNIX offer a graphical user interface (Figure 7-11). Today, a version of UNIX is available for most computers of all sizes. Power users often work with UNIX because of its flexibility and power.

Figure 7-11 Many versions of UNIX have a graphical user interface.

Linux

For more information, visit the Computer Concepts CourseMate Web site at www.cengagebrain.com, navigate to the Chapter 7 Web Link resource for this book, and then click Linux.

Linux

Linux is one of the faster growing operating systems. **Linux** (pronounced LINN-uks), introduced in 1991, is a popular, multitasking UNIX-type operating system. In addition to the basic operating system, Linux also includes many free programming languages and utility programs. Linux is not proprietary software like the operating systems discussed thus far. Instead, Linux is open source software, which means its code is available to the public for use, modification, and redistribution. Read Ethics & Issues 7-1 for a related discussion.

Linux is available in a variety of forms, known as distributions. Some distributions of Linux are command-line. Others are GUI (Figure 7-12). Users obtain Linux in a variety of ways. Some people download it free from the Web. Others purchase it from vendors, who bundle their own software with the operating system. Linux optical discs are included in many Linux books and also are available for purchase from vendors. For purchasers of new personal computers, some retailers such as Dell will preinstall Linux on the hard disk on request. If you want to preview the Linux operating system, you can obtain a Live CD or Live USB.

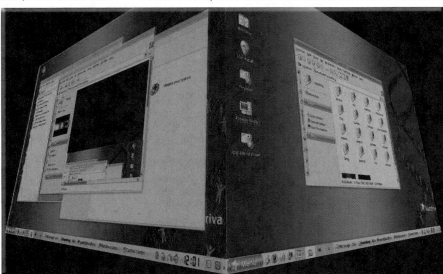

Figure 7-12 This distribution of Linux has a graphical user interface.

ETHICS & ISSUES 7-1

Closed Source vs. Open Source Operating Systems

One of the features that make Linux different from other operating systems is that Linux is open source and its source code, along with any changes, remains public. Often, when closed source operating system developers refuse to share some or all of the operating system code, third-party software developers become hindered when developing application software for the operating system. Supporters of open source maintain that source code should be open to the public so that it can be scrutinized, corrected, and enhanced. In light of concerns about security and fears of possible virus problems, however, some people are not sure open source software is a good idea. Besides, they argue, companies and programmers should be able to control, and profit from, the operating systems they create. On the other hand, open source software can be scrutinized for errors by a much larger group of people and changes can be made immediately, resulting in better software.

Are open source operating systems a good idea? Why or why not? How can the concerns about open source software be addressed? What are the advantages and disadvantages of open versus closed source operating systems? Does the open source model lead to better software?

Ethics & Issues

For the complete text of the Ethics & Issues boxes found in this chapter, visit the Computer Concepts CourseMate Web site at www.cengagebrain.com and then navigate to the Chapter 7 Ethics & Issues resource for this book.

Server Operating Systems

As discussed earlier in this chapter, a server operating system is an operating system that is designed specifically to support a network. A server operating system typically resides on a server. The client computers on the network rely on the server(s) for resources.

Many of the stand-alone operating systems discussed in the previous section function as clients and work in conjunction with a server operating system. Some of these stand-alone operating systems do include networking capability; however, server operating systems are designed specifically to support all sizes of networks, including medium- to large-sized businesses and Web servers.

Following are examples of server operating systems:

- Windows Server 2008 is an upgrade to Windows Server 2003.
- UNIX and Linux often are called multipurpose operating systems because they are both stand-alone and server operating systems.
- Solaris, a version of UNIX developed by Sun Microsystems, is a server operating system designed specifically for e-commerce applications.
- Novell's NetWare is a server operating system designed for client/server networks.

Embedded Operating Systems

The operating system on most mobile devices and many consumer electronics, called an **embedded operating system**, resides on a ROM chip. Popular embedded operating systems include Windows Embedded CE, Windows Phone 7, Palm OS, iPhone OS, BlackBerry, Google Android, embedded Linux, and Symbian OS.

- Windows Embedded CE is a scaled-down Windows operating system designed for use on communications, entertainment, and computing devices with limited functionality. Examples of devices that use Windows Embedded CE include VoIP telephones, digital cameras, point-of-sale terminals, automated teller machines, digital photo frames, fuel pumps, handheld navigation devices, portable media players, ticket machines, and computerized sewing machines.
- Windows Phone 7, which is a successor to Windows Mobile, works on specific types of smart phones. With the Windows Phone 7 operating system and a compatible device, users have access to the basic PIM (personal information manager) functions such as contact lists, schedules, tasks, calendars, and notes. These devices also can check e-mail, browse the Web, listen to music, take pictures or record video, watch a video, send and receive text messages and instant messages, record a voice message, manage finances, view a map, read an e-book, or play a game.
- Palm OS, a competing operating system to Windows Phone 7, runs on smart phones and PDAs. With Palm OS and a compatible device, users manage schedules and contacts, phone messages, notes, tasks and address lists, and appointments. Many Palm OS devices allow users to connect wirelessly to the Internet; browse the Web; send and receive e-mail messages, text messages, and instant messages; listen to music; record voice messages; and view digital photos.
- iPhone OS is an operating system for the iPhone and iPod touch. With finger motions, users can manage contacts and notes, send and receive e-mail and text messages, take pictures, record videos, record voice messages, view a compass, connect to the Internet wirelessly and browse the Web, check stocks, access maps and obtain directions, listen to music, watch movies and videos, and display photos. iPhone OS devices also provide Wi-Fi access to the iTunes Music Store.
- The BlackBerry operating system runs on handheld devices supplied by RIM (Research In Motion), shown in Figure 7-13. BlackBerry devices provide PIM, phone, and wireless capabilities such as sending e-mail messages, text messages, and instant messages; connecting to the Internet and browsing the Web; and accessing Bluetooth devices. Some also allow you to take pictures, play music, and access maps and directions.
- Google Android is an operating system designed by Google for mobile devices. Used on more than 20 different types of mobile devices, Google Android allows programmers to design programs specifically for devices supporting this operating system. Google Android contains features such as access to e-mail accounts, an alarm clock, video capture, access to Google Apps, Wi-Fi access, and easy Web browsing.
- Embedded Linux is a scaled-down Linux operating system designed for smart phones, PDAs, portable media players, Internet telephones, and many other types of devices and computers requiring an embedded operating system. Devices with embedded Linux offer calendar and address book and other PIM functions, touch screens, and handwriting recognition.
- Symbian OS is an open source multitasking operating system designed for smart phones. Users enter data by pressing keys on the keypad or keyboard, touching the screen, and writing on the screen with a stylus.

Figure 7-13 A smart phone that uses the BlackBerry operating system.

✔ **QUIZ YOURSELF 7-2**

Instructions: Find the true statement below. Then, rewrite the remaining false statements so that they are true.

1. Pocket PCs use Palm OS as their operating system.
2. Examples of embedded operating systems include Windows Server 2008, UNIX, Linux, Solaris, and NetWare.
3. Windows 7 Starter uses Windows Aero.
4. Mac OS X is a multitasking operating system available only for computers manufactured by Apple.
5. Aero Flip 3D is a UNIX-type operating system that is open source software.

⊡ **Quiz Yourself Online:** To further check your knowledge of pages 279 through 283, visit the Computer Concepts CourseMate Web site at www.cengagebrain.com, navigate to the Chapter 7 Quiz Yourself resource for this book, and then click Objectives 3 – 5.

Utility Programs

A **utility program**, also called a **utility**, is a type of system software that allows a user to perform maintenance-type tasks, usually related to managing a computer, its devices, or its programs. Most operating systems include several built-in utility programs (Figure 7-14). Users often buy stand-alone utilities, however, because they offer improvements over those included with the operating system.

Functions provided by utility programs include the following: managing files, searching for files, uninstalling programs, viewing images, cleaning up disks, defragmenting disks, backing up files and disks, setting up screen savers, securing a computer from unauthorized access, protecting against viruses, removing spyware and adware, filtering Internet content, compressing files, playing media files, burning optical discs, and maintaining a personal computer. The following sections briefly discuss each of these utilities. Read Innovative Computing 7-1 to find out about utility programs that can help you recover deleted files.

Figure 7-14 To display the utilities available in the Windows System Tools list, click the Start button, click All Programs, click Accessories, and then click System Tools.

Labels in figure: System Tools command; utility for managing files; utility for removing unwanted files; utility for defragmenting disks; utility for restoring backed up files

! **INNOVATIVE COMPUTING 7-1**

Utility Programs Locate Deleted Files

If you delete a file mistakenly from a USB flash drive, removable flash memory device, or hard disk, you easily can recover that erased file with utility programs. A few of the more popular utility programs have names that explain their purpose: Recuva, Recover My Files, FreeUndelete, FileMakerRecovery, R-Studio, and Recovery Toolbox. Most can be downloaded from the Web, often free of charge.

Data recovery experts offer advice on actions to take immediately when you realize you have erased files, even if you have emptied the Recycle Bin.

Although the file name does not appear in the list of files on that storage medium, the file actually remains intact on the storage medium. The computer marks the space on the disk as free so that another file can overwrite the contents of the deleted file. As long as you do not save any file, no matter how small, the utility program generally can locate the marked space and then retrieve the contents of the file.

⊡ For more information, visit the Computer Concepts CourseMate Web site at www.cengagebrain.com, navigate to the Chapter 7 Innovative Computing resource for this book, and then click Recovering Deleted Files.

File Manager

A **file manager** is a utility that performs functions related to file management. Some of the file management functions that a file manager performs are displaying a list of files on a storage medium (Figure 7-15); organizing files in folders; and copying, renaming, deleting, moving, and sorting files. A **folder** is a specific named location on a storage medium that contains related documents. Operating systems typically include a file manager.

Search Utility

A **search utility** is a program that attempts to locate a file on your computer based on criteria you specify (Figure 7-16). The criteria could be a word or words contained in a file, date the file was created or modified, size of the file, location of the file, file name, author/artist, and other similar properties. Search utilities can look through documents, photos, music, and other files. Operating systems typically include a built-in search utility.

Uninstaller

An **uninstaller** is a utility that removes a program, as well as any associated entries in the system files. When you install a program, the operating system records the information it uses to run the software in the system files. The uninstaller deletes files and folders from the hard disk, as well as removes program entries from the system files.

Image Viewer

An **image viewer** is a utility that allows users to display, copy, and print the contents of a graphics file. With an image viewer, users can see images without having to open them in a paint or image editing program. Most operating systems include an image viewer. Windows image viewer is called Windows Photo Viewer (Figure 7-17).

thumbnail

Figure 7-15
Windows includes file managers that allow you to view documents, photos, and music. In this case, thumbnails of photos are displayed.

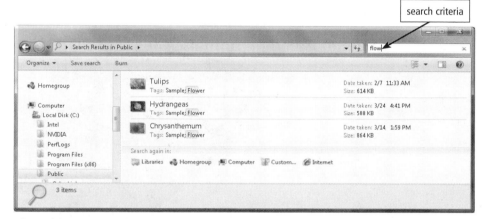

search criteria

Figure 7-16 This search displays files whose name or contents contain the text, flow.

Figure 7-17
Windows Photo Viewer allows users to see the contents of a photo file.

Disk Cleanup

A **disk cleanup** utility searches for and removes unnecessary files. Unnecessary files may include downloaded program files, temporary Internet files, deleted files, and unused program files. Operating systems, such as Windows, include a disk scanner utility.

Disk Defragmenter

A **disk defragmenter** is a utility that reorganizes the files and unused space on a computer's hard disk so that the operating system accesses data more quickly and programs run faster. When an operating system stores data on a disk, it places the data in the first available sector on the disk. It attempts to place data in sectors that are contiguous (next to each other), but this is not always possible. When the contents of a file are scattered across two or more noncontiguous sectors, the file is fragmented.

Fragmentation slows down disk access and thus the performance of the entire computer. **Defragmenting** the disk, or reorganizing it so that the files are stored in contiguous sectors, solves this problem (Figure 7-18). Operating systems usually include a disk defragmenter. Windows Disk Defragmenter is available in the System Tools list.

Figure 7-18 A fragmented disk has many files stored in noncontiguous sectors. Defragmenting reorganizes the files so that they are located in contiguous sectors, which speeds access time.

Backup and Restore Utilities

A **backup utility** allows users to copy, or back up, selected files or an entire hard disk to another storage medium such as another hard disk, optical disc, USB flash drive, or tape. During the backup process, the backup utility monitors progress and alerts you if it needs additional media, such as another disc. Many backup programs compress, or shrink the size of, files during the backup process. By compressing the files, the backup program requires less storage space for the backup files than for the original files.

Because they are compressed, you usually cannot use backup files in their backed up form. In the event you need to use a backup file, a **restore utility** reverses the process and returns backed up files to their original form. Backup utilities work with a restore utility.

You should back up files and disks regularly in the event your originals are lost, damaged, or destroyed. Operating systems include backup and restore utilities. Instead of backing up to a local disk storage device, some users opt to use cloud storage to back up their files. Cloud storage is a service on the Web that provides storage to computer users, usually for free or for a minimal monthly fee.

Screen Saver

A **screen saver** is a utility that causes a display device's screen to show a moving image or blank screen if no keyboard or mouse activity occurs for a specified time. When you press a key on the keyboard or move the mouse, the screen saver disappears and the screen returns to the previous state.

Screen savers originally were developed to prevent a problem called ghosting, in which images could be etched permanently on a monitor's screen. Although ghosting is not as severe of a problem with today's displays, manufacturers continue to recommend that users install screen savers for this reason. Screen savers also are popular for security, business, and entertainment purposes. To secure a computer, users configure their screen saver to require a password to deactivate. In addition to those included with the operating system, many screen savers are available for a minimal fee in stores and on the Web.

Personal Firewall

A **personal firewall** is a utility that detects and protects a personal computer from unauthorized intrusions. Personal firewalls constantly monitor all transmissions to and from a computer.

When connected to the Internet, your computer is vulnerable to attacks from a hacker. A hacker is someone who tries to access a computer or network illegally. Users with broadband Internet connections, such as through DSL and cable Internet service, are even more susceptible than those with dial-up access because the Internet connection always is on.

Operating systems often include a personal firewall. Windows automatically enables its built-in personal firewall, called Windows Firewall, upon installation of the operating system. If your operating system does not include a personal firewall or you want additional protection, you can purchase a stand-alone personal firewall utility (Figure 7-19) or a hardware firewall, which is a device such as a router that has a built-in firewall.

Figure 7-19 A stand-alone personal firewall utility.

Antivirus Programs

The term, computer **virus**, describes a potentially damaging computer program that affects, or infects, a computer negatively by altering the way the computer works without the user's knowledge or permission. Once the virus is in a computer, it can spread throughout and may damage your files and operating system.

Computer viruses do not generate by chance. The programmer of a virus, known as a virus author, intentionally writes a virus program. Some virus authors find writing viruses a challenge. Others write them to cause destruction. Writing a virus program usually requires significant programming skills.

Some viruses are harmless pranks that simply freeze a computer temporarily or display sounds or messages. The Music Bug virus, for example, instructs the computer to play a few chords of music. Other viruses destroy or corrupt data stored on the hard disk of the infected computer. If you notice any unusual changes in your computer's performance, it may be infected with a virus (Figure 7-20).

A **worm** copies itself repeatedly, for example, in memory or over a network, using up system resources and possibly shutting the system down. A **Trojan horse** hides within or looks like a legitimate program such as a screen saver. A certain condition or action usually triggers the Trojan horse. Unlike a virus or worm, a Trojan horse does not replicate itself to other computers. Currently, more than one million known threats to your computer exist.

To protect a computer from virus attacks, users should install an antivirus program and update it frequently. An **antivirus program** protects a computer against viruses by identifying and removing any computer viruses found in memory, on storage media, or on incoming files (Figure 7-21). Most antivirus programs also protect against worms and Trojan horses. When you purchase a new computer, it often includes antivirus software.

Three more popular antivirus programs are McAfee VirusScan, Norton AntiVirus, and Windows Live OneCare, most of which also contains spyware removers, Internet filters, and other utilities. As an alternative to purchasing these products on disc, both McAfee and Norton offer Web-based antivirus programs.

? FAQ 7-3

What steps should I take to prevent virus infections on my computer?

Set up the antivirus program to scan on a regular basis. Never open an e-mail attachment unless you are expecting the attachment and it is from a trusted source. Set macro security in programs such as word processing and spreadsheet so that you can enable or disable macros. Write-protect your recovery disk. Back up files regularly.

For more information, visit the Computer Concepts CourseMate Web site at www.cengagebrain.com, navigate to the Chapter 7 FAQ resource for this book, and then click Virus Infections.

Signs of Virus Infection

- An unusual message or image is displayed on the computer screen
- An unusual sound or music plays randomly
- The available memory is less than what should be available
- A program or file suddenly is missing
- An unknown program or file mysteriously appears
- The size of a file changes without explanation
- A file becomes corrupted
- A program or file does not work properly
- System properties change
- The computer operates much slower than usual

Figure 7-20 Viruses attack computers in a variety of ways. This list indicates some of the more common signs of virus infection.

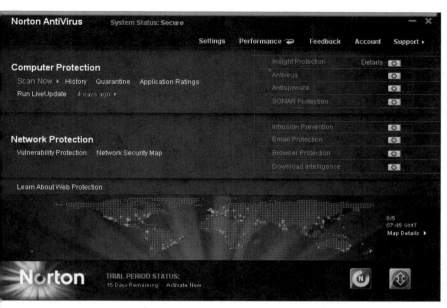

Figure 7-21 An antivirus program scans memory, disks, and incoming e-mail messages and attachments for viruses and attempts to remove any viruses it finds.

Spyware and Adware Removers

Spyware is a program placed on a computer without the user's knowledge that secretly collects information about the user, often related to Web browsing habits. The spyware program communicates information it collects to some outside source while you are online. Adware is a program that displays an online advertisement in a banner or pop-up window on Web pages, e-mail, or other Internet services. Sometimes, spyware is hidden in adware.

A **spyware remover** is a program that detects and deletes spyware, and similar programs. An **adware remover** is a program that detects and deletes adware. Most spyware and adware removers cost less than $50; some are available on the Web at no cost. Some operating systems include spyware and adware removers.

Internet Filters

Filters are programs that remove or block certain items from being displayed. Four widely used Internet filters are anti-spam programs, Web filters, phishing filters, and pop-up blockers.

Anti-Spam Programs **Spam** is an unsolicited e-mail message or newsgroup posting sent to many recipients or newsgroups at once. Spam is Internet junk mail. An **anti-spam program** is a filtering program that attempts to remove spam before it reaches your inbox. Internet access providers often filter spam as a service for their subscribers.

FAQ 7-4

Where does spam originate?

Research indicates that spam originates from various countries throughout the world. Symantec Corporation found that in a 30-day period, the United States was responsible for more spam than any other country. The chart to the right illustrates the countries responsible for the most spam worldwide.

For more information, visit the Computer Concepts CourseMate Web site at www.cengagebrain.com, navigate to the Chapter 7 FAQ resource for this book, and then click Spam.

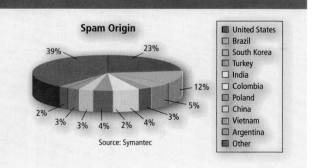

Spam Origin

39% · 23% · 12% · 5% · 3% · 4% · 2% · 4% · 3% · 3% · 2%

- United States
- Brazil
- South Korea
- Turkey
- India
- Colombia
- Poland
- China
- Vietnam
- Argentina
- Other

Source: Symantec

Web Filters **Web filtering software** is a program that restricts access to certain material on the Web. Some restrict access to specific Web sites; others filter sites that use certain words or phrases. Many businesses use Web filtering software to limit employee's Web access. Some schools, libraries, and parents use this software to restrict access to minors. Windows 7 contains parental controls, which allow parents to record and control the types of content their children can access on the Internet.

Phishing Filters **Phishing** is a scam in which a perpetrator attempts to obtain your personal and/or financial information. A **phishing filter** is a program that warns or blocks you from potentially fraudulent or suspicious Web sites. Some Web browsers include phishing filters.

Pop-Up Blockers A pop-up ad is an Internet advertisement that suddenly appears in a new window in the foreground of a Web page displayed in your browser. A **pop-up blocker** is a filtering program that stops pop-up ads from displaying on Web pages. Many Web browsers include a pop-up blocker. You also can download pop-up blockers from the Web at no cost.

File Compression

A **file compression utility** shrinks the size of a file(s). A compressed file takes up less storage space than the original file. Compressing files frees up room on the storage media and improves system performance. Attaching a compressed file to an e-mail message, for example, reduces the time needed for file transmission. Uploading and downloading compressed files to and from the Internet reduces the file transmission time.

Compressed files sometimes are called **zipped files**. When you receive or download a compressed file, you must uncompress it. To **uncompress**, or unzip, a file, you restore it to its original form. Some operating systems such as Windows include file compression and uncompression capabilities. Two popular stand-alone file compression utilities are PKZIP and WinZip.

WinZip

For more information, visit the Computer Concepts CourseMate Web site at www.cengagebrain.com, navigate to the Chapter 7 Web Link resource for this book, and then click WinZip.

Media Player

A **media player** is a program that allows you to view images and animation, listen to audio, and watch video files on your computer (Figure 7-22). Media players may also include the capability to organize media files, convert them to different formats, connect to and purchase media from an online media store, download podcasts and vodcasts, burn audio CDs, and transfer media to portable media players. Windows includes Windows Media Player. Three other popular media players are iTunes, RealPlayer, and Rhapsody. Read Ethics & Issues 7-2 for a related discussion.

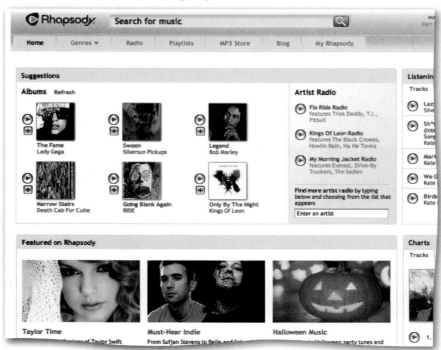

Figure 7-22
A popular media player.

Should the Government Tax Media Downloads?

When you purchase a DVD or Blu-ray Disc that contains a season or two of your favorite television show, chances are that you also pay a state and/or local sales tax. If you purchase and download the same material online in a digital format, however, chances are that you do not pay a sales tax. Some government taxing bodies seek to change that discrepancy. Two main reasons for the pressure to tax include: state and local governments feeling the pinch of lost revenue to legally downloaded digital content because consumers purchase less taxable, physical media; and pressure from the media industry to recoup lost sales due to illegally downloaded digital content. Some governments go as far as funneling collected taxes directly to the multimedia industry as compensation for illegally downloaded content that occurs in a region. Critics of the new taxes claim that government should not tax the greenest form of media purchases. Digitally downloaded content eliminates packaging, optical discs, trips to the store, and use of delivery vehicles. Critics also claim that governments single out multimedia content due to pressure from the multimedia industry. For example, some governments tax the purchase of newspapers, magazines and books, but often the same content is sold online and is not taxed. Typically, government taxing bodies tax goods, but not food and services.

Should the government tax media downloads, such as music, video, e-books, newspaper articles, and magazine articles? Why or why not? Should digital content delivery be considered a service rather than a good by taxing bodies? Why?

Disc Burning

Disc burning software writes text, graphics, audio, and video files on a recordable or rewritable CD, DVD, or Blu-ray Disc. This software enables the home user easily to back up contents of their hard disk on an optical disc and make duplicates of uncopyrighted music or movies. Disc burning software usually also includes photo editing, audio editing, and video editing capabilities (Figure 7-23). To learn about burning files to a disc, complete the Learn How To 1 exercise on page 298.

When you buy a recordable or rewritable disc, it typically includes burning software. You also can buy disc burning software for a cost of less than $100.

Figure 7-23 You can copy text, graphics, audio, and video files to discs using the digital media suite shown here, provided you have the correct type of drive and media.

Personal Computer Maintenance

Operating systems typically include a diagnostic utility that diagnoses computer problems but does not repair them. A **personal computer maintenance utility** identifies and fixes operating system problems, detects and repairs disk problems, and includes the capability of improving a computer's performance. Additionally, some personal computer maintenance utilities continuously monitor a computer while you use it to identify and repair problems before they occur. Norton SystemWorks is a popular personal computer maintenance utility designed for Windows operating systems (Figure 7-24).

Figure 7-24 A popular maintenance program for Windows users.

Instructions: Find the true statement below. Then, rewrite the remaining false statements so that they are true.

1. A pop-up blocker shrinks the size of a file(s).
2. An anti-spam program protects a computer against viruses.
3. A personal firewall is a utility that detects and protects a personal computer from unauthorized intrusions.
4. You should uninstall files and disks regularly in the event your originals are lost, damaged, or destroyed.
5. Web filtering software writes text, graphics, audio, and video files to a recordable or rewritable disc.

Quiz Yourself Online: To further check your knowledge of pages 284 through 291, visit the Computer Concepts CourseMate Web site at www.cengagebrain.com, navigate to the Chapter 7 Quiz Yourself resource for this book, and then click Objective 6.

Chapter Summary

This chapter defined an operating system and then discussed the functions common to most operating systems. The chapter introduced a variety of stand-alone operating systems, server operating systems, and embedded operating systems. Finally, the chapter described several utility programs.

Computer Usage @ Work

Education

Teachers and students have been using computers in education for many years. Teachers have been taking advantage of advances in computer technology to help provide a better educational experience for their students.

Many grade schools throughout the United States, as well as other countries, enable parents to track their child's performance online. In the past, parents would rely solely on their child bringing home graded assignments and tests to know how he or she was doing. In some cases, parents would be surprised when they saw their child's grades on report cards every two to three months. Teachers now have the opportunity to engage parents in their child's education not only by giving them an up-to-the-minute snapshot of grades, but also by posting lesson plans online so that parents know what their child is learning.

Computers and technology also benefit students in the classroom. Schools now have one or more computers in almost every classroom, enabling students to access the Internet to do research that they otherwise would have had to visit the library to perform. Schools also are able to offer additional technology courses such as Web page design, digital media, and computer programming.

At the college level, many instructors today rely heavily on e-learning systems to provide students with Web-based access to course materials and assessments, discussion forums, chat rooms, and e-mail. Once used mainly in online classes, e-learning systems provide instructors with an easy way to allow students access to the class at any time of the day.

Most instructors go beyond e-learning systems and use additional technologies to enhance their classes. For example, digital media instructors might require students to upload their assignments to a photo sharing community, and an English instructor might save paper by requiring students to upload research papers to Google Docs and share them with the instructor.

Computer use in education not only enhances the teaching experience for instructors and learning experience for students, it also provides students with technological knowledge that will benefit them for the rest of their lives.

For more information, visit the Computer Concepts CourseMate Web site at www.cengagebrain.com, navigate to the Chapter 7 Computer Usage @ Work resource for this book, and then click Education.

Companies on the Cutting Edge

VERISIGN Internet Infrastructure Services

Technology users desire immediate access to information and services. Their ability to communicate and conduct commerce securely is aided in large part by VeriSign. More than 30 billion times a day, people interact on the Internet, and their purchases, text messages, downloads, and other transactions are enabled and protected by VeriSign's infrastructure services.

Computer security company Semantic acquired VeriSign's Authentication division business in 2010 to strengthen encryption and identity services and help protect businesses and consumers by protecting information and detecting online fraud. Its domain name services department registers all .com, .net, .cc, and .tv domain names. The VeriSign Secured Seal, which has been issued to more than 100,000 domains in 145 countries, ensures companies and consumers that the Web site is secure.

The California-based company was founded in 1995 and has more than 2,200 employees worldwide.

RESEARCH IN MOTION (RIM) Wireless Mobile Communications Devices Manufacturer

By 2012, 800 million people worldwide are expected to access social networking Web sites on smart phones, up from 82 million in 2007. Research in Motion (RIM) helped fuel this networking frenzy by partnering with MySpace in 2008 to help connect networkers on the go. They can access MySpace Mobile on a BlackBerry smart phone, which is RIM's key product.

The Canadian company was founded in 1984 by Mike Lazaridis, who serves as its president and co-CEO. Lazaridis's vision for wireless technology developed in high school when he was a member of the local amateur radio and television club. He developed RIM's first major product, the Inter@active Pager, which was integrated in the first BlackBerry product in 1998. The BlackBerry gained attention for having the capability to combine a wireless mailbox with a corporate mailbox so that users could assess e-mail continuously.

Recently, Research in Motion launched BlackBerry App World, an application store that allows BlackBerry users to download personal and business programs.

For more information, visit the Computer Concepts CourseMate Web site at www.cengagebrain.com and then navigate to the Chapter 7 Companies on the Cutting Edge resource for this book.

Technology Trailblazers

STEVE WOZNIAK Apple Cofounder

Mixing fun with work comes naturally for Steve Wozniak. As Apple's cofounder, he says his computer designing career began and still continues to be a hobby filled with creativity, humor, games, and education. In his opinion, Apple's success evolved because he designed computers that had minimal parts and maximum performance.

Wozniak designed the original Apple computer in 1975 with Apple's current CEO, Steve Jobs, and wrote most of the software. Ten years later he cofounded Pixar, the award winning animation studio. He left Apple in 1985 to spend time with his family, work on community projects, and teach, but he still serves as an advisor to the corporation.

Wozinak was inducted into the Consumer Electronics Hall of Fame and the National Inventors Hall of Fame. One of his current passions is applying artificial intelligence to the area of robotics. He also is a member of the Silicon Valley Aftershocks, a polo team that plays using Segway electric transportation devices.

LINUS TORVALDS Linux Creator

Inductees to the Computer History Museum in Mountain View, CA, are noted for their contribution to computer technology. Linus Torvalds joined the Museum's Hall of Fellows in 2008 for his creation of the open source operating system, Linux.

When he developed an operating system in 1991, he announced his project in an Internet newsgroup. He made the source code available and asked readers for suggestions to enhance the product. Computer users responded by reviewing the system and offering enhancements. Three years later he released a greatly enhanced version he called Linux.

Torvalds developed this innovative operating system when he was a 21-year-old computer science student in Finland. Today, he leads the development of Linux as a fellow at OSDL (Open Source Development Labs), a not-for-profit consortium of companies dedicated to developing and promoting the operating system. Torvalds says his daily involvement with Linux involves coordinating and merging the lines of code submitted by users so that the software runs smoothly.

For more information, visit the Computer Concepts CourseMate Web site at www.cengagebrain.com and then navigate to the Chapter 7 Technology Trailblazers resource for this book.

Chapter Review

The Chapter Review reinforces the main concepts presented in this chapter.

To listen to an audio version of this Chapter Review, visit the Computer Concepts CourseMate Web site at www.cengagebrain.com and then navigate to the Chapter 7 Chapter Review resource for this book.

1. What Is System Software, and What Are the Two Types of System Software? **System software** consists of the programs that control or maintain the operations of a computer and its devices. Two types of system software are operating systems and utility programs. System software serves as the interface between the user, the application software, and the computer's hardware. An **operating system (OS)** is a set of programs that contains instructions that work together to coordinate all the activities among computer hardware resources. Different sizes of computers typically use different operating systems because operating systems generally are written to run on a specific type of computer. A **utility program**, or **utility**, performs maintenance-type tasks, usually related to managing a computer, its devices, or its programs.

2. What Are the Functions of an Operating System? The operating system starts and shuts down a computer, provides a user interface, manages programs, manages memory, coordinates tasks, configures devices, establishes an Internet connection, monitors performance, provides file management and other utilities, updates automatically, controls a network, and administers security. The **user interface** controls how data and instructions are entered and how information is displayed. Two types of user interfaces are a **graphical user interface (GUI)** and a **command-line interface**. Managing programs refers to how many users, and how many programs, an operating system can support at one time. An operating system can be single user/single tasking, single user/multitasking, **multiuser**, or **multiprocessing**. **Memory management** optimizes the use of random access memory (RAM). **Virtual memory** is a concept in which the operating system allocates a portion of a storage medium, usually the hard disk, to function as additional RAM. Coordinating tasks determines the order in which tasks are processed. Configuring devices involves loading each device's driver when a user boots the computer. A **driver** is a small program that tells the operating system how to communicate with a specific device. Establishing an Internet connection sets up a connection between a computer and an Internet access provider. A **performance monitor** is a program that assesses and reports information about computer resources and devices. Operating systems often provide the capability of managing and searching for files, viewing images, securing a computer from unauthorized access, uninstalling programs, and other tasks. Most operating systems include an **automatic update** feature that provides updates to the program. A **server operating system** is an operating system that organizes and coordinates how multiple users access and share network resources. Network administrators typically have an **administrator account** that enables them to access files, install programs, and specify network settings.

Visit the Computer Concepts CourseMate Web site at www.cengagebrain.com, navigate to the Chapter 7 Quiz Yourself resource for this book, and then click Objectives 1 – 2.

3. What Are Features of Windows 7, Mac OS X, UNIX, and Linux Operating Systems? **Windows 7** is Microsoft's fastest, most efficient operating system to date, offering quicker program start up, built-in diagnostics, automatic recovery, improved security, enhanced searching and organizing capabilities, and an easy-to-use interface. Most users choose between Windows 7 Starter, Windows 7 Home Premium, Windows 7 Ultimate, or Windows 7 Professional editions. **Mac OS X** is a multitasking GUI operating system available only for Apple computers. **UNIX** is a multitasking operating system that is flexible and powerful. **Linux** is a popular, multitasking UNIX-type operating system that is open source software, which means its code is available to the public for use, modification, and redistribution.

4. What Are the Various Server Operating Systems? Server operating systems are designed to support all sizes of networks, including medium- to large-sized businesses and Web servers. An example of a server operating system is Windows Server 2008. UNIX and Linux often are called multipurpose operating systems because they are both stand-alone and server operating systems. Solaris is a server operating system designed specifically for e-commerce applications. Novell's NetWare is a server operating system designed for client/server networks.

5. What Are Several Embedded Operating Systems? Most mobile devices and many consumer electronics have an **embedded operating system** that resides on a ROM chip. Popular embedded operating systems include the following. Windows Embedded CE is a scaled-down Windows operating system designed for use on communications, entertainment, and computing devices with limited functionality, such as VoIP telephones, digital cameras, point-of-sale terminals, automated teller machines, digital photo frames, handheld navigation devices, and portable media players. Windows Phone 7, which is a successor to Windows Mobile, works on specific types of smart phones. Palm OS is an operating system used

on smart phones and PDAs. iPhone OS is an operating system for iPhone and iPod touch. The BlackBerry operating system runs on handheld devices supplied by RIM. Google Android is an operating system developed by Google for mobile devices. Embedded Linux is a scaled-down Linux operating system for smart phones, PDAs, portable media players, and other devices. Symbian OS is an open source multitasking operating system designed for smart phones.

Visit the Computer Concepts CourseMate Web site at www.cengagebrain.com, navigate to the Chapter 7 Quiz Yourself resource for this book, and then click Objectives 3 – 5.

6. What Is the Purpose of Several Utility Programs? Most operating systems include several built-in utility programs. A **file manager** performs functions related to file management. A **search utility** attempts to locate a file on your computer based on criteria you specify. An **image viewer** displays, copies, and prints the contents of a graphics file. An **uninstaller** removes a program and any associated entries in the system files. A **disk cleanup** utility searches for and removes unnecessary files. A **disk defragmenter** reorganizes the files and unused space on a computer's hard disk. A **backup utility** is used to copy, or back up, selected files or an entire hard disk to another storage medium. A **restore utility** reverses the backup process and returns backed up files to their original form. A **screen saver** displays a moving image or blank screen if no keyboard or mouse activity occurs for a specified time. A **personal firewall** detects and protects a personal computer from unauthorized intrusions. An **antivirus program** protects computers against a **virus**, or potentially damaging computer program, by identifying and removing any computer viruses. A **spyware remover** detects and deletes spyware and similar programs. An **adware remover** detects and deletes adware. An **anti-spam program** attempts to remove **spam** before it reaches your inbox. **Web filtering software** restricts access to certain material on the Web. A **phishing filter** warns or blocks you from potentially fraudulent or suspicious Web sites. A **pop-up blocker** stops pop-up ads from displaying on Web pages. A **file compression utility** shrinks the size of a file. A **media player** allows you to view images and animation, listen to audio, and watch video files on a computer. **Disc burning software** writes on a recordable or rewritable CD, DVD, or Blu-ray Disc. A **personal computer maintenance utility** identifies and fixes operating system or disk problems and improves a computer's performance.

Visit the Computer Concepts CourseMate Web site at www.cengagebrain.com, navigate to the Chapter 7 Quiz Yourself resource for this book, and then click Objective 6.

Key Terms

You should know each key term. The list below helps focus your study.

To see an example of and a definition for each term, and to access current and additional information from the Web, visit the Computer Concepts CourseMate Web site at www.cengagebrain.com and then navigate to the Chapter 7 Key Terms resource for this book.

administrator account (278)
adware remover (289)
anti-spam program (289)
antivirus program (288)
automatic update (277)
backup utility (286)
booting (272)
buffer (275)
cold boot (272)
command-line interface (273)
defragmenting (286)
disc burning software (291)
disk cleanup (286)
disk defragmenter (286)
driver (276)
embedded operating system (283)
file compression utility (290)
file manager (285)

folder (285)
graphical user interface (GUI) (273)
hibernate (272)
image viewer (285)
Linux (282)
log on (278)
Mac OS X (281)
Macintosh operating system (281)
media player (290)
memory management (275)
multiprocessing (275)
multiuser (275)
operating system (OS) (271)
password (278)
performance monitor (277)
personal computer maintenance utility (291)

personal firewall (287)
phishing (290)
phishing filter (290)
Plug and Play (276)
pop-up blocker (290)
queue (276)
restore utility (286)
screen saver (287)
search utility (285)
server operating system (277)
service pack (277)
sleep mode (272)
spam (289)
spooling (275)
spyware remover (289)
stand-alone operating system (280)
system software (270)
Trojan horse (288)

uncompress (290)
uninstaller (285)
UNIX (281)
user ID (278)
user interface (272)
user name (278)
utility (284)
utility program (284)
virtual memory (275)
virus (288)
warm boot (272)
Web filtering software (290)
Windows 7 (280)
Windows Aero (273)
Windows ReadyBoost (275)
worm (288)
zipped files (290)

Checkpoint

The Checkpoint exercises test your knowledge of the chapter concepts. The page number containing the answer appears in parentheses after each exercise.

To complete the Checkpoint exercises interactively, visit the Computer Concepts CourseMate Web site at www.cengagebrain.com and then navigate to the Chapter 7 Checkpoint resource for this book.

Multiple Choice Select the best answer.

1. In the Windows 7 operating system, _____ provides an enhanced visual look, additional navigation options, and animation. (273)
 a. Windows Aero
 b. Plug and Play
 c. Mac OS X
 d. Windows 7 Starter

2. Windows users can increase the size of memory through _____, which can allocate available storage space on removable flash memory devices as additional memory cache. (275)
 a. Windows Aero
 b. Plug and Play
 c. Windows ReadyBoost
 d. a disk defragmenter

3. A _____ is a small program that tells the operating system how to communicate with a specific device. (276)
 a. buffer
 b. driver
 c. performance monitor
 d. device

4. Computer and network administrators typically have a(n) _____ that enables them to access all files and programs on the computer or network, install programs, and specify settings that affect all users on a computer or network. (278)
 a. file manager
 b. personal computer maintenance utility
 c. administrator account
 d. graphical user interface

5. The operating system on most mobile devices and many consumer electronics, called a(n) _____, resides on a ROM chip. (283)
 a. network operating system
 b. embedded operating system
 c. stand-alone operating system
 d. stand-alone utility program

6. A _____ is a specific named location on a storage medium that contains related documents. (285)
 a. file
 b. buffer
 c. utility
 d. folder

7. A(n) _____ is a program that warns or blocks you from potentially fraudulent or suspicious Web sites. (290)
 a. phishing filter
 b. adware remover
 c. Web filter
 d. Trojan horse

8. A(n) _____ is a program that allows you to view images and animation, listen to audio, and watch video files on your computer. (290)
 a. file manager
 b. media player
 c. service pack
 d. image viewer

Matching Match the terms with their definitions.

_____ 1. sleep mode (272)

_____ 2. hibernate (272)

_____ 3. virus (288)

_____ 4. worm (288)

_____ 5. spam (289)

a. a potentially damaging computer program that affects, or infects, a computer negatively by altering the way the computer works without the user's knowledge or permission

b. copies itself repeatedly using up system resources and possibly shutting the system down

c. saves any open documents and programs to a hard disk before removing power from the computer

d. hides within or looks like a legitimate program such as a screen saver

e. saves any open documents and programs to RAM, turns off all unneeded functions, and then places the computer in a low-power state

f. an unsolicited e-mail message or newsgroup posting sent to many recipients or newsgroups at once

Short Answer Write a brief answer to each of the following questions.

1. How is a cold boot different from a warm boot? _____ How is a memory-resident part of an operating system different from a nonresident part of an operating system? _____

2. What is the purpose of an automatic update feature? _____ Why and when might a user receive a service pack? _____

3. How does a file become fragmented? _____ How does a disk defragmenter work? _____

4. What are the differences between Windows 7 Starter and Windows 7 Home Premium? _____ What is the difference between Windows 7 Ultimate and Windows 7 Professional? _____

5. What is a backup utility, and what happens during a backup? _____ What is the purpose of a restore utility? _____

Problem Solving

The Problem Solving exercises extend your knowledge of the chapter concepts by seeking solutions to practical computer problems that you may encounter at home, school, or work. The Collaboration exercise should be completed with a team.

In the real world, practical problems often can be solved in multiple ways. Provide one solution to each of the following problems using available resources, such as articles on the Web or in print, blogs, podcasts, videos, television, user guides, other individuals, and electronics and computer stores. You may need to use multiple resources to obtain an answer. Present your solutions in the form requested by your instructor (brief report, presentation, discussion, or other means).

@ Home

1. **Computer Cannot Boot** You recently purchased a computer from your friend. When you turn on the computer, a message displays that says, "Operating system not found." What steps will you take before calling technical support?

2. **Incorrect Display Settings** You have been using the same display settings since purchasing your computer several months ago. You recently turn on your computer and notice that the screen resolution, desktop background, and color scheme has changed, even though you have not changed the display settings. What might have caused Windows to change your display settings? What are your next steps?

3. **Maximum CPU Usage** Because your computer is performing slowly, you start the Windows Task Manager to investigate. You see that the CPU usage is near 100%. You are not aware of any other programs currently running. What might be causing this?

4. **Unwanted Programs** The new computer that you ordered online arrived today. You anxiously unpack it, connect all the components, and then turn it on. After answering a series of questions to set up the computer, you notice it includes programs that you do not want. How will you remove these unwanted programs?

@ Work

5. **Password Required** After turning on your computer, it prompts you to type a password to continue the boot process; however, you forgot the password. What are your next steps to allow the computer to continue the boot process, start Windows, and access the files on the hard disk?

6. **Automatic Updates** Two or three times per month, your coworker receives a notification on his computer that the computer recently has been updated. You ask your coworker about these messages, and he says that Microsoft periodically installs updates automatically to protect the computer from various threats, as well as to improve performance. You never have seen this message appear on your computer. Does this mean that your computer does not update automatically? How can you configure your computer to update automatically?

7. **Antivirus Schedule** You recently changed your work schedule so that you work until 6:00 p.m. instead of 5:00 p.m. At 5:00 p.m. each day, you notice that the antivirus program on your computer automatically begins scanning all files on your hard disk. This process slows your computer, and the program usually still is scanning when you leave the office. How can you change the configuration so that the antivirus program does not start until after you leave?

8. **Minimum Battery Power** When you use your notebook computer and it is not plugged in, the battery lasts for only one hour, but the documentation states that the computer can last for two hours on battery power. What are some ways that you can increase the battery life?

Collaboration

9. **Computers in Education** A private elementary school in your neighborhood has received a grant to create a computer lab with Internet access so that students can learn about computers and related technologies. Your neighbor, who also is a teacher at the school, asks for advice regarding how they should spend the grant money. Form a team of three people to determine the best configuration for the lab. One team member should research whether a PC or Mac is more beneficial. Another team member should research the application software that should be installed on these computers, and the other team member should determine what, if any, peripheral devices should be attached to the computers in the lab. Compile your findings and submit them to your instructor.

Learn How To

The Learn How To activities step you through fundamental technology skills when using a computer. The Learn How To exercises enable you to become more proficient with these skills.

Premium Activity: To relate this Learn How To activity to your everyday life, see a visual demonstration of the activity, and complete a short assessment, visit the Computer Concepts CourseMate Web site at www.cengagebrain.com and then navigate to the Chapter 7 Learn How To resource for this book.

Learn How To 1: Burn Files to an Optical Disc

Many people use USB flash drives to transport files from one location to another. If they wish to share files with someone else, however, they might choose to distribute these files on an optical disc. To learn how to burn files to an optical disc using Windows 7, complete the following steps:

1. Insert a blank optical disc into the optical disc drive.
2. When the AutoPlay dialog box is displayed, click the Burn files to disc using Windows Explorer link.
3. If necessary, change the Disc title, click the 'Like a USB flash drive' option button, and then click the Next button in the Burn a Disc dialog box to prepare the blank disc.
4. Drag the files you wish to burn to the empty window that opens.
5. Click the 'Burn to disk' button.
6. Click the Next button to burn the files to the disc. When the disc has finished burning, remove the disc from the optical disc drive.

Exercise

1. Locate photos on your computer that you are willing to share with others. If you are unable to locate any photos or are using someone else's computer, download at least three photos from the Internet. Insert a blank optical disc into your optical disc drive and then burn the photos to the disc. Once you have finished burning the disc, eject it, write your name on it, and then submit it to your instructor.

Learn How To 2: Keep Windows Up-to-Date

All Programs list

Windows Update

Figure 7-25

Keeping Windows up-to-date is a critical part of keeping your computer in working order. The updates made available by Microsoft for no charge over the Internet can help to keep errors from occurring on your computer and attempt to ensure that all security safeguards are in place. To update Windows, complete the next steps:

1. Click the Start button on the Windows taskbar, click All Programs, and then click Windows Update in the All Programs list (Figure 7-25) to open the Windows Update window.
2. Click the link indicating that updates are available.
3. If necessary, select those updates you wish to install and then click the OK button. Be aware that some updates might take 20 minutes or more to download and install, based primarily on your Internet access speed.
4. Often, after installation of updates, you must restart your computer to allow those updates to take effect. Be sure to save any open files before restarting your computer.

You also can schedule automatic updates for your computer. To do so, complete the following steps:

1. Click the Start button on the Windows taskbar and then click Control Panel on the Start menu.
2. In the Control Panel window, click System and Security to open the System and Security window.
3. In the System and Security window, click 'Turn automatic updating on or off' to open the Change settings window (Figure 7-26).
4. Select the option you want to use for Windows updates. Microsoft, together with all security and operating system experts, strongly recommends you select 'Install updates automatically' so that updates will be installed on your computer automatically. Notice that if you select 'Install updates automatically', you also should select a time when your computer will be on and be connected to the Internet. A secondary choice is to download the suggested updates and then choose when you want to install them, and a third choice allows you to check for updates and then choose when you want to download and install them.
5. When you have made your selection, click the OK button in the Change settings window.

Updating Windows on your computer is vital to maintain security and operational integrity.

Exercises

1. Open the Windows Update window. Make a list of the important updates to Windows on the computer you are using. Add to the list the optional updates that are available. If you are using your own computer, install the updates of your choice on your computer. Submit the list of updates to your instructor.

2. **Optional: If you are not using your own computer, do not complete this exercise.** Open the Control Panel, click System and Security, and then click 'Turn automatic updating on or off'. Select the level of automatic updates you want to use. Write a report justifying your choice of automatic updates and then submit the report to your instructor.

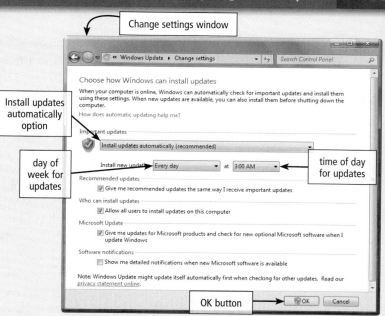

Figure 7-26

Learn It Online

The Learn It Online exercises are interactive Web exercises designed to reinforce and expand your understanding of the chapter concepts. The descriptions below briefly summarize each exercise.

To complete the Learn It Online exercises, visit the Computer Concepts CourseMate Web site at www.cengagebrain.com, navigate to the Chapter 7 resources for this book, click the link for the exercise you want to complete, and then read the instructions.

❶ At the Movies — Free Online Antivirus
Watch a movie to learn why it is important to run antivirus software on your computer and how to scan your computer for malware online for no cost and then answer questions about the movie.

❷ Student Edition Labs — Installing and Uninstalling Software and Keeping Your Computer Virus Free
Enhance your understanding and knowledge about installing and uninstalling software and keeping your computer virus free by completing the Installing and Uninstalling Software and Keeping Your Computer Virus Free Labs.

❸ Practice Test
Take a multiple choice test that checks your knowledge of the chapter concepts and review the resulting study guide.

❹ Who Wants To Be a Computer Genius²?
Play the Shelly Cashman Series version of this popular game by answering questions to find out if you are a computer genius. Panic buttons are available to provide assistance during game play.

❺ Crossword Puzzle Challenge
Complete an interactive crossword puzzle to reinforce concepts presented in this chapter.

❻ Windows Exercises
Step through the Windows 7 exercises to learn about Windows, using a screen saver, changing desktop colors, customizing the desktop for multiple users, and backing up a computer.

❼ Exploring Computer Careers
Read about a career as a systems programmer, search for related employment advertisements, and then answer related questions.

❽ Web Apps — Photoshop Express
Learn how to use Photoshop Express to upload new photos as well as photos stored on other photo sharing communities, edit photos, create new pictures, and share them with others.

Web Research

The Web Research exercises broaden your understanding of chapter concepts by presenting questions that require you to search the Web for answers.

1 Search Sleuth

Use one of the search engines listed in Figure 2-8 in Chapter 2 on page 65 or your own favorite search engine to find the answers to the following questions. Copy and paste the Web address from the Web page where you found the answer. Some questions may have more than one answer. If required, submit your answers to your instructor. (1) Who are the "goons" who attend DEFCON? What color shirts do they wear? (2) Which product does IBM propose in its "Reincarnating PCs with Portable SoulPads" paper? (3) Which bird is the mascot for Linux? What is the mascot's name? (4) Why do some computer experts consider the term, spool, a backronym? (5) Who invented the Control-Alt-Delete (CTRL+ALT+DEL) key combination used to reboot a computer? (6) Which virus did the Farooq Alvi brothers invent? (7) Why would a programmer use the EICAR test file? (8) Why are UNIX programmers concerned about the "Year 2038 problem"?

2 Green Computing

Operating systems can help monitor computer energy use and suggest methods of reducing electricity through efficient power management. Experts claim monitoring systems can save each computer user at least $60 per year in electricity costs. Suggestions include not using a screen saver, turning down a monitor's brightness level, maximizing the standby and sleep settings, and using a power saver or high performance power setting that balances processing power with notebook computer battery life. View online Web sites that provide information about power management. Which methods are effective in reducing power consumption, especially for notebook computers? Which sleep state setting gives significant power savings? Which power management settings are recommended for balanced, power saver, and high performance? Write a report summarizing your findings, and include a table of links to Web sites that provide additional details.

3 Social Networking

Social networking Web site advertisers in the United States spent $108 million in 2009, an increase of 119 percent in one year. General Motors and Proctor & Gamble are two of the larger marketers exploring the placement of advertising on social networking Web sites. Millions of registered online social networking users have posted demographic information about themselves, including age, gender, and geographical location. This data helps marketing managers deliver specific advertisements to each user in an attempt to raise revenue to support their Web sites. Adknowledge (adknowledge.com) is one of the primary companies that gathers and studies data regarding online users and then sells targeted ads on social networking, e-mail, and gaming Web sites. Visit the Adknowledge Web site, view the information about targeting social network consumers, and then read articles in the About Us and Press Room sections. How are advertisers using virtual currency? How do traffic networks help advertisers create marketing campaigns? View the posts in the Adverblog Web site (adverblog.com) to read about interactive marketing trends. Summarize the information you read and viewed.

4 Blogs

Search engines help locate Web pages about certain topics based on the search text specified. A number of the search engine Web sites feature blogs describing popular search topics. For example, Ask.com's blog (blog.ask.com) lists its Blogroll, which gives recommended research and search engine Web sites. The Yahoo! Search blog (ysearchblog.com) includes news about consumer search trends (Yahoo! Buzz) and innovations in Web search technology. Google Blog Search (blogsearch.google.com) has search engines to help users find blogs about particular topics, including politics, technology, sports, and business. Visit these sites and read the posts. What topics are discussed? Compose search queries about issues and products discussed in this chapter, such as personal firewalls or antivirus programs, and read a few of the blogs describing these topics. Summarize the information you read and viewed.

5 Ethics in Action

Several automobile insurers, including Progressive Casualty Insurance Company, are promising drivers insurance premium discounts if they install a data recorder in their cars to track their driving and then exercise good driving behavior. Progressive customers voluntarily using the MyRate wireless device hope to decrease their insurance bills by a maximum of 25 percent. Privacy experts predict more insurance companies will offer this monitoring system and that it eventually will become mandatory. These critics fear that negative data will be used against poor drivers and possibly be subpoenaed in litigation. View online sites that provide information about vehicle monitoring devices. Write a report summarizing your findings, and include a table of links to Web sites that provide additional details.

Buyer's Guide:
How to Purchase Computers and Mobile Devices

AT SOME POINT, perhaps while you are taking this course, you may decide to buy a computer or mobile device (Figure 1). The decision is an important one and will require an investment of both time and money. Like many buyers, you may have little experience with technology and find yourself unsure of how to proceed. You can start by talking to your friends, coworkers, and instructors about their computers and mobile devices. What type of computers and mobile devices did they buy? Why? For what purposes do they use their computers and mobile devices?

desktop computer

portable media player

notebook computer

smart phone

digital camera

Figure 1 Computers and mobile devices.

How to Purchase a Desktop Computer

A desktop computer sits on or below a desk or table in a stationary location such as a home, office, or dormitory room. Desktop computers are a good option if you work mostly in one place and have plenty of space in a work area. Desktop computers generally provide more performance for your money. Today, manufacturers are placing more emphasis on style by offering bright colors, stylish displays, and theme-based displays so that the computer looks attractive if it is in an area of high visibility. Once you have decided that a desktop computer is most suited to your computing needs, the next step is to determine specific software, hardware, peripheral devices, and services to purchase, as well as where to buy the computer.

❶ Determine the specific software to use on your computer.

Before deciding to purchase software, be sure it contains the features necessary for the tasks you want to perform. Rely on the computer users in whom you have confidence to help you decide on the software to use. In addition, consider purchasing software that might help you perform tasks at home that you otherwise would perform at another location, such as at school or at work. The minimum requirements of the software you select may determine the operating system (Microsoft Windows, Mac OS, Linux) you need. If you decide to use a particular operating system that does not support software you want to use, you may be able to purchase similar software from other manufacturers.

Many Web sites and trade magazines provide reviews of software products. These Web sites frequently have articles that rate computers and software on cost, performance, and support.

Your hardware requirements depend on the minimum requirements of the software you will run on your computer. Some software requires more memory and disk space than others, as well as additional input, output, and storage devices. For example, suppose you want to run software that can copy one optical disc's contents directly to another optical disc, without first copying the data to the hard disk. To support that, you should consider a desktop computer or a high-end notebook computer, because the computer will need two optical disc drives: one that reads from an optical disc, and one that writes on an optical disc. If you plan to run software that allows your computer to function as an entertainment system, then you will need an optical disc drive, quality speakers, and an upgraded sound card.

❷ Know the system requirements of the operating system.

After determining the software you want to run on your new computer, the next step is to determine the operating system to use. If, however, you purchase a new computer, chances are it will have the latest version of your preferred operating system (Windows, Mac OS, Linux).

❸ Look for bundled software.

When you purchase a computer, it may include bundled software. Some sellers even let you choose which software you want. Remember, however, that bundled software has value only if you would have purchased the software even if it had not been included with the computer. At the very least, you probably will want word processing software and an antivirus program. If you need additional programs, such as a spreadsheet, a database, or presentation software, consider purchasing or downloading Microsoft Office, Microsoft Works, OpenOffice.org, or Sun StarOffice, which include several programs at a reduced price or at no cost.

❹ Avoid buying the least powerful computer available.

Once you know the application software you want to use, then consider the following important criteria about the computer's components: (1) processor speed, (2) size and types of memory (RAM) and storage, (3) types of input/output devices, (4) types of ports and adapter cards, and (5) types of communications devices. You also should consider if the computer is upgradeable and to what extent you are able to upgrade. For example, all manufacturers limit the amount of memory you can add. The information in Figure 2 on pages 303 and 304 can help you determine which computer components are best for you and outlines considerations for specific hardware components. For a sample Base Components worksheet that lists PC recommendations for each category of user discussed in this

Considerations for Hardware Components

Card Reader/Writer: A card reader/writer is useful for transferring data directly to and from a memory card, such as the type used in a digital camera, smart phone, or portable media player. Make sure the card reader/writer can read from and write on the memory cards that you use.

Digital Video Capture Device: A digital video capture device allows you to connect a computer to a video camera or VCR and record, edit, manage, and then write video back on an optical disc or VCR tape. To create quality video (true 30 frames per second, full-sized TV), the digital video capture device should have a USB or FireWire port.

External Hard Disk: An external hard disk can serve many purposes: it can serve as extra storage for your computer, provide a way to store and transport large files or large quantities of files, and provide a convenient way to back up data on other internal and external hard disks. External hard disks can be purchased with the same capacity as any internal disk.

Fingerprint Reader: For added security, you may want to consider purchasing a fingerprint reader. It helps prevent unauthorized access to your computer and also allows you to log onto Web sites quickly via your fingerprint, rather than entering a user name and password each time you access the site. Most use a USB connection and require software installation.

Hard Disk: It is recommended that you buy a computer with at least a 320 GB hard disk if your primary interests are browsing the Web and using e-mail and Office suite-type programs; 1 TB if you also want to edit digital photos or if you plan to edit digital video or manipulate large audio files even occasionally; and 2 TB if you will edit digital video, movies, or photos often; store audio files and music; or consider yourself to be a power user. Internal hard disk controllers are available with the RAID option for added data protection.

Joystick/Wheel: If you use the computer to play games, then you will want to purchase a joystick or a wheel. These devices, especially the more expensive ones, provide for realistic game play with force feedback, programmable buttons, and specialized levers and wheels.

Keyboard: The keyboard is one of the more important devices used to communicate with the computer. For this reason, make sure the keyboard you purchase has 101 to 105 keys, is comfortable and easy to use, and has a USB connection. A wireless keyboard should be considered, especially if you have a small desk area.

Microphone: If you plan to record audio or use speech recognition to enter text and commands, then purchase a close-talk headset with gain adjustment support.

Modem: Most computers include a modem so that you can use a telephone line to access the Internet. Some modems also have fax capabilities. Your modem should be rated at 56 Kbps.

Monitor: The monitor is where you will view documents, read e-mail messages, and view pictures. A minimum of a 19" LCD flat-panel monitor is recommended, but if you plan to use the computer for graphic design or game playing, then you may want to purchase a 22" or 27" monitor. Instead of a single large, widescreen monitor, you may want to consider a side-by-side monitor setup.

Mouse: While working with a desktop computer, you use the mouse constantly. Make sure the mouse has a wheel, which acts as a third button in addition to the top two buttons on the left and right. An ergonomic design also is important because your hand is on the mouse most of the time when you are using the computer. A wireless mouse should be considered to eliminate the cord and allow you to work at short distances from the computer.

Optical Disc Drives: Most computers include a DVD±RW combination drive and/or DVD/Blu-ray Disc drive. A DVD±RW or a Blu-ray Disc drive allows you to read optical discs and to write data on (burn) an optical disc. It also will allow you to store and share video files, digital photos, and other large files with other people who have access to a DVD/Blu-ray Disc drive. A Blu-ray Disc has a capacity of at least 25 GB, and a DVD has a capacity of at least 4.7 GB, versus the 650 MB capacity of a CD.

Figure 2 Hardware guidelines. *(continues)*

Considerations for Hardware Components

Ports: Depending on how you are using the computer, you may need anywhere from 4 to 10 USB ports. USB ports have become the connection of choice in the computer industry. They offer an easy way to connect peripheral devices such as printers, digital cameras, and portable media players. Many computers intended for home or professional audio/video use have built-in FireWire ports. Most personal computers include a minimum of six USB ports, two FireWire ports, and an Ethernet port.

Printer: Your two basic printer choices are ink-jet and laser. Color ink-jet printers cost on average between $50 and $300. Laser printers cost from $200 to $2,000. In general, the less expensive the printer, the lower the resolution and speed, and the more often you are required to change the ink cartridges or toner. Laser printers print faster and with a higher quality than an ink-jet, and their toner on average costs less.

Processor: For a personal computer, an Intel Core i7 processor at 2.93 GHz is more than enough processor power for most home and small office/home office users. Game home, enterprise, and power users should upgrade to faster, more powerful processors.

RAM: RAM plays a vital role in the speed of a computer. Make sure the computer you purchase has at least 2 GB of RAM. If you have extra money to invest in a computer, consider increasing the RAM. The extra money for RAM will be well spent because more RAM typically translates into more speed.

Scanner: The most popular scanner purchased with a computer today is the flatbed scanner. When evaluating a flatbed scanner, check the color depth and resolution. Do not buy anything less than a color depth of 48 bits and a resolution of 1200 x 2400 dpi. The higher the color depth, the more accurate the color. A higher resolution picks up the more subtle gradations of color.

Sound Card: Many computers include a standard sound card that supports Dolby 5.1 surround and are capable of recording and playing digital audio. Make sure they are suitable in the event you decide to use the computer as an entertainment or gaming system.

Speakers: Once you have a good sound card, quality speakers and a separate subwoofer that amplifies the bass frequencies of the speakers can turn the computer into a premium stereo system.

USB Flash Drive: If you work on different computers and need access to the same data and information, then this portable flash memory device is ideal. USB flash drive capacity varies from 1 GB to 16 GB.

USB Hub: If you plan to connect several peripheral devices to the computer at the same time, then you need to be concerned with the number of ports available on the computer. If the computer does not have enough ports, then you should purchase a USB hub. A USB hub plugs into a single USB port and provides several additional ports.

Video Card: Most standard video cards satisfy the monitor display needs of most home and small office users. If you are a game home user or a graphic designer, you will want to upgrade to a higher quality video card. The higher refresh rates will further enhance the display of games, graphics, and movies.

Web Cam: A Web cam is a small digital video camera that can capture and display live video on a Web page. You also can capture, edit, and share video and still photos. Recommended minimum specifications include 640 x 480 resolution, a video with a rate of 30 frames per second, and a USB or FireWire port. Some Web cams are built into computer monitors.

Wireless LAN Access Point: A wireless LAN access point allows you to network several computers, so that multiple users can share files and access the Internet through a single broadband connection. Each device that you connect requires a wireless card. A wireless LAN access point can offer a range of operations up to several hundred feet, so be sure the device has a high-powered antenna.

Figure 2 Hardware guidelines. *(continued)*

book, visit the Computer Concepts CourseMate Web site at www.cengagebrain.com and then navigate to the Buyer's Guide Feature resource for this book. In the worksheet, the Home User category is divided into two groups: Application Home User and Game Home User.

Computer technology changes rapidly, meaning a computer that seems powerful enough today may not serve your computing needs in several years. In fact, studies show that many users regret not buying a more powerful computer. To avoid this, plan to buy a computer that will last for at least two to three years. You can help delay obsolescence by purchasing the fastest processor, the most memory, and the largest hard disk you can afford. If you must buy a less powerful computer, be sure you can upgrade it with additional memory, components, and peripheral devices as your computer requirements grow.

⑤ Consider upgrades to the mouse, keyboard, monitor, printer, microphone, and speakers.

You use these peripheral devices to interact with the computer, so make sure they are up to your standards. Review the peripheral devices listed in Figure 2 and then visit both local computer dealers and large retail stores to test the computers and devices on display. Ask the salesperson which input and output devices would be best for you and whether you should upgrade beyond the standard product. Consider purchasing a wireless keyboard and wireless mouse to eliminate wires on your desktop. A few extra dollars spent on these components when you initially purchase a computer can extend its usefulness by years.

⑥ Determine whether to use a broadband or dial-up connection to access the Internet.

If your computer has a modem, you can access the Internet using a standard telephone line. Ordinarily, you call a local or toll-free 800 number to connect to an Internet access provider. Using a dial-up Internet connection usually is relatively inexpensive but slow.

Broadband connections provide much faster Internet connections, which are ideal if you want faster file download speeds for software, digital photos, digital video, and music. As you would expect, they can be more expensive than a dial-up connection. If you want to use a broadband connection, your computer should have an Ethernet card installed, unless you are using a wireless broadband connection such as WiMax or 3G. If you will be using a dial-up connection, your computer should have a modem installed.

⑦ Use a worksheet to compare computers, services, and other considerations.

You can use a separate sheet of paper to take notes about each vendor's computer and then summarize the information on a worksheet. For a sample worksheet that compares prices for a PC or a Mac, visit the Computer Concepts CourseMate

Web site at www.cengagebrain.com and then navigate to the Buyer's Guide Feature resource for this book. Most companies advertise a price for a base computer that includes components housed in the system unit (processor, RAM, sound card, video card, network card), hard disks, optical disc drives, a keyboard, mouse, monitor, printer, speakers, and modem. Be aware, however, that some advertisements list prices for computers with only some of these components. Monitors and printers, for example, often are not included in a base computer's price. Depending on how you plan to use the computer, you may want to invest in additional or more powerful components. When comparing the prices of computers, make sure you are comparing identical or similar configurations.

⑧ If you are buying a new computer, you have several purchasing options: buying from a school bookstore, a local computer dealer, a local large retail store, or ordering by mail via telephone or the Web.

Each purchasing option has certain advantages. Many college bookstores, for example, sign exclusive pricing agreements with computer manufacturers and, thus, can offer student discounts. Local dealers and local large retail stores, however, more easily can provide hands-on support. Mail-order companies that sell computers by telephone or online via the Web (Figure 3) often provide the lowest prices, but extend less personal service. Some major mail-order companies, however, have started to provide next-business-day, on-site services. A credit card usually is required to buy from a mail-order company.

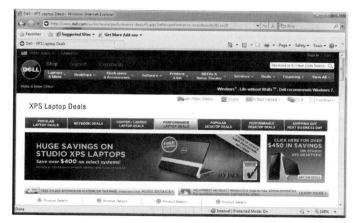

Figure 3 Mail-order companies, such as Dell, sell computers online.

⑨ If you are buying a used computer, stay with name brands such as Dell, Apple, HP, and Gateway.

Although brand-name equipment can cost more, most brand-name computers have longer, more comprehensive warranties, are better supported, and have more authorized

centers for repair services. As with new computers, you can purchase a used computer from local computer dealers, local large retail stores, or mail order via the telephone or the Web. Classified ads and used computer sellers offer additional outlets for purchasing used computers.

10 If you have a computer and are upgrading to a new one, then consider selling or trading in the old one.

If you are a replacement buyer, your older computer still may have value. If you cannot sell the computer through the classified ads, via a Web site, or to a friend, then ask if the computer dealer will buy your old computer.

An increasing number of companies are taking trade-ins, but do not expect too much money for your old computer. Other companies offer to recycle your old computer free or for a fee.

11 Be aware of hidden costs.

Before purchasing, be sure to consider any additional costs associated with buying a computer, such as an additional telephone line, a broadband modem, an uninterruptible power supply (UPS), computer furniture, a USB flash drive, paper, and computer training classes you may want to take. Depending on where you buy the computer, the seller may be willing to include some or all of these in the computer purchase price.

12 Consider more than just price.

The lowest-cost computer may not be the best long-term buy. Consider such intangibles as the vendor's time in business, regard for quality, and reputation for support. If you need to upgrade a computer often, you may want to consider a leasing arrangement, in which you pay monthly lease fees, but can upgrade or add on to your computer as your equipment needs change. No matter what type of buyer you are, insist on a 30-day, no-questions-asked return policy on the computer.

13 Avoid restocking fees.

Some companies charge a restocking fee of 10 to 20 percent as part of their money-back return policy. In some cases, no restocking fee for hardware is applied, but it is applied for software. Ask about the existence and terms of any restocking policies before you buy.

14 Use a credit card to purchase a new computer.

Many credit cards offer purchase protection and extended warranty benefits that cover you in case of loss of or damage to purchased goods. Paying by credit card also gives you time to install and use the computer before you have to pay for it. Finally, if you are dissatisfied with the computer and are unable to reach an agreement with the seller, paying by credit card gives you certain rights regarding withholding payment until the dispute is resolved. Check your credit card terms for specific details.

15 Consider purchasing an extended warranty or service plan.

If you use your computer for business or require fast resolution to major computer problems, consider purchasing an extended warranty or a service plan through a local dealer or third-party company. Most extended warranties cover the repair and replacement of computer components beyond the standard warranty. Most service plans ensure that your technical support calls receive priority response from technicians. You also can purchase an on-site service plan that states that a technician will arrive at your home, work, or school within 24 hours. If your computer includes a warranty and service agreement for a year or less, consider extending the service for two or three years when you buy the computer.

How to Purchase a Notebook Computer

If you need computing capability when you travel or to use in lectures or meetings, you may find a notebook computer to be an appropriate choice. The guidelines mentioned in the previous section also apply to the purchase of a notebook computer. The following are additional considerations unique to notebook computers, including netbooks and Tablet PCs.

1 Determine which computer fits your mobile computing needs.

Before purchasing a notebook computer, you need to determine whether a traditional notebook computer, netbook, or Tablet PC will meet your needs. If you spend most of your time working on spreadsheets, writing and/or editing documents, e-mail, or using the Internet, then a traditional notebook computer will suffice. If your primary use will be to access the Internet while traveling and you are not concerned as much with processing power or hard disk capacity, consider a netbook. If you find yourself in need of a computer in class or that you spend more time in meetings than

in your office, then the Tablet PC may be the answer. Before you invest money in a Tablet PC, however, determine which programs you plan to use on it. You should not buy a Tablet PC simply because it is an interesting type of computer.

2 Purchase a notebook computer with a sufficiently large screen.

Active-matrix screens display high-quality color that is viewable from all angles. Less expensive, passive-matrix screens sometimes are difficult to see in low-light conditions and cannot be viewed from an angle.

Notebook computers typically include a 12.1-inch, 13.3-inch, 14.1-inch, 15.4-inch, or 17-inch display. Netbooks have screens as small as 7 inches. For most users, a 14.1-inch display is satisfactory. If you intend to use the notebook computer as a desktop computer replacement, however, you may opt for a 15.4-inch or 17-inch display. The WSXGA+ standard (1680 × 1050) is popular with 17-inch displays, so if you intend to watch HD movies on the computer, take this into consideration. Dell offers a notebook computer with a 20.1-inch display that looks like a briefcase when closed. Some notebook computers with these larger displays weigh more than 10 pounds, however, so if you travel a lot and portability is essential, you might want a lighter computer with a smaller display. The lightest notebook computers, which weigh less than 3 pounds, are equipped with a 12.1-inch display.

Regardless of size, the resolution of the display should be at least 1024 × 768 pixels. To compare the screen size on various notebook computers, including netbooks and Tablet PCs, visit the company Web sites. Tablet PCs use a digitizer below a standard 10.4-inch motion-sensitive LCD display to make the writing experience on the screen feel like writing on paper. To ensure you experience the maximum benefits from the ClearType technology, make sure the LCD display has a resolution of 800 × 600 in landscape mode and a 600 × 800 in portrait mode.

3 Experiment with different keyboards, pointing devices, and digital pens.

Notebook computer keyboards, especially netbook keyboards, are far less standardized than those for desktop computers. Some notebook computers, for example, have wide wrist rests, while others have none, and keyboard layouts on notebook computers often vary. Notebook computers also use a range of pointing devices, including touchpads, pointing sticks, trackballs, and, in the case of Tablet PCs, digital pens.

Before purchasing a notebook computer, try various types of keyboards and pointing devices to determine which is easiest for you to use. Regardless of the device you select, you also may want to purchase a standard mouse to use when you are working at a desk or other large surface. Figure 4 compares the standard point-and-click of a mouse with the gestures made with a digital pen. Other gestures with the digital pen replicate some of the commonly used keys on a keyboard.

Mouse and Digital Pen Operations

Mouse	Digital Pen
Point	Point
Click	Tap
Double-click	Double-tap
Right-click	Tap and hold
Click and drag	Drag

Figure 4 Standard point-and-click of a mouse compared with the gestures made with a digital pen.

4 Make sure the notebook computer you purchase has an optical disc drive.

Most mobile computers include an optical disc drive. Although DVD/Blu-ray Disc drives are slightly more expensive, they allow you to play CDs, DVDs, and Blu-ray Discs using your notebook computer and hear the sound through earbuds. If you decide to purchase a netbook, it might not include an optical disc drive. Instead, you might need to purchase an external optical disc drive.

5 If necessary, upgrade the processor, memory, and disk storage at the time of purchase.

As with a desktop computer, upgrading a notebook computer's memory and disk storage usually is less expensive at the time of initial purchase. Some disk storage is custom designed for notebook computer manufacturers, meaning an upgrade might not be available in the future. If you are purchasing a lightweight notebook computer or Tablet PC, then it should include at least an Intel Core 2 Quad processor, 2 GB RAM, and 250 GB of storage. If you are purchasing a netbook, it should have an Intel Atom processor, at least 1 GB RAM, and 120 GB of storage.

6 The availability of built-in ports and slots and a USB hub on a notebook computer is important.

A notebook computer does not have much room to add adapter cards. If you know the purpose for which you plan to use the notebook computer, then you can determine the ports you will need. Netbooks typically have fewer ports than traditional notebook computers and Tablet PCs. Most notebook computers include common ports, such as a video port, audio port, network port, FireWire port, and multiple USB ports. If you plan to connect the notebook computer to a television, however, then you will need a PC to TV port. To optimize television viewing, you may want to consider DisplayPort, DVI, or HDMI ports. If you want to connect to networks at school or in various offices via a network cable, make sure the notebook computer you purchase has a network port. If the notebook computer does not contain a network port, you will

have to purchase an external network card that slides into an expansion slot in your computer, as well as a network cable. You also may want to consider adding a card reader.

⑦ If you plan to use your notebook computer for note-taking at school or in meetings, consider a convertible Tablet PC.

Some computer manufacturers have developed convertible Tablet PCs that allow the screen to rotate 180 degrees on a central hinge and then fold down to cover the keyboard (Figure 5). You then can use a digital pen to enter text or drawings into the computer by writing on the screen. Some notebook computers have wide screens for better viewing and editing, and some even have a screen on top of the unit in addition to the regular screen. If you spend much of your time attending lectures or meetings, then the slate Tablet PC is ideal. With a slate Tablet PC, users can attach a removable keyboard.

Figure 5
A convertible Tablet PC.

⑧ If you purchase a Tablet PC, determine whether you require multi-touch technology.

Newer operating systems now support hardware with multi-touch technology. If you choose an operating system that supports this technology, the Tablet PC also must support this technology.

⑨ Purchase a notebook computer with an integrated Web cam.

If you will be using a notebook computer to connect to the Internet and chat with friends online, consider purchasing one with an integrated Web cam.

⑩ Check with your wireless carrier to see if it offers netbooks for sale.

Most wireless carriers now offer wireless data plans allowing you to connect to the Internet from almost anywhere with a cell phone signal. Some wireless carriers now are selling netbooks with built-in capability to connect wirelessly to the Internet using a wireless data plan.

⑪ Purchase a notebook computer with a built-in wireless network connection.

A wireless network connection (Bluetooth, Wi-Fi a/b/g/n, WiMAX, etc.) can be useful when you travel or as part of a home network. Increasingly more airports, hotels, schools, and cafés have wireless networks that allow you to connect to the Internet. Many users today are setting up wireless home networks. With a wireless home network, your notebook computer can access the Internet, as well as other computers in the house, from any location to share files and hardware, such as a printer, and browse the Web. Most home wireless networks allow connections from distances of 150 to 800 feet.

⑫ If you plan to use your notebook computer for long periods without access to an electrical outlet, purchase a second battery.

The trend among notebook computer users today is power and size over battery life. Many notebook computer users today are willing to give up longer battery life for a larger screen, faster processor, and more storage. In addition, some manufacturers typically sell the notebook computer with the lowest capacity battery. For this reason, be careful in choosing a notebook computer if you plan to use it without access to electrical outlets for long periods, such as an airplane flight. You also might want to purchase a second battery as a backup. If you anticipate running the notebook computer on batteries frequently, choose a computer that uses lithium-ion batteries, which last longer than nickel cadmium or nickel hydride batteries.

⑬ Purchase a well-padded and well-designed carrying case.

An amply padded carrying case will protect your notebook computer from the bumps it will receive while traveling. A well-designed carrying case will have room for accessories such as spare optical discs, pens, and paperwork (Figure 6). Although a netbook may be small enough to fit in a handbag, make sure that the bag has sufficient padding to protect the computer.

Figure 6
A well-designed notebook computer carrying case.

⑭ If you plan to connect your notebook computer to a video projector, make sure the notebook computer is compatible with the video projector.

You should check, for example, to be sure that your notebook computer will allow you to display an image on the computer screen and projection device at the same time. Also, ensure that the notebook computer has the ports required to connect to the video projector. You also may consider purchasing a notebook computer with a built-in Web cam for video conferencing purposes.

⑮ For improved security and convenience, consider a fingerprint reader.

More than half a million notebook computers are stolen or lost each year. If you have critical information stored on your notebook computer, consider purchasing one with a fingerprint reader (Figure 7) to protect the data if your computer is stolen or lost. Fingerprint security offers a level of protection that extends well beyond the standard password protection. If your notebook computer is stolen, the odds of recovering it improve dramatically with anti-theft tracking software. Manufacturers claim recovery rates of 90 percent or more for notebook computers using their product. For convenience, fingerprint readers also allow you to log onto several Web sites in lieu of entering user name and password information.

Figure 7 Fingerprint reader technology offers greater security than passwords.

⑯ Review the docking capabilities of the Tablet PC.

The Tablet Technology in the Windows operating system supports a grab-and-go form of docking, so that you can pick up and take a docked Tablet PC with you, just as you would pick up a notepad on your way to a meeting (Figure 8).

Figure 8 A Tablet PC docked to create a desktop computer with the Tablet PC as the monitor.

How to Purchase a Smart Phone

You probably will use a smart phone more often than other mobile devices. For this reason, it is important to choose a phone that is available through your preferred wireless carrier, available in your price range, and offers access to the features you will use most frequently. This section lists guidelines you should consider when purchasing a smart phone.

❶ Choose a wireless carrier and plan that satisfies your needs and budget.

Multiple wireless carriers exist today, and each one offers a different line of smart phones. For example, the Samsung Alias is available only through Verizon Wireless. Alternatively, some smart phones, such as the BlackBerry line of smart phones, are available from multiple wireless carriers. Before deciding on a smart phone, you first should research the wireless carriers in your area, and be sure to ascertain whether the coverage is acceptable. Additionally, compare the calling plans for the various carriers and determine which one best meets your needs. Once you have determined the wireless carrier to use, you then can choose from one of their available smart phones. Once you purchase a smart phone, most carriers allow you to perform a risk-free evaluation for 30 days. If you are not satisfied with the phone or its performance, you can return the phone and pay only for the service you have used.

❷ Decide on the size, style, and weight of the smart phone that will work best for you.

Smart phones are available in various sizes, weights, shapes, and colors. Some people prefer larger, heavier phones because they feel that they are more durable, while others prefer smaller, lightweight phones for easy portability. Some smart phones are flip phones, meaning that you have to open the phone (like a clamshell) to display the screen and keypad, some open by sliding the phone, and others do not need to be opened to use them. Figure 9 shows the various smart phone styles.

Figure 9 Various smart phone styles.

③ Determine whether you prefer a touch screen, keypad, or mini-keyboard.

Modern smart phones provide various ways to enter text. During the past several years, smart phones with touch screens as their primary input device have been penetrating the market. Some smart phone users prefer touch screens because the phone does not require additional space for a keypad or mini-keyboard, but others find it more difficult to type on a touch screen. Most newer smart phones with touch screens also include handwriting recognition. Smart phones with keypads might make it easier to type for some users, but others do not like the unfamiliar feeling of keys arranged in alphabetical order. In addition, you often have to press the keys multiple times before reaching the letter you want to type. Mini-keyboards are available on some smart phones, such as the BlackBerry and Samsung Alias. Mini-keyboards provide a key for each letter, but the keys are significantly smaller than those on a standard keyboard. Most smart phone users type on mini-keyboards using their thumbs.

④ If you will be synchronizing your smart phone with a program on your computer, select a smart phone that is compatible with the program you wish to use.

Programs such as Microsoft Outlook allow you to synchronize your e-mail messages, contacts, and calendar with your smart phone. If you would like this functionality, purchase a smart phone that can synchronize with Microsoft Outlook. Similarly, if your company uses a BlackBerry Enterprise server or Microsoft Exchange server, you should consider purchasing a smart phone that can synchronize, either using wires or wirelessly, with those servers.

⑤ Compare battery life.

Any smart phone is useful only if it has the power required to run. Talking and using the Internet on your smart phone will shorten battery life more quickly than when the phone is powered on but not in use. If you have a choice, be sure to purchase a battery that will allow the phone to function all day. Pay particular attention to the talk time and standby time. If you plan to talk on the phone more than the advertised talk time, you might consider purchasing a second battery or an extended battery if your phone supports it.

⑥ Make sure your smart phone has enough memory and storage.

If you are using the smart phone to send and receive picture, video, and e-mail messages, and to store music, purchase a memory card that not only is compatible with your computer and smart phone, but also has adequate storage space for your messages and files. If you purchase a memory card and eventually fill it, you easily can transfer the data to a larger memory card.

⑦ Check out the accessories.

Determine which accessories you want for the smart phone. Accessories include carrying cases, screen protectors, synchronization cradles and cables, and car chargers.

How to Purchase a Portable Media Player

Portable media players are becoming the preferred device for listening to music and watching videos on the go. When choosing a portable media player, it is important to consider features and characteristics other than the physical size and amount of storage space. This section lists guidelines you should consider when purchasing a portable media player.

① Choose a device with sufficient storage capacity.

Audio and video files can consume a great deal of storage space, so be sure to purchase a portable media player that has enough capacity to store your audio and video files. You also should consider approximately how many media files you acquire each year, and make sure that your device has enough storage space to accommodate these files for years to come.

② Determine which file formats your new portable media player should support and how you will add files to your library.

Some portable media players are designed to accept new audio and video files only through a program installed on a computer. For example, it is easiest to add media files to an iPod using the iTunes program. Other portable media players connect to a computer using a cable and are displayed in Windows as a removable disk. You then can add files to the media player by dragging the files to the removable disk icon in Windows. The portable media player must support the file formats you are using. You can determine the file format by looking at the file extension on the media files you wish to transfer to your portable media player. Before purchasing a portable media player, make sure that it can support the file formats you are using.

③ Consider a portable media player that can play video.

Some users prefer to watch videos on their portable media player in addition to playing music. You typically can download videos for portable media players less expensively than purchasing the movie on a DVD/Blu-ray Disc. Although the display on a portable media player is small, many still find

entertainment value because they are able to watch videos and stay occupied while waiting for a bus, on an airplane, or at other locations where they otherwise might not have anything to occupy them.

4 Read reviews about the sound quality on the portable media players you are considering.

Sound quality may vary greatly among portable media players. If you are unable to try the portable media player before buying it, read reviews and make sure that those reviewing the devices find the sound quality to be acceptable. You also may consider purchasing higher-quality earbuds or headphones to enhance the sound quality.

5 Select a size and style that works best for you.

Portable media players are available in various shapes and styles. For example, Apple offers the iPod shuffle, iPod nano, iPod classic, and iPod touch (Figure 10). Each type of iPod varies in size and style, and some have capabilities (such as video) that others do not. Choose a size and style that meets your needs and fits your personality.

Figure 10 Portable media players are available in different shapes, styles, and colors.

6 Check out additional memory cards.

Most portable media players have internal storage for your media files. If you wish to increase the available storage, consider purchasing a portable media player that allows you to increase storage capacity by inserting memory cards. Similar to most computers, it is less expensive initially to purchase the largest amount of storage that you can afford, but it is helpful to be able to increase your storage at a later date.

7 Consider rechargeable batteries.

Although most portable media players include rechargeable batteries, some still use traditional alkaline batteries. Portable media players sometimes can last for only a few hours on alkaline batteries, and battery replacement can be costly. Rechargeable batteries often last longer and create less waste. If you are not near a power source, you are unable to recharge the batteries when they die. With alkaline batteries, you simply can insert new ones and continue enjoying your player.

8 Stay within your budget.

As previously mentioned, portable media players are available in a variety of shapes and sizes, and they also are available with various storage capacities. When shopping for a portable media player, be realistic when you consider how you will use the device, as well as how much storage you require. Purchasing the latest and greatest device is not always the best option, and the cost can exceed what you care to spend.

How to Purchase a Digital Camera

Both amateur and professional photographers now are mostly purchasing digital cameras to meet their photography needs. Because digital cameras with new and improved features regularly are introduced to the marketplace, consumers should know how to compare the differences among the multiple cameras that are available. This section lists guidelines you should consider when purchasing a digital camera.

1 Determine the type of digital camera that meets your needs.

Various types of digital cameras exist, including point-and-shoot cameras, field cameras, and studio cameras. Point-and-shoot cameras typically fit in your pocket and meet the needs of most general consumers. Field cameras, which often are used by photojournalists, are portable but flexible. Field cameras allow photographers to change lenses and use other attachments, and also are more customizable than point-and-shoot cameras. Studio cameras are used in photo studios and are stationary. These cameras give you the widest range of lenses and settings.

2 The digital camera with the highest resolution is not always the best.

Many consumers mistakenly believe that the digital camera with the highest resolution is the best camera for their needs. A higher resolution increases quality and clarity of your photos, as well as the size at which you can print the photos before noticing degradation in quality. If you never plan to print photos larger than 8" × 10", for example, you do not need a camera with a resolution greater than 5 megapixels. Many cameras available today advertise higher resolutions, but taking pictures at these high resolutions can use valuable storage space. Just

because your camera can take a 10-megapixel photo does not mean that you always should set the resolution to 10 megapixels.

❸ Consider size and weight.

Digital cameras are available in various sizes and weights. Some people prefer smaller, lighter cameras because they are easier to transport and take up less space. Others prefer bulkier, heavier cameras because the weight helps steady them to take a clearer picture. Many digital cameras also include an image stabilization feature that reduces the possibility of a blurry picture if you move your hands slightly while taking the picture. Some also believe that heavier cameras are of better quality, although that seldom is true. When choosing a digital camera, practice taking pictures with it and select one that feels comfortable and natural.

❹ Different cameras require different memory cards.

When purchasing a digital camera, pay careful attention to the type of memory card the camera uses. Many use SD cards, some use xD Picture cards, and some use CompactFlash memory cards. Some memory cards are more expensive to replace than others, and some have a higher capacity than other cards. If you take a lot of pictures, purchase a camera that supports a memory card with a higher storage capacity so that you can avoid carrying multiple memory cards. You also might consider purchasing a camera that uses a memory card that is compatible with your other mobile devices.

❺ Photo editing features can save you time.

Some digital cameras have integrated tools that allow you to edit photos directly from the camera. For instance, you may be able to crop photos, change the brightness, or remove red eye effects. Editing photos directly on the camera after taking them can save you from editing multiple photos at once when you transfer them to a computer. The photo editing capabilities available on digital cameras are limited when compared to photo editing programs, but in many cases they can edit a photo to your satisfaction.

❻ Make sure that you can see the LCD screen easily.

LCD screens on digital cameras allow you to configure the settings, frame a shot before taking it, and preview photos after taking them. LCD screens vary by inches, so select a camera with a screen that does not require you to strain your eyes to view. This is especially important if the camera you are considering does not have a viewfinder, because you then will be required to use the display to frame your shots.

❼ Determine whether your pictures will require you to zoom.

If you plan to take pictures of people or objects that require you to zoom in, select a digital camera that has a high optical zoom. An optical zoom enlarges the subject by adjusting the camera lens, whereas a digital zoom uses algorithms built into the camera to magnify images. Optical zooms, as opposed to digital zooms, often result in a higher quality photo. While a digital zoom might be capable of magnifying objects that are 100 feet away, the photo will suffer a loss of quality.

❽ Price is important.

As with all other devices, locate a digital camera that does not exceed your budget. If you find a great camera that is available for more than you are willing to spend, consider locating a camera with a slightly lower resolution, an alternate brand, or a smaller screen. Digital cameras can last well beyond five years if properly maintained, so consider this a longer-term investment that will create memories lasting you a lifetime.

❾ Know your batteries.

Some digital cameras require replaceable alkaline or rechargeable batteries (often AA or AAA), and others have a rechargeable battery. Similar to batteries in portable media players, using disposable batteries in digital cameras can get expensive, and they may not last as long as rechargeable battery packs. Digital camera battery life is not measured in hours (as is the case with smart phones and portable media players); instead, it is measured in how many pictures can be taken on a single charge or set of batteries. Turning off the LCD screen and flash when you take pictures can help to extend battery life.

❿ Purchase accessories.

Accessories that are available for digital cameras include carrying cases, extra batteries and battery chargers, and extra memory cards (Figure 11). Carrying cases can help protect your digital camera, especially while traveling, and the extra batteries and chargers can stay inside your carrying case so that they are readily available should you need them. Screen protectors can help protect the LCD screen on your digital camera.

Figure 11 Digital camera accessories include memory cards, cases, batteries, and battery chargers.

Multiple Web sites on the Internet allow you to purchase computers and mobile devices. For a list of Web sites that sell computers and mobile devices, visit the Computer Concepts CourseMate Web site at www.cengagebrain.com and then navigate to the Buyer's Guide Feature resource for this book.

Communications and Networks

Objectives

After completing this chapter, you will be able to:

1 Discuss the purpose of the components required for successful communications: sending device, communications device, communications channel, and receiving device

2 Describe these uses of computer communications: wireless messaging services, wireless Internet access points, cybercafés, global positioning systems, collaboration, groupware, voice mail, and Web services

3 Differentiate among types of networks: LANs, MANs, and WANs

4 Explain the purpose of communications software

5 Describe various types of lines for communications over the telephone network: dial-up, ISDN, DSL, FTTP, T-carrier, and ATM

6 Describe commonly used communications devices: dial-up modems, digital modems, wireless modems, network cards, wireless access points, and routers

7 Discuss different ways to set up a home network

8 Describe various physical and wireless transmission media: twisted-pair cable, coaxial cable, fiber-optic cable, infrared, broadcast radio, cellular radio, microwaves, and communications satellite

Communications

Computer **communications** describes a process in which two or more computers or devices transfer data, instructions, and information. Figure 8-1 shows a sample communications system. Some communications involve cables and wires; others are sent wirelessly through the air. As illustrated in this figure, communications systems contain all types of computers and computing devices. For successful communications, you need the following:

- A **sending device** that initiates an instruction to transmit data, instructions, or information.
- A communications device that connects the sending device to a communications channel.
- A **communications channel**, or transmission media on which the data, instructions, or information travel.
- A communications device that connects the communications channel to a receiving device.
- A **receiving device** that accepts the transmission of data, instructions, or information.

communications system

Figure 8-1 An example of a communications system. The communications channel consists of telephone and power lines, cable television and other underground lines, microwave stations, and satellites.

All types of computers and mobile devices serve as sending and receiving devices in a communications system. This includes mainframe computers, servers, desktop computers, notebook computers, smart phones, portable media players, handheld game consoles, and GPS receivers. One type of communications device that connects a communications channel to a sending or receiving device such as a computer is a modem. Two examples of communications channels are cable television lines and telephone lines.

Uses of Computer Communications

Computer communications are everywhere. Many require that users subscribe to an Internet access provider. With other computer communications, an organization such as a business or school provides communications services to employees, students, or customers. The following pages discuss a variety of computer communications.

Blogs, Chat Rooms, E-Mail, Fax, FTP, Instant Messaging, Internet, Newsgroups, RSS, Video Conferencing, VoIP, Web, Web 2.0, Web Folders, and Wikis

Previous chapters discussed many uses of computer communications as they related to a particular topic. In the course of a day, it is likely you use, or use information generated by, one or more of the previously discussed communications technologies, which are outlined in Figure 8-2.

The following pages discuss a variety of other uses of communications that have not been discussed in depth previously. These include wireless messaging services, wireless Internet access points, cybercafés, global positioning systems, collaboration, groupware, voice mail, and Web services.

Summary of Communications Discussed in Previous Chapters

Communications Type	Brief Description
Blogs	Time-stamped articles on a network that reflect the author's interests, opinions, and personality
Chat Rooms	Real-time typed conversation among two or more people that takes place on a computer connected to a network that also may allow the exchange of messages, photos, files, audio, and video
E-Mail	Transmission of messages and files via a computer network
Fax	Transmits and receives documents over telephone lines
FTP	Internet standard that permits users to upload and download files to and from FTP servers on the Internet
Instant Messaging	Real-time one-on-one Internet communications service that notifies you when one or more people are online and then allows you to exchange messages, photos, files, and video
Internet	Worldwide collection of networks that links millions of businesses, government agencies, educational institutions, and individuals
Newsgroups	Online areas in which users have written discussions about a particular subject
RSS	Specification that enables Web content to be distributed to subscribers
Video Conferencing	Real-time meeting between two or more geographically separated people who use a network to transmit audio and video data
VoIP	Conversation that takes place over the Internet using a telephone connected to a computer, mobile device, or telephone adapter
Web	Worldwide collection of electronic documents on the Internet that users access through a Web browser
Web 2.0	Web sites that provide a means for users to share personal information, allow users to modify Web site content, and/or have application software built into the site for visitors to use
Web Folders	Location on a Web server to which users publish documents and other files
Wikis	Collaborative Web sites that allow users to create, add to, modify, or delete Web site content

Figure 8-2 Uses of communications discussed in earlier chapters.

Wikis
For more information, visit the Computer Concepts CourseMate Web site at www.cengagebrain.com, navigate to the Chapter 8 Web Link resource for this book, and then click Wikis.

? | **FAQ 8-1**

How many households are using cell phones as their primary telephone?

A recent study indicates that approximately 20 percent of households use cell phones as their primary telephone. Some families choose to save money by disconnecting their home telephone and using their cell phone for all calls, although they tend to make more telephone calls than families with a traditional telephone line.

For more information, visit the Computer Concepts CourseMate Web site at www.cengagebrain.com, navigate to the Chapter 8 FAQ resource for this book, and then click Wireless Households.

Wireless Messaging Services

Users can send and receive wireless messages to and from smart phones, cell phones, handheld game consoles, and other mobile devices and computers using three techniques: text messaging, picture/video messaging, and wireless instant messaging (Figure 8-3).

picture/video message

text message

wireless instant message

Figure 8-3 Users can send and receive text messages, picture/video messages, and wireless instant messages to and from their smart phones and other computers and devices.

Text Messaging A mobile device with **text messaging**, also called SMS (short message service), capability allows users to send and receive short text messages, typically fewer than 300 characters, on a phone or other mobile device or computer. Text messaging services typically provide users with several options for sending and receiving messages:

- Mobile to Mobile: send a message from your mobile device to another mobile device
- Mobile to E-Mail: send a message from your mobile device to an e-mail address anywhere in the world
- Web to Mobile: send a message from a text messaging Web site to a mobile device, or request that a Web site alert a mobile device with breaking news and other updates, such as sports scores, stock prices, and weather forecasts
- Mobile to Provider: send a message by entering a four- or five-digit number assigned to a specific content or wireless service provider, followed by the message, such as a vote for a television program contestant

Video Messaging

For more information, visit the Computer Concepts CourseMate Web site at www.cengagebrain.com, navigate to the Chapter 8 Web Link resource for this book, and then click Video Messaging.

Picture/Video Messaging With **picture messaging**, users can send pictures and sound files, as well as short text messages, to a phone or other mobile device, or a computer. With **video messaging**, users can send short video clips, usually about 30 seconds in length, in addition to all picture messaging services. Picture/video messaging service, also called MMS (multimedia message service), typically provides users these options for sending and receiving messages:

- Mobile to Mobile: send the picture/video from your mobile device to another mobile device
- Mobile to E-Mail: send the picture/video from your mobile device to an e-mail address anywhere in the world

Wireless Instant Messaging Wireless instant messaging (IM) is a real-time Internet communications service that allows wireless mobile devices to exchange messages with one or more mobile devices or online users. Some wireless Internet service providers partner with IM services so that you can use your smart phone or other mobile device to send and receive wireless instant messages. With a compatible IM service, users have these IM options:

- Mobile to Mobile: use a wireless instant messenger to communicate between two mobile devices
- Mobile to Personal Computer: use a wireless instant messenger to communicate between a mobile device and a desktop or notebook computer
- Web to Mobile: send or forward messages from a desktop or notebook computer's instant messenger to a mobile device

Wireless Internet Access Points

At home, work, school, and in many public locations, people connect wirelessly to the Internet through a **wireless Internet access point** using notebook computers, smart phones, handheld game consoles, or other devices. Users access wireless Internet access points with computers or devices that have the necessary built-in wireless capability or the appropriate wireless network card, USB network adapter, ExpressCard module, or PC Card (Figure 8-4). Two types of wireless Internet access points are hot spots and mobile wireless networks.

A **hot spot** is a wireless network that provides Internet connections to mobile computers and devices. Through the hot spot, mobile users check e-mail, browse the Web, and access any service on the Internet. Three hot spot technologies are Wi-Fi, WiMAX, and Bluetooth. Wi-Fi hot spots provide wireless network connections to users in public locations such as airports and airplanes, train stations, hotels, convention centers, schools, campgrounds, shopping malls, bookstores, libraries, restaurants, and coffee shops. The coverage range for WiMAX hot spots, can be much wider than Wi-Fi; for example, they can cover an entire city. Bluetooth hot spots provide location-based services such as sending coupons or menus, to users whose enabled devices enter the coverage range. Sections later in this chapter discuss Wi-Fi, WiMAX, and Bluetooth in more detail. Read Ethics & Issues 8-1 for a related discussion.

Ethics & Issues

For the complete text of the Ethics & Issues boxes found in this chapter, visit the Computer Concepts CourseMate Web site at www.cengagebrain.com and then navigate to the Chapter 8 Ethics & Issues resource for this book.

▼ ETHICS & ISSUES 8-1

Will Widespread Wireless Broadband Connections Kill Print Media?

Airlines around the world recently started offering Wi-Fi hot spots on some flights. Communications companies also began offering WiMax coverage throughout entire cities. Even smart phones deliver high-speed Web browsing. With the proliferation of high-speed wireless Internet access, some experts believe that the end is near for print media, such as newspapers and magazines. The traditional airport and city newspaper and magazine stands' days may be numbered. Instead of buying a newspaper

and a couple of magazines before a flight, travelers choose from thousands of searchable publications on their mobile devices while traveling. Even the morning newspaper delivery is at risk as more people choose to use mobile devices to wirelessly access their favorite newspapers from home. Some experts dispute this claim, stating that the print media industry perfected the centuries-old hard copy delivery of newspapers and magazines, and that, when given the choice, most people prefer print reading.

For now, people prefer the style, quality, and portability of print media.

Will widespread wireless broadband connections, such as Wi-Fi, put an end to printed newspapers and magazines? Why or why not? Would you prefer to read newspapers and magazines in print or on a mobile device that provides similar or better readability as compared to print media? Why or why not? How can the media industry take advantage of the wireless Internet trend?

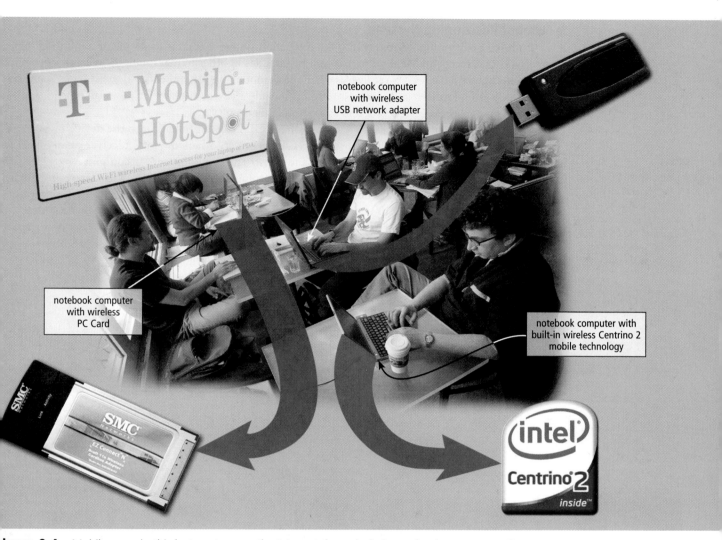

Figure 8-4 Mobile users in this hot spot access the Internet through their notebook computers. One computer uses a wireless USB network adapter; another uses a wireless PC Card. Others have Intel's built-in wireless Centrino 2 mobile technology.

Some hot spots provide free Internet access, some charge a per-use fee, and others require users to subscribe to a wireless Internet service provider, to which they pay per-access fees, daily fees, or a monthly fee. Per-access fees average $3, daily fees range from $5 to $20, and monthly fees range from $20 to $60 for unlimited access, with the higher monthly fee providing greater coverage areas.

A mobile wireless network provides users with high-speed Internet connections, as long as they are in the network's range. A mobile wireless network usually includes most major cities and airports. Subscription fees for unlimited monthly Internet access to a mobile wireless network through a cell phone usually range from $30 to $50. Fees for notebook computer access are higher, usually ranging from $60 to $80 per month.

Cybercafés

When mobile users travel without their notebook computer or Internet-enabled mobile device, they can visit a cybercafé to access e-mail, the Web, and other Internet services. A **cybercafé**, or Internet cafe, is a coffeehouse, restaurant, or other location that provides personal computers with Internet access to its customers. Cybercafés exist in cities around the world. Although some provide free Internet access, most charge a per-hour or per-minute fee. Some cybercafés also are hot spots.

Global Positioning Systems

A **global positioning system** (**GPS**) is a navigation system that consists of one or more earth-based receivers that accept and analyze signals sent by satellites in order to determine the receiver's geograph location (Figure 8-5). A GPS receiver is a handheld, mountable, or embedded device that contains an antenna, a radio receiver, and a processor. Many include a screen display that shows an individual's location on a map. Some also function as a portable media player.

Many mobile devices such as smart phones have GPS capability built into the device or as an add-on feature. Some users carry a handheld GPS receiver; others mount a receiver to an object such as an automobile, boat, airplane, farm and construction equipment, or computer.

The first and most used application of GPS technology is to assist people with determining when they are located. The data obtained from a GPS, however, can be applied to a variety of other uses creating a map, ascertaining the best route between two points, locating a lost person or stolen object, monitoring the movement of a person or object, determining altitude, and calculating speed Many vehicles use GPSs to provide drivers with directions or other information. Read Innovative Computing 8-1 to find out about a hobby that uses GPS technology.

GPS

For more information, visit the Computer Concepts CourseMate Web site at www.cengagebrain.com, navigate to the Chapter 8 Web Link resource for this book, and then click GPS.

How a GPS Works

Step 1
GPS satellites orbit Earth. Every thousandth of a second, each satellite sends a signal that indicates its current position to the GPS receiver.

Step 2
A GPS receiver (such as in a car, a wearable device, a smart phone, a handheld device, or a collar) determines its location on Earth by analyzing at least 3 separate satellite signals from the 24 satellites in orbit.

Figure 8-5 This figure shows how a GPS works.

Geocaching for Hidden Treasure

Treasure hunting for all ages has gone high-tech. Geocaching is a form of outdoor recreation, discovery, and fun, and the only requirements are a GPS receiver, Internet access, and a sense of adventure.

Participants bury or hide a small container, called a cache, that has a logbook and writing instrument and usually a small novelty trinket such as a coin, button, toy, or CD. They then log on to a geocaching Web site and post details of the container's location using latitudinal and longitudinal coordinates. Cachers then use their GPS receivers to find the container, note their discovery in the logbook, and write about their adventure on the Web site.

The first cache with GPS coordinates was documented in 2000. Today, more than 900,000 geocaches in more than 100 countries and on all 7 continents are registered on a variety of Web sites, such as geocaching.com. The locations range from under water to mountain peaks. Cachers generally follow the Geocacher's Creed, which encourages ethical behavior and preservation of natural resources.

For more information, visit the Computer Concepts CourseMate Web site at www.cengagebrain.com, navigate to the Chapter 8 Innovative Computing resource for this book, and then click Geocaching.

Collaboration

Many software products provide a means to **collaborate**, or work online, with other users connected to a server. Two methods of collaboration include collaborative software and document management systems. **Collaborative software** includes tools that enable users to share documents via online meetings and communicate with other connected users. An online meeting allows users to share documents with others in real time (Figure 8-6). When the online meeting takes place on the Web, it is called a **Web conference**. In an online meeting, all participants see a document(s) at the same time. As someone changes the document, everyone in the meeting sees the changes being made. Collaborative software often has chat, whiteboard, and video/audio conferencing capabilities.

Some organizations use document management systems to make collaboration possible among employees. A **document management system** provides for storage and management of a company's documents, such as word processing documents, presentations, and spreadsheets. Users then access these documents, depending on their needs. A document management system can track all changes made to a document. It also can store additional information such as the document's creation date, the user who created the document, a summary of the document, and any keywords associated with the document. Google Docs is a Web-based document management system that provides basic services to its subscribers at no cost. With Google Docs, multiple users can work on the same document at the same time, viewing each others edits as they are entered.

Figure 8-6 Through an online meeting, all participants see a document at the same time.

Groupware

Groupware is software that helps groups of people work together on projects and share information over a network. Groupware is a component of a broad concept called workgroup computing, which includes network hardware and software that enables group members to communicate, manage projects,

schedule meetings, and make group decisions. To assist with these activities, most groupware provides personal information manager (PIM) functions, such as an electronic appointment calendar, an address book, and a notepad. A major feature of groupware is group scheduling, in which a group calendar can track the schedules of multiple users and help coordinate appointments and meeting times.

Voice Mail

Voice mail, which functions much like an answering machine, allows someone to leave a voice message for one or more people. Unlike answering machines, however, a computer in the voice mail system converts an analog voice message into digital form. Once digitized, the message is stored in a voice mailbox. A voice mailbox is a storage location on a hard disk in the voice mail system.

To help users manage voice mail messages, some systems offer visual voice mail. With **visual voice mail**, users can view message details such as the length of calls and, in some cases, read message content instead of listening to them. Some voice mail systems can send digital voice mail files to e-mail addresses. Others can convert a voice mail message to a text message for display on a computer or mobile device.

Web Services

Web services describe standardized software that enables programmers to create applications that communicate with other remote computers over the Internet or over an internal business network. Businesses are the primary users of Web services because this technology provides a means for departments to communicate with each other, suppliers, vendors, and with clients. For example, third-party vendors can use Web services to communicate with their online retailer's Web site to manage their inventory levels.

Web services often provide content for mashups. A **mashup** is a Web application that combines services from two or more sources, creating a new application. An e-commerce business, for example, might determine the address of its closest retail store from its Web site and combine (mash) the location with a map from a travel and mapping Web site to provide the Web site visitor with driving directions.

✔ QUIZ YOURSELF 8-1

Instructions: Find the true statement below. Then, rewrite the remaining false statements so that they are true.

1. A cybercafé is a wireless network that provides Internet connections to mobile computers and devices.
2. GPS is a navigation system that consists of one or more earth-based receivers that accept and analyze signals sent by satellites in order to determine the receiver's geographic location.
3. Receiving devices initiate an instruction to transmit data, instructions, or information.
4. Users can send pictures and sound files, as well as short text messages, with text messaging.

Quiz Yourself Online: To further check your knowledge of pages 314 through 322, visit the Computer Concepts CourseMate Web site at www.cengagebrain.com, navigate to the Chapter 8 Quiz Yourself resource for this book, and then click Objectives 1 – 2.

Networks

As discussed in Chapter 1, a **network** is a collection of computers and devices connected together via communications devices and transmission media. Many businesses network their computers together to facilitate communications, share hardware, share data and information, share software, and transfer funds.

A network can be internal to an organization or span the world by connecting to the Internet. Instead of using the Internet or an internal network, some companies hire a value-added network provider for network functions. A **value-added network** (**VAN**) is a third-party business that provides networking services for a fee.

Networks facilitate communications among users and allow users to share resources with other users. Some examples of resources are data, information, hardware, and software.

LANs, MANs, and WANs

Networks usually are classified as a local area network, metropolitan area network, or wide area network. The main differentiation among these classifications is their area of coverage, as described in the following pages. Read Looking Ahead 8-1 for a look at another type of network.

LAN A **local area network (LAN)** is a network that connects computers and devices in a limited geographical area such as a home, school computer laboratory, office building, or closely positioned group of buildings. Each computer or device on the network, called a node, often shares resources such as printers, large hard disks, and programs. Often, the nodes are connected via cables. A **wireless LAN (WLAN)** is a LAN that uses no physical wires. Very often, a WLAN communicates with a wired LAN for access to its resources (Figure 8-7).

Figure 8-7 Computers and mobile devices on a wireless LAN often communicate via an access point with a wired LAN to access its software, printer, the Internet, and other resources.

MAN A **metropolitan area network** (**MAN**) is a high-speed network that connects local area networks in a metropolitan area such as a city or town and handles the bulk of communications activity across that region. A MAN typically includes one or more LANs, but covers a smaller geographic area than a WAN.

A MAN usually is managed by a consortium of users or by a single network provider that sells the service to the users. Local and state governments, for example, regulate some MANs. Telephone companies, cable television operators, and other organizations provide users with connections to the MAN.

WAN A **wide area network** (**WAN**) is a network that covers a large geographic area (such as a city, country, or the world) using a communications channel that combines many types of media such as telephone lines, cables, and radio waves (Figure 8-8). A WAN can be one large network or can consist of two or more LANs connected together. The Internet is the world's largest WAN.

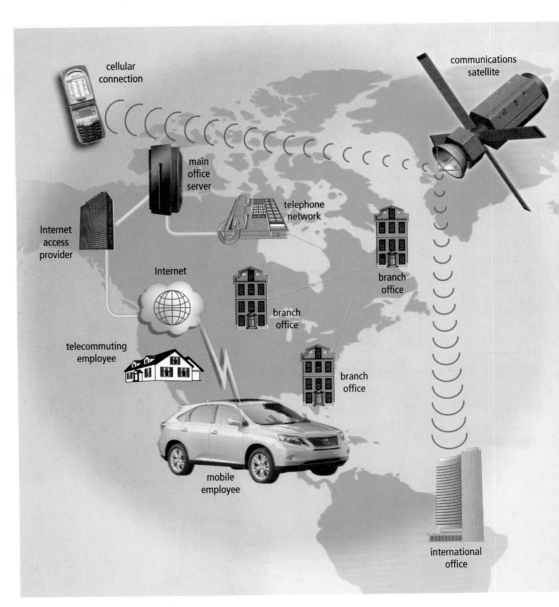

Figure 8-8 An example of a WAN.

Network Architectures

The design of computers, devices, and media in a network, sometimes called the network architecture, is categorized as either client/server or peer-to-peer.

Client/Server On a **client/server network**, one or more computers act as a server; the other computers on the network request services from the server (Figure 8-9). A **server** controls access to the hardware, software, and other resources on the network and provides a centralized storage area for programs, data, and information. The **clients** are other computers and mobile devices on the network that rely on the server for its resources. For example, a server might store a database of customers. Clients on the network (company employees) access the customer database on the server.

Some servers, called dedicated servers, perform a specific task and can be placed with other dedicated servers to perform multiple tasks. For example, a file server stores and manages files. A print server manages printers and documents being printed. A database server stores and provides access to a database. A network server manages network traffic (activity). A Web server is a computer that delivers requested Web pages to your computer.

A client/server network typically provides an efficient means to connect 10 or more computers. Most client/server networks require a person to serve as a network administrator because of the large size of the network.

Peer-to-Peer One type of **peer-to-peer network** is a simple, inexpensive network that typically connects fewer than 10 computers. Each computer, called a peer, has equal responsibilities and capabilities, sharing hardware (such as a printer), data, or information with other computers on the peer-to-peer network (Figure 8-10). Each computer stores files on its own storage devices. Thus, each computer on the network contains both the server operating system and application software. All computers on the network share any peripheral device(s) attached to any computer. For example, one computer may have a laser printer and a scanner, while another has an ink-jet printer and an external hard disk. Peer-to-peer networks are ideal for very small businesses and home users.

Figure 8-9 On a client/server network, one or more computers act as a server, and the clients access the server(s).

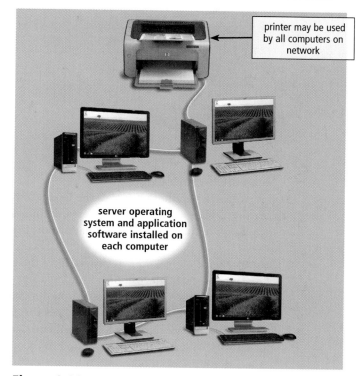

printer may be used by all computers on network

server operating system and application software installed on each computer

Figure 8-10 Each computer on a peer-to-peer network shares its hardware and software with other computers on the network.

P2P

For more information, visit the Computer Concepts CourseMate Web site at www.cengagebrain.com, navigate to the Chapter 8 Web Link resource for this book, and then click P2P.

Internet Peer-to-Peer Another type of peer-to-peer, called **P2P**, describes an Internet network on which users access each other's hard disks and exchange files directly (Figure 8-11). This type of peer-to-peer network sometimes is called a file sharing network because users with compatible software and an Internet connection copy files from someone else's hard disk to their hard disks. As more users connect to the network, each user has access to shared files on other users' hard disks. When users log off, others no longer have access to their hard disks.

Examples of networking software that support P2P are BitTorrent, Gnutella, Kazaa, and LimeWire, which allow users to swap music and other files via the Web.

Figure 8-11 P2P describes an Internet network on which users connect to each other's hard disks and exchange files directly.

Network Topologies

A **network topology** refers to the layout of the computers and devices in a communications network. Three commonly used network topologies are star, bus, and ring. Most networks, including the Internet, use combinations of these topologies.

Star Network On a **star network**, all of the computers and devices (nodes) on the network connect to a central device, thus forming a star (Figure 8-12). Two types of devices that provide a common central connection point for nodes on the network are a hub and a switch. All data that transfers from one node to another passes through the hub or switch.

Star networks are fairly easy to install and maintain. Nodes can be added to and removed from the network with little or no disruption to the network.

On a star network, if one node fails, only that node is affected. The other nodes continue to operate normally. If the hub or switch fails, however, the entire network is inoperable until the device is repaired.

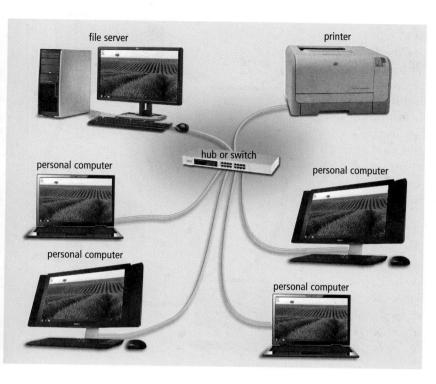

Figure 8-12 A star network contains a single, centralized hub or switch through which all the devices in the network communicate.

Bus Network A **bus network** consists of a single central cable, to which all computers and other devices connect (Figure 8-13). The bus is the physical cable that connects the computers and other devices. The bus in a bus network transmits data, instructions, and information in both directions. When a sending device transmits data, the address of the receiving device is included with the transmission so that the data is routed to the appropriate receiving device.

Bus networks are popular on LANs because they are inexpensive and easy to install. One advantage of the bus network is that computers and other devices can be attached and detached at any point on the bus without disturbing the rest of the network. Another advantage is that failure of one device usually does not affect the rest of the bus network. The greatest risk to a bus network is that the bus itself might become inoperable. If that happens, the network remains inoperative until the bus is back in working order.

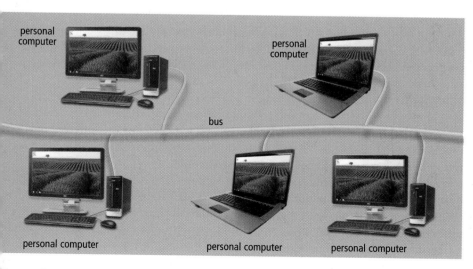

Figure 8-13 Devices in a bus network share a single data path.

Ring Network On a **ring network**, a cable forms a closed loop (ring) with all computers and devices arranged along the ring (Figure 8-14). Data transmitted on a ring network travels from device to device around the entire ring, in one direction. When a computer or device sends data, the data travels to each computer on the ring until it reaches its destination.

If a computer or device on a ring network fails, the entire network potentially could stop functioning. A ring network can span a larger distance than a bus network, but it is more difficult to install. The ring topology primarily is used for LANs, but also is used in WANs.

Figure 8-14 On a ring network, all connected devices form a continuous loop.

Intranets

Recognizing the efficiency and power of the Internet, many organizations apply Internet and Web technologies to their internal networks. An **intranet** (intra means within) is an internal network that uses Internet technologies. Intranets generally make company information accessible to employees and facilitate working in groups.

Simple intranet applications include electronic publishing of organizational materials such as telephone directories, event calendars, procedure manuals, employee benefits information, and job postings. Additionally, an intranet typically includes a connection to the Internet. More sophisticated uses of intranets include groupware applications such as project management, chat rooms, newsgroups, group scheduling, and video conferencing.

An intranet essentially is a small version of the Internet that exists within an organization. Users update information on the intranet by creating and posting a Web page, using a method similar to that used on the Internet.

Sometimes a company uses an extranet, which allows customers or suppliers to access part of its intranet. Package shipping companies, for example, allow customers to access their intranet to print air bills, schedule pickups, and even track shipped packages as the packages travel to their destinations.

Network Communications Standards

Today's networks connect terminals, devices, and computers from many different manufacturers across many types of networks, such as wide area, local area, and wireless. For the different devices on various types of networks to be able to communicate, the network must use similar techniques of moving data through the network from one application to another.

To alleviate the problems of incompatibility and ensure that hardware and software components can be integrated into any network, various organizations such as ANSI and IEEE (pronounced I triple E) propose, develop, and approve network standards. A **network standard** defines guidelines that specify the way computers access the medium to which they are attached, the type(s) of medium used, the speeds used on different types of networks, and the type(s) of physical cable and/or the wireless technology used. A standard that outlines characteristics of how two network devices communicate is called a protocol. Hardware and software manufacturers design their products to meet the guidelines specified in a particular standard, so that their devices can communicate with the network.

The following sections discuss some of the more widely used network communications standards for both wired and wireless networks including Ethernet, token ring, TCP/IP, Wi-Fi, Bluetooth, UWB, IrDA, RFID, WiMAX, and WAP. As data moves through a network from one program to another, it may use one or more of these standards.

Ethernet **Ethernet** is a network standard that specifies no central computer or device on the network (nodes) should control when data can be transmitted; that is, each node attempts to transmit data when it determines the network is able to receive communications. If two computers on an Ethernet network attempt to send data at the same time, a collision occurs, and the computers must attempt to send their messages again.

Ethernet is based on a bus topology, but Ethernet networks can be wired in a star pattern. The Ethernet standard defines guidelines for the physical configuration of the network, e.g., cabling, network cards, and nodes. Today, Ethernet is the most popular LAN standard because it is relatively inexpensive and easy to install and maintain. Ethernet networks often use cables to transmit data.

Token Ring The **token ring** standard specifies that computers and devices on the network share or pass a special signal, called a token, in a unidirectional manner and in a preset order. A token is a special series of bits that function like a ticket. The device with the token can transmit data over the network. Only one token exists per network. This ensures that only one computer transmits data at a time. Token ring is based on a ring topology (although it can use a star topology). The token ring standard defines guidelines for the physical configuration of a network. Some token ring networks connect up to 72 devices. Others use a special type of wiring that allows up to 260 connections.

TCP/IP Short for Transmission Control Protocol/Internet Protocol, **TCP/IP** is a network standard, specifically a protocol, that defines how messages (data) are routed from one end of a network to the other. TCP/IP describes rules for dividing messages into small pieces, called packets; providing addresses for each packet; checking for and detecting errors; sequencing packets; and regulating the flow of messages along the network.

TCP/IP has been adopted as a network standard for Internet communications. Thus, all hosts on the Internet follow the rules defined in this standard. Internet communications also use other standards, such as the Ethernet standard, as data is routed to its destination.

When a computer sends data over the Internet, the data is divided into packets. Each packet contains the data, as well as the recipient (destination), the origin (sender), and the sequence information used to reassemble the data at the destination. Each packet travels along the fastest individual available path to the recipient's computer via communications devices called routers.

Wi-Fi Computers and devices that have the appropriate wireless capability can communicate via radio waves with other computers or devices using **Wi-Fi** (wireless fidelity), which identifies any network based on the 802.11 standards. Developed by IEEE, **802.11** is a series of network standards that specifies how two wireless devices communicate over the air with each other. Wi-Fi uses techniques similar to the Ethernet standard to specify how physically to configure a wireless network. Most of today's computers and many mobile devices, such as smart phones and handheld game consoles, are Wi-Fi enabled.

One popular use of the Wi-Fi standard is in hot spots that offer mobile users the ability to connect to the Internet with their Wi-Fi enabled wireless computers and devices. Many homes and small businesses also use Wi-Fi to network computers and devices together wirelessly.

Bluetooth **Bluetooth** is a standard, specifically a protocol, that defines how two Bluetooth devices use short-range radio waves to transmit data. To communicate with each other, Bluetooth devices often must be within about 10 meters (about 33 feet) but can be extended to 100 meters with additional equipment. Examples of Bluetooth devices can include desktop computers, notebook computers, handheld computers, smart phones, headsets, microphones, digital cameras, GPS receivers, and printers.

Ethernet
For more information, visit the Computer Concepts CourseMate Web site at www.cengagebrain.com, navigate to the Chapter 8 Web Link resource for this book, and then click Ethernet.

UWB UWB, which stands for **ultra-wideband**, is a network standard that specifies how two UWB devices use short-range radio waves to communicate at high speeds with each other. For optimal communications, the devices should be within 2 to 10 meters (about 6.5 to 33 feet) of each other. Examples of UWB uses include wirelessly transferring video from a digital video camera, printing pictures from a digital camera, downloading media to a portable media player, or displaying a slide show on a projector.

IrDA Some computers and devices use the **IrDA** specification to transmit data wirelessly to each other via infrared (IR) light waves. Infrared requires a line-of-sight transmission; that is, the sending device and the receiving device must be in line with each other so that nothing obstructs the path of the infrared light wave.

RFID

For more information, visit the Computer Concepts CourseMate Web site at www.cengagebrain.com, navigate to the Chapter 8 Web Link resource for this book, and then click RFID.

RFID **RFID** (radio frequency identification) is a standard, specifically a protocol, that defines how a network uses radio signals to communicate with a tag placed in or attached to an object, an animal, or a person. The tag consists of an antenna and a memory chip that contains the information to be transmitted via radio waves. Through an antenna, an RFID reader reads the radio signals and transfers the information to a computer or computing device. Readers can be handheld or embedded in an object such as a doorway or tollbooth.

WiMAX **WiMAX** (Worldwide Interoperability for Microwave Access), also known as **802.16**, is a newer network standard developed by IEEE that specifies how wireless devices communicate over the air in a wide area. Using the WiMAX standard, computers or devices with the appropriate WiMAX wireless capability communicate via radio waves with other computers or devices via a WiMAX tower. The WiMAX tower, which can cover up to a 30-mile radius, connects to the Internet or to another WiMAX tower.

Two types of WiMAX specifications are fixed wireless and mobile wireless. With fixed wireless WiMAX, a customer accesses the Internet from a desktop computer at home or other permanent location. Mobile wireless WiMAX, by contrast, enables users to access the WiMAX network with mobile computers and mobile devices such as smart phones.

The WiMAX standard provides wireless broadband Internet access at a reasonable cost over long distances to business and home users. WiMAX, similar to Wi-Fi, connects mobile users to the Internet via hot spots. Some game consoles also support the WiMAX standard.

WAP The **Wireless Application Protocol** (**WAP**) is a standard, specifically a protocol, that specifies how some mobile devices such as smart phones can display the content of Internet services such as the Web, e-mail, and chat rooms. To display a Web page on a smart phone, the phone should contain a microbrowser. WAP uses a client/server network. The wireless device contains the client software, which connects to the Internet access provider's server.

Communications Software

Communications software consists of programs that (1) help users establish a connection to another computer or network; (2) manage the transmission of data, instructions, and information; and (3) provide an interface for users to communicate with one another. The first two are system software and the third is application software. Chapter 3 presented a variety of examples of application software for communications: e-mail, FTP, Web browser, newsgroup/message boards, chat rooms, instant messaging, video conferencing, and VoIP.

Some communications devices are preprogrammed to accomplish communications tasks. Other communications devices require separate communications software to ensure proper transmission of data. Communications software works with the network standards and protocols defined earlier to ensure data moves correctly through a network. Communications software usually is bundled with the operating system or purchased network devices.

Often, a computer has various types of communications software, each serving a different purpose. One type of communications software helps users establish a connection to the Internet using wizards, dialog boxes, and other on-screen messages. Communications software also allows home and small office users to configure wired and wireless networks and connect devices to an existing network.

Communications over the Telephone Network

The public switched telephone network (PSTN) is the worldwide telephone system that handles voice-oriented telephone calls (Figure 8-15). Nearly the entire telephone network today uses digital technology, with the exception of the final link from the local telephone company to a home, which often is analog.

The telephone network is an integral part of computer communications. Data, instructions, and information are transmitted over the telephone network using dial-up lines or dedicated lines. The following sections discuss various types of lines that use the telephone network for data communications.

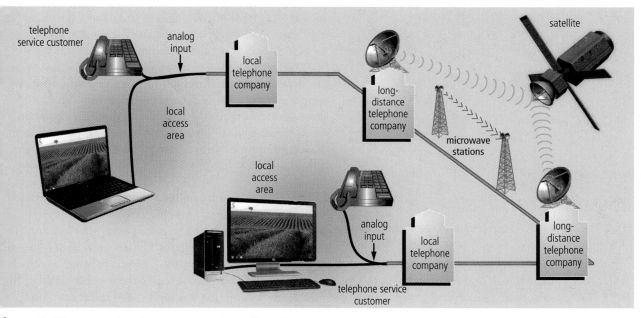

Figure 8-15 A sample telephone network configuration.

Dial-Up Lines

A **dial-up line** is a temporary connection that uses one or more analog telephone lines for communications. A dial-up connection is not permanent. Using a dial-up line to connect computers costs no more than making a regular telephone call.

Dedicated Lines

A **dedicated line** is a type of always-on connection that is established between two communications devices (unlike a dial-up line where the connection is reestablished each time it is used). The quality and consistency of the connection on a dedicated line are better than a dial-up line because dedicated lines provide a constant connection.

Businesses often use dedicated lines to connect geographically distant offices. Dedicated lines can be either analog or digital. Digital lines increasingly are connecting home and business users to networks around the globe because they transmit data and information at faster rates than analog lines.

Five types of digital dedicated lines are ISDN lines, DSL, FTTP, T-carrier lines, and ATM. Although cable television (CATV) lines and fixed wireless are not a type of telephone line, they

are very popular ways for the home user to connect to the Internet. Fixed wireless Internet connections use an antenna on your house or business to communicate with a tower location via radio signals. Later sections in this chapter discuss the use of CATV lines and radio signals to connect to the Internet.

The table in Figure 8-16 lists the approximate monthly costs of various types of Internet connections and transfer rates (speeds), as compared with dial-up lines. The following sections discuss ISDN lines, DSL, FTTP, T-carrier lines, and ATM.

Speeds of Various Internet Connections

Type of Line	Approximate Monthly Cost	Transfer Rates*
Dial-up	Local or long-distance rates	Up to 56 Kbps
ISDN	$10 to $40	Up to 1.54 Mpbs
DSL	$13 to $70	128 Kbps to 8.45 Mbps
Cable TV (CATV)	$20 to $50	128 Kbps to 52 Mbps
FTTP	$35 to $180	5 Mbps to 100 Mbps
Fixed Wireless	$35 to $80	256 Kbps to 10 Mbps
Fractional T1	$200 to $700	128 Kbps to 768 Kbps
T1	$400 to $1,600	1.544 Mbps
T3	$5,000 to $15,000	44.736 Mbps
ATM	$3,000 or more	155 Mbps to 622 Mbps, can reach 10 Gbps

*Kbps = thousand bits per second
Mbps = million bits per second
Gbps = billion bits per second

Figure 8-16 The speeds of various lines that can be used to connect to the Internet.

ISDN Lines For the small business and home user, an ISDN line provides faster transfer rates than dial-up telephone lines. Not as widely used today as in the past, **ISDN** (Integrated Services Digital Network) is a set of standards for digital transmission of data over standard copper telephone lines.

DSL DSL is a popular digital line alternative for the small business or home user. **DSL** (Digital Subscriber Line) transmits at fast speeds on existing standard copper telephone wiring. Some DSL installations include a dial tone, providing users with both voice and data communications.

ADSL is one of the more popular types of DSLs. ADSL (asymmetric digital subscriber line) is a type of DSL that supports faster transfer rates when receiving data (the downstream rate) than when sending data (the upstream rate). ADSL is ideal for Internet access because most users download more information from the Internet than they upload.

FTTP **FTTP**, which stands for **Fiber to the Premises**, uses fiber-optic cable to provide extremely high-speed Internet access to a user's physical permanent location. Two specific types of FTTP are FTTH (Fiber to the Home) and FTTB (Fiber to the Building). With FTTP service, an optical terminal at your premises receives the signals and transfers them to a router connected to your computer. As the cost of installing fiber decreases, increasingly more homes and businesses will opt for this high-speed Internet access.

T-Carrier Lines A **T-carrier line** is any of several types of long-distance digital telephone lines that carry multiple signals over a single communications line. T-carrier lines provide very fast data transfer rates. Only medium to large companies usually can afford the investment in T-carrier lines because these lines are so expensive.

The most popular T-carrier line is the **T1 line**. Businesses often use T1 lines to connect to the Internet. Many Internet access providers use T1 lines to connect to the Internet backbone. Home and small business users purchase fractional T1, in which they share a connection to the T1 line with other users. Fractional T1 is slower than a dedicated T1 line, but it also is less expensive.

A T3 line is equal in speed to 28 T1 lines. T3 lines are quite expensive. Main users of T3 lines include large corporations, telephone companies, and Internet access providers connecting to the Internet backbone. The Internet backbone itself also uses T3 lines.

ATM **ATM** (Asynchronous Transfer Mode) is a service that carries voice, data, video, and multimedia at extremely high speeds. Telephone networks, the Internet, and other networks with large amounts of traffic use ATM. Some experts predict that ATM eventually will become the Internet standard for data transmission, replacing T3 lines.

Communications Devices

A **communications device** is any type of hardware capable of transmitting data, instructions, and information between a sending device and a receiving device. One type of communications device that connects a communications channel to a sending or receiving device such as a computer is a modem. Computers process data as digital signals. Data, instructions, and information travel along a communications channel in either analog or digital form, depending on the communications channel.

The following pages describe the following types of communications devices: dial-up modems, digital modems, wireless modems, network cards, wireless access points, and routers.

Dial-Up Modems

A **dial-up modem** is a communications device that can convert digital signals to analog signals and analog signals to digital signals, so that data can travel along an analog telephone line. An analog signal consists of a continuous electrical wave, and a digital signal consists of individual electrical pulses that represent bits grouped together into bytes. A dial-up modem usually is in the form of an adapter card that you insert in an expansion slot on a computer's motherboard. One end of a standard telephone cord attaches to a port on the modem card and the other end plugs into a telephone outlet.

Digital Modems: ISDN, DSL, and Cable

A **digital modem** is a communications device that sends and receives data and information to and from a digital line. Three types of digital modems are ISDN modems, DSL modems, and cable modems.

An **ISDN modem** sends digital data and information from a computer to an ISDN line and receives digital data and information from an ISDN line. A **DSL modem** sends digital data and information from a computer to a DSL line and receives digital data and information from a DSL line. ISDN and DSL modems usually are external devices, in which one end connects to the telephone line and the other end connects to a port on the system unit.

A **cable modem** is a digital modem that sends and receives digital data over the cable television (CATV) network (Figure 8-17). With more than 110 million homes wired for cable television, cable modems provide a faster Internet access alternative to dial-up for the home user and can have speeds similar to DSL.

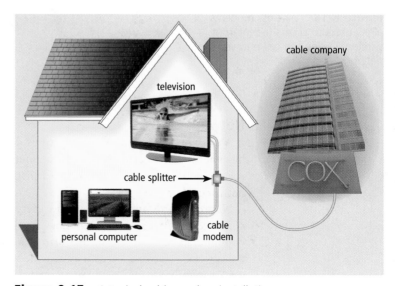

Figure 8-17 A typical cable modem installation.

Wireless Modems

Some mobile users have a **wireless modem** that uses the cell phone network to connect to the Internet wirelessly from a notebook computer, a smart phone, or other mobile device (Figure 8-18). Wireless modems, which have an external or built-in antenna, are available as USB flash drive, ExpressCard modules, PC Cards, and flash cards. Some smart phones also can function as a wireless modem when connected with a special cable to a personal computer.

wireless modem communicates with wireless Internet access provider

wireless modem inserted in notebook computer

Figure 8-18 Wireless modems allow users to access the Internet wirelessly using the cell phone network.

Network Cards

A **network card** is a communications device that enables a computer or device that does not have networking capability to access a network. The network card coordinates the transmission and receipt of data, instructions, and information to and from the computer or device containing the network card.

Network cards are available in a variety of styles (Figure 8-19). A network card for a desktop computer is an adapter card that has a port to which a cable connects. A network card for mobile computers and devices is in the form of a USB network adapter, ExpressCard module, PC Card, or a flash card. Network cards that provide wireless data transmission also are available. This type of card, sometimes called a wireless network card, often has an antenna.

A network card follows the guidelines of a particular network communications standard, such as Ethernet or token ring. An Ethernet card is the most common type of network card.

network card for desktop computer, for wired network communications

ExpressCard module, for wireless network communications

Figure 8-19 Network cards are available for both desktop and notebook computers.

Wireless Access Points

A **wireless access point** is a central communications device that allows computers and devices to transfer data wirelessly among themselves or to transfer data wirelessly to a wired network (Figure 8-7 on page 323). Wireless access points have high-quality antennas for optimal signals.

Routers

A **router** is a communications device that connects multiple computers or other routers together and transmits data to its correct destination on a network. A router can be used on any size of network. On the largest scale, routers along the Internet backbone forward data packets to their destination using the fastest available path. For smaller business and home networks, a router allows multiple computers to share a single high-speed Internet connection such as a cable modem or DSL modem (Figure 8-20). These routers connect from 2 to 250 computers.

To prevent unauthorized users from accessing files and computers, many routers are protected by a built-in firewall, called a hardware firewall. Some also have built-in antivirus protection. Today's routers or combination wireless access point/routers are easy to configure and secure against unauthorized access.

Internet

router

cable or DSL modem

Figure 8-20 Through a router, home and small business networks can share access to a high-speed Internet connection such as through a cable or DSL modem.

Home Networks

Many home users are connecting multiple computers and devices together in a **home network**. Each networked computer in the house has the following capabilities:

- Connect to the Internet at the same time
- Share a single high-speed Internet connection
- Access files and programs on the other computers in the house
- Share peripherals such as a printer, scanner, external hard disk, or optical disc drive
- Play multiplayer games with players on other computers in the house
- Connect game consoles to the Internet
- Subscribe to and use VoIP

Many vendors offer home networking packages that include all the necessary hardware and software to network your home using wired or wireless techniques. Some of these packages also offer intelligent networking capabilities. An intelligent home network extends the basic home network to include features such as lighting control, thermostat adjustment, and a security system. You no longer need extensive knowledge of networks to set up a home network. For example, the latest version of Windows allows you to connect all computers in your house to a home network easily.

Wired Home Networks

As with other networks, a home network can use wires, be wireless, or use a combination of wired and wireless. Three types of wired home networks are Ethernet, powerline cable, and phoneline.

Ethernet Network As discussed earlier in this chapter, traditional Ethernet networks require that each computer have built-in networking capabilities or contain a network card, which connects to a central network hub or similar device with a physical cable. This may involve running cable through walls, ceilings, and floors in the house. For the average home user, the hardware and software of an Ethernet network can be difficult to configure.

Powerline Cable Network A home powerline cable network is a network that uses the same lines that bring electricity into the house. This network requires no additional wiring. One end of a cable plugs in the computer's USB port and the other end of the cable plugs in a wall outlet. The data transmits through the existing power lines in the house.

Phoneline Network A phoneline network is an easy-to-install and inexpensive network that uses existing telephone lines in the home. With this network, one end of a cable connects to an adapter card or PC Card in the computer and the other end plugs in a wall telephone jack. The phoneline network does not interfere with voice and data transmissions on the telephone lines. That is, you can talk on the telephone and use the same line to connect to the Internet.

Wireless Home Networks

To network computers and devices that span multiple rooms or floors in a home, it may be more convenient to use a wireless strategy. One advantage of wireless networks is that you can take a mobile computer outside, for example in the backyard, and connect to the Internet through the home network as long as you are in the network's range.

Most home networks use a Wi-Fi network, which sends signals through the air at distances of up to 1,500 feet in some configurations. Wi-Fi networks are fairly easy to configure. Each computer that accesses the network must have the appropriate built-in wireless networking capabilities or a wireless network card, which communicates with a wireless access point or a combination router/wireless access point (Figure 8-21). To learn more about setting up a Wi-Fi network, complete the Learn How To 1 activity on pages 348 and 349.

Home Networks
For more information, visit the Computer Concepts CourseMate Web site at www.cengagebrain.com, navigate to the Chapter 8 Web Link resource for this book, and then click Home Networks.

How to Set Up Hardware for a Wi-Fi Home Network

Step 1
Sign up for high-speed Internet service, such as through a cable or DSL modem.

Internet

Step 2
Using a cable, connect the network card in a desktop computer to the combination router/wireless access point.

Step 3
Using a cable, connect the combination router/wireless access point to the cable/DSL modem.

smart phone

cable/DSL modem

desktop computer

router/wireless access point

Step 6
Purchase a smart phone with built-in wireless capabilities.

wireless desktop computer

wireless notebook computer

Step 4
Install a wireless network card or network adapter in other desktop computers in the home network.

Step 5
Insert a wireless USB network adapter, ExpressCard module, or PC Card in each notebook computer that will access the home network or purchase a notebook computer with built-in wireless networking capabilities.

Figure 8-21 This figure shows how to set up hardware for a Wi-Fi home network.

Communications Channel

As described at the beginning of the chapter, a communications channel is the transmission media on which data, instructions, or information travel in a communications system. The amount of data, instructions, and information that can travel over a communications channel sometimes is called the **bandwidth**. The higher the bandwidth, the more the channel transmits. For example, a cable modem has more bandwidth than a dial-up modem.

For transmission of text only, a lower bandwidth is acceptable. For transmission of music, graphics, photos, virtual reality images, or 3-D games, however, you need a higher bandwidth. When the bandwidth is too low for the application, you will notice a considerable slow-down in system performance.

A communications channel consists of one or more transmission media. **Transmission media** consist of materials or substances capable of carrying one or more signals. When you send data from a computer, the signal that carries the data may travel over various transmission media. This is especially true when the transmission spans a long distance.

Figure 8-22 illustrates a typical communications channel and shows the variety of transmission media used to complete the connection.

Broadband media transmit multiple signals simultaneously. Home and business users today opt for broadband Internet access because of the fast transfer rates. Two previously discussed services that offer broadband transmission are DSL and the cable television Internet service. Satellites also offer broadband transmission.

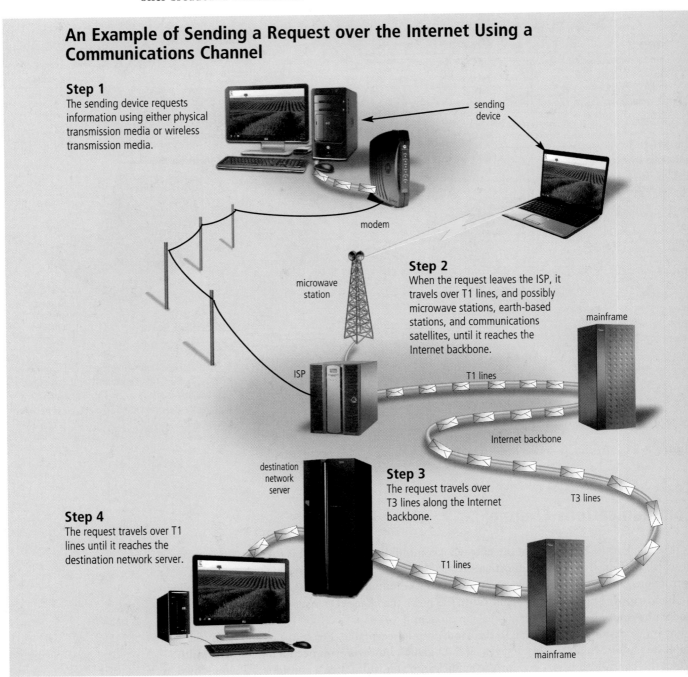

An Example of Sending a Request over the Internet Using a Communications Channel

Step 1
The sending device requests information using either physical transmission media or wireless transmission media.

sending device

modem

microwave station

Step 2
When the request leaves the ISP, it travels over T1 lines, and possibly microwave stations, earth-based stations, and communications satellites, until it reaches the Internet backbone.

mainframe

ISP

T1 lines

Internet backbone

destination network server

Step 3
The request travels over T3 lines along the Internet backbone.

T3 lines

Step 4
The request travels over T1 lines until it reaches the destination network server.

T1 lines

mainframe

Figure 8-22 This figure shows an example of sending a request over the Internet using a communications channel.

Transmission media are one of two types: physical or wireless. Physical transmission media use wire, cable, and other tangible materials to send communications signals. Wireless transmission media send communications signals through the air or space using radio, microwave, and infrared signals. The following sections discuss these types of media.

Physical Transmission Media

Physical transmission media used in communications include twisted-pair cable, coaxial cable, and fiber-optic cable. These cables typically are used within or underground between buildings. Ethernet and token ring LANs often use physical transmission media.

Twisted-Pair Cable

One of the more commonly used transmission media for network cabling and telephone systems is twisted-pair cable. **Twisted-pair cable** consists of one or more twisted-pair wires bundled together (Figure 8-23). Each twisted-pair wire consists of two separate insulated copper wires that are twisted together. The wires are twisted together to reduce noise. **Noise** is an electrical disturbance that can degrade communications.

Coaxial Cable

Coaxial cable, often referred to as coax (pronounced KO-ax), consists of a single copper wire surrounded by at least three layers: (1) an insulating material, (2) a woven or braided metal, and (3) a plastic outer coating (Figure 8-24).

Cable television (CATV) network wiring often uses coaxial cable because it can be cabled over longer distances than twisted-pair cable. Most of today's computer networks, however, do not use coaxial cable because other transmission media such as fiber-optic cable transmit signals at faster rates.

Figure 8-23 A twisted-pair cable consists of one or more twisted-pair wires. Each twisted-pair wire usually is color coded for identification. Telephone networks and LANs often use twisted-pair cable.

Figure 8-24 On a coaxial cable, data travels through a copper wire. This illustration shows computers networked together with coaxial cable.

Fiber-Optic Cable

The core of a **fiber-optic cable** consists of dozens or hundreds of thin strands of glass or plastic that use light to transmit signals. Each strand, called an optical fiber, is as thin as a human hair. Inside the fiber-optic cable, an insulating glass cladding and a protective coating surround each optical fiber (Figure 8-25).

Figure 8-25 A fiber-optic cable consists of hair-thin strands of glass or plastic that carry data as pulses of light.

Fiber-optic cables have the following advantages over cables that use wire, such as twisted-pair and coaxial cables:
- Capability of carrying significantly more signals than wire cables
- Faster data transmission
- Less susceptible to noise (interference) from other devices such as a copy machine
- Better security for signals during transmissio because they are less susceptible to noise
- Smaller size (much thinner and lighter weight)

Disadvantages of fiber-optic cable are it costs more than twisted-pair or coaxial cable and can b difficult to install and modify. Despite these limi tations, many local and long-distance telephone companies are replacing existing telephone lines with fiber-optic cables, enabling them to offer fil Internet access to home and business users.

Wireless Transmission Media

Many users opt for wireless transmission media because it is more convenient than installing cables. In addition, businesses use wireless transmission media in locations where it is impossible to install cables. Types of wireless transmission media used in communications include infrared, broadcast radio, cellular radio, microwaves, and communications satellites. Read Ethics & Issues 8-2 for a related discussion.

ETHICS & ISSUES 8-2

Should You Worry about Cell Phone, Cellular Antenna, and Wi-Fi Device Radiation?

Billions of people use cell phones, and more than 80 percent of the world's population has access to cell phone service from cellular antennas. Wi-Fi signals permeate businesses, public areas, and homes everywhere. These numbers are expected to rise sharply in coming years, and many are concerned about potential health effects from cell phones, cellular antennas, and Wi-Fi devices. Some cell phone users who suffered rare illnesses have filed lawsuits against cell phone companies, but the cases usually are lost due to lack of scientific evidence linking the use of the phones to the illnesses. While debates rage

in communities over placement of cellular antennas, the consideration of health effects on residents is muted because the federal government's Telecommunications Act of 1996 prohibits local governments from considering health effects when making decisions about cellular antenna placement. The law does not apply to Wi-Fi antennas, and some municipalities reject municipal Wi-Fi deployments due to residents' health concerns. It generally is agreed that no studies conclusively demonstrate negative health effects from cell phones, cellular antennas, and Wi-Fi devices, but skeptics claim that the

technology is too new to have endured long-term studies on humans. Long-term studies that are underway may not provide results for decades.

Are you concerned about cell phone, cellular antenna, and Wi-Fi radiation? Why or why not? Do you or does anyone you know minimize use of cell phones or other wireless devices due to health concerns? Should governments be required to consider health concerns when making decisions about wireless deployments? Why? Would you live next to a cellular antenna? Why or why not?

Infrared

As discussed earlier in the chapter, infrared (IR) is a wireless transmission medium that sends signals using infrared light waves. Mobile computers and devices, such as a mouse, printer, and smart phone, often have an IrDA port that enables the transfer of data from one device to another using infrared light waves.

Broadcast Radio

Broadcast radio is a wireless transmission medium that distributes radio signals through the air over long distances such as between cities, regions, and countries and short distances such as within an office or home. Bluetooth, UWB, Wi-Fi, and WiMAX communications technologies discussed earlier in this chapter use broadcast radio signals.

Cellular Radio

Cellular radio is a form of broadcast radio that is used widely for mobile communications, specifically wireless modems and cell phones. A cell phone is a telephone device that uses high-frequency radio waves to transmit voice and digital data messages.

Some mobile users connect their notebook computer or other mobile computer to a cell phone to access the Web, send and receive e-mail, enter a chat room, or connect to an office or school network while away from a standard telephone line. Others watch mobile TV, which is a service that provides television programs over the cellular network.

Personal Communications Services (**PCS**) is the term used by the United States Federal Communications Commission (FCC) to identify all wireless digital communications. Devices that use PCS include cell phones, PDAs, pagers, and fax machines.

Mobile TV

For more information, visit the Computer Concepts CourseMate Web site at www.cengagebrain.com, navigate to the Chapter 8 Web Link resource for this book, and then click Mobile TV.

Microwaves

Microwaves are radio waves that provide a high-speed signal transmission. Microwave transmission, often called fixed wireless, involves sending signals from one microwave station to another (shown in Figure 8-1 on page 314). Microwaves can transmit data at rates up to 4,500 times faster than a dial-up modem.

A microwave station is an earth-based reflective dish that contains the antenna, transceivers (which both send and receive signals from wireless devices), and other equipment necessary for microwave communications. Microwaves use line-of-sight transmission. To avoid possible obstructions, such as buildings or mountains, microwave stations often sit on the tops of buildings, towers, or mountains.

Microwave transmission is used in environments where installing physical transmission media is difficult or impossible and where line-of-sight transmission is available. For example, microwave transmission is used in wide-open areas such as deserts or lakes; between buildings in a close geographic area; or to communicate with a satellite. Current users of microwave transmission include universities, hospitals, city governments, cable television providers, and telephone companies. Home and small business users who do not have other high-speed Internet connections available in their area also opt for lower-cost fixed wireless plans.

Communications Satellite

A **communications satellite** is a space station that receives microwave signals from an earth-based station, amplifies (strengthens) the signals, and broadcasts the signals back over a wide area to any number of earth-based stations (shown in Figure 8-1).

These earth-based stations often are microwave stations. Other devices, such as smart phones and GPS receivers, also can function as earth-based stations. Transmission from an earth-based station to a satellite is an uplink. Transmission from a satellite to an earth-based station is a downlink.

Applications such as air navigation, television and radio broadcasts, weather forecasting, video conferencing, paging, global positioning systems, and Internet connections use communications satellites. With the proper satellite dish and a satellite modem card, consumers access the Internet using satellite technology. With satellite Internet connections, however, uplink transmissions usually are slower than downlink transmissions. This difference in speeds usually is acceptable to most Internet satellite users because they download much more data than they upload. Although a satellite Internet connection is more expensive than cable Internet or DSL connections, sometimes it is the only high-speed Internet option in remote areas.

✔ QUIZ YOURSELF 8-3

Instructions: Find the true statement below. Then, rewrite the remaining false statements so that they are true.

1. A cable modem converts a computer's digital signals to analog signals before they are transmitted over standard telephone lines.

2. A network card is an adapter card, USB network adapter, ExpressCard module, PC Card, or flash card that enables the computer or device to access a network.

3. Analog signals consist of individual electrical pulses that represent bits grouped together into bytes.

4. Physical transmission media send communications signals through the air or space using radio, microwave, and infrared signals.

5. Most wireless home networks use powerline cables.

Quiz Yourself Online: To further check your knowledge of pages 333 through 341, visit the Computer Concepts CourseMate Web site at www.cengagebrain.com, navigate to the Chapter 8 Quiz Yourself resource for this book, and then click Objectives 6 – 8.

Chapter Summary

This chapter provided an overview of communications terminology and applications. It also discussed how to join computers into a network, allowing them to communicate and share resources such as hardware, software, data, and information. It also explained various types of communications devices, media, and procedures as they relate to computers.

Computer Usage @ Work

Agriculture

The world's dependence on the agriculture industry is enormous. The demand to keep food prices affordable encourages those working in this industry to operate as efficiently as possible. Although people have worked in agriculture for more than 10,000 years, advances in technology assist with maintaining and protecting land, crops, and animals.

Almost all companies in this industry have many acres of land that they must maintain, and it is not always feasible for farmers to take frequent trips around the property to perform basic tasks such as watering soil in the absence of rain. The number of people-hours required to water soil manually on several thousand acres of land might result in businesses spending thousands of dollars in labor and utility costs. If an irrigation system is installed instead, one or more individuals still are responsible for deciding when to water and how long to water. If the irrigation process is automated, sensors detect how much rain has fallen recently, as well as whether the soil is in need of watering. The sensors then send this data to a computer that processes it and decides when and how much to water. Many automated home irrigation systems also are programmable and use rain sensors, which keep the irrigation system from turning on, or turn it off when rainfall occurs.

In addition to keeping the soil moist and reducing maintenance costs, computers also can utilize sensors to analyze the condition of crops in the field and determine whether pests or diseases are affecting the crops. If sensors detect pests and/or diseases, computers send a notification to the appropriate individual to take corrective action. In some cases, the discovery of pests might trigger a pesticide to discharge in the affected area automatically.

Until recently, the lack of adequate cellular and wireless network signals in the fields made communications difficult for farmers. Mobile cellular antennas and amplifiers stretch mobile broadband coverage across entire farms, enabling farmers to receive wireless signals up to eight times farther from the cellular tower than they would without the antennas and amplifiers. Wireless access throughout the farm also allows farmers to monitor their farms and communicate with colleagues from remote locations.

The next time you take a bite of a delicious carrot or juicy cucumber, you can appreciate how technology has helped to maintain an ideal environment for these vegetables to grow and protected them from unwanted pests, all for a reasonable price when you purchase them from your local supermarket.

For more information, visit the Computer Concepts CourseMate Web site at www.cengagebrain.com, navigate to the Chapter 8 Computer Usage @ Work resource for this book, and then click Agriculture.

Companies on the Cutting Edge

CISCO SYSTEMS Networking the Internet

Green networking practices have given Cisco Systems top ranking on the Vendor Matrix, a research tool used to assess companies' innovation and implementation of environmentally sound initiatives. Low power consumption, green power supplies and switching tools, and sound recycling efforts are part of the reason for Cisco's high marks and for the company's success.

Cisco manufactures a broad line of networking equipment for transporting data within a building, across a campus, and across the globe. A group of computer scientists at Stanford University founded Cisco in 1984. From the start,

the company focused on communicating over networks. Today, Cisco's Internet Protocol-based (IP) networking equipment is the basis of the Internet and most private networks.

The company's TelePresence video conferencing system is installed in more than 100 cities worldwide and serves a variety of audiences, ranging from corporate board members to soldiers stationed at military bases overseas. More than 2.5 million students in 160 countries have received certification credentials through the company's Cisco Academy.

Modems/Gateways

VERIZON Communications Network Leader

One of the largest mergers in United States' history occurred when Bell Atlantic acquired GTE in 2000. The company was renamed Verizon, a combination of the words Veritas, the Roman goddess of truth, and horizon. Verizon's famous "Can you hear me now?" tagline has become synonymous with the cell phone industry's connectivity issues.

More than 87 million customers nationwide subscribe to Verizon's wireless network, which is managed through the company's Wireless division. Its other units are Verizon Telecom and Verizon Business, which offer local telephone, nationwide long distance, broadband

Internet services, networking, and security services. The company's global fiber-optic network serves more than 150 countries on 6 continents, and its United States network, FiOS, was the first in the country to offer Internet, television, and telephone service.

Verizon is the only telecommunications company that has been named repeatedly to *Working Mother* magazine's 100 Best Companies for Working Mothers list. Recently, it was ranked 17th among FORTUNE 500 companies. Verizon Wireless also boasts the highest customer loyalty, profitability, and cost efficiency.

Secure, Local to Global
Business Solutions

For more information, visit the Computer Concepts CourseMate Web site at www.cengagebrain.com and then navigate to the Chapter 8 Companies on the Cutting Edge resource for this book.

Technology Trailblazers

ROBERT METCALFE Ethernet Inventor

Robert Metcalfe promised to eat his words if his prediction of the Internet's collapse in 1996 was wrong. During his keynote speech at the WWW International Conference in 1997, he placed the paper containing his prediction in a blender, mixed it with liquid, and drank the pulp. Metcalfe certainly has been correct in predicting many other aspects of the Internet, however, primarily the vision that his Ethernet invention would one day connect millions of computers worldwide.

Metcalfe's fascination with linking computers developed while he was in college. At Harvard's Project

MAC, he connected the university's computers to the ARPANET. Then, at Xerox's Palo Alto Research Center (PARC), he coinvented Ethernet in 1973. Xerox managers did not see how the Ethernet fit with the company's primary business of photocopying, so he left the company in 1979 to found 3Com Corporation and make Ethernet the standard for computer communications.

After his retirement from 3Com, he became a general partner in Polaris Venture Partners, a venture capital firm that invests in the early stages of information technology and life sciences companies.

PATRICIA RUSSO Communications Industry Leader

The ability to lead teams and solve problems is important for any top corporate leader, and Patricia Russo has used these skills in her career in the communications industry.

After graduating from Georgetown University, she held positions in sales and marketing at IBM and then in management at AT&T for more than 20 years. She also served as CEO and president of Eastman Kodak. Forbes.com has listed Russo as one of the most powerful

women in the world and noted that she has the skills to lead a company through difficult financial times.

Russo was instrumental in forming Lucent Technologies in 1996 and was appointed CEO in 2002. Under her leadership, Lucent merged with Alcatel in 2006 to become a major worldwide communications services equipment manufacturer. She served as CEO until 2008, and during her tenure Alcatel-Lucent was one of the largest corporations in the world run by a woman.

For more information, visit the Computer Concepts CourseMate Web site at www.cengagebrain.com and then navigate to the Chapter 8 Technology Trailblazers resource for this book.

Chapter Review

The Chapter Review reinforces the main concepts presented in this chapter.

To listen to an audio version of this Chapter Review, visit the Computer Concepts CourseMate Web site at www.cengagebrain.com and then navigate to the Chapter 8 Chapter Review resource for this book.

1. What Is the Purpose of the Components Required for Successful Communications? Computer **communications** describes a process in which two or more computers or devices transfer data, instructions, and information. Successful communications require a **sending device** that initiates a transmission instruction, a communications device that connects the sending device to a communications channel, a **communications channel** on which the data travels, a communications device that connects the communications channel to a receiving device, and a **receiving device** that accepts the transmission.

2. How Are Computer Communications Used? Communications technologies include blogs, chat rooms, e-mail, instant messaging, Internet, newsgroups, RSS, video conferencing, VoIP, Web, Web folders, and wikis. People also use communications for other purposes. Users send and receive wireless messages to and from smart phones, cell phones, handheld game consoles, and other mobile devices using **text messaging, picture messaging, video messaging,** and wireless instant messaging. At home, work, school, and in many public locations, people connect wirelessly to the Internet through a **wireless Internet access point,** either a **hot spot** or a mobile wireless network. A **cybercafé** is a coffeehouse, restaurant, or other location that provides personal computers with Internet access. A **global positioning system (GPS)** analyzes signals sent by satellites to determine an earth-based receiver's geographic location. Many software products allow users to **collaborate,** or work online, with other users connected to a server. **Groupware** is software that helps groups of people work together and share information over a network. **Voice mail** allows someone to leave a voice message for one or more people. **Web services** describe standardized software that enables programmers to create applications that communicate with other remote computers over a network.

Visit the Computer Concepts CourseMate Web site at www.cengagebrain.com, navigate to the Chapter 8 Quiz Yourself resource for this book, and then click Objectives 1 – 2.

3. What Are Different Types of Networks? A **network** is a collection of computers and devices connected together via communications devices and media. Networks usually are classified as a local area network, metropolitan area network, or wide area network. A **local area network (LAN)** connects computers and devices in a limited geographical area or closely positioned group of buildings. A **wireless LAN (WLAN)** is a LAN that uses no physical wires. A **metropolitan area network (MAN)** connects local area networks in a metropolitan area and handles the bulk of communications activity across that region. A **wide area network (WAN)** covers a large geographic area using a communications channel that combines many types of media.

4. What Is the Purpose of Communications Software? **Communications software** helps users establish a connection to another computer or network, manages the transmission of data, and provides an interface for users to communicate with one another.

5. What Are Various Types of Lines for Communications Over the Telephone Network? The telephone network uses dial-up lines or dedicated lines. A **dial-up line** is a temporary connection that uses one or more analog telephone lines for communications. A **dedicated line** is an always-on connection established between two communications devices. Dedicated lines include ISDN lines, DSL, FTTP, T-carrier lines, and ATM. **ISDN** is a set of standards for digital transmission over standard copper telephone lines. **DSL** transmits at fast speeds on existing standard copper telephone wiring. **FTTP (Fiber to the Premises)** uses fiber-optic cable to provide extremely high-speed Internet access to a user's physical permanent location. A **T-carrier line** is a long-distance digital telephone line that carries multiple signals over a single communications line. **ATM** (Asynchronous Transfer Mode) is a service that carries voice, data, video, and multimedia at extremely high speeds.

Visit the Computer Concepts CourseMate Web site at www.cengagebrain.com, navigate to the Chapter 8 Quiz Yourself resource for this book, and then click Objectives 3 – 5.

6. What Are Commonly Used Communications Devices? A **communications device** is any hardware capable of transmitting data between a sending device and a receiving device. A **dial-up modem** converts digital signals to analog signals and analog signals to digital signals so that data can travel along an analog telephone line. A **digital modem** sends and receives data and information to and from a digital line. An **ISDN modem** transmits digital data to and from an ISDN line, while a **DSL**

modem transmits digital data to and from a DSL line. A **cable modem** is a digital modem that sends and receives digital data over the cable television network. A **wireless modem** uses the cell phone network to connect to the Internet wirelessly from a mobile device. A **network card** enables a computer or device that does not have networking capability to access a network. A **wireless access point** allows computers and devices to transfer data wirelessly. A **router** connects multiple computers or routers together and transmits data to its correct destination on the network.

7. How Can a Home Network Be Set Up? A **home network** connects multiple computers and devices in a home. An Ethernet network connects each computer to a central hub with a physical cable. A home powerline cable network uses the same lines that bring electricity into the house. A phoneline network uses existing telephone lines in a home. Most home networks use a Wi-Fi network, which sends signals through the air at distances of up to 1,500 feet in some configurations.

8. What Are Various Physical and Wireless Transmission Media? **Transmission media** consist of materials or substances capable of carrying one or more signals. Physical transmission media use tangible materials to send communications signals. **Twisted-pair cable** consists of one or more twisted-pair wires bundled together. **Coaxial cable** consists of a single copper wire surrounded by at least three layers: an insulating material, a woven or braided metal, and a plastic outer coating. **Fiber-optic cable** consists of thin strands of glass or plastic that use light to transmit signals. Wireless transmission media send communications signals through the air or space. Infrared (IR) sends signals using infrared light waves. **Broadcast radio** distributes radio signals through the air over long and short distances. **Cellular radio** is a form of broadcast radio that is used widely for mobile communications. **Microwaves** are radio waves that provide a high-speed signal transmission. A **communications satellite** is a space station that receives microwave signals from an earth-based station, amplifies the signals, and broadcasts the signals back over a wide area.

Visit the Computer Concepts CourseMate Web site at www.cengagebrain.com, navigate to the Chapter 8 Quiz Yourself resource for this book, and then click Objectives 6 – 8.

Key Terms

You should know each key term. The list below helps focus your study.

To see an example of and a definition for each term, and to access current and additional information from the Web, visit the Computer Concepts CourseMate Web site at www.cengagebrain.com and then navigate to the Chapter 8 Key Terms resource for this book.

802.11 (329)
802.16 (330)
ATM (332)
bandwidth (337)
Bluetooth (329)
broadband (338)
broadcast radio (341)
bus network (327)
cable modem (333)
cellular radio (341)
client/server network (325)
clients (325)
coaxial cable (339)
collaborate (321)
collaborative software (321)
communications (314)
communications channel (314)
communications device (333)
communications satellite (341)
communications software (330)
cybercafé (319)

dedicated line (331)
dial-up line (331)
dial-up modem (333)
digital modem (333)
document management system (321)
DSL (332)
DSL modem (333)
Ethernet (329)
fiber-optic cable (340)
FTTP (Fiber to the Premises) (332)
global positioning system (GPS) (320)
groupware (321)
home network (336)
hot spot (318)
intranet (328)
IrDA (330)
ISDN (332)
ISDN modem (333)
local area network (LAN) (323)
mashup (322)

metropolitan area network (MAN) (324)
microwaves (341)
network (322)
network card (334)
network standard (328)
network topology (326)
noise (339)
P2P (326)
PCS (341)
peer-to-peer network (325)
picture messaging (318)
receiving device (314)
RFID (330)
ring network (328)
router (335)
sending device (314)
server (325)
star network (326)
T1 line (332)
T-carrier line (332)
TCP/IP (329)
text messaging (317)
token ring (329)

transmission media (338)
twisted-pair cable (339)
UWB (ultra-wideband) (330)
value-added network (VAN) (322)
video messaging (318)
visual voice mail (322)
voice mail (322)
Web conference (321)
Web services (322)
wide area network (WAN) (324)
Wi-Fi (329)
WiMAX (330)
wireless access point (335)
Wireless Application Protocol (WAP) (330)
wireless Internet access point (318)
wireless LAN (WLAN) (323)
wireless modem (334)

Checkpoint

The Checkpoint exercises test your knowledge of the chapter concepts. The page number containing the answer appears in parentheses after each exercise.

To complete the Checkpoint exercises interactively, visit the Computer Concepts CourseMate Web site at www.cengagebrain.com and then navigate to the Chapter 8 Checkpoint resource for this book.

Multiple Choice Select the best answer.

1. When an online meeting takes place on the Web, it is called _____. (321)
 a. video messaging
 b. a peer-to-peer network
 c. a Web meeting
 d. a Web conference

2. With _____, users can view message details such as the length of calls and, in some cases, read message contents instead of listening to them. (322)
 a. Web services
 b. Internet telephony
 c. video messaging
 d. visual voice mail

3. A _____ network is a third-party business that provides networking services for a fee. (322)
 a. value-added
 b. client/server
 c. star
 d. file sharing

4. A _____ is a Web application that combines services from two or more sources, creating a new application. (322)
 a. document management system
 b. peer-to-peer network
 c. Web service
 d. mashup

5. _____ is a standard, specifically a protocol, that defines how a network uses radio signals to communicate with a tag placed in or attached to an object, an animal, or a person. (330)
 a. RFID
 b. WiMAX
 c. Bluetooth
 d. UWB

6. _____ is a newer network standard developed by IEEE that specifies how wireless devices communicate over the air in a wide area. (330)
 a. Wi-Fi
 b. WiMAX
 c. 802.16
 d. Both b and c

7. DSL, cable television Internet service, and satellites offer _____ transmission. (338)
 a. baseband
 b. IrDA
 c. microwave
 d. broadband

8. _____ consists of a single copper wire surrounded by at least three layers. (339)
 a. Fiber-optic cable
 b. Twisted-pair cable
 c. Coaxial cable
 d. Infrared

Matching Match the terms with their definitions.

_____ 1. collaborate (321)
_____ 2. Bluetooth (329)
_____ 3. dedicated line (331)
_____ 4. dial-up modem (333)
_____ 5. noise (339)

a. online area in which users have written discussions about a subject
b. electrical disturbance that can degrade communications
c. work online with other users connected to a server
d. type of always-on connection that is established between two communications device
e. communications device that can convert digital signals to analog signals and analo signals to digital signals, so that data can travel along an analog telephone line
f. a protocol that defines how two devices use short-range radio waves to transmit da

Short Answer Write a brief answer to each of the following questions.

1. What is text messaging? _____ What are some options for sending and receiving text messages? _____

2. Describe how the global positioning system (GPS) works. _____ How do individuals use GPS technology? _____

3. What is a network topology? _____ How are a star network, a bus network, and a ring network different? _____

4. What is UWB and what are its benefits? _____ What are some uses of UWB? _____

5. What are three different types of digital modems? _____ How does each one function? _____

Problem Solving

The Problem Solving exercises extend your knowledge of the chapter concepts by seeking solutions to practical computer problems that you may encounter at home, school, or work. The Collaboration exercise should be completed with a team.

In the real world, practical problems often can be solved in multiple ways. Provide one solution to each of the following problems using available resources, such as articles on the Web or in print, blogs, podcasts, videos, television, user guides, other individuals, and electronics and computer stores. You may need to use multiple resources to obtain an answer. Present your solutions in the form requested by your instructor (brief report, presentation, discussion, or other means).

@ Home

1. **Text Messages Not Received** Although you have sent your friend multiple text messages from a cell phone, he is not receiving them. What might be the problem?

2. **Intermittent Network Connection** While using your computer, you intermittently lose the network connection. The computer is connected to a wired network using an Ethernet cable. What might be causing this loss of connection?

3. **Telephone Noise** Recently, you installed DSL service in your house. Your computers can connect to the Internet successfully, but your home telephone now experiences noise. Before the DSL service was installed, your telephone had no noise problem. What steps will you take to eliminate the noise?

4. **No Network Activity** Your computer has a network card installed to access the wired network in your house. Upon plugging the Ethernet cable into the network card and the network port on the wall, the activity lights on the network card do not illuminate. What might be causing this?

@ Work

5. **Slow Network Connection** You subscribed to an Internet service for your home business. After performing several tests, you realize that the Internet connection speed you were promised by your Internet access provider is higher than the speed you currently are experiencing. What might be causing this? What are your next steps?

6. **WEP Key Required** The information technology team has provided you with a new notebook computer. When you attempt to connect to the wireless network, Windows asks you for a WEP key. How will you proceed?

7. **Trouble Accessing Wired Network** In an effort to save money spent in commuting to and from your office, your boss has agreed to provide you with a notebook computer so that you can work from home. When you work in the office, you bring the notebook computer and regularly retrieve files from your desktop computer. When you attempt to use the corporate network to connect to the notebook computer to the desktop computer, an error message appears stating that the connection is unsuccessful. What might be wrong?

8. **No GPS Signal** As a traveling sales representative for a startup company, your boss provided you with a GPS receiver so that you can locate your customers when driving to meet them at various locations. When you travel to certain areas, the GPS receiver has a difficult time receiving signals from the GPS satellites. What might be wrong? How can you make sure that you are able to locate your customers' addresses?

Collaboration

9. **Computers in Agriculture** Your employer owns hundreds of acres of orange groves and realizes that labor and utility costs can be decreased by installing automated systems to manage the property. As a computer-literate employee of the organization, your supervisor asks you to research automated systems that can help decrease expenses. Form a team of three people to research automated agricultural solutions. One team member should research automated irrigation systems that water the trees only as needed. Another team member should research solutions that can keep the trees healthy and free from pests, and the third team member should create a list of reasons why these automated systems can decrease costs, bolster efficiency, and increase profit. Compile your findings and submit them to your instructor.

Learn How To

The Learn How To activities step you through fundamental technology skills when using a computer. The Learn How To exercises enable you to become more proficient with these skills.

Premium Activity: To relate this Learn How To activity to your everyday life, see a visual demonstration of the activity, and complete a short assessment, visit the Computer Concepts CourseMate Web site at www.cengagebrain.com and then navigate to the Chapter 8 Learn How To resource for this book.

Learn How To 1: Set Up and Install a Wi-Fi Home Network

In this chapter you learned about home networks and their advantages (see page 336, Home Networks). Creating a Wi-Fi home network consists of four phases: 1) subscribe to a high-speed Internet access provider, 2) purchase the Wi-Fi equipment, 3) connect the physical devices, and 4) create the network through the use of software.

Subscribe to a High-Speed Internet Access Provider A high-speed Internet access provider is advisable to connect all computers on the home network to the Internet. The three primary ways for home users to obtain a fast connection to the Internet are DSL, cable, and satellite. DSL is provided by telephone companies, cable is provided by cable TV companies, and satellite connections are provided by satellite TV providers. Each has its advantages and disadvantages, including the minimum and maximum speed of Internet access, cost, and availability.

Determining the optimal high-speed Internet access provider depends largely on where the network will be located, local costs, and service availability. The way to obtain the best high-speed Internet access provider is to research the options available in your area.

Purchase the Wi-Fi Equipment As part of the service when you subscribe to a high-speed Internet access provider, you receive a modem that is capable of connecting to the Internet. In most cases, the modem is not a wireless transmitter. So, in order to establish a wireless connection between the Internet and the home network, you will need a wireless router that establishes the wireless access point.

You can visit any retail electronics store and find a wide variety of wireless routers. A key to purchasing the correct router is to ensure it will work with your modem and Internet access provider. Some Internet access providers support only certain brands of routers and, while it is true that other routers may work, you might be taking a risk if you purchase an unsupported router. With the popularity of wireless home networks, though, some Internet access providers now provide a wireless router as part of the subscription service, often for an additional fee. You should investigate closely the needs for the Wi-Fi router to ensure compatibility with your Internet access provider.

In addition to the router, each computer that is to be part of the Wi-Fi network needs a wireless network adapter. This device allows the computers to communicate with one another. Most external wireless network adapters plug in either a PC Card slot, ExpressCard slot, or a USB connection. Many notebook computers have a built-in wireless network adapter.

Finally, some home networks have a combination of wired and wireless devices. In these networks, the modem connects to the wireless router, and computers on the network either connect to the wireless router using a wireless or wired connection.

Once the Wi-Fi equipment is assembled, you are ready to connect your home network.

Connect the Physical Devices Once you have assembled your equipment, you can connect the devices in the network. Usually, the modem will be connected to the source of the Internet transmission (DSL, cable, or satellite). Then the modem is connected to the wireless router, which in turn is connected to the computers on your network.

After these connections are completed, each of the computers that will be used in the network that do not have a built-in wireless network adapter must have the adapter attached, often by using a USB connection. Once these connections are made, the computers can join the network.

Create the Homegroup To establish a homegroup and share files with other computers on your network, complete the following steps:

1. Click the Start button on the Windows taskbar and then click Control Panel on the Start menu.
2. Click the 'Choose homegroup and sharing options' link below the Network and Internet heading to display the HomeGroup dialog box.
3. Click the 'Create a homegroup' button to display the Create a Homegroup dialog box.
4. In the Create a Homegroup dialog box, place a check mark next to each item you wish to share with other computers connected to the same homegroup and then click the Next button.
5. Once Windows sets up the homegroup, it will display a password that other computer users will need to know to join your homegroup.

6. Click the 'Print password and instructions' link to open the 'View and print your homegroup password' window, which contains your homegroup password and instructions about how other computers on your network can join your homegroup.

7. Ready the printer according to the printer instructions and then click the 'Print this page' button to display the Print dialog box. Select the printer to which you want to print and then click the Print button to print these instructions.

8. Click the Close button on the title bar to close the 'View and print your homegroup password' window.

9. Click the Finish button to open the HomeGroup window.

10. If necessary, make changes to your homegroup settings and then click the Save changes button. If you have no changes, click the Close button on the title bar to close the HomeGroup window.

11. Follow the instructions you printed in Step 7 to join other computers to the homegroup.

Exercise

1. Assume you live near Coeur d'Alene, Idaho. You have decided that a high-speed Internet access provider and a Wi-Fi network would be advantageous for your at-home business. Find answers to the following questions for this Idaho town or a town specified by your instructor: What high-speed Internet access providers are available? Which provides the best service? Which is the cheapest? Based on the information you gather, write a plan for subscribing to a high-speed Internet access provider. Submit the answers to the questions and your plan to your instructor.

Learn It Online

The Learn It Online exercises are interactive Web exercises designed to reinforce and expand your understanding of the chapter concepts. The descriptions below briefly summarize each exercise.

To complete the Learn It Online exercises, visit the Computer Concepts CourseMate Web site at www.cengagebrain.com, navigate to the Chapter 8 resources for this book, click the link for the exercise you want to complete, and then read the instructions.

1 At the Movies — Got Your Video Right Here
Watch a movie to see why the Sling Media Slingbox is the best way to beam your favorite shows to any broadband-connected computer or Windows Mobile device in the world and then answer questions about the movie.

2 Student Edition Labs — Networking Basics and Wireless Networking
Enhance your understanding and knowledge about networking basics and wireless networking by completing the Networking Basics and Wireless Networking Labs.

3 Practice Test
Take a multiple choice test that checks your knowledge of the chapter concepts and review the resulting study guide.

4 Who Wants To Be a Computer Genius²?
Play the Shelly Cashman Series version of this popular game by answering questions to find out if you are a computer genius. Panic buttons are available to provide assistance during game play.

5 Crossword Puzzle Challenge
Complete an interactive crossword puzzle to reinforce concepts presented in this chapter.

6 Windows Exercises
Step through the Windows 7 exercises to learn about understanding your modem, Windows Firewall, viewing network connections, and using Help and Support to understand networks.

7 Exploring Computer Careers
Read about a career as a network specialist, search for related employment advertisements, and then answer related questions.

8 Web Apps — Gmail
Learn how to use Gmail to send and receive e-mail messages, label e-mail messages, chat with others, and search for e-mail messages.

Web Research

The Web Research exercises broaden your understanding of chapter concepts by presenting questions that require you to search the Web for answers.

1 Search Sleuth

Use one of the search engines listed in Figure 2-8 in Chapter 2 on page 65 or your own favorite search engine to find the answers to the following questions. Copy and paste the Web address from the Web page where you found the answer. Some questions may have more than one answer. If required, submit your answers to your instructor. (1) Which product is manufactured in the modified chemical vapor deposition (MCVD) process? (2) In what city is the IrDA corporate office located? How many companies are IrDA members? (3) Which agency funds and controls the global positioning system? In how many hours does one satellite orbit the earth? (4) Which California county built a crime lab in 2008 that uses passive RFID tags to track evidence? (5) Who sent the first text message in 1989?

2 Green Computing

As the speed of Ethernet routers, switches, and servers increases, so does the amount of electricity consumed. Engineers are working to reduce the power requirements in various ways, including a technology called Rapid PHY Selection (RPS), which could save $1.2 billion during computer systems' lifetimes. Critics say RPS would slow the networks' performance and cause connectivity problems. Consumers, too, can benefit from using green Wi-Fi routers that adjust power consumption and shut down automatically. View online Web sites that provide information about reducing networks' electricity consumption. How does RPS adjust Ethernet speed and corresponding power usage? What technological challenges are engineers facing when developing this RPS technology? Which companies are manufacturing Wi-Fi routers for home networks? How much energy do they claim to save? Write a report summarizing your findings, and include a table of links to Web sites that provide additional details.

3 Social Networking

Conversations, experiences, photos, videos, and other aspects of a person's life can be preserved for future generations using LifeNaut, an online social network funded by the Terasem Movement Foundation, Inc. More than 9,000 people have created a personal space, called a mindfile, to create a profile, build a 3-D virtual avatar, upload files, and then share these personal life memories. Members can meet new people by browsing the online mindfiles. As biotechnology advances, scientists predict that these preserved memories could be added to a person's mind, not necessarily the mind of the person who originally created these mindfiles. Visit the LifeNaut Web site (lifenaut.com) and then click the About and FAQ links on the left side of the home page. Could viewing the LifeNaut mindfiles be useful to people who have lost their memory? Would parents desire to preserve aspects of their lives for their children to view and hear? Would you desire to record your life? Summarize the information you read and viewed.

4 Blogs

Avoiding information overload is difficult in today's world, with more than 80 million live Web sites available at all times of the day. Managing blogs, news feeds, and podcasts can be accomplished by subscribing to Bloglines, a free service that tracks Web sites tailored to a person's specific interests. More than 10,000 subscribers monitor an average of 20 news feeds, which are updated hourly. Visit Bloglines (bloglines.com) and then read the information in the About link at the bottom of the home page. What are Bloglines' key features? How does Bloglines examine RSS feeds? How does the Web site help readers organize their subscriptions? What is the purpose of a Clip Blog? Summarize the information you read and viewed.

5 Ethics in Action

Consumers may welcome customized advertisements, but they may be unaware of how they have become targeted to receive these messages. When people visit some Web sites, their IP address, browser software, operating system, and viewing habits are tracked and recorded along with their wish lists and purchase histories. These details are collected and shared among advertisers without the users' consent. The Center for Digital Democracy (CDD) filed a complaint with the Federal Trade Commission stating that these targeted advertisements and user profiles can constitute an invasion of privacy. Visit the CDD Web site (democraticmedia.org) and other Web sites discussing online ads and privacy concerns. How are the CDD and other organizations working to protect consumers from being exploited by digital advertisers? What steps can Web users take to avoid sharing personal data with marketers? Write a report summarizing your findings, and include a table of links to Web sites that provide additional details.

Information System Development and Programming Languages

Objectives

After completing this chapter, you will be able to:

1 Discuss the importance of project management, feasibility assessment, documentation, and data and information gathering techniques

2 Discuss the purpose of each system development phase

3 Differentiate between low-level languages and procedural languages

4 Identify the benefits of object-oriented programming languages and program development tools

5 List other programming languages and other program development tools

6 Describe various ways to develop Web pages

7 List the six program development steps

8 Explain the basic control structures used in designing solutions to programming problems

System Development

A **system** is a set of components that interact to achieve a common goal. Businesses use many types of systems. A billing system allows a company to send invoices and receive payments from customer Through a payroll system, employees receive paychecks. A manufacturing system produces the goo that customers order. An inventory system keeps track of the items in a warehouse. Very often, thes systems also are information systems.

An **information system** (**IS**) is a collection of hardware, software, data, people, and procedures that work together to produce quality information. An information system supports daily, short-ter and long-range activities of users.

The type of information that users need often changes. When this occurs, the information system must meet the new requirements. In some cases, members of the system development team modify the current information system. In other cases, they develop an entirely new information system.

As a computer user in a business, you someday may participate in the modification of an existing system or the development of a new system. Thus, it is important that you understand system developmen **System development** is a set of activities used to build an information system.

System development activities often are grouped into larger categories called **phases**. This collection of phases sometimes is called the **system development life cycle** (**SDLC**). Many SDLCs contain five phases:

1. Planning
2. Analysis
3. Design
4. Implementation
5. Operation, Support, and Security

As shown in Figure 11-1, each system development phase consists of a series of activities, and the phases form a loop. In theory, the five system development phases often appear sequentially, as show in Figure 11-1. In reality, activities within adjacent phases often interact with one another — making system development a dynamic iterative process.

System Development

Figure 11-1
System development often consists of five phases that form a loop. Several ongoing activities also take place throughout system development.

System development should follow three general guidelines: group activities into phases, involve the users, and define standards.

1. Group activities into phases: Many SDLCs contain the same phases shown in Figure 11-1. Others have more or fewer phases. Regardless, all system development cycles have similar activities and tasks.

2. Involve users: **Users** include anyone for whom the system is being built. Customers, employees, students, data entry clerks, accountants, sales managers, and owners all are examples of users. Users are more apt to accept a new system if they contribute to its design.

3. Define standards: **Standards** are sets of rules and procedures an organization expects employees to accept and follow. Standards help people working on the same project produce consistent results.

Who Participates in System Development?

System development should involve representatives from each department in which the proposed system will be used. This includes both nontechnical users and IT professionals. During system development, the systems analyst meets and works with a variety of people (Figure 11-2). A **systems analyst** is responsible for designing and developing an information system. The systems analyst is the users' primary contact person.

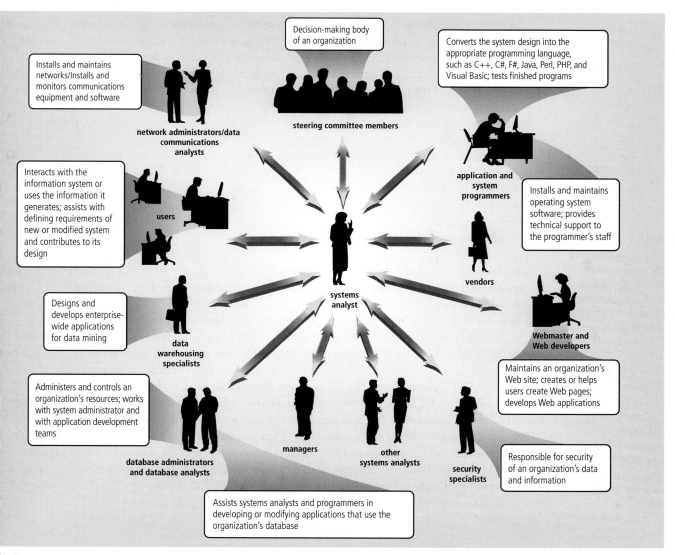

Figure 11-2 A systems analyst meets with a variety of people during a system development project.

Smaller organizations may have one systems analyst or even one person who assumes the roles of both systems analyst and programmer. Larger organizations often have multiple systems analysts. Some refer to a systems analyst as a **system developer**.

Systems analysts are the liaison between the users and the IT professionals. They convert user requests into technical specifications. They must be familiar with business operations, be able to solve problems, have the ability to introduce and support change, and possess excellent communications and interpersonal skills. Systems analysts prepare many reports, drawings, and diagrams. They discuss various aspects of the development project with users, management, other analysts, database analysts, database administrators, network administrators, Web developers, programmers, vendors, and the steering committee. The **steering committee** is a decision-making body in an organization.

For each system development project, an organization usually forms a **project team** to work on the project from beginning to end. The project team consists of users, the systems analyst, and other IT professionals.

Project Management

Project management is the process of planning, scheduling, and then controlling the activities during system development. The goal of project management is to deliver an acceptable system to the user in an agreed-upon time frame, while maintaining costs.

In smaller organizations or projects, one person manages the entire project. For larger projects, the project management activities often are separated between a project manager and a project leader. In this case, the **project leader** manages and controls the budget and schedule of the project, and the **project manager** controls the activities during system development. Project leaders and/or project managers are part of the project team. If the systems analyst is not the project manager, he or she works closely with the project manager.

To plan and schedule a project effectively, the project leader identifies the following elements for the project:

- Goal, objectives, and expectations of the project, collectively called the **scope**
- Required activities
- Time estimates for each activity
- Cost estimates for each activity
- Order of activities
- Activities that can take place at the same time

Gantt Charts

For more information, visit the Computer Concepts CourseMate Web site at www.cengagebrain.com, navigate to the Chapter 11 Web Link resource for this book, and then click Gantt Charts.

PERT Charts

For more information, visit the Computer Concepts CourseMate Web site at www.cengagebrain.com, navigate to the Chapter 11 Web Link resource for this book, and then click PERT Charts.

After these items are identified, the project leader usually records them in a project plan. Project leaders can use **project management software** to assist them in planning, scheduling, and controlling development projects (Figure 11-3).

A popular tool used to plan and schedule the time relationships among project activities is a Gantt chart (Figure 11-3a). A Gantt chart, developed by Henry L. Gantt, is a bar chart that uses horizontal bars to show project phases or activities. The left side, or vertical axis, displays the list of required activities. A horizontal axis across the top or bottom of the chart represents time.

A tool used for planning and scheduling large, complex projects is the PERT chart (Figure 11-3b). A PERT chart, short for Program Evaluations and Review Technique chart, analyzes the time required to complete a task and identifies the minimum time required for an entire project.

When the project features and deadlines have been determined, the project leader monitors and controls the project. Some activities take less time than originally planned. Others take longer. Project leaders should use **change management**, which is the process of recognizing when a change in the project has occurred and taking actions to react to the change. It is crucial that everyone is aware of and agrees on any changes made to the project plan.

Figure 11-3a (Gantt chart)

Figure 11-3b (PERT chart)

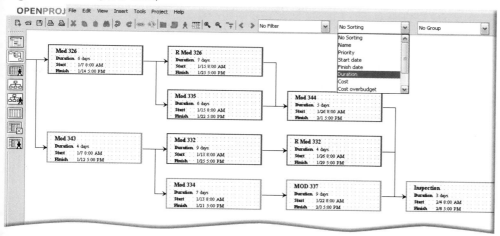

Figure 11-3 Project management software.

Feasibility Assessment

Feasibility is a measure of how suitable the development of a system will be to the organization. A project that is feasible at one point during system development might become infeasible at a later point. Thus, systems analysts frequently reevaluate feasibility during the system development project.

Four tests to evaluate feasibility are:

- Operational feasibility: Measures how well the proposed information system will work. Will the users like the new system? Will they use it? Will it meet their requirements? Is it secure?
- Schedule feasibility: Measures whether the established deadlines for the project are reasonable. If a deadline is not reasonable, the project leader might make a new schedule. If a deadline cannot be extended, then the scope of the project might be reduced to meet a mandatory deadline.
- Technical feasibility: Measures whether the organization has or can obtain the hardware, software, and people needed to deliver and then support the proposed information system.
- Economic feasibility, also called cost/benefit feasibility: Measures whether the lifetime benefits of the proposed information system will be greater than its lifetime costs.

Documentation

During system development, project members produce much documentation. **Documentation** is the collection and summarization of data and information. It includes reports, diagrams, programs, or any other information generated during system development.

It is important that all documentation be well written, thorough, consistent, and understandable. The final information system should be reflected accurately and completely in documentation developed throughout the development project. Maintaining up-to-date documentation should be an ongoing part of system development.

Data and Information Gathering Techniques

Systems analysts and other IT professionals use several techniques to gather data and information. They review documentation, observe, survey, interview, conduct joint-application design sessions, and research.

- Review Documentation — By reviewing documentation such as an organization chart, memos, and meeting minutes, systems analysts learn about the history of a project. Documentation also provides information about the organization such as its operations, weaknesses, and strengths.
- Observe — Observing people helps systems analysts understand exactly how they perform a task. Likewise, observing a machine allows you to see how it works. Read Ethics & Issues 11-1 for a related discussion.
- Survey — To obtain data and information from a large number of people, systems analysts distribute surveys.
- Interview — The interview is the most important data and information gathering technique for the systems analyst. It allows the systems analyst to clarify responses and probe during face-to-face feedback. To learn more about how to conduct an interview, complete the Learn How To 1 activity on pages 460 and 461.

𝖸 ETHICS & ISSUES 11-1

Do You Work Harder When Someone Is Watching?

While gathering data and information during system development, employees are involved actively in the process. They complete surveys, participate in interviews, and are observed while performing their jobs. Many researchers suggest that during observation, employees may not exhibit everyday behavior and may perform above and beyond their normal workday activities. They base this premise on the Hawthorne Effect, which is the result of a study performed in the 1920s in the Western Electric Company plant in Hawthorne, Illinois. The study discovered that productivity improved during observation, whether the conditions were made better or worse. Researchers concluded that productivity seemed to improve whenever the workers knew they were being observed.

Do you believe that you work harder when someone is watching? Why or why not? What is your opinion of the Hawthorne Effect? Do you agree with the research? Is such observation ethical, and can it have other psychological effects on employees? If productivity increases during observation, is observation a good data gathering technique in a system study? Why or why not?

JAD Sessions — Instead of a single one-on-one interview, analysts often use joint-application design sessions to gather data and information. **Joint-application design (JAD)** sessions, or **focus groups**, are a series of lengthy, structured, group meetings in which users and IT professionals work together to design or develop an application (Figure 11-4).

Research — Newspapers, computer magazines, reference books, trade shows, the Web, vendors, and consultants are excellent sources of information. These sources can provide the systems analyst with information such as the latest hardware and software products and explanations of new processes and procedures.

What Initiates System Development?

A user may request a new or modified information system for a variety of reasons. The most obvious reason is to correct a problem such as an incorrect calculation or a security breach. Another reason is to improve the information system. Organizations may want to improve hardware, software, or other technology to enhance an information system.

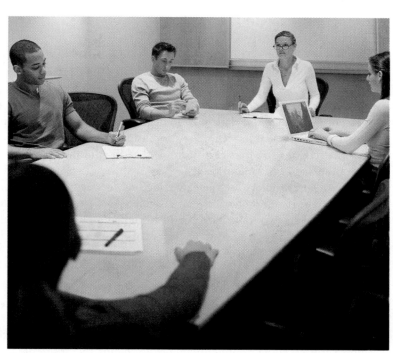

Figure 11-4 During a JAD session, the systems analyst is the moderator, or leader, of the discussion. Another member, called the scribe, records facts and action items assigned during the session.

Sometimes situations outside the control of an organization require a modification to an information system. Corporate management or some other governing body may mandate a change. Competition also can lead to change. Another source of change results from one organization merging with or acquiring another.

A user may request a new or modified information system verbally in a telephone conversation or written as an e-mail message. Read Ethics & Issues 11-2 for a related discussion. In larger organizations, users write a formal request for a new or modified information system, which is called a request for system services or **project request**. The project request becomes the first item of documentation for the project. It also triggers the first phase of the SDLC: planning.

Horizon Community College — A Case Study

This chapter includes a case study to help you understand real-world system development applications. The case study appears shaded in light orange immediately after the discussion of each phase in the chapter. The case is about Horizon Community College (HCC), a fictitious school.

Approximately 15,000 students are enrolled at HCC each year in its varied programs. Students can earn A.S. (Associate of Science) or A.A. (Associate of Arts) degrees in many areas: accounting, anthropology, childcare, computer technology, electronics, construction technology, forensic science, graphic design, history, management, marketing, nursing, and sociology. The school also offers certificates and adult education classes in each of these areas. Some classes are taken on campus while others are offered online.

Currently, instructors use their own method for recording assignment grades and calculating semester grades. At semester end, the registration department distributes via e-mail a class semester grade form, which contains a list of all students in a class and an area for the instructor to record each student's final semester grade. As instructors send in their class semester grade forms, registration clerks enter each student's grade into the school's database program. After grades are entered, the quality control group compares the original class semester grade forms with the entered grades to check for any errors that may have occurred during the data entry process. Then, report cards are printed and mailed to students.

With the number of enrolled students on the rise, Chad Goldstein, registrar, has noticed that it takes a considerable amount of time for the registration clerks to enter semester grades and for quality control to verify entered grades for accuracy. Lately, quality control has been finding an excessive number of data entry errors, in part due to the excessive workload on the registration clerks. For this reason, Chad would like the instructors to use an online grade book, so that report cards could be printed directly from the instructor's grade book. This change in procedure would save the registration department a great deal of time and money and eliminate data entry errors.

Chad realizes this task will require substantial school resources. He believes a systems study is necessary. He sends an e-mail message to the IT director (Figure 11-5a). She agrees and asks him to fill out a Request for System Services form (Figure 11-5b) and submit it to Juanita Mendez, chair of the steering committee at HCC.

Figure 11-5a (informal project request)

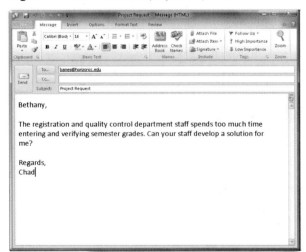

Figure 11-5b
(formal project request)

Horizon Community College
REQUEST FOR SYSTEM SERVICES

SUBMITTED BY: Chad Goldstein Form IT-102A

DEPARTMENT: Registration DATE: 12-15-2011

TYPE OF REQUEST:
 New System
 X Existing System Enhancement
 Existing System Modification

BRIEF STATEMENT OF PROBLEM:
The registration and quality control department staff spends too much time entering and verifying semester grades.

BRIEF STATEMENT OF EXPECTED SOLUTION:
Modify our current grade reporting system to enable instructors to use an online grade book, so that semester report cards could be printed directly from each instructor's online grade book.

ACTION (to be completed by steering committee member):
 ☐ Request Approved
 ☐ Request Delayed Analyst Assigned:
 ☐ Request Rejected Start Date: _____
 Signature: _____ Until: _____
 Reason: _____

 Date: _____

Figure 11-5
Sometimes users informally communicate a project request verbally or as an e-mail message. In larger organizations, requests often are documented on a form such as this Request for System Services.

Planning Phase

The **planning phase** for a project begins when the steering committee receives a project request. This committee usually consists of five to nine people. It typically includes a mix of vice presidents, managers, nonmanagement users, and IT personnel.

During the planning phase, four major activities are performed: (1) review and approve the project requests; (2) prioritize the project requests; (3) allocate resources such as money, people, and equipment to approved projects; and (4) form a project development team for each approved project.

The projects that receive the highest priority are those mandated by management or some other governing body. These requests are given immediate attention. The steering committee evaluates the remaining project requests based on their value to the organization. The steering committee approves some projects and rejects others. Of the approved projects, it is likely that only a few will begin system development immediately. Others will have to wait for additional funds or resources to become available.

Planning at Horizon Community College

After receiving the project request (Figure 11-5b) from Chad, Juanita Mendez distributes it to all members of the steering committee. They will discuss the request at their next meeting. The steering committee members of HCC are Juanita Mendez, controller and chair of the steering committee; Milan Sciranka, professor; Suzy Zhao, Web developer; Donnell Carter, training specialist; Karl Schmidt, systems analyst; and Bethany Ames, IT director. Juanita also invites Chad Goldstein to the next steering committee meeting. Because he originated the project request, Chad will have the knowledge to answer questions.

During the meeting, the committee decides the project request identifies an improvement to the system, instead of a problem. They feel the nature of the improvement (to print report cards directly from instructors' online grade books) could lead to considerable savings for the school. It also will reduce data entry errors made by registration clerks.

The steering committee approves the request. Juanita points out that the school has enough funds in its budget to begin the project immediately. Thus, Bethany assembles a system development project team. She assigns Karl Schmidt, systems analyst, as the project leader. Karl and his team immediately begin the next phase: analysis.

Analysis Phase

The **analysis phase** consists of two major activities: (1) conduct a preliminary investigation and (2) perform detailed analysis. The following sections discuss these activities.

The Preliminary Investigation The main purpose of the **preliminary investigation**, sometimes called the **feasibility study**, is to determine the exact nature of the problem or improvement and decide whether it is worth pursuing. Should the organization continue to assign resources to this project? To answer this question, the systems analyst conducts a general study of the project.

The first activity in the preliminary investigation is to interview the user who submitted the project request. Depending on the nature of the request, project team members may interview other users, too.

In addition to interviewing, members of the project team may use other data gathering techniques, such as reviewing existing documentation. Often, the preliminary investigation is completed in just a few days.

Upon completion of the preliminary investigation, the systems analyst writes the feasibility report. This report presents the team's findings to the steering committee. The feasibility report contains these major sections: introduction, existing system, benefits of a new or modified system, feasibility of a new or modified system, and the recommendation (Figure 11-6).

In some cases, the project team may recommend not to continue the project. If the steering committee agrees, the project ends at this point. If the project team recommends continuing and the steering committee approves this recommendation, then detailed analysis begins.

Horizon Community College
MEMORANDUM

To:	Steering Committee
From:	Karl Schmidt, Project Leader
Date:	December 29, 2011
Subject:	Feasibility Report of Grade Reporting System

Following is the feasibility report in response to the request for a modification to our Grade Reporting System. Your approval is necessary before the next phase of the project will begin.

Introduction

The purpose of this feasibility report is to determine whether it is beneficial for Horizon Community College to continue studying the Grade Reporting System. The registrar has indicated registration and quality control department staff spends too much time entering and verifying semester grades. This project would affect the registration department, quality control, and instructors. Students also will notice a change.

Existing System

Background

Currently, instructors use their own method for recording assignment grades and calculating semester grades. At semester end, the registration department distributes via e-mail a class semester grade form, which contains a list of all students in a class and an area for the instructor to record each student's final semester grade. As instructors send in their class semester grade forms, registration clerks enter each student's grade using the school's database. After grades are entered, the quality control group compares the original semester grade forms with the entered grades to check for any errors that may have occurred during the data entry process. Then, report cards are printed and mailed to students.

Problems

As the number of enrolled students continues to rise, the following problems have been identified with the current Grade Reporting System at Horizon Community College:

- Registration clerks and quality control spend too much time entering semester grades and verifying entered grades.

- Quality control has been finding an excessive number of data entry errors in part due to the increased workload on the registration clerks.

FEASIBILITY REPORT
Page 2

Benefits of a New or Modified System

Following is a list of benefits that could be realized if the Grade Reporting System at H Community College were modified to enable instructors to use an online grade book, sc report cards could be printed directly from each instructor's grade book:

- Data entry errors of semester grades by registration clerks would be eliminated.

- Cost of supplies, such as paper and ink, would be reduced by 10 percent.

- Through a more efficient use of registration and quality control staff time, the college achieve a 50 percent reduction in temporary clerks in the registration department.

Feasibility of a New or Modified System

Operational

A modified Grade Reporting System will require instructors enter all semester grades onli addition to report cards being generated automatically from each instructor's grade students will be able to check their class progress throughout the semester.

Schedule

The established deadline for the Grade Reporting System is reasonable.

Technical

Horizon Community College already has a functional database and server. To handl increased volume and usage of data, however, it will need to purchase a larger database ser

Economic

A detailed summary of the costs and benefits, including all assumptions, is available on o server. The potential costs of the proposed solution could range from $15,000 to $20,00 estimated savings in temporary clerks and supplies will exceed $30,000.

If you have any questions about the detailed cost/benefit summary or require f information, please contact me.

Recommendation

Based on the findings presented in this report, we recommend a continued study of the Reporting System.

Figure 11-6 A feasibility report presents the results of the preliminary investigation. The report must be prepared professionally and be well organized to be effective.

Preliminary Investigation at Horizon Community College

Karl Schmidt, systems analyst and project leader, meets with Chad Goldstein to discuss the project request. During the interview, Karl looks at the class semester grade forms. He asks Chad how many data entry errors that quality control identified during the last batch of report cards. Then Karl interviews the controller, Juanita Mendez, to obtain some general cost and benefit figures for the feasibility report. He also talks to several registration clerks, quality control clerks, instructors, and students. He wants to know their opinion of the current report card process.

Next, Karl prepares the feasibility report (Figure 11-6). After the project team members review it, Karl submits it to the steering committee. The report recommends proceeding to the detailed analysis phase of this project. The steering committee agrees. Karl and his team begin detailed analysis.

Detailed Analysis Detailed analysis involves three major activities: (1) study how the current system works; (2) determine the users' wants, needs, and requirements; and (3) recommend a solution. Detailed analysis sometimes is called logical design because the systems analysts develop the proposed solution without regard to any specific hardware or software. That is, they make no attempt to identify the procedures that should be automated and those that should be manual.

During these activities, systems analysts use all of the data and information gathering techniques. They review documentation, observe employees and machines, distribute surveys, interview employees, conduct JAD sessions, and research.

While studying the current system and identifying user requirements, the systems analyst collects a great deal of data and information. A major task for the systems analyst is to document these findings in a way that can be understood by everyone. Systems analysts use diagrams to describe the processes that transform inputs into outputs and diagrams that graphically show the flow of data in the system. Both users and IT professionals refer to this documentation.

The System Proposal After the systems analyst has studied the current system and determined all user requirements, the next step is to communicate possible solutions for the project in a system proposal. The purpose of the **system proposal** is to assess the feasibility of each alternative solution and then recommend the most feasible solution for the project, which often involves modifying or building on the current system. The systems analyst presents the system proposal to the steering committee. If the steering committee approves a solution, the project enters the design phase.

When the steering committee discusses the system proposal and decides which alternative to pursue, it considers whether to modify the existing system, buy packaged software from an outside source, build its own custom software, and/or outsource some or all of its IT needs to an outside firm. The final decision often is a mix of these options.

- **Packaged software** is mass-produced, copyrighted, prewritten software available for purchase. Packaged software is available for different types of computers. Chapter 3 presented many types of application software available for personal computers. These include word processing, spreadsheet, database, document management, note taking, desktop publishing, paint/image editing, Web page authoring, personal finance, legal, tax preparation, educational/reference, e-mail, and Web browser software.

 Vendors offer two types of packaged software: horizontal and vertical. Horizontal market software meets the needs of many different types of organizations. The programs discussed in Chapter 3 were horizontal. If an organization has a unique way of accomplishing activities, then it also may require vertical market software. Vertical market software specifically is designed for a particular business or industry. Examples of organizations that use vertical market software include banks, schools, hospitals, real estate offices, libraries, and insurance companies. Each of these industries has unique information processing requirements.

 Instead of buying packaged software, some organizations write their own applications using programming languages such as C++, C#, F#, Java, JavaScript, and Visual Basic. Application software developed by the user or at the user's request is called **custom software**.

Vertical Market Software

For more information, visit the Computer Concepts CourseMate Web site at www.cengagebrain.com, navigate to the Chapter 11 Web Link resource for this book, and then click Vertical Market Software.

The main advantage of custom software is that it matches the organization's requirements exactly. The disadvantages usually are that it is more expensive and takes longer to design and implement than packaged software.

- Organizations can develop custom software in-house using their own IT personnel or **outsource** its development, which means having an outside source develop it for them. Some organizations outsource just the software development aspect of their IT operation. Others outsource more or all of their IT operation. Depending on an organization's needs, outside firms can handle as much or as little of the IT requirements as desired. A trend that has caused much controversy relates to organizations that outsource to firms located outside their homeland.

Detailed Analysis at Horizon Community College

Karl and his team begin performing the activities in the detailed analysis phase of the Grade Reporting System. As part of the study and requirements activities, they use several of the data and information gathering techniques available to them. They interview employees throughout the school and meet with some students. They observe instructors recording grade. They prepare documents that become part of the project documentation. Members of the project team refer to these documents during the remainder of system development.

After two months of studying the existing system and obtaining user requirements, Karl discusses his findings with his supervisor, Bethany Ames. In addition to semester grades being printed from the online grade book, Karl recommends th. students be granted access to the online grade book so that they can check their progress in a class at any given time.

Based on Karl's findings, Bethany writes a system proposal for the steering committee to review. Suzy Zhao, Web developer at Horizon Community College, developed the current Web site. Thus, Bethany recommends that Suzy's staff modify the We site in-house. Bethany also recommends that the school invest in a larger database server to handle the additional grade book information.

The steering committee agrees with Bethany's proposal. Karl and his team begin the design phase of the project.

Design Phase

The **design phase** consists of two major activities: (1) if necessary, acquire hardware and software and (2) develop all of the details of the new or modified information system. The systems analyst often performs these two activities at the same time instead of sequentially.

Acquiring Necessary Hardware and Software When the steering committee approves a solution, the systems analyst begins the activity of obtaining additional hardware or software or evaluating cloud providers that offer the hardware or software to meet the organization's needs. The systems analyst may skip this activity if the approved solution does not require new hardware or software. I this activity is required, it consists of four major tasks: (1) identify technical specifications, (2) solicit vendor proposals, (3) test and evaluate vendor proposals, and (4) make a decision.

Identifying Technical Specifications The first step in acquiring necessary hardware and software is to identify all the hardware and software requirements of the new or modified system. To do this, systems analysts use a variety of research techniques. They talk with other systems analysts, visit vendors' stores, and search the Web. Many trade journals, newspapers, and magazines provide some or all of their printed content as e-zines. An **e-zine** (pronounced ee-zeen), or **electronic magazine** is a publication available on the Web.

E-Zines
For more information, visit the Computer Concepts CourseMate Web site at www.cengagebrain.com, navigate to the Chapter 11 Web Link resource for this book, and then click E-Zines.

After the systems analyst defines the technical requirements, the next step is to summarize these requirements for potential vendors. The systems analyst can use three basic types of documents for this purpose: an RFQ, an RFP, or an RFI. A request for quotation (RFQ) identifies the required product(s). With an RFQ, the vendor quotes a price for the listed product(s). With a request for proposal (RFP), the vendor selects the product(s) that meets specified requirements and then quote the price(s). A request for information (RFI) is a less formal method that uses a standard form to request information about a product or service.

Soliciting Vendor Proposals Systems analysts send the RFQ, RFP, or RFI to potential hardware and software vendors. Another source for hardware and software products is a value-added reseller. A **value-added reseller (VAR)** is an organization that purchases products from manufacturers and then resells these products to the public — offering additional services with the product (Figure 11-7).

Instead of using vendors, some organizations hire an IT consultant or a group of IT consultants. An **IT consultant** is a professional who is hired based on computer expertise, including service and advice. IT consultants often specialize in configuring hardware and software for businesses of all sizes.

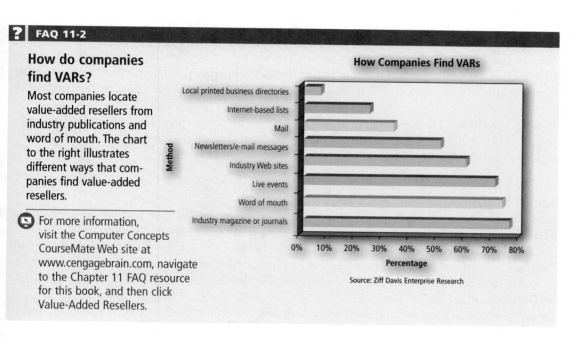

? FAQ 11-2

How do companies find VARs?

Most companies locate value-added resellers from industry publications and word of mouth. The chart to the right illustrates different ways that companies find value-added resellers.

For more information, visit the Computer Concepts CourseMate Web site at www.cengagebrain.com, navigate to the Chapter 11 FAQ resource for this book, and then click Value-Added Resellers.

How Companies Find VARs

Method / Percentage chart showing:
- Local printed business directories
- Internet-based lists
- Mail
- Newsletters/e-mail messages
- Industry Web sites
- Live events
- Word of mouth
- Industry magazine or journals

(0% to 80% scale)

Source: Ziff Davis Enterprise Research

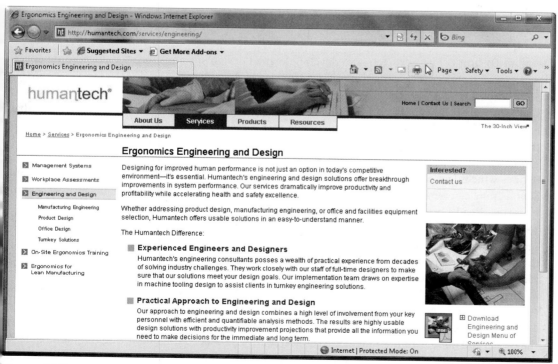

Figure 11-7 Many VARs provide complete systems, often called turnkey solutions.

Testing and Evaluating Vendor Proposals After sending RFQs and RFPs to potential vendors, the systems analyst will receive completed quotations and proposals. Evaluating the proposals and then selecting the best one often is a difficult task. It is important to be as objective as possible while evaluating each proposal.

Systems analysts use many techniques to test the various software products from vendors. They obtain a list of user references from the software vendors. They also talk to current users of the software to solicit their opinions. Some vendors will give a demonstration of the product(s) specified. Other vendors provide demonstration copies or trial versions, allowing the organizations to test the software themselves.

Sometimes it is important to know whether the software can process a certain volume of transactions efficiently. In this case, the systems analyst conducts a benchmark test. A **benchmark test** measures the performance of hardware or software. For example, a benchmark test could measure the time it takes a payroll program to print 50 paychecks. Comparing the time it takes various accounting programs to print the same 50 paychecks is one way of measuring each program's performance.

Making a Decision Having rated the proposals, the systems analyst presents a recommendation to the steering committee. The recommendation could be to award a contract to a vendor or to not make any purchases at this time.

Hardware Acquisition at Horizon Community College

Karl and his team compile a requirements list for the database server. They prepare an RFP and submit it to twelve vendors, eight through the Web and four local computer stores. Ten vendors reply within the three-week deadline.

Of the ten replies, the development team selects two to evaluate. They eliminate the other eight because these vendors did not offer adequate warranties for the database server. The project team members ask for benchmark test results for each server. In addition, they contact two current users of this database server for their opinions about its performance. After evaluating these two servers, the team selects the best one.

Karl summarizes his team's findings in a report to the steering committee. The committee gives Karl authorization to award a contract to the proposed vendor. As a courtesy and to maintain good working relationships, Karl sends a letter to all twelve vendors informing them of the committee's decision.

Detailed Design The next step is to develop detailed design specifications for the components in the proposed solution. The activities to be performed include developing designs for the databases, inputs, outputs, and programs.

- During database design, the systems analyst works closely with the database analysts and database administrators to identify those data elements that currently exist within the organization and those that are new.

 The systems analyst also addresses user access privileges. This means that the systems analyst defines which data elements each user can access, when they can access the data elements, what actions they can perform on the data elements, and under what circumstances they can access the elements. Read Looking Ahead 11-1 for a look at a future database design.

- During detailed design of inputs and outputs, the systems analyst carefully designs every menu, screen, and report specified in the requirements. The outputs often are designed first because they help define the requirements for the inputs. Thus, it is very important that outputs are identified correctly and that users agree to them.

 The systems analyst typically develops two types of designs for each input and output: a mockup and a layout chart. A mockup is a sample of the input or output that contains actual data (Figure 11-8). The systems analyst shows mockups to users for their approval. Because users will work with the inputs and outputs of the system, it is crucial to involve users during input and output design.

 After users approve the mockup, the systems analyst develops a layout chart for the programmer. A layout chart is more technical and contains programming-like notations. Many database programs provide tools for technical design (Figure 11-9).

↗ **LOOKING AHEAD 11-1**

Remote Solar System Objects Mapped in Database

Exploding supernovas, neutron stars, and black holes will become more than faint astronomical objects when the Large Synoptic Survey Telescope (LSST) becomes fully operable in 2016. The LSST is being constructed atop an 8,800-foot mountain in Chile.

Managing the telescope's 200,000 images of the billions of remote galaxies is a massive undertaking. A single minute of observation time generates 72 GB of data, which will be saved in a 150 PB database. Each year, 60 PB of the stored images in this world's largest nonproprietary database will be released to researchers. Each night, 30 TB of data will be sent to the United States so that astronomy buffs can view the night sky via their computers. In addition, astronomers will be able to log on to the Data Access Center at any time to view all the data collected.

Software billionaires Bill Gates and Charles Simonyi have donated $30 million for the project. Researchers are hopeful the LSST ultimately will give a graphical view of the universe's evolution from its birth to the present day.

For more information, visit the Computer Concepts CourseMate Web site at www.cengagebrain.com, navigate to the Chapter 11 Looking Ahead resource for this book, and then click LSST.

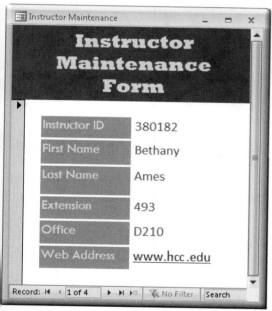

Figure 11-8 Users must give their approval on all inputs and outputs. This input screen is a mockup (containing actual sample data) for users to review.

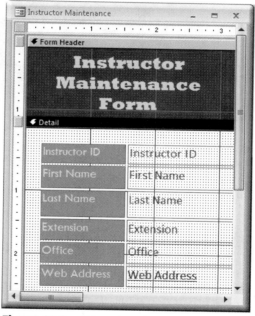

Figure 11-9 Shown here is a technical view in Access of the mockup in Figure 11-8.

Other issues that must be addressed during input and output design include the types of media to use (paper, video, audio); formats (graphical or narrative); and data entry validation techniques, which include making sure the entered data is correct (for example, a state code has to be one of the fifty valid two-letter state abbreviations).

• During program design, the systems analyst prepares the program specification package, which identifies required programs and the relationship among each program, as well as the input, output, and database specifications.

Prototyping Many systems analysts today use prototypes during detailed design. A **prototype** is a working model of the proposed system. The systems analyst actually builds a functional form of the solution during design. The main advantage of a prototype is users can work with the system before it is completed — to make sure it meets their needs. As soon as users approve a prototype, system analysts can implement a solution more quickly than without a prototype.

Case Tools Many systems analysts use computer software to assist during system development. **Computer-aided software engineering** (**CASE**) software tools are designed to support one or more activities of system development (Figure 11-10).

Figure 11-10
Computer-aided software engineering (CASE) programs assist analysts in the development of an information system. Visible Analyst by Visible Systems Corporation enables analysts to create diagrams, as well as to build the project dictionary.

Quality Review Techniques Many people should review the detailed design specifications before they are given to the programming team. Reviewers should include users, systems analysts, managers, IT staff, and members of the system development team. If the steering committee decides the project still is feasible, which usually is the case, the project enters the implementation phase.

Detailed Design at Horizon Community College

As approved by the steering committee, Karl and his team begin designing the Grade Reporting System. After studying current vendor information and interviewing more users and vendors, the team designs changes to the school's database, Web site, and the associated programs. They prepare several documents including a mockup (Figure 11-8 on the previous page) and a technical view in Access (Figure 11-9 on the previous page).

After completing the detailed design, Karl meets with several users and IT personnel to walk through the design. They locate two errors. He corrects the errors and then presents the design to the steering committee. The committee agrees with the design solution and consents to implement it.

Implementation Phase

The purpose of the **implementation phase** is to construct, or build, the new or modified system and then deliver it to the users. Members of the system development team perform four major activities in this phase: (1) develop programs, (2) install and test the new system, (3) train users, and (4) convert to the new system.

Develop Programs If the organization purchases packaged software and no modifications to the software are required, the development team may skip this activity. For custom software or packaged software that requires modification, however, programs are developed or modified either by an outside firm or in-house. Programmers write or modify programs from the program specification package created during the analysis phase. Just as system development follows an organized set of activities, so does program development. These program development activities are known as the program development life cycle.

The last sections of this chapter identify various programming languages and explain program development. An important concept to understand is that program development is part of the implementation phase.

Install and Test the New System If the organization acquires new hardware or software, someone must install and test it. The systems analysts should test individual programs. They also should be sure that all the programs work together in the system.

Systems analysts and users develop test data so that they can perform various tests. A unit test verifies that each individual program or object works by itself. A systems test verifies that all programs in an application work together properly. An integration test verifies that an application works with other applications. An acceptance test is performed by end-users and checks the new system to ensure that it works with actual data.

Train Users **Training** involves showing users exactly how they will use the new hardware and software in the system. Some training takes place as one-on-one sessions or classroom-style lectures (Figure 11-11). Other organizations use Web-based training, which is a self-directed, self-paced online instruction method. Whichever technique is used, it should include hands-on sessions with realistic sample data. Users should practice on the actual system during training. Users also should receive user manuals for reference. It is the systems analyst's responsibility to create user manuals, both printed and electronic.

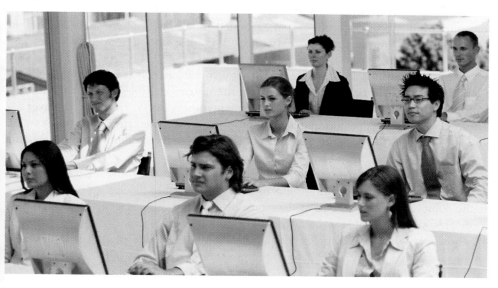

Figure 11-11
Organizations must ensure that users are trained properly on the new system. One training method uses hands-on classes to learn the new system.

Convert to the New System The final implementation activity is to change from the old system to the new system. This change can take place using one or more of the following conversion strategies: direct, parallel, phased, or pilot.

With **direct conversion**, the user stops using the old system and begins using the new system on a certain date. The advantage of this strategy is that it requires no transition costs and is a quick implementation technique. The disadvantage is that it is extremely risky and can disrupt operations seriously if the new system does not work correctly the first time.

Parallel conversion consists of running the old system alongside the new system for a specified time. Results from both systems are compared. The advantage of this strategy is that you can fix any problems in the new system before you terminate the old system. The disadvantage is that it is costly to operate two systems at the same time.

Larger systems with multiple sites may use a phased conversion. In a **phased conversion**, each location converts at a separate time. For example, an accounting system might convert its accounts receivable, accounts payable, general ledger, and payroll sites in separate phases. Each site can use a direct or parallel conversion.

With a **pilot conversion**, only one location in the organization uses the new system — so that it can be tested. After the pilot site approves the new system, other sites convert using one of the other conversion strategies.

Implementation at Horizon Community College

Upon receiving the program specification package, Karl forms an implementation team of Suzy Zhao, Web developer; Adam Rosen, programmer; and Stephan Davis, data modeler. The team works together to implement the Grade Reporting System.

Karl works closely with the team to answer questions about the design and to check the progress of their work. When the team completes its work, they ask Karl to test it. He does and it works great!

Karl arranges a training class for all instructors and also the employees of the registration department. During the training session, he shows them how to use the new online grade book on the school's Web site. Karl gives each attendee a printed user guide and indicates that he will e-mail them the electronic file. Karl also modifies the Web site informing students of the new online grade checking service.

Operation, Support, and Security Phase

The purpose of the **operation, support, and security phase** is to provide ongoing assistance for an information system and its users after the system is implemented. The support phase consists of three major activities: (1) perform maintenance activities, (2) monitor system performance, and (3) assess system security.

Information system maintenance activities include fixing errors in, as well as improving, a system's operations. To determine initial maintenance needs, the systems analyst should meet with users. The purpose of this meeting, called the post-implementation system review, is to discover whether the information system is performing according to the users' expectations. In some cases, users would like the system to do more. Maybe they have enhancements or additional requirements that involve modifying or expanding an existing information system.

During this phase, the systems analyst monitors performance of the new or modified information system. The purpose of performance monitoring is to determine whether the system is inefficient or unstable at any point. If it is, the systems analyst must investigate solutions to make the information system more efficient and reliable — back to the planning phase.

Most organizations must deal with complex computer security issues. All elements of an information system — hardware, software, data, people, and procedures — must be secure from threats both inside and outside the enterprise.

Organizations today often have a **chief security officer** (CSO) who is responsible for the physical security of an organization's property and people and also is in charge of securing its computing resources. It is critical that the CSO is included in all system development projects to ensure that all projects adequately address information security. The CSO uses many of the techniques discussed in Chapter 10 to maintain confidentiality or limited access to information, ensure integrity and reliability of systems, ensure uninterrupted availability of systems, ensure compliance with laws, and cooperate with law enforcement agencies.

An important responsibility of the CSO is to develop a computer security plan. A **computer security plan** summarizes in writing all of the safeguards that are in place to protect an organization's information assets. The CSO should evaluate the computer security plan annually or more frequently for major changes in information assets, such as the addition of a new computer or the implementation of a new application. In developing the plan, the CSO should recognize that some degree of risk is unavoidable; further, the more secure a system is, the more difficult it is for everyone to use. The goal of a computer security plan is to match an appropriate level of safeguards against the identified risks. Fortunately, most organizations never will experience a major information system disaster.

? FAQ 11-3

Are financial Web sites vulnerable?

Yes. Research indicates that vulnerabilities are common among financial Web sites. Some vulnerabilities include insecure login forms, confidential information displayed on insecure pages, and weak rules for user name and password selection. Before performing a transaction on a financial Web site, you should make sure that the Web site is secure and that the Web site has no known problems or vulnerabilities.

For more information, visit the Computer Concepts CourseMate Web site at www.cengagebrain.com, navigate to the Chapter 11 FAQ resource for this book, and then click Web Site Vulnerabilities.

Operation, Support, and Security at Horizon Community College

During the post-implementation system review, Karl learns that the new Grade Reporting System is working well. Instructors find it easy to use, and students appreciate being able to check grades online. The registration department is saving time and money because they no longer have to enter or check class semester grades. Chad says his staff is working efficiently on other registration tasks, now that the Grade Reporting System has been automated. Data in the system has been accessed only by authorized users, leading him to conclude security measures work as planned.

Six months after the Grade Reporting System has been in operation, Chad would like to add the capability for students to request transcripts online. He sends an e-mail message to Karl requesting the change. Karl asks him to fill out a Request for System Services and puts him on the agenda of the next steering committee meeting. Back to the planning phase again!

✔ QUIZ YOURSELF 11-1

Instructions: Find the true statement below. Then, rewrite the remaining false statements so that they are true.

1. A computer security plan summarizes in writing all of the safeguards that are in place to protect an organization's information assets.
2. Feasibility is the process of planning, scheduling, and then controlling the activities during system development.
3. The five phases in most SDLCs are programming, analysis, design, sampling, and recording.
4. The purpose of the design phase is to provide ongoing assistance for an information system and its users after the system is implemented.
5. Upon completion of the preliminary investigation, the systems analyst writes the system proposal.
6. Users should not be involved throughout system development.

Quiz Yourself Online: To further check your knowledge of pages 418 through 435, visit the Computer Concepts CourseMate Web site at www.cengagebrain.com, navigate to the Chapter 11 Quiz Yourself resource for this book, and then click Objectives 1 – 2.

Programming Languages and Program Development Tools

The previous sections discussed the system development phases. One activity during the implementation phase is to develop programs. Although you may never write a computer program, information you request may require a programmer to create or modify a program. Thus, you should understand how programmers develop programs to meet information requirements. A **computer program** is a series of instructions that directs a computer to perform tasks. A computer **programmer**, often called a **developer**, creates and modifies computer programs.

To create a program, programmers sometimes write, or code, a program's instructions using a programming language. A **programming language** is a set of words, abbreviations, and symbols that enables a programmer to communicate instructions to a computer. Other times, programmers

use a program development tool to create a program. A program that provides a user-friendly environment for building programs often is called a **program development tool**. Programmers use a variety of programming languages and tools to create programs (Figure 11-12).

Several hundred programming languages exist today. Each language has its own rules for writing the instructions. Languages often are designed for specific purposes, such as scientific applications, business solutions, or Web page development. When solving a problem or building a solution, programmers often use more than one language; that is, they integrate the languages.

Two types of languages are low-level and high-level. A low-level language is a programming language that is machine dependent. A machine-dependent language runs on only one particular type of computer. Each instruction in a low-level language usually equates to a single machine instruction, discussed further in the next section. With a high-level language, by contrast, each instruction typically equates to multiple machine instructions. High-level languages often are machine independent. A machine-independent language can run on many different types of computers and operating systems.

The following pages discuss low-level languages, as well as several types of high-level languages.

Figure 11-12 Programmers must decide which programming languages and program development tools to use when they create programs.

0000DE	5A50	35AA			015AC
0000E2	47F0	2100		00102	
000102	1B77				
000104	5870	304E			01050
000108	1C47				
00010A	4E50	30D6			010D8
00010E	F075	30D6	003E	010D8	0003E
000114	4F50	30D6			010D8
000118	5050	3052			01054
00011C	58E0	30B6			010B8
000120	07FE				
					00122
000122	50E0	30BA			010BC
000126	1B55				
000128	5A50	304E			01050
00012C	5B50	3052			01054
000130	5050	305A			0105C
000134	58E0	30BA			010BC
000138	07FE				

Low-Level Languages

Two types of low-level languages are machine languages and assembly languages. **Machine language**, known as the first generation of programming languages, is the only language the computer directly recognizes (Figure 11-13). Machine language instructions use series of binary digits (1s and 0s) or a combination of numbers and letters that represents binary digits. The binary digits correspond to the on and off electrical states. As you might imagine, coding in machine language is tedious and time-consuming.

Figure 11-13 A sample machine language program, coded using the hexadecimal number system. A hexadecimal number system can be used to represent binary numbers using letters of the alphabet and decimal numbers.

With an **assembly language**, the second generation of programming languages, a programmer writes instructions using symbolic instruction codes (Figure 11-14). Examples of these codes include A for addition, C for compare, L for load, and M for multiply.

Assembly languages also use symbolic addresses. A symbolic address is a meaningful name that identifies a storage location. For example, a programmer can use the name RATE to refer to the storage location that contains a pay rate.

Despite these advantages, assembly languages can be difficult to learn. In addition, programmers must convert an assembly language program into machine language before the computer can execute, or run, the program. That is, the computer cannot execute the assembly source program. A **source program** is the program that contains the language instructions, or code, to be converted to machine language. To convert the assembly language source program into machine language, programmers use a program called an assembler.

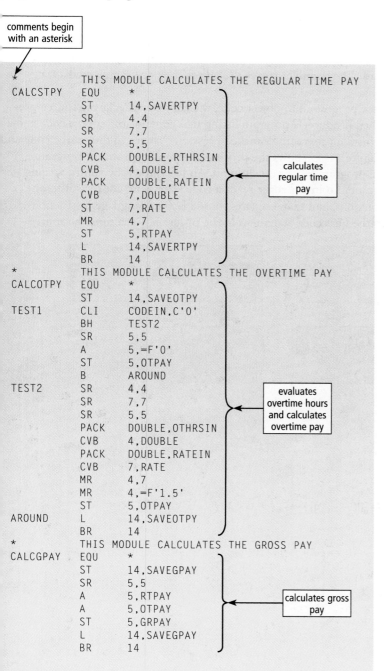

comments begin with an asterisk

```
*          THIS MODULE CALCULATES THE REGULAR TIME PAY
CALCSTPY   EQU    *
           ST     14,SAVERTPY
           SR     4,4
           SR     7,7
           SR     5,5
           PACK   DOUBLE,RTHRSIN          calculates
           CVB    4,DOUBLE                regular time
           PACK   DOUBLE,RATEIN           pay
           CVB    7,DOUBLE
           ST     7,RATE
           MR     4,7
           ST     5,RTPAY
           L      14,SAVERTPY
           BR     14
*          THIS MODULE CALCULATES THE OVERTIME PAY
CALCOTPY   EQU    *
           ST     14,SAVEOTPY
TEST1      CLI    CODEIN,C'O'
           BH     TEST2
           SR     5,5
           A      5,=F'0'
           ST     5,OTPAY
           B      AROUND
TEST2      SR     4,4                     evaluates
           SR     7,7                     overtime hours
           SR     5,5                     and calculates
           PACK   DOUBLE,OTHRSIN          overtime pay
           CVB    4,DOUBLE
           PACK   DOUBLE,RATEIN
           CVB    7,RATE
           MR     4,7
           MR     4,=F'1.5'
           ST     5,OTPAY
AROUND     L      14,SAVEOTPY
           BR     14
*          THIS MODULE CALCULATES THE GROSS PAY
CALCGPAY   EQU    *
           ST     14,SAVEGPAY
           SR     5,5
           A      5,RTPAY                 calculates gross
           A      5,OTPAY                 pay
           ST     5,GRPAY
           L      14,SAVEGPAY
           BR     14
```

Figure 11-14 An excerpt from an assembly language payroll program. The code shows the computations for regular time pay, overtime pay, and gross pay and the decision to evaluate the overtime hours.

Procedural Languages

The disadvantages of machine and assembly (low-level) languages led to the development of procedural languages in the late 1950s and 1960s. In a **procedural language**, the programmer writes instructions that tell the computer what to accomplish and how to do it.

With a procedural language, often called a **third-generation language** (**3GL**), a programmer uses a series of English-like words to write instructions. For example, ADD stands for addition or PRINT means to print. Many 3GLs also use arithmetic operators such as * for multiplication and + for addition. These English-like words and arithmetic symbols simplify the program development process for the programmer.

As with an assembly language program, the 3GL code (instructions) is called the source program. Programmers must convert this source program into machine language before the computer can execute the program. This translation process often is very complex, because one 3GL source program instruction translates into many machine language instructions. For 3GLs, programmers typically use either a compiler or an interpreter to perform the translation.

A **compiler** is a separate program that converts the entire source program into machine language before executing it. The machine language version that results from compiling the 3GL is called the object code or object program. The compiler stores the object code on storage media for execution later.

While it is compiling the source program into object code, the compiler checks the source program for errors. The compiler then produces a program listing that contains the source code and a list of any errors. This listing helps the programmer make necessary changes to the source code and correct errors in the program. Figure 11-15 shows the process of compiling a source program.

A compiler translates an entire program before executing it. An interpreter, by contrast, translates and executes one statement at a time. An **interpreter** reads a code statement, converts it to one or more machine language instructions, and then executes those machine language instructions. It does this all before moving to the next code statement in the program. Each time the source

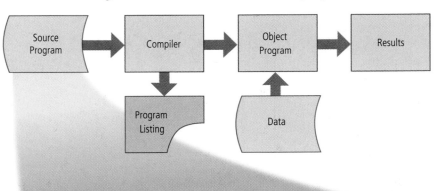

Figure 11-15 A compiler converts the source program into a machine language object program. If the compiler encounters any errors, it records them in a program-listing file, which the programmer may print when the entire compilation is complete. When a user wants to run the program, the object program is loaded into the memory of the computer and the program instructions begin executing.

```
*    COMPUTE REGULAR TIME PAY
     MULTIPLY REGULAR-TIME-HOURS BY HOURLY-PAY-RATE
          GIVING REGULAR-TIME-PAY.

*    COMPUTE OVERTIME PAY
     IF OVERTIME-HOURS > 0
        COMPUTE OVERTIME-PAY = OVERTIME-HOURS * 1.5 * HOURLY-PAY-RATE
     ELSE
        MOVE 0 TO OVERTIME-PAY.

*    COMPUTE GROSS PAY
     ADD REGULAR-TIME-PAY TO OVERTIME-PAY
          GIVING GROSS-PAY.
```

program runs, the interpreter translates and executes it, statement by statement. An interpreter does not produce an object program. Figure 11-16 shows the process of interpreting a program.

One advantage of an interpreter is that when it finds errors, it displays feedback immediately. The programmer can correct any errors before the interpreter translates the next line of code. The disadvantage is that interpreted programs do not run as fast as compiled programs.

Hundreds of procedural languages exist. Only a few, however, are used widely enough for the industry to recognize them as standards. These include C and COBOL. To illustrate the similarities and differences among these programming languages, the figures on the following pages show program code in these languages. The code solves a simple payroll problem — computing the gross pay for an employee.

The process used to compute gross pay can vary from one system to another. The examples on the following pages use a simple algorithm, or set of steps, to help you easily compare one programming language with another. Read Innovative Computing 11-1 to find out about some useful and fun online programs.

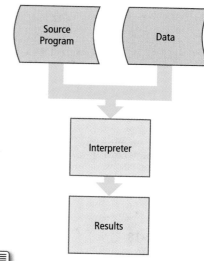

Figure 11-16 With an interpreter, one line of the source program at a time is converted into machine language and then immediately executed by the computer. If the interpreter encounters an error while converting a line of code, an error message immediately is displayed on the screen and the program stops.

⚠️ **INNOVATIVE COMPUTING 11-1**

Online Calculators Answer Life's Questions

At practically every phase of life, people can benefit from some sort of calculator. For example, one program can help expectant parents calculate the date their child will be born, and another can generate possible baby names. Once the child is born, they can use another calculator that attempts to estimate the total cost of raising the child through the teenage years.

One Web site has collected a wide variety of calculators: Your Life, Calculated. This MSN-sponsored site organizes the calculators in a variety of categories. The Career section includes a millionaire calculator to determine how much money will need to be saved each month to reach $1 million, and it also includes amortization tables and mortgage and car loan calculators.

Other tools are the tip calculator, a calculator that determines the chances of a successful personal relationship, the body mass index to measure body fat based on height and weight, the college cost calculator, and the financial aid calculator. When using online calculators, keep in mind that some are subjective in nature, and the results reflect the thoughts and/or opinions of the calculator's author.

📷 For more information, visit the Computer Concepts CourseMate Web site at www.cengagebrain.com, navigate to the Chapter 11 Innovative Computing resource for this book, and then click Online Calculators.

C The **C** programming language, developed in the early 1970s by Dennis Ritchie at Bell Laboratories, originally was designed for writing system software. Today, many programs are written in C (Figure 11-17). C runs on almost any type of computer with any operating system, but it is used most often with the UNIX and Linux operating systems.

comments begin with a slash followed by an asterisk

calculates regular time pay

evaluates overtime hours and calculates overtime pay

```
/* Compute Regular Time Pay                            */
rt_pay = rt_hrs * pay_rate;

/* Compute Overtime Pay                                */
if (ot_hrs > 0)
    ot_pay = ot_hrs * 1.5 * pay_rate;
else
    ot_pay = 0;

/* Compute Gross Pay                                   */
gross = rt_pay + ot_pay;

/* Print Gross Pay                                     */
printf("The gross pay is %d\n", gross);
```

prints gross pay

calculates gross pay

Figure 11-17 An excerpt from a C payroll program. The code shows the computations for regular time pay, overtime pay, and gross pay; the decision to evaluate the overtime hours; and the output of the gross pay.

COBOL COBOL (**CO**mmon **B**usiness-**O**riented **L**anguage) evolved out of a joint effort between the United States government, businesses, and major universities in the early 1960s. Naval officer Grace Hopper, a pioneer in computer programming, was a prime developer of COBOL.

COBOL is a programming language designed for business applications. Although COBOL programs often are lengthy, their English-like statements make the code easy to read, write, and maintain (Figure 11-18). COBOL especially is useful for processing transactions, such as payroll and billing, on mainframe computers.

comments begin with an asterisk

calculates regular time pay

calculates gross pay

evaluates overtime hours and calculates overtime pay

prints gross pay

```
*    COMPUTE REGULAR TIME PAY
     MULTIPLY REGULAR-TIME-HOURS BY HOURLY-PAY-RATE
         GIVING REGULAR-TIME-PAY.

  *  COMPUTE OVERTIME PAY
     IF OVERTIME-HOURS > 0
         COMPUTE OVERTIME-PAY = OVERTIME-HOURS * 1.5 * HOURLY-PAY-RATE
     ELSE
         MOVE 0 TO OVERTIME-PAY.

  *  COMPUTE GROSS PAY
     ADD REGULAR-TIME-PAY TO OVERTIME-PAY
         GIVING GROSS-PAY.

  *  PRINT GROSS PAY
     MOVE GROSS-PAY TO GROSS-PAY-OUT.
     WRITE REPORT-LINE-OUT FROM DETAIL-LINE
         AFTER ADVANCING 2 LINES.
```

Figure 11-18
An excerpt from a COBOL payroll program. The code shows the computations for regular time pay, overtime pay, and gross pay; the decision to evaluate the overtime hours; and the output of the gross pay.

Object-Oriented Programming Languages and Program Development Tools

Programmers use an **object-oriented programming (OOP) language** or object-oriented program development tool to implement objects in a program. An object is an item that can contain both data and the procedures that read or manipulate that data. An object represents a real person, place, even or transaction.

A major benefit of OOP is the ability to reuse and modify existing objects. For example, once a programmer creates an Employee object, it is available for use by any other existing or future program. Thus, programmers repeatedly reuse existing objects. For example, the payroll program and health benefits program both use the Employee object. That is, the payroll program would use it to process employee paychecks and the health benefits program would use it to process health insurance payment.

Programs developed using the object-oriented approach have several advantages. The objects can be reused in many systems, are designed for repeated use, and become stable over time. In addition, programmers create applications faster because they design programs using existing objects. Programming languages, such as Java, C#, F#, C++, and the latest versions of Visual Basic are complete object-oriented languages.

Object-oriented programming languages and program development tools work well in a RAD environment. **RAD** (rapid application development) is a method of developing software, in which the programmer writes and implements a program in segments instead of waiting until the entire program is completed. An important concept in RAD is the use of prebuilt components. For example, programmers do not have to write code for buttons and text boxes on Windows forms because they already exist in the programming language or tools provided with the language.

Most object-oriented program development tools are IDEs. An **IDE** (**integrated development environment**) includes tools for building graphical interfaces, an editor for entering program code, a compiler and/or interpreter, and a debugger (to remove errors, which is discussed later in the chapter). Some IDEs work with a single programming language, others support multiple languages.

Java Java is an object-oriented programming language developed by Sun Microsystems. Figure 11-19 shows a portion of a Java program and the window that the program displays.

When programmers compile a Java program, the resulting object code is machine independent. Java uses a just-in-time (JIT) compiler to convert the machine-independent code into

machine-dependent code that is executed immediately. Programmers use various Java Platform implementations, developed by Sun Microsystems, which provide development tools for creating programs for all sizes of computers.

Java Platforms

For more information, visit the Computer Concepts CourseMate Web site at www.cengagebrain.com navigate to the Chapter 11 Web Lin resource for this book, and then clic Java Platforms.

```
public class BodyMassApplet extends Applet implements ActionListener
{
        //declare variables
        Image logo; //declare an Image object
        int inches, pounds;
        double meters, kilograms, index;

        //construct components
        Label companyLabel = new Label("THE SUN FITNESS CENTER BODY MASS INDEX CALCUL
        Label heightLabel = new Label("Enter your height to the nearest inch  ");
            TextField heightField = new TextField(10);
        Label weightLabel = new Label ("Enter your weight to the nearest pound  ");
            TextField weightField = new TextField(10);
        Button calcButton = new Button("Calculate");
        Label outputLabel = new Label(
        "Click the Calculate button to see your Body Mass Index.");

        inches = Integer.parseInt(heightField.getText());
        pounds = Integer.parseInt(weightField.getText());
        meters = inches / 39.36;
        kilograms = pounds / 2.2;
        index = kilograms / Math.pow(meters,2);
        outputLabel.setText("YOUR BODY MASS INDEX IS " + Math.round(index) + ".")
    }

    public void paint(Graphics g)
    {
        g.drawImage(logo,125,160,this);
    }
}
```

Applet

THE SUN FITNESS CENTER BODY MASS INDEX CALCULATOR

Enter your height to the nearest inch 67

Enter your weight to the nearest pound 145

Calculate

YOUR BODY MASS INDEX IS 23.

Applet started.

Figure 11-19 A portion of a Java program and the window the program displays.

.NET The Microsoft .NET Framework, or **.NET** (pronounced dot net), is a set of technologies that allows almost any type of program to run on the Internet or an internal business network, as well as stand-alone computers and mobile devices. Similarly, ASP.NET is a Web application framework that provides the tools necessary for the creation of dynamic Web sites.

Using .NET and/or ASP.NET, programmers easily can develop Web applications, Web services, and Windows programs. Examples of languages that support .NET include C++, C#, F#, Visual Basic, Delphi, and PowerBuilder. The following sections discuss each of these languages.

C++ Developed in the 1980s by Bjarne Sroustrup at Bell Laboratories, **C++** (pronounced SEE-plus-plus) is an object-oriented programming language that is an extension of the C programming language. C++ includes all the elements of the C language (shown in Figure 11-17 on page 439), plus it has additional features for working with objects. Programmers commonly use C++ to develop database and Web applications.

C# Based on C++, **C#** (pronounced SEE-sharp) is an object-oriented programming language that was developed primarily by Anders Hejlsberg, Microsoft chief architect and distinguished engineer. C# has been accepted as a standard for Web applications and XML-based Web services.

F# **F#** (pronounced EFF-sharp), which is included with the latest version of Visual Studio (discussed in the next section), is a programming language that combines the benefits of an object-oriented language with the benefits of a functional language. A functional language is a programming language whose natural programming structure is useful in mathematical programs. Benefits of programs written in F# include easy access to .NET libraries and performance similar to that of C# programs.

Visual Studio **Visual Studio** is Microsoft's suite of program development tools that assists programmers in building programs for Windows, Windows Mobile, or any operating systems that support .NET. Visual Studio includes enhanced support for building security and reliability into applications through its programming languages, RAD tools, IDE, a specialized query language,

and other resources that reduce development time. For example, Visual Studio includes **code snippets**, which are prewritten code and templates associated with common programming tasks. Visual Studio also includes a set of tools for developing programs that work with Microsoft's Office suite. The following paragraphs discuss these programming languages in the Visual Studio suite: Visual Basic, Visual C++, and Visual C#.

- Visual Basic is based on the BASIC programming language, which was developed by Microsoft Corporation in the early 1990s. This language is easy to learn and use. Thus, Visual Basic is ideal for beginning programmers.

 The first step in building a Visual Basic program often is to design the graphical user interface using Visual Basic objects (Steps 1 and 2 in Figure 11-20). Visual Basic objects include items such as buttons, text boxes, and labels. Next, the programmer writes instructions (code) to define any actions that should occur in response to specific events (Step 3 in Figure 11-20). Finally, the programmer generates and tests the final program (Step 4 in Figure 11-20).

Creating a Visual Basic Program

Step 1

The developer designs the user interface, such as for the mobile device shown here. Linear Feet is a text box in which the user enters data. Pine, Oak, and Cherry are option buttons the user can click to choose the wood type. Calculate and Clear are buttons. All other objects are labels.

Step 2

The developer assigns properties to each object. Objects include text boxes, option buttons, buttons, labels, and the form itself.

Step 4

The developer tests the program. The Cost Estimate is displayed after the user clicks the Calculate button.

Step 3

The developer writes code to define the action of each event the user triggers.

Figure 11-20 This figure shows how to create a Visual Basic program.

- Visual C++ is a programming language based on C++. Not only is Visual C++ a powerful object-oriented programming language, it enables programmers to write Windows, Windows Mobile, and .NET applications quickly and efficiently.
- Visual C# combines the programming elements of C++ with an easier visual programming environment. The purpose of Visual C# is to take the complexity out of Visual C++.

Visual Programming Languages A **visual programming language** is a language that uses a visual or graphical interface for creating all source code. The graphical interface, called a **visual programming environment** (**VPE**), allows programmers to drag and drop objects to build programs. Examples of visual programming languages include Alice, Mindscript, and Prograph.

Delphi Borland's **Delphi** is a powerful program development tool that is ideal for building large-scale enterprise and Web applications in a RAD environment. Programmers use Delphi to develop programs quickly for Windows, Linux, and .NET platforms.

PowerBuilder **PowerBuilder**, developed by Sybase, is another powerful program development RAD tool best suited for Web-based, .NET, and large-scale enterprise object-oriented applications. Programmers also use PowerBuilder to develop small- and medium-scale client/server applications.

Other Programming Languages and Development Tools

The following sections discuss a variety of other programming languages and program development tools.

4GLs A **4GL** (fourth-generation language) is a nonprocedural language that enables users and programmers to access data in a database. With a **nonprocedural language**, the programmer writes English-like instructions or interacts with a graphical environment to retrieve data from files or a database. Many object-oriented program development tools use 4GLs.

One popular 4GL is SQL. **SQL** is a query language that allows users to manage, update, and retrieve data in a relational DBMS (Figure 11-21).

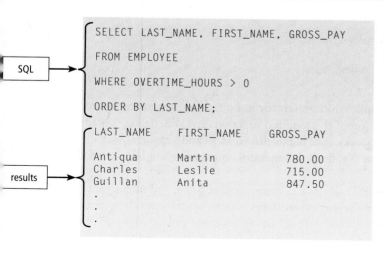

Figure 11-21 SQL is a 4GL that can be used to query database tables. This query produces an alphabetical list of those employees who receive overtime pay; that is, their overtime hours are greater than 0.

Classic Programming Languages In addition to the programming languages discussed on the previous pages, programmers sometimes use the languages listed in Figure 11-22, which were more popular in the past than today.

Ada	Derived from Pascal, developed by the U.S. Department of Defense, named after Augusta Ada Lovelace Byron, who is thought to be the first female computer programmer
ALGOL	ALGOrithmic Language, the first structured procedural language
APL	A Programming Language, a scientific language designed to manipulate tables of numbers
BASIC	Beginners All-purpose Symbolic Instruction Code, developed by John Kemeny and Thomas Kurtz as a simple, interactive problem-solving language
Forth	Similar to C, used for small computerized devices
FORTRAN	FORmula TRANslator, one of the first high-level programming languages used for scientific applications
HyperTalk	An object-oriented programming language developed by Apple to manipulate cards that can contain text, graphics, and sound
LISP	LISt Processing, a language used for artificial intelligence applications
Logo	An educational tool used to teach programming and problem solving to children
Modula-2	A successor to Pascal used for developing system software
Pascal	Developed to teach students structured programming concepts, named in honor of Blaise Pascal, a French mathematician who developed one of the earliest calculating machines
PILOT	Programmed Inquiry Learning Or Teaching, used to write computer-aided instruction programs
PL/1	Programming Language One, a business and scientific language that combines many features of FORTRAN and COBOL
Prolog	PROgramming LOGic, used for development of artificial intelligence applications
RPG	Report Program Generator, used to assist businesses with generating reports and to access/update data in databases
Smalltalk	Object-oriented programming language

Figure 11-22 Classic programming languages.

Application Generators An **application generator** is a program that creates source code or machine code from a specification of the required functionality. When using an application generator, a programmer or user works with menu-driven tools and graphical user interfaces to define the desired specifications. Application generators most often are bundled with or are included as part of a DBMS.

An application generator typically consists of a report writer, form, and menu generator. A report writer allows you to design a report on the screen, retrieve data into the report design, and then display or print the report. Figure 11-23 shows a sample form design and the resulting form it generates showing sample data a user may enter in the form. A menu generator enables you to create a menu for the application options.

Figure 11-23a (form design)

Figure 11-23b (resulting filled-in form)

Figure 11-23 A form design and the resulting filled-in form created with Microsoft Access.

Macros A **macro** is a series of statements that instructs a program how to complete a task. Macros allow users to automate routine, repetitive, or difficult tasks in application software such as word processing, spreadsheet, or database programs. That is, users can create simple programs within the software by writing macros. You usually create a macro in one of two ways: (1) record the macro or (2) write the macro.

If you want to automate a routine or repetitive task such as formatting or editing, you would record a macro. A macro recorder is similar to a movie camera because both record all actions until turned off. To record a macro, start the macro recorder in the software. Then, perform the steps to be part of the macro, such as clicks of the mouse or keystrokes. Once the macro is recorded, you can run it anytime you want to perform that same sequence of actions. For example, if you always print three copies of certain documents, you could record the actions required to print three copies. To print three copies, you would run the macro called PrintThreeCopies.

When you become familiar with programming techniques, you can write your own macros instead of recording them. Read Ethics & Issues 11-3 for a related discussion.

Macros

For more information, visit the Computer Concepts CourseMate Web site at www.cengagebrain.com, navigate to the Chapter 11 Web Link resource for this book, and then click Macros.

ETHICS & ISSUES 11-3

Who Should Be Held Accountable for Macro Security Threats?

Years ago, an individual downloaded and opened a small document that contained a virus from an Internet newsgroup. Upon opening the document, a macro was executed that sent the same document to the first 50 e-mail addresses in the person's e-mail contact list. The simple action of opening the document started a chain reaction that resulted in more than 100,000 infected computers and more than $80 million in damage. Today, such viruses, known as macro viruses, are the most common type of virus. Malware authors find that one of the easiest ways to spread viruses and worms is by distributing

documents containing macro viruses. The convenience and simplicity of macros are both their greatest strengths and weaknesses. These are weaknesses because hackers find it easy to exploit technologies with such traits.

As a result of damaging macro viruses, antivirus companies and software companies have strengthened their efforts against macro viruses. Companies often prohibit employees from running macros on their computers. Both responses have made the use of macros more difficult and confusing for users, who prefer the convenience and simplicity of the earlier days. Many claim that software

companies that include the capability to use macros should be responsible for making it impossible for malware authors to take advantage of security problems in the software. Software companies and others blame users who open documents from unknown sources.

Should users or software companies be held accountable for macro security threats? Why? Should a macro in a word processing document have the capability to access a person's e-mail contact list? Why or why not? How can users best be educated regarding handling documents from unknown sources?

Web Page Development

The designers of Web pages, known as **Web developers**, use a variety of techniques to create Web pages. The following sections discuss these techniques.

HTML and XHTML **HTML** (Hypertext Markup Language) is a special formatting language that programmers use to format documents for display on the Web. You view a Web page written with HTML in a Web browser such as Internet Explorer, Mozilla, Safari, Firefox, Opera, or Google Chrome. Similarly, **XHTML** (extensible HTML) is a markup language that enables Web sites to be displayed more easily on microbrowsers in smart phones and other mobile devices, as well as on desktop and notebook computers. Figure 11-24a shows part of the XHTML code used to create the Web page shown in Figure 11-24b. XHTML includes features of HTML and XML, which is discussed in the next section.

HTML and XHTML are not actually programming languages. They are, however, languages that have specific rules for defining the placement and format of text, graphics, video, and audio on a Web page. HTML and XHTML use tags or elements, which are words, abbreviations, and symbols that specify links to other documents and indicate how a Web page is displayed when viewed on the Web.

Figure 11-24a (portion of XHTML program)

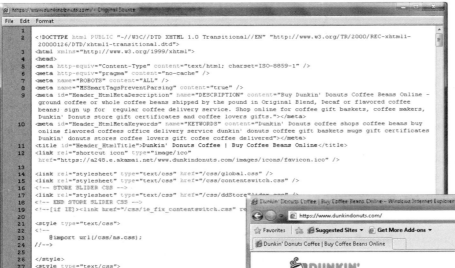

Figure 11-24b
(portion of resulting Web page)

Figure 11-24 The portion of the XHTML code in the top figure generates a portion of a Web page shown in the bottom figure.

XML and WML **XML** (Extensible Markup Language) is an increasingly popular format for sharing data that allows Web developers to create customized tags, as well as use predefined tags, used for developing a single Web site whose content can be formatted to display appropriately on various devices. XML separates the Web page content from its format, allowing the Web browser to display the contents of a Web page in a form appropriate for the display device. For example, a

smart phone, a PDA, and a notebook computer all could display the same XML page or use different formats or sections of the XML page.

Wireless devices use a subset of XML called WML. **WML** (wireless markup language) allows Web developers to design pages specifically for microbrowsers. Many smart phones and other mobile devices use WML as their markup language.

Two applications of XML are the RSS 2.0 and ATOM specifications. **RSS 2.0**, which stands for Really Simple Syndication, and **ATOM** are specifications that content aggregators use to distribute content to subscribers. The online publisher creates an RSS or ATOM document, called a Web feed, that is made available to Web sites for publication. News Web sites, blogs, and podcasts often use Web feeds to publish headlines and stories. Most Web browsers can read Web feeds, meaning they automatically download updated content from Web pages identified in the feed.

XML

For more information, visit the Computer Concepts CourseMate Web site at www.cengagebrain.com, navigate to the Chapter 11 Web Link resource for this book, and then click XML.

Scripts, Applets, Servlets, and ActiveX Controls Markup languages tell a browser how to display text and images, set up lists and option buttons, and establish links on a Web page. By adding dynamic content and interactive elements such as scrolling messages, animated graphics, forms, pop-up windows, and interaction, Web pages become much more interesting. To add these elements, Web developers write small programs called scripts, applets, servlets, and ActiveX controls. These programs run inside of another program. This is different from programs discussed thus far, which are executed by the operating system. In this case, the Web browser executes these short programs.

One reason for using scripts, applets, servlets, and ActiveX controls is to add special multimedia effects to Web pages. Examples include animated graphics, scrolling messages, calendars, and advertisements. Another reason to use these programs is to include interactive capabilities on Web pages.

Scripting Languages Programmers write scripts, applets, servlets, or ActiveX controls using a variety of languages. These include some of the languages previously discussed, such as Java, C++, C#, F#, and Visual Basic. Some programmers use scripting languages. A **scripting language** is an interpreted language that typically is easy to learn and use. Popular scripting languages include JavaScript, Perl, PHP, Rexx, Tcl, and VBScript.

- **JavaScript** is an interpreted language that allows a programmer to add dynamic content and interactive elements to a Web page (Figure 11-25). These elements include alert messages, scrolling text, animations, drop-down menus, data input forms, pop-up windows, and interactive quizzes.

Figure 11-25a (JavaScript code)

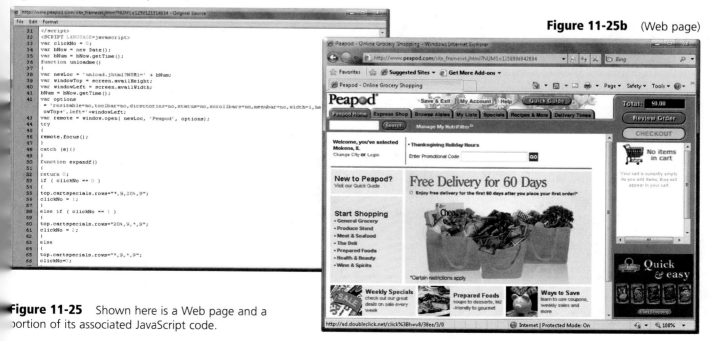

Figure 11-25b (Web page)

Figure 11-25 Shown here is a Web page and a portion of its associated JavaScript code.

PHP

For more information, visit the Computer Concepts CourseMate Web site at www.cengagebrain.com, navigate to the Chapter 11 Web Link resource for this book, and then click PHP.

- **Perl** (Practical Extraction and Report Language) originally was developed by Larry Wall at NASA's Jet Propulsion Laboratory as a procedural language similar to C and C++. The latest release of Perl, however, is an interpreted scripting language. Because Perl has powerful text processing capabilities, it has become a popular language for writing scripts.
- **PHP**, which stands for PHP: Hypertext Preprocessor, is a free, open source scripting language. PHP is similar to C, Java, and Perl.
- **Rexx** (REstructured eXtended eXecutor) was developed by Mike Cowlishaw at IBM as a procedural interpreted scripting language for both the professional programmer and the nontechnical user.
- **Tcl** (Tool Command Language) is an interpreted scripting language created by Dr. John Ousterhout and maintained by Sun Microsystems Laboratories.
- **VBScript** (Visual Basic, Scripting Edition) is a subset of the Visual Basic language that allows programmers to add intelligence and interactivity to Web pages. As with JavaScript, Web developers embed VBScript code directly into an HTML document.

Dynamic HTML Dynamic HTML (**DHTML**) is a newer type of HTML that allows Web developers to include more graphical interest and interactivity in a Web page. Typically, Web pages created with DHTML are more animated and responsive to user interaction. Colors change, font sizes grow, objects appear and disappear as a user moves the mouse, and animations dance around the screen.

Ruby on Rails **Ruby on Rails** is an open source framework that provides technologies for developing object-oriented, database-driven Web sites. Ruby on Rails is designed to make Web developers more productive by providing them an easy-to-use environment and eliminating time-consuming steps in the Web development process.

As previously discussed, Web 2.0 refers to Web sites that provide a means for users to share personal information, allow users to modify Web site content, and have application software built into the site for visitors to use. Web 2.0 sites include social networking sites, wikis, blogs, online auctions, and Web applications such as Google Docs.

Web 2.0 Program Development Web 2.0 sites often use RSS, previously discussed, and Ajax. **Ajax**, which stands for Asynchronous JavaScript and XML, is a method of creating interactive Web applications designed to provide immediate response to user requests. Instead of refreshing entire Web pages, Ajax works with the Web browser to update only changes to the Web page. This technique saves time because the Web application does not spend time repeatedly sending unchanged information across the network.

Ajax combines several programming tools: JavaScript or other scripting language, HTML or XHTML, and XML. Examples of Web sites that use Ajax are Google Maps and Flickr.

Most Web 2.0 sites also use APIs so that Web developers can create their own Web applications. An **API** (application programming interface) is a collection of tools that programmers use to interact with an environment such as a Web site or operating system. Mapping Web sites, for example, include APIs that enable programmers to integrate maps into their Web sites (Figure 11-26).

Figure 11-26 Google Maps provides tools for programmers to integrate APIs into their Web sites.

? **FAQ 11-5**

What are the popular Web programming languages?

The chart to the right shows the popularity of selected Web programming languages when compared to all programming languages.

> For more information, visit the Computer Concepts CourseMate Web site at www.cengagebrain.com, navigate to the Chapter 11 FAQ resource for this book, and then click Web Programming Languages.

Web Programming Language Popularity

Source: TIOBE Programming Community Index

Web Page Authoring Software As discussed in Chapter 3, you do not need to learn HTML to develop a Web page. You can use **Web page authoring software** to create sophisticated Web pages that include graphical images, video, audio, animation, and other special effects. Web page authoring software generates HTML and XHTML tags from your Web page design.

Four popular Web page authoring programs are Dreamweaver, Expression Web, Flash, and SharePoint Designer.

- **Dreamweaver**, by Adobe Systems, is a Web page authoring program that allows Web developers to create, maintain, and manage professional Web sites.
- **Expression Web** is Microsoft's Web page authoring program that enables Web developers to create professional, dynamic, interactive Web sites. Expression Web integrates with Visual Studio.
- **Flash**, by Adobe Systems, is a Web page authoring program that enables Web developers to combine interactive content with text, graphics, audio, and video.
- **SharePoint Designer** is a Web page authoring program that is part of the Microsoft Office and SharePoint families of products.

Multimedia Program Development

Multimedia authoring software allows programmers to combine text, graphics, animation, audio, and video into an interactive presentation. Many developers use multimedia authoring software for computer-based training (CBT) and Web-based training (WBT). Popular multimedia authoring software includes ToolBook and Director. Many businesses and colleges use ToolBook to create content for distance learning courses (Figure 11-27).

Figure 11-27
A sample ToolBook application.

Program Development

Program development consists of a series of steps programmers use to build computer programs. As discussed, the system development life cycle guides information technology (IT) professionals through the development of an information system. Likewise, the **program development life cycle** (PDLC) guides computer programmers through the development of a program. The program development life cycle consists of six steps (Figure 11-28):

1. Analyze Requirements
2. Design Solution
3. Validate Design
4. Implement Design
5. Test Solution
6. Document Solution

As shown in Figure 11-28, the steps in the program development life cycle form a loop. Program development is an ongoing process within system development. Each time someone identifies errors in or improvements to a program and requests program modifications, the Analyze Requirements step begins again. When programmers correct errors (called bugs) or add enhancements to an existing program, they are said to be **maintaining** the program. Program maintenance is a ongoing activity that occurs after a program has been delivered to users. Read Ethics & Issues 11-4 for a related discussion.

Ɣ **ETHICS & ISSUES 11-4**

Who Is Responsible for Bugs?

The consequences of bugs, or errors, in computer programs can be staggering. A software error in a missile defense system resulted in the deaths of 29 U.S. soldiers. An error in the code controlling a Canadian nuclear facility caused more than 3,000 gallons of radioactive water to be spilled. A bug in long-distance switching software cost AT&T more than $60 million. Sometimes, employees or students who report security-related bugs are disciplined because by finding the bug, they accidently accessed secure information. Experts estimate that there are 20 to 30 bugs per 1,000 lines of code in an average program. Given that many programs contain hundreds of thousands, even millions, of code lines, bugs are not surprising. Most software licenses absolve the software creator of any responsibility for the end user getting the wrong information from a bug-riddled program.

Who should be responsible for mistakes in software? Why? If users find bugs, such as security bugs, should they be disciplined after reporting the bugs? Why? Should those who design a system or write programs for a system be legally responsible if their product results in errors or damages? Why?

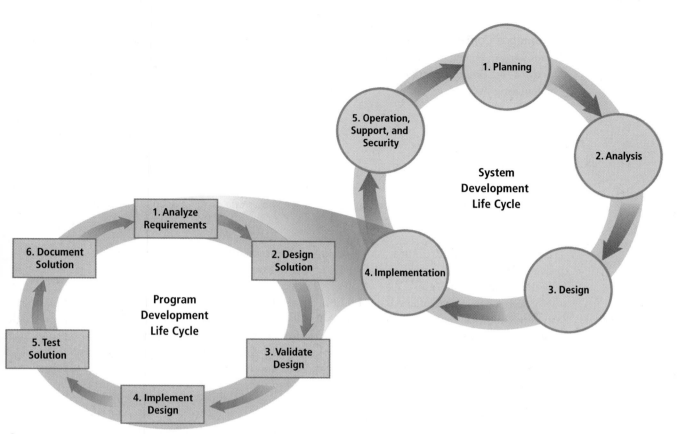

Figure 11-28 The program development life cycle consists of six steps that form a loop. The program development life cycle is part of the implementation phase of the system development life cycle.

What Initiates Program Development?

As discussed, system development consists of five phases: planning; analysis; design; implementation; and operation, support, and security. During the analysis phase, the development team recommends how to handle software needs. Choices include modifying existing programs, purchasing packaged software, building custom software in-house, or outsourcing some or all of the IT operation.

If the organization opts for in-house development, the design and implementation phases of system development become quite extensive. In the design phase, the analyst creates a detailed set of requirements for the programmers. Once the programmers receive the requirements, the implementation phase begins. At this time, the programmer analyzes the requirements of the problem to be solved. Thus, program development begins at the start of the implementation phase in system development.

The scope of the requirements largely determines how many programmers work on the program development. If the scope is large, a **programming team** that consists of a group of programmers may develop the programs. If the specifications are simple, a single programmer might complete all the development tasks. Whether a single programmer or a programming team, all the programmers involved must interact with users and members of the development team throughout program development.

By following the steps in program development, programmers create programs that are correct (produce accurate information) and maintainable (easy to modify).

Control Structures

When programmers are required to design the logic of a program, they typically use control structures to describe the tasks a program is to perform. A **control structure**, also known as a construct, depicts the logical order of program instructions. Three basic control structures are sequence, selection, and repetition.

Sequence Control Structure A **sequence control structure** shows one or more actions following each other in order (Figure 11-29). Actions include inputs, processes, and outputs. All actions must be executed; that is, none can be skipped. Examples of actions are reading a record, calculating averages or totals, and printing totals.

Sequence Control Structure

Figure 11-29 The sequence control structure shows one or more actions followed by another.

Selection Control Structure A **selection control structure** tells the program which action to take, based on a certain condition. Two common types of selection control structures are the if-then-else and the case.

When a program evaluates the condition in an if-then-else control structure, it yields one of two possibilities: true or false. Figure 11-30 shows the condition as a diamond symbol. If the result of the condition is true, then the program performs one action. If the result is false, the program performs a different action. For example, the if-then-else control structure can determine if an employee should receive overtime pay. A possible condition might be the following: Is Hours Worked greater than 40? If the response is yes (true), then the action would calculate overtime pay. If the response is no (false), then the action would set overtime pay equal to 0.

In some cases, a program should perform no action if the result of a condition is false. This variation of the if-then-else is called the if-then control structure because the program performs an action only if the result of the condition is true.

With the **case control structure,** a condition can yield one of three or more possibilities (Figure 11-31). The size of a beverage, for example, might be one of these options: small, medium, large, or extra large. A case control structure would determine the price of the beverage based on the size purchased.

If-Then-Else Control Structure

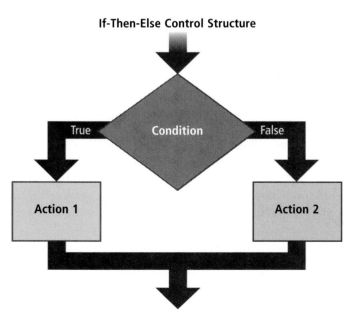

Figure 11-30 The if-then-else control structure directs the program toward one course of action or another based on the evaluation of a condition.

Case Control Structure

Condition

Condition 1 Condition 2 Condition 3 Condition 4

Action 1 Action 2 Action 3 Action 4

Figure 11-31 The case control structure allows for more than two alternatives when a condition is evaluated.

Repetition Control Structure The **repetition control structure** enables a program to perform one or more actions repeatedly as long as a certain condition is met. Many programmers refer to this construct as a loop. Two forms of the repetition control structure are the do-while and do-until.

A do-while control structure repeats one or more times as long as a specified condition is true (Figure 11-32). This control structure tests a condition at the beginning of the loop. If the result of the condition is true, the program executes the action(s) inside the loop. Then, the program loops back and tests the condition again. If the result of the condition still is true, the program executes the action(s) inside the loop again. This looping process continues until the condition being tested becomes false. At that time, the program stops looping and moves to another set of actions.

The do-while control structure normally is used when the occurrence of an event is not quantifi-able or predictable. For example, programmers frequently use the do-while control structure to process all records in a file. A payroll program using a do-while control structure loops once for each employee. This program stops looping after it processes the last employee's record.

The do-until control structure is similar to the do-while but has two major differences: where it tests the condition and when it stops looping. First, the do-until control structure tests the condition at the end of the loop (Figure 11-33).

The action(s) in a do-until control structure thus always will execute at least once. The loop in a do-while control structure, by contrast, might not execute at all. That is, if the condition immediately is false, the action or actions in the do-while loop never execute. Second, a do-until control structure continues looping until the condition is true — and then stops. This is different from the do-while control structure, which continues to loop while the condition is true.

An understanding of these control structures provides an insight into the steps performed by a computer when the computer is used to solve a problem or process data.

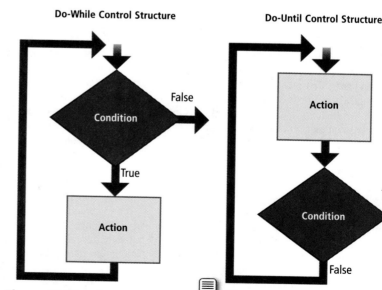

Do-While Control Structure

Condition — False

True

Action

Do-Until Control Structure

Action

Condition — True

False

Figure 11-32 The do-while control structure tests the condition at the beginning of the loop. It exits the loop when the result of the condition is false.

Figure 11-33 The do-until control structure tests the condition at the end of the loop. It exits the loop when the result of the condition is true.

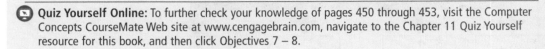

✔ QUIZ YOURSELF 11-3

Instructions: Find the true statement below. Then, rewrite the remaining false statements so that they are true.

1. Program development is an ongoing activity within system development.

2. The program development life cycle consists of these six steps: analyze requirements, design solution, validate design, implement design, test solution, and hardcode solution.

3. Three basic control structures are sequence, selection, and maintenance.

Quiz Yourself Online: To further check your knowledge of pages 450 through 453, visit the Computer Concepts CourseMate Web site at www.cengagebrain.com, navigate to the Chapter 11 Quiz Yourself resource for this book, and then click Objectives 7 – 8.

Chapter Summary

This chapter discussed the system development phases. The guidelines for system development also were presented. Activities that occur during system development, including project management, feasibility assessment, documentation, and data and information gathering, also were addressed.

This chapter discussed various programming languages and program development tools used to create and modify computer programs. It described a variety of Web development and multimedia development tools. Finally, the chapter discussed program development and the tools used in this process.

Computer Usage @ Work

Manufacturing

Manufacturing plays a crucial role in today's society. To keep up with our growing population's increasing demand for various products, organizations explore ways to streamline manufacturing processes while simultaneously minimizing costs. These organizations often find that using computers in the manufacturing process requires fewer people-hours, and products and parts are manufactured with greater accuracy and less waste.

Automakers, for example, manufacture cars on an assembly line. In the early years of car manufacturing, people were involved at all stages of the manufacturing process, and it was not uncommon to find hundreds or thousands of individuals working along the line. Although the assembly line allowed individuals to manufacture cars as quickly as they could, companies soon realized that computer-aided manufacturing (CAM) would increase output and decrease labor costs. In fact, CAM proved to be most effective when used in conjunction with computer-aided design (CAD). CAD designs an item, such as a car, to manufacture; CAM then manufactures the car according to the original design. Computers also determine the exact amount of material necessary to build the car, as well as the expected output.

Communications during the assembly process is critical. Computers automatically communicate with each other along the assembly line and provide alerts when factors arise that can interrupt the process. For example, running out of hinges that attach the door to the rest of the car's body will halt the line until someone replenishes the hinges. Computers, however, often alert individuals to low supplies before they run out and the assembly halts. Failure to detect the absence of hinges might result in the machinery that is manufacturing the car to think that it is attaching hinges when in fact it is not. This might result in damage to the door and/or the car's body further along the assembly line.

Today, computers assist with manufacturing many types of items. Although some might argue that computers perform jobs that people once held, their introduction has helped to meet our increased demand and desire for low prices.

For more information, visit the Computer Concepts CourseMate Web site at www.cengagebrain.com, navigate to the Chapter 11 Computer Usage @ Work resource for this book, and then click Manufacturing.

Companies on the Cutting Edge

COMPUTER SCIENCES CORPORATION (CSC) Global IT Services Company

When the space shuttle blasted into space and docked with the International Space Station, Computer Sciences Corporation (CSC) played a major role in the mission. NASA has partnered with CSC to provide support for its Center for Computational Sciences, which contains simulators and supercomputing resources for high-performance aerospace activities.

CSC's three primary lines of services are Business Solutions & Services, Global Outsourcing Services, and the North American Public Sector. Its information technology projects include managing the nation's air traffic control system, providing logistics for the U.S. Army's equipment, stopping security breaches, simplifying the U.S. Patent and Trademark Office's application process, and helping the California Department of Forestry fight wildfires.

The company has grown from a two-person operation in 1959 to an international corporation based in Falls Church, Virginia. Recently, it won the "BEST Award" from the American Society for Training and Development for its global learning and employee talent development programs.

ELECTRONIC ARTS (EA) Entertainment Software Developer

Video gaming is one of the more popular forms of recreation among people of all ages. Game sales are increasing among all age groups, and demand for Wii products is especially high among adult gamers.

Electronic Arts (EA) is an entertainment software publishing company that develops video games for game consoles, computers, mobile devices, and the Internet. The company had thirty-one products that sold more than one million copies in a recent year, three of which sold more than five million copies: FIFA, Madden NFL, and Need for Speed Undercover.

Electronic Arts has been developing video games since 1982. From the beginning, EA has referred to its programmers as software artists who can evoke emotions from game enthusiasts. Its yearly revenues of more than $3 billion are generated from its sales of action, fantasy, sports, and strategy software for the PlayStation, Xbox, Wii, and Game Boy systems.

For more information, visit the Computer Concepts CourseMate Web site at www.cengagebrain.com and then navigate to the Chapter 11 Companies on the Cutting Edge resource for this book.

Technology Trailblazers

ED YOURDON Project Management Consultant

Much of today's structured system development life cycle is due to the methodologies Ed Yourdon developed more than 40 years ago. Yourdon's work in the computer industry ranges from predicting technology megatrends to recruiting and retaining employees, and much of his current research focuses on developing Web 2.0 and 3.0 strategies, products, and services.

Yourdon is considered one of the ten most influential people in the software field and was inducted into the Computer Hall of Fame. He has written 27 books; the latest, *Outsource: Competing in the Global Productivity Race* and *Death March*, provide guidance to corporate managers facing constrained resources and budgets.

Yourdon began his computer career as a programmer and then founded a consulting firm to provide advice in modern software engineering technology and project management techniques. Today, he maintains his blog, The Yourdon Report, and the Structured Analysis Wiki, and serves as a consultant in his firm, NODRUOY Inc.

JAMES GOSLING Java Engineer and Architect

Songwriter and musician Neil Young has teamed with Sun Microsystems' James Gosling to develop a hybrid 1959 Lincoln Continental that will compete for the Automotive X prize, a contest for vehicles getting at least 100 mpg. The two Canadian-born innovators have named their car the Linc Volt, and its performance system is monitored by Java technology.

Gosling is the mastermind behind Java, and he affectionately is called the "father of Java." He was raised near Calgary, Alberta, and spent much of his free time turning spare machine parts into games. At 15, he wrote software for the University of Calgary's physics department. When he was hired at Sun, he built a multiprocessor version of UNIX, developed compilers to convert program code into machine language, and wrote a UNIX text editor.

He served as Sun's vice president and Oracle's chief technology officer until resigning in 2010. He was named an officer of the Order of Canada for demonstrating an outstanding level of talent and service to Canadians.

For more information, visit the Computer Concepts CourseMate Web site at www.cengagebrain.com and then navigate to the Chapter 11 Technology Trailblazers resource for this book.

Chapter Review

The Chapter Review reinforces the main concepts presented in this chapter.

To listen to an audio version of this Chapter Review, visit the Computer Concepts CourseMate Web site at www.cengagebrain.com and then navigate to the Chapter 11 Chapter Review resource for this book.

1. **Why Are Project Management, Feasibility Assessment, Documentation, and Data and Information Gathering Techniques Important during System Development?** **Project management** is the process of planning, scheduling, and then controlling the activities during system development. The goal of project management is to deliver an acceptable system to the user in an agreed-upon time frame. **Feasibility** is a measure of how suitable the development of a system will be to the organization. **Documentaton** is the collection and summarization of data and information. To gather data and information, IT professionals can review documentation, observe, distribute surveys, interview, participate in a **joint-application design** (**JAD**) session, and research.

2. **What Is the Purpose of Each System Development Phase?** A **system** is a set of components that interact to achieve a common goal. **System development** is a set of activities used to build an **information system**. Most system development cycles contain five **phases**. During the **planning phase**, a **project request** is reviewed and approved, project requests are prioritized, resources are allocated, and a project development team is formed for each approved project. During the **analysis phase**, a **preliminary investigation**, also called the **feasibility study**, is conducted to determine the exact nature of the problem or improvement, and detailed analysis is performed to study how the current system works, determine users' requirements, and recommend a solution. During the **design phase**, any necessary hardware and software are acquired, and the details of the new or modified information system are developed. In the **implementation phase**, the new or modified system is constructed and delivered to the users. During the **operation, support, and security phase**, ongoing assistance is provided for the information system and its users after the system is implemented.

Visit the Computer Concepts CourseMate Web site at www.cengagebrain.com, navigate to the Chapter 11 Quiz Yourself resource for this book, and then click Objectives 1 – 2.

3. **How Are Low-Level Languages Different from Procedural Languages?** A **programming language** is a set of words, abbreviations, and symbols that enables a **programmer** to communicate instructions to a computer. A low-level language is a programming language that runs on only one type of computer. Each instruction in a low-level language usually equates to a single machine instruction. Procedural languages are high-level languages that can run on many different types of computers and operating systems. In a **procedural language**, often called a **third-generation language** (**3GL**), a programmer writes instructions that tell the computer what to accomplish and how to do it.

4. **What Are the Benefits of Object-Oriented Programming Languages and Program Development Tools?** Programmers use an **object-oriented programming** (**OOP**) **language** or object-oriented program development tool to implement object-oriented design. A major benefit of OOP is the ability to reuse and modify existing objects, allowing programmers to create applications faster. OOP languages include **Java**, **C#**, **F#**, and **C++**. Often used in conjunction with OOP, **RAD** (rapid application development) is a method of developing software, in which a programmer writes and implements a program in segments instead of waiting until the entire program is completed. **Visual Studio** is Microsoft's suite of program development tools and includes Visual Basic, Visual C++, and Visual C#.

5. **What Are Other Programming Languages and Other Program Development Tools?** A **4GL** (fourth generation language) is a **nonprocedural language** that users and programmers use to access the data in a database. One popular 4GL is **SQL**. Other program development tools include an **application generator**, which creates source code or machine code from a specification of the required functionality, and a **macro**, which is a series of statements that instructs a program how to complete a task.

6. **How Are Web Pages Developed?** **Web developers** use a variety of techniques to develop Web pages. **HTML** (Hypertext Markup Language) is a special formatting language used to format documents for display on the Web. **XHTML**, **XML**, and **WML** also are used to develop Web pages. To add interactivity to Web pages, some programmers use a scripting language or **dynamic HTML** (**DHTML**). Other popular languages and tools include **Ruby on Rails**, **Ajax**, and **API**. Web developers also use **Web page authoring software** to create sophisticated Web pages, including **Dreamweaver**, **Expression Web**, **Flash**, and **SharePoint Designer**.

Visit the Computer Concepts CourseMate Web site at www.cengagebrain.com, navigate to the Chapter 11 Quiz Yourself resource for this book, and then click Objectives 3 – 6.

7. What Are the Six Program Development Steps? **Program development** is a series of steps programmers use to build computer programs. The **program development life cycle** (PDLC) consists of six steps: (1) analyze requirements, (2) design solution, (3) validate design, (4) implement design, (5) test solution, and (6) document solution. The steps in the program development life cycle form a loop.

8. What Are the Basic Control Structures Used in Designing Solutions to Programming Problems? A **control structure** depicts the logical order of program instructions. Three basic control structures are the **sequence control structure**, **selection control structure**, and **repetition control structure**.

Visit the Computer Concepts CourseMate Web site at www.cengagebrain.com, navigate to the Chapter 11 Quiz Yourself resource for this book, and then click Objectives 7 – 8.

Key Terms

You should know each key term. The list below helps focus your study.

To see an example of and a definition for each term, and to access current and additional information from the Web, visit the Computer Concepts CourseMate Web site at www.cengagebrain.com and then navigate to the Chapter 11 Key Terms resource for this book.

4GL (443)
Ajax (448)
analysis phase (425)
API (448)
application generator (444)
assembly language (437)
ATOM (447)
benchmark test (430)
C (439)
C# (441)
C++ (441)
case control structure (452)
change management (420)
chief security officer (434)
COBOL (COmmon Business-Oriented Language) (440)
code snippets (442)
compiler (438)
computer program (435)
computer security plan (434)
computer-aided software engineering (CASE) (432)
control structure (451)
custom software (427)
Delphi (443)
design phase (428)
developer (435)
direct conversion (433)
documentation (422)
Dreamweaver (449)
dynamic HTML (DHTML) (448)
electronic magazine (428)

Expression Web (449)
e-zine (428)
F# (441)
feasibility (421)
feasibility study (425)
Flash (449)
focus groups (423)
HTML (446)
IDE (integrated development environment) (440)
implementation phase (432)
information system (IS) (418)
interpreter (438)
IT consultant (429)
Java (440)
JavaScript (447)
joint-application design (JAD) (423)
machine language (436)
macro (445)
maintaining (450)
multimedia authoring software (449)
.NET (441)
nonprocedural language (443)
object-oriented programming (OOP) language (440)
operation, support, and security phase (434)
outsource (428)
packaged software (427)
parallel conversion (433)
Perl (448)

phased conversion (433)
phases (418)
PHP (448)
pilot conversion (434)
planning phase (425)
PowerBuilder (443)
preliminary investigation (425)
procedural language (438)
program development (450)
program development life cycle (450)
program development tool (436)
programmer (435)
programming language (435)
programming team (451)
project leader (420)
project management (420)
project management software (420)
project manager (420)
project request (423)
project team (420)
prototype (431)
RAD (440)
repetition control structure (453)
Rexx (448)
RSS 2.0 (447)
Ruby on Rails (448)
scope (420)
scripting language (447)
selection control structure (452)

sequence control structure (452)
SharePoint Designer (449)
source program (437)
SQL (443)
standards (419)
steering committee (420)
system (418)
system developer (420)
system development (418)
system development life cycle (SDLC) (418)
system proposal (427)
systems analyst (419)
Tcl (448)
third-generation language (3GL) (438)
training (433)
users (419)
value-added reseller (VAR) (429)
VBScript (448)
visual programming environment (VPE) (443)
visual programming language (443)
Visual Studio (441)
Web developers (446)
Web page authoring software (449)
WML (447)
XHTML (446)
XML (446)

Checkpoint

The Checkpoint exercises test your knowledge of the chapter concepts. The page number containing the answer appears in parentheses after each exercise.

To complete the Checkpoint exercises interactively, visit the Computer Concepts CourseMate Web site at www.cengagebrain.com and then navigate to the Chapter 11 Checkpoint resource for this book.

Multiple Choice Select the best answer.

1. The _____ manages and controls the budget and schedule of the project. (420)
 a. project team
 b. steering committee
 c. project leader
 d. system developer

2. _____ measures whether the lifetime benefits of the proposed information system will be greater than its lifetime costs. (421)
 a. Operational feasibility
 b. Technical feasibility
 c. Economic feasibility
 d. Schedule feasibility

3. In larger organizations, users write a formal request for a new or modified information system, which is called a _____. (423)
 a. prototype
 b. joint-application design (JAD)
 c. project request
 d. system proposal

4. The purpose of the _____ is to assess the feasibility of each alternative solution and then recommend the most feasible solution for the project. (427)
 a. project plan
 b. system proposal
 c. project request
 d. system review

5. A(n) _____ reads a code statement, converts it to one or more machine language instructions, and then executes those machine language instructions. (438)
 a. compiler
 b. nonprocedural language
 c. source program
 d. interpreter

6. _____ is a subset of the Visual Basic language that allows programmers to add intelligence and interactivity to Web pages. (448)
 a. Ajax
 b. Flash
 c. VBScript
 d. Rexx

7. _____ is an open source framework that provides technologies for developing object-oriented, database-driven Web sites. (448)
 a. PHP
 b. Ruby on Rails
 c. Flash
 d. Ajax

8. _____ is a Web page authoring program that is part of the Microsoft Office and SharePoint families of products. (449)
 a. PHP
 b. Ajax
 c. SharePoint Designer
 d. Flash

Matching Match the terms with their definitions.

_____ 1. project manager (420)
_____ 2. benchmark test (430)
_____ 3. source program (437)
_____ 4. macro (445)
_____ 5. API (448)

a. set of rules and procedures a company expects employees to follow
b. collection of tools that programmers use to interact with an environment such as a Web site or operating system
c. series of statements that instructs an application how to complete a task
d. the language instructions, or code, to be converted to machine language
e. controls the activities during system development
f. measures the performance of hardware or software

Short Answer Write a brief answer to each of the following questions.

1. What is system development? _____ Describe the five phases of the system development life cycle (SDLC). _____

2. Why is feasibility evaluated during system development? _____ How are operational feasibility, schedule feasibility, technical feasibility, and economic feasibility different? _____

3. What activities take place during the operations, support, and security phase? _____ How do the roles of the systems analyst and chief security officer differ in this phase? _____

4. How is a compiler different from an interpreter? _____ What is the advantage, and disadvantage, of an interpreter? _____

5. How is XML used? _____ Describe two applications of XML. _____

Problem Solving

The Problem Solving exercises extend your knowledge of the chapter concepts by seeking solutions to practical computer problems that you may encounter at home, school, or work. The Collaboration exercise should be completed with a team.

In the real world, practical problems often can be solved in multiple ways. Provide one solution to each of the following problems using available resources, such as articles on the Web or in print, blogs, podcasts, videos, television, user guides, other individuals, and electronics and computer stores. You may need to use multiple resources to obtain an answer. Present your solutions in the form requested by your instructor (brief report, presentation, discussion, or other means).

@ Home

1. **Trial Period Expired** While installing a 60-day trial of the latest version of Microsoft Office, your computer displays a message stating that the trial period already has expired. What might be causing this error message to appear?

2. **Security Questions** Each time you log into your bank's Web site, it asks you to answer a series of security questions you selected when you set up your account. The Web site also asks whether you want it to request the answers to those security questions the next time you log in. You do not want the Web site to ask these questions in the future, so you place a check mark in the appropriate check box. The very next day, however, the Web site asks you the security questions. Why might this be happening?

3. **Problem with Macro** You created a macro in one document and made it available to other documents on your computer. When you run the macro in another document, however, it does not function properly. What might be wrong?

4. **Web Page Syntax Error** When you attempt to display a Web page, an error message appears and the Web page does not display properly on your screen. The error message cites a syntax error and asks you if you would like to debug. How will you respond?

@ Work

5. **Schedule Delay** You are working as a project manager in charge of developing a new information system. Halfway through the project, you realize that you will not meet your deadline. This delay is sure to cost your company additional money. How might you approach your manager about this?

6. **Problem Installing Custom Program** After using an application generator to create a program, you save it on a USB flash drive and give the USB flash drive to your colleague so that she can install the program on her computer. She claims, however, that the program does not work on her computer. Why might the program work on your computer, but not on her computer?

7. **Program Appears Frozen** The human resources department has just released a new program used to calculate payroll for each employee. After you enter the payroll data for each employee, you click a button to calculate everyone's pay for that pay period. After clicking the button, the program becomes unresponsive and appears frozen. What might be wrong?

8. **Unknown Language** Several years ago, a programmer who no longer is with the company wrote a program for your company using an older programming language. Your colleague has discovered a bug in the program, but nobody knows the language to be able to fix the bug. What are your options?

Collaboration

9. **Computers in Manufacturing** Today, computers are used in the manufacturing of nearly every type of item. Your instructor would like everyone to realize the importance of computers in today's society and requests that each person find an item and determine how computers might have been used to assist in the manufacturing process. Form a team of three people. Each team member should locate one item that he or she believes was manufactured with the help of a computer. Then, team members should research exactly how computers were used and record their findings. Finally, the three team members should compare their research to discover similarities and differences and then compile their findings into a brief report.

Learn How To

The Learn How To activities step you through fundamental technology skills when using a computer. The Learn How To exercises enable you to become more proficient with these skills.

Learn How To 1: Conduct an Effective Interview

As you learned in this chapter, gathering information is a critical element in system development, because without accurate facts, it is unlikely that the finished system will perform in the desired manner. An important means of gathering information is the personal interview. Interviews are used in several stages throughout system development, and they must be thorough and comprehensive.

Prior to conducting an interview, you must determine that an interview is the best means for obtaining the information you seek. You have learned a variety of ways to obtain information, and you should use each of them appropriately. Because an interview interrupts a person's work and takes time, you must be sure the information gained in the interview justifies this interruption. Once you have determined you should conduct an interview to gather information required for system development, a variety of factors become relevant.

Goal: The most important element of a successful interview is for you to determine exactly what knowledge you hope to gain as a result of the interview. If you do not have a goal, you are unlikely to emerge from the interview with much useful information.

Do Your Homework: You should complete a variety of preparatory steps that will help ensure a successful interview. These steps include the following:

1. Gather as much information as you can from the fact-gathering processes that do not require an interview.
2. Be sure you plan to interview the best person to obtain the information you need.
3. Prepare the questions you want to ask prior to setting up the interview.
4. Prior to setting an appointment for an interview, be sure the management personnel of the people you will interview have approved.

Make an Appointment: An appointment almost always is required. By making an appointment, you ensure the person to be interviewed will be available. Normally you should request an appointment in writing, often through the use of e-mail. In this written request, you should set a time and place for the interview, inform the interviewee what you need to know, and establish an agenda with an estimated time. You must recognize that most people do not like to be interviewed, so often you will not be seen as friendly. In addition, it might be possible that the system being developed could eliminate or change the person's job, and clearly this can establish an adversarial relationship. Your task when making an appointment, then, is to establish credibility with the interviewee and set the stage for a successful interview.

Conduct the Interview: When conducting an interview, remember that you are the "intruder." Therefore, you should be polite, prompt, and attentive in the interview. Always understand the perspective of the person being interviewed and understand his or her fears, doubts, and potential hostilities. Sometimes, the interviewee might feel he or she is in conflict with you, so by listening closely and being aware of the body language, you should be able to discern the amount of truth and the amount of hedging that is occurring. Some of the details of the interview of which you should be aware are as follows:

1. If possible, the interview should be conducted in a quiet environment with a minimum of interruptions.
2. The demeanor should be open and friendly, but as noted you should not expect to be welcomed with open arms.
3. Your questions should directly address the goals of the interview.
4. Your questions should be thought-provoking.
5. Listen carefully, with both your ears and your eyes.
6. As you listen, concentrate on the interviewee — when points are being made, do not take notes because that will distract from what the person is saying — stay focused.
7. Throughout the interview, offer reinforcing comments, such as, "The way I understand what you just said is ..." Make sure when you leave the interview there are no misunderstandings between you and the person you interviewed.
8. Before you conclude the interview, be sure all your goals have been met.

Follow-Up: After the interview, it is recommended you send a follow-up letter or e-mail message to the person you interviewed to review the information you learned. This document should invite the interviewee to correct any errors you made in summing up your findings. In addition, for all the people you interview, keep a log of the time and place of the interview. In this way, if any questions arise regarding the interview, you will have a log.

Exercise

1. Using the techniques in this activity, conduct interviews with three students on your campus. Your interview goal is to find out about both the most successful class and the least successful class the student has completed. Why was the class successful or unsuccessful? Discuss the instructor, textbook, subject matter, and other relevant items. After the interviews, write a one-page paper summarizing your findings and identify common elements found in successful classes and in unsuccessful classes. Submit this paper to your instructor.

Learn It Online

The Learn It Online exercises are interactive Web exercises designed to reinforce and expand your understanding of the chapter concepts. The descriptions below briefly summarize each exercise.

To complete the Learn It Online exercises, visit the Computer Concepts CourseMate Web site at www.cengagebrain.com, navigate to the Chapter 11 resources for this book, click the link for the exercise you want to complete, and then read the instructions.

1 At the Movies — Electronic Arts Going Mobile
Watch a movie to learn about how Electronic Arts is tackling the mobile video game market and then answer questions about the movie.

2 Student Edition Labs — Project Management and Visual Programming
Enhance your understanding and knowledge about project management and visual programming by completing the Project Management and Visual Programming Labs.

3 Practice Test
Take a multiple choice test that checks your knowledge of the chapter concepts and review the resulting study guide.

4 Who Wants To Be a Computer Genius²?
Play the Shelly Cashman Series version of this popular game by answering questions to find out if you are a computer genius. Panic buttons are available to provide assistance during game play.

5 Crossword Puzzle Challenge
Complete an interactive crossword puzzle to reinforce concepts presented in this chapter.

6 Windows Exercises
Step through the Windows 7 exercises to search for executable files, use the Movie Box Office simulation, adjust keyboard speed, and use the Loan Payment Calculator.

7 Exploring Computer Careers
Read about a career as a programmer, search for related employment advertisements, and then answer related questions.

8 Web Apps — Google Earth
Learn how to download and use Google Earth on your computer, fly to your neighborhood and zoom in, view satellite images of your favorite nearby businesses, and show and hide various layers.

Web Research

The Web Research exercises broaden your understanding of chapter concepts by presenting questions that require you to search the Web for answers.

1 Search Sleuth

Use one of the search engines listed in Figure 2-8 in Chapter 2 on page 65 or your own favorite search engine to find the answers to the following questions. Copy and paste the Web address from the Web page where you found the answer. Some questions may have more than one answer. If required, submit your answers to your instructor. (1) Who are the winners of the most recent Worldwide UML Jokes Contest? What story does the first-place winner tell in UML notation? (2) What is the name of the document Karol Adamiecki developed in 1896? (3) What model was created from the merger of the Objectory Process, the Booch Method, and the Object-Modeling Technique? (4) Which programming language uses a mouse pointer shaped in the form of a turtle? (5) Who gave the keynote address at the latest Microsoft MIX Conference? (6) What is the purpose of a browser sniffer?

2 Green Computing

Corporations are touting their efforts to go green in their computing environments, but a survey of computer professionals found that less than seven percent of companies have implemented their green IT initiatives. One-third still are in the planning stages. Corporations may be choosing to practice green computing, but many times their efforts are driven by a financial goal to save electricity, not an ecological goal to reduce carbon dioxide emissions. Visit the Web sites of several companies profiled in this textbook and locate their environmentally friendly practices. For example, which green practices are featured? What outdated equipment has been replaced with energy-efficient machines? Is virtualization technology implemented? How are they conserving power? Write a report summarizing your findings, and include a table of links to Web sites that provide additional details.

3 Social Networking

Members of online social communities face the responsibility to act civilly and follow proper etiquette rules. *The Ultimate Social Media Etiquette Handbook*, which is posted on the techipedia Web site, states the rules for managing and maintaining online social relationships. In addition, several experts offer advice, including Philipp Lenssen (antispamnews.com), Tim O'Reilly (radar.oreilly.com), and Reihan Salam (slate.com/id/2174439). Read their columns and view the techipedia Web site (techipedia.com/social-media-etiquette-handbook) to learn about the best practices to follow when participating in online social networks. How should a networker create a personalized message giving a compelling reason why someone should join? How can a sender's background information be verified? When is sharing contact lists considered appropriate? Summarize the information you read and viewed.

4 Blogs

Creating a blog and then attracting people to read it requires a keen sense of design, marketing, and editing skills. Blogging services provide assistance in attracting visitors to a Web site and then holding their interest while they are viewing a page. Six Apart owns four blogging services: Blogs.com (blogs.com), Movable Type (movabletype.com), Vox (vox.com), and TypePad (typepad.com). Microsoft Windows Live Spaces (spaces.live.com) and Yahoo 360 (360.yahoo.com) are basic blog editors with a few features. WordPress (wordpress.com) is a blogging service with convenient editing tools. Visit these blog design Web sites and read about the features provided. Which services have blogging tools that seem easy to use? What customization tools are available? What features, such as word counters, are shown? Which Web sites allow users to upload photos?

5 Ethics in Action

Millions of VeriChip microchips have been implanted in pets for identification purposes, but the move to humans has alarmed security experts. VeriChip's Xmark subsidiary distributes the Hugs and the Halo systems of infant protection, the RoamAlert system of wandering protection, the MyCall emergency response system, and the Assetrac asset tracking system. The chips release a code when a scanner is passed over them, and this code is linked to a database that retains the person's information and can be updated. View online sites that discuss using implanted chips in humans. How can they be used to breach the confidentiality of medical records? How are they being used in nonmedical applications? Write a report summarizing your findings, and include a table of links to Web sites that provide additional details about implantable chips.

Computer Security and Safety, Ethics, and Privacy

Objectives

After completing this chapter, you will be able to:

1 Describe various types of Internet and network attacks (computer viruses, worms, Trojan horses, rootkits, botnets, denial of service attacks, back doors, and spoofing), and identify ways to safeguard against these attacks, including firewalls and intrusion detection software

2 Discuss techniques to prevent unauthorized computer access and use

3 Identify safeguards against hardware theft and vandalism

4 Explain the ways to protect against software theft and information theft

5 Discuss the types of devices available that protect computers from system failure

6 Identify risks and safeguards associated with wireless communications

7 Discuss ways to prevent health-related disorders and injuries due to computer use

8 Discuss issues surrounding information privacy, including electronic profiles, cookies, spyware and adware, spam, phishing, privacy laws, social engineering, employee monitoring, and content filtering

Computer Security Risks

Today, people rely on computers to create, store, and manage critical information. Thus, it is crucial that users take measures to protect their computers and data from loss, damage, and misuse.

A **computer security risk** is any event or action that could cause a loss of or damage to computer hardware, software, data, information, or processing capability. While some breaches to computer security are accidental, many are intentional. Some intruders do no damage; they merely access data, information, or programs on the computer. Other intruders indicate some evidence of their presence either by leaving a message or by deliberately altering or damaging data.

An intentional breach of computer security often involves a deliberate act that is against the law. Any illegal act involving a computer generally is referred to as a **computer crime**. The term **cybercrime** refers to online or Internet-based illegal acts. Today, cybercrime is one of the FBI's top three priorities.

Perpetrators of cybercrime and other intrusions fall into seven basic categories: hacker, cracker, script kiddie, corporate spy, unethical employee, cyberextortionist, and cyberterrorist.

- The term **hacker**, although originally a complimentary word for a computer enthusiast, now has a derogatory meaning and refers to someone who accesses a computer or network illegally. Some hackers claim the intent of their security breaches is to improve security.

- A **cracker** also is someone who accesses a computer or network illegally but has the intent of destroying data, stealing information, or other malicious action. Both hackers and crackers have advanced computer and network skills.

- A **script kiddie** has the same intent as a cracker but does not have the technical skills and knowledge. Script kiddies often use prewritten hacking and cracking programs to break into computers.

- Some corporate spies have excellent computer and networking skills and are hired to break into a specific computer and steal its proprietary data and information. Unscrupulous companies hire corporate spies, a practice known as corporate espionage, to gain a competitive advantage.

- Unethical employees break into their employers' computers for a variety of reasons. Some simply want to exploit a security weakness. Others seek financial gains from selling confidential information. Disgruntled employees may want revenge.

- A **cyberextortionist** is someone who uses e-mail as a vehicle for extortion. These perpetrators send an organization a threatening e-mail message indicating they will expose confidential information, exploit a security flaw, or launch an attack that will compromise the organization's network — if they are not paid a sum of money.

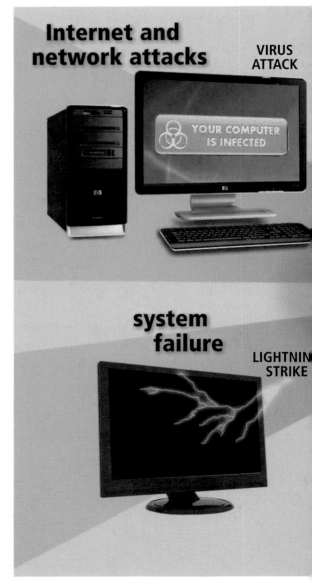

Internet and network attacks
VIRUS ATTACK
YOUR COMPUTER IS INFECTED

system failure
LIGHTNING STRIKE

- A **cyberterrorist** is someone who uses the Internet or network to destroy or damage computers for political reasons. The cyberterrorist might target the nation's air traffic control system, electricity-generating companies, or a telecommunications infrastructure. Cyberterrorism usually requires a team of highly skilled individuals, millions of dollars, and several years of planning.

Business and home users must protect, or safeguard, their computers from breaches of security and other computer security risks. Some organizations hire individuals previously convicted of computer crimes to help identify security risks and implement safeguards because these individuals know how criminals attempt to breach security.

The more common computer security risks include Internet and network attacks, unauthorized access and use, hardware theft, software theft, information theft, and system failure (Figure 10-1). The following pages describe these computer security risks and also discuss safeguards users might take to minimize or prevent their consequences.

Figure 10-1 Computers and computer users are exposed to several types of security risks.

Internet and Network Attacks

Information transmitted over networks has a higher degree of security risk than information kept on an organization's premises. In an organization, network administrators usually take measures to protect a network from security risks. On the Internet, where no central administrator is present, the security risk is greater.

Internet and network attacks that jeopardize security include computer viruses, worms, Trojan horses, and rootkits; botnets; denial of service attacks; back doors; and spoofing. The following sections address these computer security risks and suggest measures organizations and individuals can take to protect their computers while on the Internet or connected to a network.

Computer Viruses, Worms, Trojan Horses, and Rootkits

Every unprotected computer is susceptible to the first type of computer security risk — a computer virus, worm, Trojan horse, and/or rootkit.

- A computer **virus** is a potentially damaging computer program that affects, or infects, a computer negatively by altering the way the computer works without the user's knowledge or permission. Once the virus infects the computer, it can spread throughout and may damage files and system software, including the operating system.
- A **worm** is a program that copies itself repeatedly, for example in memory or on a network, using up resources and possibly shutting down the computer or network.
- A **Trojan horse** (named after the Greek myth) is a program that hides within or looks like a legitimate program. A certain condition or action usually triggers the Trojan horse. Unlike a virus or worm, a Trojan horse does not replicate itself to other computers.
- A **rootkit** is a program that hides in a computer and allows someone from a remote location to take full control of the computer. Once the rootkit is installed, the rootkit author can execute programs, change settings, monitor activity, and access files on the remote computer.

Computer viruses, worms, Trojan horses, and rootkits are classified as **malware** (short for malicious software), which are programs that act without a user's knowledge and deliberately alter the computer's operations. Unscrupulous programmers write malware and then test it to ensure it can deliver its payload. The **payload** is the destructive event or prank the program is intended to deliver. A computer infected by a virus, worm, Trojan horse, or rootkit often has one or more of the following symptoms:

- Operating system runs much slower than usual
- Available memory is less than expected
- Files become corrupted
- Screen displays unusual message or image
- Unknown programs or files mysteriously appear
- Music or unusual sound plays randomly
- Existing programs and files disappear
- Programs or files do not work properly
- System properties change
- Operating system does not start up
- Operating system shuts down unexpectedly

Currently, more than 300,000 Web sites can infect your computer with known viruses, worms, Trojan horses, rootkits, and other malware. These malicious programs deliver their payload on a computer in a variety of ways: when a user (1) opens an infected file, (2) runs an infected program, (3) boots the computer with infected removable media inserted in a drive or plugged in a port, (4) connects an unprotected computer to a network, or (5) when a certain condition or event occurs, such as the computer's clock changing to a specific date. A common way computers become infected with viruses and other malware is through users opening infected e-mail attachments (Figure 10-2).

How a Virus Can Spread through an E-Mail Message

Step 1
Unscrupulous programmers create a virus program that deletes all files. They hide the virus in a word processing document and attach the document to an e-mail message.

Step 2
They send the e-mail message to thousands of users around the world.

Step 3a
me users open the attachment and their computers come infected with the virus.

Step 3b
Other users do not recognize the name of the sender of the e-mail message. These users do not open the e-mail message — instead they immediately delete the e-mail message and continue using the computers. These users' computers are not infected with the virus.

Figure 10-2 This figure shows how a virus can spread through an e-mail message.

? | FAQ 10-1

Can multimedia files be infected with a virus?

Yes. The increase in popularity of media sharing Web sites provides a great opportunity to distribute malicious programs. During one year, approximately 500,000 people downloaded what they thought was a media file from the Internet. In fact, the file was a Trojan horse that infected many computers with spyware. For this reason, it is important to scan all media files for malware before playing them.

For more information, visit the Computer Concepts CourseMate Web site at www.cengagebrain.com, navigate to the Chapter 10 FAQ resource for this book, and then click Infected Media Files.

Safeguards against Computer Viruses and Other Malware

Users can take several precautions to protect their home and work computers and mobile devices from these malicious infections. The following paragraphs discuss these precautionary measures.

Do not start a computer with removable media, such as optical discs and USB flash drives, in the drives or ports — unless you are certain the media are uninfected or from a trusted source. A **trusted source** is an organization or person you believe will not send a virus infected file knowingly. Never open an e-mail attachment unless you are expecting the attachment *and* it is from a trusted source. If the e-mail message is from an unknown source, delete the e-mail message immediately — without opening or executing any attachments. If the e-mail message is from a trusted source, but you were

not expecting an attachment, carefully check the spelling of the e-mail address and contents of the message for errors because perpetrators often make typographical errors. If the message is error-free, verify with the source that they intended to send you an attachment — before opening it.

Some viruses are hidden in macros, which are instructions saved in software such as a word processing or spreadsheet program. In programs that allow users to write macros, you should set the macro security level so that the application software warns users that a document they are attempting to open contains a macro. From this warning, a user chooses to disable or enable the macro. If the document is from a trusted source, the user can enable the macro. Otherwise, it should be disabled.

Users should install an antivirus program and update it frequently. An **antivirus program** protects a computer against viruses by identifying and removing any computer viruses found in memory, on storage media, or on incoming files. Most antivirus programs also protect against other malware. When you purchase a new computer, it often includes antivirus software. Many e-mail servers also have antivirus programs installed to check incoming and outgoing e-mail messages for malware.

An antivirus program scans for programs that attempt to modify the boot program, the operating system, and other programs that normally are read from but not modified. In addition, many antivirus programs automatically scan files downloaded from the Web, e-mail attachments, opened files, and all removable media inserted in the computer.

One technique that antivirus programs use to identify a virus is to look for virus signatures. A **virus signature**, also called a **virus definition**, is a known specific pattern of virus code. Computer users should update their antivirus program's signature files regularly (Figure 10-3). This extremely important activity allows the antivirus program to protect against viruses written since the antivirus program was released and/or its last update. Most antivirus programs contain an automatic update feature that regularly prompts users to download the virus signature, usually at least once a week. The vendor usually provides this service to registered users at no cost for a specified time.

If an antivirus program identifies an infected file, it attempts to remove the malware. If the antivirus program cannot remove the infection, it often quarantines the infected file. A **quarantine** is a separate area of a hard disk that holds the infected file until the infection can be removed. This step ensures other files will not become infected. Quarantined files remain on your computer until you delete them or restore them.

Some users also install a personal firewall program to protect a computer and its data from unauthorized intrusions. A section later in this chapter discusses firewalls.

Figure 10-3
This antivirus program, which protects a computer from a variety of malware, regularly checks for the latest virus signatures and other important updates.

Finally, stay informed about new virus alerts and virus hoaxes. A **virus hoax** is an e-mail message that warns users of a nonexistent virus or other malware. Often, these virus hoaxes are in the form of a chain letter that requests the user to send a copy of the e-mail message to as many people as possible. The content of the hoax message, for example, may inform users that an important operating system file on their computer is a virus and encourage them to delete the file, which could make their computer unusable. Instead of forwarding the message, visit a Web site that publishes a list of virus alerts and virus hoaxes.

The list in Figure 10-4 summarizes important tips for protecting your computer from viruses and other malware.

Tips for Preventing Viruses and Other Malware

1. Never start a computer with removable media inserted in the drives or plugged in the ports, unless the media are uninfected.

2. Never open an e-mail attachment unless you are expecting it *and* it is from a trusted source.

3. Set the macro security in programs so that you can enable or disable macros. Enable macros only if the document is from a trusted source and you are expecting it.

4. Install an antivirus program on all of your computers. Update the software and the virus signature files regularly.

5. Scan all downloaded programs for viruses and other malware.

6. If the antivirus program flags an e-mail attachment as infected, delete or quarantine the attachment immediately.

7. Before using any removable media, scan the media for malware. Follow this procedure even for shrink-wrapped software from major developers. Some commercial software has been infected and distributed to unsuspecting users.

8. Install a personal firewall program.

9. Stay informed about new virus alerts and virus hoaxes.

Figure 10-4 With the growing number of new viruses and other malware, it is crucial that users take steps to protect their computers.

Botnets

A **botnet** is a group of compromised computers connected to a network such as the Internet that are used as part of a network that attacks other networks, usually for nefarious purposes. A compromised computer, known as a **zombie**, is one whose owner is unaware the computer is being controlled remotely by an outsider. Cybercriminals use botnets to send spam via e-mail, spread viruses and other malware, or commit a denial of service attack.

FAQ 10-2

How can I tell if my computer is a zombie or in a botnet?

The number of zombie computers is increasing at a rapid rate. Your computer may be a zombie or part of a botnet if you notice unusually high disk activity, a slower than normal Internet connection, or devices connected to your computer becoming increasingly unresponsive. The chances of your computer becoming a zombie or part of a botnet greatly increase if you do not have an effective firewall.

For more information, visit the Computer Concepts CourseMate Web site at www.cengagebrain.com, navigate to the Chapter 10 FAQ resource for this book, and then click Zombies and Botnets.

Denial of Service Attacks

A **denial of service attack**, or **DoS attack**, is an assault whose purpose is to disrupt computer access to an Internet service such as the Web or e-mail. Perpetrators carry out a DoS attack in a variety of ways. For example, they may use an unsuspecting computer to send an influx of confusing data messages or useless traffic to a computer network. The victim computer network slows down considerably and eventually becomes unresponsive or unavailable, blocking legitimate visitors from accessing the network.

Perpetrators have a variety of motives for carrying out a DoS attack. Those who disagree with the beliefs or actions of a particular organization claim political anger motivates their attacks. Some perpetrators use the attack as a vehicle for extortion. Others simply want the recognition, even though it is negative.

DoS Attacks

For more information, visit the Computer Concepts CourseMate Web site at www.cengagebrain.com, navigate to the Chapter 10 Web Link resource for this book, and then click DoS Attacks.

Back Doors

A **back door** is a program or set of instructions in a program that allow users to bypass security controls when accessing a program, computer, or network. Once perpetrators gain access to unsecure computers, they often install a back door or modify an existing program to include a back door, which allows them to continue to access the computer remotely without the user's knowledge.

Spoofing

Spoofing is a technique intruders use to make their network or Internet transmission appear legitimate to a victim computer or network. E-mail spoofing occurs when the sender's address or other components of the e-mail header are altered so that it appears the e-mail originated from a different sender. E-mail spoofing commonly is used for virus hoaxes, spam, and phishing scams. IP spoofing occurs when an intruder computer fools a network into believing its IP address is associated with a trusted source. Perpetrators of IP spoofing trick their victims into interacting with a phony Web site.

Safeguards against Botnets, DoS Attacks, Back Doors, and Spoofing

To defend against botnets, DoS attacks, improper use of back doors, and spoofing, users can implement firewall solutions and install intrusion detection software. The following sections discuss these safeguards.

Firewalls

A **firewall** is hardware and/or software that protects a network's resources from intrusion by users on another network such as the Internet (Figure 10-5). All networked and online computer users should implement a firewall solution.

Figure 10-5 A firewall is hardware and/or software that protects a network's resources from intrusion by users on another network such as the Internet.

Organizations use firewalls to protect network resources from outsiders and to restrict employees' access to sensitive data such as payroll or personnel records. They can implement a firewall solution themselves or outsource their needs to a company specializing in providing firewall protection. Large organizations often route all their communications through a proxy server, which is a component of the firewall. A proxy server is a server outside the organization's network that controls which communications pass into the organization's network.

Home and small office/home office users often protect their computers with a personal firewall utility. A **personal firewall** is a utility program that detects and protects a personal computer and its data from unauthorized intrusions. Some operating systems, such as Windows, include personal firewalls.

Some small office/home office users purchase a hardware firewall, such as a router or other device that has a built-in firewall, in addition to or instead of personal firewall software. Hardware firewalls stop intrusions before they attempt to affect your computer maliciously.

Firewalls

For more information, visit the Computer Concepts CourseMate Web site at www.cengagebrain.com, navigate to the Chapter 10 Web Link resource for this book, and then click Firewalls.

Intrusion Detection Software

To provide extra protection against hackers and other intruders, large organizations sometimes use intrusion detection software to identify possible security breaches. **Intrusion detection software** automatically analyzes all network traffic, assesses system vulnerabilities, identifies any unauthorized access (intrusions), and notifies network administrators of suspicious behavior patterns or system breaches.

To utilize intrusion detection software requires the expertise of a network administrator because the programs are complex and difficult to use and interpret. These programs also are quite expensive.

Unauthorized Access and Use

Another type of computer security risk is unauthorized access and use. **Unauthorized access** is the use of a computer or network without permission. **Unauthorized use** is the use of a computer or its data for unapproved or possibly illegal activities. Unauthorized use includes a variety of activities: an employee using an organization's computer to send personal e-mail messages, an employee using the organization's word processing software to track his or her child's soccer league scores, or someone gaining access to a bank computer and performing an unauthorized transfer.

Safeguards against Unauthorized Access and Use

Organizations take several measures to help prevent unauthorized access and use. At a minimum, they should have a written acceptable use policy (AUP) that outlines the computer activities for which the computer and network may and may not be used. An organization's AUP should specify the acceptable use of computers by employees for personal reasons. Some organizations prohibit such use entirely. Others allow personal use on the employee's own time such as a lunch hour.

Other measures that safeguard against unauthorized access and use include firewalls and intrusion detection software, which were discussed in the previous section, and identifying and authenticating users.

Identifying and Authenticating Users

Many organizations use access controls to minimize the chance that a perpetrator intentionally may access or an employee accidentally may access confidential information on a computer. An **access control** is a security measure that defines who can access a computer, when they can access it, and what actions they can take while accessing the computer. In addition, the computer should maintain an **audit trail** that records in a file both successful and unsuccessful access attempts. An unsuccessful access attempt could result from a user mistyping his or her password, or it could result from a hacker trying thousands of passwords.

Organizations should investigate unsuccessful access attempts immediately to ensure they are not intentional breaches of security. They also should review successful access for irregularities, such as use of the computer after normal working hours or from remote computers.

Many systems implement access controls using a two-phase process called identification and authentication. Identification verifies that an individual is a valid user. Authentication verifies that the individual is the person he or she claims to be. Three methods of identification and authentication include user names and passwords, possessed objects, and biometric devices. The technique(s) an organization uses should correspond to the degree of risk associated with the unauthorized access.

User Names and Passwords A **user name**, or user ID (identification), is a unique combination of characters, such as letters of the alphabet or numbers, that identifies one specific user. A **password** is a private combination of characters associated with the user name that allows access to certain computer resources.

Most multiuser (networked) operating systems require that users correctly enter a user name and a password before they can access the data, information, and programs stored on a computer or network (Figure 10-6).

Multiuser systems typically require that users select their own passwords. Users typically choose an easy-to-remember word or series of characters for passwords. If your password is too obvious, however, such as your initials or birthday, others can guess it easily. Easy passwords make it simple for hackers and other intruders to break into a system. Hackers use computer automated tools to assist them with guessing passwords. Thus, you should select a password carefully. Longer passwords provide greater security than shorter ones. Each character added to a password significantly increases the number of possible combinations and the length of time it might take for someone or for a hacker's computer to guess the password (Figure 10-7).

In addition to a user name and password, some systems ask users to enter one of several pieces of personal information. Such items can include a spouse's first name, a birth date, a place of birth, or a mother's maiden name. As with a password, if the user's response does not match the information on file, the system denies access.

Some Web sites use a CAPTCHA to further protect a user's password. A **CAPTCHA**, which stands for Completely Automated Public Turing test to tell Computers and Humans Apart, is a program that verifies user input is not computer generated. A CAPTCHA displays a series of distorted characters and requires the user to enter the characters correctly to continue using the Web site. For visually impaired users, the CAPTCHA text can be read aloud. Because unscrupulous individuals attempt to circumvent or decode CAPTCHAs, developers continually are seeking ways to make them more secure or develop alternative authentication techniques.

Figure 10-6 Many Web sites that maintain personal and confidential data require a user to enter a user name and password.

Password Protection

Number of Characters	Possible Combinations	AVERAGE TIME TO DISCOVER	
		Human	Computer
1	36	3 minutes	.000018 second
2	1,300	2 hours	.00065 second
3	47,000	3 days	.02 second
4	1,700,000	3 months	1 second
5	60,000,000	10 years	30 seconds
10	3,700,000,000,000,000	580 million years	59 years

- Possible characters include the letters A–Z and numbers 0–9
- Human discovery assumes 1 try every 10 seconds
- Computer discovery assumes 1 million tries per second
- Average time assumes the password would be discovered in approximately half the time it would take to try all possible combinations

Figure 10-7 This table shows the effect of increasing the length of a password that consists of letters and numbers. The longer the password, the more effort required to discover it. Long passwords, however, are more difficult for users to remember.

Possessed Objects A **possessed object** is any item that you must carry to gain access to a computer or computer facility. Examples of possessed objects are badges, cards, smart cards, and keys. The card you use in an automated teller machine (ATM) is a possessed object that allows access to your bank account.

Possessed objects often are used in combination with personal identification numbers. A **personal identification number (PIN)** is a numeric password, either assigned by a company or selected by a user. PINs provide an additional level of security. An ATM card typically requires a four-digit PIN. PINs are passwords. Select them carefully and protect them as you do any other password.

Biometric Devices A **biometric device** authenticates a person's identity by translating a personal characteristic, such as a fingerprint, into a digital code that is compared with a digital code stored in the computer verifying a physical or behavioral characteristic. If the digital code in the computer does not match the personal characteristic code, the computer denies access to the individual.

Biometric devices grant access to programs, computers, or rooms using computer analysis of some biometric identifier. Examples of biometric devices and systems include fingerprint readers (Figure 10-8), hand geometry systems, face recognition systems, voice verification systems, signature verification systems, iris recognition systems, and retinal scanners. Many grocery stores, retail stores, and gas stations now use **biometric payment**, where the customer's fingerprint is read by a fingerprint reader that is linked to a specific payment method such as a checking account or credit card.

Figure 10-8
A fingerprint reader verifies this traveler's identity.

? FAQ 10-3

How many people are victims of identity theft each year?

Studies reveal that identity theft is the fastest growing crime in the United States. In fact, identity theft costs banks, victims, and the government millions of dollars each year, with that amount continually increasing. The chart to the right illustrates the reported number of identity theft cases grouped by age.

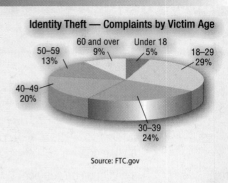

Identity Theft — Complaints by Victim Age

50–59 13%
60 and over 9%
Under 18 5%
18–29 29%
40–49 20%
30–39 24%

Source: FTC.gov

🖥 For more information, visit the Computer Concepts CourseMate Web site at www.cengagebrain.com, navigate to the Chapter 10 FAQ resource for this book, and then click Identity Theft.

Digital Forensics

Digital forensics, also called computer forensics, network forensics, or cyberforensics, is the discovery, collection, and analysis of evidence found on computers and networks. Digital forensics involves the examination of computer media, programs, data and log files on computers, servers, and networks. Many areas use digital forensics, including law enforcement, criminal prosecutors, military intelligence, insurance agencies, and information security departments in the private sector.

A digital forensics examiner must have knowledge of the law, technical experience with many types of hardware and software products, superior communication skills, familiarity with corporate structures and policies, a willingness to learn and update skills, and a knack for problem solving. For a look at the next generation of forensics, read Looking Ahead 10-1.

↗ LOOKING AHEAD 10-1

Brain Waves, Behavior Tracked to Prevent and Solve Crimes

The brain may one day become part of a crime scene investigation. When a person has committed a criminal or fraudulent act, his brain generates unique waves involuntarily when confronted with pictures, sounds, and words related to the crime scene. Computers can capture and analyze this brain fingerprint of distinctive brain waves to determine if a person has stored critical details of a particular felony or misdemeanor situation.

Similarly, behavior detection systems study a person's body language, facial expressions, speech, and emotions to isolate specific patterns that criminals commonly exhibit. The surveillance systems can recognize microexpressions, which are the split-second emotions lasting one-fifteenth of a second, on a person's face.

The U.S. Department of Homeland Security is testing its Future Attribute Screening Technologies (FAST) program, which uses cameras, infrared heat sensors, and lasers to measure pulse and breathing rates. The trial technology is being tested for use at airports and sporting and music events.

🖥 For more information, visit the Computer Concepts CourseMate Web site at www.cengagebrain.com, navigate to the Chapter 10 Looking Ahead resource for this book, and then click Brain Fingerprinting.

✔ QUIZ YOURSELF 10-1

Instructions: Find the true statement below. Then, rewrite the remaining false statements so that they are true.

1. A back door attack is an assault whose purpose is to disrupt computer access to an Internet service such as the Web or e-mail.

2. All networked and online computer users should implement a firewall solution.

3. Computer viruses, worms, Trojan horses, and rootkits are malware that acts with a user's knowledge.

4. Shorter passwords provide greater security than longer ones.

5. Updating an antivirus program's quarantine protects a computer against viruses written since the antivirus program was released.

🖥 **Quiz Yourself Online:** To further check your knowledge of pages 382 through 392, visit the Computer Concepts CourseMate Web site at www.cengagebrain.com, navigate to the Chapter 10 Quiz Yourself resource for this book, and then click Objectives 1 – 2.

Hardware Theft and Vandalism

Hardware theft and vandalism are other types of computer security risks. **Hardware theft** is the act of stealing computer equipment. **Hardware vandalism** is the act of defacing or destroying computer equipment. Hardware vandalism takes many forms, from someone cutting a computer cable to individuals breaking into a business or school computer lab and aimlessly smashing computers.

Companies, schools, and other organizations that house many computers are at risk of hardware theft and vandalism, especially those that have smaller system units that easily can fit in a backpack or briefcase. Mobile users also are susceptible to hardware theft. It is estimated that more than 600,000 notebook computers are stolen each year. The size and weight of these computers, especially netbooks, make them easy to steal.

Safeguards against Hardware Theft and Vandalism

To help reduce the chances of theft, companies and schools use a variety of security measures. Physical access controls, such as locked doors and windows, usually are adequate to protect the equipment. Many businesses, schools, and some homeowners install alarm systems for additional security. School computer labs and other areas with a large number of semifrequent users often attach additional physical security devices such as cables that lock the equipment to a desk (Figure 10-9), cabinet, or floor. Small locking devices also exist that require a key to access a hard disk or optical disc drive.

Some businesses use a **real time location system** (**RTLS**) to track and identify the location of high-risk or high-value items. One implementation of RTLS places RFID tags in items to be tracked.

RTLS
For more information, visit the Computer Concepts CourseMate Web site at www.cengagebrain.com, navigate to the Chapter 10 Web Link resource for this book, and then click RTLS.

Mobile computer users must take special care to protect their equipment. Some users attach a physical device such as a cable to lock a mobile computer temporarily to a stationary object. Other mobile users install a mini-security system in the notebook computer. Some of these security systems shut down the computer and sound an alarm if the computer moves outside a specified distance. Others can be configured to photograph the thieves when they use the computer. Notebook computer security systems and tracking software also can track the location of a stolen notebook computer.

Some notebook computers use passwords, possessed objects, and biometrics as methods of security. When you start these computers, you must enter a password, slide a card in a card reader, or press your finger on a fingerprint reader before the hard disk unlocks. This type of security does not prevent theft, but it renders the computer useless if it is stolen.

Figure 10-9 Using cables to lock computers can help prevent the theft of computer equipment.

Software Theft

Another type of computer security risk is software theft. **Software theft** occurs when someone steals software media, intentionally erases programs, illegally copies a program, or illegally registers and/or activates a program. One form of software theft involves someone physically stealing the media that contain the software or the hardware that contains the media, as described in the previous section. Another form of software theft occurs when software is stolen from software manufacturers. This type of theft, called piracy, is by far the most common form of software theft. Software **piracy** is the unauthorized and illegal duplication of copyrighted software. A related form of software theft involves users illegally obtaining registration numbers and/or activation codes.

Safeguards against Software Theft

To protect software media from being stolen, owners should keep original software boxes and media in a secure location. All computer users should back up their files and disks regularly, in the event of theft.

To protect themselves from software piracy, software manufacturers issue users license agreements. A **license agreement** is the right to use the software. That is, you do not own the software. The license agreement provides specific conditions for use of the software, which a user must accept before using the software (Figure 10-10). These terms usually are displayed when you install the software.

Figure 10-10 A user must accept the terms in the license agreement before using the software.

The most common type of license included with software purchased by individual users is a single-user license agreement, also called an end-user license agreement (EULA). A single-user license agreement typically includes many of the following conditions that specify a user's responsibility upon acceptance of the agreement.

Users are permitted to:
- Install the software on only one computer. (Some license agreements allow users to install the software on one desktop computer and one notebook computer.)
- Make one copy of the software as a backup.
- Give or sell the software to another individual, but only if the software is removed from the user's computer first.

Users are not permitted to:
- Install the software on a network, such as a school computer lab.
- Give copies to friends and colleagues, while continuing to use the software.
- Export the software.
- Rent or lease the software.

Unless otherwise specified by a license agreement, you do not have the right to copy, loan, borrow, rent, or in any way distribute software. Doing so is a violation of copyright law. It also is a federal crime. Despite this, some experts estimate for every authorized copy of software in use, at least one unauthorized copy exists. Read Ethics & Issues 10-1 for a related discussion.

In an attempt to prevent software piracy, Microsoft and other manufacturers have incorporated an activation process into many of its consumer products. During the **product activation**, which is conducted either online or by telephone, users provide the software product's 25-character identification number to receive an installation identification number unique to the computer on which the software is installed.

If you are not completely familiar with your school or employer's policies governing installation of software, check with the information technology department or your school's technology coordinator

Ethics & Issues
For the complete text of the Ethics & Issues boxes found in this chapter, visit the Computer Concepts CourseMate Web site at www.cengagebrain.com and then navigate to the Chapter 10 Ethics & Issues resource for this book.

ETHICS & ISSUES 10-1

Should Online Auctions Be Liable for Pirated Software Sales?

Currently, software companies patrol online auction sites looking for pirated copies of their software that might be for sale. When they find such activity, the software company takes legal action against the seller of the pirated software. With the explosion of online auctions, however, the companies are fighting an uphill battle given the amount of time it takes to discover the sales, find the perpetrators, and then individually bring each perpetrator to justice. Many software companies have joined forces to demand

that auction sites, such as eBay, legally be held liable for pirated software sold on their Web sites, and they have offered more than 20 suggestions as to how auction sites could better police their Web sites for pirated software. Online auction Web sites claim that the law clearly states they are not responsible for such sales, but that the software companies legally are responsible for controlling pirated sales. For its part, eBay claims already to enforce more than 13,000 rules to check for suspicious activity on its Web site, and offers

trademark holders a special program in which they can enroll and have additional rules enforced.

Should online auctions be liable for pirated software sales on their Web sites? Why or why not? Should new or clearer laws be written to force online auctions to check whether software for sale on their Web sites is pirated? Why? Would you purchase software at an online auction being sold at a substantial discount to prices offered elsewhere? Why or why not?

Information Theft

Information theft is yet another type of computer security risk. **Information theft** occurs when someone steals personal or confidential information. An unethical company executive may steal or buy stolen information to learn about a competitor. A corrupt individual may steal credit card numbers to make fraudulent purchases.

Safeguards against Information Theft

Most companies attempt to prevent information theft by implementing the user identification and authentication controls discussed earlier in this chapter. These controls are best suited for protecting information on computers located on an organization's premises. Information transmitted over networks offers a higher degree of risk because unscrupulous users can intercept it during transmission. To protect information on the Internet and networks, companies and individuals use a variety of encryption techniques.

Encryption

Encryption is the process of converting readable data into unreadable characters to prevent unauthorized access. You treat encrypted data just like any other data. That is, you can store it or send it in an e-mail message. To read the data, the recipient must **decrypt**, or decipher, it into a readable form.

In the encryption process, the unencrypted, readable data is called plaintext. The encrypted (scrambled) data is called ciphertext. An **encryption algorithm** is a set of steps that can convert readable plaintext into unreadable ciphertext. Figure 10-11 shows examples of some simple encryption algorithms. Encryption programs typically use more than one encryption algorithm, along with an encryption key. An **encryption key** is a programmed formula that the originator of the data uses to encrypt the plaintext and the recipient of the data uses to decrypt the ciphertext.

Simple Encryption Algorithms

Name	Algorithm	Plaintext	Ciphertext	Explanation
Transposition	Switch the order of characters	SOFTWARE	OSTFAWER	Adjacent characters swapped
Substitution	Replace characters with other characters	INFORMATION	WLDIMXQUWIL	Each letter replaced with another
Expansion	Insert characters between existing characters	USER	UYSYEYRY	Letter Y inserted after each character
Compaction	Remove characters and store elsewhere	ACTIVATION	ACIVTIN	Every third letter removed (T, A, O)

Figure 10-11 This table shows four simple encryption algorithms. Most encryption keys use a combination of algorithms.

Some operating systems and e-mail programs allow you to encrypt the contents of files and messages that are stored on your computer. You also can purchase an encryption program, such as Pretty Good Privacy (PGP).

A **digital signature** is an encrypted code that a person, Web site, or organization attaches to an electronic message to verify the identity of the message sender. Digital signatures often are used to ensure that an impostor is not participating in an Internet transaction. That is, digital signatures help to prevent e-mail forgery. A digital signature also can verify that the content of a message has not changed.

Many Web browsers and Web sites use encryption. A Web site that uses encryption techniques to secure its data is known as a **secure site** (Figure 10-12). Secure sites often use digital certificates. A **digital certificate** is a notice that guarantees a user or a Web site is legitimate. A **certificate authority** (CA)

indicates secure Web page

Figure 10-12 Web addresses of secure sites often begin with https instead of http. Browsers also often display a lock symbol in the window.

Digital Certificates

For more information, visit the Computer Concepts CourseMate Web site at www.cengagebrain.com, navigate to the Chapter 10 Web Link resource for this book, and then click Digital Certificates.

is an authorized person or a company that issues and verifies digital certificates. Users apply for a digital certificate from a CA. The digital certificate typically contains information such as the user's name, the issuing CA's name and signature, and the serial number of the certificate. The information in a digital certificate is encrypted.

System Failure

System failure is yet another type of computer security risk. A **system failure** is the prolonged malfunction of a computer. System failure can cause loss of hardware, software, data, or information. A variety of causes can lead to system failure. These include aging hardware; natural disasters such as fires, floods, or hurricanes; random events such as electrical power problems; and even errors in computer programs.

One of the more common causes of system failure is an electrical power variation. Electrical power variations can cause loss of data and loss of equipment. If the computer equipment is networked, a single power disturbance can damage multiple systems.

Safeguards against System Failure

To protect against electrical power variations, use a surge protector. A **surge protector** uses special electrical components to provide a stable current flow to the computer and other electronic equipment (Figure 10-13). Sometimes resembling a power strip, the computer and other devices plug in the surge protector, which plugs in the power source.

Surge Protectors

For more information, visit the Computer Concepts CourseMate Web site at www.cengagebrain.com, navigate to the Chapter 10 Web Link resource for this book, and then click Surge Protectors.

No surge protectors are 100 percent effective. Typically, the amount of protection offered by a surge protector is proportional to its cost. That is, the more expensive, the more protection the protector offers.

If your computer connects to a network or the Internet, also be sure to have protection for your modem telephone lines, DSL lines, Internet cable lines, and network lines. Many surge protectors include plug-ins for telephone lines and other cables.

For additional electrical protection, some users connect an uninterruptible power supply to the computer. An **uninterruptible power supply** (**UPS**) is a device that contains surge protection circuits and one or more batteries that can provide power during a loss of power (Figure 10-14). A UPS connects between your computer and a power source.

As another measure of protection, some companies use duplicate components or computers as a safeguard against system failure.

Figure 10-13
Circuits inside a surge protector safeguard against electrical power variations.

Figure 10-14 If power fails, an uninterruptible power supply (UPS) uses batteries to provide electricity for a limited amount of time.

Backing Up — The Ultimate Safeguard

To protect against data loss caused by a system failure or hardware/software/information theft, computer users should back up files regularly. A **backup** is a duplicate of a file, program, or disk that can be used if the original is lost, damaged, or destroyed. Thus, to **back up** a file means to make a copy of it. In the case of a system failure or the discovery of corrupted files, you **restore** the files by copying the backed up files to their original location on the computer.

You can use just about any media to store backups. A good choice for a home user might be optical discs or external hard disks. Keep backup copies in a fireproof and heatproof safe or vault, or offsite. Offsite means in a location separate from the computer site. A growing trend is to use cloud storage as an offsite location. Recall that cloud storage is an Internet service that provides storage to computer users. To learn more about how to back up files using an Internet service, complete the Learn How To 1 activity on pages 414 and 415.

Most backup programs for the home user provide for a full backup and a selective backup. A full backup copies all of the files in the computer. With a selective backup, users choose which folders and files to include in a backup.

Some users implement a three-generation backup policy to preserve three copies of important files. The grandparent is the oldest copy of the file. The parent is the second oldest copy of the file. The child is the most recent copy of the file. Others use RAID to duplicate the contents of a disk. Instead of multiple backup copies, some users choose continuous backup, where data is backed up whenever a change is made.

Most operating systems include a backup program. Backup devices, such as external disk drives, also include backup programs. Numerous stand-alone backup utilities exist. Many of these can be downloaded from the Web at no cost.

Wireless Security

Wireless technology has made dramatic changes in the way computer users communicate worldwide. Billions of home and business users have notebook computers, smart phones, and other mobile devices to access the Internet, send e-mail and instant messages, chat online, or share network connections — all without wires. Home users set up wireless home networks. Mobile users access wireless networks in hot spots at airports, hotels, shopping malls, bookstores, restaurants, and coffee shops. Schools have wireless networks so that students can access the school network using their mobile computers and devices as they move from building to building.

Although wireless access provides many conveniences to users, it also poses additional security risks. One study showed that about 80 percent of wireless networks have no security protection. Some perpetrators connect to other's wireless networks to gain free Internet access; others may try to access an organization's confidential data.

To access the network, the individual must be in range of the wireless network. Some intruders intercept and monitor communications as they transmit through the air. Others connect to a network through an unsecured wireless access point (WAP). In one technique, called **war driving**, individuals attempt to detect wireless networks via their notebook computer or mobile device while driving a vehicle through areas they suspect have a wireless network.

In addition to using firewalls, some safeguards that improve the security of wireless networks include reconfiguring the wireless access point and ensuring equipment uses one or more wireless security standards such as Wi-Fi Protected Access and 802.11i.

- A wireless access point (WAP) should be configured so that it does not broadcast a network name. The WAP also can be programmed so that only certain devices can access it.
- **Wi-Fi Protected Access** (WPA) is a security standard that improves on older security standards by authenticating network users and providing more advanced encryption techniques.
- An **802.11i** network, sometimes called WPA2, the most recent network security standard, conforms to the government's security standards and uses more sophisticated encryption techniques than WPA.

By implementing these security measures, you can help to prevent unauthorized access to wireless networks.

✔ QUIZ YOURSELF 10-2

Instructions: Find the true statement below. Then, rewrite the remaining false statements so that they are true.
1. An end-user license agreement (EULA) permits users to give copies to friends and colleagues, while continuing to use the software.
2. Encryption is a process of converting ciphertext into plaintext to prevent unauthorized access.
3. Mobile users are not susceptible to hardware theft.
4. Two wireless security standards are Wi-Fi Protected Access and 802.11i.
5. To protect against data loss caused by a system failure, computer users should restore files regularly.

Quiz Yourself Online: To further check your knowledge of pages 393 through 397, visit the Computer Concepts CourseMate Web site at www.cengagebrain.com, navigate to the Chapter 10 Quiz Yourself resource for this book, and then click Objectives 3 – 6.

Health Concerns of Computer Use

Users are a key component in any information system. Thus, protecting users is just as important as protecting hardware, software, and data.

The widespread use of computers has led to some important user health concerns. The following sections discuss health risks and preventions, along with measures users can take to keep the environment healthy.

Computers and Health Risks

A **repetitive strain injury** (**RSI**) is an injury or disorder of the muscles, nerves, tendons, ligaments, and joints. Computer-related RSIs include tendonitis and carpal tunnel syndrome. RSIs are the largest job-related injury and illness problem in the United States today.

Tendonitis is inflammation of a tendon due to some repeated motion or stress on that tendon. Carpal tunnel syndrome (CTS) is inflammation of the nerve that connects the forearm to the palm of the wrist. Repeated or forceful bending of the wrist can cause CTS or tendonitis of the wrist. Symptoms of tendonitis of the wrist include extreme pain that extends from the forearm to the hand, along with tingling in the fingers. Symptoms of CTS include burning pain when the nerve is compressed, along with numbness and tingling in the thumb and first two fingers.

Long-term computer work can lead to tendonitis or CTS. Factors that cause these disorders include prolonged typing, prolonged mouse usage, or continual shifting between the mouse and the keyboard. If untreated, these disorders can lead to permanent physical damage.

You can take many precautions to prevent these types of injuries. Take frequent breaks during the computer session to exercise your hands and arms (Figure 10-15). To prevent injury due to typing, place a wrist rest between the keyboard and the edge of your desk. To prevent injury while using a mouse, place the mouse at least six inches from the edge of the desk. In this position, your wrist is flat on the desk. Finally, minimize the number of times you switch between the mouse and the keyboard, and avoid using the heel of your hand as a pivot point while typing or using the mouse.

Another type of health-related condition due to computer usage is **computer vision syndrome** (CVS). You may have CVS if you have sore, tired, burning, itching, or dry eyes; blurred or double vision; distance blurred vision after prolonged staring at a display device; headache or sore neck; difficulty shifting focus between a display device and documents; difficulty focusing on the screen image; color fringes or after-images when you look away from the display device; and increased sensitivity to light. Eyestrain associated with CVS is not thought to have serious or long-term consequences. Figure 10-16 outlines some techniques you can follow to ease eyestrain.

People who spend their workday using the computer sometimes complain of lower back pain, muscle fatigue, and emotional fatigue. Lower back pain sometimes is caused from poor posture. Always sit

Hand Exercises

- Spread fingers apart for several seconds while keeping wrists straight.
- Gently push back fingers and then thumb.
- Dangle arms loosely at sides and then shake arms and hands.

Figure 10-15 To reduce the chance of developing tendonitis or carpal tunnel syndrome, take frequent breaks during computer sessions to exercise your hands and arms.

Techniques to Ease Eyestrain

- Every 10 to 15 minutes, take an eye break.
 - Look into the distance and focus on an object for 20 to 30 seconds.
 - Roll your eyes in a complete circle.
 - Close your eyes and rest them for at least one minute.
- Blink your eyes every five seconds.
- Place your display device about an arm's length away from your eyes with the top of the screen at eye level or below.
- Use large fonts.
- If you wear glasses, ask your doctor about computer glasses.
- Adjust the lighting.

Figure 10-16 Following these tips may help reduce eyestrain while working on a computer.

properly in the chair while you work. To alleviate back pain, muscle fatigue, and emotional fatigue, take a 15- to 30-minute break every 2 hours — stand up, walk around, stretch, and relax. Another way to help prevent these injuries is to be sure your workplace is designed ergonomically.

Ergonomics and Workplace Design

Ergonomics is an applied science devoted to incorporating comfort, efficiency, and safety into the design of items in the workplace. Ergonomic studies have shown that using the correct type and configuration of chair, keyboard, display device, and work surface helps users work comfortably and efficiently and helps protect their health. For the computer work space, experts recommend an area of at least two feet by four feet. Figure 10-17 illustrates additional guidelines for setting up the work area.

viewing angle: 20° to center of screen
viewing distance: 18 to 28 inches

arms: elbows at about 90° and arms and hands approximately parallel to floor

adjustable height chair with 4 or 5 legs for stability

keyboard height: 23 to 28 inches depending on height of user

feet flat on floor

Figure 10-17 A well-designed work area should be flexible to allow adjustments to the height and build of different individuals. Good lighting and air quality also are important considerations.

Computer Addiction

Computers can provide entertainment and enjoyment. Some computer users, however, become obsessed with the computer and the Internet. **Computer addiction** occurs when the computer consumes someone's entire social life. Computer addiction is a growing health problem but can be treated through therapy and support groups. Symptoms of a user with computer addiction include the following:

- Craves computer time
- Overjoyed when at the computer
- Neglects family and friends
- Irritable when not at the computer
- Unable to stop computer activity
- Problems at work or school

Ethics and Society

As with any powerful technology, computers can be used for both good and bad intentions. The standards that determine whether an action is good or bad are known as ethics.

Computer ethics are the moral guidelines that govern the use of computers and information systems. Six frequently discussed areas of computer ethics are unauthorized use of computers and networks, software theft (piracy), information accuracy, intellectual property rights, green computing, and information privacy.

Previous sections in this chapter discussed unauthorized use of computers and networks, and software theft (piracy). The following sections discuss issues related to information accuracy, intellectual property rights, green computing, and information privacy. The questionnaire in Figure 10-18 raises issues in each of these areas.

Your Thoughts?

	Ethical	Unethical
1. An organization requires employees to wear badges that track their whereabouts while at work.	☐	☐
2. A supervisor reads an employee's e-mail.	☐	☐
3. An employee uses his computer at work to send e-mail messages to a friend.	☐	☐
4. An employee sends an e-mail message to several coworkers and blind copies his supervisor.	☐	☐
5. An employee forwards an e-mail message to a third party without permission from the sender.	☐	☐
6. An employee uses her computer at work to complete a homework assignment for school.	☐	☐
7. The vice president of your Student Government Association (SGA) downloads a photo from the Web and uses it in a flyer recruiting SGA members.	☐	☐
8. A student copies text from the Web and uses it in a research paper for his English Composition class.	☐	☐
9. An employee sends political campaign material to individuals on her employer's mailing list.	☐	☐
10. As an employee in the registration office, you have access to student grades. You look up grades for your friends, so that they do not have to wait for delivery of grade reports from the postal service.	☐	☐
11. An employee makes a copy of software and installs it on her home computer. No one uses her home computer while she is at work, and she uses her home computer only to finish projects from work.	☐	☐
12. An employee who has been laid off installs a computer virus on his employer's computer.	☐	☐
13. A person designing a Web page finds one on the Web similar to his requirements, copies it, modifies it, and publishes it as his own Web page.	☐	☐
14. A student researches using only the Web to write a report.	☐	☐
15. In a society in which all transactions occur online (a cashless society), the government tracks every transaction you make and automatically deducts taxes from your bank account.	☐	☐
16. Someone copies a well-known novel to the Web and encourages others to read it.	☐	☐
17. A person accesses an organization's network and reports to the organization any vulnerabilities discovered.	☐	☐
18. Your friend uses a neighbor's wireless network to connect to the Internet and check e-mail.	☐	☐
19. A company uses recycled paper to print a 50-page employee benefits manual that is distributed to 425 employees.	☐	☐
20. Your friend donates her old computers and mobile devices to local schools when she purchases newer models.	☐	☐

Figure 10-18 Indicate whether you think the situation described is ethical or unethical. Discuss your answers with your instructor and other students.

Information Accuracy

Information accuracy today is a concern because many users access information maintained by other people or companies, such as on the Internet. Do not assume that because the information is on the Web that it is correct. Users should evaluate the value of a Web page before relying on its content. Be aware that the organization providing access to the information may not be the creator of the information.

In addition to concerns about the accuracy of computer input, some individuals and organizations raise questions about the ethics of using computers to alter output, primarily graphical output such as retouched photos. Using graphics equipment and software, users easily can digitize photos and then add, change, or remove images (Figure 10-19).

One group that completely opposes any manipulation of an image is the National Press Photographer Association. It believes that allowing even the slightest alteration could lead to misrepresentative photos. Others believe that digital photo retouching is acceptable as long as the significant content or meaning of the photo does not change. Digital retouching is an area in which legal precedents so far have not been established.

Figure 10-19 A digitally altered photo shows the movie character Forrest Gump (1994) meeting President John F. Kennedy (who died in 1963).

Intellectual Property Rights

Intellectual property (IP) refers to unique and original works such as ideas, inventions, art, writings, processes, company and product names, and logos. **Intellectual property rights** are the rights to which creators are entitled for their work. Certain issues arise surrounding IP today because many of these works are available digitally.

A **copyright** gives authors and artists exclusive rights to duplicate, publish, and sell their materials. A copyright protects any tangible form of expression.

A common infringement of copyright is piracy. People pirate (illegally copy) software, movies, and music. Many areas are not clear-cut with respect to the law, because copyright law gives the public fair use to copyrighted material. The issues surround the phrase, fair use, which allows use for educational and critical purposes.

This vague definition is subject to widespread interpretation and raises many questions:

- Should individuals be able to download contents of your Web site, modify it, and then put it on the Web again as their own?
- Should a faculty member have the right to print material from the Web and distribute it to all members of the class for teaching purposes only?
- Should someone be able to scan photos or pages from a book, publish them to the Web, and allow others to download them?
- Should students be able to post term papers they have written on the Web, making it tempting for other students to download and submit them as their own work?

These issues with copyright law led to the development of **digital rights management** (DRM), a strategy designed to prevent illegal distribution of movies, music, and other digital content.

Green Computing

Green computing involves reducing the electricity and environmental waste while using a computer. People use, and often waste, resources such as electricity and paper while using a computer.

The United States government developed the **ENERGY STAR program** to help reduce the amount of electricity used by computers and related devices. This program encourages manufacturers to create energy-efficient devices that require little power when they are not in use. Computers and devices that meet the ENERGY STAR guidelines display an ENERGY STAR label.

Digital Rights Management

For more information, visit the Computer Concepts CourseMate Web site at www.cengagebrain.com, navigate to the Chapter 10 Web Link resource for this book, and then click Digital Rights Management.

Green Computing Suggestions

1. **Use computers and devices that comply with the ENERGY STAR program.**
2. **Do not leave the computer running overnight.**
3. **Turn off the monitor, printer, and other devices when not in use.**
4. **Use LCD monitors instead of CRT monitors.**
5. **Use paperless methods to communicate.**
6. **Recycle paper.**
7. **Buy recycled paper.**
8. **Recycle toner cartridges.**
9. **Recycle old computers, printers, and other devices.**
10. **Telecommute (saves gas).**
11. **Use video conferencing and VoIP for meetings.**

Figure 10-20 A list of suggestions to make computing healthy for the environment.

Users should not store obsolete computers and devices in their basement, storage room, attic, warehouse, or any other location. Computers, monitors, and other equipment contain toxic materials and potentially dangerous elements including lead, mercury, and flame retardants. In a landfill, these materials release into the environment. Recycling and refurbishing old equipment are much safer alternatives for the environment.

Experts estimate that more than 700 million personal computers are obsolete. Because of the huge volumes of electronic waste, the U.S. federal government has proposed a bill that would require computer recycling across the country. Many state and local governments have methods in place to make it easy for consumers to recycle this type of equipment.

To reduce the environmental impact of computing further, users simply can alter a few habits. Figure 10-20 lists the ways you can contribute to green computing. To learn more about green computing, complete the Green Computing exercise on the Web Research page in each chapter of this book.

Information Privacy

Information privacy refers to the right of individuals and companies to deny or restrict the collection and use of information about them. In the past, information privacy was easier to maintain because information was kept in separate locations. Each retail store had its own credit files. Each government agency maintained separate records. Doctors had their own patient files.

Today, huge databases store this data online. Much of the data is personal and confidential and should be accessible only to authorized users. Many individuals and organizations, however, question whether this data really is private.

Figure 10-21 lists measures you can take to make your personal data private. The following pages address techniques companies and employers use to collect your personal data. Read Innovative Computing 10-1 to find out how merchants watch shoppers' behaviors.

⚠ INNOVATIVE COMPUTING 10-1

Customers' Behavior, Conversations Monitored

Deciding whether to display peanut butter next to jelly on a supermarket shelf is made easier with consumer-monitoring technology. Leading stores, including Best Buy, Walmart, Walgreens, Office Depot, and Abercrombie & Fitch, have installed video cameras and recorders, heat sensors, and sometimes microphones to track customers' movement throughout the store and their buying patterns.

One system, called Smartlane, counts the number of people, known as "hot blobs," entering and exiting the store and records how quickly clerks are completing transactions at cash registers. It alerts management when many hot blobs are waiting in checkout lanes or have entered the store in a short period of time so that additional clerks can be made available to reduce checkout waiting times.

Another system, BehaviorIQ, collects data on where customers walk throughout the store, when and for how long they stop to browse, and what they take from shelves and racks. Some stores claim information

gleaned from these monitoring systems has increased sales 300 percent.

Privacy experts warn that consumers might object to being recorded and analyzed. The monitoring companies, however, dispel these concerns by explaining that the data actually resembles audio recordings made when calling customer-service hotlines and when being observed for loss prevention purposes.

🔘 For more information, visit the Computer Concepts CourseMate Web site at www.cengagebrain.com, navigate to the Chapter 10 Innovative Computing resource for this book, and then click Shopping Behavior.

How to Safeguard Personal Information

1. Fill in only necessary information on rebate, warranty, and registration forms.	12. Obtain your credit report once a year from each of the three major credit reporting agencies (Equifax, Experian, and TransUnion) and correct any errors.
2. Do not preprint your telephone number or Social Security number on personal checks.	13. Request a free copy of your medical records once a year from the Medical Information Bureau.
3. Have an unlisted or unpublished telephone number.	14. Limit the amount of information you provide to Web sites. Fill in only required information.
4. If Caller ID is available in your area, find out how to block your number from displaying on the receiver's system.	15. Install a cookie manager to filter cookies.
5. Do not write your telephone number on charge or credit receipts.	16. Clear your history file when you are finished browsing.
6. Ask merchants not to write credit card numbers, telephone numbers, Social Security numbers, and driver's license numbers on the back of your personal checks.	17. Set up a free e-mail account. Use this e-mail address for merchant forms.
7. Purchase goods with cash, rather than credit or checks.	18. Turn off file and printer sharing on your Internet connection.
8. Avoid shopping club and buyer cards.	19. Install a personal firewall.
9. If merchants ask personal questions, find out why they want to know before releasing the information.	20. Sign-up for e-mail filtering through your Internet access provider or use an anti-spam program such as Brightmail.
10. Inform merchants that you do not want them to distribute your personal information.	21. Do not reply to spam for any reason.
11. Request, in writing, to be removed from mailing lists.	22. Surf the Web anonymously with a program such as Freedom WebSecure or through an anonymous Web site such as Anonymizer.com.

Figure 10-21 Techniques to keep personal data private.

Electronic Profiles

When you fill out a form such as a magazine subscription, product warranty registration card, or contest entry form, the merchant that receives the form usually enters it into a database. Likewise, every time you click an advertisement on the Web or register software online, your information and preferences enter a database. Merchants then sell the contents of their databases to national marketing firms and Internet advertising firms. By combining this data with information from public sources such as driver's licenses and vehicle registrations, these firms create an electronic profile of individuals.

Critics contend that the information in an electronic profile reveals more about an individual than anyone has a right to know. They also claim that companies should inform people if they plan to provide personal information to others. Many companies today allow people to specify whether they want their personal information distributed.

Cookies

E-commerce and other Web applications often rely on cookies to identify users. A **cookie** is a small text file that a Web server stores on your computer. Cookie files typically contain data about you, such as your user name or viewing preferences.

Many commercial Web sites send a cookie to your browser, and then your computer's hard disk stores the cookie. The next time you visit the Web site, your browser retrieves the cookie from your hard disk and sends the data in the cookie to the Web site.

Web sites use cookies for a variety of purposes:

- Most Web sites that allow for personalization use cookies to track user preferences. On such sites, users may be asked to fill in a form requesting personal information, such as their name, postal code, or site preferences. A news Web site, for example, might allow users to customize their viewing preferences to display certain stock quotes or local weather forecasts. The Web site stores their preferences in a cookie on the users' hard disks.

- Some Web sites use cookies to store users' passwords, so that they do not need to enter it every time they log in to the Web site.
- Online shopping sites generally use a session cookie to keep track of items in a user's shopping cart. This way, users can start an order during one Web session and finish it on another day in another session. Session cookies usually expire after a certain time, such as a week or a month.
- Some Web sites use cookies to track how often users visit a site and the Web pages they visit while at the site.
- Web sites may use cookies to target advertisements. These sites store a user's interests and browsing habits in the cookie.

Cookies

For more information, visit the Computer Concepts CourseMate Web site at www.cengagebrain.com, navigate to the Chapter 10 Web Link resource for this book, and then click Cookies.

You can set a browser to accept cookies automatically, prompt you if you want to accept a cookie, or disable cookie use altogether. Keep in mind if you disable cookie use, you will not be able to use many of the e-commerce Web sites. Figure 10-22 illustrates how Web sites work with cookies.

How Cookies Work

Step 1
When you type the Web address of a Web site in a browser window, the browser program searches your hard disk for a cookie associated with the Web site.

cookies

Step 2
If the browser finds a cookie, it sends information in the cookie file to the Web site.

identification number

cookie information

INTERNET

www.omahasteaks.com

Web server for www.omahasteaks.com

Step 3
If the Web site does not receive cookie information, and is expecting it, the site creates an identification number for you in its database and sends that number to your browser. The browser in turn creates a cookie file based on that number and stores the cookie file on your hard disk. The Web site now can update information in the cookie file whenever you access the site.

Figure 10-22 This figure shows how cookies work.

Spyware and Adware

Spyware is a program placed on a computer without the user's knowledge that secretly collects information about the user. Some vendors or employers use spyware to collect information about program usage or employees. Internet advertising firms often collect information about users' Web browsing habits by hiding spyware in adware. **Adware** is a program that displays an online advertisement in a banner or pop-up window on Web pages, e-mail messages, or other Internet services. To remove spyware and adware, you can obtain a spyware and adware remover that can detect and delete spyware and adware. Some operating systems and Web browsers include spyware removers.

Spam

Spam is an unsolicited e-mail message or newsgroup posting sent to multiple recipients or newsgroups at once. Spam is Internet junk mail (Figure 10-23). The content of spam ranges from selling a product or service, to promoting a business opportunity, to advertising offensive material. One study indicates more than 92 percent of e-mail is spam.

Users can reduce the amount of spam they receive with a number of techniques. Some e-mail programs have built-in settings that allow users to delete spam automatically. Users also can sign up for e-mail filtering from their Internet access provider. **E-mail filtering** is a service that blocks e-mail messages from designated sources. An alternative to e-mail filtering is to purchase an **anti-spam program** that attempts to remove spam before it reaches your inbox. The disadvantage of e-mail filters and anti-spam programs is that sometimes they remove valid e-mail messages. Thus, users should review the contents of the spam messages periodically to ensure they do not contain valid messages.

Phishing

Phishing is a scam in which a perpetrator sends an official looking e-mail message that attempts to obtain your personal and financial information (Figure 10-24). Some phishing e-mail messages ask you to reply with your information; others direct you to a phony Web site, or a pop-up window that looks like a Web site, that collects the information.

If you receive an e-mail that looks legitimate and requests you update credit card numbers, Social Security numbers, bank account numbers, passwords, or other private information, the FTC recommends you visit the Web site directly to determine if the request is valid. Never click a link in an e-mail message; instead retype the Web address in your browser.

A **phishing filter** is a program that warns or blocks you from potentially fraudulent or suspicious Web sites. Some Web browsers include phishing filters.

Pharming is a scam, similar to phishing, where a perpetrator attempts to obtain your personal and financial information, except they do so via spoofing. That is, when you type a Web address in the Web browser, you are redirected to a phony Web site that looks legitimate. The phony Web site requests you enter confidential information.

Clickjacking is yet another similar scam. With **clickjacking**, an object that can be clicked on a Web site, such as a button, image, or link, contains a malicious program. When users click the disguised object, for example, they may be redirected to a phony Web site that requests personal information, or a virus may download to their computer.

Social Engineering

As related to the use of computers, **social engineering** is defined as gaining unauthorized access or obtaining confidential information by taking advantage of the trusting human nature of some victims and the naivety of others. Some social engineers trick their victims into revealing confidential information such as user names and passwords on the telephone, in person, or on the Internet. Techniques they use include pretending to be an administrator or other authoritative figure, feigning an emergency situation, or impersonating an acquaintance. Social engineers also obtain information from users who do not destroy or conceal information properly. These perpetrators sift through company dumpsters, watch or film people dialing telephone numbers or using ATMs, and snoop around computers looking for openly displayed confidential information.

Figure 10-23 An example of spam.

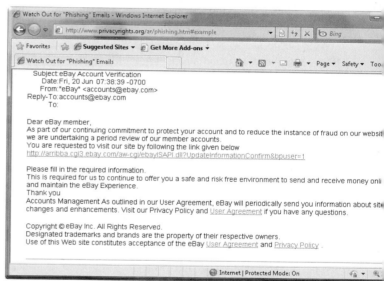

Figure 10-24 An example of a phishing e-mail message.

Privacy Laws

The concern about privacy has led to the enactment of federal and state laws regarding the storage and disclosure of personal data (Figure 10-25).

Common points in some of these laws include the following:

1. Information collected and stored about individuals should be limited to what is necessary to carry out the function of the business or government agency collecting the data.

Date	Law	Purpose
2006	Telephone Records and Privacy Protection Act	Makes it illegal to use fraudulent means to obtain someone's telephone records.
2003	CAN-SPAM Act	Gives law enforcement the right to impose penalties on people using the Internet to distribute spam.
2002	Sarbanes-Oxley Act	Requires corporate officers, auditors, and attorneys of publicly-traded companies follow strict financial reporting guidelines.
2001	Children's Internet Protection Act (CIPA)	Protects minors from inappropriate content when accessing the Internet in schools and libraries.
2001	Provide Appropriate Tools Required to Intercept and Obstruct Terrorism (PATRIOT) Act	Gives law enforcement the right to monitor people's activities, including Web and e-mail habits.
1999	Gramm-Leach-Bliley Act (GLBA) or Financial Modernization Act	Protects consumers from disclosure of their personal financial information and requires institutions to alert customers of information disclosure policies.
1998	Children's Online Privacy Protection Act (COPPA)	Requires Web sites protect personal information of children under 13 years of age.
1998	Digital Millennium Copyright Act (DMCA)	Makes it illegal to circumvent antipiracy schemes in commercial software; outlaws sale of devices that copy software illegally.
1997	No Electronic Theft (NET) Act	Closes a narrow loophole in the law that allowed people to give away copyrighted material (such as software) on the Internet without legal repercussions.
1996	Health Insurance Portability and Accountability Act (HIPAA)	Protects individuals against the wrongful disclosure of their health information.
1996	National Information Infrastructure Protection Act	Penalizes theft of information across state lines, threats against networks, and computer system trespassing.
1994	Computer Abuse Amendments Act	Amends 1984 act to outlaw transmission of harmful computer code such as viruses.
1992	Cable Act	Extends the privacy of the Cable Communications Policy Act of 1984 to include cellular and other wireless services.
1991	Telephone Consumer Protection Act	Restricts activities of telemarketers.
1988	Computer Matching and Privacy Protection Act	Regulates the use of government data to determine the eligibility of individuals for federal benefits.
1988	Video Privacy Protection Act	Forbids retailers from releasing or selling video-rental records without customer consent or a court order.
1986	Electronic Communications Privacy Act (ECPA)	Provides the same right of privacy protection for the postal delivery service and telephone companies to the new forms of electronic communications, such as voice mail, e-mail, and cell phones.
1984	Cable Communications Policy Act	Regulates disclosure of cable television subscriber records.
1984	Computer Fraud and Abuse Act	Outlaws unauthorized access of federal government computers.
1978	Right to Financial Privacy Act	Strictly outlines procedures federal agencies must follow when looking at customer records in banks.
1974	Privacy Act	Forbids federal agencies from allowing information to be used for a reason other than that for which it was collected.
1974	Family Educational Rights and Privacy Act	Gives students and parents access to school records and limits disclosure of records to unauthorized parties.
1970	Fair Credit Reporting Act	Prohibits credit reporting agencies from releasing credit information to unauthorized people and allows consumers to review their own credit records.

 Figure 10-25 Summary of the major U.S. government laws concerning privacy.

2. Once collected, provisions should be made to restrict access to the data to those employees within the organization who need access to it to perform their job duties.

3. Personal information should be released outside the organization collecting the data only when the person has agreed to its disclosure.

4. When information is collected about an individual, the individual should know that the data is being collected and have the opportunity to determine the accuracy of the data.

Employee Monitoring

Employee monitoring involves the use of computers to observe, record, and review an employee's use of a computer, including communications such as e-mail messages, keyboard activity (used to measure productivity), and Web sites visited. Many programs exist that easily allow employers to monitor employees. Further, it is legal for employers to use these programs.

A frequently debated issue is whether an employer has the right to read employee e-mail messages. Actual policies vary widely. Some companies declare that they will review e-mail messages regularly, and others state that e-mail is private. In some states, if an organization does not have a formal e-mail policy, it can read e-mail messages without employee notification. Several lawsuits have been filed against employers because many believe that such internal communications should be private. Read Ethics & Issues 10-2 for a related discussion.

Another controversial issue relates to the use of cameras to monitor employees, customers, and the public. Many people feel that this use of video cameras is a violation of privacy.

ETHICS & ISSUES 10-2

Should Text Messages Sent by Employees Be Private?

When an employee sends or receives an e-mail message using his or her employer's e-mail server, the company most likely retains a backup of the message, which can be used as evidence against the employee if the employee is suspected of engaging in unscrupulous activity. When an employee sends a text message using a company-issued smart phone for such activity, however, the smart phone provider may store a record of the message. If an employer's workplace policy requires an employee to disclose all text message communications with customers, vendors, and competitors, the employee is required legally to divulge those communications. The U.S. Supreme Court ruled that an employer can read workers' text messages if there is reason to believe the texts violate workplace rules. The Court held that employees can purchase their own cell phones if they need to make personal calls or text messages. Employees may believe they have an expectation of privacy and the right of self-expression when they use an employer's cell phone. Employers argue, however, that because they provide the devices and service to the employee, they should have a right to view the content of the messages.

Should text messages sent by employees be private? Why or why not? How can employers create and enforce policies regarding the content of text messages sent on employer-issued smart phones? Should employers demand that smart phone providers offer the option to send all employee text message communications to the company on a monthly basis? Why or why not?

Content Filtering

One of the more controversial issues that surround the Internet is its widespread availability of objectionable material, such as racist literature, violence, and obscene pictures. Some believe that such materials should be banned. Others believe that the materials should be filtered, that is, restricted. **Content filtering** is the process of restricting access to certain material on the Web. Content filtering opponents argue that banning any materials violates constitutional guarantees of free speech and personal rights.

Many businesses use content filtering to limit employees' Web access. These businesses argue that employees are unproductive when visiting inappropriate or objectionable Web sites. Some schools, libraries, and parents use content filtering to restrict access to minors.

Web filtering software is a program that restricts access to specified Web sites. Some also filter sites that use specific words. Others allow you to filter e-mail messages, chat rooms, and programs. Many Internet security programs include a firewall, antivirus program, and filtering capabilities combined (Figure 10-26).

Figure 10-26 Many Internet security programs include content filtering capabilities, where users can block specified Web sites and applications.

✔ QUIZ YOURSELF 10-3

Instructions: Find the true statement below. Then, rewrite the remaining false statements so that they are true.

1. Factors that cause CVS include prolonged typing, prolonged mouse usage, or continual shifting between the mouse and the keyboard.

2. Phishing is the discovery, collection, and analysis of evidence found on computers and networks.

3. Spam is Internet junk mail.

4. You can assume that information on the Web is correct.

Quiz Yourself Online: To further check your knowledge of pages 398 through 407, visit the Computer Concepts CourseMate Web site at www.cengagebrain.com, navigate to the Chapter 10 Quiz Yourself resource for this book, and then click Objectives 7 – 8.

Chapter Summary

This chapter identified some potential computer risks and the safeguards that organizations and individuals can implement to minimize these risks. Wireless security risks and safeguards also were discussed.

The chapter presented computer-related health issues and their preventions. The chapter ended with a discussion about ethical issues surrounding information accuracy, intellectual property rights, green computing, and information privacy.

Computer Usage @ Work

National and Local Security

Since 2001, the federal government, local governments, businesses, and individuals have been implementing aggressive new security measures because of the increase in terrorist activity. A security threat can exist anywhere, and it is nearly impossible for humans alone to protect the country. As a result, computers now assist governments, law enforcement officials, business owners, and other individuals with monitoring and maintaining security.

Advancements in computer vision enable computers to monitor indoor and outdoor areas that might be subject to a high amount of criminal activity. For example, some cities are installing cameras in problematic areas. A computer program analyzes the output from the camera and can determine whether two or more people in close proximity to one another might be engaged in a physical confrontation. If the computer detects suspicious behavior, it automatically notifies local law enforcement.

Computers also use facial recognition to identify individuals who do not belong in a particular area. For example, one theme park in Florida often takes a picture of individuals they escort out of and ban from the park. As visitors walk from their cars to the park, surveillance cameras positioned in strategic locations scan visitors' faces and compare them to the database containing images of those who are banned from the park. If the computer finds a match, it alerts a security officer who then can investigate the situation. Thousands of people visit theme parks each day, and computers make it easier to perform the otherwise impossible task of identifying those who might be trespassing.

The federal government, particularly the Department of Homeland Security, uses a computerized No Fly List to track individuals who are not authorized to travel on commercial flights within the United States. When an individual makes a reservation, a computer compares his or her name to the names on the No Fly List. If the computer finds a match, the individual must prove that he or she is not the person on the list before being allowed to board an aircraft.

Whether you are walking outside, visiting an attraction, or traveling, the chances are good that computers are, in some way, ensuring your safety.

For more information, visit the Computer Concepts CourseMate Web site at www.cengagebrain.com, navigate to the Chapter 10 Computer Usage @ Work resource for this book, and then click National and Local Security.

Companies on the Cutting Edge

MCAFEE Intrusion Prevention Products Developer

The McAfee Initiative to Fight Cybercrime is a global effort to thwart security threats and criminal activity. The world's largest dedicated security technology company has partnered with experts in law enforcement, education, government, and society to investigate, prosecute, and attempt to prevent security breaches.

McAfee products protect more than 60 million consumers, small- and medium-sized businesses, governmental agencies, and large corporations from malware, spam, and unauthorized access. In addition, more than 100 million mobile devices are protected with McAfee software. The corporation takes its name from its founder, John McAfee, who started the company in 1987 from his Santa Clara, California, home.

Recently, McAfee launched a new online backup service with unlimited capacity that allows consumers to back up and encrypt their important files such as documents, photos, music, and e-mail messages.

SYMANTEC Computer Security Solutions Leader

Symantec's programmers analyzed every line of code, rewrote programs, and developed a new security model to create its latest versions of Norton AntiVirus and Norton Internet Security. The results are programs that use less hard disk space, decrease starting and scanning time, and average less than 7 MB of memory. The more than 100 performance improvements offer advanced protection for millions of computer users worldwide.

The California-based company is one of the ten largest software corporations in the world. It was founded in 1982 and has offices in more than 40 countries. Its primary manufacturing facility is located in Dublin, Ireland.

Symantec recently released the latest version of its Norton Internet Security software. A rating service tested the level of protection provided by 10 different security products and gave Norton Internet Security the only perfect score.

For more information, visit the Computer Concepts CourseMate Web site at www.cengagebrain.com and then navigate to the Chapter 10 Companies on the Cutting Edge resource for this book.

Technology Trailblazers

RICHARD STALLMAN Software Freedom Advocate

The relationship between software and freedom is key to Richard Stallman's philosophy. Since his days as a physics student at Harvard University, he has advocated free software and campaigned against software patents and copyright laws. His pioneering work developed the concept of copyleft, which gives each person who has purchased a software product the ability to copy, adapt, and distribute the program as long as the new software also has the same lack of restrictions.

Stallman began the GNU/Linux Project in 1983 as an effort to develop and use the copyleft concept. Linux is an outgrowth of this project, which continues to be a forum for software development, ethical practices, and political campaigning. He also started the Free Software Foundation (FSF) in 1985 to promote writing free software for the GNU Project. The Free Software Directory catalogs more than 5,300 packages that run on the Linux and GNU operating systems.

GENE SPAFFORD Computer Security Expert

The Morris Worm, also called the MBDF virus, is considered the first computer worm distributed on the Internet, and Gene Spafford gained fame for deconstructing and analyzing this 1988 attack. His work led to the conviction of a Cornell University student, Robert Morris. Today, Spafford, who also is known as Spaf, is recognized as one of the world's foremost experts in the computer security, intelligence, cybercrime, and software engineering fields.

For 30 years, he has advised major corporations, including Microsoft, Intel, and Unisys, the U.S. Air Force, the Federal Bureau of Investigation, and two U.S. presidents. He is noted for several firsts in the computer security field. For example, he defined the terms, software forensics and firewall, wrote the first English-language book on the topics of viruses and malware, and founded the world's first multidisciplinary academic security awareness group: the Center for Education and Research in Information Assurance and Security (CERIAS).

For more information, visit the Computer Concepts CourseMate Web site at www.cengagebrain.com and then navigate to the Chapter 10 Technology Trailblazers resource for this book.

Chapter Review

The Chapter Review reinforces the main concepts presented in this chapter.

To listen to an audio version of this Chapter Review, visit the Computer Concepts CourseMate Web site at www.cengagebrain.com and then navigate to the Chapter 10 Chapter Review resource for this book.

1. **What Are Various Internet and Network Attacks, and How Can Users Safeguard against These Attacks?** A computer **virus** is a potentially damaging program that infects a computer and negatively affects the way the computer works. A **worm** is a program that copies itself repeatedly, using up resources and possibly shutting down the computer or network. A **Trojan horse** is a program that hides within or looks like a legitimate program. A **rootkit** is a program that hides in a computer and allows someone from a remote location to take full control of the computer. Users can take precautions to guard against this **malware**. Do not start a computer with removable media in the drives or ports unless the media are uninfected. Never open an e-mail attachment unless it is from a **trusted source**. Disable macros in documents that are not from a trusted source. Install an **antivirus program** and a personal firewall program. Stay informed about any new virus alert or **virus hoax**. To defend against a **botnet**, a **denial of service attack**, improper use of a **back door**, and **spoofing**, users can install a **firewall** and install **intrusion detection software**.

2. **What Are Techniques to Prevent Unauthorized Access and Use?** **Unauthorized access** is the use of a computer or network without permission. **Unauthorized use** is the use of a computer or its data for unapproved or illegal activities. A written acceptable use policy (AUP) outlines the activities for which the computer and network may and may not be used. Other measures include firewalls and intrusion detection software. An **access control** defines who can access a computer, when they can access it, and what actions they can take. An **audit trail** records in a file both successful and unsuccessful access attempts. Access controls include a **user name** and **password**, a **possessed object**, and a **biometric device**.

Visit the Computer Concepts CourseMate Web site at www.cengagebrain.com, navigate to the Chapter 10 Quiz Yourself resource for this book, and then click Objectives 1 – 2.

3. **What Are Safeguards against Hardware Theft and Vandalism?** **Hardware theft** is the act of stealing computer equipment. **Hardware vandalism** is the act of defacing or destroying computer equipment. Physical devices and practical security measures, passwords, possessed objects, and biometrics can reduce the risk of theft or render a computer useless if it is stolen.

4. **How Do Software Manufacturers Protect against Software Theft and Information Theft?** **Software theft** occurs when someone steals software, intentionally erases programs, illegally copies programs, or illegally registers/activates a program. Software **piracy** is the unauthorized and illegal duplication of copyrighted software. To protect themselves from software piracy, manufacturers issue a **license agreement** that provides specific conditions for use of the software. During **product activation**, users provide the product's identification number to receive an installation identification number unique to their computer. Companies attempt to prevent **information theft** through user identification and authentication controls, **encryption**, a **digital signature**, a **digital certificate**, or a **certificate authority**.

5. **What Types of Devices Are Available to Protect Computers from System Failure?** A **system failure** is the prolonged malfunction of a computer. A common cause of system failure is an electrical power variation. A **surge protector** uses special electrical components to provide a stable current flow to the computer. An **uninterruptible power supply** (UPS) contains surge protection circuits and one or more batteries that can provide power during a power loss.

6. **What Risks and Safeguards Are Associated with Wireless Communications?** Wireless access poses additional security risks. Intruders connect to other wireless networks to gain free Internet access or to access an organization's confidential data. Some individuals intercept and monitor communications as they are transmitted. Others connect to a network through an unsecured wireless access point (WAP). Some safeguards include firewalls, reconfiguring the WAP, and ensuring equipment uses a wireless security standard, such as **Wi-Fi Protected Access** and **802.11i**.

Visit the Computer Concepts CourseMate Web site at www.cengagebrain.com, navigate to the Chapter 10 Quiz Yourself resource for this book, and then click Objectives 3 – 6.

7. **How Can Health-Related Disorders and Injuries Due to Computer Use Be Prevented?** A **repetitive strain injury** (RSI) is an injury or disorder of the muscles, nerves, tendons, ligaments, and joints. Computer-related RSIs include tendonitis and carpal tunnel syndrome (CTS). Another health-related condition is eyestrain associated with **computer vision**

syndrome (CVS). To prevent health-related disorders, take frequent breaks, use precautionary exercises and techniques, and incorporate ergonomics when planning the workplace. **Computer addiction** occurs when the computer consumes someone's entire social life.

8. **What Are Issues Surrounding Information Privacy?** **Information privacy** is the right of individuals and companies to restrict the collection and use of information about them. An electronic profile combines data about an individual's Web use with data from public sources. A **cookie** is a file that a Web server stores on a computer to collect data about the user. **Spyware** is a program placed on a computer that secretly collects information about the user. **Adware** is a program that displays an online advertisement in a banner or pop-up window. **Spam** is an unsolicited e-mail message or newsgroup posting sent to many recipients. **Phishing** is a scam in which a perpetrator sends an official looking e-mail message that attempts to obtain a user's personal and financial information. The concern about privacy has led to the enactment of many federal and state laws regarding the storage and disclosure of data. As related to the use of computers, **social engineering** is defined as gaining unauthorized access or obtaining confidential information by taking advantage of the trusting human nature of some victims and the naivety of others. **Employee monitoring** uses computers to observe, record, and review an employee's computer use. **Content filtering** restricts access to certain material on the Web.

Visit the Computer Concepts CourseMate Web site at www.cengagebrain.com, navigate to the Chapter 10 Quiz Yourself resource for this book, and then click Objectives 7 – 8.

Key Terms

You should know each key term. The list below helps focus your study.

To see an example of and a definition for each term, and to access current and additional information from the Web, visit the Computer Concepts CourseMate Web site at www.cengagebrain.com and then navigate to the Chapter 10 Key Terms resource for this book.

802.11i (397)	cyberextortionist (382)	intrusion detection software (389)	spam (404)
access control (389)	cyberterrorist (383)	license agreement (394)	spoofing (388)
adware (404)	decrypt (395)	malware (384)	spyware (404)
anti-spam program (405)	denial of service attack (387)	password (390)	surge protector (396)
antivirus program (386)	digital certificate (395)	payload (384)	system failure (396)
audit trail (389)	digital forensics (392)	personal firewall (389)	Trojan horse (384)
back door (388)	digital rights management (401)	personal identification number (PIN) (391)	trusted source (385)
back up (396)	digital signature (395)	pharming (405)	unauthorized access (389)
backup (396)	DoS attack (387)	phishing (405)	unauthorized use (389)
biometric device (391)	e-mail filtering (405)	phishing filter (405)	uninterruptible power supply (UPS) (396)
biometric payment (391)	employee monitoring (407)	piracy (393)	user name (390)
botnet (387)	encryption (395)	possessed object (391)	virus (384)
CAPTCHA (390)	encryption algorithm (395)	product activation (394)	virus definition (386)
certificate authority (395)	encryption key (395)	quarantine (386)	virus hoax (387)
clickjacking (405)	ENERGY STAR program (401)	real time location system (RTLS) (393)	virus signature (386)
computer addiction (399)	firewall (388)	repetitive strain injury (RSI) (398)	war driving (397)
computer crime (382)	green computing (401)	restore (396)	Web filtering software (407)
computer ethics (399)	hacker (382)	rootkit (384)	Wi-Fi Protected Access (397)
computer security risk (382)	hardware theft (393)	script kiddie (382)	worm (384)
computer vision syndrome (398)	hardware vandalism (393)	secure site (395)	zombie (387)
content filtering (407)	information privacy (402)	social engineering (405)	
cookie (403)	information theft (395)	software theft (393)	
copyright (401)	intellectual property rights (401)		
cracker (382)			
cybercrime (382)			

Checkpoint

The Checkpoint exercises test your knowledge of the chapter concepts. The page number containing the answer appears in parentheses after each exercise.

To complete the Checkpoint exercises interactively, visit the Computer Concepts CourseMate Web site at www.cengagebrain.com and then navigate to the Chapter 10 Checkpoint resource for this book.

Multiple Choice Select the best answer.

1. A _____ is a program that hides in a computer and allows someone from a remote location to take full control of the computer. (384)
 a. worm
 b. rootkit
 c. payload
 d. cookie

2. Malware is a term that can be used to describe _____. (384)
 a. viruses
 b. rootkits
 c. Trojan horses
 d. all of the above

3. The _____ is the destructive event or prank that malware is intended to deliver. (384)
 a. hash
 b. payload
 c. cookie
 d. spam

4. A _____ is an assault whose purpose is to disrupt computer access to an Internet service such as the Web or e-mail. (387)
 a. zombie
 b. denial of service attack
 c. Trojan horse
 d. virus hoax

5. _____ involves the examination of computer media, programs, data and log files on computers, servers, and networks. (392)
 a. Encryption key
 b. E-mail filtering
 c. Digital forensics
 d. Trusted source

6. Physical access controls, such as locked doors and windows, usually are adequate to protect against _____. (393)
 a. software piracy
 b. unauthorized access
 c. hardware theft
 d. all of the above

7. A(n) _____ is a programmed formula that the originator of the data uses to encrypt the plaintext and the recipient of the data uses to decrypt the ciphertext. (395)
 a. botnet
 b. certificate authority
 c. encryption algorithm
 d. encryption key

8. As related to the use of computers, _____ is defined as gaining unauthorized access or obtaining confidential information by taking advantage of the trusting human nature of some victims and the naivety of others. (405)
 a. phishing
 b. a virus hoax
 c. social engineering
 d. pharming

Matching Match the terms with their definitions.

_____ 1. virus (384)
_____ 2. trusted source (385)
_____ 3. spoofing (388)
_____ 4. encryption algorithm (395)
_____ 5. surge protector (396)

a. organization or person you believe will not send a virus infected file knowingly
b. set of steps that can convert readable plaintext into unreadable ciphertext
c. potentially damaging computer program that affects, or infects, a computer negatively by altering the way the computer works without the user's knowledge or permission
d. technique intruders use to make their network or Internet transmission appear legitimate to a victim computer or network
e. uses special electrical components to provide a stable current flow to the computer and other electronic equipment
f. service that blocks e-mail messages from designated sources

Short Answer Write a brief answer to each of the following questions.

1. How do antivirus programs detect and identify a virus? _____ What is a virus hoax? _____
2. Describe the ENERGY STAR program. _____ How should users handle obsolete computers? _____
3. What is information privacy? _____ List five ways to safeguard your personal information. _____
4. What are two methods for avoiding phishing attacks? _____ How does clickjacking work? _____
5. What is content filtering, and who uses it? _____ Why is content filtering controversial? _____

Problem Solving

The Problem Solving exercises extend your knowledge of the chapter concepts by seeking solutions to practical computer problems that you may encounter at home, school, or work. The Collaboration exercise should be completed with a team.

In the real world, practical problems often can be solved in multiple ways. Provide one solution to each of the following problems using available resources, such as articles on the Web or in print, blogs, podcasts, videos, television, user guides, other individuals, and electronics and computer stores. You may need to use multiple resources to obtain an answer. Present your solutions in the form requested by your instructor (brief report, presentation, discussion, or other means).

@ Home

1. **Infected File Detected** A message appears on your computer screen stating that your antivirus program detected an infected file on your computer and is unable to move it to quarantine. What are your next steps?

2. **Product Key in Use** While installing the latest version of Microsoft Office, the installation program prompts you to enter the product key. Once you finish entering the product key, you receive an error message stating that the product key already is in use. What might be causing this?

3. **Questionable Fair Use** A media company's attorney has sent you a letter stating that you are violating their rights by including a short movie clip from one of their movies in one of your videos posted on YouTube. You believe that you are within fair use guidelines by including the movie clip but also feel that you should respond to the attorney's letter. What are your next steps?

4. **Verifying Photo Validity** You are writing a research paper for your history class and have found a photo on the Web that you would like to use. You are cautious about using photos on the Web because of copyright issues and photos that have been altered digitally. How might you verify the validity of a photo on the Web?

@ Work

5. **Password Management** You must remember multiple user names and passwords to access various computer resources within your company. Each time your company introduces a new system, you must remember a new user name and password, some of which you are unable to customize. What steps will you take to manage your passwords?

6. **Problem Reinstalling Software** After recovering from a computer crash, you attempt to reinstall a program that was previously installed. When you insert the installation media, begin the installation, and type the product key, you receive an indication that you are unable to continue installing the software because you have installed it the maximum number of allowable times. What are your next steps?

7. **Missing Security Cable Key** To protect your notebook computer from theft, you use a security cable to secure it to the desk in your cubicle. Your boss assigns you some work to take home and suggests that you take home your notebook computer. You discover, however, that you are unable to locate the key that releases the security cable from the computer. What are your next steps?

8. **Monitored Computer Activities** You receive an e-mail message from the IT department stating that it randomly will monitor employee computers throughout the workday to ensure that they are being used for legitimate purposes. Shortly thereafter, you begin to notice that your computer slows significantly at random times once or twice per week. You suspect the performance decrease is a result of the computer monitoring. How will you address this?

Collaboration

9. **Computers in National and Local Security** National and local security agencies often use computers to protect citizens. For example, computers are used to maintain a list of individuals not cleared to board a commercial aircraft. Form a team of three people to create a list of the various ways computers help to keep us safe. One team member should research how local agencies, such as police departments, use computers to ensure security. Another team member should research ways national security agencies use computers to protect us from threats, and the last team member should research ways that private businesses use computers to guarantee security. Compile these findings into a report and submit it to your instructor.

Learn How To

The Learn How To activities step you through fundamental technology skills when using a computer. The Learn How To exercises enable you to become more proficient with these skills.

Premium Activity: To relate this Learn How To activity to your everyday life, see a visual demonstration of the activity, and complete a short assessment, visit the Computer Concepts CourseMate Web site at www.cengagebrain.com and then navigate to the Chapter 10 Learn How To resource for this book.

Learn How To 1: Back Up Files on an Offsite Internet Server

Note: The service described in this exercise allows 15 days of free access. After that time, you may be billed automatically for service unless you cancel your service in the given time frame.

Backing up files stored on your computer on another disk or computer located in a different geographical location is the ultimate safeguard for data on your computer. A good way to back up data is to use one of the services available on the Web. A leading service is found at IBackup.com. To subscribe to the IBackup service, complete the following steps:

1. Start a Web browser, type the Web address IBackup.com in the Address bar and then press the ENTER key.
2. When the IBackup Web page is displayed, click Signup on the top horizontal toolbar.
3. Enter your e-mail address in the E-mail Address text box and then click the Continue with Registration button to display a form (Figure 10-27).
4. Fill in the form. Select the plan you want in the Select a Storage Plan list. If you want to try the service for a short period of time before subscribing, select 5 GB 15 day Free Trial Plan.
5. To continue to the next pages, you must enter credit card information. If you select the 15-day trial, your credit card will not be charged at this time, and an automatic billing at the end of 15 days will occur. After entering the required information, click the Continue button at the bottom of the page.
6. A message is displayed that confirms that you have signed up with IBackup and also provides a link for you to download the IBackup for Windows program.
7. Click the DOWNLOAD button to download the IBackup for Windows program and then follow the instructions to install the program on your computer.

After establishing an account, you can use it for the time for which you subscribed. Complete the following steps to use the service:

1. Start the IBackup for Windows program.
2. Enter your user name and password and then click the Connect button to open a window containing your files, as well as the contents of your My IBackup folder (Figure 10-28).
3. To upload a file, locate the file in the left pane of the IBackup window and drag it to the right pane. The Backup Progress dialog box will be displayed while the file is uploading. The file will be placed in the My IBackup folder.

Figure 10-27

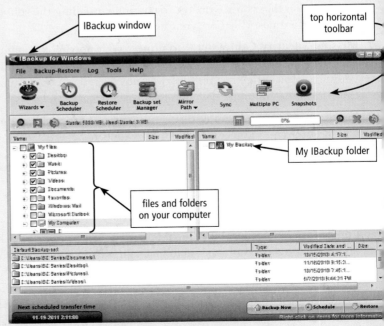

Figure 10-28

4. For further activities you can accomplish in this program for backing up your files, click the buttons on the top horizontal toolbar and experiment.

Exercises

1. Visit the IBackup Web site. Click View Demo and then follow the screen prompts to view all the services offered by IBackup. Which service is most appropriate for your home computer? Which service is most useful for the server that is used in the computer lab at your school? If you had critical data you needed to back up, would you use a service like this? Why or why not? Submit your answers to your instructor.

2. **Optional: Perform this exercise only for your own computer. Do not perform this exercise on a school computer.** Establish an account on IBackup.com. Upload two or more files from your computer. Download the files you uploaded back to your computer. Is this an efficient way to back up your files? Do you think the IBackup service would be useful for businesses? Submit your answers to your instructor.

Learn It Online

The Learn It Online exercises are interactive Web exercises designed to reinforce and expand your understanding of the chapter concepts. The descriptions below briefly summarize each exercise.

To complete the Learn It Online exercises, visit the Computer Concepts CourseMate Web site at www.cengagebrain.com, navigate to the Chapter 10 resources for this book, click the link for the exercise you want to complete, and then read the instructions.

1 At the Movies — Attack of the Mobile Viruses
Watch a movie to learn about the recent wave of viruses plaguing mobile device users and then answer questions about the movie.

2 Student Edition Labs — Protecting Your Privacy Online and Computer Ethics
Enhance your understanding and knowledge about online privacy and computer ethics by completing the Protecting Your Privacy Online and Computer Ethics Labs.

3 Practice Test
Take a multiple choice test that checks your knowledge of the chapter concepts and review the resulting study guide.

4 Who Wants To Be a Computer Genius²?
Play the Shelly Cashman Series version of this popular game by answering questions to find out if you are a computer genius. Panic buttons are available to provide assistance during game play.

5 Crossword Puzzle Challenge
Complete an interactive crossword puzzle to reinforce concepts presented in this chapter.

6 Windows Exercises
Step through the Windows 7 exercises to learn about playing audio compact discs, understanding multimedia properties, dragging and dropping Windows objects, and checking for system updates.

7 Exploring Computer Careers
Read about a career as a digital forensics examiner, search for related employment advertisements, and then answer related questions.

8 Web Apps — Dictionary.com
Learn how to use Dictionary.com to search for a dictionary entry, translate a word to other languages, and search for Web pages containing your search term.

Web Research

The Web Research exercises broaden your understanding of chapter concepts by presenting questions that require you to search the Web for answers.

❶ Search Sleuth

Use one of the search engines listed in Figure 2-8 in Chapter 2 on page 65 or your own favorite search engine to find the answers to the following questions. Copy and paste the Web address from the Web page where you found the answer. Some questions may have more than one answer. If required, submit your answers to your instructor. (1) Which five words are among the most commonly used passwords? (2) What do e-mail messages with the subject lines "Sending You All My Love," "Laughing Kitty," and "You've Received a Postcard from a Family Member" have in common? (3) T'ai chi, yoga, and the Alexander technique might offer some relief to computer users suffering from which injury? (4) For which purpose is a gas discharge arrestor used? (5) How many computers in the business world have antivirus software that has been disabled or never was installed properly?

❷ Green Computing

The more than 1 billion computers in the world each emit an average of 1,000 pounds of carbon dioxide each year. Many home computer users can help reduce their carbon footprint with the help of devices that monitor energy

consumption. Computers are not the only home devices that draw a lot of current; the average home has 27 products that always are turned on, including the television, appliances, and heating and cooling systems. Verdiem's free download, Edison, helps consumers manage their computer power usage. Smart metering devices made by Control4, Colorado vNet, and ZigBee track power usage and give automated tips on how to reduce energy costs. View online Web sites that provide information about reducing home electricity consumption. How do the monitoring devices work? How much do they cost? How do they calculate the money and energy saved per year? Write a report summarizing your findings, and include a table of links to Web sites that provide additional details.

❸ Social Networking

People with unique and special talents often desire to share their passions and pastimes with others. Online social networks provide them an opportunity to share their hobbies and creations. In fact, 69 percent of online social networking members say they have a connection with special-interest Web sites. For example, members of the Sports MatchMaker (sportsmatchmaker.com) community can find people who want to play any sport or participate in any hobby at a specific date and time. ShowOffDemo (showoffdemo.com) members spotlight their talents on a virtual stage, and the Instructables community (instructables.com) collaborates to provide instructions for arts, crafts, food, electronics, and games. Visit these Web sites and view the members' products. Which items are popular? Which are unusual? Which photos provide details on documenting the steps necessary to complete a project? How do members share project ideas and requests for information? Summarize the information you read and viewed.

❹ Blogs

More than 80,000 blogs are created daily according to Umbria Communications, a service that tracks new Internet media. Many information technology (IT) professionals maintain these blogs to tout companies' products and express personal observations. IT bloggers include Robert Scoble on video (scobleizer.com); Jeff Jaffe, Novell's chief technical officer (novell.com/ctoblog); Ed Brill on IBM (edbrill.com); and Tom Kyte on Oracle (tkyte.blogspot.com). Visit these blogs and read some of the posts. What new products are mentioned? What are the bloggers' backgrounds? What controversial topics are discussed? What personal views do the bloggers express?

❺ Ethics in Action

Radio frequency identification (RFID) tags are expected to help merchants in many ways. By placing these tags on such items as prescriptions, computer peripherals, and clothing, retailers hope to reduce theft, track inventory, reduce labor costs, and keep their shelves stocked. Privacy experts, however, claim the tags can store information about consumers' shopping habits and whereabouts. Law enforcement officials, lawyers, marketers, and even thieves could use this detailed electronic data to track people at all times of the day. View Web sites that discuss using RFID tags in stores and the privacy issues that arise from their use. Write a report summarizing your findings, and include a table of links to Web sites that provide additional details.

Enterprise Computing

Objectives

After completing this chapter, you will be able to:

1 Discuss the special information requirements of an enterprise-sized organization

2 Identify information systems and software used in the functional units of an enterprise: accounting and financial systems, human resources information systems, employee relationship management systems, computer-aided design, computer-aided engineering, computer-aided manufacturing, computer-integrated manufacturing, material requirements planning, quality control systems, marketing information systems, sales force automation, distribution systems, and customer interaction management software

3 Describe and list general purpose and integrated information systems used throughout an enterprise: office information systems, transaction processing systems, management information systems, decision support systems, expert systems, enterprise resource

planning systems, customer relationship management systems, and content management systems

4 Describe and list types of technologies used throughout an enterprise: portals, communications, data warehouses, extranets, Web services, service-oriented architecture, workflow, and virtual private networks

5 Describe virtualization, cloud computing, and grid computing

6 Discuss the computer hardware needs and solutions for an enterprise: RAID, network attached storage, storage area networks, enterprise storage systems, and blade servers

7 Determine why computer backup is important and how it is accomplished

8 Discuss the steps in a disaster recovery plan

What Is Enterprise Computing?

The term, enterprise, commonly describes a business or venture of any size. In this chapter, the term enterprise refers to large multinational corporations, universities, hospitals, research laboratories, and government organizations. **Enterprise computing** involves the use of computers in networks that encompass a variety of different operating systems, protocols, and network architectures. A typical enterprise consists of corporate headquarters, remote offices, international offices, and hundreds of individual operating entities, called functional units. The types of functional units within a typical manufacturing enterprise are accounting and finance, human resources, engineering, manufacturing, marketing, sales, distribution, customer service, and information technology. Each type of functional unit has specialized requirements for its information systems. These functional units are summarized later in this

Figure 12-1 Enterprise computing involves the management of large amounts of information over an extensive geographic area and disparate groups of people.

chapter. A **small- and medium-sized business (SMB)** is smaller in size than an enterprise and typically does not have an international presence. Such entities, however, use many of the same technologies and procedures as enterprises, but on a smaller scale.

Enterprises produce and gather enormous volumes of information about customer, supplier, and employee activity. The information flows among an assortment of entities both inside and outside of the enterprise, and users consume the information during a variety of activities (Figure 12-1). Customers, suppliers, and employees interact with the enterprise in a number of ways, and computers track each interaction. Each sale of a product, purchase of a piece of equipment, or paycheck generates activity involving information systems.

Large computers connected by vast networks allow the enterprise to manage and distribute information quickly and efficiently.

Sales Department

Remote Office

IT Department

Marketing Department

Manufacturing

Distribution

Television

Internet

Print

International Office

Types of Enterprises

Figure 12-1 on pages 464 and 465 shows an example of an enterprise whose main focus is in the manufacturing sector. Examples of some types of enterprises are listed below.

- Retail enterprises own a large number of stores in a wide geographical area and use their size to obtain discounts on the goods they purchase; they then seek to sell the goods at a lower price than smaller retailers.
- Manufacturing enterprises create goods on a large scale and then distribute and sell the goods to consumers or other organizations.
- Service enterprises typically do not create or sell goods, but provide services for consumers or other organizations. Examples include companies in the insurance, restaurant, and financial industries.
- Wholesale enterprises seek to purchase and then sell large quantities of goods to other organizations, usually at a lower cost than retail.
- Government enterprises include large city governments, state governments, and the departments and agencies of the federal government.
- Educational enterprises include large universities or school systems that include executives, instructors, and other service personnel and whose reach extends throughout a county, a state, or the entire country.
- Transportation enterprises include airlines, regional transportation authorities, freight and passenger railroads, and trucking firms. The enterprises often include a mix of such types of transportation and have a local or an international reach.

Organizational Structure of an Enterprise

Most traditional enterprises are organized in a hierarchical manner. Figure 12-2 shows an example of an organization chart of a large manufacturing company. Managers at the first two levels at the top of the chart, including the chief executive officer (CEO), mainly concern themselves with strategic decisions and long-term planning.

In Figure 12-2, the chief operating officer (COO) manages the core activities. The supporting activities include financial departments and information technology (IT) departments. The chief

Figure 12-2 Example of an organization chart for a manufacturing enterprise illustrates the hierarchy within an enterprise.

financial officer (CFO) and the chief information officer (CIO) lead these supporting roles. For example, in an airplane manufacturing company, core activity may be the production of wings and cockpits, while a supporting activity may be paying vendors for the parts needed to manufacture those parts.

Each enterprise includes its own special needs and the organizational structure of every enterprise varies. Organizations may include all or some of the managers and departments shown in Figure 12-2.

Levels of Users in the Enterprise

In an enterprise, users of information typically fall into one of four categories: executive management, middle management, operational management, and nonmanagement employees (Figure 12-3). The types of information that users require often depend on their employee level in the organization. Read Ethics & Issues 12-1 for a related discussion.

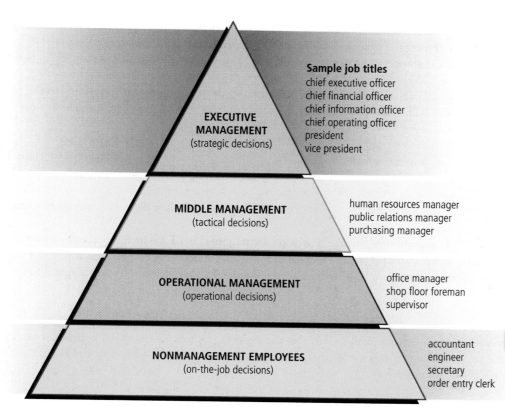

EXECUTIVE MANAGEMENT (strategic decisions)

MIDDLE MANAGEMENT (tactical decisions)

OPERATIONAL MANAGEMENT (operational decisions)

NONMANAGEMENT EMPLOYEES (on-the-job decisions)

Sample job titles
chief executive officer
chief financial officer
chief information officer
chief operating officer
president
vice president

human resources manager
public relations manager
purchasing manager

office manager
shop floor foreman
supervisor

accountant
engineer
secretary
order entry clerk

Figure 12-3 This pyramid illustrates the levels of users, sample job titles of each level of user, and the types of decisions these users make.

Should Employees Use Mobile Computers and Devices at Work?

Employers rarely enforce rules prohibiting employees from listening to their portable media players while at work. Other employers do not mind personal phone calls being made at work on employee owned cell phones. A few even allow employees to plug personally owned computers into the company network. Some people argue that some or all of these practices should and could be allowed in most office workplaces if the employer uses proper security measures. They claim that because it is impossible to prevent all employees from bringing in miniature portable media players that the company should plan for all possibilities. Many companies, however, increasingly place these practices under scrutiny. They argue that the devices make data theft unpreventable because the devices can be attached to workplace computers and backups of critical company data made to the devices. Some employers now go so far as to confiscate employees' mobile computers and devices, or to terminate employment for those caught using mobile devices in the workplace. While most employers' policies disallow such devices, the rules sometimes are difficult, if not impossible, to enforce.

Should employees be allowed to use their own mobile computers and devices at work? Why or why not? Is it possible for employers to keep all personal electronics out of the office? Why? If an employer allows employees' mobile computers and devices in the office, what rules should be in effect, how should they be enforced, and what penalties should be assessed for breaking the rules?

How Managers Use Information

Enterprise information is the information gathered in the ongoing operations of an enterprise-sized organization. Enterprise information begins with the day-to-day transactions that occur within a company, such as sales receipts or time cards. The company gathers and stores the information. Over time, employees collect, combine, and analyze the information. Ultimately, the role of information gathered in this way is to allow managers to make better decisions.

All employees, including managers, in a company need accurate information to perform their jobs effectively. **Managers** are responsible for coordinating and controlling an organization's resources. Resources include people, money, materials, and information. Managers coordinate these resources by performing four activities: planning, organizing, leading, and controlling.

- Planning involves establishing goals and objectives.
- Organizing includes identifying and combining resources, such as money and people, so that the company can reach its goals and objectives.
- Leading, sometimes referred to as directing, involves communicating instructions and authorizing others to perform the necessary work.
- Controlling involves measuring performance and, if necessary, taking corrective action.

Managers use a variety of tools and techniques to focus on information that is important to the decision-making process. These tools and techniques include business intelligence, business process management, and business process automation.

Business Process Management

For more information, visit the Computer Concepts CourseMate Web site at www.cengagebrain.com, navigate to the Chapter 12 Web Link resource for this book, and then click Business Process Management.

Business Intelligence **Business intelligence** (**BI**) includes several types of applications and technologies for acquiring, storing, analyzing, and providing access to information to help users make more sound business decisions. BI applications include decision support systems, query and reporting, online analytical processing (OLAP), statistical analysis, and data mining. These activities are described later in this chapter.

Business Process Management **Business process management** (**BPM**) includes a set of activities that enterprises perform to optimize their business processes, such as accounting and finance, hiring employees, and purchasing goods and services. BPM almost always is aided by specialized software designed to assist in these activities.

Business Process Automation **Business process automation** (**BPA**) provides easy exchange of information among business applications, reduces the need for human intervention in processes, and uses software to automate processes wherever possible. BPA offers greater efficiency and reduces risks by making processes more predictable.

Information Systems in the Enterprise

An **information system** is a set of hardware, software, data, people, and procedures that work together to produce information (Figure 12-4). A procedure is an instruction, or set of instructions, a user follows to accomplish an activity.

Information systems can be used in a variety of ways in an enterprise. Some information systems are used exclusively by only one department, or functional unit, within the enterprise. General purpose information systems include categories of information systems that can be used by almost any department within the enterprise. Integrated information systems are used by multiple departments and facilitate collaboration within the enterprise. The following sections discuss each of these three uses of information systems.

Information Systems within Functional Units

Figure 12-5 lists typical functional units, and their purpose within an enterprise, and examples of programs that each might use. The sections that follow discuss the types of information systems and software used within these units. Small- and medium-sized businesses also may use some or many of these products.

hardware

people

procedures

software

data

Figure 12-4 An information system typically contains five components: hardware, software, data, people, and procedures.

Functional Units within an Enterprise

Functional Unit	Description	Program Name
Accounting and Finance	Responsible for managing the business's money. Accounting department tracks every financial transaction that occurs within the company, including billing customers. Finance department manages the business's money as efficiently as possible.	Microsoft Dynamics GP Oracle Financials NetSuite
Human Resources (HR)	Responsible for recruiting and promoting employees, maintaining employee records, evaluating employees, training employees, and managing employee benefits and compensation.	Lawson Human Capital Management Oracle PeopleSoft Enterprise Human Capital Management Sage ABRA HRMS
Engineering or Product Development	Responsible for developing ideas into a product that can be used by customers. Ensures that the product can be manufactured effectively and designs the methods for manufacturing the product.	AutoCAD MicroStation ProductVision
Manufacturing	Responsible for converting raw materials into physical products.	CA-Plus MISys Manufacturing System Horizon Software MRP Plus Plexus Online
Marketing	Responsible for researching the market in which a business operates to determine the products and features that the business should develop. Determines the demographics to target with sales efforts and informs the target market about the company's products through advertising and education.	Aprimo Enterprise Oracle Marketing MarketingPilot
Sales	Responsible for selling the company's products and services.	OpenBOX Sales Force Automation Prophet SalesForce SFA
Distribution	Responsible for delivery of products to customers.	Activant Prophet 21 IBS's Advanced Inventory and Distribution Software Oracle Transportation Management
Customer Service	Responsible for maintaining a relationship with a customer both before and after a sale has been made.	SAP CRM Siebel CRM On Demand Syntellect Customer Interaction Management Suite
Information Technology (IT)	Responsible for designing, purchasing, implementing, testing, securing, and maintaining information systems for the rest of the organization. Sometimes called the information services (IS) department.	Microsoft System Center Configuration Manager VMware vCloud

Figure 12-5 An enterprise is composed of several functional units, each of which may use different programs to fulfill their needs.

Accounting and Finance Figure 12-6 illustrates the separate functions of accounting and financial systems used by accounting and finance departments. Accounting software manages everyday transactions, such as sales and payments to suppliers. Billing software helps the company reconcile purchases with customer payments. Financial software helps managers budget, forecast, and analyze. These types of software include comprehensive and flexible reporting tools to assist managers in making decisions, provide historical documentation, and meet regulatory requirements.

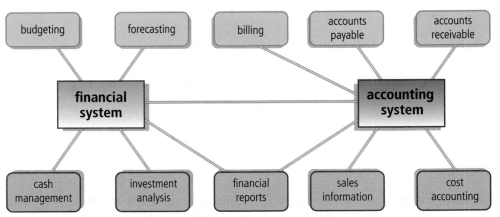

Figure 12-6 Accounting and financial systems perform different tasks but share information and produce financial reports that help management make decisions.

Human Resources A **human resources information system** (**HRIS**) manages one or more human resources functions (Figure 12-7). A human resources information system and its associated software help a company such as Walmart maintain records on its more than 2 million employees. For example, when many retail employees arrive at work, they check in using an electronic clock that automatically allows managers to know who is late, early, or on time. The payroll department then can use this information when determining employee pay.

Figure 12-7 A human resources information system (HRIS) allows human resources personnel to manage employee information, such as benefits, personal information, performance evaluations, training, and vacation time.

An employee relationship management (ERM) system automates and manages much of the communications between employees and the business. For example, an employee may interact with ERM software to gather information about the employee's retirement account. Most ERM software includes a Web interface for the employees and the human resources personnel, allowing both to interact with the system when they are in the office or at home.

Engineering or Product Development Professional workers, such as engineers, require specialized software and systems to perform their tasks. **Computer-aided design (CAD)** uses a computer and special software to aid in product design.

 Computer-aided engineering (CAE) uses computers to test product designs. Using CAE, engineers can test the design of a car or bridge before it is built. These sophisticated programs simulate the effects of wind, temperature, weight, and stress on product shapes and materials. Engineers sometimes use 3-D visualization, which allows them to interact with a product without the need to build a prototype.

Manufacturing Manufacturing information systems and software not only assist in the actual assembly process, but also assist in scheduling and managing the inventory of parts and products. **Computer-aided manufacturing (CAM)** is the use of computers to control production equipment. CAM production equipment includes software-controlled drilling, lathe, welding, and milling machines.

 Computer-integrated manufacturing (CIM) uses computers to integrate the many different operations of the manufacturing process, using technologies such as CAD, CAE, and CAM (Figure 12-8).

 Material Requirements Planning (MRP) is an approach to information management in a manufacturing environment that uses software to help monitor and control processes related to production. MRP focuses on issues related to inventory of parts and forecasting future demand so that materials needed for manufacturing can be on hand when they are needed.

ERM

For more information, visit the Computer Concepts CourseMate Web site at www.cengagebrain.com, navigate to the Chapter 12 Web Link resource for this book, and then click ERM.

Figure 12-8 Computer-integrated manufacturing (CIM) speeds the manufacturing process and reduces product defects.

Quality Control A quality control system helps an organization maintain or improve the quality of its products or services. A quality control system usually includes quality control software. Quality control software typically requires a great deal of continuous data gathering from the organization's ongoing processes. Using statistical analysis, the software can find and predict product defects and problems with the company's processes. While quality control systems often are costly and disruptive to the organization, the organization typically saves more money by producing a higher quality product or service.

Marketing A **marketing information system** serves as a central repository for the tasks of the marketing functional unit. One type of marketing information system is a market research system, which stores and analyzes data gathered from demographics and surveys. Market research software assists in target marketing by allowing marketing personnel to query databases based on criteria such as income, gender, previous purchases, and favorite recreational activities. For example, many companies use market research systems to analyze Web site visitors' use of the company's Web site, such as tracking the users that visit specific Web pages on a site and how long the user views the Web page.

Sales **Sales force automation** (**SFA**) software equips traveling salespeople with the electronic tools they need to be more productive. Sales force automation software helps salespeople manage customer contacts, schedule customer meetings, log customer interactions, manage product information, and take orders from customers.

Sales force automation software (Figure 12-9) often runs on notebook computers or other mobile devices. The notebook computer or other mobile device may connect wirelessly to the central office, allowing the salesperson to access up-to-date corporate information in real time no matter where he or she is located.

Some sales force automation programs allow the salesperson to upload information to the central office at the end of the day or end of the week. The programs also allow salespeople to download updated product and pricing information.

Figure 12-9
Sales force automation (SFA) software allows the sales force to manage customer and prospective customer relationships more effectively.

Distribution **Distribution systems** provide forecasting for inventory control, manage and track shipping of products, and provide information and analysis on inventory in warehouses. Some distribution systems rely on GPS and other navigation technologies to track shipping in real time. Many companies now employ RFID to track inventory and shipping. Because of the complexity of the tasks of inventory management and shipping, distribution systems often integrate with quality control systems.

Customer Service **Customer interaction management** (**CIM**) software manages the day-to-day interactions with customers, such as telephone calls, e-mail interactions, Web interactions, and instant messaging sessions. These interactions are logged so that a historical record of interactions with the customer can be viewed or analyzed at any time. A customer interaction management program routes support queries to the most appropriate support person depending on the customer's situation. For example, a call from a pilot with a problem regarding an airplane during a flight

requires a different level of service than an airline technician who needs to fix a simple problem with an airplane on the ground. Customer interaction management software also assists support personnel in providing the best solutions for customers.

? | FAQ 12-1

When should I supply personal information to a company?

Companies gather personal information about consumers for a variety of reasons. Companies can gather information when you make a purchase, complete a survey, or enter a sweepstakes. Unless you are sure you want the company to communicate with you in some way, few reasons exist to supply personal information to a company. Ask the company why it needs the information and use your judgment. Most companies can supply you with a privacy policy upon request.

For more information, visit the Computer Concepts CourseMate Web site at www.cengagebrain.com, navigate to the Chapter 12 FAQ resource for this book, and then click Sharing Personal Information.

Information Technology The information technology (IT) department makes technology decisions for the enterprise, such as a decision whether to build or buy new customer interaction management information systems or when a computer or information system has outlived its useful life. Many organizations elevate the importance of information technology by including a **chief information officer** (**CIO**) executive position that reports to the CEO.

IT Departments
For more information, visit the Computer Concepts CourseMate Web site at www.cengagebrain.com, navigate to the Chapter 12 Web Link resource for this book, and then click IT Departments.

General Purpose Information Systems

Some information systems in an enterprise cross the boundaries of functional units. These general purpose, or enterprise-wide, systems become necessary in an enterprise for two reasons. First, functional units within an enterprise have a significant need to share data among the units. Second, enterprise-wide systems can collect and combine data more quickly and provide executive management access to a more up-to-date and accurate view of what is happening in the organization. Advances in computing speed, storage capacity, security, and networking have made enterprise-wide systems more attractive to organizations in recent years.

General purpose information systems generally fall into one of five categories: office information systems, transaction processing systems, management information systems, decision support systems, and expert systems. The following sections present each type of these general purpose information systems.

Office Information Systems An **office information system** (**OIS**) is an information system that enables employees to perform tasks using computers and other electronic devices, instead of manually. An office information system increases employee productivity and assists with communications among employees. Some people describe an office information system as office automation.

An office information system uses many common software products to support its activities. Typical software in an office information system includes word processing, spreadsheet, database, presentation graphics, e-mail, Web browser, Web page authoring, personal information management, and groupware. To send text, graphics, audio, and video to others, an office information system uses communications technology such as voice mail, fax, and video conferencing.

Transaction Processing Systems A **transaction processing system** (**TPS**) is an information system that captures and processes data from day-to-day business activities.

Transaction processing systems were among the first computerized systems that processed business data. Many people initially referred to the functions of a transaction processing system as data processing. The first transaction processing systems computerized an existing manual system. The intent of these transaction processing systems was to process transactions faster, reduce clerical costs, and improve customer service.

When you make a purchase with a credit card at a store, you are interacting with a transaction processing system. A transaction is an individual business activity. Examples of transactions are deposits, payments, orders, and reservations. Transactions take place in real time, meaning that as

soon as you make a purchase with a credit card, you can visit your credit card company's Web site and view the transaction. In an organization, clerical staff typically uses computers and special software to perform activities associated with a transaction processing system.

Early TPSs mostly used batch processing. With batch processing, the computer collects data over time and processes all transactions later, as a group. As computers became more powerful, system developers created online transaction processing information systems. With online transaction processing (OLTP), the computer processes each transaction as it is entered. Today, most transaction processing systems use OLTP. Figure 12-10 shows an example of the difference between batch processing and OLTP.

For example, when you book a flight using an airline's Web site, the airline probably uses OLTP. You use the airline's Web site to schedule your desired flights. The Web site immediately displays your itinerary and sends you a copy of your itinerary.

Figure 12-10 With batch processing, all airline reservations are processed together at the end of the day. With OLTP, reservations are processed immediately.

Management Information Systems A **management information system** (**MIS**) is an information system that generates accurate, timely, and organized information, so that managers and other users can make decisions, solve problems, supervise activities, and track progress.

Management information systems often are integrated with transaction processing systems. To process a sales order, the transaction processing system records the sale, updates the customer's account balance, and reduces the inventory count. Using this information, the related management information system produces reports that recap daily sales activities, summarize weekly and monthly sales activities, list customers with past due account balances, chart slow- or fast-selling products, and highlight inventory items that need reordering.

A management information system creates three basic types of reports: detailed, summary, and exception (Figure 12-11). A detailed report usually lists just transactions. For example, a Detailed Flight Report lists the number of passengers booked for a given flight. A summary report consolidates data usually with totals, tables, or graphs, so that managers can review it quickly and easily.

An exception report identifies data outside of a normal condition. These out-of-the-ordinary conditions, called the exception criteria, define the normal activity or status range. For example, a Premier Club Booking Exception Report notifies the airline marketing department that some flights have not met goals for booking Premier Club members.

Exception reports save managers time. Instead of searching through a detailed report, managers simply review the exception report. These reports help managers focus on situations that require immediate decisions or actions. Most information systems support all three types of reports shown in Figure 12-11

Figure 12-11a (detailed report)

Detailed Flight Report for March 30			
Flight #	Origin/ Destination	Class – Number of Passengers	Premier Club Members
1048	ORD – RSW	A – 5 B – 14 C – 89	A – 1 B – 12 C – 20
543	ORD – BMI	A – 2 B – 7 C – 15	A – 2 B – 5 C – 5
715	ORD – LAX	A – 12 B – 25 C – 123	A – 8 B – 15 C – 39
701	ORD – JFK	A – 9 B – 10 C – 7	A – 7 B – 0 C – 3

Figure 12-11 Three basic types of information generated in an MIS are detailed, summary, and exception.

Figure 12-11b (summary report)

Summary Flight Report for March 30			
Flight #	Origin/ Destination	Passengers	Premier Club Members
1048	ORD – RSW	108	33
543	ORD – BMI	24	12
715	ORD – LAX	160	62
701	ORD – JFK	26	10

Figure 12-11c (exception report)

Exception Flight Report for March 30				
Flight #	Class	Origin/ Destination	Premier Club Members	Premier Club Member Goal
1048	A	ORD – RSW	1	4
701	C	ORD – JFK	3	5

Decision Support Systems A **decision support system (DSS)** helps users analyze information and make decisions. Often, a transaction processing system or management information system does not generate the type of report a manager needs to make a decision.

Programs that analyze data, such as those in a decision support system, sometimes are called online analytical processing (OLAP) programs. A decision support system uses data from internal and external sources. Internal sources of data might include sales orders, Material Requirements Planning results, inventory records, or financial data from accounting and financial analyses. Data from external sources could include interest rates, population trends, costs of new housing construction, or raw material pricing.

Some decision support systems include their own query languages, statistical analyses, spreadsheets, and graphics that help users retrieve data and analyze the results. Some also allow managers to create a model of the factors affecting a decision. A product manager might need to decide on a price for a new product. A simple model for finding the best price would include factors for the expected sales volume at various price levels. The model allows the user to ask what-if questions and view the expected results.

A special type of decision support system, called an executive information system (EIS), supports the strategic information needs of executive management. An EIS presents information as charts and tables that show trends, ratios, and statistics that aid in the decision making process (Figure 12-12).

Figure 12-12 An executive information system (EIS) gathers and presents information to senior management in the form of graphics and reports used to assist in decision making.

Expert Systems An **expert system** is an information system that captures and stores the knowledge of human experts and then imitates human reasoning and decision making. Figure 12-13 shows how one expert system assists with diagnosing a computer problem in Windows 7.

Expert systems consist of two main components: a knowledge base and inference rules. A knowledge base is the combined subject knowledge and experiences of the human experts. The inference rules are a set of logical judgments that are applied to the knowledge base each time a user describes a situation to the expert system.

Expert systems are one aspect of an exciting branch of computer science called artificial intelligence. **Artificial intelligence** (**AI**) is the application of human intelligence to computers. Artificial intelligence technology senses a person's actions and, based on logical assumptions and prior experience, takes the appropriate action to complete the task. Artificial intelligence has a variety of capabilities, including speech recognition, logical reasoning, and creative responses. New research in the field of artificial intelligence tries to mimic the way that human memory works in order to expedite searches for information.

A Sample Expert System in Windows 7 Help and Support

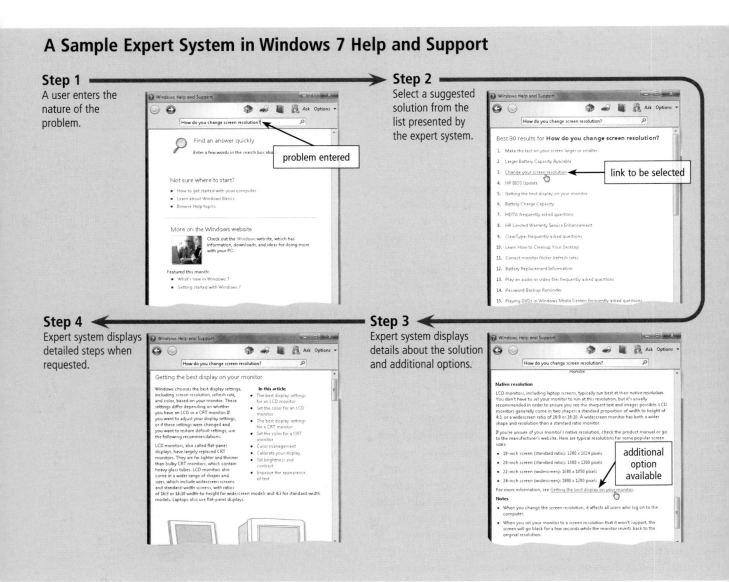

Step 1
A user enters the nature of the problem.

problem entered

Step 2
Select a suggested solution from the list presented by the expert system.

link to be selected

Step 4
Expert system displays detailed steps when requested.

Step 3
Expert system displays details about the solution and additional options.

additional option available

Figure 12-13 This figure shows a sample expert system in Windows 7 Help and Support.

Enterprises employ expert systems in a variety of roles, such as answering customer questions, training new employees, and analyzing data.

Integrated Information Systems

It often is difficult to classify an information system as belonging to only one of the five general types of information systems. Much of today's application software supports transaction processing and creates management information system reports. Other applications provide transaction processing, management information, and decision support.

Enterprise Resource Planning **Enterprise resource planning** (**ERP**) provides centralized, integrated software applications to help manage and coordinate the ongoing activities of the enterprise, including manufacturing and distribution, accounting, finance, sales, product planning, and human resources. Figure 12-14 shows how ERP fits into the operations of an enterprise.

The ERP system installed at each organization must be customized to match the business requirements of the enterprise. At a large company, an ERP system may take four to six years to implement and cost hundreds of millions of dollars. The organization hopes to regain the investment through the advantages offered by ERP.

Figure 12-14 Enterprise resource planning (ERP) encompasses all of the major activities throughout a business.

ERP

For more information, visit the Computer Concepts CourseMate Web site at www.cengagebrain.com, navigate to the Chapter 12 Web Link resource for this book, and then click ERP.

Advantages of enterprise resource planning include complete integration of information systems across departments, better project management, and improved customer service. Enterprise resource planning also helps to manage better the global nature of many enterprises. The reliance on one information system, rather than up to several hundred systems, allows the IT department to focus on one type of technology and simplifies relationships with information technology vendors.

Customer Relationship Management A **customer relationship management (CRM)** system manages information about customers, interactions with customers, past purchases, and interests. Customer relationship management mainly is used across sales, marketing, and customer service departments. Customer relationship management software tracks leads and inquiries from customers, stores a history of all correspondence and sales to a customer, and allows for tracking of outstanding issues with customers.

Content Management Systems A **content management system (CMS)** is an information system that is a combination of databases, software, and procedures that organizes and allows access to various forms of documents and other files, including images and multimedia content. The content management system also provides security controls for the content, such as who is allowed to add, view, and modify content and on which content the user is allowed to perform those operations (Figure 12-15). Publishing entities, such as news services, use content management systems to keep Web sites and RSS feeds up-to-date.

Figure 12-15 A content management system (CMS) helps a company classify and manage volumes of documents and media for future retrieval and use.

Instructions: Find the true statement below. Then, rewrite the remaining false statements so that they are true.

1. The main task of executive managers is to make tactical decisions.
2. An information system is a set of hardware, software, and people that work together to produce information.
3. A human resources information system serves as a central repository for the tasks of the marketing functional unit.
4. Customer interaction management software manages the day-to-day interactions with customers.
5. Decision support systems capture and store the knowledge of human experts and then imitate human reasoning and decision making.
6. Enterprise resource planning is a combination of databases, software, and procedures that organizes and allows access to various forms of documents and files.

Quiz Yourself Online: To further check your knowledge of pages 464 through 478, visit the Computer Concepts CourseMate Web site at www.cengagebrain.com, navigate to the Chapter 12 Quiz Yourself resource for this book, and then click Objectives 1 – 3.

Enterprise-Wide Technologies and Methodologies

Data Centers
For more information, visit the Computer Concepts CourseMate Web site at www.cengagebrain.com, navigate to the Chapter 12 Web Link resource for this book, and then click Data Centers.

Several technologies adopted by enterprises allow them the flexibility and the ability to move swiftly in a business environment. Some of the common technologies used in enterprises include portals, electronic data interchange, data warehouses, extranets, Web services, workflow, and virtual private networks. Most of the hardware and software that contains these technologies is located in a **data center**, which is a centralized location for managing and housing those items. Read Innovative Computing 12-1 to find out about unique data center solutions. The following sections discuss each of these technologies.

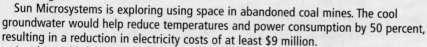

! **INNOVATIVE COMPUTING 12-1**

Unique Data Center Storage Solutions

As data centers' sizes expand, companies are searching for groundbreaking storage solutions that do not necessarily break ground. Google, for example, is considering sea-based centers on barges docked up to seven miles offshore. Energy generated from the waves' motions could help cool and power the supercomputers running the company's search engines.

Sun Microsystems is exploring using space in abandoned coal mines. The cool groundwater would help reduce temperatures and power consumption by 50 percent, resulting in a reduction in electricity costs of at least $9 million.

Another unlikely data center location, Siberia's frozen tundra, looks promising for Microsoft's expansion plans. Currently the company is building centers adjacent to hydroelectric plants, where recycled water will cool the tens of thousands of servers. This water does not need to be drinkable, so no energy is needed to purify it at waste water treatment sites. In another energy-saving measure, Microsoft is using cool outside air instead of air conditioning systems to reduce the computers' operating temperatures.

For more information, visit the Computer Concepts CourseMate Web site at www.cengagebrain.com, navigate to the Chapter 12 Innovative Computing resource for this book, and then click Data Centers.

Portals

A **portal** is a collection of links, content, and services presented on a Web page and designed to guide users to information they likely are to find interesting for their particular job function. A portal often includes searching capabilities or a link to a search engine, such as Google. Organizations often deploy **enterprise search** technology that allows users to perform searches across many enterprise-wide information systems and databases. Users typically can customize the portal Web site to meet their needs.

Information from external sources included on a portal Web page can include weather, news, reference tools, and instant messaging (Figure 12-16).

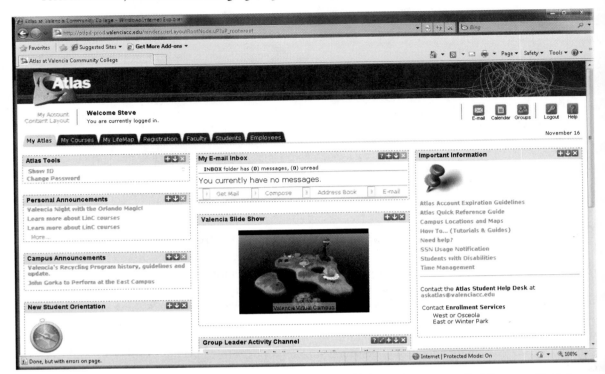

Figure 12-16 Portals allow users quick access to a multitude of information sources that they access on a regular basis.

Communications

The IT department, headed by the CIO, builds and maintains the electronic communications infrastructure of the enterprise. The communications infrastructure consists of hardware, software, and procedures. Examples of hardware include wired network connections, wireless network devices, routers, firewalls, servers, and a variety of long distance communications connections. Software can include e-mail, instant messaging, VoIP, and software applications to manage servers and end users' computers remotely. Procedures include the methods for using and managing the hardware and software. To learn about installing VoIP software on your computer, complete the Learn How To 1 activity on pages 498 and 499.

In addition to the communications software accessed by end users in the enterprise, the IT department manages the software on servers to support the end users' programs. For example, the IT department manages e-mail servers that are accessed by the end users' e-mail programs.

For e-commerce, specialized software often is used to communicate with other computers. **EDI (electronic data interchange)** is a set of standards that controls the transfer of business data and information among computers both within and among enterprises. Today, businesses use these standards to communicate with industry partners over the Internet and telephone lines.

Data Warehouses

A **data warehouse** is a huge database that stores and manages the data required to analyze historical and current transactions. Software applications such as ERP programs store and access data in a data warehouse. A data warehouse may be stored in a cloud computing environment. Cloud computing is discussed later in this chapter.

Most data warehouses include one or more databases and one or more information systems storing data in the data warehouse. The data in the databases consists of transaction data required for

decision making. This data may come from internal or external sources (Figure 12-17). Some data warehouses use Web farming for their external data. Web farming is the process of collecting data from the Internet as a source for the data warehouse.

Another growing external source of information is a click stream. A click stream is a collection of every action that users make as they move through a Web site. By analyzing visitors' click streams, companies identify consumer preferences and determine which Web pages are most attractive to visitors.

Figure 12-17 A data warehouse can receive data from a variety of sources, including company transactions, the Internet, and Web site visitor click streams.

Extranets

An **extranet** is the portion of a company's network that allows customers or suppliers of a company to access parts of an enterprise's intranet. An extranet provides a secure, physical connection to the company's network. Customers may use the extranet to place and monitor orders electronically or to make payments. Suppliers may check inventory levels of the parts they supply to the company and receive orders and payments from the company. Extranets improve efficiency by replacing the postal service, faxes, or telephone calls as the communications medium of choice.

Web Services

Web services include a relatively new set of software technologies that allows businesses to create products and B2B (business-to-business) interactions over the Internet. Web services do not include traditional user interfaces, such as a Web page. Rather, users build their own interfaces to the Web services when necessary. Two popular platforms for building and running Web services are the Sun Microsystems Java EE platform and the Microsoft .NET Framework.

For example, an airline company may provide up-to-the-minute flight status information as a Web service (Figure 12-18). Travel Web sites, such as Expedia or Orbitz, can query the Web service and then display the information on their own Web pages for their customers. The travel Web site may ask for the status of a particular flight and receive back a scheduled departure or arrival time from the Web service. How the travel Web site then uses that information is of no concern to the Web service. The travel Web site may display the information to a customer who requested the information, or it may send an e-mail notification with the information to the customer. Typically, the customer or consumer of the Web service — the travel Web site in this example — must write a program to use the Web service. Many enterprises now employ a service-oriented architecture because the company requires more communication between diverse information systems. In a service-oriented architecture (SOA), information systems provide services to other information systems in a well-defined manner over a network. One benefit to using an SOA is that services from multiple information systems can be combined to create new services or programs.

Web Services

For more information, the Computer Concepts CourseMate Web site at www.cengagebrain.com, navigate to the Chapter 12 Web Link resource for this book, and then click Web Services.

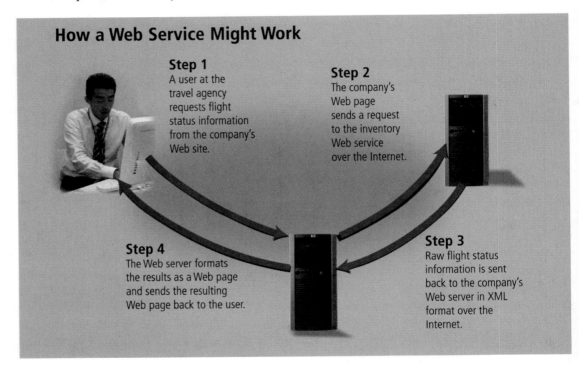

How a Web Service Might Work

Step 1
A user at the travel agency requests flight status information from the company's Web site.

Step 2
The company's Web page sends a request to the inventory Web service over the Internet.

Step 4
The Web server formats the results as a Web page and sends the resulting Web page back to the user.

Step 3
Raw flight status information is sent back to the company's Web server in XML format over the Internet.

Figure 12-18
This figure shows how a Web service might work.

Workflow

A **workflow** is a defined process that identifies the specific set of steps involved in completing a particular project or business process. A workflow may be a written set of rules or a set of rules that exists in an information system.

A **workflow application** is a program that assists in the management and tracking of all the activities in a business process from start to finish. Enterprises use workflow applications to assist in defining complex workflows.

Virtual Private Network

Many companies today allow access to their company networks through a virtual private network. When a mobile user, remote office, vendor, or customer connects to a company's network using the Internet, a **virtual private network** (**VPN**) provides them with a secure connection to the company network server, as if they had a private line. VPNs help to ensure that transmitted data is safe from being intercepted by unauthorized people (Figure 12-19). VPNs securely extend the company's internal network beyond the physical boundaries of the company. The secure connection created over the Internet between the user's computer and the company's network is called a VPN tunnel. Many companies allow external access to their internal networks only via a VPN connection.

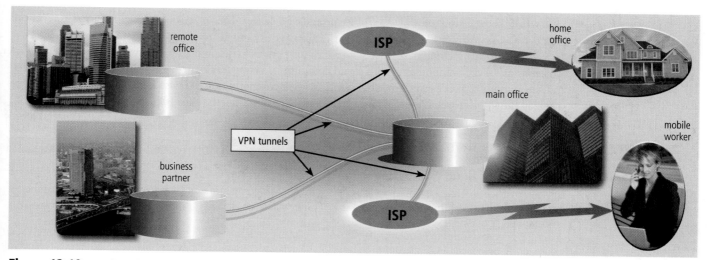

Figure 12-19 A virtual private network (VPN) allows a company to extend its internal network securely.

Virtualization and Cloud Computing

As the cost of hardware and networking services dramatically decreases, the cost of skilled specialists to maintain complex information systems increases. These opposing trends have led to an increase in the use of virtualization and cloud computing. These technologies provide for centralized and/or outsourced management of information system infrastructure, such as servers, security, and networking. The following sections describe virtualization, cloud computing, and grid computing.

Virtualization

Due to the often dynamic nature of enterprise computing needs, IT administrators often use virtualization to adapt quickly to the change. Virtualization is the practice of sharing or pooling computing resources, such as servers and storage devices. Server virtualization provides the capability to divide a physical server logically into many virtual servers. From the end user's point of view, a virtual server behaves just like a physical server. The advantages of server virtualization are that a virtual server can be created and configured quickly, does not require a new physical server, and is easier to manage.

Storage virtualization provides the capability to create a single logical storage device from many physical storage devices. For example, hard disks from many different servers located in geographically disparate areas can be combined to appear as a single hard disk to the users of the storage. The advantages of storage virtualization are that the storage can be configured quickly, may not require the purchase of additional storage devices because the necessary capacity already may exist, and is easier to manage than traditional storage.

Cloud and Grid Computing

As demand for computing resources increases, companies often find that using outside computing resources is more economical than building new computing capacity internally. Cloud and grid computing are two new technologies that provide flexible and massive online computing power. **Cloud computing** is an Internet service that provides computing needs to computer users. When the company uses the computing resources, they pay a fee based on the amount of computing time and other resources that they consume. Cloud computing allows a company to diversify its network and server infrastructure. Some cloud computing services automatically add more network and server capacity to a company's Web site, as demand for services of the Web site increases. The network and server capacity may be duplicated around

Virtualization
For more information, visit the Computer Concepts CourseMate Web site at www.cengagebrain.com, navigate to the Chapter 12 Web Link resource for this book, and then click Virtualization.

the world so that, for example, a single outage of a server does not affect the company's operations. Read Looking Ahead 12-1 for a look at the future of cloud computing.

Grid computing combines many servers and/or personal computers on a network, such as the Internet, to act as one large computer. As with cloud computing, a company may pay for the use of a grid based on the amount of processing time that it needs. Grid computing often is used in research environments, such as climate research and life science problems. For example, the SETI@home project uses a grid of millions of personal computers around the world to search radio signals for signs of extraterrestrial life.

↗ **LOOKING AHEAD 12-1**

Variable Winds Forecasted for Cloud Computing

The forecast for enterprise computing calls for partly cloudy skies. The winds of change in computing are coming to businesses in various degrees, but how and when companies and consumers will adopt the infrastructure is not clear. Most analysts agree that this revolutionary storm is brewing on the horizon and will reach just about everyone before long. Microsoft and Google are predicting cloud computing's future and are developing different business models. Microsoft is focusing on enterprise tools, while Google is working on consumer-based applications.

Small businesses should be the first widespread adopters because of cost-saving measures. Their organizational needs for occasional computing power, storage, and services make the Web applications ideal. Startup companies increasingly will use pay-as-you-go assistance, such as Amazon's Web Services. Some forecasts predict that the only required hardware will be a monitor, keyboard, and mouse because all computing and storage will be performed offsite.

Large corporations, by contrast, will be slower to adopt cloud computing. Their more specific needs and concerns of security might delay their entry into this newer resource.

 For more information, visit the Computer Concepts CourseMate Web site at www.cengagebrain.com, navigate to the Chapter 12 Looking Ahead resource for this book and then click Cloud Computing.

E-Commerce

Several market sectors have taken advantage of business opportunities on the Web. The more popular market segments include retail, finance, health, entertainment and media, and travel. Figure 12-20 briefly reviews some of the more popular e-commerce market segments.

Examples of E-Commerce

Type	Purpose	Example Web Site
E-Retail	**E-retail**, also called e-tail, occurs when retailers use the Web to sell their products and services.	amazon.com shopping.yahoo.com shopzilla.com
Finance	**Online banking** allows users to pay bills from their computer or mobile device, that is, transfer money electronically from their account to a payee's account such as the electric company or telephone company. With **online trading**, users invest in stocks, options, bonds, treasuries, certificates of deposit, money markets, annuities, mutual funds, and so on — without using a broker.	vanguard.com fidelity.com e-trade.com
Travel	The Web provides many travel-related services. If you need directions, you simply enter a starting point and destination, and many Web sites provide detailed directions along with a map. Users can make airline reservations and reserve a hotel or car.	orbitz.com priceline.com kayak.com
Entertainment and Media	Music, videos, news, sporting events, and 3-D multiplayer games are a growing part of the Web's future. Newsprint on the Web is not replacing the newspaper, but enhancing it and reaching different populations.	itunes.com youtube.com nytimes.com
Health	Many Web sites provide up-to-date medical, fitness, nutrition, or exercise information. Some Web sites offer the capability to listen in on health-related seminars and discussion.	webmd.com health.gov familydoctor.com drugstore.com

Figure 12-20 E-commerce allows a variety of industries to extend their relationships to their customers via the Internet.

Enterprises use the Web to provide services to consumers and other businesses. Public relations, online advertising, direct mail, recruiting, credit, sales, market research, technical support, training, software consulting, and Internet access represent a few of the areas of service. Read Ethics & Issues 12-2 for additional information.

ETHICS & ISSUES 12-2

Who Can You Trust When Making Purchases Online?

When you walk into a store, at some point in your shopping experience you almost always interact with a person directly. The online shopping experience, however, distances you from a seller who may be five hundred or five thousand miles away. For many consumers, this type of nonhuman transaction can be a source of stress and concern about the trustworthiness of the merchant. For some merchants, the distance and anonymity of the Internet is an ideal climate for finding unknowing victims for unscrupulous activity, such as fraud. Consumer advocates and government agencies recommend many ways to avoid a bad online shopping experience. When you provide personal information, make sure that you are dealing with a secure Web site whose address begins with https:// rather than http://. Check the site's credentials, which may include seals from TRUSTe, the

Better Business Bureau (BBB), or other certifying organizations. Make sure that the price you pay matches the price listed on the site and that you are not paying too much for shipping your order. When available, check reviews of the merchant offered by other consumers, but be aware that many merchants try to offer phony, positive reviews of themselves. Finally, make it a habit to rate merchants as often as possible so that others can learn from your experience.

When you shop online, how do you go about determining which online merchants are trustworthy? How do the methods that you use differ from merchants you visit when you walk into a store for the first time? Are consumer advocacy groups or the government the better choice for regulating online transactions? Why?

Ethics & Issues
For the complete text of the Ethics & Issues boxes found in this chapter, visit the Computer Concepts CourseMate Web site at www.cengagebrain.com and then navigate to the Chapter 12 Ethics & Issues resource for this book.

QUIZ YOURSELF 12-2

Instructions: Find the true statement below. Then, rewrite the remaining false statements so that they are true.

1. A portal is the portion of a company's network that allows customers or suppliers of a company to access parts of an enterprise's intranet.

2. A data warehouse is a huge database that stores and manages the data required to analyze historical and current transactions.

3. A VPN is a server that is placed on a network with the sole purpose of providing storage to users and information systems attached to the network.

4. A workflow application helps an enterprise collect, archive, index, and retrieve its resources.

Quiz Yourself Online: To further check your knowledge of pages 479 through 485, visit the Computer Concepts CourseMate Web site at www.cengagebrain.com, navigate to the Chapter 12 Quiz Yourself resource for this book, and then click Objectives 4 – 5.

Enterprise Hardware

Enterprise hardware allows large organizations to manage and store information and data using devices geared for heavy use, maximum availability, and maximum efficiency.

Enterprises often rely on legacy systems. A **legacy system** is an information system that has existed within the organization for an extended length of time and is relied upon heavily. Enterprises often struggle with the decision to replace legacy systems with newer technology.

The following sections discuss a variety of enterprise hardware solutions.

RAID

For applications that depend on reliable data access, users must have the data available when they attempt to access it. Some manufacturers provide a type of hard disk system that connects several smaller disks into a single unit that acts like a single large hard disk. As discussed in Chapter 6, a group of two or more integrated hard disks is called a **RAID (redundant array of independent disks)**. Although quite expensive for large computers, RAID is more reliable than traditional hard disks (Figure 12-21). Networks and Internet servers often use RAID.

A RAID system duplicates data, instructions, and information to improve data reliability. The simplest RAID storage design, called mirroring, writes data on two disks at the same time to duplicate the data. This configuration enhances storage reliability because, if a disk should fail, a duplicate of the requested item is available elsewhere within the array of disks. Some personal computers now include RAID storage.

Figure 12-21 A group of two or more integrated hard disks, called a RAID (redundant array of independent disks), often is used with network servers. Shown here is a rack-mounted RAID chassis including the hard disks.

Network Attached Storage and Storage Area Networks

Network attached storage (NAS) is a server that is placed on a network with the sole purpose of providing storage to users and information systems attached to the network (Figure 12-22a). A network attached storage server often is called a storage appliance because it is a piece of equipment with only one function — to provide additional storage. Administrators quickly add storage to an existing network simply by attaching a new network attached storage server to the network.

A **storage area network (SAN)** is a high-speed network with the sole purpose of providing storage to other servers to which it is attached (Figure 12-22b). A storage area network is a network that includes only storage devices. High-speed fiber-optic cable connects other networks and servers to the storage area network, so the networks and servers have fast access to large storage capacities.

Figure 12-22a (network attached storage on a LAN)

Figure 12-22b (a SAN provides centralized storage for servers and networks)

Figure 12-22 Network attached storage (NAS) and a storage area network (SAN) connect to existing servers and networks in different ways.

Enterprise Storage Systems

Many organizations use networks. Data, information, and instructions stored on the network must be easily accessible to all authorized users. The data, information, and instructions also must be secure, so that unauthorized users cannot access the network. An **enterprise storage system** is a strategy that focuses on the availability, protection, organization, and backup of storage in a company.

The goal of an enterprise storage system is to consolidate storage so that operations run as efficiently as possible. Most enterprise storage systems manage extraordinary amounts of data.

For example, one large retailer manages a several-hundred TB storage system to store sales data. Read Ethics & Issues 12-3 for a related discussion.

To implement an enterprise storage system, an organization uses a combination of techniques. As shown in Figure 12-23, an enterprise storage system may use servers, RAID, a tape library, optical disc jukeboxes, Internet backup, network attached storage devices, and/or a storage area network. Enterprises often use **Fibre Channel** technology to connect to storage systems at data rates up to 4 Gbps.

Some organizations manage an enterprise storage system in-house. Other enterprises elect to offload all (or at least the backup) storage management to an outside organization or online Web service. This practice is known as outsourcing. Some vendors focus on providing enterprise storage systems to clients. A data warehouse might seek this type of outside service.

RAID

optical disc jukeboxes

servers

Fibre Channel

tape libraries

SAN

Internet backup

NAS device

Figure 12-23 An enterprise storage system uses many types of storage.

How Much Data Should Companies Be Required to Keep?

After a string of corporate scandals, the Sarbanes-Oxley Act was signed into law in 2002, providing a myriad of financial reporting requirements and guidelines for public companies. A main focus of the law is the retention of business records. As provisions of the law slowly have come into effect, companies have been faced with massive new data storage requirements for these records. For example, all e-mail messages within a company are considered to be business records and must be retained. Deleting stored e-mail messages constitutes a destruction of evidence infraction. Penalties include 20 years in prison for any employee who alters or destroys records or documents. IT departments are faced not only with understanding this complex law, but also with ensuring accuracy of financial data, determining policies for record retention, and building storage capacity to hold all of the data. Supporters of the law cite its need due to the recent wave of corporate scandals. Opponents say that the law is over-reaching and costs too much for the added benefits.

Is the Sarbanes-Oxley Act an unfair burden on companies? Why or why not? Should companies be able to engage in internal communications without the fear that those communications could be used as evidence against them later? Why or why not? Should employees or employers be held accountable if laws are violated? Why? Are such laws necessary in order to protect the public? Why or why not?

Blade Servers

A **blade server**, sometimes called an ultradense server, packs a complete computer server, such as a Web server or network server, on a single card, or blade, rather than a system unit. Each blade server includes a processor, memory, hard disk, network card, and ports on the card. The individual blades insert in a blade server chassis that can hold many blades. Using blade servers allows an organization to fit 16 or more blades in the physical space occupied by a typical, single server. Figure 12-24 shows a blade and a chassis that holds many blades.

Besides the savings in space offered by blade servers, blade servers require less maintenance, use less energy, generate less heat, and easily are replaced or upgraded.

Blade Servers

For more information, visit the Computer Concepts CourseMate Web site at www.cengagebrain.com, navigate to the Chapter 12 Web Link resource for this book, and then click Blade Servers.

Figure 12-24 A blade server contains several very small servers, each on its own blade within the server.

High Availability, Scalability, and Interoperability

Enterprises measure the quality of their operations in a numbers of ways. Often systems have specific requirements for availability, the ability to grow (scalability), and interoperability with other systems. One of the goals of an enterprise's hardware is to maintain a high level of availability to end users. The availability of hardware to users is a measure of how often it is online. The following sections discuss these needs in an enterprise.

High-Availability Systems

A **high-availability system** continues running and performing tasks for at least 99 percent of the time. Some users demand that high-availability systems be available for 99.99 percent of the time. A system that has uptime of 99.99 percent is nonfunctional for less than one hour per year. That one hour, called downtime, includes any time that the computer crashes, needs repairs, or requires installation of replacement or upgrade parts. A system with 99.9 percent availability is said to have three nines of availability, and a system with 99.99 percent availability is said to have four nines of availability.

Telecommunications companies, such as local telephone companies, rely on high-availability systems to deliver telephone service. Emergency 911 communications centers require almost 100 percent uptime for their hardware and software applications as mandated by law. Centralized accounting or financial systems must be available to gather sales and other accounting information from locations scattered around the globe.

High-availability systems often include a feature called hot-swapping. Hot-swapping allows components, such as a RAID hard disk or power supplies, to be replaced while the rest of the

Figure 12-25
This heavy duty battery rack provides reliable backup power for enterprise hardware.

system continues to perform its tasks. A high-availability system also may include redundant components. **Redundant components**, such as redundant power supplies (Figure 12-25), allow for a functioning component to take over automatically the tasks of a similar component that fails. When a component fails, the system administrator is notified, but the computer continues to perform its tasks because a redundant component has taken its place automatically in the system.

Scalability

As an enterprise grows, its information systems either must grow with it or must be replaced. **Scalability** is a measure of how well a computer hardware system, software application, or information system can grow to meet increasing performance demands. A system that is designed, built, or purchased when the company is small may be inadequate when the company doubles in size. When making decisions for computing solutions, managers must be careful to consider the growth plans of the company.

A company may find that its Web site is becoming overwhelmed by customers and prospective customers. If the Web site is scalable, then the Web administrator can add more Web servers to handle the additional visitors to the Web site. Similarly, an enterprise's storage needs usually grow daily, meaning that storage systems should be scalable to store the ever-growing data generated by users.

Adding more hardware often is the easiest method to grow, or scale, an information system. Often, at some point, a system no longer scales and must be replaced with a new system.

Interoperability

Enterprises typically build and buy a diverse set of information systems. An information system often must share information, or have **interoperability**, with other information systems within the enterprise. Information systems that more easily share information with other information systems are said to be open. Information systems that are more difficult to interoperate with other information systems are said to be closed, or proprietary. Recent open systems employ XML and Web services to allow a greater level of interoperability.

Backup Procedures

Business and home users can perform four types of backup: full, differential, incremental, or selective. A fifth type, continuous data protection, typically is used only by large enterprises. A full backup, sometimes called an archival backup, copies all of the files in the computer. A full backup provides the best protection against data loss because it copies all program and data files. Performing a full backup can be time-consuming. A differential backup copies only the files that have changed since the last full backup. An incremental backup copies only the files that have changed since the last full or last incremental backup. A selective backup, sometimes called a partial backup, allows the user to choose specific files to back up, regardless of whether or not the files have changed since the last incremental backup. Continuous data protection (CDP), or continuous backup, is a system in which all data is backed up whenever a change is made. A continuous data protection plan keeps a journal of every transaction — reads, writes, and deletes — made to a server or servers.

Whatever backup procedures a company adopts, they should be stated clearly, documented in writing, and followed consistently.

? FAQ 12-3

Can I use CDP at home?

Yes. The price of storage devices is decreasing, and companies that provide continuous data protection are able to offer their services at rates much lower than what once were offered. For instance, one company allows you to back up 2 GB of data continuously for less than $60 per year.

For more information, visit the Computer Concepts CourseMate Web site at www.cengagebrain.com, navigate to the Chapter 12 FAQ resource for this book, and then click CDP.

Disaster Recovery Plan

A **disaster recovery plan** is a written plan describing the steps a company would take to restore computer operations in the event of a disaster. A disaster recovery plan contains four major components: the emergency plan, the backup plan, the recovery plan, and the test plan.

The Emergency Plan An emergency plan specifies the steps to be taken immediately after a disaster strikes. All emergency plans should contain the following information:

1. Names and telephone numbers of people and organizations to notify (e.g., management, fire department, police department)
2. Procedures to follow with the computer equipment (e.g., equipment shutdown, power shutoff, file removal)
3. Employee evacuation procedures
4. Return procedures; that is, who can reenter the facility and what actions they are to perform

The Backup Plan Once the procedures in the emergency plan have been executed, the next step is to follow the backup plan. The backup plan specifies how an organization uses backup files and equipment to resume information processing. The backup plan should specify the location of an alternate computer facility in the event the organization's normal location is destroyed or unusable.

When operations are so important that an organization cannot afford to lose the operations to a disaster, the organization often maintains a hot site, which is a separate facility that mirrors the systems and operations of the critical site. The hot site always operates concurrently with the main site, so that if either site becomes unavailable, the other site continues to meet the organization's needs. The process of one system automatically taking the place of a failed system is called **failover**.

The backup plan identifies these items:

1. The location of backup data, supplies, and equipment
2. The personnel responsible for gathering backup resources and transporting them to the alternate computer facility
3. A schedule indicating the order in which, and approximate time by which, each application should be up and running

For a backup plan to be successful, the organization must back up all critical resources. Also, additional people, including possibly nonemployees, must be trained in the backup and recovery procedures because the organization's personnel could be injured in a disaster.

The Recovery Plan The recovery plan specifies the actions to be taken to restore full information processing operations. To prepare for disaster recovery, an organization should establish planning committees, with each one responsible for different forms of recovery. For example, one committee is in charge of hardware replacement. Another is responsible for software replacement.

The Test Plan To provide assurance that the disaster plan is complete, it should be tested. A disaster recovery test plan contains information for simulating various levels of disasters and recording an organization's ability to recover. In a simulation, all personnel follow the steps in the disaster recovery plan.

Disaster Recovery Plan
For more information, visit the Computer Concepts CourseMate Web site at www.cengagebrain.com, navigate to the Chapter 12 Web Link resource for this book, and then click Disaster Recovery Plan.

Instructions: Find the true statement below. Then, rewrite the remaining false statements so that they are true.

1. Network attached storage is a high-speed network with the sole purpose of providing storage to other servers to which it is attached.
2. Scalability refers to the ability of an information system to share information with other information systems.
3. A differential backup copies only the files that have changed since the last full or last incremental backup.
4. An emergency plan specifies how a company uses backup files and equipment to resume information processing.
5. The recovery plan specifies the actions to be taken to restore full information processing operations.

Quiz Yourself Online: To further check your knowledge of pages 485 through 491, visit the Computer Concepts CourseMate Web site at www.cengagebrain.com, navigate to the Chapter 12 Quiz Yourself resource for this book, and then click Objectives 6 – 8.

Chapter Summary

This chapter reviewed the special computing requirements present in an enterprise-sized organization. Various types of users within an organization require different types of information systems. Large information systems become more valuable when they communicate with each other and offer users a great deal of flexibility in interacting with the information system and other users. The chapter discussed the benefits of virtualization, cloud computing, and grid computing.

Enterprises manage complex hardware, including storage area networks, RAID, and blade servers. Requirements for this enterprise hardware often include high-availability, scalability, and interoperability. The chapter also discussed the backup procedures present in a large organization.

Computer Usage @ Work

Municipal Services

You stayed up late last night and woke up late this morning. Because you take the bus to work, you hurry to get ready and arrive at the bus stop at 7:45 a.m., the exact time that the bus is scheduled to arrive. Ten minutes elapse and you are unsure whether you missed the bus or if the bus merely is running late. You call the city's transportation department to inquire about the bus, but they are unable to provide you with any information. Fortunately, the person with whom you are speaking informs you that the city currently is investing in a system that will provide exact bus arrival times at bus stops; it also will allow management to track the location of buses on their route. This technology uses a global positioning system to determine each bus's exact location and transmits that information back to a server. The server then can transmit relevant information to displays located at various bus stops throughout the city. Management also can use this information to dispatch additional buses if traffic conditions are poor, determine whether bus drivers are staying on their assigned routes, and discover whether they are obeying speed limits and other traffic laws.

After work, you arrive home to find an electrician installing a new electrical meter on your house. Your curiosity prompts you to approach the electrician to find out about the new meter, because you have had no problems with the old one. The electrician explains that in an effort to increase efficiency and save money, the power companies in the area are installing new meters that record power usage data electronically and then transmit the data wirelessly to the billing office. This new technology eliminates the need for employees to visit each house individually and reduces the possibility of human error in calculating your power consumption.

As the day ends, you watch a news story about how your city is installing sirens in strategic areas that will sound when dangerous weather approaches. These sirens either can be activated manually, or they can sound automatically when the National Weather Service issues a severe weather warning for your immediate area.

Computers have enhanced municipal services greatly during the past several years. Not only do computers provide increased opportunities for efficiency, they also provide a wealth of information to which one might not have access otherwise.

For more information, visit the Computer Concepts CourseMate Web site at www.cengagebrain.com, navigate to the Chapter 12 Computer Usage @ Work resource for this book, and then click Municipal Services.

RUSSELL SQUARE
HOLBORN
OXFORD CIRCUS
KING'S CROSS

Companies on the Cutting Edge

EMC Information Management and Storage Provider

Data protection and storage are keys to running a successful business and preserving family memories. EMC specializes in producing innovative solutions for storing, safeguarding, and managing information so that it readily is available, searchable, and sharable.

EMC is the world leader in external storage and storage management systems. It is best known for its large-scale enterprise storage systems, and customers include financial services firms, health-care organizations,

transportation companies, educational institutions, and manufacturers. Its RAID systems, networked storage systems, and storage management software are ranked at the top of the industry revenue shares.

EMC's Proven Professional certification program, aimed at validating knowledge about various IT topics, recently granted more than 45,000 certifications. EMC also has received numerous top awards for its network storage, software, and environmental practices.

IBM World's Largest Information Technology Company

Data centers consume tremendous amounts of electricity, but IBM is working to reduce energy consumption in these centralized locations. Its energy-efficient Active Energy Manager (AEM) tracks electricity usage and allows businesses to set a cap on total energy use for storing, networking, serving, and cooling operations.

IBM's services, consulting, and infrastructure components have helped companies develop new business ventures. Its systems supply nearly one-half of the world's supercomputing processing power, and the company is

noted for its enterprise business focus in financial services, public, industrial, distribution, communications, and small- and medium-sized businesses.

The corporation was founded in 1911 when three companies merged to sell business-related gadgets, including a machine that used punched cards to catalog data. Nine years later, the company changed its name to International Business Machines (IBM). The company recently announced that more than 200 customers switched to IBM servers from Sun and HP servers.

For more information, visit the Computer Concepts CourseMate Web site at www.cengagebrain.com and then navigate to the Chapter 12 Companies on the Cutting Edge resource for this book.

Technology Trailblazers

CHAD HURLEY YouTube Cofounder and CEO

Twenty hours of video are uploaded every minute to YouTube, and much of this Web site's popularity is due to the efforts of Chad Hurley. He and two work colleagues at PayPal cofounded YouTube in 2005, and it grew quickly to become one of the larger Web sites. One year later they sold YouTube to Google for $1.65 billion.

Hurley says he is a user interface expert and that his interests in fine arts and business have been evident since childhood. In first grade he painted photos on plywood and attempted to sell them on his front lawn.

He graduated from Indiana University of Pennsylvania with a degree in fine art, and he used his design skills in one of his first jobs after graduation to create eBay's PayPal logo.

At eBay, he envisioned the concept of adding video to the online auctions. He abandoned that idea when sellers seemed disinterested and then turned his attention to developing the YouTube concept. His goal is to allow every person worldwide to upload video content to YouTube easily and view content on any device that has a screen.

ANITA BORG Champion for Women in Technology

Women from across the globe have been inspired and encouraged to pursue a career in technology with the help of Anita Borg. The Anita Borg Institute for Women and Technology and the Google Anita Borg Scholarship provide programs and resources to help women develop technological innovations.

Borg died in 2003, but her accomplishments throughout her career laid the foundation for advancing women in computer science today. In 1987, she went to a technology conference that had only a few women in

attendance, and shortly thereafter she formed Systers, an electronic mailing list for female engineers to exchange technology ideas. Today, the Systers list has grown to more than 3,000 members in 54 countries.

Borg's computer science research in college focused on operating systems principles, and she earned her Ph.D. degree from New York University in 1981. She then held top research positions at Nixdorf, Digital Equipment Corporation, and Xerox until her death.

For more information, visit the Computer Concepts CourseMate Web site at www.cengagebrain.com and then navigate to the Chapter 12 Technology Trailblazers resource for this book.

Chapter Review

The Chapter Review reinforces the main concepts presented in this chapter.

To listen to an audio version of this Chapter Review, visit the Computer Concepts CourseMate Web site at www.cengagebrain.com and then navigate to the Chapter 12 Chapter Review resource for this book.

1. What Are the Special Information Requirements of an Enterprise-Sized Corporation? A large organization, or enterprise, requires special computing solutions because of its size and geographical extent. **Enterprise computing** uses computers in networks or a series of interconnected networks to satisfy the information needs of an enterprise. The types of information employees require depend on their level in the company. **Managers** utilize tools and techniques such as **business intelligence (BI)**, **business process management (BPM)**, and **business process automation (BPA)** to focus on information that is important to the decision-making process.

2. What Information Systems and Software Are Used in the Functional Units of an Enterprise? An **information system** is a set of hardware, software, data, people, and procedures that work together to produce information. In an enterprise, each type of functional unit has specialized requirements for their information systems. Accounting and financial systems manage everyday transactions and help budget, forecast, and analyze. A **human resources information system (HRIS)** manages one or more human resources functions. An **employee relationship management (ERM)** system automates and manages much of the communications between employees and the business. Engineers use **computer-aided design (CAD)** and **computer-aided engineering (CAE)**. **Computer-aided manufacturing (CAM)** and **computer-integrated manufacturing (CIM)** speed manufacturing. **Material Requirements Planning (MRP)** is an information management approach that uses software to help monitor and control processes related to production. A quality control system helps an organization maintain or improve the quality of its products or services. A **marketing information system** serves as a central repository for marketing tasks. **Sales force automation (SFA)** software equips traveling salespeople with the tools they need. **Distribution systems** control inventory and manage shipping. **Customer interaction management (CIM)** software manages interactions with customers.

3. What Information Systems Are Used throughout an Enterprise? Some general purpose information systems, or enterprise-wide systems, are used throughout an enterprise. An **office information system (OIS)** enables employees to perform tasks using computers and other electronic devices, instead of manually. A **transaction processing system (TPS)** captures and processes data from day-to-day business activities. A **management information system (MIS)** generates accurate, timely, and organized information, so users can make decisions, solve problems, and track progress. A **decision support system (DSS)** helps users analyze data and make decisions. An **expert system** captures and stores the knowledge of human experts and then imitates human reasoning and decision making. **Enterprise resource planning (ERP)** provides applications to help manage and coordinate ongoing activities. **Customer relationship management (CRM)** systems manage information about customers. A **content management system (CMS)** organizes and allows access to various forms of documents and files.

Visit the Computer Concepts CourseMate Web site at www.cengagebrain.com, navigate to the Chapter 12 Quiz Yourself resource for this book, and then click Objectives 1 – 3.

4. What Are Types of Technologies Used throughout an Enterprise? Technologies used throughout an enterprise include portals, communications, data warehouses, extranets, Web services, service-oriented architectures, workflow, and virtual private networks. A **portal** is a collection of links, content, and services on a Web page designed to guide users to information related to their jobs. An enterprise's communications infrastructures consists of hardware (such as wired and wireless connections and devices, routers, firewalls, and servers), software (such as e-mail, instant messaging, VoIP, and server management), and procedures for using and managing hardware and software. A **data warehouse** stores and manages the data required to analyze transactions. An **extranet** allows customers or suppliers to access part of an enterprise's intranet. **Web services** allow businesses to create products and B2B interactions. Many enterprises employ a service-oriented architecture, which helps increase communications between diverse information systems. A **workflow application** assists in the management and tracking of the activities in a business process. A **virtual private network (VPN)** provides users with a secure connection to a company's network server.

5. What Are Virtualization, Cloud Computing, and Grid Computing? Virtualization is the practice of sharing or pooling computing resources, such as servers and storage devices. Server virtualization provides the capability to divide a physical server logically into many virtual servers; storage virtualization provides the capability to create a single logical storage device from many physical storage devices. **Cloud computing** is an Internet service that provides computing needs to computer users. **Grid computing**, which often is used in research environments, combines many servers and/or personal

computers on a network to act as one large computer. Both cloud and grid computing usually require a company to pay a fee based on usage or processing time.

Visit the Computer Concepts CourseMate Web site at www.cengagebrain.com, navigate to the Chapter 12 Quiz Yourself resource for this book, and then click Objectives 4 – 5.

6. What Are the Computer Hardware Needs and Solutions for an Enterprise? **Enterprise hardware** allows large organizations to manage and share information and data using devices geared for maximum availability and efficiency. A **RAID (redundant array of independent disks)** is a group of integrated disks that duplicates data, instructions, and information to improve data reliability. **Network attached storage (NAS)** is a server that provides storage for users and information systems. A **storage area network (SAN)** provides storage to other servers. An **enterprise storage system** consolidates storage so that operations run efficiently. **Blade servers** pack a complete computer server on a single card, or blade, rather than a system unit.

7. Why Is Computer Backup Important, and How Is It Accomplished? A backup duplicates a file or program to protect an enterprise if the original is lost or damaged. A full backup copies all of the files in a computer. A differential backup copies only files that have changed since the last full backup. An incremental backup copies only files that have changed since the last full or incremental backup. A selective backup, sometimes called a partial backup, allows users to back up specific files. With continuous data protection (CDP), all data is backed up whenever a change is made.

8. What Are the Steps in a Disaster Recovery Plan? A **disaster recovery plan** describes the steps a company would take to restore computer operations in the event of a disaster. A disaster recovery plan contains four components. The emergency plan specifies the steps to be taken immediately after a disaster strikes. The backup plan specifies how a company uses backup files and equipment to resume information processing. The recovery plan identifies the actions to be taken to restore full information processing operations. The test plan contains information for simulating disasters and recording an organization's ability to recover.

Visit the Computer Concepts CourseMate Web site at www.cengagebrain.com, navigate to the Chapter 12 Quiz Yourself resource for this book, and then click Objectives 6 – 8.

Key Terms

You should know the Key Terms. The list below helps focus your study.

To see an example of and a definition for each term, and access current and additional information from the Web, visit the Computer Concepts CourseMate Web site at www.cengagebrain.com and then navigate to the Chapter 12 Key Terms resource for this book.

artificial intelligence (AI) (476)
blade server (489)
business intelligence (BI) (468)
business process automation (BPA) (468)
business process management (BPM) (468)
chief information officer (CIO) (473)
cloud computing (483)
computer-aided design (CAD) (471)
computer-aided engineering (CAE) (471)
computer-aided manufacturing (CAM) (471)
computer-integrated manufacturing (CIM) (471)

content management system (CMS) (478)
customer interaction management (CIM) (472)
customer relationship management (CRM) (478)
data center (479)
data warehouse (480)
decision support system (DSS) (475)
disaster recovery plan (491)
distribution systems (472)
EDI (electronic data interchange) (480)
enterprise computing (464)
enterprise hardware (485)
enterprise information (468)
enterprise resource planning (ERP) (477)
enterprise search (479)
enterprise storage system (487)

e-retail (484)
expert system (476)
extranet (481)
failover (491)
Fibre Channel (488)
grid computing (484)
high-availability system (489)
human resources information system (HRIS) (470)
information system (468)
interoperability (490)
legacy system (485)
management information system (MIS) (474)
managers (468)
marketing information system (472)
Material Requirements Planning (MRP) (471)
network attached storage (NAS) (486)

office information system (OIS) (473)
online banking (484)
online trading (484)
portal (479)
RAID (redundant array of independent disks) (486)
redundant components (490)
sales force automation (SFA) (472)
scalability (490)
small- and medium-sized business (SMB) (465)
storage area network (SAN) (486)
transaction processing system (TPS) (473)
virtual private network (VPN) (482)
Web services (481)
workflow (482)
workflow application (482)

Checkpoint

The Checkpoint exercises test your knowledge of the chapter concepts. The page number containing the answer appears in parentheses after each exercise.

To complete the Checkpoint exercises interactively, visit the Computer Concepts CourseMate Web site at www.cengagebrain.com and then navigate to the Chapter 12 Checkpoint resource for this book.

Multiple Choice Select the best answer.

1. _____ are smaller in size than enterprises and typically do not have an international presence. (465)
 a. Data centers
 b. Portals
 c. SMBs
 d. Web services

2. _____ includes several types of applications and technologies for acquiring, storing, analyzing, and providing access to information to help users make more sound business decisions. (468)
 a. Business process management
 b. Business intelligence
 c. Business process automation
 d. None of the above

3. Many companies elevate the importance of information technology by including a _____ executive position that reports to the CEO. (473)
 a. chief operations officer (COO)
 b. chief information officer (CIO)
 c. chief security officer (CSO)
 d. chief financial officer (CFO)

4. An advantage of ERP is _____. (478)
 a. complete integration of information systems across departments
 b. better project management
 c. better customer service
 d. all of the above

5. A(n) _____ is an information system that has existed within the organization for an extended length of time and is relied upon heavily. (485)
 a. expert system
 b. high-availability system
 c. office information system
 d. legacy system

6. The _____ of hardware to users is a measure of how often it is online. (489)
 a. redundancy
 b. availability
 c. scalability
 d. interoperability

7. _____ continue running and performing tasks for at least 99 percent of the time. (489)
 a. Distribution systems
 b. High-availability systems
 c. Blade servers
 d. Virtual private networks

8. A(n) _____ can be time-consuming but provides the best protection against data loss. (490)
 a. full backup
 b. incremental backup
 c. differential backup
 d. selective backup

Matching Match the terms with their definitions.

_____ 1. computer-aided engineering (471)

_____ 2. decision support system (DSS) (475)

_____ 3. EDI (electronic data interchange) (480)

_____ 4. extranet (481)

_____ 5. RAID (486)

a. portion of a company's network that allows customers or suppliers of a company to access parts of an enterprise's intranet

b. helps users analyze data and make decisions

c. a group of two or more integrated hard disks

d. allows a business to create products and B2B interactions

e. uses computers to test product designs

f. set of standards that controls the transfer of business data and information among computers both within and among enterprises

Short Answer Write a brief answer to each of the following questions.

1. What are managers? _____ What four activities do managers perform to coordinate resources? _____

2. What is a content management system (CMS)? _____ What type of content may be processed by a content management system? _____

3. Describe two types of virtualization. _____ What are cloud and grid computing, and why do companies use them? _____

4. What are five types of e-commerce? _____ Describe three of the five types that you listed. _____

5. What does a backup plan identify? _____ What factors contribute to the success of a backup plan? _____

Problem Solving

The Problem Solving exercises extend your knowledge of the chapter concepts by seeking solutions to practical computer problems that you may encounter at home, school, or work. The Collaboration exercise should be completed with a team.

In the real world, practical problems often can be solved in multiple ways. Provide one solution to each of the following problems using available resources, such as articles on the Web or in print, blogs, podcasts, videos, television, user guides, other individuals, and electronics and computer stores. You may need to use multiple resources to obtain an answer. Present your solutions in the form requested by your instructor (brief report, presentation, discussion, or other means).

@ Home

1. **Invalid Password** After typing your user name and password to log onto your school's portal, an error message displays stating that the password is incorrect. What are your next steps?

2. **Suspicious Account Transactions** After successfully signing up for PayPal's online payment service, you verify the balance in your checking account and notice that two suspicious transactions were conducted, each crediting your account a few pennies. Unsure of whether you now are vulnerable to identity theft, how will you proceed?

3. **Invalid Credit Card Information** Near the conclusion of an e-commerce transaction, you enter your credit card information, and the Web site reports that your credit card information is invalid. After double-checking your credit card number, expiration date, and security code, it appears that you have entered everything properly. What are your next steps?

4. **Late Fees Assessed** Your bank recently set up an online bill payment service. You begin paying your bills online and set up each bill's payment information. One credit card company has been applying late fees to your account, although you configured the online bill payment service to pay the balances on time. What might be causing this?

@ Work

5. **Unable to Update** Your company hosts a portal that enables you to perform tasks such as checking the information stored by the human resources department and viewing electronic paychecks. Having recently married, you access the portal to change your marital status, but the option buttons allowing you to select marital status are disabled. What might be wrong?

6. **Compromised Credit Card** An e-mail message arrives in your e-mail account stating that a Web site with which you perform a significant amount of business has been compromised. You regularly use a corporate credit card to purchase supplies from this Web site, and you are concerned that someone might have obtained your credit card information. What are your next steps?

7. **Incorrect Pay Rate** Recently, you received a promotion that included a pay raise. You log into your company portal and verify that your rate of pay has increased. After receiving your next paycheck, however, you realize that you were paid at the previous rate of pay. Why might you not be receiving the new rate of pay?

8. **Missing CRM Entry** As a customer service representative for a well-known computer manufacturer, you receive a telephone call from an irritated customer who states that he has called five times about the same problem. In an effort to resolve his problem, you search for his call history using your company's CRM program. Much to your surprise, you are unable to locate any information about this customer's previous telephone calls. What might be wrong?

Collaboration

9. **Computers in Municipal Services** Municipalities are incorporating technology into most, if not all, of their services. As a student in a computer technology class, your instructor provides you with a document that lists various municipal services available in the area. Your instructor requests that teams of three people determine how computers have enhanced various services. One team member should research how computers have enhanced cable television services. Another team member should research how power and water companies benefit from computer technology, and the third team member should identify ways that municipalities can save money by using computer technology.

Learn How To

The Learn How To activities step you through fundamental technology skills when using a computer. The Learn How To exercises enable you to become more proficient with these skills.

 Premium Activity: To relate this Learn How To activity to your everyday life, see a visual demonstration of the activity, and complete a short assessment, visit the Computer Concepts CourseMate Web site at www.cengagebrain.com and then navigate to the Chapter 12 Learn How To resource for this book.

Learn How To 1: Use VoIP (Voice over Internet Protocol)

Every enterprise and organization depends on reliable communications. An important means of communication is voice, or telephone, communications. In most organizations today, a telephone company is the primary vendor for providing telephone communications. In the near future, however, the Internet might be the largest provider of telephone communications.

You learned in a previous chapter about VoIP, which provides for voice communications using the Internet instead of standard telephone connections. Two advantages claimed for VoIP are improved reliability and much lower costs. Both of these advantages are attractive to businesses, and VoIP is forecasted to become the standard voice communications method within the next 5 – 10 years.

VoIP also is available to individual users. One primary means to use VoIP is through the service offered by Skype, a company that offers free, unlimited calls through an Internet connection. The Skype software also is free. Using Skype, you can talk to another Skype user via the Internet anywhere in the world for no cost whatsoever. If the person you call is not a Skype user, you can use Skype to call their ordinary landline or mobile telephone quite inexpensively. For example, to call someone on a landline telephone in the United Kingdom from anywhere in the world, the cost is approximately 2 cents per minute.

To download Skype, complete the following steps:
1. Start your Internet browser, type skype.com in the Address bar and then press the ENTER key.
2. When the Skype home page is displayed, explore the Web site for information about using Skype. When you are ready, click the Get Skype now button.
3. When the File Download - Security Warning dialog box is displayed, click the Save button.
4. In the Save As dialog box, select the Desktop for the location of the saved file. Then, click the Save button. The Skype Setup file will download. This may take a few minutes, depending on the speed of your Internet connection, because of the large file size.
5. If the Download complete window opens click the Close button. The SkypeSetup icon is displayed on the desktop.
6. Double-click the SkypeSetup icon on the desktop. If the User Account Control dialog box appears, click the Yes button.
7. In the Skype - Install window, select the language you would like to use, and then click the 'I agree - install' button.
8. If you do not wish to install the Google Toolbar, remove the check mark from the appropriate check box. Click the Continue installing Skype button.
9. When the installation is completed, click the Finish button.

Skype now is installed on your computer. The Skype icon should appear on your desktop. To start and use Skype, complete the following steps:
1. Drag the SkypeSetup icon on the desktop to the Recycle Bin.
2. Double-click the Skype icon on your desktop. The first time you start Skype, the Skype - Create account dialog box is displayed (Figure 12-26). In this dialog box, you enter your full name, Skype name, and password. The Skype name is the name you will use to start Skype each time, together with the password. You can use any name and password that has not already been used on Skype. Also, be sure to check the Skype End User License Agreement check box, and then click the Next button to display the next dialog box requesting your E-mail address, Country/Region, and City.
3. Enter your E-mail address, Country/Region, and City, and then click the Sign in button.

Figure 12-26

4. If your Skype name and password have not been used, Skype automatically will sign into your account and open the Skype window (Figure 12-27). If your Skype name or password already have been used by another user, you must select another Skype name or password.

5. After installing Skype, you can make calls to other Skype users anywhere in the world for no cost.

6. To learn the techniques for calling another Skype user, click Help on the menu bar in the Skype window, click Get Help: Answers and Support on the Help menu, and then select the subject about which you want to learn.

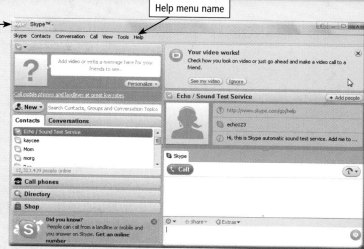

Figure 12-27

Exercise

1. Visit the Skype Web site. Examine the various screens and examples shown on the Web site. Do you think this type of service can be useful to you? Why? What are the advantages and disadvantages of using Skype? If you were calling a friend in Australia on a regular telephone, how much per minute would you have to pay? Submit your answers to your instructor.

Learn It Online

The Learn It Online exercises are interactive Web exercises designed to reinforce and expand your understanding of the chapter concepts. The descriptions below briefly summarize each exercise.

To complete the Learn It Online exercises, visit the Computer Concepts CourseMate Web site at www.cengagebrain.com, navigate to the Chapter 12 resources for this book, click the link for the exercise you want to complete, and then read the instructions.

❶ At the Movies — A Tour of Lucasfilm Data Center
Watch a movie to take a tour of the Lucasfilm Data Center, the high-tech center of IT operations for a movie production company, and then answer questions about the movie.

❷ Student Edition Labs — Project Management and Web Design Principles
Enhance your understanding and knowledge about project management and Web design principles by completing the Project Management and Web Design Principles Labs.

❸ Practice Test
Take a multiple choice test that checks your knowledge of the chapter concepts and review the resulting study guide.

❹ Who Wants To Be a Computer Genius²?
Play the Shelly Cashman Series version of this popular game by answering questions to find out if you are a computer genius. Panic buttons are available to provide assistance during game play.

❺ Crossword Puzzle Challenge
Complete an interactive crossword puzzle to reinforce concepts presented in this chapter.

❻ Windows Exercises
Step through the Windows 7 exercises to learn about changing views in Windows 7, using Windows Update, creating a desktop shortcut to the printer, and determining the brand and model of sound cards or audio devices in your computer.

❼ Exploring Computer Careers
Read about a career as a CIO, search for related employment advertisements, and then answer related questions.

❽ Web Apps — Microsoft Office Web Apps
Learn how to create, edit, and share documents, workbooks, presentations, and notes using Microsoft Office Web Apps.

Web Research

The Web Research exercises broaden your understanding of chapter concepts by presenting questions that require you to search the Web for answers.

❶ Search Sleuth

Use one of the search engines listed in Figure 2-8 in Chapter 2 on page 65 or your own favorite search engine to find the answers to the following questions. Copy and paste the Web address from the Web page where you found the answer. Some questions may have more than one answer. If required, submit your answers to your instructor. (1) What was the location of the latest International Supercomputing Conference? Who gave the opening keynote address, and what was the topic of this speech? (2) Where is the TSUBAME supercomputer installed? Why is it called "everybody's supercomputer"? (3) What are the primary purposes of the Virtual Private Network Consortium? (4) Which organization sponsors the Envirofacts data warehouse? (5) How many RAID levels exist?

❷ Green Computing

The carbon footprint of computers running the Internet is expected to exceed that of air travel by 2020. The world's data centers emit more gas than do people living in Argentina and the Netherlands, which have a combined population of 57.2 million. As you learned in Innovative Computing 12-1 on page 479, companies are developing unique data center solutions to cope with the massive electricity demands. View online Web sites that provide information about green data centers. Which countries can profit from IBM's Liebert SiteScan? How can companies benefit by adopting the Corporate Average Data Efficiency (CADE) metric? Which countries have the world's lowest and the highest electricity rates? How are companies adopting solar power? Write a report summarizing your findings, and include a table of links to Web sites that provide additional details.

❸ Social Networking

People who are at least 45 years old comprise approximately 34 percent of Internet users and quickly are becoming the largest demographic age group online. These "silver surfers" are online more than six hours per week and are making their presence known on online social networks. Monster's founder Jeff Taylor created Eons (eons.com), which is promoted as an "online gathering place for people lovin' life on the flip side of 50!" BoomerGirl Diary (boomergirl.com) and Not Over The Hill (notoverthehill.com) feature entertainment, health, financial, and travel information. Visit these Web sites and other online social networks aimed exclusively at a mature audience. Compare the content. Which groups and forums are present? What are the members' interests? Which topics are targeted toward this age group? Summarize the information you read and viewed.

❹ Blogs

The brain's 100 billion cells work best when both halves of the brain work together. The left half, often called the judicial mind, controls logical and reasoning tasks, and the right half, referred to as the creative mind, interprets and gives meaning to stimuli. Building right-brain skills is the key to achieving professional and personal success. Many blogs contain exercises and research on developing the right brain. They include The Thinking Blog (www.thethinkingblog.com), Creative Generalist (creativegeneralist.blogspot.com), Creative Think (blog.creativethink.com), and InnovationTools (innovationtools.com). Which creativity tools and strategies are suggested on these blogs? How are enterprises incorporating creative thinking? Which mind mapping and brainstorming resources are listed? Which creativity software and books are promoted? Summarize the information you read and viewed.

❺ Ethics in Action

Using grid computing, researchers at the University of Chicago, Northern Illinois University, Argonne National Laboratory, and the Max Planck Institute for Gravitational Physics in Germany simulated how black hole collisions affect gravity. Personal computers also can join millions of other computers throughout the world when they are connected to the Internet and have idle processing time. While grid computing turns inactive computer time into computational power, some critics believe some grid projects are immoral, may compromise intellectual property, and may undertake work that for-profit companies should perform. Visit Grid.org, the Open Grid Forum (ogf.org), the Globus Alliance (globus.org), and other Web sites to learn about current grid computing projects. Should for-profit companies pay grid participants for their computer time? Is data security compromised? Who sets standardization guidelines? How will companies track network resources? Write a report summarizing your findings, and include a table of links to Web sites that provide additional details.

Living Digitally

OUR DIGITAL LIVES are filled with a variety of products. We listen on portable media players to audio files we create or download. We record and view video content that matches our viewing interests. We play recorded files wherever and whenever we desire. We play games solo or with multiple friends across the globe. Our home networks link security, energy monitoring, and leisure activities throughout the house. Wherever we go in our lives, technology is a pervasive part of our daily existence.

Microsoft Xbox 360

PSPgo

3-D video display

avatar

Slingbox

Sony PlayStation 3

Nintendo Wii

flat-screen TV

head-mounte display

Rock Band

iPod/iPod touch

TiVo

igital products
our lives often
lude features that
erlap in various
tertainment and
me automation
tegories.

Audio

Video

Recording

Gaming

Digital Home

Nintendo DSi

video camera

speakers

chumby

smart phone

Studio Instruments software

Nero optical disc burning software

combination drive

Dolby logo

digital frames

Netflix

home automation dashboard

multi-room audio system

docking station

Audio

THE MUSIC INDUSTRY is a major part of our everyday lives, and digital music sales generate more than $10 billion each year. Audio files can be played on iPods and other portable media players and mobile devices. Musicians of all skill levels can create their own music with Rock Band and Guitar Hero handheld instruments.

Figure 1 Apple has sold hundreds of millions of iPods. The iPod accessory market has grown to a billion-dollar industry, with inventors developing earbuds, cases, and docking stations.

Figure 3 Rock the night away playing set lists from some of the biggest artists and bands of all times. Customize the concert experience by selecting venues and original band members or your own personalized superstars.

Figure 2 Music downloading services allow you to purchase individual tracks or entire albums and then download the music to a computer or portable media player. More than 500 downloading services are available; Apple iTunes and Amazon MP3 are the sales leaders.

Figure 4 Ray Dolby founded Dolby Laboratories in 1965. His company has become the world leader in defining high-quality products, including audio and surround sound in theaters, home entertainment systems, and broadcasting.

Video

WHETHER IN A COMFY CHAIR or on the go, watching television and movies has changed dramatically. Viewers download content and then watch the programs when and where they desire on devices ranging from large flat-screen display devices to compact smart phones. Glasses and 3-D displays add a new dimension to the viewing experience.

Figure 5 A multitude of video streaming devices is infiltrating the marketplace as companies expand their services to add subscribers and bring movies and television programs to homes via a broadband Internet connection. Apple TV takes control of your home theater system by streaming HD movies, television programs, iTunes music, podcasts, and photos to display devices.

Figure 6 Experience a private video viewing with a personal head-mounted display (HMD). Video glasses can be connected to a DVD player, iPod, or game console.

Figure 8 True 3-D video images can be seen on cell phones and video displays without special glasses or goggles. Applications include medical imaging, CAD drawings, mapping, and entertainment.

Figure 7 View your favorite television programs anywhere in the world as long as you have a broadband connection and a Slingbox. This device streams video and audio from your home to any Internet-connected device.

Figure 9 High-definition (HD) digital video recorders (DVRs), such as the TiVo, let you locate and record current and off-air digital broadcasts, pause and rewind live television programs, and create your own instant replays with slow motion.

Recording

WHETHER YOU ARE WORKING OUT at the gym or driving to Grandma's house for dinner, you might want to download or record your favorite audio, video, and photos to transport them from one location to another or upload them to share with friends and family. You also can record movies or television programs when you are not at home and then play them at your convenience on a home entertainment system or portable media player.

Figure 10
Use optical disc burning software to create optical discs quickly and easily with multiformat burners and rewritable drives to store your movies, photos, music, and digital data.

Figure 12 Turn your computer into a virtual bass guitar, drum set, electric piano, or string section with Cakewalk's Studio Instruments software. Then, record, edit, and mix your song created with these virtual and real instruments and create streaming music players and playlists on your Web site.

Figure 11
Capture video using your video camera and then, with the press of a button, upload recorded clips to social networking Web sites. Each minute, more than 20 hours of video are uploaded to YouTube.

Figure 13 Capture video of friends and family, upload the clips to your computer, and use video editing software to rearrange the sequence of events, add music and titles, and record narration.

Gaming

REVENUE GENERATED BY THE VIDEO GAMING INDUSTRY quickly is approaching $100 billion. The areas experiencing the fastest growth are online and mobile gaming as new game consoles and advanced networking become mainstream.

Figure 14 The three gaming consoles — Nintendo Wii, Sony PlayStation 3, and Microsoft Xbox 360 — offer a variety of game titles.

Figure 16 In a computer role-playing game (CRPG), players interact with one another and generally attempt to accomplish a quest. Massively multiplayer online games (MMOGs) unite millions of gamers worldwide.

Figure 17 Handheld game consoles have large, high-resolution screens and incredible sound to play audio and video files and can display photos. Bluetooth and Wi-Fi technology allows networked gaming and synchronizing with other handheld units or personal computers.

Figure 15 Gaming reaches all generations. The Wii game console's interactive quality appeals to players of all ages. The iPod touch's accelerometer, which detects movement and changes the display accordingly, and 3-D graphics immerse players in the action.

Figure 18 Outdoor treasure hunters use their GPS receivers and navigational skills to create and locate hidden caches throughout the world.

Digital Home

THE AVERAGE HOUSEHOLD has 21 consumer electronics devices, and many of them are linked via home networks and broadband connections that simplify our lives and provide entertainment in innovative ways. Digital music and video are recorded and streamed to multiple devices. Meanwhile, automation systems monitor security, energy usage, and room temperatures to provide optimal conditions.

Figure 19 Set-top boxes stream movies from the Web to your televisions, computers, and mobile devices. On average, Netflix ships approximately two million DVDs each day.

Figure 21 LED screens provide information about home electricity, gas, and water use, and they compare the rates with previous consumption.

Figure 20 Program an entire home to fit your lifestyle and needs. A home automation system can set room temperatures, open and close window shades, water the grass, watch for intruders, and play music to wake you or relax you to sleep.

Figure 22 Digital picture frames, some as large as 40 inches wide, are among the more popular consumer electronic devices; more than 3 million are sold each year. They provide a convenient method of displaying the billions of digital photos taken each day and may play songs and Web broadcasts.

Figure 23 The wireless chumby connects to the Internet and streams news, entertainment, sports scores, video clips, interactive games, photos, and hundreds of favorite widgets.

Computer technology impacts virtually every facet of our lives. From the largest media rooms to the smallest portable media players, we can watch our favorite television programs and movies any place at any time. We can browse the Web, play games with partners on the other side of the world, listen to music we created with handheld instruments, and have fun wherever life takes us. No matter where we are, our digital lives are filled with information and entertainment.

TUTORIAL 1

OBJECTIVES

Session 1.1
- Explore the history of the Internet, the Web, and HTML
- Compare the different versions of HTML
- Study the syntax of HTML tags and attributes
- Define a Web page head, body, and title
- Work with the HTML5 structural elements

Session 1.2
- Mark page headings, paragraphs, block quotes, and addresses
- Create unordered and ordered lists
- Apply an external style sheet to a Web page
- Run a JavaScript program
- Mark text-level elements including strong and emphasized text
- Insert inline images and line breaks
- Insert special characters from extended character sets

Getting Started with HTML5

Creating a Product Page for a Small Business

Case | *The J-Prop Shop*

Dave Vinet owns a small business called the J-Prop Shop that builds and sells circus props and equipment. Dave is looking to expand his business and his visibility by upgrading his Web site. Dave has already written the text for the Web site's home page and has generated some of the graphic images for it. He has come to you for help in designing a Web page and writing the code. Dave hopes to build on his Web page in the future as his business expands, so he would like you to write code that takes advantage of the latest Web standards, including HTML5. Your job will be to create a sample home page that Dave can use as a foundation for his new Web site.

STARTING DATA FILES

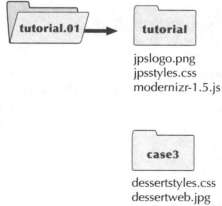

tutorial.01 → **tutorial**

jpslogo.png
jpsstyles.css
modernizr-1.5.js

review

basiclogo.png
basicstick.png
basicstyles.css
stick.txt
modernizr-1.5.js

case1

mhlogo.jpg
mhstyles.css
mhtxt.htm
modernizr-1.5.js

case2

macbeth.jpg
macbethtxt.htm
macstyles.css
modernizr-1.5.js

case3

dessertstyles.css
dessertweb.jpg
modernizr-1.5.js
torte.jpg
tortetxt.htm

case4

logo.jpg
smith.jpg
smith.txt

demo

cengage.jpg
demo.gif
demo_characters.htm
demo_html.htm
demo2.gif
modernizr-1.5.js

SESSION 1.1 VISUAL OVERVIEW

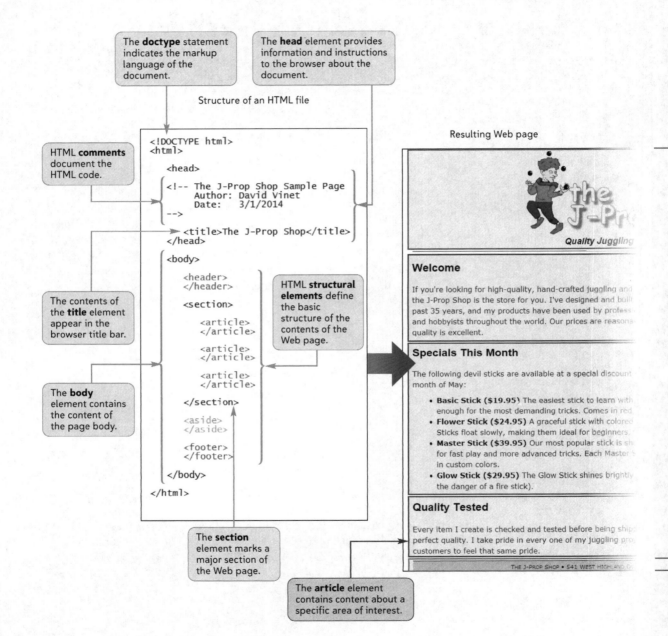

The **doctype** statement indicates the markup language of the document.

The **head** element provides information and instructions to the browser about the document.

Structure of an HTML file

HTML **comments** document the HTML code.

The contents of the **title** element appear in the browser title bar.

The **body** element contains the content of the page body.

```
<!DOCTYPE html>
<html>

    <head>

    <!-- The J-Prop Shop Sample Page
         Author: David Vinet
         Date:   3/1/2014
    -->

        <title>The J-Prop Shop</title>
    </head>

    <body>

        <header>
        </header>

        <section>

            <article>
            </article>

            <article>
            </article>

            <article>
            </article>

        </section>

        <aside>
        </aside>

        <footer>
        </footer>

    </body>

</html>
```

HTML **structural elements** define the basic structure of the contents of the Web page.

Resulting Web page

Welcome

If you're looking for high-quality, hand-crafted juggling and the J-Prop Shop is the store for you. I've designed and built past 35 years, and my products have been used by profess and hobbyists throughout the world. Our prices are reasona quality is excellent.

Specials This Month

The following devil sticks are available at a special discount month of May:

- **Basic Stick ($19.95)** The easiest stick to learn with enough for the most demanding tricks. Comes in red
- **Flower Stick ($24.95)** A graceful stick with colored Sticks float slowly, making them ideal for beginners.
- **Master Stick ($39.95)** Our most popular stick is sh for fast play and more advanced tricks. Each Master S in custom colors.
- **Glow Stick ($29.95)** The Glow Stick shines brightly the danger of a fire stick).

Quality Tested

Every item I create is checked and tested before being ship perfect quality. I take pride in every one of my juggling pro customers to feel that same pride.

THE J-PROP SHOP • 541 WEST HIGHLAND D

The **section** element marks a major section of the Web page.

The **article** element contains content about a specific area of interest.

THE STRUCTURE OF AN HTML5 DOCUMENT

The **head**er element contains an introduction to the page.

Markup Tags

Document elements are marked using **tags**.

```
<h2>Welcome</h2>
<p>If you're looking for high-
juggling and circus product
the store for you. I've des
for the past 35 years, and
used by professional entert
throughout the world. Our p
our quality is excellent.
</p>
```

Resulting Web page

Welcome

If you're looking for high-quali
the J-Prop Shop is the store fo
past 35 years, and my produc
and hobbyists throughout the
quality is excellent.

Two-sided tags mark elements that contain textual content or other elements

```
<h2>Welcome</h2>
```

opening tag element content closing tag

One-sided tags mark elements that contain no textual content

```
<br />
```

the J-Prop Shop
Props Quality Juggling and Circus Props

ucts, ted juggling and circus products,
ne esigned and built props for the
iners used by professional entertainers
 ices are reasonable and our

re special discount for the entire

y" tick to learn with, but "grippy"
blue. s. Comes in red, green, and blue.
wer tick with colored tassels. Flower
 l for beginners.

avier opular stick is shorter and heavier
able ks. Each Master Stick is available

thout k shines brightly at night (without

ssure efore being shipped out to assure
nt my my juggling props and I want my

Customer Comments

Here are a few select quotes from our happy family of customers and associates:

"I'm more than happy to recommend Dave Vinet's products. I came upon his work 10 years ago and was immediately impressed by his craftsmanship. He provides well-balanced and attractive props which are the perfect complement to my performances."
— Thomas Gage, Circus England

"Dave Vinet makes the best juggling equipment on the planet. Period."
— Douglas Pederson, Street-Wise Shows

"David has been my main supplier for 20 years. I have never had a problem with his equipment and his service is impeccable."
— Linda Unger, Linda & Louis

04210 1 WEST HIGHLAND DRIVE • AUBURN, ME 04210 • (207) 555 - 9001

The **footer** element contains address and summary information.

The **aside** element contains extra content on the page.

Exploring the History of the World Wide Web

Before you start creating a Web page for Dave, it will be helpful to first look at the history of the Web and the development of HTML. You'll start by reviewing networks and learn how they led to the creation of the World Wide Web.

Networks

A **network** is a structure that allows devices known as **nodes** or **hosts** to be linked together to share information and services. Hosts can include devices such as computers, printers, and scanners because they are all capable of sending and receiving data electronically over a network.

A host that provides information or a service is called a **server**. For example, a **print server** is a network host that provides printing services to the network; a **file server** is a host that provides storage space for saving and retrieving files. A computer or other device that receives a service is called a **client**. Networks can follow several different designs based on the relationship between the servers and the clients. One of the most commonly used designs is the **client-server network** in which several clients access information provided by one or more servers. You might be using such a network to access your data files for this tutorial.

Networks can also be classified based on the range they cover. A network confined to a small geographic area, such as within a building or department, is referred to as a **local area network** or **LAN**. A network that covers a wider area, such as several buildings or cities, is called a **wide area network** or **WAN**. Wide area networks typically consist of two or more interconnected local area networks.

The largest WAN in existence is the **Internet**, which incorporates an almost uncountable number of networks and hosts involving computers, mobile phones, PDAs, MP3 players, gaming systems, and television stations. Like many business owners, Dave uses the Internet to advertise his business to potential customers.

Locating Information on a Network

One of the biggest obstacles to effectively using the Internet is the network's sheer scope and size. Most of the early Internet tools required users to master a bewildering array of terms, acronyms, and commands. Because network users had to be well versed in computers and network technology, Internet use was limited to universities and the government. To make the Internet accessible to the general public, it needed to be easier to use. The solution turned out to be the World Wide Web.

The foundations for the **World Wide Web**, or the **Web** for short, were laid in 1989 by Timothy Berners-Lee and other researchers at the CERN nuclear research facility near Geneva, Switzerland. They needed an information system that would make it easy for their researchers to locate and share data on the CERN network with minimal training and support. To meet this need, they developed a system of hypertext documents that enabled users to easily navigate from one topic to another. **Hypertext** is a method of organization in which data sources are interconnected through a series of **links** or hyperlinks that users can activate to jump from one piece of information to another. Hypertext is ideally suited for the Internet because end users do not need to know where a particular document, information source, or service is located—they need to know only how to activate the link. The fact that the Internet and the World Wide Web are synonymous in many users' minds is a testament to the success of the hypertext approach.

Web Pages and Web Servers

Each document on the World Wide Web is referred to as a **Web page** and is stored on a **Web server**. When you access a Web page, a **Web browser** retrieves the page from its Web server and renders it on your computer or other device.

The earliest browsers, known as **text-based browsers**, were limited to displaying only text. Today's browsers are capable of handling text, images, audio, video, and interactive programs. In the early days of the Internet, Web browsing was limited to computers. Now browsers are installed on devices such as mobile phones, cars, handheld media devices, and gaming systems, to name only a few. How does a Web page work with so many combinations of browsers and devices? To understand, you need to look at how Web pages are created.

Introducing HTML

Web pages are text files written in **Hypertext Markup Language** (**HTML**). We've already discussed hypertext, but what is a markup language? A **markup language** is a language that describes the content and structure of a document by identifying, or **tagging**, different elements in the document. For example, this tutorial contains paragraphs, figure captions, page headings, and so forth; each of these items could be tagged as a distinct element using a markup language. Thus, HTML is a markup language that supports both hypertext and the tagging of distinct document elements.

The History of HTML

HTML evolved as the Web itself evolved. Thus, in order to fully appreciate the nuances of HTML, it's a good idea to review the language's history. The first popular markup language was the **Standard Generalized Markup Language** (**SGML**). Introduced in the 1980s, SGML is device- and system-independent, meaning that it can be applied to almost any type of document stored in almost any format. While powerful, SGML is also quite complex; for this reason, SGML is limited to those organizations that can afford the cost and overhead of maintaining complex SGML environments. However, SGML can also be used to create other markup languages that are tailored to specific tasks and are simpler to use and maintain. HTML is one of the languages created with SGML.

In the early years after HTML was created, no single organization was responsible for the language. Web developers were free to define and modify HTML in whatever ways they thought best. This led to incompatibilities between the various browsers and, as a result, Web page authors faced the challenge of writing HTML code that would satisfy different browsers and browser versions.

Ultimately, a group of Web designers and programmers called the **World Wide Web Consortium**, or the **W3C**, created a set of standards or specifications for all browser manufacturers to follow. The W3C has no enforcement power; but because using a uniform language is in everyone's best interest, the W3C's recommendations are usually followed, though not always immediately. For more information on the W3C and the services it offers, see its Web site at *www.w3.org*.

As HTML evolves, earlier features of the language are often **deprecated**, or phased out. While deprecated features might not be part of the current specification for HTML, that doesn't mean that you won't encounter them in your work—indeed, if you are maintaining older Web sites, you will often need to be able to interpret code from earlier versions of HTML.

XHTML and the Development of HTML5

Near the end of the 1990s, the W3C released the final specifications for the 4th version of HTML, called HTML 4, and began charting a course for the next version. The path chosen by the W3C was to reformulate HTML in terms of XML. **XML** (**Extensible Markup Language**) is a compact offshoot of SGML and is used to define new markup languages, known as **XML vocabularies**. A document based on an XML vocabulary is forced to obey specific rules for content and structure to avoid being rejected as invalid. By contrast, HTML allows for a wide variety in syntax between one HTML document and another. Another important aspect of XML is that several XML vocabularies can be combined within a single document, making it easier to extend XML into different areas of application.

The W3C developed an XML vocabulary that was a stricter version of HTML4, known as **XHTML** (**Extensible Hypertext Markup Language**). XHTML was designed to confront some of the problems associated with the various competing versions of HTML and to better integrate HTML with other markup languages. Because XHTML was an XML version of HTML, most of what Web designers used with HTML could be applied to XHTML with only a few modifications, and many tools and features associated with XML could be easily applied to XHTML.

By 2002, the W3C had released the specifications for XHTML 1.1. This version was intended to be only a minor upgrade on the way to **XHTML 2.0**, which would contain a set of XML vocabularies moving HTML into the future with robust support for multimedia, social networking, interactive Web forms, and other features needed by Web designers. One problem was that XHTML 2.0 would not be backward compatible with earlier versions of HTML and thus older Web sites could not be easily integrated with the proposed new standard.

Web designers rebelled at this development. In 2004, Ian Hickson, who was working for Opera Software at the time, proposed a different path. Hickson's proposal would have allowed for the creation of new Web applications while still maintaining backward compatibility with HTML 4. He argued that HTML was whatever the browser market determined it to be, and that trying to enforce a new specification that did not accommodate the needs and limitations of the market was a fruitless exercise.

Hickson's proposal was rejected by the W3C and, in response, a new group of Web designers and browser manufacturers formed the **Web Hypertext Application Technology Working Group (WHATWG)** with the mission to develop a rival version to XHTML 2.0, called **HTML5**. For several years, it was unclear which specification would represent the future of the Web; but by 2006, work on XHTML 2.0 had completely stalled. The W3C issued a new charter for an HTML Working Group to develop HTML5 as the next HTML specification. Work on XHTML 2.0 was halted in 2009, leaving HTML5 as the de facto standard for the next generation of HTML.

Figure 1-1	Versions of HTML

Version	Date	Description
HTML1.0	1989	The first public version of HTML.
HTML 2.0	1995	Added interactive elements including Web forms.
HTML 3.0	1996	A proposed replacement for HTML 2.0 that was never widely adopted.
HTML 3.2	1997	Included additional support for Web tables and expanded the options for interactive form elements and a scripting language.
HTML 4.01	1999	Added support for style sheets to give Web designers greater control over page layout and appearance, and provided support for multimedia elements such as audio and video. Current browsers support almost all of HTML 4.01.
XHTML 1.0	2001	A reformulation of HTML 4.01 in the XML language in order to provide enforceable standards for HTML content and to allow HTML to interact with other XML languages.
XHTML 1.1	2002	A minor update to XHTML 1.0 that allows for modularity and simplifies writing extensions to the language.
XHTML 2.0	discontinued	The follow-up version to XHTML 1.1 designed to fix some of the problems inherent in HTML 4.01 syntax. Work on this version was discontinued in 2009 due to lack of browser support.
HTML 5.0	In development	An update to HTML 4.01 that provides support for a variety of new features including semantic page elements, column layout, form validation, offline storage, and enhanced multimedia.
XHTML 5.0	In development	A version of HTML 5.0 written under the XML language; unlike XHTML 2.0, XHTML 5.0 will be backward compatible with XHTML 1.1.

Figure 1-1 summarizes the various versions of HTML that have been developed over the past 20 years. You may be wondering how on Earth anything can be written with so many versions of HTML to consider. At the time of this writing, you can write your code following the standards of HTML 4.01 or XHTML 1.1 and be assured that it will be supported by all major browsers. Many features of HTML5 are also being rapidly adopted by the market even as work continues on developing the language. HTML5 is the future, but the challenges for Web designers today lie in knowing which parts of HTML5 are supported by which browsers, and in developing strategies for supporting older browsers even as HTML5 is being implemented.

In this book you'll use HTML5 code for those features that have already achieved support among current browsers, but you'll also learn the standards used for HTML 4.01 and XHTML 1.1 and practice writing code that will support both current and older browsers.

HTML and Style Sheets

HTML marks the different parts of a document, but it does not indicate how document content should be displayed by browsers. This is a necessary facet of HTML because a Web page author has no control over what device will actually view his or her document. An end user might be using a large-screen television monitor, a mobile phone, or even a device that renders Web pages in Braille or in aural speech.

For this reason, the exact appearance of each page element is described in a separate document known as a **style sheet**. Each browser has its own **internal style sheet** that specifies the appearance of different HTML elements. For example, content that is marked as containing the text of an address is rendered by most Web browsers in italic, while major headings usually appear in large bold-faced fonts.

A Web page author can also create a style sheet that takes precedence over the internal style sheets of browsers. In addition, an author can create multiple style sheets for different output devices: one for rendering a page on a computer screen, another for printed output, and another for rendering the page aurally. In each case, the markup of the document content is the same, but the presentation is determined by the style sheet.

Tools for Creating HTML Documents

Because HTML documents are simple text files, you can create them using nothing more than a basic text editor such as Windows Notepad. Other software programs that enable you to create documents in different formats, such as Microsoft Word or Adobe Acrobat, include tools to convert their documents into HTML for quick and easy publishing on the Web.

If you intend to create a large Web site incorporating dozens of Web pages, you should invest in specialized Web publishing software to manage all of the code and extended features of your site. Programs such as Adobe Dreamweaver and Microsoft Expression Web are among the leaders in this field.

Since this book is focused on the HTML language itself and not how to work with different software programs, you'll need nothing more than a text editor and a Web browser to complete the assignments that follow.

Entering Elements and Attributes

Now that you've had a chance to review a brief history of the Web and the role of HTML in its development, you are ready to write your first HTML document for the J-Prop Shop. You'll start by studying the rules for entering HTML code.

Introducing HTML Tags

An HTML document is composed of **elements** that represent distinct items in the Web page, such as a paragraph, the page heading, or even the entire body of the page itself. Each element is marked within the HTML file by one or more **tags**. If an element contains text or another element, it is marked using a **two-sided tag set** in which an **opening tag** and a **closing tag** enclose the element content. The syntax of a two-sided tag set is

```
<element>content</element>
```

where *element* is the name of the element and *content* is the content of the element. For example, the following code marks a paragraph using a two-sided tag set:

```
<p>Welcome to the J-Prop Shop.</p>
```

In this example, the `<p>` tag marks the beginning of the paragraph, the text *Welcome to the J-Prop Shop.* is the content of the paragraph element, and the `</p>` tag marks the end of the paragraph. Elements can also contain other elements. For example, in the code

```
<p>Welcome to <em>Dave's Devil Sticks</em>.</p>
```

the paragraph tags enclose both the text of the paragraph and the tag set `<em> ... </em>`, which is used to mark content that should be treated by the browser as emphasized text. Note that the `<em>` tag set must be completely enclosed, or **nested**, within the `<p>` tags. It's improper to have tags overlap as in the following code sample:

```
<p>Welcome to <em>Dave's Devil Sticks.</p></em>
```

In this example, the closing `</em>` tag is placed *after* the closing `</p>` tag, which is improper because one element must be completely contained within another.

An element that does not enclose content is an **empty element** and it is marked with a **one-sided tag** using the syntax

```
<element />
```

where `element` is the name of the element. For example, you can mark a line break using the `br` element, which has the following syntax:

```
<br />
```

Since empty elements don't contain content, they're often employed to send directives to browsers regarding how a page should be rendered. A browser encountering the `br` element would insert a line break, causing the text of the next element in the document to be placed on a new line.

Specifying an Element Attribute

In addition to content, elements also support **attributes** that specify the use, the behavior, and in some cases the appearance of an element. Attribute values don't appear in the rendered Web page; rather, they provide information to the browser about the properties of the element.

To add an attribute to an element, you insert the attribute within the element's opening tag. For a two-sided tag, the syntax is:

```
<element attribute1="value1" attribute2="value2" ...>
   content
</element>
```

Attributes are added to one-sided tags in the same way:

```
<element attribute1="value1" attribute2="value2" ... />
```

In these examples, `attribute1`, `attribute2`, etc. are the names of attributes associated with the element, and `value1`, `value2`, etc. are the values of those attributes. For instance, the following code adds the `id` attribute to a paragraph marked with the `p` element:

```
<p id="opening">Welcome to the J-Prop Shop.</p>
```

A browser interpreting this code would recognize that the text *Welcome to the J-Prop Shop.* should be treated as a paragraph and given the id value *opening*.

REFERENCE

Adding an Attribute to an Element

• To add an element attribute, use the format

```
<element attribute1="value1"
        attribute2="value2" ...>content</element>
```

where `attribute1`, `attribute2`, etc. are the names of attributes associated with the element, and `value1`, `value2`, etc. are the values of those attributes.

White Space and HTML

Since an HTML file is a text file, it's composed of text characters and white space. **White space** includes the blank spaces, tabs, and line breaks found within the file. As far as a browser is concerned, there is no difference between a blank space, a tab, or a line break. Browsers also ignore consecutive occurrences of white space, collapsing extra

white space characters into a single blank space. Thus, browsers treat the following para-
graph elements in the same way:

```
<p>Welcome to the J-Prop Shop.</p>

<p>
    Welcome to the J-Prop Shop.
</p>

<p>Welcome
to the J-Prop Shop.</p>

<p>Welcome    to    the    J-Prop    Shop.</p>
```

Because HTML handles white space in this way, you can make your code easier for
others to read by indenting lines and adding extra blank lines to separate one tag from
another in the file.

INSIGHT

HTML5 and XHTML Syntax

The rules that govern how code should be entered are called **syntax**. The way that HTML
has been implemented by most browsers through the Web's history has allowed for
minor variations in syntax. One reason for the success of the Web is that HTML has made
it easy for non-programmers to write and edit code without being ensnarled by syntax
violations.

On the other hand, XHTML forces strict syntax on page authors. If an author's code
does not follow the rules, browsers do not render the page. One advantage of this
approach is that it forces authors to write clear and more concise code; indeed, one of
the driving forces behind the development of XHTML was the desire to clean up some of
the messy and inconsistent code found on the Web.

For example, XHTML requires that all tag names be placed in lowercase letters and
that all attribute values be enclosed within quotation marks. HTML allows either upper-
case or lowercase tag names and does not require attribute values to be quoted. In
addition, XHTML requires that every one-sided tag be entered with a closing slash: for
instance, the br element must be entered as `<br />` for XHTML compatibility. Most
browsers, however, accept HTML code in which one-sided tags are entered without clos-
ing slashes; thus, the br element could be entered either as `<br>` or as `<br />`.

HTML5 supports the informal standards accepted by most browsers and will continue
to allow for minor variations in syntax. However, it is still good practice to write all code
to be XHTML compliant whenever possible, since it will allow that code to be easily
transferred to XHTML environments if necessary.

Exploring the Structure of an HTML Document

The structure of an HTML document consists of different elements nested within each
other in a hierarchy of elements. The top element in that hierarchy is the **html element**,
which contains all of the other elements within an HTML file. Directly below the html
element in the hierarchy are the head and body elements. The **head element** contains
general information about the document—for example, the document's title, or a list of

keywords that would aid search engines in directing interested users to the page. The **body element** contains all of the content that appears in the rendered Web page. Thus, the general structure of an HTML file is

```
<html>
    <head>
        head content
    </head>
    <body>
        body content
    </body>
</html>
```

where *head content* and *body content* are the content you want to place within the document's head and body. Note that the `body` element is always placed after the `head` element.

The Document Type Declaration

Prior to the opening `<html>` tag, many HTML files also include a **Document Type Declaration**, or **doctype**, to indicate the type of markup language used in the document. The doctype is used by **validators**, which are programs that examine document code to ensure that it meets all the syntax requirements of the specified language. All XHTML files require a doctype because those documents must be validated against a set of standards.

Most current browsers also use the presence or absence of a doctype to decide which mode they should use to render a document in a process known as **doctype switching**. If a doctype is included, such browsers render the Web page in **standards mode**, in accordance with the most current specifications of the language. If no doctype is provided, these browsers render the document in **quirks mode** based on practices followed in the 1990s. The differences can be striking. Figure 1-2 shows an example of two documents rendered by Internet Explorer under standards mode and quirks mode. The only difference in the code between these two documents is the presence or absence of a doctype, but the browser renders the two documents very differently.

Figure 1-2 **A Web page rendered in standards mode and quirks mode**

Standards mode

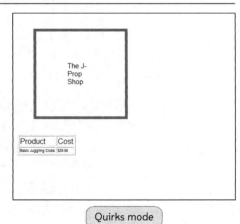

Quirks mode

Different HTML versions have different doctypes. The doctype for HTML 4.01 is:

```
<!DOCTYPE HTML PUBLIC "-//W3C//DTD HTML 4.01/EN"
   "http://www.w3.org/TR/html4/strict.dtd">
```

The doctype for XHTML is:

```
<!DOCTYPE html PUBLIC "-//W3C//DTD XHTML 1.0 Strict//EN"
   "http://www.w3.org/TR/xhtml1/DTD/xhtml1-strict.dtd">
```

Finally, the doctype for HTML5 is much simpler than what was required for HTML 4.01 or XHTML:

```
<!DOCTYPE html>
```

HTML5 documents should always be opened in standards mode because they are based on the latest specifications for the HTML language.

You can learn more about standards mode and quirks mode by searching the Web for examples of the differences between the two modes.

Creating the Initial Document

Now that you've seen the basic structure of an HTML document, you are ready to begin creating the sample Web page for Dave's Web site.

REFERENCE

Creating the Basic Structure of an HTML Document

Enter the HTML tags

```
doctype
<html>
   <head>
      head content
   </head>
   <body>
      body content
   </body>
</html>
```

where *doctype* is the Document Type Declaration, and *head content* and *body content* are the content of the document's head and body.

You can start creating Dave's Web page using a basic editor such as Windows Notepad. Since Dave wants his document to be based on HTML5, you'll use the HTML5 doctype in your file.

To create the basic structure of an HTML document:

▶ **1.** Start your text editor, opening a blank text document.

Trouble? If you don't know how to start or use your text editor, ask your instructor or technical support person for help. Note that some editors do not save files in text file format by default, so check your editor's documentation to ensure that you are creating a basic text document.

Make sure you include the exclamation point (!) within the doctype; otherwise, browsers will not recognize the doctype.

2. Type the following lines of code in your document. Press the **Enter** key after each line. Press the **Enter** key twice for a blank line between lines of code. See Figure 1-3.

```
<!DOCTYPE html>
<html>

    <head>
    </head>

    <body>
    </body>

</html>
```

Figure 1-3	Basic structure of an HTML file

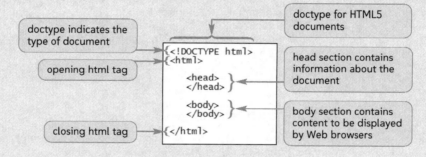

3. Save the file as **jprop.htm** in the tutorial.01\tutorial folder included with your Data Files.

Trouble? If you are using the Windows Notepad text editor to create your HTML file, make sure you don't save the file with the extension *.txt*, which is the default file extension for Notepad. Instead, save the file with the file extension *.htm* or *.html*. Using the incorrect file extension might make the file unreadable to Web browsers, which require file extensions of *.htm* or *.html*.

TIP

To make it easier to link to your Web pages, follow the Internet convention of naming HTML files and folders using only lowercase letters with no spaces.

Now that you've entered the basic structure of your HTML file, you can start entering the content of the head element.

Marking the Head Element

In general, the head element is where you provide browsers with information about your document. This can include the page's title, the location of any style sheets used with the document, the location of any programs that browsers should run when they load the page, and information for use by search engines to aid users in locating the Web site.

Defining the Page Title

The first element you'll add to the head of Dave's document is the title element, which has the syntax

```
<title>document title</title>
```

where *document title* is the text of the document title. The document title is not displayed within the page, but is usually displayed in a browser's title bar or on a browser

tab. The document title is also used by search engines like Google or Yahoo! when compiling an index of search results.

TIP

Indent your markup tags and insert extra blank spaces as shown in this book to make your code easier to read. These indentations and spaces do not affect how the page is rendered by browsers.

To add a title to your Web page:

1. Click at the end of the opening <head> tag, and then press the **Enter** key to insert a new line in your text editor.

2. Press the **Spacebar** several times to indent the new line of code, and then type <title>The J-Prop Shop</title> as shown in Figure 1-4.

Figure 1-4 Specifying the page title

```
<!DOCTYPE html>
<html>

    <head>
       <title>The J-Prop Shop</title>
    </head>

    <body>
    </body>

</html>
```

text will appear in browser title bar or on browser tab

Adding Comments

As you write your HTML file, you can add notes or comments about your code. These comments might include the name of the document's author and the date the document was created. Such notes are not intended to be displayed by browsers, but are instead used to help explain your code to yourself and others. To add notes or comments, insert a **comment tag** using the syntax

```
<!-- comment -->
```

where *comment* is the text of the comment or note. For example, the following code inserts a comment describing the page you'll create for Dave's business:

```
<!-- Sample page for the J-Prop Shop -->
```

A comment can also be spread out over several lines as follows:

```
<!-- Sample page for the J-Prop Shop.
    Created by Dave Vinet -->
```

Because they are ignored by the browser, comments can be added anywhere within the html element.

REFERENCE

Adding an HTML Comment

To insert an HTML comment anywhere within your document, enter

```
<!-- comment -->
```

where *comment* is the text of the HTML comment.

You'll add a comment to the *jprop.htm* file, identifying the author and purpose of this document.

To add a comment to the document head:

1. Click at the end of the opening `<head>` tag, and then press the **Enter** key to insert a new line in your text editor directly above the opening `<title>` tag.

2. Type the following lines of code as shown in Figure 1-5:

```
<!-- The J-Prop Shop Sample Page
     Author: your name
     Date:   the date
-->
```

where *your name* is your name and *the date* is the current date.

Figure 1-5 Adding comments to the HTML file

```
<!DOCTYPE html>
<html>

   <head>
      <!-- The J-Prop Shop Sample Page
           Author: David Vinet
           Date:   3/1/2014
      -->
      <title>The J-Prop Shop</title>
   </head>

   <body>
   </body>

</html>
```

multi-line comment describing the document

Displaying an HTML File

As you continue modifying the HTML code, you should occasionally view the page with your Web browser to verify that you have not introduced any errors. You might even want to view the results using different browsers to check for compatibility. In this book, Web pages are displayed using the Windows Internet Explorer 9 browser. Be aware that if you are using a different browser or a different operating system, you might see slight differences in the layout and appearance of the page.

To view Dave's Web page:

1. Save your changes to the **jprop.htm** file.

2. Start your Web browser. You do not need to be connected to the Internet to view local files stored on your computer.

 Trouble? If you start your browser and are not connected to the Internet, you might get a warning message. Click the OK button to ignore the message and continue.

3. After your browser loads its home page, open the **jprop.htm** file from the tutorial.01\tutorial folder.

 Trouble? If you're not sure how to open a local file with your browser, check for an Open or Open File command under the browser's File menu. If you are still having problems accessing the *jprop.htm* file, talk to your instructor or technical resource person.

Your browser displays the Web page shown in Figure 1-6. Note that in this case, the page title appears in the browser tab; in other cases, it will appear in the browser's title bar. The page itself is empty because you have not yet added any content to the body element.

Figure 1-6 Viewing the initial HTML file in a Web browser

document title appears in the browser tab

no content appears in the page body

Converting an HTML Document into XHTML

INSIGHT

There is considerable overlap between HTML and XHTML. You can quickly change an HTML document into an XHTML document just by altering the first three lines of code. To convert an HTML file into an XHTML file, replace the doctype and the opening `<html>` tag with the following:

```
<?xml version="1.0" encoding="UTF-8" standalone="no" ?>
<!DOCTYPE html PUBLIC "-//W3C//DTD XHTML 1.0 Strict//EN"
   "http://www.w3.org/TR/xhtml1/DTD/xhtml1-strict.dtd">
<html xmlns="http://www.w3.org/1999/xhtml">
```

Since XHTML is an XML vocabulary, the first line notifies browsers that the document is an XML file. The version number—1.0—tells the browser that the file is written in XML 1.0. The second line provides the doctype for an XHTML document written under a strict interpretation of XHTML syntax. The third line of the file contains the opening `<html>` tag. In XHTML, the `<html>` tag must include what is known as a **namespace declaration** indicating that any markup tags in the document should, by default, be considered part of the XHTML language. Because XML documents can contain a mixture of several different vocabularies, the namespace declaration is necessary to specify the default language of the document. With these three lines in place, browsers will recognize the file as an XHTML document.

Defining the Structure of the Page Body

Now that you've marked the document head and inserted a page title, you'll turn to the contents of the body of the Web page. It's always a good idea to plan your Web page before you start coding it. You can do this by drawing a sketch or by creating a sample document within a word processor. Your preparatory work can weed out textual errors or point to potential problems in your page layout. In this case, Dave has already drawn up a flyer that he's passed out at juggling and circus conventions. Figure 1-7 shows the handout, which provides information about Dave's company and his products.

Figure 1-7	Dave's flyer

Welcome

If you're looking for high-quality, hand-crafted juggling and circus products, the J-Prop Shop is the store for you. I've designed and built props for the past 35 years, and my products have been used by professional entertainers and hobbyists throughout the world. Our prices are reasonable and our quality is excellent.

Specials This Month

The following devil sticks are available at a special discount for the entire month of May:

- **Basic Stick ($19.95)** The easiest stick to learn with, but "grippy" enough for the most demanding tricks. Comes in red, green, and blue.
- **Flower Stick ($24.95)** A graceful stick with colored tassels. Flower Sticks float slowly, making them ideal for beginners.
- **Master Stick ($39.95)** Our most popular stick is shorter and heavier for fast play and more advanced tricks. Each Master Stick is available in custom colors.
- **Glow Stick ($29.95)** The Glow Stick shines brightly at night (without the danger of a fire stick).

Quality Tested

Every item I create is checked and tested before being shipped out to assure perfect quality. I take pride in every one of my juggling props and I want my customers to feel that same pride.

Customer Comments

Here are a few select quotes from our happy family of customers and associates:

"I'm more than happy to recommend Dave Vinet's products. I came upon his work 10 years ago and was immediately impressed by his craftsmanship. He provides well-balanced and attractive props which are the perfect complement to my performances."
— *Thomas Gage, Circus England*

"Dave Vinet makes the best juggling equipment on the planet. Period."
— *Douglas Pederson, Street-Wise Shows*

"David has been my main supplier for 20 years. I have never had a problem with his equipment and his service is impeccable."
— *Linda Unger, Linda & Louis*

THE J-PROP SHOP • 541 WEST HIGHLAND DRIVE • AUBURN, ME 04210 • (207) 555 - 9001

Dave's flyer contains several elements that are common to many Web pages, as shown in Figure 1-8. A header displays the company's logo and a footer displays contact information for the J-Prop Shop. The main section, which describes Dave's business, includes several subsections, also known as articles. A second section that appears as a sidebar displays quotes from some J-Prop customers.

Figure 1-8	Structure of Dave's Web page

Working with HTML5 Structural Elements

Each of these parts of Dave's document can be marked using HTML5 **structural elements**, which are the elements that define the major sections of a Web page. Figure 1-9 describes some of these elements.

Figure 1-9	HTML5 structural elements

Structural Element	Description
article	A subsection covering a single topic
aside	Content containing tangential or side issues to the main topic of the page
footer	Content placed at the bottom of the page
header	Content placed at the top of the page
nav	A navigation list of hypertext links
section	A major topical area in the page

For example, to mark the header of your Web page, you would enter a `header` element within the page body, using the syntax

```
<header>
    header content
</header>
```

where *header content* is the page content that you want displayed within the page header. One of the reasons we want to define these structural elements is that we can write styles for them and define the layout of the Web page content.

REFERENCE

Marking Structural Elements in HTML5

- To mark the page header, use the `header` element.
- To mark the page footer, use the `footer` element.
- To mark a main section of page content, use the `section` element.
- To mark a sidebar, use the `aside` element.
- To mark an article, use the `article` element.

Based on Dave's sample document shown in Figure 1-8, you'll add the `header`, `section`, `aside`, and `footer` structural elements to your HTML file.

To insert the HTML5 structural elements:

1. Return to the **jprop.htm** file in your text editor.

2. Within the `body` element, insert the following tags as shown in Figure 1-10:

```
<header>
</header>

<section>
</section>

<aside>
</aside>

<footer>
</footer>
```

Figure 1-10 **Inserting structural elements**

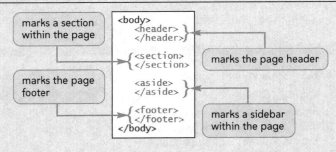

3. Save your changes to the file.

Structural elements can also be nested within one another. In the structure of Dave's page from Figure 1-8, notice that the section element contains three article elements. Add this content to your HTML file by nesting three `article` elements within the `section` element.

To add three article elements:

1. Within the `section` element, insert the following code as shown in Figure 1-11:

```
<article>
</article>

<article>
</article>

<article>
</article>
```

Figure 1-11 **Inserting nested elements**

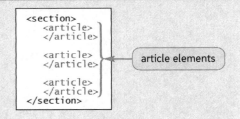

2. Save your changes to the file.

Marking a Section with the `div` Element

The structural elements are part of the current specifications for HTML5, but they are not part of HTML 4.01 or XHTML. Pages written to those languages instead use the **div element** to identify different page divisions. The syntax of the `div` element is

```
<div id="id">
   content
</div>
```

where *id* is a unique name assigned to the division and *content* is page content contained within the division. While not required, the id attribute is useful to distinguish one `div` element from another. This becomes particularly important if you apply different styles to different page divisions.

Figure 1-12 shows how the same page layout marked up using structural elements under HTML5 would be marked up in HTML 4.01 using the `div` element.

Figure 1-12 **Structural elements in HTML5 and HTML 4.01**

HTML5

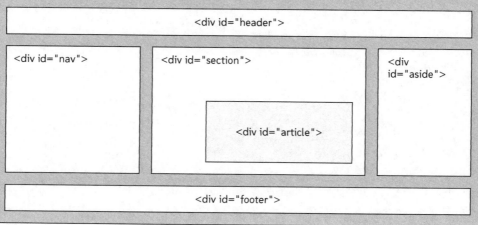

HTML 4.01

You can use either HTML5's structural elements or HTML 4.01's `div` elements to identify the major sections of your document. The HTML5 approach is preferred because it represents the future standard of the Web, and structural elements are more descriptive than the generic `div` element. One problem with the `div` element is that there are no rules for id names. One Web designer might identify the page heading with the id name *header* while another designer might use *heading* or *top*. This makes it harder for Web search engines to identify the main topics of interest in each Web page.

PROSKILLS

Written Communication: Writing Effective HTML Code

Part of writing good HTML code is being aware of the requirements of various browsers and devices, as well as understanding the different versions of the language. Here are a few guidelines for writing good HTML code:

- *Become well versed in the history of HTML and the various versions of HTML and XHTML.* Unlike other languages, HTML's history does impact how you write your code.
- *Know your market.* Do you have to support older browsers, or have your clients standardized on one particular browser or browser version? Will your Web pages be viewed on a single device such as a computer, or do you have to support a variety of devices?
- *Test your code on several different browsers and browser versions.* Don't assume that if your page works in one browser it will work in other browsers, or even in earlier versions of the same browser. Also check on the speed of the connection. A large file that performs well with a high-speed connection might be unusable with a dial-up connection.
- *Read the documentation on the different versions of HTML and XHTML at the W3C Web site and keep up to date with the latest developments in the language.*

In general, any HTML code that you write should be compatible with the current versions of the following browsers: Internet Explorer (Windows), Firefox (Windows and Macintosh), Safari (Windows and Macintosh), Chrome (Windows and Macintosh), and Opera (Windows and Macintosh). In addition, you should also view your pages on a variety of devices including laptops, mobile phones, and tablets. To effectively communicate with customers and users, you need to make sure your Web site is always readable.

At this point, you've created the basic framework of Dave's Web page. In the next session, you'll insert the page content and learn how to apply a visual style to that content to create a nicely formatted Web page. If you want to take a break before starting the next session, you can close any open files or applications.

REVIEW

Session 1.1 Quick Check

1. What is a markup language?
2. What is XHTML? How does XHTML differ from HTML?
3. What is the W3C? What is the WHATWG?
4. What is a doctype? What are two uses of the doctype?
5. What is incorrect about the syntax of the following code?

```
<p>Welcome to the <em>J-Prop Shop</p></em>
```

6. What is white space? How does HTML treat consecutive occurrences of white space?
7. What structural element would you use to mark a sidebar?
8. What structural element would you use to mark the page footer?

SESSION 1.2 VISUAL OVERVIEW

The **h2** element marks a heading.

HTML code

Resulting Web page

```
<h2>Welcome</h2>
<p>If you're looking for high-qu
     juggling and circus products,
     the store for you. I've desig
     for the past 35 years, and my
     used by professional entertai
     throughout the world. Our pri
     our quality is excellent.
</p>
```

The **p** element marks a paragraph.

The **ul** element marks an unordered list.

```
<ul>
     <li><strong>Basic Stick ($19
          The easiest stick to lea
          for the most demanding t
          and blue.
     </li>
     <li><strong>Flower Stick ($2
          A graceful stick with co
          float slowly, making the
     </li>
     <li><strong>Master Stick ($3
          Our most popular stick i
          fast play and more advan
          is available in custom c
     </li>
     <li><strong>Glow Stick ($29.
          The Glow Stick shines br
          the danger of a fire sti
     </li>
</ul>
```

The **li** element marks an item in the list.

The **strong** element is a text-level element that marks strong or bold text.

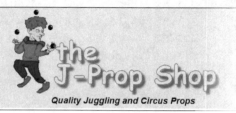

Welcome

If you're looking for high-quality, hand-crafted juggling and circus products, the J-Prop Shop is the store for you. I've designed and built props for the past 35 years, and my products have been used by professional entertainers and hobbyists throughout the world. Our prices are reasonable and our quality is excellent.

Specials This Month

The following devil sticks are available at a special discount for the entire month of May:

- **Basic Stick ($19.95)** The easiest stick to learn with, but "grippy" enough for the most demanding tricks. Comes in red, green, and blue.
- **Flower Stick ($24.95)** A graceful stick with colored tassels. Flower Sticks float slowly, making them ideal for beginners.
- **Master Stick ($39.95)** Our most popular stick is shorter and heavier for fast play and more advanced tricks. Each Master Stick is available in custom colors.
- **Glow Stick ($29.95)** The Glow Stick shines brightly at night (without the danger of a fire stick).

Quality Tested

Every item I create is checked and tested before being shipped out to assure perfect quality. I take pride in every one of my juggling props and I want my customers to feel that same pride.

THE J-PROP SHOP • 541 WEST HIGHLAND DRIVE • AUBURN, ME 04210 • [207] 555 - 9

The **address** element marks an address or contact info.

```
<address>The J-Prop Shop &bull;
          541 West Highland Drive &bull;
          Auburn, ME 04210 &bull;
          (207) 555 - 9001
</address>
```

The **•** entity represents the bullet character.

PAGE CONTENT ELEMENTS

HTML code

The **hgroup** element groups main headings and subheadings.

The **img** element is used to insert images into the Web page.

```
<hgroup>
    <h1>
        <img src="jpslogo.png" alt="The J-Prop Shop" />
    </h1>
    <h2>
        Quality Juggling and Circus Props
    </h2>
</hgroup>
```

```
<blockquote>
    <p>"I'm more than happy to reco
        products. I came upon his wo
        was immediately impressed by
        He provides well-balanced an
        props which are the perfect
        performances."
    <br />
    — <cite>Thomas Gage, C
    </p>
```

The **blockquote** element marks large blocks of quoted material.

The **cite** element marks a citation.

The **—** entity represents the em-dash character.

A page rendered with the default browser style sheet

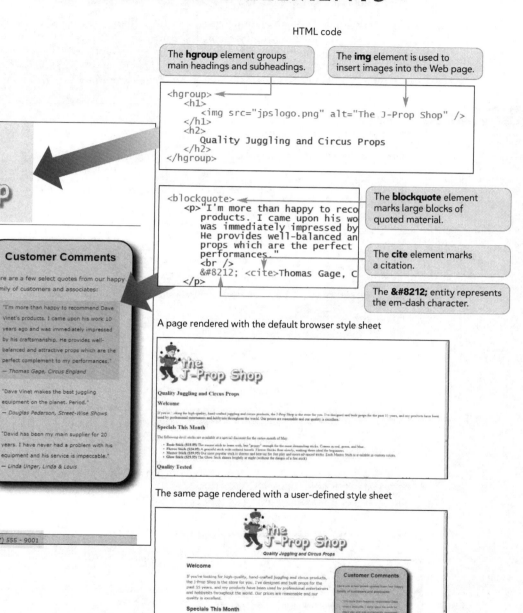

The same page rendered with a user-defined style sheet

```
<link href="jpsstyles.css" rel="stylesheet" type="text/css" />
```

The **link** element connects the Web page to the style sheet.

The href attribute indicates the name of the style sheet file.

The type attribute indicates the language of the style sheet.

Working with Grouping Elements

You're now ready to begin entering content into the body of Dave's Web page. The first elements you'll add are **grouping elements**, which are elements that contain content that is viewed as a distinct block within the Web page. Paragraphs, which were presented in the last session, are one example of a grouping element, as are page divisions marked using the div element. Figure 1-13 lists some of the commonly used grouping elements.

Figure 1-13	Grouping elements

Grouping Element	Description
address	Contact information (usually rendered as *italicized* text)
blockquote	An extended quotation (usually indented from the left and right margins)
dd	A definition from a description list
div	A generic grouping element
dl	A description list
dt	A definition term from a description list
figure	A figure or illustration (HTML5 only)
figcaption	The caption of a figure, which must be nested within the figure element (HTML5 only)
h*n*	A heading, where *n* is a value from 1 to 6, with h1 as the most prominent heading and h6 the least prominent (usually displayed in **bold** text)
li	A list item from an ordered or unordered list
ol	An ordered list
p	A paragraph
pre	Preformatted text, retaining all white space and special characters (usually displayed in a `fixed width` font)
ul	An unordered list

To explore how grouping elements are typically rendered by your Web browser, a demo page has been prepared for you.

To open the HTML Tags demo page:

1. Use your browser to open the **demo_html.htm** file from the tutorial.01\demo folder.

2. If your browser prompts you to allow code from the Web page to be run, click the **Allow blocked content** button.

Marking Content Headings

The first grouping elements you'll explore are **heading elements**, which contain the text of main headings on a Web page. They're often used for introducing new topics or for dividing the page into topical sections. The syntax to mark a heading element is

```
<hn>content</hn>
```

where *n* is an integer from 1 to 6. Content marked with <h1> tags is considered a major heading, and is usually displayed in large bold text. Content marked with <h2> through <h6> tags is used for subheadings, and is usually displayed in progressively smaller bold text.

Marking Grouping Content

- To mark a heading, enter
 `<hn>content</hn>`
 where *n* is an integer from 1 to 6 and *content* is the text of the heading.
- To mark a paragraph, enter
 `<p>content</p>`
- To mark a block quote, enter
 `<blockquote>content</blockquote>`

To see how these headings appear on your computer, use the demo page.

To view heading elements:

1. Click in the blue box in the lower-left corner of the demo page, type `<h1>The J-Prop Shop</h1>` and then press the **Enter** key to go to a new line.

2. Type `<h2>Quality Juggling and Circus Props</h2>`.

3. Click the **Preview Code** button located below the blue code window. Your browser displays a preview of how this code would appear in your Web browser (see Figure 1-14).

Figure 1-14 Previewing h1 and h2 headings

h1 and h2 headings

click to preview the HTML code

Preview Code

h1 and h2 headings as rendered by the browser

Trouble? If you are using a browser other than Internet Explorer 9 running on Windows 7, your screen might look slightly different from that shown in Figure 1-14.

4. To see how an h3 heading would look, change the opening tag for the store description from `<h2>` to `<h3>` and change the closing tag from `</h2>` to `</h3>`. Click the **Preview Code** button again.

Your browser renders the code again, this time with the store information displayed in a smaller font. If you continued to change the heading element from h3 to each of the elements down to h6, you would see the second line in the Preview box get progressively smaller.

It's important not to treat markup tags as simply a way of formatting the Web page. The h1 through h6 elements are used to identify headings, but the exact appearance of these headings depends on the browser and the device being used. While most browsers display an h1 heading in a larger font than an h2 heading, remember that the headings might not even be displayed at all. A screen reader, for example, doesn't display text, but rather conveys the presence of an h1 heading with increased volume or with special emphasis preceded by an extended pause.

Now that you've seen how to mark page headings, you can add them to Dave's Web page. The first heading Dave wants to add is an h1 heading containing the company's name. He also wants you to insert h2 headings in several places—as titles for the three articles on the page, as a title for the sidebar containing the customer comments, and as a subheading to the main heading on the page.

To add headings to Dave's document:

1. Return to the **jprop.htm** file in your text editor.

 Trouble? If you are using the Macintosh TextEdit program, you must select the *Ignore rich text commands* check box when reopening the file.

2. Within the header element, insert the following tags:

   ```
   <h1>The J-Prop Shop</h1>
   <h2>Quality Juggling and Circus Props</h2>
   ```

3. Within the first article element, insert the following h2 heading:

   ```
   <h2>Welcome</h2>
   ```

4. Within the second article element, insert

   ```
   <h2>Specials This Month</h2>
   ```

5. Within the third and final article element, insert

   ```
   <h2>Quality Tested</h2>
   ```

6. Finally, within the aside element, insert

   ```
   <h2>Customer Comments</h2>
   ```

 Figure 1-15 highlights the revised code in the file.

Figure 1-15	Inserting h1 and h2 headings

```
<body>
   <header>
      <h1>The J-Prop Shop</h1>
      <h2>Quality Juggling and Circus Props</h2>
   </header>

   <section>
      <article>
         <h2>Welcome</h2>
      </article>

      <article>
         <h2>Specials This Month</h2>
      </article>

      <article>
         <h2>Quality Tested</h2>
      </article>
   </section>

   <aside>
      <h2>Customer Comments</h2>
   </aside>

   <footer>
   </footer>
</body>
```

7. Save your changes to the file and then reload or refresh the **jprop.htm** file in your Web browser. Figure 1-16 shows the initial view of the page body content.

Figure 1-16	Viewing h1 and h2 headings in Dave's document

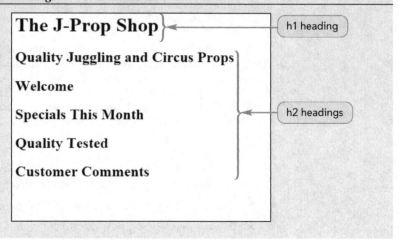

Grouping Headings

The interpretation of a particular heading depends on how it's used. For example, the h2 headings you just entered were used either to provide a title for articles or sections in the Web page or as a subtitle to the main title of the page. You can indicate that an h2 heading acts as a subtitle by grouping it with a main title heading using the **hgroup element**. The hgroup element uses the syntax

```
<hgroup>
   heading elements
</hgroup>
```

TIP

The hgroup element can contain only h1 through h6 elements or other hgroup elements.

where *heading elements* are elements marked with the <h1> through <h6> heading tags. The hgroup element was introduced in HTML5 and is not part of older HTML or XHTML specifications.

Group the first two headings in Dave's document to indicate that they should be interpreted as a main title and a subtitle.

To group the first two headings in the document:

1. Return to the **jprop.htm** file in your text editor.

2. Indent the first two headings in the document and then enclose them within <hgroup> tags as shown in Figure 1-17.

Figure 1-17 **Grouping the h1 and h2 headings**

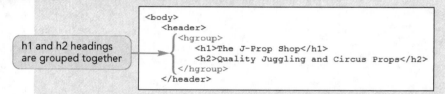

```
<body>
    <header>
        <hgroup>
            <h1>The J-Prop Shop</h1>
            <h2>Quality Juggling and Circus Props</h2>
        </hgroup>
    </header>
```

h1 and h2 headings are grouped together

3. Save your changes to the file.

Marking Paragraph Elements

As you saw earlier, you can mark a paragraph element using the <p> tag, which has the syntax

```
<p>content</p>
```

where *content* is the content of the paragraph. In older HTML code, you might occasionally see paragraphs marked with only the opening <p> tags, omitting closing tags. In those situations, a <p> tag marks the start of each new paragraph. While this convention is still accepted by many browsers, it violates HTML's syntax rules. In addition, if you want XHTML-compliant code, you must always include closing tags.

Many articles on the J-Prop Shop page are enclosed within paragraphs. You'll add these paragraphs now.

To add four paragraphs to Dave's Web page:

1. Return to the **jprop.htm** file in your text editor.

2. Directly below the h2 heading *Welcome*, insert the following paragraph code, indented as shown in Figure 1-18:

```
<p>If you're looking for high-quality, hand-crafted
    juggling and circus products, the J-Prop Shop is
    the store for you. I've designed and built props
    for the past 35 years, and my products have been
    used by professional entertainers and hobbyists
    throughout the world. Our prices are reasonable and
    our quality is excellent.
</p>
```

3. Directly below the h2 heading *Specials This Month*, insert the following:

```
<p>The following devil sticks are available at a
    special discount for the entire month of May:
</p>
```

4. Directly below the h2 heading *Quality Tested*, insert the following:

```
<p>Every item I create is checked and tested before
    being shipped out to assure perfect quality. I take
    pride in every one of my juggling props and I want
    my customers to feel that same pride.
</p>
```

5. Finally, below the h2 heading *Customer Comments*, insert the following:

```
<p>Here are a few select quotes from our happy family
    of customers and associates:
</p>
```

Figure 1-18 highlights the newly added paragraphs in the document.

Figure 1-18 **Adding paragraph elements**

```
<section>
    <article>
        <h2>Welcome</h2>
        <p>If you're looking for high-quality, hand-crafted
            juggling and circus products, the J-Prop Shop is
            the store for you. I've designed and built props
            for the past 35 years, and my products have been
            used by professional entertainers and hobbyists
            throughout the world. Our prices are reasonable and
            our quality is excellent.
        </p>
    </article>

    <article>
        <h2>Specials This Month</h2>
        <p>The following devil sticks are available at a
            special discount for the entire month of May:
        </p>
    </article>

    <article>
        <h2>Quality Tested</h2>
        <p>Every item I create is checked and tested before
            being shipped out to assure perfect quality. I take
            pride in every one of my juggling props and I want
            my customers to feel that same pride.
        </p>
    </article>
</section>

<aside>
    <h2>Customer Comments</h2>
    <p>Here are a few select quotes from our happy family
        of customers and associates:
    </p>
</aside>
```

Trouble? Don't worry if your lines do not wrap at the same locations shown in Figure 1-18. Where the line wraps in the HTML code does not affect how the page is rendered by the browser.

6. Save your changes to the file and then refresh the **jprop.htm** file in your Web browser. Figure 1-19 shows the new paragraphs added to the Web page.

| Figure 1-19 | Paragraphs in the Web page |

The J-Prop Shop

Quality Juggling and Circus Props

Welcome

If you're looking for high-quality, hand-crafted juggling and circus products, the J-Prop Shop is the store for you. I've designed and built props for the past 35 years, and my products have been used by professional entertainers and hobbyists throughout the world. Our prices are reasonable and our quality is excellent.

Specials This Month

The following devil sticks are available at a special discount for the entire month of May:

Quality Tested

Every item I create is checked and tested before being shipped out to assure perfect quality. I take pride in every one of my juggling props and I want my customers to feel that same pride.

Customer Comments

Here are a few select quotes from our happy family of customers and associates:

paragraphs

Marking a Block Quote

Next, Dave wants you to enter a few select quotes from his satisfied customers. You mark extended quotes with the HTML blockquote element, which uses the syntax

```
<blockquote>content</blockquote>
```

where *content* is the text of the quote. Most browsers render block quotes by indenting them to make it easier for readers to separate quoted material from the author's own words. You'll add the customer comments as block quotes.

To create the customer comment block quotes:

1. Return to the **jprop.htm** file in your text editor.

2. Scroll down to the aside element, and after the paragraph within that element, insert the following block quote, as shown in Figure 1-20:

```
<blockquote>
    <p>"I'm more than happy to recommend Dave Vinet's
        products. I came upon his work 10 years ago and
        was immediately impressed by his craftsmanship.
        He provides well-balanced and attractive
        props which are the perfect complement to my
        performances."
    </p>
    <p>"Dave Vinet makes the best juggling equipment on
        the planet. Period."
    </p>
    <p>"David has been my main supplier for 20 years. I
        have never had a problem with his equipment and
        his service is impeccable."
    </p>
</blockquote>
```

Figure 1-20 Adding a block quote

```
<aside>
   <h2>Customer Comments</h2>
   <p>Here are a few select quotes from our happy family
      of customers and associates:
   </p>
   <blockquote>
      <p>"I'm more than happy to recommend Dave Vinet's
         products. I came upon his work 10 years ago and
         was immediately impressed by his craftsmanship.
         He provides well-balanced and attractive
         props which are the perfect complement to my
         performances."
      </p>
      <p>"Dave Vinet makes the best juggling equipment on
         the planet. Period."
      </p>
      <p>"David has been my main supplier for 20 years. I
         have never had a problem with his equipment and
         his service is impeccable."
      </p>
   </blockquote>
</aside>
```

3. Save your changes to the file, and then reload **jprop.htm** in your Web browser. Figure 1-21 shows the revised page with the quoted material.

Figure 1-21 Block quote in the Web page

Customer Comments

Here are a few select quotes from our happy family of customers and associates:

quoted paragraphs
are indented in
the page

"I'm more than happy to recommend Dave Vinet's products. I came upon his work 10 years ago and was immediately impressed by his craftsmanship. He provides well-balanced and attractive props which are the perfect complement to my performances."

"Dave Vinet makes the best juggling equipment on the planet. Period."

"David has been my main supplier for 20 years. I have never had a problem with his equipment and his service is impeccable."

Note that the customer quote also included three paragraph elements nested within the blockquote element. The indentation applied by the browser to the block quote was also applied to any content within that element, so those paragraphs were indented even though browsers do not indent paragraphs by default.

Marking an Address

Dave wants to display the company's address at the bottom of the body of his page. Contact information such as addresses can be marked using the address element, which uses the syntax

```
<address>content</address>
```

where *content* is the contact information. Most browsers render addresses in italic. You'll use the address element to display the address of the J-Prop Shop.

To add the J-Prop Shop address:

1. Return to the **jprop.htm** file in your text editor.

2. Scroll down to the bottom of the file, and then within the `footer` element insert the following code, as shown in Figure 1-22:

```
<address>The J-Prop Shop
         541 West Highland Drive
         Auburn, ME 04210
         (207) 555 - 9001
</address>
```

Figure 1-22	Adding an address

```
<footer>
    <address>The J-Prop Shop
             541 West Highland Drive
             Auburn, ME 04210
             (207) 555 - 9001
    </address>
</footer>
</body>
```

3. Save your changes to the file, and then refresh **jprop.htm** in your Web browser. Figure 1-23 shows the revised page with the address text.

Figure 1-23	Address as rendered in the Web page

Customer Comments

Here are a few select quotes from our happy family of customers and associates:

"I'm more than happy to recommend Dave Vinet's products. I came upon his work 10 years ago and was immediately impressed by his craftsmanship. He provides well-balanced and attractive props which are the perfect complement to my performances."

"Dave Vinet makes the best juggling equipment on the planet. Period."

"David has been my main supplier for 20 years. I have never had a problem with his equipment and his service is impeccable."

> address text is displayed in italic by default

The J-Prop Shop 541 West Highland Drive Auburn, ME 04210 (207) 555 - 9001

The address text appears in italic at the bottom of the page. Note that even though you entered the company name, street address, city, state, and phone number on multiple lines, in the browser they all appear to run together on a single line. Remember that the browser ignores the occurrence of line breaks, tabs, and other white space in your text document. Shortly, you'll learn how to make this text more readable by adding a character symbol to separate the different parts of the address. For now, you'll leave the address text as it is.

Marking a List

Dave wants to display a list of products on this sample page. This information is presented on his flyer as a bulleted list. He wants something similar on the Web site. HTML supports three kinds of lists: ordered, unordered, and description.

REFERENCE

Marking Lists

- To mark an ordered list, enter

```
<ol>
    <li>item1</li>
    <li>item2</li>
...
</ol>
```

 where *item1*, *item2*, and so forth are the items in the list.
- To mark an unordered list, enter

```
<ul>
    <li>item1</li>
    <li>item2</li>
...
</ul>
```

- To mark a description list, enter

```
<dl>
    <dt>term1</dt>
    <dd>description1</dd>
    <dt>term2</dt>
    <dd>description2a</dd>
    <dd>description2b</dd>
...
</dl>
```

where *term1*, *term2*, etc. are the terms in the list and *description1*, *description2a*, *description2b*, etc. are descriptions associated with the preceding terms.

Ordered Lists

Ordered lists are used for items that follow some defined sequential order, such as lists ordered from smallest to greatest or from oldest to youngest. The beginning of an ordered list is marked by the `<ol>` (ordered list) tag. Each item within an ordered list is marked using the `<li>` (list item) tag. The structure of an ordered list is therefore

```
<ol>
    <li>item1</li>
    <li>item2</li>
...
</ol>
```

where *item1*, *item2*, and so forth are the items in the list. To explore creating an ordered list, you'll return to the HTML demo page.

To create an ordered list:

1. Return to the **demo_html.htm** file in your Web browser.

2. Delete the HTML code in the left box and replace it with the following:

```
<ol>
    <li>First Item</li>
    <li>Second Item</li>
    <li>Third Item</li>
</ol>
```

> **3.** Click the **Preview Code** button. Figure 1-24 shows how the browser renders the ordered list contents.

Figure 1-24 **Viewing an ordered list**

By default, entries in an ordered list are numbered, with the numbers added automatically by the browser.

Unordered Lists

To mark a list in which the items are not expected to occur in any specific order, you create an **unordered list**. The structure of ordered and unordered lists is the same, except that the list items for an unordered list are nested within the ul element, as follows:

```
<ul>
    <li>item1</li>
    <li>item2</li>
...
</ul>
```

You'll practice creating an unordered list with the demo page.

To create an unordered list:

> **1.** Delete the HTML code in the left box and replace it with the following:

```
<ul>
    <li>Basic Stick</li>
    <li>Flower Stick</li>
    <li>Master Stick</li>
    <li>Glow Stick</li>
</ul>
```

> **2.** Click the **Preview Code** button. Figure 1-25 shows how the browser renders the unordered list.

Figure 1-25 **Viewing an unordered list**

Trouble? In some browsers, the list appears with diamond shapes rather than circular bullets.

By default, most browsers display unordered lists using a bullet symbol. The exact bullet symbol depends on the browser, but most browsers use a filled-in circle.

Nesting Lists

You can place one list inside of another to create several levels of list items. The top level of a nested list contains the major items, with each sublevel containing items of lesser importance. Most browsers differentiate the various levels by increasing the indentation and using a different list symbol at each level. You'll use the demo page to see how this works with unordered lists.

To create a nested list:

1. Click after the word *Stick* in the `<li>Basic Stick</li>` line, and then press the **Enter** key to insert a new blank line.

2. Indent the following code between the code `<li>Basic Stick` and the closing `</li>` tag:

```
<ul>
    <li>Red</li>
    <li>Blue</li>
    <li>Green</li>
</ul>
```

3. Click the **Preview Code** button. Figure 1-26 shows the resulting nested list in the browser.

Figure 1-26 | Viewing a nested list

Trouble? Depending on your browser, the nested list of basic stick colors might appear with solid bullets rather than open circles.

The lower level of items is displayed using an open circle as the list bullet and additional indentation on the page. Once again, the exact format applied to these lists is determined by each browser's internal style sheet.

Description Lists

A third type of list is the **description list**, which contains a list of terms, each followed by its description. The structure of a description list is

```
<dl>
   <dt>term1</dt>
   <dd>description1</dd>
   <dt>term2</dt>
   <dd>description2a</dd>
   <dd>description2b</dd>
...
</dl>
```

where *term1*, *term2*, etc. are the terms in the list and *description1*, *description2a*, *description2b*, etc. are the descriptions associated with the terms. Note that description lists must follow a specified order, with each dt (definition term) element followed by one or more dd (definition description) elements.

You'll study how to work with description lists by returning to the demo page.

To create a description list:

1. Replace the code in the left box of the HTML demo page with

```
<dl>
   <dt>Basic Stick</dt>
   <dd>Easiest stick to learn</dd>
   <dt>Flower Stick</dt>
   <dd>A graceful stick with tassels</dd>
   <dt>Master Stick</dt>
   <dd>Our most popular stick</dd>
</dl>
```

2. Click the **Preview Code** button. Figure 1-27 shows the appearance of the description list in the browser.

Figure 1-27	Viewing a description list

```
HTML Code

<dl>
   <dt>Basic Stick</dt>
   <dd>Easiest stick to learn</dd>
   <dt>Flower Stick</dt>
   <dd>A graceful stick with tassels</dd>
   <dt>Master Stick</dt>
   <dd>Our most popular stick</dd>
</dl>
```

code for a description list

Preview

Basic Stick
 Easiest stick to learn
Flower Stick
 A graceful stick with tassels
Master Stick
 Our most popular stick

by default, browsers indent the description associated with each term

The demo page shows each term followed by its description, which is placed in a new block below the term and indented on the page. If you had included multiple dd elements for a single dt element, each description would have been contained within its own block and indented.

Now that you've experimented with the three types of HTML lists, you'll add an unordered list of products to Dave's Web page. By default, the product names will appear as a bulleted list.

To add an unordered list to Dave's Web page:

1. Return to the **jprop.htm** file in your text editor.

2. Within the Specials This Month article, directly below the p element, insert the following code, as shown in Figure 1-28:

```
<ul>
   <li>Basic Stick ($19.95)
      The easiest stick to learn with, but "grippy" enough
      for the most demanding tricks. Comes in red, green,
      and blue.
   </li>
   <li>Flower Stick ($24.95)
      A graceful stick with colored tassels. Flower Sticks
      float slowly, making them ideal for beginners.
   </li>
   <li>Master Stick ($39.95)
      Our most popular stick is shorter and heavier for
      fast play and more advanced tricks. Each Master Stick
      is available in custom colors.
   </li>
   <li>Glow Stick ($29.95)
      The Glow Stick shines brightly at night (without
      the danger of a fire stick).
   </li>
</ul>
```

Figure 1-28	Adding an unordered list

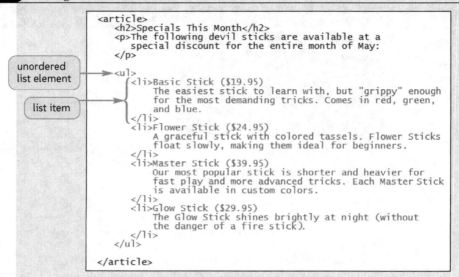

```
<article>
   <h2>Specials This Month</h2>
   <p>The following devil sticks are available at a
      special discount for the entire month of May:
   </p>
   <ul>
      <li>Basic Stick ($19.95)
         The easiest stick to learn with, but "grippy" enough
         for the most demanding tricks. Comes in red, green,
         and blue.
      </li>
      <li>Flower Stick ($24.95)
         A graceful stick with colored tassels. Flower Sticks
         float slowly, making them ideal for beginners.
      </li>
      <li>Master Stick ($39.95)
         Our most popular stick is shorter and heavier for
         fast play and more advanced tricks. Each Master Stick
         is available in custom colors.
      </li>
      <li>Glow Stick ($29.95)
         The Glow Stick shines brightly at night (without
         the danger of a fire stick).
      </li>
   </ul>

</article>
```

unordered
list element

list item

3. Save your changes to the file, and then refresh the **jprop.htm** file in your Web browser. As shown in Figure 1-29, the list of products appears as a bulleted list in the middle of the page.

Figure 1-29	Unordered list as rendered in the Web page

Specials This Month

The following devil sticks are available at a special discount for the entire month of May:

- Basic Stick ($19.95) The easiest stick to learn with, but "grippy" enough for the most demanding tricks. Comes in red, green, and blue.
- Flower Stick ($24.95) A graceful stick with colored tassels. Flower Sticks float slowly, making them ideal for beginners.
- Master Stick ($39.95) Our most popular stick is shorter and heavier for fast play and more advanced tricks. Each Master Stick is available in custom colors.
- Glow Stick ($29.95) The Glow Stick shines brightly at night (without the danger of a fire stick).

unordered list items
are displayed with
bullet markers

Although you've added much of the text content to Dave's sample page, the page as rendered by the browser still looks nothing like the flyer shown in Figure 1-7. That's because all of the page elements have been rendered using your browser's internal style sheet. To change the page's appearance, you need to substitute your own style sheet for the browser's internal one.

Applying an External Style Sheet

Style sheets are written in the **Cascading Style Sheet (CSS)** language. Like HTML files, CSS files are text files and can be created and edited using a simple text editor. A style sheet file has the file extension *.css*, which distinguishes it from an HTML file. Dave already has a style sheet for his Web page stored in the file *jpsstyles.css*.

Linking to an External Style Sheet

To apply an external style sheet to a Web page, you create a link within the document head to the style sheet file using the `link` element

```
<link href="file" rel="stylesheet" type="text/css" />
```

where `file` is the filename and location of the style sheet file. When a browser loads the page, it substitutes the style from the external style sheet file for its own internal style sheet.

See how the format and layout of Dave's sample page change when the page is linked to the *jpsstyles.css* file.

To apply Dave's external style sheet:

▶ **1.** Return to the **jprop.htm** file in your text editor.

▶ **2.** Within the head element at the top of the file, insert the following link element, as shown in Figure 1-30:

```
<link href="jpsstyles.css" rel="stylesheet" type="text/css" />
```

Figure 1-30 **Linking to the jpsstyles.css style sheet**

```
<!DOCTYPE html>
<html>

    <head>
    <!-- The J-Prop Shop Sample Page
        Author: David Vinet
        Date:   3/1/2014
    -->
        <title>The J-Prop Shop</title>
        <link href="jpsstyles.css" rel="stylesheet" type="text/css" />
    </head>
```

link element

filename of style sheet

style sheet language

▶ **3.** Save your changes to the file.

▶ **4.** Reload the **jprop.htm** file in your Web browser. As shown in Figure 1-31, the format and the layout change to reflect the styles in Dave's style sheet.

Figure 1-31

Figure 1-31 Web page rendered with the jpsstyles.css style sheet

The J-Prop Shop
Quality Juggling and Circus Props

Welcome

If you're looking for high-quality, hand-crafted juggling and circus products, the J-Prop Shop is the store for you. I've designed and built props for the past 35 years, and my products have been used by professional entertainers and hobbyists throughout the world. Our prices are reasonable and our quality is excellent.

Specials This Month

The following devil sticks are available at a special discount for the entire month of May:

- Basic Stick ($19.95) The easiest stick to learn with, but "grippy" enough for the most demanding tricks. Comes in red, green, and blue.
- Flower Stick ($24.95) A graceful stick with colored tassels. Flower Sticks float slowly, making them ideal for beginners.
- Master Stick ($39.95) Our most popular stick is shorter and heavier for fast play and more advanced tricks. Each Master Stick is available in custom colors.
- Glow Stick ($29.95) The Glow Stick shines brightly at night (without the danger of a fire stick.)

Quality Tested

Every item I create is checked and tested before being shipped out to assure perfect quality. I take pride in every one of my juggling props and I want my customers to feel that same pride.

Customer Comments

Here are a few select quotes from our happy family of customers and associates:

"I'm more than happy to recommend Dave Vinet's products. I came upon his work 10 years ago and was immediately impressed by his craftsmanship. He provides well-balanced and attractive props which are the perfect complement to my performances."

"Dave Vinet makes the best juggling equipment on the planet. Period."

"David has been my main supplier for 20 years. I have never had a problem with his equipment and his service is impeccable."

THE J-PROP SHOP 541 WEST HIGHLAND DRIVE AUBURN, ME 04210 (207) 555 - 9001

Trouble? Many elements in HTML5 are still not completely supported in current browsers, so the appearance of your Web page might differ slightly from that shown in Figure 1-31. If you are running Internet Explorer 8 or earlier, you'll see a significant difference. You'll learn how to correct this problem shortly.

Using the new style sheet, Dave's Web page is much more readable. The page is displayed in a two-column layout with the main content of the `section` element displayed in the left column. The content of the `aside` element is shown as a sidebar in the right column with a light purple background, rounded corners, and a drop shadow. The content of the `footer` element is styled with a smaller font, a top border line, and a light purple background.

Styles for HTML5 Elements

The `section`, `aside`, and `footer` elements used in the code of the *jprop.htm* file are new HTML5 elements that were not part of earlier HTML specifications. For most browsers this is not a problem, and the Web page should be rendered with a format and layout close to what Dave requested. An important exception, though, is the Internet Explorer browser. Internet Explorer version 8 and earlier versions provide almost no support for HTML5 and do not recognize styles applied to HTML5 elements. For example, as Figure 1-32 shows, even with the new style sheet, Internet Explorer 8 displays Dave's Web page with a few of the styles shown in Figure 1-31.

Figure 1-32 Web page as it appears in Internet Explorer 8

The J-Prop Shop

Quality Juggling and Circus Props

Welcome

If you're looking for high-quality, hand-crafted juggling and circus products, the J-Prop Shop is the store for you. I've designed and built props for the past 35 years, and my products have been used by professional entertainers and hobbyists throughout the world. Our prices are reasonable and our quality is excellent.

Specials This Month

The following devil sticks are available at a special discount for the entire month of May:

- Basic Stick ($19.95) The easiest stick to learn with, but "grippy" enough for the most demanding tricks. Comes in red, green, and blue.
- Flower Stick ($24.95) A graceful stick with colored tassels. Flower Sticks float slowly, making them ideal for beginners.
- Master Stick ($39.95) Our most popular stick is shorter and heavier for fast play and more advanced tricks. Each Master Stick is available in custom colors.
- Glow Stick ($29.95) The Glow Stick shines brightly at night (without the danger of a fire stick).

Quality Tested

Every item I create is checked and tested before being shipped out to assure perfect quality. I take pride in every one of my juggling props and I want my customers to feel that same pride.

Customer Comments

Here are a few select quotes from our happy family of customers and associates:

"I'm more than happy to recommend Dave Vinet's products. I came upon his work 10 years ago and was immediately impressed by his craftsmanship. He provides well-balanced and attractive props which are the perfect complement to my performances."

"Dave Vinet makes the best juggling equipment on the planet. Period."

"David has been my main supplier for 20 years. I have never had a problem with his equipment and his service is impeccable."

The J-Prop Shop 541 West Highland Drive Auburn, ME 04210 (207) 555 - 9001

Dave needs this problem fixed because he can't assume that users will always be running the latest version of Internet Explorer. Workarounds for this problem involve running an external program known as a **script**. The most often used program language for the Web is **JavaScript**. Like HTML and CSS files, JavaScript files are text files that require no special software other than a Web browser to run. At this point, you don't need to know how to write a JavaScript program to correct Internet Explorer's problem with HTML5 elements; someone else has already done that. You just need to know how to access and run their program.

One of the most useful programs to enable HTML5 support in older browsers is Modernizr. **Modernizr** is a free, open-source, MIT-licensed JavaScript library of functions that provides support for many HTML5 elements and for the newest CSS styles. One of the many uses of Modernizr is to enable support for HTML5 in older browsers. Modernizr is distributed in a single JavaScript file that you can download from *www.modernizr.com* and add to your Web site. To link a Web page to a JavaScript file, you add the `script` element

```
<script src="file"></script>
```

to the document head, where *file* is the name of the JavaScript file. The current version of Modernizr at the time of this writing is stored in the file *modernizr-1.5.js*. To link to this file, you add the following to the document head:

```
<script src="modernizr-1.5.js"></script>
```

The *modernizr-1.5.js* file has already been added to your data folder. Link to this file now to apply it to Dave's Web page.

To link to the Modernizr file:

1. Return to the **jprop.htm** file in your text editor.

2. Scroll to the top of the file and add the following tag pair above the link element, as shown in Figure 1-33:

   ```
   <script src="modernizr-1.5.js"></script>
   ```

Figure 1-33	Linking to the Modernizr script

```
<!DOCTYPE html>
<html>

    <head>
    <!-- The J-Prop Shop Sample Page
         Author: David Vinet
         Date:   3/1/2014
    -->
        <title>The J-Prop Shop</title>
        <script src="modernizr-1.5.js"></script>
        <link href="jpsstyles.css" rel="stylesheet" type="text/css" />
    </head>
```

Modernizr script file

3. Save your changes to the file.

4. If you have access to Internet Explorer 8, use that browser to open the **jprop.htm** file. As shown in Figure 1-34, the browser renders the Web page employing the page layout and many of the formats shown earlier in Figure 1-29.

Figure 1-34	Web page as it appears in Internet Explorer 8 with Modernizr

The J-Prop Shop
Quality Juggling and Circus Props

Welcome

If you're looking for high-quality, hand-crafted juggling and circus products, the J-Prop Shop is the store for you. I've designed and built props for the past 35 years, and my products have been used by professional entertainers and hobbyists throughout the world. Our prices are reasonable and our quality is excellent.

Specials This Month

The following devil sticks are available at a special discount for the entire month of May:

- Basic Stick ($19.95) The easiest stick to learn with, but "grippy" enough for the most demanding tricks. Comes in red, green, and blue.
- Flower Stick ($24.95) A graceful stick with colored tassels. Flower Sticks float slowly, making them ideal for beginners.
- Master Stick ($39.95) Our most popular stick is shorter and heavier for fast play and more advanced tricks. Each Master Stick is available in custom colors.
- Glow Stick ($29.95) The Glow Stick shines brightly at night (without the danger of a fire stick).

Quality Tested

Every item I create is checked and tested before being shipped out to assure perfect quality. I take pride in every one of my juggling props and I want my customers to feel that same pride.

Customer Comments

Here are a few select quotes from our happy family of customers and associates:

"I'm more than happy to recommend Dave Vinet's products. I came upon his work 10 years ago and was immediately impressed by his craftsmanship. He provides well-balanced and attractive props which are the perfect complement to my performances."

"Dave Vinet makes the best juggling equipment on the planet. Period."

"David has been my main supplier for 20 years. I have never had a problem with his equipment and his service is impeccable."

rounded corners and drop shadows are not supported in IE8

THE J-PROP SHOP 541 WEST HIGHLAND DRIVE AUBURN, ME 04210 (207) 555 - 9001

The rendering done by Internet Explorer 8 does not completely match what was shown under Internet Explorer 9 or many of the other competing browsers such as Firefox, Safari, or Google Chrome. For example, Internet Explorer 8 doesn't support styles for rounded corners and drop shadows. All of this underscores an important point: You may find variations between one browser and another in how your page is rendered, especially when using the newest HTML5 elements and CSS styles. This means you have to test your page under multiple browsers and devices, and make sure that any differences in format or layout do not impact your users' ability to read and understand your page.

Marking Text-Level Elements

Grouping elements like paragraphs and headings start their content on a new line. Another type of element is a **text-level element**, which marks content within a grouping element. A text-level element is like a phrase or a collection of characters within a paragraph or heading. Text-level elements do not start out on a new line, but instead flow alongside of, or **inline** with, the rest of the characters in the grouping element. Figure 1-35 lists some of the text-level elements in HTML.

Figure 1-35	Text-level elements

Text-Level Element	Description
a	A hypertext link
abbr	An abbreviation
b	Text offset from the surrounding content (usually displayed in **boldface** text)
cite	A citation (usually displayed in *italics*)
code	Program code (usually displayed in a `fixed width` font)
del	Deleted text (usually displayed with a ~~strikethrough~~ line)
dfn	A definition term (usually displayed in *italics*)
em	Emphasized content (usually displayed in *italics*)
i	Text representing an alternate voice or mood (usually displayed in *italics*)
ins	Inserted text (usually displayed with an <u>underline</u>)
kbd	Keyboard text (usually displayed in a `fixed width` font)
mark	Highlighted or marked text (usually displayed with a highlight. HTML5 only)
q	Quoted text (occasionally enclosed in "quotes")
samp	Sample computer code (usually displayed in a `fixed width` font)
small	Text displayed in a smaller font than surrounding content
span	A span of generic text
strong	Strongly emphasized content (usually displayed in **boldface** text)
sub	Subscripted text
sup	Superscripted text
time	A date and time value (HTML5 only)
var	Programming variables (usually displayed in *italic*)

TIP

Text-level elements should always be nested within grouping elements such as paragraphs or headings.

To practice using text-level elements in conjunction with grouping elements, you'll return to the HTML demo page.

To explore the use of inline elements:

▶ **1.** Return to the **demo_html.htm** file in your Web browser.

▶ **2.** Replace the code in the HTML Code box with the following:

```
<p>Welcome to the J-Prop Shop, owned and operated by David
Vinet</p>
```

▶ **3.** Click the **Preview Code** button to display this paragraph in the Preview box.

To mark *J-Prop Shop* as strongly emphasized text, you can enclose that phrase within a set of `<strong>` tags.

▶ **4.** Insert the `<strong>` opening tag directly before the word *J-Prop* in the box on the left. Insert the closing `</strong>` tag directly after the word *Shop*. Click the **Preview Code** button to confirm that *J-Prop Shop* is now displayed in a bold-faced font.

Another text-level element is the `cite` element used to make citations. Explore how citations are rendered by your browser by enclosing *David Vinet* within a set of `<cite>` tags.

▶ **5.** Insert an opening `<cite>` tag directly before the word *David* and insert the closing `</cite>` tag directly after *Vinet*. Click the **Preview Code** button to view the revised code. Figure 1-36 shows the result of applying the `<strong>` and `<cite>` tags to the paragraph text.

Figure 1-36	Applying the strong and cite text-level elements

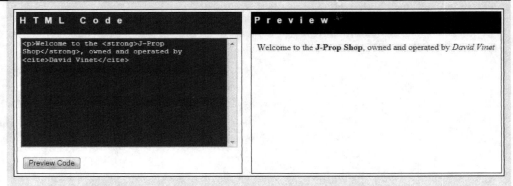

▶ **6.** Continue exploring other HTML elements listed in Figure 1-35 to see their effects on the rendered text. Close the demo file when you're done.

You can nest text-level tags to mark a single text string with more than one element. For example, the HTML code

```
<p>Welcome to the <strong><em>J-Prop Shop</em></strong>.</p>
```

marks the text string *J-Prop Shop* as both strong and emphasized text. In most browsers it appears in a ***bold italic*** font.

Dave wants the names of all of the items in his product list to be marked as strong text. Revise the code for the product names now.

To mark strong text:

1. Return to the **jprop.htm** file in your text editor.

2. Scroll down to the unordered list and enclose the name and price of each product within a set of `<strong>` tags as shown in Figure 1-37.

Figure 1-37 Marking product names using the strong element

```
<article>
    <h2>Specials This Month</h2>
    <p>The following devil sticks are available at a
        special discount for the entire month of May:
    </p>

    <ul>
        <li><strong>Basic Stick ($19.95)</strong>
            The easiest stick to learn with, but "grippy" enough
            for the most demanding tricks. Comes in red, green,
            and blue.
        </li>
        <li><strong>Flower Stick ($24.95)</strong>
            A graceful stick with colored tassels. Flower Sticks
            float slowly, making them ideal for beginners.
        </li>
        <li><strong>Master Stick ($39.95)</strong>
            Our most popular stick is shorter and heavier for
            fast play and more advanced tricks. Each Master Stick
            is available in custom colors.
        </li>
        <li><strong>Glow Stick ($29.95)</strong>
            The Glow Stick shines brightly at night (without
            the danger of a fire stick).
        </li>
    </ul>

</article>
```

3. Save your changes to the file and then reload the **jprop.htm** file in your Web browser. Figure 1-38 shows the revised appearance of the bulleted list of products.

Figure 1-38 Product names rendered in a boldfaced font

Specials This Month

The following devil sticks are available at a special discount for the entire month of May:

- **Basic Stick ($19.95)** The easiest stick to learn with, but "grippy" enough for the most demanding tricks. Comes in red, green, and blue.
- **Flower Stick ($24.95)** A graceful stick with colored tassels. Flower Sticks float slowly, making them ideal for beginners.
- **Master Stick ($39.95)** Our most popular stick is shorter and heavier for fast play and more advanced tricks. Each Master Stick is available in custom colors.
- **Glow Stick ($29.95)** The Glow Stick shines brightly at night (without the danger of a fire stick).

PROSKILLS

Written Communication: Logical and Physical Interpretation of Elements

As you learn more HTML, you'll notice some overlap in how browsers display certain elements. To display italicized text, you could use the <dfn>, , <i>, or <var> tags; or if you wanted to italicize an entire block of text, you could use the <address> tag. However, browsers differ in how they display elements, so you should not rely on the way any browser or group of browsers commonly displays an element.

In addition, it's important to distinguish between the way a browser displays an element, and the purpose of the element in the document. Although it can be tempting to ignore this difference, your HTML code benefits when you respect that distinction because search engines often look within specific elements for information. For example, a search engine may look for the address element to find contact information for a particular Web site. It would be confusing to end users if you used the address element to simply italicize a block of text. Web programmers can also use elements to extract information from a page. For example, a JavaScript program could automatically generate a bibliography from all of the citations listed within a Web site by looking for occurrences of the cite element.

The best practice for communicating the purpose of your document is to use HTML to mark content but not to rely on HTML to format that content. Formatting should be done solely through style sheets, using either the internal style sheets built into browsers or through your own customized styles.

Using the Generic Elements div and span

Most of the page elements you've examined have a specific meaning. However, sometimes you want to add an element that represents a text block or a string of inline text without it having any other meaning. HTML supports two such generic elements: div and span. The div element is used to mark general grouping content and has the following syntax:

```
<div>content</div>
```

The span element, which is used to mark general text-level content, has the following syntax:

```
<span>content</span>
```

Browsers recognize both elements but do not assign any default format to content marked with these elements. This frees Web authors to develop styles for these elements without worrying about overriding any styles imposed by browsers. Note that the main use of the div element to mark sections of the page has been superseded in HTML5 by the sectional elements such as header and article; however, you will still encounter the div element in many current and older Web sites.

Presentational Attributes

Early versions of HTML were used mostly by scientists and researchers who, for the most part, didn't need flashy graphics, decorative text fonts, or even much color on a page. The earliest Web pages weren't fancy and didn't require much from the browsers that displayed them. This changed as the Web became more popular and attracted the attention of commercial businesses, graphic designers, and artists.

One way that HTML changed to accommodate this new class of users was to introduce **presentational elements** and **presentational attributes** designed to describe how each element should be rendered by Web browsers. For example, to align text on a page, Web authors would use the `align` attribute

```
<element align="alignment">content</element>
```

where *alignment* is either *left*, *right*, *center*, or *justify*. Thus, to center an `h1` heading on a page, you could apply the following `align` attribute to the `<h1>` tag:

```
<h1 align="center">The J-Prop Shop</h1>
```

Almost all presentational elements and attributes are now deprecated in favor of style sheets, but you may still see them used in older Web sites. Using a deprecated attribute like `align` would probably not cause a Web page to fail, but it's still best to focus your HTML code on describing the content of a document and not its appearance.

Marking a Line Break

After examining your work, Dave notices that the list of customer comments lacks the names of the customers who made them. He asks you to add this information to the Web page, marking the customer information as citations.

To append customer names to the Customer Comments section:

1. Return to the **jprop.htm** file in your text editor.

2. Locate the first customer comment and then add the following code at the end of the paragraph, directly before the closing `</p>` tag:

   ```
   <cite>Thomas Gage, Circus England</cite>
   ```

3. At the end of the paragraph for the second customer comment, insert

   ```
   <cite>Douglas Pederson, Street-Wise Shows</cite>
   ```

4. Finally, at the end of the paragraph for the third customer comment, insert

   ```
   <cite>Linda Unger, Linda & Louis</cite>
   ```

 Figure 1-39 shows the revised code in the file.

Figure 1-39 Providing citations for the customer quotes

```
<aside>
   <h2>Customer Comments</h2>
   <p>Here are a few select quotes from our happy family
      of customers and associates:
   </p>
   <blockquote>
      <p>"I'm more than happy to recommend Dave Vinet's
         products. I came upon his work 10 years ago and
         was immediately impressed by his craftsmanship.
         He provides well-balanced and attractive
         props which are the perfect complement to my
         performances."
         <cite>Thomas Gage, Circus England</cite>
      </p>
      <p>"Dave Vinet makes the best juggling equipment on
         the planet. Period."
         <cite>Douglas Pederson, Street-Wise Shows</cite>
      </p>
      <p>"David has been my main supplier for 20 years. I
         have never had a problem with his equipment and
         his service is impeccable."
         <cite>Linda Unger, Linda & Louis</cite>
      </p>
   </blockquote>
</aside>
```

▶ **5.** Save your changes to the file and then refresh the **jprop.htm** file in your Web
browser. Figure 1-40 shows the revised text of the Customer Comments sidebar.

Figure 1-40 Revised Customer Comments sidebar

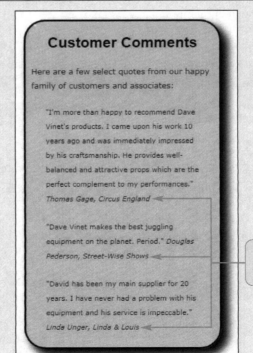

citations,
displayed by the
browser in italic

Dave thinks the comments are difficult to read when the text of a comment runs into the citation. He suggests that you start each citation on a new line. To do this, you can insert a line break into the Web page using the following empty element tag:

```
<br />
```

Line breaks must be placed within grouping elements such as paragraphs or headings. Some browsers accept line breaks placed anywhere within the body of a Web page; however, this is not good coding technique. A browser displaying an XHTML document will reject code in which a text-level element such as br is placed outside of any grouping element.

You'll use the br element to mark a line break between each customer comment and its associated citation in Dave's Web page.

To insert line breaks in the comments:

▶ **1.** Return to the **jprop.htm** file in your text editor.

▶ **2.** Insert the tag **
** between the comment and the citation for each of the three customer comments in the file. See Figure 1-41.

Figure 1-41 **Inserting line breaks**

```
<blockquote>
    <p>"I'm more than happy to recommend Dave Vinet's
       products. I came upon his work 10 years ago and
       was immediately impressed by his craftsmanship.
       He provides well-balanced and attractive
       props which are the perfect complement to my
       performances."
       <br />
       <cite>Thomas Gage, Circus England</cite>
    </p>
    <p>"Dave Vinet makes the best juggling equipment on
       the planet. Period."
       <br />
       <cite>Douglas Pederson, Street-Wise Shows</cite>
    </p>
    <p>"David has been my main supplier for 20 years. I
       have never had a problem with his equipment and
       his service is impeccable."
       <br />
       <cite>Linda Unger, Linda & Louis</cite>
    </p>
</blockquote>
```

line break element

▶ **3.** Save your changes to the file and then refresh the **jprop.htm** file in your Web browser. Verify that each citation starts on a new line below the associated customer comment.

INSIGHT

Marking a Horizontal Rule

Another empty element is hr, the horizontal rule element, which marks a major topic change within a section. The syntax of the hr element is as follows:

```
<hr />
```

The exact appearance of the hr element is left to the browser. Most browsers display a gray-shaded horizontal line a few pixels in height. The hr element was originally used as a quick way of inserting horizontal lines within a Web page. Although that task now should be left to style sheets, you will still see the hr element in older Web pages.

Inserting an Inline Image

Dave wants you to replace the name of the company at the top of his Web page with an image of the company logo. Because HTML files are simple text files, non-textual content such as graphics must be stored in separate files, which are then loaded by browsers as they render pages. To add a graphic image to a Web page, you have to insert an inline image into your code.

The img Element

Inline images are inserted into a Web page using the one-sided img element with the syntax

```
<img src="file" alt="text" />
```

where *file* is the name of the graphic image file and *text* is text displayed by browsers in place of the graphic image. In this tutorial, you'll assume that the graphic image file is located in the same folder as the Web page, so you don't have to specify the location of the file. In the next tutorial, you'll learn how to reference files placed in other folders or locations on the Web.

Browsers retrieve the specified image file and display the image alongside the rest of the Web page content. The size of the image is based on the dimensions of the image itself; however, you can specify a different size using the width and height attributes

```
width="value" height="value"
```

where the width and height values are expressed in pixels. If you specify only the width, browsers automatically set the height to maintain the proportions of the image; similarly, if you define the height, browsers automatically set the width to maintain the image proportions. Thus, by setting the width and height values yourself, you can enlarge or reduce the size of the rendered image.

Inline images are considered text-level elements and thus must be placed within a grouping element such as a heading or a paragraph. An inline image is most commonly stored in one of three formats: GIF (Graphics Interchange Format), JPEG (Joint Photographic Experts Group), or PNG (Portable Network Graphics). Dave has already created his graphic image in PNG format and stored it with his other files using the filename *jpslogo.png*. You'll replace the text of the h1 heading with this inline image.

To insert the company logo at the top of the page:

1. Return to the **jprop.htm** file in your text editor.

2. Go to the h1 heading element at the top of the body section, delete the text *The J-Prop Shop* from between the opening and closing <h1> tags, and then replace it with

   ```
   <img src="jpslogo.png" alt="The J-Prop Shop" />
   ```

 Figure 1-42 highlights the revised code in the **jprop.htm** file.

Figure 1-42 Adding an inline image

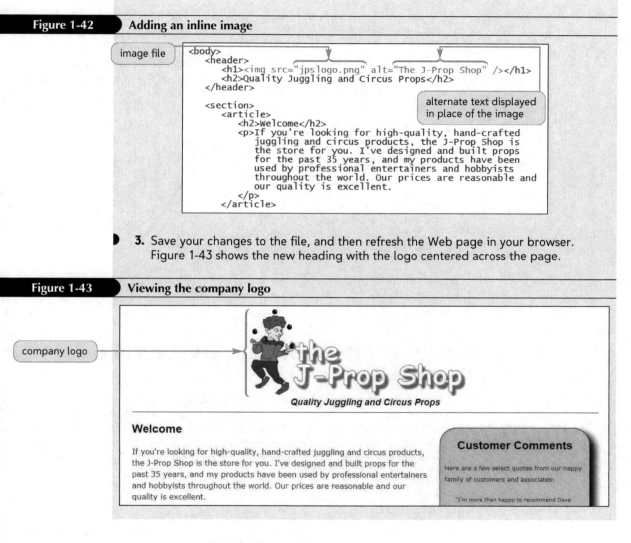

image file

```
<body>
    <header>
        <h1><img src="jpslogo.png" alt="The J-Prop Shop" /></h1>
        <h2>Quality Juggling and Circus Props</h2>
    </header>

    <section>
        <article>
            <h2>Welcome</h2>
            <p>If you're looking for high-quality, hand-crafted
               juggling and circus products, the J-Prop Shop is
               the store for you. I've designed and built props
               for the past 35 years, and my products have been
               used by professional entertainers and hobbyists
               throughout the world. Our prices are reasonable and
               our quality is excellent.
            </p>
        </article>
```

alternate text displayed in place of the image

3. Save your changes to the file, and then refresh the Web page in your browser. Figure 1-43 shows the new heading with the logo centered across the page.

Figure 1-43 Viewing the company logo

company logo

Welcome

If you're looking for high-quality, hand-crafted juggling and circus products, the J-Prop Shop is the store for you. I've designed and built props for the past 35 years, and my products have been used by professional entertainers and hobbyists throughout the world. Our prices are reasonable and our quality is excellent.

Customer Comments

Here are a few select quotes from our happy family of customers and associates:

"I'm more than happy to recommend Dave

Figures and Figure Captions

In books and magazines, figures and figure captions are often placed within boxes that stand aside from the main content of an article. HTML5 introduced this type of object to Web page markup with the figure and figcaption elements

```
<figure>
    content
    <figcaption>caption</figcaption>
</figure>
```

where *content* is the content that will appear in the figure box and *caption* is the text of the figure caption. The figcaption element is optional; but if the figcaption element is used, it must be nested within a set of <figure> tags either directly after the opening <figure> tag or directly before the closing </figure> tag. For example, the

following HTML5 code creates a figure box containing an inline image of one of the J-Prop Shop's products and a caption:

```
<figure>
   <img src="stick03.png" alt="Master Stick" />
   <figcaption>Master Stick ($39.95)</figcaption>
</figure>
```

The figure element doesn't necessarily need to contain an inline image. It can be used to mark any content that stands aside from a main article but is referenced by it. For instance, it could be used to contain an excerpt of a poem, as the following code demonstrates:

```
<figure>
   <p>'Twas brillig, and the slithy toves<br />
      Did gyre and gimble in the wabe;<br />
      All mimsy were the borogoves,<br />
      And the mome raths outgrabe.
   </p>
   <figcaption>
      <cite>Jabberwocky,
      Lewis Carroll, 1832-98</cite>
   </figcaption>
</figure>
```

As with other HTML elements, the exact appearance of a figure box is determined by a style sheet. At this time, Dave does not need to create a figure box for his company's home page.

Working with Character Sets and Special Characters

Dave likes the work you've done so far on the Web page. He has only one remaining concern: The company's address in the page footer is difficult to read because the street address, city name, zip code, and phone number all run together on one line. Dave would like to have the different parts of the address separated by a solid circular marker (•). However, this marker is not represented by any keys on your keyboard. How, then, do you insert this symbol into the Web page?

Character Sets

Every character that your browser is capable of rendering belongs to a collection of characters and symbols called a **character set**. Character sets come in a wide variety of sizes. For English, no more than about 127 characters are needed to represent all of the upper- and lowercase letters, numbers, punctuation marks, spaces, and special typing symbols in the language. Other languages, such as Japanese or Chinese, require character sets containing thousands of symbols. Beyond the basic characters used by a language are special characters such as ©, ½, π, and ®. Thus, a complete character set that includes all possible printable characters is made up of hundreds of symbols.

The character set used for the alphabet of English characters is called **ASCII (American Standard Code for Information Interchange)**. A more extended character set, called **Latin-1** or the **ISO 8859-1** character set, supports 255 characters and can be used by most languages that employ the Latin alphabet, including English, French, Spanish, and Italian. **Unicode**, the most extended character set, supports up to 65,536 symbols and can be used for any of the world's languages. The most commonly used character set on the Web is **UTF-8**, which is a compressed version of Unicode and is probably the default character set assumed by your browser. You can learn more about character sets by visiting the W3C Web site and the Web site for the Internet Assigned Numbers Authority at *www.iana.org*.

Character Encoding

Character encoding associates each symbol from a character set with a numeric value called the **numeric character reference**. For example, the copyright symbol © from the UTF-8 character set is encoded with the number 169. If you know the character encoding number, you can insert the corresponding character directly into your Web page using the entity

 &#code;

where *code* is the encoding number. Thus, to display the © symbol in your Web page, you would enter

 ©

into your HTML file.

Character Entity References

Another way to insert a special symbol is to use a **character entity reference**, which is a short memorable name used in place of the encoding number. Character entity references are inserted using the syntax

 &char;

where *char* is the character's entity reference. The character entity reference for the copyright symbol is *copy*. So to display the © symbol in your Web page, you could insert

 ©

into your HTML code.

REFERENCE

Inserting Symbols from a Character Set

- To insert a symbol based on the encoding number, use the entity
 &#code;
 where *code* is the encoding number.
- To insert a symbol based on a character entity reference, use the entity
 &char;
 where *char* is the name assigned to the character.
- To insert a nonbreaking space, use the following entity:

- To insert the < symbol, use the following entity:
 <
- To insert the > symbol, use the following entity:
 >

You can explore various encoding numbers and character entity references by opening the demo page supplied with your Data Files.

To view the demo page:

1. Use your Web browser to open the **demo_characters.htm** file from the tutorial.01\demo data folder.

2. Type £ in the input box and then click the **Show** button. The Web browser displays the £ symbol in the ivory-colored box below.

3. Replace the value in the input box with `®` and then click the **Show** button. The browser now displays the ® symbol, the symbol for registered trademarks, which you specified using a character entity reference.

You can also view a collection of numeric character references and character entity references by selecting a table from the list box on the page.

4. Verify that General Symbols is displayed in the selection list box, and then click the **Show Table** button. As shown in Figure 1-44, the browser displays a list of 35 symbols with the character entity reference and the numeric character reference displayed beneath each symbol.

Figure 1-44	HTML characters demo page

5. Take some time to explore the variety of numeric character references and character entity references supported by your browser. Close the demo page when you're finished, but leave your browser open.

Special Characters

One use of character codes is to insert text about HTML itself. For example, if you want your Web page to describe the use of the `<h1>` tag, you cannot simply type

```
The <h1> tag is used to mark h1 headings.
```

because browsers would interpret the `<h1>` text as marking the beginning of an h1 heading! Instead, you have to use the `<` and `>` entity references to insert the < and > symbols. The text would then be:

```
The &lt;h1&gt; tag is used to mark h1 headings.
```

Another use of character codes is to add extra spaces to your Web page. Remember that browsers ignore extra blank spaces in an HTML file. To insert an additional space, use the ` ` entity reference (*nbsp* stands for *nonbreaking space*), which forces browsers to insert an extra space.

On Dave's Web page, you decide to use the bullet symbol (•) to break up the address text into sections. The symbol has a character encoding number of 8226 and the character entity reference name *bull*. Dave suggests that you also add a long horizontal line known as an em-dash (—) to mark the customer names in the customer comments section. The character encoding number for an em-dash is 8212 and the entity reference is *mdash*.

To add bullets and an em-dash to Dave's Web page:

1. Return to the **jprop.htm** file in your text editor.

2. Locate the customer comment from Thomas Gage, and then directly before the opening <cite> tag insert the character code — followed by a space.

3. Repeat Step 2 for the two remaining customer comments.

> Always include a semi-colon so that browsers recognize the entry as a character code.

4. Scroll down to the address element within the page footer. At the end of each line within the address (except the last line), insert a space followed by the • character entity. Figure 1-45 highlights the revised code in the Web page.

Figure 1-45	Adding symbols from a character set

```
<aside>
  <h2>Customer Comments</h2>
  <p>Here are a few select quotes from our happy family
     of customers and associates:
  </p>
  <blockquote>
    <p>"I'm more than happy to recommend Dave Vinet's
       products. I came upon his work 10 years ago and
       was immediately impressed by his craftsmanship.
       He provides well-balanced and attractive
       props which are the perfect complement to my
       performances."
       <br />
       — <cite>Thomas Gage, Circus England</cite>
    </p>
    <p>"Dave Vinet makes the best juggling equipment on
       the planet. Period."
       <br />
       — <cite>Douglas Pederson, Street-Wise Shows</cite>
    </p>
    <p>"David has been my main supplier for 20 years. I
       have never had a problem with his equipment and
       his service is impeccable."
       <br />
       — <cite>Linda Unger, Linda & Louis</cite>
    </p>
  </blockquote>
</aside>

<footer>
  <address>The J-Prop Shop &bull;
           541 West Highland Drive &bull;
           Auburn, ME 04210 &bull;
           (207) 555 - 9001
  </address>
</footer>
</body>
```

character encoding number

character entity reference

5. Save your changes to the file.

6. Refresh the **jprop.htm** file in your Web browser. Figure 1-46 shows the final content of Dave's Web page.

Figure 1-46	Completed Web page

Welcome

If you're looking for high-quality, hand-crafted juggling and circus products, the J-Prop Shop is the store for you. I've designed and built props for the past 35 years, and my products have been used by professional entertainers and hobbyists throughout the world. Our prices are reasonable and our quality is excellent.

Specials This Month

The following devil sticks are available at a special discount for the entire month of May:

- **Basic Stick ($19.95)** The easiest stick to learn with, but "grippy" enough for the most demanding tricks. Comes in red, green, and blue.
- **Flower Stick ($24.95)** A graceful stick with colored tassels. Flower Sticks float slowly, making them ideal for beginners.
- **Master Stick ($39.95)** Our most popular stick is shorter and heavier for fast play and more advanced tricks. Each Master Stick is available in custom colors.
- **Glow Stick ($29.95)** The Glow Stick shines brightly at night (without the danger of a fire stick).

Quality Tested

Every item I create is checked and tested before being shipped out to assure perfect quality. I take pride in every one of my juggling props and I want my customers to feel that same pride.

Customer Comments

Here are a few select quotes from our happy family of customers and associates:

"I'm more than happy to recommend Dave Vinet's products. I came upon his work 10 years ago and was immediately impressed by his craftsmanship. He provides well-balanced and attractive props which are the perfect complement to my performances."
— Thomas Gage, Circus England

"Dave Vinet makes the best juggling equipment on the planet. Period."
— Douglas Pederson, Street-Wise Shows

"David has been my main supplier for 20 years. I have never had a problem with his equipment and his service is impeccable."
— Linda Unger, Linda & Louis

THE J-PROP SHOP • 541 WEST HIGHLAND DRIVE • AUBURN, ME 04210 • (207) 555 - 9001

Specifying the Character Set

To render a numeric character reference correctly, a browser must apply the correct character set to a Web page. This information is typically sent by the Web server as it transfers an HTML page to a browser. However, to be doubly certain that browsers employ the correct character set, you can specify the character set within the head element of your HTML document. For HTML 4.01 and XHTML, you add the meta element

```
<meta http-equiv="Content-Type"
      content="text/html; charset=character_set" />
```

to the document head, where *character_set* is the name of the character set you want the browser to employ when interpreting your HTML code. Under HTML5, the meta element is simply:

```
<meta charset="character_set" />
```

HTML5 also supports the syntax of the HTML 4.01 and XHTML meta element. You should always specify the character encoding in your document, even if you are not using any special symbols. It relieves the browser from having to guess about the correct encoding; and in certain situations, not specifying the encoding can lead to a security hole in the transfer of a page from the Web server to the client.

You'll add the meta element to Dave's document to specify that his file has been encoded using the UTF-8 character set.

To specify the character encoding for Dave's document:

1. Return to the **jprop.htm** file in your text editor.

2. Scroll to the top of the file. Directly below the comment in the head section, insert the following meta element as shown in Figure 1-47:

```
<meta charset="UTF-8" />
```

Figure 1-47 Specifying the character encoding

```
<!DOCTYPE html>
<html>

   <head>
      <!-- The J-Prop Shop Sample Page
           Author: David Vinet
           Date:   3/1/2014                          character set
      -->
      <meta charset="UTF-8" />
      <title>The J-Prop Shop</title>
      <script src="modernizr-1.5.js"></script>
      <link href="jpsstyles.css" rel="stylesheet" type="text/css" />
   </head>
```

3. Close the **jprop.htm** file, saving your changes.

4. Refresh the **jprop.htm** file in your browser and verify that the browser renders the page with no errors.

Written Communication: Publishing Your Web Page

Once you've completed your Web page, your next step is to get it on the Web. You first need to find a Web server to host the page. In choosing a Web server, you'll need to consider how much you want to pay, how much space you need, and how much traffic you expect at your Web site. If you'd prefer a free or low-cost option and don't need much space, you might first look toward the company that provides your Internet access. Most **Internet service providers** (ISPs) offer space on their Web servers as part of their regular service or for a small fee. However, they usually limit the amount of space available to you, unless you pay an extra fee to host a larger site. There are also free Web hosts, which provide space on servers for personal or noncommercial use. Once again, the amount of space you get is limited. Free Web hosting services make their money from selling advertising space on your site, so you should be prepared to act as a billboard in return for space on their servers. Finally, you can pay a monthly fee to an ISP to host your Web site to get more space and bandwidth.

Once you identify a Web host, you next need to consider the domain name that identifies your site. If you're planning to create a commercial site to advertise a product or service, you'll want the domain name to reflect your business. Free Web hosts usually include their names in your Web address. Thus, instead of having a Web address like

 thejpropshop.com

you might have something like

 freewebhosting.net/members/thejpropshop.html

If you're running a site for personal use, this might not be a problem—but it would look unprofessional on a commercial site. If you are planning a commercial site and simply want to advertise your product by publishing an online brochure, you can usually find an inexpensive host and pay a nominal yearly fee to reserve a Web address that reflects your company's name.

Session 1.2 Quick Check

1. Specify the code you would enter to mark the text *The J-Prop Shop* as an `h1` heading and the text *Product List* as an `h2` heading. Add code to group these two headings so browsers recognize them as a heading and subheading, respectively.
2. Specify the code you would enter to mark the text *Hamlet by William Shakespeare* as an `h1` heading, with a line break after the word *Hamlet*.
3. Create an ordered list of the following items: Packers, Bears, Lions, Vikings.
4. Specify the code to access the CSS style sheet file *uwstyles.css*. Where should you place this code within an HTML file?
5. Mark the graphic file *portrait.gif* as an inline image, setting the dimensions to 250 pixels wide by 300 pixels high. Specify the text *David Vinet* as alternate text to be displayed in place of the image for non-graphical browsers.
6. Specify the code to place the *portrait.gif* image from the previous question within a figure box with the caption *David Vinet, owner of the J-Prop Shop*.
7. The trademark symbol (™) has the character encoding number 8482. Provide the HTML code to enter this symbol into your Web page.
8. The Greek letter ß has the character entity name *beta*. How would you enter this symbol into your Web page?

Review Assignments

**Data Files needed for the Review Assignments: basiclogo.png, basicstick.png,
basicstyles.css, modernizr-1.5.js, stick.txt**

Dave has found a host for his Web page and has published the document you helped
him create on the Internet. Now he wants to start adding more pages to his Web site.
He's come to you for help in creating a page describing his basic stick. He's already
written the text for the Web page; he needs you to mark up that text with HTML code.
Figure 1-48 shows a preview of the page you'll create for Dave.

Figure 1-48 **The Basic Stick product page**

Specials This Month

The Basic Stick

The Basic Stick is the perfect stick for beginners. The stick rotates slowly to provide
extra time for performing stick tricks, but is flashy enough to impress your friends.
Enjoy the following:

Our Basic Stick

Patented Dura-Coat® finish ensures sticks can withstand all weather
conditions. More durable than other sticks, these props will keep looking like
new for as long as you own them.

Enhanced stick flexibility provides more bounce, allowing for better tricks. A
soft rubber core adds a whole new element to the sticking experience that you
have to feel to believe!

Full customization will give you the chance to own a pair of sticks unlike any
others out there. I make exactly what you want, with your colors and your
designs.

A personal touch through both my customization options and hand-crafted designs.

Specifications

- Main Stick
 - Weight: 7 oz.
 - Length: 24 inches
 - Tape: Dura-Coat® finish with laser-style color choices
- Handle Sticks (one pair)
 - Weight: 2 oz.
 - Length: 18 inches
 - Tape: Soft ivory tape with rubber core

THE J-PROP SHOP ♦ 541 WEST HIGHLAND DRIVE ♦ AUBURN, ME 04210 ♦ (207) 555 - 9001

Complete the following:

1. Use your text editor to create a new file named **basic.htm**, and then save it in the
 tutorial.01\review folder included with your Data Files.
2. Add the doctype for an HTML5 document.
3. Create the root `html` element and nest the `head` and `body` elements within it.

4. Within the `head` element, insert the comment

   ```
   The J-Prop Shop
   Sample Page for the Basic Stick
   Author: your name
   Date:   the date
   ```

 where *your name* is your name and *the date* is the current date.

5. Add code to specify that the page uses the UTF-8 character set.

6. Set the page title as **Basic Sticks**.

7. Link the file to the **modernizr-1.5.js** script file to enable HTML5 support for older browsers.

8. Link the file to the **basicstyles.css** style sheet file.

9. Within the `body` element, create structural elements for the page header, main section, and footer.

10. Within the page header, insert an `h1` heading containing the inline image file **basiclogo.png**. Specify the following alternate text for the image: **The J-Prop Shop**. Below the `h1` heading, insert an `h2` heading containing the text **Specials This Month**. Group the `h1` and `h2` headings using the `hgroup` element.

11. Within the `section` element, insert an `aside` element. The `aside` element should contain an inline image pointing to the *basicstick.png* file and having the text string **photo** as the alternate text. Below the inline image within the `aside` element, insert a paragraph containing the text string **Our Basic Stick**.

12. Add two `article` elements to the `section` element.

13. Within the first article, insert an `h2` heading containing the text **The Basic Stick**. Add a paragraph containing the following text:

 The Basic Stick is the perfect stick for beginners. The stick rotates slowly to provide extra time for performing stick tricks, but is flashy enough to impress your friends. Enjoy the following:

14. Add a block quote containing the following four paragraphs (you can copy this text from the *stick.txt* file):

 Patented Dura-Coat finish ensures sticks can withstand all weather conditions. More durable than other sticks, these props will keep looking like new for as long as you own them.

 Enhanced stick flexibility provides more bounce, allowing for better tricks. A soft rubber core adds a whole new element to the sticking experience that you have to feel to believe!

 Full customization will give you the chance to own a pair of sticks unlike any others out there. I make exactly what you want, with your colors and your designs. A personal touch through both my customization options and hand-crafted designs.

15. Mark the first few words of each of the four paragraphs as strong text, as shown in Figure 1-48.

16. Within the second article element, insert an `h2` heading with the title **Specifications**.

17. Directly below the `h2` heading, insert an unordered list. The list should contain two items: **Main Stick** and **Handle Sticks (one pair)**.

18. Within the *Main Stick* list item, insert a nested unordered list containing the following items:
 - **Weight: 7 oz.**
 - **Length: 24 inches**
 - **Tape: Dura-Coat finish with laser-style color choices**

19. Within the *Handle Sticks (one pair)* list item, insert a nested unordered list containing the following items:
 - **Weight: 2 oz.**
 - **Length: 18 inches**
 - **Tape: Soft ivory tape with rubber core**

20. Locate the two occurrences of *Dura-Coat* in the document. Directly after the word *Dura-Coat*, insert the registered trademark symbol ®. The character entity name of the ® symbol is *reg*. Display the ® symbol as a superscript by placing the character within the sup element.

21. Within the page footer, insert the company's address:
 The J-Prop Shop
 541 West Highland Drive
 Auburn, ME 04210
 (207) 555 - 9001

22. Separate the different sections of the address using a solid diamond (character code 9830).

23. Save your changes to the file, open it in your Web browser, and then compare your Web page to Figure 1-48 to verify that it was rendered correctly. Older browsers may display some slight differences in the design.

24. Submit your completed files to your instructor, in either printed or electronic form, as requested.

Case Problem 1

Apply your knowledge of HTML5 to create a Web page for a mathematics Web site.

APPLY

Data Files needed for the Case Problem: mhlogo.jpg, mhstyles.css, mhtxt.htm, modernizr-1.5.js

Math High Professor Lauren Coe of the Mathematics Department of Coastal University in Anderson, South Carolina, is one of the founders of *Math High*, a Web site containing articles and course materials for high school and college math instructors. She has written a series of biographies of famous mathematicians for the Web site and would like you to transfer content she's already written to an HTML5 file. You'll create the first one in this exercise. Figure 1-49 shows a preview of the page you'll create, which profiles the mathematician Leonhard Euler.

Figure 1-49 Math High Web page

Leonhard Euler (1707-1783)

The greatest mathematician of the eighteenth century, **Leonhard Euler** was born in Basel, Switzerland. There, he studied under another giant of mathematics, **Jean Bernoulli**. In 1731 Euler became a professor of physics and mathematics at St. Petersburg Academy of Sciences. Euler was the most prolific mathematician of all time, publishing over *800 different books and papers*. His influence was felt in physics and astronomy as well.

He is perhaps best known for his research into mathematical analysis. Euler's work, *Introductio in analysin infinitorum (1748)*, remained a standard textbook in the field for well over a century. For the princess of Anhalt-Dessau he wrote *Lettres à une princesse d'Allemagne (1768-1772)*, giving a clear non-technical outline of the main physical theories of the time.

One can hardly write a mathematical equation without copying Euler. Notations still in use today, such as *e* and π, were introduced in Euler's writings. Leonhard Euler died in 1783, leaving behind a legacy perhaps unmatched, and certainly unsurpassed, in the annals of mathematics.

The Most Beautiful Theorem?

Euler's Equation:

$$cos(x) + i sin(x) = e^{(ix)}$$

demonstrates the relationship between algebra, complex analysis, and trigonometry. From this equation, it's easy to derive the identity:

$$e^{(\pi i)} + 1 = 0$$

which relates the fundamental constants: 0, 1, π, *e*, and *i* in a single beautiful and elegant statement. A poll of readers conducted by *The Mathematical Intelligencer* magazine named Euler's Identity as the most beautiful theorem in the history of mathematics.

MATH HIGH: A SITE FOR EDUCATORS AND RESEARCHERS

Complete the following:

1. In your text editor, open the **mhtxt.htm** file from the tutorial.01\case1 folder included with your Data Files. Save the file as **mathhigh.htm** in the same folder.

2. Enclose the contents of the file within a set of opening and closing `<html>` tags. Set the doctype of the file to indicate that this is an HTML5 document.

3. Add `head` and `body` elements to the file, enclosing the page contents within the body element.

4. Within the document head, insert the comment

 Math High: Leonhard Euler

 Author: *your name*

 Date: *the date*

 where *your name* is your name and *the date* is the current date.

5. Set the character set of the document to **UTF-8**.

6. Add the page title **Math High: Leonhard Euler** to the document head.

7. Link to the **modernizr-1.5.js** script file.

8. Link to the **mhstyles.css** style sheet.

9. Within the page body, create a `header` element. Within this element, insert an inline image using the **mhlogo.jpg** file as the source and **Math High** as the alternate text.

10. Mark the page text from the line *Leonhard Euler (1707 - 1783)* up to (but not including) the line *The Most Beautiful Theorem?* as an article.

11. Mark the first line in the article element, containing *Leonhard Euler (1707 - 1783)*, as an `h1` heading.

12. Mark the next three blocks of text describing Euler's life as paragraphs.

13. Within the first paragraph, mark the names *Leonhard Euler* and *Jean Bernoulli* using the `strong` element. Mark the phrase *800 different books and papers* as emphasized text using the `em` element.

14. In the second paragraph, mark the phrase *Introductio in analysin infinitorum (1748)* as a citation.

15. In the phrase *Lettres a une princesse d'Allemagne*, replace the one-letter word *a* with *à* (the character entity name is *agrave*). Mark the entire publication name as a citation.

16. In the third paragraph, mark the notation for *e* as a `var` element and replace *pi* with the character π (the character reference name is *pi*).

17. Enclose the next section of text from the line *The Most Beautiful Theorem?* up to (but not including) the line *Math High: A Site for Educators and Researchers* as an aside.

18. Mark the text *The Most Beautiful Theorem?* as an `h1` heading.

19. Mark the next five blocks of text as individual paragraphs.

20. In the first equation, mark the letters *e*, *i*, and *x* using the `var` element (but do not italicize the *i* in *sin*). Mark the term (ix) as a superscript.

21. In the second equation, replace *pi* with the character π. Mark the letters *e* and *i* using the `var` element. Mark (πi) as a superscript.

22. In the last paragraph, mark the notations for *e* and *i* with the `var` element and replace *pi* with π.

23. Mark the journal name *The Mathematical Intelligencer* as a citation.

24. Mark the final line in the file as a footer.

25. Save your changes to the file, and then verify that the page appears correctly in your Web browser.

26. Submit your completed files to your instructor, in either printed or electronic form, as requested.

Apply your knowledge of HTML to create a page showing text from a scene of a Shakespeare play.

APPLY

Case Problem 2

Data Files needed for the Case Problem: macbeth.jpg, macbethtxt.htm, macstyles.css, modernizr-1.5.js

Mansfield Classical Theatre Steve Karls is the director of Mansfield Classical Theatre, a theatre company for young people located in Mansfield, Ohio. This summer the company is planning to perform the Shakespeare play *Macbeth*. Steve wants to put the text of the play on the company's Web site and has asked for your help in designing and completing the Web page. Steve wants a separate page for each scene from the play. A preview of the page you'll create for Act I, Scene 1 is shown in Figure 1-50. Steve has already typed the text of the scene. He needs you to supply the HTML code.

Figure 1-50 Macbeth Act I, Scene 1 Web page

Presented by: Mansfield Classical Theatre

ACT I

SCENE 1

Summary A thunderstorm approaches and three witches convene. They agree to confront the great Scot general Macbeth upon his victorious return from a war between Scotland and Norway. Soon, heroic Macbeth will receive the title of Thane of Cawdor from King Duncan. However, Macbeth learns from the witches that he is fated for greater things and he will be led down the path of destruction by his unquenchable ambition.

A desert place.

Thunder and lightning. Enter three Witches.

First Witch
> When shall we three meet again
> In thunder, lightning, or in rain?

Second Witch
> When the hurlyburly's done,
> When the battle's lost and won.

Third Witch
> That will be ere the set of sun.

First Witch
> Where the place?

Second Witch
> Upon the heath.

Third Witch
> There to meet with Macbeth.

First Witch
> I come, Graymalkin!

Second Witch
> Paddock calls.

Third Witch
> Anon.

ALL
> Fair is foul, and foul is fair:
> Hover through the fog and filthy air.

Exeunt

Go to Scene 2 ⇒

TEXT PROVIDED BY ONLINE SHAKESPEARE

Complete the following:

1. Open the **macbethtxt.htm** file from the tutorial.01\case2 folder included with your Data Files. Save the file as **macbeth.htm** in the same folder.

2. Enclose the entire Macbeth text within the structure of an HTML document including the `html`, `head`, and `body` elements. Add a doctype to the document head to indicate that the page is written in HTML5.

3. Within the head section, insert a comment containing the following text:

 Macbeth: Act I, Scene 1

 Author: *your name*

 Date: *the date*

4. Add the page title **Macbeth: Act I, Scene 1**.

5. Link the file to the **modernizr-1.5.js** script file and to the **macstyles.css** style sheet. Set the character set to **UTF-8**.

6. Within the `body` element, insert a heading group consisting of an `h1` heading and an `h2` heading. Within the `h1` heading, insert an inline image containing the *macbeth.jpg* image file. Specify **Macbeth** as the alternate text. Within the `h2` heading, enter the text **Presented by: Mansfield Classical Theatre**.

7. Enclose the text of the play within a `section` element.

8. Mark the text *ACT I* as an `h2` heading. Mark *SCENE 1* as an `h3` heading. Group the two headings within an `hgroup` element.

9. Mark the summary of the scene as a paragraph. Mark the word *Summary* using the strong element.

10. In the text of the play, mark the descriptions of setting, scene, and exits as separate paragraphs and italicize the text using the i element, as shown in Figure 1-50.

⊕ **EXPLORE** 11. Mark the dialog as a description list, with each character's name marked as a description term and each speech marked as a description. When a speech includes two lines, add a line break at the end of the first line to keep the speech on separate lines, as shown in the figure.

⊕ **EXPLORE** 12. Directly below the paragraph containing the text *Exeunt*, insert the line **Go to Scene 2**. Mark this line as a `div` element with the id value *direction*. At the end of this line, insert a **right arrow character** using the 8658 character number. Add horizontal rules directly above and below this statement.

13. Mark the line *Text provided by Online Shakespeare* as a footer. Make sure the `footer` element is below the `section` element.

14. Save your changes to the file, and then confirm the layout and content of the page in your Web browser.

15. Submit the completed files to your instructor, in either printed or electronic form, as requested.

Explore how to use HTML to create a recipe page.

CHALLENGE

Case Problem 3

Data Files needed for the Case Problem: dessertstyles.css, dessertweb.jpg, modernizr-1.5.js, torte.jpg, tortetxt.htm

dessertWEB Amy Wu wants to take her enjoyment of cooking and her love of sharing recipes to the World Wide Web. She's interested in creating a new Web site called *dessertWEB* where other cooks can submit and review dessert recipes. Each page within her site will contain a photo and description of a dessert, along with a list of ingredients, cooking directions, and a list of reviews. Each recipe will be rated on a five-star scale. She already has information on one recipe: Apple Bavarian Torte. She's asked for your help in creating a Web page from the data she's collected. A preview of the completed page is shown in Figure 1-51.

Figure 1-51 dessertWeb menu page

dessertWEB

Apple Bavarian Torte (★★★★)

A classic European torte baked in a springform pan. Cream cheese, sliced almonds, and apples make this the perfect holiday treat (12 servings).

INGREDIENTS
- ½ cup butter
- ⅓ cup white sugar
- ¼ teaspoon vanilla extract
- 1 cup all-purpose flour
- 1 (8 ounce) package cream cheese
- ¼ cup white sugar
- 1 egg
- ½ teaspoon vanilla extract
- 6 apples - peeled, cored, and sliced
- ⅓ cup white sugar
- ½ teaspoon ground cinnamon
- ¼ cup sliced almonds

DIRECTIONS
1. Preheat oven to 450° F (230° C).
2. Cream together butter, sugar, vanilla, and flour.
3. Press crust mixture into the flat bottom of a 9-inch springform pan. Set aside.
4. In a medium bowl, blend cream cheese and sugar. Beat in egg and vanilla. Pour cheese mixture over crust.
5. Toss apples with sugar and cinnamon. Spread apple mixture over all.
6. Bake for 10 minutes. Reduce heat to 400° F (200° C) and continue baking for 25 minutes.
7. Sprinkle almonds over top of torte. Continue baking until lightly browned. Cool before removing from pan.

REVIEWS

★★★★
I loved the buttery taste of the crust which complements the apples very nicely.
— Reviewed on Sep. 22, 2014 by MMASON.

★★
Nothing special. I like the crust, but there was a little too much of it for my taste, and I liked the filling but there was too little of it. I thought the crunchy apples combined with the sliced almonds detracted from the overall flavor.
— Reviewed on Sep. 1, 2014 by GLENDACHEF.

★★★★★
Delicious!! I recommend microwaving the apples for 3 minutes before baking, to soften them. Great dessert - I'll be making it again for the holidays.
— Reviewed on August 28, 2014 by BBABS.

Complete the following:

1. Open the **tortetxt.htm** file from the tutorial.01\case3 folder included with your Data Files. Save the file as **torte.htm** in the same folder.
2. Add the structure of an HTML5 document around the recipe text. Within the head element, insert a comment containing the following text:
 Apple Bavarian Torte
 Author: *your name*
 Date: *the date*
3. Set the character set of the document to **ISO-8859-1**.
4. Link the document to the **modernizr-1.5.js** script file and the **dessertstyles.css** style sheet file.
5. Specify **Apple Bavarian Torte Recipe** as the page title.
6. Within the body element, add a header element. Within the header element, insert an h1 heading containing the inline image **dessertweb.jpg** with the alternate text **dessertWEB**.

7. Enclose the recipe description, ingredients list, and directions within a `section` element. Enclose the recipe reviews within an `aside` element.

8. Mark the text *Apple Bavarian Torte* as an `h1` heading.

⊕EXPLORE
9. Replace the text *(4 stars)* in the `h1` heading with a set of four **star symbols** (character number 9733).

⊕EXPLORE
10. Directly below the `h1` heading, insert the inline image **torte.jpg**. Specify the alternate text **Torte image**. Set the width of the image to **250** pixels.

11. Mark the description of the dessert as a paragraph.

12. Mark *INGREDIENTS* and *DIRECTIONS* as `h2` headings.

13. Mark the list of ingredients as an unordered list. Mark the list of directions as an ordered list.

⊕EXPLORE
14. Within the ingredients, replace the occurrences of 1/2 with the character symbol ½ (reference number 189), the occurrences of 1/4 with the symbol ¼ (reference number 188), and the occurrences of 1/3 with the symbol ⅓ (reference number 8531.)

⊕EXPLORE
15. Replace each occurrence of the word *degrees* in the directions with the degree symbol (°) (character name *deg*).

16. Mark *REVIEWS* within the `aside` element as an `h1` heading.

17. Change the text of each customer star rating to a set of **star symbols** using character number 9733 placed within a paragraph.

⊕EXPLORE
18. Enclose the text of each customer review in a paragraph nested within a `blockquote` element. Place the name of the reviewer and the date on a new line within that paragraph. Insert an **em-dash** (character name *mdash*) before the word *Reviewed* in each of the reviews. Enclose the date of each review within a `time` element and enclose by *reviewer* within a `cite` element where *reviewer* is the name of the reviewer.

19. Save your changes to the file, and then verify the layout and content of the page in your Web browser.

20. Submit the completed files to your instructor, in either printed or electronic form, as requested.

Test your knowledge of HTML and use your creativity to design a Web page for an exercise equipment company.

RESEARCH

Case Problem 4

Data Files needed for the Case Problem: logo.jpg, smith.jpg, and smith.txt

Body Systems Body Systems is a leading manufacturer of home gyms. The company recently hired you to assist in developing its Web site. Your first task is to create a Web page for the LSM400, a popular weight machine sold by the company. You've been given a text file describing the features of the LSM400. You've also received two image files: one of the company's logo and one of the LSM400. You are free to supplement these files with any other resources available to you. You are responsible for the page's content and appearance.

Complete the following:

1. Create a new HTML5 file named **smith.htm** and save it in the tutorial.01\case4 folder included with your Data Files.

2. Add the appropriate doctype for HTML5 to the beginning of the file.

3. Add a comment to the document head describing the document's content and containing your name and the date.

4. Add an appropriate page title to the document head.

5. Set the character set of the file to **UTF-8**.

6. Use the contents of the **smith.txt** document (located in the tutorial.01\case4 folder) as the basis of the document body. Include at least one example of each of the following:

- structural elements such as the `header`, `footer`, `section`, and `aside` elements
- grouping elements including a heading and a paragraph
- an ordered or unordered list
- a text-level element
- an inline image
- a character entity reference or a character encoding number

7. Structure your HTML5 code so that it's easy for others to read and understand.

8. Save your changes to the file, and then open it in your Web browser to verify that it is readable.

9. Submit your completed files to your instructor, in either printed or electronic form, as requested.

ENDING SOLUTION FILES

tutorial.01 → **tutorial**

jprop.htm
jpslogo.png
jpsstyles.css
modernizr-1.5.js

review

basic.htm
basiclogo.png
basicstick.png
basicstyles.css
modernizr-1.5.js

case1

mathhigh.htm
mhlogo.jpg
mhstyles.css
modernizr-1.5.js

case2

macbeth.htm
macbeth.jpg
macstyles.css
modernizr-1.5.js

case3

dessertstyles.css
dessertweb.jpg
modernizr-1.5.js
torte.htm
torte.jpg

case4

logo.jpg
smith.jpg
smith.htm

TUTORIAL **2**

Developing a Web Site

Creating a Web Site for Amateur Photographers

Case | *CAMshots*

Gerry Hayward is an amateur photographer and digital camera enthusiast. He's creating a Web site named *CAMshots*, where he can offer advice and information to people who are just getting started with digital photography, or who are long-time hobbyists like himself and are looking to share tips and ideas. Gerry's Web site will contain several pages, with each page dedicated to a particular topic. He has created a few sample pages for the Web site, but he hasn't linked them together. He has asked for your help in designing his site and creating links between the pages.

OBJECTIVES

Session 2.1
- Explore how to storyboard a Web site
- Create navigation lists
- Create links between documents in a Web site
- Understand absolute and relative folder paths
- Set a base path
- Mark a location with the id attribute
- Create a link to an id

Session 2.2
- Mark an image as a link
- Create an image map
- Understand URLs
- Link to a resource on the Web
- Link to an e-mail address
- Work with hypertext attributes
- Work with metadata

HTML

STARTING DATA FILES

tutorial.02 →

tutorial
glosstxt.htm
hometxt.htm
tipstxt.htm
+ 1 style sheet
+ 5 graphic files
modernizr-1.5.js

review
camhome.htm
childtxt.htm
contesttxt.htm
flowertxt.htm
photogloss.htm
scenictxt.htm

tipweek.htm
+ 1 style sheet
+ 23 graphic files
modernizr-1.5.js

case1
uwlisttxt.htm
+ 1 style sheet
+ 1 graphic file
+ 1 text file
modernizr-1.5.js

case2
hometxt.htm
slide1txt.htm
slide2txt.htm
slide3txt.htm
slide4txt.htm

slide5txt.htm
slide6txt.htm
+ 1 style sheet
+ 18 graphic files
modernizr-1.5.js

case3
dist1txt.htm
dist2txt.htm
dist3txt.htm
dist4txt.htm
kansastxt.htm

+ 1 style sheet
+ 2 graphic files
+ 1 text file
modernizr-1.5.js

case4
characters.txt
notes.txt
tempest.txt
tempest.jpg

SESSION 2.1 VISUAL OVERVIEW

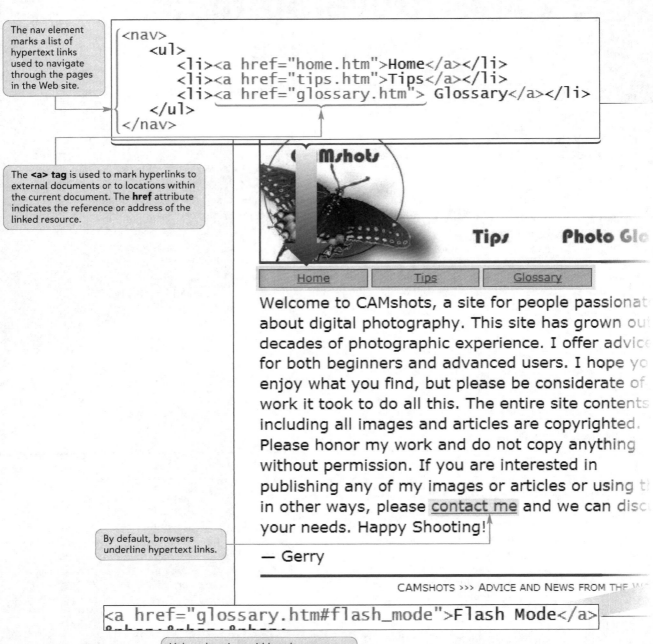

The nav element marks a list of hypertext links used to navigate through the pages in the Web site.

```
<nav>
    <ul>
        <li><a href="home.htm">Home</a></li>
        <li><a href="tips.htm">Tips</a></li>
        <li><a href="glossary.htm"> Glossary</a></li>
    </ul>
</nav>
```

The **<a> tag** is used to mark hyperlinks to external documents or to locations within the current document. The **href** attribute indicates the reference or address of the linked resource.

Home Tips Glossary

Welcome to CAMshots, a site for people passionat about digital photography. This site has grown ou decades of photographic experience. I offer advic for both beginners and advanced users. I hope yo enjoy what you find, but please be considerate of work it took to do all this. The entire site content including all images and articles are copyrighted. Please honor my work and do not copy anything without permission. If you are interested in publishing any of my images or articles or using t in other ways, please contact me and we can disc your needs. Happy Shooting!

— Gerry

By default, browsers underline hypertext links.

CAMSHOTS >>> ADVICE AND NEWS FROM THE W

```
<a href="glossary.htm#flash_mode">Flash Mode</a>
```

Links to locations within a document are referenced using the form *file#id*, where file is the name of the file and id is the id marking the location within the file.

CREATING HYPERLINKS

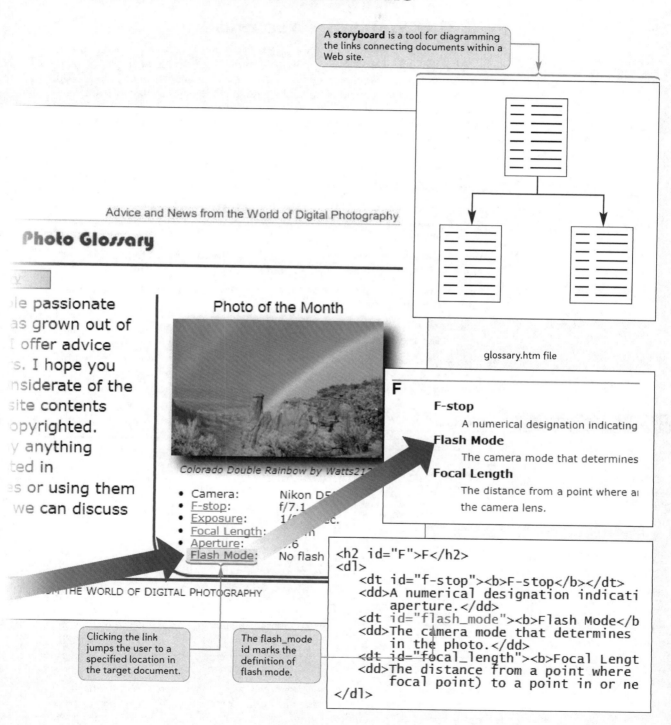

A **storyboard** is a tool for diagramming the links connecting documents within a Web site.

glossary.htm file

Advice and News from the World of Digital Photography

Photo Glossary

le passionate
as grown out of
I offer advice
s. I hope you
nsiderate of the
site contents
opyrighted.
y anything
ted in
s or using them
we can discuss

Photo of the Month

Colorado Double Rainbow by Watts212

- Camera: Nikon D5
- F-stop: f/7.1
- Exposure: 1/ ec.
- Focal Length: n
- Aperture: .6
- Flash Mode: No flash

M THE WORLD OF DIGITAL PHOTOGRAPHY

F

F-stop
 A numerical designation indicating

Flash Mode
 The camera mode that determines

Focal Length
 The distance from a point where a
 the camera lens.

Clicking the link jumps the user to a specified location in the target document.

The flash_mode id marks the definition of flash mode.

```html
<h2 id="F">F</h2>
<dl>
   <dt id="f-stop"><b>F-stop</b></dt>
   <dd>A numerical designation indicati
      aperture.</dd>
   <dt id="flash_mode"><b>Flash Mode</b
   <dd>The camera mode that determines
      in the photo.</dd>
   <dt id="focal_length"><b>Focal Lengt
   <dd>The distance from a point where
      focal point) to a point in or ne
</dl>
```

Exploring Web Site Structures

You meet with Gerry to discuss his plans for the CAMshots Web site. Gerry has already created a prototype for the Web site containing three pages written in HTML5: One page is the site's home page and contains general information about CAMshots; the second page contains tips about digital photography; and the third page contains a partial glossary of photographic terms. The pages are not complete, nor are they linked to one another. You'll begin your work for Gerry by viewing these files in your text editor and browser.

To view Gerry's Web pages:

1. Start your text editor, and then open the **hometxt.htm**, **tipstxt.htm**, and **glosstxt.htm** files, located in the tutorial.02\tutorial folder included with your Data Files.

2. Within each file, go to the comment section at the top of the file and add **your name** and **the date** in the space provided.

3. Save the files as **home.htm**, **tips.htm**, and **glossary.htm**, respectively, in the tutorial.02\tutorial folder.

4. Take some time to review the HTML code within each document so that you understand the structure and content of the files.

5. Start your Web browser and open the **home.htm**, **tips.htm**, and **glossary.htm** files. Figure 2-1 shows the current layout and appearance of Gerry's three Web pages.

| Figure 2-1 | Versions of HTML |

| home.htm | tips.htm | glossary.htm |
| the CAMshots home page | the CAMshots tips of the week | partial glossary of photography terms |

Gerry wants to create links among the three pages so that users can easily navigate from one page to another. Before you write code for the links, it's worthwhile to use a technique known as storyboarding to map out exactly how you want the pages to relate to each other. A storyboard is a diagram of a Web site's structure, showing all the pages in the site and indicating how they are linked together. Because Web sites use a variety of structures, it's important to storyboard your Web site before you start creating your

pages. This helps you determine which structure works best for the type of information your site contains. A well-designed structure ensures that users will be able to navigate the site without getting lost or missing important information.

Every Web site should begin with a single **home page** that acts as a focal point for the Web site. It is usually the first page that users see. From that home page, you add links to other pages in the site, defining the site's overall structure. The Web sites you commonly encounter as you navigate the Web employ several different Web structures. You'll examine some of these structures to help you decide how to design your own sites.

Linear Structures

If you wanted to create an online version of a famous play, like Shakespeare's *Hamlet*, one method would be to link the individual scenes of the play in a long chain. Figure 2-2 shows the storyboard for this **linear structure**, in which each page is linked with the pages that follow and precede it. Readers navigate this structure by moving forward and backward through the pages, much as they might move forward and backward through the pages of a book.

Figure 2-2 **A linear structure**

Linear structures work for Web sites that are small in size and have a clearly defined order of pages. However, they can be difficult to work with as the chain of pages increases in length. An additional problem is that in a linear structure, you move farther and farther away from the home page as you progress through the site. Because home pages often contain important general information about a site and its author, this is usually not the best design technique.

You can modify this structure to make it easier for users to return immediately to the home page or other main pages. Figure 2-3 shows this online play with an **augmented linear structure**, in which each page contains an additional link back to the opening page of each act.

Figure 2-3 **An augmented linear structure**

Hierarchical Structures

Another popular structure is the **hierarchical structure**, in which the home page links to pages dedicated to specific topics. Those pages, in turn, can be linked to even more specific topics. A hierarchical structure allows users to easily move from general to specific and back again. In the case of the online play, you could link an introductory page containing general information about the play to pages that describe each of the play's acts, and within each act you could include links to individual scenes. See Figure 2-4. Within this structure, a user could move quickly to a specific scene within the play, bypassing the need to move through each scene that precedes it.

Figure 2-4	A hierarchical structure

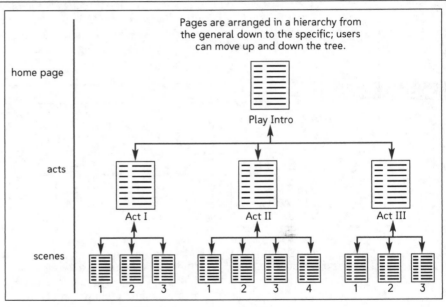

Mixed Structures

With larger and more complex Web sites, you often need to use a combination of structures. Figure 2-5 shows the online play using a mixture of hierarchical and linear structures. The overall form is hierarchical, as users can move from a general introduction down to individual scenes; however, users can also move through the site in a linear fashion, going from act to act and scene to scene. Finally, each individual scene contains a link to the home page, allowing users to jump to the top of the hierarchy without moving through the different levels.

| Figure 2-5 | A mixed structure |

As these examples show, a little foresight can go a long way toward making your Web site easier to use. Also keep in mind that search results from a Web search engine such as Google or Yahoo! can point users to any page in your Web site—not just your home page—so they will need to be able to quickly understand what your site contains and how to navigate it. At a minimum, each page should contain a link to the site's home page or to the relevant main topic page. In some cases, you might want to supply your users with a **site index**, which is a page containing an outline of the entire site and its contents. Unstructured Web sites can be difficult and frustrating to use. Consider the storyboard of the site displayed in Figure 2-6.

Figure 2-6 Web site with no coherent structure

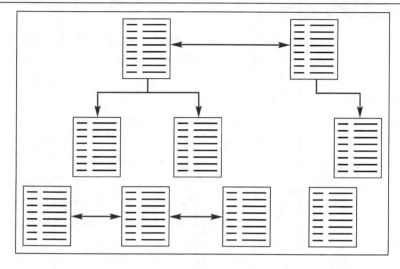

This confusing structure makes it difficult for users to grasp the site's contents and scope. The user might not even be aware of the presence of some pages because there are no connecting links, and some of the links point in only one direction. The Web is a competitive place; studies have shown that users who don't see how to get what they want within the first few seconds often leave a Web site. How long would a user spend on a site like the one shown in Figure 2-6?

Protected Structures

Sections of most commercial Web sites are off-limits except to subscribers and registered customers. As shown in Figure 2-7, these sites have a password-protected Web page that users must go through to get to the off-limits areas. The same Web site design principles apply to the protected section as the regular, open section of the site.

Figure 2-7 A protected structure

Storyboarding a protected structure is particularly important to ensure that no unauthorized access to the protected area is allowed in the site design.

Creating a Navigation List

Every Web site should include a **navigation list**, which is a list containing links to the main topic areas of the site. Ideally, this same list should appear prominently on every page, usually near the top of the page as part of the header or as a sidebar to the main content.

HTML5 introduced the `nav` structural element to make it easier to mark up navigation lists. The syntax of the element is

```
<nav>
    list of navigation links
</nav>
```

where `list of navigation links` is a list of elements that are linked to other pages on the Web site. Prior to HTML5, such lists would often be inserted within the generic `div` element as

```
<div id="id">
    list of navigation links
</div>
```

where `id` is whatever id the page author would supply to identify the navigation list.

Gerry suggests you add the topics for his three sample pages as an unordered list within the `nav` element as follows:

```
<nav>
    <ul>
        <li>Home</li>
        <li>Tips</li>
        <li>Glossary</li>
    </ul>
</nav>
```

Gerry has already designed styles for these new elements and placed them within the camstyles.css style sheet. The style sheet will format the elements so that the list appears as a horizontally aligned set of boxes. As Gerry adds more sample pages, he can easily extend this list to include the new topics, but for now he needs only these three.

Add this navigation list to each of the three sample pages that Gerry has given you.

To create the navigation list:

1. Return to the **home.htm** file in your text editor.

2. At the top of the file directly below the header element, insert the following code as shown in Figure 2-8:

```
<nav>
    <ul>
        <li>Home</li>
        <li>Tips</li>
        <li>Glossary</li>
    </ul>
</nav>
```

Figure 2-8 Marking a navigation list

navigation list marked
with the nav element

```
<body>

    <header>
        <img src="camshots.jpg" alt="CAMshots" />
    </header>

    <nav>
        <ul>
            <li>Home</li>
            <li>Tips</li>
            <li>Glossary</li>
        </ul>
    </nav>
```

3. Save your changes to the file.

4. Go to the **tips.htm** file in your text editor and then repeat Steps 2 and 3, placing the navigation list in the same place as you did in the home.htm file and saving your changes.

5. Go to the **glossary.htm** file in your text editor and then repeat Steps 2 and 3 to add a navigation list to that file.

6. Open or refresh the **home.htm** file in your Web browser. Verify that the navigation list appears directly below the page header as shown in Figure 2-9.

Figure 2-9 Navigation list in the CAMshots home page

navigation list
formatted as a
horizontal set
of boxes

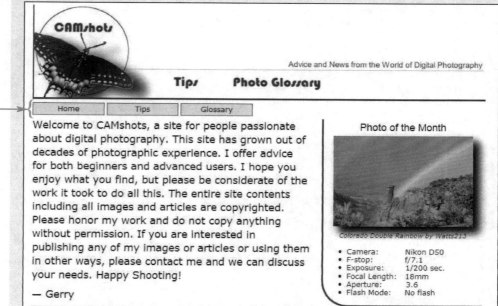

7. Open or refresh the **tips.htm** and **glossary.htm** files in your Web browser and verify that a similar navigation list appears at the top of those pages.

INSIGHT

Navigation Lists and Web Accessibility

One challenge of Web design is creating Web documents that are accessible to users with disabilities. Studies indicate that about 20% of the population has some type of disability. Many of these disabilities don't affect users' capacity to interact with the Web. But in some cases, users may need specialized Web browsers, such as screen readers that provide Web content aurally for visually impaired users.

To accommodate these users, Web page authors can take advantage of the structural elements provided by HTML5. For example, the nav element can allow users to either quickly jump to a list of links or bypass such a list if they are more interested in the content of the current document. Prior to HTML5 and the nav element, there was no way of differentiating one list from another, and thus disabled users would be forced to wait through a rendering of the same navigation list for each page they visited.

Because support for HTML5 is still in its infancy at the time of this writing, most specialized browsers have not incorporated features that enable users to quickly access the structural elements of most interest to them. However, as the specifications for HTML5 are finalized and fully supported by the browser market, this ability will become more commonly supported. Thus you should use the nav element and other structural elements from HTML5 to provide more information to browsers about the content and structure of your Web documents.

Working with Hypertext Links

Now that you've added a navigation list to each of the three sample pages, you will change each item in those lists into a hypertext link so that users can easily move between the three sample pages. Figure 2-10 shows the storyboard for the simple structure you have in mind.

Figure 2-10 **Storyboard for the CAMshots sample Web site**

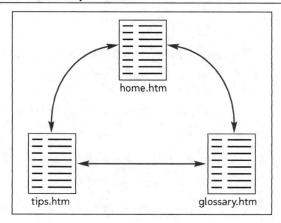

Hypertext links are created by enclosing some document content within a set of opening and closing <a> tags. The general syntax to create a hypertext link is

```
<a href="reference">content</a>
```

where *reference* is the location being linked to and *content* is the document content that is being marked as a link. The *reference* value can be a page on the World Wide

Web, a local file, an e-mail address, or a network server. For example, to create a hypertext link to the tips.htm file, you could enter the following code:

```
<a href="tips.htm">Photography Tips</a>
```

This code marks the text *Photography Tips* as a hypertext link. If a user clicks the text, the browser will load the linked resource (tips.htm). Note that filenames are case sensitive on some operating systems, such as the UNIX operating system. Web servers running on those systems differentiate between files named tips.htm and Tips.htm. For this reason, you might find that links you create on your computer do not work when you transfer your files to a Web server. To avoid this problem, the current standard is to always use lowercase filenames for all Web site files and to avoid using special characters and blank spaces.

Most browsers underline hypertext links unless a different style is specified in a user-defined style sheet. The font color of a link also changes based on whether or not the user has also visited the linked resource. By default, most browsers display hypertext links as follows:

TIP

Keep your filenames short and descriptive so that users are less apt to make a typing error when accessing your Web site.

- An unvisited link is underlined and blue.
- A previously visited link is underlined and purple.
- A link currently being clicked or activated is underlined and red.

However, Web page authors can use CSS to override these default settings.

REFERENCE

Marking a Hypertext Link

- To mark content as a hypertext link, use

```
<a href="reference">content</a>
```

where `reference` is the location being linked to and `content` is the document content that is being marked as a link.

You'll mark the names of the three sample pages in the navigation list you just created as hypertext links.

To create a hypertext link to a document:

1. Return to the **home.htm** file in your text editor and go to the navigation list at the top of the page.

2. Mark the text *Home* as a hypertext link using a set of <a> tags as follows:

```
<a href="home.htm">Home</a>
```

3. Mark the text *Tips* as a hypertext link using the following code:

```
<a href="tips.htm">Tips</a>
```

4. Mark the text *Glossary* as a hypertext link as follows:

```
<a href="glossary.htm">Glossary</a>
```

Figure 2-11 highlights the revised text in the home.htm file.

Figure 2-11 | Marking hypertext links in the navigation list

reference of the hypertext link

```
<nav>
    <ul>
        <li><a href="home.htm">Home</a></li>
        <li><a href="tips.htm">Tips</a></li>
        <li><a href="glossary.htm">Glossary</a></li>
    </ul>
</nav>
```

5. Save your changes to the file.

6. Go to the **tips.htm** file in your text editor and then repeat Steps 2 through 5 to change the text of the navigation list to hypertext links, saving your changes.

7. Go to the **glossary.htm** file in your text editor and then repeat Steps 2 through 5, saving your changes.

Now that you've added hypertext links to each of the three documents, you'll test those links in your browser.

8. Reload or refresh the **home.htm** file in your Web browser. As shown in Figure 2-12, the entries in the navigation list are underlined, providing a visual clue to the user that they are hypertext links.

Figure 2-12 | Viewing hypertext links in the navigation list

hypertext links underlined by default

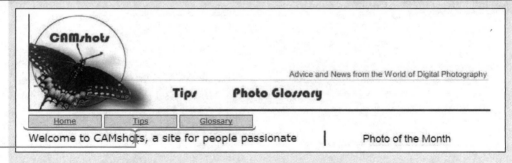

9. Click the **Tips** link in the navigation list. The Tips page should open in your browser.

10. Within the Tips page, click the **Glossary** link in the navigation list and then verify that the Glossary page opens.

11. Within the Glossary page, click the **Home** link in the navigation list to return to the CAMshots home page.

Trouble? If the links do not work, check the spelling of the filenames in the href attributes of the <a> tags. Because some Web servers require you to match capitalization in a filename, you should verify this in your attributes as well.

INSIGHT

Interpreting the <a> Tag in Different Versions of HTML

The <a> tag is treated slightly differently in versions of HTML prior to HTML5. In HTML 4.01 and XHTML, the <a> tag can be used to enclose only text-level elements and should not be used to group content or structural elements. This means that the code

```
<a href="home.htm">
   <p>Go to the home page</p>
</a>
```

would not be allowed because the hyperlink is applied to an entire paragraph. HTML5 does not make this distinction, allowing the <a> tag to enclose text-level, grouping, and structural elements.

A second important difference is that in HTML 4.01 and XHTML, the <a> tag can also be used as an anchor to mark specific locations within the document. For that reason, the <a> tag is commonly referred to as the tag for the anchor element. HTML5 does not support this interpretation; the <a> tag can be used only to mark hypertext links.

Attributes of the a Element

The a element supports several attributes in addition to the href attribute. Some of these attributes are listed in Figure 2-13.

Figure 2-13 Attributes of the anchor (a) element

Attribute	Description
charset="encoding"	Specifies the character encoding used in the linked resource (not supported in HTML5)
href="url"	Indicates the resource targeted by the hypertext link
media="media type"	Indicates the media device in which the linked resource should be viewed (HTML5)
name="name"	Assigns a name for the section anchored by the <a> tag (not supported in HTML5)
rel="relationship"	Specifies the relationship between the current document and the linked resource
ping="url"	A space-separated list of resources that get notified when the user follows the hyperlink (HTML5)
target="target_type"	Specifies where to open the linked resource
type="mime-type"	Specifies the content (the mime-type) of the linked resource

For example, the following code uses the `media` attribute to indicate to browsers that the linked resource is suitable for printing:

```
<a href="orderform.htm" media="print">
   View an Order Form
</a>
```

The `media` attribute doesn't instruct the browser to print the linked file; it just tells the browser for what kind of output media the file has been designed. On the other hand, the following code uses the `type` attribute to indicate the file format of the linked file:

```
<a href="photo.png" mime-type="image/png">
   View the photo of the month
</a>
```

In this case, the browser is forewarned that the linked file is a graphic image file in the PNG format. Some browsers can use the `mime-type` attribute to load applications and programs to view the linked document. But in most cases, the browser determines the file format as it receives the document from the Web server, and thus no `mime-type` attribute is required.

Specifying a Folder Path

In the links you just created, you specified the filename but not the location of the file. When you specify only the filename, the browser assumes that the file is in the same folder as the document containing the hypertext link. However, large Web sites containing hundreds of documents often place documents in separate folders to make them easier to manage.

As Gerry adds more files to his Web site, he will probably want to use folders to organize the files. Figure 2-14 shows a preview of how Gerry might employ those folders. In this case, the top folder containing all of the content of the Web site is named *camshots*. Gerry might place some of his HTML files within the *pages* folder, which he would then divide into three subfolders, named *tips*, *glossary*, and *articles*. He could also create separate folders for the images and video clips used on his Web site.

Figure 2-14 A sample folder structure

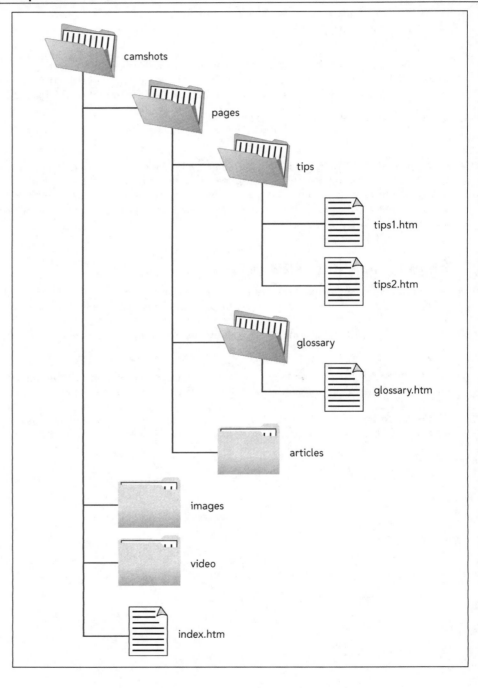

To create a link to a file located in a folder other than the current document's folder, you must specify that file's location, or **path**. HTML supports two kinds of paths: absolute and relative.

Absolute Paths

An **absolute path** specifies a file's precise location within the entire folder structure of a computer. Absolute paths employ the syntax

```
/folder1/folder2/folder3/file
```

where `folder1` is the top folder in the hierarchy, followed by `folder2`, `folder3`, and so forth, down to the file you want to link to. Figure 2-15 shows how you would express absolute paths to the four files listed in Figure 2-14.

| Figure 2-15 | Absolute paths |

Absolute Path	Interpretation
/camshots/pages/tips/tips1.htm	The tips1.htm file located in the pages/tips subfolder
/camshots/pages/tips/tips2.htm	The tips2.htm file located in the pages/tips subfolder
/camshots/pages/glossary/glossary.htm	The glossary.htm file located in the pages/glossary subfolder
/camshots/index.htm	The index.htm file located in the camshots folder

If files are located on different drives as well as in different folders, you must include the drive letter in the path

```
/drive|/folder1/folder2/folder3/file
```

where `drive` is the letter assigned to the drive. For example, the tips1.htm file located on drive C in the */camshots/pages/tips* folder would have the absolute path

```
/C|/camshots/pages/tips/tips1.htm
```

Note that you don't have to include a drive letter if the linked document is located on the same drive as the current file.

Relative Paths

When many folders and subfolders are involved, absolute paths can be cumbersome and confusing to use. For this reason, most Web designers prefer to use relative paths. A **relative path** specifies a file's location in relation to the location of the current document. If the file is in the same location as the current document, the relative path is simply the filename. If the file is in a subfolder of the current document, include the name of the subfolder without the forward slash, as follows

```
folder/file
```

where `folder` is the name of the subfolder, which is also known as a **child folder**. Note that folders used in relative paths are often referenced using relative names, such as parent, child, sibling, and so forth. For example, to go farther down the folder tree to other subfolders, include those folder names in the relative path separated by forward slashes, as in

```
folder1/folder2/folder3/file
```

where *folder1*, *folder2*, *folder3*, and so forth are subfolders, or **descendent folders**, of the current folder. Going in the opposite direction, a relative path moving up the folder tree to a **parent folder** is indicated by starting the path with a double period (..) followed by a forward slash and the name of the file. Thus, the relative path

```
../file
```

TIP

You can reference the current folder using a single period (.) character.

references the *file* document located in the parent folder. Finally, to reference a different folder on the same level as the current folder, known as a **sibling folder**, you move up the folder tree using the double period (..) to the parent and then back down to a different folder. The general syntax is

```
../folder/file
```

where *folder* is the name of the sibling folder. Figure 2-16 shows the relative paths to the six files in the tree from Figure 2-14, starting from the *camshots/pages/tips* subfolder.

Figure 2-16 Relative paths

Relative Path from the /camshots/pages/tips Subfolder	Interpretation
tips1.htm	The tips1.htm file located in the current folder
tips2.htm	The tips2.htm file located in the current folder
../glossary/glossary.htm	The glossary.htm file located in the sibling glossary folder
../../index.htm	The index.htm file located in the parent camshots folder

You should almost always use relative paths in your links. If you have to move your files to a different computer or server, you can move the entire folder structure without having to edit the relative paths you've created. If you use absolute paths, you will probably have to revise each link to reflect the new location of the folder tree on the computer.

Setting the Base Path

As you've just seen, a browser resolves relative paths based on the location of the current document. You can change this behavior by using the `base` element to specify a different starting location for all relative paths. The `base` element has the syntax

```
<base href="path" />
```

where *path* is the folder location that you want the browser to use when resolving relative paths in the current document. The `base` element must be nested within the `head` element of the HTML file so it can be applied to all hypertext links found within the document.

REFERENCE

Using the base *Element*

• To set the default location for a relative path, add the element

```
<base href="path" />
```

to the document head, where *path* is the folder location that you want browsers to use when resolving relative paths in the current document.

The base element is useful when a single document is moved to a new folder. Rather than rewriting all of the relative paths to reflect the document's new location, the base element redirects browsers to the document's old location, allowing any relative paths to be resolved as they were before.

PROSKILLS

Problem Solving: Managing Your Web Site

Web sites can quickly grow from a couple of pages to dozens or hundreds of pages. As the size of a site increases, it becomes more difficult to get a clear picture of the site's structure and content. Imagine deleting or moving a file in a Web site that contains dozens of folders and hundreds of files. Could you easily project the effect of this change? Would all of your hypertext links still work after you moved or deleted the file?

To effectively manage a Web site, you should follow a few important rules. The first is to be consistent in how you structure the site. If you decide to collect all image files in one folder, you should continue that practice as you add more pages and images. Web sites are more likely to break down if files and folders are scattered throughout the server without a consistent rule or pattern. Decide on a structure early and stick with it.

The second rule is to create a folder structure that matches the structure of the Web site itself. If the pages can be easily categorized into different groups, those groupings should also be reflected in the groupings of the subfolders. The names you assign to your files and folders should also reflect their uses on the Web site. This makes it easier for you to predict how modifying a file or folder might impact other pages on the site.

Finally, you should document your work by adding comments to each new Web page. Comments are useful not only for colleagues who may be working on the site, but also for the author who must revisit those files months or even years after creating them. The comments should include:

- The page's filename and location
- The page's author and the date the page was initially created
- A list of any supporting files used in the document, such as image and audio files
- A list of the files that link to the page, and their locations
- A list of the files that the page links to, and their locations

By following these rules, you can reduce a lot of the headaches associated with maintaining a large and complicated Web site.

Linking to Locations within a Document

Gerry has studied the navigation lists you created and would like you to add another navigation list to the Glossary page. Recall that the Glossary page contains a list of digital photography terms. The page is very long, requiring users to scroll through the document to find a term of interest. Gerry would like you to create a navigation list containing the letters A through Z. From this list, Gerry wants to give users the ability to jump to a specific section in the glossary matching the clicked letter.

See Figure 2-17.

Figure 2-17 **Jumping to a location within a document**

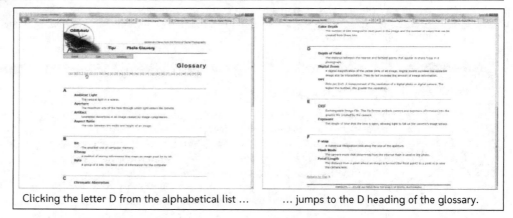

Clicking the letter D from the alphabetical list jumps to the D heading of the glossary.

Add the navigation list to the glossary page now.

To create the navigation list:

1. Return to the **glossary.htm** file in your text editor.

2. Scroll down to the section element. Directly below the h1 *Glossary* heading, insert the following navigation list (see Figure 2-18):

```
<nav>
    [A] [B] [C]
    [D] [E] [F]
    [G] [H] [I]
    [J] [K] [L]
    [M] [N] [O]
    [P] [Q] [R]
    [S] [T] [U]
    [V] [W] [X]
    [Y] [Z]
</nav>
```

Figure 2-18 **Adding a navigation element to the glossary**

3. Save your changes to the file.

Marking Locations with the id Attribute

To enable users to jump to a specific location within a document, you first need to mark that location. One way of doing this is to add the id attribute to an element at that location in the document. Recall that the syntax of the id attribute is

```
id="text"
```

where *text* is the name you want to assign to the id. For example, the following code marks an h2 element with an id of H:

```
<h2 id="H">H</h2>
```

Note that id names must be unique. If you assign the same id name to more than one element on a Web page, browsers use the first occurrence of the id name. XHTML documents are rejected if they contain elements with duplicate ids. Id names are also case sensitive and most browsers other than Internet Explorer differentiate between ids named, for example, *top* and *TOP*.

REFERENCE

Defining an Element id

- To define the id of a specific element in a Web document, use the attribute

  ```
  id="text"
  ```

 where *text* is the value of the element id.

The Glossary page contains only a partial list of the photography terms that Gerry will eventually add to his Web site. For now, you'll mark only sections in the glossary corresponding to the letters A through F.

To add the id attribute to h2 headings:

1. Scroll down the file and locate the h2 heading for the letter A. Within the opening <h2> tag, insert the following attribute:

   ```
   id="A"
   ```

2. Locate the h2 heading for the letter B and insert the following attribute in the opening <h2> tag:

   ```
   id="B"
   ```

 Figure 2-19 highlights the revised code.

Figure 2-19 Adding the id attribute to h2 headings

h2 heading marked with an id value of "A"

h2 heading marked with an id value of "B"

```
<h2 id="A">A</h2>
<dl>
    <dt><b>Ambient Light</b></dt>
    <dd>The natural light in a scene.</dd>
    <dt><b>Aperture</b></dt>
    <dd>The maximum size of the hole through which light
        enters the camera.</dd>
    <dt><b>Artifact</b></dt>
    <dd>Unwanted distortions in an image caused by image
        compression.</dd>
    <dt><b>Aspect Ratio</b></dt>
    <dd>The ratio between the width and height of an
        image.</dd>
</dl>

<h2 id="B">B</h2>
<dl>
    <dt><b>Bit</b></dt>
    <dd>The smallest unit of computer memory.</dd>
    <dt><b>Bitmap</b></dt>
    <dd>A method of storing information that maps an image
        pixel bit by bit.</dd>
    <dt><b>Byte</b></dt>
    <dd>A group of 8 bits, the basic unit of information
        for the computer.</dd>
</dl>
```

▶ **3.** Continue going down the file, adding id attributes to the opening <h2> heading tags for C, D, E, and F corresponding to the letters of those headings.

For longer documents like the Glossary page, it's also helpful for users to be able to jump directly from the bottom to the top of the page, rather than having to scroll back up. With that in mind, you'll also add an id attribute marking the element at the top of the page.

To mark the top of the page:

▶ **1.** Scroll up the **glossary.htm** file in your text editor and locate the header element directly below the opening <body> tag.

▶ **2.** Insert the following attribute within the opening <header> tag, as shown in Figure 2-20:

 id="top"

Figure 2-20 Adding the id attribute to the page header

header marked with an id value of "top"

```
<body>
    <header id="top">
        <img src="camshots.jpg" alt="CAMshots" />
    </header>
```

▶ **3.** Save your changes to the file.

Linking to an id

Once you've marked an element using the id attribute, you can create a hypertext link to that element using the a element

```
<a href="#id">content</a>
```

where *id* is the value of the id attribute of the element. For example, to create a link to the h2 heading for the letter A in the glossary document, you would enter the following code:

```
<a href="#A">A</a>
```

You'll change each entry on the Glossary page to a hypertext link pointing to the section of the glossary corresponding to the selected letter.

To change the list of letters to hypertext links:

1. Locate the letter A in the list of letters at the top of the **glossary.htm** file.

2. After the [character, insert the following opening tag:

```
<a href="#A">
```

3. Between the letter A and the] character, insert the closing tag. Figure 2-21 shows the revised code.

| Figure 2-21 | Marking a hypertext link for "A" |

Make sure you include the pound symbol (#) in the hypertext link, and ensure that the id text matches both upper- and lowercase letters in the linked id.

4. Mark the letters B through F in the list as hypertext links pointing to the appropriate h2 headings in the document. Figure 2-22 shows the revised code for the list of letters.

| Figure 2-22 | Hypertext links for the list of letters |

Gerry also wants you to create a hypertext link at the bottom of the file that points to the top. You'll use the id attribute you created in the last set of steps.

5. Scroll to the bottom of the file and locate the text *Return to Top*.

6. Mark the text as a hyperlink, pointing to the element with an id value of *top*. See Figure 2-23.

Figure 2-23 **Hypertext link to jump to the top**

link to the element with the id *top*

```
<div><a href="#top">Return to Top</a> &#8657;</div>
</section>

<footer>
    <address>
        CAMshots &#8250;&#8250;&#8250; Advice and News from
        the World of Digital Photography
    </address>
</foooter>
```

7. Save your changes to the file and then reload or refresh the **glossary.htm** file in your Web browser. As shown in Figure 2-24, the letters A through F in the alphabetical list are displayed as hypertext links.

8. Click the link for **F** and verify that you jump down to the end of the document, where the photographic terms starting with the letter F are listed.

Figure 2-24 **Hypertext links in the glossary page**

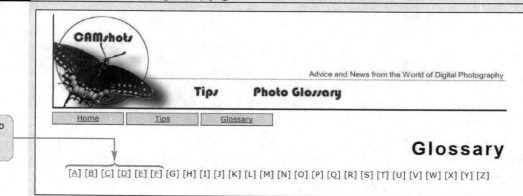

hypertext links to sections within the glossary

9. Click the **Return to Top** hypertext link and verify that you jump back to the top of the document.

10. Click the other links within the document and verify that you jump to the correct sections of the glossary.

Trouble? The browser cannot scroll farther than the end of the page. As a result, you might not see any difference between jumping to the E section of the glossary and jumping to the F section.

Anchors and the name Attribute

Early Web pages did not support the use of the id attribute as a way of marking locations within a document. Instead, they used the <a> tag as an **anchor** or bookmark using the name attribute

```
<a name="anchor">content</a>
```

where *anchor* is the name of the anchor that marks the location of the document content. For example, to add an anchor to an h2 heading, you would enter the following code:

```
<h2><a name="A">A</a></h2>
```

Marking a location with an anchor does not change your document's appearance in any way; it merely creates a destination within your document. You use the same syntax to link to locations marked with an anchor as you would with locations marked with id attributes. To link to the above anchor, you could use the following code:

```
<a href="#A">A</a>
```

The use of anchors is a deprecated feature of HTML and is not supported in strict applications of XHTML. The name attribute is not part of HTML5, but you will still see anchors used in older code and in code generated by HTML editors and converters.

Creating Links to ids in Other Documents

Gerry knows that the glossary will be one of the most useful parts of his Web site, especially for novice photographers. However, he's also aware that most people do not read through glossaries. He would like to create links from the words he uses in his articles to glossary entries so that readers of his articles can quickly access definitions for terms they don't understand. His articles are not on the same page as his Glossary page, so he'll have to create a link between those pages and specific glossary entries.

To create a link to a specific location within a document, mark the hypertext link as follows

```
<a href="reference#id">content</a>
```

where *reference* is a reference to an HTML or XHTML file and *id* is the id of an element marked with the *id* attribute within that file. For example, the HTML code

```
<a href="glossary.htm#D">"D" terms in the Glossary</a>
```

creates a hypertext link to the D entries in the glossary.htm file. Note that this assumes that the glossary.htm file is located in the same folder as the document containing the hypertext link. If not, you have to include either the absolute or relative path information along with the filename, as described earlier.

Linking to an id

• To link to a specific location within the current file, use

```
<a href="#id">content</a>
```

where *id* is the id value of an element within the document.
• To link to a specific location in another file, use

```
<a href="reference#id">content</a>
```

where *reference* is a reference to an external file and *id* is the id value of an element in that file.

On Gerry's home page, he wants to showcase a Photo of the Month, displaying a photo that his readers might find interesting or useful in their own work. Along with the photo, he has included the digital camera settings used in taking the photo. Many of the camera settings are described on the Glossary page. Gerry suggests that you create a link between the setting name and the glossary entry. The five entries he wants to link to are F-stop, Exposure, Focal Length, Aperture, and Flash Mode. Your first step is to mark these entries in the glossary using the id attribute.

To mark the glossary entries:

1. Return to the **glossary.htm** file in your text editor.

2. Scroll through the file and locate the *Aperture* definition term.

3. As shown in Figure 2-25, within the opening <dt> tag, insert the following attribute:

   ```
   id="aperture"
   ```

Figure 2-25 Adding the id attribute to the aperture definition

```
<h2 id="A">A</h2>
<dl>
    <dt><b>Ambient Light</b></dt>
    <dd>The natural light in a scene.</dd>
    <dt id="aperture"><b>Aperture</b></dt>
    <dd>The maximum size of the hole through which light
        enters the camera.</dd>
    <dt><b>Artifact</b></dt>
    <dd>Unwanted distortions in an image caused by image
        compression.</dd>
    <dt><b>Aspect Ratio</b></dt>
    <dd>The ratio between the width and height of an
        image.</dd>
</dl>
```

4. Scroll down the file and locate the *Exposure* definition term.

5. Within the opening <dt> tag, insert the following attribute:

   ```
   id="exposure"
   ```

6. Go to the F section of the glossary and mark the terms with the following ids (see Figure 2-26):

 F-stop with the id **f-stop**

 Flash Mode with the id **flash_mode**

 Focal Length with the id **focal_length**

Figure 2-26 Adding ids to the other photographic definitions

```
<h2 id="E">E</h2>
<dl>
    <dt><b>EXIF</b></dt>
    <dd>Exchangeable Image File. This file format embeds camera
        and exposure information into the graphic file created
        by the camera.</dd>
    <dt id="exposure"><b>Exposure</b></dt>
    <dd>The length of time that the lens is open, allowing light
        to fall on the camera's image sensor.</dd>
</dl>

<h2 id="F">F</h2>
<dl>
    <dt id="f-stop"><b>F-stop</b></dt>
    <dd>A numerical designation indicating the size of the
        aperture.</dd>
    <dt id="flash_mode"><b>Flash Mode</b></dt>
    <dd>The camera mode that determines how the internal flash is used
        in the photo.</dd>
    <dt id="focal_length"><b>Focal Length</b></dt>
    <dd>The distance from a point where an image is formed (the
        focal point) to a point in or near the camera lens.</dd>
</dl>
```

7. Save your changes to the **glossary.htm** file.

Next you'll go to the Home page and create links from these terms in the Photo of the Month description to their entries on the Glossary page.

To create links to the glossary entries:

1. Open the **home.htm** file in your text editor.

2. Scroll down the file and locate the *F-stop* term in the unordered list.

3. Mark *F-stop* as a hypertext link using the following code:

```
<a href="glossary.htm#f-stop">F-stop</a>
```

4. Mark *Exposure* as a hypertext link using the following code:

```
<a href="glossary.htm#exposure">Exposure</a>
```

5. Mark the remaining three entries in the unordered list as hypertext pointing to their corresponding entries on the Glossary page. Figure 2-27 highlights the revised code in the file.

Figure 2-27 **Linking to a location within another document**

```
<aside>
    <h1>Photo of the Month</h1>

    <figure>
        <img src="rainbow.png" alt="Photo" />
        <figcaption>Colorado Double Rainbow by Watts213</i></figcaption>
    </figure>

    <ul>
        <li>Camera:

            Nikon D50
        </li>
        <li><a href="glossary.htm#f-stop">F-stop</a>:

            f/7.1
        </li>
        <li><a href="glossary.htm#exposure">Exposure</a>:

            1/200 sec.
        </li>
        <li><a href="glossary.htm#focal_length">Focal Length</a>:

            18mm
        </li>
        <li><a href="glossary.htm#aperture">Aperture</a>:

            3.6
        </li>
        <li><a href="glossary.htm#flash_mode">Flash Mode</a>:

            No flash
        </li>
    </ul>
</aside>
```

document · element id

▶ **6.** Save your changes to the file.

▶ **7.** Refresh the **home.htm** file in your Web browser. As shown in Figure 2-28, the settings from the Photo of the Month description are now displayed as hypertext links.

Figure 2-28 **Linked photography terms**

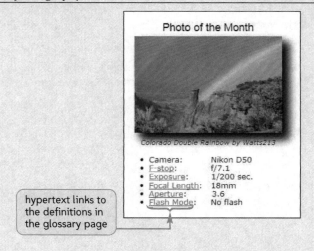

Photo of the Month

Colorado Double Rainbow by Watts213

- Camera: Nikon D50
- F-stop: f/7.1
- Exposure: 1/200 sec.
- Focal Length: 18mm
- Aperture: 3.6
- Flash Mode: No flash

hypertext links to the definitions in the glossary page

▶ **8.** Click the **F-stop** hypertext link and verify that you jump to the Glossary page with the F-stop entry displayed in the browser window.

9. Return to the CAMshots home page and click the hypertext links for the other terms in the list of photo settings, verifying that you jump to the section of the glossary that displays each term's definition.

PROSKILLS

Written Communication: Creating Effective Hypertext Links

To make it easier for users to navigate your Web site, the text of your hypertext links should tell readers exactly what type of document the link points to. For example, the link text

> *Click here for more information.*

doesn't tell the user what type of document will appear when *here* is clicked. In place of phrases like *click here*, use descriptive link text such as

> *For more information, view our list of frequently asked questions.*

If the link points to a non-HTML file, such as a PDF document, include that information in the link text. If the linked document is extremely large and will take a while to download to the user's computer, include that information in your link text so that users can decide whether or not to initiate the transfer. For example, the following link text informs users of both the type of document and its size before they initiate the link:

> *Download our complete manual (PDF 2 MB).*

Finally, when designing the style of your Web site, make your links easy to recognize. Because most browsers underline hypertext links, don't use underlining for other text elements; use italic or boldface fonts instead. Users should never be confused about what is a link and what is not. Also, if you apply a color to your text, do not choose colors that make your hyperlinks harder to pick out against the Web page background.

You've completed your initial work linking the three files in Gerry's Web site. In the next session, you'll learn how to work with linked images and how to create links to external Web sites and Internet resources. If you want to take a break before starting the next session, you can close your files and your Web browser now.

REVIEW

Session 2.1 Quick Check

1. What is a navigation list? How would you mark up a navigation list in HTML5? How would you mark up a navigation list prior to HTML5?
2. What is a linear structure? What is a hierarchical structure?
3. What code would you enter to link the text *Sports Info* to the sports.htm file? Assume that the current document and sports.htm are in the same folder.
4. What's the difference between an absolute path and a relative path?
5. What is the purpose of the `base` element?
6. Specify the code for marking the text *CAMshots FAQ* as an `h2` heading with the id *faq*.
7. Specify the code for marking the text *Read our FAQ* as a hypertext link to an element in the current document with the id *faq*.
8. Specify the code for marking the text *Read our FAQ* as a hypertext link pointing to an element with the id *faq* in the help.htm file. Assume that help.htm lies in the same folder as the current document.

SESSION 2.2 VISUAL OVERVIEW

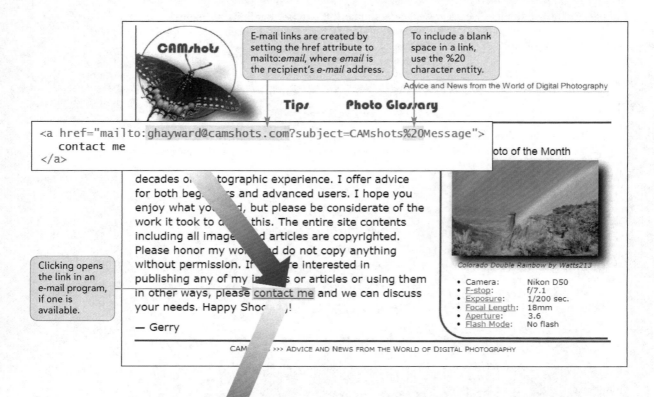

E-mail links are created by setting the href attribute to mailto:*email*, where *email* is the recipient's *e-mail* address.

To include a blank space in a link, use the %20 character entity.

Advice and News from the World of Digital Photography

Tips **Photo Glossary**

```
<a href="mailto:ghayward@camshots.com?subject=CAMshots%20Message">
   contact me
</a>
```

...oto of the Month

decades o... ...tographic experience. I offer advice for both beg... ...rs and advanced users. I hope you enjoy what yo... ...d, but please be considerate of the work it took tothis. The entire site contents including all image... ...d articles are copyrighted. Please honor my wo... ...d do not copy anything without permission. Ifre interested in publishing any of my i... ...s or articles or using them in other ways, please contact me and we can discuss your needs. Happy Shoo... ...!

— Gerry

Clicking opens the link in an e-mail program, if one is available.

Colorado Double Rainbow by Watts213

- Camera: Nikon D50
- F-stop: f/7.1
- Exposure: 1/200 sec.
- Focal Length: 18mm
- Aperture: 3.6
- Flash Mode: No flash

CAM... ...>>> Advice and News from the World of Digital Photography

```
<a href="glossary.htm#flash_mode"
   title="View Definition">
   Flash Mode
</a>:
```

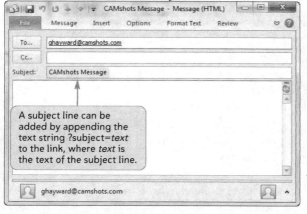

A subject line can be added by appending the text string ?subject=*text* to the link, where *text* is the text of the subject line.

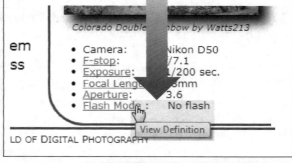

Colorado Double... ...nbow by Watts213

em
ss

- Camera: ...Nikon D50
- F-stop: ...7.1
- Exposure: ...1/200 sec.
- Focal Leng... ...mm
- Aperture: ...3.6
- Flash Mode : No flash

View Definition

LD of Digital Photography

Use the **title** attribute to add descriptive **tooltips** to hypertext links.

IMAGE MAPS AND EXTERNAL LINKS

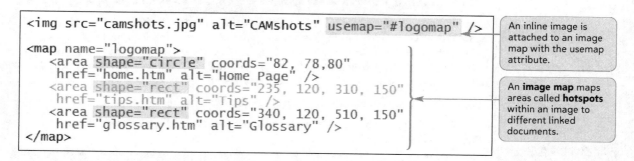

```
<img src="camshots.jpg" alt="CAMshots" usemap="#logomap" />

<map name="logomap">
   <area shape="circle" coords="82, 78,80"
     href="home.htm" alt="Home Page" />
   <area shape="rect" coords="235, 120, 310, 150"
     href="tips.htm" alt="Tips" />
   <area shape="rect" coords="340, 120, 510, 150"
     href="glossary.htm" alt="Glossary" />
</map>
```

An inline image is attached to an image map with the usemap attribute.

An **image map** maps areas called **hotspots** within an image to different linked documents.

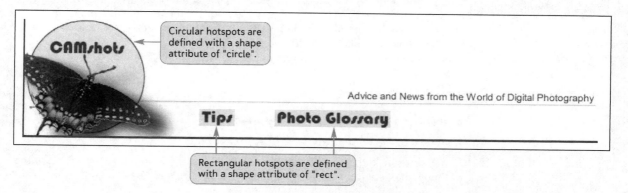

Circular hotspots are defined with a shape attribute of "circle".

CAMshots

Advice and News from the World of Digital Photography

Tips Photo Glossary

Rectangular hotspots are defined with a shape attribute of "rect".

Sample URLs to link to Internet resources

URL	Description
file:///C\server\camshots.htm	Links to the camshots.htm file in the server folder on the C drive
ftp://ftp.microsoft.com	Links to the FTP server at ftp.microsoft.com
http://www.camshots.com	Links to the Web site www.camshots.com
https://www.camshots.com	Links to the Web site www.camshots.com over a secure connection

Working with Linked Images and Image Maps

Inline images can be marked as hyperlinks using the same techniques you employed in the last session. For example, a standard practice on the Web is to turn a Web site's logo into a hyperlink pointing to the home page. This gives users quick access to the home page rather than spending time searching for a link. To mark an inline image as a hyperlink, you enclose the `<img>` tag within a set of `<a>` tags as follows:

```
<a href="reference"><img src="file" alt="text" /></a>
```

Once the image has been marked as hypertext, clicking anywhere within the image jumps the user to the linked file.

The target of the link need not be a Web page; it can also be another image file. This is commonly done for **thumbnail images** that are small representations of larger image files. Gerry has done this for his image of the photo of the month. The image on the site's home page is a thumbnail of the larger photo. Gerry wants users to be able to view the larger image file by clicking the thumbnail.

You'll turn the Photo of the Month image into a hyperlink pointing to the larger image file.

TIP

Always include alternate text for your linked images to allow non-graphical browsers to display a text link in place of the linked image.

To link the Photo of the Month image:

1. Return to the **home.htm** file in your text editor.

2. Scroll down to the `img` element for the Photo of the Month and then enclose the inline image within a set of `<a>` tags as follows (see Figure 2-29):

```
<a href="rainbow_lg.png">
   <img src="rainbow.png" alt="Photo" />
</a>
```

Figure 2-29 Linking an inline image

link to a large image of the photo

```
<aside>
   <h1>Photo of the Month</h1>

   <figure>
      <a href="rainbow_lg.png">
         <img src="rainbow.png" alt="Photo" />
      </a>
      <figcaption>Colorado Double Rainbow by Watts213</i></figcaption>
   </figure>
```

3. Save your changes to the file.

4. Reload the **home.htm** file in your Web browser. Click the Photo of the Month image and verify that the browser displays a larger, more detailed version of the image.

Removing Image Borders

By default, Web browsers underline hypertext links. If an image is linked, browsers usually display the image with a colored border. To remove the border, you can add the following `style` attribute to the `img` element:

```
<img src="file" alt="text" style="border-width: 0px" />
```

This attribute sets the width of the border to 0 pixels, effectively removing it from the rendered Web page. You can also set the border width to 0 by using the following `border` attribute:

```
<img src="file" alt="text" border="0" />
```

Note that the `border` attribute is not supported in HTML5 but you will still see it used in many Web sites. Despite the fact that many browsers still support the use of the `border` attribute, you should not use it, relying instead on either the style attribute or styles set within an external style sheet.

Introducing Image Maps

When you mark an inline image as a hyperlink, the entire image is linked to the same destination file. However, HTML also allows you to divide an image into different zones, or **hotspots,** each linked to a different destination. Gerry is interested in doing this with the current image in the CAMshots header. He would like you to create hotspots for the logo so that if a user clicks anywhere within the CAMshots circle on the left side of the logo, the user jumps to the Home page; and if the user clicks either Tips or Photo Glossary in the logo, the user jumps to the Tips page or to the Glossary page, respectively. See Figure 2-30.

Figure 2-30	Hotspots within the CAMshots header image

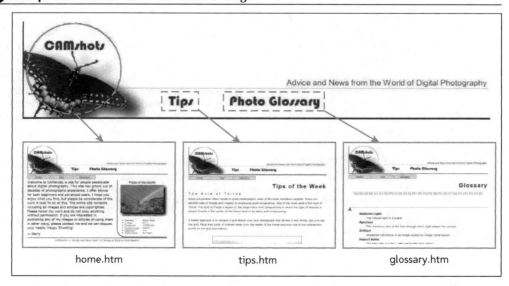

To define these hotspots, you create an **image map** that links a specified region of the inline image to a specific document. HTML supports two kinds of image maps: client-side image maps and server-side image maps. A **client-side image map** is an image map that is defined within the Web page and handled entirely by the Web browser running on a user's computer, while a **server-side image map** relies on a program running on the Web server to create and administer the map. For the CAMshots Web site, you'll create a client-side image map.

Client-Side Image Maps

Client-side image maps are defined with the `map` element

```
<map name="text">
   hotspots
</map>
```

where `text` is the name of the image map and `hotspots` are the locations of the hotspots within the image. For example, the following `map` element creates a client-side image map named *logomap*:

```
<map name="logomap">
   ...
</map>
```

TIP

For XHTML documents, use the `id` attribute in place of the `name` attribute to identify an image map.

Client-side image maps can be placed anywhere within the body of a Web page because they are not actually displayed by browsers, but simply used as references for mapping hotspots to inline images. The most common practice is to place a `map` element below the corresponding inline image.

Defining Hotspots

An individual hotspot is defined using the `area` element

```
<area shape="shape" coords="coordinates" href="reference"
  alt="text" />
```

where *shape* is the shape of the hotspot region, *coordinates* are the list of points that define the boundaries of the region, *reference* is the file or location that the hotspot is linked to, and *text* is alternate text displayed for non-graphical browsers. Hotspots can be created in the shapes of rectangles, circles, or polygons (multisided figures). You use a shape value of `rect` for rectangular hotspots, `circle` for circular hotspots, and `poly` for polygonal or multisided hotspots. A fourth possible value for the `shape` attribute, `default`, represents the remaining area of the inline image not covered by any hotspots. There is no limit to the number of hotspots you can add to an image map. Hotspots can also overlap. If they do and the user clicks an overlapping area, the browser opens the link of the first hotspot listed in the map.

Hotspot coordinates are measured in **pixels**, which are the smallest unit or dot in a digital image or display. Your computer monitor might have a size of 1024 x 768 pixels, which means that the display is 1024 dots wide by 768 dots tall. For example, the header image that Gerry uses in his Web site has dimensions of 780 pixels wide by 167 pixels tall. When used with the `coords` attribute of the `area` element, pixel values exactly define the location and size of a hotspot region.

Each hotspot shape has a different set of coordinates that define it. To define a rectangular hotspot, apply the `area` element

```
<area shape="rect" coords="x1, y1, x2, y2" ... />
```

where *x1, y1* are the coordinates of the upper-left corner of the rectangle and *x2, y2* are the coordinates of the rectangle's lower-right corner. Figure 2-31 shows the coordinates of the rectangular region surrounding the Photo Glossary hotspot.

Figure 2-31 Defining a rectangular hotspot

The upper-left corner of the rectangle has the image coordinates (235, 120), indicating that it is 235 pixels to the right and 120 pixels down from the upper-left corner of the image. The lower-right corner is found at the image coordinates (310, 150), placing it 310 pixels to the right and 150 pixels down from the upper-left corner of the image. Note that coordinates are always expressed relative to the upper-left corner of the image, regardless of the position of the image on the page.

Circular hotspots are defined using the coordinates

```
<area shape="circle" coords="x, y, r" ... />
```

where x and y are the coordinates of the center of the circle and r is the circle's radius. Figure 2-32 shows the coordinates for a circular hotspot around the CAMshots image from the Web site logo. The center of the circle is located at the coordinates (92, 82) and the circle has a radius of 80 pixels.

Figure 2-32 Defining a circular hotspot

Polygonal hotspots are defined with

```
<area shape="poly" coords="x1, y1, x2, y2, x3, y3, ..." ... />
```

where $(x1, y1)$, $(x2, y2)$, $(x3, y3)$ and so forth define the coordinates of each corner in the multisided shape. Figure 2-33 shows the coordinates for a polygonal region that covers the CAMshots logo, including the butterfly wings.

Figure 2-33 Defining a polygonal hotspot

Finally, to define the default hotspot for an image, use

```
<area shape="default" coords="0, 0, x, y" ... />
```

where x is the width of the inline image in pixels and y is the height of the image. Any spot in an inline image that is not covered by another hotspot activates the default hotspot link.

REFERENCE

Creating a Client-Side Image Map

- To create a client-side image map, insert the map element

```
<map name="text">
   hotspots
</map>
```

anywhere within the Web page body, where *text* is the name of the image map and *hotspots* is a list of hotspot areas defined within the image map. (Note: For XHTML, use the id attribute in place of the name attribute.)
- To add a hotspot to the image map, place the area element

```
<area shape="shape" coords="coordinates" href="reference"
 alt="text" />
```

within the map element, where *shape* is the shape of the hotspot region, *coordinates* is the list of points that defines the boundaries of the region, *reference* is the file or location that the hotspot is linked to, and *text* is alternate text displayed for non-graphical browsers.
- To define a rectangular-shaped hotspot, use

```
<area shape="rect" coords="x1, y1, x2, y2" ... />
```

where *x1*, *y1* are the coordinates of the upper-left corner of the rectangle and *x2*, *y2* are the coordinates of the lower-right corner of the rectangle.
- To define a circular hotspot, use

```
<area shape="circle" coords="x, y, r" ... />
```

where x and y are the coordinates of the center of the circle and r is the radius of the circle.
- To define a polygonal hotspot, use

```
<area shape="poly" coords="x1, y1, x2, y2, x3, y3, ..." ... />
```

where (*x1*, *y1*), (*x2*, *y2*), (*x3*, *y3*), and so forth define the coordinates of each corner in the multisided shape.
- To define the default hotspot, use

```
<area shape="default" coords="0, 0, x, y" ... />
```

where x is the width of the inline image in pixels and y is the height in pixels.
- To apply an image map to an inline image, add the usemap attribute

```
<img src="file" alt="text" usemap="#map" />
```

to the inline image, where *map* is the name assigned to the image map.

To determine the coordinates of a hotspot, you can use either a graphics program such as Adobe Photoshop or image map software that automatically generates the HTML code for the hotspots you define.

In this case, assume that Gerry has already determined the coordinates for the hotspots in his image map and provided them for you. He wants you to create three hotspots, which are shown earlier in Figure 2-30. The first is a circular hotspot linked to the home.htm file, centered at the point (92, 82) and with a radius of 80 pixels. The second is a rectangular hotspot linked to the tips.htm file, with corners at (235, 120) and (310, 150). The third is also rectangular, linked to the glossary.htm file, with corners at (340, 120) and (510, 150). You do not have to create a polygonal hotspot.

You'll name the image map containing these hotspots *logomap*.

To create an image map:

1. Return to the **home.htm** file in your text editor.

2. Directly below the `<img>` tag for the CAMshots header image, insert the following `map` element:

   ```
   <map name="logomap">
   </map>
   ```

3. Within the `map` element, insert a circular hotspot that points to the home.htm file using the following `area` element:

   ```
   <area shape="circle" coords="82, 82, 80"
    href="home.htm" alt="Home Page" />
   ```

4. Directly below the `<area>` tag for the circular hotspot, insert the following two rectangular hotspots pointing to the tips.htm and glossary.htm files:

   ```
   <area shape="rect" coords="235, 120, 310, 150"
    href="tips.htm" alt="Tips" />
   ```

   ```
   <area shape="rect" coords="340, 120, 510, 150"
    href="glossary.htm" alt="Glossary" />
   ```

 Figure 2-34 highlights the new code in the file.

Figure 2-34 **Creating the logomap image map**

```
<header>
    <img src="camshots.jpg" alt="CAMshots" />

    <map name="logomap">
        <area shape="circle" coords="82, 78,80"
        href="home.htm" alt="Home Page" />
        <area shape="rect" coords="235, 120, 310, 150"
        href="tips.htm" alt="Tips" />
        <area shape="rect" coords="340, 120, 510, 150"
        href="glossary.htm" alt="Glossary" />
    </map>

</header>
```

circular and rectangular hotspots

5. Save your changes to the file.

With the image map defined, your next task is to apply that map to the CAMshots header.

Applying an Image Map

To apply an image map to an image, you add the `usemap` attribute

```
<img src="file" alt="text" usemap="#map" />
```

to the inline image, where *map* is the name assigned to the image map.

Apply the *logomap* image map to the CAMshots logo and then test it in your Web browser.

To apply the *logomap* image map:

▶ **1.** Add the following attribute to the `<img>` tag for the CAMshots logo, as shown in Figure 2-35:

```
usemap="#logomap"
```

Figure 2-35 Applying the logomap image map

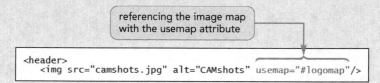

referencing the image map with the usemap attribute

```
<header>
    <img src="camshots.jpg" alt="CAMshots" usemap="#logomap"/>
```

▶ **2.** Save your changes to the file and then reload or refresh the **home.htm** file in your Web browser.

▶ **3.** Click anywhere within the word **Tips** in the header image and verify that the browser opens the Tips page.

▶ **4.** Return to the home page and click anywhere within the words **Photo Glossary** in the header image to verify that the browser opens the Glossary page.

Now that you've created an image map for the logo on the home page, you can create similar image maps for the logos on the Tips and Glossary pages.

To add image maps to the other Web pages:

▶ **1.** Return to the **tips.htm** file in your text editor.

▶ **2.** Replace the code within the header element with the code shown earlier in Figure 2-34. (Hint: You can use the copy and paste feature of your text editor to copy the code from the home.htm file into the tips.htm file.)

▶ **3.** Save your changes to the file.

▶ **4.** Go to the **glossary.htm** file in your text editor.

▶ **5.** As you did for the tips.htm file, replace the code within the header element for the inline image with the code from the home.htm file. Save your changes to the file.

▶ **6.** Reload the **home.htm** file in your Web browser and verify that you can switch among the three Web pages by clicking the hotspots in the CAMshots header image.

INSIGHT

Server-Side Image Maps

The other type of image map you might encounter on the Web is a server-side image map, in which information about the hotspots is stored on the Web server rather than entered into the HTML code of a Web page. When you click a hotspot on a server-side image map, the coordinates of the mouse click are sent to the server, which activates the corresponding link, sending the linked page to your Web browser.

The server-side image map was the original HTML standard and is still supported on the Web. However, server-side maps have some limitations compared to client-side image maps. Because the map is located on the server, you need server access to test your image map code. Also, server-side image maps might be slower because information must be sent to the server with each mouse click. Finally, unlike client-side image maps, server-side image maps require the use of a mouse to send the information to the server. This makes them unsuitable for users with disabilities or users running non-graphical browsers.

To create a server-side image map, you enclose an inline image within a hypertext link such as

```
<a href="map">
   <img src="file" alt="text" ismap="ismap" />
</a>
```

where *map* is the name of a program or file running on the Web server that handles the image map. The `ismap` attribute tells the Web browser to treat the inline image as an image map.

Linking to Resources on the Internet

In the tips.htm file, Gerry has listed some of the Web sites he finds useful in his study of photography. He would like to change the entries in this list to hypertext links that his readers can click to quickly access the sites.

Introducing URLs

To create a link to a resource on the Internet, you need to know its URL. A **Uniform Resource Locator** (**URL**) specifies the location and type of a resource on the Internet. Examples of URLs include *www.whitehouse.gov*, the home page of the President of the United States, and *www.w3.org*, the home page of the World Wide Web consortium. All URLs share the general structure

```
scheme:location
```

where *scheme* indicates the type of resource referenced by the URL and *location* is the location of that resource. For Web pages, the location refers to the location of the HTML file; but for other resources, the location might simply be the name of the resource. For example, a link to an e-mail account has the recipient's e-mail address as the location.

The name of the scheme is taken from the network protocol used to access the resource. A **protocol** is a set of rules defining how information is passed between two devices. Your Web browser communicates with Web servers using the **Hypertext Transfer Protocol** (**HTTP**). Therefore, the URLs for all Web pages must start with the http scheme. Other Internet resources, described in Figure 2-36, use different communication protocols and thus have different scheme names.

Figure 2-36	Internet protocols

Protocol	Used To
file	Access documents stored locally on a user's computer
ftp	Access documents stored on an FTP server
http	Access Web pages
https	Access Web pages over a secure encrypted connection
mailto	Open a user's e-mail client and address a new message

Linking to a Web Site

The URL for a Web page has the general form

```
http://server/path/filename#id
```

where *server* is the name of the Web server, *path* is the path to the file on that server, *filename* is the name of the file, and if necessary, *id* is the name of an id or anchor within the file. A Web page URL can also contain specific programming instructions for a browser to send to the Web server (a topic beyond the scope of this tutorial). Figure 2-37 identifies the different parts of a sample URL for a sample Web page.

Figure 2-37	Parts of a URL

You might have noticed that a URL like *http://www.camshots.com* doesn't include any pathname or filename. If a URL doesn't specify a path, then it indicates the top folder in the server's directory tree. If a URL doesn't specify a filename, the server returns the default home page. Many servers use index.html as the filename for the default home page, so the URL *http://www.camshots.com/index.html* would be equivalent to *http://www.camshots.com*.

INSIGHT

Understanding Domain Names

The server name portion of a URL is also called the **domain name**. By studying a domain name, you learn about the server hosting the Web site. Each domain name contains a hierarchy of names separated by periods (.), with the top level appearing at the end. The top level, called an **extension**, indicates the general audience supported by the Web server. For example, *.edu* is the extension reserved for educational institutions, *.gov* is used for agencies of the United States government, and *.com* is used for commercial sites or general-use sites.

The next lower level appearing before the extension displays the name of the individual or organization hosting the site. The domain name *camshots.com* indicates a commercial or general-use site owned by CAMshots. To avoid duplicating domain names, the top two levels of the domain must be registered with the IANA (Internet Assigned Numbers Authority) before they can be used. You can usually register your domain name through your Web host. Be aware that you must pay an annual fee to keep a domain name.

The lowest levels of the domain, which appear farthest to the left in the domain name, are assigned by the individual or company hosting the site. Large Web sites involving hundreds of pages typically divide their domain names into several levels. For example, a large company like Microsoft might have one domain name for file downloads—*downloads.microsoft.com*—and another for customer service—*service.microsoft.com*. Finally, the first part of the domain name displays the name of the hard drive or resource storing the Web site files. Many companies have standardized on *www* as the initial part of their domain names.

Gerry has listed four Web pages that he wants his readers to be able to access. He's also provided you with the URLs for these pages, which are shown in Figure 2-38.

Figure 2-38 **Photography URLs**

Web Site	URL
Apogee Photo	http://www.apogeephoto.com
Outdoor Photographer	http://www.outdoorphotographer.com
Digital Photo	http://www.dpmag.com
Popular Photography and Imaging	http://www.popphoto.com

You'll link the names of the Web sites that Gerry has listed in the Tips page to the URLs listed in Figure 2-38. For example, to link the text *Apogee Photo* to the Apogee Photo Web site, you would use the following <a> tag:

```
<a href="http://www.apogeephoto.com">Apogee Photo</a>
```

REFERENCE

Linking to Internet Resources

- The URL for a Web page is

 `http://server/path/filename#id`

 where *server* is the name of the Web server, *path* is the path to a file on that server, *filename* is the name of the file, and if necessary, *id* is the name of an id or anchor within the file.
- The URL for an FTP site is

 `ftp://server/path/filename`

 where *server* is the name of the FTP server, *path* is the folder path, and *filename* is the name of the file.
- The URL for an e-mail address is

 `mailto:address?header1=value1&header2=value2&...`

 where *address* is the e-mail address; *header1*, *header2*, etc. are different e-mail headers; and *value1*, *value2*, and so on are the values of the headers.
- The URL to reference a local file is

 `file://server/path/filename`

 where *server* is the name of the local server or computer, *path* is the path to the file on that server, and *filename* is the name of the file. If you are accessing a file on your own computer, the server name is replaced by a third slash (/).

You'll use the information that Gerry has given you to create links to all four of the Web sites listed on his Tips page.

To create links to sites on the Web:

1. Return to the **tips.htm** file in your text editor.

2. Scroll to the bottom of the file and locate the definition list containing the list of Web sites.

3. Mark the entry for Apogee Photo as a hypertext link using the following code:

 `<a href="http://www.apogeephoto.com">Apogee Photo</a>`

4. Mark the remaining three entries in the list as hypertext links pointing to each company's Web site. Figure 2-39 highlights the revised code in the file.

Figure 2-39	Linking to sites on the Web

```
<article>
   <h1>Photography Sites on the Web</h1>
   <p>The Web is an excellent resource for articles on photography and
       digital cameras. Here are a few of my favorites.
   </p>

   <dl>
       <dt>&#9758; <a href="http://www.apogeephoto.com">Apogee Photo</a></dt>
       <dd>An established online photography magazine with articles by
           top pros, discussion forums, workshops, and more.
       </dd>
       <dt>&#9758; <a href="http://www.outdoorphotographer.com">Outdoor Photographer</a></dt>
       <dd>The premier magazine for outdoor photography. The site
           includes extensive tips on photographing wildlife, action
           sports, scenic vistas, and travel sites.
       </dd>
       <dt>&#9758; <a href="http://www.dpmag.com">Digital Photo</a></dt>
       <dd>An excellent site for novices and professionals with
           informative reviews and buying guides for the latest equipment
           and software.
       </dd>
       <dt>&#9758; <a href="http://www.popphoto.com">Popular Photography and Imaging</a></dt>
       <dd>A useful and informative site with articles from the
           long-established magazine of professional and amateur
           photographers.
       </dd>
   </dl>
</article>
```

5. Save your changes to the file.

6. Reload or refresh the **tips.htm** file in your Web browser. Figure 2-40 shows the revised list with each entry appearing as a hypertext link.

Figure 2-40	Links on the Tips page

Photography Sites on the Web

The Web is an excellent resource for articles on photography and digital cameras. Here are a few of my favorites.

☞ Apogee Photo
 An established online photography magazine with articles by top pros, discussion forums, workshops, and more.
☞ Outdoor Photographer
 The premier magazine for outdoor photography. The site includes extensive tips on photographing wildlife, action sports, scenic vistas, and travel sites.
☞ Digital Photo
 An excellent site for novices and professionals with informative reviews and buying guides for the latest equipment and software.
☞ Popular Photography and Imaging
 A useful and informative site with articles from the long-established magazine of professional and amateur photographers.

7. Click each link on the page and verify that the appropriate Web site opens.

Trouble? To open these sites, you must be connected to the Internet. If you are still having problems after connecting to the Internet, compare your code to the URLs listed in Figure 2-38 to confirm that you have not made a typing error. Also keep in mind that because the Web is constantly changing, the Web sites for some of these links might have changed, or a site might have been removed since this book was published.

Web pages are only one type of resource that you can link to. Before continuing work on the CAMshots Web site, you'll explore how to access some of these other resources.

Linking to FTP Servers

Another method of storing and sharing files on the Internet is through FTP servers. **FTP servers** are file servers that act like virtual file cabinets in which users can store and retrieve data files, much as they store files on and retrieve files from their own computers. FTP servers transfer information using a communication protocol called **File Transfer Protocol** (**FTP**). The URL to access an FTP server follows the general format

```
ftp://server/path/
```

where `server` is the name of the FTP server and `path` is the folder path on the server that contains the files you want to access. When you access an FTP site, you can navigate through its folder tree as you would navigate the folders on your own hard disk. Figure 2-41 shows an example of an FTP site viewed as a directory listing within the Internet Explorer browser, and viewed as a collection of folders that can be navigated as if they were on the user's local machine.

Figure 2-41	Accessing an FTP site over the Web

FTP servers require each user to enter a password and a username to gain access to the server's files. The standard username is *anonymous* and requires no password. Your browser supplies this information automatically, so in most situations you don't have to worry about passwords and usernames. However, some FTP servers do not allow anonymous access. In these cases, either your browser prompts you for the username and password, or you can supply a username and password within the URL using the format

```
ftp://username:password@server/path
```

where `username` and `password` are a username and password that the FTP server recognizes. It is generally *not* a good idea, however, to include usernames and passwords in URLs, as it can allow others to view your sensitive login information. It's better to let the

browser send this information or to use a special program called an **FTP client**, which can encrypt or hide this information during transmission.

Linking to a Local File

HTML is a very useful language for creating collections of linked documents. Many software developers have chosen to distribute their online help in the form of HTML files. The Web sites for these help files then exist locally on a user's computer or network. If a Web site needs to reference local files (as opposed to files on the Internet or another wide area network), the URLs need to reflect this fact. The URL for a local file has the general form

```
file://server/path/filename
```

where *server* is the name of the local network server, *path* is the path on that server to the file, and *filename* is the name of the file. If you're accessing a file from your own computer, the server name can be omitted and replaced by an extra slash (/). Thus, a file from the *documents/articles* folder might have the following URL:

```
file:///documents/articles/tips.htm
```

If the file is on a different disk within your computer, the hard drive letter would be included in the URL as follows:

```
file://D:/documents/articles/tips.htm
```

Unlike the other URLs you've examined, the file scheme in this URL does not imply any particular communication protocol; instead, browsers retrieve the document using whatever method is the local standard for the type of file specified in the URL.

Linking to an E-Mail Address

Many Web sites use e-mail to allow users to communicate with a site's owner, sales representative, or technical support staff. You can turn an e-mail address into a hypertext link; when a user clicks the link, the user's e-mail program opens and automatically inserts the e-mail address into the *To* field of a new outgoing message. The URL for an e-mail address follows the form

```
mailto:address
```

where *address* is the e-mail address. To create a hypertext link to the e-mail address *ghayward@camshots.com*, you could use the following URL:

```
mailto:ghayward@camshots.com
```

The mailto protocol also allows you to add information to the e-mail, including the subject line and the text of the message body. To add this information to the link, you use the form

```
mailto:address?header1=value1&header2=value2&...
```

where *header1*, *header2*, etc. are different e-mail headers and *value1*, *value2*, and so on are the values of the headers. Thus, to create a link containing the e-mail message

```
TO: ghayward@camshots.com
SUBJECT: Test
BODY: This is a test message
```

you would use the following URL:

```
mailto:ghayward@camshots.com?subject=Test&Body=This%20is%20a%
20test%20message
```

Notice that the spaces in the message body *This is a test message* have been replaced with the %20 character code. This is necessary because URLs cannot contain blank spaces.

Although the mailto protocol is not technically an approved communication protocol, it is supported by almost every Web browser. However, note that a user's browser may not automatically access Web-based mail clients, such as Hotmail or Gmail, when the user clicks an e-mail link. End users accessing their mail from a Web-based mail client must configure their browsers to automatically open those Web sites in response to a mailto link.

Gerry wants you to add a link to his e-mail address on the CAMshots home page. This will give people who view his site the ability to contact him with additional questions or ideas.

To link to an e-mail address on Gerry's home page:

▶ **1.** Return to the **home.htm** file in your text editor.

▶ **2.** Go to the first paragraph and locate the text *contact me*.

▶ **3.** Mark *contact me* as a hypertext link using the following code, as shown in Figure 2-42:

```
<a href="mailto:ghayward@camshots.com?subject=CAMshots%20Message">
   contact me
</a>
```

Figure 2-42 **Linking to an e-mail address**

```
<p>Welcome to CAMshots, a site for people passionate about
   digital photography. This site has grown out of decades
   of photographic experience. I offer advice for both
   beginners and advanced users. I hope you enjoy what you find,
   but please be considerate of the work it took to do all this.
   The entire site contents including all images and articles
   are copyrighted. Please honor my work and do not copy anything
   without permission. If you are interested in publishing any
   of my images or articles or using them in other ways,
   please <a href="mailto:ghayward@camshots.com?subject=CAMshots%20Message">contact me</a>
   and we can discuss your needs. Happy Shooting!</p>
<p>— Gerry</p>
```

e-mail address e-mail subject heading

▶ **4.** Save your changes to the file.

▶ **5.** Refresh the **home.htm** file in your browser. Verify that the text *contact me* in the opening paragraph now appears as a hypertext link.

▶ **6.** Click **contact me** and verify that your e-mail program displays a message with *ghayward@camshots.com* as the recipient and *CAMshots Message* as the subject.

 Trouble? If you are using a Web-based e-mail client such as Gmail or Hotmail, the browser will not open your e-mail client. You can view online documentation for your browser to determine whether it supports linking to Web-based e-mail clients.

▶ **7.** Close your message window without saving the message.

Problem Solving: E-Mail Links and Spam

Use caution when adding e-mail links to your Web site. While it may make it more convenient for users to contact you, it also might make you more vulnerable to spam. **Spam** is unsolicited e-mail sent to large numbers of people, promoting products, services, and in some cases inappropriate Web sites. Spammers create their e-mail lists by scanning discussion groups, stealing Internet mailing lists, and using programs called **e-mail harvesters** to scan HTML code for the e-mail addresses contained in mailto URLs. Many Web developers have removed e-mail links from their Web sites in order to foil these harvesters, replacing the links with Web forms that submit e-mail requests to a secure server. If you need to include an e-mail address as a link on your Web page, you can take a few steps to reduce your exposure to spammers:

• Replace the text of the e-mail addresses with inline images that are more difficult for e-mail harvesters to read.

• Write a program to scramble any e-mail addresses in the HTML code, unscrambling the e-mail address only when a user clicks it.

• Replace the characters of the e-mail address with escape characters. For example, you can replace the @ symbol with the escape sequence %40.

There is no quick and easy solution to this problem. Fighting spammers is an ongoing battle, and they have proved very resourceful in overcoming some of the defenses people have created. As you develop your Web site, you should carefully consider how to handle e-mail addresses and review the most current methods for safeguarding that information.

Working with Hypertext Attributes

TIP

All of the hypertext attributes associated with the <a> tag can also be applied to the <area> tags within your image maps.

HTML provides several attributes to control the behavior and appearance of your links. Gerry suggests that you study a few of these to see whether they would be effective in his Web site.

Opening a Secondary Window or Tab

By default, each page you open replaces the contents of the current page in the browser window. This means that when Gerry's readers click on one of the four external links listed on the Tips page, they leave the CAMshots Web site. To return to the Web site, a user would have to click the browser's Back button.

Gerry wants his Web site to stay open when a user clicks one of the links to the external Web sites. Most browsers allow users to open multiple browser windows or multiple tabs within the same browser window. Gerry suggests that links to external sites be opened in a second browser window or tab. This arrangement allows continual access to his Web site, even as users are browsing other sites.

To force a document to appear in a new window or tab, you add the `target` attribute to the <a> tag. The general syntax is

```
<a href="url" target="window">content</a>
```

where *window* is a name assigned to the new browser window or browser tab. The value you use for the `target` attribute doesn't affect the appearance or content of the page being opened; the target simply identifies the different windows or tabs that are currently open. You can choose any name you wish for the target. If several links have the same target name, they all open in the same location, replacing the previous content in the browser window or tab. HTML also supports the special target names described in Figure 2-43.

Figure 2-43 **Target names for browser windows and tabs**

Target Name	Description
target	Opens the link in a new window or tab named *target*
_blank	Opens the link in a new, unnamed window or tab
_self	Opens the link in the current browser window or tab

Whether the new page is opened in a tab or in a browser window is determined by the browser settings. It cannot be set by the HTML code.

REFERENCE

Opening a Link in a New Window or Tab

• To open a link in a new browser window or browser tab, add the attribute

 target="*window*"

to the <a> tag, where *window* is a name assigned to the new browser window or tab. The target attribute can also be set to _blank for a new, unnamed browser window or tab, or to _self for the current browser window or tab.

Gerry suggests that all of the external links from his page be opened in a browser window or tab identified with the target name *new*.

To specify a link target:

1. Return to the **tips.htm** file in your text editor.

2. Scroll to the bottom of the file and locate the four links to the external Web sites.

3. Within each of the opening <a> tags, insert the following attribute, as shown in Figure 2-44:

 target="new"

Figure 2-44 **Setting a target for hyperlinks**

```
<dl>
    <dt>&#9758; <a href="http://www.apogeephoto.com" target="new">Apogee Photo</a></dt>
    <dd>An established online photography magazine with articles by
        top pros, discussion forums, workshops, and more.
    </dd>
    <dt>&#9758; <a href="http://www.outdoorphotographer.com" target="new">Outdoor Photographer</a></dt>
    <dd>The premier magazine for outdoor photography. The site
        includes extensive tips on photographing wildlife, action
        sports, scenic vistas, and travel sites.
    </dd>
    <dt>&#9758; <a href="http://www.dpmag.com" target="new">Digital Photo</a></dt>
    <dd>An excellent site for novices and professionals with
        informative reviews and buying guides for the latest equipment
        and software.
    </dd>
    <dt>&#9758; <a href="http://www.popphoto.com" target="new">Popular Photography and Imaging</a></dt>
    <dd>A useful and informative site with articles from the
        long-established magazine of professional and amateur
        photographers.
    </dd>
</dl>
</article>
```

> **4.** Save your changes to the file.
>
> **5.** Refresh the **tips.htm** file in your browser. Click each of the four links to external Web sites and verify that each opens in the same new browser window or tab.
>
> **6.** Close the secondary browser window or tab.

You should use the `target` attribute sparingly in your Web site. Creating secondary windows can clutter up a user's desktop. Also, because the page is placed in a new window, users cannot use the Back button to return to the previous page in that window; they must click the browser's program button or the tab for the original Web site. This confuses some users and annoys others. Many Web designers now advocate not using the target attribute at all, leaving the choice of opening a link in a new tab or window to users. Note that the target attribute is not supported in strict XHTML-compliant code.

Creating a Tooltip

If you want to provide additional information about a link on your Web page, you can add a tooltip to the link. A **tooltip** is descriptive text that appears when a user positions the mouse pointer over a link. Figure 2-45 shows an example of a tooltip applied to one of Gerry's links.

Figure 2-45	**Viewing a tooltip**

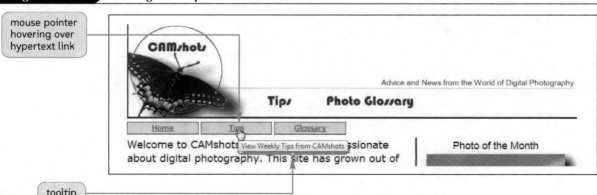

mouse pointer hovering over hypertext link

tooltip

To create the tooltip, add the title attribute to the opening <a> tag in the form

```
<a href="url" title="text">content</a>
```

where `text` is the text that appears in the tooltip. To create the tooltip shown in Figure 2-45, you would enter the following HTML code:

```
<a href="tips.htm"
   title="View Weekly Tips from CAMshots">
   Tips
</a>
```

Tooltips can also be added to image map hotspots to provide more useful feedback to the user.

Creating a Semantic Link

The text of a hypertext link should always describe to users the type of document that the link opens. You can also use the `rel` attribute to indicate the type of document that a link calls. For example, in the links to the site's home page, Gerry could insert the following `rel` attribute, setting its value to *first* to indicate that the home page is the first document in the CAMshots Web site:

```
<a href="home.htm" rel="first">Home Page</a>
```

A hypertext link containing the `rel` attribute is called a **semantic link** because the tag contains information about the relationship between the link and its destination. This information is not intended for the user, but for the browser. For example, a browser could be set up to mark the first Web page in a site with a special icon or to provide scripts that allow quick access to a site's first page.

Although the `rel` attribute is not limited to a fixed set of values, the specifications for HTML and XHTML include a proposed list of special values. Figure 2-46 shows some of these proposed relationship values.

Figure 2-46	Proposed values for the rel attribute

rel Attribute	Link To ...
alternate	An alternate version of the document
archives	A collection of historical documents
author	Information about the author of the document
external	An external document
first	The first document in a selection
help	A help document
index	An index for the document
last	The last document in a selection
license	Copyright information for the document
next	The next document in a selection
prev	The previous document in a selection
search	A search tool for the selection
sidebar	A document that should be shown in the browser's sidebar
stylesheet	An external style sheet

HTML 4.01 and XHTML also support the `rev` attribute to describe the reverse relationship: how a linked document views the current document. For example, if you're linking to the Glossary page from the home page, the reverse relation is *first* (because that is how the Glossary page views the home page). The HTML code would be

```
<a href="glossary.htm" rel="glossary" rev="first">Glossary</a>
```

The `rev` attribute is not supported in HTML5.

At this point, Gerry decides against using the `rel` and `rev` attributes on his Web site. However, he'll keep them in mind as an option as his Web site expands in size and complexity.

Using the `link` Element

Another way to add a hypertext link to your document is to add a `link` element to the document's head with the syntax

```
<link href="url" rel="text" rev="text" target="window" />
```

where the *href*, *rel*, *rev*, and *target* attributes serve the same purpose as in the `<a>` tag. You've already used the `link` element to link your Web pages to external style sheets, but you can use it to link to other types of documents as well. For example, to use the `link` element to create semantic links to the three pages of Gerry's Web site, you could add the following link elements to the `head` element of each document:

```
<link rel="first" href="home.htm" />
<link rel="help" href="tips.htm" />
<link rel="index" href="glossary.htm" />
```

Because they are placed within a document's head, `link` elements do not appear as part of the Web page. Instead, if a browser supports it, the links can be displayed in a browser toolbar. The advantage of the `link` element used in this way is that it places the list of links outside of the Web page, freeing up page space for other content. Also, because the links appear in a browser toolbar, they are always easily accessible to users. Currently, Opera is one of the few browsers with built-in support for the `link` element. Third-party software exists to provide this support for Internet Explorer and Firefox. Because no single list of relationship names is widely accepted, you must check with each browser's documentation to find out what relationship names it supports. Until semantic links are embraced by more browsers, you should use them only if you duplicate that information elsewhere on the page.

Working with Metadata

Gerry is happy with the work you've done on the design for his CAMshots Web site. Now he wants to start working on getting the site noticed. When someone searches for "digital photography tips" or "camera buying guide," will they find Gerry's Web site? There are thousands of photography sites on the Web. Gerry knows he needs to add a few extra touches to his home page to make it more likely that the site will be picked up by major search engines such as Yahoo! and Google.

Optimizing a Web site for search engines can be a long and involved process. For the best results, Web authors often turn to **search engine optimization** (**SEO**) tools to make their sites appear more prominently in search engines. Because CAMshots is a hobby site, Gerry does not want to invest any money in improving the site's visibility; but he would like to do a few simple things that would help.

Using the `meta` Element

To be noticed on the Web, a site needs to include information about itself for search engines to read and add to their search indices. Information about a site is called **metadata**. You can add metadata to your Web pages by adding a `meta` element to the document head. In the last tutorial, you saw how to use the `meta` element to store information about the character set used by the page; but you can also use it to store other information about the document. The syntax of the `meta` element is

```
<meta name="text" content="text" scheme="text" http-equiv="text" />
```

where the `name` attribute specifies the type of metadata, the `content` attribute stores the metadata value, the `scheme` attribute defines the metadata format, and the `http-equiv` attribute is used to attach metadata or commands to the communication stream between

the Web server and the browser. Note that the `scheme` attribute is not supported under HTML5, while the `charset` attribute (not listed above) is supported only under HTML5.

There are three uses of the `meta` element:

- To store information about a document that can be read by the author, other users, and Web browsers
- To control how browsers handle a document, including forcing browsers to automatically refresh the page at timed intervals
- To assist Web search engines in adding a document to their search index

For example, the following `meta` element stores the name of the Web page's author:

```
<meta name="author" content="Gerry Hayward" />
```

For search engines, you should include metadata describing the site and the topics it covers. This is done by adding a `meta` element containing the site description and another meta element with a list of keywords. The following two elements would summarize the CAMshots Web site for search engines:

```
<meta name="description" content="CAMshots provides advice on
digital cameras and photography" />

<meta name="keywords" content="photography, cameras, digital
imaging" />
```

Figure 2-47 lists some other examples of metadata that you can use to describe your documents.

Figure 2-47	Examples of the uses of the meta element

Meta Name	Example	Description
author	`<meta name="author" content="Gerry Hayward" />`	Supplies the name of the document author
classification	`<meta name="classification" content="photography" />`	Classifies the document category
copyright	`<meta name="copyright" content="© 2014 CAMshots" />`	Provides a copyright statement
description	`<meta name="description" content="Digital photography and advice" />`	Provides a description of the document
generator	`<meta name="generator" content="Dreamweaver" />`	Indicates the name of the program that created the HTML code for the document
keywords	`<meta name="keywords" content="photography, cameras, digital imaging" />`	Provides a list of keywords describing the document
owner	`<meta name="owner" content="CAMshots" />`	Indicates the owner of the document
rating	`<meta name="rating" content="general" />`	Provides a rating of the document in terms of its suitability for minors
reply-to	`<meta name="reply-to" content="ghayward@camshots.com (G. Hayward)" />`	Supplies a contact e-mail address and name for the document

In recent years, search engines have become more sophisticated in evaluating Web sites. In the process, the meta element has decreased in importance. However, it is still used by search engines when adding a site to their indices. Because adding metadata requires very little effort, you should still include meta elements in your Web documents.

REFERENCE

Working with Metadata

- To document the contents of a Web page, use the meta element

 `<meta name="text" content="text" />`

 where the name attribute specifies the type of metadata and the content attribute stores the metadata value.
- To add metadata or a command to the communication stream between the Web server and Web browsers, use

 `<meta http-equiv="text" content="text" />`

 where the http-equiv attribute specifies the type of data or command attached to the communication stream and the content attribute specifies the data value or command.

Having discussed metadata issues with you, Gerry asks that you include a few meta elements to describe his new site.

To add metadata to Gerry's document:

1. Return to the **home.htm** file in your text editor.
2. Directly below the meta element that defines the document's character set, insert the following meta elements, as shown in Figure 2-48:

   ```
   <meta name="author" content="your name" />
   <meta name="description" content="A site for sharing information on
   digital photography and cameras" />
   <meta name="keywords" content="photography, cameras, digital
   imaging" />
   ```

Figure 2-48 Adding meta elements to the CAMshots home page

```
<meta charset="UTF-8" />
<meta name="author" content="Gerry Hayward" />
<meta name="description" content="A site for sharing information on
            digital photography and cameras" />
<meta name="keywords" content="photography, cameras, digital imaging" />

<title>CAMshots Home Page</title>
<script src="modernizr-1.5.js"></script>
<link href="camstyles.css" rel="stylesheet" type="text/css" />
</head>
```

metadata category metadata value

3. Close the file, saving your changes.
4. Close any open files or applications.

Using the meta Element to Reload a Web Page

Describing your document is not the only use of the meta element. As you learned earlier, servers transmit Web pages using a communication protocol called HTTP. You can add information and commands to this communication stream with the http-equiv attribute of the meta element. One common use of the http-equiv attribute is to force browsers to refresh a Web page at timed intervals, which is useful for Web sites that publish scoreboards or stock tickers. For example, to automatically refresh a Web page every 60 seconds, you would apply the following meta element:

```
<meta http-equiv="refresh" content="60" />
```

Another use of the meta element is to redirect the browser from the current document to a new document. This might prove useful to Gerry someday if he changes the URL of his site's home page. As his readers get accustomed to the new Web address, he can keep the old address online, automatically redirecting readers to the new site. The meta element to perform an automatic redirect has the general form

```
<meta http-equiv="refresh" content="sec;url=url" />
```

TIP

When redirecting a Web site to a new URL, avoid confusion by always including text notifying users that the page is being redirected, and provide users several seconds to read the text.

where *sec* is the time in seconds before the browser redirects the user and *url* is the URL of the new site. To redirect users after five seconds to the Web page at *http://www. camshots.com*, you could enter the following meta element:

```
<meta http-equiv="refresh" content="5;url=http://www.camshots.com" />
```

At this point, Gerry does not need to use the meta element to send data or commands through the HTTP communication protocol. However, he will keep this option in mind if he moves the site to a new address.

Gerry is happy with the Web site you've started. He'll continue to work on the site and will come back to you for more assistance as he adds new pages and elements.

REVIEW

Session 2.2 Quick Check

1. The CAMmap image map has a circular hotspot centered at the point (50, 75) with a radius of 40 pixels pointing to the faq.htm file. Specify the code to create a map element containing this circular hotspot.
2. An inline image based on the logo.jpg file with the alternate text *CAMshots* needs to use the CAMmap image map. Specify the code to apply the image map to the image.
3. What are the five parts of a URL?
4. Specify the code to link the text *White House* to the URL *http://www. whitehouse.gov*, with the destination document displayed in a new unnamed browser window.
5. Specify the code to link the text *University of Washington* to the FTP server at *ftp.uwash.edu*.
6. Specify the code to link the text *President of the United States* to the e-mail address *president@whitehouse.gov*.
7. What attribute would you add to a hypertext link to display the tooltip *Tour the White House*?
8. Specify the code to add the description *United States Office of the President* as metadata to a document.
9. Specify the code to automatically refresh your Web document every 5 minutes.

Practice the skills you learned in the tutorial using the same case scenario.

PRACTICE

Review Assignments

Data Files needed for the Review Assignments: camhome.htm, child1.jpg–child3.jpg, childtxt.htm, conlogo.jpg, constyles.css, contest1.png–contest3.png, contesttxt.htm, flower1.jpg–flower3.jpg, flowertxt.htm, modernizr-1.5.js, photogloss.htm, scenic1.jpg–scenic3.jpg, scenictxt.htm, thirdstip.jpg, thumb1.jpg–thumb9.jpg, tipweek.htm

Gerry has been working on the CAMshots Web site for a while. During that time, the site has grown in popularity with amateur photographers. Now he wants to host a monthly photo contest to highlight the work of his colleagues. Each month Gerry will pick the three best photos from different photo categories. He's asked for your help in creating the collection of Web pages highlighting the winning entries. Gerry has already created four pages. The first page contains information about the photo contest; the remaining three pages contain the winning entries for child photos, scenic photos, and flower photos. Although Gerry has already entered much of the page content, he needs you to work on creating the links between and within each page. Figure 2-49 shows a preview of the photo contest's home page.

Figure 2-49	CAMshots Contest Winners page

Complete the following:

1. Use your text editor to open the **contesttxt.htm**, **childtxt.htm**, **scenictxt.htm**, and **flowertxt.htm** files from the tutorial.02\review folder included with your Data Files. Enter *your name* and *the date* within each file, and then save them as **contest.htm**, **child.htm**, **scenic.htm**, and **flower.htm**, respectively, in the same folder.

2. Go to the **child.htm** file in your text editor. Directly below the `header` element, create a navigation list containing an unordered list with the following list items as hyperlinks:
 a. **Home** linked to the camhome.htm file
 b. **Tips** linked to the tipweek.htm file
 c. **Contest** linked to the contest.htm file
 d. **Glossary** linked to the photogloss.htm file

3. Go to the `section` element and locate the contest1.png inline image. Directly below the inline image, insert an image map with the following properties:
 a. Set the name of the image map as **contestmap**.
 b. Add a polygonal hotspot pointing to the child.htm file containing the points (427, 5), (535, 20), (530, 59), and (421, 43). Enter **Child Photos** as the alternate text for the hotspot.
 c. Add a polygonal hotspot pointing to the flower.htm file containing the points (539, 57), (641, 84), (651, 46), and (547, 26). Enter **Flower Photos** as the alternate text for the hotspot.
 d. Add a polygonal hotspot pointing to the scenic.htm file containing the points (650, 86), (753, 125), (766, 78), and (662, 49). Enter **Scenic Photos** as the alternate text for the hotspot.

4. Apply the contestmap image map to the contest1 inline image.

5. Locate the three `h2` elements naming the three child photo winners. Assign the `h2` elements the ids **photo1**, **photo2**, and **photo3**, respectively.

6. Save your changes to the file.

7. Go to the **flower.htm** file in your text editor. Repeat Steps 2 through 6, applying the image map to the contest2.png image at the top of the `section` element.

8. Go to the **scenic.htm** file in your text editor. Repeat Steps 2 through 6 applying the image map to the contest3.png image at the top of the `section` element.

9. Go to the **contest.htm** file in your text editor. Repeat Step 2 to insert a navigation list at the top of the page.

10. Scroll down to the second article. Link the text *Child Photos* to the child.htm file. Link *Flower Photos* to the flower.htm file. Link *Scenic Photos* to the scenic.htm file.

11. Scroll down to the nine thumbnail images (named *thumb1.jpg* through *thumb9.jpg*). Link each inline image to the corresponding `h2` heading in the child.htm, flower.htm, or scenic.htm file you identified in Step 5.

12. Scroll down to the aside element. Mark the text *Gerry Hayward* as a hypertext link to an e-mail address with **ghayward@camshots.com** as the e-mail address and **Photo Contest** as the subject line.

13. Mark the text *BetterPhoto.com* as a hypertext link pointing to the URL **http://www.betterphoto.com**. Set the attribute of the link so that it opens in a new browser window or tab.

14. Save your changes to the file.

15. Open **contest.htm** in your Web browser. Verify that the e-mail link opens a new mail message window with the subject line *Photo Contest*. Verify that the link to BetterPhoto.com opens that Web site in a new browser window or tab. Verify that you can navigate through the Web site using the hypertext links in the navigation list. Finally, click each of the nine thumbnail images at the bottom of the page and verify that each connects to the larger image of the photo on the appropriate photo contest page.

16. Go to the **child.htm** file in your Web browser. Verify that you can navigate forward and backward through the three photo contest pages by clicking the hotspots in the image map.

17. Submit your completed files to your instructor, in either printed or electronic form, as requested.

Apply your knowledge of hypertext links to create a directory of universities and colleges.

APPLY

Case Problem 1

Data Files needed for this Case Problem: colleges.txt, hestyles.css, highered.jpg, modernizr-1.5.js, uwlisttxt.htm

HigherEd Adella Coronel is a guidance counselor for Eagle High School in Waunakee, Wisconsin. She wants to take her interest in helping students choose colleges to the Web by starting a Web site called HigherEd. She's come to you for help in creating the site. The first page she wants to create is a simple directory of Wisconsin colleges and universities. She's created the list of schools, but has not yet marked the entries in the list as hypertext links. The list is very long, so she has broken it down into three categories: private colleges and universities, technical colleges, and public universities. Because of the length of the page, she wants to include hypertext links that allow students to jump down to a specific college category. Figure 2-50 shows a preview of the page you'll create for Adella.

Figure 2-50	HigherEd Web site

Higher ◆ Ed

The Directory of Higher Education Opportunities

Wisconsin Colleges and Universities

Private Colleges and Universities	Technical College System	University of Wisconsin System

Private Colleges and Universities

Alverno College
Beloit College
Cardinal Stritch University
Carroll College
Concordia University Wisconsin
Edgewood College
Lakeland College
Lawrence University
Marian University
Medical College of Wisconsin
Milwaukee Institute of Art and Design
Milwaukee School of Engineering

Complete the following:

1. In your text editor, open the **uwlisttxt.htm** file from the tutorial.02\case1 folder included with your Data Files. Enter *your name* and *the date* in the file comments. Save the file as **uwlist.htm** in the same folder.

2. Directly below the `h1` heading, insert a navigation list containing an unordered list with following list items: **Private Colleges and Universities**, **Technical College System**, and **University of Wisconsin System**.

3. Add the ids **private**, **technical**, and **public** to the three `h2` headings that categorize the list of schools.

4. Mark each of the school entries on the page as a hypertext link. Use the URLs provided in the colleges.txt file. (Hint: Use the copy and paste feature of your text editor to efficiently copy and paste the URL text.)

⊕ **EXPLORE**

5. Adella wants the links to the school Web sites to appear in a new tab or window. Because there are so many links on the page, add a `base` element to the document head specifying that all links open by default in a new browser window or tab named **collegeWin**.

6. Link the three items in your navigation list to the corresponding `h2` headings.

⊕ **EXPLORE**

7. For each of the hypertext links you marked in Step 6, set the link to open in the current browser window and not in a new browser window or tab.

8. Save your changes to the file.

9. Open **uwlist.htm** in your Web browser and verify that the school links all open in the same browser window or tab, and that the links within the document to the different school categories bring the user to those locations on the page but not in a new window or tab.

10. Submit your completed files to your instructor, in either printed or electronic form, as requested.

Apply your knowledge of HTML to create a slide show Web site.

APPLY

Case Problem 2

Data Files needed for this Case Problem: fiddler.jpg, fidstyles.css, first.png, home.png, hometxt.htm, last.png, modernizr-1.5.js, next.png, prev.png, slide1.jpg–slide6.jpg, slide1txt.htm–slide6txt.htm, thumb1.jpg–thumb6.jpg

Lakewood School Tasha Juroszek is a forensics teacher at Lakewood School, a small private school in Moultrie, Georgia. Tasha has just finished directing her students in *Fiddler on the Roof, Jr.* and wants to place a slide show of the performances on the Web. She has already designed the layout and content of the pages, but needs help to finish the slide show. She has asked you to add hypertext links between the slide pages and the site's home page. Figure 2-51 shows a preview of one of the slide pages on the Web site.

Figure 2-51 Fiddler on the Roof, Jr. slide page

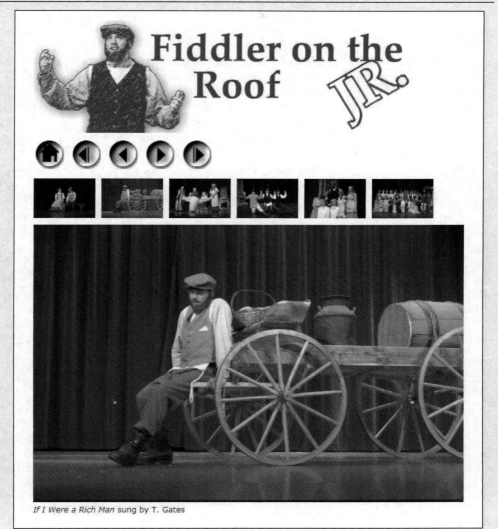

If I Were a Rich Man sung by T. Gates

Complete the following:

1. Use your text editor to open the **hometxt.htm** file and the **slide1txt.htm** through **slide6txt.htm** files from the tutorial.02\case2 folder included with your Data Files. Enter *your name* and *the date* in the comment section of each file. Save the files as **home.htm** and **slide1.htm** through **slide6.htm**, respectively.

2. Return to the **slide1.htm** file in your text editor. At the top of the page are five buttons used to navigate through the slide show. Locate the inline image for the home button (home.png) and mark it as a hypertext link pointing to the home.htm file. Add the tooltip **Home Page** to the hyperlink.

3. There are six slides in Tasha's slide show. Mark the First Slide button as a hypertext link pointing to the slide1.htm file. Mark the Last Slide button as a link to the slide6.htm file. Link the Previous Slide button to slide1.htm, the first slide in the show. Link the Next Slide button to the slide2.htm file. Add an appropriate tooltip to each hyperlink.

4. Directly below the slide show buttons are thumbnail images of the six slides. Link each thumbnail image to its slide page.

5. Save your changes to the file.

6. Repeat Steps 2 through 5 for the five remaining slide pages. Within each page, set the navigation buttons to go back and forth through the slide show. For the slide6.htm file, the Next Slide button should point to the slide6.htm file because it is the last slide in the show.

7. Go to the **home.htm** file in your text editor. Go to the first paragraph in the article and mark the text string *slide show* as a hypertext link pointing to the slide1.htm file.

8. Go to the end of the second paragraph and mark the phrase *contact me* as a hypertext link pointing to the e-mail address **tashajur@lakewood.edu**, with the subject heading **Digital Photo**.

9. Save your changes to the file.

10. Load the **home.htm** file in your Web browser. Test the links in the Web site and verify that they allow the user to easily move back and forth through the slide show.

11. Submit your completed files to your instructor, in either printed or electronic form, as requested.

Explore how to use HTML to create an election results Web site.

Case Problem 3

Data Files needed for this Case Problem: dcoords.txt, dist1txt.htm–dist4txt.htm, ewlogo.png, ewstyles.css, kansasmap.png, kansastxt.htm, modernizr-1.5.js

ElectionWeb Allison Hawks is a political science student at the University of Kansas. As part of a project for one of her courses, she is setting up a Web site to report results from the upcoming elections. She's asked for your help in designing and writing the hypertext links and image maps to be used throughout her site. She has created a set of sample files detailing hypothetical results for the races for governor, senator, and the four Kansas congressional districts. A preview of the site's home page is shown in Figure 2-52.

CHALLENGE

Figure 2-52 **Kansas results from ElectionWeb**

Kansas Statewide Races

The Kansas Election polls have officially been closed now for two hours and results are being constantly updated. As of 10pm with 65% of the ballots counted, leaders in the state-wide races for governor and senator are as follows:

News Sources

Yahoo! News
FOX News
CNN
MSNBC
Google News
New York Times
digg
Washington Post
LATimes
Reuters
ABCNews
USA Today

Governor (65% reporting)

Charles Young (R) - 371,885 (47%)
Karen Drew (D) - 356,060 (45%)
Barry Davis (I) - 39,562 (5%)

U.S. Senate (65% reporting)

✔ Helen Sanchez (D) - 387,710 (49%)
Linda Epstein (R) - 348,147 (44%)
Hunter Ryan (I) - 47,474 (6%)

Get up-to-the-minute election results from the Kansas Secretary of State.

Click to view congressional district results

ElectionWeb: *Your Source for Online Election Results*

Complete the following:

1. Use your text editor to open the **kansastxt.htm** file and the **dist1txt.htm** through **dist4txt.htm** files from the tutorial.02\case3 folder included with your Data Files. Enter *your name* and *the date* in the comment section of each file. Save the files as **kansas.htm** and **district1.htm** through **district4.htm,** respectively.

⊕ EXPLORE 2. Go to the **kansas.htm** file in your text editor. Use the `meta` element to specify *your name* as the document author, and **Kansas** and **elections** as keywords for Web search engines.

⊕ EXPLORE 3. Create a semantic link in the document head linking this document to the Office of the Kansas Secretary of State at the following address:
http://www.kssos.org/elections/elections_statistics.html
Use a `rel` attribute value of **external** for the link.

4. Set the base target of the Web page to **new** so that links on the page open, by default, in a new browser window or tab.

5. Go to the page body, and then directly below the header element insert a navigation list with the following content:

 a. An `h2` heading with the text **News Sources**

 b. An unordered list containing the following entries: **Yahoo! News**, **FOX News**, **CNN**, **MSNBC**, **Google News**, **New York Times**, **digg**, **Washington Post**, **LATimes**, **Reuters**, **ABCNews**, and **USA Today**.

 c. Look up the Web addresses of the 12 news sources and link your list entries to the appropriate Web sites. Set the `rel` attribute of each link to **external**.

6. Scroll down to the last paragraph before the figure box and link the text *Secretary of State* to the Office of the Kansas Secretary of State Web site.

7. Directly below the figure box, create an image map named **kansasdistricts** containing four polygonal hotspots for each of the four Kansas congressional districts. Use the coordinates found in the dcoords.txt file as the coordinates of the hotspots.

⊕ EXPLORE 8. Set the hotspots in your image map to access the district1.htm, district2.htm, district3.htm, and district4.htm files, using the target attribute value of **_self** so that those Web pages open within the current browser window or tab.

9. Apply the kansasdistricts image map to the kansasmap.png inline image.

10. Save your changes to the file.

11. Go to the **district1.htm** file in your text editor.

12. Directly below the opening `<section>` tag, insert a navigation list containing an unordered list with the items **District 1**, **District 2**, **District 3**, and **District 4**. Link each entry to its corresponding Web page in the ElectionWeb Web site.

13. Scroll down to the last paragraph before the figure box and link the text *statewide races* to the kansas.htm file.

14. Apply the same image map you created in Step 7 for the kansas.htm file to the kansasmap.png inline image.

15. Save your changes to the file.

16. Open the **district2.htm**, **district3.htm**, and **district4.htm** files in your text editor and repeat Steps 12 through 15 for each file.

17. Open the **kansas.htm** file in your Web browser and verify that you can navigate through Allison's sample pages by clicking the hypertext links within the page body and within the image maps. Verify that you can access the external Web sites listed in the news sources and the Office of the Kansas Secretary of State.

18. Submit your completed project to your instructor, in either printed or electronic form, as requested.

Test your knowledge of HTML and use your creativity to design a Web site documenting a Shakespeare play.

RESEARCH

Case Problem 4

Data Files needed for this Case Problem: characters.txt, notes.txt, tempest.jpg, tempest.txt

Mansfield Classical Theatre Steve Karls continues to work as the director of Mansfield Classical Theatre in Mansfield, Ohio. The next production he plans to direct is *The Tempest*. Steve wants to put the text of this play on the Web, but he also wants to augment the dialog of the play with notes and commentary. However, he doesn't want his commentary to get in the way of a straight-through reading of the text, so he has hit on the idea of linking his commentary to key phrases in the dialog. Steve has created text files containing an excerpt from *The Tempest* as well as his commentary and other supporting documents. He would like you to take his raw material and create a collection of linked pages.

Complete the following:

1. Create HTML files named **tempest.htm**, **commentary.htm**, and **cast.htm**, saving them in the tutorial.02\case4 folder included with your Data Files. Add comment tags to the head section of each document containing your name and the date. Add an appropriate page title to each document.

2. Using the contents of the tempest.txt, notes.txt, and characters.txt text files, create the body of the three Web pages in Steve's Web site. You can supplement the material on the page with appropriate material you find on your own.

3. Use the tempest.jpg file as a logo for the page. Create an image map from the logo pointing to the tempest.htm, commentary.htm, and cast.htm files. The three rectangular boxes on the logo have the following coordinates for their upper-left and lower-right corners:

 The Play: (228, 139) (345, 173)

 Commentary: (359, 139) (508, 173)

 The Cast: (520, 139) (638, 173)

4. Use this image map in all three of the Web pages for this Web site.

5. Create links between the dialog on the play page and the notes on the commentary page. The notes contain line numbers to aid you in linking each line of dialog to the appropriate note.

6. Create a link between the first appearance of each character's name in the tempest.htm page and the character's description on the cast.htm page.

7. Include a link to Steve Karls' e-mail address on the tempest.htm page. Steve's e-mail address is **stevekarls@mansfieldct.com**. E-mail sent to Steve's account from this Web page should have the subject line **Comments on the Tempest**.

8. Add appropriate `meta` elements to each of the three pages documenting the page's contents and purpose.

9. Search the Web for sites that would provide additional material about the play. Add links to these pages on the tempest.htm page. The links should open in a new browser window or tab.

10. Submit your completed files to your instructor, in either printed or electronic form, as requested.

ENDING DATA FILES

tutorial

glossary.htm
home.htm
tips.htm
+ 1 style sheet
+ 5 graphic files
modernizr-1.5.js

review

camhome.htm
child.htm
contest.htm
flower.htm
photogloss.htm
scenic.htm
tipweek.htm
+ 1 style sheet
+ 23 graphic files
modernizr-1.5.js

case1

uwlist.htm
+ 1 style sheet
+ 1 graphic file
modernizr-1.5.js

case2

home.htm
slide1.htm
slide2.htm
slide3.htm
slide4.htm
slide5.htm
slide6.htm
+ 1 style sheet
+ 18 graphic files
modernizr-1.5.js

case3

district1.htm
district2.htm
district3.htm
district4.htm
kansas.htm
+ 1 style sheet
+ 2 graphic files
modernizr-1.5.js

case4

cast.htm
commentary.htm
tempest.htm
+ 1 graphic file

 # Written Communication

Avoiding Common Mistakes in Written Communication

Most written communication errors can be easily avoided, yet are often overlooked. It's particularly important to catch writing errors on a personal Web site or online resume, which often help determing the first impression that a colleague or potential employer forms of you. Whether you are pressed for time, don't pay attention to detail, or have never learned the basics of good writing in the first place, these guidelines should help turn your writing into works you can be proud to claim.

Plan and Focus Your Writing

- Think about your audience. Who will read what you write? What knowledge do they already possess, and what attitudes might they have about your subject? Who will be viewing your Web documents, and what will they expect to see?

- Be clear about why you are writing in the first place. Are you writing to inform, or do you want action to be taken? Do you hope to change a belief or simply state your position? For a personal Web site or resume, make sure you understand what information potential employers and professional contacts will mostly likely be looking for.

- Research your topic. Provide all the necessary information the reader will need to make a decision or take action, if needed. If facts are included, be sure you can substantiate them. For a resume, ensure all your dates are accurate, and look up the exact names of organizations, institutions, and endorsements.

- Don't be afraid to rewrite or revise. If it's an important document, consider having someone else read it so you can determine whether your meaning is clear. At a minimum, read what you have written out loud to determine whether the message and impact come across as you intended. For online documents, continue the revision process on a regular basis so your documents do not become inaccurate or outdated.

Check Grammar and Spelling

Text editing programs remove all excuses for not checking your spelling and grammar in written communications. Keep in mind that spellchecking doesn't catch every error, so be sure to review your work carefully. Hiring managers are often inundated with resumes for a job opening, and an error in spelling or grammar is sometimes all it takes for an otherwise promising application to be rejected.

Set the Right Tone

When you write informal communications, you may use abbreviated or incomplete sentences and phrases or slang. In the workplace, however, you must carefully consider the tone of your written communication so you don't unintentionally offend your readers. Using contractions is considered friendly and is usually all right, but it is never acceptable to use offensive language. Anything you post about yourself online may be viewed by colleagues or a prospective employer, no matter how informal the context, so be sure that anything you write reflects well on you.

Write Clearly and Accessibly

When you write, your language should be free of buzzwords and jargon that will weaken your message, or make it difficult for your reader to understand your meaning.

Create Your Own Web Site

The Web has become an important medium for advertising yourself. By making your resume available online, you can quickly get prospective employers the information they need to make a hiring decision. There are many sites that will assist you in writing and posting your resume. They will also, for a fee, present your online resume to employers in your chosen field. Assuming you don't want to pay to use such a site, you can also create your own Web site containing your employment history and talents. In this exercise, you'll use the skills you learned in Tutorials 1 and 2 to design your own Web site and create an online resume.

Note: Please be sure *not* to include any personal information of a sensitive nature in the documents you create to be submitted to your instructor for this exercise. Later on, you can update the documents with such information for your own personal use.

1. Collect material about yourself that would be useful in an online resume. You should include material for a page on your employment history, talents and special interests, a general biography, and a summary of the main points of your resume.

2. Create a storyboard outlining the pages on your Web site. Clearly indicate the links between the pages. Make sure that your site is easy to navigate no matter which page users start on.

3. Collect or create graphical image files to make your site interesting to viewers. If you obtain graphics from the Web, be sure to follow all copyright restrictions on the material.

4. Start designing your site's home page. It should include an interesting and helpful logo. The home page should be brief and to the point, summarizing the main features of your resume. Its height should not be greater than two screens.

5. Add other pages containing more detailed information. Each page should have a basic theme and topic. The pages should follow a unified theme and design.

6. Use the `em` and `strong` elements to highlight important ideas. Do not overuse these page elements; doing so can detract from your page's readability rather than enhancing it.

7. Use numbered and bulleted lists to list the main points in your resume.

8. Use block quotes to highlight recommendations from colleagues and former employers.

9. Use the `hr` element to divide longer pages into topical sections.

10. If sites on the Web would be relevant to your online resume (such as the Web sites of former or current employers), include links to those sites.

11. Include a link to your e-mail address. Write the e-mail address link so that it automatically adds an appropriate subject line to the e-mail message it creates.

12. Save your completed Web site and present it to your instructor.

1 Creating, Formatting, and Editing a Word Document with a Picture

Microsoft product screen shots used with permission from Microsoft Corporation.

Objectives

You will have mastered the material in this chapter when you can:

- Enter text in a Word document
- Check spelling as you type
- Format paragraphs
- Format text
- Undo and redo commands or actions
- Change theme colors
- Insert digital pictures in a Word document
- Format pictures
- Add a page border
- Adjust spacing
- Change document properties
- Correct errors and revise a document
- Print and read a document

1 Creating, Formatting, and Editing a Word Document with a Picture

Introduction

To advertise a sale, promote a business, publicize an event, or convey a message to the community, you may want to create a flyer and hand it out in person or post it in a public location. Libraries, schools, religious organizations, grocery stores, coffee shops, and other places often provide bulletin boards or windows for flyers. You also see flyers posted on webpages or as email messages.

Flyers announce personal items for sale or rent (car, boat, apartment); garage or block sales; services being offered (animal care, housecleaning, lessons, tours); membership, sponsorship, or donation requests (club, religious organization, charity); and other messages, such as a lost or found pet.

Project — Flyer with a Picture

Individuals and businesses create flyers to gain public attention. Flyers, which usually are a single page in length, are an inexpensive means of reaching the community. Many flyers, however, go unnoticed because they are designed poorly.

The project in this chapter follows general guidelines and uses Word to create the flyer shown in Figure 1–1. This colorful, eye-catching flyer announces tour adventures. The picture of the tour group on the mountain trail, taken with a digital camera, entices passersby or viewers to stop and look at the flyer. The headline on the flyer is large and colorful to draw attention into the text. The body copy below the picture briefly describes the tours, along with a bulleted list that concisely highlights important tour information. The signature line of the flyer calls attention to the contact phone number. The word, breathtaking, and the signature line are in a different color so that they stand apart from the rest of the text on the flyer. Finally, the graphical page border nicely frames and complements the contents of the flyer.

For an introduction to Office and instruction about how to perform basic tasks in Office apps, read the Office and Windows chapter at the beginning of this book, where you can learn how to run an application, use the ribbon, save a file, open a file, exit an application, use Help, and much more.

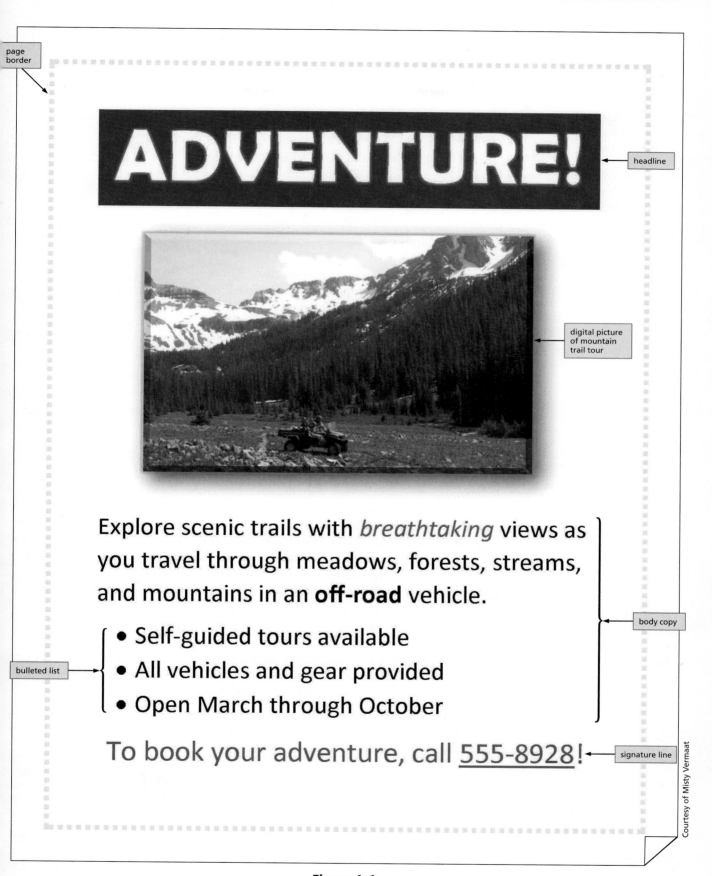

page border

headline

digital picture of mountain trail tour

body copy

bulleted list

signature line

Courtesy of Misty Vermaat

ADVENTURE!

Explore scenic trails with *breathtaking* views as you travel through meadows, forests, streams, and mountains in an **off-road** vehicle.

- Self-guided tours available
- All vehicles and gear provided
- Open March through October

To book your adventure, call 555-8928!

Figure 1–1

Roadmap

For an introduction to Windows and instruction about how to perform basic Windows tasks, read the Office and Windows chapter at the beginning of this book, where you can learn how to resize windows, change screen resolution, create folders, move and rename files, use Windows Help, and much more.

In this chapter, you will learn how to create the flyer shown in Figure 1–1. The following roadmap identifies general activities you will perform as you progress through this chapter:

1. ENTER TEXT in a new document.
2. FORMAT the TEXT in the flyer.
3. INSERT a PICTURE, called Mountain Trail, in the flyer.
4. FORMAT the PICTURE in the flyer.
5. ENHANCE the PAGE with a border and spacing.
6. CORRECT errors AND REVISE text in the flyer.
7. PRINT OR READ the flyer.

At the beginning of step instructions throughout the chapter, you will see an abbreviated form of this roadmap. The abbreviated roadmap uses colors to indicate chapter progress: gray means the chapter is beyond that activity, blue means the task being shown is covered in that activity, and black means that activity is yet to be covered. For example, the following abbreviated roadmap indicates the chapter would be showing a task in the 2 FORMAT TEXT activity.

1 ENTER TEXT | **2 FORMAT TEXT** | 3 INSERT PICTURE | 4 FORMAT PICTURE
5 ENHANCE PAGE | 6 CORRECT & REVISE | 7 PRINT OR READ

Use the abbreviated roadmap as a progress guide while you read or step through the instructions in this chapter.

To Run Word and Create a Blank Document

If you are using a computer to step through the project in this chapter and you want your screens to match the figures in this book, you should change your screen's resolution to 1366×768. For information about how to change a computer's resolution, refer to the Office and Windows chapter at the beginning of this book.

The following steps, which assume Windows 8 is running, use the Start screen or the Search box to run Word based on a typical installation. You may need to ask your instructor how to run Word on your computer. For a detailed example of the procedure summarized below, refer to the Office and Windows chapter.

One of the few differences between Windows 7 and Windows 8 occurs in the steps to run Word. If you are using Windows 7, click the Start button, type **Word** in the 'Search programs and files' box, click Word 2013, and then, if necessary, maximize the Word window. For detailed steps to run Word in Windows 7, refer to the Office and Windows chapter at the beginning of this book. For a summary of the steps, refer to the Quick Reference located at the back of this book.

1 Scroll the Start screen for a Word 2013 tile. If your Start screen contains a Word 2013 tile, tap or click it to run Word and then proceed to Step 5; if the Start screen does not contain the Word 2013 tile, proceed to the next step to search for the Word app.

2 Swipe in from the right edge of the screen or point to the upper-right corner of the screen to display the Charms bar and then tap or click the Search charm on the Charms bar to display the Search menu.

3 Type **Word** as the search text in the Search box and watch the search results appear in the Apps list.

4 Tap or click Word 2013 in the search results to run Word.

5 Tap or click the Blank document thumbnail on the Word start screen to create a blank document and display it in the Word window.

6 If the Word window is not maximized, tap or click the Maximize button on its title bar to maximize the window.

7 If the Print Layout button on the status bar is not selected (shown in Figure 1–2), tap or click it so that your screen is in Print Layout view.

Q&A What is Print Layout view?
The default (preset) view in Word is **Print Layout view**, which shows the document on a mock sheet of paper in the document window.

8 If Normal (HOME tab | Styles group) is not selected in the Styles gallery (shown in Figure 1–2), tap or click it so that your document uses the Normal style.

Q&A What is the Normal style?
When you create a document, Word formats the text using a particular style. The default style in Word is called the **Normal style**, which is discussed later in this book.

What if rulers appear on my screen?
Tap or click VIEW on the ribbon to display the VIEW tab and then remove the check mark from the View Ruler check box (VIEW tab | Show group).

Entering Text

The first step in creating a document is to enter its text. With the projects in this book, you enter text by typing on the keyboard. By default, Word positions text you type at the left margin. In a later section of this chapter, you will learn how to format, or change the appearance of, the entered text.

BTW
The Word Window
The chapters in this book begin with the Word window appearing as it did at the initial installation of the software. Your Word window may look different depending on your screen resolution and other Word settings.

To Type Text

1 ENTER TEXT | 2 FORMAT TEXT | 3 INSERT PICTURE | 4 FORMAT PICTURE
5 ENHANCE PAGE | 6 CORRECT & REVISE | 7 PRINT OR READ

To begin creating the flyer in this chapter, type the headline in the document window. *Why? The headline is the first line of text in the Adventure Flyer.* The following steps type the first line of text in the document.

1
• Type **Adventure!** as the headline (Figure 1–2).

Figure 1–2

Q&A

What if I make an error while typing?
You can press the BACKSPACE key until you have deleted the text in error and then retype the text correctly.

What is the purpose of the Spelling and Grammar Check icon on the status bar?
The **Spelling and Grammar Check icon** displays either a check mark to indicate the entered text contains no spelling or grammar errors, or an X to indicate that it found potential errors. Word flags potential errors in the document with a red, green, or blue wavy underline. Later in this chapter, you will learn how to fix flagged errors.

2

- Press the ENTER key to move the insertion point to the beginning of the next line (Figure 1–3).

Why did blank space appear between the headline and the insertion point?
Each time you press the ENTER key, Word creates a new paragraph and inserts blank space between the two paragraphs. Later in this chapter, you will learn how to increase and decrease the spacing between paragraphs.

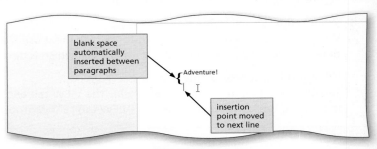

Figure 1–3

CONSIDER THIS

How do you use the touch keyboard with a touch screen?
To display the on-screen touch keyboard, tap the Touch Keyboard button on the Windows taskbar. When finished using the touch keyboard, tap the X button on the touch keyboard to close the keyboard.

To Display Formatting Marks

1 ENTER TEXT | 2 FORMAT TEXT | 3 INSERT PICTURE | 4 FORMAT PICTURE
5 ENHANCE PAGE | 6 CORRECT & REVISE | 7 PRINT OR READ

You may find it helpful to display formatting marks while working in a document. *Why? Formatting marks indicate where in a document you press the* ENTER *key,* SPACEBAR, *and other nonprinting characters.* A **formatting mark** is a character that Word displays on the screen but is not visible on a printed document. For example, the paragraph mark (¶) is a formatting mark that indicates where you pressed the ENTER key. A raised dot (·) shows where you pressed the SPACEBAR. Formatting marks are discussed as they appear on the screen.

Depending on settings made during previous Word sessions, your Word screen already may display formatting marks (Figure 1–4). The following step displays formatting marks, if they do not show already on the screen.

1

- If the HOME tab is not the active tab, tap or click HOME on the ribbon to display the HOME tab.

- If it is not selected already, tap or click the 'Show/Hide ¶' button (HOME tab | Paragraph group) to display formatting marks on the screen (Figure 1–4).

BTW

Zooming

If text is too small for you to read on the screen, you can zoom the document by dragging the Zoom slider on the status bar or tapping or clicking the Zoom Out or Zoom In buttons on the status bar. Changing the zoom has no effect on the printed document.

Figure 1–4

Q&A **What if I do not want formatting marks to show on the screen?**
You can hide them by tapping or clicking the 'Show/Hide ¶' button (HOME tab | Paragraph group) again. It is recommended that you display formatting marks so that you visually can identify when you press the ENTER key, SPACEBAR, and other keys associated with nonprinting characters. Most of the document windows presented in this book, therefore, show formatting marks.

Other Ways

1. Press CTRL+SHIFT+*

To Insert a Blank Line

1 ENTER TEXT | 2 FORMAT TEXT | 3 INSERT PICTURE | 4 FORMAT PICTURE
5 ENHANCE PAGE | 6 CORRECT & REVISE | 7 PRINT OR READ

In the flyer, the digital picture of the mountain trail appears between the headline and body copy. You will not insert this picture, however, until after you enter and format all text. *Why? Although you can format text and insert pictures in any order, for illustration purposes, this chapter formats all text first before inserting the picture. Thus, you leave a blank line in the document as a placeholder for the picture.*

To enter a blank line in a document, press the ENTER key without typing any text on the line. The following step inserts one blank line below the headline.

1
- Press the ENTER key to insert a blank line in the document (Figure 1–5).

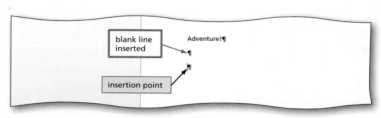

Figure 1–5

To Zoom Page Width

1 ENTER TEXT | 2 FORMAT TEXT | 3 INSERT PICTURE | 4 FORMAT PICTURE
5 ENHANCE PAGE | 6 CORRECT & REVISE | 7 PRINT OR READ

The next step in creating this flyer is to enlarge the contents that appear on the screen. *Why? You would like the text on the screen to be larger so that it is easier to read.* The document currently displays at 100% (shown in Figure 1–6). With Word, you can zoom page width, which zooms (enlarges or shrinks) the mock sheet of paper on the screen so that it is the width of the Word window. The following steps zoom page width.

1
- Tap or click VIEW on the ribbon to display the VIEW tab.

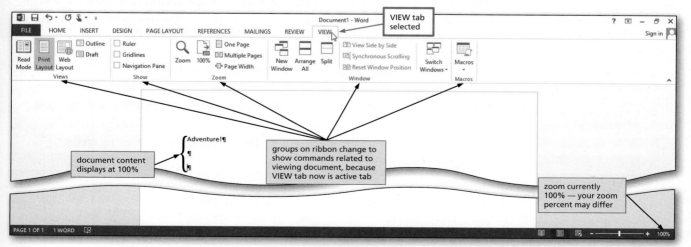

Figure 1–6

2

- Tap or click the Page Width button (VIEW tab | Zoom group) to display the page the same width as the document window (Figure 1–7).

Q&A

If I change the zoom, will the document print differently?
Changing the zoom has no effect on the printed document.

What are the other predefined zoom options?
Through the VIEW tab | Zoom group or the Zoom dialog box (Zoom button in Zoom group), you can zoom to one page (an entire single page appears in the document window), many pages (multiple pages appear at once in the document window), page width, text width, and a variety of set percentages. Whereas page width zoom places the edges of the page at the edges of the document window, text width zoom places the document contents at the edges of the document window.

Figure 1–7

Other Ways

1. Tap or click Zoom button (VIEW tab | Zoom group), tap or click Page width (Zoom dialog box), tap or click OK button

BTW
The Ribbon and Screen Resolution
Word may change how the groups and buttons within the groups appear on the ribbon, depending on the computer's screen resolution. Thus, your ribbon may look different from the ones in this book if you are using a screen resolution other than 1366 × 768.

Wordwrap

Wordwrap allows you to type words in a paragraph continually without pressing the ENTER key at the end of each line. As you type, if a word extends beyond the right margin, Word also automatically positions that word on the next line along with the insertion point.

Word creates a new paragraph each time you press the ENTER key. Thus, as you type text in the document window, do not press the ENTER key when the insertion point reaches the right margin. Instead, press the ENTER key only in these circumstances:

1. To insert a blank line(s) in a document (as shown in the previous steps)

2. To begin a new paragraph

3. To terminate a short line of text and advance to the next line

4. To respond to questions or prompts in Word dialog boxes, task panes, and other on-screen objects

To Wordwrap Text as You Type

1 ENTER TEXT | 2 FORMAT TEXT | 3 INSERT PICTURE | 4 FORMAT PICTURE
5 ENHANCE PAGE | 6 CORRECT & REVISE | 7 PRINT OR READ

The next step in creating the flyer is to type the body copy. *Why?* *In many flyers, the body copy text appears below the headline.* The following steps illustrate how the body copy text wordwraps as you enter it in the document.

1

- Type the first sentence of the body copy: `Explore scenic trails with breathtaking views as you travel through meadows, forests, streams, and mountains in an off-road vehicle.`

Q&A Why does my document wrap on different words?
The printer connected to a computer is one factor that can control where wordwrap occurs for each line in a document. Thus, it is possible that the same document could wordwrap differently if printed on different printers.

2

- Press the ENTER key to position the insertion point on the next line in the document (Figure 1–8).

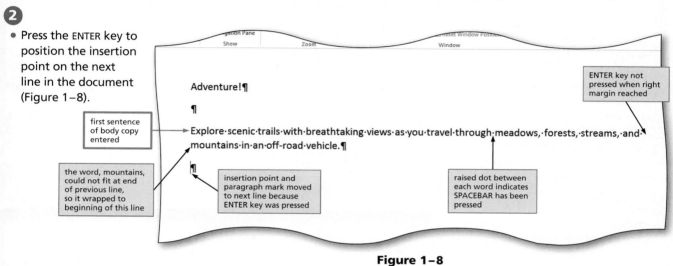

Figure 1–8

Spelling and Grammar Check

As you type text in a document, Word checks your typing for possible spelling and grammar errors. If all of the words you have typed are in Word's dictionary and your grammar is correct, as mentioned earlier, the Spelling and Grammar Check icon on the status bar displays a check mark. Otherwise, the icon shows an X. In this case, Word flags the potential error in the document window with a red, green, or blue wavy underline. A red wavy underline means the flagged text is not in Word's dictionary (because it is a proper name or misspelled). A green wavy underline indicates the text may be incorrect grammatically. A blue wavy underline indicates the text may contain a contextual spelling error, such as the misuse of homophones (words that are pronounced the same but that have different spellings or meanings, such as one and won). Although you can check the entire document for spelling and grammar errors at once, you also can check flagged errors as they appear on the screen.

A flagged word is not necessarily misspelled. For example, many names, abbreviations, and specialized terms are not in Word's main dictionary. In these cases, you can instruct Word to ignore the flagged word. As you type, Word also detects duplicate words while checking for spelling errors. For example, if your document contains the phrase, to the the store, Word places a red wavy underline below the second occurrence of the word, the.

BTW
Automatic Spelling Correction
As you type, Word automatically corrects some misspelled words. For example, if you type recieve, Word automatically corrects the misspelling and displays the word, receive, when you press the SPACEBAR or type a punctuation mark. To see a complete list of automatically corrected words, click FILE on the ribbon to open the Backstage view, click Options in the Backstage view, click Proofing in the left pane (Word Options dialog box), click the AutoCorrect Options button, and then scroll through the list near the bottom of the dialog box.

To Check Spelling and Grammar as You Type

In the following steps, the word, tours, has been misspelled intentionally as tuors. *Why? These steps illustrate Word's check spelling as you type feature. If you are completing this project on a computer, your flyer may contain different or no misspelled words, depending on the accuracy of your typing.*

1

- Type `Self-guided tuors` and then press the SPACEBAR, so that a red wavy line appears below the misspelled word (Figure 1–9).

Q&A What if Word does not flag my spelling and grammar errors with wavy underlines?

To verify that the check spelling and grammar as you type features are enabled, tap or click FILE on the ribbon to open the Backstage view and then tap or click Options in the Backstage view. When the Word Options dialog box is displayed, tap or click Proofing in the left pane, and then ensure the 'Check spelling as you type' and 'Mark grammar errors as you type' check boxes contain check marks. Also ensure the 'Hide spelling errors in this document only' and 'Hide grammar errors in this document only' check boxes do not contain check marks. Tap or click the OK button.

Adventu... | space between misspelled word and insertion point

¶

Explore·scenic·trails·with·breathtaking·views·as·you·travel·through·meadows,·forests,·st mountains·in·an·off-road·vehicle.¶

text entered with misspelled word

Self-guided·tuors·¶ | insertion point

misspelled word flagged with red wavy underline

'Spelling and Grammar Check' icon contains X, indicating Word detected a possible spelling or grammar error

RDS

Figure 1–9

2

- Press and hold or right-click the flagged word (tuors, in this case) to display a shortcut menu that presents a list of suggested spelling corrections for the flagged word (Figure 1–10).

Q&A What if, when I press and hold or right-click the misspelled word, my desired correction is not in the list on the shortcut menu?

You can tap or click outside the shortcut menu to close the shortcut menu and then retype the correct word.

What if a flagged word actually is, for example, a proper name and spelled correctly?

Press and hold or right-click it and then tap or click Ignore All on the shortcut menu to instruct Word not to flag future occurrences of the same word in this document.

¶

Explore·scenic·trails·with·breathtaking·views·as·you·travel·through·meadows,·t mountains·in·an·off-road | insertion point

Self-guided·tuors·¶

tours
tutors
tour's
tumors
tours'

list of suggested corrections for flagged word

word, tours, to be selected

Ignore All
Add to Dictionary
Hyperlink...
New Comment

Ignore All command

shortcut menu

Figure 1–10

3

- Tap or click tours on the shortcut menu to replace the misspelled word in the document with a correctly spelled word (Figure 1–11).

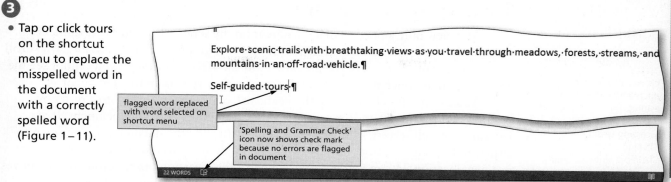

Explore·scenic·trails·with·breathtaking·views·as·you·travel·through·meadows,·forests,·streams,·and mountains·in·an·off-road·vehicle.¶

Self-guided·tours·¶

flagged word replaced with word selected on shortcut menu

'Spelling and Grammar Check' icon now shows check mark because no errors are flagged in document

22 WORDS

Figure 1–11

Other Ways

1. Tap or click 'Spelling and Grammar Check' icon on status bar, tap or click desired word in Spelling pane, tap or click Change button, tap or click OK button

To Enter More Text

In the flyer, the text yet to be entered includes the remainder of the body copy, which will be formatted as a bulleted list, and the signature line. The next steps enter the remainder of text in the flyer.

1 Press the END key to move the insertion point to the end of the current line.

2 Type `available` and then press the ENTER key.

3 Type `Open March through October` and then press the ENTER key.

4 Type `All vehicles and gear provided` and then press the ENTER key.

5 Type the signature line in the flyer (Figure 1–12): `To book your adventure, call 555-8928!`

If requested by your instructor, enter your phone number instead of 555-8928 in the signature line.

BTW

Character Widths
Many word processing documents use variable character fonts, where some characters are wider than others; for example, the letter w is wider than the letter i.

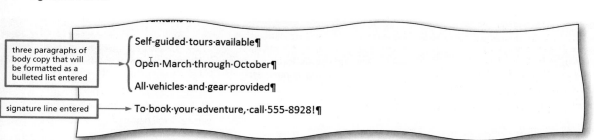

three paragraphs of body copy that will be formatted as a bulleted list entered

Self-guided·tours·available¶

Open·March·through·October¶

All·vehicles·and·gear·provided¶

signature line entered

To·book·your·adventure,·call·555-8928!¶

Figure 1–12

How should you organize text in a flyer?

The text in a flyer typically is organized into three areas: headline, body copy, and signature line.

- The **headline** is the first line of text on the flyer. It conveys the product or service being offered, such as a car for sale, personal lessons, or sightseeing tours, or the benefit that will be gained, such as a convenience, better performance, greater security, higher earnings, or more comfort, or it can contain a message, such as a lost or found pet.

- The **body copy** consists of text between the headline and the signature line. This text highlights the key points of the message in as few words as possible. It should be easy to read and follow. While emphasizing the positive, the body copy must be realistic, truthful, and believable.

- The **signature line**, which is the last line of text on the flyer, contains contact information or identifies a call to action.

CONSIDER THIS

Navigating a Document

You view only a portion of a document on the screen through the document window. At some point when you type text or insert graphics, Word probably will **scroll** the top or bottom portion of the document off the screen. Although you cannot see the text and graphics once they scroll off the screen, they remain in the document.

You can use touch gestures, the keyboard, or a mouse to scroll to a different location in a document and/or move the insertion point around a document. If you are using a touch screen, simply use your finger to slide the document up or down to display a different location in the document and then tap to move the insertion point to a new location. When you use the keyboard, the insertion point automatically moves when you press the desired keys. For example, the previous steps used the END key to move the insertion point to the end of the current line. Table 1–1 outlines various techniques to navigate a document using the keyboard.

With the mouse, you can use the scroll arrows or the scroll box on the scroll bar to display a different portion of the document in the document window and then click the mouse to move the insertion point to that location. Table 1–2 explains various techniques for using the scroll bar to scroll vertically with the mouse.

Table 1–1 Moving the Insertion Point with the Keyboard

Insertion Point Direction	Key(s) to Press	Insertion Point Direction	Key(s) to Press
Left one character	LEFT ARROW	Up one paragraph	CTRL+UP ARROW
Right one character	RIGHT ARROW	Down one paragraph	CTRL+DOWN ARROW
Left one word	CTRL+LEFT ARROW	Up one screen	PAGE UP
Right one word	CTRL+RIGHT ARROW	Down one screen	PAGE DOWN
Up one line	UP ARROW	To top of document window	ALT+CTRL+PAGE UP
Down one line	DOWN ARROW	To bottom of document window	ALT+CTRL+PAGE DOWN
To end of line	END	To beginning of document	CTRL+HOME
To beginning of line	HOME	To end of document	CTRL+END

© 2014 Cengage Learning

Table 1–2 Using the Scroll Bar to Scroll Vertically with the Mouse

Scroll Direction	Mouse Action	Scroll Direction	Mouse Action
Up	Drag the scroll box upward.	Down one screen	Click anywhere below the scroll box on the vertical scroll bar.
Down	Drag the scroll box downward.	Up one line	Click the scroll arrow at the top of the vertical scroll bar.
Up one screen	Click anywhere above the scroll box on the vertical scroll bar.	Down one line	Click the scroll arrow at the bottom of the vertical scroll bar.

© 2014 Cengage Learning

To Save a Document

You have performed many tasks while creating this document and do not want to risk losing work completed thus far. Accordingly, you should save the document on your hard disk, SkyDrive, or a location that is most appropriate to your situation.

The following steps assume you already have created folders for storing your files, for example, a CIS 101 folder (for your class) that contains a Word folder (for your assignments). Thus, these steps save the document in the Word folder in the

CIS 101 folder on your desired save location. For a detailed example of the procedure for saving a file in a folder or saving a file on SkyDrive, refer to the Office and Windows chapter at the beginning of this book.

1 Tap or click the Save button on the Quick Access Toolbar, which depending on settings, will display either the Save As gallery in the Backstage view or the Save As dialog box.

2 To save on a hard disk or other storage media on your computer, proceed to Step 2a. To save on SkyDrive, proceed to Step 2b.

2a If your screen opens the Backstage view and you want to save on storage media on your computer, tap or click Computer in the left pane, if necessary, to display options in the right pane related to saving on your computer. If your screen already displays the Save As dialog box, proceed to Step 4.

2b If your screen opens the Backstage view and you want to save on SkyDrive, tap or click SkyDrive in the left pane to display SkyDrive saving options or a Sign In button. If your screen displays a Sign In button, tap or click it and then sign in to SkyDrive.

3 Tap or click the Browse button in the right pane to display the Save As dialog box associated with the selected save location (i.e., Computer or SkyDrive).

4 Type **Adventure Flyer** in the File name box to change the file name. Do not press the ENTER key after typing the file name because you do not want to close the dialog box at this time.

5 Navigate to the desired save location (in this case, the Word folder in the CIS 101 folder [or your class folder] on your computer or SkyDrive).

6 Tap or click the Save button (Save As dialog box) to save the document in the selected folder on the selected save location with the entered file name.

BTW
Organizing Files and Folders
You should organize and store files in folders so that you easily can find the files later. For example, if you are taking an introductory computer class called CIS 101, a good practice would be to save all Word files in a Word folder in a CIS 101 folder. For a discussion of folders and detailed examples of creating folders, refer to the Office and Windows chapter at the beginning of this book.

Formatting Paragraphs and Characters

With the text for the flyer entered, the next step is to **format**, or change the appearance of, its text. A paragraph encompasses the text from the first character in the paragraph up to and including its paragraph mark (¶). **Paragraph formatting** is the process of changing the appearance of a paragraph. For example, you can center or add bullets to a paragraph. Characters include letters, numbers, punctuation marks, and symbols. **Character formatting** is the process of changing the way characters appear on the screen and in print. You use character formatting to emphasize certain words and improve readability of a document. For example, you can color, italicize, or underline characters. Often, you apply both paragraph and character formatting to the same text. For example, you may center a paragraph (paragraph formatting) and underline some of the characters in the same paragraph (character formatting).

Although you can format paragraphs and characters before you type, many Word users enter text first and then format the existing text. Figure 1–13a on the next page shows the flyer in this chapter before formatting its paragraphs and characters. Figure 1–13b on the next page shows the flyer after formatting. As you can see from the two figures, a document that is formatted is easier to read and looks more professional. The following pages discuss how to format the flyer so that it looks like Figure 1–13b.

If you are using your finger on a touch screen and are having difficulty completing the steps in this chapter, consider using a stylus. Many people find it easier to be precise with a stylus than with a finger. In addition, with a stylus you see the pointer. If you still are having trouble completing the steps with a stylus, try using a mouse.

(a) Unformatted Flyer

(b) Formatted Flyer

Figure 1–13

Font, Font Sizes, and Themes

Characters that appear on the screen are a specific shape and size. The **font**, or typeface, defines the appearance and shape of the letters, numbers, and special characters. In Word, the default font usually is Calibri (shown in Figure 1–14). You can leave characters in the default font or change them to a different font. **Font size** specifies the size of the characters and is determined by a measurement system called points. A single **point** is about 1/72 of one inch in height. The default font size in Word typically is 11 (Figure 1–14). Thus, a character with a font size of 11 is about 11/72 or a little less than 1/6 of one inch in height. You can increase or decrease the font size of characters in a document.

A document **theme** is a set of unified formats for fonts, colors, and graphics. Word includes a variety of document themes to assist you with coordinating these visual elements in a document. The default theme fonts are Calibri Light for headings and Calibri for body text. By changing the document theme, you quickly can give your document a new look. You also can define your own document themes.

BTW
Formatting Marks
With some fonts, the formatting marks will not be displayed properly on the screen. For example, the raised dot that signifies a blank space between words may be displayed behind a character instead of in the blank space, causing the characters to look incorrect.

CONSIDER THIS

How do I know which formats to use in a flyer?
In a flyer, consider the following formatting suggestions.

- **Increase the font size of characters.** Flyers usually are posted on a bulletin board or in a window. Thus, the font size should be as large as possible so that passersby easily can read the flyer. To give the headline more impact, its font size should be larger than the font size of the text in the body copy. If possible, make the font size of the signature line larger than the body copy but smaller than the headline.

- **Change the font of characters.** Use fonts that are easy to read. Try to use only two different fonts in a flyer; for example, use one for the headline and the other for all other text. Too many fonts can make the flyer visually confusing.

- **Change the paragraph alignment.** The default alignment for paragraphs in a document is **left-aligned**, that is, flush at the left margin of the document with uneven right edges. Consider changing the alignment of some of the paragraphs to add interest and variety to the flyer.

- **Highlight key paragraphs with bullets.** A bulleted paragraph is a paragraph that begins with a dot or other symbol. Use bulleted paragraphs to highlight important points in a flyer.

- **Emphasize important words.** To call attention to certain words or lines, you can underline them, italicize them, or bold them. Use these formats sparingly, however, because overuse will minimize their effect and make the flyer look too busy.

- **Use color.** Use colors that complement each other and convey the meaning of the flyer. Vary colors in terms of hue and brightness. Headline colors, for example, can be bold and bright. Signature lines should stand out more than body copy but less than headlines. Keep in mind that too many colors can detract from the flyer and make it difficult to read.

To Center a Paragraph

The headline in the flyer currently is left-aligned (Figure 1–14). *Why? Word, by default left-aligns text, unless you specifically change the alignment.* You want the headline to be **centered**, that is, positioned horizontally between the left and right margins on the page. Recall that Word considers a single short line of text, such as the one-word headline, a paragraph. Thus, you will center the paragraph containing the headline. The following steps center a paragraph.

1

- Tap or click HOME on the ribbon to display the HOME tab.

- Tap or click somewhere in the paragraph to be centered (in this case, the headline) to position the insertion point in the paragraph to be formatted (Figure 1–14).

Figure 1–14

2

- Tap or click the Center button (HOME tab | Paragraph group) to center the paragraph containing the insertion point (Figure 1–15).

Q&A What if I want to return the paragraph to left-aligned?
You would tap or click the Center button again or tap or click the Align Left button (HOME tab | Paragraph group).

Figure 1–15

Other Ways

1. Tap 'Show Context Menu' button on mini toolbar or right-click paragraph, tap or click Paragraph on shortcut menu, tap or click Indents and Spacing tab (Paragraph dialog box), tap or click Alignment arrow, tap or click Centered, tap or click OK button

2. Tap or click Paragraph Settings Dialog Box Launcher (HOME tab or PAGE LAYOUT tab | Paragraph group), tap or click Indents and Spacing tab (Paragraph dialog box), tap or click Alignment arrow, tap or click Centered, tap or click OK button

3. Press CTRL+E

To Center Another Paragraph

In the flyer, the signature line is to be centered to match the paragraph alignment of the headline. The following steps center the signature line.

1 Tap or click somewhere in the paragraph to be centered (in this case, the signature line) to position the insertion point in the paragraph to be formatted.

2 Tap or click the Center button (HOME tab | Paragraph group) to center the paragraph containing the insertion point (shown in Figure 1–16 on the next page).

BTW

File Type
Depending on your Windows settings, the file type .docx may be displayed on the title bar immediately to the right of the file name after you save the file. The file type .docx identifies a Word 2013 document.

BTW
Touch Screen
Differences
The Office and Windows interfaces may vary if you are using a touch screen. For this reason, you might notice that the function or appearance of your touch screen differs slightly from this chapter's presentation.

Formatting Single versus Multiple Paragraphs and Characters

As shown on the previous pages, to format a single paragraph, simply move the insertion point in the paragraph to make it the current paragraph, and then format the paragraph. Similarly, to format a single word, position the insertion point in the word to make it the current word, and then format the word.

To format multiple paragraphs or words, however, you first must select the paragraphs or words you want to format and then format the selection.

1 ENTER TEXT | 2 FORMAT TEXT | 3 INSERT PICTURE | 4 FORMAT PICTURE
5 ENHANCE PAGE | 6 CORRECT & REVISE | 7 PRINT OR READ

To Select a Line

The default font size of 11 point is too small for a headline in a flyer. To increase the font size of the characters in the headline, you first must select the line of text containing the headline. *Why? If you increase font size of text without selecting any text, Word will increase the font size only of the word containing the insertion point.* The following steps select a line.

- If you are using a mouse, move the pointer to the left of the line to be selected (in this case, the headline) until the pointer changes to a right-pointing block arrow (Figure 1–16).

Figure 1–16

- If you are using a touch screen, double-tap to the left of the line to be selected to select the line; if you are using a mouse, while the pointer is a right-pointing block arrow, click the mouse to select the entire line to the right of the pointer (Figure 1–17).

Figure 1–17

Q&A Why is the selected text shaded gray?

If your screen normally displays dark letters on a light background, which is the default setting in Word, then selected text displays with a light shading color, such as gray, on the dark letters. Note that the selection that appears on the text does not print.

Other Ways

1. Drag pointer through line

2. With insertion point at beginning of desired line, press SHIFT+DOWN ARROW

To Change the Font Size of Selected Text

The next step is to increase the font size of the characters in the selected headline. ***Why?*** *You would like the headline to be as large as possible and still fit on a single line, which in this case is 72 point.* The following steps increase the font size of the headline from 11 to 72 point.

● With the text selected, tap or click the Font Size arrow (HOME tab | Font group) to display the Font Size gallery (Figure 1–18).

Q&A
Why are the font sizes in my Font Size gallery different from those in Figure 1–18?
Font sizes may vary depending on the current font and your printer driver.

What happened to the mini toolbar?
The mini toolbar disappears if you do not use it. These steps use the Font Size arrow on the HOME tab instead of the Font Size arrow on the mini toolbar.

Figure 1–18

● If you are using a mouse, point to 72 in the Font Size gallery to display a live preview of the selected text at the selected point size (Figure 1–19).

Q&A
Can I use live preview on a touch screen?
Live preview is not available on a touch screen.

🔍 **Experiment**

● If you are using a mouse, point to various font sizes in the Font Size gallery and watch the font size of the selected text change in the document window.

Figure 1–19

● Tap or click 72 in the Font Size gallery to increase the font size of the selected text.

Other Ways			
1. Tap or click Font Size arrow on mini toolbar, tap or click desired font size in Font Size gallery	2. Tap 'Show Context Menu' button on mini toolbar or right-click selected text, tap or click Font on shortcut menu, tap or click Font tab (Font dialog box), select desired font size in Size list, tap or click OK button	3. Tap or click Font Dialog Box Launcher, tap or click Font tab (Font dialog box), select desired font size in Size list, tap or click OK button	4. Press CTRL+D, tap or click Font tab (Font dialog box), select desired font size in Size list, tap or click OK button

To Change the Font of Selected Text

The default theme font for headings is Calibri Light and for all other text, called body text in Word, is Calibri. Many other fonts are available, however, so that you can add variety to documents.

The following steps change the font of the headline from Calibri to Berlin Sans FB Demi. *Why? To draw more attention to the headline, you change its font so that it differs from the font of other text in the flyer.*

1

- With the text selected, tap or click the Font arrow (HOME tab | Font group) to display the Font gallery (Figure 1–20).

Q&A

Will the fonts in my Font gallery be the same as those in Figure 1–20?
Your list of available fonts may differ, depending on the type of printer you are using and other settings.

What if the text no longer is selected?
Follow the steps on page WD 16 to select a line.

Figure 1–20

2

- If necessary, scroll through the Font gallery to display Berlin Sans FB Demi (or a similar font).

- If you are using a mouse, point to Berlin Sans FB Demi (or a similar font) to display a live preview of the selected text in the selected font (Figure 1–21).

 Experiment

- If you are using a mouse, point to various fonts in the Font gallery and watch the font of the selected text change in the document window.

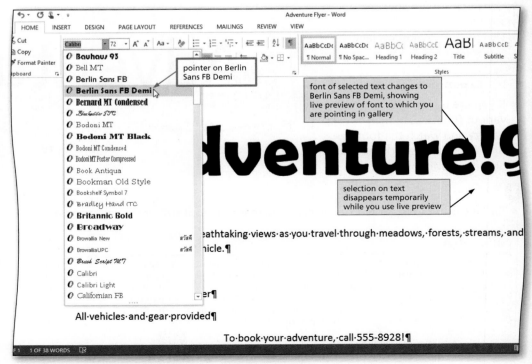

Figure 1–21

3

- Tap or click Berlin Sans FB Demi (or a similar font) to change the font of the selected text.

Q&A If the font I want to use appears in the Recently Used Fonts list in the Font gallery, could I tap or click it there instead?

Yes.

Other Ways

1. Tap or click Font arrow on mini toolbar, tap or click desired font in Font gallery	2. Tap 'Show Context Menu' button on mini toolbar or right-click selected text, tap or click Font on shortcut menu, tap or click Font tab (Font dialog box), select desired font in Font list, tap or click OK button	3. Tap or click Font Dialog Box Launcher (HOME tab	Font group), tap or click Font tab (Font dialog box), select desired font in Font list, tap or click OK button	4. Press CTRL+D, tap or click Font tab (Font dialog box), select desired font in Font list, tap or click OK button

To Change the Case of Selected Text

1 ENTER TEXT | 2 FORMAT TEXT | 3 INSERT PICTURE | 4 FORMAT PICTURE
5 ENHANCE PAGE | 6 CORRECT & REVISE | 7 PRINT OR READ

The headline currently shows the first letter in each word capitalized, which sometimes is referred to as initial cap. The following steps change the headline to uppercase. *Why?* *To draw more attention to the headline, you would like the entire line of text to be capitalized, or in uppercase letters.*

1

- With the text selected, tap or click the Change Case button (HOME tab | Font group) to display the Change Case gallery (Figure 1–22).

Figure 1–22

2

- Tap or click UPPERCASE in the Change Case gallery to change the case of the selected text (Figure 1–23).

Q&A What if a ruler appears on the screen or the pointer shape changes?

If you are using a mouse, depending on the position of your pointer and locations you click on the screen, a ruler may automatically appear or the pointer's shape may change. Simply move the mouse and the ruler should disappear and/or the pointer shape will change.

Figure 1–23

Other Ways

1. Tap 'Show Context Menu' button on mini toolbar or right-click selected text, tap or click Font on shortcut menu, tap or click Font tab (Font dialog box), select All caps in Effects area, tap or click OK button	2. Tap or click Font Dialog Box Launcher (HOME tab	Font group), tap or click Font tab (Font dialog box), select All caps in Effects area, tap or click OK button	3. Press SHIFT+F3 repeatedly until text is desired case

To Apply a Text Effect to Selected Text

Word provides many text effects to add interest and variety to text. The following steps apply a text effect to the headline. **Why?** *You would like the text in the headline to be even more noticeable.*

1

- With the text selected, tap or click the 'Text Effects and Typography' button (HOME tab | Font group) to display the Text Effects and Typography gallery (Figure 1–24).

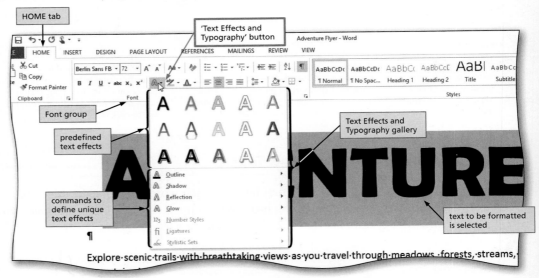

Figure 1–24

2

- If you are using a mouse, point to 'Fill - White, Outline - Accent 1, Glow - Accent 1' (fourth text effect in second row) to display a live preview of the selected text in the selected text effect (Figure 1–25).

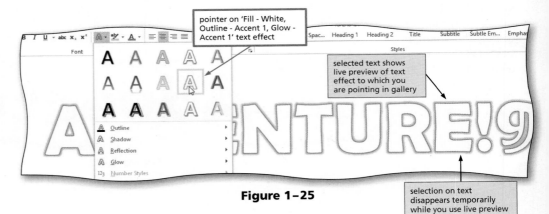

Figure 1–25

Experiment

- If you are using a mouse, point to various text effects in the Text Effects and Typography gallery and watch the text effects of the selected text change in the document window.

3

- Tap or click 'Fill - White, Outline - Accent 1, Glow - Accent 1' to change the text effect of the selected text.

4

- Tap or click anywhere in the document window to remove the selection from the selected text.

Other Ways

1. Tap 'Show Context Menu' button on mini toolbar or right-click selected text, tap or click Font on shortcut menu, tap or click Font tab (Font dialog box), tap or click Text Effects button, expand TEXT FILL or TEXT OUTLINE section and then select the desired text effect(s) (Format Text Effects dialog box), tap or click OK button, tap or click OK button

2. Tap or click Font Dialog Box Launcher (HOME tab | Font group), tap or click Font tab (Font dialog box), tap or click Text Effects button, expand TEXT FILL or TEXT OUTLINE section and then select desired text effect (Format Text Effects dialog box), tap or click OK button, tap or click OK button

To Shade a Paragraph

When you **shade** text, Word colors the rectangular area behind any text or graphics. If the text to shade is a paragraph, Word shades the area from the left margin to the right margin of the current paragraph. To shade a paragraph, place the insertion point in the paragraph. To shade any other text, you must first select the text to be shaded.

This flyer uses green as the shading color for the headline. *Why? To make the headline of the flyer more eye-catching, you shade it.* The following steps shade a paragraph.

1

- Tap or click somewhere in the paragraph to be shaded (in this case, the headline) to position the insertion point in the paragraph to be formatted.

- Tap or click the Shading arrow (HOME tab | Paragraph group) to display the Shading gallery (Figure 1–26).

Figure 1–26

Q&A If I am using a mouse, what if I click the Shading button by mistake?
Click the Shading arrow and proceed with Step 2. If you are using a touch screen, you may not have a separate Shading button.

Experiment

- If you are using a mouse, point to various colors in the Shading gallery and watch the shading color of the current paragraph change.

2

- Tap or click 'Green, Accent 6, Darker 25%' (rightmost color in fifth row) to shade the current paragraph (Figure 1–27).

Q&A What if I apply a dark shading color to dark text?
When the font color of text is Automatic, it usually is black. If you select a dark shading color, Word automatically may change the text color to white so that the shaded text is easier to read.

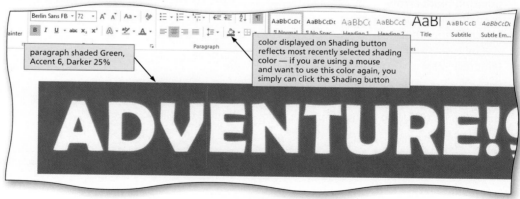

Figure 1–27

Other Ways

1. Tap or click Borders arrow (HOME tab | Paragraph group), tap or click Borders and Shading, tap or click Shading tab (Borders and Shading dialog box), tap or click Fill arrow, select desired color, tap or click OK button

To Select Multiple Lines

The next formatting step for the flyer is to increase the font size of the characters between the headline and the signature line. *Why? You want this text to be easier to read from a distance.*

To change the font size of the characters in multiple lines, you first must select all the lines to be formatted. The following steps select multiple lines.

1

- Scroll, if necessary, so that all text below the headline is displayed on the screen.

- If you are using a touch screen, tap to position the insertion point in the text to select; if you are using a mouse, move the pointer to the left of the first paragraph to be selected until the pointer changes to a right-pointing block arrow (Figure 1–28).

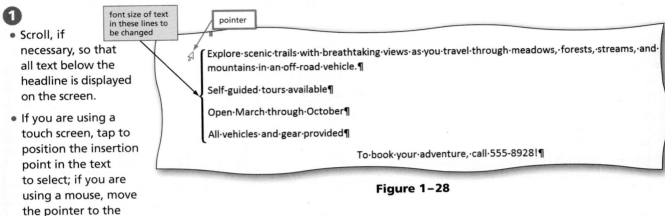

Figure 1–28

2

- If you are using a touch screen, drag the selection handle(s) as necessary to select the text that will be formatted; if you are using a mouse, while the pointer is a right-pointing block arrow, drag downward to select all lines that will be formatted (Figure 1–29).

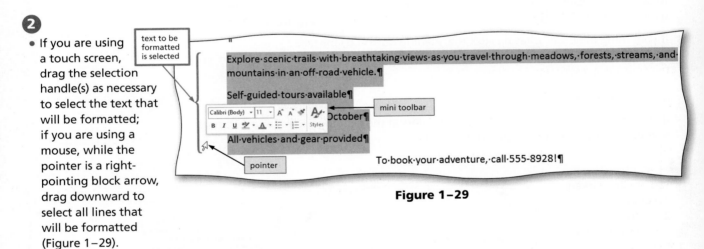

Figure 1–29

Q&A What is a selection handle?

When working on a touch screen, a **selection handle** (small circle) appears below the insertion point. Using a fingertip, you drag a selection handle to select text.

Other Ways

1. With insertion point at beginning of desired line, press SHIFT+DOWN ARROW repeatedly until all lines are selected

To Change the Font Size of Selected Text

The characters between the headline and the signature line in the flyer currently are 11 point. To make them easier to read from a distance, this flyer uses a 24-point font size for these characters. The following steps change the font size of the selected text.

1 With the text selected, tap or click the Font Size arrow (HOME tab | Font group) to display the Font Size gallery.

2 Tap or click 24 in the Font Size gallery to increase the font size of the selected text.

3 Tap or click anywhere in the document window to remove the selection from the text.

4 If necessary, scroll so that you can see all the resized text on the screen (Figure 1–30).

Figure 1–30

To Bullet a List of Paragraphs

1 ENTER TEXT | 2 FORMAT TEXT | 3 INSERT PICTURE | 4 FORMAT PICTURE
5 ENHANCE PAGE | 6 CORRECT & REVISE | 7 PRINT OR READ

A **bulleted list** is a series of paragraphs, each beginning with a bullet character. The next step is to format the three paragraphs about the tours that are above the signature line in the flyer as a bulleted list.

To format a list of paragraphs with bullets, you first must select all the lines in the paragraphs. ***Why?*** *If you do not select all paragraphs, Word will place a bullet only in the paragraph containing the insertion point.* The following steps bullet a list of paragraphs.

1
- If you are using a touch screen, tap to position the insertion point in the text to select; if you are using a mouse, move the pointer to the left of the first paragraph to be selected until the pointer changes to a right-pointing block arrow.

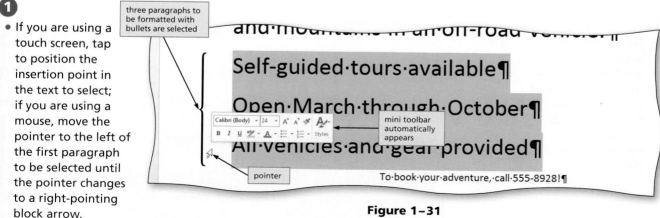

Figure 1–31

- If you are using a touch screen, drag the selection handle(s) as necessary to select the text that will be formatted; if you are using a mouse, drag downward until all paragraphs that will be formatted with a bullet character are selected (Figure 1–31).

2

• Tap or click the Bullets button (HOME tab | Paragraph group) to place a bullet character at the beginning of each selected paragraph (Figure 1–32).

Q&A

What if my screen displays a Bullets gallery?
If you are using a touch screen, you may not have a separate Bullets button and Bullets arrow. In this case, select the desired bullet style in the Bullets gallery.

If I am using a mouse, what if I accidentally click the Bullets arrow?
Press the ESCAPE key to remove the Bullets gallery from the screen and then repeat Step 2. If you are using a touch screen, you may not have a separate Bullets button and Bullets arrow.

How do I remove bullets from a list or paragraph?
Select the list or paragraph and then tap or click the Bullets button again.

Figure 1–32

Other Ways

1. Press and hold or right-click selected paragraphs, tap or click Bullets button on mini toolbar, if necessary select bullet style in Bullets gallery

1 ENTER TEXT | 2 FORMAT TEXT | 3 INSERT PICTURE | 4 FORMAT PICTURE
5 ENHANCE PAGE | 6 CORRECT & REVISE | 7 PRINT OR READ

To Undo and Redo an Action

Word provides a means of canceling your recent command(s) or action(s). For example, if you format text incorrectly, you can undo the format and try it again. When you point to the Undo button, Word displays the action you can undo as part of a ScreenTip.

If, after you undo an action, you decide you did not want to perform the undo, you can redo the undone action. Word does not allow you to undo or redo some actions, such as saving or printing a document. The following steps undo the bullet format just applied and then redo the bullet format. *Why? These steps illustrate the undo and redo actions.*

1

• Tap or click the Undo button on the Quick Access Toolbar to reverse your most recent action (in this case, remove the bullets from the paragraphs) (Figure 1–33).

Figure 1–33

- Tap or click the Redo button on the Quick Access Toolbar to reverse your most recent undo (in this case, place a bullet character on the paragraphs again) (shown in Figure 1–32).

Other Ways

1. Press CTRL+Z to undo; press CTRL+Y to redo

To Italicize Text

1 ENTER TEXT | 2 FORMAT TEXT | 3 INSERT PICTURE | 4 FORMAT PICTURE
5 ENHANCE PAGE | 6 CORRECT & REVISE | 7 PRINT OR READ

Italic text has a slanted appearance. The next step is to italicize the word, breathtaking, in the flyer to further emphasize it. As with a single paragraph, if you want to format a single word, you do not need to select it. *Why? To format a single word, you simply position the insertion point somewhere in the word and apply the desired format.* The following step italicizes a word.

- Tap or click somewhere in the word to be italicized (breathtaking, in this case) to position the insertion point in the word to be formatted.

- Tap or click the Italic button (HOME tab | Font group) to italicize the word containing the insertion point (Figure 1–34).

Q&A

How would I remove an italic format?
You would tap or click the Italic button a second time, or you immediately could tap or click the Undo button on the Quick Access Toolbar or press CTRL+Z.

Figure 1–34

How can I tell what formatting has been applied to text?
The selected buttons and boxes on the HOME tab show formatting characteristics of the location of the insertion point. With the insertion point in the word, breathtaking, the HOME tab shows these formats: 24-point Calibri italic font.

Why did the appearance of the Redo button change?
It changed to a Repeat button. When it is a Repeat button, you can tap or click it to repeat your last action. For example, you can select different text and then click the Repeat button to apply (repeat) the italic format to the selected text.

Other Ways

1. Tap or click Italic button on mini toolbar	2. Tap 'Show Context Menu' button on mini toolbar or right-click selected text, tap or click Font on shortcut menu, tap or click Font tab (Font dialog box), tap or click Italic in Font style list, tap or click OK button	3. Tap or click Font Dialog Box Launcher (HOME tab \| Font group), tap or click Font tab (Font dialog box), tap or click Italic in Font style list, tap or click OK button	4. Press CTRL+I

To Color Text

The following steps change the color of the word, breathtaking. *Why? To emphasize the word even more, you change its color to a shade of orange.*

 1

- With the insertion point in the word to format, tap or click the Font Color arrow (HOME tab | Font group) to display the Font Color gallery (Figure 1–35).

Q&A If I am using a mouse, what if I click the Font Color button by mistake? Click the Font Color arrow and then proceed with Step 2. If you are using a touch screen, you may not have a separate Font Color button.

Figure 1–35

 Experiment

- If you are using a mouse, point to various colors in the Font Color gallery and watch the color of the current word change.

2

- Tap or click 'Orange, Accent 2, Darker 25%' (sixth color in fifth row) to change the color of the text (Figure 1–36).

Q&A How would I change the text color back to black? You would position the insertion point in the word or select the text, tap or click the Font Color arrow (HOME tab | Font group) again, and then tap or click Automatic in the Font Color gallery.

Figure 1–36

Other Ways

1. Tap or click Font Color arrow on mini toolbar, tap or click desired color

2. Tap 'Show Context Menu' button on mini toolbar or right-click selected text, tap or click Font on shortcut menu, tap or click Font tab (Font dialog box), tap or click Font color arrow, tap or click desired color, tap or click OK button

3. Tap or click Font Dialog Box Launcher (HOME tab | Font group), tap or click Font tab (Font dialog box), tap or click Font color arrow, tap or click desired color, tap or click OK button

To Use the Mini Toolbar to Format Text

Recall from the Office and Windows chapter at the beginning of this book that the mini toolbar automatically appears based on certain tasks you perform. *Why? Word places commonly used buttons and boxes on the mini toolbar for your convenience. If you do not use the mini toolbar, it disappears from the screen.* All commands on the mini toolbar also exist on the ribbon.

The following steps use the mini toolbar to change the color and font size of text in the signature line of the flyer.

1

• If you are using a touch screen, double-tap to the left of the line to be selected to select the line, and then tap the selection to display the mini toolbar; if you are using a mouse, move the pointer to the left of the line to be selected until the pointer changes to a right-pointing block arrow and then click to select the line and display the mini toolbar (Figure 1–37).

Figure 1–37

Q&A Why does my mini toolbar look different than the one in Figure 1–37?
If you are using a touch screen, the buttons and boxes on the mini toolbar differ. For example, it contains a 'Show Context Menu' button at the far-right edge, which you tap to display a shortcut menu.

2

• Tap or click the Font Size arrow on the mini toolbar to display the Font Size gallery.

• If you are using a mouse, point to 28 in the Font Size gallery to display a live preview of the selected font size (Figure 1–38).

3

• Tap or click 28 in the Font Size gallery to increase the font size of the selected text.

Figure 1–38

- With the text still selected and the mini toolbar still displayed, tap or click the Font Color arrow on the mini toolbar to display the Font Color gallery.

- If you are using a mouse, point to 'Orange, Accent 2, Darker 25%' (sixth color in the fifth row) to display a live preview of the selected font color (Figure 1–39).

Figure 1–39

- Tap or click 'Orange, Accent 2, Darker 25%' to change the color of the selected text.

- Tap or click anywhere in the document window to remove the selection from the text.

To Select a Group of Words

1 ENTER TEXT | 2 FORMAT TEXT | 3 INSERT PICTURE | 4 FORMAT PICTURE
5 ENHANCE PAGE | 6 CORRECT & REVISE | 7 PRINT OR READ

To emphasize the contact phone number (555-8928), this text is underlined in the flyer. Because the phone number is separated with a hyphen, Word considers it a group of words. To format a group of words, you first must select them. ***Why?*** *If you underline text without selecting any text first, Word will underline only the word containing the insertion point.* The following steps select a group of words.

- If you are using a touch screen, tap to position the insertion point in the text you want to select; if you are using a mouse, position the pointer immediately to the left of the first character of the text to be selected, in this case, the 5 in 555 (Figure 1–40).

Figure 1–40

Q&A | Why did the shape of the pointer change?
The pointer's shape is an I-beam when positioned in unselected text in the document window.

- If you are using a touch screen, drag the selection handle(s) to select the text to be formatted; if you are using a mouse, drag the pointer through the last character of the text to be selected, in this case, the 8 in the phone number (Figure 1–41).

Figure 1–41

Q&A | Why did the pointer shape change again?
When the pointer is positioned in selected text, its shape is a left-pointing block arrow.

Other Ways

1. With insertion point at beginning of first word in group, press CTRL+SHIFT+RIGHT ARROW repeatedly until all words are selected

To Underline Text

1 ENTER TEXT | **2** FORMAT TEXT | **3** INSERT PICTURE | **4** FORMAT PICTURE | **5** ENHANCE PAGE | **6** CORRECT & REVISE | **7** PRINT OR READ

Underlined text prints with an underscore (_) below each character. In the flyer, the contact phone number, 555-8928, in the signature line is underlined. *Why? Underlines are used to emphasize or draw attention to specific text.* The following step formats selected text with an underline.

1

- With the text selected, tap or click the Underline button (HOME tab | Font group) to underline the selected text (Figure 1–42).

Q&A

What if my screen displays an Underline gallery? If you are using a touch screen, you may not have a separate Underline button and Underline arrow. In this case, select the desired underline style in the Underline gallery.

If a button exists on the mini toolbar, can I tap or click that instead of using the ribbon? Yes.

HOME tab

Underline arrow displays Underline gallery, which contains a variety of underline styles and colors (touch screens may not have separate Underline button and Underline arrow)

Underline button selected

Font group

Explore·scenic·trails·with·*breathtaking*·vie
you·travel·through·meadows,·forests,·stre
and·mountains·in·an·off-road·vehicle.¶

·Self-guided·tours·available¶
·Open·March·through·October¶
All·vehicles·and·gear·provided¶
·book·your·adventure,·call·555-8928!¶

selected text underlined

Figure 1–42

How would I remove an underline?
You would tap or click the Underline button a second time, or you immediately could tap or click the Undo button on the Quick Access Toolbar.

Other Ways

| 1. Tap or click Underline button on mini toolbar | 2. Tap 'Show Context Menu' button on mini toolbar or right-click text, tap or click Font on shortcut menu, tap or click Font tab (Font dialog box), tap or click Underline style box arrow, tap or click desired underline style, tap or click OK button | 3. Tap or click Font Dialog Box Launcher (HOME tab | Font group), tap or click Font tab (Font dialog box), tap or click Underline style arrow, tap or click desired underline style, tap or click OK button | 4. Press CTRL+U |
|---|---|---|---|

To Bold Text

1 ENTER TEXT | **2** FORMAT TEXT | **3** INSERT PICTURE | **4** FORMAT PICTURE | **5** ENHANCE PAGE | **6** CORRECT & REVISE | **7** PRINT OR READ

Bold characters appear somewhat thicker and darker than those that are not bold. The steps on the next page format the text, off-road, in bold characters. *Why? To further emphasize this text, it is bold in the flyer.* Recall that if you want to format a single word, you simply position the insertion point in the word and then format the word. To format text that consists of more than one word, as you have learned previously, you select the text first.

1

- Select the text to be formatted (the text, off-road, in this case); that is, if you are using a touch screen, tap to position the insertion point in the text you want to select and then drag the selection handle(s) to select the text to be formatted; if you are using a mouse, position the pointer immediately to the left of the first character of the text to be selected and then drag the pointer through the last character of the text to be selected.

- With the text selected, tap or click the Bold button (HOME tab | Font group) to bold the selected text (Figure 1–43).

Q&A How would I remove a bold format?
You would tap or click the Bold button a second time, or you immediately could tap or click the Undo button on the Quick Access Toolbar.

Figure 1–43

- Tap or click anywhere in the document window to remove the selection from the screen.

Other Ways

1. Tap or click Bold button on mini toolbar
2. Tap 'Show Context Menu' button on mini toolbar or right-click selected text, tap or click Font on shortcut menu, tap or click Font tab (Font dialog box), tap or click Bold in Font style list, tap or click OK button
3. Tap or click Font Dialog Box Launcher (HOME tab | Font group), tap or click Font tab (Font dialog box), tap or click Bold in Font style list, tap or click OK button
4. Press CTRL+B

1 ENTER TEXT | 2 FORMAT TEXT | 3 INSERT PICTURE | 4 FORMAT PICTURE
5 ENHANCE PAGE | 6 CORRECT & REVISE | 7 PRINT OR READ

To Zoom One Page

Earlier in this chapter, you changed the zoom to page width so that the text on the screen was larger and easier to read. In the next set of steps, you want to see the entire page (mock sheet of paper) on the screen at once. **Why?** *You want be able to see the effect of adjusting colors in the document as a whole.* The next step displays a single page in its entirety in the document window as large as possible.

1

- Tap or click VIEW on the ribbon to display the VIEW tab.

- Tap or click the One Page button (VIEW tab | Zoom group) to display the entire page in the document window as large as possible (Figure 1–44).

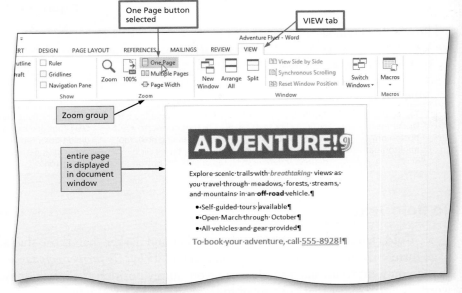

Figure 1–44

Other Ways

1. Tap or click Zoom button (VIEW tab | Zoom group), tap or click Whole page (Zoom dialog box), tap or click OK button

What colors should I choose when creating documents?

When choosing color, associate the meaning of the color with your message:

• Red expresses danger, power, or energy and often is associated with sports or physical exertion.

• Brown represents simplicity, honesty, and dependability.

• Orange denotes success, victory, creativity, and enthusiasm.

• Yellow suggests sunshine, happiness, hope, liveliness, and intelligence.

• Green symbolizes growth, healthiness, harmony, blooming, and healing and often is associated with safety or money.

• Blue indicates integrity, trust, importance, confidence, and stability.

• Purple represents wealth, power, comfort, extravagance, magic, mystery, and spirituality.

• White stands for purity, goodness, cleanliness, precision, and perfection.

• Black suggests authority, strength, elegance, power, and prestige.

• Gray conveys neutrality and, thus, often is found in backgrounds and other effects.

To Change Theme Colors

1 ENTER TEXT | 2 FORMAT TEXT | 3 INSERT PICTURE | 4 FORMAT PICTURE
5 ENHANCE PAGE | 6 CORRECT & REVISE | 7 PRINT OR READ

A **color scheme** in Word is a document theme that identifies 12 complementary colors for text, background, accents, and links in a document. With more than 20 predefined color schemes, Word provides a simple way to coordinate colors in a document.

The default color scheme is called Office. In the flyer, you will change the color scheme from Office to Green. *Why? You want the colors in the flyer to suggest growth, harmony, blooming, trust, and stability, which are conveyed by shades of greens and blues. In Word, the Green color scheme uses these colors.* The following steps change theme colors.

1

• Tap or click DESIGN on the ribbon to display the DESIGN tab.

• Tap or click the Theme Colors button (DESIGN tab | Document Formatting group) to display the Theme Colors gallery.

• If you are using a mouse, point to Green in the Theme Colors gallery to display a live preview of the selected theme color (Figure 1–45).

Figure 1–45

 Experiment

• If you are using a mouse, point to various color schemes in the Theme Colors gallery and watch the colors change in the document.

- Tap or click Green in the Colors gallery to change the document theme colors.

Q&A What if I want to return to the original color scheme?
You would tap or click the Theme Colors button again and then tap or click Office in the Theme Colors gallery.

BTW
Selecting Nonadjacent Items
In Word, you can use keyboard keys to select nonadjacent items, that is, items not next to each other. This is helpful when you are applying the same formatting to multiple items. To select nonadjacent items (text or graphics), select the first item, such as a word or paragraph, as usual; then, press and hold down the CTRL key. While holding down the CTRL key, select additional items.

To Zoom Page Width

Because the document contents are small when displayed at one page, the next steps zoom page width again.

1 Tap or click VIEW on the ribbon to display the VIEW tab.

2 Tap or click the Page Width button (VIEW tab | Zoom group) to display the page the same width as the document window (shown in Figure 1–46 on page WD 34).

Selecting Text

In many of the previous steps, you have selected text. Table 1–3 summarizes the techniques used to select various items.

Table 1–3 Techniques for Selecting Text

Item to Select	Touch	Mouse	Keyboard (where applicable)
Block of text	Tap to position insertion point in text to select and then drag selection handle(s) to select text.	Click at beginning of selection, scroll to end of selection, position pointer at end of selection, hold down SHIFT key, and then click; or drag through text.	
Character(s)	Tap to position insertion point in text to select and then drag selection handle(s) to select text.	Drag through character(s).	SHIFT+RIGHT ARROW or SHIFT+LEFT ARROW
Document		Move pointer to left of text until pointer changes to right-pointing block arrow and then triple-click.	CTRL+A
Graphic	Tap the graphic.	Click the graphic.	
Line	Double-tap to left of line to be selected.	Move pointer to left of line until pointer changes to right-pointing block arrow and then click.	HOME, then SHIFT+END or END, then SHIFT+HOME
Lines	Tap to position insertion point in text to select and then drag selection handle(s) to select text.	Move pointer to left of first line until pointer changes to right-pointing block arrow and then drag up or down.	HOME, then SHIFT+DOWN ARROW or END, then SHIFT+UP ARROW
Paragraph	Tap to position insertion point in text to select and then drag selection handle(s) to select text.	Triple-click paragraph; or move pointer to left of paragraph until pointer changes to right-pointing block arrow and then double-click.	CTRL+SHIFT+DOWN ARROW or CTRL+SHIFT+UP ARROW
Paragraphs	Tap to position insertion point in text to select and then drag selection handle(s) to select text.	Move pointer to left of paragraph until pointer changes to right-pointing block arrow, double-click, and then drag up or down.	CTRL+SHIFT+DOWN ARROW or CTRL+SHIFT+UP ARROW repeatedly
Sentence	Tap to position insertion point in text to select and then drag selection handle(s) to select text.	Press and hold down CTRL key and then click sentence.	
Word	Double-tap word.	Double-click word.	CTRL+SHIFT+RIGHT ARROW or CTRL+SHIFT+LEFT ARROW
Words	Tap to position insertion point in text to select and then drag selection handle(s) to select text.	Drag through words.	CTRL+SHIFT+RIGHT ARROW or CTRL+SHIFT+LEFT ARROW repeatedly

To Save an Existing Document with the Same File Name

You have made several modifications to the document since you last saved it. Thus, you should save it again. The following step saves the document again. For an example of the step listed below, refer to the Office and Windows chapter at the beginning of this book.

1 Tap or click the Save button on the Quick Access Toolbar to overwrite the previously saved file.

Break Point: If you wish to take a break, this is a good place to do so. You can exit Word now (refer to page WD 46 for instructions). To resume at a later time, run Word (refer to pages WD 46 to WD 47 for instructions), open the file called Adventure Flyer (refer to page WD 47 for instructions), and continue following the steps from this location forward.

Inserting and Formatting a Picture in a Word Document

With the text formatted in the flyer, the next step is to insert a digital picture in the flyer and format the picture. Flyers usually contain a graphical image(s), such as a picture, to attract the attention of passersby. In the following pages, you will perform these tasks:

1. Insert a digital picture into the flyer and then reduce its size.
2. Enlarge the size of the picture.
3. Change the look of the picture.

How do I locate a graphic file to use in a document?

To use a graphic in a Word document, the image must be stored digitally in a file. Files containing graphics are available from a variety of sources:

- Microsoft has free digital images on the web for use in a document. Other websites also have images available, some of which are free, while others require a fee.
- You can take a picture with a digital camera or camera phone and **download** it, which is the process of copying the digital picture from the camera or phone to your computer.
- With a scanner, you can convert a printed picture, drawing, or diagram to a digital file.

If you receive a picture from a source other than yourself, do not use the file until you are certain it does not contain a virus. A **virus** is a computer program that can damage files and programs on your computer. Use an antivirus program to verify that any files you use are virus free.

To Center Another Paragraph

In the flyer, the digital picture of a mountain trail tour group should be centered on the blank line below the headline. The blank paragraph below the headline currently is left-aligned. The following steps center this paragraph.

1 Tap or click HOME on the ribbon to display the HOME tab.

2 Tap or click somewhere in the paragraph to be centered (in this case, the blank line below the headline) to position the insertion point in the paragraph to be formatted.

3 Tap or click the Center button (HOME tab | Paragraph group) to center the paragraph containing the insertion point (shown in Figure 1–46 on the next page).

BTW

BTWs

For a complete list of the BTWs found in the margins of this book, visit the BTW resource on the Student Companion Site located on www.cengagebrain.com. For detailed instructions about accessing available resources, visit www.cengage.com/ct/studentdownload or contact your instructor for information about accessing the required files.

To Insert a Picture

The next step in creating the flyer is to insert a digital picture of a mountain trail tour group in the flyer on the blank line below the headline. The picture, which was taken with a digital camera, is available on the Data Files for Students. Visit www.cengage.com/ct/studentdownload for detailed instructions or contact your instructor for information about accessing the required files.

The following steps insert a picture, which, in this example, is located in the Chapter 01 folder in the Word folder in the Data Files for Students folder. *Why? It is good practice to organize and store files in folders so that you easily can find the files at a later date.*

❶

• If necessary, position the insertion point at the location where you want to insert the picture (in this case, on the centered blank paragraph below the headline).

• Tap or click INSERT on the ribbon to display the INSERT tab (Figure 1–46).

Figure 1–46

❷

• Tap or click the From File button (INSERT tab | Illustrations group) (shown in Figure 1–46) to display the Insert Picture dialog box (shown in Figure 1–47).

❸

• Navigate to the desired picture location (in this case, the Chapter 01 folder in the Word folder in the Data Files for Students folder). For a detailed example of this procedure, refer to Steps 4a and 4b in the To Save a File in a Folder section in the Office and Windows chapter at the beginning of this book.

Figure 1–47

• Tap or click Mountain Trail to select the file (Figure 1–47).

4

● Tap or click the Insert button (Insert Picture dialog box) to insert the picture at the location of the insertion point in the document (Figure 1–48).

Q&A What are the symbols around the picture?
A selected graphic appears surrounded by a **selection rectangle**, which has small squares and circles, called **sizing handles,** at each corner and middle location.

What is the purpose of the Layout Options button?
When you tap or click the Layout Options button, Word provides options for changing how the graphic is positioned with text in the document.

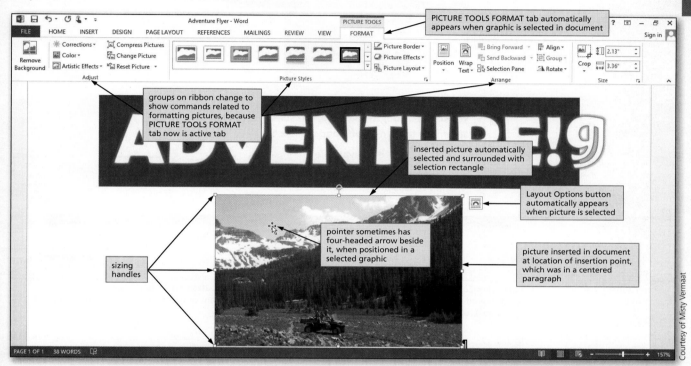

Figure 1–48

Courtesy of Misty Vermaat

How do you know where to position a graphic on a flyer?
The content, size, shape, position, and format of a graphic should capture the interest of passersby, enticing them to stop and read the flyer. Often, the graphic is the center of attention and visually the largest element on a flyer. If you use colors in the graphical image, be sure they are part of the document's color scheme.

CONSIDER THIS

1 ENTER TEXT | 2 FORMAT TEXT | 3 INSERT PICTURE | **4 FORMAT PICTURE**
5 ENHANCE PAGE | 6 CORRECT & REVISE | 7 PRINT OR READ

To Zoom the Document

In the steps on the following pages, you will work with the picture just inserted. The next task is to adjust the zoom percentage. *Why? Currently, you can see only a small amount of text with the picture. Seeing more of the document at once helps you determine the appropriate size for the picture.* The following step zooms the document.

1

 Experiment

● If you are using a mouse, repeatedly click the Zoom Out and Zoom In buttons on the status bar and watch the size of the document change in the document window.

● If you are using a touch screen, repeatedly pinch (move two fingers together) and stretch (move two fingers apart) and watch the size of the document change in the document window.

- Pinch and stretch or click the Zoom Out or Zoom In button as many times as necessary until the Zoom button on the status bar displays 80% on its face (Figure 1–49).

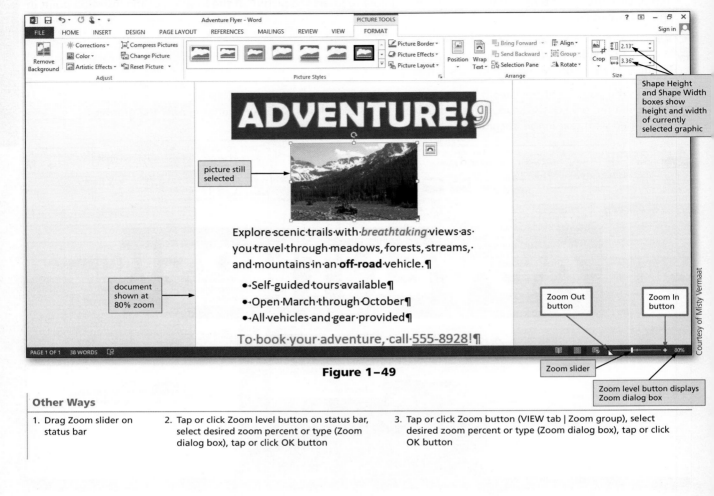

Figure 1–49

Other Ways

1. Drag Zoom slider on status bar	2. Tap or click Zoom level button on status bar, select desired zoom percent or type (Zoom dialog box), tap or click OK button	3. Tap or click Zoom button (VIEW tab \| Zoom group), select desired zoom percent or type (Zoom dialog box), tap or click OK button

To Resize a Graphic

Resizing includes both increasing and reducing the size of a graphic. The next step is to resize the picture so that it is larger in the flyer. *Why? You want the graphic as large as possible on a single page flyer to draw the attention of passersby.* The following steps resize a selected graphic.

1

- Be sure the graphic still is selected.

Q&A What if my graphic (picture) is not selected?

To select a graphic, tap or click it.

- If you are using a mouse, point to the lower-left corner sizing handle on the picture so that the pointer shape changes to a two-headed arrow (Figure 1–50).

Figure 1–50

2

- Drag the sizing handle diagonally outward until the lower-left corner of the picture is positioned approximately as shown in Figure 1–51. Do not lift your finger or release the mouse button at this point.

3

- Release your finger or the mouse button to resize the graphic, which in this case, should have a height of about 3.26" and a width of about 5.04".

Q&A

How can I see the height and width measurements?

Look in the Size group on the PICTURE TOOLS FORMAT tab to see the height and width measurements of the currently selected graphic (shown in Figure 1–49).

What if the graphic is the wrong size?

Repeat Steps 1, 2, and 3, or enter the desired height and width values in the Shape Height and Shape Width boxes (PICTURE TOOLS FORMAT tab | Size group).

What if I want to return a graphic to its original size and start again?

With the graphic selected, tap or click the Size Dialog Box Launcher (PICTURE TOOLS FORMAT tab | Size group), tap or click the Size tab (Layout dialog box), tap or click the Reset button, and then tap or click the OK button.

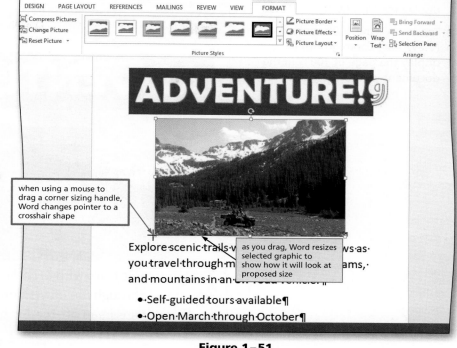

when using a mouse to drag a corner sizing handle, Word changes pointer to a crosshair shape

as you drag, Word resizes selected graphic to show how it will look at proposed size

Courtesy of Misty Vermaat

Figure 1–51

Other Ways

1. Enter height and width of graphic in Shape Height and Shape Width boxes (PICTURE TOOLS FORMAT tab | Size group)
2. Tap or click Advanced Layout: Size Dialog Box Launcher (PICTURE TOOLS FORMAT tab | Size group), tap or click Size tab (Layout dialog box), enter desired height and width values in boxes, tap or click OK button

To Zoom 100%

1 ENTER TEXT | 2 FORMAT TEXT | 3 INSERT PICTURE | **4 FORMAT PICTURE**
5 ENHANCE PAGE | **6 CORRECT & REVISE** | **7 PRINT OR READ**

In the next series of steps, you will format the picture. Earlier in this chapter, you changed the zoom to 80% so that you could see more of the page while resizing the graphic. The step on the next page zooms the screen to 100%. *Why? You want the contents of the image to be enlarged a bit, while still seeing some of the text in the document.*

1

- Tap or click VIEW on the ribbon to display the VIEW tab.

- Tap or click the 100% button (VIEW tab | Zoom group) to display the page at 100% in the document window (Figure 1–52).

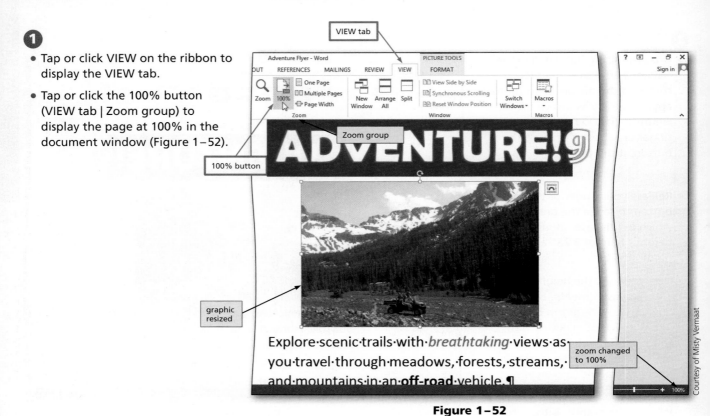

Figure 1–52

Other Ways

1. Tap or click Zoom button (VIEW tab | Zoom group), tap or click 100% (Zoom dialog box), tap or click OK button

To Apply a Picture Style

1 ENTER TEXT | 2 FORMAT TEXT | 3 INSERT PICTURE | 4 FORMAT PICTURE
5 ENHANCE PAGE | 6 CORRECT & REVISE | 7 PRINT OR READ

A **style** is a named group of formatting characteristics. Word provides more than 25 picture styles. *Why? Picture styles enable you easily to change a picture's look to a more visually appealing style, including a variety of shapes, angles, borders, and reflections.* The flyer in this chapter uses a style that applies a drop shadow to the picture. The following steps apply a picture style to a picture.

1

- Tap or click PICTURE TOOLS FORMAT on the ribbon to display the PICTURE TOOLS FORMAT tab.

- Be sure the graphic still is selected (Figure 1–53).

Q&A

What if my graphic (picture) is not selected?
To select a graphic, tap or click it.

What is the white circle attached to top of the selected graphic?
It is called a rotate handle. When you drag a graphic's **rotate handle**, the graphic moves in either a clockwise or counterclockwise direction.

Figure 1–53

2

- Tap or click the More button in the Picture Styles gallery (PICTURE TOOLS FORMAT tab | Picture Styles group) (shown in Figure 1–53) to expand the gallery.

- If you are using a mouse, point to 'Drop Shadow Rectangle' in the Picture Styles gallery to display a live preview of that style applied to the picture in the document (Figure 1–54).

 Experiment

- If you are using a mouse, point to various picture styles in the Picture Styles gallery and watch the style of the picture change in the document window.

3

- Tap or click 'Drop Shadow Rectangle' in the Picture Styles gallery (fourth style in first row) to apply the style to the selected picture.

expanded gallery shows more options—your list may be arranged differently

pointer on 'Drop Shadow Rectangle' picture style

picture format changes to Drop Shadow Rectangle, showing live preview of style to which you are pointing in expanded gallery

Courtesy of Misty Vermaat

Figure 1–54

Other Ways

1. Press and hold or right-click picture, tap or click 'Picture Quick Styles' on mini toolbar, select desired style

To Apply Picture Effects

1 ENTER TEXT | 2 FORMAT TEXT | 3 INSERT PICTURE | 4 FORMAT PICTURE
5 ENHANCE PAGE | 6 CORRECT & REVISE | 7 PRINT OR READ

Word provides a variety of picture effects, such as shadows, reflections, glow, soft edges, bevel, and 3-D rotation. The difference between the effects and the styles is that each effect has several options, providing you with more control over the exact look of the image.

In this flyer, the picture has a slight green glow effect and beveled edges. The following steps apply picture effects to the selected picture. *Why? Picture effects enable you to further customize the a picture.*

1

- With the picture still selected, tap or click the Picture Effects button (PICTURE TOOLS FORMAT tab | Picture Styles group) to display the Picture Effects menu.

- Tap or point to Glow on the Picture Effects menu to display the Glow gallery.

- If you are using a mouse, point to 'Turquoise, 5 pt glow, Accent color 6' in the Glow Variations area (rightmost glow in first row) to display a live preview of the selected glow effect applied to the picture in the document window (Figure 1–55).

 Experiment

- If you are using a mouse, point to various glow effects in the Glow gallery and watch the picture change in the document window

PICTURE TOOLS FORMAT tab

Picture Effects button

Picture Styles gallery

Glow gallery

Glow command

Glow Variations area

pointer on 'Turquoise, 5 pt glow, Accent color 6'

Picture Effects menu

selected picture shows live preview of glow effect to which you are pointing in gallery

Courtesy of Misty Vermaat

Figure 1–55

2

- Tap or click 'Turquoise, 5 pt glow, Accent color 6' in the Glow gallery to apply the selected picture effect.

Q&A What if I wanted to discard formatting applied to a picture?
You would tap or click the Reset Picture button (PICTURE TOOLS FORMAT tab | Adjust group). To reset formatting and size, you would tap or click the Reset Picture arrow (PICTURE TOOLS FORMAT tab | Adjust group) and then tap or click 'Reset Picture & Size' on the Reset Picture menu.

3

- Tap or click the Picture Effects button (PICTURE TOOLS FORMAT tab | Picture Styles group) to display the Picture Effects menu again.

- Tap or point to Bevel on the Picture Effects menu to display the Bevel gallery.

- If you are using a mouse, point to Angle in the Bevel area (first effect in second row) to display a live preview of the selected bevel effect applied to the picture in the document window (Figure 1–56).

🔍 Experiment

- If you are using a mouse, point to various bevel effects in the Bevel gallery and watch the picture change in the document window.

4

- Tap or click Angle in the Bevel gallery to apply the selected picture effect.

Figure 1–56

Courtesy of Misty Vermaat

Other Ways

1. Tap 'Show Context Menu' button on mini toolbar or right-click picture, tap or click Format Object or Format Picture on shortcut menu, tap or click Effects button (Format Picture task pane), select desired options, tap or click Close button

2. Tap or click Format Shape Dialog Box Launcher (PICTURE TOOLS FORMAT tab | Picture Styles group), tap or click Effects button (Format Picture task pane), select desired options, tap or click Close button

Enhancing the Page

BTW

Word Help
At any time while using Word, you can find answers to questions and display information about various topics through Word Help. Used properly, this form of assistance can increase your productivity and reduce your frustrations by minimizing the time you spend learning how to use Word. For instruction about Word Help and exercises that will help you gain confidence in using it, read the Office and Windows chapter at the beginning of this book.

With the text and graphics entered and formatted, the next step is to look at the page as a whole and determine if it looks finished in its current state. As you review the page, answer these questions:

- Does it need a page border to frame its contents, or would a page border make it look too busy?

- Is the spacing between paragraphs and graphics on the page adequate? Do any sections of text or graphics look as if they are positioned too closely to the items above or below them?

- Does the flyer have too much space at the top or bottom? Should the contents be centered vertically?

You determine that a graphical, color-coordinated border would enhance the flyer. You also notice that the flyer would look better proportioned if it had a little more space above and below the picture. You also want to ensure that the contents are centered vertically. The following pages make these enhancements to the flyer.

To Add a Page Border

In Word, you can add a border around the perimeter of an entire page. The flyer in this chapter has a light green border. *Why? This border color complements the color of the flyer contents.* The following steps add a page border.

- Tap or click DESIGN on the ribbon to display the DESIGN tab.

- Tap or click the 'Borders and Shading' button (DESIGN tab | Page Background group) to display the Borders and Shading dialog box (Figure 1–57).

Figure 1–57

- Tap or click the second border style in the Style list (Borders and Shading dialog box) to select the style.

- Tap or click the Color arrow to display a Color palette (Figure 1–58).

Figure 1–58

- Tap or click 'Lime, Accent 2, Lighter 80%' (sixth color in second row) in the Color palette to select the color for the page border.

- Tap or click the Width arrow to display the Width list and then tap or click 4 ½ pt to select the thickness of the page border (Figure 1–59).

- Tap or click the OK button to add the border to the page (shown in Figure 1–60).

Q&A What if I wanted to remove the border?
You would tap or click None in the Setting list in the Borders and Shading dialog box.

Figure 1–59

To Zoom One Page

1 ENTER TEXT | 2 FORMAT TEXT | 3 INSERT PICTURE | 4 FORMAT PICTURE
5 ENHANCE PAGE | 6 CORRECT & REVISE | 7 PRINT OR READ

The next steps zoom one page so that you can see the entire page on the screen at once.

1 Tap or click VIEW on the ribbon to display the VIEW tab.

2 Tap or click the One Page button (VIEW tab | Zoom group) to display the entire page in the document window as large as possible.

To Change Spacing before and after Paragraphs

1 ENTER TEXT | 2 FORMAT TEXT | 3 INSERT PICTURE | 4 FORMAT PICTURE
5 ENHANCE PAGE | 6 CORRECT & REVISE | 7 PRINT OR READ

The default spacing above (before) a paragraph in Word is 0 points and below (after) is 8 points. In the flyer, you want to increase the spacing below the paragraph containing the headline and above the signature line. **Why?** *The flyer spacing will look more balanced with spacing increased above and below these paragraphs.* The following steps change the spacing above and below a paragraph.

1

- Position the insertion point in the paragraph to be adjusted, in this case, the paragraph containing the headline.

Q&A What happened to the PICTURE TOOLS FORMAT tab?
When you tap or click outside of a graphic or press a key to scroll through a document, Word deselects the graphic and removes the PICTURE TOOLS FORMAT tab from the screen. That is, this tab appears only when a graphic is selected.

- Tap or click PAGE LAYOUT on the ribbon to display the PAGE LAYOUT tab.

- If you are using a touch screen, tap the Spacing After box (PAGE LAYOUT tab | Paragraph group) and then type 12 to change the spacing below the paragraph; if you are using a mouse, click the Spacing After up arrow (PAGE LAYOUT tab | Paragraph group) so that 12 pt is displayed in the Spacing After box to increase the space below the current paragraph (Figure 1–60).

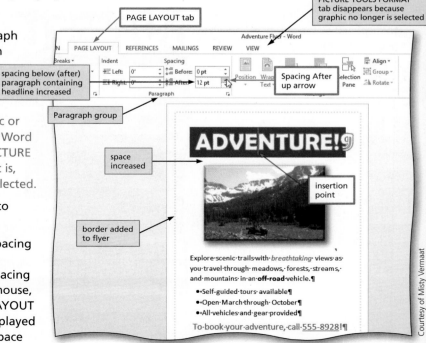

Figure 1–60

2

- Position the insertion point in the paragraph to be adjusted, in this case, the paragraph containing the signature line.

- If you are using a touch screen, tap the Spacing Before box (PAGE LAYOUT tab | Paragraph group) and then type 12 to change the spacing above the paragraph; if you are using a mouse, click the Spacing Before up arrow (PAGE LAYOUT tab | Paragraph group) as many times as necessary so that 12 pt is displayed in the Spacing Before box to increase the space above the current paragraph (Figure 1–61).

- If the text flows to two pages, reduce the spacing above and below paragraphs as necessary.

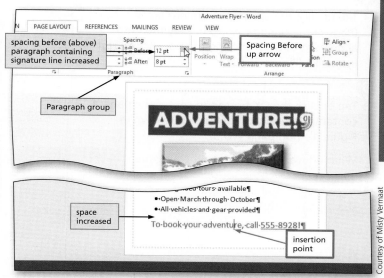

Figure 1–61

Courtesy of Misty Vermaat

Other Ways

1. Tap 'Show Context Menu' button on mini toolbar or right-click paragraph, tap or click Paragraph on shortcut menu, tap or click Indents and Spacing tab (Paragraph dialog box), enter spacing before and after values, tap or click OK button

2. Tap or click Paragraph Settings Dialog Box Launcher (HOME tab or PAGE LAYOUT tab | Paragraph group), tap or click Indents and Spacing tab (Paragraph dialog box), enter spacing before and after values, tap or click OK button

To Center Page Contents Vertically

1 ENTER TEXT | 2 FORMAT TEXT | 3 INSERT PICTURE | 4 FORMAT PICTURE
5 ENHANCE PAGE | 6 CORRECT & REVISE | 7 PRINT OR READ

In Word, you can center the page contents vertically. **Why?** *This places the same amount of space at the top and bottom of the page.* The following steps center page contents vertically.

1

- If necessary, tap or click PAGE LAYOUT on the ribbon to display the PAGE LAYOUT tab.

- Tap or click the Page Setup Dialog Box Launcher (PAGE LAYOUT tab | Page Setup group) to display the Page Setup dialog box.

- Tap or click the Layout tab (Page Setup dialog box) to display the Layout sheet (Figure 1–62).

Figure 1–62

2

- Tap or click the Vertical alignment arrow (Page Setup dialog box) to display the list of alignment options and then tap or click Center in the list (Figure 1–63).

3

- Tap or click the OK button to center the page contents vertically on the screen (shown in Figure 1–1 on page WD 3).

Q&A What if I wanted to change the alignment back? You would select the Top vertical alignment from the Vertical alignment list in the Layout sheet (Page Setup dialog box).

Figure 1–63

To Save an Existing Document with the Same File Name

You have made several modifications to the document since you last saved it. Thus, you should save it again. The following step saves the document again. For an example of the step listed below, refer to the Office and Windows chapter at the beginning of this book.

1 Tap or click the Save button on the Quick Access Toolbar to overwrite the previously saved file.

Document Properties

Word helps you organize and identify your files by using **document properties**, which are the details about a file such as the project author, title, and subject. For example, a class name or document topic can describe the file's purpose or content.

Why would you want to assign document properties to a document?

Document properties are valuable for a variety of reasons:

- Users can save time locating a particular file because they can view a file's document properties without opening the document.

- By creating consistent properties for files having similar content, users can better organize their documents.

- Some organizations require Word users to add document properties so that other employees can view details about these files.

The more common document properties are standard and automatically updated properties. **Standard properties** are associated with all Microsoft Office files and include author, title, and subject. **Automatically updated properties** include file system properties, such as the date you create or change a file, and statistics, such as the file size.

To Change Document Properties

To change document properties, you would follow these steps.

1. Tap or click FILE on the ribbon to open the Backstage view and then, if necessary, tap or click the Info tab in the Backstage view to display the Info gallery.

2. If the property you wish to change is displayed in the Properties list in the right pane of the Info gallery, try to tap or click to the right of the property. If a text box appears to the right of the property, type the text for the property in the text box, and then tap or click the Back button in the upper-left corner of the Backstage view to return to the Word window. Skip the remaining steps.

3. If the property you wish to change is not displayed in the Properties list in the right pane of the Info gallery or you cannot change it in the Info gallery, tap or click the Properties button in the right pane to display the Properties menu, and then tap or click 'Show Document Panel' on the Properties menu to close the Backstage view and display the Document Information Panel in the Word document window.

Q&A Why are some of the document properties in my Document Information Panel already filled in?
The person who installed Office 2013 on your computer or network may have set or customized the properties.

4. Type the desired text in the appropriate property text boxes.

Q&A What if the property I want to change is not displayed in the Document Information Panel?
Tap or click the Document Properties button in the Document Information Panel and then tap or click Advanced Properties on the menu to display the Properties dialog box. If necessary, tap or click the Summary tab (Properties dialog box) to display the Summary sheet, fill in the appropriate text boxes, and then tap or click the OK button.

5. Tap or click the 'Close the Document Information Panel' button at the right edge of the Document Information Panel so that the panel no longer appears in the Word document window.

To Sign Out of a Microsoft Account

If you are signed in to a Microsoft account and are using a public computer or otherwise wish to sign out of your Microsoft account, you should sign out of the account from the Account gallery in the Backstage view before exiting Word. Signing out of the account is the safest way to make sure that nobody else can access SkyDrive files or settings stored in your Microsoft account. The following steps sign out of a Microsoft account from Word. For a detailed example of the procedure summarized below, refer to the Office and Windows chapter at the beginning of this book.

1 If you wish to sign out of your Microsoft account, tap or click FILE on the ribbon to open the Backstage view and then tap or click the Account tab to display the Account gallery.

2 Tap or click the Sign out link, which displays the Remove Account dialog box. If a Can't remove Windows accounts dialog box appears instead of the Remove Account dialog box, tap or click the OK button and skip the remaining steps.

Q&A Why does a Can't remove Windows accounts dialog box appear?
If you signed in to Windows using your Microsoft account, then you also must sign out from Windows, rather than signing out from within the Word. When you are finished using Windows, be sure to sign out at that time.

3 Tap or click the Yes button (Remove Account dialog box) to sign out of your Microsoft account on this computer.

Q&A Should I sign out of Windows after signing out of my Microsoft account?
When you are finished using the computer, you should sign out of your account for maximum security.

4 Tap or click the Back button in the upper-left corner of the Backstage view to return to the document.

BTW
Q&As
For a complete list of the Q&As found in many of the step-by-step sequences in this book, visit the Q&A resource on the Student Companion Site located on www.cengagebrain.com. For detailed instructions about accessing available resources, visit www.cengage.com/ct/studentdownload or contact your instructor for information about accessing the required files.

To Exit Word

Although you still need to make some edits to this document, you want to exit Word and resume working on the project at a later time. Thus, the following steps exit Word. For a detailed example of the procedure summarized below, refer to the Office and Windows chapter at the beginning of this book.

1a If you have one Word document open, tap or click the Close button on the right side of the title bar to close the open document and exit Word.

1b If you have multiple Word documents open, press and hold or right-click the Word app button on the taskbar and then tap or click 'Close all windows' on the shortcut menu to close all open documents and exit Word.

Q&A Could I press and hold or repeatedly click the Close button to close all open documents and exit Word?
Yes.

2 If a Microsoft Word dialog box appears, tap or click the Save button to save any changes made to the document since the last save.

Break Point: If you wish to take a break, this is a good place to do so. To resume at a later time, continue following the steps from this location forward.

Correcting Errors and Revising a Document

After creating a document, you may need to change it. For example, the document may contain an error, or new circumstances may require you to add text to the document.

Types of Changes Made to Documents

The types of changes made to documents normally fall into one of the three following categories: additions, deletions, or modifications.

Additions Additional words, sentences, or paragraphs may be required in a document. Additions occur when you omit text from a document and want to insert it later. For example, you may want to add your email address to the flyer.

Deletions Sometimes, text in a document is incorrect or no longer is needed. For example, you may discover that the tours no longer provide gear. In this case, you would delete the words, and gear, from the flyer.

Modifications If an error is made in a document or changes take place that affect the document, you might have to revise a word(s) in the text. For example, the tours may start in April instead of March.

BTW
Certification
The Microsoft Office Specialist (MOS) program provides an opportunity for you to obtain a valuable industry credential — proof that you have the Word 2013 skills required by employers. For more information, visit the Certification resource on the Student Companion Site located on www.cengagebrain.com. For detailed instructions about accessing available resources, visit www.cengage.com/ct/studentdownload or contact your instructor for information about accessing the required files.

To Run Word

Once you have created and saved a document, you may need to retrieve it from your storage medium. For example, you might want to revise the document or print it. The following steps, which assume Windows 8 is running, use the Start screen or the Search box to run Word based on a typical installation. You may need to ask your instructor how to run Word on your computer. For a detailed example of the procedure summarized below, refer to the Office and Windows chapter.

1 Scroll the Start screen for a Word 2013 tile. If your Start screen contains a Word 2013 tile, tap or click it to run Word and then proceed to Step 5; if the Start screen does not contain the Word 2013 tile, proceed to the next step to search for the Word app.

2 Swipe in from the right edge of the screen or point to the upper-right corner of the screen to display the Charms bar and then tap or click the Search charm on the Charms bar to display the Search menu.

3 Type `Word` as the search text in the Search box and watch the search results appear in the Apps list.

4 Tap or click Word 2013 in the search results to run Word.

5 Tap or click the Blank document thumbnail on the Word start screen to create a blank document and display it in the Word window.

6 If the Word window is not maximized, tap or click the Maximize button on its title bar to maximize the window.

To Open a Document from Word

Earlier in this chapter you saved your flyer using the file name, Adventure Flyer. The following steps open the Adventure Flyer file from the Word folder in the CIS 101 folder. For a detailed example of the procedure summarized below, refer to the Office and Windows chapter at the beginning of this book.

1 Tap or click FILE on the ribbon to open the Backstage view and then tap or click the Open tab in the Backstage view to display the Open gallery.

2 If the file you wish to open is displayed in the Recent Documents list, tap or click the file name to open the file and display the opened document in the Word window; then, skip the remaining steps. If the file you wish to open is not displayed in the Recent Documents list, proceed to the next step to locate the file.

3 Tap or click Computer, SkyDrive, or another location in the left pane, tap or click the Browse button, and then navigate to the location of the file to be opened (in this case the Word folder in the CIS 101 folder).

4 Tap or click Adventure Flyer to select the file to be opened.

5 Tap or click the Open button (Open dialog box) to open the selected file and display the opened document in the Word window.

To Zoom the Document

While modifying the document, you prefer the document at 100% so that it is easier to read. Thus, the following step changes the zoom back to 100%.

1 Tap or click VIEW on the ribbon to display the VIEW tab.

2 Tap or click the 100% button (VIEW tab | Zoom group) to display the page at 100% in the document window.

BTW
Quick Reference
For a table that lists how to complete the tasks covered in this book using touch gestures, the mouse, ribbon, shortcut menu, and keyboard, see the Quick Reference Summary at the back of this book, or visit the Quick Reference resource on the Student Companion Site located on www.cengagebrain.com. For detailed instructions about accessing available resources, visit www.cengage.com/ct/studentdownload or contact your instructor for information about accessing the required files.

To Insert Text in an Existing Document

Word inserts text to the left of the insertion point. The text to the right of the insertion point moves to the right and downward to fit the new text. The following steps insert the word, today, to the left of the word, with, in the flyer. *Why? These steps illustrate the process of inserting text.*

1

- Scroll through the document and then tap or click to the left of the location of text to be inserted (in this case, the w in with) to position the insertion point where text should be inserted (Figure 1–64).

Figure 1–64

2

- Type **today** and then press the SPACEBAR to insert the word to the left of the insertion point (Figure 1–65).

Q&A

Why did the text move to the right as I typed?
In Word, the default typing mode is **insert mode**, which means as you type a character, Word moves all the characters to the right of the typed character one position to the right.

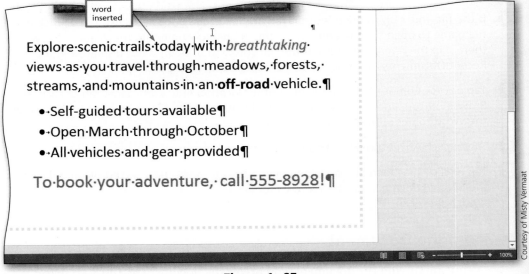

Figure 1–65

To Delete Text

It is not unusual to type incorrect characters or words in a document. As discussed earlier in this chapter, you can tap or click the Undo button on the Quick Access Toolbar to undo a command or action immediately — this includes typing. Word also provides other methods of correcting typing errors.

To delete an incorrect character in a document, simply tap or click next to the incorrect character and then press the BACKSPACE key to erase to the left of the insertion point, or press the DELETE key to erase to the right of the insertion point.

To delete a word or phrase, you first must select the word or phrase. The following steps select the word, today, which was just added in the previous steps and then delete the selection. *Why? These steps illustrate the process of selecting a word and then deleting selected text.*

1

- Double-tap or double-click the word to be selected (in this case, today) to select the word (Figure 1–66).

2

- If you are using a touch screen, tap the selected text to display the mini toolbar and then tap the Cut button on the mini toolbar to delete the selected text; if you are using a keyboard, with the text selected, press the DELETE key to delete the selected text.

Figure 1–66

Courtesy of Misty Vermaat

Other Ways

1. Press and hold or right-click selected item, tap Cut on mini toolbar or click Cut on shortcut menu	2. Select item, press BACKSPACE to delete to left of insertion point or press DELETE to delete to right of insertion point	3. Select item, press CTRL+X

To Move Text

1 ENTER TEXT | 2 FORMAT TEXT | 3 INSERT PICTURE | 4 FORMAT PICTURE
5 ENHANCE PAGE | 6 CORRECT & REVISE | 7 PRINT OR READ

An efficient way to move text a short distance is drag-and-drop editing. With **drag-and-drop editing**, you select the item to be moved, drag the selected item to the new location, and then drop, or insert, it in the new location. Another technique for moving text is the cut-and-paste technique, which is discussed in the next chapter.

The following steps use drag-and-drop editing to move text. *Why? While proofreading the flyer, you realize that the body copy would read better if the last two bulleted paragraphs were reversed.*

1

- If you are using a mouse, position the pointer in the paragraph to be moved (in this case, the last bulleted item) and then triple-click to select the paragraph.

- If you are using a mouse, with the pointer in the selected text, press and hold down the mouse button, which displays a small dotted box with the pointer (Figure 1–67).

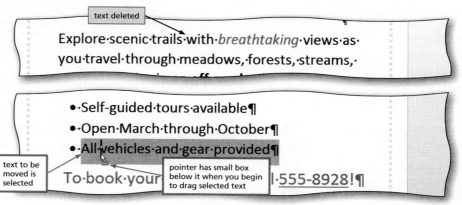

Figure 1–67

2

- If you are using a mouse, drag the insertion point to the location where the selected text is to be moved, as shown in Figure 1–68.

Figure 1–68

- If you are using a mouse, release the mouse button to move the selected text to the location of the dotted insertion point (Figure 1–69).

Q&A What if I accidentally drag text to the wrong location?

Tap or click the Undo button on the Quick Access Toolbar and try again.

Can I use drag-and-drop editing to move any selected item?

Yes, you can select words, sentences, phrases, and graphics and then use drag-and-drop editing to move them.

What is the purpose of the Paste Options button?

If you are using a mouse and click the Paste Options button, a menu appears that allows you to change the format of the item that was moved. The next chapter discusses the Paste Options menu.

- Tap or click anywhere in the document window to remove the selection from the bulleted item.

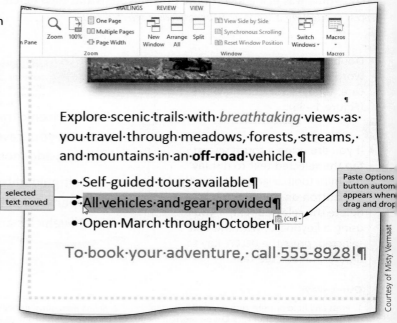

Figure 1–69

Q&A What if I am using a touch screen?

If you have a stylus, you can follow Steps 1 through 3 using the stylus. If you are using your finger, you will need to use the cut-and-paste technique: tap to position the insertion point in the text to be moved and then drag the selection handles as necessary to select the text that you want to move; tap the selection to display the mini toolbar and then tap the Cut button on the mini toolbar to remove the text; tap to position the insertion point at the location where you want to move the text; display the HOME tab and then tap the Paste button on the HOME tab to place the text at the location of the insertion point. The next chapter discusses this procedure in more depth.

Other Ways

1. Tap or click Cut button (HOME tab | Clipboard group), tap or click where text or object is to be pasted, tap or click Paste button (HOME tab | Clipboard group)

2. Press and hold or right-click selected text, tap or click Cut on mini toolbar or shortcut menu, press and hold or right-click where text or object is to be pasted, tap Paste on mini toolbar or click Keep Source Formatting on shortcut menu

3. Press CTRL+X, position insertion point where text or object is to be pasted, press CTRL+V

To Save an Existing Document with the Same File Name

You have made several modifications to the document since you last saved it. Thus, you should save it again. The following step saves the document again. For an example of the step listed below, refer to the Office and Windows chapter at the beginning of this book.

 Tap or click the Save button on the Quick Access Toolbar to overwrite the previously saved file.

Printing or Reading a Document

After creating a document, you may want to print it or read it on-screen. Printing a document enables you to distribute it to others in a form that can be read or viewed but typically not edited. It is a good practice to save a document before printing it, in the event you experience difficulties printing. Some users prefer reading a document on-screen instead of on paper.

What is the best method for distributing a document?

The traditional method of distributing a document uses a printer to produce a hard copy. A **hard copy** or **printout** is information that exists on a physical medium such as paper. Hard copies can be useful for the following reasons:

- Some people prefer proofreading a hard copy of a document rather than viewing it on the screen to check for errors and readability.

- Hard copies can serve as a backup reference if your storage medium is lost or becomes corrupted and you need to recreate the document.

Instead of distributing a hard copy of a document, users can distribute the document as an electronic image that mirrors the original document's appearance. The electronic image of the document can be sent as an email attachment, posted on a website, or copied to a portable storage medium such as a USB flash drive. Two popular electronic image formats, sometimes called fixed formats, are PDF by Adobe Systems and XPS by Microsoft. In Word, you can create electronic image files through the Save As dialog box and the Export, Share, and Print tabs in the Backstage view. Electronic images of documents, such as PDF and XPS, can be useful for the following reasons:

- Users can view electronic images of documents without the software that created the original document (e.g., Word). Specifically, to view a PDF file, you use a program called Adobe Reader, which can be downloaded free from Adobe's website. Similarly, to view an XPS file, you use a program called XPS Viewer, which is included in the latest versions of Windows and Internet Explorer.

- Sending electronic documents saves paper and printer supplies. Society encourages users to contribute to **green computing**, which involves reducing the electricity consumed and environmental waste generated when using computers, mobile devices, and related technologies.

To Print a Document

1 ENTER TEXT | 2 FORMAT TEXT | 3 INSERT PICTURE | 4 FORMAT PICTURE
5 ENHANCE PAGE | 6 CORRECT & REVISE | 7 PRINT OR READ

With the completed document saved, you may want to print it. *Why? Because this flyer is being posted, you will print a hard copy on a printer.* The following steps print a hard copy of the contents of the saved Adventure Flyer document.

1

- Tap or click FILE on the ribbon to open the Backstage view.

- Tap or click the Print tab in the Backstage view to display the Print gallery (Figure 1–70).

How can I print multiple copies of my document?
Increase the number in the Copies box in the Print gallery.

What if I decide not to print the document at this time?
Tap or click the Back button in the upper-left corner of the Backstage view to return to the document window.

2

- Verify that the printer listed on the Printer Status button will print a hard copy of the document. If necessary, click the Printer Status button to display a list of available printer options and then click the desired printer to change the currently selected printer.

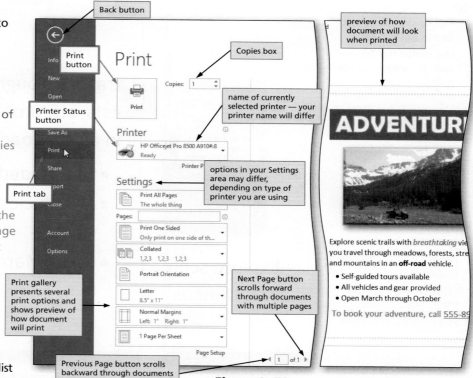

Figure 1–70

Courtesy of Misty Vermaat

- Tap or click the Print button in the Print gallery to print the document on the currently selected printer.

- When the printer stops, retrieve the hard copy (Figure 1–71).

Q&A

Do I have to wait until my document is complete to print it?
No, you can follow these steps to print a document at any time while you are creating it.

What if I want to print an electronic image of a document instead of a hard copy?
You would click the Printer Status button in the Print gallery and then select the desired electronic image option, such as Microsoft XPS Document Writer, which would create an XPS file.

What if one or more of my borders do not print?
Tap or click the Page Borders button (DESIGN tab | Page Background group), tap or click the Options button (Borders and Shading dialog box), tap or click the Measure from arrow and click Text, change the four text boxes to 15 pt, and then tap or click the OK button in each dialog box. Try printing the document again. If the borders still do not print, adjust the boxes in the dialog box to a number smaller than 15 point.

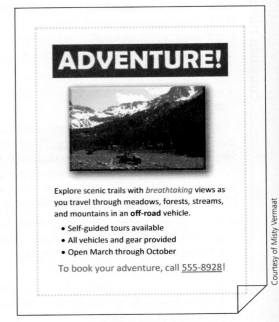

Figure 1–71

To Switch to Read Mode

The next steps switch from Print Layout view to Read mode. *Why? If you are not composing a document, you can switch to **Read mode,** which hides the ribbon and other writing tools so that more content fits on the screen. Read mode is intended to make it easier to read a document.* The following step switches to Read mode.

- Tap or click the Read Mode button on the status bar to switch to Read mode (Figure 1–72).

Experiment

- Tap or click the arrows to advance forward and then move backward through the document.

Q&A

Besides reading, what can I do in Read mode?
You can zoom, copy text, highlight text, search, add comments, and more.

Figure 1–72

Other Ways

1. Tap or click Read Mode button (VIEW tab | Views group)
2. Tap or click VIEW on the ribbon, tap or click Edit Document

To Switch to Print Layout View

The next steps switch back to Print Layout view. *Why? If you want to show the document on a mock sheet of paper in the document window, along with the ribbon and other writing tools, you should switch to Print Layout view.* The following step switches to Print Layout view.

1

- Tap or click the Print Layout button on the status bar to switch to Print Layout view (Figure 1–73).

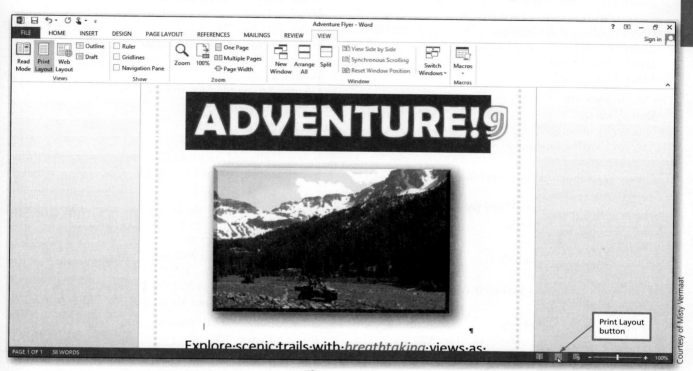

Figure 1–73

Other Ways

1. Tap or click Print Layout button (VIEW tab | Views group)

To Exit Word

This project now is complete. The following steps exit Word. For a detailed example of the procedure summarized below, refer to the Office and Windows chapter at the beginning of this book.

1a If you have one Word document open, tap or click the Close button on the right side of the title bar to close the open document and exit Word.

1b If you have multiple Word documents open, press and hold or right-click the Word app button on the taskbar and then tap or click 'Close all windows' on the shortcut menu to close all open documents and exit Word.

2 If a Microsoft Word dialog box appears, tap or click the Save button to save any changes made to the document since the last save.

Chapter Summary

In this chapter, you have learned how to enter text in a document, format text, insert and format a picture, add a page border, adjust paragraph and page spacing, and print and read a document. The items listed below include all the new Word skills you have learned in this chapter, with the tasks grouped by activity.

Enter and Edit Text
Type Text (WD 5)
Insert a Blank Line (WD 7)
Wordwrap Text as You Type (WD 9)
Check Spelling and Grammar as You Type (WD 10)
Insert Text in an Existing Document (WD 48)
Delete Text (WD 48)
Move Text (WD 49)

File Management
Run Word (WD 4)
Save a Document (WD 12)
Save an Existing Document with the Same File Name (WD 33)
Change Document Properties (WD 44)
Exit Word (WD 46)
Open a Document from Word (WD 47)
Print a Document (WD 51)

Format a Page
Change Theme Colors (WD 31)
Add a Page Border (WD 41)
Center Page Contents Vertically (WD 43)

Format Text
Center a Paragraph (WD 15)
Change the Font Size of Selected Text (WD 17)
Change the Font of Selected Text (WD 18)
Change the Case of Selected Text (WD 19)
Apply a Text Effect to Selected Text (WD 20)

Shade a Paragraph (WD 21)
Bullet a List of Paragraphs (WD 23)
Undo and Redo an Action (WD 24)
Italicize Text (WD 25)
Color Text (WD 26)
Use the Mini Toolbar to Format Text (WD 27)
Underline Text (WD 29)
Bold Text (WD 29)
Change Spacing before and after Paragraphs (WD 42)

Select Text
Select a Line (WD 16)
Select Multiple Lines (WD 22)
Select a Group of Words (WD 28)

Word Settings
Display Formatting Marks (WD 6)
Zoom Page Width (WD 7)
Zoom One Page (WD 30)
Zoom the Document (WD 35)
Zoom 100% (WD 37)
Switch to Read Mode (WD 52)
Switch to Print Layout View (WD 53)

Work with Graphics (Pictures)
Insert a Picture (WD 34)
Resize a Graphic (WD 36)
Apply a Picture Style (WD 38)
Apply Picture Effects (WD 39)

CONSIDER THIS: PLAN AHEAD

What decisions will you need to make when creating your next flyer?
Use these guidelines as you complete the assignments in this chapter and create your own flyers outside of this class.

1. Choose the text for the headline, body copy, and signature line — using as few words as possible to make a point.

2. Format various elements of the text.

 a) Select appropriate font sizes for text in the headline, body copy, and signature line.

 b) Select appropriate fonts for text in the headline, body copy, and signature line.

 c) Adjust paragraph alignment, as appropriate.

 d) Highlight key paragraphs with bullets.

 e) Emphasize important words.

 f) Use color to convey meaning and add appeal.

3. Find an eye-catching graphic(s) that conveys the overall message and meaning of the flyer.

4. Establish where to position and how to format the graphical image(s) so that the image grabs the attention of passersby and draws them into reading the flyer.

5. Determine whether the flyer needs enhancements such as a graphical, color-coordinated border or spacing adjustments to improve readability or overall appearance.

6. Correct errors and revise the document as necessary.

 a) Post the flyer on a wall and make sure all text and images are legible from a distance.

 b) Ask someone else to read the flyer and give you suggestions for improvements.

7. Determine the best method for distributing the document such as printing, sending via email, or posting on the web.

How should you submit solutions to questions in the assignments identified with a ✳ symbol?

Every assignment in this book contains one or more questions identified with a ✳ symbol. These questions require you to think beyond the assigned document. Present your solutions to the questions in the format required by your instructor. Possible formats may include one or more of these options: write the answer; create a document that contains the answer; present your answer to the class; discuss your answer in a group; record the answer as audio or video using a webcam, smartphone, or portable media player; or post answers on a blog, wiki, or website.

Apply Your Knowledge

Reinforce the skills and apply the concepts you learned in this chapter.

Modifying Text and Formatting a Document

Note: To complete this assignment, you will be required to use the Data Files for Students. Visit www.cengage.com/ct/studentdownload for detailed instructions or contact your instructor for information about accessing the required files.

Instructions: Run Word. Open the document, Apply 1-1 County Park Flyer Unformatted, from the Data Files for Students. The document you open is an unformatted flyer. You are to modify text, format paragraphs and characters, and insert a picture in the flyer to create the flyer shown in Figure 1–74.

Perform the following tasks:

1. Delete the word, below, in the sentence below the headline.

2. Insert the word, Valley, between the words, Green County, in the second to last line of the flyer.

3. Change the period to an exclamation point in the last line so that the text reads: Thank You!

4. If requested by your instructor, change the phone number in the flyer to your phone number.

5. Center the headline and the last two paragraphs of the flyer.

6. Select the third, fourth, and fifth paragraphs in the flyer and add bullets to the selected paragraphs.

7. Change the theme colors to the Red Orange color scheme.

8. Change the font and font size of the headline to 48-point Franklin Gothic Heavy, or a similar font. Change the case of the headline text to uppercase letters. Apply the text effect called Fill - Black, Text 1, Outline - Background 1, Hard Shadow - Background 1 to the headline. Change the font color of the headline text to Dark Red, Accent 6.

headline →

bulleted list →

Courtesy of Misty Vermaat

Figure 1–74

Continued >

Apply Your Knowledge continued

9. Change the font size of the sentence below the headline, the bulleted list, and the last line of flyer to 26 point.

10. Use the mini toolbar to change the font size of the sentence below the bulleted list to 18 point.

11. Select the words, Follow these guidelines, in the paragraph below the headline and underline them.

12. Bold the word, not, in the first bulleted paragraph. Change the font color of this same word to Dark Red, Accent 6.

13. Italicize the word, all, in the second bulleted item. Undo this change and then redo the change.

14. Switch the last two bulleted paragraphs. That is, select the 'Never leave food unattended' bullet and move it so that it is the second bulleted paragraph.

15. Bold the text, Thank You!, in the last line of the flyer. Shade this same paragraph Dark Red, Accent 6, Darker 25%. If the font color does not automatically change to a lighter color, change its color to White, Background 1.

16. Change the zoom so that the entire page is visible in the document window.

17. Insert the picture of the squirrel eating the sucker centered on the blank line below the headline. The picture is called Squirrel and is available on the Data Files for Students. Apply the Soft Edge Oval picture style to the inserted picture.

18. Change the spacing before the first bulleted paragraph to 12 point and the spacing after the last bulleted paragraph to 24 point.

19. The entire flyer should fit on a single page. If it flows to two pages, resize the picture or decrease spacing before and after paragraphs until the entire flyer text fits on a single page.

20. Change the zoom to text width, then page width, then 100% and notice the differences.

21. If requested by your instructor, enter the text, Green Valley, as the keywords in the document properties. Change the other document properties, as specified by your instructor.

22. Click FILE on the ribbon and then click Save As. Save the document using the file name, Apply 1-1 County Park Flyer Formatted.

23. Print the document. Switch to Read Mode and browse pages through the document. Switch to Print Layout view.

24. Submit the revised document, shown in Figure 1–74, in the format specified by your instructor.

25. Exit Word.

26. ✹ If this flyer were announcing the park reopening instead of including a warning, which color scheme would you apply and why?

Extend Your Knowledge

Extend the skills you learned in this chapter and experiment with new skills. You may need to use Help to complete the assignment.

Modifying Text and Picture Formats and Adding Page Borders

Note: To complete this assignment, you will be required to use the Data Files for Students. Visit www.cengage.com/ct/studentdownload for detailed instructions or contact your instructor for information about accessing the required files.

Instructions: Run Word. Open the document, Extend 1-1 Baseball Tryouts Flyer Draft, from the Data Files for Students. You will enhance the look of the flyer shown in Figure 1–75.
Hint: Remember, if you make a mistake while formatting the picture, you can reset it by using the Reset Picture button or Reset Picture arrow (PICTURE TOOLS FORMAT tab | Adjust group).

Perform the following tasks:

1. Use Help to learn about the following: remove bullets, grow font, shrink font, art page borders, decorative underline(s), picture bullets, picture border shading, picture border color, shadow picture effects, and color saturation and tone.

2. Remove the bullet from the last line of the flyer.

3. Select the text, August 30, and use the 'Increase Font Size' button (HOME tab | Font group) to increase its font size.

4. Add an art page border to the flyer. If the border is not in color, add color to it.

5. Change the solid underline below the word, Travel, to a decorative underline. Change the color of the underline.

6. Change the style of the bullets to picture bullet(s). Adjust the hanging indent, if necessary, to align the text in bulleted list.

7. Change the color of the picture border. Add the Perspective Right 3-D Rotation picture effect to the picture.

8. Change the color saturation and color tone of the picture.

9. If requested by your instructor, change the name of the field (High Crop) to your last name.

10. Save the revised document with the file name, Extend 1-1 Baseball Tryouts Flyer Final, and then submit it in the format specified by your instructor.

11. ✴ In this assignment you added an art page border to the flyer. Which border did you select and why?

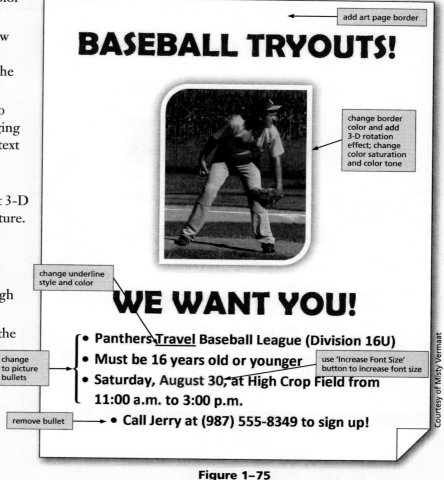

Figure 1–75

Analyze, Correct, Improve

Analyze a document, correct all errors, and improve it.

Correcting Spelling and Grammar Errors and Adding Color

Note: To complete this assignment, you will be required to use the Data Files for Students. Visit www.cengage.com/ct/studentdownload for detailed instructions or contact your instructor for information about accessing the required files.

Instructions: Run Word. Open the document, Analyze 1-1 Beauty Salon Flyer Draft, from the Data Files for Students. The document is a flyer that contains spelling and grammar errors, as shown in Figure 1–76 on the next page. It also could include color to make it more visually appealing.

Continued >

Analyze, Correct, Improve *continued*

1. Correct You are to correct each spelling (red wavy underline) and grammar (green and blue wavy underlines) error by pressing and holding or right-clicking the flagged text and then clicking the appropriate correction on the shortcut menu.

If your screen does not display the wavy underlines, tap or click FILE on the ribbon and then tap or click Options in the Backstage view. When the Word Options dialog box is displayed, tap or click Proofing in the left pane, be sure the 'Hide spelling errors in this document only' and 'Hide grammar errors in this document only' check boxes do not contain check marks, and then tap or click the OK button. If your screen still does not display the wavy underlines, redisplay the Word Options dialog box, tap or click Proofing, and then tap or click the Recheck Document button.

2. Improve Enhance the flyer by (a) adding a shading color to the first and last lines (paragraphs) on the flyer, (b) changing the color of the text in the first line and last line of the flyer, and (c) adding a color glow effect to the three pictures in the flyer.

If requested by your instructor, change the street name in the flyer to your first name. Save the revised document with the file name, Extend 1-1 Beauty Salon Flyer Final, and then submit it in the format specified by your instructor.

3. ✻ In this assignment, you selected color to add to the flyer. Which color(s) did you select and why?

Figure 1–76

Courtesy of Misty Vermaat

In the Labs

Design and/or create a document using the guidelines, concepts, and skills presented in this chapter. Labs 1 and 2, which increase in difficulty, require you to create solutions based on what you learned in the chapter; Lab 3 requires you to create a solution, which uses cloud and web technologies, by learning and investigating on your own from general guidance.

Lab 1: Creating a Flyer with a Picture

Problem: Your friend asked you to prepare a flyer that advertises the puppy she has for sale. First, you prepare the unformatted flyer shown in Figure 1–77a, and then you format it so that it looks like Figure 1–77b on page WD 60. *Hint:* Remember, if you make a mistake while formatting the flyer, you can use the Undo button on the Quick Access Toolbar to undo your last action.

Note: To complete this assignment, you will be required to use the Data Files for Students. Visit www.cengage.com/ct/studentdownload for detailed instructions or contact your instructor for information about accessing the required files.

Instructions: Perform the following tasks:

1. Run Word. Display formatting marks on the screen.

2. Type the flyer text, unformatted, as shown in Figure 1–77a, inserting a blank line between the headline and the body copy. If Word flags any misspelled words as you type, check their spelling and correct them.

3. Save the document using the file name, Lab 1-1 Puppy for Sale Flyer.

4. Center the headline and the signature line.

5. Change the theme colors to Aspect.

6. Change the font size of the headline to 72 point and the font to Gil Sans Ultra Bold Condensed, or a similar font. Apply the text effect called Fill - Dark Purple, Accent 1, Outline - Background, Hard Shadow - Accent 1.

7. Change the font size of body copy between the headline and the signature line to 22 point.

8. Change the font size of the signature line to 20 point.

9. Change the font of the body copy and signature line to Comic Sans MS.

10. Bullet the three lines (paragraphs) of text above the signature line.

11. Change the color of the words, purebred American Cocker Spaniel, to Dark Green, Accent 4, Darker 50%.

12. Italicize the word, and, in the third bulleted paragraph.

13. Bold the text in the signature line. Shade this paragraph containing the signature line in Dark Purple, Accent 5, Lighter 80%.

14. Underline the phone number in the signature line.

15. Change the zoom so that the entire page is visible in the document window.

16. Insert the picture centered on a blank line below the headline. The picture is called Puppy and is available on the Data Files for Students.

17. Apply the Rotated, White picture style to the inserted picture. Apply the glow effect called Dark Purple, 5 pt glow, Accent color 5 to the picture.

Puppy for Sale

blank line →

Own this six-month-old male, potty-trained, purebred American Cocker Spaniel puppy.

Fun, smart, cuddly, and playful

Needs a loving home

Knows these commands: sit, down, stay, heel, and leave it

If interested, call Vivian at (356) 555-7733.

(a) Unformatted Text
Figure 1–77 (Continued)

Continued >

In the Labs continued

Courtesy of Misty Vermaat

(b) Formatted Document
Figure 1–77 (Continued)

18. Change the spacing after the paragraph containing the headline to 0 pt. Change the spacing above (before) the signature line to 18 pt. The entire flyer should fit on a single page. If it flows to two pages, resize the picture or decrease spacing before and after paragraphs until the entire flyer text fits on a single page.

19. Add a 6-pt Dark Green, Accent 4, Lighter 60% page border, as shown in Figure 1–77b.

20. If requested by your instructor, change the contact name in the flyer to your first name.

21. Save the flyer again with the same file name. Submit the document, shown in Figure 1–77b, in the format specified by your instructor.

22. ☀ Why do you think this flyer used shades of purple and green?

Lab 2: **Creating a Flyer with a Resized Pictures**

Problem: Your boss at Junior's Wedding Bakery has asked you to prepare a flyer that promotes its business. You prepare the flyer shown in Figure 1–78. *Hint:* Remember, if you make a mistake while formatting the flyer, you can use the Undo button on the Quick Access Toolbar to undo your last action.

Note: To complete this assignment, you will be required to use the Data Files for Students. Visit www.cengage.com/ct/studentdownload for detailed instructions or contact your instructor for information about accessing the required files.

Instructions: Perform the following tasks:

1. Run Word. Type the flyer text, unformatted. If Word flags any misspelled words as you type, check their spelling and correct them.

2. Save the document using the file name, Lab 1-2 Wedding Bakery Flyer.

3. Change the theme colors to the Marquee color scheme.

4. Add bullets to the three paragraphs shown in the figure. Center all paragraphs, except the paragraphs containing the bulleted list.

5. Change the font size of the headline to 36 point and the font to Franklin Gothic Heavy, or a similar font. Apply the text effect called Fill - Orange, Accent 3, Sharp Bevel.

6. Change the font size of body copy between the headline and signature line to 20 point, except for line above the bulleted list, which is 24 point.

7. Change the font size of the signature line to 22 point. Bold the text in the signature line. Change the font color of the text in the signature line to Orange, Accent 3.

8. Italicize the word, personalize.

9. Bold the text above the bulleted list.

10. Underline the text, Junior's Wedding Bakery.

11. Shade the line above the bulleted list to the Orange, Accent 3 color. If the font color does not automatically change to a lighter color, change it to White, Background 1.

12. Change the zoom so that the entire page is visible in the document window.

13. Insert the first picture on a blank line below the headline and the second picture on a blank line below the bulleted list. The pictures are called Bakery 1 and Bakery 2, respectively, and are available on the Data Files for Students.

14. Resize the top picture so that it is approximately 2.8" × 5.39". Apply the Soft Edge Oval picture style to the top inserted picture. Apply the Offset Right Shadow picture effect to the top picture. Resize the bottom picture so that it is approximately 1.5" × 4.05". Apply the Simple Frame, Black picture style to the bottom inserted picture.

15. Change the spacing after the paragraph containing the bakery name to 0 pt and the spacing after the last bulleted paragraph to 12 pt. The entire flyer should fit on a single page. If it flows to two pages, resize the picture or decrease spacing before and after paragraphs until the entire flyer text fits on a single page.

16. Add the page border shown in Figure 1–78, using the color Gold, Accent 5.

17. Center the page contents vertically.

18. If requested by your instructor, change the bakery name to your last name.

19. Save the flyer again with the same file name. Submit the document, shown in Figure 1–78, in the format specified by your instructor.

20. ☼ Why do you think this flyer used shades of orange and yellow?

Figure 1–78

Lab 3: Expand Your World: Cloud and Web Technologies
Using the Word Web App to Create a Flyer with a Picture

Problem: You have a side business where you build bean bag toss boards. You would like to create a flyer that promotes this business. You will use the Word Web App to prepare a flyer. The text for the unformatted flyer is shown in Figure 1–79.

Note: To complete this assignment, you will be required to use the Data Files for Students. Visit www.cengage.com/ct/studentdownload for detailed instructions or contact your instructor for information about accessing the required files.

Instructions: Perform the following tasks:

1. Run a browser. Search for the text, Word Web App, using a search engine. Visit several websites to learn about the Word Web App. Navigate to the Office Web Apps website. You will need to sign in to your SkyDrive account.

2. Use the Create button to begin creating a Word document using the Word Web App. Name the document Lab 1-3 Bean Bag Toss Flyer.

3. Notice the differences between the Word Web App and the Word desktop app you used to create the project in this chapter.

4. Enter the text in the flyer, shown in Figure 1–79, checking spelling as you type.

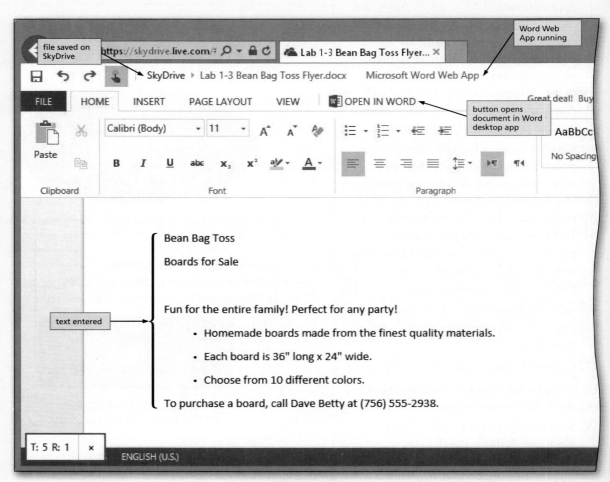

Figure 1–79

5. Insert the picture called Bean Bag Toss, which is located on the Data Files for Students.

6. Use the features available in the Word Web App, along with the concepts and techniques presented in this chapter, to format this flyer. Be sure to change the font and font size of text, center a paragraph(s), italicize text, color text, underline text, and apply a picture style. Adjust spacing above and below paragraphs as necessary. Resize the picture, if necessary.

7. If requested by your instructor, replace the contact name in the flyer with your name.

8. Save the document again. Tap or click the button to open the document in the Word desktop app. If necessary, sign in to your Microsoft account when prompted. Notice how the document appears in the Word desktop app.

9. Using either the Word Web App or Word desktop app, submit the document in the format requested by your instructor. Exit the Word Web App (FILE tab | Exit). Sign out of your SkyDrive account. Sign out of the Microsoft account in Word.

10. ✳ What is the Word Web App? Which features that are covered in this chapter are not available in the Word Web App? Do you prefer using the Word Web App or the Word desktop app? Why?

✳ Consider This: Your Turn

Apply your creative thinking and problem solving skills to design and implement a solution.

Note: To complete these assignments, you may be required to use the Data Files for Students. Visit www.cengage.com/ct/studentdownload for detailed instructions or contact your instructor for information about accessing the required files.

1: Design and Create a Photography Club Flyer
Personal

Part 1: As secretary of your school's Photography Club, you are responsible for creating and distributing flyers announcing the club. The flyer should contain two digital pictures appropriately resized; the Data Files for Students contains two pictures called Photography 1 and Photography 2, or you can use your own digital pictures if they are appropriate for the topic of the flyer. The flyer should contain the headline, Photography Club, and this signature line: Questions? Call Emily at (883) 555-0901. The body copy consists of the following text, in any order: Do you love photography? This is the club for you! All skill levels are welcome. Meetings every Tuesday at 5:00 p.m. in the Student Center (room 232). Bring your camera. We look forward to seeing you at our next meeting!

Use the concepts and techniques presented in this chapter to create and format this flyer. Be sure to check spelling and grammar. Submit your assignment and answers to the critical thinking questions in the format specified by your instructor.

Part 2: ✳ You made several decisions while creating the flyer in this assignment: where to place text, how to format the text (i.e., font, font size, paragraph alignment, bulleted paragraphs, underlines, italics, bold, color, etc.), which graphics to use, where to position the graphics, how to format the graphics, and which page enhancements to add (i.e., borders and spacing). What was the rationale behind each of these decisions? When you proofread the document, what further revisions did you make and why? How would you recommend distributing this flyer?

2: Design and Create a Hot Air Balloon Rides Flyer
Professional

Part 1: As a part-time employee at Galaxy Recreations, your boss has asked you to create and distribute flyers announcing hot air balloon rides. The flyer should contain two digital pictures appropriately resized; the Data Files for Students contains two pictures called Hot Air Balloon 1

Continued >

STUDENT ASSIGNMENTS

Consider This: Your Turn *continued*

and Hot Air Balloon 2, or you can use your own digital pictures if they are appropriate for the topic of the flyer. The flyer should contain the headline, Hot Air Balloon Rides, and this signature line: For reservations, call (485) 555-2295. The body copy consists of the following text, in any order: Amazing sights from incredible heights! The experience of a lifetime. Fun for the whole family. No pets. Bring your camera. Open seven days a week from 10:00 a.m. to 4:00 p.m. Book your private tour with Galaxy Recreations today!

Use the concepts and techniques presented in this chapter to create and format this flyer. Be sure to check spelling and grammar. Submit your assignment in the format specified by your instructor.

Part 2: ☀ You made several decisions while creating the flyer in this assignment: where to place text, how to format the text (i.e., font, font size, paragraph alignment, bulleted paragraphs, underlines, italics, bold, color, etc.), which graphics to use, where to position the graphics, how to format the graphics, and which page enhancements to add (i.e., borders and spacing). What was the rationale behind each of these decisions? When you proofread the document, what further revisions did you make and why? How would you recommend distributing this flyer?

3: Design and Create a Water Park Flyer
Research and Collaboration

Part 1: As a part-time employee at a local water park, your boss has asked you and two other employees to create and distribute flyers for the upcoming water park season. Form a three-member team to compose and create this flyer. Research a local water park: its location, hours, prices, rules, specials, etc. As a group, determine the text for the flyer's headline, body copy, and signature line. Your team also will need to obtain at least two digital pictures appropriate for the content of this flyer. You could take the pictures with a digital camera or search for public-domain images on the web.

Use the concepts and techniques presented in this chapter to create and format this flyer. Be sure to check spelling and grammar. Submit your team assignment in the format specified by your instructor.

Part 2: ☀ You made several decisions while creating the flyer in this assignment: text to use, where to place text, how to format the text (i.e., font, font size, paragraph alignment, bulleted paragraphs, underlines, italics, bold, color, etc.), which graphics to use, where to position the graphics, how to format the graphics, and which page enhancements to add (i.e., borders and spacing). What was the rationale behind each of these decisions? When you proofread the document, what further revisions did you make and why? What research methods did you use to create the flyer? Where did you obtain your pictures? How would you recommend distributing this flyer?

Learn Online

Reinforce what you learned in this chapter with games, exercises, training, and many other online activities and resources.

Student Companion Site Reinforcement activities and resources are available at no additional cost on www.cengagebrain.com. Visit www.cengage.com/ct/studentdownload for detailed instructions about accessing the resources available at the Student Companion Site.

SAM Put your skills into practice with SAM Projects! If you have a SAM account, go to www.cengage.com/sam2013 to access SAM assignments for this chapter.

2 Creating a Research Paper with References and Sources

Microsoft product screen shots used with permission from Microsoft Corporation.

Objectives

You will have mastered the material in this chapter when you can:

- Describe the MLA documentation style for research papers
- Modify a style
- Change line and paragraph spacing in a document
- Use a header to number pages of a document
- Apply formatting using keyboard shortcuts
- Modify paragraph indentation
- Insert and edit citations and their sources

- Add a footnote to a document
- Insert a manual page break
- Create a bibliographical list of sources
- Cut, copy, and paste text
- Find text and replace text
- Find a synonym
- Check spelling and grammar at once
- Look up information

2 | Creating a Research Paper with References and Sources

Introduction

In both academic and business environments, you will be asked to write reports. Business reports range from proposals to cost justifications to five-year plans to research findings. Academic reports focus mostly on research findings.

A **research paper** is a document you can use to communicate the results of research findings. To write a research paper, you learn about a particular topic from a variety of sources (research), organize your ideas from the research results, and then present relevant facts and/or opinions that support the topic. Your final research paper combines properly credited outside information along with personal insights. Thus, no two research papers — even if they are about the same topic — will or should be the same.

Project — Research Paper

When preparing a research paper, you should follow a standard documentation style that defines the rules for creating the paper and crediting sources. A variety of documentation styles exists, depending on the nature of the research paper. Each style requires the same basic information; the differences in styles relate to requirements for presenting the information. For example, one documentation style uses the term bibliography for the list of sources, whereas another uses references, and yet a third prefers the title works cited. Two popular documentation styles for research papers are the **Modern Language Association of America (MLA)** and **American Psychological Association (APA)** styles. This chapter uses the MLA documentation style because it is used in a wide range of disciplines.

The project in this chapter follows research paper guidelines and uses Word to create the short research paper shown in Figure 2–1. This paper, which discusses biometric devices, follows the MLA documentation style. Each page contains a page number. The first two pages present the name and course information (student name, instructor name, course name, and paper due date), paper title, an introduction with a thesis statement, details that support the thesis, and a conclusion. This section of the paper also includes references to research sources and a footnote. The third page contains a detailed, alphabetical list of the sources referenced in the research paper. All pages include a header at the upper-right edge of the page.

BTW
APA Appendix
If your version of this book includes the Word APA Appendix and you are required to create a research paper using the APA documentation style instead of the MLA documentation style, the appendix shows the steps required to create the research paper in this chapter using following APA guidelines. If your version of this book does not include the Word APA Appendix, see online or print publications for the APA guidelines or see your instructor.

Bailey 3

Works Cited

Allensmith, Samantha Clare. *Understanding Face Recognition Systems*. n.d. Course Technology. Web. 16 Sept. 2014.

Nadeer, Aisha Sati and Jonathon Richard White. *Biometric Security*. Chicago: Windy City Press, 2014. Print.

Rossi, Marcell Enrico. "How To Use Fingerprint Readers." *Digital Security Review* Aug. 2014: n. pag. Web. 3 Oct. 2014.

alphabetical list of sources

Bailey 2

device. Face recognition systems are becoming more sophisticated and can recognize people with or without glasses, hats, facial hair, makeup, or jewelry, and with new hairstyles (Allensmith).

Home and business users alike are using biometric security. Through a biometric identifier, such as a fingerprint, biometric devices can deny or grant access to programs, devices, computers, rooms, and other locations. Biometric devices are an effective security technology.

header contains last name followed by page number

Bailey 1

Teddy Bailey

Ms. Pedro

English 101

October 15, 2014

Access Granted

Biometric devices authenticate a person's identity by verifying unique personal characteristics. These devices translate a biometric identifier, such as a fingerprint, into a digital code that is compared with a digital code stored in a computer. If the digital code in the computer matches the personal characteristic code, the computer grants access. Examples of biometric devices include fingerprint readers and face recognition systems.

A fingerprint reader, or scanner, captures curves and indentations of a fingerprint. Organizations use fingerprint readers to secure doors, computers, and software. For example, a fingerprint reader can be set up to authenticate users before they can access a computer (Rossi). External fingerprint readers usually plug into a USB port. To save on desk space, some laptops include built-in fingerprint readers.[1]

parenthetical reference

superscripted note reference mark

A face recognition system captures a live face image and compares it with a stored image to determine if the person is a legitimate user. Some buildings use face recognition systems to secure access to rooms. Law enforcement, surveillance systems, and airports use face recognition systems to protect the public. Some mobile devices use face recognition systems to unlock the

[1] Nadeer and White state that fingerprint readers can perform different functions for different fingers; for example, one finger runs a program and another finger shuts down the computer (62-63).

content note positioned as footnote

Figure 2–1

For an introduction to Windows and instruction about how to perform basic Windows tasks, read the Office and Windows chapter at the beginning of this book, where you can learn how to resize windows, change screen resolution, create folders, move and rename files, use Windows Help, and much more.

Roadmap

In this chapter, you will learn how to create the research paper shown in Figure 2–1 on the previous page. The following roadmap identifies general activities you will perform as you progress through this chapter:

1. CHANGE the DOCUMENT SETTINGS.
2. CREATE the HEADER for each page of the research paper.
3. TYPE the RESEARCH PAPER text WITH CITATIONS.
4. CREATE an ALPHABETICAL WORKS CITED page.
5. PROOFREAD AND REVISE the RESEARCH PAPER.

At the beginning of step instructions throughout the chapter, you will see an abbreviated form of this roadmap. The abbreviated roadmap uses colors to indicate chapter progress: gray means the chapter is beyond that activity, blue means the task being shown is covered in that activity, and black means that activity is yet to be covered. For example, the following abbreviated roadmap indicates the chapter would be showing a task in the 2 CREATE HEADER activity.

1 CHANGE DOCUMENT SETTINGS | **2 CREATE HEADER** | 3 TYPE RESEARCH PAPER WITH CITATIONS

4 CREATE ALPHABETICAL WORKS CITED | 5 PROOFREAD & REVISE RESEARCH PAPER

Use the abbreviated roadmap as a progress guide while you read or step through the instructions in this chapter.

MLA Documentation Style

The research paper in this project follows the guidelines presented by the MLA. To follow the MLA documentation style, use a 12-point Times New Roman or similar font. Double-space text on all pages of the paper using one-inch top, bottom, left, and right margins. Indent the first word of each paragraph one-half inch from the left margin. At the right margin of each page, place a page number one-half inch from the top margin. On each page, precede the page number with your last name.

The MLA documentation style does not require a title page. Instead, place your name and course information in a block at the left margin beginning one inch from the top of the page. Center the title one double-spaced line below your name and course information.

In the text of the paper, place author references in parentheses with the page number(s) of the referenced information. The MLA documentation style uses in-text **parenthetical references** instead of noting each source at the bottom of the page or at the end of the paper. In the MLA documentation style, notes are used only for optional content or bibliographic notes.

If used, content notes elaborate on points discussed in the paper, and bibliographic notes direct the reader to evaluations of statements in a source or provide a means for identifying multiple sources. Use a superscript (raised number) both to signal that a note exists and to sequence the notes (shown in Figure 2–1). Position notes at the bottom of the page as footnotes or at the end of the paper as endnotes. Indent the first line of each note one-half inch from the left margin. Place one space following the superscripted number before beginning the note text. Double-space the note text (shown in Figure 2–1).

The MLA documentation style uses the term, **works cited,** to refer to the bibliographic list of sources at the end of the paper. The works cited page

BTW

APA Documentation Style

In the APA style, a separate title page is required instead of placing name and course information on the paper's first page. Double-space all pages of the paper with one-inch top, bottom, left, and right margins. Indent the first word of each paragraph one-half inch from the left margin. In the upper-right margin of each page, including the title page, place a running head that consists of the page number preceded by a brief summary of the paper title.

alphabetically lists sources that are referenced directly in the paper. Place the list of sources on a separate numbered page. Center the title, Works Cited, one inch from the top margin. Double-space all lines. Begin the first line of each source at the left margin, indenting subsequent lines of the same source one-half inch from the left margin. List each source by the author's last name, or, if the author's name is not available, by the title of the source.

Changing Document Settings

The MLA documentation style defines some global formats that apply to the entire research paper. Some of these formats are the default in Word. For example, the default left, right, top, and bottom margin settings in Word are one inch, which meets the MLA documentation style. You will modify, however, the font, font size, and line and paragraph spacing.

To Run Word and Create a Blank Document

If you are using a computer to step through the project in this chapter and you want your screens to match the figures in this book, you should change your screen's resolution to 1366 × 768. For information about how to change a computer's resolution, refer to the Office and Windows chapter at the beginning of this book.

The following steps, which assume Windows 8 is running, use the Start screen or the Search box to run Word based on a typical installation. You may need to ask your instructor how to run Word on your computer. For a detailed example of the procedure summarized below, refer to the Office and Windows chapter.

1 Scroll the Start screen for a Word 2013 tile. If your Start screen contains a Word 2013 tile, tap or click it to run Word and then proceed to Step 5; if the Start screen does not contain the Word 2013 tile, proceed to the next step to search for the Word app.

2 Swipe in from the right edge of the screen or point to the upper-right corner of the screen to display the Charms bar and then tap or click the Search charm on the Charms bar to display the Search menu.

3 Type **Word** as the search text in the Search box and watch the search results appear in the Apps list.

4 Tap or click Word 2013 in the search results to run Word.

5 Tap or click the Blank document thumbnail on the Word start screen to create a blank document and display it in the Word window.

6 If the Word window is not maximized, tap or click the Maximize button on its title bar to maximize the window.

7 If the Print Layout button on the status bar is not selected (shown in Figure 2–2 on the next page), tap or click it so that your screen is in Print Layout view.

8 If Normal (HOME tab | Styles group) is not selected in the Styles gallery (shown in Figure 2–2), tap or click it so that your document uses the Normal style.

9 To display the page the same width as the document window, if necessary, tap or click the Page Width button (VIEW tab | Zoom group).

For an introduction to Office and instruction about how to perform basic tasks in Office apps, read the Office and Windows chapter at the beginning of this book, where you can learn how to run an application, use the ribbon, save a file, open a file, exit an application, use Help, and much more.

One of the few differences between Windows 7 and Windows 8 occurs in the steps to run Word. If you are using Windows 7, click the Start button, type **Word** in the 'Search programs and files' box, click Word 2013, and then, if necessary, maximize the Word window. For detailed steps to run Word in Windows 7, refer to the Office and Windows chapter at the beginning of this book. For a summary of the steps, refer to the Quick Reference located at the back of this book.

To Display Formatting Marks

BTW

Style Formats
To see the formats assigned to a particular style in a document, tap or click the Styles Dialog Box Launcher (HOME tab | Styles group) and then tap or click the Style Inspector button in the Styles task pane. Position the insertion point in the style in the document and then point to the Paragraph formatting or Text level formatting areas in the Style Inspector task pane to display a ScreenTip describing formats assigned to the location of the insertion point. You also can tap or click the Reveal Formatting button in the Style Inspector task pane or press SHIFT+F1 to display the Reveal Formatting task pane.

As discussed in Chapter 1, it is helpful to display formatting marks that indicate where in the document you press the ENTER key, SPACEBAR, and other keys. The following steps display formatting marks.

1 If the HOME tab is not the active tab, tap or click HOME on the ribbon to display the HOME tab.

2 If the 'Show/Hide ¶' button (HOME tab | Paragraph group) is not selected already, tap or click it to display formatting marks on the screen.

Styles

When you create a document, Word formats the text using a particular style. A **style** is a named group of formatting characteristics, including font and font size. The default style in Word is called the **Normal style**, which most likely uses an 11-point Calibri font. If you do not specify a style for text you type, Word applies the Normal style to the text. In addition to the Normal style, Word has many other built-in, or predefined, styles that you can use to format text. Styles make it easy to apply many formats at once to text. You can modify existing styles and create your own styles. Styles are discussed as they are used in this book.

To Modify a Style

1 CHANGE DOCUMENT SETTINGS | 2 CREATE HEADER | 3 TYPE RESEARCH PAPER WITH CITATIONS
4 CREATE ALPHABETICAL WORKS CITED | 5 PROOFREAD & REVISE RESEARCH PAPER

The MLA documentation style requires that all text in the research paper use a 12-point Times New Roman or similar font. If you change the font and font size using buttons on the ribbon, you will need to make the change many times during the course of creating the paper. *Why? Word formats various areas of a document based on the Normal style, which uses an 11-point Calibri font. For example, body text, headers, and bibliographies all display text based on the Normal style.*

Thus, instead of changing the font and font size for various document elements, a more efficient technique is to change the Normal style for this document to use a 12-point Times New Roman font. *Why? By changing the Normal style, you ensure that all text in the document will use the format required by the MLA.* The following steps change the Normal style.

1

• Press and hold or right-click Normal in the Styles gallery (HOME tab | Styles group) to display a shortcut menu related to styles (Figure 2–2).

Figure 2–2

- Tap or click Modify on the shortcut menu to display the Modify Style dialog box (Figure 2–3).

Figure 2–3

- Tap or click the Font arrow (Modify Style dialog box) to display the Font list. Scroll to and then click Times New Roman in the list to change the font for the style being modified.

- Tap or click the Font Size arrow (Modify Style dialog box) and then tap or click 12 in the Font Size list to change the font size for the style being modified.

- Ensure that the 'Only in this document' option button is selected (Figure 2–4).

Q&A Will all future documents use the new font and font size?
No, because the 'Only in this document' option button is selected. If you wanted all future documents to use a new setting, you would select the 'New documents based on this template' option button.

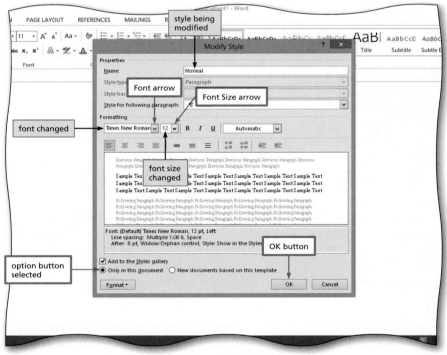

Figure 2–4

- Tap or click the OK button (Modify Style dialog box) to update the Normal style to the specified settings.

Other Ways

1. Tap or click Styles Dialog Box Launcher, tap or click arrow next to style name, tap or click Modify on menu, change settings (Modify Style dialog box), tap or click OK button

2. Press ALT+CTRL+SHIFT+S, tap or click arrow next to style name, tap or click Modify on menu, change settings (Modify Style dialog box), tap or click OK button

BTW
Line Spacing
If the top of a set of characters or a graphical image is chopped off, then line spacing may be set to Exactly. To remedy the problem, change line spacing to 1.0, 1.15, 1.5, 2.0, 2.5, 3.0, or At least (in the Paragraph dialog box), all of which accommodate the largest font or image.

Adjusting Line and Paragraph Spacing

Line spacing is the amount of vertical space between lines of text in a paragraph. **Paragraph spacing** is the amount of space above and below a paragraph. By default, the Normal style places 8 points of blank space after each paragraph and inserts a vertical space equal to 1.08 lines between each line of text. It also automatically adjusts line height to accommodate various font sizes and graphics.

The MLA documentation style requires that you **double-space** the entire research paper. That is, the amount of vertical space between each line of text and above and below paragraphs should be equal to one blank line. The next sets of steps adjust line spacing and paragraph spacing according to the MLA documentation style.

To Change Line Spacing

1 CHANGE DOCUMENT SETTINGS | 2 CREATE HEADER | 3 TYPE RESEARCH PAPER WITH CITATIONS
4 CREATE ALPHABETICAL WORKS CITED | 5 PROOFREAD & REVISE RESEARCH PAPER

The following steps change the line spacing to 2.0 to double-space lines in a paragraph. *Why? The lines of the research paper should be double-spaced, according to the MLA documentation style.*

- Tap or click the 'Line and Paragraph Spacing' button (HOME tab | Paragraph group) to display the Line and Paragraph Spacing gallery (Figure 2–5).

Q&A What do the numbers in the Line and Paragraph Spacing gallery represent?
The options 1.0, 2.0, and 3.0 set line spacing to single, double, and triple, respectively. Similarly, the 1.15, 1.5, and 2.5 options set line spacing to 1.15, 1.5, and 2.5 lines. All of these options adjust line spacing automatically to accommodate the largest font or graphic on a line.

Figure 2–5

- Tap or click 2.0 in the Line and Paragraph Spacing gallery to change the line spacing at the location of the insertion point.

Q&A Can I change the line spacing of existing text?
Yes. Select the text first and then change the line spacing as described in these steps.

Other Ways

1. Tap 'Show Context Menu' on mini toolbar or right-click paragraph, tap or click Paragraph on shortcut menu, tap or click Indents and Spacing tab (Paragraph dialog box), tap or click Line spacing arrow, select desired spacing, tap or click OK button

2. Tap or click Paragraph Settings Dialog Box Launcher (HOME tab or PAGE LAYOUT tab | Paragraph group), tap or click Indents and Spacing tab (Paragraph dialog box), tap or click Line spacing arrow, select desired spacing, tap or click OK button

3. Press CTRL+2 for double-spacing

To Remove Space after a Paragraph

The following steps remove space after a paragraph. *Why? The research paper should not have additional blank space after each paragraph, according to the MLA documentation style.*

1

- Tap or click the 'Line and Paragraph Spacing' button (HOME tab | Paragraph group) to display the Line and Paragraph Spacing gallery (Figure 2–6).

 Why is there a check mark to the left of 2.0 in the gallery?
The check mark indicates the currently selected line spacing.

2

- Tap or click 'Remove Space After Paragraph' in the Line and Paragraph Spacing gallery so that no blank space appears after paragraphs.

Figure 2–6

Can I remove space after existing paragraphs?
Yes. Select the paragraphs first and then remove the space as described in these steps.

Other Ways

1. Adjust Spacing After arrows (PAGE LAYOUT tab | Paragraph group) until 0 pt is displayed

2. Tap 'Show Context Menu' on mini toolbar or right-click paragraph, tap or click Paragraph on shortcut menu, tap or click Indents and Spacing tab (Paragraph dialog box), adjust After arrows until 0 pt is displayed, tap or click OK button

3. Tap or click Paragraph Settings Dialog Box Launcher (HOME tab or PAGE LAYOUT tab | Paragraph group), tap or click Indents and Spacing tab (Paragraph dialog box), adjust After arrows until 0 pt is displayed, tap or click OK button

To Update a Style to Match a Selection

To ensure that all paragraphs in the paper will be double-spaced and do not have space after the paragraphs, you want the Normal style to include the line and paragraph spacing changes made in the previous two sets of steps. The following steps update the Normal style. *Why? You can update a style to reflect the settings of the location of the insertion point or selected text. Because no text has yet been typed in the research paper, you do not need to select text prior to updating the Normal style.*

1

- Press and hold or right-click Normal in the Styles gallery (HOME tab | Styles group) to display a shortcut menu (Figure 2–7).

2

- Tap or click 'Update Normal to Match Selection' on the shortcut menu to update the selected (or current) style to reflect the settings at the location of the insertion point.

Figure 2–7

Other Ways

1. Tap or click Styles Dialog Box Launcher, tap or click arrow next to style name, tap or click 'Update Normal to Match Selection'

2. Press ALT+CTRL+SHIFT+S, tap or click arrow next to style name, tap or click 'Update Normal to Match Selection'

Creating a Header

BTW
The Ribbon and Screen Resolution
Word may change how the groups and buttons within the groups appear on the ribbon, depending on the computer's screen resolution. Thus, your ribbon may look different from the ones in this book if you are using a screen resolution other than 1366 × 768.

A **header** is text and/or graphics that print at the top of each page in a document. Similarly, a **footer** is text and/or graphics that print at the bottom of every page. In Word, headers print in the top margin one-half inch from the top of every page, and footers print in the bottom margin one-half inch from the bottom of each page, which meets the MLA documentation style. In addition to text and graphics, headers and footers can include document information such as the page number, current date, current time, and author's name.

In this research paper, you are to precede the page number with your last name placed one-half inch from the upper-right edge of each page. The procedures on the following pages enter your name and the page number in the header, as specified by the MLA documentation style.

To Switch to the Header

1 CHANGE DOCUMENT SETTINGS | 2 CREATE HEADER | 3 TYPE RESEARCH PAPER WITH CITATIONS
4 CREATE ALPHABETICAL WORKS CITED | 5 PROOFREAD & REVISE RESEARCH PAPER

The following steps switch from editing the document text to editing the header. *Why? To enter text in the header, you instruct Word to edit the header.*

1
- Tap or click INSERT on the ribbon to display the INSERT tab.

- Tap or click the 'Add a Header' button (INSERT tab | Header & Footer group) to display the Add a Header gallery (Figure 2–8).

🔎 **Experiment**
- Tap or click the down scroll arrow in the Add a Header gallery to see the available built-in headers.

Q&A Can I use a built-in header for this research paper?
None of the built-in headers adheres to the MLA documentation style. Thus, you enter your own header content instead of using a built-in header for this research paper.

How would I remove a header from a document?
You would tap or click Remove Header in the Add a Header gallery. Similarly, to remove a footer, you would tap or click Remove Footer in the Add a Footer gallery.

Figure 2–8

2

- Tap or click Edit Header in the Add a Header gallery to switch from the document text to the header, which allows you to edit the contents of the header (Figure 2–9).

Q&A How do I remove the HEADER & FOOTER TOOLS DESIGN tab from the ribbon? When you are finished editing the header, you will close it, which removes the HEADER & FOOTER TOOLS DESIGN tab.

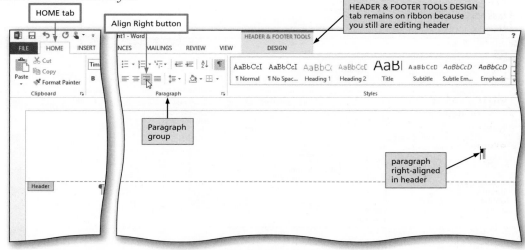

Figure 2–9

Other Ways

1. Double-tap or double-click dimmed header
2. Press and hold or right-click header in document, tap or click Edit Header button that appears

To Right-Align a Paragraph

1 CHANGE DOCUMENT SETTINGS | 2 CREATE HEADER | 3 TYPE RESEARCH PAPER WITH CITATIONS
4 CREATE ALPHABETICAL WORKS CITED | 5 PROOFREAD & REVISE RESEARCH PAPER

The paragraph in the header currently is left-aligned (Figure 2–9). The following steps right-align this paragraph. *Why? Your last name and the page number should print **right-aligned;** that is, they should print at the right margin, according to the MLA documentation style.*

1

- Tap or click HOME on the ribbon to display the HOME tab.

2

- Tap or click the Align Right button (HOME tab | Paragraph group) to right-align the current paragraph (Figure 2–10).

Q&A What if I wanted to return the paragraph to left-aligned? Tap or click the Align Right button again, or tap or click the Align Left button (HOME tab | Paragraph group).

Figure 2–10

Other Ways

1. Tap 'Show Context Menu' button on mini toolbar or right-click paragraph, tap or click Paragraph on shortcut menu, tap or click Indents and Spacing tab (Paragraph dialog box), tap or click Alignment arrow, tap or click Right, tap or click OK button
2. Tap or click Paragraph Settings Dialog Box Launcher (HOME tab or PAGE LAYOUT tab | Paragraph group), tap or click Indents and Spacing tab (Paragraph dialog box), tap or click Alignment arrow, tap or click Right, tap or click OK button
3. Press CTRL+R

BTW
Footers
If you wanted to create a footer, you would click the Footer button (INSERT tab | Header & Footer group) and then select the desired built-in footer or click Edit Footer to create a customized footer; or, you could double-tap or double-click the dimmed footer.

To Enter Text

The following step enters the last name right-aligned in the header area.

 Type **Bailey** and then press the SPACEBAR to enter the last name in the header. If requested by your instructor, enter your last name instead of Bailey in the header.

To Insert a Page Number

1 CHANGE DOCUMENT SETTINGS | 2 CREATE HEADER | 3 TYPE RESEARCH PAPER WITH CITATIONS
4 CREATE ALPHABETICAL WORKS CITED | 5 PROOFREAD & REVISE RESEARCH PAPER

The following steps insert a page number at the location of the insertion point. *Why?* *The MLA documentation style requires a page number following the last name in the header.*

- Tap or click HEADER & FOOTER TOOLS DESIGN on the ribbon to display the HEADER & FOOTER TOOLS DESIGN tab.
- Tap or click the 'Add Page Numbers' button (HEADER & FOOTER TOOLS DESIGN tab | Header & Footer group) to display the Add Page Numbers menu.

Q&A Why does the button name in the step differ from the name on the face of the button in the figure?
The text that appears on the face of the button may vary, depending on screen resolution. The name that appears in the ScreenTip (when you point to the button), however, never changes. For this reason, this book uses the name that appears in the ScreenTip to identify buttons, boxes, and other on-screen elements.

- Tap or point to Current Position on the Add Page Numbers menu to display the Current Position gallery (Figure 2–11).

Experiment

- Tap or click the down scroll arrow in the Current Position gallery to see the available page number formats.

Figure 2–11

2

- If necessary, scroll to the top of the Current Position gallery.

- Tap or click Plain Number in the Current Position gallery to insert an unformatted page number at the location of the insertion point (Figure 2–12).

Figure 2–12

To Close the Header

1 CHANGE DOCUMENT SETTINGS | 2 CREATE HEADER | 3 TYPE RESEARCH PAPER WITH CITATIONS
4 CREATE ALPHABETICAL WORKS CITED | 5 PROOFREAD & REVISE RESEARCH PAPER

The next task is to switch back to the document text. **Why?** *You are finished entering text in the header.* The following step closes the header.

1

- Tap or click the 'Close Header and Footer' button (HEADER & FOOTER TOOLS DESIGN tab | Close group) (shown in Figure 2–12) to close the header and switch back to the document text (Figure 2–13).

Q&A How do I make changes to existing header text?
Switch to the header using the steps described on page WD 74, edit the header as you would edit text in the document window, and then switch back to the document text.

Figure 2–13

Typing the Research Paper Text

The text of the research paper in this chapter encompasses the first two pages of the paper. You will type the text of the research paper and then modify it later in the chapter, so that it matches Figure 2–1 on page WD 67.

CONSIDER THIS

What should you consider when writing the first draft of a research paper?

As you write the first draft of a research paper, be sure it includes the proper components, uses credible sources, and does not contain any plagiarized material.

- **Include an introduction, body, and conclusion.** The first paragraph of the paper introduces the topic and captures the reader's attention. The body, which follows the introduction, consists of several paragraphs that support the topic. The conclusion summarizes the main points in the body and restates the topic.

- **Evaluate sources for authority, currency, and accuracy.** Be especially wary of information obtained on the web. Any person, company, or organization can publish a webpage on the Internet. Ask yourself these questions about the source:

 - Authority: Does a reputable institution or group support the source? Is the information presented without bias? Are the author's credentials listed and verifiable?

 - Currency: Is the information up to date? Are dates of sources listed? What is the last date revised or updated?

 - Accuracy: Is the information free of errors? Is it verifiable? Are the sources clearly identified?

- **Acknowledge all sources of information; do not plagiarize.** Sources of research include books, magazines, newspapers, and the Internet. As you record facts and ideas, list details about the source: title, author, place of publication, publisher, date of publication, etc. When taking notes, be careful not to **plagiarize**. That is, do not use someone else's work and claim it to be your own. If you copy information directly, place it in quotation marks and identify its source. Not only is plagiarism unethical, but it is considered an academic crime that can have severe punishments such as failing a course or being expelled from school.

When you summarize, paraphrase (rewrite information in your own words), present facts, give statistics, quote exact words, or show a map, chart, or other graphic, you must acknowledge the source. Information that commonly is known or accessible to the audience constitutes common knowledge and does not need to be acknowledged. If, however, you question whether certain information is common knowledge, you should document it — just to be safe.

To Enter Name and Course Information

As discussed earlier in this chapter, the MLA documentation style does not require a separate title page for research papers. Instead, place your name and course information in a block at the top of the page, below the header, at the left margin. The following steps enter the name and course information in the research paper.

BTW
Date Formats
The MLA style prefers the day-month-year (15 October 2014) or month-day-year (October 15, 2014) format.

1 Type **Teddy Bailey** as the student name and then press the ENTER key.

2 Type **Ms. Pedro** as the instructor name and then press the ENTER key.

3 Type **English 101** as the course name and then press the ENTER key.

4 Type **October 15, 2014** as the paper's due date and then press the ENTER key (Figure 2–14).

If requested by your instructor, enter your name and course information instead of the information shown above.

Q&A Why did the word, October, appear on the screen as I began typing the month name?

Word has an AutoComplete feature, where it predicts some words or phrases as you are typing and displays its prediction in a ScreenTip. If the AutoComplete prediction is correct, you can tap the ScreenTip or press the ENTER key to instruct Word to finish your typing with the word or phrase that appears in the ScreenTip.

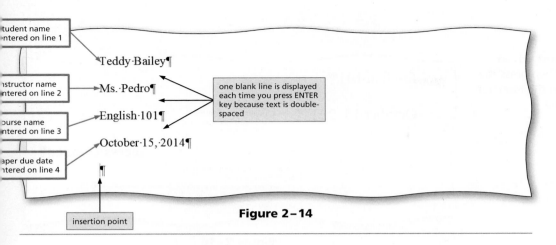

student name entered on line 1

instructor name entered on line 2

course name entered on line 3

paper due date entered on line 4

Teddy·Bailey¶

Ms.·Pedro¶

English·101¶

October·15,·2014¶

one blank line is displayed each time you press ENTER key because text is double-spaced

insertion point

Figure 2–14

To Click and Type

1 CHANGE DOCUMENT SETTINGS | 2 CREATE HEADER | 3 TYPE RESEARCH PAPER WITH CITATIONS
4 CREATE ALPHABETICAL WORKS CITED | 5 PROOFREAD & REVISE RESEARCH PAPER

The next task is to enter the title of the research paper centered between the page margins. In Chapter 1, you used the Center button (HOME tab | Paragraph group) to center text and graphics. As an alternative, if you are using a mouse, you can use Word's Click and Type feature to format and enter text, graphics, and other items. *Why? With **Click and Type**, you can double-click a blank area of the document window and Word automatically formats the item you type or insert according to the location where you double-clicked.* If you are using a mouse, the following steps use Click and Type to center and then type the title of the research paper. If you are using a touch screen, you will use a different method.

- If you are using a touch screen, tap the Center button (HOME tab | Paragraph group) and then proceed to Step 3 because the Click and Type feature does not work with a touch screen.

Experiment

- If you are using a mouse, move the pointer around the document below the entered name and course information and observe the various icons that appear with the I-beam.

- If you are using a mouse, position the pointer in the center of the document at the approximate location for the research paper title until a center icon appears below the I-beam (Figure 2–15).

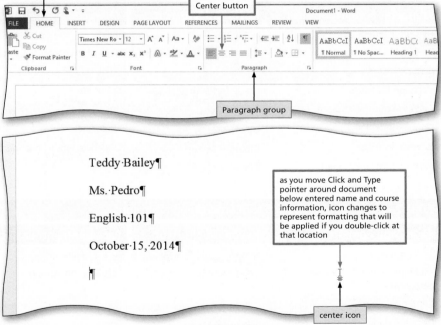

HOME tab

Center button

Document1 - Word

Paragraph group

Teddy·Bailey¶

Ms.·Pedro¶

English·101¶

October·15,·2014¶

¶

as you move Click and Type pointer around document below entered name and course information, icon changes to represent formatting that will be applied if you double-click at that location

center icon

Figure 2–15

Q&A

What are the other icons that appear in the Click and Type pointer?

A left-align icon appears to the right of the I-beam when the Click and Type pointer is in certain locations on the left side of the document window. A right-align icon appears to the left of the I-beam when the Click and Type pointer is in certain locations on the right side of the document window.

- If you are using a mouse, double-click to center the paragraph mark and insertion point between the left and right margins.

3

- Type **Access Granted** as the paper title and then press the ENTER key to position the insertion point on the next line (Figure 2–16).

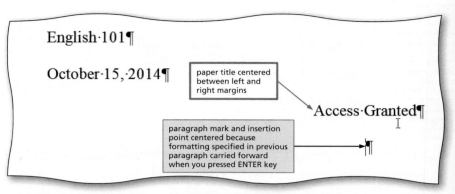

English·101¶

October·15,·2014¶

paper title centered between left and right margins

Access·Granted¶

paragraph mark and insertion point centered because formatting specified in previous paragraph carried forward when you pressed ENTER key

Figure 2–16

Keyboard Shortcuts

Word has many **keyboard shortcuts**, sometimes called shortcut keys or keyboard key combinations, for your convenience while typing. Table 2–1 lists the common keyboard shortcuts for formatting characters. Table 2–2 lists common keyboard shortcuts for formatting paragraphs.

Table 2–1 Keyboard Shortcuts for Formatting Characters

Character Formatting Task	Keyboard Shortcut	Character Formatting Task	Keyboard Shortcut
All capital letters	CTRL+SHIFT+A	Italic	CTRL+I
Bold	CTRL+B	Remove character formatting (plain text)	CTRL+SPACEBAR
Case of letters	SHIFT+F3	Small uppercase letters	CTRL+SHIFT+K
Decrease font size	CTRL+SHIFT+<	Subscript	CTRL+EQUAL SIGN
Decrease font size 1 point	CTRL+[	Superscript	CTRL+SHIFT+PLUS SIGN
Double-underline	CTRL+SHIFT+D	Underline	CTRL+U
Increase font size	CTRL+SHIFT+>	Underline words, not spaces	CTRL+SHIFT+W
Increase font size 1 point	CTRL+]		

Table 2–2 Keyboard Shortcuts for Formatting Paragraphs

Paragraph Formatting	Keyboard Shortcut	Paragraph Formatting	Keyboard Shortcut
1.5 line spacing	CTRL+5	Justify paragraph	CTRL+J
Add/remove one line above paragraph	CTRL+0 (ZERO)	Left-align paragraph	CTRL+L
Center paragraph	CTRL+E	Remove hanging indent	CTRL+SHIFT+T
Decrease paragraph indent	CTRL+SHIFT+M	Remove paragraph formatting	CTRL+Q
Double-space lines	CTRL+2	Right-align paragraph	CTRL+R
Hanging indent	CTRL+T	Single-space lines	CTRL+1
Increase paragraph indent	CTRL+M		

To Format Text Using a Keyboard Shortcut

The paragraphs below the paper title should be left-aligned, instead of centered. Thus, the next step is to left-align the paragraph below the paper title. When your fingers are already on the keyboard, you may prefer using keyboard shortcuts to format text as you type it.

The following step left-aligns a paragraph using the keyboard shortcut CTRL+L. (Recall from Chapter 1 that a notation such as CTRL+L means to press the letter L on the keyboard while holding down the CTRL key.)

1 Press CTRL+L to left-align the current paragraph, that is, the paragraph containing the insertion point (shown in Figure 2–17 on the next page).

Q&A Why would I use a keyboard shortcut instead of the ribbon to format text?
Switching between the mouse and the keyboard takes time. If your hands are already on the keyboard, use a keyboard shortcut. If your hand is on the mouse, use the ribbon.

To Save a Document

You have performed many tasks while creating this research paper and do not want to risk losing work completed thus far. Accordingly, you should save the document. The following steps assume you already have created folders for storing your files, for example, a CIS 101 folder (for your class) that contains a Word folder (for your assignments). Thus, these steps save the document in the Word folder in the CIS 101 folder using the file name, Biometric Devices Paper.

1 Tap or click the Save button on the Quick Access Toolbar, which depending on settings, will display either the Save As gallery in the Backstage view or the Save As dialog box.

2 To save on a hard disk or other storage media on your computer, proceed to Step 2a. To save on SkyDrive, proceed to Step 2b.

2a If your screen opens the Backstage view and you want to save on storage media on your computer, tap or click Computer in the left pane, if necessary, to display options in the right pane related to saving on your computer. If your screen already displays the Save As dialog box, proceed to Step 4.

2b If your screen opens the Backstage view and you want to save on SkyDrive, tap or click SkyDrive in the left pane to display SkyDrive saving options or a Sign In button. If your screen displays a Sign In button, tap or click it and then sign in to SkyDrive.

3 Tap or click the Browse button in the right pane to display the Save As dialog box associated with the selected save location (i.e., Computer or SkyDrive).

4 Type `Biometric Devices Paper` in the File name box to change the file name. Do not press the ENTER key after typing the file name because you do not want to close the dialog box at this time.

5 Navigate to the desired save location (in this case, the Word folder in the CIS 101 folder [or your class folder] on your computer or SkyDrive).

6 Tap or click the Save button (Save As dialog box) to save the research paper in the selected folder on the selected save location with the entered file name.

BTW

Keyboard Shortcuts
To print a complete list of keyboard shortcuts in Word, tap or click the Microsoft Word Help button near the upper-right corner of the Word window, type **keyboard shortcuts** in the 'Search online help' text box at the top of the Word Help window, press the ENTER key, tap or click the Keyboard shortcuts for Microsoft Word link, tap or click the Show All link in the upper-right corner of the Help window, tap or click the Print button in the Help window, and then tap or click the Print button in the Print dialog box.

BTW

Organizing Files and Folders
You should organize and store files in folders so that you easily can find the files later. For example, if you are taking an introductory computer class called CIS 101, a good practice would be to save all Word files in a Word folder in a CIS 101 folder. For a discussion of folders and detailed examples of creating folders, refer to the Office and Windows chapter at the beginning of this book.

To Display the Rulers

According to the MLA documentation style, the first line of each paragraph in the research paper is to be indented one-half inch from the left margin. Although you can use a dialog box to indent paragraphs, Word provides a quicker way through the **horizontal ruler**. This ruler is displayed at the top edge of the document window just below the ribbon. Word also provides a **vertical ruler** that is displayed along the left edge of the Word window. The following step displays the rulers. **Why?** *You want to use the horizontal ruler to indent paragraphs.*

- If necessary, scroll the document so that the research paper title is at the top of the document window.

- Tap or click VIEW on the ribbon to display the VIEW tab.

- If the rulers are not displayed, tap or click the View Ruler check box (VIEW tab | Show group) to place a check mark in the check box and display the horizontal and vertical rulers on the screen (Figure 2–17).

Q&A What tasks can I accomplish using the rulers?
You can use the rulers to indent paragraphs, set tab stops, change page margins, and adjust column widths.

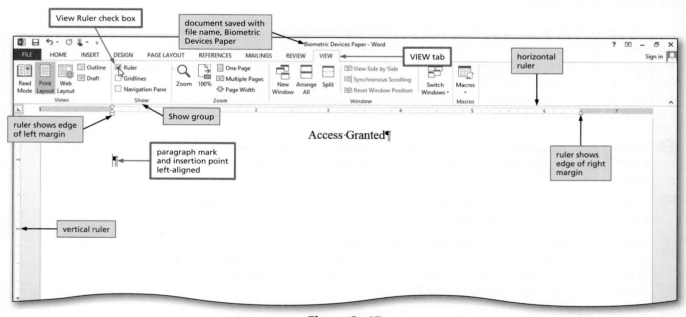

Figure 2–17

To First-Line Indent Paragraphs

If you are using a mouse, you can use the horizontal ruler, usually simply called the **ruler**, to indent just the first line of a paragraph, which is called a **first-line indent**. The left margin on the ruler contains two triangles above a square. The **'First Line Indent' marker** is the top triangle at the 0" mark on the ruler (Figure 2–18). The bottom triangle is discussed later in this chapter. The small square at the 0" mark is the Left Indent marker. The **Left Indent marker** allows you to change the entire left margin, whereas the 'First Line Indent' marker indents only the first line of the paragraph.

The next steps first-line indent paragraphs in the research paper. **Why?** *The first line of each paragraph in the research paper is to be indented one-half inch from the left margin, according to the MLA documentation style.*

1

- If you are using a mouse, with the insertion point on the paragraph mark below the research paper title, point to the 'First Line Indent' marker on the ruler (Figure 2–18).

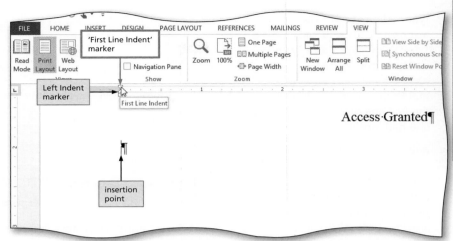

Figure 2–18

2

- If you are using a mouse, drag the 'First Line Indent' marker to the .5" mark on the ruler to display a vertical dotted line in the document window, which indicates the proposed indent location of the first line of the paragraph (Figure 2–19).

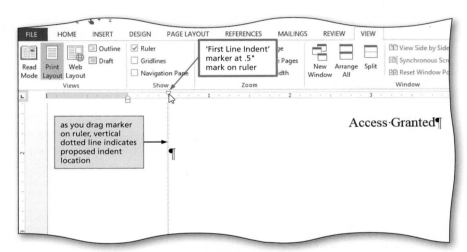

Figure 2–19

3

- If you are using a mouse, release the mouse button to place the 'First Line Indent' marker at the .5" mark on the ruler, or one-half inch from the left margin (Figure 2–20).

- If you are using a touch screen, you cannot drag the 'First Line Indent' marker and must follow these steps instead: tap the Paragraph Settings Dialog Box Launcher (HOME tab or PAGE LAYOUT tab | Paragraph group) to display the Paragraph dialog box, tap the Indents and Spacing tab (Paragraph dialog box), tap the Special arrow, tap First line, and then tap the OK button.

Figure 2–20

- Type **Biometric devices authenticate a person's identity by verifying unique personal characteristics.** and notice that Word automatically indented the first line of the paragraph by one-half inch (Figure 2–21).

Q&A Will I have to set a first-line indent for each paragraph in the paper?
No. Each time you press the ENTER key, paragraph formatting in the previous paragraph carries forward to the next paragraph. Thus, once you set the first-line indent, its format carries forward automatically to each subsequent paragraph you type.

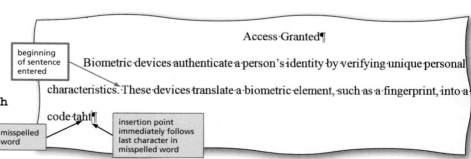

Figure 2–21

Other Ways

1. Tap 'Show Context Menu' button on mini toolbar or right-click paragraph, tap or click Paragraph on shortcut menu, tap or click Indents and Spacing tab (Paragraph dialog box), tap or click Special arrow, tap or click First line, tap or click OK button

2. Tap or click Paragraph Settings Dialog Box Launcher (HOME tab or PAGE LAYOUT tab | Paragraph group), tap or click Indents and Spacing tab (Paragraph dialog box), tap or click Special arrow, tap or click First line, tap or click OK button

To AutoCorrect as You Type

1 CHANGE DOCUMENT SETTINGS | 2 CREATE HEADER | 3 TYPE RESEARCH PAPER WITH CITATIONS
4 CREATE ALPHABETICAL WORKS CITED | 5 PROOFREAD & REVISE RESEARCH PAPER

Word has predefined many commonly misspelled words, which it automatically corrects for you. ***Why?*** *As you type, you may make typing, spelling, capitalization, or grammar errors. Word's **AutoCorrect** feature automatically corrects these kinds of errors as you type them in the document. For example, if you type ahve, Word automatically changes it to the correct spelling, have, when you press the SPACEBAR or a punctuation mark key such as a period or comma.*

The following steps intentionally misspell the word, that, as taht to illustrate the AutoCorrect feature.

1

- Press the SPACEBAR.

- Type the beginning of the next sentence, misspelling the word, that, as follows: **These devices translate a biometric element, such as a fingerprint, into a digital code taht** (Figure 2–22).

Figure 2–22

2

- Press the SPACEBAR and watch Word automatically correct the misspelled word.

- Type the rest of the sentence (Figure 2–23): **is compared with a digital code stored in a computer.**

Figure 2–23

To Use the AutoCorrect Options Button

The following steps illustrate the AutoCorrect Options button and menu. *Why? If you are using a mouse, when you position the pointer on text that Word automatically corrected, a small blue box appears below the text. If you point to the small blue box, Word displays the AutoCorrect Options button. When you tap or click the* **AutoCorrect Options button***, Word displays a menu that allows you to undo a correction or change how Word handles future automatic corrections of this type.* If you are using a touch screen, read these steps without performing them.

- If you are using a mouse, position the pointer in the text automatically corrected by Word (the word, that, in this case) to display a small blue box below the automatically corrected word (Figure 2–24).

Figure 2–24

- Point to the small blue box to display the AutoCorrect Options button.

- Click the AutoCorrect Options button to display the AutoCorrect Options menu (Figure 2–25).

- Press the ESCAPE key to remove the AutoCorrect Options menu from the screen.

Q&A
Do I need to remove the AutoCorrect Options button from the screen?
No. When you move the pointer, the AutoCorrect Options button will disappear from the screen. If, for some reason, you wanted to remove the AutoCorrect Options button from the screen, you could press the ESCAPE key a second time.

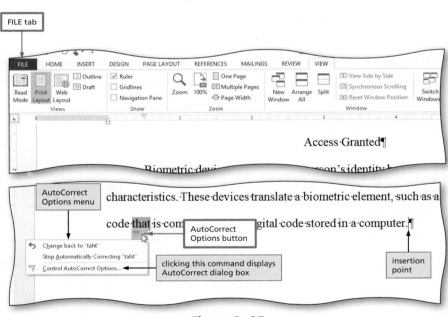

Figure 2–25

To Create an AutoCorrect Entry

The next steps create an AutoCorrect entry. *Why? In addition to the predefined list of AutoCorrect spelling, capitalization, and grammar errors, you can create your own AutoCorrect entries to add to the list. For example, if you tend to mistype the word computer as comptuer, you should create an AutoCorrect entry for it.*

1

- Tap or click FILE on the ribbon (shown in Figure 2–25 on the previous page) to open the Backstage view (Figure 2–26).

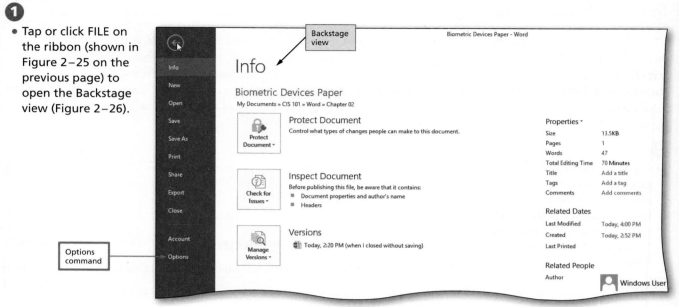

Figure 2–26

2

- Tap or click Options in the Backstage view to display the Word Options dialog box.

- Tap or click Proofing in the left pane (Word Options dialog box) to display proofing options in the right pane.

- Tap or click the AutoCorrect Options button in the right pane to display the AutoCorrect dialog box.

- When Word displays the AutoCorrect dialog box, type **comptuer** in the Replace text box.

- Press the TAB key and then type **computer** in the With text box (Figure 2–27).

Q&A | How would I delete an existing AutoCorrect entry?
You would select the entry to be deleted in the list of defined entries in the AutoCorrect dialog box and then tap or click the Delete button (AutoCorrect dialog box).

Figure 2–27

- Tap or click the Add button (AutoCorrect dialog box) to add the entry alphabetically to the list of words to correct automatically as you type. (If your dialog box displays a Replace button instead, tap or click it and then tap or click the Yes button in the Microsoft Word dialog box to replace the previously defined entry.)

- Tap or click the OK button (AutoCorrect dialog box) to close the dialog box.

- Tap or click the OK button (Word Options dialog box) to close the dialog box.

The AutoCorrect Dialog Box

In addition to creating AutoCorrect entries for words you commonly misspell or mistype, you can create entries for abbreviations, codes, and so on. For example, you could create an AutoCorrect entry for asap, indicating that Word should replace this text with the phrase, as soon as possible.

If, for some reason, you do not want Word to correct automatically as you type, you can turn off the Replace text as you type feature by tapping or clicking Options in the Backstage view, tapping or clicking Proofing in the left pane (Word Options dialog box), tapping or clicking the AutoCorrect Options button in the right pane (Figure 2–27), removing the check mark from the 'Replace text as you type' check box, and then tapping or clicking the OK button in each open dialog box.

The AutoCorrect sheet in the AutoCorrect dialog box (Figure 2–27) contains other check boxes that correct capitalization errors if the check boxes are selected:

- If you type two capital letters in a row, such as TH, Word makes the second letter lowercase, Th.

- If you begin a sentence with a lowercase letter, Word capitalizes the first letter of the sentence.

- If you type the name of a day in lowercase letters, such as tuesday, Word capitalizes the first letter in the name of the day, Tuesday.

- If you leave the CAPS LOCK key on and begin a new sentence, such as aFTER, Word corrects the typing, After, and turns off the CAPS LOCK key.

If you do not want Word to automatically perform any of these corrections, simply remove the check mark from the appropriate check box in the AutoCorrect dialog box.

Sometimes you do not want Word to AutoCorrect a particular word or phrase. For example, you may use the code WD. in your documents. Because Word automatically capitalizes the first letter of a sentence, the character you enter following the period will be capitalized (in the previous sentence, it would capitalize the letter i in the word, in). To allow the code WD. to be entered into a document and still leave the AutoCorrect feature turned on, you would set an exception. To set an exception to an AutoCorrect rule, tap or click Options in the Backstage view, tap or click Proofing in the left pane (Word Options dialog box), tap or click the AutoCorrect Options button in the right pane, tap or click the Exceptions button (Figure 2–27), tap or click the appropriate tab in the AutoCorrect Exceptions dialog box, type the exception entry in the text box, tap or click the Add button, tap or click the Close button (AutoCorrect Exceptions dialog box), and then tap or click the OK button in each of the remaining dialog boxes.

BTW
Automatic Corrections
If you do not want to keep a change automatically made by Word and you immediately notice the automatic correction, you can undo the change by clicking the Undo button on the Quick Access Toolbar or pressing CTRL+Z. You also can undo a correction through the AutoCorrect Options button, which was shown on page WD 85.

BTW
Touch Screen Differences
The Office and Windows interfaces may vary if you are using a touch screen. For this reason, you might notice that the function or appearance of your touch screen differs slightly from this chapter's presentation.

To Enter More Text

The next task is to continue typing text in the research paper up to the location of the in-text parenthetical reference. The following steps enter this text.

1 With the insertion point positioned at the end of the first paragraph in the paper, as shown in Figure 2–25 on page WD 85, press the SPACEBAR and then type these two sentences, intentionally misspelling the word readers as raders: `If the digital code in the computer matches the personal characteristic code, the computer grants access. Examples of biometric devices include fingerprint raders and face recognition systems.`

Q&A Why is the word, readers, misspelled?
Later in this chapter, you will use Word's check spelling and grammar at once feature to check the entire document for errors.

2 Press the ENTER key to start a new paragraph.

3 Type `A fingerprint reader, or scanner, captures curves and indentations of a fingerprint. Organizations use fingerprint readers to secure doors, computers, and software. For example, a fingerprint reader can be set up to authenticate users before they can access a computer` and then press the SPACEBAR (Figure 2–28).

BTW
Spacing after Punctuation
Because word processing documents use variable character fonts, it often is difficult to determine in a printed document how many times someone has pressed the SPACEBAR between sentences. Thus, the rule is to press the SPACEBAR only once after periods, colons, and other punctuation marks.

Figure 2–28

Citations

Both the MLA and APA guidelines suggest the use of in-text parenthetical references (placed at the end of a sentence), instead of footnoting each source of material in a paper. These parenthetical references, called citations in Word, guide the reader to the end of the paper for complete information about the source.

Word provides tools to assist you with inserting citations in a paper and later generating a list of sources from the citations. With a documentation style selected, Word automatically formats the citations and list of sources according to that style. The process for adding citations in Word is as follows:

1. Modify the documentation style, if necessary.
2. Insert a citation placeholder.
3. Enter the source information for the citation.

You can combine Steps 2 and 3, where you insert the citation placeholder and enter the source information at once. Or, you can insert the citation placeholder as you write and then enter the source information for the citation at a later time. While creating the research paper in this chapter, you will use both methods.

BTW
BTWs
For a complete list of the BTWs found in the margins of this book, visit the BTW resource on the Student Companion Site located on www.cengagebrain.com. For detailed instructions about accessing available resources, visit www.cengage.com/ct/studentdownload or contact your instructor for information about accessing the required files.

To Change the Bibliography Style

The first step in inserting a citation is to be sure the citations and sources will be formatted using the correct documentation style, called the bibliography style in Word. **Why?** *You want to ensure that Word is using the MLA documentation style for this paper.* The following steps change the specified documentation style.

1

- Tap or click REFERENCES on the ribbon to display the REFERENCES tab.

- Tap or click the Bibliography Style arrow (REFERENCES tab | Citations & Bibliography group) to display the Bibliography Style gallery, which lists predefined documentation styles (Figure 2–29).

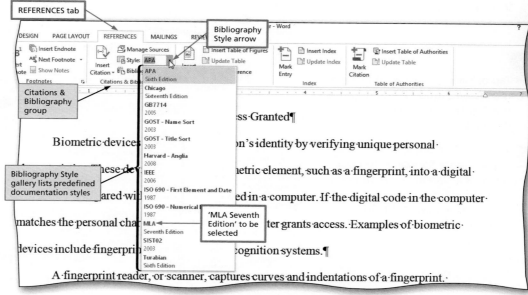

Figure 2–29

2

- Tap or click 'MLA Seventh Edition' in the Bibliography Style gallery to change the documentation style to MLA.

 Q&A What if I am using a different edition of a documentation style shown in the Bibliography Style gallery?
Select the closest one and then, if necessary, perform necessary edits before submitting the paper.

What details are required for sources?

During your research, be sure to record essential publication information about each of your sources. Following is a sample list of types of required information for the MLA documentation style.

- Book: full name of author(s), complete title of book, edition (if available), volume (if available), publication city, publisher name, publication year, and publication medium

- Magazine: full name of author(s), complete title of article, magazine title, issue number (if available), date of magazine, page numbers of article, publication medium, and date viewed (if medium is a website)

- Website: full name of author(s), title of website, website publisher or sponsor (if none, write N.p.), publication date (if none, write n.d.), publication medium, and date viewed

CONSIDER THIS

To Insert a Citation and Create Its Source

With the documentation style selected, the next task is to insert a citation at the location of the insertion point and enter the source information for the citation. You can accomplish these steps at once by instructing Word to add a new source. The steps on the next page add a new source for a magazine (periodical) article on the web. **Why?** *The material preceding the insertion point was summarized from an online magazine article.*

1

- Tap or click the Insert Citation button (REFERENCES tab | Citations & Bibliography group) to display the Insert Citation menu (Figure 2–30).

Figure 2–30

2

- Tap or click 'Add New Source' on the Insert Citation menu to display the Create Source dialog box (Figure 2–31).

Q&A What are the Bibliography Fields in the Create Source dialog box? A **field** is a placeholder for data whose contents can change. You enter data in some fields; Word supplies data for others. In this case, you enter the contents of the fields for a particular source, for example, the author name in the Author field.

Figure 2–31

Experiment

- Tap or click the 'Type of Source' arrow and then tap or click one of the source types in the list, so that you can see how the list of fields changes to reflect the type of source you selected.

3

- If necessary, tap or click the 'Type of Source' arrow (Create Source dialog box) and then tap or click 'Article in a Periodical', so that the list shows fields required for a magazine (periodical).

- Tap or click the Author text box. Type **Rossi, Marcell Enrico** as the author.

- Tap or click the Title text box. Type **Understanding How to Use Fingerprint Readers** as the article title.

- Press the TAB key and then type **Digital Security Review** as the periodical title.

- Press the TAB key and then type **2014** as the year.

- Press the TAB key and then type **Aug.** as the month.

- Press the TAB key twice and then type **n. pag.** as the number of pages.

- Press the TAB key and then type **Web** as the medium (Figure 2–32).

Figure 2–32

Q&A Why is the month abbreviated? The MLA documentation style abbreviates all months, except May, June, and July, when they appear in a source.

What does the n. pag. entry mean in the Pages text box? The MLA documentation style uses the abbreviation n. pag. for no pagination, which indicates the source has no page references. This is common for web sources.

4

- Place a check mark in the 'Show All Bibliography Fields' check box so that Word displays all fields available for the selected source, including the date viewed (accessed) fields.

- If necessary, scroll to the bottom of the Bibliography Fields list to display the date viewed (accessed) fields.

- Tap or click the Year Accessed text box. Type **2014** as the year.

- Press the TAB key and then type **Oct.** as the month accessed.

- Press the TAB key and then type **3** as the day accessed (Figure 2–33).

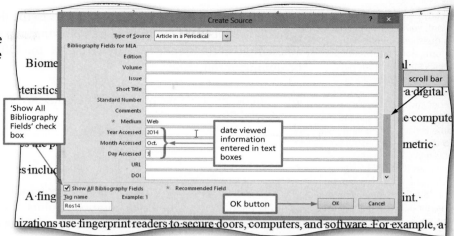

Figure 2–33

What if some of the text boxes disappear as I enter the fields?

With the 'Show All Bibliography Fields' check box selected, the dialog box may not be able to display all fields at the same time. In this case, some may scroll up off the screen.

5

- Tap or click the OK button to close the dialog box, create the source, and insert the citation in the document at the location of the insertion point.

- Press the END key to move the insertion point to the end of the line, which also deselects the citation.

- Press the PERIOD key to end the sentence (Figure 2–34).

Figure 2–34

To Enter More Text

The next task is to continue typing text in the research paper up to the location of the footnote. The following steps enter this text.

1 Press the SPACEBAR.

2 Type the next sentences (Figure 2–35): **External fingerprint readers usually plug into a USB port. To save on desk space, some laptops include built-in fingerprint readers.**

Figure 2–35

To Save an Existing Document with the Same File Name

You have made several modifications to the document since you last saved it. Thus, you should save it again. The following step saves the document again. For an example of the step listed below, refer to the Office and Windows chapter at the beginning of this book.

1 Tap or click the Save button on the Quick Access Toolbar to overwrite the previously saved file.

Footnotes

As discussed earlier in this chapter, notes are optional in the MLA documentation style. If used, content notes elaborate on points discussed in the paper, and bibliographic notes direct the reader to evaluations of statements in a source or provide a means for identifying multiple sources. The MLA documentation style specifies that a superscript (raised number) be used for a **note reference mark** to signal that a note exists either at the bottom of the page as a **footnote** or at the end of the document as an **endnote**.

In Word, **note text** can be any length and format. Word automatically numbers notes sequentially by placing a note reference mark both in the body of the document and to the left of the note text. If you insert, rearrange, or remove notes, Word renumbers any subsequent note reference marks according to their new sequence in the document.

To Insert a Footnote Reference Mark

1 CHANGE DOCUMENT SETTINGS | 2 CREATE HEADER | 3 TYPE RESEARCH PAPER WITH CITATIONS
4 CREATE ALPHABETICAL WORKS CITED | 5 PROOFREAD & REVISE RESEARCH PAPER

The following step inserts a footnote reference mark in the document at the location of the insertion point and at the location where the footnote text will be typed. *Why? You will insert a content note elaborating on fingerprint reader functions, which you want to position as a footnote.*

- With the insertion point positioned as shown in Figure 2–35 on the previous page, tap or click the Insert Footnote button (REFERENCES tab | Footnotes group) to display a note reference mark (a superscripted 1) in two places: (1) in the document window at the location of the insertion point and (2) at the bottom of the page where the footnote will be positioned, just below a separator line (Figure 2–36).

Q&A What if I wanted notes to be positioned as endnotes instead of as footnotes?
You would tap or click the Insert Endnote button (REFERENCES tab | Footnotes group), which places the separator line and the endnote text at the end of the document, instead of the bottom of the page containing the reference.

Insert Footnote button

Insert Endnote button

REFERENCES tab

Biometric Devices Paper - Word

INSERT DESIGN PAGE LAYOUT REFERENCES MAILINGS REVIEW VIEW

Insert Endnote
Next Footnote
Show Notes
Insert Footnote

Manage Sources
Style: MLA
Bibliography
Insert Citation

Insert Table of Figures
Update Table
Cross-reference
Insert Caption

Mark Entry
Insert Index
Update Index

Mark Citation
Insert Ta
Update

Footnotes Citations & Bibliography Captions Index Table of Aut

Footnotes group

include built-in fingerprint readers

note reference mark is displayed, by default, superscripted in document window and in note text area

separator line, which automatically is inserted, divides document text from note text

footnote text will be typed here

Figure 2–36

Other Ways

1. Press ALT+CTRL+F

To Enter Footnote Text

The following step types the footnote text to the right of the note reference mark below the separator line.

1 Type the footnote text up to the citation (shown in Figure 2–37): **Nadeer and White state that fingerprint readers can perform different functions for different fingers; for example, one finger runs a program and another finger shuts down the computer** and then press the SPACEBAR.

To Insert a Citation Placeholder

1 CHANGE DOCUMENT SETTINGS | 2 CREATE HEADER | 3 TYPE RESEARCH PAPER WITH CITATIONS
4 CREATE ALPHABETICAL WORKS CITED | 5 PROOFREAD & REVISE RESEARCH PAPER

Earlier in this chapter, you inserted a citation and its source at once. In Word, you also can insert a citation without entering the source information. *Why? Sometimes, you may not have the source information readily available and would prefer to enter it at a later time.*

The following steps insert a citation placeholder in the footnote, so that you can enter the source information later.

1

• With the insertion point positioned as shown in Figure 2–37, tap or click the Insert Citation button (REFERENCES tab | Citations & Bibliography group) to display the Insert Citation menu (Figure 2–37).

Figure 2–37

2

• Tap or click 'Add New Placeholder' on the Insert Citation menu to display the Placeholder Name dialog box.

• Type **Nadeer** as the tag name for the source (Figure 2–38).

Q&A What is a tag name?
A tag name is an identifier that links a citation to a source. Word automatically creates a tag name when you enter a source. When you create a citation placeholder, enter a meaningful tag name, which will appear in the citation placeholder until you edit the source.

Figure 2–38

• Tap or click the OK button (Placeholder Name dialog box) to close the dialog box and insert the entered tag name in the citation placeholder in the document (shown in Figure 2–39).

• Press the PERIOD key to end the sentence.

Q&A
What if the citation is in the wrong location?
Tap or click the citation to select it and then drag the citation tab (on the upper-left corner of the selected citation) to any location in the document.

Footnote Text Style

If you are using your finger on a touch screen and are having difficulty completing the steps in this chapter, consider using a stylus. Many people find it easier to be precise with a stylus than with a finger. In addition, with a stylus you see the pointer. If you still are having trouble completing the steps with a stylus, try using a mouse.

When you insert a footnote, Word formats it using the Footnote Text style, which does not adhere to the MLA documentation style. For example, notice in Figure 2–37 on the previous page that the footnote text is single-spaced, left-aligned, and a smaller font size than the text in the research paper. According to the MLA documentation style, notes should be formatted like all other paragraphs in the paper.

You could change the paragraph formatting of the footnote text to first-line indent and double-spacing and then change the font size from 10 to 12 point. If you use this technique, however, you will need to change the format of the footnote text for each footnote you enter into the document.

A more efficient technique is to modify the format of the Footnote Text style so that every footnote you enter in the document will use the formats defined in this style.

To Modify a Style Using a Shortcut Menu

1 CHANGE DOCUMENT SETTINGS | 2 CREATE HEADER | 3 TYPE RESEARCH PAPER WITH CITATIONS
4 CREATE ALPHABETICAL WORKS CITED | 5 PROOFREAD & REVISE RESEARCH PAPER

The Footnote Text style specifies left-aligned single-spaced paragraphs with a 10-point font size for text. The following steps modify the Footnote Text style. *Why? To meet MLA documentation style, the footnotes should be double-spaced with a first line indent and a 12-point font size for text.*

1

• If you are using a touch screen, press and hold the note text in the footnote and then tap the 'Show Context Menu' button on the mini toolbar; if you are using a mouse, right-click the note text in the footnote to display a shortcut menu related to footnotes (Figure 2–39).

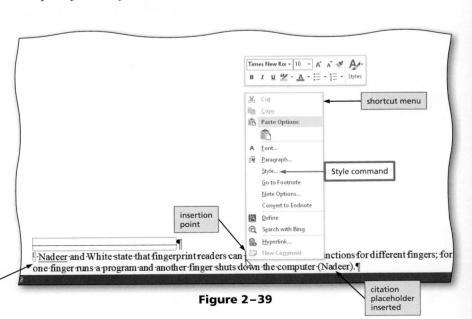

Figure 2–39

2

- Tap or click Style on the shortcut menu to display the Style dialog box. If necessary, tap or click the Category arrow, tap or click All styles in the Category list, and then tap or click Footnote Text in the Styles list to select the style to modify.

- Tap or click the Modify button (Style dialog box) to display the Modify Style dialog box.

- Tap or click the Font Size arrow (Modify Style dialog box) to display the Font Size list and then tap or click 12 in the Font Size list to change the font size.

- Tap or click the Double Space button to change the line spacing.

- Tap or click the Format button to display the Format menu (Figure 2–40).

Figure 2–40

3

- Tap or click Paragraph on the Format menu (Modify Style dialog box) to display the Paragraph dialog box.

- Tap or click the Special arrow (Paragraph dialog box) and then tap or click First line (Figure 2–41).

Figure 2–41

- Tap or click the OK button (Paragraph dialog box) to close the dialog box.

- Tap or click the OK button (Modify Style dialog box) to close the dialog box.

- Tap or click the Apply button (Style dialog box) to apply the style changes to the footnote text (Figure 2–42).

Figure 2–42

Q&A Will all footnotes use this modified style?
Yes. Any future footnotes entered in the document will use a 12-point font with the paragraphs first-line indented and double-spaced.

Other Ways

1. Tap or click Styles Dialog Box Launcher (HOME tab | Styles group), tap or point to style name in list, tap or click style name arrow, tap or click Modify, change settings (Modify Style dialog box), tap or click OK button

2. Tap or click Styles Dialog Box Launcher (HOME tab | Styles group), tap or click Manage Styles button in task pane, select style name in list, tap or click Modify button (Manage Styles dialog box), change settings (Modify Style dialog box), tap or click OK button in each dialog box

To Edit a Source

1 CHANGE DOCUMENT SETTINGS | 2 CREATE HEADER | 3 TYPE RESEARCH PAPER WITH CITATIONS
4 CREATE ALPHABETICAL WORKS CITED | 5 PROOFREAD & REVISE RESEARCH PAPER

When you typed the footnote text for this research paper, you inserted a citation placeholder for the source. The following steps edit a source. ***Why?*** *Assume you now have the source information and are ready to enter it.*

- Tap or click somewhere in the citation placeholder to be edited, in this case (Nadeer), to select the citation placeholder.

- Tap or click the Citation Options arrow to display the Citation Options menu (Figure 2–43).

Figure 2–43

Q&A What is the purpose of the tab to the left of the selected citation?
If, for some reason, you wanted to move a citation to a different location in the document, you would select the citation and then drag the citation tab to the desired location.

2

- Tap or click Edit Source on the Citation Options menu to display the Edit Source dialog box.

- If necessary, tap or click the 'Type of Source' arrow (Edit Source dialog box) and then tap or click Book, so that the list shows fields required for a book.

- Because this source has two authors, tap or click the Edit button to display the Edit Name dialog box, which assists you with entering multiple author names.

- Type **Nadeer** as the first author's last name; press the TAB key and then type **Aisha** as the first name; press the TAB key and then type **Sati** as the middle name (Figure 2–44).

Q&A What if I already know how to punctuate the author entry properly?
You can enter the name directly in the Author box.

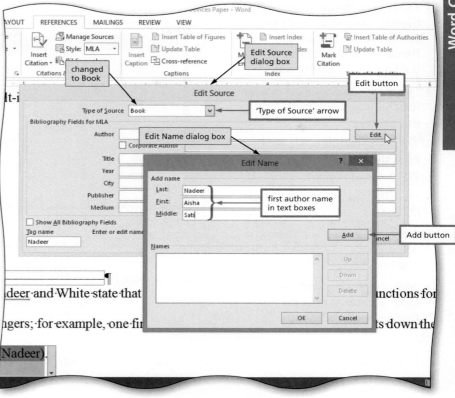

Figure 2–44

3

- Tap or click the Add button (Edit Name dialog box) to add the first author name to the Names list.

- Type **White** as the second author's last name; press the TAB key and then type **Jonathon** as the first name; press the TAB key and then type **Richard** as the middle name.

- Tap or click the Add button to add the second author name to the Names list (Figure 2–45).

Figure 2–45

- Tap or click the OK button (Edit Name dialog box) to add the author names that appear in the Names list to the Author box in the Edit Source dialog box.

- Tap or click the Title text box (Edit Source dialog box). Type **Biometric Security** as the book title.

- Press the TAB key and then type **2014** as the year.

- Press the TAB key and then type **Chicago** as the city.

- Press the TAB key and then type **Windy City Press** as the publisher.

- Press the TAB key and then type **Print** as the medium (Figure 2–46).

Figure 2–46

- Tap or click the OK button to close the dialog box, create the source, and update the citation to display both author last names (shown in Figure 2–47).

Other Ways

1. Tap or click Manage Sources button (REFERENCES tab | Citations & Bibliography group), tap or click placeholder source in Current List, tap or click Edit button (Source Manager dialog box)

To Edit a Citation

1 CHANGE DOCUMENT SETTINGS | 2 CREATE HEADER | **3 TYPE RESEARCH PAPER WITH CITATIONS**
4 CREATE ALPHABETICAL WORKS CITED | **5 PROOFREAD & REVISE RESEARCH PAPER**

In the MLA documentation style, if a source has page numbers, you should include them in the citation. Thus, Word provides a means to enter the page numbers to be displayed in the citation. Also, if you reference the author's name in the text, you should not list it again in the parenthetical citation. Instead, just list the page number(s) in the citation. To do this, you instruct Word to suppress author and title. **Why?** *If you suppress the author, Word automatically displays the title, so you need to suppress both the author and title if you want just the page number(s) to be displayed.* The following steps edit the citation, suppressing the author and title but displaying the page numbers.

- If necessary, tap or click somewhere in the citation to be edited, in this case somewhere in (Nadeer and White), which selects the citation and displays the Citation Options arrow.

- Tap or click the Citation Options arrow to display the Citation Options menu (Figure 2–47).

Figure 2–47

- Tap or click Edit Citation on the Citation Options menu to display the Edit Citation dialog box.
- Type **62-63** in the Pages text box (Edit Citation dialog box).
- Tap or click the Author check box to place a check mark in it.
- Tap or click the Title check box to place a check mark in it (Figure 2–48).

Figure 2–48

- Tap or click the OK button to close the dialog box, remove the author names from the citation in the footnote, suppress the title from showing, and add page numbers to the citation.
- Press the END key to move the insertion point to the end of the line, which also deselects the citation (Figure 2–49).

Figure 2–49

Working with Footnotes and Endnotes

You edit footnote text just as you edit any other text in the document. To delete or move a note reference mark, however, the insertion point must be in the document text (not in the footnote text).

To delete a note, select the note reference mark in the document text (not in the footnote text) by dragging through the note reference mark and then tap or click the Cut button (HOME tab | Clipboard group). Or, tap or click immediately to the right of the note reference mark in the document text and then press the BACKSPACE key twice, or tap or click immediately to the left of the note reference mark in the document text and then press the DELETE key twice.

To move a note to a different location in a document, select the note reference mark in the document text (not in the footnote text), tap or click the Cut button (HOME tab | Clipboard group), tap or click the location where you want to move the note, and then tap or click the Paste button (HOME tab | Clipboard group). When you move or delete notes, Word automatically renumbers any remaining notes in the correct sequence.

If you are using a mouse and position the pointer on the note reference mark in the document text, the note text is displayed above the note reference mark as a ScreenTip. To remove the ScreenTip, move the pointer.

If, for some reason, you wanted to change the format of note reference marks in footnotes or endnotes (i.e., from 1, 2, 3, to A, B, C), you would tap or click the Footnote & Endnote Dialog Box Launcher (REFERENCES tab | Footnotes group) to display the Footnote and Endnote dialog box, tap or click the Number format arrow (Footnote and Endnote dialog box), tap or click the desired number format in the list, and then tap or click the Apply button.

If, for some reason, you wanted to change a footnote number, you would tap or click the Footnote & Endnote Dialog Box Launcher (REFERENCES tab | Footnotes group) to display the Footnote and Endnote dialog box, enter the desired number in the Start at box, and then tap or click the Apply button (Footnote and Endnote dialog box).

If, for some reason, you wanted to convert footnotes to endnotes, you would tap or click the Footnote & Endnote Dialog Box Launcher (REFERENCES tab | Footnotes group) to display the Footnote and Endnote dialog box, tap or click the

BTW
Footnote and Endnote Location
You can change the location of footnotes from the bottom of the page to the end of the text by tapping or clicking the Footnote & Endnote Dialog Box Launcher (REFERENCES tab | Footnotes group), tapping or clicking the Footnotes arrow (Footnote and Endnote dialog box), and then tapping or clicking Below text. Similarly, tapping or clicking the Endnotes arrow (Footnote and Endnote dialog box) enables you to change the location of endnotes from the end of the document to the end of a section.

Convert button (Footnote and Endnote dialog box), select the 'Convert all footnotes to endnotes' option button, tap or click the OK button, and then tap or click the Close button (Footnote and Endnote dialog box).

To Enter More Text

The next task is to continue typing text in the body of the research paper. The following steps enter this text.

1 Position the insertion point after the note reference mark in the document and then press the ENTER key.

2 Type the first three sentences in the third paragraph of the research paper (shown in Figure 2–50): `A face recognition system captures a live face image and compares it with a stored image to determine if the person is a legitimate user. Some buildings use face recognition systems to secure access to rooms. Law enforcement, surveillance systems, and airports use face recognition systems to protect the public.`

To Count Words

1 CHANGE DOCUMENT SETTINGS | 2 CREATE HEADER | 3 TYPE RESEARCH PAPER WITH CITATIONS
4 CREATE ALPHABETICAL WORKS CITED | 5 PROOFREAD & REVISE RESEARCH PAPER

Often when you write papers, you are required to compose the papers with a minimum number of words. The minimum requirement for the research paper in this chapter is 275 words. You can look on the status bar and see the total number of words thus far in a document. For example, Figure 2–50 shows the research paper has 214 words, but you are not sure if that count includes the words in your footnote. The following steps display the Word Count dialog box. **Why?** *You want to verify that the footnote text is included in the count.*

1
- Tap or click the Word Count indicator on the status bar to display the Word Count dialog box.
- If necessary, place a check mark in the 'Include textboxes, footnotes and endnotes' check box (Word Count dialog box) (Figure 2–50).

Q&A | Why do the statistics in my Word Count dialog box differ from those in Figure 2–50?
Depending on the accuracy of your typing, your statistics may differ.

Figure 2–50

2

- Tap or click the Close button to close the dialog box.

Q&A Can I display statistics for just a section of the document?
Yes. Select the section and then click the Word Count indicator on the status bar to display statistics about the selected text.

Other Ways

1. Tap or click Word Count button (REVIEW tab | Proofing group) 2. Press CTRL+SHIFT+G

Automatic Page Breaks

As you type documents that exceed one page, Word automatically inserts page breaks, called **automatic page breaks** or **soft page breaks**, when it determines the text has filled one page according to paper size, margin settings, line spacing, and other settings. If you add text, delete text, or modify text on a page, Word recalculates the location of automatic page breaks and adjusts them accordingly.

Word performs page recalculation between the keystrokes, that is, in between the pauses in your typing. Thus, Word refers to the automatic page break task as **background repagination**. An automatic page break will occur in the next set of steps.

To Enter More Text and Insert a Citation Placeholder

The next task is to type the remainder of the third paragraph in the body of the research paper. The following steps enter this text and a citation placeholder at the end of the paragraph.

1 With the insertion point positioned at the end of the third sentence in the third paragraph, as shown in Figure 2–50, press the SPACEBAR.

2 Type the rest of the third paragraph: `Some mobile devices use face recognition systems to unlock the device. Face recognition systems are becoming more sophisticated and can recognize people with or without glasses, hats, facial hair, makeup, or jewelry, and with new hairstyles` and then press the SPACEBAR.

Q&A Why does the text move from the second page to the first page as I am typing?
Word, by default, will not allow the first line of a paragraph to be by itself at the bottom of a page (an **orphan**) or the last line of a paragraph to be by itself at the top of a page (a **widow**). As you type, Word adjusts the placement of the paragraph to avoid orphans and widows.

3 Tap or click the Insert Citation button (REFERENCES tab | Citations & Bibliography group) to display the Insert Citation menu. Tap or click 'Add New Placeholder' on the Insert Citation menu to display the Placeholder Name dialog box.

4 Type `Allensmith` as the tag name for the source.

5 Tap or click the OK button to close the dialog box and insert the tag name in the citation placeholder.

6 Press the PERIOD key to end the sentence.

BTW

Page Break Locations
As you type, your page break may occur at different locations depending on Word settings and the type of printer connected to the computer.

To Hide and Show White Space

With the page break and header, it is difficult to see the entire third paragraph at once on the screen. With the screen in Print Layout view, you can hide white space, which is the space that is displayed at the top and bottom of pages (including headers and footers) and also the space between pages. The following steps hide white space, if your screen displays it, and then shows white space. *Why? You want to see the as much of the third paragraph as possible at once, which spans the bottom of the first page and the top of the second page.*

1

- If you are using a mouse, position the pointer in the document window in the space between pages so that the pointer changes to a 'Hide White Space' button (Figure 2–51).

2

- If you are using a touch screen, double-tap in the space between pages; if you are using a mouse, double-click while the pointer is a 'Hide White Space' button to hide white space.

Figure 2–51

Q&A Does hiding white space have any effect on the printed document?
No.

3

- If you are using a mouse, position the pointer in the document window on the page break between pages so that the pointer changes to a 'Show White Space' button (Figure 2–52).

4

- If you are using a touch screen, double-tap the page break; if you are using a mouse, double-click while the pointer is a 'Show White Space' button to show white space.

Figure 2–52

Other Ways

1. Tap or click FILE on ribbon, tap or click Options in Backstage view, tap or click Display in left pane (Word Options dialog box), remove or select check mark from 'Show white space between pages in Print Layout view' check box, tap or click OK button

To Edit a Source

When you typed the third paragraph of the research paper, you inserted a citation placeholder, Allensmith, for the source. You now have the source information, which is for a website, and are ready to enter it. The following steps edit the source for the Allensmith citation placeholder.

1 Tap or click somewhere in the citation placeholder to be edited, in this case (Allensmith), to select the citation placeholder.

2 Tap or click the Citation Options arrow to display the Citation Options menu.

3 Tap or click Edit Source on the Citation Options menu to display the Edit Source dialog box.

4 If necessary, tap or click the Type of Source arrow (Edit Source dialog box); scroll to and then click Web site, so that the list shows fields required for a Web site.

5 Place a check mark in the 'Show All Bibliography Fields' check box to display more fields related to Web sites.

6 Tap or click the Author text box. Type `Allensmith, Samantha Clare` as the author.

7 Tap or click the Name of Web Page text box. Type `Understanding Face Recognition Systems` as the webpage name.

8 Tap or click the Production Company text box. Type `Course Technology` as the production company.

9 Tap or click the Year Accessed text box. Type `2014` as the year accessed (Figure 2–53).

10 Press the TAB key and then type `Sept.` as the month accessed.

11 Press the TAB key and then type `16` as the day accessed.

12 Press the TAB key and then type `Web` as the Medium.

Q&A Do I need to enter a web address (URL)?
The latest MLA documentation style update does not require the web address in the source.

13 Tap or click the OK button to close the dialog box and create the source.

BTW

Q&As
For a complete list of the Q&As found in many of the step-by-step sequences in this book, visit the Q&A resource on the Student Companion Site located on www.cengagebrain.com. For detailed instructions about accessing available resources, visit www.cengage.com/ct/studentdownload or contact your instructor for information about accessing the required files.

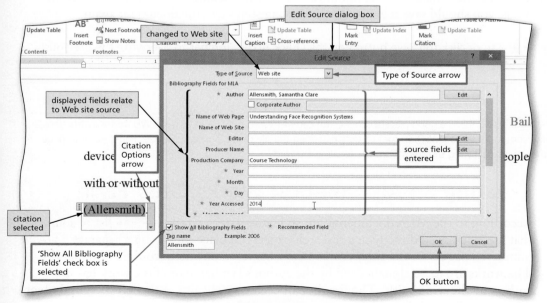

Figure 2–53

BTW
Printing Document Properties
To print document properties, tap or click FILE on the ribbon to open the Backstage view, tap or click the Print tab in the Backstage view to display the Print gallery, tap or click the first button in the Settings area to display a list of options specifying what you can print, tap or click Document Info in the list to specify you want to print the document properties instead of the actual document, and then tap or click the Print button in the Print gallery to print the document properties on the currently selected printer.

To Enter More Text

The next task is to type the last paragraph of text in the research paper. The following steps enter this text.

1 Press the END key to position the insertion point at the end of the third paragraph and then press the ENTER key.

2 Type the last paragraph of the research paper (Figure 2–54): **Home and occupational users alike are using biometric security. Through a biometric element, such as a fingerprint, devices can deny or grant access to programs, devices, computers, rooms, and other locations. Biometric devices are an effective security technology.**

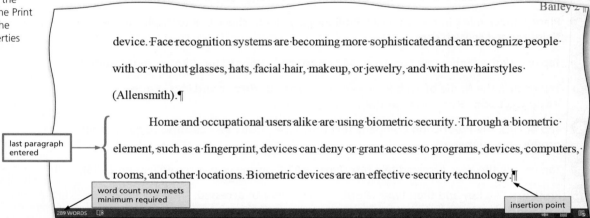

device. Face recognition systems are becoming more sophisticated and can recognize people with or without glasses, hats, facial hair, makeup, or jewelry, and with new hairstyles (Allensmith).¶

Home and occupational users alike are using biometric security. Through a biometric element, such as a fingerprint, devices can deny or grant access to programs, devices, computers, rooms, and other locations. Biometric devices are an effective security technology.¶

Bailey 2

last paragraph entered

word count now meets minimum required

289 WORDS

insertion point

Figure 2–54

To Save an Existing Document with the Same File Name

You have made several modifications to the document since you last saved it. Thus, you should save it again. The following step saves the document again.

1 Tap or click the Save button on the Quick Access Toolbar to overwrite the previously saved file.

Break Point: If you wish to take a break, this is a good place to do so. You can exit Word now (refer to page WD 46 for instructions). To resume at a later time, run Word (refer to page WD 46 for instructions), open the file called Biometric Devices Paper (refer to page WD 47 for instructions), and continue following the steps from this location forward.

Creating an Alphabetical Works Cited Page

According to the MLA documentation style, the **works cited page** is a list of sources that are referenced directly in a research paper. You place the list on a separate numbered page with the title, Works Cited, centered one inch from the top margin. The works are to be alphabetized by the author's last name or, if the work has no author, by the work's title. The first line of each entry begins at the left margin. Indent subsequent lines of the same entry one-half inch from the left margin.

What is a bibliography?

A **bibliography** is an alphabetical list of sources referenced in a paper. Whereas the text of the research paper contains brief references to the source (the citations), the bibliography lists all publication information about the source. Documentation styles differ significantly in their guidelines for preparing a bibliography. Each style identifies formats for various sources, including books, magazines, pamphlets, newspapers, websites, television programs, paintings, maps, advertisements, letters, memos, and much more. You can find information about various styles and their guidelines in printed style guides and on the web.

To Page Break Manually

1 CHANGE DOCUMENT SETTINGS | 2 CREATE HEADER | 3 TYPE RESEARCH PAPER WITH CITATIONS
4 CREATE ALPHABETICAL WORKS CITED | 5 PROOFREAD & REVISE RESEARCH PAPER

The next step is to insert a manual page break following the body of the research paper. *Why? According to the MLA documentation style, the works cited are to be displayed on a separate numbered page.*

A **manual page break**, or **hard page break**, is one that you force into the document at a specific location. Word never moves or adjusts manual page breaks. Word, however, does adjust any automatic page breaks that follow a manual page break. Word inserts manual page breaks immediately above or to the left of the location of the insertion point. The following step inserts a manual page break after the text of the research paper.

1

- Verify that the insertion point is positioned at the end of the text of the research paper, as shown in Figure 2–54.

- Tap or click INSERT on the ribbon to display the INSERT tab.

- Tap or click the 'Insert a Page Break' button (INSERT tab | Pages group) to insert a manual page break immediately to the left of the insertion point and position the insertion point immediately below the manual page break (Figure 2–55).

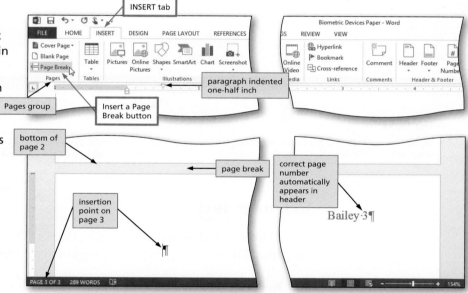

Figure 2–55

Other Ways

1. Press CTRL+ENTER

To Apply a Style

1 CHANGE DOCUMENT SETTINGS | 2 CREATE HEADER | 3 TYPE RESEARCH PAPER WITH CITATIONS
4 CREATE ALPHABETICAL WORKS CITED | 5 PROOFREAD & REVISE RESEARCH PAPER

The works cited title is to be centered between the margins of the paper. If you simply issue the Center command, the title will not be centered properly. *Why? It will be to the right of the center point because earlier you set the first-line indent for paragraphs to one-half inch.*

To properly center the title of the works cited page, you could drag the 'First Line Indent' marker back to the left margin before centering the paragraph, or you could apply the Normal style to the location of the insertion point. Recall that you modified the Normal style for this document to 12-point Times New Roman with double-spaced, left-aligned paragraphs that have no space after the paragraphs.

To apply a style to a paragraph, first position the insertion point in the paragraph and then apply the style. The step on the next page applies the modified Normal style to the location of the insertion point.

- Tap or click HOME on the ribbon to display the HOME tab.

- With the insertion point on the paragraph mark at the top of page 3 (as shown in Figure 2–55 on the previous page) even if Normal is selected, tap or click Normal in the Styles gallery (HOME tab | Styles group) to apply the Normal style to the paragraph containing the insertion point (Figure 2–56).

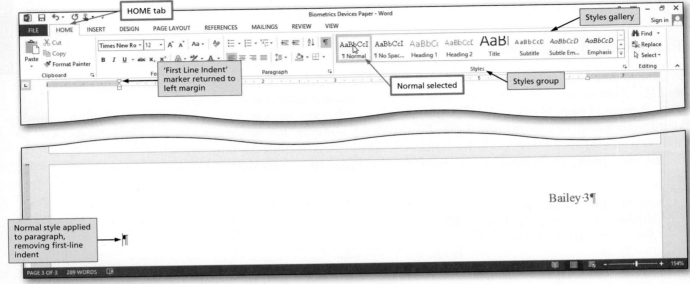

Figure 2–56

Other Ways

1. Tap or click Styles Dialog Box Launcher (HOME tab | Styles group), select desired style in Styles task pane

2. Press CTRL+SHIFT+S, tap or click Style Name arrow in Apply Styles task pane, select desired style in list

To Center Text

The next task is to enter the title, Works Cited, centered between the margins of the paper. The following steps use a keyboard shortcut to format the title.

1 Press CTRL+E to center the paragraph mark.

2 Type **Works Cited** as the title.

3 Press the ENTER key.

4 Press CTRL+L to left-align the paragraph mark (shown in Figure 2–57).

To Create a Bibliographical List

1 CHANGE DOCUMENT SETTINGS | 2 CREATE HEADER | 3 TYPE RESEARCH PAPER WITH CITATIONS
4 CREATE ALPHABETICAL WORKS CITED | 5 PROOFREAD & REVISE RESEARCH PAPER

While typing the research paper, you created several citations and their sources. The next task is to use Word to format the list of sources and alphabetize them in a **bibliographical list**. *Why? Word can create a bibliographical list with each element of the source placed in its correct position with proper punctuation, according to the specified style, saving you time looking up style guidelines. For example, in this research paper, the book source will list, in this order, the author name(s), book title, publisher city, publishing company name, and publication year with the correct punctuation between each element according to the MLA documentation style.* The next steps create an MLA-styled bibliographical list from the sources previously entered.

1

- Tap or click REFERENCES on the ribbon to display the References tab.

- With the insertion point positioned as shown in Figure 2–56, tap or click the Bibliography button (REFERENCES tab | Citations & Bibliography group) to display the Bibliography gallery (Figure 2–57).

Q&A Will I select the Works Cited option from the Bibliography gallery?
No. The title it inserts is not formatted according to the MLA documentation style. Thus, you will use the Insert Bibliography command instead.

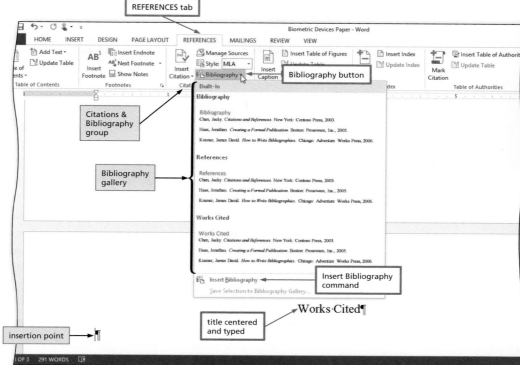

Figure 2–57

2

- Tap or click Insert Bibliography in the Bibliography gallery to insert a list of sources at the location of the insertion point.

- If necessary, scroll to display the entire list of sources in the document window (Figure 2–58).

Q&A What is the n.d. in the first work?
The MLA documentation style uses the abbreviation n.d. for no date (for example, no date appears on the webpage).

Figure 2–58

To Format Paragraphs with a Hanging Indent

Notice in Figure 2–58 on the previous page that the first line of each source entry begins at the left margin, and subsequent lines in the same paragraph are indented one-half inch from the left margin. In essence, the first line hangs to the left of the rest of the paragraph; thus, this type of paragraph formatting is called a **hanging indent**. The Bibliography style in Word automatically formats the works cited paragraphs with a hanging indent.

If you wanted to format paragraphs with a hanging indent, you would use one of the following techniques.

* With the insertion point in the paragraph to format, drag the **Hanging Indent marker** (the bottom triangle) on the ruler to the desired mark on the ruler (i.e., .5") to set the hanging indent at that location from the left margin.

or

* Tap the 'Show Context Menu' button on the mini toolbar or right-click the paragraph to format, tap or click Paragraph on shortcut menu, tap or click the Indents and Spacing tab (Paragraph dialog box), tap or click the Special arrow, tap or click Hanging, and then tap or click the OK button.

or

* Tap or click the Paragraph Dialog Box Launcher (HOME tab or PAGE LAYOUT tab | Paragraph group), tap or click the Indents and Spacing tab (Paragraph dialog box), tap or click the Special arrow, tap or click Hanging, and then tap or click the OK button.

or

* With the insertion point in the paragraph to format, press CTRL+T.

To Save an Existing Document with the Same File Name

You have made several modifications to the document since you last saved it. Thus, you should save it again. The following step saves the document again. For an example of the step listed below, refer to the Office and Windows chapter at the beginning of this book.

 Tap or click the Save button on the Quick Access Toolbar to overwrite the previously saved file.

Proofreading and Revising the Research Paper

As discussed in Chapter 1, once you complete a document, you might find it necessary to make changes to it. Before submitting a paper to be graded, you should proofread it. While **proofreading**, ensure all the source information is correct and look for grammatical errors and spelling errors. Also ensure that transitions between sentences flow smoothly and the sentences themselves make sense.

To assist you with the proofreading effort, Word provides several tools. You can go to a page, copy text, find text, replace text, insert a synonym, check spelling and grammar, and look up information. The following pages discuss these tools.

BTW
Certification
The Microsoft Office Specialist (MOS) program provides an opportunity for you to obtain a valuable industry credential — proof that you have the Word 2013 skills required by employers. For more information, visit the Certification resource on the Student Companion Site located on www.cengagebrain.com. For detailed instructions about accessing available resources, visit www.cengage.com/ct/studentdownload or contact your instructor for information about accessing the required files.

What should you consider when proofreading and revising a paper?

As you proofread the paper, look for ways to improve it. Check all grammar, spelling, and punctuation. Be sure the text is logical and transitions are smooth. Where necessary, add text, delete text, reword text, and move text to different locations. Ask yourself these questions:

- Does the title suggest the topic?
- Is the thesis clear?
- Is the purpose of the paper clear?
- Does the paper have an introduction, body, and conclusion?
- Does each paragraph in the body relate to the thesis?
- Is the conclusion effective?
- Are sources acknowledged correctly?
- Are all sources acknowledged?

To Modify a Source

1 CHANGE DOCUMENT SETTINGS | 2 CREATE HEADER | 3 TYPE RESEARCH PAPER WITH CITATIONS
4 CREATE ALPHABETICAL WORKS CITED | **5 PROOFREAD & REVISE RESEARCH PAPER**

While proofreading the paper, you notice an error in the magazine title; specifically, the first word (Understanding) should be removed. If you modify the contents of any source, the list of sources automatically updates. *Why? Word automatically updates the contents of fields, and the bibliography is a field.* The following steps delete a word from the title of the magazine article.

1

- Tap or click the Manage Sources button (REFERENCES tab | Citations & Bibliography group) to display the Source Manager dialog box.

- Tap or click the source you wish to edit in the Current List, in this case the article by Rossi, to select the source.

- Tap or click the Edit button (Source Manager dialog box) to display the Edit Source dialog box.

- In the Title text box, delete the word, Understanding, from the beginning of the title (Figure 2–59).

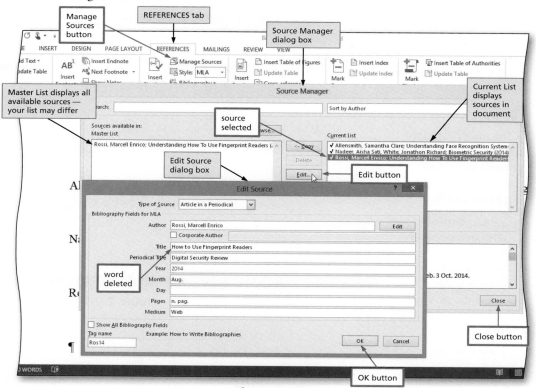

Figure 2–59

2

- Tap or click the OK button (Edit Source dialog box) to close the dialog box.

- If a Microsoft Word dialog box appears, tap or click its Yes button to update all occurrences of the source.

- Tap or click the Close button (Source Manager dialog box) to update the list of sources and close the dialog box.

To Update a Field

Depending on settings, the bibliography field may not automatically reflect the edited magazine title. Thus, the following steps update the bibliography field. ***Why?*** *Because the bibliography is a field, you may need to instruct Word to update its contents.*

- If you are using a touch screen, press and hold anywhere in the bibliography text and then tap the 'Show Context Menu' button on the mini toolbar; if you are using a mouse, right-click anywhere in the bibliography text to display a shortcut menu related to fields (Figure 2–60).

Q&A Why are all the words in the bibliography shaded gray?
By default, Word shades selected fields gray.

What if the bibliography field is not shaded gray?
Tap or click FILE on the ribbon to open the Backstage view, tap or click Options in the Backstage view, tap or click Advanced in the left pane (Word Options dialog box), scroll to the 'Show document content' area, tap or click the Field shading arrow, tap or click When selected, and then tap or click the OK button.

Figure 2–60

- Tap or click Update Field on the shortcut menu to update the selected field (Figure 2–61).

Q&A Can I update all fields in a document at once?
Yes. Select the entire document and then follow these steps.

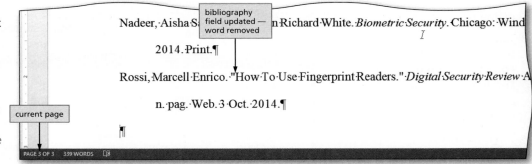

Figure 2–61

Other Ways

1. Select the field, press F9

TO CONVERT A FIELD TO REGULAR TEXT

If, for some reason, you wanted to convert a field, such as the bibliography field, to regular text, you would perform the following steps. Keep in mind, though, once you convert the field to regular text, it no longer is a field that can be updated.

1. Tap or click somewhere in the field to select it, in this case, somewhere in the bibliography.
2. Press CTRL+SHIFT+F9 to convert the selected field to regular text.

To Go to a Page

The next task in revising the paper is to modify text on the second page of the document. *Why? You want to copy text from one location to another on the second page.* You could scroll to the desired location in the document, or you can use the Navigation Pane to browse through pages in a document. The following steps display the top of the second page in the document window and position the insertion point at the beginning of that page.

❶

- Tap or click VIEW on the ribbon to display the VIEW tab.

- Place a check mark in the 'Open the Navigation Pane' check box (VIEW tab | Show group) to open the Navigation Pane on the left side of the Word window.

- If necessary, tap or click the PAGES tab in the Navigation Pane to display thumbnails of the pages in the document.

- Scroll to and then tap or click the thumbnail of the second page to display the top of the selected page in the top of the document window (Figure 2–62).

Q&A What is the Navigation Pane?
The **Navigation Pane** is a window that enables you to browse through headings in a document, browse through pages in a document, or search for text in a document.

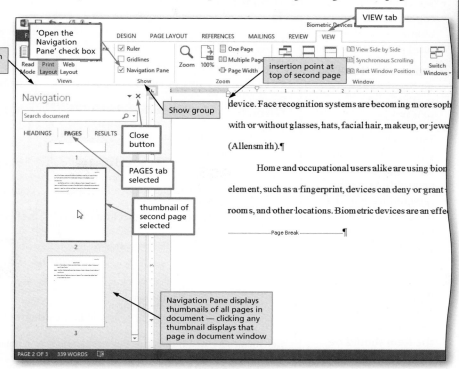

Figure 2–62

❷

- Tap or click the Close button in the Navigation Pane to close the pane.

Other Ways

1. Tap or click Find arrow (HOME tab | Editing group), tap or click Go To on Find menu, tap or click Go To tab (Find and Replace dialog box), enter page number, tap or click Go To button

2. Tap or click Page Number indicator on status bar, tap or click PAGES tab in Navigation Pane, tap or click thumbnail of desired page (Navigation Pane)

3. Press CTRL+G, enter page number, tap or click Go To button

Copying, Cutting, and Pasting

While proofreading the research paper, you decide it would read better if the word, biometric, in the second sentence of the last paragraph also appeared in front of the word, devices, in the same sentence. You could type the word at the desired location, but because this is a difficult word to spell and type, you decide to use the Office Clipboard. The **Office Clipboard** is a temporary storage area that holds up to 24 items (text or graphics) copied from any Office program. The Office Clipboard works with the copy, cut, and paste commands:

- **Copying** is the process of placing items on the Office Clipboard, leaving the item in the document.

- **Cutting** removes the item from the document before placing it on the Office Clipboard.

- **Pasting** is the process of copying an item from the Office Clipboard into the document at the location of the insertion point.

BTW
Quick Reference
For a table that lists how to complete the tasks covered in this book using touch gestures, the mouse, ribbon, shortcut menu, and keyboard, see the Quick Reference Summary at the back of this book, or visit the Quick Reference resource on the Student Companion Site located on www.cengagebrain .com. For detailed instructions about accessing available resources, visit www.cengage.com/ct/ studentdownload or contact your instructor for information about accessing the required files.

To Copy and Paste

In the research paper, you copy a word from one location to another. *Why? The sentence reads better with the word,* biometric, *inserted before the word,* devices. The following steps copy and paste a word.

- Select the item to be copied (the word, biometric, in this case).
- Tap or click HOME on the ribbon to display the HOME tab.
- Tap or click the Copy button (HOME tab | Clipboard group) to copy the selected item in the document to the Office Clipboard (Figure 2–63).

Figure 2–63

- Position the insertion point at the location where the item should be pasted (immediately to the left of the word, devices, in this case) (Figure 2–64).

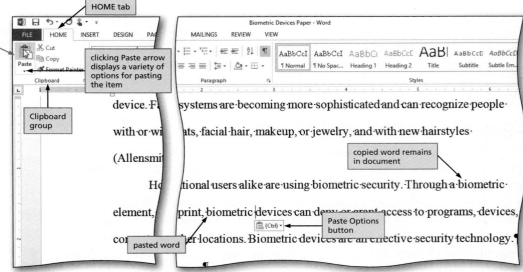

Figure 2–64

- Tap or click the Paste button (HOME tab | Clipboard group) to paste the copied item in the document at the location of the insertion point (Figure 2–65).

Q&A What if I click the Paste arrow by mistake?
Click the Paste arrow again to remove the Paste menu and repeat Step 3.

Figure 2–65

Other Ways

1. Press and hold or right-click selected item, tap Copy on mini toolbar or click Copy on shortcut menu, press and hold or right-click where item is to be pasted, tap Paste on mini toolbar or click Keep Source Formatting in Paste Options area on shortcut menu

2. Select item, press CTRL+C, position insertion point at paste location, press CTRL+V

To Display the Paste Options Menu

When you paste an item or move an item using drag-and-drop editing, which was discussed in the previous chapter, Word automatically displays a Paste Options button near the pasted or moved text (Figure 2–65). *Why? The Paste Options button allows you to change the format of a pasted item. For example, you can instruct Word to format the pasted item the same way as where it was copied (the source), or format it the same way as where it is being pasted (the destination).* The following steps display the Paste Options menu.

- Tap or click the Paste Options button to display the Paste Options menu (Figure 2–66).

Q&A

What are the functions of the buttons on the Paste Options menu?
In general, the left button indicates the pasted item should look the same as it did in its original location (the source).

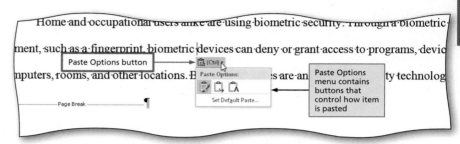

Figure 2–66

The second button formats the pasted text to match the rest of the item where it was pasted (the destination). The third button removes all formatting from the pasted item. The Set Default Paste command displays the Word Options dialog box. Keep in mind that the buttons shown on a Paste Options menu will vary, depending on the item being pasted.

- Tap or click anywhere to remove the Paste Options menu from the window.

Other Ways

1. CTRL (to remove the Paste Options menu)

To Find Text

While proofreading the paper, you would like to locate all occurrences of the word, element. *Why? You are contemplating changing occurrences of this word to the word, identifier.* The following steps find all occurrences of specific text in a document.

- If you are using a touch screen, tap the Find button (HOME tab | Editing group) and then tap Find on the menu; if you are using a mouse, click the Find button (HOME tab | Editing group) to display the Navigation Pane.

- If necessary, tap or click the RESULTS tab in the Navigation Pane, which displays a Search box where you can type text for which you want to search (Figure 2–67).

Figure 2–67

2
- Type **element** in the Navigation Pane Search box to display all occurrences of the typed text, called the search text, in the Navigation Pane and to highlight the occurrences of the search text in the document window (Figure 2–68).

Figure 2–68

3

 Experiment
- Tap or click both occurrences in the Navigation Pane and watch Word display the associated text in the document window.
- Type various search text in the Navigation Pane Search box, and watch Word both list matches in the Navigation Pane and highlight matches in the document window.
- Tap or click the Close button in the Navigation Pane to close the pane.

Other Ways
1. Tap or click Find arrow (HOME tab \| Editing group), tap or click Find on Find menu, enter search text in Navigation Pane 2. Tap or click Page Number indicator on status bar, enter search text in Navigation Pane 3. Press CTRL+F, enter search text in Navigation Pane

To Replace Text

1 CHANGE DOCUMENT SETTINGS | 2 CREATE HEADER | 3 TYPE RESEARCH PAPER WITH CITATIONS
4 CREATE ALPHABETICAL WORKS CITED | 5 PROOFREAD & REVISE RESEARCH PAPER

You decide to change all occurrences of element to identifier. **Why?** *The text, biometric identifier, is a better description than biometric element.* Word's find and replace feature locates each occurrence of a word or phrase and then replaces it with text you specify. The following steps find and replace text.

1
- Tap or click the Replace button (HOME tab | Editing group) to display the Replace sheet in the Find and Replace dialog box.
- If necessary, type **element** in the Find what box (Find and Replace dialog box).
- Type **identifier** in the Replace with box (Figure 2–69).

Figure 2–69

2

- Tap or click the Replace All button to instruct Word to replace all occurrences of the Find what text with the Replace with text (Figure 2–70). If Word displays a dialog box asking if you want to continue searching from the beginning of the document, tap or click the Yes button.

Q&A

Does Word search the entire document?

If the insertion point is at the beginning of the document, Word searches the entire document; otherwise, Word searches from the location of the insertion point to the end of the document and then displays a dialog box asking if you want to continue searching from the beginning. You also can search a section of text by selecting the text before tapping or clicking the Replace button.

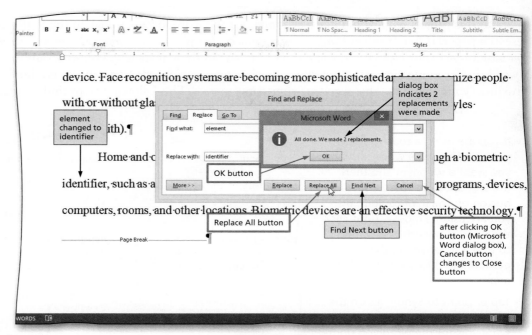

Figure 2–70

3

- Tap or click the OK button (Microsoft Word dialog box) to close the dialog box.
- Tap or click the Close button (Find and Replace dialog box) to close the dialog box.

Other Ways

1. Press CTRL+H

Find and Replace Dialog Box

The Replace All button (Find and Replace dialog box) replaces all occurrences of the Find what text with the Replace with text. In some cases, you may want to replace only certain occurrences of a word or phrase, not all of them. To instruct Word to confirm each change, tap or click the Find Next button (Find and Replace dialog box) (Figure 2–70), instead of the Replace All button. When Word locates an occurrence of the text, it pauses and waits for you to tap or click either the Replace button or the Find Next button. Tapping or clicking the Replace button changes the text; tapping or clicking the Find Next button instructs Word to disregard the replacement and look for the next occurrence of the Find what text.

If you accidentally replace the wrong text, you can undo a replacement by tapping or clicking the Undo button on the Quick Access Toolbar. If you used the Replace All button, Word undoes all replacements. If you used the Replace button, Word undoes only the most recent replacement.

BTW
Finding Formatting
To search for formatting or a special character, tap or click the More button in the Find and Replace dialog box (shown in Figure 2–69). To find formatting, use the Format button in the Find dialog box. To find a special character, use the Special button.

To Find and Insert a Synonym

In this project, you would like a synonym for the word, occupational, in the fourth paragraph of the research paper. *Why? When writing, you may discover that you used the same word in multiple locations or that a word you used was not quite appropriate, which is the case here.* In these instances, you will want to look up a **synonym**, or a word similar in meaning, to the duplicate or inappropriate word. A **thesaurus** is a book of synonyms. Word provides synonyms and a thesaurus for your convenience. The following steps find a suitable synonym.

- If you are using a touch screen, press and hold the word for which you want a synonym and then tap the 'Show Context Menu' button on the mini toolbar; if you are using a mouse, right-click the word for which you want to find a synonym (in this case, occupational) to display a shortcut menu.

- Tap or point to Synonyms on the shortcut menu to display a list of synonyms for the word you right-clicked (Figure 2–71).

Figure 2–71

- Tap or click the synonym you want (in this case, business) on the Synonyms submenu to replace the selected word in the document with the selected synonym (Figure 2–72).

Q&A What if the synonyms list on the shortcut menu does not display a suitable word?
You can display the thesaurus in the Thesaurus task pane by tapping or clicking Thesaurus on the Synonyms submenu. The Thesaurus task pane displays a complete thesaurus, in which you can look up synonyms for various meanings of a word. You also can look up an **antonym,** or word with an opposite meaning.

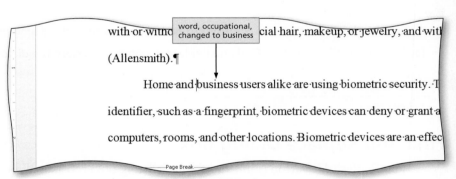

Figure 2–72

Other Ways

1. Click Thesaurus button (REVIEW tab | Proofing group) 2. Press SHIFT+F7

To Check Spelling and Grammar at Once

As discussed in Chapter 1, Word checks spelling and grammar as you type and places a wavy underline below possible spelling or grammar errors. Chapter 1 illustrated how to check these flagged words immediately. The next steps check spelling and grammar at once. *Why? Some users prefer to wait and check their entire document for spelling and grammar errors at once.*

Note: In the following steps, the word, readers, has been misspelled intentionally as raders to illustrate the use of Word's check spelling and grammar at once feature. If you are completing this project on a personal computer, your research paper may contain different misspelled words, depending on the accuracy of your typing.

- Press CTRL+HOME because you want the spelling and grammar check to begin from the top of the document.

- Tap or click REVIEW on the ribbon to display the REVIEW tab.

- Tap or click the Spelling & Grammar button (REVIEW tab | Proofing group) to begin the spelling and grammar check at the location of the insertion point, which, in this case, is at the beginning of the document.

- Tap or click the desired word in the list of suggestions in the Spelling pane (readers, in this case) (Figure 2–73).

Figure 2–73

- With the word, reader, selected in the list of suggestions, tap or click the Change button (Spelling task pane) to change the flagged word to the selected suggestion and then continue the spelling and grammar check until the next error is identified or the end of the document is reached (Figure 2–74).

- Because the flagged word is a proper noun and spelled correctly, tap or click the Ignore All button (Spelling task pane) to ignore this and future occurrences of the flagged proper noun and then continue the spelling and grammar check until the next error is identified or the end of the document is reached.

Figure 2–74

- When the spelling and grammar check is finished and Word displays a dialog box, tap or click its OK button.

Q&A Can I check spelling of just a section of a document?

Yes, select the text before starting the spelling and grammar check.

Other Ways

1. Tap or click 'Spelling and Grammar Check' icon on status bar 2. Press F7

The Main and Custom Dictionaries

As shown in the previous steps, Word may flag a proper noun as an error because the proper noun is not in its main dictionary. To prevent Word from flagging proper nouns as errors, you can add the proper nouns to the custom dictionary. To add a correctly spelled word to the custom dictionary, tap or click the Add button (Spelling task pane) or press and hold and then tap 'Show Context Menu' button on mini toolbar or right-click the flagged word and then tap or click Add to Dictionary on the shortcut menu. Once you have added a word to the custom dictionary, Word no longer will flag it as an error.

To View or Modify Entries in a Custom Dictionary

To view or modify the list of words in a custom dictionary, you would follow these steps.

1. Tap or click FILE on the ribbon and then tap or click Options in the Backstage view.
2. Tap or click Proofing in the left pane (Word Options dialog box).
3. Tap or click the Custom Dictionaries button.
4. When Word displays the Custom Dictionaries dialog box, place a check mark next to the dictionary name to view or modify. Tap or click the 'Edit Word List' button (Custom Dictionaries dialog box). (In this dialog box, you can add or delete entries to and from the selected custom dictionary.)
5. When finished viewing and/or modifying the list, tap or click the OK button in the dialog box.
6. Tap or click the OK button (Custom Dictionaries dialog box).
7. If the 'Suggest from main dictionary only' check box is selected in the Word Options dialog box, remove the check mark. Tap or click the OK button (Word Options dialog box).

To Set the Default Custom Dictionary

If you have multiple custom dictionaries, you can specify which one Word should use when checking spelling. To set the default custom dictionary, you would follow these steps.

1. Tap or click FILE on the ribbon and then tap or click Options in the Backstage view.
2. Tap or click Proofing in the left pane (Word Options dialog box).
3. Tap or click the Custom Dictionaries button.
4. When the Custom Dictionaries dialog box is displayed, place a check mark next to the desired dictionary name. Tap or click the Change Default button (Custom Dictionaries dialog box).
5. Tap or click the OK button (Custom Dictionaries dialog box).
6. If the 'Suggest from main dictionary only' check box is selected in the Word Options dialog box, remove the check mark. Tap or click the OK button (Word Options dialog box).

To Look Up Information

If you are signed in to your Microsoft account, you can look up a definition by tapping or clicking the Define button (REVIEW tab | Proofing group). If you are not signed in to your Microsoft account but are connected to the Internet, you can use the Research task pane to search through various forms of reference information on the web. The following steps use the Research task pane to look up a definition of a word. *Why? Assume you want to know more about the word, legitimate, but are not signed in to your Microsoft account.*

1

- While holding down the ALT key, tap or click the word you want to look up (in this case, legitimate) to open the Research task pane and display a dictionary entry for the ALT+clicked word (Figure 2–75). Release the ALT key.

Q&A | Why does my Research task pane look different?

Depending on your settings and Microsoft's website search settings, your Research task pane may appear different from the figures shown here.

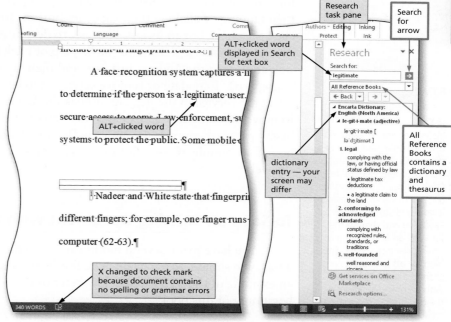

Figure 2–75

2

- Tap or click the Source arrow in the Research task pane to display a list of search locations and then tap or click 'All Research Sites' in the list (Figure 2–76).

Q&A | Can I copy information from the Research task pane into my document?

Yes, you can use the Copy and Paste commands. When using Word to insert material from the Research task pane or any other online reference, however, be careful not to plagiarize.

3

- Tap or click the Close button in the Research task pane.

Figure 2–76

Other Ways

1. Press ALT+SHIFT+F7

Research Task Pane Options

When you install Word, it selects a series of services (reference books and websites) that it searches through when you use the Research task pane. You can view, modify, and update the list of services at any time.

Tapping or clicking the Research options link at the bottom of the Research task pane (shown in Figure 2–76 on the previous page) displays the Research Options dialog box, where you can view or modify the list of installed services. You can view information about any installed service by tapping or clicking the service in the list and then tapping or clicking the Properties button. To activate an installed service, tap or click the check box to its left; likewise, to deactivate a service, remove the check mark. To add a particular website to the list, tap or click the Add Services button, enter the web address in the Address text box, and then tap or click the Add button (Add Services dialog box). To update or remove services, tap or click the Update/Remove button, select the service in the list, tap or click the Update (or Remove) button (Update or Remove Services dialog box), and then tap or click the Close button. You also can install parental controls through the Parental Control button (Research Options dialog box), for example, if you want to prevent minor children who use Word from accessing the web.

BTW
**Distributing
a Document**
Instead of printing and distributing a hard copy of a document, you can distribute the document electronically. Options include sending the document via email; saving it on cloud storage (such as SkyDrive) and sharing the file with others; posting it on a social networking site, blog, or other website; and sharing a link associated with an online location of the document. You also can create and share a PDF or XPS image of the document, so that users can view the file in Acrobat Reader or XPS Viewer instead of in Word.

To Save an Existing Document with the Same File Name

You have made several modifications to the document since you last saved it. Thus, you should save it again. The following step saves the document again. For an example of the step listed below, refer to the Office and Windows chapter at the beginning of this book.

 Tap or click the Save button on the Quick Access Toolbar to overwrite the previously saved file.

To Zoom Multiple Pages

1 CHANGE DOCUMENT SETTINGS | 2 CREATE HEADER | 3 TYPE RESEARCH PAPER WITH CITATIONS
4 CREATE ALPHABETICAL WORKS CITED | 5 PROOFREAD & REVISE RESEARCH PAPER

The next steps display multiple pages in the document window at once. *Why? You want be able to see all pages in the research paper on the screen at the same time. You also hide formatting marks and the rulers so that the display is easier to view.*

- Tap or click HOME on the ribbon to display the HOME tab.
- If the 'Show/Hide ¶' button (HOME tab | Paragraph group) is selected, tap or click it to hide formatting marks.
- Tap or click VIEW on the ribbon to display the VIEW tab.
- If the rulers are displayed, tap or click the View Ruler check box (VIEW tab | Show group) to remove the check mark from the check box and remove the horizontal and vertical rulers from the screen.
- Tap or click the Multiple Pages button (VIEW tab | Zoom group) to display the all three pages at once in the document window (Figure 2–77).

Figure 2–77

 2

- When finished, tap or click the Page Width button (VIEW tab | Zoom group) to return to the page width zoom.

To Change Read Mode Color

1 CHANGE DOCUMENT SETTINGS | 2 CREATE HEADER | 3 TYPE RESEARCH PAPER WITH CITATIONS
4 CREATE ALPHABETICAL WORKS CITED | 5 PROOFREAD & REVISE RESEARCH PAPER

You would like to read the entire research paper using Read mode but would like to change the background color of the Read mode screen. *Why? You prefer a background that is easier on your eyes when reading on the screen.* The following steps change the color of the screen in Read mode.

1

- Tap or click the Read Mode button on the status bar to switch to Read mode.
- Tap or click the VIEW tab to display the VIEW menu.
- Tap or point to Page Color on the VIEW menu to display the Page Color menu (Figure 2–78).

Figure 2–78

- Tap or click Sepia on the Page Color submenu to change the color of the Read mode screen to sepia (Figure 2–79).

Figure 2–79

- When finished, tap or click the Print Layout button (shown in Figure 2–78 on the previous page) on the status bar to return to Print Layout view.

BTW
Conserving Ink and Toner
If you want to conserve ink or toner, you can instruct Word to print draft quality documents by tapping or clicking FILE on the ribbon to open the Backstage view, tapping or clicking Options in the Backstage view, tapping or clicking Advanced in the left pane (Word Options dialog box), sliding or scrolling to the Print area in the right pane, placing a check mark in the 'Use draft quality' check box, and then tapping or clicking the OK button. Then, use the Backstage view to print the document as usual.

To Print a Document

If you want a hard copy of the research paper, perform the following steps.

1. Tap or click FILE on the ribbon to open the Backstage view.

2. Tap or click the Print tab in the Backstage view to display the Print gallery.

3. Verify that the printer listed on the Printer Status button will print a hard copy of the document. If necessary, tap or click the Printer Status button to display a list of available printer options and then tap or click the desired printer to change the currently selected printer.

4. Tap or click the Print button in the Print gallery to print the document on the currently selected printer.

5. When the printer stops, retrieve the hard copy (shown in Figure 2–1 on page WD 67).

To Exit Word

This project now is complete. The following steps exit Word. For a detailed example of the procedure summarized below, refer to the Office and Windows chapter at the beginning of this book.

1a. If you have one Word document open, tap or click the Close button on the right side of the title bar to close the open document and exit Word.

1b. If you have multiple Word documents open, press and hold or right-click the Word app button on the taskbar and then tap or click 'Close all windows' on the shortcut menu to close all open documents and exit Word.

2. If a Microsoft Word dialog box appears, tap or click the Save button to save any changes made to the document since the last save.

Chapter Summary

In this chapter, you have learned how to change document settings, use headers to number pages, modify a style, insert and edit citations and their sources, add footnotes, create a bibliographical list of sources, and use proofreading tools. The items listed below include all the new Word skills you have learned in this chapter, with the tasks grouped by activity.

Enter and Edit Text
AutoCorrect as You Type (WD 84)
Use the AutoCorrect Options Button (WD 85)
Create an AutoCorrect Entry (WD 85)
Count Words (WD 100)
Update a Field (WD 110)
Copy and Paste (WD 112)
Find Text (WD 113)
Replace Text (WD 114)
Find and Insert a Synonym (WD 115)
Check Spelling and Grammar at Once (WD 116)
View or Modify Entries in a Custom Dictionary (WD 118)
Set the Default Custom Dictionary (WD 118)

Format a Page
Switch to the Header (WD 74)
Insert a Page Number (WD 76)
Close the Header (WD 77)
Page Break Manually (WD 105)

Format Text
Modify a Style (WD 70)
Change Line Spacing (WD 72)
Remove Space after a Paragraph (WD 73)
Update a Style to Match a Selection (WD 73)

Right-Align a Paragraph (WD 75)
Click and Type (WD 79)
First-Line Indent Paragraphs (WD 82)
Modify a Style Using a Shortcut Menu (WD 94)
Apply a Style (WD 105)
Format Paragraphs with a Hanging Indent (WD 108)
Convert a Field to Regular Text (WD 110)
Display the Paste Options Menu (WD 113)

Word Settings
Display the Rulers (WD 82)
Hide and Show White Space (WD 102)
Go to a Page (WD 111)
Look Up Information (WD 119)
Zoom Multiple Pages (WD 120)
Change Read Mode Color (WD 121)

Work with Citations, Sources, and Footnotes
Change the Bibliography Style (WD 89)
Insert a Citation and Create Its Source (WD 89)
Insert a Footnote Reference Mark (WD 92)
Insert a Citation Placeholder (WD 93)
Edit a Source (WD 96)
Edit a Citation (WD 98)
Create a Bibliographical List (WD 106)
Modify a Source (WD 109)

What decisions will you need to make when creating your next research paper?
Use these guidelines as you complete the assignments in this chapter and create your own research papers outside of this class.

1. Select a topic.

 a) Spend time brainstorming ideas for a topic.

 b) Choose a topic you find interesting.

 c) For shorter papers, narrow the scope of the topic; for longer papers, broaden the scope.

 d) Identify a tentative thesis statement, which is a sentence describing the paper's subject matter.

2. Research the topic and take notes, being careful not to plagiarize.

3. Organize your notes into related concepts, identifying all main ideas and supporting details in an outline.

4. Write the first draft from the outline, referencing all sources of information and following the guidelines identified in the required documentation style.

5. Create the list of sources, using the formats specified in the required documentation style.

6. Proofread and revise the paper.

CONSIDER THIS: PLAN AHEAD

How should you submit solutions to questions in the assignments identified with a symbol?
Every assignment in this book contains one or more questions identified with a symbol. These questions require you to think beyond the assigned document. Present your solutions to the questions in the format required by your instructor. Possible formats may include one or more of these options: write the answer; create a document that contains the answer; present your answer to the class; discuss your answer in a group; record the answer as audio or video using a webcam, smartphone, or portable media player; or post answers on a blog, wiki, or website.

Apply Your Knowledge

Reinforce the skills and apply the concepts you learned in this chapter.

Revising Text and Paragraphs in a Document

Note: To complete this assignment, you will be required to use the Data Files for Students. Visit www.cengage.com/ct/studentdownload for detailed instructions or contact your instructor for information about accessing the required files.

Instructions: Run Word. Open the document, Apply 2 - 1 Virtual Reality Paragraph Draft, from the Data Files for Students. The document you open contains a paragraph of text. You are to revise the document as follows: move a word, move another word and change the format of the moved word, change paragraph indentation, change line spacing, find all occurrences of a word, replace all occurrences of a word with another word, locate a synonym, and edit the header.

Perform the following tasks:

1. Copy the text, VR, from the first sentence and paste it in the last sentence after the underlined word, potential.

2. Select the underlined word, potential, in the paragraph. If you are using a mouse, use drag-and-drop editing to move the selected word, potential, so that it is before the word, buyers, in the same sentence. If you are using a touch screen, use the cut and paste commands to move the word. Tap or click the Paste Options button that displays to the right of the moved word, potential. Remove the underline format from the moved sentence by tapping or clicking 'Keep Text Only' on the Paste Options menu.

3. Display the ruler, if necessary. If you are using a mouse, use the ruler to indent the first line of the paragraph one-half inch; otherwise, use the Paragraph dialog box.

4. Change the line spacing of the paragraph to double.

5. Use the Navigation Pane to find all occurrences of the word, VR. How many are there?

6. Use the Find and Replace dialog box to replace all occurrences of the word, 3D, with the word, 3-D. How many replacements were made?

7. Use the Navigation Pane to find the word, endless. Use Word's thesaurus to change the word, endless, to the word, infinite. What other words are in the list of synonyms?

8. Switch to the header so that you can edit it. In the first line of the header, change the word, Draft, to the word, Modified, so that it reads: VR Paragraph Modified.

9. In the second line of the header, insert the page number (with no formatting) one space after the word, Page.

10. Change the alignment of both lines of text in the header from left-aligned to right-aligned. Switch back to the document text.

11. If requested by your instructor, enter your first and last name on a separate line below the page number in the header.

12. Tap or click FILE on the ribbon and then tap or click Save As. Save the document using the file name, Apply 2 - 1 Virtual Reality Paragraph Modified.

13. Submit the modified document, shown in Figure 2–80, in the format specified by your instructor.

14. Use the Research task pane to look up the definition of the word, simulate, in the paragraph. Which dictionary was used? If you have a Microsoft account and are signed into it, use the Define button (REVIEW tab | Proofing group) to look up a definition of the word.

15. Change the search location to All Research Sites. Submit an article from one of the sites.

16. Display the Research Options dialog box. How many currently active Reference Books and Research Sites are in the list? If your instructor approves, activate one of the services.

17. ✳ Answer the questions posed in #5, #6, #7, #14, and #16. How would you find and replace a special character, such as a paragraph mark?

Figure 2–80

Extend Your Knowledge

Extend the skills you learned in this chapter and experiment with new skills. You may need to use Help to complete the assignment.

Working with References and Proofing Tools

Note: To complete this assignment, you will be required to use the Data Files for Students. Visit www.cengage.com/ct/studentdownload for detailed instructions or contact your instructor for information about accessing the required files.

Instructions: Run Word. Open the document, Extend 2 - 1 Cybercrime Paper Draft, from the Data Files for Students. You will add another footnote to the paper, convert the footnotes to endnotes, modify the Endnote Text style, change the format of the note reference marks, use Word's readability statistics, translate the document to another language (Figure 2–81 on the next page), and convert the document from MLA to APA documentation style.

Perform the following tasks:

1. Use Help to learn more about footers, footnotes and endnotes, readability statistics, bibliography styles, AutoCorrect, and the Mini Translator.

2. Delete the footer from the document.

Continued >

Extend Your Knowledge *continued*

Figure 2–81

3. Insert a second footnote at an appropriate place in the research paper. Use the following footnote text: Unscrupulous companies hire corporate spies, a practice known as corporate espionage, to gain a competitive advantage.

4. Change the location of the footnotes from bottom of page to below text. How did the placement of the footnotes change?

5. Convert the footnotes to endnotes. Where are the endnotes positioned?

6. Modify the Endnote Text style to 12-point Times New Roman font, double-spaced text with a hanging-line indent.

7. Change the format of the note reference marks to capital letters (A, B, etc.).

8. Add an AutoCorrect entry that replaces the word, perpetraters, with the word, perpetrators. Add this sentence as the last sentence in the paper, misspelling the word perpetrators to test the AutoCorrect entry: These perpetraters present a growing threat to society. Delete the AutoCorrect entry that replaces perpetraters with the word, perpetrators.

9. Display the Word Count dialog box. How many words, characters without spaces, characters with spaces, paragraphs, and lines are in the document? Be sure to include footnote and endnote text in the statistics.

10. Check spelling of the document, displaying readability statistics. What are the Flesch-Kincaid Grade Level, the Flesch Reading Ease score, and the percent of passive sentences? Modify the paper to lower the grade level, increase the reading ease score, and lower the percent of passive sentences. How did you modify the paper? What are the new statistics?

11. If requested by your instructor, change the student name at the top of the paper to your name, including the last name in the header.

12. Save the revised document with the file name, Extend 2-1 Cybercrime Paper Modified, and then submit it in the format specified by your instructor.

13. If you have an Internet connection, translate the research paper into a language of your choice using the Translate button (REVIEW tab | Language group). Submit the translated document in the format specified by your instructor. Use the Mini Translator to hear how to pronounce three words in your paper.

14. Select the entire document and then change the documentation style from MLA to APA. Save the APA version of the document with a new file name. Compare the APA version to the MLA version. If you have a hard copy of each and your instructor requests it, circle the differences between the two documents.

15. ❋ Answer the questions posed in #4, #5, #9, and #10. Where did you insert the second footnote and why?

Analyze, Correct, Improve
Analyze a document, correct all errors, and improve it.

Inserting Missing Elements in an MLA-Styled Research Paper
Note: To complete this assignment, you will be required to use the Data Files for Students. Visit www.cengage.com/ct/studentdownload for detailed instructions or contact your instructor for information about accessing the required files.

Instructions: Run Word. Open the document, Analyze 2-1 Internet Filters Paper Draft, from the Data Files for Students. The document is a research paper that is missing several elements. You are to insert these missing elements, all formatted according to the MLA documentation style: header with a page number, name and course information, paper title, footnote, and source information for a citation.

1. Correct In the research paper, correct the following items:
(a) Insert a header with a your own last name and page number and then type the course information (your name, your instructor's name, your course name, and today's date), and an appropriate paper title, all formatted according to the MLA documentation style.
(b) The Clark citation placeholder is missing its source information (shown in Figure 2-82 on the next page). Use the following information to edit the source: book titled *Internet Protection*, written by Addison Lee Clark, publication year is 2014, publication city is New York, publisher is Journey Press, medium is Print. Edit the citation so that it displays the author name and the page numbers of 35–37 for this reference.
(c) Modify the website author name to include his middle name: Robert Timothy Lane. Also, change the medium in this same source from Print to Web.
(d) Use the Navigation Pane to display page 2. Insert a page break before the Works Cited heading. Use Word to insert the bibliographical list (bibliography) below the Works Cited heading.

2. Improve Enhance the paper by inserting a footnote with the note reference at an appropriate place in the paper, formatted according to the MLA documentation style, that gives a statistic about spam. (You will need to do research to obtain this statistic.) Change the Footnote Text style to 12-point Times New Roman, double-spaced paragraphs with a first-line indent. Add a citation and source for your new footnote. Be sure to update the works cited page after you add the citation and source. Save the modified document with the file name, Analyze 2-1 Internet Filters Paper Modified, and then submit it in the format specified by your instructor.

3. ❋ In this assignment you inserted a statistic from a web source. Why did you select that website?

Continued >

Analyze, Correct, Improve *continued*

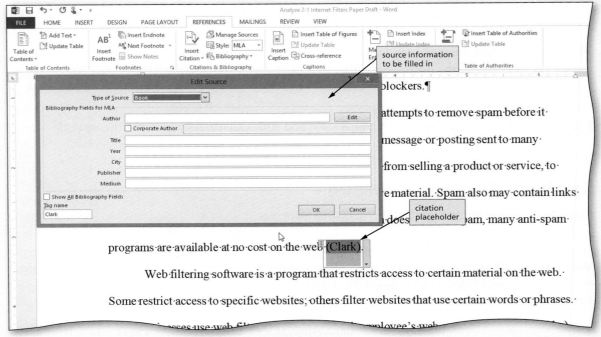

Figure 2–82

In the Labs

Design and/or create a document using the guidelines, concepts, and skills presented in this chapter. Labs 1 and 2, which increase in difficulty, require you to create solutions based on what you learned in the chapter; Lab 3 requires you to create a solution, which uses cloud and web technologies, by learning and investigating on your own from general guidance.

Lab 1: **Preparing a Short Research Paper**

Problem: You are a college student currently enrolled in an introductory English class. Your assignment is to prepare a short research paper (350–450 words) in any area of interest to you. The requirements are that the paper be presented according to the MLA documentation style and have three references. At least one of the three references must be from the web. You prepare the paper shown in Figure 2–83, which discusses health risks associated with technology.

Instructions: Perform the following tasks:

1. Run Word. If necessary, display formatting marks on the screen.
2. Modify the Normal style to the 12-point Times New Roman font.
3. Adjust line spacing to double.
4. Remove space below (after) paragraphs.
5. Update the Normal style to reflect the adjusted line and paragraph spacing.
6. Create a header to number pages.
7. Type the name and course information at the left margin. If requested by your instructor, use your name and course information instead of the information shown in Figure 2–83a. Center and type the title.
8. Set a first-line indent to one-half inch for paragraphs in the body of the research paper.

Delhi 1

Rajesh Delhi

Ms. June

English 102

November 9, 2014

Health Risks Associated with Technology

The widespread use of technology has led to some important user health concerns. Some of the more common physical health risks are repetitive strain injuries, computer vision syndrome, and muscular pain. These injuries are on the rise for users of technology.

A repetitive strain injury (RSI) is an injury or disorder of the muscles, nerves, tendons, ligaments, and joints. Technology-related RSIs include tendonitis and carpal tunnel syndrome (CTS). Tendonitis is inflammation of a tendon due to repeated motion or stress on that tendon. CTS is inflammation of the nerve that connects the forearm to the palm. Repeated or forceful bending of the wrist can cause tendonitis or CTS of the wrist. Factors that cause these disorders include prolonged typing or mouse usage and continual shifting between a mouse and keyboard (Jones 45-48). If untreated, these disorders can lead to permanent physical damage.

Computer vision syndrome (CVS) affects eyesight. Symptoms of CVS are sore, tired, burning, itching, or dry eyes; blurred or double vision; distance blurred vision after prolonged staring at a display device; headache or sore neck; difficulty shifting focus between a display device and documents; difficulty focusing on a screen image; color fringes or afterimages when looking away from a display device; and increased sensitivity to light. Eyestrain associated with CVS is not thought to have serious or long-term consequences (Anderson and Dean).

People who spend their workday using the computer sometimes complain of lower back pain, muscle fatigue, and emotional fatigue. Lower back pain sometimes is caused from poor

(a) Page 1

Figure 2–83

Continued >

In the Labs *continued*

Delhi 2

posture. It is advisable to sit properly in a chair while working and take periodic breaks. Users

also should be sure their workplace is designed ergonomically. Ergonomic studies have shown

that using the correct type and configuration of chair, keyboard, display device, and work surface

helps users work comfortably and efficiently and helps protect their health (Sanchez).

Many physical health risks are associated with using technology. These risks include

repetitive strain injuries, computer vision syndrome, and muscular pain. Users should take as

many preventive measures as possible to avoid these risks.

(b) Page 2
Figure 2–83 (Continued)

9. Type the research paper as shown in Figures 2–83a and 2–83b. Change the bibliography style to MLA. As you insert citations, enter their source information (shown in Figure 2–83c). Edit the citations so that they are displayed according to Figures 2–83a and 2–83b.

10. At the end of the research paper text, press the ENTER key and then insert a manual page break so that the Works Cited page begins on a new page. Enter and format the works cited title (Figure 2–83c). Use Word to insert the bibliographical list (bibliography).

11. Check the spelling and grammar of the paper at once.

12. Save the document using Lab 2 - 1 Technology Health Risks Paper as the file name. Submit the document, shown in Figure 2–83, in the format specified by your instructor.

13. ✷ Read the paper in Print Layout view. Switch to Read mode and scroll through the pages. Do you prefer reading in Print Layout view or Read mode. Why? In Read mode, which of the page colors do you like best and why?

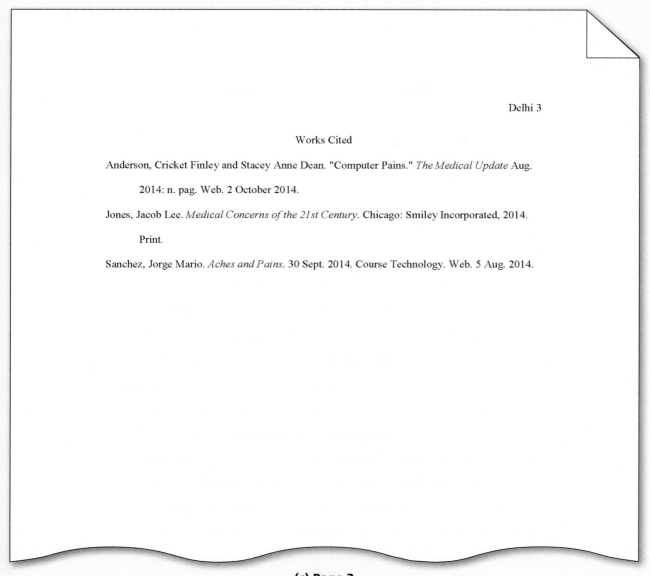

Delhi 3

Works Cited

Anderson, Cricket Finley and Stacey Anne Dean. "Computer Pains." *The Medical Update* Aug.

2014: n. pag. Web. 2 October 2014.

Jones, Jacob Lee. *Medical Concerns of the 21st Century*. Chicago: Smiley Incorporated, 2014.

Print.

Sanchez, Jorge Mario. *Aches and Pains*. 30 Sept. 2014. Course Technology. Web. 5 Aug. 2014.

(c) Page 3
Figure 2–83 (Continued)

Lab 2: **Preparing a Research Report with a Footnote**

Problem: You are a college student enrolled in an introductory technology class. Your assignment is to prepare a short research paper (350–450 words) in any area of interest to you. The requirements are that the paper be presented according to the MLA documentation style, contain at least one note positioned as a footnote, and have three references. At least one ne of the three references must be from the Internet. You prepare a paper about protecting mobile devices (Figure 2–84).

Instructions: Perform the following tasks:
1. Run Word. Modify the Normal style to the 12-point Times New Roman font. Adjust line spacing to double and remove space below (after) paragraphs. Update the Normal style to include the adjusted line and paragraph spacing. Create a header to number pages. Type the name and course information at the left margin. If requested by your instructor, use your name and course information instead of the information shown in Figure 2–84a on the next page. Center and type the title. Set a first-line indent for paragraphs in the body of the research paper.

Continued >

In the Labs *continued*

Tanner 1

Camryn Tanner

Dr. Bai

Technology 101

October 16, 2014

Mobile Device Protection

The consequences of losing a smartphone or other mobile device are significant because these devices store personal and business data. The goal, therefore, for mobile device users is to make their data as secure as possible. Techniques include avoiding unsafe links, using caution when downloading apps, turning off GPS tracking, and installing mobile security software.

A high percentage of users follow unknown links, which can lead to a malicious website. Malicious links can inject malware on a mobile device. The malware may steal personal information or create toll fraud, which secretly contacts wireless messaging services that impose steep fees on a monthly bill (Bao). Users should avoid tapping or clicking unknown links.

Any device that connects to the Internet is susceptible to mobile malware.[1] Popular games are likely candidates to house malware, and it often is difficult to distinguish the legitimate apps from the fake apps. Users should check the reliability of the seller, the descriptions and reviews of the app, and the requested permissions before downloading.

GPS technology can track the mobile device's location as long as it is transmitting and receiving signals to and from satellites. Although this feature may be helpful, serious privacy concerns can arise when the technology is used in malicious ways, such as to stalk individuals or trace their whereabouts (Fields). It is best to keep this feature disabled until needed.

───────────────────

[1] According to Jameson and Bennett, cyberthieves target apps on popular devices (72).

(a) Page 1

Figure 2–84

2. Type the research paper as shown in Figures 2–84a and 2–84b. Insert the footnote as shown in Figure 2–84a. Change the Footnote Text style to the format specified in the MLA documentation style. Change the bibliography style to MLA. As you insert citations, use the following source information, entering it according to the MLA style:

a. Type of Source: Article in a Periodical
 Author: He Gao Bao
 Article Title: Securing Mobile Devices
 Periodical Title: Technology Today
 Year: 2014
 Month: Sept.
 Pages: no pages used
 Medium: Web
 Year Accessed: 2014
 Month Accessed: Oct.
 Day Accessed: 1

b. Type of Source: Web site
 Author: Charlotte Fields
 Name of webpage: Secure Your Mobile Device
 Year/Month/Date: none given
 Medium: Web
 Year Accessed: 2014
 Month Accessed: Sept.
 Day Accessed: 22

c. Type of Source: Book
 Author: Lewis Taylor Jameson and Kathryn Leona Bennett
 Title: Mobile Technologies
 Year: 2014
 City: New York
 Publisher: Maxwell Press
 Medium: Print

3. At the end of the research paper text, press the ENTER key once and insert a manual page break so that the Works Cited page begins on a new page. Enter and format the works cited title. Use Word to insert the bibliographical list.

4. Check the spelling and grammar of the paper.

5. Save the document using Lab 2-2 Mobile Devices Protection Paper as the file name. Submit the document, shown in Figure 2–84, in the format specified by your instructor.

6. ✻ This paper uses web sources. What factors should you consider when selecting web sources?

Tanner 2

Users can enable the password feature on their mobile device as the first step in stopping prying eyes from viewing contents. More protection is necessary, however, to stop viruses and spyware and to safeguard personal and business data. Mobile security apps can lock a mobile device remotely, erase its memory, and activate its GPS function (Bao).

Some techniques users can take to protect their mobile devices include avoiding unsafe links, using caution when downloading, turning off GPS tracking, and using mobile security software. Users should take these measures to protect their mobile devices.

(b) Page 2
Figure 2–84 (Continued)

Continued >

In the Labs *continued*

Lab 3: Expand Your World: Cloud and Web Technologies
Using an Online Bibliography Tool to Create a List of Sources

Problem: Assume you are using a mobile device or computer that does not have Word but has Internet access. To make use of time between classes, you will use an online bibliography tool to create a list of sources that you can copy and paste into the Works Cited pages of a research paper due tomorrow.

Instructions: Perform the following tasks:

1. Run a browser. Search for the text, online bibliography tool, using a search engine. Visit several of the online bibliography tools and determine which you would like to use to create a list of sources. Navigate to the desired online bibliography tool.

2. Use the online bibliography tool to enter list of sources shown below (Figure 2–85):

 Dayton, Lacey Marie and Sally Louise Walsh. *The Wireless Revolution*. New York: New Artists Press, 2014. Print.

 Dover, Guy Sean. *Communications of Today*. Los Angeles: Sunshine Works, 2014. Print.

Figure 2–85

Howard, Timothy James. "The Wireless Era." *Computers and Networks* Aug. 2014. Web. 29 Aug. 2014.

Matthews, Carl James. *Wireless Trends.* Aug. 2014. Course Technology. Web. 8 Sept. 2014.

Newby, Trisha Lynn and Howard Lou Hopper. "Wireless Communications." *Communications News* Aug. 2014. Web. 4 Oct. 2014.

Newman, William Jared. *The Amazing Wireless World.* Sept. 2014. Course Technology. Web. 28 Sept. 2014.

3. If requested by your instructor, replace the name in one of the sources above with your name.

4. Search for another source that discusses wireless communications. Add that source.

5. Copy and paste the list of sources into a Word document.

6. Save the document with the name Lab 1-3 Wireless Communications Sources. Submit the document in the format specified by your instructor.

7. ✸ Which online bibliography tools did you evaluate? Which one did you select to use and why? Do you prefer using the online bibliography tool or Word to create sources? Why? What differences, if any, did you notice between the list of sources created with the online bibliography tool and the lists created when you use Word?

✸ Consider This: Your Turn

Apply your creative thinking and problem solving skills to design and implement a solution.

Note: To complete these assignments, you may be required to use the Data Files for Students. Visit www.cengage.com/ct/studentdownload for detailed instructions or contact your instructor for information about accessing the required files.

1: Create a Research Paper about Laptops, Tablets, and Desktops
Personal

Part 1: As a student in an introductory computer class, your instructor has assigned a brief research paper that discusses types of computers. The source for the text in your research paper is in a file called Your Turn 2 - 1 Computer Notes, which is located on the Data Files for Students. If your instructor requests, use the Research task pane to obtain information from another source and include that information as a note positioned as a footnote in the paper, along with entering its corresponding source information as appropriate. Add an AutoCorrect entry to correct a word you commonly mistype. If necessary, set the default dictionary. Add one of the source last names to the dictionary.

Using the concepts and techniques presented in this chapter, organize the notes in the text in the file on the Data Files for Students, rewording as necessary, and then create and format this research paper according to the MLA documentation style. Be sure to check spelling and grammar of the finished paper. Submit your assignment and answers to the critical thinking questions in the format specified by your instructor.

Part 2: ✸ You made several decisions while creating the research paper in this assignment: how to organize the notes, where to place citations, how to format sources, and which source on the web to use for the footnote text (if requested by your instructor). What was the rationale behind each of these decisions? When you proofread the document, what further revisions did you make and why?

Continued >

Consider This: Your Turn *continued*

2: Create a Research Paper about POS Terminals, ATMs, and Self-Service Kiosks
Professional

Part 1: As a part-time employee at an advertising firm that specializes in marketing for technology, your boss has asked you to write a brief research paper that discusses types of terminals. The source for the text in your research paper is in a file called Your Turn 2 - 2 Terminals Notes, which is located on the Data Files for Students. If your instructor requests, use the Research task pane to obtain information from another source and include that information as a note positioned as a footnote in the paper, and enter its corresponding source information as appropriate. Add an AutoCorrect entry to correct a word you commonly mistype. If necessary, set the default dictionary. Add one of the source last names to the dictionary.

Using the concepts and techniques presented in this chapter, organize the notes in the file on the Data Files for Students, rewording as necessary, and then create and format this research paper according to the MLA documentation style. Be sure to check spelling and grammar of the finished paper. Submit your assignment and answers to the critical thinking questions in the format specified by your instructor.

Part 2: ✹ You made several decisions while creating the research paper in this assignment: how to organize the notes, where to place citations, how to format sources, and which source on the web to use for the footnote text (if requested by your instructor). What was the rationale behind each of these decisions? When you proofread the document, what further revisions did you make and why?

3: Create a Research Paper about Social Media Sites
Research and Collaboration

Part 1: Because all local youth groups will be creating a page on a social media site, you and two other leaders of local youth groups have been asked to prepare a research paper comparing and contrasting three different social media sites. Form a three-member team to research, compose, and create this paper. Research three separate social media sites: features, capabilities, typical uses, privacy settings, etc. Each team member should write the supporting paragraphs for the social media site he or she researched, including all citations and sources. As a group, write the introduction and conclusion. Be sure to include your team's recommendation in the conclusion.

Use the concepts and techniques presented in this chapter to create and format this paper according to the MLA documentation style. Be sure to check spelling and grammar of the finished paper. Submit your team notes and research paper in the format specified by your instructor.

Part 2: ✹ You made several decisions while creating the research paper in this assignment: the sources to use, which notes to take from the sources, how to organize the notes, how to organize each team member's submissions, what text to write for the introduction and conclusion, where to place citations, and how to format sources. What was the rationale behind each of these decisions? When you proofread the document, what further revisions did you make and why?

Learn Online

Reinforce what you learned in this chapter with games, exercises, training, and many other online activities and resources.

Student Companion Site Reinforcement activities and resources are available at no additional cost on www.cengagebrain.com. Visit www.cengage.com/ct/studentdownload for detailed instructions about accessing the resources available at the Student Companion Site.

SAM Put your skills into practice with SAM! If you have a SAM account, go to www.cengage.com/sam2013 to access SAM assignments for this chapter.

1 Creating a Worksheet and a Chart

Microsoft product screenshots used with permission from Microsoft Corporation.

Objectives

You will have mastered the material in this chapter when you can:

- Describe the Excel worksheet
- Enter text and numbers
- Use the Sum button to sum a range of cells
- Enter a simple function
- Copy the contents of a cell to a range of cells using the fill handle
- Apply cell styles
- Format cells in a worksheet

- Create a 3-D pie chart
- Change a worksheet name and worksheet tab color
- Change document properties
- Preview and print a worksheet
- Use the AutoCalculate area to display statistics
- Correct errors on a worksheet

1 | Creating a Worksheet and a Chart

Introduction

Almost any organization collects vast amounts of data. Often, data is consolidated into a summary so that people in the organization better understand the meaning of the data. An Excel worksheet allows data to be summarized and charted easily. A chart conveys a visual representation of data. In this chapter, you will create a worksheet that includes a chart. The data in the worksheet and chart includes data for a personal budget worksheet that contains monthly estimates on budget amounts.

Project — Worksheet and a Chart

The project in this chapter follows proper design guidelines and uses Excel to create the worksheet and chart shown in Figure 1–1a and Figure 1–1b. The worksheet contains budget data for Bob Gleamin. He wants to estimate what his personal budget will look like for the year, so he has gathered together the information on how much he pays for various expenses and has a list of his current incomes. Now, he wants an easy-to-read worksheet using this information to see how much he will be ahead or behind each month to aid him in planning his budget. In addition, a 3-D pie chart is required that shows the estimated expenses portion for each of the 12 months.

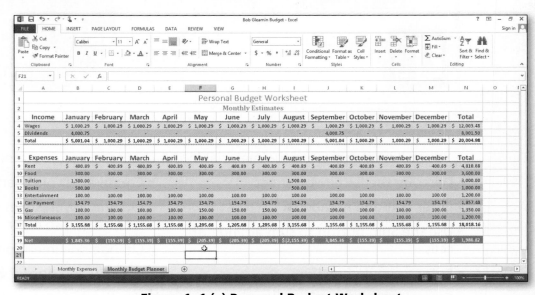

Figure 1–1 (a) Personal Budget Worksheet

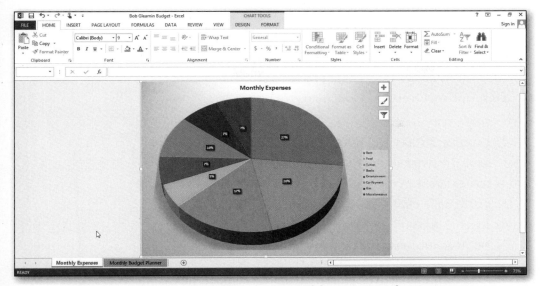

Figure 1–1 (b) Pie Chart Showing Monthly Expenses by Category

The first step in creating an effective worksheet is to make sure you understand what is required. The person or persons requesting the worksheet should supply their requirements in a requirements document. A requirements document includes a needs statement, a source of data, a summary of calculations, and any other special requirements for the worksheet, such as charting and web support. Figure 1–2 shows the requirements document for the new workbook to be created in this chapter.

Worksheet Title	Personal Budget Worksheet
Needs	A yearly projection of Bob Gleamin's personal budget
Source of data	The data supplied by Bob Gleamin includes monthly estimates, including income and expenses
Calculations	The following calculations must be made: 1. For each month, a total for incomes and expenses 2. For each budget item, a total for the item 3. A total for all incomes and expenses 4. Net = income – expenses

Figure 1–2

Roadmap

In this chapter, you will learn how to perform basic workbook tasks using Excel. The following roadmap identifies general activities you will perform as you progress through this chapter:

Descriptive, Overview Roadmap

1. ENTER TEXT in a blank worksheet.
2. CALCULATE SUMS AND USE FORMULAS in the worksheet.
3. SAVE the WORKBOOK using the file name, Bob Gleamin Budget.
4. FORMAT TEXT in the worksheet.
5. INSERT a pie CHART into the worksheet.
6. Assign a NAME to the worksheet TAB.
7. PREVIEW AND PRINT the WORKSHEET.

At the beginning of step instructions throughout the chapter, you will see an abbreviated form of this roadmap. The abbreviated roadmap uses colors to indicate chapter progress: gray means the chapter is beyond that activity, blue means the task being shown is covered in that activity, and black means that activity is yet to be covered. For example, the following abbreviated roadmap indicates the chapter would be showing a task in the Save Workbook activity.

1 ENTER TEXT | 2 CALCULATE SUMS & USE FORMULAS | 3 SAVE WORKBOOK | 4 FORMAT TEXT
5 INSERT CHART | 6 NAME TAB | 7 PREVIEW & PRINT WORKSHEET

CONSIDER THIS

The key to developing a useful worksheet is careful planning. Careful planning can reduce your effort significantly and result in a worksheet that is accurate, easy to read, flexible, and useful. When analyzing a problem and designing a worksheet solution, what steps should you follow?

- Define the problem, including need, source of data, calculations, charting, and web or special requirements.
- Design the worksheet.
- Enter the data and formulas.
- Test the worksheet.

For an introduction to Windows and instruction about how to perform basic Windows tasks, read the Office and Windows chapter at the beginning of this book, where you can learn how to resize windows, change screen resolution, create folders, move and rename files, use Windows Help, and much more.

After carefully reviewing the requirements document (Figure 1– 2 on the previous page) and making the necessary decisions, the next step is to design a solution or draw a sketch of the worksheet based on the requirements, including titles, column and row headings, the location of data values, and the 3-D pie chart, as shown in Figure 1– 3. The dollar signs and commas that you see in the sketch of the worksheet indicate formatted numeric values.

With a good understanding of the requirements document, an understanding of the necessary decisions, and a sketch of the worksheet, the next step is to use Excel to create the worksheet and chart.

Personal Budget Worksheet

Income	January	December	Total
Wages	$99,999.99	$99,999.99	$99,999.99
Dividend			
Total	$99,999.99	$99,999.99	$99,999.99
Expenses	January	December	Total
Rent	$99,999.99	$99,999.99	$99,999.99
Food			
Tuition			
Books			
Entertainment			
Car payment			
Gas			
Miscellaneous			
Total	$99,999.99	$99,999.99	$99,999.99
Net	$99,999.99	$99,999.99	$99,999.99

Monthly Expenses

Legend of Expenses

Figure 1–3

To Run Excel and Create a Blank Workbook

If you are using a computer to step through the project in this chapter and you want your screens to match the figures in this book, you should change your screen's resolution to 1366 × 768. For information about how to change a computer's resolution, refer to the Office and Windows chapter at the beginning of this book.

The following steps, which assume Windows is running, use the Start screen or the Search box to run Excel based on a typical installation. You may need to ask your instructor how to run Excel on your computer. For a detailed example of the procedure summarized below, refer to the Office and Windows chapter.

1 Scroll the Start screen for an Excel 2013 tile. If your Start screen contains an Excel 2013 tile, tap or click it to run Excel and then proceed to Step 5; if the Start screen does not contain the Excel 2013 tile, proceed to the next step to search for the Excel app.

2 Swipe in from the right edge of the screen or point to the upper-right corner of the screen to display the Charms bar and then tap or click the Search charm on the Charms bar to display the Search menu.

3 Type **Excel** as the search text in the Search box and watch the search results appear in the Apps list.

4 Tap or click Excel 2013 in the search results to run Excel.

5 Tap or click the Blank workbook thumbnail on the Excel start screen to create a blank workbook and display it in the Excel window.

6 If the Excel window is not maximized, tap or click the Maximize button on its title bar to maximize the window.

One of the few differences between Windows 7 and Windows 8 occurs in the steps to run Excel. If you are using Windows 7, click the Start button, type **Excel** in the 'Search programs and files' text box, click Excel 2013, and then, if necessary, maximize the Excel window. For detailed steps to run Excel in Windows 7, refer to the Office and Windows chapter at the beginning of this book. For a summary of the steps, refer to the Quick Reference located at the back of this book.

BTW
BTWs
For a complete list of the BTWs found in the margins of this book, visit the BTW resource on the Student Companion Site located on www.cengagebrain.com. For detailed instructions about accessing available resources, visit www.cengage.com/ct/studentdownload or contact your instructor for information about accessing the required files.

If you are using your finger on a touch screen and are having difficulty completing the steps in this chapter, consider using a stylus. Many people find it easier to be precise with a stylus than with a finger. In addition, with a stylus you see the pointer. If you still are having trouble completing the steps with a stylus, try using a mouse.

BTW

Touch Screen Differences

The Office and Windows interfaces may vary if you are using a touch screen. For this reason, you might notice that the function or appearance of your touch screen differs slightly from this chapter's presentation.

BTW

Q&As

For a complete list of the Q&As found in many of the step-by-step sequences in this book, visit the Q&A resource on the Student Companion Site located on www.cengagebrain.com. For detailed instructions about accessing available resources, visit www.cengage.com/ct/studentdownload or contact your instructor for information about accessing the required files.

Selecting a Cell

To enter data into a cell, you first must select it. The easiest way to **select** a cell (make it active) is to tap it or use the mouse to move the block plus sign pointer to the cell and then click.

An alternative method is to use the arrow keys that are located just to the right of the alphanumeric keys on a standard keyboard. An arrow key selects the cell adjacent to the active cell in the direction of the arrow on the key.

You know a cell is selected, or active, when a heavy border surrounds the cell and the active cell reference appears in the Name box on the left side of the formula bar. Excel also changes the active cell's column heading and row heading to a shaded color.

Entering Text

In Excel, any set of characters containing a letter, hyphen (as in a telephone number), or space is considered text. **Text** is used to place titles, such as worksheet titles, column titles, and row titles, on the worksheet.

Worksheet titles and subtitles should be as brief and meaningful as possible. A worksheet title could include the name of the organization, department, or a description of the content of the worksheet. A worksheet subtitle, if included, could include a more detailed description of the content of the worksheet. Examples of worksheet titles are December 2014 Payroll and Year 2015 Projected Budget, and examples of subtitles are Marketing Department and Rent and Utilities, respectively.

As shown in Figure 1–4, data in a worksheet often is identified by row and column titles so that the user of a worksheet easily can identify the meaning of the data. Rows typically contain information that is similar to items in a list. Columns typically contain descriptive information about items in rows or contain information that helps to group the data in the worksheet. Examples of row titles are Income and Total, and examples of column titles are Wages and Gas.

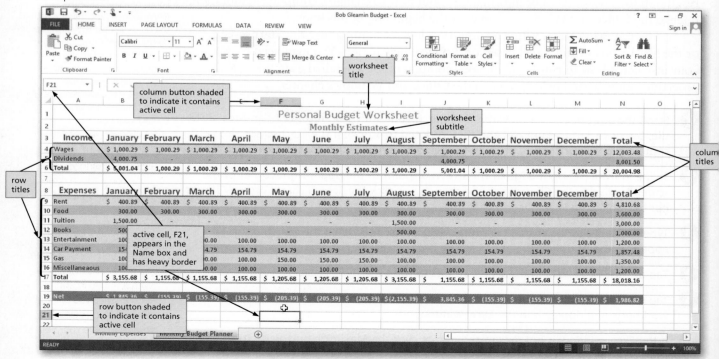

Figure 1–4

To Enter the Worksheet Titles

As shown in Figure 1–4, the worksheet title, Personal Budget Worksheet, identifies the purpose for which the worksheet is being created in Chapter 1. The worksheet subtitle, Monthly Estimates, identifies the type of data contained in the worksheet. **Why?** *A title and subtitle help the reader to understand clearly what the worksheet contains.*

The following steps enter the worksheet titles in cells A1 and A2. Later in this chapter, the worksheet titles will be formatted so that they appear as shown in Figure 1–4.

1

• If necessary, tap or click cell A1 to make cell A1 the active cell (Figure 1–5).

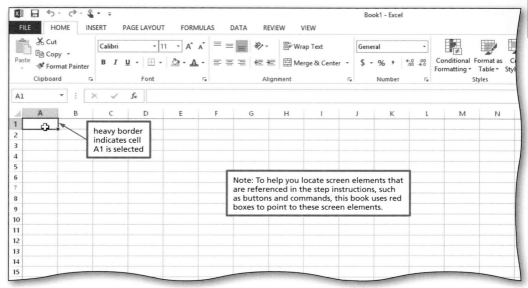

Figure 1–5

2

• Type **Personal Budget Worksheet** in cell A1 and then point to the Enter box in the formula bar to prepare to enter text in the active cell (Figure 1–6).

Q&A Why did the appearance of the formula bar change? Excel displays the title in the formula bar and in cell A1. When you begin typing a cell entry, Excel displays two additional boxes in the formula bar: the Cancel box and the Enter box. Tapping or clicking the **Enter box** completes an entry. Tapping or clicking the **Cancel box** cancels an entry.

Figure 1–6

❸
- Tap or click the Enter box to complete the entry and enter the worksheet title (Figure 1–7).

Q&A Why does the entered text appear in three cells?
When the text is longer than the width of a cell, Excel displays the overflow characters in adjacent cells to the right as long as those adjacent cells contain no data. If the adjacent cells contain data, Excel hides the overflow characters. Excel displays the overflow characters in the formula bar whenever that cell is the active cell.

Figure 1–7

❹
- Tap or click cell A2 to select it.
- Type **Monthly Estimates** as the cell entry.
- Tap or click the Enter box to complete the entry and enter the worksheet subtitle (Figure 1–8).

Q&A What happens when I tap or click the Enter box?
When you complete an entry by tapping or clicking the Enter box, the insertion point disappears and the cell in which the text is entered remains the active cell.

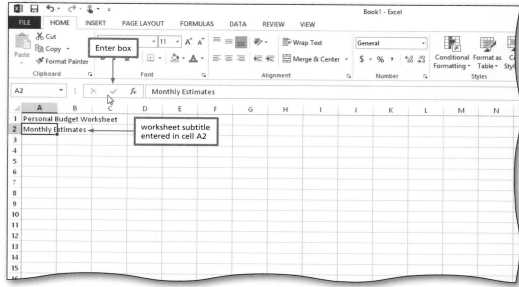

Figure 1–8

Other Ways

1. To complete entry, tap or click any cell other than active cell	2. To complete entry, press ENTER	3. To complete entry, press HOME, PAGE UP, PAGE DOWN, or END	4. To complete entry, press UP ARROW, DOWN ARROW, LEFT ARROW, or RIGHT ARROW

AutoCorrect

The **AutoCorrect feature** of Excel works behind the scenes, correcting common mistakes when you complete a text entry in a cell. AutoCorrect makes three types of corrections for you:

1. Corrects two initial uppercase letters by changing the second letter to lowercase.

2. Capitalizes the first letter in the names of days.

3. Replaces commonly misspelled words with their correct spelling. For example, it will change the misspelled word *recieve* to *receive* when you complete the entry. AutoCorrect will correct the spelling of hundreds of commonly misspelled words automatically.

BTW
The Ribbon and Screen Resolution
Excel may change how the groups and buttons within the groups appear on the ribbon, depending on the computer's screen resolution. Thus, your ribbon may look different from the ones in this book if you are using a screen resolution other than 1366 × 768.

To Enter Column Titles

1 ENTER TEXT | 2 CALCULATE SUMS & USE FORMULAS | 3 SAVE WORKBOOK | 4 FORMAT TEXT
5 INSERT CHART | 6 NAME TAB | 7 PREVIEW & PRINT WORKSHEET

The column titles in row 3 shown in Figure 1–4 (Income, January, February, March, April, May, June, July, August, September, October, November, December, and Total) identify the numbers in each column in the first part of the worksheet. The column titles in row 8 (Expenses, January, February, March, April, May, June, July, August, September, October, November, December, and Total) identify the numbers in each column in the second part of the worksheet. In the case of the Personal Budget Worksheet data, the month names identify the estimates for the budget for each month using the income or expense type, depending on which part you are reviewing.

To enter the column titles in row 3, select the appropriate cell and then enter the text. The following steps enter the column titles in row 3. **Why?** *Data entered in columns should be identified using column titles to identify what the column contains.*

1

- Tap or click cell A3 to make it the active cell.

- Type **Income** to begin entry of a column title in the active cell (Figure 1–9).

Q&A What is the vertical line in cell A1?
The text in cell A1 is followed by the insertion point. The **insertion point** is a blinking vertical line that indicates where the next typed character will appear.

Figure 1–9

2

- If you are using a touch screen, tap cell B3; if you are using a mouse, press the RIGHT ARROW key to enter a column title and make the cell to the right the active cell (Figure 1–10).

Q&A Why is the RIGHT ARROW key used to complete the entry in the cell?

If the next entry you want to enter is in an adjacent cell, use the arrow keys to complete the entry in a cell. When you press an arrow key to complete an entry, the adjacent cell in the direction of the arrow (up, down, left, or right) becomes the active cell. If the next entry is in a nonadjacent cell, complete the current entry by tapping or clicking the next cell in which you plan to enter data. You also can tap or click the Enter box or press the ENTER key and then tap or click the appropriate cell for the next entry.

Figure 1–10

3

- Repeat Steps 1 and 2 to enter the remaining column titles; that is, enter **January** in cell B3, **February** in cell C3, **March** in cell D3, **April** in cell E3, **May** in cell F3, **June** in cell G3, **July** in cell H3, **August** in cell I3, **September** in cell J3, **October** in cell K3, **November** in cell L3, **December** in cell M3, and **Total** in cell N3 (complete the last entry in cell N3 by tapping or clicking the Enter box in the formula bar).

Figure 1–11

- Tap or click cell A8 to select it.

- Repeat Steps 1 and 2 to enter the remaining column titles; that is, enter **Expenses** in cell A8, **January** in cell B8, **February** in cell C8, **March** in cell D8, **April** in cell E8, **May** in cell F8, **June** in cell G8, **July** in cell H8, **August** in cell I8, **September** in cell J8, **October** in cell K8, **November** in cell L8, **December** in cell M8, and **Total** in cell N8 (complete the last entry in cell N8 by tapping or clicking the Enter box in the formula bar) (Figure 1–11).

To Enter Row Titles

The next step in developing the worksheet for this project is to enter the row titles in column A. For the Personal Budget Worksheet data, the list of income types and expense types make up the row titles. It is likely that in the future, Bob Gleamin may add more income or expense items. Each income or expense item, therefore, should be placed in its own row. The row titles in column A for income (Wages, Dividends, and Total), expenses (Rent, Food, Tuition, Books, Entertainment, Car Payment, Gas, Miscellaneous, and Total), and net income (Net) identify the numbers in each row.

This process for entering row titles is similar to the process for entering column titles. The following steps enter the row titles in the worksheet.

- Tap or click cell A4 to select it.

- Type **Wages** and then tap cell A5 or press the DOWN ARROW key to enter a row title (Figure 1–12).

Figure 1–12

2

- Repeat Step 1 to enter the remaining row titles in column A; that is, enter **Dividends** in cell A5, **Total** in cell A6, **Rent** in cell A9, **Food** in cell A10, **Tuition** in cell A11, **Books** in cell A12, **Entertainment** in cell A13, **Car Payment** in cell A14, **Gas** in cell A15, **Miscellaneous** in cell A16, **Total** in cell A17, and **Net** in cell A19 (Figure 1–13).

Figure 1–13

Q&A Why is the text left-aligned in the cells?
When you enter text, Excel automatically left-aligns the text in the cell. Excel treats any combination of numbers, spaces, and nonnumeric characters as text. For example, Excel recognizes the following entries as text: 401AX21, 921–231, 619 321, 883XTY
You can change the text alignment in a cell by realigning it. Other alignment techniques are discussed later in this chapter.

Entering Numbers

In Excel, you can enter numbers into cells to represent amounts. A **number** can contain only the following characters:

0 1 2 3 4 5 6 7 8 9 + − () , / . $ % E e

If a cell entry contains any other keyboard character (including spaces), Excel interprets the entry as text and treats it accordingly. The use of special characters is explained when they are used in this book.

To Enter Numbers

1 ENTER TEXT | 2 CALCULATE SUMS & USE FORMULAS | 3 SAVE WORKBOOK | 4 FORMAT TEXT
5 INSERT CHART | 6 NAME TAB | 7 PREVIEW & PRINT WORKSHEET

The Personal Budget Worksheet numbers used in Chapter 1 are summarized in Table 1–1. These numbers, which represent yearly income and expenses amounts, must be entered in rows 4–5 and 9–16.

Table 1–1 Personal Budget Worksheet

Income	January	February	March	April	May	June	July	August	September	October	November	Dec
Wages	1000.29	1000.29	1000.29	1000.29	1000.29	1000.29	1000.29	1000.29	1000.29	1000.29	1000.29	100
Dividends	4000.75	0	0	0	0	0	0	0	4000.75	0	0	0

Expenses	January	February	March	April	May	June	July	August	September	October	November	Dec
Rent	400.89	400.89	400.89	400.89	400.89	400.89	400.89	400.89	400.89	400.89	400.89	400
Food	300	300	300	300	300	300	300	300	300	300	300	300
Tuition	1500	0	0	0	0	0	0	1500	0	0	0	0
Books	500	0	0	0	0	0	0	500	0	0	0	0
Entertainment	100	100	100	100	100	100	100	100	100	100	100	100
Car Payment	154.79	154.79	154.79	154.79	154.79	154.79	154.79	154.79	154.79	154.79	154.79	154.
Gas	100	100	100	100	150	150	150	100	100	100	100	100
Miscellaneous	100	100	100	100	100	100	100	100	100	100	100	100

The following steps enter the numbers in Table 1–1 one row at a time.

1

- Tap or click cell B4 to select it.

- Type 1000.29 and then if you are using a touch screen, tap cell C4. If you are using a mouse, press the RIGHT ARROW key to enter the data in the selected cell and make the cell to the right (cell C4) the active cell (Figure 1–14).

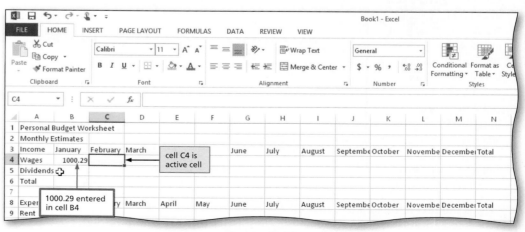

Figure 1–14

Q&A Do I need to enter dollar signs, commas, or trailing zeros for the amounts?

You are not required to type dollar signs, commas, or trailing zeros. When you enter a dollar value that has cents, however, you must add the decimal point and the numbers representing the cents. Later in this chapter, the numbers will be formatted to use dollar signs, commas, and trailing zeros to improve the appearance and readability of the numbers.

2

- Enter 1000.29 in cells C4, D4, E4, F4, G4, H4, I4, J4, K4, L4, and M4 to complete the first row of numbers in the worksheet (Figure 1–15).

Q&A Why are the numbers right-aligned?

When you enter numeric data in a cell, Excel recognizes the values as numbers and right-aligns the values in order to properly vertically align decimal and integer values. For example, values entered below those entered in this step automatically will be right-aligned so that the decimals of the values properly align.

Figure 1–15

3

- Tap or click cell B5 to select it and complete the entry in the previously selected cell.

- Enter the remaining personal budget numbers provided in Table 1–1 on page EX 12 for each of the nine remaining budget items in rows 5 and 9–16 to finish entering numbers in the worksheet (Figure 1–16).

Q&A Why did tapping or clicking cell B5 complete the entry in cell M4?

Figure 1–16

Selecting another cell completes the entry in the previously selected cell in the same way as pressing the ENTER key, pressing an arrow key, or tapping or clicking the Enter box in the formula bar. In the next set of steps, the entry of the number in cell B5 will be completed by selecting another cell.

Calculating a Sum

The next step in creating the worksheet is to perform any necessary calculations, such as calculating the column and row totals. When you use functions, Excel performs the calculations for you, which helps to prevent errors and allows you to work more efficiently.

To Sum a Column of Numbers

1 ENTER TEXT | 2 CALCULATE SUMS & USE FORMULAS | 3 SAVE WORKBOOK | 4 FORMAT TEXT | 5 INSERT CHART | 6 NAME TAB | 7 PREVIEW & PRINT WORKSHEET

As stated in the requirements document in Figure 1–2 on page EX 3, totals are required for each month and each budget item. The first calculation is to determine the total income for the Wages and Dividends in the month of January in column B. To calculate this value in cell B6, Excel must add, or sum, the numbers in cells B4 and B5. The **SUM function** adds all the numbers in a range of cells. *Why? Excel's SUM function provides a convenient means to accomplish this task.*

A **range** is a series of two or more adjacent cells in a column or row or a rectangular group of cells. For example, the group of adjacent cells B4 and B5 is called a range. Many Excel operations, such as summing numbers, are performed on a range of cells.

After the total income for a month in column B is determined, the totals for the remaining months for income, the totals for the expenses, and the totals for budget item will be determined. The following steps sum the numbers in column B.

1

- Tap or click cell B6 to make it the active cell and complete the entry in the previously selected cell.

- Tap or click the Sum button (HOME tab | Editing group) to display a formula in the formula bar and in the active cell (Figure 1–17).

What if my screen displays a Sum menu?

If you are using a touch screen, you may not have a separate Sum button and Sum arrow. In this case, select the desired option on the Sum menu.

How does Excel know which cells to sum?

When you enter the SUM function using the Sum button on the ribbon, Excel automatically selects what it considers to be your choice of the range to sum. When proposing the range to sum, Excel first looks for a range of cells with numbers above the active cell and then to the left. If Excel proposes the wrong range, you can correct it by dragging through the correct range before pressing the ENTER key. You also can enter the correct range by typing the beginning cell reference, a colon (:), and the ending cell reference.

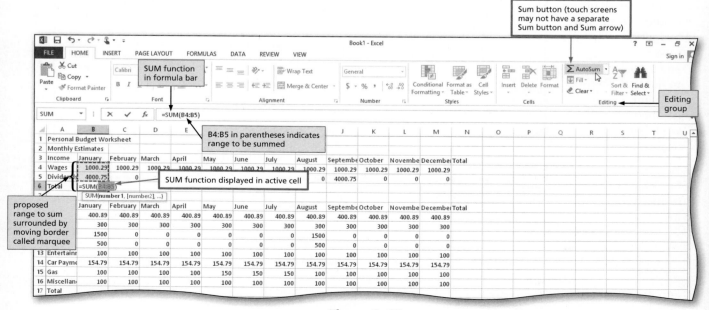

Figure 1–17

2

- Tap or click the Enter box in the formula bar to enter a sum in the active cell.

Q&A | What is the purpose of the Sum arrow?
If you tap or click the Sum arrow on the right side of the Sum button (HOME tab | Editing group) (shown in Figure 1–17), Excel displays a list of often-used functions from which you can choose. The list includes functions that allow you to determine the average, the number of items in the selected range, the maximum value, or the minimum value of a range of numbers.

3

- Repeat Steps 1 and 2 to enter the SUM function in cell B17 (Figure 1–18).

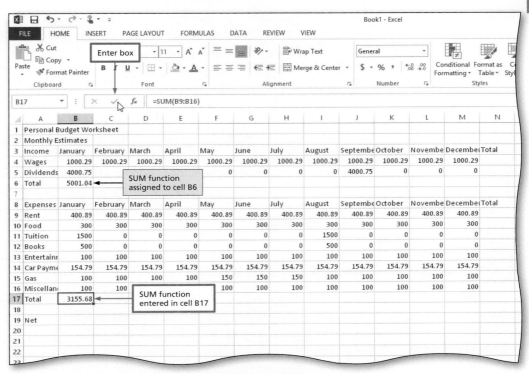

Figure 1–18

Other Ways

1. Tap or click Insert Function button in formula bar, select SUM in Select a function list, tap or click OK button (Insert Function dialog box),

 tap or click OK button (Function Arguments dialog box)

2. Tap or click Sum arrow (HOME tab | Editing group), tap or click More Functions in list, tap

 or click SUM (Insert Function dialog box), tap or click OK button, select range (Function Arguments dialog box), tap or click OK button

3. Type **=s** in cell, select SUM in list, select range, tap or click Enter box

4. Press ALT+EQUAL SIGN (=) twice

Using the Fill Handle to Copy a Cell to Adjacent Cells

Excel also must calculate the totals for income during each month in cells C6:M6. Table 1–2 on the next page illustrates the similarities between the entry in cell B6 and the entries required to sum the totals in cells C6, D6, E6, F6, G6, H6, I6, J6, K6, L6, and M6.

To place the SUM functions in range C6:M6, you could follow the same steps shown previously in Figure 1–17 and Figure 1–18. A second, more efficient method, however, is to copy the SUM function from cell B6 to the range C6:M6. The cell being copied is called the **source area** or **copy area**. The range of cells receiving the copy is called the **destination area** or **paste area**.

Table 1–2 Sum Function Entries in Row 6		
Cell	**SUM Function Entries**	**Result**
B6	=SUM(B4:B5)	Sums cells B4 and B5
C6	=SUM(C4:C5)	Sums cells C4 and C5
D6	=SUM(D4:D5)	Sums cells D4 and D5
E6	=SUM(E4:E5)	Sums cells E4 and E5
F6	=SUM(F4:F5)	Sums cells F4 and F5
G6	=SUM(G4:G5)	Sums cells G4 and G5
H6	=SUM(H4:H5)	Sums cells H4 and H5
I6	=SUM(I4:I5)	Sums cells I4 and I5
J6	=SUM(J4:J5)	Sums cells J4 and J5
K6	=SUM(K4:K5)	Sums cells K4 and K5
L6	=SUM(L4:L5)	Sums cells L4 and L5
M6	=SUM(M4:M5)	Sums cells M4 and M5

Although the SUM function entries in Table 1–2 are similar, they are not exact copies. The range in each SUM function entry uses cell references that are one column to the right of the previous column. When you copy formulas that include cell references, Excel automatically adjusts them for each new position, resulting in the SUM function entries illustrated in Table 1–2. Each adjusted cell reference is called a **relative reference**.

To Copy a Cell to Adjacent Cells in a Row

1 ENTER TEXT | 2 CALCULATE SUMS & USE FORMULAS | 3 SAVE WORKBOOK | 4 FORMAT TEXT
5 INSERT CHART | 6 NAME TAB | 7 PREVIEW & PRINT WORKSHEET

The easiest way to copy the SUM formula from cell B6 to cells C6:M6 is to use the fill handle. *Why?* *Using the fill handle means that Excel creates the formulas for you.* The **fill handle** is the small black square located in the lower-right corner of the heavy border around the active cell. The following steps use the fill handle to copy cell B6 to the adjacent cells C6:M6.

1

- With cell B6 active, if you are using a touch screen, press and hold cell B6 to display the mini toolbar, then tap AutoFill on the mini toolbar; if you are using a mouse, point to the fill handle to activate it (Figure 1–19).

Q&A Why is my fill handle not a black square? If you are using a touch screen, the fill handle appears as a black and white rectangle with a blue down arrow in it.

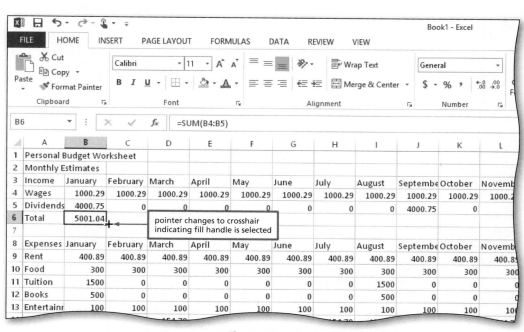

Figure 1–19

2

- Drag the fill handle to select the destination area, range C6:M6, to display a shaded border around the source area and the destination area (Figure 1–20). Do not lift your finger from the screen or release the mouse button.

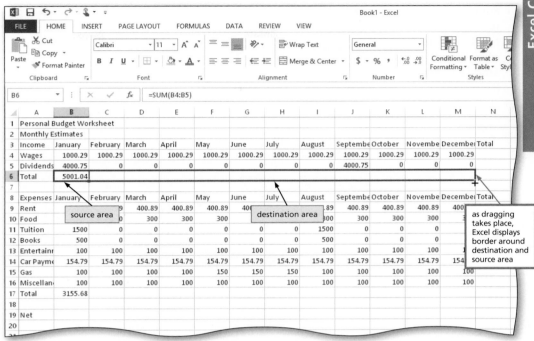

Figure 1–20

3

- Lift your finger from the screen or release the mouse button to copy the SUM function from the active cell to the destination area and calculate the sums (Figure 1–21).

Q&A What is the purpose of the 'Auto Fill Options' button? When you copy one range to another, Excel displays an 'Auto Fill Options' button (Figure 1–21). The 'Auto Fill Options' button allows you to choose whether you want to copy the values from the source area to the destination area with formatting, do so without formatting, or copy only the format. To view the available fill options, tap or click the 'Auto Fill Options' button. The 'Auto Fill Options' button disappears when you begin another activity in Excel, such as typing data in another cell or applying formatting to a cell or range of cells.

Figure 1–21

- Repeat Steps 1–3 to copy the SUM function from cell B17 to the range C17:M17 (Figure 1–22).

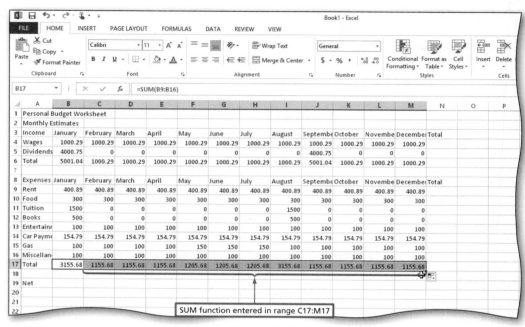

Figure 1–22

Other Ways

1. Select source area, tap or click Copy button (HOME tab | Clipboard group), select destination area, tap or click Paste button (HOME tab | Clipboard group)

2. Press and hold or right-click source area, tap or click Copy on shortcut menu; press and hold or right-click destination area, tap or click Paste on shortcut menu

To Determine Multiple Totals at the Same Time

1 ENTER TEXT | 2 CALCULATE SUMS & USE FORMULAS | 3 SAVE WORKBOOK | 4 FORMAT TEXT
5 INSERT CHART | 6 NAME TAB | 7 PREVIEW & PRINT WORKSHEET

The next step in building the worksheet is to determine the budget item totals for each budget item and total income and expenses in column N. To calculate these totals, you can use the SUM function much as it was used to total the budget items for each month in rows 6 and 17.

In this example, however, Excel will determine totals for all of the rows at the same time. *Why? By determining multiple totals at the same time, the number of steps to add totals is reduced.* The following steps sum multiple totals at once.

- Tap or click cell N4 to make it the active cell (Figure 1–23).

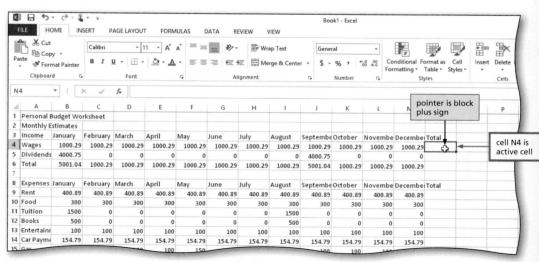

Figure 1–23

2

- If you are using a touch screen, drag the lower-right selection handle down to cell N6; if you are using a mouse, with the pointer in cell N4 and in the shape of a block plus sign, drag the pointer down to cell N6 to highlight the range with a transparent view (Figure 1–24).

Figure 1–24

3

- Tap or click the Sum button (HOME tab | Editing group) to calculate and display the sums of the corresponding rows (Figure 1–25).

Q&A How does Excel create unique totals for each row?
If each cell in a selected range is next to a row of numbers, Excel assigns the SUM function to each cell when you tap or click the Sum button.

Figure 1–25

4

• Repeat Steps 1–3 to select cells N9 to N17 and calculate and display the sums of the corresponding rows (Figure 1–26).

Figure 1–26

To Enter a Formula Using the Keyboard

1 ENTER TEXT | 2 CALCULATE SUMS & USE FORMULAS | 3 SAVE WORKBOOK | 4 FORMAT TEXT
5 INSERT CHART | 6 NAME TAB | 7 PREVIEW & PRINT WORKSHEET

The formulas needed in the worksheet are noted in the requirements document as follows:

Net (row 19) = Income – Expenses

The net for each month, which appears in row 19, is equal to the income total in row 6 minus the expense total in row 17. The following steps enter the initial net formula in cell B19 using the keyboard. *Why? Sometimes a predefined function does not fit your needs; therefore, you enter a formula of your own.*

1

• Select cell B19 to deselect the selected range.

• Type **=b6-b17** in the cell to display the formula in the formula bar and in the current cell and to display colored borders around the cells referenced in the formula (Figure 1–27).

Q&A What occurs on the worksheet as I enter the formula?

The **equal sign** (=) preceding b6–b17 in the formula alerts Excel that you are entering a

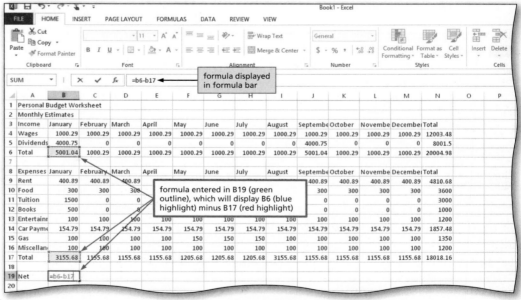

Figure 1–27

formula or function and not text. Because the most common error when entering a formula is to reference the wrong cell in a formula, Excel colors the borders of the cells referenced in the formula. The coloring helps in the reviewing process to ensure the cell references are correct. The **minus sign** (–) following b6 in the formula is the arithmetic operator that directs Excel to perform the subtraction operation.

2

- Tap or click cell C19 to complete the arithmetic operation indicated by the formula, to display the result in the worksheet, and to select the cell to the right (Figure 1–28).

Figure 1–28

To Copy a Cell to Adjacent Cells in a Row

The easiest way to copy the SUM formula from cell B19 to cells C19, D19, E19, F19, G19, H19, I19, J19, K19, L19, M19, and N19 is to use the fill handle. The following steps use the fill handle to copy the formula in cell B19 to the adjacent cells C19:N19.

1 Select cell B19.

2 Drag the fill handle to select the destination area, range C19:N19, to display a shaded border around the source area and the destination area. Do not lift your finger or release the mouse button.

3 Lift your finger or release the mouse button to copy the simple formula function from the active cell to the destination area and calculate the results.

To Save a Workbook with a New File Name

You have performed many tasks while creating this workbook and do not want to risk losing work completed thus far. Accordingly, you should save the workbook on your hard disk, SkyDrive, or a location that is most appropriate to your situation.

The following steps assume you already have created folders for storing your files, for example, a CIS 101 folder (for your class) that contains an Excel folder (for your assignments). Thus, these steps save the workbook in the Excel folder in the CIS 101 folder on your desired save location. For a detailed example of the procedure for saving a file in a folder or saving a file on SkyDrive, refer to the Office and Windows chapter at the beginning of this book.

1 Tap or click the Save button on the Quick Access Toolbar, which depending on settings, will display either the Save As gallery in the Backstage view or the Save As dialog box.

2 To save on a hard disk or other storage media on your computer, proceed to Step 2a. To save on SkyDrive, proceed to Step 2b.

2a If your screen opens the Backstage view and you want to save on storage media on your computer, tap or click Computer in the left pane, if necessary, to display options in the right pane related to saving on your computer. If your screen already displays the Save As dialog box, proceed to Step 3.

2b If your screen opens the Backstage view and you want to save on SkyDrive, tap or click SkyDrive in the left pane to display SkyDrive saving options or a Sign In button. If your screen displays a Sign In button, tap or click it and then sign in to SkyDrive.

3 Tap or click the Browse button in the right pane to display the Save As dialog box associated with the selected save location (i.e., Computer or SkyDrive).

4 Type `Bob Gleamin Budget` in the File name box to change the file name. Do not press the ENTER key after typing the file name because you do not want to close the dialog box at this time.

5 Navigate to the desired save location (in this case, the Excel folder in the CIS 101 folder [or your class folder] on your computer or SkyDrive).

6 Tap or click the Save button (Save As dialog box) to save the workbook in the selected folder on the selected save location with the entered file name.

Break Point: If you wish to take a break, this is a good place to do so. You can exit Excel. To resume at a later time, run Excel, open the file called Bob Gleamin Budget, and continue following the steps from this location forward.

Formatting the Worksheet

The text, numeric entries, and functions for the worksheet now are complete. The next step is to format the worksheet. You **format** a worksheet to emphasize certain entries and make the worksheet easier to read and understand.

Figure 1–29a shows the worksheet before formatting. Figure 1–29b shows the worksheet after formatting. As you can see from the two figures, a worksheet that is formatted not only is easier to read but also looks more professional.

CONSIDER THIS

The key to formatting a worksheet is to consider the ways you can enhance the worksheet so that it appears professional. When formatting a worksheet, what steps should you consider?

• Identify how to format various elements of the worksheet.

• Increase the font size of cells.

• Change the font color of cells.

• Center the worksheet titles, subtitles, and column headings.

• Modify column widths to best fit text in cells.

• Change the font style of cells.

To change the unformatted worksheet in Figure 1–29a so that it appears like the formatted worksheet in Figure 1–29b, the following tasks must be completed:

1. Change the font, change the font style to bold, increase the font size, and change the font color of the worksheet titles in cells A1 and A2.

2. Center the worksheet titles in cells A1 and A2 across columns A through N.

(a) Unformatted Worksheet

(b) Formatted Worksheet

Figure 1–29

3. Format the body of the worksheet. The body of the worksheet, range A3:N19, includes the column titles, row titles, and numbers. Formatting the body of the worksheet changes the numbers to use a dollars-and-cents format, with dollar signs in rows 4 and 9 and the total rows (row 6 and 17); changes the styles of some rows; adds underlining that emphasizes portions of the worksheet; and modifies the column widths to fit the text in the columns and make the text and numbers readable.

The remainder of this section explains the process required to format the worksheet. Although the formatting procedures are explained in the order described above, you should be aware that you could make these format changes in any order. Modifying the column widths, however, usually is done last because other formatting changes may affect the size of data in the cells in the column.

Font Style, Size, and Color

The characters that Excel displays on the screen are a specific font, style, size, and color. The **font**, or font face, defines the appearance and shape of the letters, numbers, and special characters. Examples of fonts include Calibri, Cambria, Times New Roman, Arial, and Courier. **Font style** indicates how the characters are emphasized. Common font styles include regular, bold, underline, and italic. The **font size** specifies the size of the characters on the screen. Font size is gauged by a measurement system called points. A single point is about 1/72 of one inch in height. Thus, a character with a **point size** of 10 is about 10/72 of one inch in height. The **font color** defines the color of the characters. Excel can display characters in a wide variety of colors.

When Excel first runs, the preset font for the entire workbook is Calibri, with a font size, font style, and font color of 11–point regular black. Excel allows you to change the font characteristics in a single cell, a range of cells, the entire worksheet, or the entire workbook.

BTW

Organizing Files and Folders
You should organize and store files in folders so that you easily can find the files later. For example, if you are taking an introductory computer class called CIS 101, a good practice would be to save all Excel files in a Excel folder in a CIS 101 folder. For a discussion of folders and detailed examples of creating folders, refer to the Office and Windows chapter at the beginning of this book.

To Change a Cell Style

Excel includes the capability of changing several characteristics of a cell, such as the font, font size, and font color, all at once by assigning a predefined cell style to a cell. *Why? Using the predefined styles that Excel includes provides a consistent appearance to common portions of your worksheets, such as worksheet titles, worksheet subtitles, column headings, and total rows.* The following steps assign the Title cell style to the worksheet title in cell A1.

1
- Tap or click cell A1 to make cell A1 the active cell.
- Tap or click the Cell Styles button (HOME tab | Styles group) to display the Cell Styles gallery (Figure 1–30).

Figure 1–30

2
- If you are using a mouse, point to the Title cell style in the Titles and Headings area of the Cell Styles gallery to see a live preview of the cell style in the active cell (Figure 1–31).

Q&A Can I use live preview on a touch screen?
Live preview is not available on a touch screen.

Experiment
- If you are using a mouse, point to several other cell styles in the Cell Styles gallery to see a live preview of other cell styles in cell A1.

Figure 1–31

3

- Tap or click the Title cell style to apply the cell style to the active cell (Figure 1– 32).

Q&A
Why do several items in the Font group on the ribbon change?
The changes to the Font box and Font Size box indicate the font changes applied to the active cell, cell A1, as a result of applying the Title cell style.

Figure 1–32

To Change the Font

1 ENTER TEXT | 2 CALCULATE SUMS & USE FORMULAS | 3 SAVE WORKBOOK | 4 FORMAT TEXT
5 INSERT CHART | 6 NAME TAB | 7 PREVIEW & PRINT WORKSHEET

Why? *Different fonts often are used in a worksheet to make it more appealing to the reader and to relate or distinguish data in the worksheet.* The following steps change the worksheet subtitle's font to Cambria.

1

- Tap or click cell A2 to make it the active cell.

- Tap or click the Font arrow (HOME tab | Font group) to display the Font gallery. If necessary, scroll to display Cambria.

- If you are using a mouse, point to Cambria in the Font gallery to see a live preview of the selected font in the active cell (Figure 1–33).

Experiment

- If you are using a mouse, point to several other fonts in the Font gallery to see a live preview of other fonts in the selected cell.

Figure 1–33

2

• Tap or click Cambria in the Font gallery to change the font of the worksheet subtitle to Cambria (Figure 1– 34).

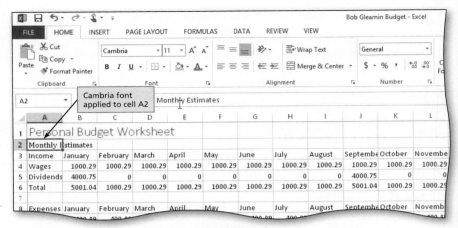

Figure 1–34

Other Ways

1. Tap or click Font Settings Dialog Box Launcher, tap or click Font tab (Format Cells dialog box), tap or click desired font in Font list, tap or click OK button

2. If you are using a mouse, click Font box arrow on mini toolbar, click desired font in Font gallery

3. Tap 'Show Context Menu' button on mini toolbar or right-click selected cell, tap or click Format Cells on shortcut menu, tap or click Font tab (Format Cells dialog box), tap or click desired font, tap or click OK button

To Bold a Cell

1 ENTER TEXT | 2 CALCULATE SUMS & USE FORMULAS | 3 SAVE WORKBOOK | **4 FORMAT TEXT**
5 INSERT CHART | 6 NAME TAB | 7 PREVIEW & PRINT WORKSHEET

Bold text has a darker appearance than normal text. *Why? You bold an entry in a cell to emphasize it or make it stand out from the rest of the worksheet.* The following steps bold the worksheet title and subtitle.

1

• Tap or click cell A1 to make it active and then tap or click the Bold button (HOME tab | Font group) to change the font style of the active cell to bold (Figure 1–35).

Q&A

What if a cell already includes a bold style?
If the active cell already is bold, then Excel displays the Bold button with a transparent green background.

How do I remove the bold style from a cell?
Tapping or clicking the Bold button (HOME tab | Font group) a second time removes the bold style.

Figure 1–35

2

• Repeat Step 1 to bold cell A2.

Other Ways

1. Tap or click Font Settings Dialog Box Launcher, tap or click Font tab (Format Cells dialog box), tap or click Bold in Font style list, tap or click OK button

2. If you are using a mouse, click Bold button on mini toolbar

3. Tap 'Show Context Menu' button on mini toolbar or right-click selected cell, tap or click Format Cells on shortcut menu, tap or click Font tab (Format Cells dialog box), tap or click Bold, tap or click OK button

4. Press CTRL+B

To Increase the Font Size of a Cell Entry

Increasing the font size is the next step in formatting the worksheet subtitle. *Why? You increase the font size of a cell so that the entry stands out and is easier to read.* The following steps increase the font size of the worksheet subtitle in cell A2.

1

- With cell A2 selected, tap or click the Font Size arrow (HOME tab | Font group) to display the Font Size gallery.

- If you are using a mouse, point to 14 in the Font Size gallery to see a live preview of the active cell with the selected font size (Figure 1–36).

Experiment

- If you are using a mouse, point to several other font sizes in the Font Size list to see a live preview of other font sizes in the selected cell.

Figure 1–36

2

- Tap or click 14 in the Font Size gallery to change the font size in the active cell (Figure 1–37).

Q&A Can I assign a font size that is not in the Font Size gallery?
Yes. An alternative to tapping or clicking a font size in the Font Size gallery is to tap or click the Font Size box (HOME tab | Font group), type the font size, and then press the ENTER key. This procedure allows you to assign a font size not available in the Font Size gallery to a selected cell entry.

Figure 1–37

Other Ways

1. Tap or click 'Increase Font Size' button (HOME tab | Font group) or 'Decrease Font Size' button (HOME tab | Font group)

2. Tap or click Font Settings Dialog Box Launcher, tap or click Font tab (Format Cells dialog box), tap or click desired size in Size list, tap or click OK button

3. Tap or click Font Size arrow on mini toolbar, tap or click desired font size in Font Size gallery

4. Tap 'Show Context Menu' button on mini toolbar or right-click selected cell, tap or click Format Cells on shortcut menu, tap or click Font tab (Format Cells dialog box), select font size in Size box, tap or click OK button

EX 28 **Excel Chapter 1** Creating a Worksheet and a Chart

1 ENTER TEXT | 2 CALCULATE SUMS & USE FORMULAS | 3 SAVE WORKBOOK | 4 FORMAT TEXT
5 INSERT CHART | 6 NAME TAB | 7 PREVIEW & PRINT WORKSHEET

To Change the Font Color of a Cell Entry

The next step is to change the color of the font in cells A1 and A2 to blue. *Why? Changing the font color of cell entries can help the text stand out more.* The following steps change the font color of a cell entry.

1
- Tap or click cell A1 and then tap or click the Font Color arrow (HOME tab | Font group) to display the Font Color gallery.

- If you are using a mouse, point to 'Blue, Accent 1' (column 5, row 1) in the Theme Colors area of the Font Color gallery to see a live preview of the font color in the active cell (Figure 1–38).

 Experiment
- If you are using a mouse, point to several other colors in the Font Color gallery to see a live preview of other font colors in the active cell.

Figure 1–38

Q&A Which colors does Excel make available in the Font Color gallery?
You can choose from more than 60 different font colors in the Font Color gallery. Your Font Color gallery may have more or fewer colors, depending on color settings of your operating system. The Theme Colors area contains colors that are included in the current workbook's theme.

2
- Tap or click 'Blue, Accent 1' (column 5, row 1) in the Font Color gallery to change the font color of the worksheet title in the active cell (Figure 1–39).

Q&A Why does the Font Color button change after I select the new font color?
When you choose a color on the Font Color gallery, Excel changes the Font Color button (HOME tab | Font group) to the chosen color. Thus, to change the font color of the cell entry in another cell to the same color, you need only to select the cell and then tap or click the Font Color button (HOME tab | Font group).

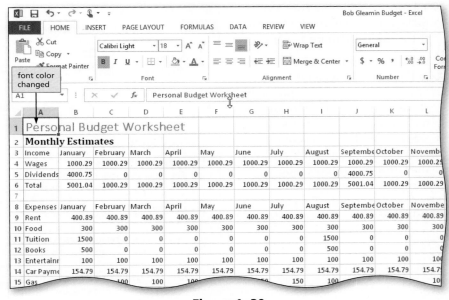

Figure 1–39

3
- Repeat Steps 1 and 2 to apply Blue, Accent 1 (column 5, row 1) to cell A2.

Other Ways

1. Tap or click Font Settings Dialog Box Launcher, tap or click Font tab (Format Cells dialog box), tap or click desired color in Color list, tap or click OK button

2. Tap or click Font Color arrow on mini toolbar, tap or click desired font color in the Font Color gallery

3. Tap 'Show Context Menu' button on mini toolbar or right-click selected cell, tap or click Format Cells on shortcut menu, tap or click Font tab (Format Cells dialog box), select color in Font Color gallery, tap or click OK button

To Center Cell Entries across Columns by Merging Cells

The final step in formatting the worksheet title and subtitle is to center them across columns A through N. *Why? Centering a title across the columns used in the body of the worksheet improves the worksheet's appearance.* To do this, the 14 cells in the range A1:N1 are combined, or merged, into a single cell that is the width of the columns in the body of the worksheet. The 14 cells in the range A2:N2 are merged in a similar manner. **Merging** cells involves creating a single cell by combining two or more selected cells. The following steps center the worksheet title and subtitle across columns by merging cells.

1

- Select cell A1 and then if you are using a touch screen, drag the selection handles as necessary to cell N1; if you are using a mouse, drag to cell N1 to highlight the range to be merged and centered (Figure 1–40).

Q&A What if a cell in the range B1:N1 contains data?
For the 'Merge & Center' button (HOME tab | Alignment group) to work properly, all the cells except the leftmost cell in the selected range must be empty.

Figure 1–40

2

- Tap or click the 'Merge & Center' button (HOME tab | Alignment group) to merge cells A1 through N1 and center the contents of the leftmost cell across the selected columns (Figure 1–41).

Q&A What if my screen displays a Merge & Center menu?
If you are using a touch screen, you may not have a separate 'Merge & Center' button and 'Merge & Center' arrow. In this case, select the desired option on the Merge & Center menu.

What happened to cells B1 through N1?
After the merge, cells B1 through N1 no longer exist. The new cell A1 now extends across columns A through N.

Figure 1–41

3

- Repeat Steps 1 and 2 to merge and center the worksheet subtitle across cells A2 through N2 (Figure 1–42).

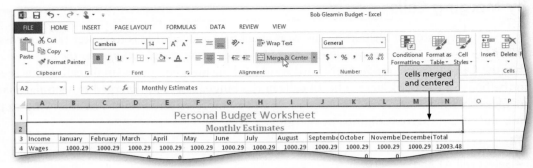

Figure 1–42

Q&A

Are cells B1 through N1 and B2 through N2 lost forever?

No. The opposite of merging cells is **splitting** a merged cell. After you have merged multiple cells to create one merged cell, you can unmerge, or split, the merged cell to display the original cells on the worksheet. You split a merged cell by selecting it and tapping or clicking the 'Merge & Center' button. For example, if you tap or click the 'Merge & Center' button a second time in Step 2, it will split the merged cell A1 into cells A1, B1, C1, D1, E1, F1, G1, H1, I1, J1, K1, L1, M1, and N1.

Other Ways

1. If you are using a mouse, right-click selection, click 'Merge & Center' button on mini toolbar

2. Tap 'Show Context Menu' button on mini toolbar or right-click selected cell, tap or click Format Cells on shortcut menu, tap or click Alignment tab (Format Cells dialog box), select 'Center Across Selection' in Horizontal list, tap or click OK button

To Format Rows Using Cell Styles

1 ENTER TEXT | 2 CALCULATE SUMS & USE FORMULAS | 3 SAVE WORKBOOK | **4 FORMAT TEXT**
5 INSERT CHART | 6 NAME TAB | 7 PREVIEW & PRINT WORKSHEET

The next step to format the worksheet is to format the rows. *Why? Row titles and the total row should be formatted so that anyone who views the worksheet can distinguish quickly the column titles and total row from the data in the body of the worksheet. Data rows can be formatted to make them easier to read, as well.* The following steps format the column titles and total row using cell styles in the default worksheet theme.

1

- Tap or click cell A3 and then drag to cell N3 to select the range.
- Tap or click the Cell Styles button (HOME tab | Styles group) to display the Cell Styles gallery.
- If you are using a mouse, point to the Heading 1 cell style in the Titles and Headings area of the Cell Styles gallery to see a live preview of the cell style in the selected range (Figure 1–43).

Experiment

- If you are using a mouse, point to other cell styles in the Titles and Headings area of the Cell Styles gallery to see a live preview of other cell styles in the selected range, A3:N3.

Figure 1–43

2

- Tap or click the Heading 1 cell style to apply the cell style to the selected range.

- Tap or click the Center button (HOME tab | Alignment group) to center the column headings in the selected range.

- Tap or click cell A8 and then drag the pointer to cell N8 to select the range (Figure 1–44).

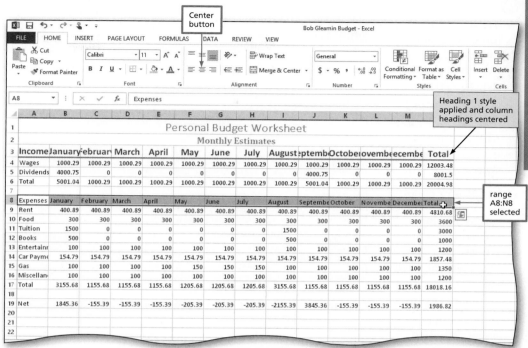

Figure 1–44

3

- Use Steps 1 and 2 to center the column headings and format the range A8:N8 with the Heading 1 cell style format (Figure 1–45).

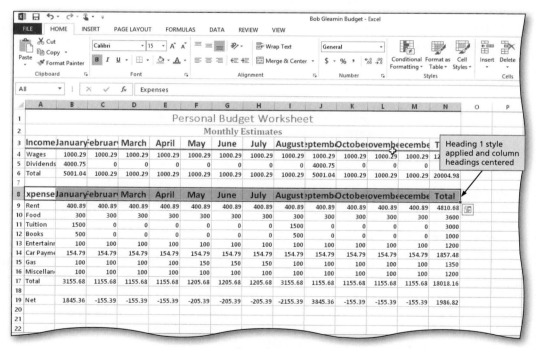

Figure 1–45

4

- Use Steps 1 and 2 to format the range A6:N6 and A17:N17 with the Total cell style format.

- Use Steps 1 and 2 to format the range A19:N19 with the Accent 1 cell style format.

- Use Steps 1 and 2 to format the range A4:N4, A9:N9, A11:N11, A13:N13, A15:N15 with the 20% - Accent 1 cell style format.

- Use Steps 1 and 2 to format the range A5:N5, A10:N10, A12:N12, A14:N14, A16:N16 with the 40% - Accent 1 cell style format (Figure 1–46).

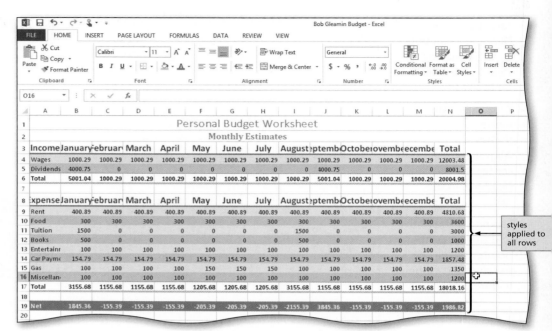

Figure 1–46

To Format Numbers in the Worksheet

1 ENTER TEXT | 2 CALCULATE SUMS & USE FORMULAS | 3 SAVE WORKBOOK | 4 FORMAT TEXT
5 INSERT CHART | 6 NAME TAB | 7 PREVIEW & PRINT WORKSHEET

Why? *As previously noted, the numbers in the first row and last row of each section should be formatted to use a dollar-and-cents format, while the others use a comma format.* Excel allows you to format numbers in a variety of ways, and these methods are discussed in other chapters in this book. The following steps use buttons on the ribbon to format the numbers in the worksheet.

1

- Select the range B4:N4.

- Tap or click the 'Accounting Number Format' button (HOME tab | Number group) to apply the accounting number format to the cells in the selected range.

Q&A What if my screen displays an Accounting Number Format menu?
If you are using a touch screen, you may not have a separate 'Accounting Number Format' button and 'Accounting Number Format' arrow. In this case, select the desired option on the Accounting Number Format menu.

- Select the range B5:N5 (Figure 1– 47).

Figure 1–47

Q&A What effect does the accounting number format have on the selected cells?
The accounting number format causes the cells to be displayed with two decimal places so that decimal places in cells below the selected cells align vertically. Cell widths are adjusted automatically to accommodate the new formatting.

2

- Tap or click the Comma Style button (HOME tab | Number group) to apply the comma style format to the selected range.
- Select the range B6:N6 to make it the active range (Figure 1– 48).

Q&A What effect does the comma style format have on the selected cells?
The comma style format causes the cells to be displayed with two decimal places and commas as thousands separators.

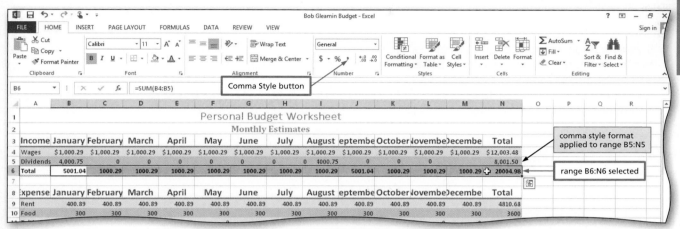

Figure 1–48

3

- Tap or click the 'Accounting Number Format' button (HOME tab | Number group) to apply the accounting number format to the cells in the selected range.
- Select cell A7.

4

- Use Steps 1–3 to format the ranges B9:N9, B17:N17, and B19:N19 with the accounting number format.
- Use Steps 1–3 to format the range B10:N16 with the comma style format (Figure 1– 49).

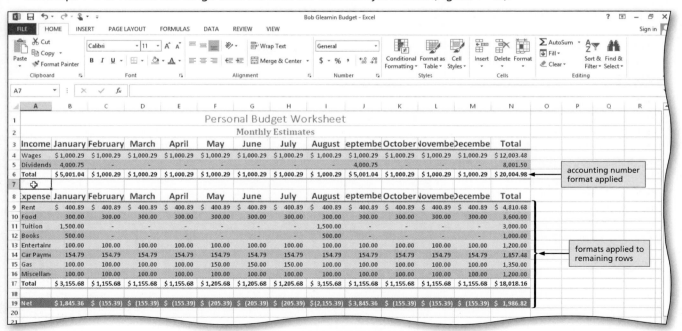

Figure 1–49

Other Ways

1. Tap or click 'Accounting Number Format' or Comma Style button on mini toolbar

2. Tap 'Show Context Menu' button on mini toolbar or right-click selected cell, tap or click Format Cells on shortcut menu, tap or click Number tab (Format Cells dialog box), select Accounting in Category list or select Number and tap or click 'Use 1000 Separator', tap or click OK button

To Adjust the Column Width

The last step in formatting the worksheet is to adjust the width of the columns so that all the titles can be seen clearly. **Why?** *To make a worksheet easy to read, the column widths should be adjusted appropriately.* Excel includes several methods for adjusting cell widths and row heights, and these methods are discussed later in this book. The following steps adjust the width of columns A through N so that the contents of the columns are seen clearly.

1
- If you are using a mouse, point to the boundary on the right side of the column A heading above row 1 to change the pointer to a split double arrow (Figure 1–50).

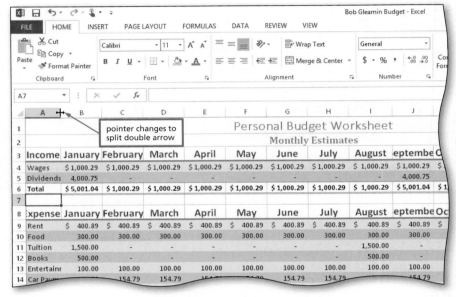

Figure 1–50

2
- If you are using a mouse, double-click the boundary to adjust the width of the column to the width of the largest item in the column (Figure 1–51).

Q&A

What if none of the items in column A extends through the entire width of the column?
If all of the items in column A were shorter in length than the width of the column when you double-tap or double-click the right side of the column A heading, then Excel still would adjust the column width to the largest item in the column. That is, Excel would reduce the width of the column to the largest item.

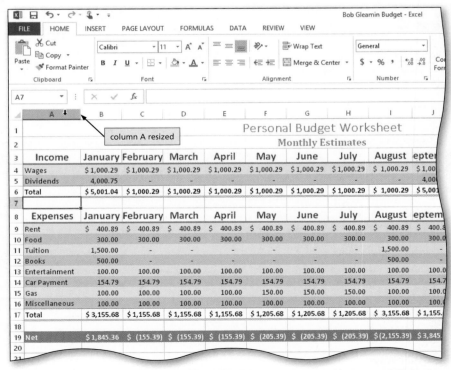

Figure 1–51

3

- Repeat Steps 1 and 2 to adjust the column width of columns B through N (Figure 1–52).

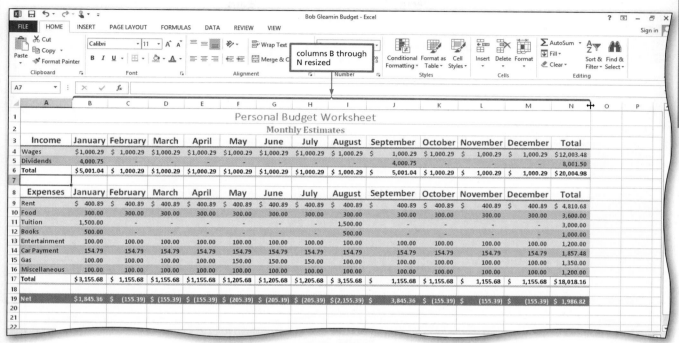

Figure 1–52

To Use the Name Box to Select a Cell

1 ENTER TEXT | 2 CALCULATE TOTALS | 3 SAVE WORKBOOK | 4 FORMAT TEXT
5 INSERT CHART | 6 NAME TAB | 7 PREVIEW & PRINT WORKSHEET

The next step is to chart the monthly expenses. To create the chart, you first must select the cell in the upper-left corner of the range to chart (cell A3). Rather than tapping or clicking cell A3 to select it, the next section describes how to use the Name box to select the cell. The Name box is located on the left side of the formula bar. **Why?** *To select any cell, tap or click the Name box and enter the cell reference of the cell you want to select.* The following steps select cell A3 using the Name box.

1

- Tap or click the Name box in the formula bar and then type **a3** as the cell you want to select (Figure 1–53).

Q&A Why is cell A7 still selected?
The current cell will remain selected until you press the ENTER key.

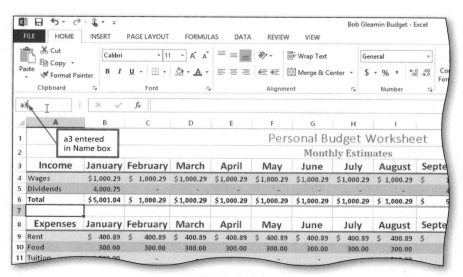

Figure 1–53

2

- Press the ENTER key to change the active cell in the Name box and make cell A3 the active cell (Figure 1–54).

Figure 1–54

Other Ways to Select Cells

As you will see in later chapters, in addition to using the Name box to select any cell in a worksheet, you also can use it to assign names to a cell or range of cells. Excel supports several additional ways to select a cell, as summarized in Table 1–3.

Table 1–3 Selecting Cells in Excel	
Key, Box, or Command	**Function**
ALT+PAGE DOWN	Selects the cell one worksheet window to the right and moves the worksheet window accordingly.
ALT+PAGE UP	Selects the cell one worksheet window to the left and moves the worksheet window accordingly.
ARROW	Selects the adjacent cell in the direction of the arrow on the key.
CTRL+ARROW	Selects the border cell of the worksheet in combination with the arrow keys and moves the worksheet window accordingly. For example, to select the rightmost cell in the row that contains the active cell, press CTRL+RIGHT ARROW. You also can press the END key, release it, and then press the appropriate arrow key to accomplish the same task.
CTRL+HOME	Selects cell A1 or the cell one column and one row below and to the right of frozen titles and moves the worksheet window accordingly.
Find command on Find and Select menu or SHIFT+F5	Finds and selects a cell that contains specific contents that you enter in the Find and Replace dialog box. If necessary, Excel moves the worksheet window to display the cell. You also can press CTRL+F to display the Find dialog box.
Go To command on Find and Select menu or F5	Selects the cell that corresponds to the cell reference you enter in the Go To dialog box and moves the worksheet window accordingly. You also can press CTRL+G to display the Go To dialog box.
HOME	Selects the cell at the beginning of the row that contains the active cell and moves the worksheet window accordingly.
Name box	Selects the cell in the workbook that corresponds to the cell reference you enter in the Name box.
PAGE DOWN	Selects the cell down one worksheet window from the active cell and moves the worksheet window accordingly.
PAGE UP	Selects the cell up one worksheet window from the active cell and moves the worksheet window accordingly.

Break Point: If you wish to take a break, this is a good place to do so. Be sure to save the Bob Gleamin Budget file again and then you can exit Excel. To resume at a later time, run Excel, open the file called Bob Gleamin Budget, and continue following the steps from this location forward.

Adding a Pie Chart to the Worksheet

Excel includes 10 chart types from which you can choose, including column, line, pie, bar, area, X Y (scatter), stock, surface, bubble, and radar. The type of chart you choose depends on the type of data that you have, how much data you have, and the message you want to convey.

A line chart often is used to illustrate changes in data over time. Pie charts show the contribution of each piece of data to the whole, or total, of the data. Area charts, like line charts, illustrate changes over time, but often are used to compare more than one set of data, and the area below the lines is filled in with a different color for each set of data. An X Y (scatter) chart is used much like a line chart, but each piece of data is represented by a dot and is not connected with a line. A stock chart provides a number of methods commonly used in the financial industry to show stock market data. A surface chart compares data from three columns and/or rows in a three-dimensional manner. A bubble chart is much like an X Y (scatter) chart, but a third set of data results indicates how large each individual dot, or bubble, is on the chart. A radar chart can compare several sets of data in a manner that resembles a radar screen, with each set of data represented by a different color. A column or cylinder chart is a good way to compare values side by side. A pie chart can go even further in comparing values across categories by showing each pie piece in comparison with the others.

As outlined in the requirements document in Figure 1–2 on page EX 3, the worksheet should include a pie chart to represent graphically the yearly expenses totals for the expenses budget items for Bob Gleamin's budget. The pie chart shown in Figure 1–55 is on its own sheet in the workbook. The pie chart resides on a separate sheet, called a **chart sheet**, which contains only the chart.

BTW

Excel Help
At any time while using Excel, you can find answers to questions and display information about various topics through Excel Help. Used properly, this form of assistance can increase your productivity and reduce your frustrations by minimizing the time you spend learning how to use Excel. For instruction about Excel Help and exercises that will help you gain confidence in using it, read the Office and Windows chapter at the beginning of this book.

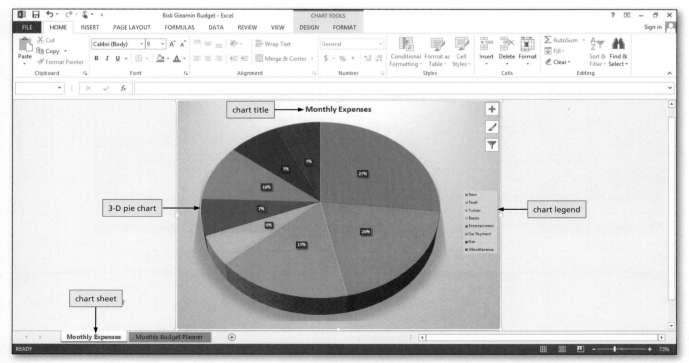

Figure 1–55

In this worksheet, the ranges to chart are the nonadjacent ranges A9:A16 (category names) and N9:N16 (yearly expense totals). The expense titles in the range A9:A16 will identify the slices of the pie chart; these entries are called **category names**. The range N9:N16 contains the data that determines the size of the slices in the pie; these entries are called the **data series**. Because eight budget items are being charted, the 3-D pie chart contains eight slices.

To Add a 3-D Pie Chart

1 ENTER TEXT | 2 CALCULATE SUMS & USE FORMULAS | 3 SAVE WORKBOOK | 4 FORMAT TEXT
5 INSERT CHART | 6 NAME TAB | 7 PREVIEW & PRINT WORKSHEET

Why? *When you want to see how each part relates to the whole, you use a pie chart.* The following steps draw the 3-D pie chart.

1

- Select the range A9:A16 to identify the range of the category names for the 3-D pie chart.

- While holding down the CTRL key, select the range N9:N16.

- Tap or click INSERT on the ribbon to display the INSERT tab.

- Tap or click the 'Insert Pie or Doughnut Chart' button (INSERT tab | Charts group) to display the Insert Pie or Doughnut Chart gallery (Figure 1–56).

 Why does the ribbon display extra tabs?
Excel displays additional tabs that provide options for use when you are working with certain objects, such as charts.

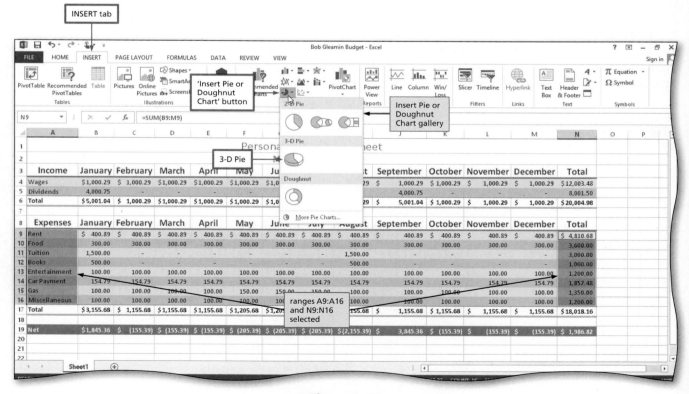

Figure 1–56

2

● Tap or click 3-D Pie in the Insert Pie or Doughnut Chart gallery to insert the chart in the worksheet (Figure 1–57).

Figure 1–57

3

● Tap or click the chart title to select it.

● Type **Monthly Expenses** and then press the ENTER key to change the title.

● Deselect the chart title (Figure 1–58).

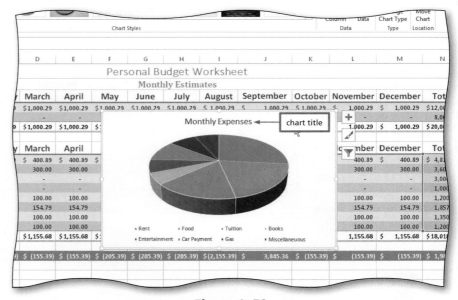

Figure 1–58

To Apply a Style to a Chart

Why? *If you want to make it clear how much of the pie each slice represents, you can use a style to include a percentage.* The following steps apply Style 3 to the 3-D pie chart.

1

• Tap or click the Chart Styles button to display the Chart Styles gallery (Figure 1–59).

Figure 1–59

2

• Tap or click Style 3 in the Chart Styles gallery to change the chart style to Style 3 (Figure 1–60).

3

• Tap or click the Chart Styles button to close the Chart Styles gallery.

Figure 1–60

Changing the Sheet Tab Names

The sheet tabs at the bottom of the window allow you to view any worksheet in the workbook. You tap or click the sheet tab of the worksheet you want to view in the Excel window. By default, Excel presets the names of the worksheets to Sheet1, Sheet2, and so on. The worksheet names become increasingly important as you move toward more sophisticated workbooks, especially workbooks in which you reference cells between worksheets.

BTW

Exploding a Pie Chart
If you want to draw attention to a particular slice in a pie chart, you can offset the slice so that it stands out from the rest. A pie chart with one or more slices offset is referred to as an exploded pie chart. To offset a slice, tap or click the slice two times to select it (do not double-tap or double-click) and then drag the slice outward.

To Move a Chart to a New Sheet

1 ENTER TEXT | 2 CALCULATE SUMS & USE FORMULAS | 3 SAVE WORKBOOK | 4 FORMAT TEXT
5 INSERT CHART | 6 NAME TAB | 7 PREVIEW & PRINT WORKSHEET

Why? By moving a chart to its own sheet, the size will increase, which allows better viewing. The following steps move the 3-D pie chart to a chart sheet named, Monthly Expenses.

1

- Tap or click the Move Chart button (CHART TOOLS DESIGN tab | Location group) to display the Move Chart dialog box (Figure 1–61).

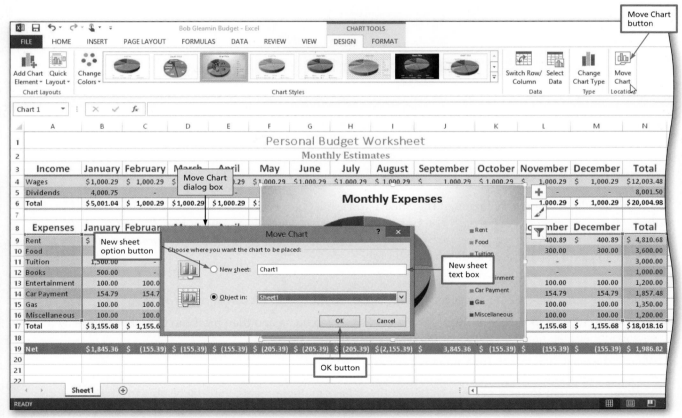

Figure 1–61

2

- Tap or click New sheet to select it (Move Chart dialog box) and then type **Monthly Expenses** in the New sheet text box to enter a sheet tab name for the worksheet that will contain the chart.

- Tap or click the OK button (Move Chart dialog box) to move the chart to a new chart sheet with a new sheet tab name, Monthly Expenses in this case (Figure 1–62).

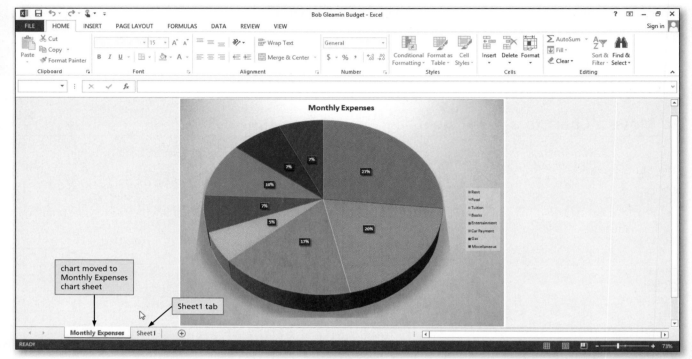

chart moved to Monthly Expenses chart sheet

Sheet1 tab

Figure 1–62

To Change the Worksheet Tab Name

1 ENTER TEXT | 2 CALCULATE SUMS & USE FORMULAS | 3 SAVE WORKBOOK | 4 FORMAT TEXT
5 INSERT CHART | **6 NAME TAB** | 7 PREVIEW & PRINT WORKSHEET

You decide to change the name of the Sheet1 worksheet tab to Monthly Budget Planner. *Why? Use simple, meaningful names for each worksheet tab. Worksheet tab names often match the worksheet title. If a worksheet includes multiple titles in multiple sections of the worksheet, use a sheet tab name that encompasses the meaning of all of the sections.*

The following steps rename the worksheet tab.

1

- Double-tap or double-click the sheet tab labeled Sheet1 in the lower-left corner of the window.

- Type **Monthly Budget Planner** as the worksheet tab name and then press the ENTER key to display the new worksheet tab name on the sheet tab (Figure 1–63).

Q&A

What is the maximum length for a sheet tab name?
Worksheet tab names can be up to 31 characters (including spaces) in length. Longer worksheet names, however, mean that fewer sheet tabs will show. If you have multiple sheets, you will be able to scroll through sheet tabs.

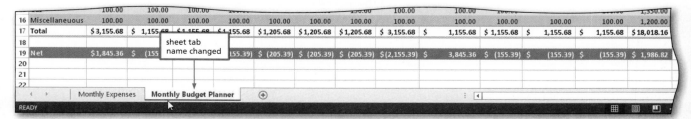

sheet tab name changed

Figure 1–63

2

- Press and hold or right-click the sheet tab labeled, Monthly Budget Planner, in the lower-left corner of the window to display a shortcut menu.

- Tap or point to Tab Color on the shortcut menu to display the Tab Color gallery (Figure 1–64).

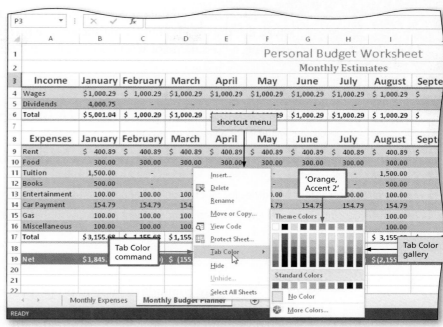

Figure 1–64

3

- Tap or click the color of your shirt in the Theme Colors area to change the color of the tab (Figure 1–65).

- If necessary, tap or click HOME on the ribbon to display the HOME tab.

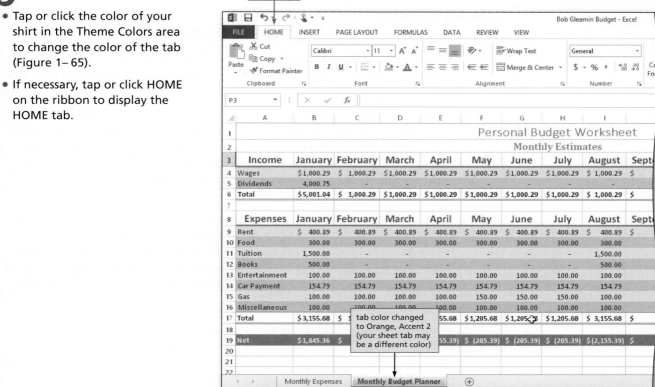

Figure 1–65

Document Properties

Excel helps you organize and identify your files by using **document properties**, which are the details about a file such as the project author, title, and subject. For example, a class name or workbook topic can describe the file's purpose or content.

Why would you want to assign document properties to a workbook?
Document properties are valuable for a variety of reasons:

- Users can save time locating a particular file because they can view a file's document properties without opening the workbook.
- By creating consistent properties for files having similar content, users can better organize their workbooks.
- Some organizations require Excel users to add document properties so that other employees can view details about these files.

The more common document properties are standard and automatically updated properties. **Standard properties** are associated with all Microsoft Office files and include author, title, and subject. **Automatically updated properties** include file system properties, such as the date you create or change a file, and statistics, such as the file size.

TO CHANGE DOCUMENT PROPERTIES

To change document properties, you would follow these steps.

1. Tap or click FILE on the ribbon to open the Backstage view and then, if necessary, tap or click the Info tab in the Backstage view to display the Info gallery.

2. If the property you wish to change is displayed in the Properties list in the right pane of the Info gallery, try to tap or click to the right of the property. If a text box appears to the right of the property, type the text for the property in the text box and then tap or click the Back button in the upper-left corner of the Backstage view to return to the Excel window. Skip the remaining steps.

3. If the property you wish to change is not displayed in the Properties list in the right pane of the Info gallery or you cannot change it in the Info gallery, tap or click the Properties button in the right pane to display the Properties menu, and then tap or click 'Show Document Panel' on the Properties menu to close the Backstage view and display the Document Information Panel in the Excel workbook window.

Q&A
Why are some of the document properties in my Document Information Panel already filled in?
The person who installed Office 2013 on your computer or network may have set or customized the properties.

4. Type the desired text in the appropriate property text boxes.

Q&A What if the property I want to change is not displayed in the Document Information Panel?

Tap or click the Document Properties button in the Document Information Panel and then tap or click Advanced Properties on the menu to display the Properties dialog box. If necessary, tap or click the Summary tab (Properties dialog box) to display the Summary sheet, fill in the appropriate text boxes, and then tap or click the OK button.

5. Tap or click the 'Close the Document Information Panel' button at the right edge of the Document Information Panel so that the panel no longer appears in the Excel workbook window.

To Save an Existing Workbook with the Same File Name

You have made several modifications to the workbook since you last saved it. Thus, you should save it again. The following step saves the workbook again. For an example of the step listed below, refer to the Office and Windows chapter at the beginning of this book.

 Tap or click the Save button on the Quick Access Toolbar to overwrite the previously saved file.

Printing a Worksheet

After creating a worksheet, you may want to print it. Printing a worksheet enables you to distribute the worksheet to others in a form that can be read or viewed but typically not edited. It is a good practice to save a workbook before printing a worksheet, in the event you experience difficulties printing.

BTW
Conserving Ink and Toner
If you want to conserve ink or toner, you can instruct Excel to print draft quality documents by tapping or clicking FILE on the ribbon to open the Backstage view, tapping or clicking Options in the Backstage view to display the Excel Options dialog box, tapping or clicking Advanced in the left pane (Excel Options dialog box), sliding or scrolling to the Print area in the right pane, placing a check mark in the 'Use draft quality' check box, and then tapping or clicking the OK button. Then, use the Backstage view to print the document as usual.

CONSIDER THIS

What is the best method for distributing a workbook?
The traditional method of distributing a workbook uses a printer to produce a hard copy. A **hard copy** or **printout** is information that exists on a physical medium such as paper. Hard copies can be useful for the following reasons:

• Some people prefer proofreading a hard copy of a workbook rather than viewing it on the screen to check for errors and readability.

• Hard copies can serve as a backup reference if your storage medium is lost or becomes corrupted and you need to recreate the workbook.

Instead of distributing a hard copy of a workbook, users can distribute the workbook as an electronic image that mirrors the original workbook's appearance. The electronic image of the workbook can be sent as an email attachment, posted on a website, or copied to a portable storage medium such as a USB flash drive. Two popular electronic image formats, sometimes called fixed formats, are PDF by Adobe Systems and XPS by Microsoft. In Excel, you can create electronic image files through the Save As dialog box and the Export, Share, and Print tabs in the Backstage view. Electronic images of workbooks, such as PDF and XPS, can be useful for the following reasons:

• Users can view electronic images of workbooks without the software that created the original workbook (e.g., Excel). Specifically, to view a PDF file, you use a program called Adobe Reader, which can be downloaded free from Adobe's website. Similarly, to view an XPS file, you use a program called XPS Viewer, which is included in the latest versions of Windows and Internet Explorer.

• Sending electronic workbooks saves paper and printer supplies. Society encourages users to contribute to **green computing**, which involves reducing the electricity consumed and environmental waste generated when using computers, mobile devices, and related technologies.

To Preview and Print a Worksheet in Landscape Orientation

Pages printed in portrait orientation have the short (8½") edge at the top of the printout; the printed page is taller than it is wide. Landscape orientation prints the long (11") edge at the top of the paper; the printed page is wider than it is tall. With the completed workbook saved, you may want to print it. *Why? Because the worksheet is included in a report, you will print a hard copy on a printer.* The following steps print a hard copy of the contents of the worksheet.

- Tap or click FILE on the ribbon to open the Backstage view.
- Tap or click the Print tab in the Backstage view to display the Print gallery (Figure 1–66).

Q&A

How can I print multiple copies of my worksheet?
Increase the number in the Copies box in the Print gallery.

What if I decide not to print the worksheet at this time?
Tap or click the Back button in the upper-left corner of the Backstage view to return to the workbook window.

Figure 1–66

- Verify that the printer listed on the Printer Status button will print a hard copy of the workbook. If necessary, tap or click the Printer Status button to display a list of available printer options and then tap or click the desired printer to change the currently selected printer.

3

- Tap or click the Portrait Orientation button in the Settings area and then select Landscape Orientation to change the orientation of the page to landscape.
- Tap or click the No Scaling button and then select 'Fit Sheet on One Page' to print the entire worksheet on one page (Figure 1–67).

Figure 1–67

4

- Tap or click the Print button in the Print gallery to print the worksheet in landscape orientation on the currently selected printer.

- When the printer stops, retrieve the hard copy (Figure 1– 68).

Q&A Do I have to wait until my worksheet is complete to print it?

No, you can follow these steps to print a document at any time while you are creating it.

Personal Budget Worksheet
Monthly Estimates

Income	January	February	March	April	May	June	July	August	September	October	November	December	Total
Wages	$1,000.29	$ 1,000.29	$1,000.29	$1,000.29	$1,000.29	$1,000.29	$1,000.29	$ 1,000.29	$ 1,000.29	$1,000.29	$ 1,000.29	$ 1,000.29	$12,003.48
Dividends	4,000.75	-	-	-	-	-	-	-	4,000.75	-	-	-	8,001.50
Total	**$5,001.04**	**$ 1,000.29**	**$1,000.29**	**$1,000.29**	**$1,000.29**	**$1,000.29**	**$1,000.29**	**$ 1,000.29**	**$ 5,001.04**	**$1,000.29**	**$ 1,000.29**	**$ 1,000.29**	**$ 20,004.98**

Expenses	January	February	March	April	May	June	July	August	September	October	November	December	Total
Rent	$ 400.89	$ 400.89	$ 400.89	$ 400.89	$ 400.89	$ 400.89	$ 400.89	$ 400.89	$ 400.89	$ 400.89	$ 400.89	$ 400.89	$ 4,810.68
Food	300.00	300.00	300.00	300.00	300.00	300.00	300.00	300.00	300.00	300.00	300.00	300.00	3,600.00
Tuition	1,500.00	-	-	-	-	-	-	1,500.00	-	-	-	-	3,000.00
Books	500.00	-	-	-	-	-	-	500.00	-	-	-	-	1,000.00
Entertainment	100.00	100.00	100.00	100.00	100.00	100.00	100.00	100.00	100.00	100.00	100.00	100.00	1,200.00
Car Payment	154.79	154.79	154.79	154.79	154.79	154.79	154.79	154.79	154.79	154.79	154.79	154.79	1,857.48
Gas	100.00	100.00	100.00	100.00	150.00	150.00	150.00	100.00	100.00	100.00	100.00	100.00	1,350.00
Miscellaneous	100.00	100.00	100.00	100.00	100.00	100.00	100.00	100.00	100.00	100.00	100.00	100.00	1,200.00
Total	**$3,155.68**	**$ 1,155.68**	**$1,155.68**	**$1,155.68**	**$1,205.68**	**$1,205.68**	**$1,205.68**	**$ 3,155.68**	**$ 1,155.68**	**$1,155.68**	**$ 1,155.68**	**$ 1,155.68**	**$ 18,018.16**

| Net | $1,845.36 | $ (155.39) | $ (155.39) | $ (155.39) | $ (205.39) | $ (205.39) | $ (205.39) | $(2,155.39) | 3,845.36 | $ (155.39) | $ (155.39) | (155.39) | $ 1,986.82 |

Figure 1–68

Other Ways

1. Press CTRL+P, press ENTER

To Open a Document from Excel

Earlier in this chapter you saved your workbook using the file name, Bob Gleamin Budget. The following steps open the Bob Gleamin Budget file from the Excel folder in the CIS 101 folder. For a detailed example of the procedure summarized below, refer to the Office and Windows chapter at the beginning of this book.

1 Tap or click FILE on the ribbon to open the Backstage view and then tap or click the Open tab in the Backstage view to display the Open gallery.

2 If the file you wish to open is displayed in the Recent Workbooks list, tap or click the file name to open the file and display the opened workbook in the Excel window; then skip the remaining steps. If the file you wish to open is not displayed in the Recent Workbooks list, proceed to the next step to locate the file.

3 Tap or click Computer, SkyDrive, or another location in the left pane and then navigate to the location of the file to be opened (in this case, the Excel folder in the CIS 101 folder).

4 Tap or click Bob Gleamin Budget to select the file to be opened.

5 Tap or click the Open button (Open dialog box) to open the selected file and display the opened workbook in the Excel window.

AutoCalculate

You easily can obtain a total, an average, or other information about the numbers in a range by using the **AutoCalculate area** on the status bar. First, select the range of cells containing the numbers you want to check. Next, press and hold or right-click the AutoCalculate area to display the Customize Status Bar shortcut menu (Figure 1–69). The check marks indicate that the calculations are included in the status bar; more than one may be selected. The functions of the AutoCalculate commands on the Customize Status Bar shortcut menu are described in Table 1–4.

Table 1–4 Commonly Used Status Bar Commands	
Command	Function
Average	AutoCalculate area displays the average of the numbers in the selected range
Count	AutoCalculate area displays the number of nonblank cells in the selected range
Numerical Count	AutoCalculate area displays the number of cells containing numbers in the selected range
Minimum	AutoCalculate area displays the lowest value in the selected range
Maximum	AutoCalculate area displays the highest value in the selected range
Sum	AutoCalculate area displays the sum of the numbers in the selected range

To Use the AutoCalculate Area to Determine a Maximum

1 ENTER TEXT | 2 CALCULATE SUMS & USE FORMULAS | 3 SAVE WORKBOOK | 4 FORMAT TEXT
5 INSERT CHART | 6 NAME TAB | **7 PREVIEW & PRINT WORKSHEET**

The following steps display the largest total for the months in the budget. **Why?** *Sometimes, you want to see a quick analysis, which can be shown in the AutoCalculate area on the status bar.*

1

- Select the range B19:M19. Press and hold or right-click the status bar to display the Customize Status Bar shortcut menu (Figure 1–69).

Q&A What is displayed on the Customize Status Bar shortcut menu?

This shortcut menu includes several commands that allow you to control the items displayed on the Customize Status Bar shortcut menu. The AutoCalculate area includes six commands as well as the result of the associated calculation on the right side of the menu.

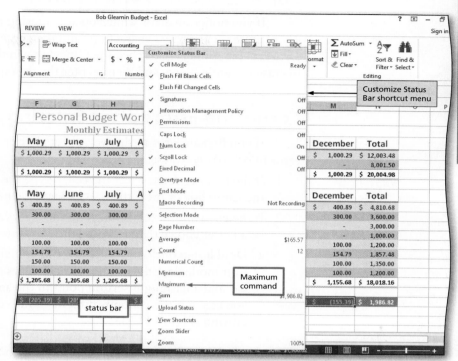

Figure 1–69

2

- Tap or click Maximum on the shortcut menu to display the Maximum value in the range B19:M19 in the AutoCalculate area of the status bar.

- Tap or click anywhere on the worksheet to cause the shortcut menu to disappear (Figure 1–70).

3

- Press and hold or right-click the AutoCalculate area and then tap or click Maximum on the shortcut menu to cause the Maximum value to no longer appear in the AutoCalculate area.

- Tap or click anywhere in the worksheet to cause the shortcut menu to disappear.

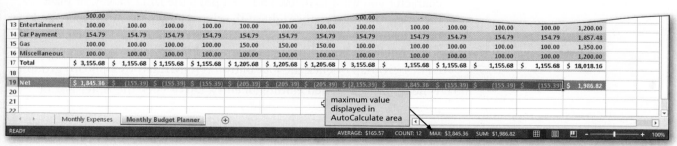

Figure 1–70

Correcting Errors

You can correct errors on a worksheet using one of several methods. The method you choose will depend on the extent of the error and whether you notice it while entering the data or after you have entered the incorrect data into the cell.

Correcting Errors while Entering Data into a Cell

If you notice an error while you are entering data into a cell, press the BACKSPACE key to erase the incorrect character(s) and then enter the correct character(s). If the error is a major one, tap or click the Cancel box in the formula bar or press the ESC key to erase the entire entry and then reenter the data from the beginning.

Correcting Errors after Entering Data into a Cell

If you find an error in the worksheet after entering the data, you can correct the error in one of two ways:

1. If the entry is short, select the cell, retype the entry correctly, and then tap or click the Enter box or press the ENTER key. The new entry will replace the old entry.

2. If the entry in the cell is long and the errors are minor, using Edit mode may be a better choice than retyping the cell entry. Use Edit mode as described below.

 a. Double-tap or double-click the cell containing the error to switch Excel to Edit mode. In **Edit mode**, Excel displays the active cell entry in the formula bar and a flashing insertion point in the active cell. With Excel in Edit mode, you can edit the contents directly in the cell — a procedure called **in-cell editing** (Figure 1–71).

Figure 1–71

 b. Make changes using in-cell editing, as indicated below.

 (1) To insert new characters between two characters, place the insertion point between the two characters and begin typing. Excel inserts the new characters to the left of the insertion point.

 (2) To delete a character in the cell, move the insertion point to the left of the character you want to delete and then press the DELETE key, or place the insertion point to the right of the character you want to delete and then press the BACKSPACE key. You also can drag to select the character or adjacent characters you want to delete and then press the DELETE key or CTRL+X, or tap or click the Cut button (HOME tab | Clipboard group).

 (3) When you are finished editing an entry, tap or click the Enter box or press the ENTER key.

When Excel enters Edit mode, the keyboard usually is in Insert mode. In **Insert mode**, as you type a character, Excel inserts the character and moves all characters to the right of the typed character one position to the right. You can change to Overtype mode by pressing the INSERT key. In **Overtype mode**, Excel overtypes, or replaces, the character to the right of the insertion point. The INSERT key toggles the keyboard between Insert mode and Overtype mode.

While in Edit mode, you may have reason to move the insertion point to various points in the cell, select portions of the data in the cell, or switch from inserting characters to overtyping characters. Table 1–5 summarizes the more common tasks performed during in-cell editing.

Table 1–5 Summary of In-Cell Editing Tasks		
Task	**Touch / Mouse**	**Keyboard**
1. Move the insertion point to the beginning of data in a cell.	Point to the left of the first character and tap or click.	Press HOME
2. Move the insertion point to the end of data in a cell.	Point to the right of the last character and tap or click.	Press END
3. Move the insertion point anywhere in a cell.	Point to the appropriate position and tap or click the character.	Press RIGHT ARROW or LEFT ARROW
4. Highlight one or more adjacent characters.	Drag through adjacent characters.	Press SHIFT+RIGHT ARROW or SHIFT+LEFT ARROW
5. Select all data in a cell.	Double-tap or double-click the cell with the insertion point in the cell if the data in the cell contains no spaces.	
6. Delete selected characters.	Tap or click the Cut button (HOME tab \| Clipboard group).	Press DELETE
7. Delete characters to the left of the insertion point.		Press BACKSPACE
8. Delete characters to the right of the insertion point.		Press DELETE
9. Toggle between Insert and Overtype modes.		Press INSERT

Undoing the Last Cell Entry

Excel provides the Undo button on the Quick Access Toolbar (Figure 1–72), which allows you to erase recent cell entries. Thus, if you enter incorrect data in a cell and notice it immediately, tap or click the Undo button and Excel changes the cell entry to what it was prior to the incorrect data entry.

Figure 1–72

Excel remembers the last 100 actions you have completed. Thus, you can undo up to 100 previous actions by tapping or clicking the Undo arrow to display the Undo list and then tapping or clicking the action to be undone (Figure 1–72). You can drag through several actions in the Undo list to undo all of them at once. If no actions are available for Excel to undo, then the Undo button is unavailable; its dimmed appearance indicates that it is unavailable.

The Redo button, next to the Undo button on the Quick Access Toolbar, allows you to repeat previous actions; that is, if you accidentally undo an action, you can use the Redo button to redo it.

Clearing a Cell or Range of Cells

If you enter data into the wrong cell or range of cells, you can erase, or clear, the data using one of the first four methods listed below. The fifth method clears the formatting from the selected cells. To clear a cell or range of cells, you would perform the following steps:

TO CLEAR CELL ENTRIES USING THE FILL HANDLE

1. Select the cell or range of cells and then point to the fill handle so that the pointer changes to a crosshair.
2. Drag the fill handle back into the selected cell or range until a shadow covers the cell or cells you want to erase.

TO CLEAR CELL ENTRIES USING THE SHORTCUT MENU

1. Select the cell or range of cells to be cleared.
2. Press and hold or right-click the selection.
3. Tap or click Clear Contents on the shortcut menu.

TO CLEAR CELL ENTRIES USING THE DELETE KEY

1. Select the cell or range of cells to be cleared.
2. Press the DELETE key.

TO CLEAR CELL ENTRIES AND FORMATTING USING THE CLEAR BUTTON

1. Select the cell or range of cells to be cleared.
2. Tap or click the Clear button (HOME tab | Editing group).
3. Tap or click Clear Contents on the menu.

TO CLEAR FORMATTING USING THE CELL STYLES BUTTON

1. Select the cell or range of cells from which you want to remove the formatting.
2. Tap or click the Cell Styles button (HOME tab | Styles group) and point to Normal.
3. Tap or click Normal in the Cell Styles gallery.

The Clear All command on the Clear menu is the only command that clears both the cell entry and the cell formatting. As you are clearing cell entries, always remember that you should *never press the SPACEBAR to clear a cell*. Pressing the SPACEBAR enters a blank character. A blank character is text and is different from an empty cell, even though the cell may appear empty.

Clearing the Entire Worksheet

If the required worksheet edits are extremely extensive or if the requirements drastically change, you may want to clear the entire worksheet and start over. To clear the worksheet or delete an embedded chart, you would use the following steps.

TO CLEAR THE ENTIRE WORKSHEET

1. Tap or click the Select All button on the worksheet.
2. Tap or click the Clear button (HOME tab | Editing group) and then tap or click Clear All on the menu to delete both the entries and formats.

BTW
Certification
The Microsoft Office Specialist (MOS) program provides an opportunity for you to obtain a valuable industry credential — proof that you have the Excel 2013 skills required by employers. For more information, visit the Certification resource on the Student Companion Site located on www.cengagebrain.com. For detailed instructions about accessing available resources, visit www.cengage.com/ct/studentdownload or contact your instructor for information about accessing the required files.

The Select All button selects the entire worksheet. Instead of tapping or clicking the Select All button, you can press CTRL+A. To clear an unsaved workbook, tap or click the Close Window button on the workbook's title bar or tap or click the Close button in the Backstage view. Tap or click the No button if the Microsoft Excel dialog box asks if you want to save changes. To start a new, blank workbook, tap or click the New button in the Backstage view.

To Sign Out of a Microsoft Account

If you are signed in to a Microsoft account and are using a public computer or otherwise wish to sign out of your Microsoft account, you should sign out of the account from the Account gallery in the Backstage view before exiting Excel. Signing out of the account is the safest way to make sure that nobody else can access SkyDrive files or settings stored in your Microsoft account. The following steps sign out of a Microsoft account from Excel. For a detailed example of the procedure summarized below, refer to the Office and Windows chapter at the beginning of this book.

1 If you wish to sign out of your Microsoft account, tap or click FILE on the ribbon to open the Backstage view and then tap or click the Account tab to display the Account gallery.

2 Tap or click the Sign out link, which displays the Remove Account dialog box. If a Can't remove Windows accounts dialog box appears instead of the Remove Account dialog box, click the OK button and skip the remaining steps.

Q&A Why does a Can't remove Windows accounts dialog box appear?
If you signed in to Windows using your Microsoft account, then you also must sign out from Windows, rather than signing out from within Excel. When you are finished using Windows, be sure to sign out at that time.

3 Tap or click the Yes button (Remove Account dialog box) to sign out of your Microsoft account on this computer.

Q&A Should I sign out of Windows after signing out of my Microsoft account?
When you are finished using the computer, you should sign out of your account for maximum security.

4 Tap or click the Back button in the upper-left corner of the Backstage view to return to the worksheet.

To Exit Excel

This project now is complete. The following steps exit Excel. For a detailed example of the procedure summarized below, refer to the Office and Windows chapter at the beginning of this book.

1a If you have one Excel workbook open, tap or click the Close button on the right side of the title bar to close the open workbook and exit Excel.

1b If you have multiple Excel workbooks open, press and hold or right-click the Excel app button on the taskbar and then tap or click 'Close all windows' on the shortcut menu, or press ALT+F4 to close all open workbooks and exit Excel.

Q&A Could I press and hold or repeatedly click the Close button to close all open documents and exit Excel?
Yes.

2 If a Microsoft Excel dialog box appears, tap or click the Save button to save any changes made to the workbook since the last save.

BTW
Quick Reference
For a table that lists how to complete the tasks covered in this book using touch gestures, the mouse, ribbon, shortcut menu, and keyboard, see the Quick Reference Summary at the back of this book, or visit the Quick Reference resource on the Student Companion Site located on www.cengagebrain.com. For detailed instructions about accessing available resources, visit www.cengage.com/ct/studentdownload or contact your instructor for information about accessing the required files.

Chapter Summary

In this chapter you have learned how to enter text and numbers to create a worksheet, select a range, use the Sum button, format cells, insert a chart, and preview and print a worksheet. The items listed below include all the new Excel skills you have learned in this chapter, with the tasks grouped by activity.

Clear Cells
Clear Cell Entries Using the Fill Handle (EX 52)
Clear Cell Entries Using the Shortcut Menu (EX 52)
Clear Cell Entries Using the DELETE Key (EX 52)
Clear Cell Entries and Formatting Using the Clear Button (EX 52)
Clear Cell Formatting Using the Cell Styles Button (EX 52)
Clear the Entire Worksheet (EX 52)

Display AutoCalculate Functions
Use the AutoCalculate Area to Determine a Maximum (EX 48)

Enter Data
Enter the Worksheet Titles (EX 7)
Enter Column Titles (EX 9)
Enter Row Titles (EX 11)
Enter Numbers (EX 12)

Enter Functions and Formulas
Sum a Column of Numbers (EX 14)
Copy a Cell to Adjacent Cells in a Row (EX 16)
Determine Multiple Totals at the Same Time (EX 18)
Enter a Formula Using the Keyboard (EX 20)

File Management
Change Document Properties (EX 44)

Format a Worksheet
Change a Cell Style (EX 24)
Change the Font (EX 25)
Bold a Cell (EX 26)
Increase the Font Size of a Cell Entry (EX 27)
Change the Font Color of a Cell Entry (EX 28)
Center Cell Entries across Columns by Merging Cells (EX 29)
Format Rows Using Cell Styles (EX 30)
Format Numbers in the Worksheet (EX 32)
Adjust the Column Width (EX 34)
Use the Name Box to Select a Cell (EX 35)

Insert a Chart
Add a 3-D Pie Chart (EX 38)
Apply a Style to a Chart (EX 40)

Manage Worksheets
Move a Chart to a New Sheet (EX 41)
Change the Worksheet Tab Name (EX 42)

Preview and Print Worksheets
Preview and Print a Worksheet in Landscape Orientation (EX 46)

CONSIDER THIS

What decisions will you need to make when creating workbooks and charts in the future?

1. Determine the workbook structure.

 a) Determine the data you will need for your workbook.

 b) Sketch a layout of your data and your chart.

2. Create the worksheet.

 a) Enter titles, subtitles, and headings.

 b) Enter data, functions, and formulas.

3. Format the worksheet.

 a) Format the titles, subtitles, and headings using styles.

 b) Format the totals.

 c) Format the numbers.

 d) Format the text.

4. Create the chart.

 a) Determine the type of chart to use.

 b) Determine the chart title and data.

 c) Format the chart.

CONSIDER THIS **STUDENT ASSIGNMENTS Excel Chapter 1**

How should you submit solutions to questions in the assignments identified with a ✸ symbol?
Every assignment in this book contains one or more questions identified with a ✸ symbol. These questions require you to think beyond the assigned file. Present your solutions to the questions in the format required by your instructor. Possible formats may include one or more of these options: write the answer; create a document that contains the answer; present your answer to the class; discuss your answer in a group; record the answer as audio or video using a webcam, smartphone, or portable media player; or post answers on a blog, wiki, or website.

Apply Your Knowledge

Reinforce the skills and apply the concepts you learned in this chapter.

Changing the Values in a Worksheet

Note: To complete this assignment, you will be required to use the Data Files for Students. Visit www.cengage.com/ct/studentdownload for detailed instructions or contact your instructor for information about accessing the required files.

Instructions: Run Excel. Open the workbook Apply 1–1 Treagle Market (Figure 1–73a on the next page).

1. Make the changes to the worksheet described in Table 1–6 so that the worksheet appears as shown in Figure 1–73b on the next page. As you edit the values in the cells containing numeric data, watch the totals in row 8, the totals in column G, and the chart change.

2. Change the worksheet title in cell A1 to the Title cell style and then merge and center it across columns A through G. Use buttons in the Font group on the HOME tab on the ribbon to change the worksheet subtitle in cell A2 to 14-point font and then center it across columns A through G. Use the Aqua, Accent 5 color (column 9, row 1 in the Font Color gallery) for the aqua font color.

3. Apply the worksheet name, Yearly Analysis, to the sheet tab and apply the Aqua, Accent 5 theme color to the sheet tab.

4. Move the chart to a new sheet called Sales Analysis Chart. Apply the Style 2 chart style to the chart (Figure 1–73c on the next page). Change the chart title to SALES ANALYSIS.

5. Replace Treagle in cell A1 with your last name. Save the workbook using the file name, Apply 1–1 Treagle Market Sales Analysis. Submit the revised workbook as specified by your instructor.

6. Exit Excel.

7. ✸ Besides the styles used in the worksheet, what other changes could you make to enhance the worksheet?

Table 1–6 New Worksheet Data	
Cell	**Change Cell Contents To**
A2	Yearly Sales Analysis
B7	3895.23
C5	26125.75
D6	30589.14
E7	35450.82
F6	6352.78

Continued >

Apply Your Knowledge *continued*

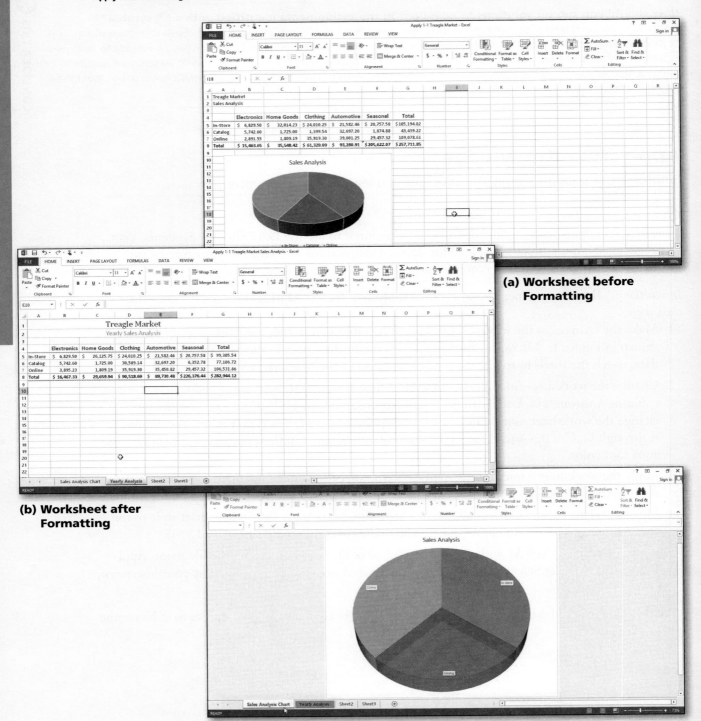

(a) Worksheet before Formatting

(b) Worksheet after Formatting

(c) 3-D Pie Chart on Separate Sheet

Figure 1–73

Extend Your Knowledge

Extend the skills you learned in this chapter and experiment with new skills. You may need to use Help to complete the assignment.

Creating Styles and Formatting a Worksheet

Note: To complete this assignment, you will be required to use the Data Files for Students. Visit www.cengage.com/ct/studentdownload for detailed instructions or contact your instructor for information about accessing the required files.

Instructions: Run Excel. Open the workbook Extend 1–1 Kaseey Vehicles (Figure 1–74). Perform the following tasks to create styles and format a worksheet using them.

1. Select cell A4. Use the New Cell Style command in the Cell Styles gallery to create a style that fills only cell A4 using the Orange, Accent 2, Lighter 40% color (row 4, column 6). Name the style, MyHeadings.

2. Select cell A5. Use the New Cell style dialog box to create a style that fills only cell A5 using the Orange, Accent 2, Lighter 80% color. Name the style, MyRows.

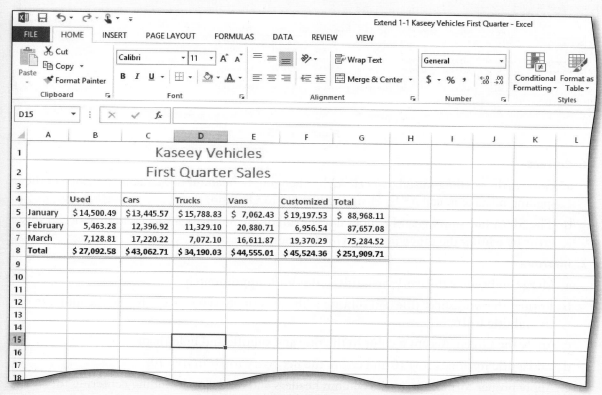

Figure 1–74

3. Select cell ranges B4:G4 and A5:A8. Apply the MyHeadings style to the cell ranges.

4. Select cell ranges B5:G5 and B7:G7. Apply the MyRows style to the cell ranges.

5. Apply a worksheet name to the sheet tab and apply a color of your choice to the sheet tab.

6. Change the font color for the text in cells A1 and A2 to the color of your eyes. Save the workbook using the file name, Extend 1–1 Kaseey Vehicles First Quarter. Submit the revised workbook as specified by your instructor.

7. Exit Excel.

8. ❀ What other styles would you create to improve the worksheet's appearance?

Analyze, Correct, Improve

Analyze a workbook and correct all errors and/or improve the design.

Fixing Formatting Problems and Data Errors in a Worksheet

Note: To complete this assignment, you will be required to use the Data Files for Students. Visit www.cengage.com/ct/studentdownload for detailed instructions or contact your instructor for information about accessing the required files.

Instructions: Run Excel. Open the workbook Analyze 1–1 CPJ Clothing. Correct the following formatting problems and data in the worksheet, while keeping in mind the guidelines presented in this chapter. Your worksheet should look like Figure 1–75 when it is corrected.

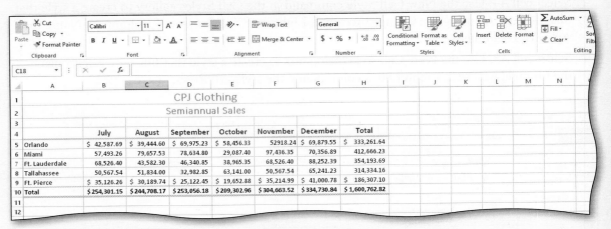

Figure 1–75

1. Correct

 a. Correct the spelling mistake in cell A2 by changing Semiannul to Semiannual. Correct the spelling mistake in cell A5 by changing Orlndo to Orlando.

 b. The SUM function in cell H7 does not sum all of the numbers in the column. Correct this error by editing the range for the SUM function in the cell.

2. Improve

 a. Merge and center the worksheet title and subtitle appropriately.

 b. Format the worksheet title and subtitle with appropriate cell styles. Change the font size of the subtitle to 16.

 c. Apply the Green, Accent 6 color to the title and subtitle and bold them.

 d. Add a title for totals row 10 and create the necessary totals in row 10.

 e. Apply proper formatting to the column headers and total row, including centering the column headers.

 f. Adjust the column sizes so that all data in each column is visible.

 g. Create the grand total for the annual cost of goods.

 h. Apply a worksheet name to the sheet tab and apply the Green, Accent 6 color to the sheet tab.

 i. Change the document properties as specified by your instructor. Save the workbook using the file name, Analyze 1–1 CPJ Clothing Sales. Submit the revised workbook as specified by your instructor.

 j. Change the city in cell A5 to the city you were born.

3. ✴ If you were going to create a pie chart of the expenses for each city, what data would you use?

In the Labs

Design and/or create a workbook using the guidelines, concepts, and skills presented in this chapter. Labs 1 and 2, which increase in difficulty, require you to create solutions based on what you learned in the chapter; Lab 3 requires you to create a solution, which uses cloud and web technologies, by learning and investigating on your own from general guidance.

Lab 1: **Fourth Quarter Revenue Analysis Worksheet**

Problem: You work as a spreadsheet specialist for Caitlyn's Candles, which has four regional shops in the state of California. Your manager has asked you to develop a fourth quarter revenue analysis similar to the one shown in Figure 1–76.

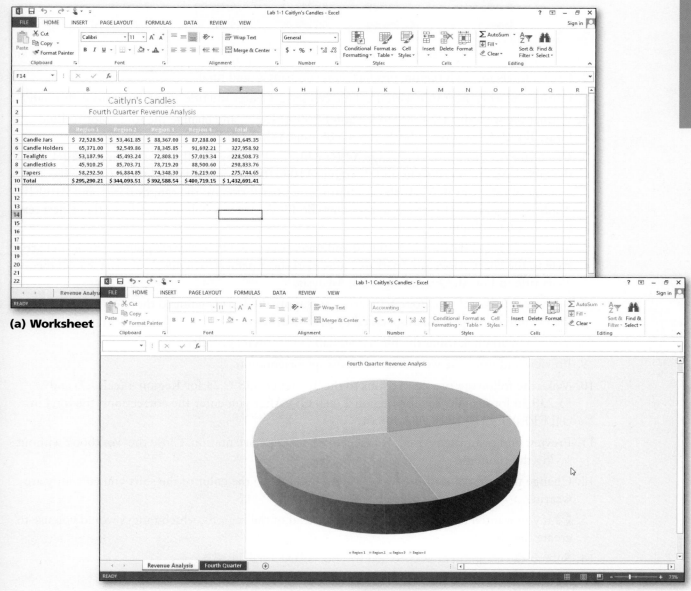

(a) Worksheet

(b) Pie Chart

Figure 1–76

Continued >

In the Labs *continued*

Instructions: Perform the following tasks.

1. Run Excel and create a new blank workbook. Enter the worksheet title, Caitlyn's Candles, in cell A1 and the worksheet subtitle, Fourth Quarter Revenue Analysis, in cell A2. Beginning in row 4, enter the region data shown in Table 1–7.

Table 1–7 Caitlyn's Candles				
	Region 1	**Region 2**	**Region 3**	**Region 4**
Candle Jars	72,528.50	53,461.85	88,367.00	87,288.00
Candle Holders	65,371.00	92,549.86	78,345.85	91,692.21
Tealights	53,187.96	45,493.24	72,808.19	57,019.34
Candlesticks	45,910.25	85,703.71	78,719.20	88,500.60
Tapers	58,292.50	66,884.85	74,348.30	76,219.00

2. Create totals for each region, product, and company grand total.

3. Format the worksheet title with the Title cell style. Center the title across columns A through F.

4. Format the worksheet subtitle to 14-point Calibri Light, and change the font color to Blue-Gray, Text 2. Center the subtitle across columns A through F.

5. Use Cell Styles to format the range A4:F4 with the Heading 2 cell style, the range B4:F4 with the 60% - Accent 4 cell style, and the range A10:G10 with the Total cell style. Center the column titles in row 4. Apply the accounting number format to the ranges B5:F5 and B10:F10. Apply the comma style format to the range B6:F9. Adjust any column widths to the widest text entry in each column.

6. Select the ranges B4:E4 and B10:E10 and then insert a 3-D pie chart. Apply the Style 4 chart style to the chart. Move the chart to a new worksheet named Revenue Analysis. Change the chart title to Fourth Quarter Revenue Analysis.

7. Rename the Sheet1 tab, Fourth Quarter, and apply the Purple color to the sheet tab. Change the document properties, as specified by your instructor.

8. Save the workbook using the file name, Lab 1-1 Caitlyn's Candles.

9. Preview and print the worksheet in landscape orientation.

10. Make the following two corrections to the Tealights: 55899.23 for Region 4 (cell E7) and 55,238.56 for Candle Jars for Region 2 (cell C5). After you enter the corrections, the total in cell F10 should equal $1,433,348.01.

11. Preview and print the revised worksheet in landscape orientation. Close the workbook without saving the changes.

12. Change the font color of the text in cells A1 and A2 to the color of the shirt you currently are wearing.

13. ✸ If you wanted to chart the item totals instead of the regions, which ranges would you use to create the chart?

14. Submit the assignment as specified by your instructor.

Lab 2: **Sales Analysis Worksheet**

Problem: As the chief accountant for CinCar Satellite, a satellite service serving seven states, you have been asked by the vice president to create a worksheet to analyze the yearly sales for each state (Figure 1–77). The packages and corresponding sales by state for the year are shown in Table 1–8 on the next page.

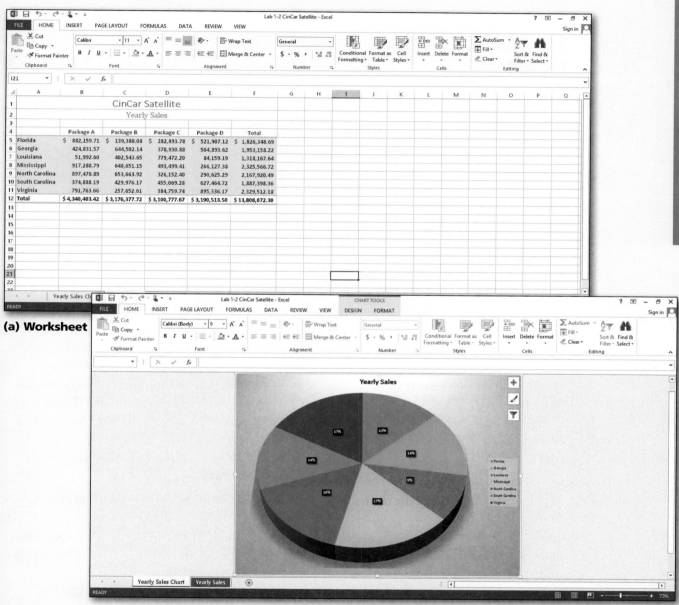

(a) Worksheet

(b) Pie Chart

Figure 1–77

Continued >

In the Labs *continued*

Instructions: Perform the following tasks.

1. Create the worksheet shown in Figure 1–77a on the previous page using the data in Table 1–8.

2. Use the SUM function to determine total revenue for the four packages, the totals for each state, and the company total. Add column and row headings for the totals row and totals column, as appropriate.

Table 1–8 CinCar Satellite				
	Package A	**Package B**	**Package C**	**Package D**
Florida	$882,159.71	$139,388.08	$282,893.78	$521,907.12
Georgia	424,831.57	644,502.14	378,930.88	504,893.62
Louisiana	51,992.60	402,543.65	779,472.20	84,159.19
Mississippi	917,288.79	648,651.15	493,499.41	266,127.38
North Carolina	897,478.89	653,663.92	326,152.40	290,625.29
South Carolina	374,888.19	429,976.17	455,069.28	627,464.72
Virginia	$791,763.66	$257,652.61	$384,759.74	$895,336.17

3. Format the worksheet title and subtitle with the Title cell style and center them across columns A through F. Use the Font group on the ribbon to format the worksheet subtitle as 14-point Cambria red. Format the title with Dark Red, bold font color. Center the titles across columns A through F.

4. Format the range B4:F4 with the Heading 3 cell style and center the text in the cells. Format the range A5:F11 with the 20% - Accent 1 cell style, and the range A12:F12 with the Total cell style. Format cells B5:F5 and B12:F12 with the accounting number format and cells B6:F11 with the comma style format.

5. Create a 3-D pie chart that shows the sales contributions of each state. Chart the state names (A5:A11) and corresponding totals (F5:F11). Insert the 3-D pie chart by using the 'Insert Pie or Doughnut Chart' button (INSERT tab | Charts group). Use the sheet tab name, Yearly Sales Chart. Apply a chart style of your choosing.

6. Change the Sheet1 tab name to Yearly Sales, and apply the Purple color to the sheet tab. Change the document properties, as specified by your instructor.

7. Save the workbook using the file name, Lab 1-2 CinCar Satellite. Print the worksheet in landscape orientation.

8. Two corrections to the figures were sent in from the accounting department. The correct sales figure is $151,992.60 for Package A sold in Louisiana (cell B7) and $183,573.67 for Package B sold in Virginia (cell C11). Print the revised worksheet in landscape orientation.

9. Use the Undo button to change the worksheet back to the original numbers in Table 1–8. Use the Redo button to change the worksheet back to the revised state.

10. Exit Excel without saving the latest changes to the workbook.

11. Change the state in cell A11 to the state in which you were born. If your state already is listed in the spreadsheet, choose a different state.

12. ✳ If you wanted to make a distinction between the rows in the table, what could you do?

13. Submit the assignment as specified by your instructor.

Lab 3: Expand Your World: Cloud and Web Technologies Online

Problem: You are tasked with creating a travel expense report for two trips you made to conferences during the past six months. You decide to download and use one of Excel's templates to create your worksheet.

Instructions Part 1: Tap or click the New tab in the Backstage view and then search for and tap or click the Travel expense report template to download it. Enter data for two trips, one to Las Vegas and one for San Diego, using the web to search for data. Save the file as Lab 1-3 Part 1 Travel Expenses. Print the worksheet. Submit the assignment as specified by your instructor.

Instructions Part 2: ✺ Which template would you use if you wanted to create a workout plan or a training plan for employees?

✺ Consider This: Your Turn

Apply your creative thinking and problem solving skills to design and implement a solution.

1: Create a Personal Budget
Personal

Part 1: To estimate your budget, you decide to create a worksheet listing your income and expenses. Create a worksheet that lists your incomes and your expenses using estimates for the next six months. Total your income and expenses. Calculate your net value using a simple formula. Use the concepts and techniques presented in this chapter to format your worksheet and create a 3-D pie chart for your net result for the six months. Submit your assignment in the format specified by your instructor.

Part 2: ✺ Now that you have looked over your results, did you neglect to include any income? How did you determine the values you used in your estimates? Did you anticipate possible changes in the near future?

2: Create a Sales Worksheet
Professional

Part 1: You are working for a popular sports restaurant that has five branches. Your boss has asked you to create a worksheet to show results for drinks, meals, games, and souvenir sales. Using estimates, create the worksheet for Sports & You. Include totals and averages. Use the concepts and techniques presented in this chapter to format the workbook. Include a chart to compare your revenues. Submit your assignment in the format specified by your instructor.

Part 2: ✺ What steps did you use to create your estimates? Based upon your knowledge of restaurants, do you think seasonal sales would be different, and if so, why?

3: Compare Car Prices
Research and Collaboration

Part 1: Working in a group, research current cars for sale. Create a worksheet that compares the type of cars and the base price for each model, as well as the costs to add various additional options. Calculate the average price for the cars and averages of the additional options. Use the concepts and techniques presented in this chapter to format the worksheet. Include a chart to compare the different car costs. Submit your assignment in the format specified by your instructor.

Part 2: ✺ Based upon the data you found, how could you chart the information to show the comparisons? Which chart would be the best to use?

Learn Online

Reinforce what you learned in this chapter with games, exercises, training, and many other online activities and resources.

Student Companion Site Reinforcement activities and resources are available at no additional cost on www.cengagebrain.com. Visit www.cengage.com/ct/studentdownload for detailed instructions about accessing the resources available at the Student Companion Site.

SAM Put your skills into practice with SAM! If you have a SAM account, go to www.cengage.com/sam2013 to access SAM assignments for this chapter.

2 Formulas, Functions, and Formatting

Microsoft product screenshots used with permission from Microsoft Corporation.

Objectives

You will have mastered the material in this chapter when you can:

- Enter formulas using the keyboard
- Enter formulas using Point mode
- Apply the MAX, MIN, and AVERAGE functions
- Verify a formula using Range Finder
- Apply a theme to a workbook
- Apply a date format to a cell or range

- Add conditional formatting to cells
- Change column width and row height
- Check the spelling on a worksheet
- Change margins and headers in Page Layout view
- Preview and print versions and sections of a worksheet

2 | Formulas, Functions, and Formatting

Introduction

In Chapter 1, you learned how to enter data, sum values, format a worksheet to make it easier to read, and draw a chart. This chapter continues to illustrate these topics and presents some new ones.

The new topics covered in this chapter include using formulas and functions to create a worksheet. A **function** is a prewritten formula that is built into Excel. Other new topics include option buttons, verifying formulas, applying a theme to a worksheet, borders, formatting numbers and text, conditional formatting, changing the widths of columns and heights of rows, spell checking, alternative types of worksheet displays and printouts, and adding page headers and footers to a worksheet. One alternative worksheet display and printout shows the formulas in the worksheet instead of the values. When you display the formulas in the worksheet, you see exactly what text, data, formulas, and functions you have entered into it.

Project — Worksheet with Formulas and Functions

The project in this chapter follows proper design guidelines and uses Excel to create the worksheet shown in Figure 2–1. HyperMass Online Storage established its online website to provide online storage for its customers. The owners pay employees to maintain the servers and handle customer requests. Before the owners pay the employees, they summarize the hours worked, pay rate, and tax information for each employee to ensure that the business properly compensates its employees. This summary includes information such as the employee names, number of dependents, hours worked, hourly pay rate, tax information, net pay, and hire date. As the complexity of the task of creating the summary increases, the owners want to use Excel to create a salary report.

Figure 2–1

Recall that the first step in creating an effective worksheet is to make sure you understand what is required. The people who will use the worksheet usually provide the requirements. The requirements document for the HyperMass Online Storage Salary Report worksheet includes the following needs: source of data, summary of calculations, and other facts about its development (Figure 2–2).

Worksheet Title	HyperMass Online Storage Salary Report
Needs	An easy-to-read worksheet that summarizes the company's salary report (Figure 2–3 on the next page). For each employee, the worksheet is to include the employee's name, dependents, hours worked, hourly pay rate, gross pay, federal tax, state tax, total tax percent, net pay, and hire date. The worksheet also should include totals and the highest value, lowest value, and average for the columns of numbers specified below.
Source of Data	The data supplied includes the employee names, dependents, hours worked, hourly pay rate, and hire dates.
Calculations	The following calculations must be made for each of the employees: 1. Gross Pay = Hours Worked × Hourly Pay Rate 2. Federal Tax = 0.22 × (Gross Pay − Dependents * 24.32) 3. State Tax = 0.04 × Gross Pay 4. Tax % = (Federal Tax + State Tax) / Gross Pay 5. Net Pay = Gross Pay − (Federal Tax + State Tax) 6. Compute the totals for hours worked, gross pay, federal tax, state tax, and net pay 7. Compute the total tax percent 8. Use the MAX and MIN functions to determine the highest and lowest values for dependents, hours worked, hourly pay rate, gross pay, federal tax, state tax, total tax percent, and net pay 9. Use the AVERAGE function to determine the average for hours worked, dependents, hourly pay rate, gross pay, federal tax, state tax, and net pay

Figure 2–2

In addition, using a sketch of the worksheet can help you visualize its design. The sketch for the HyperMass Online Storage Salary Report worksheet includes a title, a subtitle, column and row headings, and the location of data values (Figure 2–3). It also uses specific characters to define the desired formatting for the worksheet, as follows:

1. The row of Xs below the leftmost column heading defines the cell entries as text, such as employee names.

2. The rows of Zs and 9s with slashes, dollar signs, decimal points, commas, and percent signs in the remaining columns define the cell entries as numbers. The Zs indicate that the selected format should instruct Excel to suppress leading 0s. The 9s indicate that the selected format should instruct Excel to display any digits, including 0s.

3. The decimal point means that a decimal point should appear in the cell entry and indicates the number of decimal places to use.

4. The slashes in the last column identify the cell entry as a date.

5. The dollar signs that are adjacent to the Zs below the totals row signify a floating dollar sign, or one that appears next to the first significant digit.

6. The commas indicate that the selected format should instruct Excel to display a comma separator only if the number has sufficient digits (values in the thousandths) to the left of the decimal point.

7. The percent sign (%) in the Tax % column indicates a percent sign should appear after the number.

sketch of worksheet

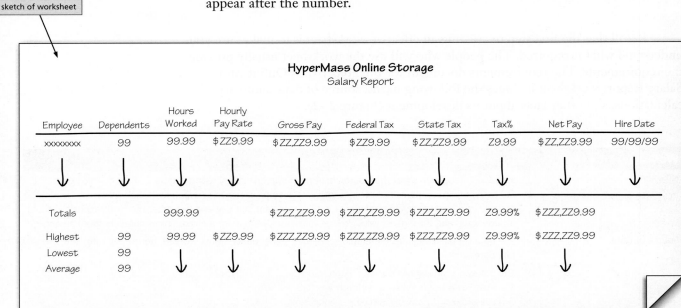

Employee	Dependents	Hours Worked	Hourly Pay Rate	Gross Pay	Federal Tax	State Tax	Tax%	Net Pay	Hire Date
xxxxxxxx	99	99.99	$ZZ9.99	$ZZ,ZZ9.99	$ZZ9.99	$ZZ,ZZ9.99	Z9.99	$ZZ,ZZ9.99	99/99/99
↓	↓	↓	↓	↓	↓	↓	↓	↓	↓
Totals		999.99		$ZZZ,ZZ9.99	$ZZZ,ZZ9.99	$ZZZ,ZZ9.99	Z9.99%	$ZZZ,ZZ9.99	
Highest	99	99.99	$ZZ9.99	$ZZZ,ZZ9.99	$ZZZ,ZZ9.99	$ZZZ,ZZ9.99	Z9.99%	$ZZZ,ZZ9.99	
Lowest	99	↓	↓	↓	↓	↓	↓	↓	
Average	99								

HyperMass Online Storage
Salary Report

Figure 2–3

Roadmap

In this chapter, you will learn how to use functions and create formulas. The following roadmap identifies general activities you will perform as you progress through this chapter:

1. **ENTER FORMULAS** in the worksheet.
2. **ENTER FUNCTIONS** in the worksheet.

3. **VERIFY FORMULAS** in the worksheet.

4. **FORMAT** the **WORKSHEET**.

5. **CHECK SPELLING**.

6. **PRINT** the **WORKSHEET**.

At the beginning of step instructions throughout the chapter, you will see an abbreviated form of this roadmap. The abbreviated roadmap uses colors to indicate chapter progress: gray means the chapter is beyond that activity, blue means the task being shown is covered in that activity, and black means that activity is yet to be covered. For example, the following abbreviated roadmap indicates the chapter would be showing a task in the 2 ENTER FUNCTIONS activity.

1 ENTER FORMULAS | 2 ENTER FUNCTIONS | 3 VERIFY FORMULAS
4 FORMAT WORKSHEET | 5 CHECK SPELLING | 6 PRINT WORKSHEET

The function, or purpose, of a worksheet is to provide a user with direct ways to accomplish tasks. In designing a worksheet, functional considerations should supersede visual aesthetics. When designing your worksheet, what steps should be taken to ensure this?

- Avoid the temptation to use flashy or confusing visual elements within the worksheet.

- Understand the requirements document.

- Choose the proper functions and formulas.

- Build the worksheet.

CONSIDER THIS

To Run Excel and Create a Blank Workbook

If you are using a computer to step through the project in this chapter and you want your screens to match the figures in this book, you should change your screen's resolution to 1366 × 768. For information about how to change a computer's resolution, refer to the Office and Windows chapter at the beginning of this book.

The following steps, which assume Windows 8 is running, use the Start screen or the search box to run Excel based on a typical installation. You may need to ask your instructor how to run Excel on your computer. For a detailed example of the procedure summarized below, refer to the Office and Windows chapter.

1 Scroll the Start screen for an Excel 2013 tile. If your Start screen contains an Excel 2013 tile, tap or click it to run Excel and then proceed to Step 5; if the Start screen does not contain the Excel 2013 tile, proceed to the next step to search for the Excel app.

2 Swipe in from the right edge of the screen or point to the upper-right corner of the screen to display the Charms bar and then tap or click the Search charm on the Charms bar to display the Search menu.

3 Type `Excel` as the search text in the Search box and watch the search results appear in the Apps list.

4 Tap or click Excel 2013 in the search results to run Excel.

5 Tap or click the Blank workbook thumbnail on the Excel start screen to create a blank workbook and display it in the Excel window.

6 If the Excel window is not maximized, tap or click the Maximize button on its title bar to maximize the window.

For an introduction to Windows and instruction about how to perform basic Windows tasks, read the Office and Windows chapter at the beginning of this book, where you can learn how to resize windows, change screen resolution, create folders, move and rename files, use Windows Help, and much more.

For an introduction to Office and instruction about how to perform basic tasks in Office programs, read the Office and Windows chapter at the beginning of this book, where you can learn how to run a program, use the ribbon, save a file, open a file, exit a program, use Help, and much more.

Entering the Titles and Numbers into the Worksheet

The first step in creating the worksheet is to enter the titles and numbers into the worksheet. The following sets of steps enter the worksheet title and subtitle and then the salary report data shown in Table 2–1 on page EX 71.

To Enter the Worksheet Title and Subtitle

With a good comprehension of the requirements document, an understanding of the necessary decisions, and a sketch of the worksheet, the next step is to use Excel to create the worksheet.

The following steps enter the worksheet title and subtitle into cells A1 and A2.

1 If necessary, select cell A1. Type **HyperMass Online Storage** in the selected cell and then press the DOWN ARROW key to enter the worksheet title.

2 Type **Salary Report** in cell A2 and then press the DOWN ARROW key to enter the worksheet subtitle.

To Enter the Column Titles

The employee names and the row titles Totals, Average, Highest, and Lowest in the leftmost column begin in cell A4 and continue down to cell A16. The employee data is entered into rows 4 through 12 of the worksheet. The remainder of this section explains the steps required to enter the column titles, payroll data, and row titles, as shown in Figure 2–4, and then save the workbook.

The column titles in row 3 begin in cell A3 and extend through cell J3. Some of the column titles in Figure 2–4 include multiple lines of text, such as Hours Worked in cell C3. To start a new line in a cell, press ALT+ENTER after each line, except for the last line, which is completed by tapping or clicking the Enter box, pressing the ENTER key, or pressing one of the arrow keys. When you see ALT+ENTER in a step, press the ENTER key while holding down the ALT key and then release both keys. The following steps enter the column titles.

1 With cell A3 selected, type **Employee** and then press the RIGHT ARROW key to enter the column heading.

2 Type **Dependents** and then press the RIGHT ARROW key to enter the column heading.

3 In cell C3, type **Hours** and then press ALT+ENTER to enter the first line of the column heading. Type **Worked** and then press the RIGHT ARROW key to enter the column heading.

4 Type **Hourly** in cell D3 and then press ALT+ENTER to begin a new line in the cell. Type **Pay Rate** and then press the RIGHT ARROW key to enter the column heading.

5 Type **Gross Pay** in cell E3 and then press the RIGHT ARROW key to enter the column heading.

6 Type **Federal Tax** in cell F3 and then press the RIGHT ARROW key to enter the column heading.

7 Type **State Tax** in cell G3 and then press the RIGHT ARROW key to enter the column heading.

8 Type **Tax %** in cell H3 and then press the RIGHT ARROW key to enter the column heading.

9 Type **Net Pay** in cell I3 and then press the RIGHT ARROW key to enter the column heading.

10 Type **Hire Date** in cell J3 and then press the RIGHT ARROW key to enter the column heading.

To Enter the Salary Data

The salary data in Table 2–1 includes a hire date for each employee. Excel considers a date to be a number and, therefore, it displays the date right-aligned in the cell. The following steps enter the data for each employee: name, dependents, hours worked, hourly pay rate, and hire date.

1 Select cell A4. Type **Carl, Michael** and then press the RIGHT ARROW key to enter the employee name.

2 Type **3** in cell B4 and then press the RIGHT ARROW key to enter a number in the selected cell.

3 Type **60.45** in cell C4 and then press the RIGHT ARROW key to enter a number in the selected cell.

4 Type **19.50** in cell D4 and then press the RIGHT ARROW key to enter a number in the selected cell.

5 Type **4/5/10** in cell J4 and then tap or click cell A5 to select the cell.

6 Enter the payroll data in Table 2–1 for the eight remaining employees in rows 5 through 12 (shown in Figure 2–4 on page 72).

Q&A In Step 5, why did the date that was entered change from 4/5/10 to 4/5/2010?
When Excel recognizes that you entered a date in mm/dd/yy format, it automatically formats the date as mm/dd/yyyy for you. Most professionals prefer to view dates in mm/dd/yyyy format as opposed to mm/dd/yy format because the latter can cause confusion regarding the intended year. For example, a date displayed as 3/3/50 could imply a date of 3/3/1950 or 3/3/2050. The use of a four-digit year eliminates this confusion.

Table 2–1 HyperMass Online Storage Salary Report Data

Employee	Dependents	Hours Worked	Hourly Pay Rate	Hire Date
Carl, Michael	3	60.45	19.50	4/5/10
Green, Sue	0	81.50	22.85	7/15/11
Fekir, Sith	1	69.50	17.36	1/13/09
Lane, Jon	2	65.25	19.45	3/1/12
Nichols, Peter	3	71.25	12.60	4/15/11
Pearson, Ada	3	44.65	22.45	10/31/08
Rodriquez, Juan	2	55.50	20.15	7/15/09
Williams, Sean	0	80.00	20.85	5/14/09
Yau, Xin	4	70.00	18.75	6/17/02

To Enter the Row Titles

The following steps add row titles for the rows that will contain the totals, highest, lowest, and average amounts.

1 Select cell A13. Type `Totals` and then press the DOWN ARROW key to enter a row header.

2 Type `Highest` in cell A14 and then press the DOWN ARROW key to enter a row header.

3 Type `Lowest` in cell A15 and then press the ENTER key to enter a row header.

4 Type `Average` in cell A16 and then press the DOWN ARROW key to enter a row header (Figure 2–4).

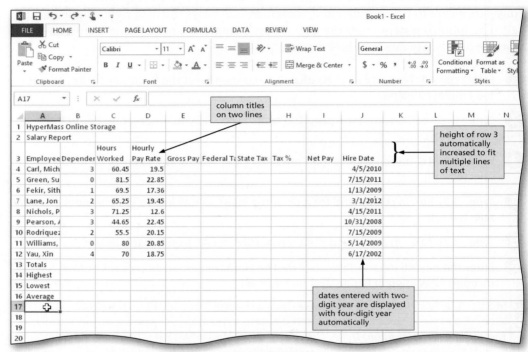

Figure 2–4

To Change the Worksheet Tab Name and Color and Save the Workbook

The following steps change the worksheet tab name to Salary Report, change the sheet tab color, and save the workbook in the Excel folder (for your assignments) using the file name, HyperMass Online Storage Salary Report.

1 Double-tap or double-click the Sheet1 tab and then enter `Salary Report` as the sheet tab name and then press the ENTER key.

2 Press and hold or right-click the sheet tab to display the shortcut menu.

3 Tap or point to Tab Color on the shortcut menu to display the Tab Color gallery. Tap or click Green, Accent 6, Darker 25% (column 10, row 5) in the Theme Colors area to apply a new color to the sheet tab.

4 Tap or click the Save button on the Quick Access Toolbar, which depending on settings, will display either the Save As gallery in the Backstage view or the Save As dialog box.

5 To save on a hard disk or other storage media on your computer, proceed to Step 5a. To save on SkyDrive, proceed to Step 5b.

5a If your screen opens the Backstage view and you want to save on storage media on your computer, tap or click Computer, if necessary, to display options in the right pane related to saving on your computer. If your screen already displays the Save As dialog box, proceed to Step 6.

5b If your screen opens the Backstage view and you want to save on SkyDrive, tap or click SkyDrive to display SkyDrive saving options or a Sign In button. If your screen displays a Sign In button, tap or click it and then sign in to SkyDrive.

6 Tap or click the Browse button in the right pane to display the Save As dialog box associated with the selected Save As Place (i.e., Computer or SkyDrive).

7 Type `HyperMass Online Storage Salary Report` in the File name box to change the file name. Do not press the ENTER key after typing the file name because you do not want to close the dialog box at this time.

8 Navigate to the desired save location (in this case, the Excel folder in the CIS 101 folder [or your class folder] on your computer or SkyDrive).

9 Tap or click the Save button (Save As dialog box) to save the document in the selected folder on the selected location with the entered file name.

Entering Formulas

One of the reasons Excel is such a valuable tool is that you can assign a **formula** to a cell, and Excel will calculate the result. Consider, for example, what would happen if you had to multiply 60.45 by 19.5 and then manually enter the product for Gross Pay, 1,178.78, in cell E4. Every time the values in cells C4 or D4 changed, you would have to recalculate the product and enter the new value in cell E4. By contrast, if you enter a formula in cell E4 to multiply the values in cells C4 and D4, Excel recalculates the product whenever new values are entered into those cells and displays the result in cell E4.

 A formula in a cell that contains a reference back to itself is called a **circular reference**. Excel often warns you when you create a circular reference. In almost all cases, circular references are the result of an incorrect formula. A circular reference can be direct or indirect. For example, placing the formula =A1 in cell A1 results in a direct circular reference. An **indirect circular reference** occurs when a formula in a cell refers to another cell or cells that include a formula that refers back to the original cell.

To Enter a Formula Using the Keyboard

1 ENTER FORMULAS | 2 ENTER FUNCTIONS | 3 VERIFY FORMULAS
4 FORMAT WORKSHEET | 5 CHECK SPELLING | 6 PRINT WORKSHEET

The formulas needed in the worksheet are noted in the requirements document as follows:

1. Gross Pay (column E) = Hours Worked × Hourly Pay Rate
2. Federal Tax (column F) = 0.22 × (Gross Pay − Dependents × 24.32)
3. State Tax (column G) = 0.04 × Gross Pay
4. Tax % (column H) = (Federal Tax + State Tax) / Gross Pay
5. Net Pay (column I) = Gross Pay − (Federal Tax + State Tax)

The gross pay for each employee, which appears in column E, is equal to hours worked in column C times hourly pay rate in column D. Thus, the gross pay for Michael Carl in cell E4 is obtained by multiplying 60.45 (cell C4) by 19.50 (cell D4) or =C4 × D4. The following steps enter the initial gross pay formula in cell E4 using the keyboard. *Why? In order for Excel to perform the calculations, you must create formulas.*

1

- With cell E4 selected, type **=c4*d4** in the cell to display the formula in the formula bar and in the current cell and to display colored borders around the cells referenced in the formula (Figure 2–5).

Q&A

What occurs on the worksheet as I enter the formula?

The **equal sign** (=) preceding c4*d4 alerts Excel that you are entering a formula or function and not text. Because the most common error when entering a formula is to reference the wrong cell in a formula mistakenly, Excel colors the borders of the cells referenced in the formula. The coloring helps in the reviewing process to ensure the cell references are correct. The **asterisk** (*) following c4 is the arithmetic operator that directs Excel to perform the multiplication operation.

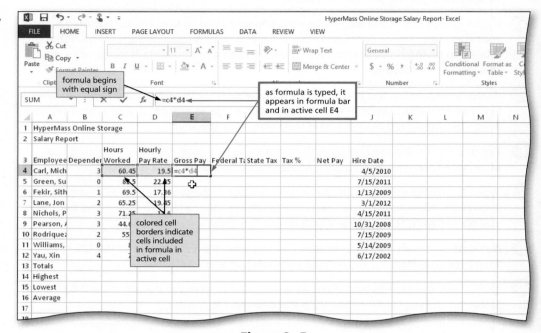

Figure 2–5

2

- Press the RIGHT ARROW key to complete the arithmetic operation indicated by the formula, to display the result in the worksheet, and to select the cell to the right (Figure 2–6). The number of decimal places shown in cell E4 may be different, but these values will be adjusted later in this chapter.

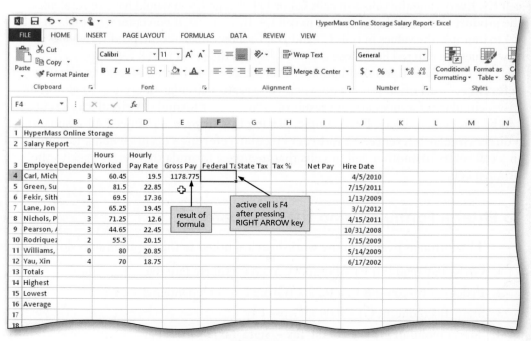

Figure 2–6

Arithmetic Operations

Excel provides powerful functions and capabilities that allow you to perform arithmetic operations easily and efficiently. Table 2–2 describes multiplication and other valid Excel arithmetic operators.

Table 2–2 Summary of Arithmetic Operators			
Arithmetic Operator	**Meaning**	**Example of Usage**	**Result**
–	Negation	–78	Negative 78
%	Percentage	=23%	Multiplies 23 by 0.01
^	Exponentiation	=3 ^ 4	Raises 3 to the fourth power
*	Multiplication	=61.5 * C5	Multiplies the contents of cell C5 by 61.5
/	Division	=H3 / H11	Divides the contents of cell H3 by the contents of cell H11
+	Addition	=11 + 9	Adds 11 and 9
–	Subtraction	=22 – F15	Subtracts the contents of cell F15 from 22

Order of Operations

When more than one arithmetic operator is involved in a formula, Excel follows the same basic order of operations that you use in algebra. Moving from left to right in a formula, the **order of operations** is as follows: first negation (–), then all percentages (%), then all exponentiations (^), then all multiplications (*) and divisions (/), and finally, all additions (+) and subtractions (–).

As in algebra, you can use parentheses to override the order of operations. For example, if Excel follows the order of operations, 8 * 3 + 2 equals 26. If you use parentheses, however, to change the formula to 8 * (3 + 2), the result is 40, because the parentheses instruct Excel to add 3 and 2 before multiplying by 8. Table 2–3 illustrates several examples of valid Excel formulas and explains the order of operations.

Table 2–3 Examples of Excel Formulas	
Formula	**Result**
=G15	Assigns the value in cell G15 to the active cell.
=2^4 + 7	Assigns the sum of 16 + 7 (or 23) to the active cell.
=100 + D2 or =D2 +100 or =(100 + D2)	Assigns 100 plus the contents of cell D2 to the active cell.
=25% * 40	Assigns the product of 0.25 times 40 (or 10) to the active cell.
– (K15 * X45)	Assigns the negative value of the product of the values contained in cells K15 and X45 to the active cell. You do not need to type an equal sign before an expression that begins with minus signs, which indicates a negation.
=(U8 – B8) * 6	Assigns the difference between the values contained in cells U8 and B8 times 6 to the active cell.
=J7 / A5 + G9 * M6 – Z2 ^ L7	Completes the following operations, from left to right: exponentiation (Z2 ^ L7), then division (J7 / A5), then multiplication (G9 * M6), then addition (J7 / A5) + (G9 * M6), and finally subtraction (J7 / A5 + G9 * M6) – (Z2 ^ L7). If cells A5 = 6, G9 = 2, J7 = 6, L7 = 4, M6 = 5, and Z2 = 2, then Excel assigns the active cell the value –5; that is, 6 / 6 + 2 * 5 – 2 ^ 4 = –5.

To Enter Formulas Using Point Mode

The sketch of the worksheet in Figure 2–3 on page EX 68 calls for the federal tax, state tax, tax percent, and net pay for each employee to appear in columns F, G, H, and I, respectively. All four of these values are calculated using formulas in row 4:

Federal Tax (cell F4) = 0.22 × (Gross Pay – Dependents × 24.32) or =0.22 * (E4 – B4 * 24.32)
State Tax (cell G4) = 0.04 × Gross Pay or =0.04 * E4
Tax % (cell H4) = (Federal Tax + State Tax) / Gross Pay or =(F4 + G4)/E4
Net Pay (cell I4) = Gross Pay – (Federal Tax + State Tax) or =E4 – (F4 + G4)

An alternative to entering the formulas in cells F4, G4, H4, and I4 using the keyboard is to enter the formulas using the pointer and Point mode. **Point mode** allows you to select cells for use in a formula by using your finger or the pointer. The following steps enter formulas using Point mode. *Why? Using Point mode makes it easier to create formulas without worrying about typographical errors when entering cell references.*

1

• With cell F4 selected, type =0.22*(to begin the formula and then tap or click cell E4 to add a cell reference in the formula (Figure 2–7).

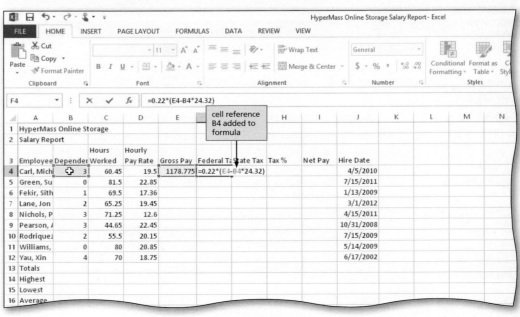

Figure 2–7

2

• Type – (minus sign) and then tap or click cell B4 to add a subtraction operator and a reference to another cell to the formula.

• Type *24.32) to complete the formula (Figure 2–8).

Figure 2–8

3

- Tap or click the Enter box in the formula bar and then select cell G4 to prepare to enter the next formula.

- Type =0.04* and then tap or click cell E4 to add a cell reference to the formula (Figure 2–9).

Q&A Why should I use Point mode to enter formulas? Using Point mode to enter formulas often is faster and more accurate than using the keyboard to type the entire formula when the cell you want to select does not require you to scroll. In many instances, as in these steps, you may want to use both the keyboard and touch gestures or the pointer when entering a formula in a cell. You can use the keyboard to begin the formula, for example, and then use touch gestures or the pointer to select a range of cells.

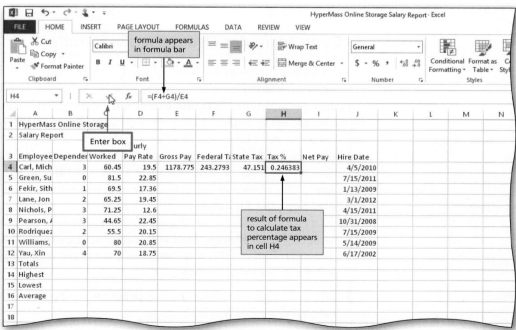

Figure 2–9

4

- Tap or click the Enter box in the formula bar to enter the formula in cell G4.

- Select cell H4. Type =((equal sign followed by an open parenthesis) and then tap or click cell F4 to add a reference to the formula.

- Type + (plus sign) and then tap or click cell G4 to add a cell reference to the formula.

- Type)/ (close parenthesis followed by a forward slash), and then tap or click cell E4 to add a cell reference to the formula.

- Tap or click the Enter box in the formula bar to enter the formula in cell H4 (Figure 2–10).

Figure 2–10

5

- Tap or click cell I4 to select cell I4 to prepare to enter the next formula.

- Type = (equal sign) and then tap or click cell E4 to begin the formula and add a cell reference to the formula.

- Type − ((minus sign followed by an open parenthesis) and then tap or click cell F4 to add a subtraction operator, open parenthesis, and cell reference to the formula.

- Type + (plus sign) and then tap or click cell G4 to add an addition operator and cell reference to the formula.

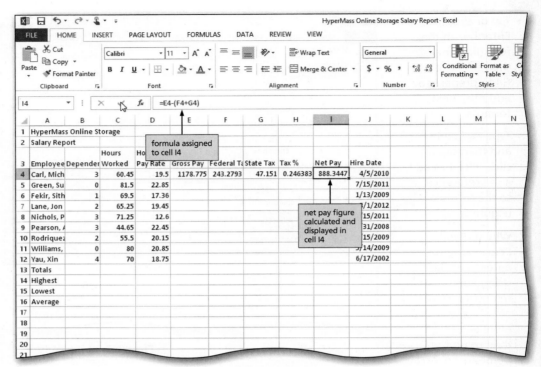

Figure 2–11

- Type) (close parenthesis) to complete the formula (Figure 2–11).

- Tap or click the Enter box in the formula bar to enter the formula.

To Copy Formulas Using the Fill Handle

The five formulas for Michael Carl in cells E4, F4, G4, H4, and I4 now are complete. The next step is to copy them to the range E5:I12. When performing copying operations in Excel, the source area is the cell, or range, from which data or formulas are being copied. When a range is used as a source, it sometimes is called the source range. The destination area is the cell, or range, to which data or formulas are being copied. When a range is used as a destination, it sometimes is called the destination range. Recall from Chapter 1 that the fill handle is a small black square in the lower-right corner of the active cell or active range. The following steps copy the formulas using the fill handle.

1 Select the source range, E4:I4 in this case, activate the fill handle, drag the fill handle down through cell I12, and then continue to hold your finger or the mouse button to select the destination range.

2 Lift your finger or release the mouse button to copy the formulas to the destination range (Figure 2–12).

Q&A How does Excel adjust the cell references in the formulas in the destination area?
Recall that when you copy a formula, Excel adjusts the cell references so that the new formulas contain references corresponding to the new location and perform calculations using the appropriate values. Thus, if you copy downward, Excel adjusts the row portion of cell references. If you copy across, then Excel adjusts the column portion of cell references. These cell references are called **relative cell references**.

Figure 2–12

Option Buttons

Excel displays Option buttons in a workbook while you are working on it to indicate that you can complete an operation using automatic features such as AutoCorrect, Auto Fill, error checking, and others. For example, the 'Auto Fill Options' button shown in Figure 2–12 appears after a fill operation, such as dragging the fill handle. When an error occurs in a formula in a cell, Excel displays the Trace Error button next to the cell and identifies the cell with the error by placing a green triangle in the upper left of the cell.

Table 2–4 summarizes the Option buttons available in Excel. When one of these buttons appears on your worksheet, tap or click its arrow to produce the list of options for modifying the operation or to obtain additional information.

Table 2–4 Option Buttons in Excel	
Name	**Menu Function**
'Auto Fill Options'	Gives options for how to fill cells following a fill operation, such as dragging the fill handle
AutoCorrect Options	Undoes an automatic correction, stops future automatic corrections of this type, or causes Excel to display the AutoCorrect Options dialog box
Insert Options	Lists formatting options following an insertion of cells, rows, or columns
Paste Options	Specifies how moved or pasted items should appear (for example, with original formatting, without formatting, or with different formatting)
Trace Error	Lists error-checking options following the assignment of an invalid formula to a cell

The Paste Options button provides powerful functionality. When performing copy and paste operations, the button allows you great freedom in specifying what it is you want to paste. You can choose from the following options:

- Paste an exact copy of what you copied, including the cell contents and formatting.
- Copy only formulas.
- Copy only formatting.
- Copy only values.
- Copy a combination of these options.
- Copy a picture of what you copied.

To Determine Totals Using the Sum Button

The next step is to determine the totals in row 13 for the hours worked in column C, gross pay in column E, federal tax in column F, state tax in column G, and net pay in column I. To determine the total hours worked in column C, the values in the range C4 through C12 must be summed. To do so, enter the function =sum(c4:c12) in cell C13 or select cell C13, tap or click the Sum button (HOME tab | Editing group), and then press the ENTER key. Recall that a function is a prewritten formula that is built into Excel. Similar SUM functions can be used in cells E13, F13, G13, and I13 to total gross pay, federal tax, state tax, and net pay, respectively. The following steps determine totals in cell C13, the range E13:G13, and cell I13.

1 Select the cell to contain the sum, cell C13 in this case. Tap or click the Sum button (HOME tab | Editing group) to sum the contents of the range C4:C12 in cell C13 and then tap or click the Enter box to display a total in the selected cell.

2 Select the range to contain the sums, range E13:G13 in this case. Tap or click the Sum button (HOME tab | Editing group) to display totals in the selected range.

3 Select the cell to contain the sum, cell I13 in this case. Tap or click the Sum button (HOME tab | Editing group) to sum the contents of the range I4:I12 in cell I13 and then tap or click the Enter box to display a total in the selected cell (Figure 2–13).

Q&A Why did I have to tap or click the Enter box?
When creating a sum for a single column, you tap or click the Enter box. If you are calculating the sum for multiple ranges, you tap or click the Sum button.

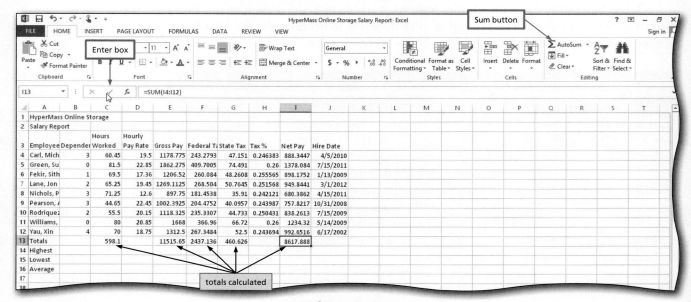

Figure 2–13

To Determine the Total Tax Percentage

With the totals in row 13 determined, the next step is to copy the tax percentage formula in cell H12 to cell H13. The following step copies the tax percentage formula.

1 Select the cell to be copied, H12 in this case, and then drag the fill handle down through cell H13 to copy the formula (Figure 2–14).

Q&A Why was the SUM function not used for tax percentage in H13?
The tax percentage is based off of the totals, not the sum, of the tax percentage column; therefore, there was no need to use the SUM function.

Figure 2–14

Using the AVERAGE, MAX, and MIN Functions

The next step in creating the HyperMass Online Storage Salary Report worksheet is to compute the highest value, lowest value, and average value for the number of dependents listed in the range B4:B12 using the MAX, MIN, and AVERAGE functions in the range B14:B16. Once the values are determined for column B, the entries can be copied across to the other columns.

With Excel, you can enter functions using one of five methods: (1) keyboard, touch gesture, or pointer; (2) the Insert Function box in the formula bar; (3) the Sum menu; (4) the Sum button (FORMULAS tab | Function Library group); and (5) the Name box area in the formula bar. The method you choose will depend on your typing skills and whether you can recall the function name and required arguments.

In the following sections, three of these methods will be used. The Insert Function box in the formula bar method will be used to determine the highest number of dependents (cell B14). The Sum menu will be used to determine the lowest number of dependents (cell B15). The keyboard and pointer will be used to determine the average number of dependents (cell B16).

To Determine the Highest Number in a Range of Numbers Using the Insert Function Box

The next step is to select cell B14 and determine the highest (maximum) number in the range B4:B12. Excel includes a function called the **MAX function** that displays the highest value in a range. The following steps use the Insert Function box in the formula bar to enter the MAX function. *Why? Although you could enter the MAX function using the keyboard and Point mode as described previously, an alternative method to entering the function is to use the Insert Function box in the formula bar.*

1

- Select the cell to contain the maximum number, cell B14 in this case.

- Tap or click the Insert Function box in the formula bar to display the Insert Function dialog box.

- If necessary, scroll to and then tap or click MAX in the Select a function list (Insert Function dialog box) to select it (Figure 2–15).

Q&A What if the MAX function is not in the Select a function list?
Click the 'Or select a category' arrow to display the list of function categories, select All, and then scroll down and select the MAX function in the Select a function list.

How can I learn about other functions?
Excel has more than 400 additional functions that perform nearly every type of calculation you can imagine. These functions are categorized in the Insert Function dialog box shown in Figure 2–15. To view the categories, tap or click the 'Or select a category' arrow. To obtain a description of a selected function, select its name in the Insert Function dialog box. Excel displays the description of the function below the Select a function list in the dialog box.

Figure 2–15

2

- Tap or click the OK button (Insert Function dialog box) to display the Function Arguments dialog box.

- Type **b4:b12** in the Number1 box (Function Arguments dialog box) to enter the first argument of the function (Figure 2–16).

Q&A | Why did numbers appear to the right of the Number 1 box in the Function Arguments dialog box?

As shown in Figure 2–16, Excel displays the value the MAX function will return to cell B14 in the Function Arguments dialog box. It also lists the first few numbers in the selected range, next to the Number1 box.

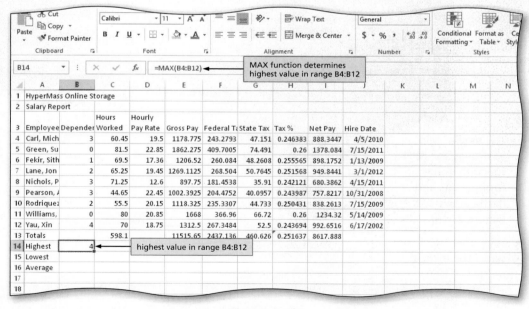

Figure 2–16

3

- Tap or click the OK button (Function Arguments dialog box) to display the highest value in the chosen range in the selected cell (Figure 2–17).

Q&A | Why should I not just enter the highest value that I see in the range B4:B12 in cell B14?

In this example, rather than entering the MAX function, you visually could scan the range B4:B12, determine that the highest number of

Figure 2–17

dependents is 4, and manually enter the number 4 as a constant in cell B14. Excel would display the number the same as in Figure 2–17. Because it contains a constant, however, Excel will continue to display 4 in cell B14, even if the values in the range change. If you use the MAX function, Excel will recalculate the highest value in the range each time a new value is entered into the worksheet.

Other Ways

1. Tap or click Sum arrow (HOME tab \| Editing group), tap or click Max	2. Tap or click Sum arrow (FORMULAS tab \| Function Library group), tap or click Max	3. Type **=MAX** in cell, fill in arguments

To Determine the Lowest Number in a Range of Numbers Using the Sum Menu

The next step is to enter the **MIN function** in cell B15 to determine the lowest (minimum) number in the range B4:B12. Although you can enter the MIN function using the method used to enter the MAX function, the following steps illustrate an alternative method using the Sum button (HOME tab | Editing group). **Why?** *The Sum menu provides another way that you can insert functions, providing a menu from which you can choose.*

• Select cell B15 and then tap or click the Sum arrow (HOME tab | Editing group) to display the Sum menu (Figure 2–18).

Q&A Why should I use the Sum menu?
Using the Sum menu allows you to enter one of five often-used functions easily into a cell, without having to memorize its name or the required arguments.

Figure 2–18

• Tap or click Min to display the MIN function in the formula bar and in the active cell (Figure 2–19).

Q&A Why does Excel select the incorrect range?
The range automatically selected by Excel is not always correct. Excel attempts to guess which cells you want to include in the function by looking for ranges that are adjacent to the selected cell and that contain numeric data.

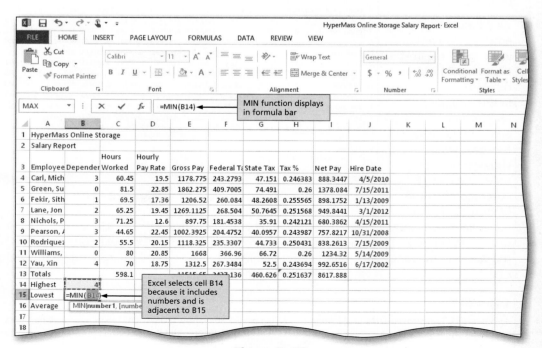

Figure 2–19

3

- Tap or click cell B4 and then drag through cell B12 to display the function with the new range in the formula bar and in the selected cell (Figure 2–20).

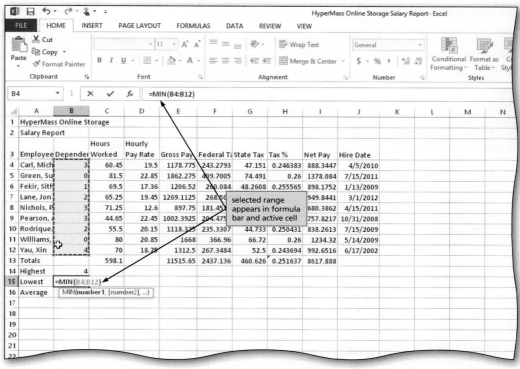

Figure 2–20

4

- Tap or click the Enter box to determine the lowest value in the range B4:B12 and display the result in the selected cell (Figure 2–21).

Figure 2–21

Other Ways

1. Tap or click Insert Function box in formula bar, if necessary, select Statistical category, tap or click MIN, specify arguments
2. Tap or click Sum arrow (FORMULAS tab | Function Library group), tap or click Min
3. Type =MIN in cell, fill in arguments

To Determine the Average of a Range of Numbers Using the Keyboard

The AVERAGE function sums the numbers in a specified range and then divides the sum by the number of cells with numeric values in the range. The following steps use the AVERAGE function to determine the average of the numbers in the range B4:B12. *Why? The AVERAGE function creates an accurate average automatically.*

- Select the cell to contain the average, cell B16 in this case.

- Type **=av** in the cell to display the Formula AutoComplete list. Press the DOWN ARROW key to highlight the required formula (Figure 2–22).

Q&A

What is happening as I type?

As you type the equal sign followed by the characters in the name of a function, Excel displays the Formula AutoComplete list. This list contains those functions that alphabetically match the letters you have typed. Because you typed =av, Excel displays all the functions that begin with the letters, av.

Figure 2–22

- Double-tap or double-click AVERAGE in the Formula AutoComplete list to select the function.

- Select the range to be averaged, B4:B12 in this case, to insert the range as the argument to the function (Figure 2–23).

Q&A

As I drag, why does the function in cell B16 change?

When you tap or click cell B4, Excel appends cell B4 to the left parenthesis in the formula bar and surrounds cell B4 with a marquee. When you begin dragging, Excel appends to the argument a colon (:) and the cell reference of the cell where the pointer is located.

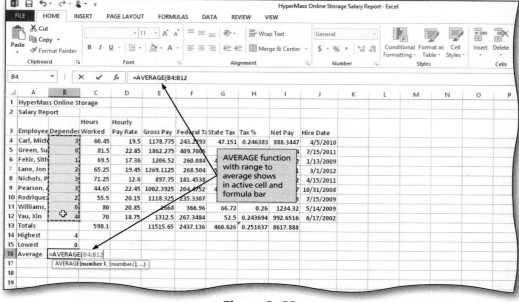

Figure 2–23

3

- Tap or click the Enter box to compute the average of the numbers in the selected range and display the result in the selected cell (Figure 2–24).

Q&A Can I use the arrow keys to complete the entry instead?
No. When you use Point mode you cannot use the arrow keys to complete the entry. While in Point mode, the arrow keys change the selected cell reference in the range you are selecting.

What is the purpose of the parentheses in the function?
The AVERAGE function requires that the argument (in this case, the range B4:B12) be included within parentheses following the function name. Excel automatically appends the right parenthesis to complete the AVERAGE function when you tap or click the Enter box or press the ENTER key.

Figure 2–24

Other Ways

1. Tap or click Insert Function box in formula bar, select Statistical category, tap or click AVERAGE

2. Tap or click Sum arrow (HOME tab | Editing group), tap or click Average

3. Tap or click Sum arrow (FORMULAS tab | Function Library group), tap or click Average

To Copy a Range of Cells Across Columns to an Adjacent Range Using the Fill Handle

The next step is to copy the AVERAGE, MAX, and MIN functions in the range B14:B16 to the adjacent range C14:I16. The following steps use the fill handle to copy the functions.

1 Select the source range from which to copy the functions, in this case B14:B16.

2 Drag the fill handle in the lower-right corner of the selected range through cell I16 to copy the three functions to the selected range.

③ Select cell H16 and then press the DELETE key to delete the average of the tax % (Figure 2–25).

Q&A

Why delete the formula in cell H16?
The average of the tax percentage in cell H16 is deleted because an average of percentages of this type is mathematically invalid.

How can I be sure that the function arguments are proper for the cells in range C14:I16?
Remember that Excel adjusts the cell references in the copied functions so that each function refers to the range of numbers above it in the same column. Review the numbers in rows 14 through 16 in Figure 2–25. You should see that the functions in each column return the appropriate values, based on the numbers in rows 4 through 12 of that column.

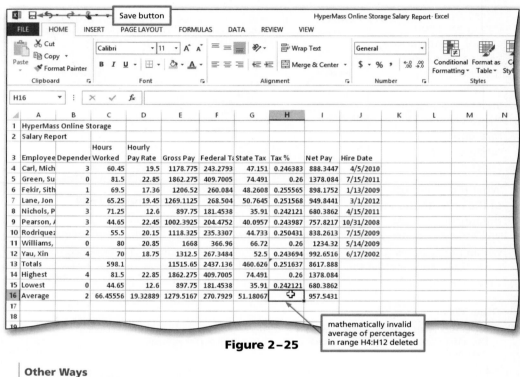

Figure 2–25

> mathematically invalid average of percentages in range H4:H12 deleted

Other Ways

1. Select source area, tap or click Copy button (HOME tab | Clipboard group), select destination area, tap or click Paste button (HOME tab | Clipboard group)

2. Press and hold or right-click source area, tap or click Copy on shortcut menu; press and hold or right-click destination area, tap or click Paste icon on shortcut menu

3. Select source area and then point to border of range; while holding down CTRL, drag source area to destination area

4. Select source area, press CTRL+C, select destination area, press CTRL+V

To Save a Workbook Using the Same File Name

Earlier in this project, an intermediate version of the workbook was saved using the file name, HyperMass Online Storage Salary Report. The following step saves the workbook a second time, using the same file name.

① Tap or click the Save button on the Quick Access Toolbar to overwrite the previously saved file.

Break Point: If you wish to take a break, this is a good place to do so. You can exit Excel now. To resume at a later time, run Excel, open the file called HyperMass Online Storage Salary Report, and continue following the steps from this location forward.

Verifying Formulas Using Range Finder

One of the more common mistakes made with Excel is to include an incorrect cell reference in a formula. An easy way to verify that a formula references the cells you want it to reference is to use Range Finder. **Range Finder** checks which cells are referenced in the formula assigned to the active cell.

To use Range Finder to verify that a formula contains the intended cell references, double-tap or double-click the cell with the formula you want to check. Excel responds by highlighting the cells referenced in the formula so that you can verify that the cell references are correct.

To Verify a Formula Using Range Finder

1 ENTER FORMULAS | 2 ENTER FUNCTIONS | 3 VERIFY FORMULAS
4 FORMAT WORKSHEET | 5 CHECK SPELLING | 6 PRINT WORKSHEET

Why? Range Finder allows you to make immediate changes to the cells referenced in a formula. The following steps use Range Finder to check the formula in cell H4.

1
- Double-tap or double-click cell H4 to activate Range Finder (Figure 2–26).

2
- Press the ESC key to quit Range Finder and then tap or click anywhere in the worksheet, such as cell A18, to deselect the current cell.

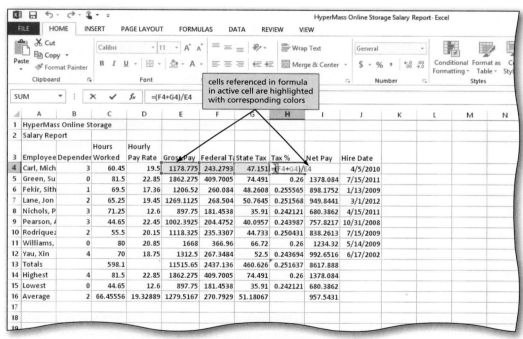

Figure 2–26

Formatting the Worksheet

Although the worksheet contains the appropriate data, formulas, and functions, the text and numbers need to be formatted to improve their appearance and readability.

In Chapter 1, cell styles were used to format much of the worksheet. This section describes how to change the unformatted worksheet in Figure 2–27a to the formatted worksheet in Figure 2–27b using a theme and other commands on the ribbon. The colors and fonts that are used in the worksheet shown in Figure 2–27b are those that are associated with the Basis theme.

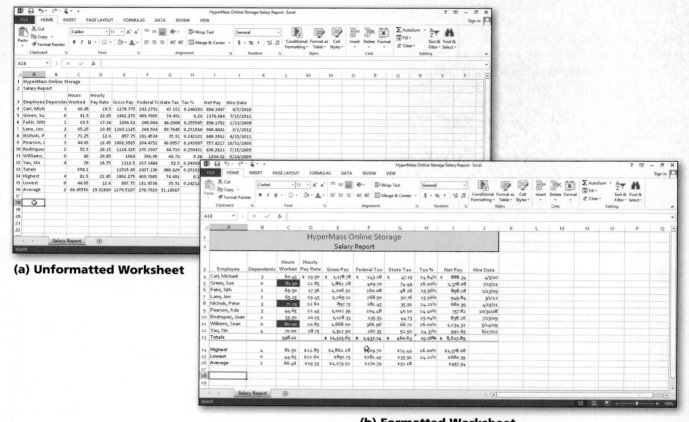

(a) Unformatted Worksheet

(b) Formatted Worksheet

Figure 2–27

The following outlines the formatting suggested in the sketch of the worksheet in Figure 2–3 on page EX 68.

1. Workbook theme — Basis
2. Worksheet title and subtitle
 a. Alignment — center across columns A through J
 b. Cell style — Title
 c. Font size — title 18; subtitle 16
 d. Background color (range A1:J2) — Green, Accent 1, Lighter 60%
 e. Border — thick box border around range A1:J2
3. Column titles
 a. Cell style — Heading 3
 b. Alignment — center
4. Data
 a. Dates in column J — mm/dd/yy format
 b. Alignment — center data in range B4:B16
 c. Numbers in column C — comma style and two decimal places; if a cell in range C4:C12 is greater than 70, then cell appears with background color of orange and a font color of white
 d. Numbers in top row (D4:G4, I4) — accounting number format
 e. Numbers below top row (D5:G12) — comma style and decimal places

5. Total line
 a. Cell style — Total
 b. Numbers — accounting number format

6. Highest, lowest, and average rows
 a. Font style of row titles in range A14:A16 — bold
 b. Numbers — currency style with floating dollar sign, comma style for Hours Worked

7. Percentages in column H
 a. Numbers — percentage style with two decimal places

8. Column widths
 a. Columns A and B — best fit
 b. Columns E, F, and I — 10.50 characters
 c. Column G — 10.25 characters
 d. Column C, D, and H — 7.50 characters

9. Row heights
 a. Row 3 — 48.00 points
 b. Row 14 — 27.00 points
 c. Remaining rows — default

To Change the Workbook Theme

1 ENTER FORMULAS | 2 ENTER FUNCTIONS | 3 VERIFY FORMULAS
4 FORMAT WORKSHEET | 5 CHECK SPELLING | 6 PRINT WORKSHEET

Why? *The Basis theme includes fonts and colors that provide the worksheet with a professional and subtly colored appearance.* The following steps change the workbook theme to the Basis theme.

1

- Display the PAGE LAYOUT tab.

- Tap or click the Themes button (PAGE LAYOUT tab | Themes group) to display the Themes gallery (Figure 2–28).

🔍 **Experiment**

- Point to several themes in the Themes gallery to see a live preview of the themes.

Q&A Why should I change the theme of a workbook?

A company or department may standardize with

Figure 2–28

a specific theme so that all of their documents have a similar appearance. Similarly, an individual may want to have a theme that sets his or her work apart from the work of others. Other Office programs, such as Word and PowerPoint, include the same themes included with Excel, meaning that all of your Microsoft Office documents can share a common theme.

2

- Tap or click Basis in the Themes gallery to change the workbook theme (Figure 2–29).

Q&A

Why did the cells in the worksheet change?

The cells in the worksheet originally were formatted with the default font for the default Office theme. The default font for the Basis theme is different from that of the default font for the Office theme and, therefore, changed on the worksheet when you changed the theme. If you had modified the font for any of the cells, those cells would not be formatted with the default font for the Basis theme.

Figure 2–29

To Format the Worksheet Titles

The following steps merge and center the worksheet titles, apply the Title cells style to the worksheet titles, and decrease the font of the worksheet subtitle.

1 Display the HOME tab.

2 Select the range to be merged, A1:J1 in this case, and then tap or click the 'Merge & Center' button (HOME tab | Alignment group) to merge and center the text in the selected range.

3 Select the range A2:J2 and then tap or click the 'Merge & Center' button (HOME tab | Alignment group) to merge and center the text in the selected range.

4 Select the range to contain the Title cell style, in this case A1:A2, tap or click the Cell Styles button (HOME tab | Styles group) to display the Cell Styles gallery, and then tap or click the Title cell style in the Cell Styles gallery to apply the Title cell style to the selected range.

5 Select cell A2 and then tap or click the 'Decrease Font Size' button (HOME tab | Font group) to decrease the font size of the selected cell to the next lowest font size (Figure 2–30).

Q&A

What is the effect of tapping or clicking the 'Decrease Font Size' button?

When you tap or click the 'Decrease Font Size' button, Excel assigns the next lowest font size in the Font Size gallery to the selected range. The 'Increase Font Size' button works in a similar manner, but causes Excel to assign the next highest font size in the Font Size gallery to the selected range.

Figure 2–30

Which colors should you select when formatting your worksheet?

Knowing how people perceive colors helps you emphasize parts of your worksheet. Warmer colors (red and orange) tend to reach toward the reader. Cooler colors (blue, green, and violet) tend to pull away from the reader. Bright colors jump out of a dark background and are easiest to see. White or yellow text on a dark blue, green, purple, or black background is ideal.

To Change the Background Color and Apply a Box Border to the Worksheet Title and Subtitle

1 ENTER FORMULAS | 2 ENTER FUNCTIONS | 3 VERIFY FORMULAS
4 FORMAT WORKSHEET | 5 CHECK SPELLING | 6 PRINT WORKSHEET

Why? A background color and border can draw attention to the title of a worksheet. The final formats assigned to the worksheet title and subtitle are the green background color and thick box border (Figure 2–27b on page EX 90). The following steps complete the formatting of the worksheet titles.

1

- Select the range A1:A2 and then tap or click the Fill Color arrow (HOME tab | Font group) to display the Fill Color gallery (Figure 2–31).

🔍 **Experiment**

- Point to a number of colors in the Fill Color gallery to display a live preview of the color in the range A1:A2.

Figure 2–31

2

- Tap or click Green, Accent 1, Lighter 60% (column 5, row 3) in the Fill Color gallery to change the background color of the range of cells (Figure 2–32).

Figure 2–32

3

- Tap or click the Borders arrow (HOME tab | Font group) to display the Borders gallery (Figure 2–33).

Figure 2–33

4

- Tap or click 'Thick Box Border' in the Borders gallery to display a thick box border around the selected range.

- Tap or click anywhere in the worksheet, such as cell A18, to deselect the current range (Figure 2–34).

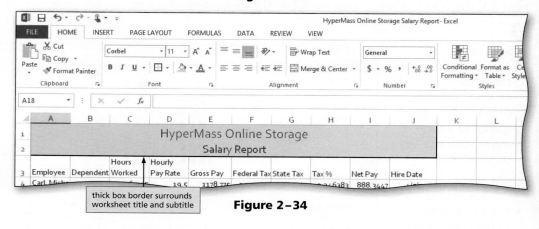

Figure 2–34

Other Ways

1. Tap or click Font Settings Dialog Box Launcher (HOME tab | Font group), tap or click Fill tab (Format Cells dialog box), tap or click desired fill, tap or click OK button

2. Press and hold or right-click range, tap or click Format Cells on shortcut menu, tap or click Fill tab (Format Cells dialog box), tap or click desired fill, tap or click OK button

3. Press CTRL+1, tap or click Fill tab (Format Cells dialog box), tap or click desired fill, tap or click OK button

To Apply a Cell Style to the Column Headings and Format the Total Rows

As shown in Figure 2–27b on page EX 90, the column titles (row 3) should have the Heading 3 cell style and the totals row (row 13) should have the Total cell style. The summary information headings in the range A14:A16 should be bold. The following steps assign these styles and formats to row 3 and row 13 and the range A14:A16.

1 Select the range to be formatted, cells A3:J3 in this case.

2 Use the Cell Styles gallery to apply the Heading 3 cell style to the range A3:J3.

3 Tap or click the Center button (HOME tab | Alignment group) to center the column headings.

4 Apply the Total cell style to the range A13:J13.

5 Bold the range A14:A16 (Figure 2–35).

Figure 2–35

To Format Dates and Center Data in Cells

Why? *With the column titles and total rows formatted, the next step is to format the dates in column J and center the dependents in column B.* The following steps format the dates in the range J4:J12 and center the data in the range B4:B16.

- Select the range to contain the new date format, cells J4:J12 in this case.

- Tap or click the Format Cells: Number Format Dialog Box Launcher (HOME tab | Number group) to display the Format Cells dialog box.

- If necessary, tap or click the Number tab (Format Cells dialog box), tap or click Date in the Category list, and then tap or click 3/14/12 in the Type list to choose the format for the selected range (Figure 2–36).

- Tap or click the OK button (Format Cells dialog box) to format the dates in the current column using the selected date format style.

Figure 2–36

- Select the range B4:B16 and then tap or click the Center button (HOME tab | Alignment group) to center the data in the selected range.

- Select cell E4 to deselect the selected range (Figure 2–37).

Q&A

Can I format an entire column at once?

Yes. Rather than selecting the range B4:B16 in Step 3, you could have tapped or clicked the column B heading immediately above cell B1, and then tapped or clicked the Center button (HOME tab | Alignment group). In this case, all cells in column B down to the last cell in the worksheet would have been formatted to use center alignment. This same procedure could have been used to format the dates in column J.

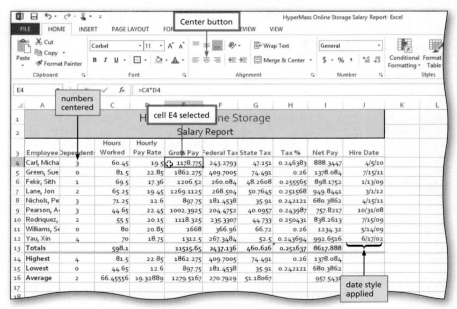

Figure 2–37

Other Ways

1. Press and hold or right-click range, tap or click Format Cells on shortcut menu, tap or click Number tab (Format Cells dialog box), tap or click desired number format, tap or click OK button

2. Press CTRL+1, tap or click Number tab (Format Cells dialog box), tap or click desired number format, tap or click OK button

Formatting Numbers Using the Ribbon

As shown in Figure 2–27b on page EX 90, the worksheet is formatted to resemble an accounting report. For example, in columns D through G and I, the numbers in the first row (row 4), the totals row (row 13), and the rows below the totals (rows 14 through 16) have dollar signs, while the remaining numbers (rows 5 through 12) in columns D through G and column I do not.

To Apply an Accounting Number Format and Comma Style Format Using the Ribbon

1 ENTER FORMULAS | 2 ENTER FUNCTIONS | 3 VERIFY FORMULAS
4 FORMAT WORKSHEET | 5 CHECK SPELLING | 6 PRINT WORKSHEET

The following steps assign formats using the 'Accounting Number Format' button and the Comma Style button. The accounting number format is applied to the currency amounts in rows 4 and 13. The comma style format is applied to the range E5:G12 and to range I5:I12, and to column C (Hours Worked). ***Why?*** *This gives the worksheet a more professional look.*

1

- Select the range to contain the accounting number format, cells D4:G4 in this case.

- While holding down the CTRL key, select cell I4, the range E13:G13, and cell I13 to select the nonadjacent ranges and cells.

- Tap or click the 'Accounting Number Format' button (HOME tab | Number group) to apply the accounting number format with fixed dollar signs to the selected nonadjacent ranges (Figure 2–38).

 What is the effect of applying the accounting number format?
The 'Accounting Number Format' button assigns a fixed dollar sign to the numbers in the ranges. In each cell in these ranges, Excel displays the dollar sign to the far left with spaces between it and the first digit in the cell.

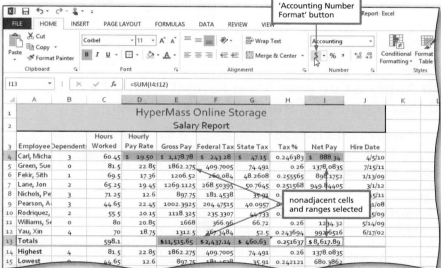

Figure 2–38

2

- Select the ranges to contain the comma style format, cells D5:G12 and I5:I12 in this case.

- Tap or click the Comma Style button (HOME tab | Number group) to assign the comma style format to the selected ranges (Figure 2–39).

Figure 2–39

❸

- Select the range to contain the comma style format, cells C4:C16 in this case.

- Tap or click the Comma Style button (HOME tab | Number group) to assign the comma style format to the selected range (Figure 2–40).

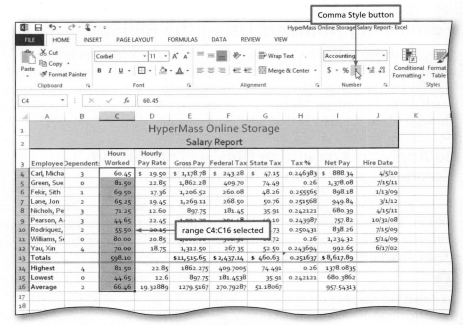

Figure 2–40

To Apply a Currency Style Format with a Floating Dollar Sign Using the Format Cells Dialog Box

1 ENTER FORMULAS | 2 ENTER FUNCTIONS | 3 VERIFY FORMULAS
4 FORMAT WORKSHEET | 5 CHECK SPELLING | 6 PRINT WORKSHEET

Why? The Format Cells dialog box can be used to apply formatting that is not available directly on the ribbon. The following steps use the Format Cells dialog box to apply the currency style format with a floating dollar sign to the numbers in the ranges D14:G16 and I14:I16.

❶

- Select the ranges (D14:G16 and I14:I16) and then tap or click the Number Format Dialog Box Launcher (HOME tab | Number group) to display the Format Cells dialog box.

- If necessary, tap or click the Number tab to display the Number sheet (Format Cells dialog box).

- Tap or click Currency in the Category list to select the necessary number format category and then tap or click the third style ($1,234.10) in the Negative numbers list to select the desired currency format for negative numbers (Figure 2–41).

 How do I select the proper format?
You can choose from 12 categories of formats. Once you select a category, you can select the number

Figure 2–41

of decimal places, whether or not a dollar sign should be displayed, and how negative numbers should appear. Selecting the appropriate negative numbers format is important, because doing so adds a space to the right of the number in order to align the numbers in the worksheet on the decimal points. Some of the available negative number formats do not align the numbers in the worksheet on the decimal points.

2

- Tap or click the OK button (Format Cells dialog box) to assign the currency style format with a floating dollar sign to the selected ranges (Figure 2–42).

Q&A What is the difference between using the accounting number style and currency style?
When using the 'Accounting Number Format' button, recall that a floating dollar sign always appears immediately to the left of the first digit, and the fixed dollar sign always appears on the left side of the cell.

Figure 2–42

Other Ways

1. Press CTRL+1, tap or click Number tab (Format Cells dialog box), tap or click Currency in Category list, select format, tap or click OK button

2. Press CTRL+SHIFT+DOLLAR SIGN ($)

To Apply a Percent Style Format and Use the Increase Decimal Button

1 ENTER FORMULAS | 2 ENTER FUNCTIONS | 3 VERIFY FORMULAS
4 FORMAT WORKSHEET | 5 CHECK SPELLING | 6 PRINT WORKSHEET

The next step is to format the tax percentage in column H. *Why? Currently, Excel displays the numbers as decimal fractions when they should appear as percentages.* The following steps format the range H4:H16 to the percent style format with two decimal places.

1

- Select the range to format, cells H4:H16 in this case.

- Tap or click the Percent Style button (HOME tab | Number group) to display the numbers in the selected range as a rounded whole percent.

Q&A What is the result of tapping or clicking the Percent Style button?
The Percent Style button instructs Excel to display a value as a percentage, determined by multiplying the cell entry by 100, rounding the result to the nearest percent, and adding a percent sign. For example, when cell H4 is formatted using the Percent Style buttons, Excel displays the actual value 0.246383 as 25%.

Figure 2–43

2

- Tap or click the Increase Decimal button (HOME tab | Number group) two times to display the numbers in the selected range with two decimal places (Figure 2–43).

Other Ways

1. Press and hold or right-click selected range, tap or click Format Cells on shortcut menu, tap or click Number tab (Format Cells dialog box), tap or click Percentage in Category list, select format, tap or click OK button

2. Press CTRL+1, tap or click Number tab (Format Cells dialog box), tap or click Percentage in Category list, select format, tap or click OK button

3. Press CTRL+SHIFT+PERCENT SIGN (%)

Conditional Formatting

The next step is to emphasize the values greater than 70 in column C by formatting them to appear with an orange background and white font color (Figure 2–44).

To Apply Conditional Formatting

The following steps assign conditional formatting to the range C4:C12. *Why? After formatting, any cell value greater than 70 will cause Excel to display the number in the cell with an orange background and a white font color.*

- Select the range C4:C12.

- Tap or click the Conditional Formatting button (HOME tab | Styles group) to display the Conditional Formatting menu (Figure 2–44).

Figure 2–44

- Tap or click New Rule on the Conditional Formatting menu to display the New Formatting Rule dialog box.

- Tap or click 'Format only cells that contain' in the Select a Rule Type area (New Formatting Rule dialog box) to change the Edit the Rule Description area.

- In the Edit the Rule Description area, tap or click the arrow in the relational operator box (second box) to display a list of relational operators, and then select greater than to select the desired operator.

Figure 2–45

- Select the rightmost box, and then type 70 to enter the second value of the rule description (Figure 2–45).

Q&A

What do the changes in the Edit the Rule Description area indicate?

The Edit the Rule Description area allows you to view and edit the rules for the conditional format. In this case, reading the area indicates that Excel should conditionally format only those cells with cell values greater than 70.

3

- Tap or click the Format button (New Formatting Rule dialog box) to display the Format Cells dialog box.

- If necessary, tap or click the Font tab (Format Cells dialog box) to display the Font sheet. Tap or click the Color arrow to display the Color gallery and then tap or click White, Background 1 (column 1, row 1) in the Color gallery to select the font color (Figure 2–46).

Figure 2–46

4

- Tap or click the Fill tab (Format Cells dialog box) to display the Fill sheet and then tap or click the orange color in column 6, row 5 to select the background color (Figure 2–47).

Figure 2–47

5

• Tap or click the OK button (Format Cells dialog box) to close the Format Cells dialog box and display the New Formatting Rule dialog box with the desired font and background colors displayed in the Preview box (Figure 2–48).

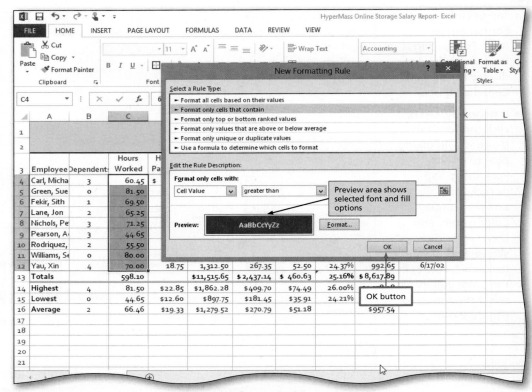

Figure 2–48

6

• Tap or click the OK button (New Formatting Rule dialog box) to assign the conditional format to the selected range.

• Tap or click anywhere in the worksheet, such as cell A18, to deselect the current range (Figure 2–49).

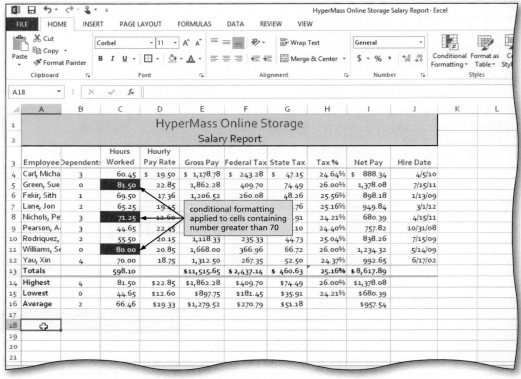

Figure 2–49

Conditional Formatting Operators

As shown in Figure 2–48, the second text box in the Edit the Rule Description area in the New Formatting Rule dialog box allows you to select a relational operator, such as less than, to use in the condition. The eight different relational operators from which you can choose for conditional formatting in the New Formatting Rule dialog box are summarized in Table 2–5.

Table 2–5 Summary of Conditional Formatting Relational Operators	
Relational Operator	**Description**
between	Cell value is between two numbers
not between	Cell value is not between two numbers
equal to	Cell value is equal to a number
not equal to	Cell value is not equal to a number
greater than	Cell value is greater than a number
less than	Cell value is less than a number
greater than or equal to	Cell value is greater than or equal to a number
less than or equal to	Cell value is less than or equal to a number

Changing Column Width and Row Height

When Excel starts and displays a blank worksheet on the screen, all of the columns have a default width of 8.43 characters, or 64 pixels. These values may change depending on the theme applied to the workbook. For example, in this chapter, the Basis theme was applied to the workbook, resulting in columns having a default width of 8.38 characters. A character is defined as a letter, number, symbol, or punctuation mark in 11-point Calibri font, the default font used by Excel. An average of 8.43 characters in 11-point Calibri font will fit in a cell.

Another measure of the height and width of cells is pixels. A **pixel**, which is short for picture element, is a dot on the screen that contains a color. The size of the dot is based on your screen's resolution. At the resolution of 1366 × 768 used in this book, 1366 pixels appear across the screen and 768 pixels appear down the screen for a total of 1,049,088 pixels. It is these 1,049,088 pixels that form the font and other items you see on the screen.

The default row height in a blank worksheet is 15 points (or 20 pixels). Recall from Chapter 1 that a point is equal to 1/72 of an inch. Thus, 15 points is equal to about 1/5 of an inch. You can change the width of the columns or height of the rows at any time to make the worksheet easier to read or to ensure that Excel displays an entry properly in a cell.

To Change Column Width

1 ENTER FORMULAS | 2 ENTER FUNCTIONS | 3 VERIFY FORMULAS
4 FORMAT WORKSHEET | 5 CHECK SPELLING | 6 PRINT WORKSHEET

When changing the column width, you can set the width manually or you can instruct Excel to size the column to best fit. **Best fit** means that the width of the column will be increased or decreased so that the widest entry will fit in the column. *Why? Sometimes, you may prefer more or less white space in a column than best fit provides. To change the white space, Excel allows you to change column widths manually.*

When the format you assign to a cell causes the entry to exceed the width of a column, Excel automatically changes the column width to best fit. If you do not assign a format to a cell or cells in a column, the column width will remain 8.43 characters. To set a column width to best fit, double-tap or double-click the right boundary of the column heading above row 1.

The steps on the following pages change the column widths as follows: column A and B to best fit; column G to 10.25 characters; columns C, D, and H to 7.50 characters; and columns E, F, and I to 10.50 characters.

1

- Drag through column headings A and B above row 1 to select the columns.

- Tap or point to the boundary on the right side of column heading B to cause the pointer to become a split double arrow (Figure 2–50).

Q&A What if I want to make a large change to the column width?
If you want to increase or decrease column width significantly, you can press and hold or right-click a column heading and then use the Column Width command on the shortcut menu to change the column's width. To use this command, however, you must select one or more entire columns.

Figure 2–50

2

- Double-tap or double-click the right boundary of column heading B to change the width of the selected columns to best fit.

- Tap or point to the right boundary of the column G heading above row 1.

- When the pointer changes to a split double arrow, drag until the ScreenTip indicates Width: 10.25 (87 pixels). Do not lift your finger or release the mouse button (Figure 2–51).

Figure 2–51

Q&A What happens if I change the column width to zero (0)?
If you decrease the column width to 0, the column is hidden. **Hiding cells** is a technique you can use to hide data that might not be relevant to a particular report or sensitive data that you do not want others to see. To instruct Excel to display a hidden column, position the mouse pointer to the right of the column heading boundary where the hidden column is located and then drag to the right.

3

- Lift your finger or release the mouse button to change the column width.

- Tap or click the column C heading above row 1 to select the column.

- While holding down the CTRL key, tap or click the column D heading and then the column H heading above row 1 so that nonadjacent columns are selected.

- Tap or point to the boundary on the right side of the column H heading above row 1.

- Drag until the ScreenTip indicates Width: 7.50 (65 pixels). Do not lift your finger or release the mouse button (Figure 2–52).

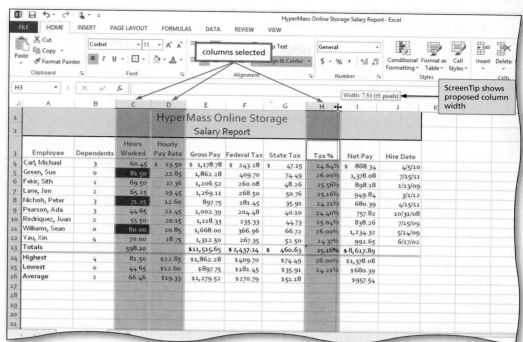

Figure 2–52

4

- Lift your finger or release the mouse button to change the column widths.

- Tap or click the column E heading and drag to select the column F heading.

- While holding down the CTRL key, tap or click the column I heading above row 1 so that nonadjacent columns are selected.

- Drag the right boundary of column F until the ScreenTip indicates Width: 10.50 (89 pixels). Lift your finger or release the mouse button to change the column widths.

- Tap or click anywhere in the worksheet, such as cell A18, to deselect the columns (Figure 2–53).

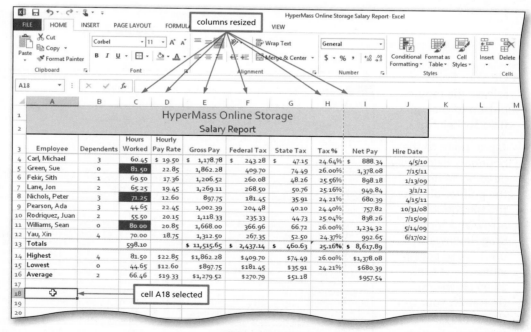

Figure 2–53

Other Ways

1. Press and hold or right-click column heading or drag through multiple column headings, press and hold or right-click selected heading, tap or click Column Width on shortcut menu, enter desired column width, tap or click OK button

To Change Row Height

Why? *You also can increase or decrease the height of a row manually to improve the appearance of the worksheet.* When you increase the font size of a cell entry, such as the title in cell A1, Excel automatically increases the row height to best fit so that it can display the characters properly. Recall that Excel did this earlier when multiple lines were entered in a cell in row 3, and when the cell style of the worksheet title and subtitle was changed. The following steps improve the appearance of the worksheet by increasing the height of row 3 to 48.00 points and increasing the height of row 14 to 27.00 points.

1

• Tap or point to the boundary below row heading 3 until the pointer displays the split double arrow.

• Drag down until the ScreenTip indicates Height: 48.00 (64 pixels). Do not apply the change yet (Figure 2–54).

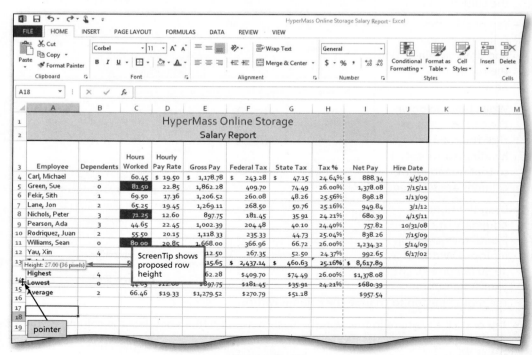

Figure 2–54

2

• Lift your finger or release the mouse button to change the row height.

• Tap or point to the boundary below row heading 14 until the pointer displays the split double arrow and then drag downward until the ScreenTip indicates Height: 27.00 (36 pixels). Do not lift your finger or release the mouse button (Figure 2–55).

Figure 2–55

3

- Lift your finger or release the mouse button to change the row height.

- Tap or click anywhere in the worksheet, such as cell A18, to deselect the current cell (Figure 2–56).

Q&A Can I hide a row?
Yes. As with column widths, when you decrease the row height to 0, the row is hidden. To instruct Excel to display a hidden row, position the pointer just below the row heading boundary where the row is hidden and then drag downward. To set a row height to best fit, double-tap or double-click the bottom boundary of the row heading.

Figure 2–56

Other Ways

1. Press and hold or right-click row heading or drag through multiple row headings, press and hold or right-click selected heading, tap or click Row Height on shortcut menu, enter desired row height, tap or click OK button

Break Point: If you wish to take a break, this is a good place to do so. Be sure to save the HyperMass Online Storage Salary Report file again and then you can exit Excel. To resume at a later time, run Excel, open the file called HyperMass Online Storage Salary Report, and continue following the steps from this location forward.

Checking Spelling

Excel includes a **spell checker** you can use to check a worksheet for spelling errors. The spell checker looks for spelling errors by comparing words on the worksheet against words contained in its standard dictionary. If you often use specialized terms that are not in the standard dictionary, you may want to add them to a custom dictionary using the Spelling dialog box.

When the spell checker finds a word that is not in either dictionary, it displays the word in the Spelling dialog box. You then can correct it if it is misspelled.

Does the spell checker catch all spelling mistakes?

While Excel's spell checker is a valuable tool, it is not infallible. You should proofread your workbook carefully by pointing to each word and saying it aloud as you point to it. Be mindful of misused words such as its and it's, through and though, and to and too. Nothing undermines a good impression more than a professional looking report with misspelled words.

CONSIDER THIS

To Check Spelling on the Worksheet

Why? *Everything on a worksheet should be spell checked to make sure it is as accurate as possible.* To illustrate how Excel responds to a misspelled word, the following steps purposely misspell the word, Employee, in cell A3 as the word, Empolyee, as shown in Figure 2–57.

• Tap or click cell A3 and then type `Empolyee` to misspell the word, Employee.

• Select cell A2 so that the spell checker begins checking at the selected cell.

• Tap or click REVIEW on the ribbon to display the REVIEW tab.

• Tap or click the Spelling button (REVIEW tab | Proofing group) to run the spell checker and display the misspelled word in the Spelling dialog box (Figure 2–57).

Q&A What happens when the spell checker finds a misspelled word?
When the spell checker identifies that a cell contains a word not in its standard or custom dictionary, it selects that cell as the active cell and displays the Spelling dialog box. The Spelling dialog box lists the word not found in the dictionary and a list of suggested corrections (Figure 2–58).

Figure 2–57

②

• Tap or click the Change button (Spelling dialog box) to change the misspelled word to the correct word (Figure 2–58).

• Tap or click the Close button to close the Spelling dialog box.

• If a Microsoft Excel dialog box is displayed, tap or click the OK button.

③

• Tap or click anywhere in the worksheet, such as cell A18, to deselect the current cell.

• Display the HOME tab.

• Tap or click the Save button on the Quick Access Toolbar to save the workbook.

Q&A What other actions can I take in the Spelling dialog box?
If one of the words in the Suggestions list is correct, tap or click it and then tap or click the Change button. If none of the suggestions is correct, type the correct word in the Not in Dictionary text box and then tap or click the Change button. To change the word throughout the worksheet, tap or click the Change All button instead of the Change button. To skip correcting the word, tap or click the Ignore Once button. To have Excel ignore the word for the remainder of the worksheet, tap or click the Ignore All button.

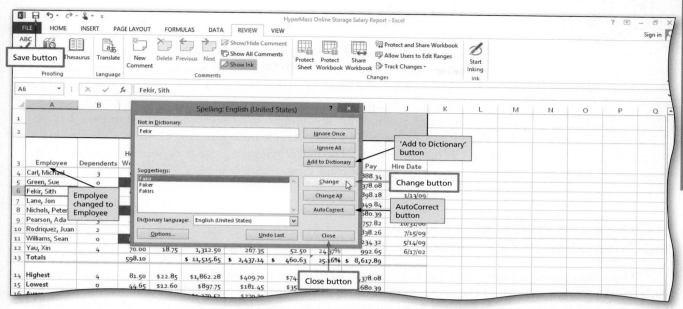

Figure 2–58

Other Ways

1. Press F7

Additional Spell Checker Considerations

Consider these additional guidelines when using the spell checker:

- To check the spelling of the text in a single cell, double-tap or double-click the cell to make the formula bar active and then tap or click the Spelling button (REVIEW tab | Proofing group).

- If you select a single cell so that the formula bar is not active and then start the spell checker, Excel checks the remainder of the worksheet, including notes and embedded charts.

- If you select a cell other than cell A1 before you start the spell checker, Excel will display a dialog box when the spell checker reaches the end of the worksheet, asking if you want to continue checking at the beginning.

- If you select a range of cells before starting the spell checker, Excel checks the spelling of the words only in the selected range.

- To check the spelling of all the sheets in a workbook, press and hold or right-click any sheet tab, tap or click 'Select All Sheets' on the sheet tab shortcut menu, and then start the spell checker.

- To add words to the dictionary, such as your last name, tap or click the 'Add to Dictionary' button in the Spelling dialog box (shown in Figure 2–58) when Excel flags the word as not being in the dictionary.

- Tap or click the AutoCorrect button (shown in Figure 2–58) to add the misspelled word and the correct version of the word to the AutoCorrect list. For example, suppose that you misspell the word, do, as the word, dox. When the spell checker displays the Spelling dialog box with the correct word, do, in the Suggestions list, tap or click the AutoCorrect button. Then, anytime in the future that you type the word, dox, Excel automatically will change it to the word, do.

Printing the Worksheet

Excel allows for a great deal of customization in how a worksheet appears when printed. For example, the margins on the page can be adjusted. A header or footer can be added to each printed page, as well. A **header** is text and graphics that print at the top of each page. Similarly, a **footer** is text and graphics that print at the bottom of each page. Excel also has the capability to work on the worksheet in Page Layout view. **Page Layout view** allows you to create or modify a worksheet while viewing how it will look in printed format. The default view that you have worked in up until this point in the book is called **Normal view**.

To Change the Worksheet's Margins, Header, and Orientation in Page Layout View

1 ENTER FORMULAS | 2 ENTER FUNCTIONS | 3 VERIFY FORMULAS
4 FORMAT WORKSHEET | 5 CHECK SPELLING | **6 PRINT WORKSHEET**

The following steps change to Page Layout view, narrow the margins of the worksheet, change the header of the worksheet, and set the orientation of the worksheet to landscape. *Why? Often, you may want to reduce margins so that the printed worksheet better fits the page. Changing the header helps to identify the content on each page, and changing the orientation can help you fit wider printouts across a sheet of paper.* **Margins** are those portions of a printed page outside the main body of the printed document and always are blank when printed. The current worksheet is too wide for a single page and requires landscape orientation to fit on one page in a readable manner.

1

- Tap or click the Page Layout button on the status bar to view the worksheet in Page Layout view (Figure 2–59).

 What are some key features of Page Layout view?
Page Layout view shows the worksheet divided into pages. A gray background separates each page. The white areas surrounding each page indicate the print margins. The top of each page includes a Header area, and the bottom of each page includes a Footer area. Page Layout view also includes a ruler at the top of the page that assists you in placing objects on the page, such as charts and pictures.

Figure 2–59

2

- Display the PAGE LAYOUT tab.

- Tap or click the Adjust Margins button (PAGE LAYOUT tab | Page Setup group) to display the Margins gallery (Figure 2–60).

Figure 2–60

3

- Tap or click Narrow in the Margins gallery to change the worksheet margins to the Narrow margin style.

- Select cell A6 to deselect the header. Tap or click above the worksheet title in cell A1 in the center area of the Header area.

- Type **John Simon** and then press the ENTER key. Type **Chief Financial Officer** to complete the worksheet header (Figure 2–61).

If requested by your instructor, type your name instead of John Simon.

- Select cell A6 to deselect the header.

Figure 2–61

 What else can I place in a header?

You can add text, page number information, date and time information, the file path of the workbook, the file name of the workbook, the sheet name of the workbook, and pictures to a header.

4

- Display the PAGE LAYOUT tab.

- Tap or click the 'Change Page Orientation' button (PAGE LAYOUT tab | Page Setup group) to display the Change Page Orientation gallery (Figure 2–62).

Figure 2–62

5

- Tap or click Landscape in the Change Page Orientation gallery to change the worksheet's orientation to landscape (Figure 2–63).

Do I need to change the orientation every time I want to print the worksheet? No. Once you change the orientation and save the workbook, Excel will save the orientation setting for that workbook until you change it. When you open a new workbook, Excel sets the orientation to portrait.

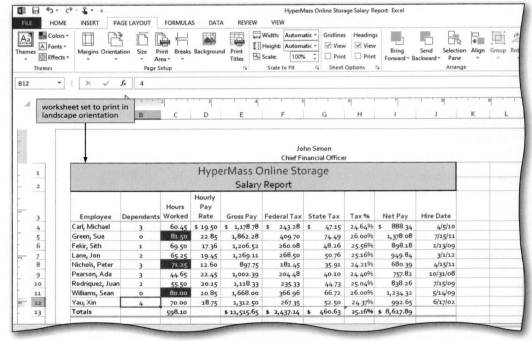

Figure 2–63

Why does the header not appear centered over the worksheet?
The header is centered between the left and right margins of the page. The worksheet contents do not extend across the page from margin to margin, which makes the header appear off center.

Other Ways

1. Tap or click Page Setup Dialog Box Launcher (PAGE LAYOUT tab | Page Setup group), tap or click Page tab (Page Setup dialog box), tap or click Portrait or Landscape, tap or click OK button

To Print a Worksheet

Excel provides other options for printing a worksheet. In the following sections, you first print the worksheet and then print a section of the worksheet. The following steps print the worksheet.

1 Tap or click FILE on the ribbon to open the Backstage view.

2 Tap or click the Print tab in the Backstage view to display the Print gallery.

3 If necessary, tap or click the Printer Status button in the Print gallery to display a list of available Printer options and then tap or click the desired printer to change the currently selected printer.

4 Tap or click the Print button in the Print gallery to print the worksheet in landscape orientation on the currently selected printer.

5 When the printer stops, retrieve the hard copy (Figure 2–64).

John Simon
Chief Financial Officer

HyperMass Online Storage
Salary Report

Employee	Dependents	Hours Worked	Hourly Pay Rate	Gross Pay	Federal Tax	State Tax	Tax %	Net Pay	Hire Date
Carl, Michael	3	60.45	$ 19.50	$ 1,178.78	$ 243.28	$ 47.15	24.64%	$ 888.34	4/5/10
Green, Sue	0	81.50	22.85	1,862.28	409.70	74.49	26.00%	1,378.08	7/15/11
Fekir, Sith	1	69.50	17.36	1,206.52	260.08	48.26	25.56%	898.18	1/13/09
Lane, Jon	2	65.25	19.45	1,269.11	268.50	50.76	25.16%	949.84	3/1/12
Nichols, Peter	3	71.25	12.60	897.75	181.45	35.91	24.21%	680.39	4/15/11
Pearson, Ada	3	44.65	22.45	1,002.39	204.48	40.10	24.40%	757.82	10/31/08
Rodriquez, Juan	2	55.50	20.15	1,118.33	235.33	44.73	25.04%	838.26	7/15/09
Williams, Sean	0	80.00	20.85	1,668.00	366.96	66.72	26.00%	1,234.32	5/14/09
Yau, Xin	4	70.00	18.75	1,312.50	267.35	52.50	24.37%	992.65	6/17/02
Totals		**598.10**		**$ 11,515.65**	**$ 2,437.14**	**$ 460.63**	**25.16%**	**$ 8,617.89**	
Highest	4	81.50	$22.85	$1,862.28	$409.70	$74.49	26.00%	$1,378.08	
Lowest	0	44.65	$12.60	$897.75	$181.45	$35.91	24.21%	$680.39	
Average	2	66.46	$19.33	$1,279.52	$270.79	$51.18		$957.54	

Figure 2–64

To Print a Section of the Worksheet

You can print portions of the worksheet by selecting the range of cells to print and then tapping or clicking the Selection option button in the Print what area in the Print dialog box. *Why? To save paper, you only want to print the portion of the worksheet you need, instead of printing the entire worksheet.* The following steps print the range A3:E16.

1

- Select the range to print, cells A3:E16 in this case.

- Tap or click FILE on the ribbon to open the Backstage view.

- Tap or click the Print tab to display the Print gallery.

- Tap or click 'Print Active Sheets' in the Settings area (Print tab | Print gallery) to display a list of options that determine what Excel should print (Figure 2–65).

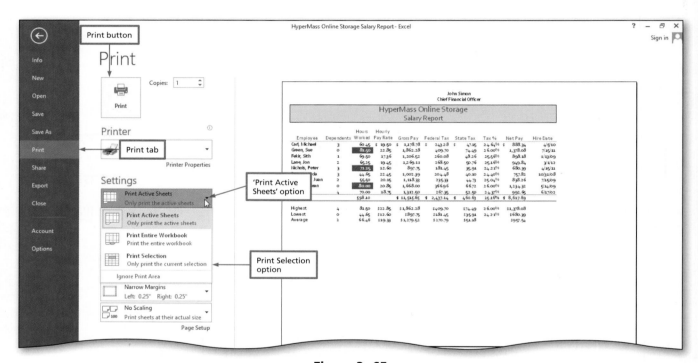

Figure 2–65

2

- Tap or click Print Selection to instruct Excel to print only the selected range.

- Tap or click the Print button in the Print gallery to print the selected range of the worksheet on the currently selected printer (Figure 2–66).

- Tap or click the Normal button on the status bar to return to Normal view.

- Tap or click cell A18 to deselect the range A3:E16.

Q&A What are my options for telling Excel what to print?

Excel includes three options to allow you to determine what should be printed (Figure 2–65). As shown in the previous steps, the Print Selection option instructs Excel to print the selected range. The 'Print Active Sheets' option instructs Excel to print the active worksheet (the worksheet currently on the screen) or the selected worksheets. Finally, the 'Print Entire Workbook' option instructs Excel to print all of the worksheets in the workbook.

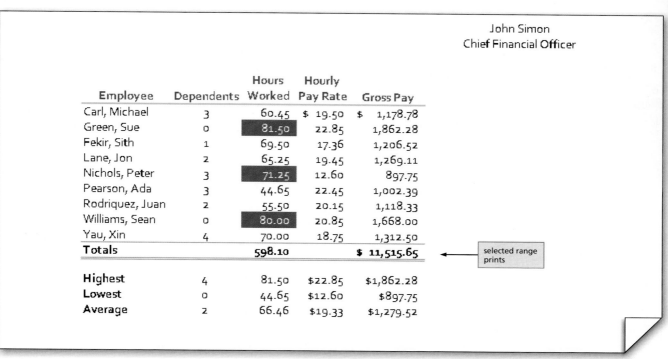

John Simon
Chief Financial Officer

Employee	Dependents	Hours Worked	Hourly Pay Rate	Gross Pay
Carl, Michael	3	60.45	$ 19.50	$ 1,178.78
Green, Sue	0	81.50	22.85	1,862.28
Fekir, Sith	1	69.50	17.36	1,206.52
Lane, Jon	2	65.25	19.45	1,269.11
Nichols, Peter	3	71.25	12.60	897.75
Pearson, Ada	3	44.65	22.45	1,002.39
Rodriquez, Juan	2	55.50	20.15	1,118.33
Williams, Sean	0	80.00	20.85	1,668.00
Yau, Xin	4	70.00	18.75	1,312.50
Totals		598.10		$ 11,515.65
Highest	4	81.50	$22.85	$1,862.28
Lowest	0	44.65	$12.60	$897.75
Average	2	66.46	$19.33	$1,279.52

selected range prints

Figure 2–66

Other Ways

1. Select range, tap or click Print Area button (PAGE LAYOUT tab | Page Setup group), tap or click 'Set Print Area', tap or click FILE tab to open Backstage view, tap or click Print tab, tap or click Print button

Displaying and Printing the Formulas Version of the Worksheet

Thus far, you have been working with the **values version** of the worksheet, which shows the results of the formulas you have entered, rather than the actual formulas. Excel also can display and print the **formulas version** of the worksheet, which shows the actual formulas you have entered, rather than the resulting values.

The formulas version is useful for debugging a worksheet. **Debugging** is the process of finding and correcting errors in the worksheet. Viewing and printing the formulas version instead of the values version makes it easier to see any mistakes in the formulas.

When you change from the values version to the formulas version, Excel increases the width of the columns so that the formulas and text do not overflow into adjacent cells on the right. The formulas version of the worksheet, thus, usually is significantly wider than the values version. To fit the wide printout on one page, you can use landscape orientation, which already has been selected for the workbook, and the Fit to option in the Page sheet in the Page Setup dialog box.

To Display the Formulas in the Worksheet and Fit the Printout on One Page

1 ENTER FORMULAS | 2 ENTER FUNCTIONS | 3 VERIFY FORMULAS
4 FORMAT WORKSHEET | 5 CHECK SPELLING | 6 PRINT WORKSHEET

The following steps change the view of the worksheet from the values version to the formulas version of the worksheet and then print the formulas version on one page. *Why? Printing the formulas in the worksheet can help you verify your formulas are correct and the worksheet is making the correct calculations.*

- Press CTRL+ACCENT MARK (`) to display the worksheet with formulas.
- Tap or click the right horizontal scroll arrow until column J appears (Figure 2–67).

Figure 2–67

- Tap or click the Page Setup Dialog Box Launcher (PAGE LAYOUT tab | Page Setup group) to display the Page Setup dialog box (Figure 2–68).

- If necessary, tap or click Landscape in the Orientation area in the Page sheet to select it.

- If necessary, tap or click Fit to in the Scaling area to select it.

Figure 2–68

- Tap or click the Print button (Page Setup dialog box) to print the formulas in the worksheet on one page in landscape orientation (Figure 2–69). If necessary, in the Backstage view, select the Print Active Sheets option in the Settings area of the Print gallery.

- When Excel opens the Backstage view, tap or click the Print button to print the worksheet.

				John Simon					
				Chief Financial Officer					
				HyperMass Online Storage					
				Salary Report					

Employee	Dependents	Hours Worked	Hourly Pay Rate	Gross Pay	Federal Tax	State Tax	Tax%	Net Pay	Hire Date
Carl, Michael	3	60.45	19.5	=C4*D4	=0.22*IE4-B4*24.32I	=0.04*E4	=IF4+G4I/E4	=E4-IF4+G4I	40273
Green, Sue	0	81.5	22.85	=C5*D5	=0.22*IE5-B5*24.32I	=0.04*E5	=IF5+G5I/E5	=E5-IF5+G5I	40739
Fekir, Sith	1	69.5	17.36	=C6*D6	=0.22*IE6-B6*24.32I	=0.04*E6	=IF6+G6I/E6	=E6-IF6+G6I	39826
Lane, Jon	2	65.25	19.45	=C7*D7	=0.22*IE7-B7*24.32I	=0.04*E7	=IF7+G7I/E7	=E7-IF7+G7I	40969
Nichols, Peter	3	71.25	12.6	=C8*D8	=0.22*IE8-B8*24.32I	=0.04*E8	=IF8+G8I/E8	=E8-IF8+G8I	40648
Pearson, Ada	3	44.65	22.45	=C9*D9	=0.22*IE9-B9*24.32I	=0.04*E9	=IF9+G9I/E9	=E9-IF9+G9I	39752
Rodriguez, Juan	2	55.5	20.15	=C10*D10	=0.22*IE10-B10*24.32I	=0.04*E10	=IF10+G10I/E10	=E10-IF10+G10I	40009
Williams, Sean	0	80	20.85	=C11*D11	=0.22*IE11-B11*24.32I	=0.04*E11	=IF11+G11I/E11	=E11-IF11+G11I	39947
Yau, Xin	4	70	18.75	=C12*D12	=0.22*IE12-B12*24.32I	=0.04*E12	=IF12+G12I/E12	=E12-IF12+G12I	37424
Totals		=SUM(C4:C12)		=SUM(E4:E12)	=SUM(F4:F12)	=SUM(G4:G12)	=IF13+G13I/E13	=SUM(I4:I12)	
Highest	=MAX(B4:B12)	=MAX(C4:C12)	=MAX(D4:D12)	=MAX(E4:E12)	=MAX(F4:F12)	=MAX(G4:G12)	=MAX(H4:H12)	=MAX(I4:I12)	
Lowest	=MIN(B4:B12)	=MIN(C4:C12)	=MIN(D4:D12)	=MIN(E4:E12)	=MIN(F4:F12)	=MIN(G4:G12)	=MIN(H4:H12)	=MIN(I4:I12)	
Average	=AVERAGE(B4:B12)	=AVERAGE(C4:C12	=AVERAGE(D4:D1	=AVERAGE(E4:E12)	=AVERAGE(F4:F12)	=AVERAGE(G4:G12)		=AVERAGE(I4:I12)	

formulas printed on one page

Figure 2–69

4

- After viewing and printing the formulas version, press CTRL+ACCENT MARK (`) to instruct Excel to display the values version.

- Tap or click the left horizontal scroll arrow until column A appears.

To Change the Print Scaling Option Back to 100%

Depending on your printer, you may have to change the Print Scaling option back to 100% after using the Fit to option. Doing so will cause the worksheet to print at the default print scaling of 100%. The following steps reset the Print Scaling option so that future worksheets print at 100%, instead of being resized to print on one page.

1 If necessary, display the PAGE LAYOUT tab and then tap or click the Page Setup Dialog Box Launcher (PAGE LAYOUT tab | Page Setup group) to display the Page Setup dialog box.

2 Tap or click Adjust to in the Scaling area to select the Adjust to setting.

3 If necessary, type 100 in the Adjust to box to adjust the print scaling to a new percentage.

4 Tap or click the OK button (Page Setup dialog box) to set the print scaling to normal.

5 Display the HOME tab.

Q&A What is the purpose of the Adjust to box in the Page Setup dialog box?
The Adjust to box allows you to specify the percentage of reduction or enlargement in the printout of a worksheet. The default percentage is 100%. When you tap or click the Fit to option, this percentage automatically changes to the percentage required to fit the printout on one page.

To Sign Out of a Microsoft Account

If you are signed in to a Microsoft account and are using a public computer or otherwise wish to sign out of your Microsoft account, you should sign out of the account from the Account gallery in the Backstage view before exiting Excel. Signing out of the account is the safest way to make sure that nobody else can access SkyDrive files or settings stored in your Microsoft account. The following steps sign out of a Microsoft account from Excel. For a detailed example of the procedure summarized below, refer to the Office and Windows chapter at the beginning of this book.

1 If you wish to sign out of your Microsoft account, tap or click FILE on the ribbon to open the Backstage view and then tap or click the Account tab to display the Account gallery.

2 Tap or click the Sign out link, which displays the Remove Account dialog box. If a Can't remove Windows accounts dialog box appears instead of the Remove Account dialog box, click the OK button and skip the remaining steps.

Q&A Why does a Can't remove Windows accounts dialog box appear?
If you signed in to Windows using your Microsoft account, then you also must sign out from Windows, rather than signing out from within Excel. When you are finished using Windows, be sure to sign out at that time.

3 Tap or click the Yes button (Remove Account dialog box) to sign out of your Microsoft account on this computer.

Q&A Should I sign out of Windows after signing out of my Microsoft account?
When you are finished using the computer, you should sign out of your account for maximum security.

4 Tap or click the Back button in the upper-left corner of the Backstage view to return to the worksheet.

To Save the Workbook and Exit Excel

With the workbook complete, the following steps save the workbook and exit Excel.

1 Tap or click the Save button on the Quick Access Toolbar.

2 Tap or click the Close button on the upper-right corner of the title bar.

3 Sign out of your account and shut down the computer as directed by your instructor.

Chapter Summary

In this chapter you have learned how to enter formulas, calculate an average, find the highest and lowest numbers in a range, verify formulas using Range Finder, add borders, align text, format numbers, change column widths and row heights, and add conditional formatting to a range of numbers. In addition, you learned to spell check a worksheet, print a section of a worksheet, and display and print the formulas version of the worksheet using the Fit to option. The items listed below include all the new Excel skills you have learned in this chapter, with the tasks grouped by activity.

Enter Formulas
Enter a Formula Using the Keyboard (EX 73)
Enter Formulas Using Point Mode (EX 76)

Enter Functions
Determine the Highest Number in a Range of Numbers Using the Insert Function Box (EX 82)
Determine the Lowest Number in a Range of Numbers Using the Sum Menu (EX 84)
Determine the Average of a Range of Numbers Using the Keyboard (EX 86)

Verify Formulas
Verify a Formula Using Range Finder (EX 89)

Format a Worksheet
Change the Workbook Theme (EX 91)
Change the Background Color and Apply a Box Border to the Worksheet Title and Subtitle (EX 93)
Format Dates and Center Data in Cells (EX 96)

Apply an Accounting Number Format and Comma Style Format Using the Ribbon (EX 97)
Apply a Currency Style Format with a Floating Dollar Sign Using the Format Cells Dialog Box (EX 98)
Apply a Percent Style Format and Use the Increase Decimal Button (EX 99)
Apply Conditional Formatting (EX 100)
Change Column Width (EX 103)
Change Row Height (EX 106)

Spell Check a Worksheet
Check Spelling on the Worksheet (EX 108)

Print a Worksheet
Change the Worksheet's Margins, Header, and Orientation in Page Layout View (EX 110)
Print a Section of the Worksheet (EX 114)
Display the Formulas in the Worksheet and Fit the Printout on One Page (EX 116)

What decisions will you need to make when creating workbooks in the future?

1. Determine the workbook structure.

 a) Determine the formulas and functions you will need for your workbook.

 b) Sketch a layout of your data and functions.

2. Create the worksheet.

 á) Enter the titles, subtitles, and headings.

 b) Enter the data, desired functions, and formulas.

3. Format the worksheet.

 a) Determine the theme for the worksheet.

 b) Format the titles, subtitles, and headings using styles.

 c) Format the totals, minimums, maximums, and averages.

 d) Format the numbers and text.

 e) Resize columns and rows.

Apply Your Knowledge

Reinforce the skills and apply the concepts you learned in this chapter.

Cost Analysis Worksheet

Note: To complete this assignment, you will be required to use the Data Files for Students. Visit www.cengage.com/ct/studentdownload for detailed instructions or contact your instructor for information about accessing the required files.

Instructions: The purpose of this exercise is to open a partially completed workbook, enter formulas and functions, copy the formulas and functions, and then format the worksheet titles and numbers. As shown in Figure 2–70, the completed worksheet analyzes the costs associated with a taxi company's fleet of vehicles.

Figure 2–70

Continued >

Apply Your Knowledge *continued*

1. Run Excel. Open the workbook Apply 2–1 Briteeny Taxi.

2. Use the following formulas in cells E4, F4, and G4:

 Mileage Cost (cell E4) = Cost per Mile * Miles Driven or = B4 * C4

 Total Cost (cell F4) = Maintenance Cost + Mileage Cost or = D4 + E4

 Total Cost per Mile (cell G4) = Total Cost / Miles Driven or = F4 / C4

 Use the fill handle to copy the three formulas in the range E4:G4 to the range E5:G12.

3. Determine totals for the miles driven, maintenance cost, mileage cost, and total cost in row 13. Copy the formula in cell G12 to G13 to assign the formula in cell G12 to G13 in the total line. If necessary, reapply the Total cell style to cell G13.

4. In the range D14:D16, determine the average value, highest value, and lowest value, respectively, for the values in the range D4:D12. Use the fill handle to copy the three functions to the range E14:G16.

5. Format the worksheet as follows:

 a. Change the workbook theme to Organic by using the Themes button (PAGE LAYOUT tab | Themes group)

 b. Cell A1 — change to Title cell style

 c. Cell A2 — change to a font size of 16

 d. Cells A1:A2 — Teal, Accent 2, Lighter 80% fill color and a thick box border

 e. Cells B4, D4:G4, and D13:G13 — accounting number format with two decimal places and fixed dollar signs by using the 'Accounting Number Format' button (HOME tab | Number group)

 f. Cells B5:B12, and D5:G12 — comma style format with two decimal places by using the Comma Style button (HOME tab | Number group)

 g. Cells C4:C13 — comma style format with no decimal places

 h. Cells G4:G12 — apply conditional formatting so that cells with a value greater than 1 appear with a gold background color

6. Switch to Page Layout view. Enter your name, course, laboratory assignment number, and any other information, as specified by your instructor, in the Header area. Preview and print the worksheet in landscape orientation. Change the document properties, as specified by your instructor. Save the workbook using the file name, Apply 2-1 Briteeny Taxi Complete.

7. Use Range Finder to verify the formula in cell G13.

8. Print the range A3:D16. Press CTRL+ACCENT MARK (`) to change the display from the values version of the worksheet to the formulas version. Print the formulas version in landscape orientation on one page by using the Fit to option in the Page sheet in the Page Setup dialog box. Press CTRL+ACCENT MARK (`) to change the display of the worksheet back to the values version. Close the workbook without saving it.

9. ✳ Besides adding a header to your document, can you think of anything else that could be added when printing the worksheet?

10. Submit the workbook and results as specified by your instructor.

Extend Your Knowledge

Extend the skills you learned in this chapter and experiment with new skills. You may need to use Help to complete the assignment.

Applying Conditional Formatting to Cells

Note: To complete this assignment, you will be required to use the Data Files for Students. Visit www.cengage.com/ct/studentdownload for detailed instructions or contact your instructor for information about accessing the required files.

Instructions: Run Excel. Open the workbook Extend 2–1 Fentine Blogworld. Perform the following tasks to apply four types of conditional formatting to cells in a worksheet:

1. Select the range C4:C16. Tap or click the Conditional Formatting button (HOME tab | Styles group) and then tap or click New Rule on the Conditional Formatting menu. Select 'Format only top or bottom ranked values' in the Select a Rule Type area (New Formatting Rules dialog box), as shown in Figure 2–71. Enter any value between 10 and 30 in the text box in the Edit the Rule Description (New Formatting Rule dialog box) area, and then tap or click the '% of the selected range' check box to select it. Tap or click the Format button, and choose a purple background in the Fill sheet to assign this conditional format. Tap or click the OK button in each dialog box and view the worksheet.

2. With range C4:C16 selected, apply a conditional format to the range that uses an orange background color to highlight cells with scores that are below average.

3. With range D4:D16 selected, apply a conditional format to the range that uses a green background to highlight cells that contain a value between 200 to 400.

4. With range E4:E16 selected, apply a conditional format to the range that uses a red background color to highlight cells that contain Art or Food. (*Hint:* You need to apply two separate formats, one for Art and one for Food.)

5. ✺ When might you want to look for values above the average in a worksheet?

6. Change the document properties as specified by your instructor. Save the workbook using the file name, Extend 2-1 Fentine Blogworld Complete. Submit the revised workbook as specified by your instructor.

Figure 2–71

Analyze, Correct, Improve

Analyze a workbook and correct all errors and/or improve the design.

Correcting Formatting, Functions, and Formulas in a Worksheet

Note: To complete this assignment, you will be required to use the Data Files for Students. Visit www.cengage.com/ct/studentdownload for detailed instructions or contact your instructor for information about accessing the required files.

Instructions: Run Excel. Open the workbook ACI 2–1 Janeese Crystals. In this exercise, you will learn how to correct formatting, functions, and formula problems in a worksheet. The completed worksheet is shown in Figure 2–72.

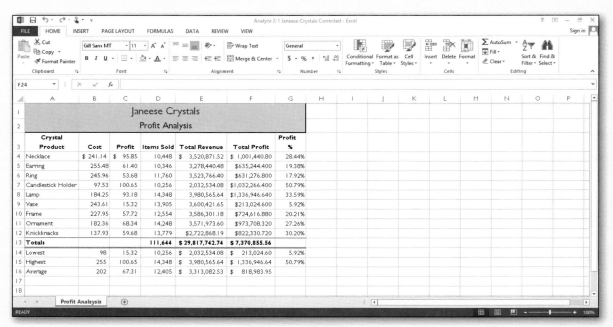

Figure 2–72

Perform the following tasks:

1. Correct

a. Spell check the worksheet and correct any spelling mistakes that are found, but ignore any spelling mistakes found in the worksheet title.

b. The averages in several columns do not include the product in row 4. Adjust the functions in these cells so that all products are included in the calculation.

c. The total profit calculations should be Total Profit = Items Sold * Profit. Adjust the formulas in the range F4:F12 so that the correct formula is used.

d. The values for the total row were entered without using a function. Replace the values with the appropriate function.

e. The currency values in rows 4 and 14 through 16 should be formatted with the 'Accounting Number Format' button (HOME tab | Number group). They are currently formatted with the Currency format (floating dollar sign). The accounting number format displays a fixed dollar sign.

f. Delete the function in the cell containing the average of % Profit.

2. Improve

a. Add a thick box border around the title and subtitle so that they appear more separated from the rest of the worksheet.

b. Adjust the column widths of columns A, D, and F to best fit.

c. Center the column headings in row 3.

d. Format the values in C5:C12 and C14:C16 using the comma format.

e. Change the document properties as specified by your instructor. Save the workbook using the file name, ACI 2–1 Janeese Crystals Corrected. Submit the revised workbook as specified by your instructor.

3. ✷ What else could you do to improve the worksheet?

In the Labs

Design and/or create a workbook using the guidelines, concepts, and skills presented in this chapter. Labs 1 and 2, which increase in difficulty, require you to create solutions based on what you learned in the chapter; Lab 3 requires you to create a solution, which uses cloud and web technologies, by learning and investigating on your own from general guidance.

Lab 1: Loan Balance Worksheet

Problem: You are a part-time assistant in the accounting department at HelpToday Personal Loans, a Cincinnati-based personal loan company supplying small loans to individuals. You have been asked to use Excel to generate a report that summarizes the existing loan balances (Figure 2–73). The customer data in Table 2–6 is available for test purposes.

Instructions: Create a worksheet similar to the one shown in Figure 2–73. Include the three columns of customer data in Table 2–6 in the report, plus two additional columns to compute a monthly fee and a current balance for each customer. Assume no negative unpaid monthly balances.

Table 2–6 HelpToday Personal Loans Data

Customer	Previous Balance	Payments
Tolliver, Ralph	1,600.72	72.15
Jennings, Howard	1,518.62	382.30
Rivera, Juan	679.29	80.69
Lance, Brad	1,060.42	107.60
Yin, Yu	1,178.83	125.63
Lang, Rose	1,280.20	79.85
Tulley, Sullivan	1,253.88	389.79
Jiminez, Jose	477.11	278.52
Adams, Bettina	821.31	153.14

Figure 2–73

Continued >

In the Labs *continued*

Perform the following tasks:

1. Enter and format the worksheet title `HelpToday Personal Loans` and worksheet subtitle `Monthly Loan Balance Analysis` in cells A1 and A2. Change the theme of the worksheet to the Metropolitan theme. Apply the Title cell style to cells A1 and A2. Change the font size in cell A1 to 28 points. Merge and center the worksheet title and subtitle across columns A through E. Change the background color of cells A1 and A2 to the Orange standard color. Change the font color of cells A1 and A2 to the White theme color. Draw a thick box border around the range A1:A2.

2. Change the width of column A to 19.00 points. Change the widths of columns B through E to 15.00 points. Change the heights of row 3 to 36.00 points and row 14 to 25.50 points.

3. Enter the column titles in row 3 and row titles in the range A13:A16, as shown in Figure 2–73. Center the column titles in the range A3:E3. Apply the Heading 3 cell style to the range A3:E3. Apply the Total cell style to the range A13:E13. Bold the titles in the range A13:A16. Change the font size in the range A3:E16 to 12 points.

4. Enter the data in Table 2–6 in the range A4:C12.

5. Use the following formulas to determine the monthly fee in column D and the current balance in column E for the first customer. Copy the two formulas down through the remaining customers.
 a. Monthly Fee (cell D4) = 5% * Previous Balance
 b. Current Balance (E4) = Previous Balance – Payments + Monthly Fee

6. Determine the totals in row 13.

7. Determine the average, minimum, and maximum values in cells B14:B16 for the range B4:B12, and then copy the range B14:B16 to C14:E16.

8. Format the numbers as follows: (a) assign the currency style with a floating dollar sign to the cells containing numeric data in the ranges B4:E4 and B13:E16, and (b) assign a number style with two decimal places and a thousand's separator (currency with no dollar sign) to the range B5:E12.

9. Use conditional formatting to change the formatting to white font on a purple background in any cell in the range D4:D12 that contains a value greater than 50.

10. Change the worksheet name from Sheet1 to Loan Balance and the sheet tab color to the Orange standard color. Change the document properties, as specified by your instructor. Change the worksheet header with your name, course number, and other information as specified by your instructor.

11. Spell check the worksheet. Preview and then print the worksheet in landscape orientation. Save the workbook using the file name, Lab 2–1 HelpToday Personal Loans Report.

12. Print the range A3:D13. Print the formulas version on another page. Close the workbook without saving the changes. Submit the assignment as specified by your instructor.

13. ✸ When you created the formula for the monthly fee, you used 5%. What would you have to do if the rate changed today to, say, 10% to update the formulas?

Lab 2: **Sales Summary Worksheet**

Problem: You have been asked to build a worksheet for a start-up company, TravelUS Campers, that analyzes the financing needs for the company's first year in business. The company plans to begin operations in January with an initial investment of $700,000.00. The expected revenue and costs for the company's first year are shown in Table 2–7. The desired worksheet is shown in Figure 2–74. The initial investment is shown as the starting balance for January (cell B4). The amount of financing required by the company is shown as the lowest ending balance (cell F18).

Instructions Part 1: Perform the following tasks to build the worksheet shown in Figure 2–74.

Table 2–7 TravelUS Campers Financing Needs Data		
Month	**Incomes**	**Expenses**
January	209081	262911
February	63811	381881
March	300660	250143
April	229207	209498
May	248369	355232
June	96118	260888
July	62970	242599
August	195824	368955
September	305669	235604
October	224741	383254
November	159644	411768
December	210000	540000

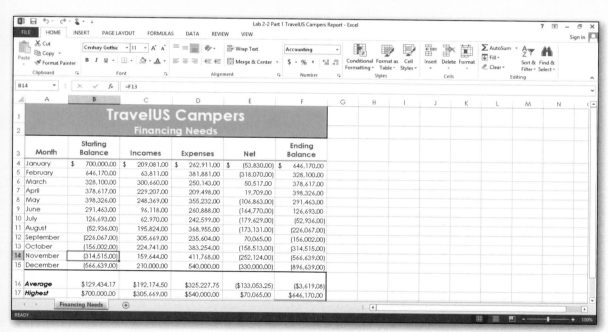

Figure 2–74

1. Run Excel. Apply the Wisp theme to a new workbook.

2. Increase the width of column A to 12.00 and the width of columns B through F to 14.50.

3. Enter the worksheet title `TravelUS Campers` in cell A1 and the worksheet subtitle `Financing Needs` in cell A2. Enter the column titles in row 3, as shown in Figure 2–74. In row 3, use ALT+ENTER to start a new line in a cell.

4. Enter the financing needs data described in Table 2–7 in columns A, C, and D in rows 4 through 15. Enter the initial starting balance (cell B4) of 700000.00. Enter the row titles in the range A16:A18, as shown in Figure 2–74.

5. For the months of February through December, the starting balance is equal to the previous month's ending balance. Obtain the starting balance for February by setting the starting balance of February to the ending balance of January. Use a cell reference rather than typing in the data. Copy the formula for February to the remaining months.

Continued >

In the Labs *continued*

6. Obtain the net amounts in column E by subtracting the expenses in column D from the incomes in column C. Enter the formula in cell E4 and copy it to the range E5:E15. Obtain the ending balance amounts in column F by adding the starting balance in column B to the net in column E. Enter the formula in cell F4 and copy it to the range F5:F15.

7. In the range B16:B18, use the AVERAGE, MAX, and MIN functions to determine the average value, highest value, and lowest value in the range B4:B15. Copy the range B16:B18 to the range C16:F18.

8. One at a time, merge and center the worksheet title and subtitle across columns A through F. Select cells A1 and A2 and change the background color to light green from standard colors (column 5). Apply the Title cell style to cells A1 and A2. Change the worksheet title in cell A1 to 28-point white (column 1, row 1 on the Font Color gallery). Change the worksheet subtitle to the same color. Bold both the title and subtitle. Assign a thick box border to the range A1:A2.

9. Center the titles in row 3, columns A through F. Apply the Heading 2 cell style to the range A3:F3. Italicize and bold the row titles in the range A16:A18.

10. Assign a thick box border to the range A16:F18. Change the background and font color for cell F18 to the same colors applied to the worksheet title in Step 8.

11. Change the row heights of row 3 to 42.00 points and row 16 to 33.00 points.

12. Assign the accounting number format to the range B4:F4. Assign the comma style format to the range B5:F15. Assign a currency format with a floating dollar sign to the range B16:F18.

13. Rename the sheet tab as Financing Needs. Apply the Green color from the standard colors (column 6) to the sheet tab. Change the document properties, as specified by your instructor. Change the worksheet header with your name, course number, and other information as specified by your instructor. Save the workbook using the file name, Lab 2–2 Part 1 TravelUS Campers Report. Print the entire worksheet in landscape orientation. Next, print only the range A3:B15.

14. Display the formulas version by pressing CTRL+ACCENT MARK (`). Print the formulas version using the Fit to option button in the Scaling area in the Page sheet (Page Setup dialog box). After printing the worksheet, reset the Scaling option by selecting the Adjust to option button in the Page sheet (Page Setup dialog box) and changing the percent value to 100%. Change the display from the formulas version to the values version by pressing CTRL+ACCENT MARK (`). Do not save the workbook.

15. Submit the revised workbook as requested by your instructor.

16. ✺ In reviewing the worksheet you created, how do you think the company could obtain a positive result without increasing income or decreasing expenses?

Instructions Part 2: In this part of the exercise, you will change the revenue amounts until the lowest ending balance is greater than zero, indicating that the company does not require financing in its first year of operation. Open the workbook created in Part 1 and save the workbook as Lab 2–2 Part 2 TravelUS Campers Report. Manually increment each of the 12 values in the Incomes column by $20,000.00 until the lowest ending balance in cell F18 is greater than zero. The value of cell F18 should equal $63,361.00. All 12 values in column C must be incremented the same number of times. Update the worksheet header and save the workbook. Print the worksheet. Submit the assignment as specified by your instructor.

Instructions Part 3: In this part of the exercise, you will change the monthly costs until the lowest ending balance is greater than zero, indicating that the company does not require financing in its first year of operation. Open the workbook created in Part 1 and then save the workbook as Lab 2–2 Part 3 TravelUS Campers Report. Manually decrement each of the 12 values in the Expenses

column by $20,000.00 until the lowest ending balance in cell F18 is greater than zero. Decrement all 12 values in column D the same number of times. Your worksheet is correct when the lowest ending balance in cell F18 is $39,361.00. Update the worksheet header and save the workbook. Print the worksheet. Submit the assignment as specified by your instructor.

Lab 3: Expand Your World: Cloud and Web Technologies Online

Problem: You want to create an estimate of the cost for attending your college for four years. You decide to create the worksheet using the Excel web app so that you can share it with your friends online.

Instructions: Perform the following tasks:
1. Sign in to your Microsoft account on the web and run the Excel web app. Create a blank workbook. In the first worksheet, use row headings for each year of college (Freshman, Sophomore, Junior, and Senior). For the column headings, use your current expenses (such as car payment, rent, tuition, and so forth). Enter estimates for each year based upon estimates you find by searching the web. Include totals for each column. Also include highest, lowest, and average values for the columns. Using the techniques taught in this chapter, create appropriate titles and format the worksheet accordingly. Submit the assignment as specified by your instructor.

✳ Consider This: Your Turn

Apply your creative thinking and problem solving skills to design and implement a solution.

1: Analyze Energy Consumption
Personal

Part 1: Your parents believe that your late-night studying sessions and household appliance usage contribute to excessive electricity bills. You have decided to try to prove them wrong by analyzing your monthly electricity consumption. You research the energy consumption of your personal items and appliance usage to obtain consumption costs per hour for each item. Table 2–8 contains the data and format for the report you will create. Use the concepts and techniques presented in this project to create and format the worksheet.

Table 2–8 Appliance Electricity Usage Costs

Appliance	Cost per Hour	Hours Used Monthly	Total Cost per Month (30 Days)
Clothes dryer	$0.447	20	
Computer	$0.08	150	
Blu-ray player	$0.061	100	
Light bulbs	$0.056	160	
Sound system	$0.05	180	
Television	$0.08	90	
Washing machine	$0.06	30	

Continued >

Consider This: Your Turn *continued*

Part 2: ✳ Now that you have looked over your results, did you neglect to include any appliances? How did you determine the costs you used in your calculations?

2: Analyze Profit Potential

Professional

Part 1: You work as an intern in the college student services department and have been asked to create a worksheet that will aid the clubs on campus in managing their budgets. Each club is allocated money at the beginning of the year and can hold fund-raisers to raise more money for events. Each club is required to save five percent of their income for use at the start of the next year. Table 2–9 shows the clubs that you are working with, as well as their initial allocation and estimated fund-raiser amounts. You will need to calculate how much they need to save as well as the average, lowest, and highest values for the clubs' budgets. Use the concepts and techniques presented in this chapter to create and format the worksheet.

Table 2–9 Student Club Data		
Club	**Allocation**	**Fund-Raisers**
Acting Club	$40,000	$10,000
Golf Club	$25,500	$5,000
Gaming Club	$12,750	$2,000
Math Club	$5,000	$1,000
Photography Club	$3,500	$2,500
Music Club	$15,00	$7,200

Part 2: ✳ How did you decide on the formula to use for the amount each club needs to save? Which formats did you use and why? Which theme did you select for your worksheet?

3: Internet Service

Research and Collaboration

Part 1: You and your friends have decided to subscribe to a new Internet service provider. You would like to maximize services while keeping costs low. As a group, research and find three to five Internet service providers in your area. For each company, find the best service package as well as the basic service package. Using the cost figures you find, calculate the cost per month for each service for a year. Include totals, minimum, maximum, and average values. Use the concepts and techniques presented in this chapter to create and format the worksheet.

Part 2: ✳ Which companies did you choose for your report? Which services offered the best deals that you would be willing to use?

Learn Online

Reinforce what you learned in this chapter with games, exercises, training, and many other online activities and resources.

Student Companion Site Reinforcement activities and resources are available at no additional cost on www.cengagebrain.com. Visit www.cengage.com/ct/studentdownload for detailed instructions about accessing the resources available at the Student Companion Site.

SAM Put your skills into practice with SAM! If you have a SAM account, go to www.cengage .com/sam2013 to access SAM assignments for this chapter.

1 Databases and Database Objects: An Introduction

Microsoft product screenshots used with permission from Microsoft Corporation.

Objectives

You will have mastered the material in this chapter when you can:

- Describe the features of the Access window
- Create a database
- Create tables in Datasheet and Design views
- Add records to a table
- Close a database
- Open a database

- Print the contents of a table
- Create and use a query
- Create and use a form
- Create and print custom reports
- Modify a report in Layout view
- Perform special database operations
- Design a database to satisfy a collection of requirements

1 | Databases and Database Objects: An Introduction

Introduction

The term **database** describes a collection of data organized in a manner that allows access, retrieval, and use of that data. Microsoft Access 2013, usually referred to as simply Access, is a database management system. A **database management system** is software that allows you to use a computer to create a database; add, change, and delete data in the database; ask and answer questions concerning the data; and create forms and reports using the data.

Project — Database Creation

Bavant Publishing Inc. is a publishing company that specializes in foreign language textbooks. Bavant sells in both the K-12 and the higher education markets. Recently, Bavant purchased a small, private publisher of Arabic, Russian, Chinese, and Japanese language textbooks. These languages are increasing in popularity with college students. All textbooks are available in hardcover and some are available as e-books. Bavant Publishing also provides ancillary materials, such as workbooks and laboratory manuals, video resources, audio resources, and companion websites.

Bavant representatives visit campuses and meet with faculty, describing the features and strengths of the textbooks and providing review materials for instructors. Bavant pays a base salary to its book reps, who can earn bonus pay based on exceeding sales goals. Customers place orders with the publisher following the organization's procedures; for example, colleges and universities place orders through their bookstores. Because institutions can cancel classes due to low enrollments, customers sometimes return unused books. At the end of an accounting period, these returns are subtracted from the current amount due.

Bavant wants to maintain records on the sales of textbooks from the newly acquired publisher separately from their other foreign language textbooks to better track profitability and market potential. Bavant organizes this data on its customers and book representatives in a database managed by Access. In this way, Bavant keeps its data current and accurate and can analyze it for trends and produce a variety of useful reports.

In a **relational database** such as those maintained by Access, a database consists of a collection of tables, each of which contains information on a specific subject. Figure 1–1 shows the database for Bavant Publishing. It consists of two tables: the Customer table (Figure 1–1a) contains information about Bavant customers, and the Book Rep table (Figure 1–1b) contains information about the book reps to whom these customers are assigned.

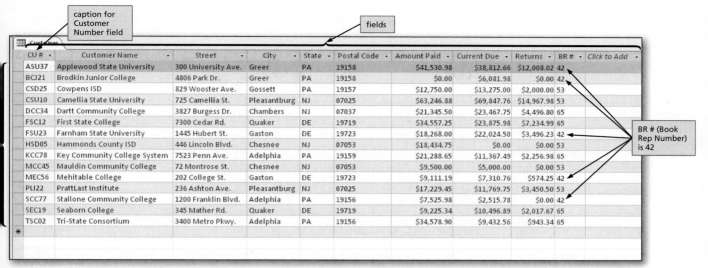

caption for Customer Number field

fields

BR # (Book Rep Number) is 42

CU #	Customer Name	Street	City	State	Postal Code	Amount Paid	Current Due	Returns	BR #	Click to Add
ASU37	Applewood State University	300 University Ave.	Greer	PA	19158	$41,530.98	$38,812.66	$12,008.02	42	
BCJ21	Brodkin Junior College	4806 Park Dr.	Greer	PA	19158	$0.00	$6,081.98	$0.00	42	
CSD25	Cowpens ISD	829 Wooster Ave.	Gossett	PA	19157	$12,750.00	$13,275.00	$2,000.00	53	
CSU10	Camellia State University	725 Camellia St.	Pleasantburg	NJ	07025	$63,246.88	$69,847.76	$14,967.98	53	
DCC34	Dartt Community College	3827 Burgess Dr.	Chambers	NJ	07037	$21,345.50	$23,467.75	$4,496.80	65	
FSC12	First State College	7300 Cedar Rd.	Quaker	DE	19719	$34,557.25	$23,875.98	$7,234.99	65	
FSU23	Farnham State University	1445 Hubert St.	Gaston	DE	19723	$18,268.00	$22,024.50	$3,496.23	42	
HSD05	Hammonds County ISD	446 Lincoln Blvd.	Chesnee	NJ	07053	$18,434.75	$0.00	$0.00	53	
KCC78	Key Community College System	7523 Penn Ave.	Adelphia	PA	19159	$21,288.65	$11,367.49	$2,256.98	65	
MCC45	Mauldin Community College	72 Montrose St.	Chesnee	NJ	07053	$9,500.00	$5,000.00	$0.00	53	
MEC56	Mehitable College	202 College St.	Gaston	DE	19723	$9,111.19	$7,310.76	$574.25	42	
PLI22	PrattLast Institute	236 Ashton Ave.	Pleasantburg	NJ	07025	$17,229.45	$11,769.75	$3,450.50	53	
SCC77	Stallone Community College	1200 Franklin Blvd.	Adelphia	PA	19156	$7,525.98	$2,515.78	$0.00	42	
SEC19	Seaborn College	345 Mather Rd.	Quaker	DE	19719	$9,225.34	$10,496.89	$2,017.67	65	
TSC02	Tri-State Consortium	3400 Metro Pkwy.	Adelphia	PA	19156	$34,578.90	$9,432.56	$943.34	65	

Figure 1–1 (a) Customer Table

BR #	Last Name	First Name	Street	City	State	Postal Code	Start Date	Salary	Bonus Rate	Click to Add
42	Perez	Melina	261 Porter Dr.	Adelphia	PA	19156	5/14/2012	$31,500.00	0.20	
48	Statnik	Michael	3135 Simpson Dr.	Pleasantburg	NJ	07025	1/15/2013	$29,000.00	0.20	
53	Ch	265 Maxwell St.	Gossett	PA	19157	6/1/2013	$26,250.00	0.19		
65	Ro	1827 Maple Ave.	Adelphia	PA	19159	7/1/2014	$7,750.00	0.18		
								$0.00	0.00	

BR # (Book Rep Number) for Melina Perez is 42

Figure 1–1 (b) Book Rep Table

The rows in the tables are called **records**. A record contains information about a given person, product, or event. A row in the Customer table, for example, contains information about a specific customer, such as the customer's name, address information, and other data.

The columns in the tables are called fields. A **field** contains a specific piece of information within a record. In the Customer table, for example, the fourth field, City, contains the name of the city where the customer is located.

The first field in the Customer table is CU #, which is an abbreviation for Customer Number. Bavant Publishing assigns each customer a number; the Bavant customer numbers consist of three uppercase letters followed by a two-digit number.

The customer numbers are unique; that is, no two customers have the same number. Such a field is a **unique identifier**. A unique identifier, as its name suggests, is a way of uniquely identifying each record in the database. A given customer number will appear only in a single record in the table. Only one record exists, for example, in which the customer number is TSC02. A unique identifier also is called a **primary key**. Thus, the Customer Number field is the primary key for the Customer table.

The next eight fields in the Customer table are Customer Name, Street, City, State, Postal Code, Amount Paid, Current Due, and Returns. The Amount Paid column contains the amount that the customer has paid Bavant Publishing year to date (YTD) prior to the current period. The Current Due column contains the amount due to Bavant for the current period. The Returns column contains the dollar value of the books or other products the customer was unable to sell and has returned to Bavant in the current period. For example, customer TSC02 is Tri-State Consortium. The address is 3400 Metro Pkwy., in Adelphia, Pennsylvania. The postal code is 19156. The customer has paid $34,578.90 for products purchased so far. The amount due for the current period is $9,432.56. The customer has returned products worth $943.34.

Bavant assigns a single book rep to work with each customer. The last column in the Customer table, BR # (an abbreviation for Book Rep Number) gives the number of the customer's book rep. The book rep number for Tri-State Consortium is 65.

The first field in the Book Rep table is also BR #, for Book Rep Number. The book rep numbers are unique, so the Book Rep Number field is the primary key of the Book Rep table.

The other fields in the Book Rep table are Last Name, First Name, Street, City, State, Postal Code, Start Date, Salary, and Bonus Rate. The Start Date field gives the date the rep began working for Bavant. The Salary field gives the salary paid to the rep thus far this year. The Bonus Rate gives the potential bonus percentage based on personal performance. The bonus rate applies when the book rep exceeds a predetermined sales goal. For example, book rep 65 is Tracy Rogers. Her address is 1827 Maple Ave., in Adelphia, Pennsylvania. The postal code is 19159. Tracy started working for Bavant on July 1, 2014. So far this year, she has been paid $7,750.00 in salary. Her bonus rate is 0.18 (18%).

The book rep number appears in both the Customer table and the Book Rep table, and relates customers and book reps. Book rep 48, Michael Statnik, recently transferred from another division of the company and has not yet been assigned any customers. His book rep number, therefore, does not appear on any row in the Customer table.

CONSIDER THIS

How would you find the name of the book rep for Tri-State Consortium?
In the Customer table, you see that the book rep number for customer Tri-State Consortium is 65. To find the name of this book rep, look for the row in the Book Rep table that contains 65 in the BR # column. After you have found it, you know that the book rep for Tri-State Consortium is Tracy Rogers.

CONSIDER THIS

How would you find all the customers assigned to Tracy Rogers?
First, look in the Book Rep table to find that her number is 65. You would then look through the Customer table for all the customers that contain 65 in the BR # column. Tracy's customers are DCC34 (Dartt Community College), FSC12 (First State College), KCC78 (Key Community College System), SEC19 (Seaborn College), and TSC02 (Tri-State Consortium).

Roadmap

In this chapter, you will learn how to create and use the database shown in Figure 1–1 on page AC 3. The following roadmap identifies general activities you will perform as you progress through this chapter:

1. CREATE the FIRST TABLE, Book Rep, using Datasheet view.
2. ADD RECORDS to the Book Rep table.
3. PRINT the CONTENTS of the Book Rep table.
4. IMPORT RECORDS into the second table, Customer.
5. MODIFY the SECOND TABLE using Design view.
6. CREATE a QUERY for the Customer table.
7. CREATE a FORM for the Customer table.
8. CREATE a REPORT for the Customer table.

At the beginning of step instructions throughout the chapter, you will see an abbreviated form of this roadmap. The abbreviated roadmap uses colors to indicate chapter progress: gray means the chapter is beyond that activity, blue means the task being shown is covered in that activity, and black means that activity is yet to be covered. For example, the following abbreviated roadmap indicates the chapter would be showing a task in the 3 PRINT CONTENTS activity.

1 CREATE FIRST TABLE | 2 ADD RECORDS | **3 PRINT CONTENTS** | 4 IMPORT RECORDS | 5 MODIFY SECOND TABLE
6 CREATE QUERY | 7 CREATE FORM | 8 CREATE REPORT

Use the abbreviated roadmap as a progress guide while you read or step through the instructions in this chapter.

To Run Access

If you are using a computer to step through the project in this chapter and you want your screens to match the figures in this book, you should change your screen's resolution to 1366 × 768. For information about how to change a computer's resolution, refer to the Office and Windows chapter at the beginning of this book.

The following steps, which assume Windows is running, use the Start screen or the search box to run Access based on a typical installation. You may need to ask your instructor how to run Access on your computer. For a detailed example of the procedure summarized below, refer to the Office and Windows chapter.

1 Scroll the Start screen for an Access 2013 tile. If your Start screen contains an Access 2013 tile, tap or click it to run Access and then proceed to Step 5; if the Start screen does not contain the Access 2013 tile, proceed to the next step to search for the Access app.

2 Swipe in from the right edge of the screen or point to the upper-right corner of the screen to display the Charms bar, and then tap or click the Search charm on the Charms bar to display the Search menu.

3 Type Access as the search text in the Search box and watch the search results appear in the Apps list.

4 Tap or click Access 2013 in the search results to run Access.

5 If the Access window is not maximized, tap or click the Maximize button on its title bar to maximize the window.

For an introduction to Windows and instruction about how to perform basic Windows tasks, read the Office and Windows chapter at the beginning of this book, where you can learn how to resize windows, change screen resolution, create folders, move and rename files, use Windows Help, and much more.

For an introduction to Office and instruction about how to perform basic tasks in Office apps, read the Office and Windows chapter at the beginning of this book, where you can learn how to run an application, use the ribbon, save a file, open a file, exit an application, use Help, and much more.

One of the few differences between Windows 7 and Windows 8 occurs in the steps to run Access. If you are using Windows 7, click the Start button, type `Access` in the 'Search programs and files' box, click Access 2013, and then, if necessary, maximize the Access window. For detailed steps to run Access in Windows 7, refer to the Office and Windows chapter at the beginning of this book. For a summary of the steps, refer to the Quick Reference located at the back of this book.

BTW

Organizing Files and Folders

You should organize and store files in folders so that you easily can find the files later. For example, if you are taking an introductory computer class called CIS 101, a good practice would be to save all Access files in an Access folder in a CIS 101 folder. For a discussion of folders and detailed examples of creating folders, refer to the Office and Windows chapter at the beginning of this book.

BTW

Q&As

For a complete list of the Q&As found in many of the step-by-step sequences in this book, visit the Q&A resource on the Student Companion Site located on www.cengagebrain.com. For detailed instructions about accessing available resources, visit www.cengage.com/ct/studentdownload or contact your instructor for information about accessing the required files.

Creating a Database

In Access, all the tables, reports, forms, and queries that you create are stored in a single file called a database. Thus, you first must create the database to hold the tables, reports, forms, and queries. You can use either the Blank desktop database option or a template to create a new database. If you already know the tables and fields you want in your database, you would use the Blank desktop database option. If not, you can use a template. Templates can guide you by suggesting some commonly used databases.

To Create a Database

Because you already know the tables and fields you want in the Bavant Publishing database, you would use the Blank desktop database option rather than using a template. The following steps assume you already have created folders for storing your files, for example, a CIS 101 folder (for your class) that contains an Access folder (for your assignments). Thus, these steps save the database in the Access folder in the CIS 101 folder on your desired save location. For a detailed example of the procedure for saving a file in a folder or saving a file on SkyDrive, refer to the Office and Windows chapter at the beginning of this book.

1 Tap or click the 'Blank desktop database' thumbnail to select the database type.

2 Type `Bavant Publishing` in the File Name text box to enter the new file name. Do not press the ENTER key after typing the file name because you do not want to create the database at this time.

3 Tap or click the 'Browse for a location to put your database' button to display the File New Database dialog box.

4 Navigate to the location for the database, for example, the Documents library, the My Documents folder, the folder identifying your class (CIS 101, in this case), and then to the Access folder.

5 Tap or click the OK button (File New Database dialog box) to select the location for the database and close the dialog box.

6 Tap or click the Create button to create the database on the selected drive in the selected folder with the file name, Bavant Publishing (Figure 1–2).

Q&A

The title bar for my Navigation Pane contains All Tables rather than All Access Objects, as in the figure. Is that a problem?

It is not a problem. The title bar indicates how the Navigation Pane is organized. You can carry out the steps in the text with either organization. To make your screens match the ones in the text, tap or click the Navigation Pane arrow and then tap or click Object Type.

I do not have the Search bar that appears on the figure. Is that a problem?

It is not a problem. If your Navigation Pane does not display a Search bar and you want your screens to match the ones in the text, press and hold or right-click the Navigation Pane title bar arrow to display a shortcut menu, and then tap or click Search Bar.

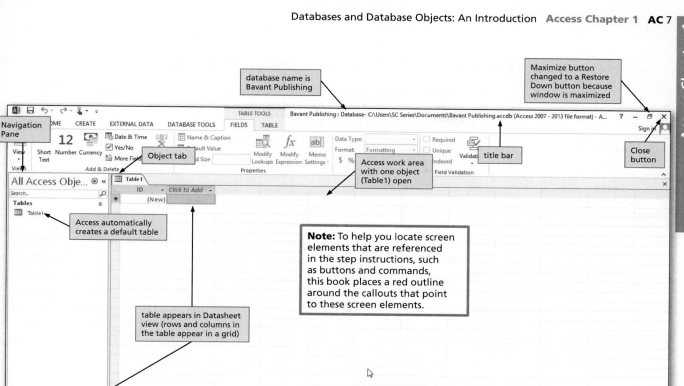

Figure 1–2

TO CREATE A DATABASE USING A TEMPLATE

Ideally, you will design your own database, create a blank database, and then create the tables you have determined that your database should contain. If you are not sure what database design you will need, you could use a template. Templates can guide you by suggesting some commonly used databases. To create a database using a template, you would use the following steps.

1. If you have another database open, close it without exiting Access by tapping or clicking FILE on the ribbon to open the Backstage view and then tapping or clicking Close.

2. If you do not see a template that you want, you can search Microsoft Office online for additional templates.

3. Tap or click the template you want to use. Be sure you have selected one that indicates it is for a desktop database.

4. Enter a file name and select a location for the database.

5. Tap or click the Create button to create the database.

The Access Window

The Access window consists of a variety of components to make your work more efficient. These include the Navigation Pane, Access work area, ribbon, shortcut menus, and Quick Access Toolbar. Some of these components are common to other Microsoft Office apps; others are unique to Access.

BTW

Naming Files
The following characters cannot be used in a file name: question mark (?), quotation mark ("), slash (/), backslash (\), colon (:), asterisk (*), vertical bar (|), greater than symbol (>), and less than symbol (<).

BTW

Available Templates
The templates gallery includes both desktop and web-based templates. If you are creating an Access database for your own use, select a desktop template. Web-based templates allow you to create databases that you can publish to a SharePoint server.

Navigation Pane and Access Work Area

You work on objects such as tables, forms, and reports in the **Access work area**. In the work area in Figure 1–2 on the previous page, a single table, Table1, is open in the work area. **Object tabs** for the open objects appear at the top of the work area. If you have multiple objects open at the same time, you can select one of the open objects by tapping or clicking its tab. To the left of the work area is the Navigation Pane. The **Navigation Pane** contains a list of all the objects in the database. You use this pane to open an object. You also can customize the way objects are displayed in the Navigation Pane.

The **status bar**, located at the bottom of the Access window, presents information about the database object, the progress of current tasks, and the status of certain commands and keys; it also provides controls for viewing the object. As you type text or perform certain commands, various indicators may appear on the status bar. The left edge of the status bar in Figure 1–2 shows that the table object is open in **Datasheet view**. In Datasheet view, the table is represented as a collection of rows and columns called a **datasheet**. Toward the right edge are View buttons, which you can use to change the view that currently appears.

Determining Tables and Fields

Once you have created the database, you need to create the tables and fields that your database will contain. Before doing so, however, you need to make some decisions regarding the tables and fields.

Naming Tables and Fields

In creating your database, you must name tables and fields. Before beginning the design process, you must understand the rules Access applies to table and field names. These rules are:

1. Names can be up to 64 characters in length.
2. Names can contain letters, digits, and spaces, as well as most of the punctuation symbols.
3. Names cannot contain periods (.), exclamation points (!), accent graves (`), or square brackets ([]).
4. Each field in a table must have a unique name.

The approach to naming tables and fields used in this text is to begin the names with an uppercase letter and to use lowercase for the other letters. In multiple-word names, each word begins with an uppercase letter, and there is a space between words (for example, Customer Number).

Determining the Primary Key

For each table, you need to determine the primary key, the unique identifier. In many cases, you will have obvious choices, such as Customer Number or Book Rep Number. If you do not have an obvious choice, you can use the primary key that Access creates automatically. It is a field called ID. It is an autonumber field, which means that Access will assign the value 1 to the first record, 2 to the second record, and so on.

Determining Data Types for the Fields

For each field in your database, you must determine the field's **data type**, that is, the type of data that can be stored in the field. Four of the most commonly used data types in Access are:

1. **Short Text** — The field can contain any characters. A maximum number of 255 characters is allowed in a field whose data type is Short Text.

2. **Number** — The field can contain only numbers. The numbers can be either positive or negative. Fields assigned this type can be used in arithmetic operations. You usually assign fields that contain numbers but will not be used for arithmetic operations (such as postal codes) a data type of Short Text.

3. **Currency** — The field can contain only monetary data. The values will appear with currency symbols, such as dollar signs, commas, and decimal points, and with two digits following the decimal point. Like numeric fields, you can use currency fields in arithmetic operations. Access assigns a size to currency fields automatically.

4. **Date & Time** — The field can store dates and/or times.

Table 1–1 shows the other data types that are available in Access.

Table 1–1 Additional Data Types

Data Type	Description
Long Text	Field can store a variable amount of text or combinations of text and numbers where the total number of characters may exceed 255.
AutoNumber	Field can store a unique sequential number that Access assigns to a record. Access will increment the number by 1 as each new record is added.
Yes/No	Field can store only one of two values. The choices are Yes/No, True/False, or On/Off.
OLE Object	Field can store an OLE object, which is an object linked to or embedded in the table.
Hyperlink	Field can store text that can be used as a hyperlink address.
Attachment	Field can contain an attached file. Images, spreadsheets, documents, charts, and other elements can be attached to this field in a record in the database. You can view and edit the attached file.
Calculated	Field specified as a calculation based on other fields. The value is not actually stored.

© 2014 Cengage Learning

In the Customer table, because the Customer Number, Customer Name, Street, City, and State all can contain letters, their data types should be Short Text. The data type for Postal Code is Short Text instead of Number because you typically do not use postal codes in arithmetic operations; you do not add postal codes or find an average postal code, for example. The Amount Paid, Current Due, and Returns fields contain monetary data, so their data types should be Currency. The Book Rep Number field contains numbers, but you will not use these numbers in arithmetic operations, so its type should be Short Text.

Similarly, in the Book Rep table, the data type for the Book Rep Number, Last Name, First Name, Street, City, State, and Postal Code fields all should be Short Text. The Start Date field should be Date & Time. The Salary field contains monetary amounts, so its data type should be Currency. The Bonus Rate field contains numbers that are not dollar amounts, so its data type should be Number.

For fields whose type is Short Text, you can change the field size, that is, the maximum number of characters that can be entered in the field. If you set the field size for the State field to 2, for example, Access will not allow the user to enter more than two characters in the field. On the other hand, fields whose data type is Number often

require you to change the field size, which is the storage space assigned to the field by Access. Table 1–2 shows the possible field sizes for Number fields.

Table 1–2 Field Sizes for Number Fields	
Field Size	**Description**
Byte	Integer value in the range of 0 to 255
Integer	Integer value in the range of -32,768 to 32,767
Long Integer	Integer value in the range of -2,147,483,648 to 2,147,483,647
Single	Numeric values with decimal places to seven significant digits — requires 4 bytes of storage
Double	Numeric values with decimal places to more accuracy than Single — requires 8 bytes of storage
Replication ID	Special identifier required for replication
Decimal	Numeric values with decimal places to more accuracy than Single or Double — requires 12 bytes of storage

© 2014 Cengage Learning

CONSIDER THIS

What is the appropriate size for the Bonus Rate field?
If the size were Byte, Integer, or Long Integer, only integers could be stored. If you try to store a value that has decimal places, such as 0.18, in fields of these sizes, the portion to the right of the decimal point would be removed, giving a result of 0. To address this problem, the bonus rate should have a size of Single, Double, or Decimal. With such small numbers involved, Single, which requires the least storage of the three, is the appropriate choice.

Creating a Table

BTW

On Screen Keyboard
To display the on-screen touch keyboard, tap the Touch Keyboard button on the Windows taskbar. When finished using the touch keyboard, tap the X button on the touch keyboard to close the keyboard.

To create a table in Access, you must define its structure. That is, you must define all the fields that make up the table and their characteristics. You also must indicate the primary key.

In Access, you can use two different views to create a table: Datasheet view and Design view. In **Datasheet view**, the data in the table is presented in rows and columns, similar to a spreadsheet. Although the main reason to use Datasheet view is to add or update records in a table, you also can use it to create a table or to later modify its structure. The other view, **Design view**, is only used to create a table or to modify the structure of a table.

As you might expect, Design view has more functionality for creating a table than Datasheet view. That is, there are certain actions that only can be performed in Design view. One such action is assigning Single as the field size for the Bonus Rate field. In this chapter, you will create the first table, the Book Rep table, in Datasheet view. Once you have created the table in Datasheet view, you will use Design view to change the field size.

Whichever view you choose to use, before creating the table, you need to know the names and data types of the fields that will make up the table. You also can decide to enter a **description** for a particular field to explain important details about the field. When you select this field, this description will appear on the status bar. You also might choose to assign a **caption** to a particular field. If you assign a caption, Access will display the value you assign, rather than the field name, in datasheets and in forms. If you do not assign a caption, Access will display the field name.

CONSIDER THIS

When would you want to use a caption?
You would use a caption whenever you want something other than the field name displayed. One common example is when the field name is relatively long and the data in the field is relatively short. In the Book Rep table, the name of the first field is Book Rep Number, but the field contains data that is only two characters long. You will change the caption for this field to BR #, which is much shorter than Book Rep Number yet still describes the field. Doing so will enable you to greatly reduce the width of the column.

The results of these decisions for the fields in the Book Rep table are shown in Table 1–3. The table also shows the data types and field sizes of the fields as well as any special properties that need to be changed. The Book Rep Number field has a caption of BR #, enabling the width of the Book Rep Number column to be reduced in the datasheet.

Table 1–3 Structure of Book Rep Table

Field Name	Data Type	Field Size	Notes
Book Rep Number	Short Text	2	Primary Key **Description:** Unique identifier of book rep **Caption:** BR #
Last Name	Short Text	15	
First Name	Short Text	15	
Street	Short Text	20	
City	Short Text	20	
State	Short Text	2	
Postal Code	Short Text	5	
Start Date	Date/Time		(This appears as Date & Time on the menu of available data types)
Salary	Currency		
Bonus Rate	Number	Single	Format: Fixed Decimal Places: 2

© 2014 Cengage Learning

If you are using your finger on a touch screen and are having difficulty completing the steps in this chapter, consider using a stylus. Many people find it easier to be precise with a stylus than with a finger. In addition, with a stylus you see the pointer. If you still are having trouble completing the steps with a stylus, try using a mouse.

CONSIDER THIS

How do you determine the field size?
You need to determine the maximum number of characters that can be entered in the field. In some cases, it is obvious. Field sizes of 2 for the State field and 5 for the Postal Code field are certainly the appropriate choices. In other cases, you need to determine how many characters you wish to allow. In the list shown in Table 1–3, Bavant evidently decided allowing 15 characters was sufficient for last names. This field size can be changed later if it proves to be insufficient.

CONSIDER THIS

What is the purpose of the Format and Decimal Places properties?
The format guarantees that bonus rates will be displayed with a fixed number of decimal places. Setting the decimal places property to 2 guarantees that the rates will be displayed with precisely two decimal places. Thus, a bonus rate of 0.2 will be displayed as 0.20.

To Modify the Primary Key

1 CREATE FIRST TABLE | 2 ADD RECORDS | 3 PRINT CONTENTS | 4 IMPORT RECORDS | 5 MODIFY SECOND TABLE
6 CREATE QUERY | 7 CREATE FORM | 8 CREATE REPORT

When you first create your database, Access automatically creates a table for you. You can immediately begin defining the fields. If, for any reason, you do not have this table or inadvertently delete it, you can create the table by tapping or clicking CREATE on the ribbon and then tapping or clicking the Table button (CREATE tab | Tables group). In either case, you are ready to define the fields.

The steps on the next page change the name, data type, and other properties of the first field to match the Book Rep Number field in Table 1–3, which is the primary key. *Why? Access has already created the first field as the primary key field, which it has named ID. Book Rep Number is a more appropriate choice.*

1

- Press and hold or right-click the column heading for the ID field to display a shortcut menu (Figure 1–3).

Q&A Why does my shortcut menu look different?
You displayed a shortcut menu for the column instead of the column heading. Be sure you press and hold or right-click the column heading.

Figure 1–3

2

- Tap or click Rename Field on the shortcut menu to highlight the current name.

- Type `Book Rep Number` to assign a name to the new field.

- Tap or click the white space immediately below the field name to complete the addition of the field (Figure 1–4).

Q&A Why does the full name of the field not appear?
The default column size is not large enough for Book Rep Number to be displayed in its entirety. You will address this issue in later steps.

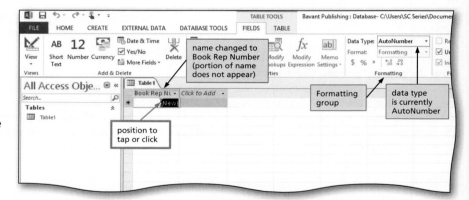

Figure 1–4

3

- Because the data type needs to be changed from AutoNumber to Short Text, tap or click the Data Type arrow (TABLE TOOLS FIELDS tab | Formatting group) to display a menu of available data types (Figure 1–5).

Figure 1–5

- Tap or click Short Text to select
 the data type for the field
 (Figure 1–6).

Figure 1–6

- Tap or click the Field Size text
 box (TABLE TOOLS FIELDS tab |
 Properties group) to select the
 current field size, use either the
 DELETE or BACKSPACE keys to erase
 the current field size, if necessary,
 and then type 2 as the new
 field size.

- Tap or click the Name & Caption
 button (TABLE TOOLS FIELDS tab
 | Properties group) to display the
 Enter Field Properties dialog box.

- Tap or click the Caption text box
 (Enter Field Properties dialog box),
 and then type BR # as the
 caption.

- Tap or click the Description text
 box, and then type Unique
 identifier of book rep
 as the description (Figure 1–7).

Figure 1–7

- Tap or click the OK button
 (Enter Field Properties dialog
 box) to change the caption and
 description (Figure 1–8).

Figure 1–8

To Define the Remaining Fields in a Table

1 CREATE FIRST TABLE | **2 ADD RECORDS** | **3 PRINT CONTENTS** | **4 IMPORT RECORDS** | **5 MODIFY SECOND TABLE**
6 CREATE QUERY | **7 CREATE FORM** | **8 CREATE REPORT**

To define an additional field, you tap or click the Click to Add column heading, select the data type, and then type the field name. This is different from the process you used to modify the ID field. The following steps define the remaining fields shown in Table 1–3 on page AC 11. These steps do not change the field size of the Bonus Rate field, however. *Why? You can only change the field size of a Number field in Design view. Later, you will use Design view to change this field size and change the format and number of decimal places.*

- Tap or click the 'Click to Add' column heading to display a menu of available data types (Figure 1–9).

Figure 1–9

- Tap or click Short Text in the menu of available data types to select the Short Text data type.

- Type `Last Name` to enter a field name.

- Tap or click the blank space below the field name to complete the change of the name. Tap or click the blank space a second time to select the field (Figure 1–10).

Q&A

After entering the field name, I realized that I selected the wrong data type. How can I correct it?
Tap or click the Data Type arrow, and then select the correct type.

I inadvertently clicked the blank space before entering the field name. How can I correct the name?
Press and hold or right-click the field name, tap or click Rename Field on the shortcut menu, and then type the new name.

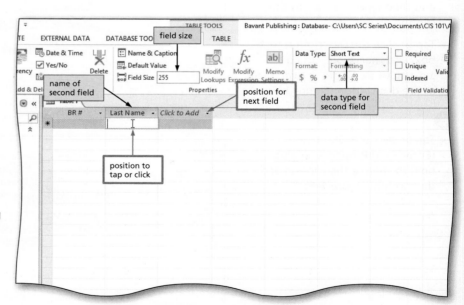

Figure 1–10

3

- Change the field size to 15 just as you changed the field size of the Book Rep Number field.

- Using the same technique, add the remaining fields in the Book Rep table. For the First Name, Street, City, State, and Postal Code fields, use the Short Text data type, but change the field sizes to match Table 1–3 on page AC 11. For the Start Date field, change the data type to Date & Time. For the Salary field, change the data type to Currency. For the Bonus Rate field, change the data type to Number (Figure 1–11).

Figure 1–11

Q&A

I have an extra row between the row containing the field names and the row that begins with the asterisk. What happened? Is this a problem? If so, how do I fix it?

You inadvertently added a record to the table by pressing a key. Even pressing the SPACEBAR would add a record. You now have an unwanted record. To fix it, press the ESC key or tap or click the Undo button to undo the action. You may need to do this more than once.

When I try to move on to specify another field, I get an error message indicating that the primary key cannot contain a null value. How do I correct this?

First, tap or click the OK button to remove the error message. Next, press the ESC key or tap or click the Undo button to undo the action. You may need to do this more than once.

BTW

Currency Symbols
To show the symbol for the Euro (€) instead of the dollar sign, change the Format property for the field whose data type is currency. To change the default symbols for currency, change the settings in Windows.

Making Changes to the Structure

When creating a table, check the entries carefully to ensure they are correct. If you discover a mistake while still typing the entry, you can correct the error by repeatedly pressing the BACKSPACE key until the incorrect characters are removed. Then, type the correct characters. If you do not discover a mistake until later, you can use the following techniques to make the necessary changes to the structure:

- To undo your most recent change, tap or click the Undo button on the Quick Access Toolbar. If there is nothing that Access can undo, this button will be dim, and tapping or clicking it will have no effect.

- To delete a field, press and hold or right-click the column heading for the field (the position containing the field name), and then tap or click Delete Field on the shortcut menu.

- To change the name of a field, press and hold or right-click the column heading for the field, tap or click Rename Field on the shortcut menu, and then type the desired field name.

- To insert a field as the last field, tap or click the 'Click to Add' column heading, tap or click the appropriate data type on the menu of available data types, type the desired field name, and, if necessary, change the field size.

- To insert a field between existing fields, press and hold or right-click the column heading for the field that will follow the new field, and then tap or click Insert

BTW

Touch Screen Differences
The Office and Windows interfaces may vary if you are using a touch screen. For this reason, you might notice that the function or appearance of your touch screen differs slightly from this chapter's presentation.

Field on the shortcut menu. Press and hold or right-click the column heading for the field, tap or click Rename Field on the shortcut menu, and then type the desired field name.

- To move a field, tap or click the column heading for the field to be moved to select the field, and then drag the field to the desired position.

As an alternative to these steps, you might want to start over. To do so, tap or click the Close button for the table, and then tap or click the No button in the Microsoft Access dialog box. Tap or click CREATE on the ribbon, and then tap or click the Table button to create a table. You then can repeat the process you used earlier to define the fields in the table.

To Save a Table

1 CREATE FIRST TABLE | 2 ADD RECORDS | 3 PRINT CONTENTS | 4 IMPORT RECORDS | 5 MODIFY SECOND TABLE

6 CREATE QUERY | 7 CREATE FORM | 8 CREATE REPORT

The Book Rep table structure is complete. The final step is to save the table within the database. As part of the process, you will give the table a name. The following steps save the table, giving it the name Book Rep. **Why?** *Bavant has decided that Book Rep is an appropriate name for the table.*

- Tap or click the Save button on the Quick Access Toolbar to display the Save As dialog box (Figure 1–12).

Figure 1–12

- Type `Book Rep` to change the name assigned to the table.
- Tap or click the OK button (Save As dialog box) to save the table (Figure 1–13).

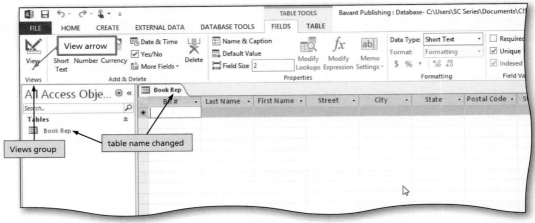

Figure 1–13

Other Ways

1. Tap or click FILE on the ribbon, tap or click Save in the Backstage view
2. Press and hold or right-click tab for table, tap or click Save on shortcut menu
3. Press CTRL+S

To View the Table in Design View

Even when creating a table in Datasheet view, Design view can be helpful. *Why? You easily can view the fields, data types, and properties to ensure you have entered them correctly. It is also easier to determine the primary key in Design view.* The following steps display the structure of the Book Rep table in Design view so that you can verify the design is correct.

1

• Tap or click the View arrow (TABLE TOOLS FIELDS tab | Views group) to display the View menu (Figure 1–14).

Q&A

Could I just tap or click the View button rather than the arrow?

Yes. Tapping or clicking the button is equivalent to tapping or clicking the command represented by the icon currently appearing on the button. Because the icon on the button in Figure 1–14 is for Design view, tapping or clicking the button would display the table in Design view. If you are uncertain, you can always tap or click the arrow and select from the menu.

Figure 1–14

2

• Tap or click Design View on the View menu to view the table in Design view (Figure 1–15).

Figure 1–15

Other Ways

1. Tap or click Design View button on status bar

Checking the Structure in Design View

You should use Design view to carefully check the entries you have made. In Figure 1–15 on the previous page, for example, you can see that the Book Rep Number field is the primary key of the Book Rep table by the key symbol in front of the field name. If your table does not have a key symbol, you can tap or click the Primary Key button (TABLE TOOLS DESIGN tab | Tools group) to designate the field as the primary key. You also can check that the data type, description, field size, and caption are all correct.

For the other fields, you can see the field name, data type, and description without taking any special action. To see the field size and/or caption for a field, tap or click the field's **row selector**, the small box that precedes the field. Tapping or clicking the row selector for the Last Name field, for example, displays the properties for the field. You then can check to see that the field size is correct. In addition, if the field has a caption, you can check to see if that is correct. If you find any mistakes, you can make the necessary corrections on this screen. When you have finished, you would tap or click the Save button to save your changes.

To Change a Field Size in Design View

1 CREATE FIRST TABLE | 2 ADD RECORDS | 3 PRINT CONTENTS | 4 IMPORT RECORDS | 5 MODIFY SECOND TABLE
6 CREATE QUERY | 7 CREATE FORM | 8 CREATE REPORT

Most field size changes can be made in either Datasheet view or Design view. However, changing the field size for Number fields, such as the Bonus Rate field, can only be made in Design view. Because the values in the Bonus Rate field have decimal places, only Single, Double, or Decimal would be possible choices for the field size. The difference between these choices concerns the amount of accuracy. Double is more accurate than Single, for example, but requires more storage space. Because the rates are only two decimal places, Single is an acceptable choice.

The following steps change the field size of the Bonus Rate field to Single, the format to Fixed, and the number of decimal places to 2. ***Why change the format and number of decimal places?*** *To ensure that each value will appear with precisely two decimal places.*

- If necessary, tap or click the vertical scroll bar to display the Bonus Rate field. Tap or click the row selector for the Bonus Rate field to select the field (Figure 1–16).

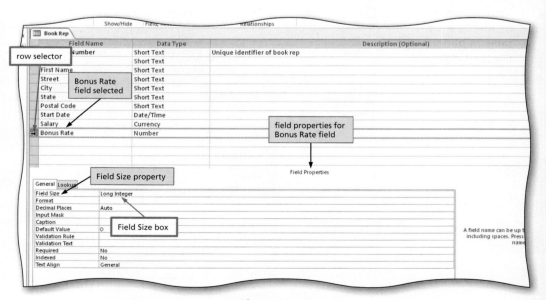

Figure 1–16

2

- Tap or click the Field Size box to display the Field Size arrow.

- Tap or click the Field Size arrow to display the Field Size menu (Figure 1–17).

Figure 1–17

Q&A

What would happen if I left the field size set to Long Integer?

If the field size is Long Integer, Integer, or Byte, no decimal places can be stored. For example, a value of .10 would be stored as 0. If you enter rates and the values all appear as 0, chances are you did not change the field size property.

3

- Tap or click Single to select single precision as the field size.

- Tap or click the Format box to display the Format arrow.

- Tap or click the Format arrow to open the Format menu (Figure 1–18).

Figure 1–18

4

- Tap or click Fixed to select fixed as the format.

- Tap or click the Decimal Places box to display the Decimal Places arrow.

- Tap or click the Decimal Places arrow to enter the number of decimal places.

- Tap or click 2 to assign the number of decimal places.

- Tap or click the Save button to save your changes (Figure 1–19).

Figure 1–19

Q&A

Why did the Property Update Options button appear?

You changed the number of decimal places. The Property Update Options button offers a quick way of making the same change everywhere Bonus Rate appears. So far, you have not added any data or created any forms or reports that use the Bonus Rate field, so no such changes are necessary.

To Close the Table

Once you are sure that your entries are correct and you have saved your changes, you can close the table. The following step closes the table.

1 Tap or click the Close button for the Book Rep table to close the table.

Other Ways

1. Press and hold or right-click tab for table, tap or click Close on shortcut menu

To Add Records to a Table

1 CREATE FIRST TABLE | 2 ADD RECORDS | 3 PRINT CONTENTS | 4 IMPORT RECORDS | 5 MODIFY SECOND TABLE
6 CREATE QUERY | 7 CREATE FORM | 8 CREATE REPORT

Creating a table by building the structure and saving the table is the first step in the two-step process of using a table in a database. The second step is to add records to the table. To add records to a table, the table must be open. When making changes to tables, you work in Datasheet view.

You often add records in phases. *Why? You might not have enough time to add all the records in one session, or you might not have all the records currently available.* The following steps open the Book Rep table in Datasheet view and then add the first two records in the Book Rep table (Figure 1–20).

BR #	Last Name	First Name	Street	City	State	Postal Code	Start Date	Salary	Bonus Rate
53	Chin	Robert	265 Maxwell St.	Gossett	PA	19157	6/1/2013	$26,250.00	0.19
42	Perez	Melina	261 Porter Dr.	Adelphia	PA	19156	5/14/2012	$31,500.00	0.20

Figure 1–20

- Press and hold or right-click the Book Rep table in the Navigation Pane to display the shortcut menu (Figure 1–21).

Figure 1–21

2

- Tap or click Open on the shortcut menu to open the table in Datasheet view.

- Tap or click the Shutter Bar Open/Close Button to close the Navigation Pane (Figure 1–22).

Figure 1–22

3

- Tap or click the first row in the BR # field if necessary to display an insertion point, and type 53 to enter the first book rep number (Figure 1–23).

Figure 1–23

- Press the TAB key to move to the next field.

- Enter the last name, first name, street, city, state, and postal code by typing the following entries, pressing the TAB key after each one: Chin as the last name, Robert as the first name, 265 Maxwell St. as the street, Gossett as the city, PA as the state, and 19157 as the postal code.

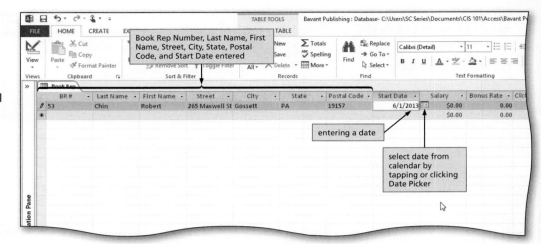

Figure 1–24

- If requested by your instructor, enter your address instead of 265 Maxwell St. as the street. If your address is longer than 20 characters, enter the first 20 characters.

- Type 6/1/2013 in the Start Date field (Figure 1–24).

- Press the TAB key and then type 26250 in the Salary field.

Q&A Do I need to type a dollar sign?
You do not need to type dollar signs or commas. In addition, because the digits to the right of the decimal point are both zeros, you do not need to type either the decimal point or the zeros.

- Press the TAB key to complete the entry for the Salary field.

Figure 1–25

- Type 0.19 in the Bonus Rate field, and then press the TAB key to complete the entry of the first record (Figure 1–25).

Q&A Do I need to type the leading zero for the Bonus Rate?
Typing the leading zero is not necessary. You could type .19 if you prefer. In addition, you would not have to type any final zeros. For example, if you needed to enter 0.20, you could simply type .2 as your entry.

How and when do I save the record?
As soon as you have entered or modified a record and moved to another record, Access saves the original record. This is different from other applications. The rows entered in an Excel worksheet, for example, are not saved until the entire worksheet is saved.

6

- Use the techniques shown in Steps 3 through 5 to enter the data for the second record (Figure 1–26).

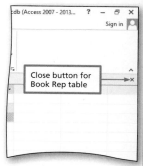

Figure 1–26

Q&A Does it matter that I entered book rep 42 after I entered book rep 53? Should the book rep numbers be in order?

The order in which you enter the records is not important. When you close and later reopen the table, the records will be in book rep number order, because the Book Rep Number field is the primary key.

When I entered the Salary field and changed the data type to Currency, I noticed that the word Currency appeared twice. Why?

The second Currency is the format, which indicates how the data will be displayed. For the Currency data type, Access automatically sets the format to Currency, which is usually what you would want. You could change it to something else, if desired, by tapping or clicking the arrow and selecting the desired format.

Experiment

- Tap or click the Salary field on either of the records. Be sure the TABLE TOOLS FIELDS tab is selected. Tap or click the Format arrow, and then tap or click each of the formats in the Format box menu to see the effect on the values in the Salary field. When finished, tap or click Currency in the Format box menu.

Making Changes to the Data

As you enter data, check your entries carefully to ensure they are correct. If you make a mistake and discover it before you press the TAB key, correct it by pressing the BACKSPACE key until the incorrect characters are removed, and then type the correct characters. If you do not discover a mistake until later, you can use the following techniques to make the necessary corrections to the data:

- To undo your most recent change, tap or click the Undo button on the Quick Access Toolbar. If there is nothing that Access can undo, this button will be dimmed, and tapping or clicking it will have no effect.

- To add a record, tap or click the New (blank) record button, tap or click the position for the Book Rep Number field on the first open record, and then add the record. Do not worry about it being in the correct position in the table. Access will reposition the record based on the primary key, in this case, the Book Rep Number.

- To delete a record, tap or click the record selector, shown in Figure 1–26, for the record to be deleted. Then press the DELETE key to delete the record, and tap or click the Yes button when Access asks you to verify that you want to delete the record.

- To change the contents of one or more fields in a record, the record must be on the screen. If it is not, use any appropriate technique, such as the UP ARROW and DOWN ARROW keys or the vertical scroll bar, to move to the record. If the field you want to correct is not visible on the screen, use the horizontal scroll bar along the bottom of the screen to shift all the fields until the one you want appears. If the value in the field is currently highlighted, you can simply type the new value. If you would rather edit the existing value, you must have an insertion point in the field. You can place the insertion point by tapping or clicking in the field or by pressing the F2 key. You then can use the arrow keys, the DELETE key, and the BACKSPACE key for making the correction. You also can use the INSERT key to switch between Insert and Overtype mode. When you have made the change, press the TAB key to move to the next field.

BTW

AutoCorrect Feature
The AutoCorrect feature of Access corrects common data entry errors. AutoCorrect corrects two capital letters by changing the second letter to lowercase and capitalizes the first letter in the names of days. It also corrects more than 400 commonly misspelled words.

BTW

Other AutoCorrect Options
Using the Office AutoCorrect feature, you can create entries that will replace abbreviations with spelled-out names and phrases automatically. To specify AutoCorrect rules, tap or click FILE on the ribbon to open the Backstage view, tap or click Options, and then tap or click Proofing in the Access Options dialog box.

If you cannot determine how to correct the data, you may find that you are "stuck" on the record, in which case Access neither allows you to move to another record nor allows you to close the table until you have made the correction. If you encounter this situation, simply press the ESC key. Pressing the ESC key will remove from the screen the record you are trying to add. You then can move to any other record, close the table, or take any other action you desire.

To Close a Table

Now that you have created and saved the Book Rep table, you can close it. The following step closes the table.

1 Tap or click the Close button for the Book Rep table, shown in Figure 1–26 on the previous page, to close the table (Figure 1–27).

Figure 1–27

To Exit Access

The following steps exit Access. For a detailed example of the procedure summarized below, refer to the Office and Windows chapter at the beginning of this book.

1 Tap or click the Close button on the right side of the title bar to exit Access.

2 If a Microsoft Access dialog box appears, tap or click the Save button to save any changes made to the object since the last save.

Break Point: If you wish to take a break, this is a good place to do so. To resume later, continue following the steps from this location forward.

Starting Access and Opening a Database

Once you have created and later closed a database, you will need to open it in the future in order to use it. Opening a database requires that Access is running on your computer.

To Run Access

1 Scroll the Start screen for an Access 2013 tile. If your Start screen contains an Access 2013 tile, tap or click it to run Access. If the Start screen does not contain the Access 2013 tile, proceed to the next step to search for the Access app.

2 Swipe in from the right edge of the screen or point to the upper-right corner of the screen to display the Charms bar, and then tap or click the Search charm on the Charms bar to display the Search menu.

3 Type Access as the search text in the Search text box and watch the search results appear in the Apps list.

4 Tap or click Access 2013 in the search results to run Access.

To Open a Database from Access

Earlier in this chapter, you created the Bavant Publishing database in an appropriate storage location. The following steps open the database from the location you specified when you first created it (for example, the Access folder in the CIS 101 folder). For a detailed example of the procedure summarized below, refer to the Office 2013 and Windows chapter at the beginning of this book.

1 Tap or click FILE on the ribbon to open the Backstage view, if necessary.

2 If the database you want to open is displayed in the Recent list, tap or click the file name to open the database and display the opened database in the Access window; then skip to Step 7. If the database you want to open is not displayed in the Recent list or if the Recent list does not appear, tap or click 'Open Other Files' to display the Open Gallery.

3 If the database you want to open is displayed in the Recent list in the Open gallery, tap or click the file name to open the database and display the opened database in the Access window; then skip to Step 7.

4 Tap or click Computer, SkyDrive, or another location in the left pane and then navigate to the location of the database to be opened (for example, the Access folder in the CIS 101 folder).

5 Tap or click Bavant Publishing to select the database to be opened.

6 Tap or click the Open button (Open dialog box) to open the selected file and display the opened database in the Access window (Figure 1–28).

7 If a Security Warning appears, tap or click the Enable Content button.

BTW

Enabling Content
If the database is one that you created, or if it comes from a trusted source, you can enable the content. You should disable the content of a database if you suspect that your database might contain harmful content or damaging macros.

Figure 1–28

To Add Records to a Table that Contains Data

1 CREATE FIRST TABLE | 2 ADD RECORDS | 3 PRINT CONTENTS | 4 IMPORT RECORDS | 5 MODIFY SECOND TABLE
6 CREATE QUERY | 7 CREATE FORM | 8 CREATE REPORT

You can add records to a table that already contains data using a process almost identical to that used to add records to an empty table. The only difference is that you place the insertion point after the last record before you enter the additional data. To position the insertion point after the last record, you can use the **Navigation buttons**, which are buttons used to move within a table, found near the lower-left corner of the screen when a table is open. *Why not just tap or click the Book Rep Number (BR #) on the first open record? You could do this, but it is a good habit to use the New (blank) record button. Once a table contains more records than will fit on the screen, it is easier to tap or click the New (blank) record button.* The purpose of each Navigation button is described in Table 1–4.

Table 1–4 Navigation Buttons in Datasheet View	
Button	**Purpose**
First record	Moves to the first record in the table
Previous record	Moves to the previous record
Next record	Moves to the next record
Last record	Moves to the last record in the table
New (blank) record	Moves to the end of the table to a position for entering a new record

© 2014 Cengage Learning

The following steps add the remaining records (Figure 1–29) to the Book Rep table.

BR #	Last Name	First Name	Street	City	State	Postal Code	Start Date	Salary	Bonus Rate
65	Rogers	Tracy	1827 Maple Ave.	Adelphia	PA	19159	7/1/2014	$7,750.00	0.18
48	Statnik	Michael	3135 Simpson Dr.	Pleasantburg	NJ	07025	1/15/2013	$29,000.00	0.20

Figure 1–29

- If the Navigation Pane is closed, tap or click the Shutter Bar Open/Close Button, shown in Figure 1–27 on page AC 24, to open the Navigation Pane (Figure 1–30).

Figure 1–30

2

- Press and hold or right-click the Book Rep table in the Navigation Pane to display a shortcut menu.

- Tap or click Open on the shortcut menu to open the table in Datasheet view.

Q&A Why do the records appear in a different order than the order in which I entered them?
When you open the table, they are sorted in the order of the primary key. In this case, that means they will appear in Book Rep Number order.

- Close the Navigation Pane by tapping or clicking the Shutter Bar Open/Close Button (Figure 1–31).

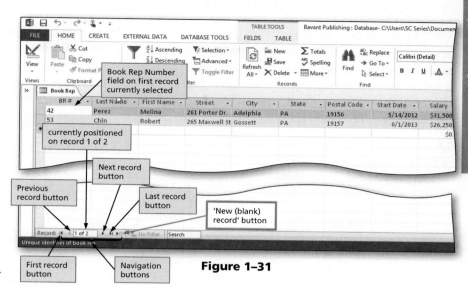

Figure 1–31

3

- Tap or click the 'New (blank) record' button to move to a position to enter a new record (Figure 1–32).

Figure 1–32

4

- Add the records shown in Figure 1–29 using the same techniques you used to add the first two records (Figure 1–33).

Figure 1–33

Other Ways

1. Tap or click New button (HOME tab | Records group) 2. Press CTRL+PLUS SIGN (+)

To Resize Columns in a Datasheet

Access assigns default column sizes, which do not always provide space to display all the data in the field. In some cases, the data might appear but the entire field name will not. You can correct this problem by **resizing** the column (changing its size) in the datasheet. In some instances, you may want to reduce the size of a column. *Why? Some fields, such as the State field, are short enough that they do not require all the space on the screen that is allotted to them.* Changing a column width changes the **layout**, or design, of a table. The following steps resize the columns in the Book Rep table and save the changes to the layout.

- Point to the right boundary of the field selector for the Book Rep Number (BR #) field (Figure 1–34) so that the pointer becomes a two-headed arrow.

Q&A
I am using touch and I cannot see the pointer. Is this a problem?

It is not a problem. Remember that if you are using your finger on a touch screen, you will not see the pointer.

Figure 1–34

- Double-tap or double-click the right boundary of the field selector to resize the field so that it best fits the data.

- Use the same technique to resize all the other fields to best fit the data.

- Save the changes to the layout by tapping or clicking the Save button on the Quick Access Toolbar (Figure 1–35).

Figure 1–35

- Tap or click the table's Close button (shown in Figure 1–33 on the previous page) to close the table.

Q&A
What if I closed the table without saving the layout changes?
You would be asked if you want to save the changes.

Other Ways

1. Press and hold or right-click field name, tap or click Field Width

What is the best method for distributing database objects?

The traditional method of distributing database objects such as tables, reports, and forms uses a printer to produce a hard copy. A **hard copy** or **printout** is information that exists on a physical medium such as paper. Hard copies can be useful for the following reasons:

- Some people prefer proofreading a hard copy of a document rather than viewing it on the screen to check for errors and readability.

- Hard copies can serve as a backup reference if your storage medium is lost or becomes corrupted and you need to recreate the document.

Instead of distributing a hard copy, users can distribute the document as an electronic image that mirrors the original document's appearance. The electronic image of the document can be emailed, posted on a website, or copied to a portable storage medium such as a USB flash drive. Two popular electronic image formats, sometimes called fixed formats, are PDF by Adobe Systems and XPS by Microsoft. In Access, you can create electronic image files through the EXTERNAL DATA tab on the ribbon. Electronic images of documents, such as PDF and XPS, can be useful for the following reasons:

- Users can view electronic images of documents without the software that created the original document (e.g., Access). Specifically, to view a PDF file, you use a program called Adobe Reader, which can be downloaded free from Adobe's website. Similarly, to view an XPS file, you use a program called XPS Viewer, which is included in the latest versions of Windows and Internet Explorer.

- Sending electronic documents saves paper and printer supplies. Society encourages users to contribute to **green computing,** which involves reducing the electricity consumed and environmental waste generated when using computers, mobile devices, and related technologies.

Previewing and Printing the Contents of a Table

When working with a database, you often will need to print a copy of the table contents. Figure 1–36 shows a printed copy of the contents of the Book Rep table. (Yours may look slightly different, depending on your printer.) Because the Book Rep table is substantially wider than the screen, it also will be wider than the normal printed page in portrait orientation. **Portrait orientation** means the printout is across the width of the page. **Landscape orientation** means the printout is across the height of the page. To print the wide database table, you might prefer to use landscape orientation. A convenient way to change to landscape orientation is to preview what the printed copy will look like by using Print Preview. This allows you to determine whether landscape orientation is necessary and, if it is, to change the orientation easily to landscape. In addition, you also can use Print Preview to determine whether any adjustments are necessary to the page margins.

BTW

Changing Printers
To change the default printer that appears in the Print dialog box, tap or click FILE on the ribbon, tap or click the Print tab in the Backstage view, tap or click Print in the Print gallery, then tap or click the Name arrow and select the desired printer.

Book Rep 9/15/2014

BR #	Last Name	First Name	Street	City	State	Postal Code	Start Date	Salary	Bonus Rate
42	Perez	Melina	261 Porter Dr.	Adelphia	PA	19156	5/14/2012	$31,500.00	0.20
48	Statnik	Michael	3135 Simpson Dr.	Pleasantburg	NJ	07025	1/15/2013	$29,000.00	0.20
53	Chin	Robert	265 Maxwell St.	Gossett	PA	19157	6/1/2013	$26,250.00	0.19
65	Rogers	Tracy	1827 Maple Ave.	Adelphia	PA	19159	7/1/2014	$7,750.00	0.18

Figure 1–36

To Preview and Print the Contents of a Table

The following steps use Print Preview to preview and then print the contents of the Book Rep table. *Why? By previewing the contents of the table in Print Preview, you can make any necessary adjustments to the orientation or to the margins before printing the contents.*

- If the Navigation Pane is closed, open the Navigation Pane by tapping or clicking the Shutter Bar Open/Close Button.

- Be sure the Book Rep table is selected.

Q&A Why do I have to be sure the Book Rep table is selected? It is the only object in the database. When the database contains only one object, you do not have to worry about selecting the object. Ensuring that the correct object is selected is a good habit to form, however, to make sure that the object you print is the one you want.

Figure 1–37

- Tap or click FILE on the ribbon to open the Backstage view.

- Tap or click the Print tab in the Backstage view to display the Print gallery (Figure 1–37).

- Tap or click the Print Preview button in the Print gallery to display a preview of what the table will look like when printed (Figure 1–38).

Q&A I cannot read the table. Can I magnify a portion of the table?
Yes. Point the pointer, whose shape will change to a magnifying glass, at the portion of the table that you want to magnify, and then tap or click. You can return to the original view of the table by tapping or clicking a second time.

Figure 1–38

3

- Tap or click the pointer in the position shown in Figure 1–38 to magnify the upper-right section of the table (Figure 1–39).

Q&A My table was already magnified in a different area. How can I see the area shown in the figure? One way is to use the scroll bars to move to the desired portion of the table. You also can tap or click the pointer anywhere in the table to produce a screen like the one shown in Figure 1–38, and then tap or click in the location shown in the figure.

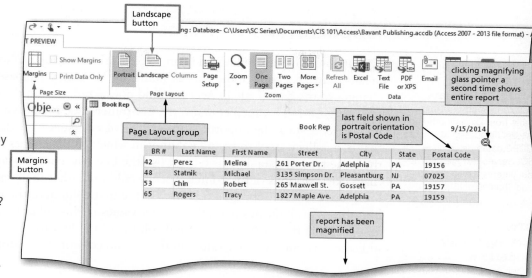

Figure 1–39

4

- Tap or click the Landscape button (PRINT PREVIEW tab | Page Layout group) to change to landscape orientation.

- Tap or click the Margins button (PRINT PREVIEW tab | Page Size group) and then click Normal if necessary to display all the fields (Figure 1–40).

 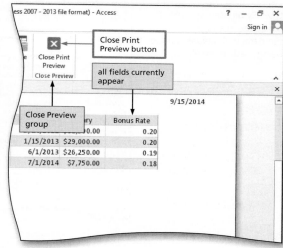

Figure 1–40

5

- Tap or click the Print button (PRINT PREVIEW tab | Print group) to display the Print dialog box.

- Tap or click the OK button (Print dialog box) to print the table.

- When the printer stops, retrieve the hard copy of the Book Rep table.

- Tap or click the Close Print Preview button (PRINT PREVIEW tab | Close Preview group) to close the Print Preview window.

Q&A Do I have to select Print Preview before printing the table?
No. If you wish to print without previewing, you would select either Print or Quick Print rather than Print Preview.

Other Ways

1. Press CTRL+P, tap or click OK button in Print dialog box

Importing or Linking Data from Other Applications to Access

If your data for a table is stored in an Excel worksheet, you can **import** the data, which means to make a copy of the data as a table in the Access database. In this case, any changes to the data made in Access would not be reflected in the Excel worksheet.

Figure 1–41, which contains the Customer data, is an example of the type of worksheet that can be imported. In this type of worksheet, the data is stored as a **list**, that is, a collection of rows and columns in which all the entries in a column represent the same type of data. In this type of list, the first row contains **column headings**, that is, descriptions of the contents of the column, rather than data. In the worksheet in Figure 1–41, for example, the entry in the first column of the first row is Customer Number. This indicates that all the other values in this column are customer numbers. The fact that the entry in the second column of the first row is Customer Name indicates that all the other values in the second column are customer names.

Figure 1–41

Does it matter how the data in the Excel workbook is formatted? If so, how can you be sure the Excel data is formatted in such a way you can import it?
The format of data in an Excel workbook is important when you want to import it into Access. To ensure the data is in an appropriate format:

1. Make sure the data is in the form of a list, a collection of rows and columns in which all the entries in a column represent the same type of data.

2. Make sure there are no blank rows within the list. If there are, remove them prior to importing or linking.

3. Make sure there are no blank columns within the list. If there are, remove them prior to importing or linking.

4. Determine whether the first row contains column headings that will make appropriate field names in the resulting table. If not, you might consider adding such a row. In general, the process is simpler if the first row in the worksheet contains appropriate column headings.

The Import process will create a table. In this table, the column headings in the first row of the worksheet become the field names. The rows of the worksheet, other than the first row, become the records in the table. In the process, each field will be assigned the data type that seems the most reasonable, given the data currently in the worksheet. When the Import process is finished, you can use Datasheet or Design view to modify these data types or to make any other changes to the structure you feel are necessary.

To Import an Excel Worksheet

1 CREATE FIRST TABLE | 2 ADD RECORDS | 3 PRINT CONTENTS | 4 IMPORT RECORDS | 5 MODIFY SECOND TABLE
6 CREATE QUERY | 7 CREATE FORM | 8 CREATE REPORT

You import a worksheet by using the Import Spreadsheet Wizard. In the process, you will indicate that the first row in the worksheet contains the column headings. *Why? You are indicating that Access is to use those column headings as the field names in the Access table.* In addition, you will indicate the primary key for the table. As part of the process, you could, if appropriate, choose not to include all the fields from the worksheet in the resulting table.

The following steps import the Customer worksheet.

1

- Tap or click EXTERNAL DATA on the ribbon to display the EXTERNAL DATA tab (Figure 1–42).

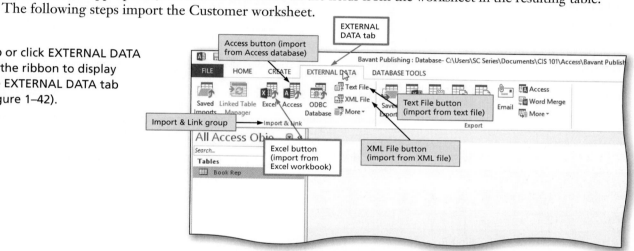

Figure 1–42

2

- Tap or click the Excel button (EXTERNAL DATA tab | Import & Link group) to display the Get External Data - Excel Spreadsheet dialog box.

- Tap or click the Browse button in the Get External Data - Excel Spreadsheet dialog box.

- Navigate to the location containing the workbook (for example, the Access folder in the CIS 101 folder). For a detailed example of this procedure, refer to Steps 4a – 4b in the To Save a File in a Folder section in the Office and Windows chapter at the beginning of this book.

- Tap or click the Customer Data workbook, and then tap or click the Open button to select the workbook (Figure 1–43).

Figure 1–43

3

- With the option button to import the data to a new table selected, tap or click the OK button to display the Import Spreadsheet Wizard dialog box (Figure 1–44).

Q&A What happens if I select the option button to append records to an existing table?

Instead of the records being placed in a new table, they will be added to an existing table that you specify, provided the value in the primary key field does not duplicate that on an existing record.

Figure 1–44

4

- If necessary, tap or click First Row Contains Column Headings to select it.

- Tap or click the Next button (Figure 1–45).

Q&A When would I use the Field Options on the Import Spreadsheet Wizard?

You would use these options if you wanted to change properties for one or more fields. You can change the name, the data type, and whether the field is indexed. You also can indicate that some fields should not be imported.

Figure 1–45

5

- Because the Field Options need not be specified, tap or click the Next button (Figure 1–46).

Figure 1–46

6

- Tap or click the 'Choose my own primary key' option button (Figure 1–47).

Q&A

How do I decide which option button to select?

If one of the fields is an appropriate primary key, choose your own primary key from the list of fields. If you are sure you do not want a primary key, choose No primary key. Otherwise, let Access add the primary key.

Figure 1–47

7

- Because the Customer Number field, which is the correct field, is already selected as the primary key, tap or click the Next button.

- Use the DELETE or BACKSPACE keys as necessary to erase the current entry, and then type Customer in the Import to Table text box.

- Tap or click the Finish button to import the data (Figure 1–48).

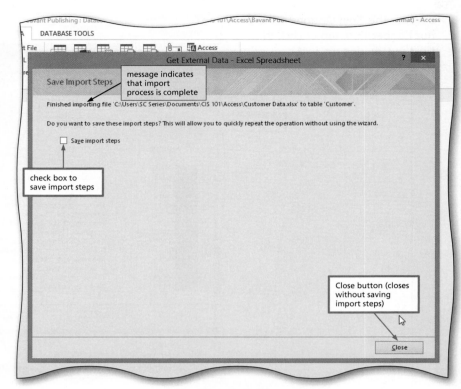

Figure 1–48

8

- Tap or click the 'Save import steps' check box to display the Save import steps options.

- If necessary, type Import-Customer Data in the Save as text box.

- Type Import data from Customer Data workbook into Customer table in the Description text box (Figure 1–49).

Q&A When would I create an Outlook task?

If the import operation is one you will repeat on a regular basis, you can create and schedule the import process just as you can schedule any other Outlook task.

Figure 1–49

9

- Tap or click the Save Import button to save the import steps (Figure 1–50).

Q&A I saved the table as Customer Data. How can I change the name?

Press and hold or right-click the table name in the Navigation Pane. Click Rename on the shortcut menu and change the table name to Customer.

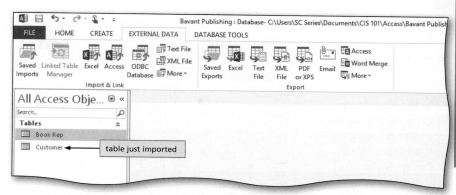

Figure 1–50

Modifying the Table

The import process has created the Customer table. The table has the correct fields and records. There are some details the process cannot handle, however. These include field sizes, descriptions, and captions. You will use Design view to make the necessary changes. The information you need is shown in Table 1–5.

BTW

Creating a Table in Design View

To create a table in Design view, display the CREATE tab, and then tap or click the Table Design button (CREATE tab | Tables group). You will then see the same screen as in Figure 1–51 on the following page, except that there will be no entries. Make all the necessary entries for the fields in your table, save the table, and assign the table a name.

Table 1–5 Structure of Customer Table

Field Name	Data Type	Field Size	Notes
Customer Number	Short Text	5	Primary Key **Description:** Customer Number (three uppercase letters followed by 2-digit number) **Caption:** CU #
Customer Name	Short Text	30	
Street	Short Text	20	
City	Short Text	20	
State	Short Text	2	
Postal Code	Short Text	5	
Amount Paid	Currency		
Current Due	Currency		
Returns	Currency		
Book Rep Number	Short Text	2	**Description:** Book Rep Number (number of book rep for customer) **Caption:** BR #

© 2014 Cengage Learning

To Modify a Table in Design View

1 CREATE FIRST TABLE | 2 ADD RECORDS | 3 PRINT CONTENTS | 4 IMPORT RECORDS | 5 MODIFY SECOND TABLE
6 CREATE QUERY | 7 CREATE FORM | 8 CREATE REPORT

You will usually need to modify the design of a table created during the import process. *Why? Some properties of a table are not specified during the import process, such as descriptions, captions, and field sizes. You also might need to change a data type.* The steps on the next page make the necessary modifications to the design of the Customer table.

1

- Open the Navigation Pane, if necessary.

- Press and hold or right-click the Customer table in the Navigation Pane to display the shortcut menu, and then tap or click Design View on the shortcut menu to open the table in Design view (Figure 1–51).

Figure 1–51

2

- Tap or click the Description (Optional) box for the Customer Number field, and then type `Customer Number (three uppercase letters followed by 2-digit number)` as the description.

- With the Customer Number field selected, tap or click the Field Size box, erase the current field size, and type 5 as the new field size.

- Tap or click the Caption box, and type CU # as the caption (Figure 1–52).

Figure 1–52

3

- Make the other changes shown in Table 1–5 on the previous page. To select a field to be changed, tap or click the field's row selector. For most fields, you only need to change the field size. For the Book Rep Number field, you also need to change the description and caption.

- Tap or click the Save button on the Quick Access Toolbar to save your changes.

- Because you know the data will satisfy the new field sizes, click the Yes button when given a message about the possibility of data loss.

Other Ways

1. Press F6 to move between upper and lower panes in Table Design window

Correcting Errors in the Structure

Whenever you create or modify a table in Design view, you should check the entries carefully to ensure they are correct. If you make a mistake and discover it before you press the TAB key, you can correct the error by repeatedly pressing the BACKSPACE key until the incorrect characters are removed. Then, type the correct characters. If you do not discover a mistake until later, you can tap or click the entry, type the correct value, and then press the ENTER key. You can use the following techniques to make changes to the structure:

- If you accidentally add an extra field to the structure, select the field by tapping or clicking the row selector (the leftmost column on the row that contains the field to be deleted). Once you have selected the field, press the DELETE key. This will remove the field from the structure.

- If you forget to include a field, select the field that will follow the one you want to add by tapping or clicking the row selector, and then press the INSERT key. The remaining fields move down one row, making room for the missing field. Make the entries for the new field in the usual manner.

- If you made the wrong field a primary key field, tap or click the correct primary key entry for the field and then tap or click the Primary Key button (TABLE TOOLS DESIGN tab | Tools group).

- To move a field, tap or click the row selector for the field to be moved to select the field, and then drag the field to the desired position.

As an alternative to these steps, you may want to start over. To do so, tap or click the Close button for the window containing the table, and then tap or click the No button in the Microsoft Access dialog box. You then can repeat the process you used earlier to define the fields in the table.

> **BTW**
>
> **Importing Data to an Existing Table**
> When you create a new table in Design view, you can import data from other sources into the table using the EXTERNAL DATA tab.

To Close the Table

Now that you have completed and saved the Customer table, you can close it. The following step closes the table.

1 Tap or click the Close button for the Customer table (see Figure 1–52) to close the table.

To Resize Columns in a Datasheet

You can resize the columns in the datasheet for the Customer table just as you resized the columns in the datasheet for the Book Rep table. The following steps resize the columns in the Customer table to best fit the data.

1 Open the Customer table in Datasheet view.

2 Double-tap or double-click the right boundary of the field selectors of each of the fields to resize the columns so that they best fit the data.

3 Save the changes to the layout by tapping or clicking the Save button on the Quick Access Toolbar.

4 Close the table.

> **BTW**
>
> **Resizing Columns**
> To resize all columns in a datasheet to best fit simultaneously, select the column heading for the first column, hold down the SHIFT key and select the last column in the datasheet. Then, double-tap or double-click the right boundary of any field selector.

Break Point: If you wish to take a break, this is a good place to do so. You can exit Access now. To resume at a later time, run Access, open the database called Bavant Publishing, and continue following the steps from this location forward.

Additional Database Objects

BTW

Tabbed Documents Versus Overlapping Windows

By default, Access 2013 displays database objects in tabbed documents instead of in overlapping windows. If your database is in overlapping windows mode, tap or click FILE on the ribbon, tap or click Options in the Backstage view, tap or click Current Database in the Access Options dialog box, and select the Display Document Tabs check box and the Tabbed Documents option button.

A database contains many types of objects. Tables are the objects you use to store and manipulate data. Access supports other important types of objects as well; each object has a specific purpose that helps maximize the benefits of a database. Through queries (questions), Access makes it possible to ask complex questions concerning the data in the database and then receive instant answers. Access also allows the user to produce attractive and useful forms for viewing and updating data. Additionally, Access includes report creation tools that make it easy to produce sophisticated reports for presenting data.

Creating Queries

Queries are simply questions, the answers to which are in the database. Access contains a powerful query feature that helps you find the answers to a wide variety of questions. Once you have examined the question you want to ask to determine the fields involved in the question, you can begin creating the query. If the query involves no special sort order, restrictions, or calculations, you can use the Simple Query Wizard.

To Use the Simple Query Wizard to Create a Query

1 CREATE FIRST TABLE | 2 ADD RECORDS | 3 PRINT CONTENTS | 4 IMPORT RECORDS | 5 MODIFY SECOND TABLE
6 CREATE QUERY | 7 CREATE FORM | 8 CREATE REPORT

The following steps use the Simple Query Wizard to create a query that Bavant Publishing might use to obtain financial information on its customers. *Why? The Simple Query Wizard is the quickest and easiest way to create a query.* This query displays the number, name, amount paid, current due, returns, and book rep number of all customers.

- If the Navigation Pane is closed, tap or click the Shutter Bar Open/Close Button to open the Navigation Pane.

- Be sure the Customer table is selected.

- Tap or click CREATE on the ribbon to display the CREATE tab.

- Tap or click the Query Wizard button (CREATE tab | Queries group) to display the New Query dialog box (Figure 1–53).

Figure 1–53

2

- Be sure Simple Query Wizard is selected, and then tap or click the OK button (New Query dialog box) to display the Simple Query Wizard dialog box (Figure 1–54).

Q&A
What would happen if the Book Rep table were selected instead of the Customer table?
The list of available fields would contain fields from the Book Rep table rather than the Customer table.

If the list contained Book Rep table fields, how could I make it contain Customer table fields?
Tap or click the arrow in the Tables / Queries box, and then tap or click the Customer table in the list that appears.

Figure 1–54

3

- With the Customer Number field selected, tap or click the Add Field button to add the field to the query.

- With the Customer Name field selected, tap or click the Add Field button a second time to add the field.

- Tap or click the Amount Paid field, and then tap or click the Add Field button to add the field.

- In a similar fashion, add the Current Due, Returns, and Book Rep Number fields (Figure 1–55).

Figure 1–55

4

- Tap or click the Next button to move to the next screen.

- Ensure that the Detail (shows every field of every record) option button is selected (Figure 1–56).

Q&A

What is the difference between Detail and Summary?
Detail shows all the records and fields. Summary only shows computations (for example, the total amount paid).

Figure 1–56

5

- Tap or click the Next button to move to the next screen.

- Confirm that the title of the query is Customer Query (Figure 1–57).

Q&A
What should I do if the title is incorrect?
Click the box containing the title to produce an insertion point. Erase the current title and then type Customer Query.

Figure 1–57

6

- Tap or click the Finish button to create the query (Figure 1–58).

7

- Tap or click the Close button for the Customer Query to remove the query results from the screen.

Q&A
If I want to use this query in the future, do I need to save the query?
Normally you would. The one exception is a query created by the wizard. The wizard automatically saves the query it creates.

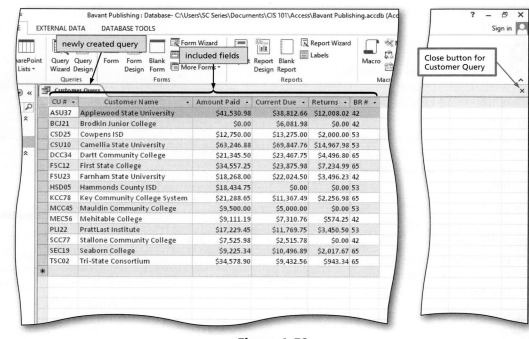

Figure 1–58

BTW

Access Help
At any time while using Access, you can find answers to questions and display information about various topics through Access Help. Used properly, this form of assistance can increase your productivity and reduce your frustrations by minimizing the time you spend learning how to use Access. For instruction about Access Help and exercises that will help you gain confidence in using it, read the Office and Windows chapter at the beginning of this book.

Using Queries

After you have created and saved a query, Access stores it as a database object and makes it available for use in a variety of ways:

- If you want to change the design of the query, press and hold or right-click the query in the Navigation Pane and then tap or click Design View on the shortcut menu to open the query in Design view.

- To view the results of the query from Design view, tap or click the Run button to instruct Access to **run** the query, that is, to perform the necessary actions to produce and display the results in Datasheet view.

- To view the results of the query from the Navigation Pane, open it by pressing and holding or right-clicking the query and tapping or clicking Open on the

shortcut menu. Access automatically runs the query and displays the results in Datasheet view.

- To print the results with the query open in either Design view or Datasheet view, tap or click FILE on the ribbon, tap or click the Print tab, and then tap or click either Print or Quick Print.

- To print the query without first opening it, be sure the query is selected in the Navigation Pane and tap or click FILE on the ribbon, tap or click the Print tab, and then tap or click either Print or Quick Print.

You can switch between views of a query using the View button (HOME tab | Views group). Tapping or clicking the arrow in the bottom of the button produces the View button menu. You then tap or click the desired view in the menu. The two query views you will use in this chapter are Datasheet view (which displays the query results) and Design view (for changing the query design). You also can tap or click the top part of the View button, in which case, you will switch to the view identified by the icon on the button. In the figure, the button contains the icon for Design view, so tapping or clicking the button would change to Design view. For the most part, the icon on the button represents the view you want, so you can usually simply tap or click the button.

BTW
Creating Queries
Although the Simple Query Wizard is a convenient way to create straightforward queries, you will find that many of the queries you create require more control than the wizard provides. In Chapter 2, you will use Design view to create customized queries.

To Use a Criterion in a Query

1 CREATE FIRST TABLE | 2 ADD RECORDS | 3 PRINT CONTENTS | 4 IMPORT RECORDS | 5 MODIFY SECOND TABLE
6 CREATE QUERY | 7 CREATE FORM | 8 CREATE REPORT

After you have determined the fields to be included in a query, you will determine whether you need to further restrict the results of the query. For example, you might want to include only those customers whose book rep number is 53. In such a case, you need to enter the number 53 as a criterion for the book rep field. *Why? A criterion is a condition that the records must satisfy in order to be included in the query results.* To do so, you will open the query in Design view, enter the criterion below the appropriate field, and then view the results of the query. The following steps enter a criterion to include only the customers of book rep 53 and then view the query results.

1

- Press and hold or right-click the Customer Query in the Navigation Pane to produce a shortcut menu (Figure 1–59).

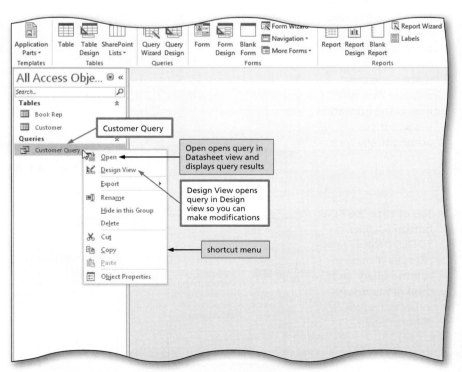

Figure 1–59

2

- Tap or click Design View on the shortcut menu to open the query in Design view (Figure 1–60).

Figure 1–60

3

- Tap or click the Criteria row in the Book Rep Number column of the grid, and then type 53 as the criterion (Figure 1–61).

Q&A
The Book Rep Number field is a text field. Do I need to enclose the value for a text field in quotation marks? You could, but it is not necessary, because Access inserts the quotation marks for you automatically.

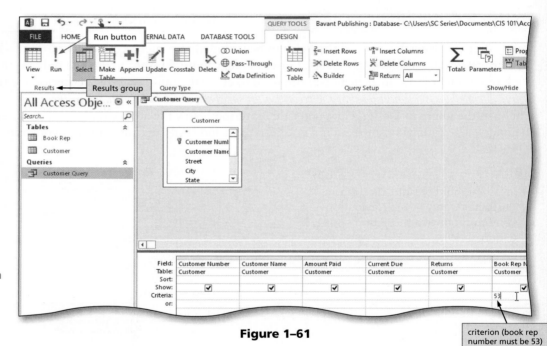

Figure 1–61

4

- Tap or click the Run button (QUERY TOOLS DESIGN tab | Results group) to run the query and display the results in Datasheet view (Figure 1–62).

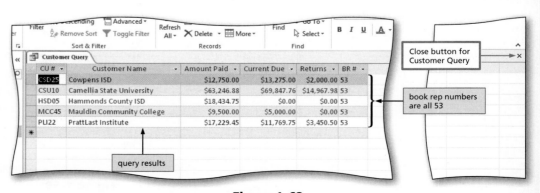

Figure 1–62

5

- Tap or click the Close button for the Customer Query to close the query.

- When asked if you want to save your changes, tap or click the No button.

Q&A

If I saved the query, what would happen the next time I ran the query?
You would see only customers of book rep 53.

Could I save a query with another name?
Yes. To save a query with a different name, tap or click FILE on the ribbon, tap or click the Save As tab, tap or click Save Object As, tap or click the Save As button, enter a new file name in the Save As dialog box, and then tap or click the OK button (Save As dialog box).

Other Ways

1. Tap or click View button (QUERY TOOLS DESIGN tab | Results group) 2. Tap or click Datasheet View button on status bar

To Print the Results of a Query

The following steps print the results of a saved query.

1 With the Customer Query selected in the Navigation Pane, tap or click FILE on the ribbon to open the Backstage view.

2 Tap or click the Print tab in the Backstage view to display the Print gallery.

3 Tap or click the Quick Print button to print the query.

Creating and Using Forms

In Datasheet view, you can view many records at once. If there are many fields, however, only some of the fields in each record might be visible at a time. In **Form view**, where data is displayed in a form on the screen, you usually can see all the fields, but only for one record.

To Create a Form

1 CREATE FIRST TABLE | 2 ADD RECORDS | 3 PRINT CONTENTS | 4 IMPORT RECORDS | 5 MODIFY SECOND TABLE
6 CREATE QUERY | **7 CREATE FORM** | **8 CREATE REPORT**

Like a paper form, a **form** in a database is a formatted document with fields that contain data. Forms allow you to view and maintain data. Forms also can be used to print data, but reports are more commonly used for that purpose. The simplest type of form in Access is one that includes all the fields in a table stacked one above the other. The following steps use the Form button to create a form. **Why?** *Using the Form button is the simplest way to create this type of form.* The steps then use the form to view records and then save the form.

1

- Select the Customer table in the Navigation Pane.

- If necessary, tap or click CREATE on the ribbon to display the CREATE tab (Figure 1–63).

Figure 1–63

2

• Tap or click the Form button (CREATE tab | Forms group) to create a simple form (Figure 1–64).

Q&A A Field list appeared on my screen. What should I do?
Tap or click the Add Existing Fields button (FORM LAYOUT TOOLS DESIGN tab | Tools group) to remove the Field list from the screen.

Figure 1–64

3

• Tap or click the Form View button on the Access status bar to display the form in Form view rather than Layout view.

Q&A What is the difference between Layout view and Form view?
Layout view allows you to make changes to the look of the form. Form view is the view you use to examine or make changes to the data.

How can I tell when I am in Layout view?
Access identifies Layout view in three ways. The left side of the status bar will contain the words Layout View; shading will appear around the outside of the selected field in the form; and the Layout View button will be selected on the right side of the status bar.

• Tap or click the Next record button three times to move to record 4 (Figure 1–65).

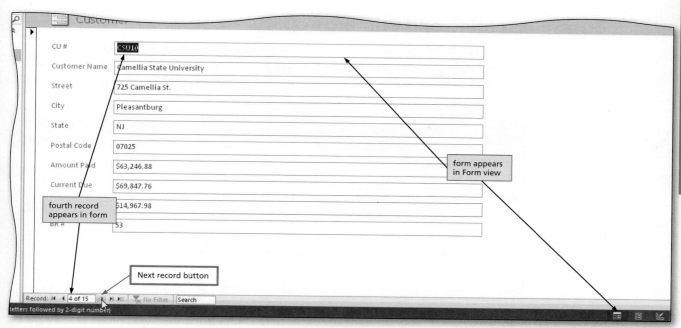

CU # **CSU10**

Customer Name Camellia State University

Street 725 Camellia St.

City Pleasantburg

State NJ

Postal Code 07025

Amount Paid $63,246.88

Current Due $69,847.76

form appears in Form view

fourth record appears in form $14,967.98

BR # 53

Next record button

Record: 14 4 4 of 15 ▶ ▶ No Filter Search

letters followed by 2-digit number)

Figure 1–65

④

• Tap or click the Save button on the Quick Access Toolbar to display the Save As dialog box (Figure 1–66).

Q&A Do I have to tap or click the Next record button before saving?
No. The only reason you were asked to tap or click the button was so that you could experience navigation within the form.

⑤

• Type Customer Form as the form name, and then tap or click the OK button to save the form.

• Tap or click the Close button for the form to close the form.

Save button

Save As dialog box

position to enter form name

OK button

Figure 1–66

Other Ways

1. Tap or click View button (FORM LAYOUT TOOLS DESIGN tab | Views group)

Using a Form

After you have saved a form, you can use it at any time by pressing and holding or right-clicking the form in the Navigation Pane and then tapping or clicking Open on the shortcut menu. In addition to viewing data in the form, you also can use it to enter or update data, a process that is very similar to updating data using a datasheet. If you plan to use the form to enter or revise data, you must ensure you are viewing the form in Form view.

Break Point: If you wish to take a break, this is a good place to do so. You can exit Access now. To resume at a later time, run Access, open the database called Bavant Publishing, and continue following the steps from this location forward.

Creating and Printing Reports

Bavant Publishing wants to create the Customer Financial Report shown in Figure 1–67. To create this report, you will first create a simple report containing all records. Then, you will modify the report to match the one shown in Figure 1–67.

Customer Financial Report						Monday, September 15, 2014
						2:23:09 PM
Customer Number	Customer Name	Amount Paid	Current Due	Returns	Book Rep Number	
ASU37	Applewood State University	$41,530.98	$38,812.66	$12,008.02	42	
BCJ21	Brodkin Junior College	$0.00	$6,081.98	$0.00	42	
CSD25	Cowpens ISD	$12,750.00	$13,275.00	$2,000.00	53	
CSU10	Camellia State University	$63,246.88	$69,847.76	$14,967.98	53	
DCC34	Dartt Community College	$21,345.50	$23,467.75	$4,496.80	65	
FSC12	First State College	$34,557.25	$23,875.98	$7,234.99	65	
FSU23	Farnham State University	$18,268.00	$22,024.50	$3,496.23	42	
HSD05	Hammonds County ISD	$18,434.75	$0.00	$0.00	53	
KCC78	Key Community College System	$21,288.65	$11,367.49	$2,256.98	65	
MCC45	Mauldin Community College	$9,500.00	$5,000.00	$0.00	53	
MEC56	Mehitable College	$9,111.19	$7,310.76	$574.25	42	
PLI22	PrattLast Institute	$17,229.45	$11,769.75	$3,450.50	53	
SCC77	Stallone Community College	$7,525.98	$2,515.78	$0.00	42	
SEC19	Seaborn College	$9,225.34	$10,496.89	$2,017.67	65	
TSC02	Tri-State Consortium	$34,578.90	$9,432.56	$943.34	65	
		$318,592.87	$255,278.86	$53,446.76		

Figure 1–67

To Create a Report

1 CREATE FIRST TABLE | 2 ADD RECORDS | 3 PRINT CONTENTS | 4 IMPORT RECORDS | 5 MODIFY SECOND TABLE
6 CREATE QUERY | 7 CREATE FORM | **8 CREATE REPORT**

You will first create a report containing all fields. *Why? It is easiest to create a report with all the fields and then delete the fields you do not want.* The following steps create and save the initial report. They also modify the report title.

- Be sure the Customer table is selected in the Navigation Pane.

- Tap or click CREATE on the ribbon to display the CREATE tab (Figure 1–68).

Q&A

Do I need to select the Customer table prior to tapping or clicking CREATE on the ribbon?
You do not need to select the table at that point. You do need to select a table prior to tapping or clicking the Report button, because Access will include all the fields in whichever table or query is currently selected.

Figure 1–68

2

- Tap or click the Report button (CREATE tab | Reports group) to create the report (Figure 1–69).

Q&A Why is the report title Customer? Access automatically assigns the name of the table or query as the title of the report. It also automatically includes the date. You can change either of these later.

Figure 1–69

3

- Tap or click the Save button on the Quick Access Toolbar to display the Save As dialog box, and then type Customer Financial Report as the name of the report (Figure 1–70).

Figure 1–70

4

- Tap or click the OK button (Save As dialog box) to save the report (Figure 1–71).

Q&A The name of the report changed. Why did the report title not change? The report title is assigned the same name as the report by default. Changing the name of the report does not

Figure 1–71

change the report title. You can change the title at any time to anything you like.

- Close the report by tapping or clicking its Close button.

Using Layout View in a Report

Access has four different ways to view reports: Report view, Print Preview, Layout view, and Design view. Report view shows the report on the screen. Print Preview shows the report as it will appear when printed. Layout view is similar to Report view in that it shows the report on the screen, but also allows you to make changes to the report. Layout view is usually the easiest way to make such changes. Design view also allows you to make changes, but does not show you the actual report. Design view is most useful when the changes you need to make are especially complex. In this chapter, you will use Layout view to modify the report.

To Modify Report Column Headings and Resize Columns

1 CREATE FIRST TABLE | 2 ADD RECORDS | 3 PRINT CONTENTS | 4 IMPORT RECORDS | 5 MODIFY SECOND TABLE
6 CREATE QUERY | 7 CREATE FORM | **8 CREATE REPORT**

To make the report match the one shown in Figure 1–67 on page AC 48, you need to change the title, remove some columns, modify the column headings, and also resize the columns. The following steps use Layout view to make the necessary modifications to the report. *Why? Working in Layout view gives you all the tools you need to make the desired modifications. You can view the results of the modifications immediately.*

- Press and hold or right-click Customer Financial Report in the Navigation Pane, and then tap or click Layout View on the shortcut menu to open the report in Layout view.

- If a Field list appears, tap or click the Add Existing Fields button (REPORT LAYOUT TOOLS DESIGN tab | Tools group) to remove the Field list from the screen.

- Close the Navigation Pane.

- Tap or click the report title once to select it.

- Tap or click the report title a second time to produce an insertion point (Figure 1–72).

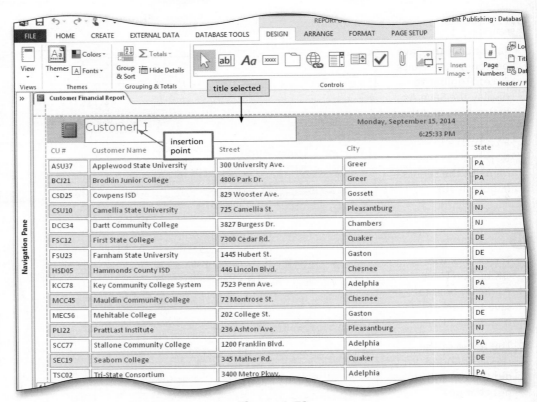

Figure 1–72

Q&A

My insertion point is in the middle of Customer. How do I produce an insertion point at the position shown in the figure?

You can use the RIGHT ARROW key to move the insertion point to the position in the figure, or you can tap or click the desired position.

2

- Press the SPACEBAR to insert a space, and then type `Financial Report` to complete the title.

- Tap or click the column heading for the Street field to select it.

- Hold the SHIFT key down and then tap or click the column headings for the City, State, and Postal Code fields to select multiple column headings.

Figure 1–73

Q&A What happens if I do not hold down the SHIFT key?

When you tap or click another column heading, it will be the only one that is selected. To select multiple objects, you need to hold the SHIFT key down for every object after the first selection.

I selected the wrong collection of objects. What should I do?

You can tap or click somewhere else on the report so that the objects you want are not selected, and then begin the process again. Alternatively, you can repeatedly tap or click the Undo button on the Quick Access Toolbar to undo your selections. Once you have done so, you can select the objects you want.

- Tap or click ARRANGE on the ribbon to display the REPORT LAYOUT TOOLS ARRANGE tab (Figure 1–73).

3

- Tap or click the Select Column button (REPORT LAYOUT TOOLS ARRANGE tab | Rows & Columns group) to select the entire columns corresponding to the column headings you selected in the previous step.

- Press the DELETE key to delete the selected columns.

- Tap or click the column heading for the Customer Number field twice, once to select it and the second time to produce an insertion point (Figure 1–74).

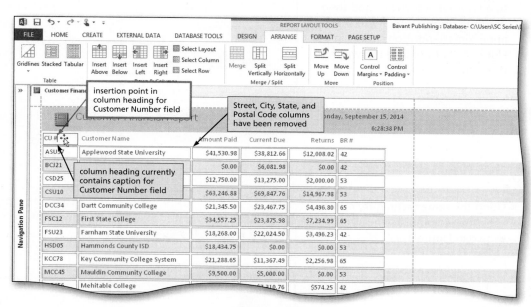

Figure 1–74

Q&A I selected the wrong field. What should I do?

Tap or click somewhere outside the various fields to deselect the one you have selected. Then, tap or click the Customer Number field twice.

- Use the DELETE or BACKSPACE keys as necessary to erase the current entry, and then type `Customer Number` as the new entry.

- Tap or click the heading for the Book Rep Number field twice, erase the current entry, and then type `Book Rep Number` as the new entry.

- Tap or click the Customer Number field heading to select it, point to the lower boundary of the heading for the Customer Number field so that the pointer changes to a two-headed arrow, and then drag the lower boundary to the approximate position shown in Figure 1–75 to expand the column headings.

Figure 1–75

Q&A I did something wrong when I dragged and now my report looks strange. What should I do?
Tap or click the Undo button on the Quick Access Toolbar to undo the change. Depending on the specific action you took, you may need to tap or click it more than once.

My screen displays Book Rep Number on one line not two. Is this a problem?
No. You will adjust the column heading in a later step.

- Point to the right boundary of the heading for the Customer Number field so that the pointer changes to a two-headed arrow, and then drag the right boundary to the approximate position shown in Figure 1–76 to reduce the width of the column.

Figure 1–76

- Using the same technique, resize the other columns to the sizes shown in Figure 1–77.

Figure 1–77

To Add Totals to a Report

The report in Figure 1–67 contains totals for the Amount Paid, Current Due, and Returns columns. You can use Layout view to add these totals. The following steps use Layout view to include totals for these three columns. *Why? In Layout view you can tap or click a single button to add totals. This button sums all the values in the field.*

1

- Tap or click the Amount Paid field heading (shown in Figure 1–77) to select the field.

Q&A Do I have to tap or click the heading? Could I tap or click the field on one of the records?
You do not have to tap or click the heading. You also could tap or click the Amount Paid field on any record.

- Tap or click DESIGN on the ribbon to display the DESIGN tab.

- Tap or click the Totals button (REPORT LAYOUT TOOLS DESIGN tab | Grouping & Totals group) to display the Totals menu containing a list of available calculations (Figure 1–78).

Figure 1–78

2

- Tap or click Sum to calculate the sum of the amount of paid values.

- Using the same technique, add totals for the Current Due and Returns columns.

Q&A When I clicked the Totals button after selecting the Returns field heading, Sum was already checked. Do I still need to tap or click Sum?
No. In fact, if you do tap or click it, you will remove the check mark, which will remove the total from the column.

Figure 1–79

- Scroll down to the bottom of the report to verify that the totals are included. If necessary, expand the size of the total controls so they appear completely by dragging the lower boundary of the controls to the approximate position shown in Figure 1–79.

- Tap or click the page number to select it, and then drag it to the approximate position shown in Figure 1–79.

Q&A Why did I need to move the page number?
The dotted line near the right-hand edge of the screen indicates the right-hand border of the available space on the printed page, based on whatever margins and orientation are currently selected. A portion of the page number extends beyond this border. By moving the page number, it no longer extends beyond the border.

3

- Tap or click the Save button on the Quick Access Toolbar to save your changes to the report layout.

- Close the report.

To Print a Report

The following steps print the report.

1 Open the Navigation Pane if necessary, confirm that the Customer Financial Report is selected, and then tap or click FILE on the ribbon to open the Backstage view.

2 Tap or click the Print tab in the Backstage view to display the Print gallery.

3 Tap or click the Quick Print button to print the report.

Q&A When I print the report, I have pound signs (####) rather than numbers where the totals should be for the Amount Paid and Current Due columns. The report looked fine on the screen. How can I correct it?
The columns are not wide enough to display the complete number. Open the report in Layout view and slightly increase the width of the Amount Paid and Current Due columns by dragging the right boundary of the column headings.

How can I print multiple copies of my report?
Tap or click FILE on the ribbon to open the Backstage view. Tap or click the Print tab, tap or click Print in the Print gallery to display the Print dialog box, increase the number in the Number of Copies box, and then tap or click the OK button (Print dialog box).

How can I print a range of pages rather than printing the whole report?
Tap or click FILE on the ribbon to open the Backstage view. Tap or click the Print tab, tap or click Print in the Print gallery to display the Print dialog box, tap or click the Pages option button in the Print Range area, enter the desired page range, and then tap or click the OK button (Print dialog box).

BTW

Exporting a Report as a PDF or XPS File
To export a report as a PDF or XPS file, display the EXTERNAL DATA tab, and then tap or click the PDF or XPS button (EXTERNAL DATA tab | Export group). Enter the appropriate information in the Publish to PDF or XPS dialog box and tap or click the Publish button.

BTW

Report Navigation
When previewing a report, you can use the Navigation buttons on the status bar to move from one page to another.

Database Properties

Access helps you organize and identify your databases by using **database properties,** which are the details about a file. Database properties, also known as **metadata,** can include such information as the project author, title, or subject. **Keywords** are words or phrases that further describe the database. For example, a class name or database topic can describe the file's purpose or content.

Five different types of database properties exist, but the more common ones used in this book are standard and automatically updated properties. **Standard properties** are associated with all Microsoft Office documents and include author, title, and subject. **Automatically updated properties** include file system properties, such as the date you create or change a file, and statistics, such as the file size.

CONSIDER THIS

Why would you want to assign database properties to a database?
Database properties are valuable for a variety of reasons:

- Users can save time locating a particular file because they can view a file's database properties without opening the database.

- By creating consistent properties for files having similar content, users can better organize their databases.

- Some organizations require Access users to add database properties so that other employees can view details about these files.

TO CHANGE DATABASE PROPERTIES

To change database properties, you would follow these steps.

1. Tap or click FILE on the ribbon to open the Backstage view and then, if necessary, tap or click the Info tab in the Backstage view to display the Info gallery.

2. Click the 'View and edit database properties' link in the right pane of the Info gallery to display the Bavant Publishing Properties dialog box.

Q&A Why are some of the database properties already filled in?
The person who installed Office 2013 on your computer or network might have set or customized the properties.

3. If the property you want to change is displayed in the Properties dialog box, click the text box for the property and make the desired change. Skip the remaining steps.

4. If the property you want to change is not displayed in the Properties dialog box, click the appropriate tab so the property is displayed and then make the desired change.

5. Click the OK button in the Properties dialog box to save your changes and remove the dialog box from the screen.

To Sign Out of a Microsoft Account

If you are signed in to a Microsoft account and are using a public computer or otherwise wish to sign out of your Microsoft account, you should sign out of the account from the Account gallery in the Backstage view before exiting Access. Signing out of the account is the safest way to make sure that nobody else can access SkyDrive files or settings stored in your Microsoft account. The following steps sign out of a Microsoft account from Access. For a detailed example of the procedure summarized below, refer to the Office and Windows chapter at the beginning of this book.

① If you wish to sign out of your Microsoft account, tap or click FILE on the ribbon to open the Backstage view and then tap or click the Account tab to display the Account gallery.

② Tap or click the Sign out link, which displays the Remove Account dialog box. If a Can't remove Windows accounts dialog box appears instead of the Remove Account dialog box, click the OK button and skip the remaining steps.

Q&A Why does a Can't remove Windows accounts dialog box appear?
If you signed in to Windows using your Microsoft account, then you also must sign out from Windows, rather than signing out from within Access. When you are finished using Windows, be sure to sign out at that time.

③ Tap or click the Yes button (Remove Account dialog box) to sign out of your Microsoft account on this computer.

Q&A Should I sign out of Windows after signing out of my Microsoft account? [End Q]
When you are finished using the computer, you should sign out of your account for maximum security.

④ Tap or click the Back button in the upper-left corner of the Backstage view to return to the database.

To Exit Access

The following steps exit Access.

1 Tap or click the Close button on the right side of the title bar to close the open database, if there is one, and exit Access.

2 If a Microsoft Access dialog box appears, tap or click the Save button to save any changes made to the database since the last save.

Special Database Operations

Additional operations involved in maintaining a database are backup, recovery, compacting, and repairing.

Backup and Recovery

It is possible to damage or destroy a database. Users can enter data that is incorrect; programs that are updating the database can end abnormally during an update; a hardware problem can occur; and so on. After any such event has occurred, the database may contain invalid data or it might be totally destroyed.

Obviously, you cannot allow a situation in which data has been damaged or destroyed to go uncorrected. You must somehow return the database to a correct state. This process is called recovery; that is, you **recover** the database.

The simplest approach to recovery involves periodically making a copy of the database (called a **backup copy** or a **save copy**). This is referred to as **backing up** the database. If a problem occurs, you correct the problem by overwriting the actual database — often referred to as the **live database** — with the backup copy.

To back up the database that is currently open, you use the Back Up Database command on the Save As tab in the Backstage view. In the process, Access suggests a name that is a combination of the database name and the current date. For example, if you back up the Bavant Publishing database on October 20, 2014, Access will suggest the name, Bavant Publishing_2014-10-20. You can change this name if you desire, although it is a good idea to use this name. By doing so, it will be easy to distinguish between all the backup copies you have made to determine which is the most recent. In addition, if you discover that a critical problem occurred on October 18, 2014, you may want to go back to the most recent backup before October 18. If, for example, the database was not backed up on October 17 but was backed up on October 16, you would use Bavant Publishing_2014-10-16.

To Back Up a Database

You would use the following steps to back up a database to a file on a hard disk or high-capacity removable disk.

1. Open the database to be backed up.
2. Tap or click FILE on the ribbon to open the Backstage view, and then tap or click the Save As tab.
3. With Save Database As selected in the File Types area, tap or click 'Back Up Database' in the Save Database As area, and then tap or click the Save As button.
4. Navigate to the desired location in the Save As box. If you do not want the name Access has suggested, enter the desired name in the File name text box.
5. Tap or click the Save button to back up the database.

Access creates a backup copy with the desired name in the desired location. Should you ever need to recover the database using this backup copy, you can simply copy it over the live version.

Compacting and Repairing a Database

As you add more data to a database, it naturally grows larger. When you delete an object (records, tables, forms, or queries), the space previously occupied by the object does not become available for additional objects. Instead, the additional objects are given new space; that is, space that was not already allocated. To remove this empty space from the database, you must **compact** the database. The same option that compacts the database also repairs problems that might have occurred in the database.

To Compact and Repair a Database

You would use the following steps to compact and repair a database.

1. Open the database to be compacted.
2. Tap or click FILE on the ribbon to open the Backstage view, and then, if necessary, select the Info tab.
3. Tap or click the Compact & Repair Database button in the Info gallery to compact and repair the database.

The database now is the compacted form of the original.

Additional Operations

Additional special operations include opening another database, closing a database without exiting Access, and saving a database with another name. They also include deleting a table (or other object) as well as renaming an object.

When you open another database, Access will automatically close the database that previously was open. Before deleting or renaming an object, you should ensure that the object has no dependent objects; that is, other objects that depend on the object you want to delete.

To Close a Database without Exiting Access

You would use the following steps to close a database without exiting Access.

1. Tap or click FILE on the ribbon to open the Backstage view.
2. Tap or click Close.

To Save a Database with Another Name

To save a database with another name, you would use the following steps.

1. Tap or click FILE on the ribbon to open the Backstage view, and then select the Save As tab.
2. With Save Database As selected in the Database File Types area and Access Database selected in the Save Database As area, tap or click the Save As button.
3. Enter a name and select a location for the new version.
4. Tap or click the Save button.

If you want to make a backup, could you just save the database with another name?
You could certainly do that. Using the backup procedure discussed earlier has the advantage that it automatically includes the current database name and the date in the name of the file it creates.

TO DELETE A TABLE OR OTHER OBJECT IN THE DATABASE

You would use the following steps to delete a database object.

1. Press and hold or right-click the object in the Navigation Pane.
2. Tap or click Delete on the shortcut menu.
3. Tap or click the Yes button in the Microsoft Access dialog box.

TO RENAME AN OBJECT IN THE DATABASE

You would use the following steps to rename a database object.

1. Press and hold or right-click the object in the Navigation Pane.
2. Tap or click Rename on the shortcut menu.
3. Type the new name and press the ENTER key.

Database Design

BTW
Database Design Language (DBDL)
Database Design Language (DBDL) is a commonly accepted shorthand representation for showing the structure of a relational database. You write the name of the table and then within parentheses you list all the columns in the table. If the columns continue beyond one line, indent the subsequent lines.

This section illustrates the **database design** process, that is, the process of determining the tables and fields that make up the database. It does so by showing how you would design the database for Bavant Publishing from a set of requirements. In this section, you will use commonly accepted shorthand to represent the tables and fields that make up the database as well as the primary keys for the tables. For each table, you give the name of the table followed by a set of parentheses. Within the parentheses is a list of the fields in the table separated by commas. You underline the primary key. For example,

Product (<u>Product Code</u>, Description, On Hand, Price) represents a table called Product. The Product table contains four fields: Product Code, Description, On Hand, and Price. The Product Code field is the primary key.

Database Requirements

BTW
Determining Database Requirements
The determination of database requirements is part of a process known as systems analysis. A systems analyst examines existing and proposed documents, and examines organizational policies to determine exactly the type of data needs the database must support.

The Bavant Publishing database must maintain information on both customers and book reps. The business currently keeps this data in two Word tables and two Excel workbooks, as shown in Figure 1–80. They use Word tables for address information and Excel workbooks for financial information.

- For customers, Bavant needs to maintain address data. It currently keeps this data in a Word table (Figure 1–80a).
- Bavant also maintains financial data for each customer. This includes the amount paid, current amount due, and return amount for the customer. It keeps these amounts, along with the customer name and number, in the Excel worksheet shown in Figure 1–80b.
- Bavant keeps book rep address data in a Word table, as shown in Figure 1–80c.
- Just as with customers, it keeps financial data for book reps, including their start date, salary, and bonus rate, in a separate Excel worksheet, as shown in Figure 1–80d.

Customer Number	Customer Name	Street	City	State	Postal Code
ASU37	Applewood State University	300 University Ave.	Greer	PA	19158
BCJ21	Brodkin Junior College	4806 Park Dr.	Greer	PA	19158
CSD25	Cowpens ISD	829 Wooster Ave.	Gossett	PA	19157
CSU10	Camellia State University	725 Camellia St.	Pleasantburg	NJ	07025
DCC34	Dartt Community College	3827 Burgess Dr.	Chambers	NJ	07037
FSC12	First State College	7300 Cedar Rd.	Quaker	DE	19719
FSU23	Farnham State University	1445 Hubert St.	Gaston	DE	19723
HSD05	Hammonds County ISD	446 Lincoln Blvd.	Chesnee	NJ	07053
KCC78	Key Community College System	7523 Penn Ave.	Adelphia	PA	19159
MCC45	Mauldin Community College	72 Montrose St.	Chesnee	NJ	07053
MEC56	Mehitable College	202 College St.	Gaston	DE	19723
PLI22	PrattLast Institute	236 Ashton Ave.	Pleasantburg	NJ	07025
SCC77	Stallone Community College	1200 Franklin Blvd.	Adelphia	PA	19156
SEC19	Seaborn College	345 Mather Rd.	Quaker	DE	19719
TSC02	Tri-State Consortium	3400 Metro Pkwy.	Adelphia	PA	19156

© 2014 Cengage Learning

Figure 1–80 (a) Customer Address Information (Word Table)

	A	B	C	D	E
1	Customer Number	Customer Name	Amount Paid	Current Due	Returns
2	ASU37	Applewood State University	$41,530.98	$38,812.66	$12,008.02
3	BCJ21	Brodkin Junior College	$0.00	$6,081.98	$0.00
4	CSD25	Cowpens ISD	$12,750.00	$13,275.00	$2,000.00
5	CSU10	Camellia State University	$63,246.88	$69,847.76	$14,967.98
6	DCC34	Dartt Community College	$21,345.50	$23,467.75	$4,496.80
7	FSC12	First State College	$34,557.25	$23,875.98	$7,234.99
8	FSU23	Farnham State University	$18,268.00	$22,024.50	$3,496.23
9	HSD05	Hammonds County ISD	$18,434.75	$0.00	$0.00
10	KCC78	Key Community College System	$21,288.65	$11,367.49	$2,256.98
11	MCC45	Mauldin Community College	$9,500.00	$5,000.00	$0.00
12	MEC56	Mehitable College	$9,111.19	$7,310.76	$574.25
13	PLI22	PrattLast Institute	$17,229.45	$11,769.75	$3,450.50
14	SCC77	Stallone Community College	$7,525.98	$2,515.78	$0.00
15	SEC19	Seaborn College	$9,225.34	$10,496.89	$2,017.67
16	TSC02	Tri-State Consortium	$34,578.90	$9,432.56	$943.34

Figure 1–80 (b) Customer Financial Information (Excel Worksheet)

Book Rep Number	Last Name	First Name	Street	City	State	Postal Code
42	Perez	Melina	261 Porter Dr.	Adelphia	PA	19156
48	Statnik	Michael	3135 Simpson Dr.	Pleasantburg	NJ	07025
53	Chin	Robert	265 Maxwell St.	Gossett	PA	19157
65	Rogers	Tracy	1827 Maple Ave.	Adelphia	PA	19159

© 2014 Cengage Learning

Figure 1–80 (c) Book Rep Address Information (Word Table)

	A	B	C	D	E	F
1	Book Rep Number	Last Name	First Name	Start Date	Salary	Bonus Rate
2	53	Chin	Robert	6/1/2013	$26,250	0.19
3	42	Perez	Melina	5/14/2012	$31,500	0.20
4	65	Rogers	Tracy	7/1/2014	$7,750	0.18
5	48	Statnik	Michael	1/15/2013	$29,000	0.20

Figure 1–80 (d) Book Rep Financial Information (Excel Worksheet)

- Finally, Bavant keeps track of which customers are assigned to which book reps. Each customer is assigned to a single book rep, but each book rep might be assigned many customers. Currently, for example, customers ASU37 (Applewood State University), BCJ21 (Brodkin Junior College), FSU23 (Farnham State University), MEC56 (Mehitable College), and SCC77 (Stallone Community College) are assigned to book rep 42 (Melina Perez). Customers CSD25 (Cowpens ISD), CSU10 (Camellia State University), HSD05 (Hammonds County ISD), MCC45 (Mauldin Community College), and PLI22 (PrattLast Institute) are assigned to book rep 53 (Robert Chin). Customers DCC34 (Dartt Community College), FSC12 (First State College), KCC78 (Key Community College System), SEC19 (Seaborn College), and TSC02 (Tri-State Consortium) are assigned to book rep 65 (Tracy Rogers). Bavant has an additional book rep, Michael Statnik, whose number has been assigned as 48, but who has not yet been assigned any customers.

Database Design Process

The database design process involves several steps.

What is the first step in the process?
Identify the tables. Examine the requirements for the database to identify the main objects that are involved. There will be a table for each object you identify.

In a database for one organization, for example, the main objects might be departments and employees. This would require two tables: one for departments and the other for employees. In the database for another organization, the main objects might be customers and book reps. In this case, there also would be two tables: one for customers and the other for book reps. In still another organization's database, the main objects might be books, publishers, and authors. This database would require three tables: one for books, a second for publishers, and a third for authors.

Identifying the Tables

For the Bavant Publishing database, the main objects are customers and book reps. This leads to two tables, which you must name. Reasonable names for these two tables are:

Customer
Book Rep

After identifying the tables, what is the second step in the database design process?
Determine the primary keys. Recall that the primary key is the unique identifier for records in the table. For each table, determine the unique identifier. In a Department table, for example, the unique identifier might be the Department Code. For a Book table, the unique identifier might be the ISBN (International Standard Book Number).

Determining the Primary Keys

The next step is to identify the fields that will be the unique identifiers, or primary keys. Customer numbers uniquely identify customers, and book rep numbers uniquely identify book reps. Thus, the primary key for the Customer table is the customer number, and the primary key for the Book Rep table is the book rep number. Reasonable names for these fields would be Customer Number and Book Rep Number, respectively. Adding these primary keys to the tables gives:

Customer (<u>Customer Number</u>)
Book Rep (<u>Book Rep Number</u>)

What is the third step in the database design process after determining the primary keys?
Determine the additional fields. The primary key will be a field or combination of fields in a table. A table typically will contain many additional fields, each of which contains a type of data. Examine the project requirements to determine these additional fields. For example, in an Employee table, additional fields might include Employee Name, Street Address, City, State, Postal Code, Date Hired, and Salary.

Determining Additional Fields

After identifying the primary keys, you need to determine and name the additional fields. In addition to the customer number, the Customer Address Information shown in Figure 1–80a on page AC 59 contains the customer name, street, city, state, and postal code. These would be fields in the Customer table. The Customer Financial Information shown in Figure 1–80b on page AC 59 also contains the customer number and customer name, which are already included in the Customer table. The financial information also contains the amount paid, current due, and returns. Adding the amount paid, current due, and returns fields to those already identified in the Customer table and assigning reasonable names gives:

Customer (<u>Customer Number</u>, Customer Name, Street, City, State, Postal Code, Amount Paid, Current Due, Returns)

Similarly, examining the Book Rep Address Information in Figure 1–80c on page AC 59 adds the last name, first name, street, city, state, and postal code fields to the Book Rep table. In addition to the book rep number, last name, and first name, the Book Rep Financial Information in Figure 1–80d on page AC 59 would add the start date, salary, and bonus rate. Adding these fields to the Book Rep table and assigning reasonable names gives:

Book Rep (<u>Book Rep Number</u>, Last Name, First Name, Street, City, State, Postal Code, Start Date, Salary, Bonus Rate)

BTW
Additional Data for Bavant Publishing
Bavant could include other types of data in the database. The Customer table could include data on a contact person at each organization, such as, name, telephone number, and email address. The Book Rep table could include the mobile telephone number, email address, and emergency contact information for the book rep.

What happens as the fourth step, after determining additional fields?
Determine relationships between the tables. A relationship is an association between objects. In a database containing information about departments and employees, there is an association between the departments and the employees. A department is associated with all the employees in the department, and an employee is associated with the department to which he or she is assigned. Technically, you say that a department is related to all the employees in the department, and an employee is related to his or her department.

The relationship between department and employees is an example of a **one-to-many relationship** because one employee is associated with one department, but each department can be associated with many employees. The Department table would be the "one" table in the relationship. The Employee table would be the "many" table in the relationship.

When you have determined that two tables are related, follow these general guidelines:

Identify the "one" table.

Identify the "many" table.

Include the primary key from the "one" table as a field in the "many" table.

CONSIDER THIS

BTW

Certification
The Microsoft Office Specialist (MOS) program provides an opportunity for you to obtain a valuable industry credential — proof that you have the Access 2013 skills required by employers. For more information, visit the Certification resource on the Student Companion Site located on www.cengagebrain.com. For detailed instructions about accessing available resources, visit www.cengage.com/ct/ studentdownload or contact your instructor for information about accessing the required files.

Determining and Implementing Relationships Between the Tables

According to the requirements, each customer has one book rep, but each book rep can have many customers. Thus, the Book Rep table is the "one" table, and the Customer table is the "many" table. To implement this one-to-many relationship between book reps and customers, add the Book Rep Number field (the primary key of the Book Rep table) to the Customer table. This produces:

Customer (<u>Customer Number</u>, Customer Name, Street, City, State, Postal Code, Amount Paid, Current Due, Returns, Book Rep Number)
Book Rep (<u>Book Rep Number</u>, Last Name, First Name, Street, City, State, Postal Code, Start Date, Salary, Bonus Rate)

CONSIDER THIS

After creating relationships between tables, what is the fifth step in the database design process?
Determine data types for the fields, that is, the type of data that can be stored in the field.

Determining Data Types for the Fields

See Pages AC 9 through AC 10 for a discussion of the available data types and their use in the Bavant Publishing database. That section also discusses other properties that can be assigned, such as captions, field size, and the number of decimal places.

Identifying and Removing Redundancy

BTW

Quick Reference
For a table that lists how to complete the tasks covered in this book using touch gestures, the mouse, ribbon, shortcut menu, and keyboard, see the Quick Reference Summary at the back of this book, or visit the Quick Reference resource on the Student Companion Site located on www.cengagebrain. com. For detailed instructions about accessing available resources, visit www.cengage.com/ct/ studentdownload or contact your instructor for information about accessing the required files.

Redundancy means storing the same fact in more than one place. It usually results from placing too many fields in a table — fields that really belong in separate tables — and often causes serious problems. If you had not realized there were two objects, such as customers and book reps, you might have placed all the data in a single Customer table. Figure 1–81 shows an example of a table that includes both customer and book rep information. Notice that the data for a given book rep (number, name, address, and so on) occurs on more than one record. The data for rep 42, Melina Perez, is repeated in the figure. Storing this data on multiple records is an example of redundancy.

name of Book Rep 42 appears more than once

Customer Number	Customer Name	Street	...	Book Rep Number	Last Name	First Name
ASU37	Applewood State University	300 University Ave.	...	42	Perez	Melina
BCJ21	Brodkin Junior College	4806 Park Dr.	...	42	Perez	Melina
CSD25	Cowpens ISD	829 Wooster Ave.	...	53	Chin	Robert
CSU10	Camellia State University	725 Camellia St.	...	53	Chin	Robert
DCC34	Dartt Community College	3827 Burgess Dr.	...	65	Rogers	Tracy
...	...	...	...	...	...	...

Book Rep numbers are 42

© 2014 Cengage Learning

Figure 1–81

What problems does this redundancy cause?

Redundancy results in several problems, including:

1. Wasted storage space. The name of book rep 42, Melina Perez, for example, should be stored only once. Storing this fact several times is wasteful.

2. More complex database updates. If, for example, Melina Perez's name is spelled incorrectly and needs to be changed in the database, her name would need to be changed in several different places.

3. Possible inconsistent data. Nothing prohibits the book rep's last name from being Perez on customer ASU37's record and Perret on customer BCJ21's record. The data would be inconsistent. In both cases, the book rep number is 42, but the last names are different.

How do you eliminate redundancy?

The solution to the problem is to place the redundant data in a separate table, one in which the data no longer will be redundant. If, for example, you place the data for book reps in a separate table (Figure 1–82), the data for each book rep will appear only once.

Customer Number	Customer Name	Street	...	Book Rep Number
ASU37	Applewood State University	300 University Ave.	...	42
BCJ21	Brodkin Junior College	4806 Park Dr.	...	42
CSD25	Cowpens ISD	829 Wooster Ave.	...	53
CSU10	Camellia State University	725 Camellia St.	...	53
DCC34	Dartt Community College	3827 Burgess Dr.	...	65

Book Rep numbers are 42

Book Rep Number	Last Name	First Name	...
42	Perez	Melina	...
48	Statnik	Michael	...
53	Chin	Robert	...
65	Rogers	Tracy	...

name of Book Rep 42 appears only once

© 2014 Cengage Learning

Figure 1–82

Notice that you need to have the book rep number in both tables. Without it, there would be no way to tell which book rep is associated with which customer. The remaining book rep data, however, was removed from the Customer table and placed in the Book Rep table. This new arrangement corrects the problems of redundancy in the following ways:

1. Because the data for each book rep is stored only once, space is not wasted.

2. Changing the name of a book rep is easy. You need to change only one row in the Book Rep table.

3. Because the data for a book rep is stored only once, inconsistent data cannot occur.

Designing to omit redundancy will help you to produce good and valid database designs. You should always examine your design to see if it contains redundancy. If it does, you should decide whether you need to remove the redundancy by creating a separate table.

If you examine your design, you will see that there is one area of redundancy (see the data in Figure 1–1 on page AC 3). Cities and states are both repeated. Every customer whose postal code is 19158, for example, has Greer as the city and PA as the state. To remove this redundancy, you would create a table with the primary key Postal Code and City and State as additional fields. City and State would be removed from the Customer table. Having City, State, and Postal Code in a table is very common, however, and usually you would not take such action. No other redundancy exists in your tables.

BTW

Postal Codes
Some organizations with customers throughout the country have a separate table of postal codes, cities, and states. When placing an order, you typically are asked for your postal code (or ZIP code), rather than city, state, and postal code. You then are asked to confirm that the city and state correspond to that postal code.

Chapter Summary

In this chapter you have learned to create an Access database, create tables and add records to a database, print the contents of tables, import data, create queries, create forms, create reports, and change database properties. You also have learned how to design a database. The items listed below include all the new Access skills you have learned in this chapter, with tasks grouped by activity.

Database Object Management
Delete a Table or Other Object in the Database (AC 58)
Rename an Object in the Database (AC 58)

Database Properties
Change Database Properties (AC 55)

File Management
Run Access (AC 5)
Create a Database (AC 6)
Create a Database Using a Template (AC 7)
Exit Access (AC 24)
Open a Database from Access (AC 25)
Back Up a Database (AC 56)
Compact and Repair a Database (AC 57)
Close a Database without Exiting Access (AC 57)
Save a Database with Another Name (AC 57)

Form Creation
Create a Form (AC 45)

Import Data
Import an Excel Worksheet (AC 33)

Print Objects
Preview and Print the Contents of a Table (AC 30)

Print the Results of a Query (AC 45)
Print a Report (AC 54)

Query Creation
Use the Simple Query Wizard to Create a Query (AC 40)
Use a Criterion in a Query (AC 43)

Report Creation
Create a Report (AC 48)
Modify Report Column Headings and Resize Columns (AC 50)
Add Totals to a Report (AC 53)

Table Creation
Modify the Primary Key (AC 11)
Define the Remaining Fields in a Table (AC 14)
Save a Table (AC 16)
View the Table in Design View (AC 17)
Change a Field Size in Design View (AC 18)
Close the Table (AC 20)
Resize Columns in a Datasheet (AC 28)
Modify a Table in Design View (AC 37)

Table Update
Add Records to a Table (AC 20)
Add Records to a Table that Contains Data (AC 26)

What decisions will you need to make when creating your next database?
Use these guidelines as you complete the assignments in this chapter and create your own databases outside of this class.

1. Identify the tables that will be included in the database.

2. Determine the primary keys for each of the tables.

3. Determine the additional fields that should be included in each of the tables.

4. Determine relationships between the tables.

 a) Identify the "one" table.

 b) Identify the "many" table.

 c) Include the primary key of the "one" table as a field in the "many" table.

5. Determine data types for the fields in the tables.

6. Determine additional properties for fields.

 a) Determine if a special caption is warranted.

 b) Determine if a special description is warranted.

 c) Determine field sizes.

 d) Determine formats.

7. Identify and remove any unwanted redundancy.

8. Determine a storage location for the database.

9. Determine the best method for distributing the database objects.

CONSIDER THIS

How should you submit solutions to questions in the assignments identified with a ✳ symbol?

Every assignment in this book contains one or more questions identified with a ✳ symbol. These questions require you to think beyond the assigned database. Present your solutions to the questions in the format required by your instructor. Possible formats may include one or more of these options: write the answer; create a document that contains the answer; present your answer to the class; discuss your answer in a group; record the answer as audio or video using a webcam, smartphone, or portable media player; or post answers on a blog, wiki, or website.

Apply Your Knowledge

Reinforce the skills and apply the concepts you learned in this chapter.

Adding a Caption, Changing a Data Type, Creating a Query, a Form, and a Report

Note: To complete this assignment, you will be required to use the Data Files for Students. Visit www.cengage.com/ct/studentdownload for detailed instructions or contact your instructor for information about accessing the required files.

Instructions: Cosmetics Naturally Inc. manufactures and sells beauty and skin care products made with only natural ingredients. The company's products do not contain any synthetic chemicals, artificial fragrances, or chemical preservatives. Cosmetics Naturally has a database that keeps track of its sales representatives and customers. Each customer is assigned to a single sales rep, but each sales rep may be assigned to many customers. The database has two tables. The Customer table contains data on the customers who purchase Cosmetics Naturally products. The Sales Rep table contains data on the sales reps. You will add a caption, change a data type, create two queries, a form, and a report, as shown in Figure 1–83 on the next page.

Perform the following tasks:

1. Start Access, open the Apply Cosmetics Naturally database from the Data Files for Students, and enable the content.

2. Open the Sales Rep table in Datasheet view, add SR # as the caption for the Sales Rep Number field, and resize all columns to best fit the data. Save the changes to the layout of the table and close the table.

3. Open the Customer table in Design view and change the data type for the Postal Code field to Short Text. Change the field size for the field to 5. Save the changes to the table and close the table.

4. Use the Simple Query Wizard to create a query for the Customer table that contains the Customer Number, Customer Name, Amount Paid, Balance, and Sales Rep Number. The query is a detail query. Use the name Customer Query for the query and close the query.

5. Create a simple form for the Sales Rep table. Save the form and use the name Sales Rep for the form. Close the form.

6. Create the report shown in Figure 1–83 for the Customer table. The report includes totals for both the Amount Paid and Balance fields. Be sure the totals appear completely. You might need to expand the size of the total controls. Move the page number so that it is within the margins. Save the report as Customer Financial Report.

7. If requested by your instructor, add your last name to the title of the report, that is, change the title to Customer Financial Report LastName where LastName is your actual last name.

8. Compact and repair the database.

9. Submit the revised database in the format specified by your instructor.

10. ✳ How would you change the field name of the Balance field in the Customer table to Current Balance?

Continued >

3. ✳ The Awards field currently has a data type of Short Text, but the only values that will be stored in that field are Yes and No to indicate whether the movie won any awards. What would be a more appropriate data type for this field?

In the Labs

Design, create, modify, and/or use a database following the guidelines, concepts, and skills presented in this chapter. Labs are listed in order of increasing difficulty. Labs 1 and 2, which increase in difficulty, require you to create solutions based on what you learned in the chapter; Lab 3 requires you to create a solution, which uses cloud and web technologies, by learning and investigating on your own from general guidance.

Lab 1: Creating Objects for the Dartt Offsite Services Database

Problem: Dartt Offsite Services is a local company that provides offsite data services and solutions. The company provides remote data backup, disaster recovery planning and services, website backup, and offsite storage of paper documents for small businesses and nonprofit organizations. Service representatives are responsible for communicating data solutions to the client, scheduling backups and other tasks, and resolving any conflicts. The company recently decided to store its client and service rep data in a database. Each client is assigned to a single service rep, but each service rep may be assigned many clients. The database and the Service Rep table have been created, but the Monthly Salary field needs to be added to the table. The records shown in Table 1–6 must be added to the Service Rep table. The company plans to import the Client table from the Excel worksheet shown in Figure 1–86. Dartt would like to finish storing this data in a database and has asked you to help.

	A	B	C	D	E	F	G	H	I	J	K
1	Client Number	Client Name	Street	City	State	Postal Code	Amount Paid	Balance Due	Service Rep Number		
2	BBF32	Babbage CPA Firm	464 Linnell Dr.	Austin	SC	28796	$3,524.00	$567.85	24		
		Theon Veterinary Services					$2,750.00	$1,200.00			
15	WEC05	Walburg Energy Company	12 Polk St.	Walburg	NC	28819	$1,567.45	$1,100.50	24		
16	WSC01	Wood Sports Complex	578 Central Ave.	Walburg	NC	28819	$2,250.00	$1,600.00	24		
17											

Figure 1–86

Note: To complete this assignment, you will be required to use the Data Files for Students. Visit www.cengage.com/ct/studentdownload for detailed instructions or contact your instructor for information about accessing the required files.

Instructions: Perform the following tasks:
1. Start Access and open the Lab 1 Dartt Offsite Services database from the Data Files for Students.
2. Open the Service Rep table in Datasheet view and add the Monthly Salary field to the end of the table. The field has the Currency data type. Assign the caption SR # to the Service Rep Number field.
3. Add the records shown in Table 1–6.
4. Resize the columns to best fit the data. Save the changes to the layout of the table.

Service Rep Number	Last Name	First Name	Street	City	State	Postal Code	Start Date	Monthly Salary
21	Kelly	Jenna	25 Paint St.	Kyle	SC	28797	5/14/2012	$3,862.45
45	Scott	Josh	1925 Pine Rd.	Byron	SC	28795	4/28/2014	$3,062.08
24	Liu	Mia	265 Marble Dr.	Kyle	SC	28797	1/7/2013	$3,666.67
37	Martinez	Mike	31 Steel St.	Georgetown	SC	28794	5/13/2013	$3,285.00

Table 1–6 Data for Service Rep Table

5. Import the Lab 1–1 Client Data workbook shown in Figure 1–86 into the database. The first row of the workbook contains the column headings. Client Number is the primary key for the new table. Assign the name Client to the table. Save the Import steps, and assign the name Import-Client Data to the steps. Assign Import Client Data as the description.

6. Open the Client table in Design view and make the following changes:

 a. Change the field size for the Client Number field to 5. Change the field size for the Client Name field to 30. Change the field size for the Street and City fields to 20. Change the field size for the State field to 2 and the field size for the Postal Code field to 5. Change the field size for the Service Rep Number field to 2.

 b. Add the caption CL # to the Client Number field.

 c. Add the caption SR # to the Service Rep Number field.

7. Save the changes to the Client table. If a Microsoft Access dialog box appears with the 'Some data may be lost' message, click the Yes button.

8. Open the Client table in Datasheet view and resize all columns to best fit the data. Save the changes to the layout of the table.

9. Create a query using the Simple Query Wizard for the Client table that displays the Client Number, Client Name, Amount Paid, Balance Due, and Service Rep Number. Save the query as Client Query.

10. Create the report shown in Figure 1–87 for the Client table. The report should include the Client Number, Client Name, Amount Paid, Balance Due, and Service Rep Number fields. Include totals for the Amount Paid and Balance Due fields. Be sure to change the column headings to those shown in Figure 1–87. Save the report as Client Financial Report.

11. If requested to do so by your instructor, change the address for Jenna Kelly in the Service Rep table to your address. If your address is longer than 20 characters, simply enter as much as you can.

12. Submit the revised database in the format specified by your instructor.

13. ✳ You entered the records for the Service Rep table in the order shown in Table 1–6 on the previous page, that is service reps 21, 45, 24, 37. What order will the records be in after you close and reopen the Service Rep table? Why?

Figure 1–87

Lab 2: Creating the Tennis Logos Database

Problem: Tennis Logos supplies customized tennis clothing and accessories for clubs and tournaments. The company purchases these items from suppliers at wholesale prices and adds the customer's logo. The final item price is determined by marking up the wholesale price and adding a fee that is based on the complexity of the logo. Tennis Logos also does graphic design work for customers. Currently, the information about the items and the suppliers is stored in two Excel workbooks. Each item is assigned to a single supplier, but each supplier may be assigned many items. You are to create a database that will store the item and supplier information. You already have determined that you need two tables, a Supplier table and an Item table, in which to store the information.

Note: To complete this assignment, you will be required to use the Data Files for Students. Visit www.cengage.com/ct/studentdownload for detailed instructions or contact your instructor for information about accessing the required files.

Continued >

In the Labs *continued*

Instructions: Perform the following tasks:

1. Use the Blank desktop database option to create a new database in which to store all objects related to the items for sale. Call the database Lab 2 Tennis Logos.

2. Import the Lab 1–2 Supplier Data Excel workbook into the database. The first row of the workbook contains the column headings. Supplier Code is the primary key for the new table. Assign the name Supplier to the table. Do not save the Import steps.

3. Open the Supplier table in Datasheet view. Change the field size for the Supplier Code field to 2; the field size for the Supplier Name field to 30; and the field size for the Telephone Number field to 12.

4. Import the Lab 1–2 Item Data Excel workbook into the database. The first row of the workbook contains the column headings. Item Number is the primary key for this table. Assign the name Item to the table. Save the Import steps, and assign the name Import-Item Data to the steps. You do not need a description.

5. Open the Item table in Design view. Change the field size for the Item Number field to 4. Change the field size for the Description field to 30. Add the caption Wholesale for the Wholesale Price field. The On Hand field should be an Integer field. Be sure that the field size for the Supplier Code in the Item table is identical to the field size for the Supplier Code in the Supplier table. Save the changes to the table and close the table.

6. Open the Item table in Datasheet view and resize the columns to best fit the data. Save the changes to the layout of the table and close the table.

7. Create a query for the Item table. Include the Item Number, Description, Wholesale Price, Base Cost, and Supplier Code. Save the query as Item Query.

8. Create a simple form for the Item table. Use the name Item for the form.

9. Create the report shown in Figure 1–88 for the Item table. Do not add any totals. Save the report as Inventory Status Report.

10. If requested to do so by your instructor, change the telephone number for Last Merchandisers to your telephone number.

11. Submit the database in the format specified by your instructor.

12. ☀ If you had designed this database, could you have used the field name, Name, for the Supplier Name? If not, why not?

Item Number	Description	On Hand	Wholesale Price
	Inventory Status Report	Monday, September 15, 2014 9:37:32 PM	
3363	Baseball Cap	110	$4.87
3673	Cotton Visor	150	$4.59
4543	Crew Sweatshirt	75	$7.29
4583			

Figure 1–88

Lab 3: Expand Your World: Cloud and Web Technologies
Exporting Query Results and Reports

Problem: You and two of your friends have started a pet sitting business. You want to be able to share query results and reports, so you have decided to store the items on the SkyDrive. You are still learning Access, so you are going to create a sample query and the report shown in Figure 1–89, export the results, and save to the SkyDrive.

Note: To complete this assignment, you will be required to use the Data Files for Students. Visit www.cengage.com/ct/studentdownload for detailed instructions or contact your instructor for information about accessing the required files.

Customer Balance Report				Monday, September 15, 2014
				9:39:02 PM
Customer Number	Last Name	First Name	Balance	Sitter Number
AB10	Alvarez	Frances	$45.00	103
BR16		Alex	$80.00	
	Santoro	Maria	$0.00	107
TR35	Trent	Gerry	$40.00	105
			$419.00	

Figure 1–89

Instructions:

1. Open the Lab 3 Pet Sitters database from the Data Files for Students.

2. Use the Simple Query Wizard to create a query that includes the Customer Number, First Name, Last Name, Balance, and Sitter Number. Save the query as Customer Query.

3. Export the Customer Query as an XPS document to your SkyDrive in the Access folder.

4. Create the report shown in Figure 1–89. Save the report as Customer Balance Report.

5. Export the Customer Balance Report as a PDF document to your Sky Drive in the Access folder. For information about how to use the Sky Drive, refer to the Office and Windows chapter at the beginning of this book.

6. If requested to do so by your instructor, open the Sitter table and change the last name and first name for sitter 103 to your last name and your first name.

7. Submit the assignment in the format specified by your instructor.

8. ✷ Based on your current knowledge of XPS and PDF documents, which one do you think you would use most frequently? Why?

✷ Consider This: Your Turn

Apply your creative thinking and problem solving skills to design and implement a solution.

1. Creating the Craft Database

Note: To complete this assignment, you will be required to use the Data Files for Students. Visit www.cengage.com/ct/studentdownload for detailed instructions or contact your instructor for information about accessing the required files.

Personal/Academic

Part 1: You attend a college that is renowned for its school of arts and crafts. Students who major in arts and crafts can sell their designs online through the college bookstore. The bookstore has used an Excel workbook to store data on wood-crafted items as well as the students who created the items. Because you are a major in computer science and also are studying woodworking, your senior project is to create a database of these wood-crafted items. The database must keep track of the wood-crafted items for sale and maintain data on the students who created the items. Each item is created by a single student, but each student may have created several items.

Based on the information in the Your Turn 1–1 Craft workbook, use the concepts and techniques presented in this chapter to design and create a database to store the craft data. Create a Wood Crafts for Sale report that lists the item number, description, price, and student code. Submit your assignment in the format specified by your instructor.

Part 2: ✷ You made several decisions while determining the table structures and adding data to the tables in this assignment. What method did you use to add the data to each table? Are there any other methods that also would have worked?

Continued >

Consider This: Your Turn *continued*

2. Creating the Mums Landscaping Database
Professional

Part 1: Mums Landscaping is a local company that provides landscaping and lawn maintenance services to commercial customers, such as businesses, housing subdivisions, and schools. You worked for Mums part-time in both high school and in college. Mums has used an Excel workbook to store financial data on its customers but now would like to create a database that includes information on its customers and crew supervisors. Each customer is assigned to a single crew supervisor, but each supervisor may be assigned many customers.

Based on the information in the Your Turn 1–2 Mums Landscaping workbook, use the concepts and techniques presented in this chapter to design and create a database to store the data that Mums needs. Submit your assignment in the format specified by your instructor.

Part 2: ✺ You made several decisions while creating the Mums Landscaping database in this assignment. What did you decide to use as the primary key for each table? Why?

3. Creating an Electronic Assets Database
Research and Collaboration

Part 1: In today's world, most college students will own at least one electronic device, such as a cell phone. Many students have multiple electronic devices. Microsoft Access includes a desktop Asset tracking template that you can modify to keep track of your electronic devices, such as cell phone, MP3 player, and computer. Get together with your group and make a list of the electronic devices that each of you own. Use the desktop Asset tracking template to create an Electronic Assets database. Watch the video to learn how the database works. As a team, review the fields in the Assets table and decide which fields to include in the database. Delete any unwanted fields. Decide how you will describe each device, for example, will you use the term cell phone, smartphone, or mobile phone? Have each team member enter at least two devices. Create a query to find one type of device, such as cell phone. Submit your assignment in the format specified by your instructor.

Part 2: ✺ You made several decisions while creating the Electronic Assets database. Which fields did you decide to delete from the Assets table? What terms did you use to describe each device? What was the rationale for these decisions?

Learn Online

Reinforce what you learned in this chapter with games, exercises, training, and many other online activities and resources.

Student Companion Site Reinforcement activities and resources are available at no additional cost on www.cengagebrain.com. Visit www.cengage.com/ct/studentdownload for detailed instructions about accessing the resources available at the Student Companion Site.

SAM Put your skills into practice with SAM! If you have a SAM account, go to www.cengage.com/sam2013 to access SAM assignments for this chapter.

2 | Querying a Database

Microsoft product screenshots used with permission from Microsoft Corporation

Objectives

You will have mastered the material in this chapter when you can:

- Create queries using Design view
- Include fields in the design grid
- Use text and numeric data in criteria
- Save a query and use the saved query
- Create and use parameter queries
- Use compound criteria in queries
- Sort data in queries

- Join tables in queries
- Create a report and a form from a query
- Export data from a query to another application
- Perform calculations and calculate statistics in queries
- Create crosstab queries
- Customize the Navigation Pane

2 | Querying a Database

Introduction

One of the primary benefits of using a database management system such as Access is having the ability to find answers to questions related to data stored in the database. When you pose a question to Access, or any other database management system, the question is called a query. A **query** is simply a question presented in a way that Access can process.

To find the answer to a question, you first create a corresponding query using the techniques illustrated in this chapter. After you have created the query, you instruct Access to run the query, that is, to perform the steps necessary to obtain the answer. Access then displays the answer in Datasheet view.

Project — Querying a Database

One of the most important benefits of using Access to manage a database is easily finding the answers to questions and requests. Figure 2–1 presents examples of such queries, which concern the data in the Bavant Publishing database.

In addition to these questions, Bavant Publishing managers need to find information about customers located in a specific city, but they want to enter a different city each time they ask the question. The company can use a parameter query to accomplish this task. Bavant Publishing managers also want to summarize data in a specific way, which might involve performing calculations, and they can use a crosstab query to present the data in the desired form.

BTW
Select Queries
The queries you create in this chapter are select queries. In a select query, you retrieve data from one or more tables using criteria that you specify and display the data in a datasheet.

BTW
BTWs
For a complete list of the BTWs found in the margins of this book, visit the BTW resource on the Student Companion Site located on www.cengagebrain.com. For detailed instructions about accessing available resources, visit www.cengage.com/ct/studentdownload or contact your instructor for information about accessing the required files.

Give me the number, name, amount paid, and current due for all customers whose name starts with S.

CU #	Customer Name	Amount Paid	Current Due
SCC77	Stallone Community College	$7,525.98	$2,515.78
SEC19	Seaborn College	$9,225.34	$10,496.89

Give me the customer number, customer name, amount paid, current due, and book rep number for all customers whose returns are greater than $0.00 and whose book rep number is 42.

CU #	Customer Name	Amount Paid	Current Due	Returns	BR #
ASU37	Applewood State University	$41,530.98	$38,812.66	$12,008.02	42
FSU23	Farnham State University	$18,268.00	$22,024.50	$3,496.23	42
MEC56	Mehitable College	$9,111.19	$7,310.76	$574.25	42

Give me the customer number, customer name, amount paid, and current due for customer CSU10.

CU #	Customer Name	Amount Paid	Current Due
CSU10	Camellia State University	$63,246.88	$69,847.76

List the customer number, customer name, book rep number, and amount paid for all customers. Sort the results by book rep number. For customers with the same book rep number, further sort the results by amount paid.

Summarize the total returns by state and by book rep.

State	Total Of Retı	42	53	65
DE	$13,323.14	$4,070.48		$9,252.66
NJ	$22,915.28		$18,418.48	$4,496.80
PA	$17,208.34	$12,008.02	$2,000.00	$3,200.32

CU #	Customer Name	BR #	Amount Paid
BCJ21	Brodkin Junior College	42	$0.00
SCC77	Stallone Community College	42	$7,525.98
MEC56	Mehitable College	42	$9,111.19
FSU23	Farnham State University	42	$18,268.00
ASU37	Applewood State University	42	$41,530.98
MCC45	Mauldin Community College	53	$9,500.00
CSD25	Cowpens ISD	53	$12,750.00
PLI22	PrattLast Institute	53	$17,229.45
HSD05	Hammonds County ISD	53	$18,434.75
CSU10	Camellia State University	53	$63,246.88
SEC19	Seaborn College	65	$9,225.34
KCC78	Key Community College System	65	$21,288.65
DCC34	Dartt Community College	65	$21,345.50
FSC12	First State College	65	$34,557.25
TSC02	Tri-State Consortium	65	$34,578.90

Give me the average amount paid by customers of each book rep.

For each book rep, list the book rep number, last name, and first name. Also, list the customer number and customer name for each of the book rep's customers.

BR #	AvgOfAmou
42	$15,287.23
53	$24,232.22
65	$24,199.13

BR #	Last Name	First Name	CU #	Customer Name
42	Perez	Melina	ASU37	Applewood State University
42	Perez	Melina	BCJ21	Brodkin Junior College
42	Perez	Melina	FSU23	Farnham State University
42	Perez	Melina	MEC56	Mehitable College
42	Perez	Melina	SCC77	Stallone Community College
48	Statnik	Michael		
53	Chin	Robert	CSD25	Cowpens ISD
53	Chin	Robert	CSU10	Camellia State University
53	Chin	Robert	HSD05	Hammonds County ISD
53	Chin	Robert	MCC45	Mauldin Community College
53	Chin	Robert	PLI22	PrattLast Institute
65	Rogers	Tracy	DCC34	Dartt Community College
65	Rogers	Tracy	FSC12	First State College
65	Rogers	Tracy	KCC78	Key Community College System
65	Rogers	Tracy	SEC19	Seaborn College
65	Rogers	Tracy	TSC02	Tri-State Consortium

List the customer number, customer name, amount paid, current due, and the total amount (amount paid plus current due) for each customer.

CL #	Client Name	Amount Paid	Current Due	Total Amour
BA53	Bavant Animal Hospital	$0.00	$7,500.00	$7,500.00
BB32	Babbage CPA Firm	$1,500.00	$500.00	$2,000.00
BC76	Buda Community Clinic	$2,500.00	$750.00	$3,250.00
CJ29	Catering by Jenna	$3,000.00	$1,000.00	$4,000.00
GA74	Grant Antiques	$5,500.00	$3,200.00	$8,700.00
GF56	Granger Foundation	$0.00	$6,500.00	$6,500.00
HC10	Hendley County Hospital	$3,100.00	$1,200.00	$4,300.00
KD21	KAL Design Studio	$6,000.00	$3,200.00	$9,200.00
KG04	Kyle Grocery Cooperative	$3,200.00	$0.00	$3,200.00
ME14	Mike's Electronic Stop	$2,500.00	$1,500.00	$4,000.00
PJ34	Patricia Jean Florist	$0.00	$5,200.00	$5,200.00
SL77	Smarter Law Associates	$3,800.00	$0.00	$3,800.00
TB17	The Bikeshop	$2,750.00	$1,200.00	$3,950.00
WE05	Walburg Energy Alternatives	$4,500.00	$1,450.00	$5,950.00
WS01	Woody Sporting Goods	$2,250.00	$1,600.00	$3,850.00

Database

Figure 2–1

Roadmap

In this chapter, you will learn how to create and use the queries shown in Figure 2–1 on the previous page. The following roadmap identifies general activities you will perform as you progress through this chapter:

1. CREATE QUERIES in Design view.
2. USE CRITERIA in queries.
3. SORT DATA in queries.
4. JOIN TABLES in queries.
5. EXPORT query RESULTS.
6. PERFORM CALCULATIONS in queries.
7. CREATE a CROSSTAB query.
8. CUSTOMIZE the NAVIGATION PANE.

At the beginning of the step instructions throughout the chapter, you will see an abbreviated form of this roadmap. The abbreviated roadmap uses colors to indicate chapter progress: gray means the chapter is beyond that activity, blue means the task being shown is covered in that activity, and black means that activity is yet to be covered. For example, the following abbreviated roadmap indicates the chapter would be showing a task in the 3 SORT DATA activity.

1 CREATE QUERIES | 2 USE CRITERIA | 3 SORT DATA | 4 JOIN TABLES | 5 EXPORT RESULTS
6 PERFORM CALCULATIONS | 7 CREATE CROSSTAB | 8 CUSTOMIZE NAVIGATION PANE

Use the abbreviated roadmap as a progress guide while you read or step through the instructions in this chapter.

To Run Access

If you are using a computer to step through the project in this chapter and you want your screens to match the figures in this book, you should change your screen's resolution to 1366 × 768. For information about how to change a computer's resolution, refer to the Office and Windows chapter at the beginning of this book.

The following steps, which assume Windows is running, use the Start screen or the search box to run Access based on a typical installation. You may need to ask your instructor how to run Access on your computer. For a detailed example of the procedure summarized below, refer to the Office and Windows chapter.

1 Scroll the Start screen for an Access 2013 tile. If your Start screen contains an Access 2013 tile, tap or click it to run Access and then proceed to Step 5; if the Start screen does not contain the Access 2013 tile, proceed to the next step to search for the Access app.

2 Swipe in from the right edge of the screen or point to the upper-right corner of the screen to display the Charms bar, and then tap or click the Search charm on the Charms bar to display the Search menu.

3 Type Access as the search text in the Search text box and watch the search results appear in the Apps list.

For an introduction to Windows and instruction about how to perform basic Windows tasks, read the Office and Windows chapter at the beginning of this book, where you can learn how to resize windows, change screen resolution, create folders, move and rename files, use Windows Help, and much more.

For an introduction to Office and instruction about how to perform basic tasks in Office programs, read the Office and Windows chapter at the beginning of this book, where you can learn how to run an app, use the ribbon, save a file, open a file, exit an app, use Help, and much more.

4 Tap or click Access 2013 in the search results to run Access.

5 If the Access window is not maximized, tap or click the Maximize button on its title bar to maximize the window.

To Open a Database from Access

In the previous chapter, you created the Bavant Publishing database in an appropriate storage location. The following steps open the database from the location you specified when you first created it (for example, the Access folder in the CIS 101 folder). For a detailed example of the procedure summarized below, refer to the Office and Windows chapter at the beginning of this book.

1 Tap or click FILE on the ribbon to open the Backstage view, if necessary.

2 If the database you want to open is displayed in the Recent list, tap or click the file name to open the database and display the opened database in the Access window; then skip to Step 7. If the database you want to open is not displayed in the Recent list or if the Recent list does not appear, tap or click 'Open Other Files' to display the Open Gallery.

3 If the database you want to open is displayed in the Recent list in the Open gallery, tap or click the file name to open the database and display the opened database in the Access window; then skip to Step 7.

4 Tap or click Computer, SkyDrive, or another location in the left pane and then navigate to the location of the database to be opened (for example, the Access folder in the CIS 101 folder).

5 Tap or click Bavant Publishing to select the database to be opened.

6 Tap or click the Open button (Open dialog box) to open the selected file and display the opened database in the Access window.

7 If a Security Warning appears, tap or click the Enable Content button.

One of the few differences between Windows 7 and Windows 8 occurs in the steps to run Access. If you are using Windows 7, click the Start button, type Access in the 'Search programs and files' box, click Access 2013, and then, if necessary, maximize the Access window. For detailed steps to run Access in Windows 7, refer to the Office and Windows chapter at the beginning of this book. For a summary of the steps, refer to the Quick Reference located at the back of this book.

Creating Queries

As you learned in Chapter 1, you can use queries in Access to find answers to questions about the data contained in the database. *Note:* In this chapter, you will save each query example. When you use a query for another task, such as to create a form or report, you will assign a specific name to a query, for example, Rep-Customer Query. In situations in which you will not use the query again, you will assign a name using a convention that includes the chapter number and a query number, for example, Ch2q01. Queries are numbered consecutively.

To Create a Query in Design View

1 CREATE QUERIES | 2 USE CRITERIA | 3 SORT DATA | 4 JOIN TABLES | 5 EXPORT RESULTS
6 PERFORM CALCULATIONS | 7 CREATE CROSSTAB | 8 CUSTOMIZE NAVIGATION PANE

In Chapter 1, you used the Simple Query Wizard to create a query. Most of the time, however, you will use Design view, which is the primary option for creating queries. *Why? Once you have created a new query in Design view, you have more options than with the wizard and can specify fields, criteria, sorting, calculations, and so on.* The following steps create a new query in Design view.

1

- Tap or click the 'Shutter Bar Open/Close Button' to close the Navigation Pane.

- Tap or click CREATE on the ribbon to display the CREATE tab (Figure 2–2).

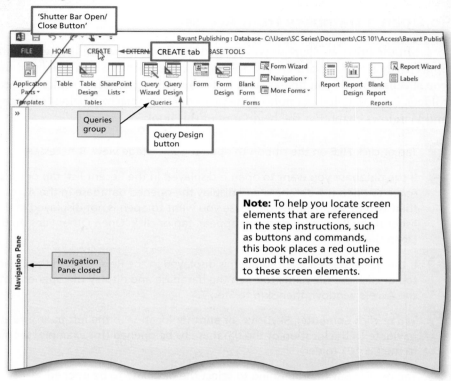

Figure 2–2

2

- Tap or click the Query Design button (CREATE tab | Queries group) to create a new query (Figure 2–3).

Q&A Is it necessary to close the Navigation Pane?
No. Closing the pane gives you more room for the query, however, so it is usually a good practice.

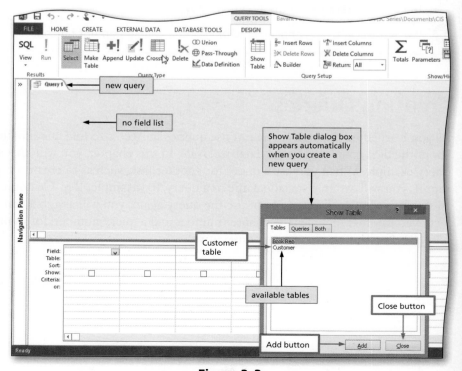

Figure 2–3

3

- Tap or click the Customer table (Show Table dialog box) to select the table.

- Tap or click the Add button to add the selected table to the query.

- Tap or click the Close button to remove the dialog box from the screen.

What if I inadvertently add the wrong table? Press and hold or right-click the table that you added in error and tap or click Remove Table on the shortcut menu. You also can just close the query, indicate that you do not want to save it, and then start over.

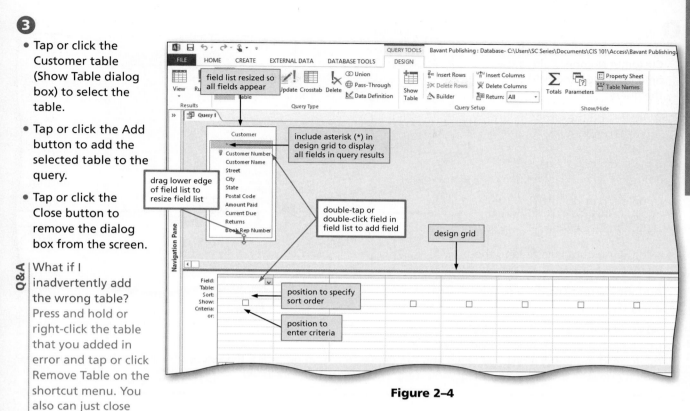

Figure 2–4

- Drag the lower edge of the field list down far enough so all fields in the table appear (Figure 2–4).

Is it essential that I resize the field list?
No. You can always scroll through the list of fields using the scroll bar. Resizing the field list so that all fields appear is usually more convenient.

To Add Fields to the Design Grid

1 CREATE QUERIES | 2 USE CRITERIA | 3 SORT DATA | 4 JOIN TABLES | 5 EXPORT RESULTS
6 PERFORM CALCULATIONS | 7 CREATE CROSSTAB | 8 CUSTOMIZE NAVIGATION PANE

Once you have a new query displayed in Design view, you are ready to make entries in the **design grid**, the portion of the window where you specify fields and criteria for the query. The design grid is located in the lower pane of the window. You add the fields you want included in the query to the Field row in the grid. ***Why add fields to the grid?*** *Only the fields that appear in the design grid will be included in the query results.* The following step begins creating a query that Bavant Publishing might use to obtain the customer number, customer name, amount paid, and current due for a particular customer.

1

- Double-tap or double-click the Customer Number field in the field list to add the field to the query.

Q&A
What if I add the wrong field?
Tap or click just above the field name in the design grid to select the column and then press the DELETE key to remove the field.

- Double-tap or double-click the Customer Name field in the field list to add the field to the query.

- Add the Amount Paid field to the query.

- Add the Current Due field to the query (Figure 2–5).

Figure 2–5

Q&A
What if I want to include all fields?
Do I have to add each field individually?
No. Instead of adding individual fields, you can double-tap or double-click the asterisk (*) to add the asterisk to the design grid. The asterisk is a shortcut indicating all fields are to be included.

If you are using your finger on a touch screen and are having difficulty completing the steps in this chapter, consider using a stylus. Many people find it easier to be precise with a stylus than with a finger. In addition, with a stylus you see the pointer. If you still are having trouble completing the steps with a stylus, try using a mouse.

BTW
Touch Screen Differences
The Office and Windows interfaces may vary if you are using a touch screen. For this reason, you might notice that the function or appearance of your touch screen differs slightly from this chapter's presentation.

Determining Criteria

When you use queries, usually you are looking for those records that satisfy some criterion. In the simple query you created in the previous chapter, for example, you entered a criterion to restrict the records to those with the book rep number 53. In another query, you might want the name, amount paid, and current due amounts for the customer whose number is CSU10, for example, or for those customers whose names start with the letters, Gr. You enter criteria in the Criteria row in the design grid below the field name to which the criterion applies. For example, to indicate that the customer number must be CSU10, you first must add the Customer Number field to the design grid. You then would type CSU10 in the Criteria row below the Customer Number field.

Running the Query

After adding the appropriate fields and defining the query's criteria, you must run the query to get the results. To view the results of the query from Design view, tap or click the Run button to instruct Access to run the query, that is, to perform the necessary actions to produce and display the results in Datasheet view.

To Use Text Data in a Criterion

To use **text data** (data in a field whose data type is Short Text) in criteria, simply type the text in the Criteria row below the corresponding field name, just as you did in Chapter 1. In Access, you do not need to enclose text data in quotation marks as you do in many other database management systems. *Why? Access will enter the quotation marks automatically, so you can simply type the desired text.* The following steps finish creating a query that Bavant Publishing might use to obtain the customer number, customer name, amount paid, and current due amount of customer CSU10. These steps add the appropriate criterion so that only the desired customer will appear in the results. The steps also save the query.

1

- Tap or click the Criteria row for the Customer Number field to produce an insertion point.

- Type `CSU10` as the criterion (Figure 2–6).

Figure 2–6

2

- Tap or click the Run button (QUERY TOOLS DESIGN tab | Results group) to run the query (Figure 2–7).

Q&A

Can I also use the View button in the Results group to run the query?

Yes. You can tap or click the View button to view the query results in Datasheet view.

Figure 2–7

• Tap or click the Save button on the Quick Access Toolbar to display the Save As dialog box.

• Type `Ch2q01` as the name of the query (Figure 2–8).

Can I also save from Design view? Yes. You can save the query when you view it in Design view just as you can save it when you view query results in Datasheet view.

Figure 2–8

• Tap or click the OK button (Save As dialog box) to save the query (Figure 2–9).

Figure 2–9

Other Ways

1. Press and hold or right-click query tab, tap or click Save on shortcut menu 2. Press CTRL + S

Using Saved Queries

After you have created and saved a query, you can use it in a variety of ways:

• To view the results of a query that is not currently open, open it by pressing and holding or right-clicking the query in the Navigation Pane and tapping or clicking Open on the shortcut menu.

• If you want to change the design of a query that is already open, return to Design view and make the changes.

• If you want to change the design of a query that is not currently open, press and hold or right-click the query in the Navigation Pane and then tap or click Design View on the shortcut menu to open the query in Design view.

• To print the results with a query open, tap or click FILE on the ribbon, tap or click the Print tab in the Backstage view, and then tap or click Quick Print.

• To print a query without first opening it, be sure the query is selected in the Navigation Pane and tap or click FILE on the ribbon, tap or click the Print tab in the Backstage view, and then tap or click Quick Print.

• You can switch between views of a query using the View button (HOME tab | Views group). Tapping or clicking the arrow at the bottom of the button produces the View button menu. You then tap or click the desired view in the menu. The two query views you use in this chapter are Datasheet view (to see the results) and Design view (to change the design). You can tap or click the top part of the

View button, in which case you will switch to the view identified by the icon on the button. In Figure 2–9, the View button displays the icon for Design view, so tapping or clicking the button would change to Design view. For the most part, the icon on the button represents the view you want, so you can usually simply tap or click the button.

BTW

On Screen Keyboard
To display the on-screen touch keyboard, tap the Touch Keyboard button on the Windows taskbar. When finished using the touch keyboard, tap the X button on the touch keyboard to close the keyboard

Wildcards

Microsoft Access supports wildcards. **Wildcards** are symbols that represent any character or combination of characters. One common wildcard, the **asterisk (*)**, represents any collection of characters. Another wildcard symbol is the **question mark (?)**, which represents any individual character.

CONSIDER THIS

What does S* represent? What does T?m represent?
S* represents the letter, S, followed by any collection of characters. T?m represents the letter, T, followed by any single character, followed by the letter, m. A search for T?m might return the names Tim or Tom.

To Use a Wildcard

1 CREATE QUERIES | 2 USE CRITERIA | 3 SORT DATA | 4 JOIN TABLES | 5 EXPORT RESULTS
6 PERFORM CALCULATIONS | 7 CREATE CROSSTAB | 8 CUSTOMIZE NAVIGATION PANE

The following steps modify the previous query to use the asterisk wildcard so that Bavant Publishing can select only those customers whose names begin with S. *Why? Because you do not know how many characters will follow the S, the asterisk wildcard symbol is appropriate.* The steps also save the query with a new name using the Save As command.

1
- Tap or click the View button (HOME tab | Views group), shown in Figure 2–9 on page AC 82, to return to Design view.

- If necessary, tap or click the Criteria row below the Customer Number field to produce an insertion point.

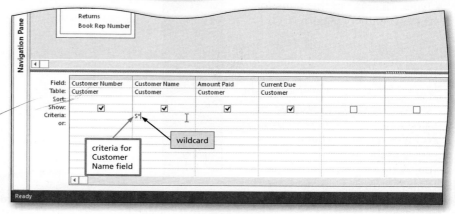

Q&A
The text I entered now has quotation marks surrounding it. What happened?
Criteria for text data needs to be enclosed in quotation marks. You do not have to type the quotation marks; Access adds them automatically.

- Use the DELETE or BACKSPACE key as necessary to delete the current entry.

- Tap or click the Criteria row below the Customer Name field to produce an insertion point.

- Type S* as the criterion (Figure 2–10).

Figure 2–10

2

- Run the query by tapping or clicking the Run button (QUERY TOOLS DESIGN tab | Results group) (Figure 2–11).

🔍 **Experiment**

- Change the letter S to lowercase in the criteria and run the query to determine whether case makes a difference when entering a wildcard.

Figure 2–11

3

- Tap or click FILE on the ribbon to open the Backstage view.

- Tap or click the Save As tab in the Backstage view to display the Save As gallery.

- Tap or click Save Object As in the File Types area (Figure 2–12).

Q&A Can I just tap or click the Save button on the Quick Access Toolbar as I did when saving the previous query?

If you tapped or clicked the Save button, you would replace the previous query with the version you just created. Because you want to save both the previous query and the new one, you need to save the new version with a different name. To do so, you must use Save Object As, which is available through the Backstage view.

Figure 2–12

4

- With Save Object As selected in the File Types gallery, tap or click the Save As button to display the Save As dialog box.

- Type `Ch2q02` as the name for the saved query (Figure 2–13).

Q&A The current entry in the As text box is Query. Could I save the query as some other type of object?

Although you usually would want to save the query as another query, you also can save it as a form or report by changing the entry in the As text box. If you do, Access would create either a simple form or a simple report for the query.

Figure 2–13

5

- Tap or click the OK button (Save As dialog box) to save the query with the new name and close the Backstage view (Figure 2–14).

Q&A How can I tell that the query was saved with the new name?
The new name will appear on the tab.

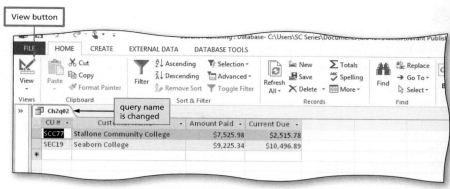

Figure 2–14

Other Ways

1. Tap or click Design View button on status bar

To Use Criteria for a Field Not Included in the Results

1 CREATE QUERIES | 2 USE CRITERIA | 3 SORT DATA | 4 JOIN TABLES | 5 EXPORT RESULTS
6 PERFORM CALCULATIONS | 7 CREATE CROSSTAB | 8 CUSTOMIZE NAVIGATION PANE

In some cases, you might require criteria for a particular field that should not appear in the results of the query. For example, you may want to see the customer number, customer name, address, and amount paid for all customers located in Gaston. The criteria involve the City field, but you do not want to include the City field in the results.

To enter a criterion for the City field, it must be included in the design grid. Normally, it would then appear in the results. To prevent this from happening, remove the check mark from its Show check box in the Show row of the grid. *Why? A check mark in the Show Check box instructs Access to show the field in the result. If you remove the check mark, you can use the field in the query but not display it in the query results.*

The following steps modify the previous query so that Bavant Publishing can select only those customers located in Gaston. Bavant does not want the city to appear in the results, however. The steps also save the query with a new name.

1

- Tap or click the View button (HOME tab | Views group), shown in Figure 2–14, to return to Design view.

Q&A The text I entered is now preceded by the word, Like. What happened?
Criteria including wildcards need to be preceded by the word, Like. However, you do not have to type it; Access adds the word automatically to any criterion involving a wildcard.

- Erase the criterion in the Criteria row of the Customer Name field.

- Add the City field to the query.

- Type Gaston as the criterion for the City field (Figure 2–15).

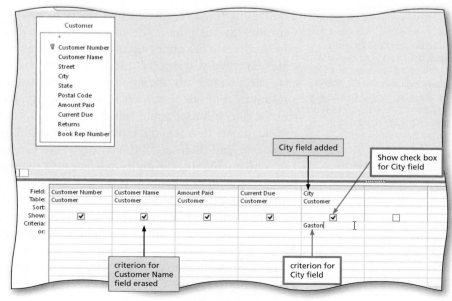

Figure 2–15

2

- Tap or click the Show check box for the City field to remove the check mark (Figure 2–16).

Q&A Could I have removed the check mark before entering the criterion?
Yes. The order in which you perform the two operations does not matter.

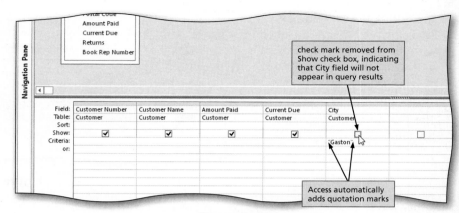

Figure 2–16

3

- Run the query (Figure 2–17).

⌕ Experiment

- Tap or click the View button to return to Design view, enter a different city name as the criterion, and run the query. Repeat this process with additional city names, including at least one city name that is not in the database. When finished, change the criterion back to Gaston.

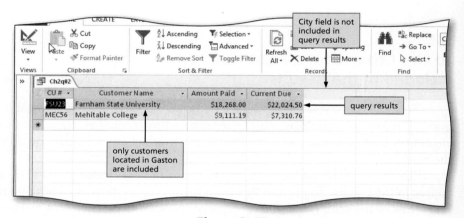

Figure 2–17

BTW
Designing Queries
Before creating queries, examine the contents of the tables involved. You need to know the data type for each field and how the data for the field is stored. If a query includes a state, for example, you need to know whether state is stored as the two-character abbreviation or as the full state name.

Creating a Parameter Query

If you wanted to find customers located in Adelphia instead of Gaston, you would either have to create a new query or modify the existing query by replacing Gaston with Adelphia as the criterion. Rather than giving a specific criterion when you first create the query, occasionally you may want to be able to enter part of the criterion when you run the query and then have the appropriate results appear. For example, you might want a query to return the customer number, customer name, and amount paid for all customers in a specific city, specifying a different city each time you run the query. A user could run the query, enter Adelphia as the city, and then see all the customers in Adelphia. Later, the user could use the same query but enter Gaston as the city, and then see all the customers in Gaston.

To enable this flexibility, you create a **parameter query**, which is a query that prompts for input whenever it is used. You enter a parameter (the prompt for the user), rather than a specific value as the criterion. You create the parameter by enclosing a value in a criterion in square brackets. It is important that the value in the brackets does not match the name of any field. If you enter a field name in square brackets, Access assumes you want that particular field and does not prompt the user for input. To prompt the user to enter the city name as the input, you could place [Enter City] as the criterion in the City field.

To Create and View a Parameter Query

The following steps create a parameter query. *Why? The parameter query will give users at Bavant the ability to enter a different city when they run the query rather than having a specific city as part of the criterion in the query.* The steps also save the query with a new name.

1

- Return to Design view.

- Erase the current criterion in the City column, and then type [Enter City] as the new criterion (Figure 2–18).

Q&A What is the purpose of the square brackets?
The square brackets indicate that the text entered is not text that the value in the column must match. Without the brackets, Access would search for records on which the city is Enter City.

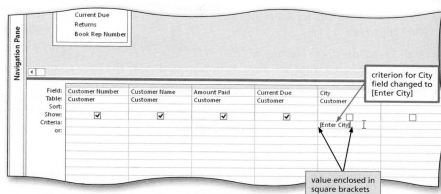

Figure 2–18

What if I typed a field name in the square brackets?
Access would simply use the value in that field. To create a parameter query, you must not use a field name in the square brackets.

2

- Tap or click the Run button (QUERY TOOLS DESIGN tab | Results group) to display the Enter Parameter Value dialog box (Figure 2–19).

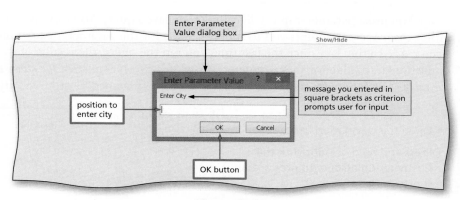

Figure 2–19

3

- Type Adelphia as the parameter value in the Enter City text box, and then tap or click the OK button (Enter Parameter Value dialog box) to close the dialog box and view the query (Figure 2–20).

Experiment

- Try using other characters between the square brackets. In each case, run the query. When finished, change the characters between the square brackets back to Enter City.

Figure 2–20

- Tap or click FILE on the ribbon to open the Backstage view.

- Tap or click the Save As tab in the Backstage view to display the Save As gallery.

- Tap or click Save Object As in the File Types area.

- With Save Object As selected in the File Types area, click the Save As button to display the Save As dialog box.

- Type `Customer-City Query` as the name for the saved query.

- Tap or click the OK button (Save As dialog box) to save the query with the new name and close the Backstage view (Figure 2–21).

Figure 2–21

- Tap or click the Close button for the Customer-City query to close the query.

Break Point: If you wish to take a break, this is a good place to do so. You can exit Access now. To resume later, run Access, open the database called Bavant Publishing, and continue following the steps from this location forward.

To Use a Parameter Query

1 CREATE QUERIES | 2 USE CRITERIA | 3 SORT DATA | 4 JOIN TABLES | 5 EXPORT RESULTS
6 PERFORM CALCULATIONS | 7 CREATE CROSSTAB | 8 CUSTOMIZE NAVIGATION PANE

You use a parameter query like any other saved query. You can open it or you can print the query results. In either case, Access prompts you to supply a value for the parameter each time you use the query. If changes have been made to the data since the last time you ran the query, the results of the query may be different, even if you enter the same value for the parameter. *Why? As with other queries, the query always uses the data that is currently in the table.* The following steps use the parameter query named Customer-City Query.

1

- Open the Navigation Pane.

- Press and hold or right-click the Customer-City Query to produce a shortcut menu.

- Tap or click Open on the shortcut menu to open the query and display the Enter Parameter Value dialog box (Figure 2–22).

Q&A
The title bar for my Navigation Pane contains Tables and Related Views rather than All Access Objects as it did in Chapter 1. What should I do?
Tap or click the Navigation Pane arrow and then tap or click All Access Objects.

I do not have the Search bar at the top of the Navigation Pane that I had in Chapter 1. What should I do?
Press and hold or right-click the Navigation Pane title bar arrow to display a shortcut menu, and then tap or click Search Bar.

Figure 2–22

2

- Type `Adelphia` in the Enter City text box, and then tap or click the OK button (Enter Parameter Value dialog box) to display the results using Adelphia as the city, as shown in Figure 2–21.

- Close the query.

To Use a Number in a Criterion

To enter a number in a criterion, type the number without any dollar signs or commas. *Why? If you enter a dollar sign, Access assumes you are entering text. If you enter a comma, Access considers the criterion invalid.* The following steps create a query that Bavant Publishing might use to display all customers whose current due amount is $0. The steps also save the query with a new name.

- Close the Navigation Pane.
- Tap or click CREATE on the ribbon to display the CREATE tab.
- Tap or click the Query Design button (CREATE tab | Queries group) to create a new query.
- Tap or click the Customer table (Show Table dialog box) to select the table.

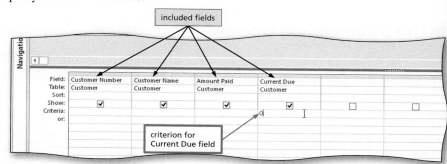

Figure 2–23

- Tap or click the Add button to add the selected table to the query.
- Tap or click the Close button to remove the dialog box from the screen.
- Drag the lower edge of the field list down far enough so all fields in the list are displayed.
- Include the Customer Number, Customer Name, Amount Paid, and Current Due fields in the query.
- Type 0 as the criterion for the Current Due field (Figure 2–23).

Q&A Do I need to enter a dollar sign and decimal point?
No. Access will interpret 0 as $0 because the data type for the Current Due field is currency.

- Run the query (Figure 2–24).

Q&A Why did Access display the results as $0.00 when I only entered 0?
Access uses the format for the field to determine how to display the result. In this case, the format indicated that Access should include the dollar sign, decimal point, and two decimal places.

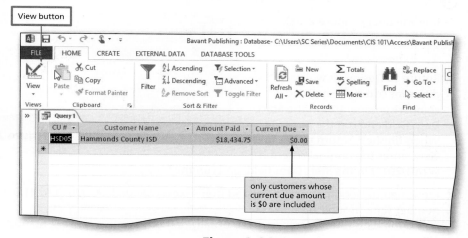

Figure 2–24

- Save the query as Ch2q03.

Q&A How do I know when to use the Save button to save a query or use the Backstage view to perform a Save As?
If you are saving a new query, the simplest way is to use the Save button on the Quick Access Toolbar. If you are saving changes to a previously saved query but do not want to change the name, use the Save button. If you want to save a previously saved query with a new name, you must use the Backstage view and perform a Save Object As.

- Close the query.

Comparison Operators

Unless you specify otherwise, Access assumes that the criteria you enter involve equality (exact matches). In the last query, for example, you were requesting those customers whose current due amount is equal to 0 (zero). In other situations, you

might want to find a range of results; for example, you could request customers whose current due is greater than $1,000.00. If you want a query to return something other than an exact match, you must enter the appropriate **comparison operator**. The comparison operators are > (greater than), < (less than), >= (greater than or equal to), <= (less than or equal to), and NOT (not equal to).

To Use a Comparison Operator in a Criterion

1 CREATE QUERIES | 2 USE CRITERIA | 3 SORT DATA | 4 JOIN TABLES | 5 EXPORT RESULTS
6 PERFORM CALCULATIONS | 7 CREATE CROSSTAB | 8 CUSTOMIZE NAVIGATION PANE

The following steps use the > operator to create a query that Bavant Publishing might use to find all book reps whose start date is after 1/1/2013. *Why? A date greater than 1/1/2013 means the date comes after 1/1/2013.* The steps also save the query with a new name.

 1

- Start a new query using the Book Rep table.

- Include the Book Rep Number, Last Name, First Name, and Start Date fields.

- Type >1/01/2013 as the criterion for the Start Date field (Figure 2–25).

Figure 2–25

Q&A Did I have to type the leading zero in the Day portion of the date?
No. You could have typed 1/1/2013. Some people often type the day using two digits, such as 1/01/2013. You also could have typed a leading zero in the month, 01/01/2013.

 2

- Run the query (Figure 2–26).

 Experiment

- Return to Design view. Try a different criterion involving a comparison operator in the Start Date field and run the query. When finished, return to Design view, enter the original criterion (>1/01/2013) in the Start Date field, and run the query.

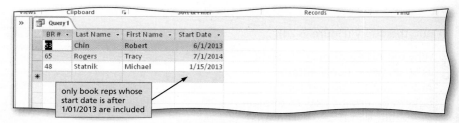

Figure 2–26

Q&A I returned to Design view and noticed that Access changed 1/01/2013 to #1/01/2013#. Why does the date now have number signs around it?
This is the date format in Access. You usually do not have to enter the number signs because in most cases Access will insert them automatically.

My records are in a different order. Is this a problem?
No. The important thing is which records are included in the results. You will see later in this chapter how you can specify the specific order you want for cases when the order is important.

Can I use the same comparison operators with text data?
Yes. Comparison operators function the same whether you use them with number fields, currency fields, date fields, or text fields.

3

- Save the query as Ch2q04.

- Close the query.

Using Compound Criteria

Often your search data must satisfy more than one criterion. This type of criterion is called a **compound criterion** and is created using the words AND or OR.

In an **AND criterion**, each individual criterion must be true in order for the compound criterion to be true. For example, an AND criterion would allow you to find customers that have returns greater than $0.00 and whose book rep is book rep 42.

An **OR criterion** is true if either individual criterion is true. An OR criterion would allow you to find customers that have returns greater than $0.00 as well as customers whose book rep is book rep 42. In this case, any customer who has returns greater than $0.00 would be included in the answer, regardless of whether the customer's book rep is book rep 42. Likewise, any customer whose book rep is book rep 42 would be included, regardless of whether the customer has returns greater than $0.00.

BTW

Queries: Query-by-Example
Query-By-Example, often referred to as QBE, was a query language first proposed in the mid-1970s. In this approach, users asked questions by filling in a table on the screen. The Access approach to queries is based on Query-By-Example.

To Use a Compound Criterion Involving AND

1 CREATE QUERIES | 2 USE CRITERIA | 3 SORT DATA | 4 JOIN TABLES | 5 EXPORT RESULTS
6 PERFORM CALCULATIONS | 7 CREATE CROSSTAB | 8 CUSTOMIZE NAVIGATION PANE

To combine criteria with AND, place the criteria on the same row of the design grid. *Why? Placing the criteria in the same row indicates that both criteria must be true in Access.* The following steps use an AND criterion to enable Bavant to find those customers who have returns greater than $0.00 and whose book rep is rep 42. The steps also save the query.

- Start a new query using the Customer table.

- Include the Customer Number, Customer Name, Amount Paid, Current Due, Returns, and Book Rep Number fields.

- Type >0 as the criterion for the Returns field.

- Type 42 as the criterion for the Book Rep Number field (Figure 2–27).

Figure 2–27

- Run the query (Figure 2–28).

- Save the query as Ch2q05.

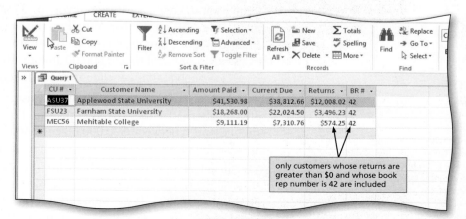

Figure 2–28

To Use a Compound Criterion Involving OR

To combine criteria with OR, each criterion must go on separate rows in the Criteria area of the grid. *Why?* *Placing criteria on separate rows indicates at least one criterion must be true in Access.* The following steps use an OR criterion to enable Bavant to find those customers who have returns greater than $0.00 or whose book rep is rep 42 (or both). The steps also save the query with a new name.

- Return to Design view.
- If necessary, tap or click the Criteria entry for the Book Rep Number field and then use the BACKSPACE key or the DELETE key to erase the entry ("42").
- Tap or click the or row (the row below the Criteria row) for the Book Rep Number field, and then type 42 as the entry (Figure 2–29).

Figure 2–29

- Run the query (Figure 2–30).

- Save the query as Ch2q06.

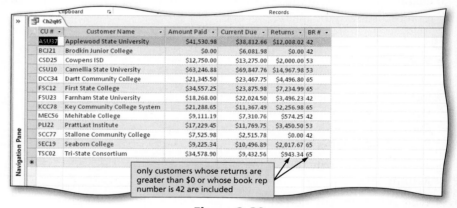

Figure 2–30

BTW
**Rearranging Fields
in a Query**
To move a field in the design grid, tap or click the column selector for the field to select the field and drag it to the appropriate location.

BTW
Q&As
For a complete list of the Q&As found in many of the step-by-step sequences in this book, visit the Q&A resource on the Student Companion Site located on www. cengagebrain.com. For detailed instructions about accessing available resources, visit www. cengage.com/ct/studentdownload or contact your instructor for information about accessing the required files.

Special Criteria

You can use three special criteria in queries:

1. If you want to create a criterion involving a range of values in a single field, you can use the **AND operator.** You place the word AND between the individual conditions. For example, if you wanted to find all customers whose amount paid is greater than or equal to $20,000.00 and less than or equal to $40,000.00, you would enter >= 20000 AND <= 40000 as the criterion in the Amount Paid column.

2. You can select values in a given range by using the **BETWEEN operator.** This is often an alternative to the AND operator. For example, to find all customers whose amount paid is between $20,000.00 and $40,000.00, inclusive, you would enter BETWEEN 20000 AND 40000 as the criterion in the Amount Paid column.

3. You can select a list of values by using the **IN operator.** You follow the word IN with the list of values in parentheses. For example, to find customers whose book rep number is 42 and customers whose book rep is 65 using the IN operator, you would enter IN ("42","65") on the Criteria row in the Book Rep Number column. Unlike when you enter a simple criterion, you must enclose text values in quotation marks.

How would you find customers whose book rep number is 42 or 65 without using the IN operator?
Place the number 42 in the Criteria row of the Book Rep Number column. Place the number 65 in the or row of the Book Rep Number column.

Sorting

In some queries, the order in which the records appear is irrelevant. All you need to be concerned about are the records that appear in the results. It does not matter which one is first or which one is last.

In other queries, however, the order can be very important. You may want to see the cities in which customers are located and would like them arranged alphabetically. Perhaps you want to see the customers listed by book rep number. Further, within all the customers of any given book rep, you might want them to be listed by amount paid from largest amount to smallest.

To order the records in a query result in a particular way, you **sort** the records. The field or fields on which the records are sorted is called the **sort key**. If you are sorting on more than one field (such as sorting by amount paid within book rep number), the more important field (Book Rep Number) is called the **major key** (also called the **primary sort key**) and the less important field (Amount Paid) is called the **minor key** (also called the **secondary sort key**).

To sort in Microsoft Access, specify the sort order in the Sort row of the design grid below the field that is the sort key. If you specify more than one sort key, the sort key on the left will be the major sort key, and the one on the right will be the minor key.

> BTW
> **Sorting Data in a Query**
> When sorting data in a query, the records in the underlying tables (the tables on which the query is based) are not actually rearranged. Instead, the DBMS determines the most efficient method of simply displaying the records in the requested order. The records in the underlying tables remain in their original order.

> BTW
> **Clearing the Design Grid**
> You also can clear the design grid using the ribbon. To do so, tap or click the HOME tab, tap or click the Advanced button to display the Advanced menu, and then tap or click Clear Grid on the Advanced menu.

To Clear the Design Grid

1 CREATE QUERIES | 2 USE CRITERIA | 3 SORT DATA | 4 JOIN TABLES | 5 EXPORT RESULTS
6 PERFORM CALCULATIONS | 7 CREATE CROSSTAB | 8 CUSTOMIZE NAVIGATION PANE

Why? *If the fields you want to include in the next query are different from those in the previous query, it is usually simpler to start with a clear grid, that is, one with no fields already in the design grid.* You always can clear the entries in the design grid by closing the query and then starting over. A simpler approach to clearing the entries is to select all the entries and then press the DELETE key. The following steps return to Design view and clear the design grid.

- Return to Design view.

- Tap or click just above the Customer Number column heading in the grid to select the column.

Q&A I clicked above the column heading, but the column is not selected. What should I do?
You did not point to the correct location. Be sure the pointer changes into a down-pointing arrow and then tap or click again.

- Hold the SHIFT key down and tap or click just above the Book Rep Number column heading to select all the columns (Figure 2–31).

Figure 2–31

- Press the DELETE key to clear the design grid.

To Sort Data in a Query

If you determine that the query results should be sorted, you will need to specify the sort key. The following steps sort the cities in the Customer table by indicating that the City field is to be sorted. The steps specify Ascending sort order. ***Why?*** *When sorting text data, Ascending sort order arranges the results in alphabetical order.*

- Include the City field in the design grid.
- Tap or click the Sort row below the City field, and then tap or click the Sort arrow to display a menu of possible sort orders (Figure 2–32).

Figure 2–32

- Tap or click Ascending to select the sort order (Figure 2–33).

Figure 2–33

- Run the query (Figure 2–34).

Experiment

- Return to Design view and change the sort order to Descending. Run the query. Return to Design view and change the sort order back to Ascending. Run the query.

Q&A Why do some cities appear more than once?
More than one customer is located in those cities.

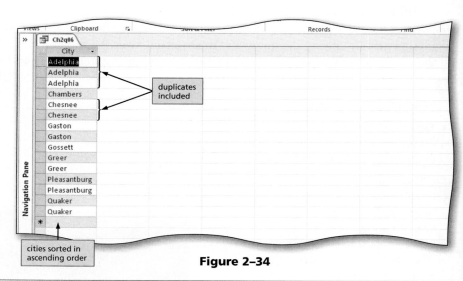

Figure 2–34

To Omit Duplicates

When you sort data, duplicates normally are included. In the query shown in Figure 2–34, for example, Adelphia appears three times. Several other cities appear twice. You eliminate duplicates using the query's property sheet. A **property sheet** is a window containing the various properties of the object. To omit duplicates, you will use the property sheet to change the Unique Values property from No to Yes.

The following steps create a query that Bavant Publishing might use to obtain a sorted list of the cities in the Customer table in which each city is listed only once. *Why? Unless you wanted to know how many customers were located in each city, the duplicates typically do not add any value.* The steps also save the query with a new name.

- Return to Design view.
- Tap or click the second field (the empty field to the right of City) in the design grid to produce an insertion point.
- If necessary, tap or click DESIGN on the ribbon to display the DESIGN tab.
- Tap or click the Property Sheet button (QUERY TOOLS DESIGN tab | Show/Hide group) to display the property sheet (Figure 2–35).

Q&A My property sheet looks different. What should I do?
If your sheet looks different, close the property sheet and repeat this step.

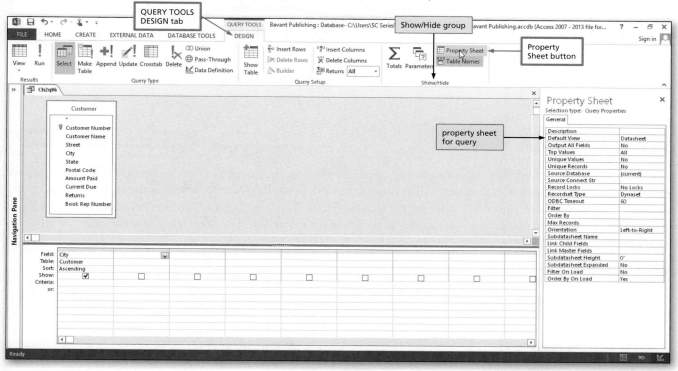

Figure 2–35

2

- Tap or click the Unique Values property box, and then tap or click the arrow that appears to display a list of available choices (Figure 2–36).

Figure 2–36

- Tap or click Yes to indicate that the query will return unique values, which means that each value will appear only once in the query results.

- Close the Query Properties property sheet by tapping or clicking the Property Sheet button (QUERY TOOLS DESIGN tab | Show/Hide group) a second time.

- Run the query (Figure 2–37).

Figure 2–37

- Save the query as Ch2q07.

Other Ways

1. Press and hold or right-click second field in design grid, tap or click Properties on shortcut menu

To Sort on Multiple Keys

1 CREATE QUERIES | 2 USE CRITERIA | 3 SORT DATA | 4 JOIN TABLES | 5 EXPORT RESULTS
6 PERFORM CALCULATIONS | 7 CREATE CROSSTAB | 8 CUSTOMIZE NAVIGATION PANE

The following steps sort on multiple keys. Specifically, Bavant needs the data to be sorted by amount paid (low to high) within book rep number, which means that the Book Rep Number field is the major key and the Amount Paid field is the minor key. The steps place the Book Rep Number field to the left of the Amount Paid field. *Why? In Access, the major key must appear to the left of the minor key.* The steps also save the query with a new name.

1

- Return to Design view. Clear the design grid by tapping or clicking the top of the first column in the grid, and then pressing the DELETE key to clear the design grid.

- In the following order, include the Customer Number, Customer Name, Book Rep Number, and Amount Paid fields in the query.

- Select Ascending as the sort order for both the Book Rep Number field and the Amount Paid field (Figure 2–38).

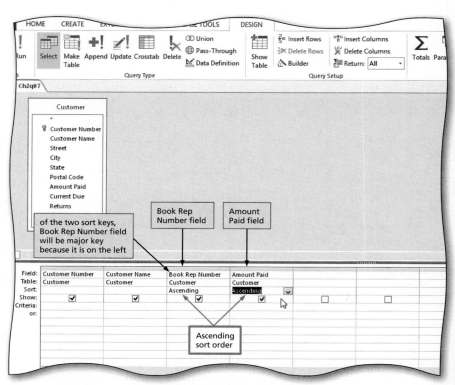

Figure 2–38

2

- Run the query (Figure 2–39).

 Experiment

- Return to Design view and try other sort combinations for the Book Rep Number and Amount Paid fields, such as Ascending for Book Rep Number and Descending for Amount Paid. In each case, run the query to see the effect of the changes. When finished, select Ascending as the sort order for both fields.

Q&A

What if the Amount Paid field is to the left of the Book Rep Number field?

It is important to remember that the major sort key must appear to the left of the minor sort key in the design grid. If you attempted to sort by amount paid within book rep number, but placed the Amount Paid field to the left of the Book Rep Number field, your results would be incorrect.

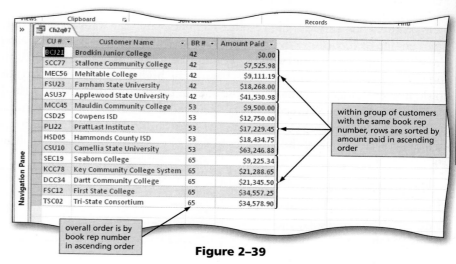

> within group of customers with the same book rep number, rows are sorted by amount paid in ascending order

> overall order is by book rep number in ascending order

Figure 2–39

3

- Save the query as Ch2q08.

 CONSIDER THIS

Is there any way to sort the records in this same order, but have the Amount Paid field appear to the left of the Book Rep Number field in the query results?

Yes. Remove the check mark from the Book Rep Number field, and then add an additional Book Rep Number field at the end of the query. The first Book Rep Number field will be used for sorting but will not appear in the results. The second will appear in the results, but will not be involved in the sorting process.

 CONSIDER THIS

How do you approach the creation of a query that might involve sorting?

Examine the query or request to see if it contains words such as *order* or *sort*. Such words imply that the order of the query results is important. If so, you need to sort the query.

If sorting is required, identify the field or fields on which the results are to be sorted. In the request, look for language such as *ordered by* or *sort the results by*, both of which would indicate that the specified field is a sort key.

If using multiple sort keys, determine the major and minor keys. If you are using two sort keys, determine which one is the more important, or the major key. Look for language such as *sort by amount paid within book rep number*, which implies that the overall order is by book rep number. In this case, the Book Rep Number field would be the major sort key and the Amount Paid field would be the minor sort key.

Determine sort order. Words such as *increasing*, *ascending*, or *low-to-high* imply Ascending order. Words such as *decreasing*, *descending*, or *high-to-low* imply Descending order. Sorting in *alphabetical order* implies Ascending order. If there were no words to imply a particular order, you would typically use Ascending.

Examine the query or request to see if there are any special restrictions. One common restriction is to exclude duplicates. Another common restriction is to list only a certain number of records, such as the first five records.

To Create a Top-Values Query

Rather than show all the results of a query, you may want to show only a specified number of records or a percentage of records. **Why?** *You might not need to see all the records, just enough to get a general idea of the results.* Creating a **top-values query** allows you to restrict the number of records that appear. When you sort records, you can limit results to those records having the highest (descending sort) or lowest (ascending sort) values. To do so, first create a query that sorts the data in the desired order. Next, use the Return box on the DESIGN tab to change the number of records to be included from All to the desired number or percentage.

The following steps create a query for Bavant Publishing that shows only the first five records that were included in the results of the previous query. The steps also save the resulting query with a new name.

1

- Return to Design view.

- If necessary, tap or click DESIGN on the ribbon to display the Design tab.

- Tap or click the Return arrow (QUERY TOOLS DESIGN tab | Query Setup group) to display the Return menu (Figure 2–40).

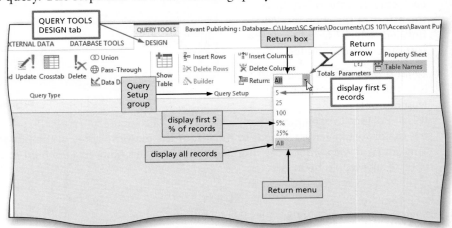

Figure 2–40

2

- Tap or click 5 in the Return menu to specify that the query results should contain the first five rows.

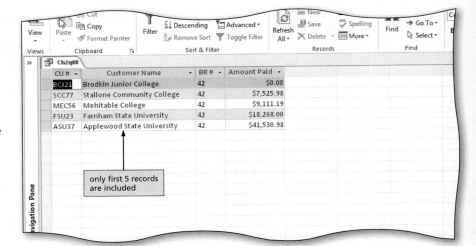

Figure 2–41

Q&A Could I have typed the 5? What about other numbers that do not appear in the list?

Yes, you could have typed the 5. For numbers not appearing in the list, you must type the number.

- Run the query (Figure 2–41).

3

- Save the query as Ch2q09.

- Close the query.

Q&A Do I need to close the query before creating my next query?

Not necessarily. When you use a top-values query, however, it is important to change the value in the Return box back to All. If you do not change the Return value back to All, the previous value will remain in effect. Consequently, you might not get all the records you should in the next query. A good practice whenever you use a top-values query is to close the query as soon as you are done. That way, you will begin your next query from scratch, which guarantees that the value is reset to All.

Break Point: If you wish to take a break, this is a good place to do so. You can exit Access now. To resume later, run Access, open the database called Bavant Publishing, and continue following the steps from this location forward.

Joining Tables

In designing a query, you need to determine whether more than one table is required. For example, if the question being asked involves data from both the Customer and Book Rep tables, then both tables are required for the query. A query might require listing the number and name of each customer (from the Customer table) along with the number and name of the customer's book rep (from the Book Rep table). Both the Customer and Book Rep tables are required for this query. You need to **join** the tables to find records in the two tables that have identical values in matching fields (Figure 2–42). In this example, you need to find records in the Customer table and the Book Rep table that have the same value in the Book Rep Number fields.

BTW

Ad Hoc Relationships
When you join tables in a query, you are creating an ad hoc relationship, that is, a relationship between tables created for a specific purpose. In Chapter 3, you will create general-purpose relationships using the Relationships window.

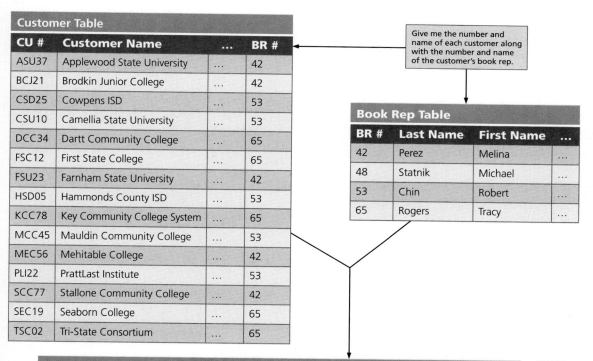

Give me the number and name of each customer along with the number and name of the customer's book rep.

Customer Table

CU #	Customer Name	...	BR #
ASU37	Applewood State University	...	42
BCJ21	Brodkin Junior College	...	42
CSD25	Cowpens ISD	...	53
CSU10	Camellia State University	...	53
DCC34	Dartt Community College	...	65
FSC12	First State College	...	65
FSU23	Farnham State University	...	42
HSD05	Hammonds County ISD	...	53
KCC78	Key Community College System	...	65
MCC45	Mauldin Community College	...	53
MEC56	Mehitable College	...	42
PLI22	PrattLast Institute	...	53
SCC77	Stallone Community College	...	42
SEC19	Seaborn College	...	65
TSC02	Tri-State Consortium	...	65

Book Rep Table

BR #	Last Name	First Name	...
42	Perez	Melina	...
48	Statnik	Michael	...
53	Chin	Robert	...
65	Rogers	Tracy	...

Customer Table

CU #	Customer Name	...	BR #	Last Name	First Name	...
ASU37	Applewood State University	...	42	Perez	Melina	...
BCJ21	Brodkin Junior College	...	42	Perez	Melina	...
CSD25	Cowpens ISD	...	53	Chin	Robert	...
CSU10	Camellia State University	...	53	Chin	Robert	...
DCC34	Dartt Community College	...	65	Rogers	Tracy	...
FSC12	First State College	...	65	Rogers	Tracy	...
FSU23	Farnham State University	...	42	Perez	Melina	...
HSD05	Hammonds County ISD	...	53	Chin	Robert	...
KCC78	Key Community College System	...	65	Rogers	Tracy	...
MCC45	Mauldin Community College	...	53	Chin	Robert	...
MEC56	Mehitable College	...	42	Perez	Melina	...
PLI22	PrattLast Institute	...	53	Chin	Robert	...
SCC77	Stallone Community College	...	42	Perez	Melina	...
SEC19	Seaborn College	...	65	Rogers	Tracy	...
TSC02	Tri-State Consortium	...	65	Rogers	Tracy	...

BTW

Join Line
If you do not get a join line automatically, there may be a problem with one of your table designs. Open each table in Design view and make sure that the data types are the same for the matching field in both tables and that one of the matching fields is the primary key in a table. Correct these errors and create the query again.

© 2014 Cengage Learning

Figure 2–42

To Join Tables

If you have determined that you need to join tables, you first will bring field lists for both tables to the upper pane of the Query window while working in Design view. Access will draw a line, called a **join line**, between matching fields in the two tables, indicating that the tables are related. You then can select fields from either table. Access joins the tables automatically.

The first step is to create a new query and add the Book Rep table to the query. Then, add the Customer table to the query. A join line should appear, connecting the Book Rep Number fields in the two field lists. **_Why might the join line not appear?_** *If the names of the matching fields differ from one table to the other, Access will not insert the line. You can insert it manually, however, by tapping or clicking one of the two matching fields and dragging the pointer to the other matching field.*

The following steps create a query to display information from both the Customer table and the Book Rep table.

- Tap or click CREATE on the ribbon to display the CREATE tab.
- Tap or click the Query Design button (CREATE tab | Queries group) to create a new query.
- If necessary, tap or click the Book Rep table (Show Table dialog box) to select the table.
- Tap or click the Add button (Show Table dialog box) to add a field list for the Book Rep Table to the query (Figure 2–43).

Figure 2–43

- Tap or click the Customer table (Show Table dialog box).
- Tap or click the Add button (Show Table dialog box) to add a field list for the Customer table.
- Close the Show Table dialog box by tapping or clicking the Close button.
- Expand the size of the two field lists so all the fields in the Book Rep and Customer tables appear (Figure 2–44).

Figure 2–44

Q&A

I did not get a join line. What should I do?

Ensure that the names of the matching fields are the same, the data types are the same, and the matching field is the primary key in one of the two tables. If all of these factors are true and you still do not have a join line, you can produce one by pointing to a matching field and dragging to the other matching field.

3

- In the design grid, include the Book Rep Number, Last Name, and First Name fields from the Book Rep Table as well as the Customer Number and Customer Name fields from the Customer table.

- Select Ascending as the sort order for both the Book Rep Number field and the Customer Number field (Figure 2–45).

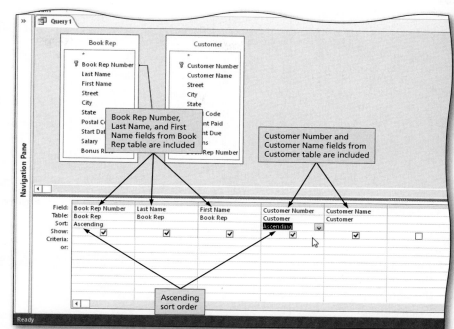

Figure 2–45

4

- Run the query (Figure 2–46).

5

- Tap or click the Save button on the Quick Access Toolbar to display the Save As dialog box.

- Type `Rep-Customer Query` as the query name.

6

- Tap or click the OK button (Save As dialog box) to save the query.

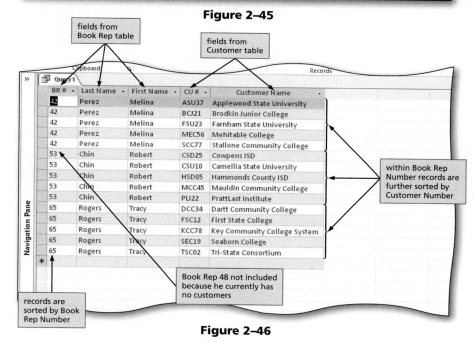

Figure 2–46

To Change Join Properties

1 CREATE QUERIES | 2 USE CRITERIA | 3 SORT DATA | 4 JOIN TABLES | 5 EXPORT RESULTS
6 PERFORM CALCULATIONS | 7 CREATE CROSSTAB | 8 CUSTOMIZE NAVIGATION PANE

Normally, records that do not match do not appear in the results of a join query. For example, the book rep named Michael Statnik does not appear in the results. *Why? He currently does not have any customers.* To cause such a record to be displayed, you need to change the **join properties**, which are the properties that indicate which records appear in a join. The following steps change the join properties of the Rep-Customer Query so that Bavant can include all book reps in the results, rather than only those reps who have already been assigned customers.

1

- Return to Design view.

- Press and hold or right-click the join line to produce a shortcut menu (Figure 2–47).

Q&A I do not see Join Properties on my shortcut menu. What should I do?
If Join Properties does not appear on your shortcut menu, you did not point to the appropriate portion of the join line. You will need to point to the correct (middle) portion and press and hold or right-click again.

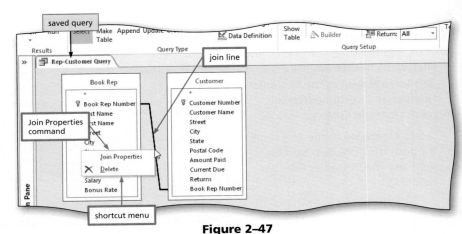

Figure 2–47

2

- Tap or click Join Properties on the shortcut menu to display the Join Properties dialog box (Figure 2–48).

Figure 2–48

3

- Tap or click option button 2 (Join Properties dialog box) to include all records from the Book Rep Table regardless of whether they match any customers.

- Tap or click the OK button (Join Properties dialog box) to modify the join properties.

- Run the query (Figure 2–49).

Experiment

- Return to Design view, change the Join properties, and select option button 3. Run the query to see the effect of this option. When done, return to Design view, change the join properties, and once again select option button 2.

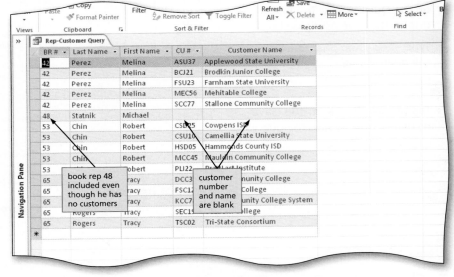

Figure 2–49

4

- Tap or click the Save button on the Quick Access Toolbar to save the changes to the query.

- Close the Rep-Customer Query.

Q&A I see a dialog box that asks if I want to save the query. What should I do?
Tap or click the OK button to save the query.

To Create a Report from a Query

You can use queries in the creation of reports. The report in Figure 2–50 involves data from more than one table. *Why? The Last Name and First Name fields are in the Book Rep table. The Customer Number and Customer Name fields are in the Customer table. The Book Rep Number field is in both tables.* The easiest way to create such a report is to base it on a query that joins the two tables. The following steps use the Report Wizard and the Rep-Customer Query to create the report.

Rep-Customer Report

BR #	Last Name	First Name	CU #	Customer Name
42	Perez	Melina	ASU37	Applewood State University
42	Perez	Melina	BCJ21	Brodkin Junior College
42	Perez	Melina	FSU23	Farnham State University
42	Perez	Melina	MEC56	Mehitable College
42	Perez	Melina	SCC77	Stallone Community College
48	Statnik	Michael		
53	Chin	Robert	CSD25	Cowpens ISD
53	Chin	Robert	CSU10	Camellia State University
53	Chin	Robert	HSD05	Hammonds County ISD
53	Chin	Robert	MCC45	Mauldin Community College
53	Chin	Robert	PLI22	PrattLast Institute
65	Rogers	Tracy	DCC34	Dartt Community College
65	Rogers	Tracy	FSC12	First State College
65	Rogers	Tracy	KCC78	Key Community College System
65	Rogers	Tracy	SEC19	Seaborn College
65	Rogers	Tracy	TSC02	Tri-State Consortium

Figure 2–50

1
- Open the Navigation Pane, and then select the Rep-Customer Query in the Navigation Pane.
- Tap or click CREATE on the ribbon to display the CREATE tab.
- Tap or click the Report Wizard button (CREATE tab | Reports group) to display the Report Wizard dialog box (Figure 2–51).

Figure 2–51

● Tap or click the Add All Fields button (Report Wizard dialog box) to add all the fields in the Rep-Customer Query.

● Tap or click the Next button to display the next Report Wizard screen (Figure 2–52).

Figure 2–52

● Because you will not specify any grouping, tap or click the Next button in the Report Wizard dialog box to display the next Report Wizard screen.

● Because you already specified the sort order in the query, tap or click the Next button again to display the next Report Wizard screen.

● Make sure that Tabular is selected as the Layout and Portrait is selected as the Orientation.

● Tap or click the Next button to display the next Report Wizard screen.

● Erase the current title, and then type `Rep-Customer Report` as the new title.

● Tap or click the Finish button to produce the report (Figure 2–53).

Figure 2–53

● Close the Rep-Customer Report.

To Print a Report

The following steps print a hard copy of the report.

1 With the Rep-Customer Report selected in the Navigation Pane, tap or click FILE on the ribbon to open the Backstage view.

2 Tap or click the Print tab in the Backstage view to display the Print gallery.

3 Tap or click the Quick Print button to print the report.

How would you approach the creation of a query that might involve multiple tables?

Examine the request to see if all the fields involved in the request are in one table. If the fields are in two (or more) tables, you need to join the tables.

If joining is required, identify the matching fields in the two tables that have identical values. Look for the same column name in the two tables or for column names that are similar.

Determine whether sorting is required. Queries that join tables often are used as the basis for a report. If this is the case, it may be necessary to sort the results. For example, the Rep-Customer Report is based on a query that joins the Book Rep and Customer tables. The query is sorted by book rep number and customer number.

Examine the request to see if there are any special restrictions. For example, the user only may want customers whose current due amount is $0.00.

Examine the request to see if you only want records from both tables that have identical values in matching fields. If you want to see records in one of the tables that do not have identical values, then you need to change the join properties.

Creating a Form for a Query

In the previous chapter, you created a form for the Customer table. You also can create a form for a query. Recall that a form in a database is a formatted document with fields that contain data. Forms allow you to view and maintain data.

To Create a Form for a Query

1 CREATE QUERIES | 2 USE CRITERIA | 3 SORT DATA | 4 JOIN TABLES | 5 EXPORT RESULTS
6 PERFORM CALCULATIONS | 7 CREATE CROSSTAB | 8 CUSTOMIZE NAVIGATION PANE

The following steps create a form, then save the form. *Why? The form will be available for future use in viewing the data in the query.*

- If necessary, select the Rep-Customer Query in the Navigation Pane.
- Tap or click CREATE on the ribbon to display the CREATE tab (Figure 2–54).

Figure 2–54

- Tap or click the Form button (CREATE tab | Forms group) to create a simple form (Figure 2–55).

Q&A I see a field list also. What should I do?
Tap or click the Close button for the Field List.

- Tap or click the Save button on the Quick Access Toolbar to display the Save As dialog box.
- Type `Rep-Customer Form` as the form name.

Figure 2–55

- Tap or click the OK button to save the form.
- Tap or click the Close button for the form to close the form.

Using a Form

After you have saved a form, you can use it at any time by pressing and holding or right-clicking the form in the Navigation Pane and then tapping or clicking Open on the shortcut menu. If you plan to use the form to enter data, you must ensure you are viewing the form in Form view.

Exporting Data from Access to Other Applications

You can **export**, or copy, tables or queries from an Access database so that another application (for example, Excel or Word) can use the data. The application that will receive the data determines the export process to be used. You can export to text files in a variety of formats. For applications to which you cannot directly export data, you often can export an appropriately formatted text file that the other application can import. Figure 2–56 shows the workbook produced by exporting the Rep-Customer Query to Excel. The columns in the workbook have been resized to best fit the data.

BTW
Distributing a Document
Instead of printing and distributing a hard copy of a document, you can distribute the document electronically. Options include sending the document via email; posting it on cloud storage (such as SkyDrive) and sharing the file with others; posting it on a social networking site, blog, or other website; and sharing a link associated with an online location of the document. You also can create and share a PDF or XPS image of the document, so that users can view the file in Acrobat Reader or XPS Viewer instead of in Access.

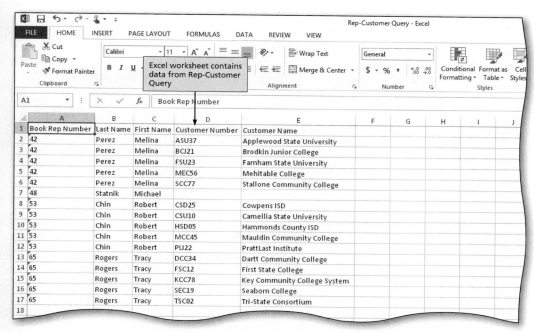

Figure 2–56

To Export Data to Excel

1 CREATE QUERIES | 2 USE CRITERIA | 3 SORT DATA | 4 JOIN TABLES | 5 EXPORT RESULTS
6 PERFORM CALCULATIONS | 7 CREATE CROSSTAB | 8 CUSTOMIZE NAVIGATION PANE

For Bavant Publishing to make the Rep-Customer Query available to Excel users, it needs to export the data. To export data to Excel, select the table or query to be exported and then tap or click the Excel button in the Export group on the EXTERNAL DATA tab. The steps on the next page export the Rep-Customer Query to Excel and save the export steps. *Why save the export steps? By saving the export steps, you could easily repeat the export process whenever you like without going through all the steps.* You would use the saved steps to export data in the future by tapping or clicking the Saved Exports button (EXTERNAL DATA tab | Export group) and then selecting the steps you saved.

1

- If necessary, tap or click the Rep-Customer Query in the Navigation Pane to select it.

- Tap or click EXTERNAL DATA on the ribbon to display the EXTERNAL DATA tab (Figure 2–57).

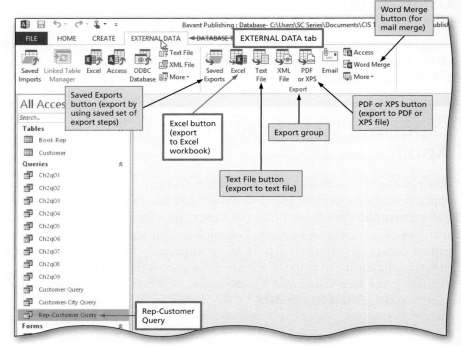

Figure 2–57

2

- Tap or click the Excel button (EXTERNAL DATA tab | Export group) to display the Export-Excel Spreadsheet dialog box.

- Tap or click the Browse button (Export-Excel Spreadsheet dialog box), and then navigate to the location where you wish to export the query (for example, the Access folder in the CIS 101 folder).

- Be sure the file name is Rep-Customer Query and then tap or click the Save button (File Save dialog box) to select the file name and location (Figure 2–58).

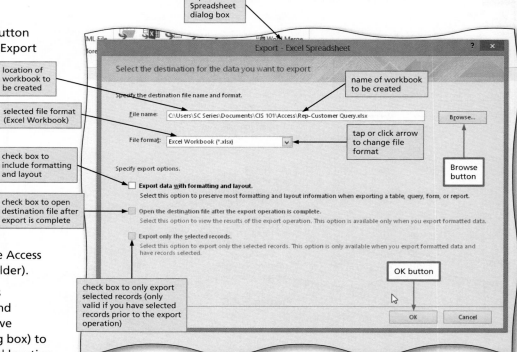

Figure 2–58

Q&A Did I need to browse?
No. You could type the appropriate file location.

Could I change the name of the file?
You could change it. Simply replace the current file name with the one you want.

What if the file I want to export already exists?
Access will indicate that the file already exists and ask if you want to replace it. If you tap or click the Yes button, the file you export will replace the old file. If you tap or click the No button, you must either change the name of the export file or cancel the process.

3

- Tap or click the OK button (Export-Excel Spreadsheet dialog box) to export the data (Figure 2–59).

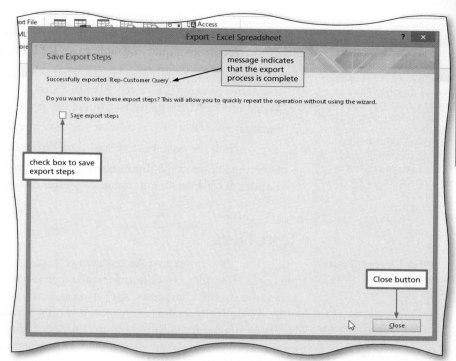

Figure 2–59

4

- Tap or click the 'Save export steps' check box (Export-Excel Spreadsheet dialog box) to display the Save Export Steps options.

- If necessary, type `Export-Rep-Customer Query` in the Save as text box.

- Type `Export the Rep-Customer Query without formatting` in the Description text box (Figure 2–60).

Q&A How could I re-use the export steps?

You can use these steps to export data in the future by tapping or clicking the Saved Exports button (EXTERNAL DATA tab | Export group) and then selecting the steps you saved.

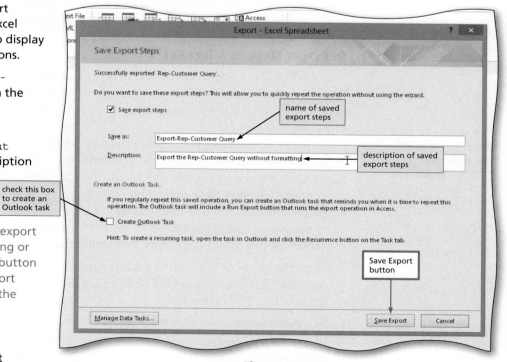

Figure 2–60

5

- Tap or click the Save Export button (Export-Excel Spreadsheet dialog box) to save the export steps.

Other Ways

1. Press and hold or right-click database object in Navigation Pane, tap or click Export

BTW
Exporting Data
You frequently need to export data so that it can be used in other applications and by other users in an organization. For example, the Accounting department might require financial data in an Excel format to perform certain financial functions. Marketing might require a list of customer names and addresses in Word or RTF format for marketing campaigns.

To Export Data to Word

It is not possible to export data from Access to the standard Word format. It is possible, however, to export the data as a rich text format (RTF) file, which Word can use. To export data from a query or table to an RTF file, you would use the following steps.

1. With the query or table to be exported selected in the Navigation Pane, tap or click the More button (EXTERNAL DATA tab | Export group) and then tap or click Word on the More menu to display the Export-RTF File dialog box.
2. Navigate to the location in which to save the file and assign a file name.
3. Tap or click the Save button, and then tap or click the OK button to export the data.
4. Save the export steps if you want, or simply tap or click the Close button in the Export-RTF File dialog box to close the dialog box without saving the export steps.

Text Files

You also can export Access data to text files, which can be used for a variety of purposes. Text files contain unformatted characters, including alphanumeric characters, and some special characters, such as tabs, carriage returns, and line feeds.

In **delimited files**, each record is on a separate line and the fields are separated by a special character, called the **delimiter**. Common delimiters are tabs, semicolons, commas, and spaces. You also can choose any other value that does not appear within the field contents as the delimiter. The comma-separated values (CSV) file often used in Excel is an example of a delimited file.

In **fixed-width files**, the width of any field is the same on every record. For example, if the width of the first field on the first record is 12 characters, the width of the first field on every other record also must be 12 characters.

BTW
Saving Export Steps
Because query results are based on the data in the underlying tables, a change to an underlying table would result in a new query answer. For example, if the last name for book rep 42 changed from Perez to Smith, the change would be made in the Book Rep table. If you run the Rep-Customer Query again and export the query using the saved export steps, the Excel workbook would show the changed name.

To Export Data to a Text File

When exporting data to a text file, you can choose to export the data with formatting and layout. This option preserves much of the formatting and layout in tables, queries, forms, and reports. For forms and reports, this is the only option for exporting to a text file.

If you do not need to preserve the formatting, you can choose either delimited or fixed-width as the format for the exported file. The most common option, especially if formatting is not an issue, is delimited. You can choose the delimiter. You also can choose whether to include field names on the first row. In many cases, delimiting with a comma and including the field names is a good choice.

To export data from a table or query to a comma-delimited file in which the first row contains the column headings, you would use the following steps.

1. With the query or table to be exported selected in the Navigation Pane, tap or click the Text File button (EXTERNAL DATA tab | Export group) to display the Export-Text File dialog box.
2. Select the name and location for the file to be created.
3. If you need to preserve formatting and layout, be sure the 'Export data with formatting and layout' check box is checked. If you do not need to preserve formatting and layout, make sure the check box is not checked. Once you have made your selection, tap or click the OK button in the Export-Text File dialog box.
4. To create a delimited file, be sure the Delimited option button is selected in the Export Text Wizard dialog box. To create a fixed-width file, be sure the Fixed Width option button is selected. Once you have made your selection, tap or click the Next button.

BTW
Organizing Files and Folders
You should organize and store files in folders so that you easily can find the files later. For example, if you are taking an introductory computer class called CIS 101, a good practice would be to save all Access files in an Access folder in a CIS 101 folder. For a discussion of folders and detailed examples of creating folders, refer to the Office and Windows chapter at the beginning of this book.

5. a. If you are exporting to a delimited file, choose the delimiter that you want to separate your fields, such as a comma. Decide whether to include field names on the first row and, if so, tap or click the 'Include Field Names on First Row' check box. If you want to select a text qualifier, select it in the Text Qualifier list. When you have made your selections, tap or click the Next button.

 b. If you are exporting to a fixed-width file, review the position of the vertical lines that separate your fields. If any lines are not positioned correctly, follow the directions on the screen to reposition them. When you have finished, tap or click the Next button.

6. Tap or click the Finish button to export the data.

7. Save the export steps if you want, or simply tap or click the Close button in the Export-Text File dialog box to close the dialog box without saving the export steps.

BTW

Join Types
The type of join that finds records from both tables that have identical values in matching fields is called an inner join. An inner join is the default join in Access. Outer joins are used to show all the records in one table as well as the common records; that is, the records that share the same value in the join field. In a left outer join, all rows from the table on the left are included. In a right outer join, all rows from the table on the right are included.

Adding Criteria to a Join Query

Sometimes you will want to join tables, but you will not want to include all possible records. For example, you would like to create a report showing only those customers whose amount paid is greater than $20,000.00. In this case, you would relate the tables and include fields just as you did before. You also will include criteria. To include only those customers whose amount paid is more than $20,000.00, you will include >20000 as a criterion for the Amount Paid field.

To Restrict the Records in a Join

1 CREATE QUERIES | 2 USE CRITERIA | 3 SORT DATA | 4 JOIN TABLES | 5 EXPORT RESULTS
6 PERFORM CALCULATIONS | 7 CREATE CROSSTAB | 8 CUSTOMIZE NAVIGATION PANE

The following steps modify the Rep-Customer Query so that the results for Bavant Publishing include a criterion. **Why?** *Bavant wants to include only those customers whose amount paid is more than $20,000.00.*

1

- Open the Navigation Pane, if necessary, and then press and hold or right-click the Rep-Customer Query to produce a shortcut menu.

- Tap or click Design View on the shortcut menu to open the Rep-Customer Query in Design view.

- Close the Navigation Pane.

- Add the Amount Paid field to the query.

- Type >20000 as the criterion for the Amount Paid field (Figure 2–61).

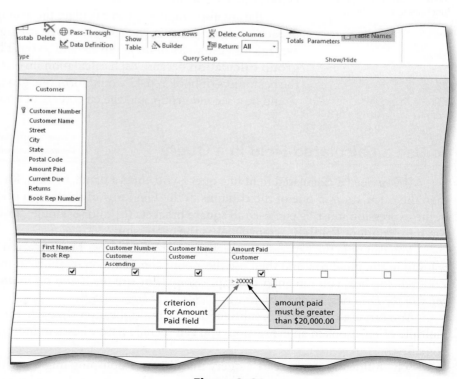

Figure 2–61

2

- Run the query (Figure 2–62).

3

- Close the query.

- When asked if you want to save your changes, tap or click the No button.

Q&A

What would happen if I saved the changes?

The next time you used this query, you would only see customers whose amount paid is more than $20,000.00.

BR #	Last Name	First Name	CU #	Customer Name	Amount Paid
42	Perez	Melina	ASU37	Applewood State University	$41,530.98
53	Chin	Robert	CSU10	Camellia State University	$63,246.88
65	Rogers	Tracy	DCC34	Dartt Community College	$21,345.50
65	Rogers	Tracy	FSC12	First State College	$34,557.25
65	Rogers	Tracy	KCC78	Key Community College System	$21,288.65
65	Rogers	Tracy	TSC02	Tri-State Consortium	$34,578.90

amount paid is greater than $20,000.00

Figure 2–62

Calculations

If a special calculation is required for a query, you need to determine whether the calculation is **an individual record calculation** (for example, adding the values in two fields) or a **group calculation** (for example, finding the total of the values in a particular field on all the records).

Bavant Publishing might want to know the total amount (amount paid and current due) from each customer. This would seem to pose a problem because the Customer table does not include a field for total amount. You can calculate it, however, because the total amount is equal to the amount paid plus the current due. A field that can be computed from other fields is called a **calculated field** or a **computed field**. A calculated field is an individual record calculation because each calculation only involves fields in a single record.

Bavant also might want to calculate the average amount paid for the customers of each book rep. That is, they may want the average for customers of book rep 42, the average for customers of book rep 53, and so on. This type of calculation is called a **group calculation** because each calculation involves groups of records. In this example, the customers of book rep 42 would form one group, the customers of book rep 53 would be a second group, and the customers of book rep 65 would form a third group.

To Use a Calculated Field in a Query

1 CREATE QUERIES | 2 USE CRITERIA | 3 SORT DATA | 4 JOIN TABLES | 5 EXPORT RESULTS
6 PERFORM CALCULATIONS | 7 CREATE CROSSTAB | 8 CUSTOMIZE NAVIGATION PANE

If you need a calculated field in a query, you enter a name, or alias, for the calculated field, a colon, and then the calculation in one of the columns in the Field row of the design grid for the query. Any fields included in the expression must be enclosed in square brackets ([]). For example, for the total amount, you will type Total Amount:[Amount Paid]+[Current Due] as the expression.

You can type the expression directly into the Field row. The preferred method, however, is to select the column in the Field row and then use the Zoom command on its shortcut menu. When Access displays the Zoom dialog box, you can enter the expression. ***Why use the Zoom command?*** *You will not be able to see the entire entry in the Field row, because the space available is not large enough.*

You can use addition (+), subtraction (−), multiplication (*), or division (/) in calculations. If you have multiple calculations in an expression, you can include parentheses to indicate which calculations should be done first.

The following steps create a query that Bavant Publishing might use to obtain financial information on its customers, including the total amount (amount paid + current due), which is a calculated field.

1

- Create a query with a field list for the Customer table.

- Add the Customer Number, Customer Name, Amount Paid, and Current Due fields to the query.

- Press and hold or right-click the Field row in the first open column in the design grid to display a shortcut menu (Figure 2–63).

Figure 2–63

2

- Tap or click Zoom on the shortcut menu to display the Zoom dialog box.

- Type `Total Amount:[Amount Paid]+[Current Due]` in the Zoom dialog box (Figure 2–64).

Q&A

Do I always need to put square brackets around field names?
If the field name does not contain spaces, square brackets are technically not required. It is a good practice, however, to get in the habit of using the brackets in field calculations.

Figure 2–64

3

- Tap or click the OK button (Zoom dialog box) to enter the expression (Figure 2–65).

Figure 2–65

4

- Run the query (Figure 2–66).

Experiment

- Return to Design view and try other expressions. In at least one case, omit the Total Amount and the colon. In at least one case, intentionally misspell a field name. In each case, run the query to see the effect of your changes. When finished, reenter the original expression.

Figure 2–66

Other Ways

1. Press SHIFT+F2

To Change a Caption

In Chapter 1, you changed the caption for a field in a table. When you assigned a caption, Access displayed it in datasheets and forms. If you did not assign a caption, Access displayed the field name. You also can change a caption in a query. Access will display the caption you assign in the query results. When you omitted duplicates, you used the query property sheet. When you change a caption in a query, you use the property sheet for the field. In the property sheet, you can change other properties for the field, such as the format and number of decimal places. The following steps change the caption of the Amount Paid field to Paid and the caption of the Current Due field to Due. *Why? These changes give shorter, yet very readable, column headings for the fields.* The steps also save the query with a new name.

- Return to Design view.

- If necessary, tap or click DESIGN on the ribbon to display the QUERY TOOLS DESIGN tab.

- Tap or click the Amount Paid field in the design grid, and then tap or click the Property Sheet button (QUERY TOOLS DESIGN tab | Show/Hide group) to display the properties for the Amount Paid field.

- Tap or click the Caption box, and then type Paid as the caption (Figure 2–67).

Q&A | My property sheet looks different. What should I do?
Close the property sheet and repeat this step.

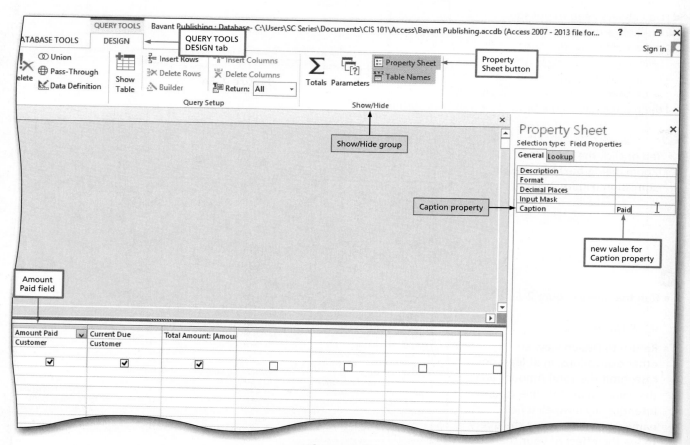

Figure 2–67

②

- Close the property sheet by tapping or clicking the Property Sheet button a second time.

- Tap or click the Current Due field in the design grid, and then tap or click the Property Sheet button (QUERY TOOLS DESIGN tab | Show/Hide group).

- Tap or click the Caption box, and then type Due as the caption.

- Close the Property Sheet by tapping or clicking the Property Sheet button a second time.

- Run the query (Figure 2–68).

③

- Save the query as Ch2q10.

- Close the query.

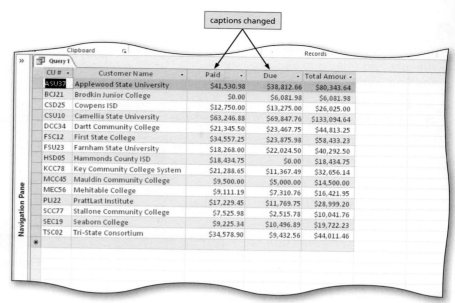

Figure 2–68

Other Ways

1. Press and hold or right-click field in design grid, tap or click Properties on shortcut menu

To Calculate Statistics

1 CREATE QUERIES | 2 USE CRITERIA | 3 SORT DATA | 4 JOIN TABLES | 5 EXPORT RESULTS
6 PERFORM CALCULATIONS | 7 CREATE CROSSTAB | 8 CUSTOMIZE NAVIGATION PANE

For group calculations, Microsoft Access supports several built-in statistics: COUNT (count of the number of records), SUM (total), AVG (average), MAX (largest value), MIN (smallest value), STDEV (standard deviation), VAR (variance), FIRST (first value), and LAST (last value). These statistics are called aggregate functions. An **aggregate function** is a function that performs some mathematical function against a group of records. To use an aggregate function in a query, you include it in the Total row in the design grid. In order to do so, you must first include the Total row by tapping or clicking the Totals button on the DESIGN tab. *Why? The Total row usually does not appear in the grid.*

The following steps create a new query for the Customer table. The steps include the Total row in the design grid, and then calculate the average amount paid for all customers.

①

- Create a new query with a field list for the Customer table.

- Tap or click the Totals button (QUERY TOOLS DESIGN tab | Show/Hide group) to include the Total row in the design grid.

- Add the Amount Paid field to the query (Figure 2–69).

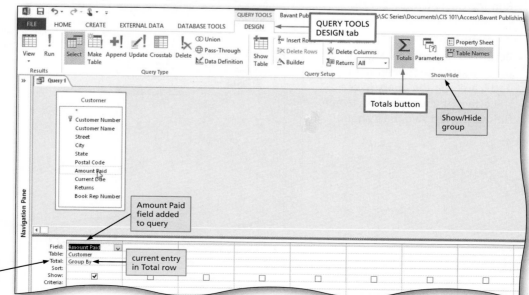

Figure 2–69

2

- Tap or click the Total row in the Amount Paid column to display the Total arrow.

- Tap or click the Total arrow to display the Total list (Figure 2–70).

Figure 2–70

3

- Tap or click Avg to select the calculation that Access is to perform (Figure 2–71).

Figure 2–71

4

- Run the query (Figure 2–72).

 Experiment

- Return to Design view and try other aggregate functions. In each case, run the query to see the effect of your selection. When finished, select Avg once again.

Figure 2–72

To Use Criteria in Calculating Statistics

Why? *Sometimes calculating statistics for all the records in the table is appropriate. In other cases, however, you will need to calculate the statistics for only those records that satisfy certain criteria.* To enter a criterion in a field, first you select Where as the entry in the Total row for the field, and then enter the criterion in the Criteria row. Access uses the word, Where, to indicate that you will enter a criterion. The following steps use this technique to calculate the average amount paid for customers of book rep 42. The steps also save the query with a new name.

- Return to Design view.
- Include the Book Rep Number field in the design grid.
- Tap or click the Total row in the Book Rep Number column.
- Tap or click the Total arrow in the Book Rep Number column to produce a Total list (Figure 2–73).

Figure 2–73

- Tap or click Where to be able to enter a criterion.
- Type 42 as the criterion for the Book Rep Number field (Figure 2–74).

Figure 2–74

- Run the query (Figure 2–75).

- Save the query as Ch2q11.

Figure 2–75

To Use Grouping

Why? *Statistics often are used in combination with grouping; that is, statistics are calculated for groups of records. For example, Bavant could calculate the average amount paid for the customers of each book rep, which would require the average for the customers of book rep 42, the average for customers of book rep 53, and so on.* **Grouping** means creating groups of records that share some common characteristic. In grouping by Book Rep Number, for example, the customers of book rep 42 would form one group, the customers of book rep 53 would form a second, and the customers of book rep 65 would form a third group. The calculations then are made for each group. To indicate grouping in Access, select Group By as the entry in the Total row for the field to be used for grouping.

The following steps create a query that calculates the average amount paid for customers of each book rep at Bavant Publishing. The steps also save the query with a new name.

1

- Return to Design view and clear the design grid.

- Include the Book Rep Number field in the query.

- Include the Amount Paid field in the query.

- Select Avg as the calculation in the Total row for the Amount Paid field (Figure 2–76).

Q&A Why was it not necessary to change the entry in the Total row for the Book Rep Number field? Group By, which is the initial entry in the Total row when you add a field, is correct. Thus, you did not need to change the entry.

Figure 2–76

2

- Run the query (Figure 2–77).

3

- Save the query as Ch2q12.

- Close the query.

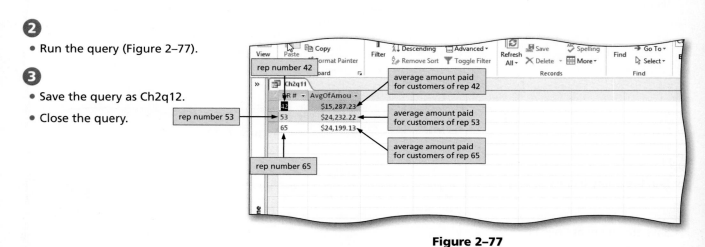

Figure 2–77

Crosstab Queries

A **crosstab query**, or simply, crosstab, calculates a statistic (for example, sum, average, or count) for data that is grouped by two different types of information. One of the types will appear down the side of the resulting datasheet, and the other will appear across the top. Crosstab queries are useful for summarizing data by category or group.

For example, if a query must summarize the sum of the returns grouped by both state and book rep number, you could have states as the row headings, that is, down the side. You could have book rep numbers as the column headings, that is, across the top. The entries within the datasheet represent the total of the returns. Figure 2–78 shows a crosstab in which the total of returns is grouped by both state and book rep number, with states down the left side and book rep numbers across the top. For example, the entry in the row labeled DE and in the column labeled 42 represents the total of the returns by all customers of book rep 42 who are located in Delaware.

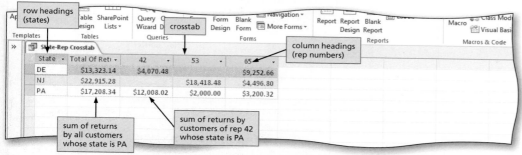

Figure 2–78

How do you know when to use a crosstab query?

If data is to be grouped by two different types of information, you can use a crosstab query. You will need to identify the two types of information. One of the types will form the row headings and the other will form the column headings in the query results.

To Create a Crosstab Query

1 CREATE QUERIES | 2 USE CRITERIA | 3 SORT DATA | 4 JOIN TABLES | 5 EXPORT RESULTS
6 PERFORM CALCULATIONS | **7 CREATE CROSSTAB** | **8 CUSTOMIZE NAVIGATION PANE**

The following steps use the Crosstab Query Wizard to create a crosstab query. **Why?** *Bavant Publishing wants to group data on returns by two types of information: state and book rep.*

 1

- Tap or click CREATE on the ribbon to display the CREATE tab.
- Tap or click the Query Wizard button (CREATE tab | Queries group) to display the New Query dialog box (Figure 2–79).

Figure 2–79

2

- Tap or click Crosstab Query Wizard (New Query dialog box).

- Tap or click the OK button to display the Crosstab Query Wizard dialog box (Figure 2–80).

Figure 2–80

3

- With the Tables option button selected, tap or click Table: Customer to select the Customer table, and then tap or click the Next button to display the next Crosstab Query Wizard screen.

- Tap or click the State field, and then tap or click the Add Field button to select the State field for row headings (Figure 2–81).

Figure 2–81

4

- Tap or click the Next button to display the next Crosstab Query Wizard screen.

- Tap or click the Book Rep Number field to select the field for column headings (Figure 2–82).

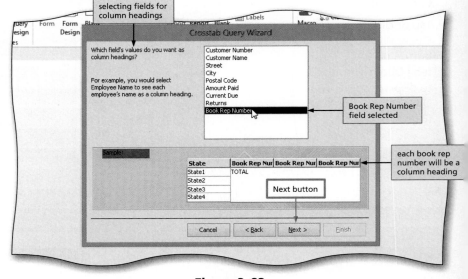

Figure 2–82

5

- Tap or click the Next button to display the next Crosstab Query Wizard screen.

- Tap or click the Returns field to select the field for calculations.

🔍 **Experiment**

- Tap or click other fields. For each field, examine the list of calculations that are available. When finished, tap or click the Returns field again.

- Tap or click Sum to select the calculation to be performed (Figure 2–83).

Q&A My list of functions is different. What did I do wrong?
Either you clicked the wrong field, or the Returns field has the wrong data type. For example, if you mistakenly assigned it the Short Text data type, you would not see Sum in the list of available calculations.

Figure 2–83

6

- Tap or click the Next button to display the next Crosstab Query Wizard screen.

- Erase the text in the name text box and type `State-Rep Crosstab` as the name of the query (Figure 2–84).

7

- If requested to do so by your instructor, name the crosstab query as FirstName LastName Crosstab where FirstName and LastName are your first and last names.

- Tap or click the Finish button to produce the crosstab shown in Figure 2–78 on page AC 119.

- Close the query.

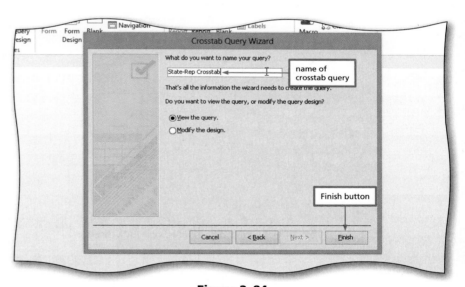

Figure 2–84

Customizing the Navigation Pane

Currently, the entries in the Navigation Pane are organized by object type. That is, all the tables are together, all the queries are together, and so on. You might want to change the way the information is organized. For example, you might want to have the Navigation Pane organized by table, with all the queries, forms, and reports associated with a particular table appearing after the name of the table. You also can use the Search bar to restrict the objects that appear to only those that have a certain collection of characters in their name. For example, if you entered the letters, Cu, only those objects containing Cu somewhere within the name will be included.

BTW
Access Help
At any time while using Access, you can find answers to questions and display information about various topics through Access Help. Used properly, this form of assistance can increase your productivity and reduce your frustrations by minimizing the time you spend learning how to use Access. For instruction about Access Help and exercises that will help you gain confidence in using it, read the Office and Windows chapter at the beginning of this book.

To Customize the Navigation Pane

The following steps change the organization of the Navigation Pane. They also use the Search bar to restrict the objects that appear. ***Why?*** *Using the Search bar, you can reduce the number of objects that appear in the Navigation Pane and just show the ones in which you are interested.*

- If necessary, tap or click the 'Shutter Bar Open/Close Button' to open the Navigation Pane.

- Tap or click the Navigation Pane arrow to produce the Navigation Pane menu (Figure 2–85).

Figure 2–85

- Tap or click 'Tables and Related Views' to organize the Navigation Pane by table rather than by the type of object (Figure 2–86).

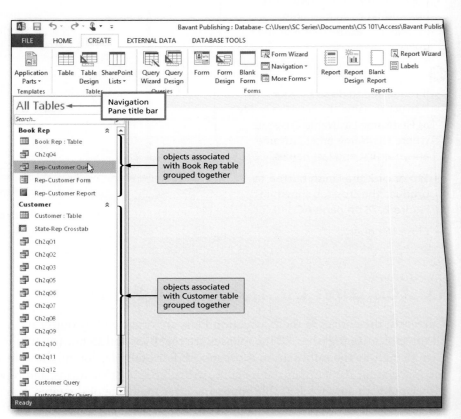

Figure 2–86

3

- Tap or click the Navigation Pane arrow to produce the Navigation Pane menu.

- Tap or click Object Type to once again organize the Navigation Pane by object type.

 Experiment

- Select different Navigate To Category options to see the effect of the option. With each option you select, select different Filter By Group options to see the effect of the filtering. When you have finished experimenting, select the 'Object Type Navigate To Category' option and the 'All Access Objects Filter By Group' option.

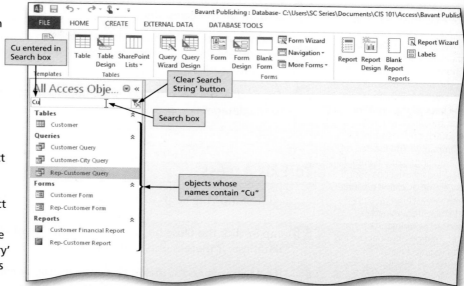

Figure 2–87

4

- If the Search bar does not appear, press and hold or right-click the Navigation Pane and tap or click Search Bar on the shortcut menu.

- Tap or click in the Search box to produce an insertion point.

- Type Cu as the search string to restrict the objects displayed to only those containing the desired string (Figure 2–87).

5

- Tap or click the 'Clear Search String' button to remove the search string and redisplay all objects.

Q&A Did I have to tap or click the button to redisplay all objects? Could I simply have erased the current string to achieve the same result?

You did not have to tap or click the button. You could have used the DELETE or BACKSPACE keys to erase the current search string.

To Sign Out of a Microsoft Account

If you are signed in to a Microsoft account and are using a public computer or otherwise wish to sign out of your Microsoft account, you should sign out of the account from the Account gallery in the Backstage view before exiting Access. Signing out of the account is the safest way to make sure that nobody else can access SkyDrive files or settings stored in your Microsoft account. The following steps sign out of a Microsoft account from Access. For a detailed example of the procedure summarized below, refer to the Office and Windows chapter at the beginning of this book.

1 If you wish to sign out of your Microsoft account, tap or click FILE on the ribbon to open the Backstage view and then tap or click the Account tab to display the Account gallery.

2 Tap or click the Sign out link, which displays the Remove Account dialog box. If a Can't remove Windows accounts dialog box appears instead of the Remove Account dialog box, click the OK button and skip the remaining steps.

Q&A Why does a Can't remove Windows accounts dialog box appear?

If you signed in to Windows using your Microsoft account, then you also must sign out from Windows, rather than signing out from within Access. When you are finished using Windows, be sure to sign out at that time.

BTW

Certification
The Microsoft Office Specialist (MOS) program provides an opportunity for you to obtain a valuable industry credential — proof that you have the Access 2013 skills required by employers. For more information, visit the Certification resource on the Student Companion Site located on www. cengagebrain.com. For detailed instructions about accessing available resources, visit www.cengage.com/ ct/studentdownload or contact your instructor for information about accessing the required files.

BTW
Quick Reference
For a table that lists how
to complete the tasks
covered in this book using
touch gestures, the mouse,
ribbon, shortcut menu, and
keyboard, see the Quick
Reference Summary at
the back of this book, or
visit the Quick Reference
resource on the Student
Companion Site located on
www.cengagebrain.com. For
detailed instructions about
accessing available resources,
visit www.cengage.com/
ct/studentdownload or
contact your instructor for
information about accessing
the required files.

3 Tap or click the Yes button (Remove Account dialog box) to sign out of your Microsoft account on this computer.

Q&A Should I sign out of Windows after signing out of my Microsoft account?
When you are finished using the computer, you should sign out of your account for maximum security.

4 Tap or click the Back button in the upper-left corner of the Backstage view to return to the database.

To Exit Access

The following steps exit Access.

1 Tap or click the Close button on the right side of the title bar to close the open database, if there is one, and exit Access.

2 If a Microsoft Access dialog box appears, tap or click the Save button to save any changes made to the database since the last save.

Chapter Summary

In this chapter you have learned to create queries, enter fields, enter criteria, use text and numeric data in queries, use wildcards, use compound criteria, create parameter queries, sort data in queries, join tables in queries, perform calculations in queries, and create crosstab queries. You also learned to create a report and a form that used a query, to export a query, and to customize the Navigation Pane. The items listed below include all the new Access skills you have learned in this chapter, with tasks grouped by activity.

Calculations in Queries
Use a Calculated Field in a Query (AC 112)
Calculate Statistics (AC 115)
Use Criteria in Calculating Statistics (AC 117)
Use Grouping (AC 118)

Crosstab Query
Create a Crosstab Query (AC 119)

Criteria in Queries
Use Text Data in a Criterion (AC 81)
Use a Wildcard (AC 83)
Use Criteria for a Field Not Included in the Results (AC 85)
Use a Number in a Criterion (AC 89)
Use a Comparison Operator in a Criterion (AC 90)
Use a Compound Criterion Involving AND (AC 91)
Use a Compound Criterion Involving OR (AC 92)

Design Grid
Clear the Design Grid (AC 93)

Export Data
Export Data to Excel (AC 107)
Export Data to Word (AC 110)
Export Data to a Text File (AC 110)

Form Creation
Create a Form for a Query (AC 105)

Join Queries
Join Tables (AC 100)
Change Join Properties (AC 101)
Restrict the Records in a Join (AC 111)

Navigation Pane
Customize the Navigation Pane (AC 122)

Parameter Query
Create and View a Parameter Query (AC 87)
Use a Parameter Query (AC 88)

Query Creation
Create a Query in Design View (AC 78)
Add Fields to the Design Grid (AC 79)
Change a Caption (AC 114)

Report Creation
Create a Report from a Query (AC 103)

Sort in Queries
Sort Data in a Query (AC 94)
Omit Duplicates (AC 94)
Sort on Multiple Keys (AC 96)
Create a Top-Values Query (AC 98)

What decisions will you need to make when creating queries?

Use these guidelines as you complete the assignments in this chapter and create your own queries outside of this class.

1. Identify the fields by examining the question or request to determine which fields from the tables in the database are involved.

2. Identify restrictions or the conditions that records must satisfy to be included in the results.

3. Determine whether special order is required.

 a) Determine the sort key(s).
 b) If using two sort keys, determine the major and minor key.
 c) Determine sort order. If there are no words to imply a particular order, you would typically use Ascending.
 d) Determine restrictions, such as excluding duplicates.

4. Determine whether more than one table is required.

 a) Determine which tables to include.
 b) Determine the matching fields.
 c) Determine whether sorting is required.
 d) Determine restrictions.
 e) Determine join properties.

5. Determine whether calculations are required.

 a) For individual record calculations, determine the calculation and a name for the calculated field.
 b) For group calculations, determine the calculation as well as the field to be used for grouping.

6. If data is to be summarized and the data is to be grouped by two different types of information, create a crosstab query.

How should you submit solutions to questions in the assignments identified with a ✳ symbol?

Every assignment in this book contains one or more questions identified with a ✳ symbol. These questions require you to think beyond the assigned database. Present your solutions to the questions in the format required by your instructor. Possible formats may include one or more of these options: write the answer; create a document that contains the answer; present your answer to the class; discuss your answer in a group; record the answer as audio or video using a webcam, smartphone, or portable media player; or post answers on a blog, wiki, or website.

Apply Your Knowledge

Reinforce the skills and apply the concepts you learned in this chapter.

Using Wildcards in a Query, Creating a Parameter Query, Joining Tables, and Creating a Report

Instructions: Start Access. Open the Apply Cosmetics Naturally database that you modified in Apply Your Knowledge in Chapter 1 on page AC 65. (If you did not complete the exercise, see your instructor for a copy of the modified database.)

Perform the following tasks:

1. Create a query for the Customer table and add the Customer Number, Customer Name, Amount Paid, and Balance fields to the design grid. Add a criterion to find all customers whose names start with the letter C. Run the query and then save it as Apply 2 Step 1 Query.

2. Create a query for the Customer table and add the Customer Number, Customer Name, Amount Paid, and Sales Rep Number fields to the design grid. Sort the records in descending order by Amount Paid. Add a criterion for the Sales Rep Number field that allows the user to enter a different sales rep each time the query is run. Run the query and enter 41 as the sales rep number to test the query. Save the query as Apply 2 Step 2 Query.

Continued >

Apply Your Knowledge *continued*

3. Create a query that joins the Sales Rep and Customer tables. Add the Sales Rep Number, Last Name, and First Name fields from the Sales Rep table and the Customer Number and Customer Name fields from the Customer table to the design grid. Sort the records in ascending order by Customer Number within Sales Rep Number. All sales reps should appear in the result, even if they currently have no customers. Run the query and save it as Rep-Customer Query.

4. Create the report shown in Figure 2–88. The report uses the Rep-Customer Query.

Rep-Customer Report

SR #	Last Name	First Name	CU #	Customer Name
34	Johnson	Bobbi	AS24	Ashley's Salon
34	Johnson	Bobbi	DB14	Della's Beauty Place
34	Johnson	Bobbi	EY07	Environmentally Yours
34	Johnson	Bobbi	NC25	Nancy's Place
34	Johnson	Bobbi	TT21	Tan and Tone
39	Gutaz	Nicholas	BL15	Blondie's on Main
39	Gutaz	Nicholas	CY12	Curlin Yoga Studio
39	Gutaz	Nicholas	JN34	Just Natural
39	Gutaz	Nicholas	LB20	Le Beauty
39	Gutaz	Nicholas	UR23	U R Beautiful
41	Orlon	Jake	BA35	Beauty for All
41	Orlon	Jake	CL09	Casual Looks
41	Orlon	Jake	FN19	Fitness Counts
41	Orlon	Jake	RD03	Rose's Day Spa
41	Orlon	Jake	TW56	The Workout Place
55	Sinson	Terry		

Figure 2–88

5. If requested to do so by your instructor, rename the Rep-Customer Report in the Navigation Pane as LastName-Customer Report where LastName is your last name.

6. Submit the revised database in the format specified by your instructor.

7. ✹ What criteria would you enter in the Customer Name field if you wanted to find all customers who had the word Beauty somewhere in their name?

Extend Your Knowledge

Extend the skills you learned in this chapter and experiment with new skills. You may need to use Help to complete the assignment.

Creating Crosstab Queries Using Criteria, and Exporting a Query

Note: To complete this assignment, you will be required to use the Data Files for Students. Visit www.cengage.com/ct/studentdownload for detailed instructions or contact your instructor for information about accessing the required files.

Instructions: Start Access. Open the Extend Janitorial Services database. Janitorial Services is a small business that provides janitorial services to commercial businesses. The owner has created an Access database in which to store information about the customers she serves and the cleaning staff she employs. You will create the crosstab query shown in Figure 2–89. You also will query the database using specified criteria, and export a query.

Figure 2–89

Perform the following tasks:

1. Create the crosstab query shown in Figure 2–89. The crosstab groups the total of customers' balance by city and employee number.

2. Create a query to find all customers who are not located in Kadrick. Include the Customer Number, Customer Name, and Balance fields in the query results. Save the query as Extend 2 Step 2 Query.

3. Create a query to find all employees whose first name is either Timmy or Tammy. Include the Employee Number, First Name, and Last Name in the query results. Save the query as Extend 2 Step 3 Query.

4. Create a query to find all customers where the employee number is either 210 or 214 and the balance is greater than $1,000.00. Include the Customer Number, Customer Name, Balance, and Employee Number fields in the design grid. Use the IN operator in your query design. Save the query as Extend 2 Step 4 Query.

5. Export the City-Employee Crosstab as a Word file with the name City-Employee Crosstab.rtf and save the export steps.

6. Open the Customer table and change the balance for customer AT23 to $755.

7. If requested to do so by your instructor, change the customer name of customer AT23 from Atlas Repair to Last Name Repair where Last Name is your last name.

8. Use the saved export steps to export the City-Employee Crosstab again. When asked if you want to replace the existing file, click Yes.

9. Submit the revised database and the exported RTF file in the format specified by your instructor.

10. ✵ How would you create the query in Step 4 without using the IN operator?

Analyze, Correct, Improve

Analyze a database, correct all errors, and improve the design.

Correcting Errors in the Table Structure

Note: To complete this assignment, you will be required to use the Data Files for Students. Visit www.cengage.com/ct/studentdownload for detailed instructions or contact your instructor for information about accessing the required files.

Instructions: Analyze Fitness is a database maintained by the Sports Science department at your university. Graduate students work with local residents as personal trainers to earn the necessary hours required for certification. The department chair has asked you to correct and improve two of the queries she created. Start Access and open the Analyze Fitness database from the Data Files for Students.

1. Correct The query shown in Figure 2–90 returns 0 results, and the department chair knows that is not correct. She wants to find all customers who live on Levick. Open the query in Design view, correct the errors, and save as Corrected Criteria Query.

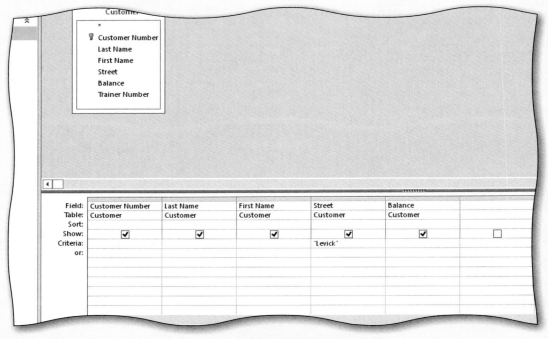

Figure 2–90

2. Improve The department chair also created the query shown in Figure 2–91. The query is sorted correctly, but she wanted Trainer Number to appear as the last field in the query result. She also would like to change the caption for the Balance field to Due. Improve the query to display the results in the desired order. Save the query as Improved Sort Query. Submit the revised database in the format specified by your instructor.

3. ✳ Why does the query shown in Figure 2–90 return 0 results?

Figure 2–91

In the Labs

Design, create, modify, and/or use a database following the guidelines, concepts, and skills presented in this chapter. Labs are listed in order of increasing difficulty. Labs 1 and 2, which increase in difficulty, require you to create solutions based on what you learned in the chapter; Lab 3 requires you to create a solution, which uses cloud and web technologies, by learning and investigating on your own from general guidance.

Lab 1: Querying the Dartt Offsite Services Database

Problem: The management of Dartt Offsite Services has determined a number of questions it wants the database management system to answer. You must obtain the answers to these questions.

Note: Use the database modified in Lab 1 of Chapter 1 on page AC 68 for this assignment, or see your instructor for information on accessing the required files.

Instructions: Perform the following tasks:

1. Start Access. Open the Lab 1 Dartt Offsite Services database and create a new query for the Client table. Add the Client Number, Client Name, Amount Paid, Balance Due, and Service Rep Number fields to the design grid, and restrict the query results to only those clients where the service rep number is 37. Save the query as Lab 2-1 Step 1 Query.

2. Create a query for the Client table that includes the Client Number, Client Name, and Balance Due fields for all clients located in North Carolina (NC) with a balance due less than $1,000.00. Save the query as Lab 2-1 Step 2 Query.

3. Create a query for the Client table that includes the Client Number, Client Name, Street, City, and State field for all clients whose names begin with Ba. Save the query as Lab 2-1 Step 3 Query.

Continued >

In the Labs continued

4. Create a query for the Client table that lists all cities in ascending order. Each city should appear only once. Save the query as Lab 2-1 Step 4 Query.

5. Create a query for the Client table that allows the user to type the name of the desired city when the query is run. The query results should display the Client Number, Client Name, Balance Due, and Amount Paid fields. Test the query by searching for those records where the client is located in Austin. Save the query as Lab 2-1 Step 5 Query.

6. Create a query for the Service Rep table that includes the First Name, Last Name, and Start Date for all service reps who started after May 1, 2013. Save the query as Lab 2-1 Step 6 Query.

7. Create a query that joins the Service Rep and Client tables. Include the Service Rep Number, Last Name, and First Name from the Service Rep table. Include the Client Number, Client Name, and Amount Paid from the Client table. Sort the records in ascending order by service rep's last name and client name. All service reps should appear in the result even if they currently have no clients. Save the query as Lab 2-1 Step 7 Query.

8. Open the Lab 2-1 Step 7 Query in Design view and remove the Service Rep table from the query. Add the Balance Due field to the design grid. Calculate the total of the balance and amount paid amounts. Assign the alias Total Amount to the calculated field. Change the caption for the Amount Paid field to Paid and the caption for the Balance Due field to Owe. Save the query as Lab 2-1 Step 8 Query.

9. Create a query for the Client table to display the total amount paid amount for service rep 24. Save the query as Lab 2-1 Step 9 Query.

10. Create a query for the Client table to display the average balance amount for each service rep. Save the query as Lab 2-1 Step 10 Query.

11. Create the crosstab query shown in Figure 2–92. The crosstab groups the average of clients' amount paid amounts by state and service rep number. Save the crosstab as State-Service Rep Crosstab.

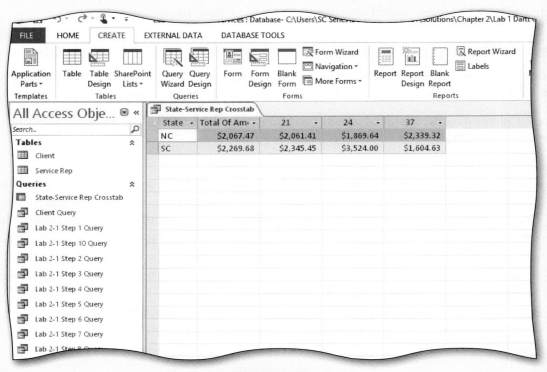

Figure 2–92

12. If requested to do so by your instructor, open the Lab 2-1 Step 1 query and change the caption for the Service Rep Number field to your last name.

13. Submit the revised database in the format specified by your instructor.

14. ☀ How would you modify the query in Step 7 to include only service reps that currently have clients?

Lab 2: **Querying the Tennis Logos Database**

Problem: The manager of Tennis Logos has determined a number of questions he wants the database management system to answer. You must obtain answers to these questions.

Note: Use the database created in Lab 2 of Chapter 1 on page AC 69 for this assignment or see your instructor for information on accessing the required files.

Instructions: Perform the following tasks:

1. Start Access. Open the Lab 2 Tennis Logos database and create a query for the Item table that includes all fields and all records in the Item table. Name the query Lab 2-2 Step 1 Query.

2. Create a query for the Item table that includes the Item Number, Description, Wholesale Price, and Supplier Code fields for all records where the supplier code is SD. Save the query as Lab 2-2 Step 2 Query.

3. Create a query for the Item table that includes the Item Number and Description fields for all items where the description starts with C. Save the query as Lab 2-2 Step 3 Query.

4. Create a query for the Item table that includes the Item Number and Description for all items with a Base Cost greater than $10.00. Save the query as Lab 2-2 Step 4 Query.

5. Create a query for the Item table that includes the Item Number, Description, and Wholesale Price fields for all items with a Wholesale Price between $1.00 and $4.00. Save the query as Lab 2-2 Step 5 Query.

6. Create a query for the Item table that includes the Item Number, Description, On Hand, and Wholesale Price fields for all items where the number on hand is less than 100 and the wholesale price is less than $3.00. Save the query as Lab 2-2 Step 6 Query.

7. Create a query for the Item table that includes the Item Number, Description, Wholesale Price, and Supplier Code for all items that have a Wholesale Price greater than $10.00 or a Supplier Code of LM. Save the query as Lab 2-2 Step 7 Query.

8. Create a query that joins the Supplier and the Item tables. Include the Supplier Code and Supplier Name from the Supplier table and the Item Number, Description, Wholesale Price, and Base Cost fields from the Item table. Sort the query in ascending order by Supplier Code and Description. Save the query as Supplier-Item Query.

9. Create a form for the Supplier-Item Query. Save the form as Supplier-Item Form.

10. If requested to do so by your instructor, rename the form in the Navigation Pane as LastName-Item Form where LastName is your last name.

11. Create the report shown in Figure 2–93. The report uses the Supplier-Item Query but does not use all the fields in the query.

12. Create a query for the Item table that includes the Item Number, Description, Base Cost, and Wholesale Price. Calculate the difference between Base Cost and Wholesale Price (Base Cost – Wholesale Price). Assign the alias Cost Difference to the calculated field. Save the query as Lab 2-2 Step 12 Query.

Continued >

In the Labs *continued*

Supplier-Item Report			
Supplier Name	Description	Wholesale	Base Cost
Last Merchandisers	Baseball Cap	$4.87	$6.10
Last Merchandisers	Cotton Visor	$4.59	$5.74
Last Merchandisers	Foam Visor	$0.79	$1.00
Last Merchandisers	V-Neck Pullover	$13.60	$15.75
Last Merchandisers	V-Neck Vest	$20.85	$25.02
Pratt Clothing	Crew Sweatshirt	$7.29	$8.75
Pratt Clothing	Crew T-Shirt	$2.81	$3.38
Pratt Clothing	Fleece Vest	$28.80	$34.50
Pratt Clothing	Golf Shirt	$10.06	$12.35
Pratt Clothing	Windbreaker	$15.17	$18.20
Pratt Clothing	Zip Hoodie	$16.67	$20.04
Scryps Distributors	Drink Holder	$0.82	$1.07
Scryps Distributors	Sports Bottle	$1.04	$1.35
Scryps Distributors	Tote Bag	$1.26	$1.75
Scryps Distributors	Travel Mug	$2.47	$3.50

Figure 2–93

13. Create a query for the Item table that displays the average Wholesale Price and the average Base Cost of all items. Save the query as Lab 2-2 Step 13 Query.

14. Submit the revised database in the format specified by your instructor.

15. ✷ There are two ways to create the query in step 1. What are they? Which one did you use?

Lab 3: Expand Your World: Cloud and Web Technologies
Creating Queries, Customizing the Navigation Pane, and Using the Excel Web App

Problem: Shopper is a small business that does personal shopping for clients. You will create two queries for the owner, customize the Navigation Pane, export a query in CSV format, open the exported file, and then modify the file using the Excel Web app.

Note: To complete this assignment, you will be required to use the Data Files for Students. Visit www.cengage.com/ct/studentdownload for detailed instructions or contact your instructor for information about accessing the required files.

Instructions: Perform the following tasks:
1. Open the Lab 3 Shopper database. Create and save a query that joins the Shopper and Client tables. Include the Last Name and First Name from the Shopper table and the Client Number, Last Name, First Name, and Balance fields from the Client table. Sort the query by shopper Last Name and Client Number.

2. Create and save a query for the Client table. The query result should display the Last Name, First Name, Amount Paid, Balance, and Shopper Number in that order. Sort the query by Last Name within Shopper Number.

3. Change the organization of the Navigation Pane so that all objects associated with the Client table are grouped together and all objects associated with the Shopper table are grouped together.

4. Export the query you created in Step 2 above as a CSV file. Do not save the export steps.

5. Upload the CSV file to your SkyDrive and open the file in the Excel Web app.

6. Delete the Shopper Number column and resize the remaining columns.

7. If requested to do so by your instructor, change the last name and first name of the first client to your last name and first name.

8. Save and close the Excel workbook.

9. Submit the revised database and Excel workbook in the format specified by your instructor.

10. ✸ Study the query result from Step 2 above. What do you notice about the first name and last name field headings? Why do they appear as they do?

✸ Consider This: Your Turn

Apply your creative thinking and problem solving skills to design and implement a solution.

1: Querying the Craft Database
Personal/Academic

Instructions: Open the Craft database you created in Chapter 1 on page AC 73. If you did not create this database, contact your instructor for information about accessing the required files.

Part 1: Use the concepts and techniques presented in this chapter to create queries for the following. Save each query.

 a. Find the item number and description of all items that contain the word, Rack.

 b. Find the item number and description of all items made by students with a student code of 3962 or 7568.

 c. Find the item number, description, and price of all items that have a price between $20.00 and $40.00.

 d. Find the total price (price * on hand) of each item available for sale. Show the item number, description, price, on hand, and total price in the result. Change the caption for the On Hand field to Quantity.

 e. Find the seller of each item. Show the student's last name and first name as well as the item number, description, price, and on hand. Sort the results by description within student last name.

 f. Create a form based on the query you created in Step e.

 g. Determine the average price of items grouped by student code.

 h. Determine the two most expensive items for sale. Show the description and price.

Submit your assignment in the format specified by your instructor.

Part 2: ✸ You made several decisions while creating the queries in this assignment, including the query in Step b. What was the rationale behind your decisions? There are two ways to create the query in Step b. What are they? Which one did you use?

Continued >

Consider This: Your Turn *continued*

2: Querying the Mums Landscaping Database
Professional

Instructions: Open the Mums Landscaping database you created in Chapter 1 on page AC 73. If you did not create this database, contact your instructor for information about accessing the required files.

Part 1: Use the concepts and techniques presented in this chapter to create queries for the following. Save each query.

 a. Find all supervisors who started prior to January 1, 2013. Show the supervisor's first name, last name, and hourly rate.

 b. Find the customer name and address of all customers located on Cantor.

 c. Find the customer number, customer name, amount paid, and balance for all customers whose amount paid is $0.00 or whose balance is $0.00.

 d. Create a parameter query for the Customer table that will allow the user to enter a different postal code each time the query is run. The user should see all fields in the query result.

 e. Create a crosstab query that groups the total of customer's balance amounts by postal code and supervisor number.

 f. Find the supervisor for each customer. List the supervisor number, last name, first name, customer number, customer name, and balance. Sort the results by customer number within supervisor number.

 g. Open the query you created in Step f above and restrict retrieval to only those customers whose balance is greater than $500.00.

 h. Estimate the weekly pay for each supervisor by multiplying the hourly rate by 40. Show the supervisor's first name, last name, hourly rate, and weekly pay.

Submit your assignment in the format specified by your instructor.

Part 2: ☀ You made several decisions while creating the queries in this assignment, including the calculation in Step h above. What was the rationale behind your decisions, and how could you modify the query in Step h if the Supervisor table included a field called Hours Worked in which the actual hours worked was stored?

3: Creating Queries to Analyze Data
Research and Collaboration

Part 1: Examine a website that contains weather data, such as weather.com or Bing weather, and, as a team, select 30 cities of interest in your state or province. Create a database that contains one table and has the following fields: City, State or Province, High Temp, Low Temp, and Conditions. Use standard weather terms for the Conditions field, such as rainy, snowy, cloudy, clear, and so on. Create queries that do the following:

 a. Display the five cities with the highest high temperature.

 b. Display the five cities with the lowest low temperature.

 c. Display the average high and low temperatures for all cities.

 d. Display the average high and low temperatures for all cities where the conditions were clear.

 e. Calculate the difference between the high and low temperatures for each city.

 f. Display the high and low temperatures for each city in both Fahrenheit and Celsius.

Submit your assignment in the format specified by your instructor.

Part 2: ✸ You made several decisions while creating the queries in this assignment, including the grouping in Steps c and d and the calculations in Steps e and f. What was the rationale behind your decisions? How would you modify the query in Step d above to show the average high and low temperatures in cities grouped by Condition?

Learn Online

Reinforce what you learned in this chapter with games, exercises, training, and many other online activities and resources.

Student Companion Site Reinforcement activities and resources are available at no additional cost on www.cengagebrain.com. Visit www.cengage.com/ct/studentdownload for detailed instructions about accessing the resources available at the Student Companion Site.

SAM Put your skills into practice with SAM! If you have a SAM account, go to www.cengage.com/sam2013 to access SAM assignments for this chapter.

1 Creating and Editing a Presentation with Pictures

Microsoft product screenshots used with permission from Microsoft Corporation.

Objectives

You will have mastered the material in this chapter when you can:

- Select and change a document theme and variant
- Create a title slide and a text slide with a multilevel bulleted list
- Add new slides and change slide layouts
- Insert photos and illustrations into slides with and without content placeholders
- Move and resize photos and illustrations

- Change font size and color
- Bold and italicize text
- Duplicate a slide
- Arrange slides
- Select slide transitions
- View a presentation in Slide Show view
- Print a presentation

1 | Creating and Editing a Presentation with Pictures

Introduction

A PowerPoint **presentation,** also called a **slide show,** can help you deliver a dynamic, professional-looking message to an audience. PowerPoint allows you to produce slides to use in an academic, business, or other environment. The collection of slides in a presentation is called a **deck**, resembling a deck of cards that are stacked on top of each other. A common use of slide decks is to enhance an oral presentation. A speaker might desire to convey information, such as urging students to volunteer at a fund-raising event, explaining changes in employee compensation packages, or describing a new laboratory procedure. The PowerPoint slides should reinforce the speaker's message and help the audience retain the information presented. Custom slides can fit your specific needs and contain diagrams, charts, tables, pictures, shapes, video, sound, and animation effects to make your presentation more effective. An accompanying handout gives audience members reference notes and review material for your presentation.

Project — Presentation with a Bulleted List, Photos, and an Illustration

In this chapter's project, you will follow proper design guidelines and learn to use PowerPoint to create, save, and print the slides shown in Figures 1–1a through 1–1e. The objective is to produce a presentation, titled Keeping Hydrated, to help athletes understand the need to drink water before, during, and after a workout. This slide show has a variety of pictures and visual elements to add interest and give facts about proper hydration. Some of the text has formatting and color enhancements. Transitions help one slide flow gracefully into the next during a slide show. In addition, you will print a handout of your slides to distribute to audience members.

(a) Slide 1 (Title Slide with Photo)

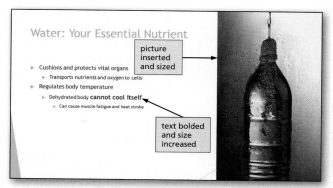

(b) Slide 2 (Multilevel Bulleted List with Photo)

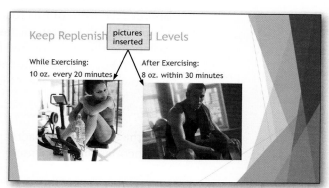

(c) Slide 3 (Title and Illustration)

(d) Slide 4 (Comparison Layout and Photos)

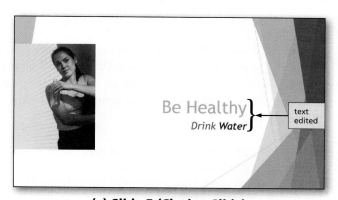

(e) Slide 5 (Closing Slide)

Figure 1–1

For an introduction to Windows and instruction about how to perform basic Windows tasks, read the Office and Windows chapter at the beginning of this book, where you can learn how to resize windows, change screen resolution, create folders, move and rename files, use Windows Help, and much more.

Roadmap

In this chapter, you will learn how to create the slides shown in Figure 1–1 on the previous page. The following roadmap identifies general activities you will perform as you progress through this chapter:

1. INSERT the four PRESENTATION SLIDES, using various layouts.
2. ENTER the TEXT for the slides.
3. FORMAT the TEXT on each slide.
4. INSERT GRAPHICAL ELEMENTS, including photos and an illustration.
5. SIZE AND POSITION the graphical elements.
6. ENHANCE the SLIDE SHOW by adding a closing slide and transition.
7. DISPLAY AND PRINT the SLIDES and a handout.

At the beginning of step instructions throughout the chapter, you will see an abbreviated form of this roadmap. The abbreviated roadmap uses colors to indicate chapter progress: gray means the chapter is beyond that activity; blue means the task being shown is covered in that activity, and black means that activity is yet to be covered. For example, the following abbreviated roadmap indicates the chapter would be showing a task in the 5 Size & Position activity.

1 INSERT PRESENTATION SLIDES | 2 ENTER TEXT | 3 FORMAT TEXT | 4 INSERT GRAPHICAL ELEMENTS
5 SIZE & POSITION | 6 ENHANCE SLIDE SHOW | 7 DISPLAY & PRINT SLIDES

Use the abbreviated roadmap as a progress guide while you read or step through the instructions in this chapter.

To Run PowerPoint

One of the few differences between Windows 7 and Windows 8 occurs in the steps to run PowerPoint. If you are using Windows 7, click the Start button, type **PowerPoint** in the 'Search programs and files' box, click PowerPoint 2013, and then, if necessary, maximize the PowerPoint window. For detailed steps to run PowerPoint in Windows 7, refer to the Office and Windows chapter at the beginning of this book. For a summary of the steps, refer to the Quick Reference located at the back of this book.

If you are using a computer to step through the project in this chapter and you want your screens to match the figures in this book, you should change your screen's resolution to 1366 × 768. For information about how to change a computer's resolution, refer to the Office and Windows chapter at the beginning of this book.

The following steps, which assume Windows 8 is running, use the Start screen or the search box to run PowerPoint based on a typical installation. You may need to ask your instructor how to run PowerPoint on your computer. For a detailed example of the procedure summarized below, refer to the Office and Windows chapter.

1 Scroll the Start screen for a PowerPoint 2013 tile. If your Start screen contains a PowerPoint 2013 tile, tap or click it to run PowerPoint and then proceed to Step 5; if the Start screen does not contain the PowerPoint 2013 tile, proceed to the next step to search for the PowerPoint app.

2 Swipe in from the right edge of the screen or point to the upper-right corner of the screen to display the Charms bar and then tap or click the Search charm on the Charms bar to display the Search menu.

3 Type **PowerPoint** as the search text in the Search box and watch the search results appear in the Apps list.

4 Tap or click PowerPoint 2013 in the search results to run PowerPoint.

5 If the PowerPoint window is not maximized, tap or click the Maximize button on its title bar to maximize the window.

Choosing a Document Theme and Variant

You easily can give the slides in a presentation a professional and integrated appearance by using a theme. A document **theme** is a specific design with coordinating colors, fonts, and special effects such as shadows and reflections. Several themes are available when you run PowerPoint, each with a specific name. Using one of the formatted themes makes creating a professional-looking presentation easier and quicker than using the Blank Presentation template, where you would need to make all design decisions.

Each theme has a set of four alternate designs, called **variants.** Each variant has the same overall composition, but the colors, fonts, and design elements differ. Once you select a theme, you then can select a variation that best fits your overall design needs. If you later decide that another theme or variant would better fit the presentation's general theme, you can change these elements while you are developing slides.

To Choose a Document Theme and Variant

1 INSERT PRESENTATION SLIDES | 2 ENTER TEXT | 3 FORMAT TEXT | 4 INSERT GRAPHICAL ELEMENTS

5 SIZE & POSITION | 6 ENHANCE SLIDE SHOW | 7 DISPLAY & PRINT SLIDES

When you begin creating a new PowerPoint presentation, you need to select a theme. You either can start with no design elements by using the Blank Presentation, or you select one of the available professionally designed themes. The following steps apply the Ion theme and then change the variant. *Why? The title slide will have text and a photo, so you want to select a theme, like Ion, with an uncluttered background. The presentation discusses the importance of drinking water while exercising, and blue is the color commonly associated with water in lakes and oceans. The default Ion theme is predominantly green and white, but one of its variants is blue and is an appropriate choice to relate to the water concept.*

- Press and hold or point to the Ion theme on the New screen (Figure 1–2).

Q&A Why are my theme images, called thumbnails, displaying in a different order?
PowerPoint places the themes you have used recently in the first rows. You may need to scroll down to locate the Ion theme.

Figure 1–2

- Tap or click the Ion theme to display a theme preview dialog box with a thumbnail view of the theme and its variants (Figure 1–3).

Q&A Can I see previews of other themes?
Yes. Tap or click the right or left arrows on the sides of the theme preview dialog box.

Figure 1–3

- Tap or click the upper-right (blue) variant to view previews of that style applied to the thumbnail.

Q&A Can I see previews of the Ion theme and blue variant applied to layouts other than the title slide?
Yes. Tap or click the right or left arrows beside the words, More Images, below the thumbnail. Three other layouts will be displayed: Title and Content, Two Content, and Photo.

- Tap or click the Create button to apply the Ion theme and blue variant to the presentation and to display Slide 1 (Figure 1–4).

Figure 1–4

Creating a Title Slide

When you open a new presentation, the default **Title Slide** layout appears. The purpose of this layout is to introduce the presentation to the audience. PowerPoint includes other standard layouts for each of the themes. The slide layouts are set up in **landscape orientation**, where the slide width is greater than its height. In landscape orientation, the slide size is preset to 10 inches wide and 7.5 inches high when printed on a standard sheet of paper measuring 11 inches wide and 8.5 inches high.

 Placeholders are boxes with dotted or hatch-marked borders that are displayed when you create a new slide. Most layouts have both a title text placeholder and at least one content placeholder. Depending on the particular slide layout selected, title and subtitle placeholders are displayed for the slide title and subtitle; a content text placeholder is displayed for text, art, or a table, chart, picture, graphic, or movie. The title slide has two text placeholders where you can type the main heading, or title, of a new slide and the subtitle.

 With the exception of the Blank slide layout, PowerPoint assumes every new slide has a title. To make creating a presentation easier, any text you type after a new slide appears becomes title text in the title text placeholder. The following steps create the title slide for this presentation.

Choose the words for the slide.

All presentations should follow the 7 × 7 rule, which states that each slide should have a maximum of seven lines, and each line should have a maximum of seven words. PowerPoint designers must choose their words carefully and, in turn, help viewers read the slides easily.

Avoid line wraps. Your audience's eyes want to stop at the end of a line. Thus, you must plan your words carefully or adjust the font size so that each point displays on only one line.

To Enter the Presentation Title

1 INSERT PRESENTATION SLIDES | 2 ENTER TEXT | 3 FORMAT TEXT | 4 INSERT GRAPHICAL ELEMENTS
5 SIZE & POSITION | 6 ENHANCE SLIDE SHOW | 7 DISPLAY & PRINT SLIDES

 The presentation title for Project 1 is Healthy Hydration. *Why? The presentation discusses the importance of drinking water while exercising, and blue is the color associated with water.* The following step creates the slide show's title.

- Tap or click the label, 'Tap to add title', or, 'Click to add title', located inside the title text placeholder to select the placeholder (Figure 1–5).

Figure 1–5

- Type **Healthy Hydration** in the title text placeholder. Do not press the ENTER key (Figure 1–6).

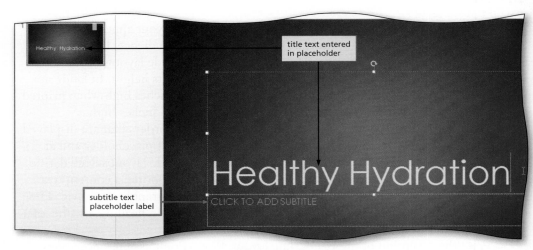

Figure 1–6

BTW

Q&As
For a complete list of the Q&As found in many of the step-by-step sequences in this book, visit the Q&A resource on the Student Companion Site located on www.cengagebrain.com. For detailed instructions about accessing available resources, visit www.cengage.com/ct/studentdownload or see the inside back cover of this book.

For an introduction to Office and instruction about how to perform basic tasks in Office apps, read the Office and Windows chapter at the beginning of this book, where you can learn how to run an application, use the ribbon, save a file, open a file, exit an application, use Help, and much more.

Correcting a Mistake When Typing

If you type the wrong letter, press the BACKSPACE key to erase all the characters back to and including the one that is incorrect. If you mistakenly press the ENTER key after typing the title and the insertion point is on the new line, simply press the BACKSPACE key to return the insertion point to the right of the letter in the word, Water.

When you install PowerPoint, the default setting allows you to reverse up to the last 20 changes by tapping or clicking the Undo button on the Quick Access Toolbar. The ScreenTip that appears when you point to the Undo button changes to indicate the type of change just made. For example, if you type text in the title text placeholder and then point to the Undo button, the ScreenTip that appears is Undo Typing. For clarity, when referencing the Undo button in this project, the name displaying in the ScreenTip is referenced. You can reapply a change that you reversed with the Undo button by tapping or clicking the Redo button on the Quick Access Toolbar. Tapping or clicking the Redo button reverses the last undo action. The ScreenTip name reflects the type of reversal last performed.

Paragraphs

Text in the subtitle text placeholder supports the title text. It can appear on one or more lines in the placeholder. To create more than one subtitle line, you press the ENTER key after typing some words. PowerPoint creates a new line, which is the second paragraph in the placeholder. A **paragraph** is a segment of text with the same format that begins when you press the ENTER key and ends when you press the ENTER key again. This new paragraph is the same level as the previous paragraph. A **level** is a position within a structure, such as an outline, that indicates the magnitude of importance. PowerPoint allows for five paragraph levels.

How do you use the touch keyboard with a touch screen?

To display the on-screen touch keyboard, tap the Touch Keyboard button on the Windows taskbar. When finished using the touch keyboard, tap the X button on the touch keyboard to close the keyboard.

To Enter the Presentation Subtitle Paragraph

1 INSERT PRESENTATION SLIDES | 2 ENTER TEXT | 3 FORMAT TEXT | 4 INSERT GRAPHICAL ELEMENTS

5 SIZE & POSITION | 6 ENHANCE SLIDE SHOW | 7 DISPLAY & PRINT SLIDES

The first subtitle paragraph links to the title. *Why? The subtitle gives additional detail that the presentation will focus on water consumption while exercising.* The following steps enter the presentation subtitle.

- Tap or click the label, 'Tap to add subtitle', or, 'Click to add subtitle', located inside the subtitle text placeholder to select the placeholder (Figure 1–7).

Figure 1–7

- Type **Drinking Water While Exercising** but do not press the ENTER key (Figure 1–8).

Q&A

Why does the text display with capital letters despite the fact I am typing uppercase and lowercase letters? The Ion theme uses the All Caps effect for the subtitle text. This effect converts lowercase letters to uppercase letters.

Figure 1–8

To Zoom a Slide

1 INSERT PRESENTATION SLIDES | 2 ENTER TEXT | 3 FORMAT TEXT | 4 INSERT GRAPHICAL ELEMENTS
5 SIZE & POSITION | 6 ENHANCE SLIDE SHOW | 7 DISPLAY & PRINT SLIDES

You will be modifying the text and other slide components as you create the presentation, so you can enlarge the slide on the screen. *Why? Zooming the slide can help you see slide elements more clearly so that you can position them precisely where desired.* The following step changes the zoom to 80 percent.

1

Figure 1–9

 Experiment

- Repeatedly tap or click the Zoom In and Zoom Out buttons on the status bar and watch the size of the slide change in the Slide pane.

- Tap or click the Zoom In or Zoom Out button as many times as necessary until the Zoom button on the status bar displays 80% on its face (Figure 1–9).

Q&A If I change the zoom percentage, will the slide display differently when I run the presentation?
No. Changing the zoom helps you develop the slide content and does not affect the slide show.

Other Ways

1. Drag Zoom slider on status bar	2. Tap or click Zoom level button on status bar, select desired zoom percent or type (Zoom dialog box), tap or click OK button	3. Tap or click Zoom button (VIEW tab \| Zoom group), select desired zoom percent or type (Zoom dialog box), tap or click OK button	4. For touch screens: Pinch two fingers together in Slide pane (zoom out) or stretch two fingers apart (zoom in)

Formatting Characters in a Presentation

BTW
BTWs
For a complete list of the BTWs found in the margins of this book, visit the BTW resource on the Student Companion Site located on www.cengagebrain.com. For detailed instructions about accessing available resources, visit www.cengage.com/ct/studentdownload or see the inside back cover of this book.

Recall that each document theme determines the color scheme, font set, and layout of a presentation. You can use a specific document theme and then change the characters' formats any time before, during, or after you type the text.

Fonts and Font Styles

Characters that appear on the screen are a specific shape and size. Examples of how you can modify the appearance, or **format**, of these typed characters on the screen and in print include changing the font, style, size, and color. The **font**, or typeface, defines the appearance and shape of the letters, numbers, punctuation marks, and symbols. **Style** indicates how the characters are formatted. PowerPoint's text font styles include regular, italic, bold, and bold italic. **Size** specifies the height of the characters and is gauged by a measurement system that uses points. A **point** is 1/72 of an inch in height. Thus, a character with a font size of 36 is 36/72 (or 1/2) of an inch in height. **Color** defines the hue of the characters.

This presentation uses the Ion document theme, which has particular font styles and font sizes. The Ion document theme default title text font is named Century Gothic. It has no special effects, and its size is 54 point. The Ion default subtitle text font also is Century Gothic with a font size of 18 point.

To Select a Paragraph

1 INSERT PRESENTATION SLIDES | 2 ENTER TEXT | 3 FORMAT TEXT | 4 INSERT GRAPHICAL ELEMENTS
5 SIZE & POSITION | 6 ENHANCE SLIDE SHOW | 7 DISPLAY & PRINT SLIDES

You can use many techniques to format characters. When you want to apply the same formats to multiple words or paragraphs, it is helpful to select these words. **Why?** *It is efficient to select the desired text and then make the desired changes to all the characters simultaneously.* The first formatting change you will make will apply to the title slide subtitle. The following step selects this paragraph.

- If you are using a touch screen, tap to position the insertion point in the text to select, and then drag the selection handles as necessary to select the entire paragraph; if you are using a mouse, triple-click the paragraph, Drinking Water While Exercising, in the subtitle text placeholder to select the paragraph (Figure 1–10).

Figure 1–10

What is the selection handle?

When working on a touch screen, a **selection handle** (small circle) appears below the insertion point. Using a fingertip, you drag the selection handle to select text.

Other Ways

1. Position pointer to left of first paragraph and drag to end of line

To Italicize Text

1 INSERT PRESENTATION SLIDES | 2 ENTER TEXT | 3 FORMAT TEXT | 4 INSERT GRAPHICAL ELEMENTS
5 SIZE & POSITION | 6 ENHANCE SLIDE SHOW | 7 DISPLAY & PRINT SLIDES

Different font styles often are used on slides. **Why?** *These style changes make the words more appealing to the reader and emphasize particular text.* **Italicized** text has a slanted appearance. Used sparingly, it draws the readers' eyes to these characters. The following step adds emphasis to the line of the subtitle text by changing regular text to italic text.

- With the subtitle text still selected, tap or click the Italic button on the mini toolbar to italicize that text on the slide (Figure 1–11).

If I change my mind and decide not to italicize the text, how can I remove this style?

Tap or click the Italic button a second time, immediately tap or click the Undo button on the Quick Access Toolbar, or press CTRL+Z.

Figure 1–11

Other Ways

1. Tap 'Show Context Menu' button on mini toolbar or right-click selected text, tap or click Font on shortcut menu, tap or click Font tab (Font dialog box), tap or click Italic in Font style list, tap or click OK button

2. Select text, tap or click Italic button (HOME tab | Font group)

3. Tap or click Font dialog box launcher (HOME tab | Font group), tap or click Font tab (Font dialog box), tap or click Italic in Font style list, tap or click OK button

4. Select text, press CTRL+I

To Increase Font Size

Why? *To add emphasis, you increase the font size for the subtitle text.* The Increase Font Size button on the mini toolbar increases the font size in preset increments. The following step uses this button to increase the font size.

- Tap or click the 'Increase Font Size' button on the mini toolbar three times to increase the font size of the selected text from 20 to 32 point (Figure 1–12).

Figure 1–12

Other Ways			
1. Tap or click Font Size arrow on mini toolbar, tap or click desired font size in Font Size gallery	2. Tap or click Increase Font Size button (HOME tab \| Font group)	3. Tap or click Font Size arrow (HOME tab \| Font group), tap or click desired font size in Font size gallery	4. Press CTRL+SHIFT+>

To Select a Word

PowerPoint designers use many techniques to emphasize words and characters on a slide. To accentuate the word, Water, on your slide, you want to increase the font size and change the font color to dark blue for the word, WATER, in the subtitle text. To make these changes, you should begin by selecting the word, WATER. *Why?* *You could perform these actions separately, but it is more efficient to select the word and then change the font attributes.* The following steps select a word.

- Position the pointer somewhere in the word to be selected (in this case, in the word, WATER) (Figure 1–13).

Figure 1–13

2

- Double-tap or double-click the word to select it (Figure 1–14).

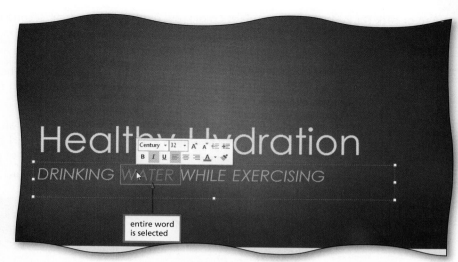

Figure 1–14

Other Ways

1. Position pointer before first character, press CTRL+SHIFT+RIGHT ARROW

To Change the Text Color

PowerPoint allows you to use one or more text colors in a presentation. You decide to change the color of the word you selected, WATER. *Why? The color, blue, is associated with water, and you want to add more emphasis, subtly, to that word in your subtitle slide text.* The following steps add emphasis to this word by changing the font color from green to blue.

1

- With the word, WATER, selected, tap or click the Font Color arrow on the mini toolbar to display the Font Color gallery, which includes Theme Colors and Standard Colors (Figure 1–15).

Q&A If the mini toolbar disappears from the screen, how can I display it once again?
Press and hold or right-click the text, and the mini toolbar should appear.

 Experiment

- If you are using a mouse, point to various colors in the gallery and watch the word's font color change.

Figure 1–15

- Tap or click Dark Blue in the Standard Colors row on the mini toolbar (second color from right) to change the font color to Dark Blue (Figure 1–16).

Q&A

Why did I select the color Dark Blue?
Dark Blue is one of the 10 standard colors associated with every document theme, and it is a universal color representing the natural resource of water. The color will emphasize the fact that the presentation focuses on water.

What is the difference between the colors shown in the Theme Colors area and the Standard Colors?
The 10 colors in the top row of the Theme Colors area are two text, two background, and six accent colors in the Ion theme; the five colors in each column under the top row display different transparencies. The Standard Colors are available in every document theme.

Figure 1–16

- Tap or click outside the selected area to deselect the word.

Other Ways

1. Tap 'Show Context Menu' button on mini toolbar or right-click selected text, tap or click Font on shortcut menu, tap or click Font Color button, tap or click Dark Blue in Standard Colors row
2. Tap or click Font Color arrow (HOME tab | Font group), tap or click Dark Blue in Standard Colors row

To Save a Presentation with a New File Name

You have performed many tasks while creating this presentation and do not want to risk losing work completed thus far. Accordingly, you should save the presentation on your hard disk, SkyDrive, or a location that is most appropriate to your situation.

The following steps assume you already have created folders for storing your files, for example, a CIS 101 folder (for your class) that contains a PowerPoint folder (for your assignments). Thus, these steps save the presentation in the PowerPoint

folder in the CIS 101 folder on your desired save location. For a detailed example of the procedure for saving a file in a folder or saving a file on SkyDrive, refer to the Office and Windows chapter at the beginning of this book.

1 Tap or click the Save button on the Quick Access Toolbar, which depending on settings, will display either the Save As gallery in the Backstage view or the Save As dialog box.

2 To save on a hard disk or other storage media on your computer, proceed to Step 2a. To save on SkyDrive, proceed to Step 2b.

2a If your screen opens the Backstage view and you want to save on storage media on your computer, tap or click Computer in the left pane, if necessary, to display options in the right pane related to saving on your computer. If your screen already displays the Save As dialog box, proceed to Step 3.

2b If your screen opens the Backstage view and you want to save on SkyDrive, tap or click SkyDrive in the left pane to display SkyDrive saving options or a Sign In button. If your screen displays a Sign In button, tap or click it and then sign in to SkyDrive.

3 Tap or click the Browse button in the right pane to display the Save As dialog box associated with the selected save location (i.e., Computer or SkyDrive).

4 Type `Keeping Hydrated` in the File name box to change the file name. Do not press the ENTER key after typing the file name because you do not want to close the dialog box at this time.

5 Navigate to the desired save location (in this case, the PowerPoint folder in the CIS 101 folder [or your class folder] on your computer or SkyDrive).

6 Tap or click the Save button (Save As dialog box) to save the presentation in the selected folder on the selected save location with the entered file name.

Adding a New Slide to a Presentation

With the text for the title slide for the presentation created, the next step is to add the first text slide immediately after the title slide. Usually, when you create a presentation, you add slides with text, pictures, graphics, or charts. Some placeholders allow you to double-tap or double-click the placeholder and then access other objects, such as videos, charts, diagrams, and organization charts. You can change the layout for a slide at any time during the creation of a presentation.

To Add a New Text Slide with a Bulleted List

1 INSERT PRESENTATION SLIDES | 2 ENTER TEXT | 3 FORMAT TEXT | 4 INSERT GRAPHICAL ELEMENTS
5 SIZE & POSITION | 6 ENHANCE SLIDE SHOW | 7 DISPLAY & PRINT SLIDES

When you add a new slide, PowerPoint uses the Title and Content slide layout. This layout provides a title placeholder and a content area for text, art, charts, and other graphics. A vertical scroll bar appears in the Slide pane when you add the second slide. *Why? The scroll bar allows you to move from slide to slide easily.* A small image of this slide also appears in the Thumbnail pane. The step on the next page adds a new slide with the Title and Content slide layout.

1

- Tap or click the New Slide button (HOME tab | Slides group) to insert a new slide with the Title and Content layout (Figure 1–17).

Q&A Why does the bullet character display a green triangle?
The Ion document theme determines the bullet characters. Each paragraph level has an associated bullet character.

I clicked the New Slide arrow instead of the New Slide button. What should I do?
Tap or click the Title and Content slide thumbnail in the Ion layout gallery.

How do I know which slide number I am viewing?
The left edge of the status bar shows the current slide number followed by the total number of slides in the document. In addition, the slide number is displayed to the left of the slide thumbnail.

What are those six icons grouped in the middle of the Slide pane?
You can tap or click one of the icons to insert a specific type of content: table, chart, SmartArt graphic, pictures, online pictures, or video.

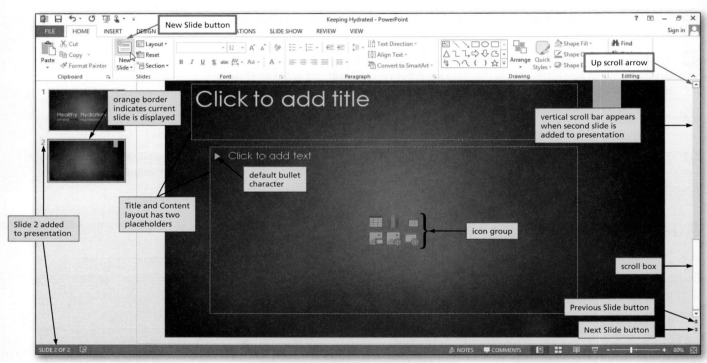

Figure 1–17

Other Ways

1. Press CTRL+M

Creating a Text Slide with a Multilevel Bulleted List

The information in the Slide 2 text placeholder is presented in a bulleted list with three levels. A **bulleted list** is a list of paragraphs, each of which may be preceded by a bullet character, such as a dot, arrow, or checkmark. Some themes, such as the Ion theme, do not display a bullet character at the start of a paragraph by default. A slide that consists of more than one level of bulleted text is called a **multilevel bulleted list slide**. In a multilevel bulleted list, a lower-level paragraph is a subset of a higher-level paragraph. It usually contains information that supports the topic in the paragraph immediately above it.

As you can see in Figure 1–1b on page PPT 3, two of the Slide 2 paragraphs appear at the same level, called the first level: Cushions and protects vital organs, and Regulates body temperature. Beginning with the second level, each paragraph indents to the right of the preceding level and is pushed down to a lower level. For example, if you increase the indent of a first-level paragraph, it becomes a second-level paragraph. The second, fourth, and fifth paragraphs on Slide 2 are second-level paragraphs. The last paragraph, Can cause muscle fatigue and heat stroke, is a third-level paragraph.

Creating a text slide with a multilevel bulleted list requires several steps. Initially, you enter a slide title in the title text placeholder. Next, you select the content text placeholder. Then, you type the text for the multilevel bulleted list, increasing and decreasing the indents as needed. The next several sections add a slide with a multilevel bulleted list.

BTW

Touch Screen Differences
The Office and Windows interfaces may vary if you are using a touch screen. For this reason, you might notice that the function or appearance of your touch screen differs slightly from this chapter's presentation.

To Enter a Slide Title

1 INSERT PRESENTATION SLIDES | 2 ENTER TEXT | 3 FORMAT TEXT | 4 INSERT GRAPHICAL ELEMENTS
5 SIZE & POSITION | 6 ENHANCE SLIDE SHOW | 7 DISPLAY & PRINT SLIDES

PowerPoint assumes every new slide has a title. *Why? The audience members read the title and then can begin to focus their attention on the information being presented on that slide.* The title for Slide 2 is Water: Your Essential Nutrient. The following step enters this title.

- Tap or click the label, 'Tap to add title', or, 'Click to add title', to select it and then type `Water: Your Essential Nutrient` in the title text placeholder. Do not press the ENTER key (Figure 1–18).

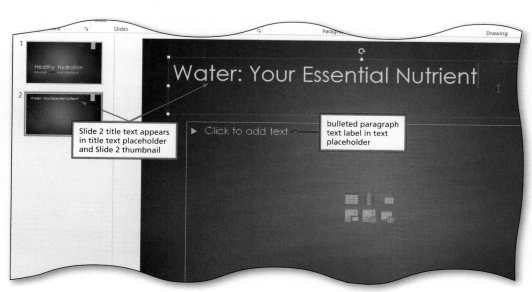

Figure 1–18

To Select a Text Placeholder

Why? *Before you can type text into a content placeholder, you first must select it.* The following step selects the text placeholder on Slide 2.

- Tap or click the label, 'Tap to add text', or 'Click to add text', to select the content placeholder (Figure 1–19).

Q&A Why does my pointer have a different shape?
If you move the pointer away from the bullet, it will change shape.

Figure 1–19

Other Ways

1. Press CTRL+ENTER

To Type a Multilevel Bulleted List

The content placeholder provides an area for the text characters. When you tap or click inside a placeholder, you then can type or paste text. As discussed previously, a bulleted list is a list of paragraphs, each of which is preceded by a bullet. A paragraph is a segment of text ended by pressing the ENTER key. The theme determines the bullets for each level. *Why?* *The bullet variations are determined by the specific paragraph levels, and they generally vary in size, shape, and color.*

The content text placeholder is selected, so the next step is to type the multilevel bulleted list that consists of six paragraphs, as shown in Figure 1–1b on page PPT 3. Creating a lower-level paragraph is called **demoting** text; creating a higher-level paragraph is called **promoting** text. The following steps create a multilevel bulleted list consisting of three levels.

- Type **Cushions and protects vital organs** and then press the ENTER key (Figure 1–20).

Figure 1–20

Creating and Editing a Presentation with Pictures **PowerPoint Chapter 1** **PPT** 19
</ant../segment>

PowerPoint Chapter 1
</ant../segment>

2

- Tap or click the 'Increase List Level' button (HOME tab | Paragraph group) to indent the second paragraph below the first and create a second-level paragraph (Figure 1–21).

Q&A Why does the bullet for this paragraph have a different size? A different bullet is assigned to each paragraph level.

Figure 1–21

3

- Type **Transports nutrients and oxygen to cells** and then press the ENTER key (Figure 1–22).

Figure 1–22

4

- Tap or click the 'Decrease List Level' button (HOME tab | Paragraph group) so that the second-level paragraph becomes a first-level paragraph (Figure 1–23).

Q&A Can I delete bullets on a slide? Yes. If you do not want bullets to display in a particular paragraph, tap or click the Bullets button (HOME tab | Paragraph group) or press and hold or right-click the paragraph and then tap or click the Bullets button on the shortcut menu.

Figure 1–23

Other Ways

1. Press TAB to promote paragraph; press SHIFT+TAB to demote paragraph

To Type the Remaining Text for Slide 2

The following steps complete the text for Slide 2.

1 Type `Regulates body temperature` and then press the ENTER key.

2 Tap or click the 'Increase List Level' button (HOME tab | Paragraph group) to demote the paragraph to the second level.

3 Type `Dehydrated body cannot cool itself` and then press the ENTER key to add a new paragraph at the same level as the previous paragraph.

4 Tap or click the 'Increase List Level' button (HOME tab | Paragraph group) to demote the paragraph to the third level.

5 Type `Can cause muscle fatigue and heat stroke` but do not press the ENTER key (Figure 1–24).

Q&A I pressed the ENTER key in error, and now a new bullet appears after the last entry on this slide. How can I remove this extra bullet?
Press the BACKSPACE key twice.

Figure 1–24

To Select a Group of Words

1 INSERT PRESENTATION SLIDES | 2 ENTER TEXT | 3 FORMAT TEXT | 4 INSERT GRAPHICAL ELEMENTS
5 SIZE & POSITION | 6 ENHANCE SLIDE SHOW | 7 DISPLAY & PRINT SLIDES

PowerPoint designers use many techniques to emphasize words and characters on a slide. To highlight your slide show's concept of the dangers of not drinking water while exercising, you want to bold and increase the font size of the words, cannot cool itself, in the body text. The following steps select three words. *Why? You could perform these actions separately, but it is more efficient to select the words and then change the font attributes.*

1

- Position the pointer immediately to the left of the first character of the text to be selected (in this case, the c in the word, cannot) (Figure 1–25).

Figure 1–25

• Drag the pointer through the last character of the text to be selected (in this case, the f in the word, itself) (Figure 1–26).

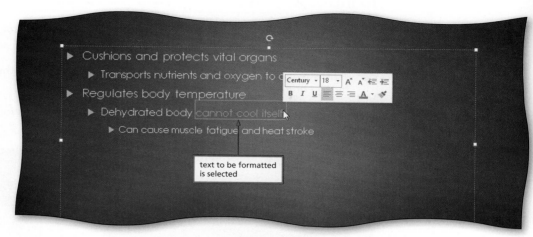

Figure 1–26

Other Ways

1. Press CTRL+SHIFT+RIGHT ARROW repeatedly until desired words are selected

To Bold Text

1 INSERT PRESENTATION SLIDES | 2 ENTER TEXT | 3 FORMAT TEXT | 4 INSERT GRAPHICAL ELEMENTS

5 SIZE & POSITION | 6 ENHANCE SLIDE SHOW | 7 DISPLAY & PRINT SLIDES

Why? Bold characters display somewhat thicker and darker than those that display in a regular font style. Tapping or clicking the Bold button on the mini toolbar is an efficient method of bolding text. To add more emphasis to the fact that the body needs water for cooling purposes, you want to bold the words, cannot cool itself. The following step bolds this text.

• With the words, cannot cool itself, selected, tap or click the Bold button on the mini toolbar to bold the three words (Figure 1–27).

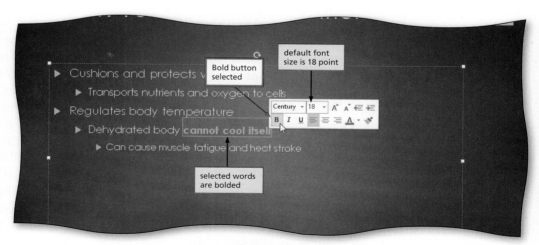

Figure 1–27

Other Ways

1. Tap 'Show Context Menu' button on mini toolbar or right-click selected text, tap or click Font on shortcut menu, tap or click Font tab (Font dialog box), tap or click Bold in Font style list, tap or click OK button	2. Select text, tap or click Bold button (HOME tab \| Font group)	3. Tap or click Font dialog box launcher (HOME tab \| Font group), tap or click Font tab (Font dialog box), tap or click Bold in Font style list, tap or click OK button	4. Select text, press CTRL+B

To Increase Font Size

Why? To add emphasis, you increase the font size for the words, *cannot cool itself.* The following steps increase the font size from 16 to 18 point.

1 With the words, cannot cool itself, still selected, tap or click the 'Increase Font Size' button on the mini toolbar once (Figure 1–28).

2 Tap or click outside the selected area to deselect the three words.

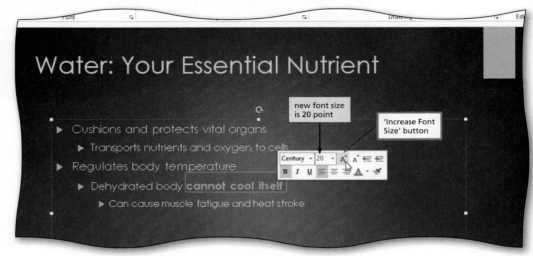

Figure 1–28

Adding New Slides, Changing Slide Layouts, and Changing the Theme

Slide 3 in Figure 1–1c on page PPT 3 contains an illustration of a character drinking water and does not contain a bulleted list. When you add a new slide, PowerPoint applies the Title and Content layout. This layout, along with the Title Slide layout for Slide 1, are the default styles. A **layout** specifies the arrangement of placeholders on a slide. These placeholders are arranged in various configurations and can contain text, such as the slide title or a bulleted list, or they can contain content, such as SmartArt graphics, photos, charts, tables, and shapes. The placement of the text, in relationship to content, depends on the slide layout. You can specify a particular slide layout when you add a new slide to a presentation or after you have created the slide.

Using the **layout gallery**, you can choose a slide layout. The nine layouts in this gallery have a variety of placeholders to define text and content positioning and formatting. Three layouts are for text: Title Slide, Section Header, and Title Only. Five are for text and content: Title and Content, Two Content, Comparison, Content with Caption, and Picture with Caption. The Blank layout has no placeholders. If none of these standard layouts meets your design needs, you can create a **custom layout**. A custom layout specifies the number, size, and location of placeholders, background content, and optional slide and placeholder-level properties.

When you change the layout of a slide, PowerPoint retains the text and objects and repositions them into the appropriate placeholders. Using slide layouts eliminates the need to resize objects and the font size because PowerPoint automatically sizes the objects and text to fit the placeholders. At any time when creating the slide content, you can change the theme and variant to give the presentation a different look and feel.

To Add a Slide with the Title Only Layout

The following steps add Slide 3 to the presentation with the Title Only slide layout style. *Why? The only text on the slide is the title, and the majority of the slide content is the illustration.*

- If necessary, tap or click HOME on the ribbon to display the HOME tab.

- Tap or click the New Slide arrow (HOME tab | Slides group) to display the Ion layout gallery (Figure 1–29).

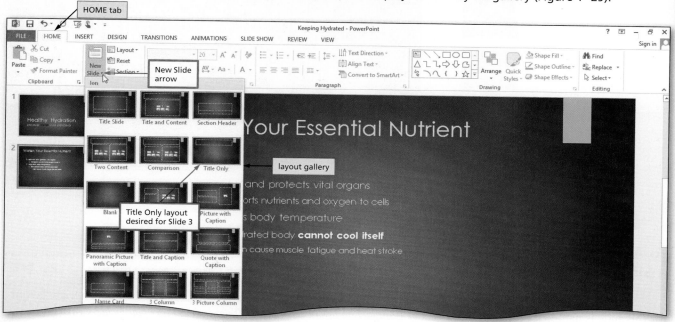

Figure 1–29

- Tap or click Title Only to add a new slide and apply that layout to Slide 3.

- If necessary, swipe up or click the Up scroll arrow several times until the title text placeholder is visible (Figure 1–30).

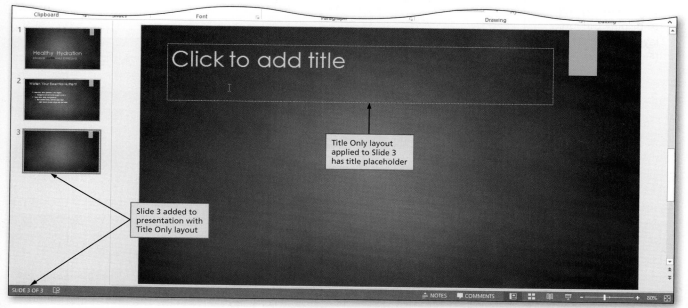

Figure 1–30

To Enter a Slide Title

The only text on Slide 3 is the title. The following step enters the title text for this slide.

 Type **Begin Workout with Plenty of Water** as the title text but do not press the ENTER key (Figure 1–31).

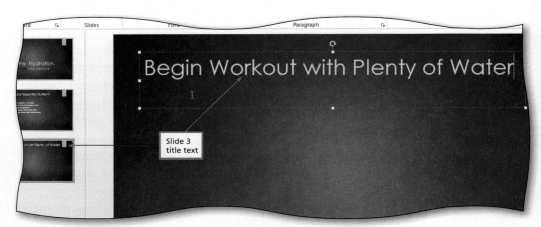

Figure 1–31

To Add a New Slide and Enter a Slide Title and Headings

1 INSERT PRESENTATION SLIDES | 2 ENTER TEXT | 3 FORMAT TEXT | **4 INSERT GRAPHICAL ELEMENTS**
5 SIZE & POSITION | 6 ENHANCE SLIDE SHOW | 7 DISPLAY & PRINT SLIDES

The text on Slide 4 in Figure 1–1d on page PPT 3 consists of a title and two headings. The appropriate layout for this slide is named Comparison. *Why? The Comparison layout has two headings and two text placeholders adjacent to each other, so an audience member easily can compare and contrast the items shown side by side.* The following steps add Slide 4 to the presentation with the Comparison layout and then enter the title and heading text for this slide.

1

- Tap or click the New Slide arrow in the Slides group to display the Ion layout gallery (Figure 1–32).

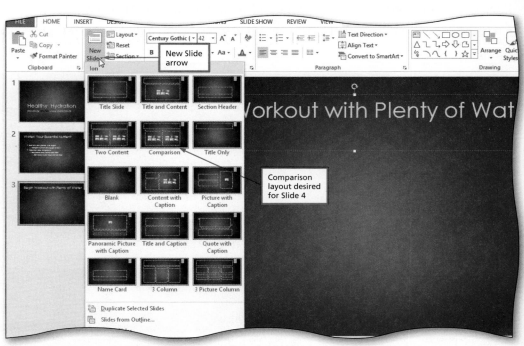

Figure 1–32

2

- Tap or click Comparison to add Slide 4 and apply that layout (Figure 1–33).

Figure 1–33

3

- Type **Keep Replenishing Fluid Levels** in the title text placeholder.

- Tap or click the left heading placeholder with the label, 'Tap to add text', or 'Click to add text', to select this placeholder (Figure 1–34).

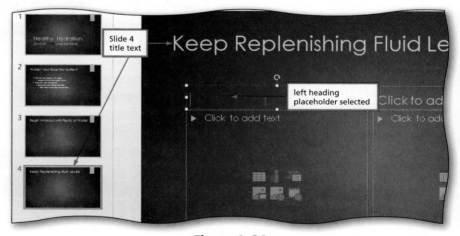

Figure 1–34

4

- Type **While Exercising:** and then press the ENTER key.

- Type **10 oz. every 20 minutes** but do not press the ENTER key.

- Select the right heading placeholder and then type **After Exercising:** and press the ENTER key.

- Type **8 oz. within 30 minutes** but do not press the ENTER key (Figure 1–35).

Figure 1–35

Q&A What is the white box with the arrow between the placeholders?

The text is too large to fit in the placeholder using the default font and paragraph attributes, so PowerPoint adjusts the text so it displays properly. That icon informs you that the font was altered.

To Change the Theme

A theme provides consistency in design and color throughout the entire presentation by setting the color scheme, font set, and layout of a presentation. This collection of formatting choices includes a set of colors (the Theme Colors group), a set of heading and content text fonts (the Theme Fonts group), and a set of lines and fill effects (the Theme Effects group). These groups allow you to choose and change the appearance of all the slides or individual slides in your presentation. *Why? At any time while creating the slide deck, you may decide to switch the theme so that the slides have a totally different appearance.* The following steps change the theme for this presentation from Ion to Facet.

- Tap or click DESIGN on the ribbon to display the DESIGN tab (Figure 1–36).

Figure 1–36

- Tap or click the More button (DESIGN tab | Themes group) to expand the gallery, which shows more theme gallery options (Figure 1–37).

Experiment

- If you are using a mouse, point to various document themes in the Themes gallery and watch the colors and fonts change on the title slide.

Figure 1–37

Q&A Are the themes displayed in a specific order?

They are listed in alphabetical order in two groups: Facet to Wisp beginning in the first row and Banded to Wood Type beginning in the second row. If you are using a mouse and point to a theme, a ScreenTip with the theme's name appears on the screen.

- Tap or click the Facet theme to apply this theme to all four slides (Figure 1–38).

Q&A The Facet theme is visible in the first row of the gallery, so why did I click the More button to expand the gallery?

While it is not necessary to view all the thumbnails, it sometimes is helpful to see all possible themes when deciding which one best fits the presentation.

If I decide at some future time that this design does not fit the theme of my presentation, can I apply a different design?
Yes. You can repeat these steps at any time while creating your presentation.

Figure 1–38

To Change the Variant

1 INSERT PRESENTATION SLIDES | 2 ENTER TEXT | 3 FORMAT TEXT | 4 INSERT GRAPHICAL ELEMENTS
5 SIZE & POSITION | 6 ENHANCE SLIDE SHOW | 7 DISPLAY & PRINT SLIDES

When you began creating this presentation, you selected the Ion theme and then chose a blue variant. You can change the color variation at any time for any theme. *Why? The new Facet theme has a default green color, but you want to emphasize the blue color associated with water, just like you initially did when you chose the blue variant for the Ion theme.* The following steps change the variant from green to blue.

1
- If you are using a mouse, point to the blue variation (DESIGN tab | Variants group) to see a preview of the blue variation on Slide 4 (Figure 1–39).

🔍 **Experiment**
- If you are using a mouse, point to the pink and black variants and watch the colors change on the slide.

Figure 1–39

2

- Tap or click the blue variant to apply this color to all four slides (Figure 1–40).

Q&A If I decide at some future time that this color variation does not fit the theme of my presentation, can I apply a different variant?

Yes. You can repeat these steps at any time while creating your presentation.

Figure 1–40

To Save an Existing Presentation with the Same File Name

You have made several modifications to the presentation since you last saved it. Thus, you should save it again. The following step saves the presentation again. For an example of the step listed below, refer to the Office and Windows chapter at the beginning of this book.

 Tap or click the Save button on the Quick Access Toolbar to overwrite the previously saved file.

Break Point: If you wish to take a break, this is a good place to do so. You can exit PowerPoint now (refer to page PPT 55 for instructions). To resume at a later time, run PowerPoint (refer to page PPT 4 for instructions), open the file called Keeping Hydrated, and continue following the steps from this location forward.

BTW
Welcome Back!
If you are designing a slide in your deck other than Slide 1 and then save and close the document, PowerPoint's new Welcome back! feature allows you to continue where you left off at the last save when you open the document. You may need to adjust the zoom if you are working at a different level than the default setting.

PowerPoint Views

The PowerPoint window display varies depending on the view. A **view** is the mode in which the presentation appears on the screen. You will use some views when you are developing slides and others when you are delivering your presentation. When creating a presentation, you most likely will use Normal, Slide Sorter, Notes Page, and Outline views. When presenting your slides to an audience, you most likely will use Slide Sorter, Presenter, and Reading views.

The default view is **Normal view**, which is composed of three areas that allow you to work on various aspects of a presentation simultaneously. The large area in the middle, called the **Slide pane**, displays the slide you currently are developing and allows you to enter text, tables, charts, graphics, pictures, video, and other elements. As you create the slides, miniature views of the individual slides, called thumbnails, are displayed in the **Thumbnail pane**. You can rearrange the thumbnails in this pane. The **Notes pane**, by default, is hidden at the bottom of the window. If you want to type notes to yourself or remarks to share with your audience, you can click the Notes button in the status bar to open the Notes pane. After you have created at least two slides, a scroll bar containing **scroll arrows** and **scroll boxes** will appear on the right edge of the window.

To Move to Another Slide in Normal View

Why? *When creating or editing a presentation in Normal view (the view you are currently using), you often want to display a slide other than the current one.* Before continuing with developing this project, you want to display the title slide. If you are using a touch screen, you can tap the desired slide in the Thumbnail pane; if you are using a mouse, you can click the desired slide in the Thumbnail pane or drag the scroll box on the vertical scroll bar. When you drag the scroll box, the **slide indicator** shows the number and title of the slide you are about to display. Releasing shows the slide. The following steps move from Slide 4 to Slide 1 using the scroll box in the Slide pane.

- Position the pointer on the scroll box.

- Press and hold down the mouse button so that Slide: 4 of 4 Keep Replenishing Fluid Levels appears in the slide indicator (Figure 1–41).

Figure 1–41

2

- Drag the scroll box up the vertical scroll bar until Slide: 1 of 4 Healthy Hydration appears in the slide indicator (Figure 1–42).

Figure 1–42

3

- Release so that Slide 1 appears in the Slide pane and the Slide 1 thumbnail has an orange border in the Thumbnail pane (Figure 1–43).

Figure 1–43

Other Ways

1. Click Next Slide button or Previous Slide button to move forward or back one slide
2. Tap or click slide in Thumbnail pane
3. Press PAGE DOWN or PAGE UP to move forward or back one slide

Inserting Photos and Illustrations into Slides

BTW
Microsoft Clip Organizer
Previous versions of Microsoft Office stored photos, illustrations, animations, videos, and other media in the Clip Organizer. Office 2013, however, has replaced this feature with the Insert Media dialog box, which allows you to search for and insert files from the Office.com Clip Art collection, Bing, Flickr, SkyDrive, Facebook, and other online sources.

A **clip** is a single media file, such as a photo, illustration, sound, or video. Adding a clip can help increase the visual and audio appeal of many slides and can offer a quick way to add professional-looking graphics and multimedia to a presentation without creating these files yourself. This material is contained in the **Office.com Clip Art** collection of drawings, photos, sounds, and other media files shared among Microsoft Office applications.

You also can add your own clips to slides. These images may include scanned photos, illustrations, and artwork from storage media, such as USB flash drives, hard disks, and memory cards. If you have a Microsoft account, you can add photos from other websites, including Flickr and SkyDrive.

You can add images from Office.com to your presentation in two ways. One way is by selecting one of the slide layouts that includes a content placeholder with an Online Pictures button. A second method is by tapping or clicking the Online Pictures button in the Images area on the INSERT tab. Tapping or clicking the Online Pictures button opens the Insert Pictures dialog box. The **Insert Pictures dialog box** allows you to search for clip art by using descriptive keywords. Clips have one or more keywords associated with various entities, activities, labels, and emotions.

If you have an active connection to the Internet, clips from the Microsoft Office.com website will display automatically as the result of your search. Microsoft constantly revises the content of Office.com, so you may not be able to locate the pictures used in this chapter. Contact your instructor if you need the photos and illustration used in the following steps.

How can you design a title slide that holds your audience's attention?

Develop a slide that reflects the content of your presentation but does so in a thought-provoking way. A title, at the very least, should prepare your audience for the material they are about to see and hear. Look for ways to focus attention on your theme and the method in which you plan to present this theme. A unique photograph or graphic can help generate interest. You may decide to introduce your topic with a startling fact, a rhetorical question, or a quotation. The device you choose depends upon your audience, the occasion, and the presentation's purpose.

To Insert a Picture from Office.com into the Title Slide

1 INSERT PRESENTATION SLIDES | 2 ENTER TEXT | 3 FORMAT TEXT | 4 INSERT GRAPHICAL ELEMENTS
5 SIZE & POSITION | 6 ENHANCE SLIDE SHOW | 7 DISPLAY & PRINT SLIDES

Slide 1 uses the Title Slide layout, which has two placeholders for text but none for graphical content. You desire to place a graphic on Slide 1. *Why? It is likely that your viewers will see an image on this slide before they read any text, so you want to include a photo to create interest in the presentation and introduce your audience to the topic. For this presentation,* you will locate a photo of a person holding a water bottle and then insert this photo in this slide. Later in this chapter, you will resize and position the photo in an appropriate location. The following steps add a photo to Slide 1.

1

- Tap or click INSERT on the ribbon to display the INSERT tab.

- Tap or click the Online Pictures button (INSERT tab | Images group) to display the Insert Pictures dialog box.

- With the insertion point in the Office.com Clip Art area, type **water bottle** in the search box (Figure 1–44).

Figure 1–44

2

- Tap or click the Search button (the magnifying glass) or press the ENTER key so that Office.com will search for and display all clips having the keywords, water bottle.

 Why does the x button display when I begin typing the search terms?
Clicking the x button deletes all letters in the box.

3

- If necessary, slide or scroll down the list to display the photo shown in Figure 1–45.

- Tap or click the photo to select it (Figure 1–45).

 What if the water bottle image displayed in Figure1–45 is not shown in my Office.com Clip Art dialog box?
Select a similar photo. Microsoft updates the files in the Office.com Clip art collection, so the images change constantly.

What are the words and numbers in the lower-left corner of the dialog box?
The words are the keywords associated with this photo, and the figures are the number of pixels associated with the width and height of the clip.

Figure 1–45

4

- Tap or click the Insert button to download the photo and insert it into the slide (Figure 1–46).

 Can I double-tap or double-click the photo instead of selecting it and then tap or click the Insert button?
Yes. Either method downloads and inserts the photo.

Why is this photo displayed in this location on the slide?
The slide layout does not have a content placeholder, so PowerPoint inserts the file in the center of the slide.

Figure 1–46

To Insert a Picture from Office.com into a Slide without a Content Placeholder

The next step is to add a water bottle photo to Slide 2. This slide has a bulleted list in the text placeholder, so the icon group does not display in the center of the placeholder. Later in this chapter, you will resize the inserted photo. The following steps add one photo to Slide 2.

1 Tap or click the Slide 2 thumbnail in the Thumbnail pane to display Slide 2.

2 Tap or click INSERT on the ribbon to display the INSERT tab and then tap or click the Online Pictures button (INSERT tab | Images group) to display the Insert Pictures dialog box.

3 Type `water bottle` in the Office.com Clip Art search box and then tap or click the Search button.

4 If necessary, slide or scroll down the list to display the water bottle photo shown in Figure 1–47, tap or click the photo to select it, and then tap or click the Insert button to download and insert the photo into Slide 2 (Figure 1–47).

Q&A Why is my photo a different size from the one shown in Figure1–1b on page PPT 3? The clip was inserted into the slide and not into a content placeholder. You will resize the photo later in this chapter.

desired photo inserted into Slide 2

Figure 1–47

To Insert an Illustration from Office.com into a Slide without a Content Placeholder

Next, you will add an illustration to Slide 3. You will not insert this file into a content placeholder, so it will display in the center of the slide. Later in this chapter, you will resize this illustration. You locate and download illustrations in the same manner you used to locate and download photos. The following steps add an illustration to Slide 3.

1 Tap or click the Slide 3 thumbnail in the Thumbnail pane.

2 Display the INSERT tab, tap or click the Online Pictures button, type `drinking water` as the search text, and then tap or click the Search button.

 If necessary, slide or scroll down the list to display the picture of a character drinking water shown in Figure 1–48 and then insert it into Slide 3 (Figure 1–48).

Figure 1–48

To Insert a Picture from Office.com into a Content Placeholder

1 INSERT PRESENTATION SLIDES | 2 ENTER TEXT | 3 FORMAT TEXT | 4 INSERT GRAPHICAL ELEMENTS

5 SIZE & POSITION | 6 ENHANCE SLIDE SHOW | 7 DISPLAY & PRINT SLIDES

Slide 4 uses the Comparison layout, which has a content placeholder below each of the two headings. You desire to insert photos into both content placeholders. *Why? You want to reinforce the concept that people should drink water during and after workouts.* The following steps insert photos of a female into the left content placeholder and a male into the right content placeholder on Slide 4.

1

- Tap or click the Slide 4 thumbnail in the Thumbnail pane to display Slide 4 (Figure 1–49).

Figure 1–49

- Tap or click the Online Pictures icon in the left content placeholder to select that placeholder and to open the Insert Pictures dialog box.

- Tap or click the search box, type **women bottled water** as the search text, and then press the ENTER key.

- If necessary, slide or scroll down the list to display the photo shown in Figure 1–50.

- Select the photo and then double-tap or double-click to download and insert it into the left content placeholder (Figure 1–50).

Figure 1–50

❸

- Tap or click the Online Pictures icon in the right content placeholder to select that placeholder and to open the Insert Pictures dialog box.

- Tap or click the search box, type **men exercises hydration** as the search text, and press or tap the ENTER key.

- If necessary, slide or scroll down the list to display the photo shown in Figure 1–51.

- Insert the photo into the right content placeholder (Figure 1–51).

Figure 1–51

Break Point: If you wish to take a break, this is a good place to do so. You can save your presentation and then exit PowerPoint now. To resume at a later time, run PowerPoint, open the file called Keeping Hydrated, and continue following the steps from this location forward.

Resizing Photos and Illustrations

Sometimes it is necessary to change the size of photos and illustrations. **Resizing** includes enlarging or reducing the size of a graphic. You can resize these images using a variety of techniques. One method involves changing the size of a picture by specifying exact dimensions in a dialog box. Another method involves sliding or dragging one of the graphic's sizing handles to the desired location. A selected graphic appears surrounded by a **selection rectangle**, which has small squares and circles, called **sizing handles** or move handles, at each corner and middle location.

BTW
PowerPoint Help
At any time while using PowerPoint, you can find answers to questions and display information about various topics through PowerPoint Help. Used properly, this form of assistance can increase your productivity and reduce your frustrations by minimizing the time you spend learning how to use PowerPoint. For instruction about PowerPoint Help and exercises that will help you gain confidence in using it, read the Office and Windows chapter at the beginning of this book.

To Proportionally Resize Pictures

Why? *On Slides 1, 2, and 3, the photo and illustration sizes are either too small or too large to display aesthetically on the slides. The photo and illustration on Slides 1 and 3 are too small, and the photo on Slide 2 is too large.* The photo on Slide 1 is of a person, so it generally is important to maintain the proportions. To change the size of a photo and keep the width and height in proportion to each other, drag the corner sizing handles to view how the image will look on the slide. Using these corner handles maintains the graphic's original proportions. If, however, the proportions do not need to be maintained, as with the water bottle on Slide 2, drag the square sizing handles to alter the proportions so that the graphic's height and width become larger or smaller. The following steps proportionally increase the size of the Slide 1 photo using a corner sizing handle.

1

- Click the Slide 1 thumbnail in the Thumbnail pane to display Slide 1.

- Tap or click the photo to select it and display the selection rectangle.

- Point to the upper-right corner sizing handle on the illustration so that the pointer changes to a two-headed arrow (Figure 1–52).

Q&A I am using a touch screen and do not see a two-headed arrow when I press and hold the upper-right sizing handle. Why?
Touch screens may not display pointers; you can just press and slide sizing handles to resize.

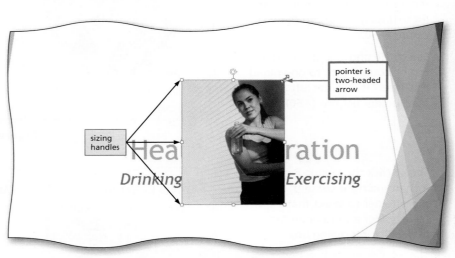

Figure 1–52

2

- Drag the sizing handle diagonally toward the upper-right corner of the slide until the upper-right sizing handle or the crosshair is positioned approximately as shown in Figure 1–53.

Q&A What if the illustration is not the same size as the one shown in Figure 1–53?
Repeat Steps 1 and 2.

Figure 1–53

3

- Release to resize the illustration.

- Tap or click outside the illustration to deselect it (Figure 1–54).

Q&A What happened to the PICTURE TOOLS FORMAT tab?

When you tap or click outside the illustration, PowerPoint deselects the illustration and removes the PICTURE TOOLS FORMAT tab from the screen.

Figure 1–54

To Nonproportionally Resize the Photograph on Slide 2

1 INSERT PRESENTATION SLIDES | 2 ENTER TEXT | 3 FORMAT TEXT | 4 INSERT GRAPHICAL ELEMENTS
5 SIZE & POSITION | 6 ENHANCE SLIDE SHOW | 7 DISPLAY & PRINT SLIDES

Why? *The height of the water bottle photo in Slide 2 extends from the top to the bottom of the slide. The width, however, will cover some of the text when the photo is positioned on the right side of the slide.* The width of this photo can be decreased slightly without negatively distorting the original image. You can decrease the width of a photo by sliding or dragging one of the square sizing handles on the sides of the image. The following steps resize the width of the water bottle photo using a sizing handle along the side of the image.

1

- Display Slide 2 and then tap or click the water bottle photo to select it and display the selection rectangle.

- Tap or click the Zoom Out button as many times as necessary until the Zoom level is 60%.

- Press or point to the sizing handle on the left side of the photo so that the pointer changes to a two-headed arrow (Figure 1–55).

Figure 1–55

• Drag the sizing handle toward the right side of the slide until the sizing handle or crosshair is positioned approximately as shown in Figure 1–56.

Q&A What if the illustration is not the same size as the one shown in Figure 1–56?
Repeat Steps 1 and 2.

Figure 1–56

• Release to resize the photo.

• Tap or click outside the photo to deselect it (Figure 1–57).

Q&A What if I want to return the photo to its original size and start again?
With the photo selected, tap or click the Reset Picture arrow (PICTURE TOOLS FORMAT tab | Adjust group) and then click Reset Picture & Size in the Reset Picture gallery.

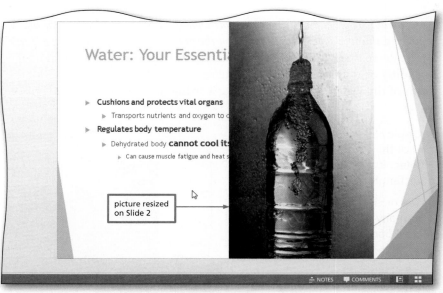

Figure 1–57

To Resize the Illustration on Slide 3

The illustration on Slide 3 can be reduced slightly to fit entirely on the slide. You resize an illustration in the same manner that you resize a photo. You want to maintain the proportions of the character and water in this illustration, so you will drag one of the corner sizing handles. The following steps resize this illustration using a corner sizing handle.

1 Display Slide 3 and then tap or click the character drinking water illustration to select it.

2 Drag the lower-left corner sizing handle on the illustration diagonally outward until the illustration is resized approximately as shown in Figure 1–58.

Figure 1–58

To Move Pictures

1 INSERT PRESENTATION SLIDES | 2 ENTER TEXT | 3 FORMAT TEXT | 4 INSERT GRAPHICAL ELEMENTS
5 SIZE & POSITION | 6 ENHANCE SLIDE SHOW | 7 DISPLAY & PRINT SLIDES

Why? *After you insert a photo or an illustration on a slide, you might want to reposition it. The female athlete photo on Slide 1 could be moved to the left side of the slide, the water bottle on Slide 2 could be moved to the right side of the slide, and the illustration on Slide 3 could be positioned in the center of the slide.* PowerPoint displays **Smart Guides** automatically when a photo, illustration, shape, or other object is close to lining up with another slide element. For example, a Smart Guide will display to help you align the right or left edge of a picture in relation to a text placeholder or to another picture. The following steps move the photos on Slides 1 and 2 and center the illustration on Slide 3.

1

• If necessary, tap or click the character illustration on Slide 3 to select it.

• Drag the illustration upward until the horizontal Smart Guide is displayed under the title text placeholder and the vertical Smart Guide is displayed through the center of the slide, as shown in Figure 1–59, and then release.

• If necessary, select the photo and then use the ARROW keys to position it precisely as shown in Figure 1–59.

Q&A The illustration still is not located exactly where I want it to display. What can I do to align the image? Press the CTRL key while you press the ARROW keys. This key combination moves the illustration in smaller increments than when you press only an ARROW key.

Figure 1–59

- Display Slide 2 and then tap or click the water bottle photo to select it.
- Drag the photo to align with the right edge of the slide (Figure 1–60).

Q&A My water bottle photo is covering some of the title text on the slide. What should I do?
Either resize the photo to make it narrower or move the photo to the right so that it is hanging slightly off the side of the slide.

Figure 1–60

- Display Slide 1 and then tap or click the athlete photo to select it.
- Drag the photo to the left and either upward or downward until the horizontal center Smart Guide is displayed, as shown in Figure 1–61, and then release.

- Tap or click outside the photo to deselect it.

Figure 1–61

Q&A The athlete photo is too wide and is covering some of the text on the slide. What should I do?
Changing the width of a photo showing a person generally is not advisable because the altered proportions make the person appear tall and thin or short and overweight. In this case, move the photo to the left so that it is hanging slightly off the side of the slide, as shown in Figure1–61.

Ending a Slide Show with a Closing Slide

All the text for the slides in the Healthy Hydration slide show has been entered. This presentation thus far consists of a title slide, one text slide with a multilevel bulleted list, a third slide for a photo, and a fourth slide with a Comparison layout. A closing slide that resembles the title slide is the final slide to create.

CONSIDER THIS

What factors should you consider when developing a closing slide for the presentation?
After the last slide appears during a slide show, the default PowerPoint setting is to end the presentation with a **black slide**. This black slide appears only when the slide show is running and concludes the slide show, so your audience never sees the PowerPoint window. It is a good idea, however, to end your presentation with a final closing slide to display at the end of the presentation. This slide ends the presentation gracefully and should be an exact copy, or a very similar copy, of your title slide. The audience will recognize that the presentation is drawing to a close when this slide appears. It can remain on the screen when the audience asks questions, approaches the speaker for further information, or exits the room.

To Duplicate a Slide

Why? *When two slides contain similar information and have the same format, duplicating one slide and then making minor modifications to the new slide saves time and increases consistency.*

Slide 5 will have the same layout and design as Slide 1. The most expedient method of creating this slide is to copy Slide 1 and then make minor modifications to the new slide. The following steps duplicate the title slide.

1

- With Slide 1 selected, tap or click the New Slide arrow (HOME tab | Slides group) to display the Facet layout gallery (Figure 1–62).

Figure 1–62

2

- Tap or click 'Duplicate Selected Slides' in the Facet layout gallery to create a new Slide 2, which is a duplicate of Slide 1 (Figure 1–63).

Figure 1–63

Break Point: If you wish to take a break, this is a good place to do so. Be sure to save the Keeping Hydrated file again and then you can exit PowerPoint. To resume at a later time, run PowerPoint, open the file called Keeping Hydrated, and continue following the steps from this location forward.

To Arrange a Slide

The new Slide 2 was inserted directly below Slide 1 because Slide 1 was the selected slide. This duplicate slide needs to display at the end of the presentation directly after the final title and content slide. *Why? It is a closing slide that reinforces the concept presented in Slide 1 and indicates to your audiences that your presentation is ending.*

Changing slide order is an easy process and is best performed in the Thumbnail pane. When you tap or click the thumbnail and begin to drag it to a new location, the remaining thumbnails realign to show the new sequence. When you release, the slide drops into the desired location. Hence, this process of sliding or dragging and then dropping the thumbnail in a new location is called **drag and drop**. You can use the drag-and-drop method to move any selected item, including text and graphics. The following step moves the new Slide 2 to the end of the presentation so that it becomes a closing slide.

- With Slide 2 selected, drag the Slide 2 slide thumbnail below the last slide in the Thumbnail pane (Figure 1–64).

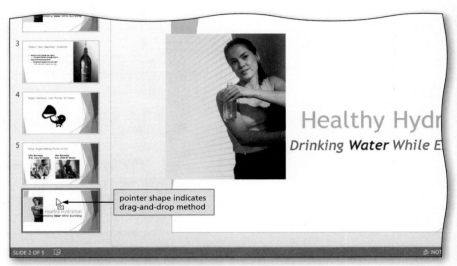

pointer shape indicates drag-and-drop method

Figure 1–64

Other Ways

1. Tap or click Slide Sorter button on status bar, drag thumbnail to new location
2. Tap or click Slide Sorter button (VIEW tab | Presentation Views group), tap or click slide thumbnail, drag thumbnail to new location

Making Changes to Slide Text Content

After creating slides in a presentation, you may find that you want to make changes to the text. Changes may be required because a slide contains an error, the scope of the presentation shifts, or the style is inconsistent. This section explains the types of changes that commonly occur when creating a presentation.

You generally make three types of changes to text in a presentation: additions, replacements, and deletions.

- Additions are necessary when you omit text from a slide and need to add it later. You may need to insert text in the form of a sentence, word, or single character. For example, you may want to add the presenter's middle name on the title slide.
- Replacements are needed when you want to revise the text in a presentation. For example, you may want to substitute the word, *their*, for the word, *there*.
- Deletions are required when text on a slide is incorrect or no longer is relevant to the presentation. For example, a slide may look cluttered. Therefore, you may want to remove one of the bulleted paragraphs to add more space.

Editing text in PowerPoint basically is the same as editing text in a word processing program. The following sections illustrate the most common changes made to text in a presentation.

Replacing Text in an Existing Slide

When you need to correct a word or phrase, you can replace the text by selecting the text to be replaced and then typing the new text. As soon as you press any key on the keyboard, the selected text is deleted and the new text is displayed.

PowerPoint inserts text to the left of the insertion point. The text to the right of the insertion point moves to the right (and shifts downward if necessary) to accommodate the added text.

Deleting Text

You can delete text using one of many methods. One is to use the BACKSPACE key to remove text just typed. The second is to position the insertion point to the left of the text you want to delete and then press the DELETE key. The third method is to drag through the text you want to delete and then tap or click the Cut button on the mini toolbar, press DELETE or BACKSPACE key, or press CTRL + X. Use the third method when deleting large sections of text.

To Delete Text in a Placeholder

1 INSERT PRESENTATION SLIDES | 2 ENTER TEXT | **3 FORMAT TEXT** | 4 INSERT GRAPHICAL ELEMENTS
5 SIZE & POSITION | 6 ENHANCE SLIDE SHOW | **7 DISPLAY & PRINT SLIDES**

Why? To keep the ending slide clean and simple, you want to delete a few words in the slide title and subtitle text. The following steps change Healthy Hydration to Be Healthy and then change Drinking Water While Exercising to Drink Water.

- With Slide 5 selected, position the pointer immediately to the right of the last character of the text to be selected in the title text placeholder (in this case, the n in the word, Hydration).

- Drag the pointer through the first character of the text to be selected (in this case, the space after the word, Healthy) (Figure 1–65).

Q&A I am having difficulty selecting the required text. Can I drag from left to right or right to left?
Yes. You may need several attempts to select the correct characters.

Could I also have selected the word, Hydration, by double-tapping or double-clicking it?
Yes. Either method works to select a word.

Figure 1–65

- Tap or click the Cut button (HOME tab | Clipboard group) to delete the selected text and space.

- Position the pointer to the left of the word, Healthy, and then type **Be** and press the SPACEBAR as the first word in the title text placeholder (Figure 1–66).

- If requested by your instructor, add your mother's first name after the word, Healthy, in the title text placeholder.

Figure 1–66

- Position the pointer immediately to the right of the last character of the text to be selected in the subtitle text placeholder (in this case, the g in the word, Exercising).

- Drag the pointer to the left through the last character of the text to be selected (in this case, the space after the word, Water) (Figure 1–67).

Figure 1–67

4

- Tap or click the Cut button.

- Select the letters, ing, in the word, Drinking.

- Tap or click the Cut button (Figure 1–68).

Figure 1–68

Other Ways

1. Tap 'Show Context Menu' button on mini toolbar or right-click selected text, tap or click Cut on shortcut menu
2. Select text, press DELETE or BACKSPACE key
3. Select text, press CTRL+X

Adding a Transition

PowerPoint includes a wide variety of visual and sound effects that can be applied to text or content. A **slide transition** is a special effect used to progress from one slide to the next in a slide show. You can control the speed of the transition effect and add a sound.

To Add a Transition between Slides

1 INSERT PRESENTATION SLIDES | 2 ENTER TEXT | 3 FORMAT TEXT | 4 INSERT GRAPHICAL ELEMENTS
5 SIZE & POSITION | 6 ENHANCE SLIDE SHOW | 7 DISPLAY & PRINT SLIDES

Why? *Transitions add interest when you advance the slides in a presentation and make a slide show presentation look professional.* In this presentation, you apply the Switch transition in the Exciting category to all slides and change the transition speed from 1.25 seconds to 2 seconds. The following steps apply this transition to the presentation.

1

- Tap or click the TRANSITIONS tab on the ribbon and then point to the More button (TRANSITIONS tab | Transition to This Slide group) in the Transition to This Slide gallery (Figure 1–69).

Figure 1–69

 Is a transition applied now?

No. None, the first slide icon in the Transition to This Slide group, is selected, which indicates no transition has been applied.

- Tap or click the More button to expand the Transitions gallery.

- Point to the Switch transition in the Exciting category in the Transitions gallery (Figure 1–70).

Figure 1–70

- Tap or click Switch in the Exciting category in the Transitions gallery to apply this transition to the closing slide.

Q&A Why does a star appear next to Slide 5 in the Thumbnail pane?
The star indicates that a transition animation effect is applied to that slide.

- Tap or click the Duration up arrow (TRANSITIONS tab | Timing group) seven times to change the transition speed from 01.25 seconds to 03.00 seconds (Figure 1–71).

Q&A Why did the time change from the default 2.00 to 1.25?
Each transition has a default duration time. The default Switch transition time is 01.25 seconds.

Figure 1–71

4

- Tap or click the Preview Transitions button (TRANSITIONS tab | Preview area) to view the transition and the new transition time (Figure 1–72).

Q&A Can I adjust the duration time I just set?

Yes. Tap or click the Duration up or down arrows or type a speed in the Duration box and preview the transition until you find the time that best fits your presentation.

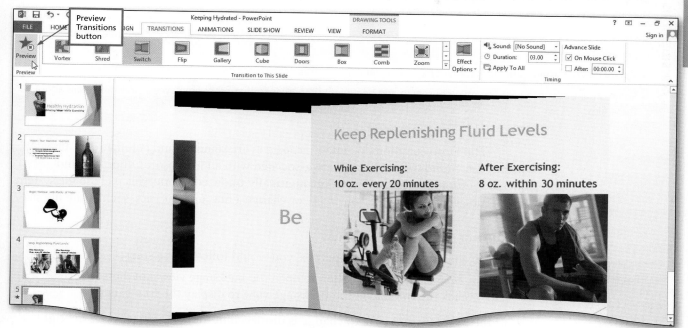

Figure 1–72

5

- Tap or click the 'Apply To All' button (TRANSITIONS tab | Timing group) to apply the Switch transition and the increased transition time to Slides 1 through 4 in the presentation (Figure 1–73).

Q&A What if I want to apply a different transition and duration to each slide in the presentation?

Repeat Steps 2 and 3 for each slide individually.

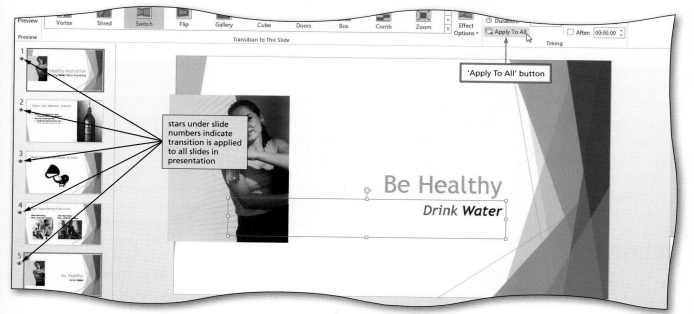

Figure 1–73

Document Properties

PowerPoint helps you organize and identify your files by using **document properties**, which are the details about a file such as the project author, title, and subject. For example, a class name or presentation topic can describe the file's purpose or content.

Why would you want to assign document properties to a presentation?

Document properties are valuable for a variety of reasons:

- Users can save time locating a particular file because they can view a file's document properties without opening the presentation.
- By creating consistent properties for files having similar content, users can better organize their presentations.
- Some organizations require PowerPoint users to add document properties so that other employees can view details about these files.

The more common document properties are standard and automatically updated properties. **Standard properties** are associated with all Microsoft Office files and include author, title, and subject. **Automatically updated properties** include file system properties, such as the date you create or change a file, and statistics, such as the file size.

To Change Document Properties

BTW
Printing Document Properties
PowerPoint 2013 does not allow you to print document properties. This feature, however, is available in other Office 2013 apps, including Word and Excel.

To change document properties, you would follow these steps.

1. Tap or click FILE on the ribbon to open the Backstage view and then, if necessary, tap or click the Info tab in the Backstage view to display the Info gallery.

2. If the property you wish to change is displayed in the Properties list in the right pane of the Info gallery, try to tap or click to the right of the property. If a box appears to the right of the property, type the text for the property in the box, and then tap or click the Back button in the upper-left corner of the Backstage view to return to the PowerPoint window. Skip the remaining steps.

3. If the property you wish to change is not displayed in the Properties list in the right pane of the Info gallery or you cannot change it in the Info gallery, tap or click the Properties button in the right pane to display the Properties menu, and then tap or click 'Show Document Panel' on the Properties menu to close the Backstage view and display the Document Information Panel in the PowerPoint presentation window.

Q&A Why are some of the document properties in my Document Information Panel already filled in?

The person who installed Office 2013 on your computer or network may have set or customized the properties.

4. Type the desired text in the appropriate property boxes.

Q&A What if the property I want to change is not displayed in the Document Information Panel?

Tap or click the Document Properties button in the Document Information Panel and then tap or click Advanced Properties on the menu to display the Properties dialog box. If necessary, tap or click the Summary tab (Properties dialog box) to display the Summary sheet, fill in the appropriate boxes, and then tap or click the OK button.

5. Tap or click the 'Close the Document Information Panel' button at the right edge of the Document Information Panel so that the panel no longer appears in the PowerPoint presentation window.

Viewing the Presentation in Slide Show View

The Start From Beginning button, located in the Quick Access Toolbar, allows you to show a presentation using a computer. As the name implies, the first slide to be displayed always will be Slide 1. You also can run a presentation starting with the slide currently displaying when you tap or click the Slide Show button on the status bar. In either case, PowerPoint displays the slides on the full screen without any of the PowerPoint window objects, such as the ribbon. The full-screen slide hides the toolbars, menus, and other PowerPoint window elements.

To Start Slide Show View

1 INSERT PRESENTATION SLIDES | 2 ENTER TEXT | 3 FORMAT TEXT | 4 INSERT GRAPHICAL ELEMENTS
5 SIZE & POSITION | 6 ENHANCE SLIDE SHOW | **7 DISPLAY & PRINT SLIDES**

Why? You run a presentation in for your audience so they can see the slides in their entirety and view any transitions or other effects added to the slides. When making a presentation, you use **Slide Show view.** You can start Slide Show view from Normal view or Slide Sorter view. Slide Show view begins when you tap or click the Start From Beginning button or the Slide Show button. The following steps start Slide Show view starting with Slide 1.

1
- If you are using a touch screen, proceed to Step 2. If you are using a mouse, point to the Start From Beginning button (Figure 1–74).

Q&A | What would have displayed if I had tapped or clicked the Slide Show button instead of the Start From Beginning button?
When you tap or click the Slide Show button to start the presentation, PowerPoint begins the show with the currently displayed slide, which in this case is Slide 5. Only Slide 5 would display during the slide show.

Figure 1–74

- Swipe forward on or click the black slide to return to Normal view in the PowerPoint window.

Other Ways

1. Press PAGE DOWN to advance one slide at a time, or press PAGE UP to go back one slide at a time	2. Press RIGHT ARROW or DOWN ARROW to advance one slide at a time, or press LEFT ARROW or UP ARROW to go back one slide at a time	3. If Slide Show toolbar is displayed, tap or click Next Slide or Previous Slide button on toolbar

Printing a Presentation

After creating a presentation, you may want to print it. Printing a presentation enables you to distribute it to others in a form that can be read or viewed but typically not edited. It is a good practice to save a presentation before printing it, in the event you experience difficulties printing.

CONSIDER THIS

What is the best method for distributing a presentation?

The traditional method of distributing a presentation uses a printer to produce a hard copy. A **hard copy** or **printout** is information that exists on a physical medium such as paper. Hard copies can be useful for the following reasons:

- Some people prefer proofreading a hard copy of a presentation rather than viewing it on the screen to check for errors and readability.

- Hard copies can serve as a backup reference if your storage medium is lost or becomes corrupted and you need to recreate the presentation.

Instead of distributing a hard copy of a presentation, users can distribute the presentation as an electronic image that mirrors the original presentation's appearance. The electronic image of the presentation can be sent as an email attachment, posted on a website, or copied to a portable storage medium such as a USB flash drive. Two popular electronic image formats, sometimes called fixed formats, are PDF by Adobe Systems and XPS by Microsoft. In PowerPoint, you can create electronic image files through the Save As dialog box and the Export, Share, and Print tabs in the Backstage view. Electronic images of presentations, such as PDF and XPS, can be useful for the following reasons:

- Users can view electronic images of presentations without the software that created the original presentation (e.g., PowerPoint). Specifically, to view a PDF file, you use a program called Adobe Reader, which can be downloaded free from Adobe's website. Similarly, to view an XPS file, you use a program called XPS Viewer, which is included in the latest versions of Windows and Internet Explorer.

- Sending electronic presentations saves paper and printer supplies. Society encourages users to contribute to **green computing**, which involves reducing the electricity consumed and environmental waste generated when using computers, mobile devices, and related technologies.

To Print a Presentation

1 INSERT PRESENTATION SLIDES | 2 ENTER TEXT | 3 FORMAT TEXT | 4 INSERT GRAPHICAL ELEMENTS | 5 SIZE & POSITION | 6 ENHANCE SLIDE SHOW | **7 DISPLAY & PRINT SLIDES**

With the completed presentation saved, you may want to print it. *Why? You could distribute a handout of the slides to your audience members, or you might want to keep a printed copy as a backup in the event you experience technical difficulties before or during your speech. You, therefore, will print a hard copy on a printer.* The following steps print a hard copy of the contents of the saved Keeping Hydrated presentation.

1

- Tap or click FILE on the ribbon to open the Backstage view.
- Tap or click the Print tab in the Backstage view to display the Print gallery (Figure 1–78).

Q&A | How do I preview Slides 2 through 5?
Tap or click the Next Page button in the Print gallery to scroll forward through pages in the document; similarly, tap or click the Previous Page button to scroll backward through pages.

How can I print multiple copies of my presentation?
Increase the number in the Copies box in the Print gallery.

What if I decide not to print the presentation at this time?
Tap or click the Back button in the upper-left corner of the Backstage view to return to the presentation window.

2

- Verify that the printer listed on the Printer Status button will print a hard copy of the presentation. If necessary, click the Printer Status button to display a list of available printer options and then click the desired printer to change the currently selected printer.

Q&A | The selected printer is a black-and-white laser printer, so the preview is grayscale and shows varying shades of gray. If I change the currently selected printer to a color printer, will the preview display in color?
Yes, the preview will match the printer output.

BTW

Conserving Ink and Toner

If you want to conserve ink or toner, you can instruct PowerPoint to print draft quality documents by tapping or clicking FILE on the ribbon to open the Backstage view, tapping or clicking Options in the Backstage view to display the PowerPoint Options dialog box, tapping or clicking Advanced in the left pane (PowerPoint Options dialog box), sliding or scrolling to the Print area in the right pane, not placing a check mark in the High quality check box, and then tapping or clicking the OK button. Then, use the Backstage view to print the document as usual.

Figure 1–78

3

- Tap or click the Print button in the Print gallery to print the presentation on the currently selected printer.
- When the printer stops, retrieve the hard copy (Figure 1–79).

◄ Do I have to wait until my presentation is complete to print it?

No, you can follow these steps to print a presentation at any time while you are creating it.

What if I want to print an electronic image of a presentation instead of a hard copy?

You would click the Printer Status button in the Print gallery and then select the desired electronic image option, such as Microsoft XPS Document Writer, which would create an XPS file.

(a) Slide 1

(b) Slide 2

(c) Slide 3

(d) Slide 4

(e) Slide 5

Figure 1–79 (Handouts printed using a black-and-white printer)

Other Ways

1. Press CTRL+P, press ENTER

To Sign Out of a Microsoft Account

If you are signed in to a Microsoft account and are using a public computer or otherwise wish to sign out of your Microsoft account, you should sign out of the account from the Accounts gallery in the Backstage view before exiting PowerPoint. Signing out of the account is the safest way to make sure that nobody else can access SkyDrive files or settings stored in your Microsoft account. The following steps sign out of a Microsoft account from PowerPoint. For a detailed example of the procedure summarized below, refer to the Office and Windows chapter at the beginning of this book.

1 If you wish to sign out of your Microsoft account, tap or click FILE on the ribbon to open the Backstage view and then tap or click the Account tab to display the Account gallery.

2 Tap or click the Sign out link, which displays the Remove Account dialog box. If a Can't remove Windows accounts dialog box appears instead of the Remove Account dialog box, click the OK button and skip the remaining steps.

Q&A Why does a Can't remove Windows accounts dialog box appear?
If you signed in to Windows using your Microsoft account, then you also must sign out from Windows, rather than signing out from within PowerPoint. When you are finished using Windows, be sure to sign out at that time.

3 Tap or click the Yes button (Remove Account dialog box) to sign out of your Microsoft account on this computer.

Q&A Should I sign out of Windows after signing out of my Microsoft account?
When you are finished using the computer, you should sign out of your account for maximum security.

4 Tap or click the Back button in the upper-left corner of the Backstage view to return to the presentation.

BTW
Certification
The Microsoft Office Specialist (MOS) program provides an opportunity for you to obtain a valuable industry credential — proof that you have the PowerPoint 2013 skills required by employers. For more information, visit the Certification resource on the Student Companion Site located on www.cengagebrain.com. For detailed instructions about accessing available resources, visit www.cengage.com/ct/studentdownload or see the inside back cover of this book.

To Exit PowerPoint

This project now is complete. The following steps exit PowerPoint. For a detailed example of the procedure summarized below, refer to the Office and Windows chapter at the beginning of this book.

1a If you have one PowerPoint presentation open, tap or click the Close button on the right side of the title bar to close the open document and exit PowerPoint.

1b If you have multiple PowerPoint presentations open, press and hold or right-click the PowerPoint app button on the taskbar and then tap or click 'Close all windows' on the shortcut menu, or press ALT+F4 to close all open presentations and exit PowerPoint.

Q&A Could I press and hold or repeatedly click the Close button to close all open documents and exit PowerPoint?
Yes.

2 If a Microsoft PowerPoint dialog box appears, tap or click the Save button to save any changes made to the presentation since the last save.

BTW
Quick Reference
For a table that lists how to complete the tasks covered in this book using touch gestures, the mouse, ribbon, shortcut menu, and keyboard, see the Quick Reference Summary at the back of this book, or visit the Quick Reference resource on the Student Companion Site located on www.cengagebrain.com. For detailed instructions about accessing available resources, visit www.cengage.com/ct/studentdownload or see the inside back cover of this book.

Chapter Summary

In this chapter you have learned how to apply and change a document theme and variant, create a title slide and text slides with a bulleted list, insert photos and an illustration and then resize and move them on a slide, format and edit text, add a slide transition, view the presentation in Slide Show view, and print slides as handouts. The items listed below include all the new PowerPoint skills you have learned in this chapter, with the tasks grouped by activity.

Enter and Edit Text
Enter the Presentation Title (PPT 7)
Enter the Presentation Subtitle Paragraph (PPT 9)
Zoom a Slide (PPT 10)
Add a New Text Slide with a Bulleted List (PPT 15)
Enter a Slide Title (PPT 17)
Type a Multilevel Bulleted List (PPT 18)
Add a Slide with the Title Only Layout (PPT 23)
Add a New Slide and Enter a Slide Title and Headings (PPT 24)
Move to Another Slide in Normal View (PPT 29)
Duplicate a Slide (PPT 41)
Arrange a Slide (PPT 42)
Delete Text in a Placeholder (PPT 43)

Format a Slide
Choose a Document Theme and Variant (PPT 5)
Change the Theme (PPT 26)
Change the Variant (PPT 27)

Format Text
Italicize Text (PPT 11)
Increase Font Size (PPT 12, 22)

Change the Text Color (PPT 13)
Bold Text (PPT 21)

Enhance Slides with Pictures and a Transition
Insert a Picture from Office.com into the Title Slide (PPT 31)
Insert a Picture from Office.com into a Content Placeholder (PPT 34)
Proportionally Resize Pictures (PPT 36)
Move Pictures (PPT 39)
Add a Transition between Slides (PPT 45)

Run and Print a Slide Show
Change Document Properties (PPT 48)
Start Slide Show View (PPT 49)
Move Manually through Slides in a Slide Show (PPT 50)
Print a Presentation (PPT 52)

Select Text and Slide Elements
Select a Paragraph (PPT 11)
Select a Word (PPT 12)
Select a Text Placeholder (PPT 18)
Select a Group of Words (PPT 20)

CONSIDER THIS

What decisions will you need to make when creating your next presentation?

Use these guidelines as you complete the assignments in this chapter and create your own slide show decks outside of this class.

1. Determine the content you want to include on your slides.

2. Determine which theme and variant are appropriate.

3. Identify the slide layouts that best communicate your message.

4. Format various text elements to emphasize important points.

 a) Select appropriate font sizes.

 b) Emphasize important words with bold or italic type and color.

5. Locate graphical elements, such as photos and illustrations, that reinforce your message.

 a) Size and position them aesthetically on slides.

6. Determine a storage location for the presentation.

7. Determine the best method for distributing the presentation.

How should you submit solutions to questions in the assignments identified with a ✷ symbol?

Every assignment in this book contains one or more questions identified with a ✷ symbol. These questions require you to think beyond the assigned presentation. Present your solutions to the questions in the format required by your instructor. Possible formats may include one or more of these options: write the answer; create a document that contains the answer; present your answer to the class; discuss your answer in a group; record the answer as audio or video using a webcam, smartphone, or portable media player; or post answers on a blog, wiki, or website.

Apply Your Knowledge

Reinforce the skills and apply the concepts you learned in this chapter.

Modifying Character Formats and Paragraph Levels and Moving an Illustration

Note: To complete this assignment, you will be required to use the Data Files for Students. Visit www.cengage.com/ct/studentdownload for detailed instructions or contact your instructor for information about accessing the required files.

Instructions: Run PowerPoint. Open the presentation, Apply 1-1 Effective Writing, from the Data Files for Students.

The two slides in the presentation discuss steps to follow when writing a persuasive essay. The document you open is an unformatted presentation. You are to modify the document theme, indent the paragraphs, resize and move the photo, and format the text so the slides look like Figure 1–80 on this page and the next page.

Perform the following tasks:

1. Change the document theme to Ion.

2. On the title slide, use your name in place of Student Name and bold and italicize your name.

3. If requested by your instructor, change your first name to your grandmother's first name on the title slide.

4. Increase the title text font size to 60 point. Size and position the photo using the Smart Guides to align the image with the bottom of the title placeholder, as shown in Figure 1–80a.

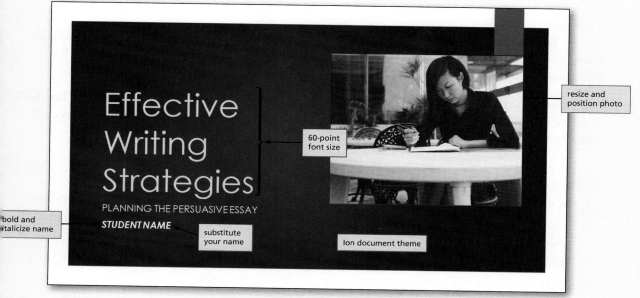

(a) Slide 1 (Title Slide with a Picture)
Figure 1–80

Continued >

Apply Your Knowledge continued

5. On Slide 2, increase the indent of the third and fourth paragraphs to second-level paragraphs. Then combine paragraphs six and seven (To change readers' minds? and To confirm opinions?) to read, To change readers' minds or confirm opinions?, as shown in Figure 1–80b. Increase the indent of this paragraph to second level.

6. Save the presentation using the file name, Apply 1-1 Effective Writing Strategies.

7. Submit the revised document in the format specified by your instructor.

8. ✻ In Step 5 you combined two paragraphs. How did this action improve the slide content?

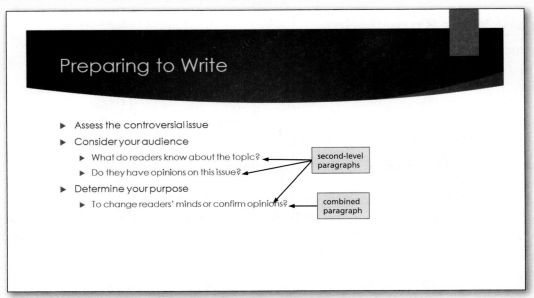

(b) Slide 2 (Multilevel Bulleted List)
Figure 1–80 (Continued)

Extend Your Knowledge

Extend the skills you learned in this chapter and experiment with new skills. You may need to use Help to complete the assignment.

Changing Slide Theme, Layout, and Text

Note: To complete this assignment, you will be required to use the Data Files for Students. Visit www.cengage.com/ct/studentdownload for detailed instructions or contact your instructor for information about accessing the required files.

Instructions: Run PowerPoint. Open the presentation that you are going to prepare for your brother's horseback riding business, Extend 1-1 Horseback Riding, from the Data Files for Students. You will choose a theme, format slides, and create a closing slide.

Perform the following tasks:

1. Apply an appropriate document theme.

2. On Slide 1 (Figure 1–81), use your name in place of Student Name. Format the text on this slide using techniques you learned in this chapter, such as changing the font size and color and bolding and italicizing words.

3. Delete the bullets in the subtitle text.

4. Resize the photo and move it to an appropriate area on the slide.

5. On Slide 2, add bullets to the paragraphs in the Beginners and Advanced boxes, and then change the look of the default bullets.

6. On Slide 3, create paragraphs and adjust the paragraph levels to create a bulleted list. Edit the text so that the slide meets the 7×7 rule, which states that each line should have a maximum of seven words, and each slide should have a maximum of seven lines.

7. Create an appropriate closing slide using the title slide as a guide. Change the title text to, See you at the Trails!

8. The slides contain a variety of pictures downloaded from Office.com. Size and move them when necessary.

9. Apply an appropriate transition to all slides.

10. Save the presentation using the file name, Extend 1-1 Horseback Riding Lessons.

11. Submit the revised document in the format specified by your instructor.

12. If requested by your instructor, replace the word, you, with your mother's first name on the closing slide.

13. ☀ In this assignment, you changed the bullet style on Slide 2. Which bullet style did you select and why?

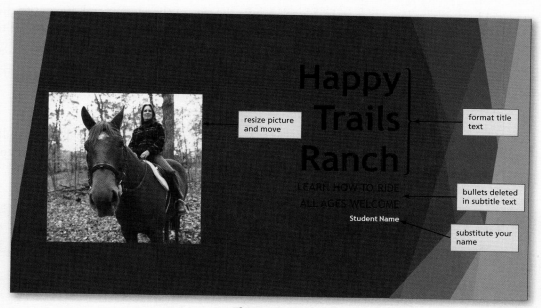

Figure 1–81

Analyze, Correct, Improve

Analyze a presentation, correct all errors, and improve it.

Correcting Formatting and List Levels

Note: To complete this assignment, you will be required to use the Data Files for Students. Visit www.cengage.com/ct/studentdownload for detailed instructions or contact your instructor for information about accessing the required files.

Instructions: Run PowerPoint. Open the presentation, Analyze 1-1 Math Tutor, from the Data Files for Students. As a part-time job while attending college, you decide to tutor students who are struggling with math. You decide to create a presentation promoting your service and begin with this document. Modify the slides by making the indicated corrections and improvements.

Continued >

Analyze, Correct, Improve *continued*

1. Correct

a. Change the document theme from Office Theme Dark, shown in Figure 1–82, to Organic with the rightmost color variant.

b. If requested by your instructor, change the Southtown Library Room number, 201, to your birth year on Slide 2.

c. Correct the spelling errors on Slides 2 and 3.

d. Use your name in place of Student Name on Slide 1.

2. Improve

a. Adjust the size of the picture on Slide 1 and move it to the left of the subtitle text.

b. Move Slide 2 to the end of the presentation so that it becomes the new Slide 3.

c. On Slide 2, increase the font size of the Slide 2 title text, A Math Tutor Is Your Answer, to 54 point. Increase the size of the picture and move it to fill the white space on the right of the bulleted list. Align the picture using the right and bottom Smart Guides.

d. On Slide 3, increase the font size of the title text, Schedule, to 60 point. Decrease the indent level for both bulleted lists to first level. Adjust the size of the picture and move it to the upper-right corner of the slide so that the upper edge of the image is aligned with the top edge of the title text placeholder.

e. Apply the same transition and duration to all slides.

f. Save the presentation using the file name, Analyze 1-1 – Math Tutor Info.

g. Submit the revised document in the format specified by your instructor.

3. ✸ Which errors existed in the starting file? How did decreasing the indent level of the bulleted lists on Slide 3 and increasing the title text on Slides 2 and 3 enhance the presentation? When you adjusted the pictures, how did you determine their final sizes?

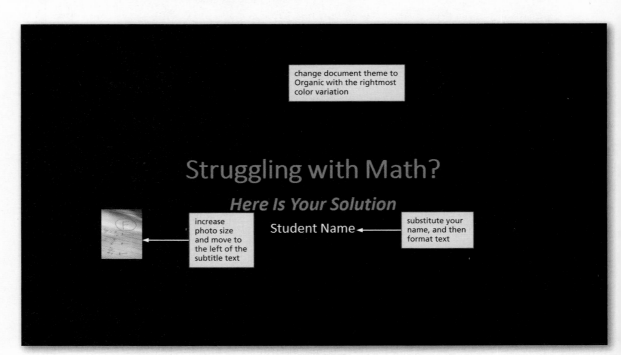

Figure 1–82

In the Labs

Design and/or create a presentation using the guidelines, concepts, and skills presented in this chapter. Labs 1 and 2, which increase in difficulty, require you to create solutions based on what you learned in the chapter; Lab 3 requires you to create a solution, which uses cloud and web technologies, by learning and investigating on your own from general guidance.

Lab 1: Creating a Presentation with Bulleted Lists, a Closing Slide, and Pictures

Problem: You are majoring in accounting and work part-time at a tax-filing service. Your clients have asked you numerous times what documents they should keep at home to support their tax returns. You decide to put together a presentation that would offer some basic guidelines about how to organize personal documents. You develop the outline shown in Figure 1–83 and then prepare the PowerPoint presentation shown in Figures 1–84a through 1–84e on pages PPT 62–64.

Files or Piles
 Document Storage and Retention at Home

Store and Retain
 In Home Office Safe
 Tax records for six years
 Pay stubs until W2 arrives
 Credit card statements
 Canceled checks
 Utility bills
 In Bank Safe Deposit Box
 Wills, deeds, and titles
 Birth and death certificates
 Passports
 Military records

Keep Indefinitely
 Personal health records
 Medical history
 Retirement benefit statements

General Rules
 Shred documents showing personal information
 Organize and store chronologically
 Keep list of important documents
 State their location
 Share with relative or friend

Figure 1–83

In the Labs *continued*

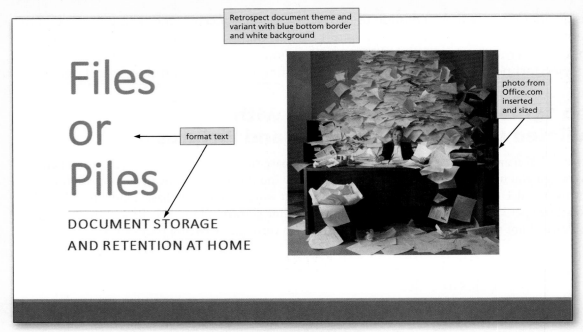

(a) Slide 1 (Title Slide)

(b) Slide 2

Figure 1–84

(c) Slide 3

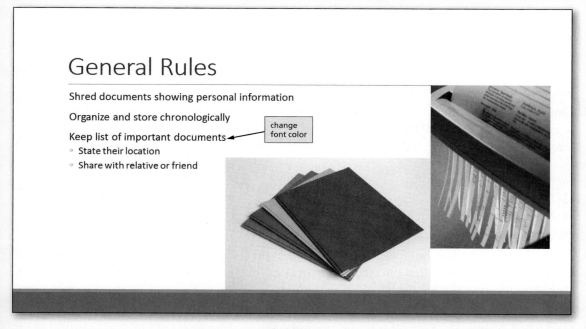

(d) Slide 4

Figure 1–84 (Continued)

Contin

In the Labs *continued*

**Files
or
Piles**

DOCUMENT STORAGE
AND RETENTION AT HOME

add closing slide by duplicating
and editing Slide 1

(e) Slide 5 (Closing Slide)
Figure 1–84 (Continued)

Instructions: Perform the following tasks:

1. Create a new presentation using the Retrospect document theme and select the variant with the blue bottom border and white background.

2. Using the typed outline illustrated in Figure 1–83 on page PPT 61, create the title slide shown in Figure 1–84a. Press the ENTER key to place each word on a separate line and divide the title into three lines, as shown in the figure. Increase the font size of the title text to 88 point and bold this text. Change the font color to Green (the sixth color from left in the Standard Colors row). Increase the font size of the subtitle text, DOCUMENT STORAGE AND RETENTION AT HOME, to 28 point and bold this text. Press the ENTER key to divide the subtitle into two lines, as shown in the figure. Find and insert the picture from the Office.com Clip Art collection. Size the picture and use the Smart Guides to position it as shown in the figure.

3. Using the typed outline in Figure 1–83, create the three text slides with lists and find and insert the pictures from the Office.com Clip Art collection. Size the pictures and use the Smart Guides to position these images, as shown in Figures 1–84b, 1–84c, and 1–84d. You may want to zoom the slides to help you align these graphic elements.

4. On Slide 2, change the font color in the left and right heading placeholders to Green and bold and italicize this text.

5. On Slides 2, 3 and 4, change the font color of the lists to Dark Blue (second color from right in the Standard Colors row).

6. Create a closing slide by duplicating Slide 1 and adding the photo using the Smart Guides to center it on top of the existing photo.

7. If requested by your instructor, use your father's first name in place of the word, Piles, and replace the word, or, with the word, for, on Slide 5.

8. Apply the Shred transition in the Exciting category to all slides. Change the duration to 4.5 seconds.

9. Tap or click the Start From Beginning button to start the show from the first slide. Then swipe or click to display each slide.

10. Save the presentation using the file name, Lab 1-1 Document Storage at Home.

11. Submit the document in the format specified by your instructor.

12. ✺ What is the significance of placing the neat file folders photo on top of the messy desk photo on the closing slide? Why did you change the font color on Slides 2, 3, and 4 to Dark Blue?

Lab 2: Creating a Presentation with Bulleted Lists and Pictures

Problem: The number of reported West Nile Virus (WNV) cases across the continental United States has been growing steadily. After a discussion in your biology class, your instructor assigned everyone in the class to research WNV and to outline the facts that were discussed. You use your class notes to create the outline shown in Figure 1–85 and then create the presentation shown in Figures 1–86a through 1–86d on pages PPT 66–68.

West Nile Virus (WNV)
Facts, Signs, and Prevention
Student Name

What Is WNV?

 Transmitted by mosquitoes that bit infected birds

 First identified in eastern Africa in 1937

 Now worldwide in tropical and temperate climates

 Appeared in United States in 1999

 Now reported in 48 states

 At risk: People with weak immune systems

What Are the Symptoms?

 Most commonly resemble the flu

 High fever

 Headache

 Body aches

 Nausea / vomiting

 Vision problems

How Can I Avoid WNV?

 Protect against mosquito bites

 Wear repellent with EPA-recommended ingredients

 Avoid being outdoors at dawn and dusk

 Wear clothes that cover skin

 Remove standing water from yard vessels

 Repair damaged window and door screens

Figure 1–85

Continued >

In the Labs *continued*

Instructions: Perform the following tasks:

1. Create a new presentation using the Facet document theme.

2. Using the outline illustrated in Figure 1–85 on the previous page, create the title slide shown in Figure 1–86a, using your name in place of Student Name.

3. If requested by your instructor, substitute the name of your hometown in place of your last name.

4. On Slide 1, bold the text, West Nile Virus (WNV). Decrease the font size of the text, Facts, Signs, and Prevention, to 44 point. Change the font color of all the title text to Red, Accent 5 (second color from right in the Theme Colors row).

5. Using the outline in Figure 1–85, create the three text slides with bulleted lists shown in Figures 1–86b, 1–86c, and 1–86d. Change the color of the title text on these three text slides to Red, Accent 5.

6. Add the pictures shown in Figures 1–86a through 1–86d from Office.com. Zoom the slide and then resize the pictures when necessary.

7. Apply the Page Curl transition in the Exciting category to all slides. Change the duration to 2.25 seconds.

8. Tap or click the Start From Beginning button to start the slide show and then display each slide.

9. Save the presentation using the file name, Lab 1–2 West Nile Virus.

10. Submit the revised document in the format specified by your instructor.

11. ✳ How does changing the font color to red help reinforce the West Nile Virus prevention concept? What is the significance of adding a mosquito illustration to every slide?

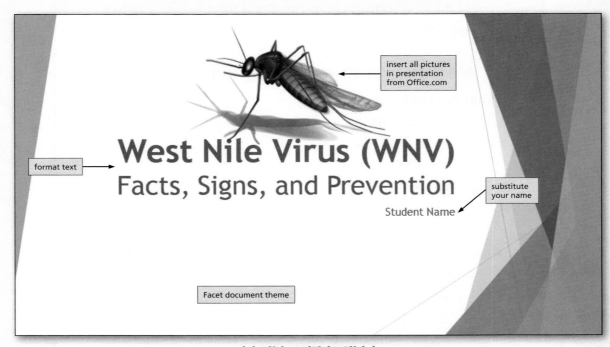

(a) Slide 1 (Title Slide)

Figure 1–86

(b) Slide 2

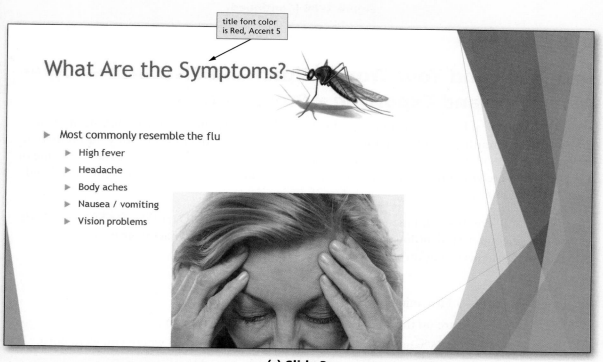

(c) Slide 3

Figure 1–86 (Continued)

Continued >

In the Labs *continued*

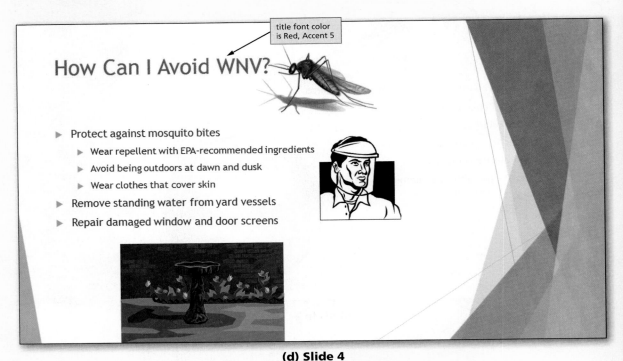

(d) Slide 4

Figure 1–86 (Continued)

Lab 3: Expand Your World: Cloud and Web Technologies
Modifying and Exporting a Presentation

Problem: Your local library is planning events to celebrate Hispanic Heritage Month, and you are part of a committee to publicize the event. You want to share the title slide of your preliminary PowerPoint presentation with fellow committee members, so you have decided to store the file on SkyDrive. You are going to modify the slide you have created thus far shown in Figure 1–87 and save it to SkyDrive.

Note: To complete this assignment, you will be required to use the Data Files for Students. Visit www.cengage.com/ct/studentdownload for detailed instructions or contact your instructor for information about accessing the required files.

Instructions:
1. Open the Lab 1–3 Hispanic Heritage file.
2. Insert another picture on the title slide in the area indicated in Figure 1–87.
3. If requested to do so by your instructor, change the city to the town where you were born.
4. Save the presentation using the file name, Lab 1–3 Heritage Month.
5. Export the file to your SkyDrive in the Chapter 01 folder in the PowerPoint folder.
6. Submit the assignment in the format specified by your instructor.
7. ✸ When would you save one of your files for school or your job to SkyDrive? Do you think using SkyDrive enhances collaboration efforts? Why?

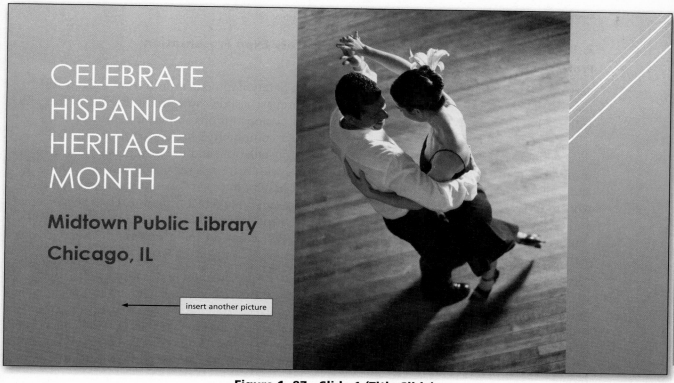

Figure 1–87 Slide 1 (Title Slide)

✳ Consider This: Your Turn

Apply your creative thinking and problem-solving skills to design and implement a solution.

1. Design and Create a Presentation about Mars Exploration

Personal

Part 1: Your astronomy class is studying the solar system, and you have been assigned the topic of the Mars Curiosity rover and its exploration of that planet. You have learned that the rover was launched from Cape Canaveral, Florida, on November 26, 2011, and landed in the Gale Crater on Mars on August 6, 2012. The mission was scheduled to last two years and had the major goal of assessing whether Mars was or is capable of supporting life. The Curiosity rover is the size of a car and has a MastCam equipped with two camera systems to take photos of the landscape as it maneuvers around the rocky surface. The rover also can scoop up samples of the Martian soil, fire a laser at rocks as far away as nine feet (2.7 meters), and make weather station readings. Use the concepts and techniques you learned in the chapter to create a PowerPoint presentation with a suitable theme, a title slide, and three text slides with bulleted lists. Add pictures from Office.com and apply a transition. Submit your assignment in the format specified by your instructor.

Part 2: ✳ You made several decisions while creating the presentation in this assignment: what theme to use, where to place text, how to format the text (font, font size, paragraph alignment, bulleted paragraphs, italics, bold, color). You also decided which graphical images to use, where to position the graphical images, if a closing slide would be useful, and which transition would be most effective. What was the rationale behind each of these decisions? When you proofed the document, what further revisions did you make and why? Where would you recommend showing this slide show?

Continued >

Consider This: Your Turn *continued*

2. Design and Create a Fire Department Safety Expo Presentation
Professional

Part 1: Your local fire department is sponsoring a Safety Expo one month from today at the local hardware store. The chief has asked you to prepare a slide show promoting the event, which will be held from noon to 5 p.m. A wide variety of demonstrations and informational booths will be present. They include: firefighters from your community's fire department, who will discuss home emergency planning, proper car seat installation, and fire extinguisher use; a local insurance agent, who will distribute tote bags filled with materials regarding adequate home and rental insurance coverage and also a nine-volt battery for a smoke alarm; and a children's workshop, where participants under 10 years of age can build a picture frame. Use the concepts and techniques presented in this chapter to develop and format this slide show with at least four slides with bulleted lists. Add pictures from Office.com and apply a transition. Submit your assignment in the format specified by your instructor.

Part 2: ✳ You made several decisions while creating the presentation in this assignment: what theme to use, where to place text, how to format the text (font, font size, paragraph alignment, bulleted paragraphs, italics, bold, color). You also decided which graphical images to use, where to position the graphical images, if a closing slide would be useful, and which transition would be most effective. What was the rationale behind each of these decisions? When you proofed the document, what further revisions did you make and why? Where would you recommend showing this slide show?

3. Design and Create a Presentation about Commemorative Postage Stamps
Research and Collaboration

Part 1: Stamp collecting is one of the world's more popular indoor hobbies. Collectors often seek postage stamps pertaining to a particular interest, such as birds, flowers, famous people, or ships. Have each member of your team gather information on these topics: stamp collecting equipment, popular commemorative stamps issued, current commemorative stamps for sale at your local post office, and rare stamps. After coordinating these facts, use the concepts and techniques presented in this chapter to prepare a presentation with a minimum of four slides that explore the subject of stamp collection. Select a suitable theme and include a title slide, bulleted lists, and a closing slide. Add pictures from Office.com and apply a transition. Submit your assignment in the format specified by your instructor.

Part 2: ✳ You made several decisions while creating the presentation in this assignment: what theme to use, where to place text, how to format the text (font, font size, paragraph alignment, bulleted paragraphs, italics, bold, color). You also decided which graphical images to use, where to position the graphical images, if a closing slide would be useful, and which transition would be most effective. What was the rationale behind each of these decisions? When you proofed the document, what further revisions did you make and why? Where would you recommend showing this slide show?

Learn Online

Reinforce what you learned in this chapter with games, exercises, training, and many other online activities and resources.

Student Companion Site Reinforcement activities and resources are available at no additional cost on www.cengagebrain.com. Visit www.cengage.com/ct/studentdownload for detailed instructions about accessing the resources available at the Student Companion Site.

SAM Put your skills into practice with SAM! If you have a SAM account, go to www.cengage.com/sam2013 to access SAM assignments for this chapter.

2 | Enhancing a Presentation with Pictures, Shapes, and WordArt

Objectives

You will have mastered the material in this chapter when you can:

- Search for and download an online theme
- Insert and format pictures
- Insert and size a shape
- Apply effects to a shape
- Add text to a shape
- Change the text font

- Insert and format WordArt
- Insert a picture to create a background
- Format slide backgrounds
- Find and replace text and check spelling
- Add and print speaker notes

2 | Enhancing a Presentation with Pictures, Shapes, and WordArt

Introduction

In our visually oriented culture, audience members enjoy viewing effective graphics. Whether reading a document or viewing a PowerPoint presentation, people increasingly want to see photographs, artwork, graphics, and a variety of typefaces. Researchers have known for decades that documents with visual elements are more effective than those that consist of only text because the illustrations motivate audiences to study the material. People remember at least one-third more information when the document they are seeing or reading contains visual elements. These graphics help clarify and emphasize details, so they appeal to audience members with differing backgrounds, reading levels, attention spans, and motivations.

Project — Presentation with Pictures, Shapes, and WordArt

The project in this chapter focuses on helping families plan for emergencies. Children need to prepare for the unexpected by collecting supplies to make an emergency supply kit, developing a communication plan, and realizing the need to be ready for any unexpected situation that may arise. The presentation shown in Figure 2 – 1 follows graphical guidelines and has a variety of illustrations and visual elements that are colorful and appealing to children. For example, the pictures have particular shapes and effects. The enhanced type has a style that blends well with the formatted background and illustrations. Pictures and type are formatted using picture styles and WordArt, which give the presentation a professional look. You plan to present the material during community safety open houses at fire stations and local hardware stores, so you want to add notes explaining concepts you will be discussing during the meeting.

BTW

BTWs

For a complete list of the BTWs found in the margins of this book, visit the BTW resource on the Student Companion Site located on www.cengagebrain.com. For detailed instructions about accessing available resources, visit www.cengage.com/ct/studentdownload or see the inside back cover of this book.

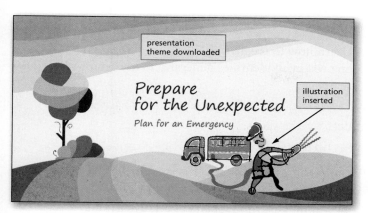

(a) Slide 1 (Title Slide)

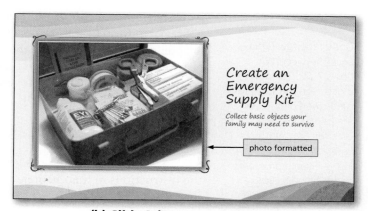

(b) Slide 2 (Formatted Picture)

(c) Slide 3 (Shapes Inserted and Formatted)

(d) Slide 4 (Picture Background)

Figure 2–1

For an introduction to Windows and instruction about how to perform basic Windows tasks, read the Office and Windows chapter at the beginning of this book, where you can learn how to resize windows, change screen resolution, create folders, move and rename files, use Windows Help, and much more.

Roadmap

In this chapter, you will learn how to create the slides shown in Figure 2–1 on the previous page. The following roadmap identifies general activities you will perform as you progress through this chapter:

1. DOWNLOAD a theme and SELECT SLIDES for the presentation.
2. INSERT and FORMAT PICTURES for the slides.
3. INSERT and FORMAT SHAPES on one slide.
4. INSERT and FORMAT WORDART by changing the shape, fill, and outline.
5. FORMAT SLIDE BACKGROUNDS with a gradient, texture, and picture fill.
6. REVIEW and REVISE SLIDES by finding a synonym and checking spelling.

At the beginning of step instructions throughout the chapter, you will see an abbreviated form of this roadmap. The abbreviated roadmap uses colors to indicate chapter progress: gray means the chapter is beyond that activity; blue means the task being shown is covered in that activity, and black means that activity is yet to be covered. For example, the following abbreviated roadmap indicates the chapter would be showing a task in the 5 FORMAT SLIDE BACKGROUNDS activity.

One of the few differences between Windows 7 and Windows 8 occurs in the steps to run PowerPoint. If you are using Windows 7, click the Start button, type **PowerPoint** in the 'Search programs and files' box, click PowerPoint 2013, and then, if necessary, maximize the PowerPoint window. For detailed steps to run PowerPoint in Windows 7, refer to the Office and Windows chapter at the beginning of this book. For a summary of the steps, refer to the Quick Reference located at the back of this book.

1 DOWNLOAD & SELECT SLIDES | 2 INSERT & FORMAT PICTURES | 3 INSERT & FORMAT SHAPES
4 INSERT & FORMAT WORDART | **5 FORMAT SLIDE BACKGROUNDS** | 6 REVIEW & REVISE SLIDES

Use the abbreviated roadmap as a progress guide while you read or step through the instructions in this chapter.

To Run PowerPoint

If you are using a computer to step through the project in this chapter and you want your screens to match the figures in this book, you should change your screen's resolution to 1366×768. For information about how to change a computer's resolution, refer to the Office and Windows chapter at the beginning of this book.

The following steps, which assume Windows 8 is running, use the Start screen or the search box to run PowerPoint based on a typical installation. You may need to ask your instructor how to run PowerPoint on your computer. For a detailed example of the procedure summarized below, refer to the Office and Windows chapter.

For an introduction to Office and instruction about how to perform basic tasks in Office apps, read the Office and Windows chapter at the beginning of this book, where you can learn how to run an application, use the ribbon, save a file, open a file, exit an application, use Help, and much more.

1 Scroll the Start screen for a PowerPoint 2013 tile. If your Start screen contains a PowerPoint 2013 tile, tap or click it to run PowerPoint and then proceed to Step 5; if the Start screen does not contain the PowerPoint 2013 tile, proceed to the next step to search for the PowerPoint app.

2 Swipe in from the right edge of the screen or point to the upper-right corner of the screen to display the Charms bar and then tap or click the Search charm on the Charms bar to display the Search menu.

3 Type **PowerPoint** as the search text in the Search box and watch the search results appear in the Apps list.

4 Tap or click PowerPoint 2013 in the search results to run PowerPoint.

5 If the PowerPoint window is not maximized, tap or click the Maximize button on its title bar to maximize the window.

Downloading a Theme and Editing Slides

In Chapter 1, you selected a theme and then typed the content for the title and text slides. In this chapter, you will type the slide content for the title and text slides, select a background, insert and format pictures and shapes, and then insert and format WordArt. To begin creating the four slides in this presentation, you will download a theme, delete unneeded slides in this downloaded presentation, and then enter text in three of the four slides.

To Search for and Download an Online Theme

1 DOWNLOAD & SELECT SLIDES | 2 INSERT & FORMAT PICTURES | 3 INSERT & FORMAT SHAPES
4 INSERT & FORMAT WORDART | 5 FORMAT SLIDE BACKGROUNDS | 6 REVIEW & REVISE SLIDES

PowerPoint displays many themes that are varied and appealing and give you an excellent start at designing a presentation. At times, however, you may have a specific topic and design concept and could use some assistance in starting to develop the presentation. Microsoft offers hundreds of predesigned themes and templates that could provide you with an excellent starting point. ***Why?*** *You can search for one of these ready-made presentations, or you can browse one of the predefined categories, such as business, medical, education, and nature. The themes and templates can save you time and help you develop content.* The following steps search for a theme that has an educational concept and is oriented toward children.

- Press and hold or point to Education in the Suggested searches list (Figure 2–2).

Q&A Why does a Recent Presentation list display on the left side of my screen?
You can specify the number of recent presentations to display in the Advanced tab of the PowerPoint Options dialog box.

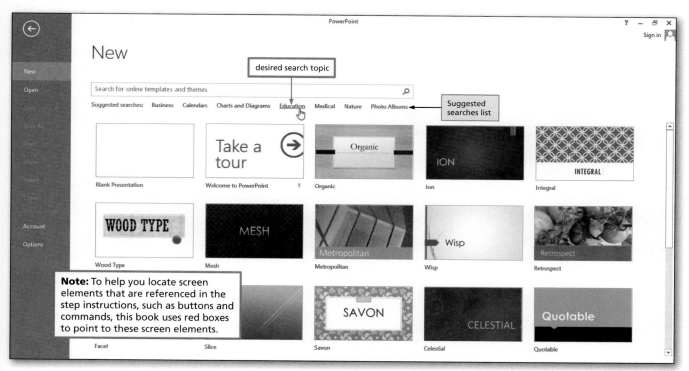

Figure 2–2

2

● Tap or click Education to search for themes with an academic subject.

Q&A ◁ Can I also use keywords to search for themes?

Yes. Tap or click the 'Search for online templates and themes' search box, type terms that relate to the topic of your presentation, and then click the Start searching button (the magnifying glass) or press the ENTER key so that Office.com will search for and display all themes with your keywords.

3

● Slide or scroll down about halfway through the theme thumbnails until the 'Colorful nature presentation, illustrated landscape design (widescreen)' theme, shown in Figure 2–3, is displayed.

Q&A ◁ Why are my theme thumbnails displaying in a different order?

Microsoft adds and modifies the themes, so the order may change.

4

● Tap or click the 'Colorful nature presentation, illustrated landscape design (widescreen)' theme to display a theme preview dialog box with a thumbnail view of the theme (Figure 2–3).

Q&A ◁ Can I see previews of the slides in this theme?

Yes. Click the right or left arrows beside the words, More Images, below the thumbnail. On some devices, a preview of all slides starts automatically after you tap the theme.

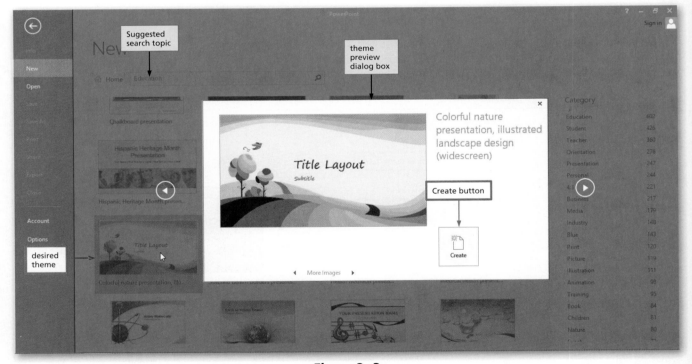

Figure 2–3

5

● Tap or click the Create button to download the theme and open a presentation with that theme in PowerPoint.

BTW
Additional Theme Information
You may see additional information regarding the theme in the theme preview dialog box if you are downloading the file for the first time. This information includes the provider (in this case, Microsoft Corporation), a description of the theme content and the intended audience, the file size (in this case, 2190 KB), and a rating.

To Delete a Slide

The downloaded theme has 13 slides with a variety of layouts. You will use four different layouts in your Be Prepared presentation, so you can delete the slides you downloaded that you will not need. *Why? Deleting the extra slides now helps reduce clutter and helps you focus on the layouts you will use.* The following steps delete the extra slides.

- If necessary, tap or click the Slide 1 thumbnail in the Thumbnail pane to select this slide.

- Swipe horizontally across each of the Slide 2, 3, and 4 thumbnails, or press and hold the SHIFT key and then click the thumbnail for Slide 4 to select slides 1 through 4 (Figure 2–4).

Q&A
Why would I select Slide 1, the Title Slide layout, for deletion if I need a title slide for my presentation?
Slide 9 also will work well to format as the title slide (Slide 1) in this presentation.

Figure 2–4

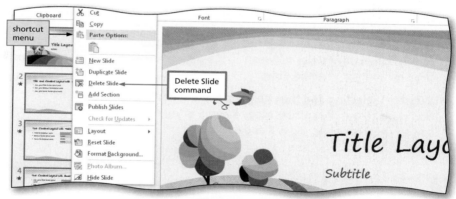

- Press and hold or right-click any selected slide to display the shortcut menu (Figure 2–5).

Figure 2–5

- Tap Delete or click Delete Slide to delete the selected slides from the presentation (Figure 2–6).

Q&A
How would I delete several slides simultaneously if they are not sequential?
Repeat this procedure except make a short swipe across each slide thumbnail you want to delete to select it, or press and hold the CTRL key while you tap or click each slide you want to delete.

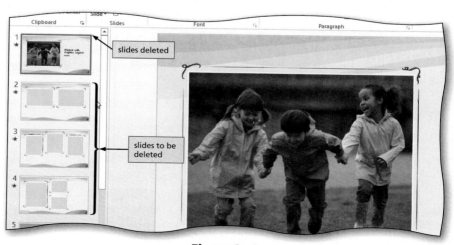

Figure 2–6

4

- Select the new Slides 2, 3, and 4, display the shortcut menu, and then delete these slides (Figure 2–7).

Q&A Why am I selecting and then deleting these slides?
You want to use the current slides 1 and 5 in your presentation, so you need to delete the slides between these two slides.

slides deleted

Figure 2–7

5

- Tap or click the Slide 3 thumbnail to select this slide.

- Scroll down and then swipe the Slide 6 thumbnail or press and hold the CTRL key and then click the thumbnail for Slide 6 to select both slides 3 and 6 (Figure 2–8).

Q&A Why did I press and hold down the CTRL key instead of the SHIFT key?
Holding down the CTRL key selects only the slides you tap or click, whereas holding the SHIFT key selects consecutive slides between the first and last selected slides.

Why am I selecting and then deleting these slides?
You want to use the current slides 4 and 5 in your presentation, so you need to delete slides 3 and 6.

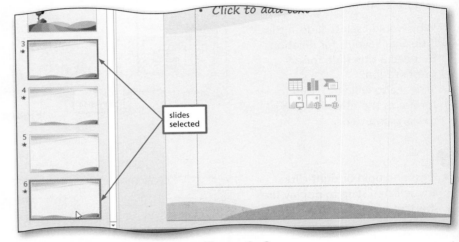

slides selected

Figure 2–8

6

- Display the shortcut menu and then delete slides 3 and 6 (Figure 2–9).

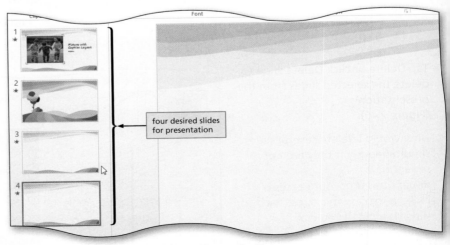

four desired slides for presentation

Figure 2–9

Other Ways

1. Select slide(s), press DELETE

To Create a Title Slide

Recall from Chapter 1 that the title slide introduces the presentation to the audience. In addition to introducing the presentation, this project uses the title slide to capture the audience's attention by using title text and an illustration. *Why? The presentation focuses on families and their need to work together to develop an emergency plan. The illustration of a fire truck and firefighter help introduce the concept.* The following steps rearrange Slide 1 and Slide 2 and then create the slide show's title slide.

1. Move Slide 2 in the Thumbnail pane above Slide 1 so that it becomes the first slide in the deck.

2. Type `Prepare` as the first text paragraph in the title text placeholder.

3. Press the ENTER key and then type `for the Unexpected` as the second paragraph in the title text placeholder.

4. Tap or click the subtitle text placeholder and then type `Plan for a Disaster` as the subtitle text (Figure 2–10).

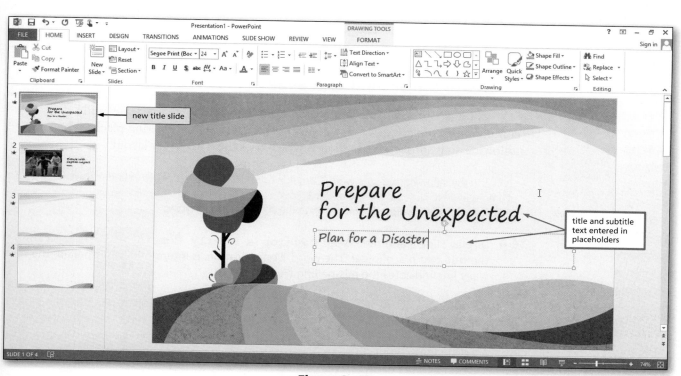

Figure 2–10

To Create the First Text Slide

The first text slide you create in Chapter 2 emphasizes the need to make an emergency supply kit that contains supplies and other necessities for survival. The following steps create the Slide 2 text slide using the Picture with Caption layout.

1. Display Slide 2, select the text in the title text placeholder, and then type `Create a Disaster Supply Kit` in the placeholder.

2. Tap or click the caption placeholder and then type `Collect basic objects your family may need to stay alive` in this placeholder (Figure 2–11).

BTW

Q&As
For a complete list of the Q&As found in many of the step-by-step sequences in this book, visit the Q&A resource on the Student Companion Site located on www.cengagebrain.com. For detailed instructions about accessing available resources, visit www.cengage.com/ct/studentdownload or see the inside back cover of this book.

Figure 2–11

To Create the Second Text Slide

The second text slide you create shows two components of the family communication plan: carrying a contact list and arranging meeting places. The following step adds a title to Slide 3, which uses the Title Only layout.

Note: In the following step, the word, Communication, has been misspelled intentionally as Comunication to illustrate the use of PowerPoint's spell check feature. Your slides may contain different misspelled words, depending upon the accuracy of your typing.

1 Display Slide 3 and then type **Develop a Family Comunication Plan** in the title text placeholder. The word, Comunication, is intentionally misspelled; the red wavy line indicates the misspelling (Figure 2–12).

Figure 2–12

BTW
The Ribbon and Screen Resolution
PowerPoint may change how the groups and buttons within the groups appear on the ribbon, depending on the computer's screen resolution. Thus, your ribbon may look different from the ones in this book if you are using a screen resolution other than 1366 × 768.

To Save a Presentation

You have performed many tasks while creating this presentation and do not want to risk losing work completed thus far. Accordingly, you should save the presentation on your hard disk, SkyDrive, or a location that is most appropriate to your situation.

The following steps assume you already have created folders for storing your files, for example, a CIS 101 folder (for your class) that contains a PowerPoint folder

(for your assignments). Thus, these steps save the presentation in the PowerPoint folder in the CIS 101 folder on your desired save location. For a detailed example of the procedure for saving a file in a folder or saving a file on SkyDrive, refer to the Office and Windows chapter at the beginning of this book.

1 Tap or click the Save button on the Quick Access Toolbar, which depending on settings, will display either the Save As gallery in the Backstage view or the Save As dialog box.

2 To save on a hard disk or other storage media on your computer, proceed to Step 2a. To save on SkyDrive, proceed to Step 2b.

2a If your screen opens the Backstage view and you want to save on storage media on your computer, tap or click Computer in the left pane, if necessary, to display options in the right pane related to saving on your computer. If your screen already displays the Save As dialog box, proceed to Step 3.

2b If your screen opens the Backstage view and you want to save on SkyDrive, tap or click SkyDrive in the left pane to display SkyDrive saving options or a Sign In button. If your screen displays a Sign In button, tap or click it and then sign in to SkyDrive.

3 Tap or click the Browse button in the right pane to display the Save As dialog box associated with the selected save location (i.e., Computer or SkyDrive).

4 Type **Emergency Plan** in the File name box to change the file name. Do not press the ENTER key after typing the file name because you do not want to close the dialog box at this time.

5 Navigate to the desired save location (in this case, the PowerPoint folder in the CIS 101 folder [or your class folder] on your computer or SkyDrive).

6 Tap or click the Save button (Save As dialog box) to save the presentation in the selected folder on the selected save location with the entered file name.

Inserting and Formatting Pictures in a Presentation

With the text entered in three of the four slides, the next step is to insert pictures into Slides 1 and 2 and then format the pictures. These graphical images draw the viewers' eyes to the slides and help them retain the information presented.

In the following pages, you will perform these tasks:

1. Insert the illustration into Slide 1.
2. Resize the illustration.
3. Change the Slide 2 photo.
4. Change the photo's brightness and contrast.
5. Change the photo's style and effect.
6. Add and modify the photo's border.

To Insert a Picture into a Slide without a Content Placeholder

1 DOWNLOAD & SELECT SLIDES | 2 INSERT & FORMAT PICTURES | 3 INSERT & FORMAT SHAPES
4 INSERT & FORMAT WORDART | 5 FORMAT SLIDE BACKGROUNDS | 6 REVIEW & REVISE SLIDES

BTW
Organizing Files and Folders
You should organize and store files in folders so that you easily can find the files later. For example, if you are taking an introductory computer class called CIS 101, a good practice would be to save all PowerPoint files in a PowerPoint folder in a CIS 101 folder. For a discussion of folders and detailed examples of creating folders, refer to the Office and Windows chapter at the beginning of this book.

In Chapter 1, you inserted photos and an illustration into slides without a content placeholder. *Why? Some slide layouts do not have a content placeholder, so you must insert and move the pictures to appropriate locations on the slide.* The illustration for Slide 1 is available on the Data Files for Students. Visit www.cengage.com/ct/studentdownload for detailed instructions or contact your instructor for information about accessing the

required files. The instructions in this chapter show the required files in the PowerPoint Chapter 2 folder in the CIS 101 folder on your computer. The following steps insert an illustration into the title slide.

1

- Display Slide 1 and then tap or click INSERT on the ribbon to display the INSERT tab.
- Tap or click the Pictures button (INSERT tab | Images group) to display the Insert Picture dialog box.

2

- If Computer is not displayed in the navigation pane, press and drag or drag the navigation pane scroll bar (Insert Picture dialog box) until Computer appears.
- Tap or click Computer in the navigation pane to display a list of available storage locations in the Insert Picture dialog box. If necessary, scroll through the dialog box until your class folder appears in the list.
- Double-tap or double-click your folder in the list of available storage locations to display a list of files and folders. Double-tap or double-click the Data Files for Students folder, double-tap or double-click the PowerPoint folder, and then double-tap or double-click the Chapter 02 folder to display a list of files in that folder.

- Slide or scroll down and then tap or click Fire Truck to select the file name (Figure 2–13).

What if the picture is not in the folder?
Use the same process, but select the location containing the Chapter 2 data file pictures or search for the picture on Office.com.

Why do I see thumbnails of the pictures along with the file names in my folder?
Your view is different from the view shown in Figure 2–13.

Figure 2–13

3

- Tap or click the Insert button (Insert Picture dialog box) to insert the illustration into Slide 1.
- Drag the upper-right sizing handle diagonally toward the upper-right corner of the slide until the crosshair is positioned approximately as shown in Figure 2–14.

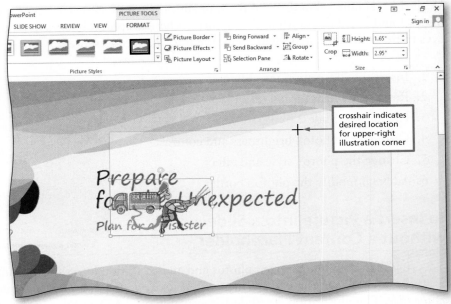

Figure 2–14

4

- Release to resize the illustration.

- Drag the illustration downward until the horizontal Smart Guide is displayed under the title text placeholder and the vertical Smart Guide is displayed near the right side of the slide, as shown in Figure 2–15, and then release.

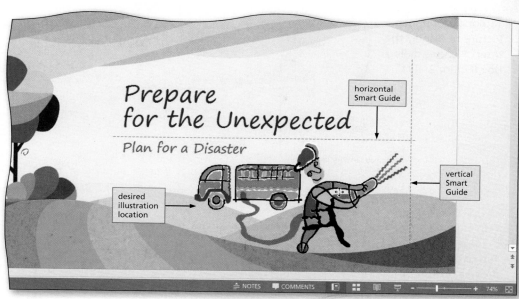

Figure 2–15

To Change a Picture

1 DOWNLOAD & SELECT SLIDES | 2 INSERT & FORMAT PICTURES | 3 INSERT & FORMAT SHAPES
4 INSERT & FORMAT WORDART | 5 FORMAT SLIDE BACKGROUNDS | 6 REVIEW & REVISE SLIDES

Why? *The downloaded theme included the photo of three children on Slide 2. You need to change the photo to reflect the emergency kit concept presented on this slide.* The next task in the presentation is to change the default picture on Slide 2 with one of the emergency pictures on the Data Files for Students. The following steps change the Slide 2 photo to the Emergency Kit photo, which, in this example, is located in the PowerPoint Chapter 02 folder that contains the saved presentation.

1

- Display Slide 2 and then press and hold or right-click the picture to display the shortcut menu (Figure 2–16).

Q&A

Why are the Style and Crop buttons displayed above the shortcut menu on my screen?
These two buttons display either above or below the shortcut menu depending upon where you press and hold or right-click on the screen.

Figure 2–16

2

- Tap or click Change Picture to display the Insert Pictures dialog box (Figure 2–17).

Figure 2–17

3

- Tap or click the Browse button in the From a file area to display the Insert Pictures dialog box.

- If necessary, navigate to the PowerPoint Chapter 02 folder, slide or scroll down, and then click First Aid Kit to select the file name (Figure 2–18).

Figure 2–18

4

- Tap or click the Insert button (Insert Picture dialog box) to insert the photo into the Slide 2 picture placeholder (Figure 2–19).

Figure 2–19

Other Ways

1. Tap or click Change Picture button (PICTURE TOOLS FORMAT tab | Adjust group)

To Correct a Picture

A photo's color intensity can be modified by changing the brightness and contrast. **Brightness** determines the overall lightness or darkness of the entire image, whereas **contrast** is the difference between the darkest and lightest areas of the image. The brightness and contrast are changed in predefined percentage increments. The following step increases the brightness and decreases the contrast. *Why? Altering the photo's brightness will coordinate with the vibrant colors in the slide design while decreasing the contrast will soften the image. It is important for the audience to recognize the first aid kit but not focus on each individual supply in the kit.*

1

- With the First Aid Kit photo on Slide 2 still selected, tap or click FORMAT on the ribbon to display the PICTURE TOOLS FORMAT tab.

- Tap or click the Corrections button (PICTURE TOOLS FORMAT tab | Adjust group) to display the Corrections gallery.

- If you are using a mouse, point to Brightness: +20% Contrast: −40% (the fourth picture in the first Brightness/Contrast row) to display a live preview of these corrections on the picture (Figure 2–20).

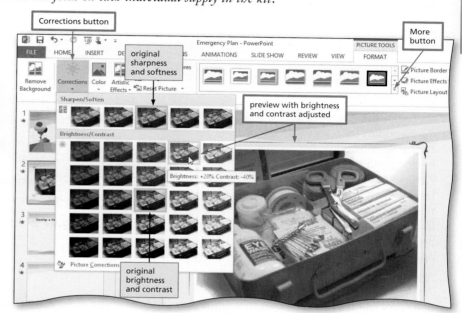

Figure 2–20

Q&A Can I use live preview on a touch screen?
Live preview is not available on a touch screen.

Why is a pink border surrounding the pictures in the center of the Sharpen/Soften and Brightness/Contrast areas of the gallery?
The image on Slide 2 currently has normal sharpness, brightness, and contrast (0%), which is represented by these center images in the gallery.

🔍 Experiment

- If you are using a mouse, point to various pictures in the Brightness and Contrast area and watch the brightness and contrast change on the picture in Slide 2.

- Tap or click Brightness: +20% Contrast: −40% to apply this correction to the First Aid Kit photo.

Q&A How can I remove all effects from the picture?
Tap or click the Reset Picture button (PICTURE TOOLS FORMAT tab | Adjust group).

Other Ways

1. Tap or click Picture Corrections Options (Corrections gallery), move Brightness or Contrast sliders or enter number in box next to slider (Format Picture task pane)

To Apply a Picture Style

A **style** is a named group of formatting characteristics. The picture on Slide 2 emphasizes the concept of assembling a supply kit, and you can increase its visual appeal by applying a style. *Why? PowerPoint provides more than 25 picture styles that enable you easily to change a picture's look to a more visually appealing style, including a variety of shapes, angles, borders, and reflections.* You want to use a style that applies a shadow to the First Aid Kit photo. The following steps apply a picture style to the Slide 2 photo.

- With the Slide 2 picture selected, if necessary tap or click the PICTURE TOOLS FORMAT tab and then tap or click the More button in the Picture Styles gallery (PICTURE TOOLS FORMAT tab | Picture Styles group) (shown in Figure 2–20) to expand the gallery.

Figure 2–21

- If you are using a mouse, point to Center Shadow Rectangle in the Picture Styles gallery (the sixth style in the second row) to display a live preview of that style applied to the picture in the document (Figure 2–21).

Experiment

- If you are using a mouse, point to various picture styles in the Picture Styles gallery and watch the style of the picture change in the document window.

2

- Tap or click Center Shadow Rectangle in the Picture Styles gallery to apply the style to the selected picture (Figure 2–22).

BTW
Touch Screen Differences
The Office and Windows interfaces may vary if you are using a touch screen. For this reason, you might notice that the function or appearance of your touch screen differs slightly from this chapter's presentation.

Figure 2–22

1 DOWNLOAD & SELECT SLIDES | 2 INSERT & FORMAT PICTURES | 3 INSERT & FORMAT SHAPES
4 INSERT & FORMAT WORDART | 5 FORMAT SLIDE BACKGROUNDS | 6 REVIEW & REVISE SLIDES

To Add a Picture Border

The next step is to add a border to the Slide 2 picture. *Why? Some picture styles do not have a border; others, such as the Center Shadow Rectangle style you applied to this picture, do have this edging. This border is small, and you want a larger edge around the photo to draw attention to the graphic.* The following steps add a border to the First Aid Kit picture.

1

- With the Slide 2 picture still selected, tap or click the Picture Border arrow (PICTURE TOOLS FORMAT tab | Picture Styles group) to display the Picture Border gallery.

Q&A | What if the PICTURE TOOLS FORMAT tab no longer is displayed on my ribbon?
Tap or click the picture to display the PICTURE TOOLS FORMAT tab.

2

- Point to Weight on the Picture Border gallery to display the Weight gallery (Figure 2–23).

3

- If you are using a mouse, point to 3 pt to display a live preview of this line weight on the picture.

Figure 2–23

Q&A | Can I make the line width more than 6 pt?
Yes. Tap or click More Lines, tap or click Solid line in the LINE section of the Format Picture task pane, and then increase the amount in the Width box.

Experiment

- If you are using a mouse, point to various line weights in the Weight gallery and watch the line thickness change.

- Tap or click 3 pt to add this line weight to the picture.

To Change a Picture Border Color

1 DOWNLOAD & SELECT SLIDES | 2 INSERT & FORMAT PICTURES | 3 INSERT & FORMAT SHAPES
4 INSERT & FORMAT WORDART | 5 FORMAT SLIDE BACKGROUNDS | 6 REVIEW & REVISE SLIDES

The default color for the border you added to the Slide 2 picture is brown, but you will change the border color to light blue. **Why?** *The light blue color coordinates with other elements on the slide, especially the blue sky.* The following steps change the Slide 2 picture border color.

1

- With the Slide 2 photo still selected, tap or click the Picture Border arrow (PICTURE TOOLS FORMAT tab | Picture Styles group) to display the Picture Border gallery.

2

- If you are using a mouse, point to Light Blue, Background 2 (the third color in the first row) in the Picture Border gallery to display a live preview of that border color on the picture (Figure 2–24).

Figure 2–24

Experiment

- If you are using a mouse, point to various colors in the Picture Border gallery and watch the border on the picture change in the slide.

3

- Tap or click Light Blue, Background 2 in the Picture Border gallery to change the picture border color.

To Apply Picture Effects

Why? *The picture effect allows you to further customize a picture.* PowerPoint provides a variety of picture effects, including shadows, reflections, glow, soft edges, bevel, and 3-D rotation. The difference between the effects and the styles is that each effect has several options, providing you with more control over the exact look of the image.

In this presentation, the photo on Slide 2 has a blue glow effect and a bevel applied to its edges. The following steps apply picture effects to the selected picture.

1

- With the Slide 2 picture selected, tap or click the Picture Effects button (PICTURE TOOLS FORMAT tab | Picture Styles group) to display the Picture Effects menu.

Q&A What if the PICTURE TOOLS FORMAT tab no longer is displayed on my ribbon?
Tap or double-click the picture to display the PICTURE TOOLS FORMAT tab.

- Point to Glow on the Picture Effects menu to display the Glow gallery.

Figure 2–25

- If you are using a mouse, point to Light Blue, 18 pt glow, Accent color 2 in the Glow Variations area (the second glow in the last row) to display a live preview of the selected glow effect applied to the picture in the document window (Figure 2–25).

Experiment

- If you are using a mouse, point to various glow effects in the Glow gallery and watch the picture change in the document window.

2

- Tap or click Light Blue, 18 pt glow, Accent color 2 in the Glow gallery to apply the selected picture effect.

3

- Tap or click the Picture Effects button (PICTURE TOOLS FORMAT tab | Picture Styles group) to display the Picture Effects menu again.

- Point to Bevel on the Picture Effects menu to display the Bevel gallery.

- If you are using a mouse, point to Relaxed Inset (the second bevel in the first row) to display a live preview of the selected bevel effect applied to the Slide 2 picture (Figure 2–26).

Experiment

- If you are using a mouse, point to various bevel effects in the Bevel gallery and watch the picture change in the slide.

Figure 2–26

4

- Tap or click Relaxed Inset in the Bevel gallery to apply the selected picture effect.

Other Ways

1. Press and hold or right-click picture, click Format Picture on shortcut menu, select desired options (Format Picture task pane), tap or click Close button

2. Tap or click Format Shape task pane launcher (PICTURE TOOLS FORMAT tab | Picture Styles group), select desired options (Format Picture task pane), tap or click Close button

Break Point: If you wish to take a break, this is a good place to do so. Be sure to save the Emergency Plan file again and then you can exit PowerPoint. To resume at a later time, run PowerPoint, open the file called Emergency Plan, and continue following the steps from this location forward.

Inserting and Formatting a Shape

One method of getting the audience's attention and reinforcing the major concepts being presented is to have graphical elements on the title slide. PowerPoint provides a wide variety of predefined shapes that can add visual interest to a slide. Shape elements include lines, basic geometrical shapes, arrows, equation shapes, flowchart symbols, stars, banners, and callouts. After adding a shape to a slide, you can change its default characteristics by adding text, bullets, numbers, and styles. You also can combine multiple shapes to create a more complex graphic.

Slide 3 in this presentation is enhanced in a variety of ways. First, a scroll and a plus shape are inserted on Slide 4. Then, a rectangle is added and copied, and text is added to each rectangle and then formatted.

To Add a Shape

Many of the shapes included in the Shapes gallery can direct the viewer to important aspects of the presentation. The following steps add a scroll shape to Slide 3. *Why? A scroll shape helps emphasize the presentation's theme of drafting and finalizing a plan for dealing with emergencies in the household.*

1

• Display Slide 3 and then display the HOME tab (Figure 2–27).

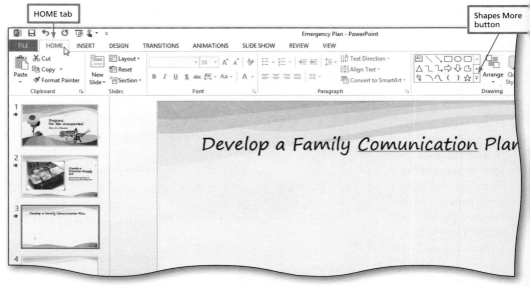

Figure 2–27

2

• Tap or click the Shapes More button (HOME tab | Drawing group) shown in Figure 2–27 to display the Shapes gallery (Figure 2–28).

 I do not see a Shapes More button and the three rows of the shapes shown in Figure 2–28. Instead, I have a Shapes button. Why? Monitor dimensions and resolution affect how buttons display on the ribbon. Tap or click the Shapes button to display the entire Shapes gallery.

Figure 2–28

- Tap or click the Vertical Scroll shape in the Stars and Banners area of the Shapes gallery.

Q&A Why did my pointer change shape?

The pointer changed to a plus shape to indicate the Vertical Scroll shape has been added to the Clipboard.

- Position the pointer (a crosshair) below the word, Develop, as shown in Figure 2–29.

- Tap or click Slide 3 to insert the Vertical Scroll shape.

Figure 2–29

Other Ways

1. Tap or click Shapes button (INSERT tab | Illustrations group)

To Resize a Shape

1 DOWNLOAD & SELECT SLIDES | 2 INSERT & FORMAT PICTURES | 3 INSERT & FORMAT SHAPES
4 INSERT & FORMAT WORDART | 5 FORMAT SLIDE BACKGROUNDS | 6 REVIEW & REVISE SLIDES

The next step is to resize the Vertical Scroll shape. *Why? The shape should be enlarged so that it fills the middle area of the left side of the slide.* The following steps resize the selected Vertical Scroll shape.

- Press and hold down the SHIFT key and then drag the lower-right corner sizing handle until the Vertical Scroll shape is resized approximately as shown in Figure 2–30.

Q&A Why did I need to press the SHIFT key while enlarging the shape?

Holding down the SHIFT key while dragging keeps the proportions of the original shape.

What if my shape is not selected?
To select a shape, click it.

If I am using a touch screen, how can I maintain the shape's original proportion?
If you drag one of the corner sizing handles, the object should stay in proportion.

Figure 2–30

2

- Release to resize the shape.

- Drag the scroll shape until the vertical Smart Guide is displayed along the left side of the slide, as shown in Figure 2–31, and then release.

What if I want to move the shape to a precise location on the slide? With the shape selected, press the ARROW keys or the CTRL+ARROW keys to move the shape to the desired location.

Figure 2–31

Other Ways

1. Enter shape height and width in Height and Width boxes (DRAWING TOOLS FORMAT tab | Size group)

2. Tap or click Size and Position task pane launcher (DRAWING TOOLS FORMAT tab | Size group), tap or click Size tab, enter desired height and width values in boxes, tap or click Close button

1 DOWNLOAD & SELECT SLIDES | 2 INSERT & FORMAT PICTURES | 3 INSERT & FORMAT SHAPES
4 INSERT & FORMAT WORDART | 5 FORMAT SLIDE BACKGROUNDS | 6 REVIEW & REVISE SLIDES

To Add Other Shapes

Circles, squares, arrows, stars, and equation shapes are among the items included in the Shapes gallery. These shapes can be combined to show relationships among the elements, and they can help illustrate the basic concepts presented in your slide show. The following steps add the Plus and Rectangle shapes to Slide 3.

1

- Tap or click the Shapes More button (HOME tab | Drawing group) to display the Shapes gallery (Figure 2–32).

Figure 2–32

2

- Tap or click the Plus shape in the Equation Shapes area of the Shapes gallery.

- Position the pointer in the center of Slide 3 and then tap or click to insert the Plus shape.

3

- Press and hold down the SHIFT key and then drag a corner sizing handle until the Plus shape is the size shown in Figure 2–33.

Q&A If I am using a touch screen, how can I maintain the Plus shape's original proportion?

The object should stay in proportion when you drag one of the corner sizing handles.

- Drag the Plus shape until the horizontal Smart Guide is displayed in the middle of the two shapes and the vertical Smart Guide is displayed between the two shapes, as shown in Figure 2–33, and then release.

Figure 2–33

4

- Display the Shapes gallery and then tap or click the Rectangle shape in the Rectangles area of the gallery.

- Position the pointer toward the upper-right side of the Plus shape and then tap or click to insert the Rectangle shape.

5

- Resize the Rectangle shape so that it is the size shown in Figure 2–34.

- Drag the Rectangle shape until the horizontal Smart Guide is displayed below the title text and the vertical Smart Guide is displayed between the Plus and the Rectangle shapes, as shown in Figure 2–34, and then release.

Figure 2–34

To Apply a Shape Style

1 DOWNLOAD & SELECT SLIDES | 2 INSERT & FORMAT PICTURES | 3 INSERT & FORMAT SHAPES
4 INSERT & FORMAT WORDART | 5 FORMAT SLIDE BACKGROUNDS | 6 REVIEW & REVISE SLIDES

Formatting text in a shape follows the same techniques as formatting text in a placeholder. You can change font, font color and size, and alignment. You later will add contact information to the scroll, but now you want to apply a shape style to the scroll. *Why? The style will give depth to the object so that it appears three-dimensional.* The Quick Styles gallery has a variety of styles that change depending upon the theme applied to the presentation. The following steps apply a style to the Vertical Scroll shape.

1

- Tap or click the Vertical Scroll shape to select it and then tap or click the Quick Styles button (HOME tab | Drawing group) (Figure 2–35).

Figure 2–35

2

- If you are using a mouse, point to Subtle Effect – Lavender, Accent 6 in the Quick Styles gallery (the last shape in the fourth row) to display a live preview of that style applied to the Vertical Scroll shape in the slide (Figure 2–36).

 Experiment

- If you are using a mouse, point to various styles in the Quick Styles gallery and watch the style of the shape change.

Figure 2–36

3

- Tap or click Subtle Effect – Lavender, Accent 6 in the Quick Styles gallery to apply the selected style to the Vertical Scroll shape.

Other Ways

1. Tap or click Shape Styles More button (DRAWING TOOLS FORMAT tab | Shape Styles group), select style

2. Press and hold or right-click shape, tap or click Format Shape on shortcut menu, select desired style (Format Shape task pane), tap or click Close button

To Apply Another Style

You later will add meeting place information to the rectangle, but now you want to format this shape. **Why?** *The formatting will add interest. In addition, the Plus shape helps join the scroll and the rectangle, both of which will contain components of the family communication plan. You can apply a coordinating shape style to the Plus sign.* The following steps apply styles to the Rectangle and Plus shapes.

1 Tap or click the Rectangle shape on Slide 3 to select it.

2 Tap or click the Quick Styles button (HOME tab | Drawing group) to display the Quick Styles gallery and then apply the Subtle Effect – Lavender, Accent 6 style to the Rectangle shape.

3 Tap or click the Plus shape on Slide 3 to select it and then tap or click the Quick Styles button.

4 Tap or click Colored Outline – Lavender, Accent 6 (the last style in the first row) to apply that style to the Plus shape (Figure 2–37).

Figure 2–37

To Add Text to a Shape

1 DOWNLOAD & SELECT SLIDES | 2 INSERT & FORMAT PICTURES | 3 INSERT & FORMAT SHAPES
4 INSERT & FORMAT WORDART | 5 FORMAT SLIDE BACKGROUNDS | 6 REVIEW & REVISE SLIDES

The scroll and rectangle shapes on Slide 3 help call attention to the key aspects of your presentation. **Why?** *Your goal is to urge families to develop a communication plan by gathering contact information and determining meeting locations.* The next step is to add this information to Slide 3. The following steps add text to the two shapes.

- Tap or click the Vertical Scroll shape to select it and then type `Contact names & phone numbers` in the shape.

- Tap or click the Rectangle shape to select it and then type `Meeting place near house` in the shape (Figure 2–38).

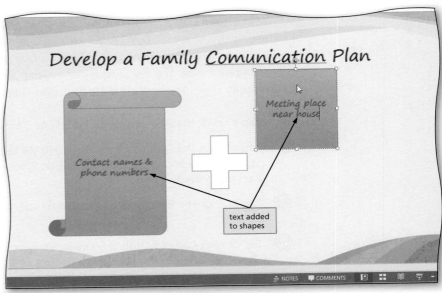

Figure 2–38

1 DOWNLOAD & SELECT SLIDES | 2 INSERT & FORMAT PICTURES | 3 INSERT & FORMAT SHAPES
4 INSERT & FORMAT WORDART | 5 FORMAT SLIDE BACKGROUNDS | 6 REVIEW & REVISE SLIDES

To Change the Font

The default theme font is Segoe Print. To draw more attention to text in the shapes and to help differentiate these slide elements from the title text, you want to change the font to Courier New. *Why? This font resembles the letters that typewriters produced.* To change the font, you must select the letters you want to format. In Chapter 1, you selected a paragraph and then formatted the characters, and you follow the same procedure to change the font. The following steps change the text font in the shape.

- Be certain the Rectangle shape is selected. If you are using a touch screen, tap to position the insertion point in the text to select and then drag the selection handles as necessary until all the characters are selected and the mini toolbar is displayed; if you are using a mouse, triple-click the text to select all the characters and display the mini toolbar (Figure 2–39).

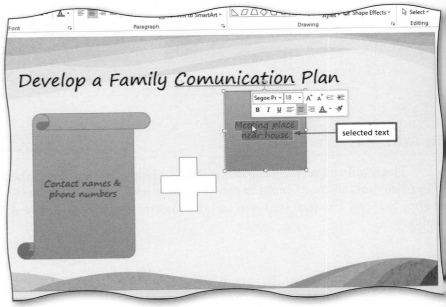

Figure 2–39

2

- Tap or click the Font arrow to display the Font gallery (Figure 2–40).

 Q&A

Will the fonts in my Font gallery be the same as those shown in Figure 2–40?

Your list of available fonts may differ, depending on what fonts you have installed and the type of printer you are using.

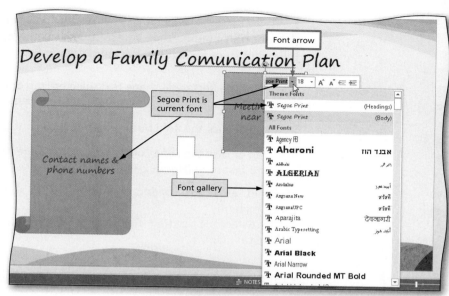

Figure 2–40

3

- If you are using a mouse, drag or scroll through the Font gallery and then point to Courier New (or a similar font) to display a live preview of the title text in the Courier New font (Figure 2–41).

🔎 **Experiment**

- If you are using a mouse, point to various fonts in the Font gallery and watch the subtitle text font change in the slide.

- Tap or click Courier New (or a similar font) to change the font of the selected text to Courier New.

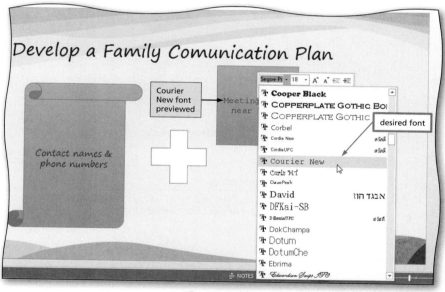

Figure 2–41

Other Ways

1. Tap or click Font arrow (HOME tab | Font group), tap or click desired font in Font gallery

2. Press and hold or right-click selected text, click Font on shortcut menu (Font dialog box), tap or click Font tab, select desired font in Font list, tap or click OK button

3. Tap or click Font dialog box launcher (HOME tab | Font group), tap or click Font tab (Font dialog box), select desired font in Font list, tap or click OK button

4. Press CTRL+SHIFT+F, click Font tab (Font dialog box), select desired font in the Font list, tap or click OK button

To Format the Text

To increase readability, you can format the Rectangle shape text by increasing the font size, bolding the characters, and changing the font color to black. The following steps format the Rectangle shape text.

1 With the Rectangle shape text selected, tap or click the Increase Font Size button (HOME tab | Font group) three times to increase the font size to 28 pt.

2 Tap or click the Bold button (HOME tab | Font group) to bold the text.

3 Tap or click the Font Color arrow and change the color to Black (the fourth color in the first row) (Figure 2–42).

Q&A Could I also add a shadow behind the text to add depth and help the letters display prominently?
Yes. Select the text and then tap or click the Text Shadow button (HOME tab | Font group).

Figure 2–42

Other Ways

1. Select text, tap 'Show Context Menu' button on mini toolbar or right-click selected text, tap or click desired text format button on mini toolbar

Format Painter

To save time and avoid formatting errors, you can use the Format Painter to apply custom formatting to other places in your presentation quickly and easily. You can use this feature in three ways:

- To copy only character attributes, such as font and font effects, select text that has these qualities.
- To copy both character attributes and paragraph attributes, such as alignment and indentation, select the entire paragraph.
- To apply the same formatting to multiple words, phrases, or paragraphs, double-tap or double-click the Format Painter button and then select each item you want to format. You then can press the ESC key or click the Format Painter button to turn off this feature.

To Format Text Using the Format Painter

Why? *To save time and duplicated effort, you quickly can use the Format Painter to copy formatting attributes from the Rectangle shape text and apply them to Vertical Scroll text.* The following steps use the Format Painter to copy formatting features.

- With the Rectangle shape text still selected, double-tap or double-click the Format Painter button (HOME tab | Clipboard group).

- Move the pointer off the ribbon (Figure 2–43).

Q&A Why did my pointer change shape?

The pointer changed shape by adding a paintbrush to indicate that the Format Painter function is active.

Figure 2–43

- Tap and drag the selection handles as necessary or triple-click the Vertical Scroll text to apply the format to all characters (Figure 2–44).

- Tap the Format Painter button or press the ESC key to turn off the Format Painter feature.

Figure 2–44

Other Ways

1. Select text, tap or click Format Painter button on mini toolbar

To Copy and Paste a Shape

When developing a communication plan, family members need to determine two meeting places: one near the house and a second outside the neighborhood. You already have created the shape stating the first meeting location. You now need to create a second shape with the instruction to decide where to meet away from the house. The following steps copy the Rectangle shape and then move the copy. ***Why?*** *You could repeat all the steps you performed to create the first rectangle, but it is much more efficient to duplicate the shape and then edit the text.*

- Select the Rectangle shape and then tap or click the Copy button (HOME tab | Clipboard group) (Figure 2–45).

Figure 2–45

2

- Tap or click the Paste button (HOME tab | Clipboard group) to insert a duplicate Rectangle shape on Slide 3.

- Drag the Rectangle shape below the first Rectangle shape (Figure 2–46).

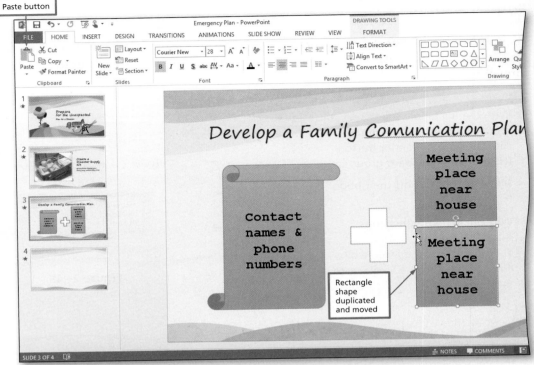

Figure 2–46

3

- In the second Rectangle shape, select the text, near house, and then type **away from vicinity** as the replacement text (Figure 2–47).

Figure 2–47

Other Ways

1. Press and hold or right-click selected shape, tap or click Copy on shortcut menu, press and hold or right-click, tap or click Paste on shortcut menu

2. Select shape, press CTRL+C, press CTRL+V

Break Point: If you wish to take a break, this is a good place to do so. Be sure to save the Emergency Plan file again and then you can exit PowerPoint. To resume at a later time, run PowerPoint, open the file called Emergency Plan, and continue following the steps from this location forward.

Inserting and Formatting WordArt

One method of adding appealing visual elements to a presentation is by using **WordArt** styles. This feature is found in other Microsoft Office applications, including Word and Excel. This gallery of decorative effects allows you to type new text or convert existing text to WordArt. You then can add elements such as fills, outlines, and effects.

WordArt **fill** in the interior of a letter can consist of a solid color, texture, picture, or gradient. The WordArt **outline** is the exterior border surrounding each letter or symbol. PowerPoint allows you to change the outline color, weight, and style. You also can add an **effect**, which helps add emphasis or depth to the characters. Some effects are shadows, reflections, glows, bevels, and 3-D rotations.

BTW

Undo Text Formatting Changes
To remove a formatting change you have made to text, such as an underline or bolding, select the text and then tap or click the button that originally applied the format. For example, to undo bolding, select the text and then click the Bold button. If you apply a format and then immediately decide to remove this effect, click the Undo button on the Quick Access Toolbar.

To Insert WordArt

1 DOWNLOAD & SELECT SLIDES | 2 INSERT & FORMAT PICTURES | 3 INSERT & FORMAT SHAPES
4 INSERT & FORMAT WORDART | 5 FORMAT SLIDE BACKGROUNDS | 6 REVIEW & REVISE SLIDES

Having a communication plan is of utmost importance to prepare for the unexpected. You want to emphasize this concept, and the last slide in the presentation is an excellent location to urge your audience to take action. *Why? Audience members remember the first and last things they see and hear.* You quickly can add a visual element to the slide by selecting a WordArt style from the WordArt Styles gallery and then applying it to some text. The following steps insert WordArt.

1
- Display Slide 4 and then display the INSERT tab.

- Tap or click the WordArt button (INSERT tab | Text group) to display the WordArt gallery (Figure 2–48).

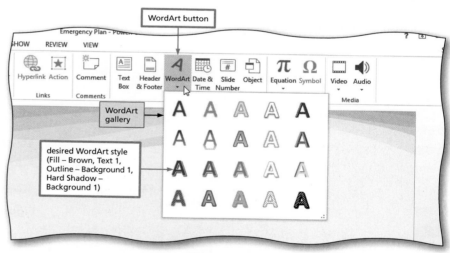

Figure 2–48

2
- Tap or click Fill – Brown, Text 1, Outline – Background 1, Hard Shadow – Background 1 (the first style in the third row) to insert the WordArt object (Figure 2–49).

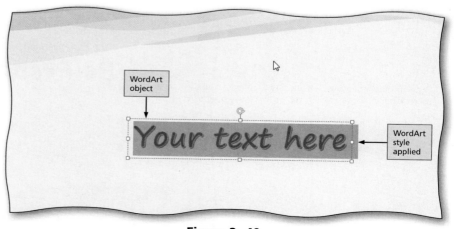

Figure 2–49

3

- Type **Be Prepared** in the object as the WordArt text (Figure 2–50).

Why did the DRAWING TOOLS FORMAT tab appear automatically in the ribbon?
It appears when you select text to which you could add a WordArt style or other effect.

Figure 2–50

To Change the WordArt Shape

1 DOWNLOAD & SELECT SLIDES | 2 INSERT & FORMAT PICTURES | 3 INSERT & FORMAT SHAPES
4 INSERT & FORMAT WORDART | 5 FORMAT SLIDE BACKGROUNDS | 6 REVIEW & REVISE SLIDES

Why? *The WordArt text is useful to emphasize the need to prepare for emergencies. You further can emphasize this text by changing its shape.* PowerPoint provides a variety of graphical shapes that add interest to WordArt text. The following steps change the WordArt shape to Inflate Bottom.

1

- With the WordArt object still selected, click the Text Effects button (DRAWING TOOLS FORMAT tab | WordArt Styles group) to display the Text Effects menu (Figure 2–51).

Figure 2–51

2

- Point to Transform in the Text Effects menu to display the WordArt Transform gallery (Figure 2–52).

Figure 2–52

3

- If you are using a mouse, point to the Inflate Bottom shape in the Warp area (the third shape in the last row) to display a live preview of that text effect applied to the WordArt object (Figure 2–53).

Experiment

- If you are using a mouse, point to various effects in the Transform gallery and watch the format of the text and borders change.

Q&A How can I see the preview of a Transform effect if the gallery is overlaying the WordArt letters? Move the WordArt box to the left or right side of the slide and then repeat Steps 1 and 2.

Figure 2–53

4

- Tap or click the Inflate Bottom shape to apply this text effect to the WordArt object.

Q&A Can I change the shape I applied to the WordArt? Yes. Position the insertion point in the box and then repeat Steps 1 and 2.

5

- Drag the upper-left sizing handle diagonally toward the upper-left corner of the slide until the crosshair is positioned approximately as shown in Figure 2–54.

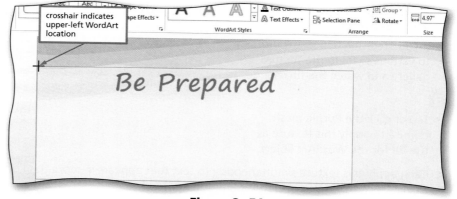

Figure 2–54

6

- Release to resize the WordArt object.

- Drag the WordArt object toward the center of the slide until it is positioned approximately as shown in Figure 2–55.

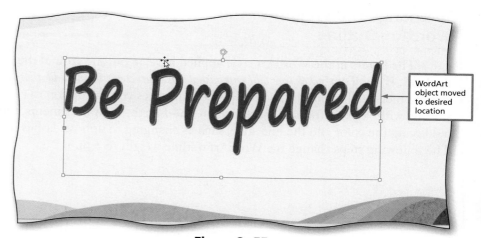

Figure 2–55

To Apply a WordArt Text Fill

Various texture fills are available to give your WordArt characters a unique look. The 24 pictures in the Texture gallery give the appearance of a physical object, such as water drops, sand, tissue paper, and a paper bag. The following steps add the Purple Mesh texture as a fill for the WordArt characters. *Why? Purple coordinates well with the shapes on Slide 3 and is similar to the color in the Slide1 flower and firefighter's hose.*

1

- With the WordArt object selected, click the Text Fill arrow (DRAWING TOOLS FORMAT tab | WordArt Styles group) to display the Text Fill gallery.

- Point to Texture in the Text Fill gallery to display the Texture gallery.

2

- If you are using a mouse, point to the Purple mesh texture (the third texture in the fifth row) to display a live preview of that texture applied to the WordArt object (Figure 2–56).

 Experiment

- If you are using a mouse, point to various styles in the Texture gallery and watch the fill change.

3

- Tap or click the Purple mesh texture to apply this texture as the fill for the WordArt object.

Q&A Can I apply this texture simultaneously to text that appears in more than one place on my slide?
Yes. If you are not using a touch screen, you can select one area of text, press and then hold the CTRL key while you select the other text, and then apply the texture.

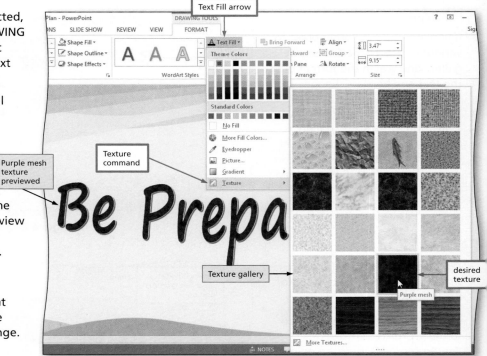

Figure 2–56

To Change the Weight of the WordArt Outline

The letters in the WordArt style applied have an outline around the edges. You can increase the width of the lines. *Why? The thicker line will emphasize this characteristic and add another visual element.* As with fonts, lines also are measured in point size, and PowerPoint gives you the option to change the line **weight**, or thickness, starting with ¼ point (pt) and increasing in one-fourth-point increments. Other outline options include modifying the color and the line style, such as changing to dots or dashes or a combination of dots and dashes. The following steps change the WordArt outline weight to 3 pt.

- With the WordArt object still selected, click the Text Outline arrow (DRAWING TOOLS FORMAT tab | WordArt Styles group) to display the Text Outline gallery.

- Point to Weight in the gallery to display the Weight list.

- If you are using a mouse, point to 3 pt to display a live preview of this line weight on the WordArt text outline (Figure 2–57).

Q&A | Can I make the line width more than 6 pt?
Yes. Tap or click More Lines and increase the amount in the Width box.

Experiment

- If you are using a mouse, point to various line weights in the Weight list and watch the line thickness change.

Figure 2–57

2

- Tap or click 3 pt to apply this line weight to the WordArt text outline.

Q&A | Must my text have an outline?
No. To delete the outline, click No Outline in the Text Outline gallery.

To Change the Color of the WordArt Outline

1 DOWNLOAD & SELECT SLIDES | 2 INSERT & FORMAT PICTURES | 3 INSERT & FORMAT SHAPES
4 INSERT & FORMAT WORDART | 5 FORMAT SLIDE BACKGROUNDS | 6 REVIEW & REVISE SLIDES

Why? The WordArt outline color and the slide background color are similar, so you can add contrast by changing one of these slide elements. The following steps change the WordArt outline color.

1

- With the WordArt object still selected, display the Text Outline gallery.

- If you are using a mouse, point to Red (the second color in the Standard Colors row) to display a live preview of this outline color.

Experiment

- If you are using a mouse, point to various colors in the gallery and watch the outline colors change.

2

- Tap or click Red to apply this color to the WordArt outline.

- Tap or click outside of the WordArt box to deselect this slide element (Figure 2–58).

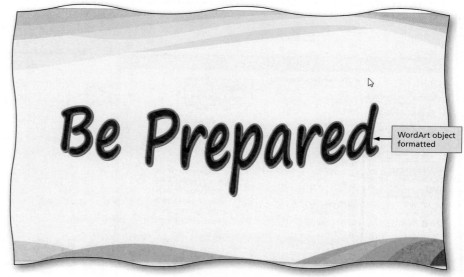

Figure 2–58

BTW
PowerPoint Help
At any time while using PowerPoint, you can find answers to questions and display information about various topics through PowerPoint Help. Used properly, this form of assistance can increase your productivity and reduce your frustrations by minimizing the time you spend learning how to use PowerPoint. For instruction about PowerPoint Help and exercises that will help you gain confidence in using it, read the Office and Windows chapter at the beginning of this book.

Formatting Slide Backgrounds

A slide's background is an integral part of a presentation because it can generate audience interest. Every slide can have the same background, or different backgrounds can be used in a presentation. This background is considered fill, which is the content that makes up the interior of a shape, line, or character. Four fills are available: solid, gradient, picture or texture, and pattern. **Solid fill** is one color used throughout the entire slide. **Gradient fill** is one color shade gradually progressing to another shade of the same color or one color progressing to another color. **Picture** or **texture fill** uses a specific file or an image that simulates a material, such as cork, granite, marble, or canvas. **Pattern fill** adds designs, such as dots or diamonds, that repeat in rows across the slide.

Once you add a fill, you can adjust its appearance. For example, you can adjust its **transparency**, which allows you to see through the background, so that any text on the slide is visible. You also can select a color that is part of the theme or a custom color. You can use **offsets**, another background feature, to move the background away from the slide borders in varying distances by percentage. **Tiling options** repeat the background image many times vertically and horizontally on the slide; the smaller the tiling percentage, the greater the number of times the image is repeated.

To Insert a Picture to Create a Background

1 DOWNLOAD & SELECT SLIDES | 2 INSERT & FORMAT PICTURES | 3 INSERT & FORMAT SHAPES
4 INSERT & FORMAT WORDART | 5 FORMAT SLIDE BACKGROUNDS | 6 REVIEW & REVISE SLIDES

Why? *For variety and interest, you want to use an illustration as the Slide 4 background.* This picture is stored on the Data Files for Students. PowerPoint will stretch the height and width of this picture to fill the slide area. The following steps insert the picture, Emergency Collage, on Slide 4 only.

1
- With Slide 4 displaying, display the DESIGN tab and then click the Format Background button (DESIGN tab | Customize group).
- With the FILL section displaying (Format Background task pane) and 'Picture or texture fill' selected, tap or click the File button to display the Insert Picture dialog box (Figure 2–59).
- If necessary, navigate to the PowerPoint Chapter 02 folder or the location where your Data Files for Students folder is located.

Figure 2–59

2

• If necessary, slide or scroll down and then click Emergency Collage to select the file name (Figure 2–60).

Figure 2–60

3

• Tap or click the Insert button (Insert Picture dialog box) to insert the Emergency Collage illustration as the Slide 4 background (Figure 2–61).

Q&A What if I do not want to use this picture?
Tap or click the Undo button on the Quick Access Toolbar or tap or click the Reset Background button at the bottom of the Format Background task pane.

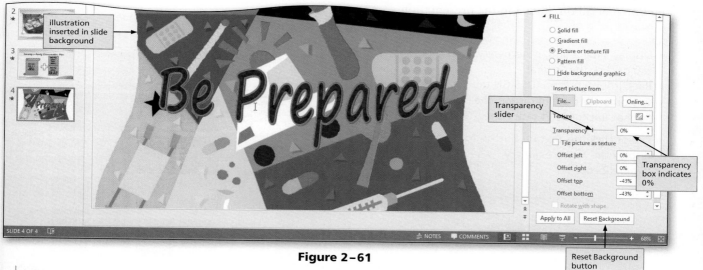

Figure 2–61

Other Ways

1. Tap or click Format Background on shortcut menu, click Picture or Texture Fill, Insert from File (Format Background pane)

To Format the Background Picture Fill Transparency

1 DOWNLOAD & SELECT SLIDES | 2 INSERT & FORMAT PICTURES | 3 INSERT & FORMAT SHAPES
4 INSERT & FORMAT WORDART | **5 FORMAT SLIDE BACKGROUNDS** | **6 REVIEW & REVISE SLIDES**

The Emergency Collage illustration on Slide 4 has vibrant colors and conflicts with the WordArt. One method of reducing this richness is to change the transparency. The **Transparency slider** indicates the amount of opaqueness. The default setting is 0, which is fully opaque. The opposite extreme is 100%, which is fully transparent. To change the transparency, you can move the Transparency slider or enter a number in the box next to the slider. The following step adjusts the transparency of the background picture to 60%.

- Tap or click the Transparency slider and drag it to the right until 60% is displayed in the Transparency box (Figure 2–62).

Q&A

Can I move the slider in small increments so that I can get a precise percentage easily?
Yes. Tap or click the up or down arrows in the Transparency box to move the slider in one-percent increments.

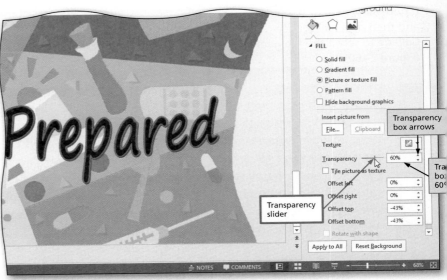

Figure 2–62

To Insert a Texture Fill

You used a texture fill to add interest to the WordArt characters. These same fills are available to add as a slide background. You also can use your own texture pictures for custom backgrounds. The following steps insert the Bouquet fill on Slide 3 in the presentation.

1

- Display Slide 3 and, if necessary, tap or click the Format Background button (DESIGN tab | Customize group) to display the Format Background task pane.

- Tap or click the Texture button to display the Texture gallery (Figure 2–63).

Figure 2–63

2

- Tap or click the Bouquet texture (the last texture in the fourth row) to insert this texture fill as the background on Slide 3 (Figure 2–64).

Q&A

Is a live preview available to see the various textures on this slide?
No. Live preview is not an option with the background textures and fills.

Could I insert this background on all four slides simultaneously?
Yes. You would click the 'Apply to All' button to insert the Bouquet background on all slides.

Figure 2–64

'Apply to All' button

Other Ways

1. Press and hold or right-click background, click Format Background on shortcut menu, select desired options (Format Background pane)

To Format the Background Texture Fill Transparency

1 DOWNLOAD & SELECT SLIDES | 2 INSERT & FORMAT PICTURES | 3 INSERT & FORMAT SHAPES
4 INSERT & FORMAT WORDART | **5 FORMAT SLIDE BACKGROUNDS** | 6 REVIEW & REVISE SLIDES

The Bouquet texture on Slide 3 may detract from the three shapes because it does not offer sufficient contrast with the symbols and text. You can adjust the transparency of a slide texture in the same manner that you change a picture transparency. The following step adjusts the texture transparency to 35%.

1
- Click the Transparency slider and drag it to the right until 35% is displayed in the Transparency box (Figure 2–65).

Figure 2–65

To Insert a Gradient Fill

1 DOWNLOAD & SELECT SLIDES | 2 INSERT & FORMAT PICTURES | 3 INSERT & FORMAT SHAPES
4 INSERT & FORMAT WORDART | 5 FORMAT SLIDE BACKGROUNDS | **6 REVIEW & REVISE SLIDES**

Although you selected Bouquet texture fill on Slide 3 and changed the transparency, you decide that another type of background may be more suitable for your presentation. *Why? The Bouquet texture is very colorful and may detract from the messages presented in the symbols.* For each theme, PowerPoint provides 30 preset **gradient fills** with five designs for each of the six major theme colors. Each fill has one dark color shade that gradually lightens to either another shade of the same color or another color. The following steps replace the texture fill on Slide 3 to a preset gradient fill.

- Tap or click Gradient fill in the Format Background pane and then click the Preset gradients button to display the Preset gradients gallery (Figure 2–66).

Q&A Are the backgrounds displayed in a specific order?

Yes. The first row has light colors at the top of the background; the middle rows have darker fills at the bottom; the bottom row has overall dark fills on all edges.

Is a live preview available to see the various gradients on this slide?

No. Live preview is not an option with the background textures and fills.

Figure 2–66

- Tap or click Bottom Spotlight – Accent 2 (the second fill in the fourth row) to apply that style to Slide 3 (Figure 2–67).

Q&A If I decide later that this background gradient does not fit the theme of my presentation, can I apply a different background?

Yes. You can repeat these steps at any time while creating your presentation.

What if I want to apply this background gradient to all slides in the presentation?

Tap or click the desired style or click the 'Apply to All' button at the bottom of the pane.

Figure 2–67

- Tap or click the Close button (Format Background pane) to close the pane and return to Slide 3.

Other Ways

1. Tap or click DESIGN tab on ribbon, tap or click Format Background button (Customize group), select desired options (Format Background pane)

2. Press and hold or right-click background, click Format Background on shortcut menu, select desired options (Format Background pane)

Reviewing and Revising Individual Slides

The text, pictures, and shapes for all slides in the Emergency Plan presentation have been entered. Once you complete a slide show, you might decide to change elements. PowerPoint provides several tools to assist you with making changes. They include finding and replacing text, inserting a synonym, and checking spelling. The following pages discuss these tools.

Replace Dialog Box

At times, you might want to change all occurrences of a word or phrase to another word or phrase. For example, an instructor may have one slide show to accompany a lecture for several introductory classes, and he wants to update slides with the particular class name and section that appear on several slides. He manually could change the characters, but PowerPoint includes an efficient method of replacing one word with another. The Find and Replace feature automatically locates specific text and then replaces it with desired text.

In some cases, you may want to replace only certain occurrences of a word or phrase, not all of them. To instruct PowerPoint to confirm each change, click the Find Next button in the Replace dialog box instead of the Replace All button. When PowerPoint locates an occurrence of the text, it pauses and waits for you to click either the Replace button or the Find Next button. Clicking the Replace button changes the text; clicking the Find Next button instructs PowerPoint to disregard that particular instance and look for the next occurrence of the Find what text.

To Find and Replace Text

1 DOWNLOAD & SELECT SLIDES | 2 INSERT & FORMAT PICTURES | 3 INSERT & FORMAT SHAPES
4 INSERT & FORMAT WORDART | 5 FORMAT SLIDE BACKGROUNDS | 6 REVIEW & REVISE SLIDES

While reviewing your slides, you realize that the word, Emergency, would be a better choice than the word, Disaster. To change these words throughout a presentation, you could view each slide, look for the word, Disaster, delete the word, and then type the replacement word, Emergency. A more efficient and effective method of performing this action is to use PowerPoint's Find and Replace feature, which automatically locates each occurrence of a word or phrase and then replaces it with specified text. The word, Disaster, displays twice in the presentation. The following steps use Find and Replace to replace all occurrences of the words, a Disaster, with the words, an Emergency.

- Display the HOME tab and then tap or click the Replace button (HOME tab | Editing group) to display the Replace dialog box.

- Type **a Disaster** in the Find what box (Replace dialog box).

- Tap or click the Replace with box and then type **an Emergency** in the box (Figure 2–68).

Figure 2–68

2

- Tap or click the Replace All button (Replace dialog box) to instruct PowerPoint to replace all occurrences of the Find what words, a Disaster, with the Replace with words, an Emergency (Figure 2–69).

Q&A
If I accidentally replaced the wrong text, can I undo this replacement?
Yes. Tap or click the Undo button on the Quick Access Toolbar to undo all replacements. If you had tapped or clicked the Replace button instead of the Replace All button, PowerPoint would undo only the most recent replacement.

3

- Tap or click the OK button (Microsoft PowerPoint dialog box).

- Tap or click the Close btton (Replace dialog box).

Figure 2–69

BTW
Finding and Replacing Text
When finding and replacing text, you do not need to display the slide that contains the word for which you are searching. You can perform this action when any slide is displayed. To see the results of the search and replace action, however, you need to display the slide where the change occurred.

Other Ways

1. Press CTRL+H

To Find and Insert a Synonym

1 DOWNLOAD & SELECT SLIDES | 2 INSERT & FORMAT PICTURES | 3 INSERT & FORMAT SHAPES
4 INSERT & FORMAT WORDART | 5 FORMAT SLIDE BACKGROUNDS | 6 REVIEW & REVISE SLIDES

When reviewing your slide show, you may decide that a particular word does not express the exact usage you intended or that you used the same word on multiple slides. In these cases, you could find a **synonym**, or word similar in meaning, to replace the inappropriate or duplicate word. PowerPoint provides a **thesaurus**, which is a list of synonyms and antonyms, to help you find a replacement word.

In this project, you want to find a synonym to replace the words, stay alive, on Slide 2. The following steps locate an appropriate synonym and replace the word.

1

- Display Slide 2 and then select the words, stay alive.

- If you are using a mouse, right-click to display a shortcut menu related to the words you right-clicked. Then, point to Synonyms on the shortcut menu to display a list of synonyms for these words (Figure 2–70).

Q&A
If I want to locate a synonym for only one word, do I need to select it?
No. You simply need to place the insertion point in the word and then press and hold or right-click to display the shortcut menu.

- If you are using a touch screen, tap the Thesaurus button (REVIEW tab | Proofing group) to display the Thesaurus task pane for the selected words. Then, in the task pane, tap the arrow next to the word survive if necessary to display a shortcut menu.

Figure 2–70

2

- Tap Insert or click the synonym you want (survive) on the Synonyms submenu to replace the words, stay alive, in the presentation with the word, survive (Figure 2–71).

Q&A What if a suitable word does not display in the Synonyms submenu?

You can display the Thesaurus task pane by tapping or clicking Thesaurus on the Synonyms submenu. A complete thesaurus with synonyms displays in the task pane along with an antonym, which is a word with an opposite meaning.

Figure 2–71

Other Ways

1. Tap or click Thesaurus (REVIEW tab | Proofing group) 2. Press SHIFT+F7

To Add Notes

1 DOWNLOAD & SELECT SLIDES | 2 INSERT & FORMAT PICTURES | 3 INSERT & FORMAT SHAPES
4 INSERT & FORMAT WORDART | 5 FORMAT SLIDE BACKGROUNDS | 6 REVIEW & REVISE SLIDES

As you create slides, you may find material you want to state verbally and do not want to include on the slide. You can type and format notes in the **Notes pane** as you work in Normal view and then print this information as **notes pages**. The Notes pane is hidden until you tap or click the Notes button on the status bar to open the pane. If you want to close the Notes pane, tap or click the Notes button again. After adding comments, you can print a set of speaker notes. These notes will print below a small image of the slide. Charts, tables, and pictures added to the Notes pane also print on these pages. The following steps add text to the Notes pane on Slides 2, 3, and 4.

Note: In the following step, the word, whistle, has been misspelled intentionally as wistle to illustrate the use of PowerPoint's spell check feature. Your slides may contain different misspelled words, depending upon the accuracy of your typing.

1

- Display Slide 2 and then if necessary tap or click the Notes button on the status bar to display the Notes pane.

Q&A Why might I need to tap or click the Notes pane?

By default, the Notes pane is closed when you begin a new presentation. Once you display the Notes pane for any slide, the Notes pane will remain open unless you tap or click the Notes button to close it.

- Tap or click the Notes pane and then type `The kit should include a flashlight, wistle, water, radio, batteries, three-day supply of food, three gallons of water for each family member, change of clothing, tools, and first aid kit.` (Figure 2–72).

Q&A What if I cannot see all the lines I typed?

You can drag the splitter bar up to enlarge the Notes pane. Clicking the Notes pane scroll arrows or swiping up or down on the Notes pane allows you to view the entire text.

Figure 2–72

2

- Display Slide 3, tap or click the Notes pane, and then type `One meeting place should be near the home, and the second should be outside the neighborhood. One out-of-state relative should be included in the contacts list.` (Figure 2–73).

Figure 2–73

3

- Display Slide 4 and then type `The Federal Emergency Management Agency (FEMA) has additional information about helping people prepare for emergency situations. Visit www.ready.gov.` in the Notes pane (Figure 2–74).

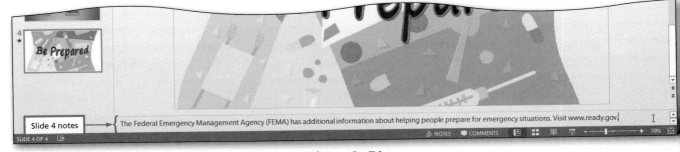

Figure 2–74

BTW

Formatting Notes Pane Text

You can format text in the Notes pane in the same manner you format text on a slide. For example, you can bold key words or change the font size and color to add emphasis.

BTW

Detecting Spelling Errors

The x in the Spell Check icon indicates PowerPoint detected a possible spelling error. A check mark in the icon indicates the entered text contains no spelling errors.

Checking Spelling

After you create a presentation, you should check it visually for spelling errors and style consistency. In addition, you use PowerPoint's Spelling tool to identify possible misspellings on the slides and in the notes. Do not rely on the spelling checker to catch all your mistakes. Although PowerPoint's spelling checker is a valuable tool, it is not infallible. You should proofread your presentation carefully by pointing to each word and saying it aloud as you point to it. Be mindful of commonly misused words such as its and it's, through and though, and to and too.

PowerPoint checks the entire presentation for spelling mistakes using a standard dictionary contained in the Microsoft Office group. This dictionary is shared with the other Microsoft Office applications such as Word and Excel. A custom dictionary is available if you want to add special words such as proper names, cities, and acronyms. When checking a presentation for spelling errors, PowerPoint opens the standard dictionary and the custom dictionary file, if one exists. When a word appears in the Spelling pane, you can perform one of several actions, as described in Table 2–1.

The standard dictionary contains commonly used English words. It does not, however, contain many proper names, abbreviations, technical terms, poetic contractions, or antiquated terms. PowerPoint treats words not found in the dictionaries as misspellings.

Table 2–1 Spelling Pane Buttons and Actions

Button Name/Action	When to Use	Action
Ignore	Word is spelled correctly but not found in dictionaries	PowerPoint continues checking rest of the presentation but will flag that word again if it appears later in document.
Ignore All	Word is spelled correctly but not found in dictionaries	PowerPoint ignores all occurrences of the word and continues checking rest of presentation.
Add	Add word to custom dictionary	PowerPoint opens custom dictionary, adds word, and continues checking rest of presentation.
Change	Word is misspelled	Click proper spelling of the word in Suggestions list. PowerPoint corrects word, continues checking rest of presentation, but will flag that word again if it appears later in document.
Change All	Word is misspelled	Click proper spelling of word in Suggestions list. PowerPoint changes all occurrences of misspelled word and continues checking rest of presentation.
Listen to the pronunciation	To hear the pronunciation of a word	Tap or click the audio speaker icon next to the properly spelled word near the bottom of the Spelling pane.
View synonyms	See some synonyms for the correctly spelled word	View the bullet list of synonyms below the correctly spelled word near the bottom of the Spelling pane.
Close	Stop spelling checker	PowerPoint closes spelling checker and returns to PowerPoint window.

© 2014 Cengage Learning

To Check Spelling

1 DOWNLOAD & SELECT SLIDES | 2 INSERT & FORMAT PICTURES | 3 INSERT & FORMAT SHAPES
4 INSERT & FORMAT WORDART | 5 FORMAT SLIDE BACKGROUNDS | 6 REVIEW & REVISE SLIDES

The following steps check the spelling on all slides in the Emergency Plan presentation.

1

• Tap or click REVIEW on the Ribbon to display the REVIEW tab.

• Tap or click the Spelling button (REVIEW Tab | Proofing group) to start the spelling checker and display the Spelling pane (Figure 2–75).

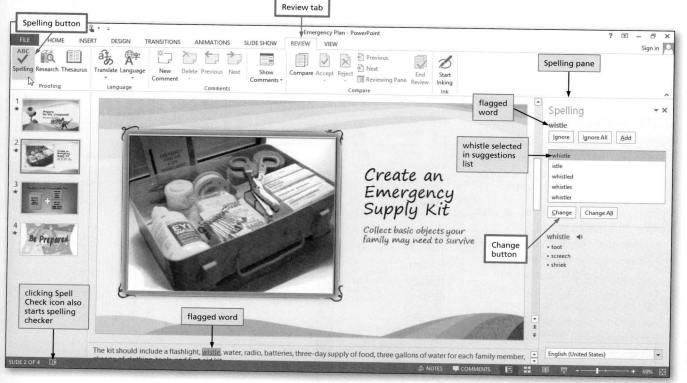

Figure 2–75

2

- With the word, wistle, selected in the list, tap or click the Change button (Spelling pane) to replace the misspelled flagged word, wistle, with the selected correctly spelled word, whistle, and then continue the spelling check (Figure 2–76).

Q&A
Could I have tapped or clicked the Change All button instead of the Change button?
Yes. When you tap or click the Change All button, you change the current and future occurrences of the misspelled word. The misspelled word, wistle, appears only once in the presentation, so tapping or clicking the Change or the Change All button in this instance produces identical results.

Occasionally a correctly spelled word is flagged as a possible misspelled word. Why?
Your custom dictionary does not contain the word, so it is seen as spelled incorrectly. You can add this word to a custom dictionary to prevent the spelling checker from flagging it as a mistake.

Figure 2–76

3

- Replace the misspelled word, Comunication, with the word, Communication.

- Continue checking all flagged words in the presentation. When the Microsoft PowerPoint dialog box appears, tap or click the OK button (Microsoft PowerPoint dialog box) to close the spelling checker and return to the slide where a possible misspelled word appeared.

Other Ways

1. Tap or click Spell Check icon on status bar 2. Press and hold or right-click flagged word, tap or click correct word 3. Press F7

1 DOWNLOAD & SELECT SLIDES | 2 INSERT & FORMAT PICTURES | 3 INSERT & FORMAT SHAPES
4 INSERT & FORMAT WORDART | 5 FORMAT SLIDE BACKGROUNDS | 6 REVIEW & REVISE SLIDES

To Insert a Slide Number

PowerPoint can insert the slide number on your slides automatically to indicate where the slide is positioned within the presentation. The number location on the slide is determined by the presentation theme. You have the option to not display this slide number on the title slide. The following steps insert the slide number on all slides except the title slide.

1

- If necessary, display Slide 3 and then display the INSERT tab.

- Tap or click the Slide Number button (INSERT tab | Text group) to display the Header and Footer dialog box (Figure 2–77).

Q&A
Why might I need to tap or click the Thumbnail pane?
If the final flagged word had been located in the Notes pane during the spell check, the insertion point would have been in the Notes pane. The page number, consequently, would have been inserted in the Notes pane instead of on the slide.

Figure 2–77

2

- Tap or click the Slide number check box (Header and Footer dialog box) to place a check mark in it.

- Tap or click the 'Don't show on title slide' check box (Header and Footer dialog box) to place a check mark in it (Figure 2–78).

Q&A | Where does the slide number display on the slide?
Each theme determines where the slide number is displayed in the footer. In this theme, the slide number location is the left side of the footer, as indicated by the black box at the bottom of the Preview area.

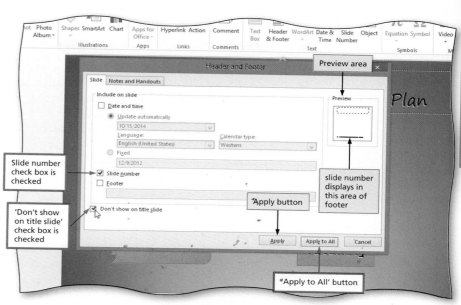

Figure 2–78

3

- Tap or click the Apply to All button (Header and Footer dialog box) to close the dialog box and insert the slide number on all slides except Slide 1 (Figure 2–79).

Q&A | How does tapping or clicking the Apply to All button differ from tapping or clicking the Apply button?
The Apply button inserts the slide number only on the currently displayed slide whereas the Apply to All button inserts the slide number on every slide.

Figure 2–79

Other Ways

1. Tap or click Header & Footer button (INSERT tab | Text group), tap or click Slide Number box (Header and Footer dialog box), tap or click 'Slide number' and 'Don't show on title slide' boxes, tap or click Apply to All button

To Add a Transition between Slides

A final enhancement you will make in this presentation is to apply the Fracture transition in the Exciting category to all slides and increase the transition duration. The following steps apply this transition to the presentation.

1 Tap or click TRANSITIONS on the ribbon. Tap or click the More button (TRANSITIONS tab | Transition to This Slide group) to expand the Transitions gallery.

2 Tap or click the Fracture transition in the Exciting category to apply this transition.

3 Tap or click the Duration up arrow in the Timing group four times to change the transition speed from 02.00 to 03.00.

BTW

Certification
The Microsoft Office Specialist (MOS) program provides an opportunity for you to obtain a valuable industry credential — proof that you have the PowerPoint 2013 skills required by employers. For more information, visit the Certification resource on the Student Companion Site located on www.cengagebrain. com. For detailed instructions about accessing available resources, visit www.cengage.com/ct/ studentdownload or see the inside back cover of this book.

4 Tap or click the Preview Transitions button (TRANSITIONS tab | Preview area) to view the new transition time.

5 Tap or click the Apply To All button (TRANSITIONS tab | Timing group) to apply this transition and speed to all four slides in the presentation (Figure 2–80).

Q&A Can I apply a particular transition or duration to one slide and then change the transition or timing for a different slide in the presentation?

Yes. Select a slide and then select a transition and duration. Do not tap or click the Apply To All button. Repeat this process to apply the transition and duration to individual slides.

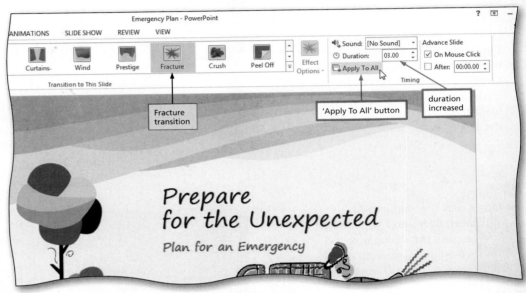

Figure 2–80

CONSIDER THIS

How can I use handouts to organize my speech?

As you develop a lengthy presentation with many visuals, handouts may help you organize your material. Print handouts with the maximum number of slides per page. Use scissors to cut each thumbnail and then place these miniature slide images adjacent to each other on a flat surface. Any type on the thumbnails will be too small to read, so the images will need to work with only the support of the verbal message you provide. You can rearrange these thumbnails as you organize your speech. When you return to your computer, you can rearrange the slides on your screen to match the order of your thumbnail printouts. Begin speaking the actual words you want to incorporate in the body of the talk. This process of glancing at the thumbnails and hearing yourself say the key ideas of the speech is one of the best methods of organizing and preparing for the actual presentation. Ultimately, when you deliver your speech in front of an audience, the images on the slides or on your note cards should be sufficient to remind you of the accompanying verbal message.

To Print Speaker Notes

Comments added to slides in the Notes pane give the speaker information that supplements the text on the slide. They will print with a small image of the slide at the top and the comments below the slide. The following steps print the speaker notes.

- Display Slide 1, tap or click FILE on the ribbon to open the Backstage view, and then tap or click the Print tab in the Backstage view to display Slide 1 in the Print gallery.

- Tap or click 'Full Page Slides' in the Settings area to display the Print gallery (Figure 2–81).

Q&A Why does the preview of my slide appear in color?
Your printer determines how the preview appears. If your printer is not capable of printing color images, the preview will not appear in color.

Figure 2–81

BTW
Distributing a Document
Instead of printing and distributing a hard copy of a document, you can distribute the document electronically. Options include sending the document via email; posting it on cloud storage (such as SkyDrive) and sharing the file with others; posting it on a social networking site, blog, or other website; and sharing a link associated with an online location of the document. You also can create and share a PDF or XPS image of the document, so that users can view the file in Acrobat Reader or XPS Viewer instead of in PowerPoint.

2

- Tap or click Notes Pages in the Print Layout area to select this option and then tap or click the Next Page button three times to display a preview of Slide 4 (Figure 2–82).

Q&A Can I preview Slides 1, 2, or 3 now?
Yes. Click the Previous Page button to preview the other slides.

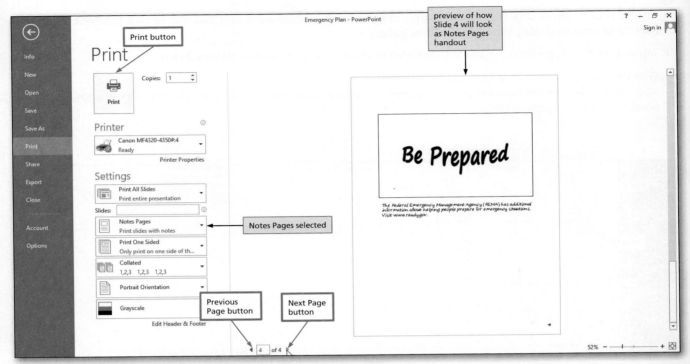

Figure 2–82

3

- Verify that the printer listed on the Printer Status button will print a hard copy of the presentation. If necessary, click the Printer Status button to display a list of available printer options and then click the desired printer to change the currently selected printer.

- Tap or click the Print button in the Print gallery to print the notes pages on the currently selected printer.

- When the printer stops, retrieve the hard copy (Figure 2–83).

Q&A Why does the background display on my printout but not in the figure?
Graphics are displayed depending upon the settings in the Print gallery. For example, the background will print if Color is specified whereas it will not with a Grayscale or Pure Black and White setting.

BTW
Printing Document Properties
To print document properties, tap or click FILE on the ribbon to open the Backstage view, tap or click the Print tab in the Backstage view to display the Print gallery, tap or click the first button in the Settings area to display a list of options specifying what you can print, tap or click Document Info in the list to specify you want to print the document properties instead of the actual document, and then tap or click the Print button in the Print gallery to print the document properties on the currently selected printer.

(a) Slide 1 – Speaker Notes

The kit should include a flashlight, whistle, water, radio, batteries, three-day supply of food, three gallons of water for each family member, change of clothing, tools, and first aid kit.

(b) Slide 2 – Speaker Notes

Figure 2–83 (Continued)

Develop a Family Communication Plan

Contact names & phone numbers

Meeting place near house

Meeting place away from vicinity

One meeting place should be near the home, and the second should be outside the neighborhood. One out-of-state relative should be included in the contacts list.

3

(c) Slide 3 – Speaker Notes

Be Prepared

The Federal Emergency Management Agency (FEMA) has additional information about helping people prepare for emergency situations. Visit www.ready.gov.

4

(d) Slide 4 – Speaker Notes

Figure 2–83 (Handouts printed using a black-and-white printer) (Continued)

BTW

Conserving Ink and Toner

If you want to conserve ink or toner, you can instruct PowerPoint to print draft quality documents by tapping or clicking FILE on the ribbon to open the Backstage view, tapping or clicking Options in the Backstage view to display the PowerPoint Options dialog box, tapping or clicking Advanced in the left pane (PowerPoint Options dialog box), sliding or scrolling to the Print area in the right pane, placing a check mark in the 'Use draft quality check box, and then tapping or clicking the OK button. Then, use the Backstage view to print the document as usual.

Other Ways

1. Press CTRL+P, press ENTER

To Save the Presentation, Sign Out of a Microsoft Account, and Exit PowerPoint

You have made several changes to the presentation since you last saved it. Thus, you should save it again. The following steps save the presentation, sign out of your Microsoft account, and exit PowerPoint.

1 Tap or click the Save button on the Quick Access Toolbar.

2 If you wish to sign out of your Microsoft account, open the Backstage view, tap or click the Account tab to display the Account gallery, and then tap or click the Sign out link, which displays the Remove Account dialog box. If a Can't remove Windows accounts dialog box appears instead of the Remove Account dialog box, click the OK button and skip the remaining steps.

3 Tap or click the Yes button (Remove Account dialog box) to sign out of your Microsoft account on this computer.

4 Tap or click the Back button in the upper-left corner of the Backstage view to return to the presentation.

5a If you have one PowerPoint presentation open, tap or click the Close button on the right side of the title bar to close the open document and exit PowerPoint.

5b If you have multiple PowerPoint presentations open, press and hold or right-click the PowerPoint app button on the taskbar and then tap or click 'Close all windows' on the shortcut menu, or press ALT+F4 to close all open presentations and exit PowerPoint.

BTW
Quick Reference
For a table that lists how to complete the tasks covered in this book using touch gestures, the mouse, ribbon, shortcut menu, and keyboard, see the Quick Reference Summary at the back of this book, or visit the Quick Reference resource on the Student Companion Site located on www.cengagebrain.com. For detailed instructions about accessing available resources, visit www.cengage.com/ct/studentdownload or see the inside back cover of this book.

Chapter Summary

In this chapter you have learned how to insert and format pictures, add and format shapes, insert and format WordArt, add slide backgrounds, find and replace text, check spelling, add notes, and print speaker notes. The items listed below include all the new PowerPoint skills you have learned in this chapter, with the tasks grouped by activity.

Download and Modify Themes
Search for and Download an Online Theme (PPT 77)
Delete a Slide (PPT 79)

Format Fonts
Change the Font (PPT 98)
Format Text Using the Format Painter (PPT 101)

Format Slide Backgrounds
Insert a Picture to Create a Background (PPT 108)
Format the Background Picture Fill Transparency (PPT 109)
Insert a Texture Fill (PPT 110)
Format the Background Texture Fill Transparency (PPT 111)
Insert a Gradient Fill (PPT 111)

Insert and Format Pictures
Insert a Picture into a Slide without a Content Placeholder (PPT 83)
Change a Picture (PPT 85)
Correct a Picture (PPT 87)
Apply a Picture Style (PPT 87)
Add a Picture Border (PPT 88)
Change a Picture Border Color (PPT 89)
Apply Picture Effects (PPT 90)

Insert and Format Shapes
Add a Shape (PPT 92)
Resize a Shape (PPT 93)
Add Other Shapes (PPT 94)
Apply a Shape Style (PPT 95)
Add Text to a Shape (PPT 97)
Copy and Paste a Shape (PPT 101)

Insert and Format WordArt
Insert WordArt (PPT 103)
Change the WordArt Shape (PPT 104)
Apply a WordArt Text Fill (PPT 106)
Change the Weight of the WordArt Outline
(PPT 106)
Change the Color of the WordArt Outline
(PPT 107)

Review and Enhance Slides and Printouts
Find and Replace Text (PPT 113)
Find and Insert a Synonym (PPT 114)
Add Notes (PPT 115)
Check Spelling (PPT 117)
Insert a Slide Number (PPT 118)
Print Speaker Notes (PPT 121)

CONSIDER THIS

What decisions will you need to make when creating your next presentation?

Use these guidelines as you complete the assignments in this chapter and create your own slide show decks outside of this class.

1. Determine if an online theme can help you design and develop the presentation efficiently and effectively.

2. Identify personal pictures that would create interest and promote the message being presented.

3. Consider modifying pictures.

 a) Add corrections.

 b) Add styles.

 c) Add effects.

 d) Add and format borders.

4. Locate shapes that supplement the verbal and written message.

 a) Size and position them aesthetically on slides.

 b) Add styles.

5. Develop WordArt that emphasizes major presentation messages.

 a) Modify the shape.

 b) Change the weight and color to coordinate with slide elements.

6. Format individual slide backgrounds.

 a) Add and modify fills.

 b) Insert a picture.

7. Change fonts to emphasize particular slide components.

8. Search for synonyms that help express your thoughts.

9. Create speaker notes.

10. Check spelling.

How should you submit solutions to questions in the assignments identified with a ✸ symbol?

Every assignment in this book contains one or more questions identified with a ✸ symbol. These questions require you to think beyond the assigned presentation. Present your solutions to the questions in the format required by your instructor. Possible formats may include one or more of these options: write the answer; create a document that contains the answer; present your answer to the class; discuss your answer in a group; record the answer as audio or video using a webcam, smartphone, or portable media player; or post answers on a blog, wiki, or website.

Apply Your Knowledge

Reinforce the skills and apply the concepts you learned in this chapter.

Changing the Background and Adding Photos and WordArt

Note: To complete this assignment, you will be required to use the Data Files for Students. Visit www.cengage.com/ct/studentdownload for detailed instructions or contact your instructor for information about accessing the required files.

Instructions: Run PowerPoint. Open the presentation, Apply 2-1 Bicycle, from the Data Files for Students.

The five slides in the presentation discuss bicycle safety. The document you open is an unformatted presentation. You are to add photos, apply picture styles, add WordArt, change slide layouts, apply a transition, and use the Format Painter so the slides look like Figures 2–84a through 2–84e on pages PPT 127 through 130.

Perform the following tasks:

1. On the title slide, use your name in place of Student Name and bold and italicize your name.

2. If requested by your instructor, change your first name to your mother's first name on the title slide.

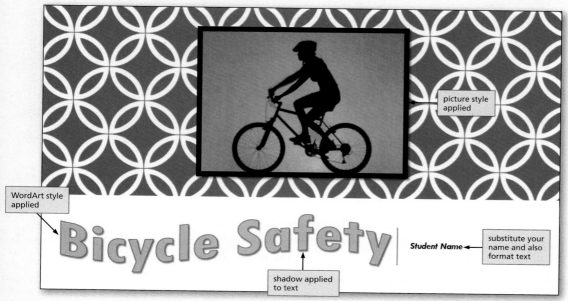

(a) Slide 1

Figure 2–84 (Continued)

Continued >

Apply Your Knowledge *continued*

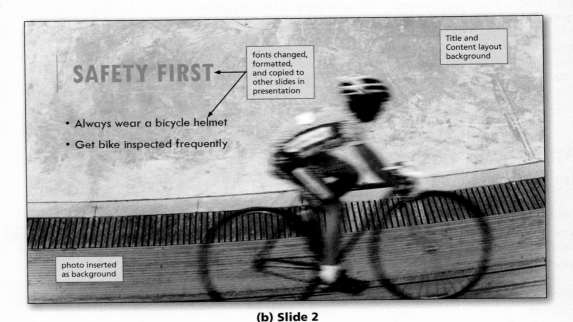

(b) Slide 2

(c) Slide 3

Figure 2–84

3. Increase the title text font size to 60 point. Apply the WordArt style, Fill – Blue, Accent 2, Outline – Accent 2 (the third style in the first row). Apply the Transform text effect, Wave 2 (the second effect in the fifth Warp area row) to this text. Also add a shadow to this text.

4. Apply the Moderate Frame, Black picture style (the fifth style in the second row) to the photo on Slide 1, as shown in Figure 2–84a on the previous page.

5. On Slide 2, change the layout to Title and Content. Increase the title text font to 54 point, change the font color to Green (the sixth color in the Standard Colors row), and then bold the text. Increase the bulleted list font to 24 point, as shown in Figure 2–84b.

6. Create a background on Slide 2 by inserting the photo called Cyclist, which is available on the Data Files for Students.

7. On Slide 2, type `The average cost for a routine bike inspection is $20.` in the Notes pane.

8. On Slides 3 through 5, change the layout to Two Content. Insert the photos, as shown in Figures 2–84c through 2–84e on the next page. The photos to be inserted are called Bicycle2, Bicycle3, and Bicycle4 and are available on the Data Files for Students. Also, change the background to Top Spotlight – Accent 2 gradient fill (the second gradient in the second row) in the Preset gradients gallery on Slides 3 through 5.

9. On Slide 3, adjust the size of the photo and apply the Reflected Bevel, Black picture style (the fourth style in the fourth row) and change the photo brightness to +20% (the fourth picture in the third row in the Brightness and Contrast area).

10. On Slide 3, type `Laws for bicycles on the road vary in every state and country.` in the Notes pane.

11. On Slide 4, adjust the size of the photo, apply the Metal Oval picture style (the seventh style in the fourth row), and then change the photo border to Black, Text 1 (the second color in the first Theme Colors row), as shown in Figure 2–84d.

12. Use the thesaurus to change the word, suitable, to appropriate.

13. Type `Hydration is critical. Make sure your bike is equipped with a bottle holder.` in the Notes pane.

14. On Slide 5, adjust the size of the photo and apply the Bevel Perspective picture style (the first style in the fourth row) to the photo, as shown in Figure 2–84e on the next page.

15. Use the Format Painter to format the title text and the bulleted lists on Slides 3 through 5 with the same features as the title text and bulleted list on Slide 2.

16. Apply the Wind transition in the Exciting category to all slides. Change the duration to 2.50 seconds.

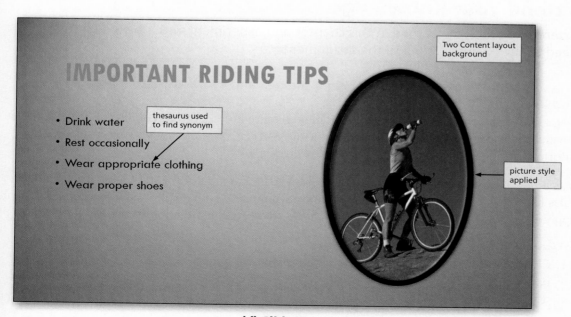

(d) Slide 4
Figure 2–84 (Continued)

Continued >

Apply Your Knowledge *continued*

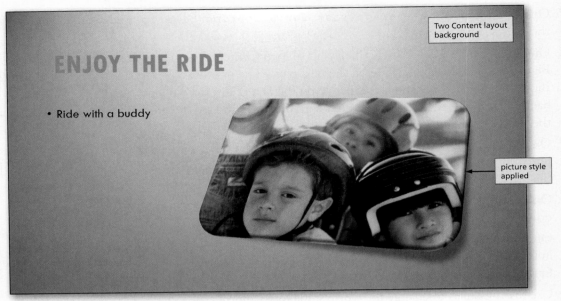

(e) Slide 5

Figure 2–84 (Continued)

17. Save the presentation using the file name, Apply 2-1 Bicycle Safety.

18. Submit the revised document in the format specified by your instructor.

19. ✸ In Step 4 you applied the Moderate Frame, Black picture style. How did this style improve the slide?

Extend Your Knowledge

Extend the skills you learned in this chapter and experiment with new skills. You may need to use Help to complete the assignment.

Changing Slide Backgrounds, Inserting Shapes and WordArt, and Finding and Replacing Text

Note: To complete this assignment, you will be required to use the Data Files for Students. Visit www.cengage.com/ct/studentdownload for detailed instructions or contact your instructor for information about accessing the required files.

Instructions: Run PowerPoint. Open the presentation, Extend 2-1 Field Archery, from the Data Files for Students. You will create backgrounds including inserting a photo to create a background, apply a WordArt Style and Effect, and add shapes to create the presentation shown in Figure 2–85.

Perform the following tasks:
1. Change the theme to Wisp and choose the second variant.

2. Find and replace the words, Bow and Arrow, with the word, Archery, on all slides.

3. On Slides 2 through 4, change the background style to Top Spotlight – Accent 5 (the fifth style in the second Preset gradients row). Also, change the title text to bold and change the font color to Orange, Accent 1 (the fifth color in the first Theme Colors row) on Slides 2 through 4.

4. On the title slide (Figure 2–85a), create a background by inserting the photo called Bow and Arrow, which is available on the Data Files for Students. Change the transparency to 50%.

5. Apply the WordArt style, Fill - Orange, Accent 1, Shadow (the second style in the first row), to the title text, center the text, and increase the font size to 72 point. Apply the WordArt Transform text effect, Arch Up (the first effect in the first Follow Path row), and then bold this text. Also, move the title text above the archer in the photo on the title slide.

6. If requested by your instructor, add your current or previous pet's name as the Slide 1 subtitle text.

7. On Slides 2 through 4, increase the font size of the first-level bulleted text to 22 point and the second-level bulleted text to 20 point.

8. On Slide 2, enlarge the illustration to the size shown in Figure 2–85b on the next page, apply the Reflected Bevel, Black picture style (the fourth style in the fourth row), and then move it to the location shown in the figure.

9. On Slide 3, apply the Soft Edge Oval picture style (the sixth style in the third row) to the photo and move the photo to the upper-right area of the slide. Also, apply the Orange, 18 pt glow, Accent color 1 glow variation (the first variation in the fourth Glow Variations row) to this photo, as shown in Figure 2–85c on the next page.

10. On Slide 4, select the Oval shape and while holding down the Shift key, draw a circle 6" × 6", as shown in Figure 2–85d on page PPT 133. Fill this shape with Black, Text 1, Lighter 15% and then change the shape outline to No Outline. Then copy and paste this shape two times. Change the shape size of the first pasted circle to 4" × 4". Hint: Use the Size and Position group on the PICTURE TOOLS FORMAT tab to enter the exact measurement of the shape. Change the Shape Fill to White and then center this shape over the original black circle using the Smart Guides. Select the second pasted circle and change the shape size to 2" × 2", the Shape Fill to Black, Text 1, Lighter 15% and then center this shape over the white circle shape using the Smart Guides.

(a) Slide 1

Figure 2–85 (Continued)

Continued >

Extend Your Knowledge *continued*

(b) Slide 2

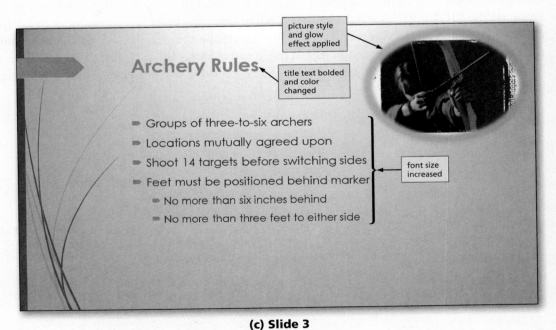

(c) Slide 3

Figure 2–85

11. Insert an arrow on Slide 4 by using the Right Arrow shape under Block Arrows. Size the arrow to 1.5" × 6" and then copy and paste this arrow shape two times. Copy and paste the three paragraphs from the bulleted list into the three arrow shapes. Select the text on one of these shapes, change the font size to 28 point, change the font color to black, center the text, and

(d) Slide 4
Figure 2–85 (Continued)

then bold the text. Use the Format Painter to format the text in the two arrows with the same features as the first arrow. Move the arrows so that each one points to the correct ring, as shown in Figure 2–85d. Delete the bulleted text in the text placeholder.

12. Apply an appropriate transition to all slides.

13. Save the presentation using the file name, Extend 2-1 Field Archery Scoring.

14. Submit the revised document in the format specified by your instructor.

15. ☀ In this assignment, you changed the transparency of the inserted background photo on the title slide to 50%. How did this transparency change enhance your title slide?

Analyze, Correct, Improve

Analyze a presentation, correct all errors, and improve it.

Correcting Formatting, Adding Slide Numbers, and Correcting Spelling

Note: To complete this assignment, you will be required to use the Data Files for Students. Visit www.cengage.com/ct/studentdownload for detailed instructions or contact your instructor for information about accessing the required files.

Instructions: Run PowerPoint. Open the presentation, Analyze 2-1 Avoid the Flu, from the Data Files for Students. This presentation contains four slides and explains why doctors recommend you should get an annual flu shot. Figure 2–86 on the next page shows the uncorrected title slide. Modify the slides by making the indicated corrections and improvements.

1. Correct

 a. Change the variant to blue (the second variant in the gallery).

 b. Decrease the font size of the Slide 1 title text and change the font color. Also, capitalize the letter F in the word, flu.

 c. Use your name in place of Student Name on Slide 1.

Continued >

Analyze, Correct, Improve *continued*

d. If requested by your instructor, change your first name on Slide 1 to your mother's first name.

e. On Slides 2 through 4, adjust the photo sizes and move them so they do not overlap text and are the appropriate dimensions for the slide content.

f. On all slides, adjust font sizes and font color so they are the appropriate size and enhance the presentation.

g. Correct the spelling errors on all slides.

2. Improve

a. Increase the size of the medical symbol on the title slide and move the symbol to the right side of the slide.

b. On Slides 2 through 4, change the color of the title text and bold all the titles.

c. Change the photo border colors on all slides to make them more visually attractive.

d. Add the slide number to all slides except the title slide.

e. Apply the same transition and duration to all slides.

f. Save the presentation using the file name, Analyze 2-1 – Get Your Flu Shot.

g. Submit the revised document in the format specified by your instructor.

3. ✳ Which errors existed in the starting file? How did changing the variant color help? When you adjusted the photo sizes, how did you determine their final sizes?

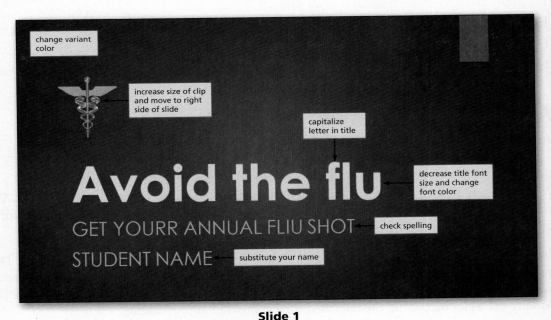

Slide 1

Figure 2–86

In the Labs

Design and/or create a presentation using the guidelines, concepts, and skills presented in this chapter. Labs 1 and 2, which increase in difficulty, require you to create solutions based on what you learned in the chapter; Lab 3 requires you to create a solution, which uses cloud and web technologies, by learning and investigating on your own from general guidance.

Lab 1: Creating a Presentation Inserting Photos, Applying Picture Styles, and Inserting Shapes

Problem: Your creative cooking class has volunteered to manage a bake sale to raise funds for victims of a tornado in a neighboring town. To encourage more students to participate in the bake sale, you decide to put together a presentation that would run in the cafeteria. You want to show your audience how easy it is to make an apple pie. Create the slides shown in Figure 2–87.

Instructions: Perform the following tasks:

1. Create a new presentation using the Retrospect theme. Do not change the brown variant.

2. On Slide 1, create a background by inserting the photo called Apple Pie from the Data Files for Students, as shown in Figure 2–87a. Change the transparency to 53%.

3. Type **Homemade Apple Pie** as the Slide 1 title text. Press the ENTER key after the word, Homemade, so the text is on two lines, and then center the text. Apply the WordArt style Fill – Orange, Accent 2, Outline – Accent 2 (the third style in the first row). Change the text fill to Dark Red (the first color in the Standard Colors row), and then change the text outline color to Green (the sixth color in the Standard Colors row) and the text outline weight to 3 pt. Also, apply the Transform text Effect, Chevron Up (the first effect in the second Warp row), to this text. Position this WordArt, as shown in Figure 2–87a. Type **BAKE SALE – SATURDAY JANUARY 20** in the subtitle placeholder. Change the font to MV Boli, increase the font size to 30 point, bold this text, and then center the text, as shown in the figure.

4. Create Slides 2 through 4 with the Two Content layout, Slide 5 with the Content with Caption layout, and Slide 6 with the Picture with Caption layout.

(a) Slide 1

Figure 2–87 (Continued)

Continued >

In the Labs *continued*

5. Type the title and content and insert all photos on Slides 2 through 5, as shown in Figures 2–87b through 2–87e. The photos to be inserted are called Apples, Ingredients, Cooks, and Apple Pie Slice, and are available on the Data Files for Students. Size the photos and then use the Smart Guides to position these images. You may want to zoom the slides to help you align these graphic elements.

6. On Slide 2, increase the title text size to 54 point, change the font color to Dark Red, and then bold this text. Use the Format Painter to apply these formatting changes to the title text on Slides 3 and 4. On Slide 2, change the list font size to 24 point. Apply the Bevel Perspective picture style (the first style in the fourth row) to the photo, change the border color to Light Green (the fifth color in the Standard Colors row), and then change the border weight to 6 pt, as shown in Figure 2–87b.

(b) Slide 2

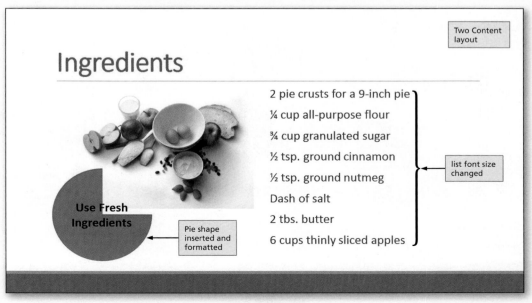

(c) Slide 3
Figure 2–87

7. On Slide 3, change the list font size to 24 point. Insert the Pie shape located in the Basic Shapes area to the lower-left corner of the slide. Apply the Colored Fill – Brown, Accent 4 (the eighth color in the first row) to the shape. Size the shape as shown in the figure. Type the text, **Use Fresh Ingredients** in the shape. Bold this text, and change the font size to 24 point, as shown in Figure 2–87c.

8. On Slide 4, change the list font size to 20 point. Apply the Snip Diagonal Corner, White picture style (the first style in the third row) to the photo, change the border color to Dark Red (the first color in the Standard Colors row), and then apply the Reflection picture effect, Tight Reflection, touching (the first effect in the first Reflection Variations row). Copy the pie shape from Slide 3 and paste it in the bottom center of the slide. Type the text, **Bake 40 to 50 Minutes**, as shown in Figure 2–87d.

(d) Slide 4

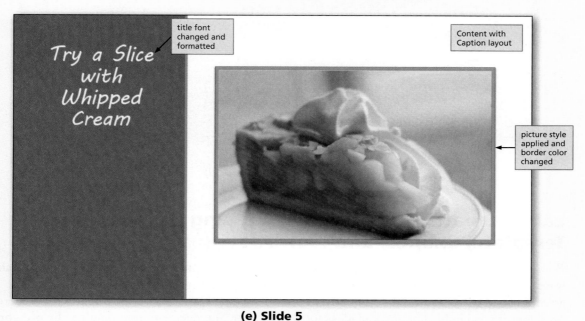

(e) Slide 5

Figure 2–87 (Continued)

Continued >

In the Labs *continued*

9. On Slide 5, change the title text font to MV Boli, change the font size to 40 point, and then center this text. Apply the Simple Frame, White picture style (the first style in the first row) to the slice of pie photo and then change the border color to Orange, Accent 1 (the fifth color in the Theme Colors row), as shown in Figure 2–87e on the previous page.

10. On Slide 6, change the caption title font to MV Boli, change the font size to 32 point, and then bold this text. Select the photo, click the Change Picture button (PICTURE TOOLS FORMAT tab | Adjust group), and then insert the Bake Sale illustration from the Data Files for Students, as shown in Figure 2–87f.

11. If requested by your instructor, type the name of the city or county in which you were born into the subtitle text placeholder on Slide 6.

12. Apply the Peel Off transition in the Exciting category to all slides. Change the duration to 2.5 seconds.

13. Check the spelling and correct any errors. Save the presentation using the file name, Lab 2-1 Homemade Apple Pie.

14. Submit the document in the format specified by your instructor.

15. ✸ What is the significance of changing the transparency of the photo on the title slide? Why did you put a red border on the photo on Slide 4? Explain why you did not follow the 7 × 7 rule on Slides 3 and 4.

(f) Slide 6

Figure 2–87 (Continued)

Lab 2: **Creating a Presentation Using an Online Theme Template, Shapes, and WordArt**

Problem: Your local Chamber of Commerce is presenting a seminar to local business owners about ways to expand their business. Because you are majoring in business, your teacher thought that attending this meeting would be a good experience for you. He asked the Chamber of Commerce president if you could submit some ideas for the seminar. You decide to put together the presentation shown in Figure 2–88.

Instructions: Perform the following tasks:

1. Create a new presentation using the Business project plan presentation (widescreen) in the Business category under Suggested searches.

2. Delete Slides 7 through 14.

3. Apply the Two Content layout to Slide 2, the Alternate Content with Caption layout to Slide 3, the Content with Caption layout to Slide 4, the Title only layout to Slide 5, and the Section Header layout to Slide 6. Delete all titles and text content from Slides 2 through 6. Type the new title and text content for Slides 2, 3, and 4, as shown in Figures 2–88b through 2–88d on the next page.

4. Insert the photos and illustration shown in Figures 2–88b through 2–88e from the Data Files for Students. The photos and illustration are called Advertising, Delivery, Customer, and Call Center. Apply the Canvas texture fill (the second texture in the first row) to Slides 2 through 5 and change the transparency to 35%.

5. On the title slide, type the new title and subtitle content, increase the font size of the subtitle text to 28 point, and then change the font color to Orange (the third color in the Standard Colors row), as shown in Figure 2–88a.

6. If requested by your instructor, add the name of your hometown after the word, Business, in the subtitle placeholder. Type the word `in` before the name of your hometown.

7. On Slide 2, increase the font size of the title to 40 point, change the font color to Indigo, Text 2, Darker 25% (the fourth color in the fifth Theme Colors row), and then bold this text. Increase the font size of the bulleted list to 24 point. Apply the Perspective Shadow, White picture style (the fourth style in the third row) and resize the photo, as shown in Figure 2–88b.

8. On Slide 3, increase the font size of the title to 40 point and then bold this text. Increase the font size of the text to 24 point. Apply the Simple Frame picture style (the first style in the first row) to the photo, as shown in Figure 2–88c.

9. On Slide 4, increase the font size of the title text to 40 point, change the font color to Indigo, Text 2, Darker 25% (the fourth color in the fifth Theme Colors row), and then bold this text. Increase the font size of the bulleted list text to 24 point. Apply the Metal Frame picture style (the third style in the first row) to the photo, as shown in Figure 2–88d.

10. On Slide 5, increase the font size of the title to 40 point, change the font color to Indigo, Text 2, Darker 25% (the fourth color in the fifth Theme Colors row), and then bold this text. Move

(a) Slide 1

Figure 2–88 (Continued)

Continued >

In the Labs *continued*

(b) Slide 2

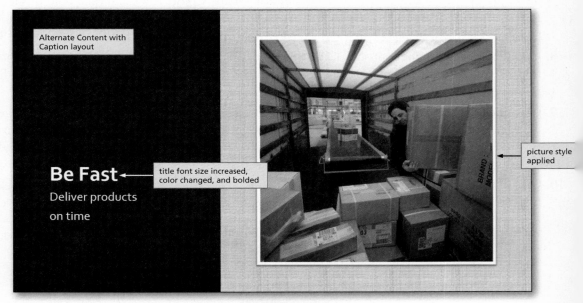

(c) Slide 3

Figure 2–88

the photo to the right side of the slide and then apply the Soft Edge Oval picture style (the sixth style in the third row) to the photo, as shown in Figure 2–88e.

11. Insert the Diamond shape located in the Basic Shapes area, resize the shape so that it is approximately 3.42" × 3.93", and then right-click the shape, click Style, and apply the Subtle Effect – Red, Accent 6 Shape Quick Style (the seventh style in the fourth row). Copy and paste the shape two times and move the shapes, as shown in Figure 2–88e. Type the text into the shape and then increase the text size to 24 point.

12. On Slide 6, type the new title and subtitle content, and create a background by inserting the Ladder photo from the Data Files for Students. Change the transparency to 40%. Decrease the title font size to 44 point, change the font color to Indigo, Text 2, Darker 25% (the fourth color in the fifth Theme Colors row), right-align the text, and then bold this text. Increase the font size of the subtitle text to 28 point, change the font color to Indigo, Text 2 (the fourth color in the first Theme

(d) Slide 4

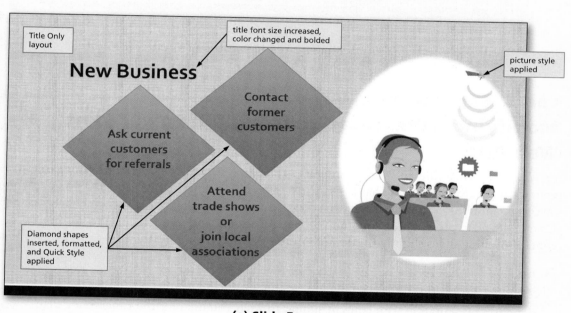

(e) Slide 5
Figure 2–88 (Continued)

Colors row), and then right-align this text, as shown in Figure 2–88f. Insert the Pentagon shape located in the Block Arrows area and then apply the Subtle Effect - Lime, Accent 1 Quick Style (the second style in the fourth row) to the shape. Type `Success` in the shape, change the font to Forte, change the font size to 60 point, and then change the font color to Gray – 80%, Text 1.

3. Change the transition to Doors in the Exciting category to all slides. Change the duration to 2.75 seconds.

4. Check spelling and correct all errors. Save the presentation using the file name, Lab 2-2 Small Business Seminar.

5. Submit the revised document in the format specified by your instructor.

6. ✺ You searched for an online theme under Business. Why? Do you think any of the other themes would have worked well for your presentation? How does changing the slide layouts help your presentation?

Continued >

In the Labs *continued*

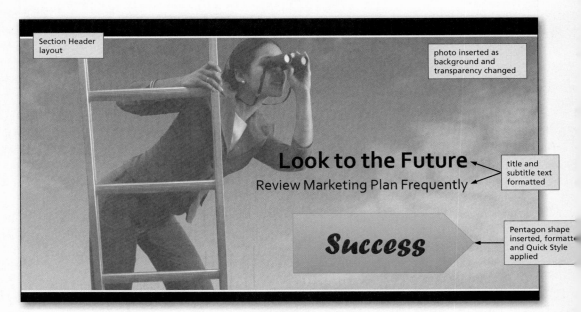

(f) Slide 6
Figure 2–88 (Continued)

Lab 3: Expand Your World: Cloud and Web Technologies
Modifying a Presentation Using the PowerPoint Web App

Problem: The fire chief in your community is planning a family security and safety workshop at your local hardware store. He has asked you to help him publicize the event, and he wants to focus on urging families to prepare for unexpected situations. You inform him that you have created an Emergency Plan presentation for your computer class, and he would like you to customize the content of these slides slightly to promote the workshop.

Instructions:

1. Sign in to your Microsoft account and run the PowerPoint web app.

2. Create a presentation with content similar to what you used for the Emergency Plan presentation.

3. On the title slide, add the name and address of the nearest hardware store. In addition, add the date that is exactly one month from today and a starting time of noon. Add the name of one of your elementary school teachers as the fire chief's name on this slide.

4. Save the presentation using the file name, Lab 2-3 Local Safety Workshop.

5. Submit the assignment in the format specified by your instructor.

6. ✷ Other than the content the chief asked you to include on the title slide, how does the presentation you created using the PowerPoint web app differ from the presentation you created in the Chapter 2 project? Which formatting features are not available in the web app? Do you think using the web app has sufficient functions to develop effective presentations? Why or why not?

Consider This: Your Turn

Apply your creative thinking and problem-solving skills to design and implement a solution.

Design and Create a Presentation about Skydiving from New Heights

Personal

Part 1: Members of your skydiving club are discussing free-falling records of new heights reached by skydivers over the past years. They've been following the news reports about the man from Austria, 43-year-old Felix Baumgartner, who broke a record by completing the highest skydive and traveling faster than the speed of sound without being in an aircraft. At a recent meeting with your fellow skydivers, many questions arose as to how this man was able to accomplish this, what risks were involved, and how long he trained for this venture. You researched facts about this record-breaking skydive and learned that the height he dove from (128,100 feet above Earth) was more than three times the cruising altitude of a passenger jet (hitting Mach 1.24 or 833.9 mph). It was the height at which water boils. If his pressurized spacesuit had malfunctioned, it would have been disastrous: a leak in his spacesuit would have caused his blood to boil instantly. Half of his nine-minute descent was a free fall of 119,846 feet. He trained for seven years. Use the concepts and techniques presented in this chapter to prepare a presentation with a minimum of four slides that explores this subject. Select a suitable theme, and include a title slide, bulleted lists, shapes, and WordArt. The presentation should contain photos and illustrations appropriately resized. Eight photos and illustrations are available on the Data Files for Students: Skydiving1, Skydiving2, Skydiving3, Skydiving4, Skydiving5, Skydiving6, Skydiving7, and Skydiving8. You can add your own digital photos or photos from Office.com if they are appropriate for this topic. Apply picture styles and effects. Add a title slide and closing slide to complete your presentation. Format the title slide with a shape. Format the background with at least one photo and apply a background texture to at least one slide. Review and revise your presentation as needed. Submit your assignment in the format specified by your instructor.

Part 2: ✳ You made several decisions while creating the presentation in this assignment: where to place text, how to format the text (such as font, font size, and where to use WordArt), which graphical image(s) to use, what styles and effects to apply, where to position the graphical image, how to format the graphical images, and which shapes to use to add interest to the presentation. What was the rationale behind each of these decisions? When you reviewed the document, what further revisions did you make and why? Where would you recommend showing this slide show?

Design and Create a Presentation about Teaching Geometry to Elementary Students

Professional

Part 1: You work part time for a tutoring agency. Because you are majoring in math, your boss asked if you would put together a teaching aid for teaching geometry to the elementary students. You decide to create a presentation with some basic shapes: squares, circles, and triangles. To make the slides appeal to your young students, you decide to use shapes and add photos and illustrations. Geometry for elementary students also can cover parallel lines, intersecting lines, and how intersecting lines form angles. You can show them shapes such as pentagons, heptagons, and octagons. They can look for shapes in their environment and draw them. You can teach them that even though a shape is turned upside down or rotated, it is still the same shape even if it looks different. Use the concepts and techniques presented in this chapter to create a presentation with at least four slides. Select a suitable theme, include a title slide, and add WordArt. Review and revise your presentation as needed. Submit your assignment in the format specified by your instructor.

Part 2: ✳ You made several decisions while creating the presentation in this assignment: where to place text, how to format the text (such as font, font size, and where to use WordArt), which graphical image(s) to use, what styles and effects to apply, where to position the graphical images,

Continued >

Consider This: Your Turn *continued*

and which shapes to use to add interest to the presentation. What was the rationale behind each of these decisions? When you reviewed the document, what further revisions did you make and why? Where would you recommend showing this slide show?

3. Design and Create a Presentation about Coyotes Roaming in Your Neighborhood
Research and Collaboration

Part 1: Many of your neighbors are concerned about the coyotes that have been spotted in your neighborhood. With the help of a friend who works part time at a local wildlife refuge, you suggest that each of you do some research about coyotes and discuss your findings and put together a presentation to share at the next town hall meeting. Your main concern is that the coyotes are finding outdoor food sources such as pet food, uncovered garbage cans, and areas near homes where rodents may be nesting. You want to make suggestions to your neighbors about how to deter the coyotes from staying in your neighborhood. You ask your friend who works at the wildlife refuge to research the habits of coyotes. You will gather information from the local newspaper where there have been articles written about the coyotes and your other neighbor will talk to other people in the neighbor about sightings of coyotes and possible photographs. After coordinating all the facts about the coyotes, use the concepts and techniques presented in this chapter to prepare a presentation with a minimum of four slides that explores the subject of coyotes. Summarize your research findings and type this information in the Notes pane of each slide. Select a suitable theme, include a title slide, bulleted lists, shapes, and WordArt. Seven photos and illustrations are available on the Data Files for Students: Coyote1, Coyote2, Coyote3, Coyote4, Coyote5, Coyote6, and Coyote7. Change the brightness and contrast for at least one photo. Insert shapes and WordArt to enhance your presentation. Apply a transition in the Subtle area to all slides and increase the duration. Review and revise your presentation as needed. Submit your assignment in the format specified by your instructor.

Part 2: ✹ You made several decisions while creating the presentation in this assignment: where to place text, how to format the text (such as font, font size, and where to use WordArt), which graphical image(s) to use, what styles and effects to apply, where to position the graphical image, what shapes to use to add interest to the presentation. What was the rationale behind each of these decisions? When you reviewed the document, what further revisions did you make and why? Where would you recommend showing this slide show?

Learn Online

Reinforce what you learned in this chapter with games, exercises, training, and many other online activities and resources.

Student Companion Site Reinforcement activities and resources are available at no additional cost on www.cengagebrain.com. Visit www.cengage.com/ct/studentdownload for detailed instructions about accessing the resources available at the Student Companion Site.

 SAM Put your skills into practice with SAM! If you have a SAM account, go to www.cengage.com sam2013 to access SAM assignments for this chapter.